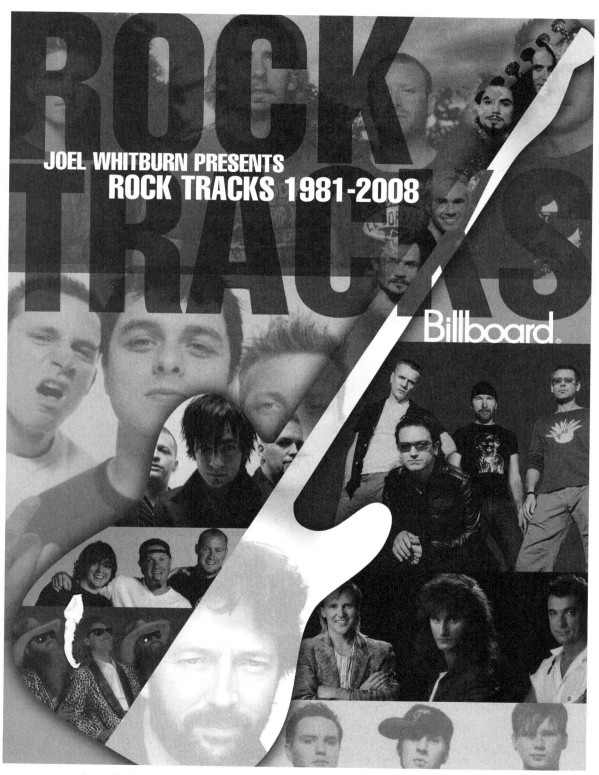

JOEL WHITBURN PRESENTS
ROCK TRACKS 1981-2008

Billboard®

Compiled from Billboard's "Mainstream Rock Tracks" charts 1981-2008
and Billboard's "Modern Rock Tracks" charts 1988-2008.

ISBN 0-89820-174-8
ISBN 978-0-89820-174-1

Record Research Inc.
P.O. Box 200
Menomonee Falls, Wisconsin 53052-0200   U.S.A.

Phone: (262) 251-5408
Fax: (262) 251-9452
E-Mail: books@recordresearch.com
Web site: www.recordresearch.com

CONTENTS

An alphabetical listing, by artist, of every track to chart on *Billboard's* **Mainstream Rock Tracks** chart from March 21, 1981, through March 29, 2008, and every track to chart on *Billboard's* **Modern Rock Tracks** chart from September 10, 1988, through March 29, 2008.

A combined alphabetical listing, by song title, of every track to chart on *Billboard's* "Mainstream Rock Tracks" and "Modern Rock Tracks" charts from 1981-2008

Top 100 Artists In Rank Order

Top 100 Artists In A-Z Order

Top 40 Artists: 1981-89 / 1990s / 2000-08

Top Artist Achievements:
   Most Charted Tracks
   Most Top 10 Tracks
   Most #1 Tracks
   Most Weeks At The #1 Position

Top Tracks: All Time / 1981-89 / 1990-99 / 2000-08

Tracks Of Longevity: 1981-89 / 1990s / 2000-08

A chronological listing, by peak date, of every title to top *Billboard's* "Mainstream Rock Tracks" chart.

MODERN ROCK TRACKS WRAP-UP

#1 MODERN ROCK TRACKS

A chronological listing, by peak date, of every title to top
Billboard's "Modern Rock Tracks" chart.

CLASSIC ROCK SECTION

AUTHOR'S NOTE

Then: Joel – 1958

Now: Joel – 2008

Welcome to the third edition of *Rock Tracks*. This is the first edition to combine both the "Mainstream Rock" and "Modern Rock" chart data into one handy artist section. We've also expanded the **Classic Rock Tracks** section to include additional tracks and album information.

Rock and roll music exploded onto the music scene in the mid-1950s, but it wasn't until March of 1981 that *Billboard* began a weekly *Top Tracks* chart devoted to rock radio airplay. During the mid-1980s an alternative rock radio format developed and by September of 1988 *Billboard* debuted the *Modern Rock Tracks* chart. After 20 years these two charts continue to evolve along with the music as each year brings more new bands to the airwaves, many of which are featured on the front and back book covers (see below).

Way back in 1958 Danny & The Juniors proclaimed that "Rock And Roll Is Here To Stay" and 50 years later that statement still stands.

JOEL WHITBURN

Artist photos on front cover (clockwise from top): Nickelback, Red Hot Chili Peppers, U2, Rush, Blink-182, Eric Clapton, ZZ Top, Limp Bizkit, Three Days Grace and Green Day.

Artist photos on back cover (top to bottom): Good Charlotte, Seether, Fall Out Boy, Van Halen, Alanis Morissette and John Mellencamp.

A special thanks to my Record Research staff: Paul Haney, Jeanne Olynick, Brent Olynick, Kim Bloxdorf and Fran Whitburn.

RESEARCHING BILLBOARD'S
ROCK TRACKS CHARTS

This is the third edition of **Rock Tracks** which is compiled from *Billboard's* "Mainstream Rock Tracks" and "Modern Rock Tracks" charts. *Billboard* published its first rock tracks chart in 1981 and titled it simply "Top Tracks." It was a weekly Top 60 airplay chart compiled from rock radio as indicated by the nation's leading album-oriented and top track stations.

What is a track? In an article explaining this new chart, *Billboard's* Mike Harrison said "Quite simply, a track is an individual song played on the raw merits of its popularity regardless of its mechanical configuration (meaning regardless of whether it is a 45 rpm single, LP cut or whatever)." *Billboard* continues to regard a track by this same definition, although today's mechanical configuration is generally CD album tracks or CD singles.

Below is a brief history of both rock tracks charts:

MAINSTREAM ROCK TRACKS

DEBUT DATE	CHART TITLE	POSITIONS	NOTES
3/21/81	**TOP TRACKS**	60	Weekly chart; first #1 track: "I Can't Stand It" by Eric Clapton
9/15/84	**TOP ROCK TRACKS**	60	Chart title changed to include Rock
10/20/84	**TOP ROCK TRACKS**	50	Chart reduced to a Top 50
4/12/86	**ALBUM ROCK TRACKS**	50	Chart title changed to include Album
11/23/91	**ALBUM ROCK TRACKS**	50	Began using actual monitored airplay (Broadcast Data Systems*) only to compile the chart
6/27/92	**ALBUM ROCK TRACKS**	40	Chart reduced to a Top 40
4/13/96	**MAINSTREAM ROCK TRACKS**	40	Chart title changed to Mainstream

MODERN ROCK TRACKS

DEBUT DATE	CHART TITLE	POSITIONS	NOTES
9/10/88	**MODERN ROCK TRACKS**	30	Weekly chart; first #1 track: "Peek-A-Boo" by Siouxsie And The Banshees
6/12/93	**MODERN ROCK TRACKS**	30	Began using a combination of actual monitored airplay (Broadcast Data Systems*) and radio station playlists to compile the chart
1/22/94	**MODERN ROCK TRACKS**	30	Began using actual monitored airplay (Broadcast Data Systems*) only to compile the chart
9/10/94	**MODERN ROCK TRACKS**	40	Chart increased to a Top 40.

*BDS is a subsidiary of *Billboard* that electronically monitors actual radio airplay. They have installed monitors throughout the country which track the airplay of songs 24 hours a day, seven days a week. These monitors can identify each song played by an encoded audio "fingerprint."

The focal point of **Rock Tracks** is contained in one thoroughly researched combined artist section. This section contains all of the songs that hit the "Mainstream Rock Tracks" and "Modern Rock Tracks" charts. Each artist's charted tracks are listed in chronological order, but there are some exceptions. In addition to listing tracks chronologically, all tracks that charted from the same album are grouped together. Listing same-album tracks together takes precedence over chronological order.

EXPLANATION OF COLUMNAR HEADINGS

Debut: Date first charted.

Cht: Chart identification: **℞** = **Mainstream Rock** / **Ⓜ** = **Modern Rock**

Peak: Highest charted position (highlighted in bold type). All #1 tracks are identified by a special #1 symbol (**❶**).

Wks: Total weeks charted.

Hot Pos: Peak position achieved on *Billboard's* "Hot 100" or "Bubbling Under The Hot 100" Pop Charts (the weeks at #1, #2 or #3 are shown as a superior number next to the position). Also includes the peak position of non-Hot 100 hits from *Billboard's* Hot 100 Airplay chart.

ALBUM TITLE: Title of the album from which the track attained its airplay appears in italics. If the track is from a movie or television **Soundtrack** album the title is preceded by **St:**. If the track is from a **Various Artistis** album, the title is preceded by **VA:**. Some tracks were only available as *(single only)* or *(download only)*.

ALBUM LABEL & NUMBER: Original label and number of album.

EXPLANATION OF SYMBOLS

2^3 Superior number to the right of the #1, #2 or #3 peak position is the total weeks the track held that position

+   Indicates that track peaked in the year after it first charted

↑   Indicates the weeks charted data is subject to change since the track was still charted as of the 3/29/2008 cut-off date

LETTERS IN BRACKETS AFTER TITLES:

[C] - Comedy Recording
[F] - Foreign Language Recording
[I] - Instrumental Recording
[L] - Live Recording

[N] - Novelty Recording
[R] - Re-entry, reissue, remix or re-recording of a previously charted track by that artist
[X] - Christmas Recording

ARTIST BIOGRAPHIES

Below every artist name is a brief biography of that artist. For this book, an extra effort was made to list each band's members, their instruments and where the band was formed. Individual birthdates are also listed for many of the major artists. With the ever-changing lineups of many bands, each band's members are listed at the time of their charted track(s). Mention is made of a band's earlier members if their history is related to or included within this book. The classifications (rock, pop, etc.) of the artists are very broad since musical labels are very subjective and these definitions evolve over time. Also true in many cases, a particular category may not fit a band whose sound changes during its career.

TITLE NOTES

Directly under some track titles are notes indicating backing vocalists, guest instrumentalists, the name of a famous songwriter or producer, etc. Duets and other important name variations are shown in bold capital letters. All movie, TV and album titles, and other major works, are shown in italics. In the title notes "Bubbled Under" refers to *Billboard's Bubbling Under The Hot 100* chart.

ARTISTS CROSS REFERENCED IN BOLD TYPE

Names of artists and groups mentioned in the biographies and title notes of other rock track artists are highlighted in bold type if they have their own track listings elsewhere in this book. For example, **Eddie Vedder** is bold in the Pearl Jam artist biography which indicates that Eddie Vedder has his own track listings. A name is only made bold the <u>first</u> time it appears in an artist's biography.

You will find this to be an extremely useful feature in tracing the integral history of many of these artists. For a good example of this, see Whitesnake.

TOP TRACKS AT A GLANCE

The following four features help quickly identify an artist's top charted tracks:

- Every #1 track is identified by a special #1 symbol (**❶**).

- Every #1 track is shaded with a light gray background.

- Artists with 5 or more charted tracks have their highest-charted track identified by a heavy underscore below the track title. Ties among an artist's top tracks are broken based on total weeks at the peak position, total weeks in the Top 10, total weeks in the Top 20 and total weeks charted.

- Listed in bold type right below the artist's biography in rank order are:
  the Top 3 track of every artist with 10 to 19 charted tracks and
  the Top 5 tracks of every artist with 20 or more charted tracks.

PICTURES OF THE TOP 50 ARTISTS

An album cover photo for each of the Top 50 artists is shown next to their listing in the artist section. Their overall ranking is listed to the right of their name.

WHAT'S NEW WITH THIS EDITION

The following new features are included in this third edition of *Rock Tracks*.

COMBINED ARTIST SECTION

Both **Mainstream Rock** and **Modern Rock** chart data has now been merged into one comprehensive, artist-by-artist listing in the main body of this book. Look for the special symbols (**®** = **Mainstream Rock** and **Ⓜ** = **Modern Rock**) to designate which chart(s) each track hit. If a track hit both charts, the highest charting will always be listed first.

ARTIST RANKINGS

Decade and All-Time artist rankings are now shown directly to the right of each artist name for easy reference.

ARTIST AND SONG AWARDS

All artist awards are now shown directly after each bio. These awards include Rock & Roll Hall of Fame, Billboard Century Award and Grammy's Best New Artist, Lifetime Achievement and Trustees awards. Individual song awards include Grammy, Oscar, Rock & Roll Hall of Fame and Rolling Stone 500 (RS500) honors.

CLASSIC ROCK TRACKS SECTION

This expanded section now includes the album titles from which the selected tracks first appeared.

COMBINED ARTIST SECTION

Lists, alphabetically by artist name, every track that <u>debuted</u> on *Billboard's* "Mainstream Rock Tracks" charts from March 21, 1981, through March 29, 2008, and "Modern Rock Tracks" charts from September 10,1988, through March 29, 2008.

Billboard				ARTIST		Hot		
Debut	Cht	Peak	Wks	Track Title	ℝ=Mainstream Rock ℳ=Modern Rock	Pos	Album Title	Album Label & Number

A

ABANDONED POOLS

Born Thomas Walter on 10/30/1970 in Pasadena, California. Male singer/songwriter/multi-instrumentalist. Former bassist for the **Eels**.

| 3/16/02 | ℳ | 27 | 11 | The Remedy | — | Humanistic | Warner 48106 |

ABC

Electro-pop band from Sheffield, Yorkshire, England: Martin Fry (vocals), Mark White (guitar), Stephen Singleton (sax), Mark Lickley (bass) and David Palmer (drums). Alan Spenner replaced Lickley in 1983. Andy Newkirk replaced Palmer in 1983.

| 10/16/82 | ℝ | 32 | 1 | 1 The Look Of Love (Part One) | 18 | The Lexicon Of Love | Mercury 4059 |
| 2/4/84 | ℝ | 35 | 2 | 2 That Was Then But This Is Now | 89 | Beauty Stab | Mercury 814661 |

ACCEPT

Hard-rock band from Solingen, Germany: Udo Dirkschneider (vocals), Wolf Hoffmann (guitar), Hermann Frank (guitar), Peter Baltes (bass) and Stefan Kaufmann (drums).

| 2/25/84 | ℝ | 21 | 5 | Balls To The Wall | — | Balls To The Wall | Portrait 39241 |

ACCEPTANCE

Alternative-rock band from Seattle, Washington: Jason Vena (vocals), Christain McAlhaney (guitar), Kaylan Cloyd (guitar), Ryan Zwiefelhofer (bass) and Nick Radovanovic (drums).

| 4/2/05 | ℳ | 25 | 12 | Different | — | Phantoms | Columbia 89016 |

AC/DC

ℝ **All-Time: #29**

Hard-rock band formed in Sydney, Australia: brothers Angus Young (guitar; born on 3/31/1955) and Malcolm Young (guitar; born on 1/6/1953), Ron Belford "Bon" Scott (vocals; born on 7/9/1946; died of alcohol abuse on 2/19/1980, age 33), Mark Evans (bass; born on 3/2/1956) and Phil Rudd (drums; born on 5/19/1954). Scott and the Young brothers were born in Scotland. Cliff Williams (born on 12/14/1949) replaced Evans in 1977. Brian Johnson (born on 10/5/1947) joined as lead singer after Scott's death. Simon Wright (born on 6/19/1963) replaced Rudd in 1985. Wright joined **Dio** in 1989, replaced by Chris Slade (born on 10/30/1946) of **The Firm**. Rudd returned in 1995; replacing Slade. Group made a cameo concert appearance in the 1997 movie *Private Parts*. Also see **Classic Rock Tracks** section.

AWARD: R&R Hall of Fame: 2003

TOP HITS: 1)Stiff Upper Lip 2)Hard As A Rock 3)Big Gun 4)Moneytalks 5)Dirty Deeds Done Dirt Cheap

3/28/81	ℝ	50	1	1 Hells Bells	—	Back In Black	Atlantic 16018
3/28/81	ℝ	51	2	2 Back In Black	37	↓	
				R&R Hall of Fame ★ RS500 #187			
4/11/81	ℝ	60	1	3 Shoot To Thrill	—	↓	
4/11/81	ℝ	4	17	4 Dirty Deeds Done Dirt Cheap	—	Dirty Deeds Done Dirt Cheap	Atlantic 16033
4/18/81	ℝ	26	7	5 Big Balls	—	↓	
				above 2 recorded in 1975 (vocals by Bon Scott)			
12/5/81+	ℝ	4	18	6 For Those About To Rock (We Salute You)	—	For Those About To Rock We Salute You	Atlantic 11111
12/19/81+	ℝ	9	15	7 Let's Get It Up	44	↓	
12/19/81+	ℝ	38	14	8 Put The Finger On You	—	↓	
9/3/83	ℝ	26	8	9 Flick Of The Switch	—	Flick Of The Switch	Atlantic 80100
9/24/83	ℝ	37	4	10 Guns For Hire	84	↓	
11/3/84	ℝ	33	11	11 Jailbreak	—	'74 Jailbreak	Atlantic 80178
				recorded in 1974 (vocals by Bon Scott)			
8/31/85	ℝ	44	4	12 Sink The Pink	—	Fly On The Wall	Atlantic 81263
5/31/86	ℝ	23	12	13 Who Made Who	—	Who Made Who	Atlantic 81650
2/6/88	ℝ	20	12	14 Heatseeker	—	Blow Up Your Video	Atlantic 81828
4/30/88	ℝ	28	7	15 That's The Way I Wanna Rock N Roll	—	↓	
9/29/90	ℝ	5	10	16 Thunderstruck	—	The Razors Edge	Atco 91413
11/10/90+	ℝ	3[1]	18	17 Moneytalks	23	↓	
3/9/91	ℝ	16	10	18 Are You Ready	—	↓	
10/31/92	ℝ	29	4	19 Highway To Hell [L]	—	Live	Atco 92215
				studio version was a #47 pop hit in 1979 (vocals by Bon Scott)			
6/5/93	ℝ	①[2]	20	20 Big Gun	65	St: Last Action Hero	Columbia 57127
9/23/95	ℝ	①[3]	24	21 Hard As A Rock	—	Ballbreaker	EastWest 61780
12/2/95+	ℝ	9	15	22 Cover You In Oil	—	↓	
3/16/96	ℝ	25	8	23 Ballbreaker	—	↓	
11/1/97	ℝ	6	15	24 Dirty Eyes	—	Bonfire	EastWest 62119
				recorded in 1977 (vocals by Bon Scott); early version of "Whole Lotta Rosie" which appeared on their 1977 album *Let There Be Rock*			
2/19/00	ℝ	①[4]	23	25 Stiff Upper Lip	115	Stiff Upper Lip	EastWest 62494
6/3/00	ℝ	7	20	26 Satellite Blues	—	↓	
9/16/00	ℝ	22	9	27 Meltdown	—	↓	
3/31/01	ℝ	21	10	28 Safe In New York City	—	↓	

ACE OF BASE

Pop-dance band from Gothenburg, Sweden: vocalists/sisters Jenny and Linn Berggren with keyboardists Jonas "Joker" Berggren (their brother) and Ulf "Buddha" Ekberg.

Debut	Cht	Peak	Wks	Track Title	Hot Pos	Album Title	Label & Number
9/18/93	Ⓜ	17	7	All That She Wants..	2³	The Sign...Arista 18740	

ADAMS, Bryan   Ⓡ 1980s: #7 / All-Time: #23

Born on 11/5/1959 in Kingston, Ontario, Canada (to British parents). Rock singer/songwriter/guitarist. Lead singer of Sweeney Todd from 1976-77. Teamed with Jim Vallance in 1978 in successful songwriting partnership. Cameo appearance as a gas station attendant in the 1989 movie *Pink Cadillac*.

TOP HITS: 1)Run To You 2)Somebody 3)Can't Stop This Thing We Started 4)Heat Of The Night 5)Lonely Nights

Debut	Cht	Peak	Wks	Track Title	Hot Pos	Album Title	Label & Number
1/23/82	Ⓡ	3¹	16	1 Lonely Nights..	84	*You Want It, You Got It*.................................A&M 4864	
4/3/82	Ⓡ	15	11	2 Fits Ya Good	—	↓	
2/12/83	Ⓡ	6	24	3 Cuts Like A Knife..	15	*Cuts Like A Knife* ....A&M 4919	
2/19/83	Ⓡ	21	14	4 Take Me Back...	—	↓	
2/19/83	Ⓡ	44	3	5 The Only One	—	↓	
3/5/83	Ⓡ	26	9	6 I'm Ready..	—	↓	
6/4/83	Ⓡ	32	7	7 Straight From The Heart	10	↓	
8/13/83	Ⓡ	21	10	8 This Time	24	↓	
1/28/84	Ⓡ	9	9	9 Heaven..	—	*St: A Night In Heaven* ....A&M 4966	
				also see #15 below			
11/3/84	Ⓡ	❶⁴	15	10 Run To You	6	*Reckless* ....A&M 5013	
11/24/84	Ⓡ	7	25	11 It's Only Love..	15	↓	
				BRYAN ADAMS & TINA TURNER			
12/8/84	Ⓡ	40	8	12 Summer Of '69	5	↓	
12/15/84+	Ⓡ	42	6	13 Kids Wanna Rock	—	↓	
1/19/85	Ⓡ	❶²	16	14 Somebody	11	↓	
4/27/85	Ⓡ	27	8	15 Heaven... [R]	❶²	↓	
				same version as #9 above			
8/31/85	Ⓡ	7	12	16 One Night Love Affair	13	↓	
7/13/85	Ⓡ	21	10	17 Diana..	—	*(single only)* ....A&M 256	
				only available as a British import single			
12/28/85+	Ⓡ	31	3	18 Christmas Time .... [X]	—	*(single only)* ....A&M 8651	
3/28/87	Ⓡ	2²	11	19 Heat Of The Night	6	*Into The Fire* ....A&M 3907	
4/11/87	Ⓡ	33	4	20 Another Day	—	↓	
4/18/87	Ⓡ	6	16	21 Into The Fire...	—	↓	
5/30/87	Ⓡ	3¹	12	22 Hearts On Fire...	26	↓	
8/8/87	Ⓡ	10	9	23 Victim Of Love	32	↓	
9/8/90	Ⓡ	7	9	24 Young Lust...	7	*VA: The Wall - Live In Berlin*.................Mercury 846611	
				recorded on 7/21/1990 at the Berlin Wall; first recorded by **Pink Floyd** *in 1979*			
6/29/91	Ⓡ	10	10	25 (Everything I Do) I Do It For You	❶⁷	*St: Robin Hood: Prince Of Thieves*...Morgan Creek 20004	
9/14/91	Ⓡ	2²	16	26 Can't Stop This Thing We Started..........................	2¹	*Waking Up The Neighbours*..........................A&M 5367	
12/7/91+	Ⓡ	6	13	27 There Will Never Be Another Tonight....................	31	↓	
3/7/92	Ⓡ	14	8	28 Thought I'd Died And Gone To Heaven.................	13	↓	
5/2/92	Ⓡ	13	8	29 Touch The Hand	—	↓	
2/7/98	Ⓡ	38	2	30 Back To You .... [L]	42ᴬ	*MTV Unplugged* ....A&M 540831	
				recorded on 9/26/1997 at the Hammerstein Ballroom in New York City			

ADDICT

Rock band from London, England: Mark Aston (vocals), Nikolaj Juel (guitar), James Denham (bass) and Luke Bullen (drums).

Debut	Cht	Peak	Wks	Track Title	Hot Pos	Album Title	Label & Number
5/23/98	Ⓡ	24	13	1 Monster Side...	—	*Stones* ....Big Cat 81845	
12/26/98	Ⓡ	39	4	2 Nobody Knows	—	↓	

ADEMA

Hard-rock band from Bakersfield, California: Mark Chavez (vocals), Mike Ransom (guitar), Tim Fluckey (guitar), Dave DeRoo (bass) and Kris Kohls (drums). Chavez is the half-brother of Jonathan Davis (of **Korn**). Ransom left in 2004. Luke Caraccioli replaced Chavez in late 2004. Bobby Reeves replaced Caraccioli in late 2005.

Debut	Cht	Peak	Wks			Hot Pos	Album Title	Label & Number
7/14/01	Ⓜ	14	25	1	Giving In	—	Adema	Arista 14696
7/14/01	Ⓡ	16	23					
12/8/01+	Ⓜ	15	25	2	The Way You Like It	—	↓	
12/15/01+	Ⓡ	21	24					
6/8/02	Ⓡ	25	10	3	Freaking Out	—	↓	
6/29/02	Ⓜ	36	6					
7/19/03	Ⓡ	25	11	4	Unstable	—	Unstable	Arista 53914
8/16/03	Ⓜ	37	4					

ADORABLE

Rock band formed in Coventry, England: Pior Fijalkowski (vocals), Robert Dillam (guitar), Wil (bass) and Kevin Gritton (drums).

Debut	Cht	Peak	Wks			Hot Pos	Album Title	Label & Number
6/26/93	Ⓜ	29	1		Sunshine Smile	—	Against Perfection	Creation 81416

ADRENALIN

Rock band from Detroit, Michigan: Marc Gilbert (vocals), brothers Mike Romeo (guitar) and Jim Romeo (sax), brothers Mark Pastoria (keyboards) and Brian Pastoria (drums), Mike "Flash" Haggerty (guitar) and Bruce Schafer (bass).

Debut	Cht	Peak	Wks			Hot Pos	Album Title	Label & Number
7/28/84	Ⓡ	28	5		Faraway Eyes	—	American Heart	Rocshire 9517

ADVENTURES, The

Pop band from Belfast, Ireland: Terry Sharpe (male vocals), husband-and-wife Patrick Gribben (guitar) and Eileen Gribben (female vocals), Gerard "Spud" Murphy (guitar), Tony Ayre (bass) and Paul Crowder (drums).

Debut	Cht	Peak	Wks			Hot Pos	Album Title	Label & Number
4/16/88	Ⓡ	39	5		Broken Land	95	The Sea Of Love	Elektra 60772

AEROSMITH

1980s: #40 / 1990s: #2 / 2000s: #37 / All-Time: #4

Hard-rock band formed in Boston, Massachusetts: **Steven Tyler** (vocals; born on 3/26/1948), **Joe Perry** (guitar; born on 9/10/1950), Brad Whitford (guitar; born on 2/23/1952), Tom Hamilton (bass; born on 12/31/1951) and Joey Kramer (drums; born on 6/21/1950). Perry left in 1979; replaced by Jimmy Crespo. Whitford left in 1981; replaced by Rick Dufay. Original band reunited in April 1984. Tyler is the father of actresses/models Liv Tyler and Mia Tyler. Liv married Royston Langdon (of **Spacehog**) on 3/25/2003. Mia was married to Dave Buckner (of **Papa Roach**) from 2003-05. Band appeared in the movies *Sgt. Pepper's Lonely Hearts Club Band* and *Wayne's World 2*. Also see **Classic Rock Tracks** section.

AWARD: R&R Hall of Fame: 2001

TOP HITS: 1)Livin' On The Edge 2)Cryin' 3)Jaded 4)Falling In Love (Is Hard On The Knees) 5)Deuces Are Wild

Debut	Cht	Peak	Wks			Hot Pos	Album Title	Label & Number
10/9/82	Ⓡ	21	9	1	Lightning Strikes	—	Rock In A Hard Place	Columbia 38061
11/2/85	Ⓡ	18	10	2	Let The Music Do The Talking	—	Done With Mirrors	Geffen 24091
12/21/85+	Ⓡ	20	10	3	Shela	—	↓	
8/29/87	Ⓡ	4	10	4	Dude (Looks Like A Lady)	14	Permanent Vacation	Geffen 24162
9/12/87	Ⓡ	12	18	5	Rag Doll	17	↓	
11/14/87	Ⓡ	14	12	6	Hangman Jury	—	↓	
1/30/88	Ⓡ	2³	14	7	Angel	3²	↓	
5/21/88	Ⓡ	42	4	8	Magic Touch	—	↓	
1/23/88	Ⓡ	44	2	9	Rocking Pneumonia And The Boogie Woogie Flu ...	—	St: Less Than Zero	Def Jam 44042
					#52 Pop hit for Huey Smith & The Clowns in 1957			
11/26/88+	Ⓡ	13	12	10	Chip Away The Stone	77	Gems	Columbia 44487
					recorded in 1978			
9/2/89	Ⓡ	❶²	11	11	Love In An Elevator	5	Pump	Geffen 24254
9/23/89	Ⓡ	2¹	18	12	Janie's Got A Gun	4	↓	
					Grammy: Rock Vocal Group			
11/25/89+	Ⓡ	14	9	13	F.I.N.E. (Fucked-up, Insecure, Neurotic, Emotional)	—	↓	
1/13/90	Ⓡ	❶¹	19	14	What It Takes	9	↓	
4/14/90	Ⓡ	17	9	15	Monkey On My Back	—	↓	
6/16/90	Ⓡ	❶²	16	16	The Other Side	22	↓	
8/25/90	Ⓡ	27	6	17	Love Me Two Times	—	St: Air America	MCA 6467
					#25 Pop hit for The Doors in 1968			
11/16/91	Ⓡ	21	4	18	Helter Skelter	—	Pandora's Box	Columbia 46209
					first recorded by The Beatles in 1968			
12/7/91	Ⓡ	36	17	19	Sweet Emotion	36	↓	
					above 2 recorded in 1975			
4/10/93	Ⓡ	❶⁹	20	20	Livin' On The Edge	18	Get A Grip	Geffen 24455
					Grammy: Rock Vocal Group			
5/1/93	Ⓡ	5	18	21	Eat The Rich	—	↓	
6/5/93	Ⓡ	❶⁶	20	22	Cryin'	12	↓	
9/4/93	Ⓡ	5	10	23	Fever	—	↓	
10/30/93	Ⓡ	3⁷	24	24	Amazing	24	↓	

Billboard				ARTIST	Track Title	Ⓡ=Mainstream Rock Ⓜ=Modern Rock	Hot Pos	Album Title	Album Label & Number
Debut	Cht	Peak	Wks						
				AEROSMITH — cont'd					
5/21/94	Ⓡ	7	14	25	Crazy		17	↓	
					Grammy: Rock Vocal Group				
1/15/94	Ⓡ	❶⁴	26	26	**Deuces Are Wild**		—	*VA: The Beavis & Butt-Head Experience*...Geffen 24613	
11/5/94	Ⓡ	3¹	16	27	Blind Man		48	*Big Ones* ...Geffen 24716	
1/28/95	Ⓡ	16	7	28	Walk On Water		—	↓	
3/1/97	Ⓡ	❶⁵	26	29	Falling In Love (Is Hard On The Knees)		35	*Nine Lives* ...Columbia 67547	
4/19/97	Ⓡ	37	1	30	Nine Lives		—	↓	
5/10/97	Ⓡ	4	17	31	Hole In My Soul		51	↓	
5/17/97	Ⓡ	❶⁴	29	32	Pink		27	↓	
					Grammy: Rock Vocal Group				
12/13/97+	Ⓡ	3²	19	33	Taste Of India		❶⁴	↓	
5/30/98	Ⓡ	4	24	34	I Don't Want To Miss A Thing		❶⁴	*St: Armageddon* ...Columbia 69440	
7/25/98	Ⓡ	4	22	35	What Kind Of Love Are You On		—	↓	
10/28/00	Ⓡ	4	14	36	Angel's Eye		—	*St: Charlie's Angels*...Columbia 61064	
1/27/01	Ⓡ	❶⁵	26	37	Jaded		7	*Just Push Play* ...Columbia 62088	
5/5/01	Ⓡ	10	15	38	Just Push Play		—	↓	
10/27/01	Ⓡ	23	10	39	Sunshine		—	↓	
6/1/02	Ⓡ	25	11	40	Girls Of Summer		—	*O, Yeah! Ultimate Aerosmith Hits* ...Columbia 86700	
3/20/04	Ⓡ	7	18	41	Baby, Please Don't Go		—	*Honkin' On Bobo*...Columbia 87025	
					blues standard written and first recorded by Big Joe Williams in 1935				
9/30/06	Ⓡ	15	15	42	Devil's Got A New Disguise		—	*Devil's Got A New Disguise: The Very Best Of Aerosmith*...Geffen 00867	

AFGHAN WHIGS, The
Rock band from Cincinnati, Ohio: Greg Dulli (vocals), Rick McCollum (guitar), John Curley (bass) and Steve Earle (drums). Paul Buchignani replaced Earle in 1995.

11/6/93	Ⓜ	18	13	1	Debonair	—	*Gentlemen* ...Elektra 61501
3/9/96	Ⓜ	29	5	2	Honky's Ladder	—	*Black Love* ...Elektra 61896

AFI   Ⓜ **2000s: #38 / All-Time: #81**
Hardcore punk-rock band formed in Ukiah, California: Davey "Havok" Marchand (vocals), Jade Puget (guitar), Hunter Burgan (bass) and Adam Carson (drums). AFI: A Fire Inside. Marchand and Puget also recorded as **Blaqk Audio**.

2/15/03	Ⓜ	7	23	1	Girl's Not Grey	114	*Sing The Sorrow*...Nitro 450380
3/15/03	Ⓡ	33	10				
7/5/03	Ⓜ	16	18	2	The Leaving Song Pt. II	—	↓
8/2/03	Ⓡ	31	10				
12/6/03+	Ⓜ	7	26	3	Silver And Cold	—	↓
1/17/04	Ⓡ	39	2				
5/6/06	Ⓜ	❶⁵	26	4	Miss Murder	24	*Decemberunderground*...Tiny Evil 006854
6/3/06	Ⓡ	13	20				
10/7/06	Ⓜ	4	22	5	Love Like Winter	68	↓
3/17/07	Ⓜ	17	11	6	The Missing Frame	—	↓

AFROMAN
Born Joseph Foreman on 7/28/1974 in Los Angeles, California; later based in Hattiesburg, Mississippi. Novelty rapper/songwriter.

8/18/01	Ⓜ	17	8		Because I Got High	[N]	13	*The Good Times*...Universal 014979

AFTER THE FIRE
Rock band from England: Andy Piercy (vocals, bass), John Russell (guitar), **Peter Banks** (keyboards) and Pete King (drums). Banks was a member of **Yes**.

3/5/83	Ⓡ	4	12		Der Kommissar	5	*ATF* ...Epic 38282
					also see **Falco**'s *original German version*		

AGAINST ME!
Punk-rock band from Gainesville, Florida: Tom Gabel (vocals, guitar), James Bowman (guitar), Andrew Seward (bass) and Warren Oakes (drums).

8/11/07	Ⓜ	11	20	1	Thrash Unreal	—	*New Wave* ...Sire 101304
2/23/08	Ⓜ	31↑	6↑	2	Stop	—	↓

AGENTS OF GOOD ROOTS
Rock band from Richmond, Virginia: Andrew Winn (vocals, guitar), J.C. Kuhl (sax), Stewart Myers (bass) and Brian Jones (drums).

4/18/98	Ⓜ	37	4		Come On	—	*One By One* ...RCA 67590

Billboard				ARTIST		Hot		
Debut	Cht	Peak	Wks	Track Title	®=Mainstream Rock ⓜ=Modern Rock	Pos	Album Title	Album Label & Number

AIRBOURNE
Rock band from Warrnambool, Victoria, Australia: brothers Joel O'Keeffe (vocals, guitar) and Ryan O'Keeffe (drums), with David Roads (guitar) and Justin Street (bass).

12/8/07+	®	16	17↑	Too Much, Too Young, Too Fast	—	Runnin' Wild	Roadrunner 7963

ALARM, The
Rock band from Rhyl, Wales: Mike Peters (vocals; born on 2/25/1959), Dave Sharp (guitar; born on 1/28/1959), Eddie MacDonald (bass; born on 11/1/1959) and Nigel Twist (drums; born on 7/18/1958).

TOP HITS: 1)Sold Me Down The River 2)Rain In The Summertime 3)The Road

3/31/84	®	39	5	1 Sixty Eight Guns	106	Declaration	I.R.S. 70608
11/2/85+	®	12	15	2 Strength	61	Strength	I.R.S. 5666
2/15/86	®	29	9	3 Spirit Of '76	—	↓	
10/31/87	®	6	15	4 Rain In The Summertime	71	Eye Of The Hurricane	I.R.S. 42061
2/20/88	®	16	11	5 Presence Of Love	77	↓	
6/18/88	®	35	5	6 Rescue Me ....[L]	—	Electric Folklore Live	I.R.S. 39108
9/9/89	®	2²	17	7 Sold Me Down The River	50	Change	I.R.S. 82018
9/16/89	ⓜ	3²	11				
12/2/89+	®	9	11	8 Devolution Workin' Man Blues	—	↓	
11/25/89	ⓜ	11	8				
2/10/90	®	33	7	9 Love Don't Come Easy	—	↓	
11/3/90	ⓜ	7	11	10 The Road	—	Standards	I.R.S. 13056
11/3/90	®	16	11				
5/11/91	ⓜ	15	5	11 Raw	—	Raw	I.R.S. 13087
5/11/91	®	29	7				

ALIAS
Rock band formed in Los Angeles, California: former **Sheriff** members Freddy Curci (vocals) and Steve DeMarchi (guitar), with former **Heart** members Roger Fisher (guitar), Steve Fossen (bass) and Mike Derosier (drums).

6/30/90	®	18	9	Haunted Heart	—	Alias	EMI 93908

ALICE IN CHAINS ® 1990s: #9 / All-Time: #42 ★ ⓜ All-Time: #86
Male hard-rock band formed in Seattle, Washington: Layne Staley (vocals; born on 8/22/1967; died of a drug overdose on 4/5/2002, age 34), **Jerry Cantrell** (guitar; born on 3/18/1966), Mike Starr (bass; born on 4/4/1966) and Sean Kinney (drums; born on 5/27/1966). Starr replaced by Mike Inez (former bassist for **Ozzy Osbourne**; born on 5/14/1966) in late 1993. Inez also recorded with **Slash's Snakepit**. Staley also recorded with **Mad Season** and **Class Of '99**. Scott Olson (guitar) joined in 1996.

TOP HITS: 1)No Excuses 2)Heaven Beside You 3)Get Born Again 4)Over Now 5)Rooster

4/13/91	®	18	20	1 Man In The Box	—	Facelift	Columbia 46075
				also see #20 below			
9/14/91	®	27	9	2 Sea Of Sorrow	—	↓	
8/8/92	®	31	8	3 Would?	—	St: Singles	Epic 52476
				also see #17 below			
10/17/92	®	24	9	4 Them Bones	—	Dirt	Columbia 52475
11/28/92	ⓜ	30	1				
1/30/93	ⓜ	27	3	5 Angry Chair	—	↓	
1/30/93	®	34	5				
3/13/93	®	7	20	6 Rooster	—	↓	
10/2/93	®	10	21	7 Down In A Hole	—	↓	
7/3/93	®	19	12	8 What The Hell Have I	—	St: Last Action Hero	Columbia 57127
2/12/94	®	❶²	26	9 No Excuses	48ᴬ	Jar Of Flies	Columbia 57628
2/12/94	ⓜ	3³	16				
5/14/94	®	10	26	10 I Stay Away	—	↓	
10/29/94	®	25	7	11 Don't Follow	—	↓	
12/31/94+	®	7	21	12 Got Me Wrong	—	St: Clerks	Columbia 66660
12/10/94+	ⓜ	22	14				
10/21/95	®	7	16	13 Grind	—	Alice In Chains	Columbia 67248
10/28/95	ⓜ	18	13				
12/23/95+	®	3¹	26	14 Heaven Beside You	52ᴬ	↓	
1/13/96	ⓜ	6	18				

Debut	Cht	Peak	Wks	ARTIST / Track Title		Hot Pos	Album Title	Album Label & Number

Billboard

| | | | | ARTIST | ⓡ=Mainstream Rock ⓜ=Modern Rock | **Hot** | | |
| Debut | Cht | Peak | Wks | Track Title | | Pos | Album Title | Album Label & Number |

ALICE IN CHAINS — cont'd

5/11/96	ⓡ	8	26	15 **Again**		—	↓	
6/15/96	ⓜ	36	6					
8/3/96	ⓡ	4	26	16 **Over Now** .... [L]		—	*MTV Unplugged* ....Columbia 67703	
8/24/96	ⓜ	24	14					
11/2/96	ⓡ	19	18	17 **Would?** .... [L-R]		—	↓	
				live version of #3 above; above 2 recorded on 4/10/1996 at the Majestic Theater in New York City				
6/12/99	ⓡ	4	19	18 **Get Born Again**		106	*Nothing Safe* ....Columbia 63649	
6/12/99	ⓜ	12	12					
10/30/99	ⓡ	11	14	19 **Fear The Voices**		—	*Music Bank* ....Columbia 69580	
12/30/00	ⓡ	39	2	20 **Man In The Box** .... [L-R]		—	*Live* ....Columbia 85274	
				live version of #1 above				

ALIEN ANT FARM

Rock band from Riverside, California: Dryden Mitchell (vocals), Terry Corso (guitar), Tye Zamora (bass) and Mike Cosgrove (drums).

2/10/01	ⓜ	18	32	1 **Movies**		—	*ANThology* ....New Noize 450293	
2/9/02	ⓡ	38	3					
6/9/01	ⓜ	❶[4]	27	2 **Smooth Criminal**		23	↓	
8/18/01	ⓡ	18	24	*#7 Pop hit for **Michael Jackson** in 1989*				
7/26/03	ⓜ	29	7	3 **These Days**		—	*truANT* ....El Tonal 000568	
8/9/03	ⓡ	38	1					

ALKALINE TRIO

Punk-rock trio from Chicago, Illinois: Matt Skiba (vocals, guitar), Daniel Andriano (bass) and Derek Grant (drums).

7/5/03	ⓜ	38	1	1 **We've Had Enough**		—	*Good Mourning* ....Vagrant 381	
7/9/05	ⓜ	40	1	2 **Time To Waste**		—	*Crimson* ....Vagrant 409	

ALL-AMERICAN REJECTS, The

Punk-rock band from Stillwater, Oklahoma: Tyson Ritter (vocals, bass), Nick Wheeler (guitar), Mike Kennerty (guitar) and Chris Gaylor (drums).

12/21/02+	ⓜ	8	23	1 **Swing, Swing**		60	*The All-American Rejects* ....Doghouse 450407	
5/24/03	ⓜ	29	8	2 **The Last Song**		—	↓	

ALLMAN, Gregg, Band

Born on 12/8/1947 in Nashville, Tennessee; raised in Daytona Beach, Florida. Rock singer/songwriter/keyboardist. Founding member of **The Allman Brothers Band**. Married to Cher from 1975-77. Played "Gaines" in the 1991 movie *Rush*. His band included brothers Dan Toler (guitar) and David Toler (drums), Tim Heding (keyboards), Chaz Trippy (percussion) and Bruce Waibel (bass; committed suicide on 9/2/2003, age 45). Also see **Classic Rock Tracks** section.

2/14/87	ⓡ	❶[1]	14	1 **I'm No Angel**		49	*I'm No Angel* ....Epic 40531	
4/18/87	ⓡ	3[1]	10	2 **Anything Goes**		—	↓	
6/20/87	ⓡ	25	8	3 **Can't Keep Running**		—	↓	
7/9/88	ⓡ	3[2]	12	4 **Can't Get Over You**		—	*Just Before The Bullets Fly* ....Epic 44033	
10/1/88	ⓡ	17	8	5 **Slip Away**		—	↓	
				#6 Pop hit for Clarence Carter in 1968				

ALLMAN BROTHERS BAND, The

Southern-rock band formed in Macon, Georgia. Original lineup: brothers **Gregg Allman** (vocals, organ) and Duane Allman (lead guitar), **Dickey Betts** (guitar), Berry Oakley (bass), with Butch Trucks and Jai Johnny Johanson (drums). Duane Allman died in a motorcycle crash on 10/29/1971 (age 24). Oakley died in a motorcycle crash on 11/11/1972 (age 24). Lineup in 1981: Gregg Allman, Betts, Trucks and Johanson, with David Goldflies (bass) and David Toler (drums). Lineup in 1990: Gregg Allman, Betts, Trucks and Johanson with Warren Hayes (guitar), Allen Woody (bass) and Johnny Neel (keyboards). Neel left in 1991; replaced by Mark Quinones. Hayes and Woody formed **Gov't Mule**. Woody died on 8/26/2000 (age 44). Also see **Classic Rock Tracks** section.

AWARD: R&R Hall of Fame: 1995

TOP HITS: 1)Good Clean Fun 2)End Of The Line 3)No One To Run With

8/15/81	ⓡ	11	15	1 **Straight From The Heart**		39	*Brothers Of The Road* ....Arista 9564	
6/24/89	ⓡ	26	5	2 **Statesboro Blues**		—	*Dreams* ....Polydor 839417	
				recorded in 1970				
7/7/90	ⓡ	❶[1]	16	3 **Good Clean Fun**		—	*Seven Turns* ....Epic 46144	
9/15/90	ⓡ	12	9	4 **Seven Turns**		—	↓	
12/22/90+	ⓡ	26	8	5 **It Ain't Over Yet**		—	↓	
7/6/91	ⓡ	2[1]	15	6 **End Of The Line**		—	*Shades Of Two Worlds* ....Epic 47877	
9/28/91	ⓡ	42	8	7 **Bad Rain**		—	↓	
5/7/94	ⓡ	7	15	8 **No One To Run With**		—	*Where It All Begins* ....Epic 64232	
9/3/94	ⓡ	29	6	9 **Back Where It All Begins**		—	↓	
4/12/03	ⓡ	37	7	10 **Firing Line**		—	*Hittin' The Note* ....Peach 84599	

Billboard				ARTIST		Hot		
Debut	Cht	Peak	Wks	Track Title	®=Mainstream Rock Ⓜ=Modern Rock	Pos	Album Title	Album Label & Number

ALMOND, Marc
Born Peter Mark Sinclair Almond on 7/9/1957 in Southport, Lancashire, England. Male singer/songwriter/multi-instrumentalist. Half of the **Soft Cell** duo.

12/10/88+	Ⓜ	8	12	Tears Run Rings		67	The Stars We Are .... Capitol 91042	

ALMOST, The
Alternative-rock band formed in Tampa Bay, Florida: Aaron Gillespie (vocals), Jay Vilardi (guitar), Alex Aponte (bass) and Kenny Bozich (drums). Gillespie is also the drummer for Underoath.

3/24/07	Ⓜ	7	26	Say This Sooner (No One Will See Things The Way I Do) .	111	Southern Weather .... Tooth & Nail 52481	
6/23/07	®	35	6				

ALTER BRIDGE
Rock band from Tallahassee, Florida: Myles Kennedy (vocals), Mark Tremonti (guitar), Brian Marshall (bass) and Scott Phillips (drums). The latter three were members of **Creed**.

7/10/04	®	2[1]	26	1 Open Your Eyes	123	One Day Remains .... Wind-Up 13097	
7/17/04	Ⓜ	24	14				
12/4/04+	®	7	17	2 Find The Real	—	↓	
4/23/05	®	29	6	3 Broken Wings	—	↓	
8/18/07	®	3[2]	26	4 Rise Today	—	Blackbird .... Universal Republic 009955	
11/10/07	Ⓜ	32	12				
2/2/08	®	19	9↑	5 Watch Over You	—	↓	

AMBROSIA
Pop band from Los Angeles, California: David Pack (vocals, guitar), Joe Puerta (vocals, bass), Christopher North (keyboards) and Burleigh Drummond (drums). Puerta later joined **Bruce Hornsby & The Range**.

5/29/82	®	44	2	For Openers (Welcome Home)	—	Road Island .... Warner 3638	

AMERICAN HI-FI
Male rock band from Boston, Massachusetts: Stacy Jones (vocals), Jaime Arentzen (guitar), Drew Parsons (bass) and Brian Nolan (drums). Jones was drummer with **Letters To Cleo**.

2/3/01	Ⓜ	5	26	1 Flavor Of The Weak	41	American Hi-Fi .... Island 542871	
7/28/01	Ⓜ	33	6	2 Another Perfect Day	—	↓	
2/1/03	Ⓜ	33	7	3 The Art Of Losing	—	The Art Of Losing .... Island 063657	

AMMONIA
Rock trio from Perth, Australia: Dave Johnstone (vocals, guitar), Simon Hensworth (bass) and Allan Balmont (drums).

3/30/96	Ⓜ	29	8	Drugs	—	Mint 400 .... Epic 67556	

AMOS, Tori
Born Myra Ellen Amos on 8/22/1963 in Newton, North Carolina; raised in Baltimore, Maryland. Adult Alternative singer/songwriter/pianist. First recorded in 1988 with rock group Y Kant Tori Read.

4/11/92	Ⓜ	27	4	1 Silent All These Years	65	Little Earthquakes .... Atlantic 82358	
6/13/92	Ⓜ	22	5	2 Crucify	—	↓	
1/29/94	Ⓜ	❶[2]	17	3 God	72	Under The Pink .... Atlantic 82567	
5/21/94	Ⓜ	12	12	4 Cornflake Girl	107	↓	
1/20/96	Ⓜ	13	13	5 Caught A Lite Sneeze	60	Boys For Pele .... Atlantic 82862	
4/25/98	Ⓜ	13	15	6 Spark	49	From The Choirgirl Hotel .... Atlantic 83095	

ANBERLIN
Alternative-rock band from Orlando, Florida: Stephen Christian (vocals), Joseph Milligan (guitar), Nathan Strayer (guitar), Deon Rexroat (bass) and Nathan Young (drums).

3/11/06	Ⓜ	38	2	Paperthin Hymn	—	Never Take Friendship .... Tooth & Nail 66607	

ANDERSON, Jon
Born on 10/25/1944 in Accrington, Lancashire, England. Rock singer/songwriter. Lead singer of **Yes**; one-half of **Jon & Vangelis** duo.

6/19/82	®	59	1	1 Olympia	—	Animation .... Atlantic 19355	
8/18/84	®	16	9	2 Cage Of Freedom	—	St: Metropolis .... Columbia 39526	

ANDERSON, Laurie
Born on 6/5/1947 in Glen Ellyn, Illinois. Avant-garde performance artist.

12/9/89+	Ⓜ	7	12	Babydoll	—	Strange Angels .... Warner 25900	

ANDERSON, Michael
Born in Grand Rapids, Michigan. Rock singer/songwriter.

6/18/88	®	17	9	Sound Alarm	—	Sound Alarm .... A&M 5203	

ANDERSON, BRUFORD, WAKEMAN, HOWE — see YES

	Cht	Peak	Wks	ARTIST / Track Title	Hot Pos	Album Title	Album Label & Number
Debut				ℝ=Mainstream Rock ⓜ=Modern Rock			

Legend note: ℝ=Mainstream Rock, ⓜ=Modern Rock

ANDREONE, Leah
Born on 5/24/1973 in San Diego, California. Female pop singer/pianist.

Debut	Cht	Peak	Wks	Track Title	Hot Pos	Album Title	Album Label & Number
11/16/96	ⓜ	39	2	It's Alright, It's OK	57	Veiled	RCA 66897

ANDREWS, Jake
Born on 4/16/1980 in Austin, Texas. Blues-rock singer/guitarist. Son of Mother Earth guitarist John Andrews.

5/8/99	ℝ	32	9	Time To Burn	—	Time To Burn	Jericho 90002

ANDREWS, Michael
Born in San Diego, California. Singer/songwriter.

2/28/04	ⓜ	30	9	Mad World	—	St: Donnie Darko	Universal 71802

MICHAEL ANDREWS Featuring Gary Jules
first recorded by **Tears For Fears** in 1983

ANGEL CITY
Hard-rock band from Sydney, Australia: Bernard "Doc" Neeson (vocals; born in Belfast, Ireland), brothers Rick Brewster and John Brewster (guitars), Jim Hilbun (bass) and Brent Eccles (drums).

1/26/85	ℝ	35	5	Underground	—	Two Minute Warning	MCA 5509

ANGELS AND AIRWAVES
Alternative-rock band formed in San Diego, California: Tom DeLonge (vocals, guitar), David Kennedy (guitar), Ryan Sinn (bass) and Adam "Atom" Willard (drums). DeLong is also a member of **Blink-182**. DeLong and Kennedy are also members of **Box Car Racer**. Sinn is also a member of **The Distillers**. Willard was a member of **The Offspring** from 2004-06. Sinn left in late 2007, replaced by Matt Wachter (of **30 Seconds To Mars**).

4/8/06	ⓜ	5	20	1 The Adventure	55	We Don't Need To Whisper	Suretone 006759
8/5/06	ⓜ	21	11	2 Do It For Me Now	—	↓	
11/4/06+	ⓜ	19	13	3 The War	—	↓	
9/22/07	ⓜ	11	20	4 Everything's Magic	104	I-Empire	Suretone 010101

ANIMAL BAG
Rock band from Charlotte, North Carolina: Luke Edwards (vocals, guitar), Rich Parris (guitar), Bill "Otis" Hughes (bass) and David "Boo" Duckworth (drums). Duckworth died of a drug overdose on 6/6/2002 (age 35).

4/17/93	ℝ	29	7	Everybody	—	Animal Bag	Stardog 512885

ANIMALS, The
Rock band from Newcastle, England: Eric Burdon (vocals), Hilton Valentine (guitar), Alan Price (keyboards), Bryan "Chas" Chandler (bass) and John Steel (drums). Chandler died of a heart attack on 7/17/1996 (age 57). Also see **Classic Rock Tracks** section.
AWARD: R&R Hall of Fame: 1994

8/27/83	ℝ	34	17	The Night	48	Ark	I.R.S. 70037

ANOTHER ANIMAL
Hard-rock band formed in Los Angeles, California: Whitfield Crane (vocals), Tony Rombola (guitar), Lee Richards (guitar), Robbie Merrill (bass) and Shannon Larkin (drums). Crane was a member of **Ugly Kid Joe**. Rombola, Merrill and Larkin are also members of **Godsmack**. Richards is also a member of **Dropbox**.

9/15/07+	ℝ	8	24	Broken Again	—	Another Animal	Universal Republic 009865

ANT, Adam
Born Stuart Goddard on 11/3/1954 in London, England. Romantic-punk rock singer/songwriter/actor. His band The Ants: Marco Pirroni (guitar), Terry Miall (percussion), Kevin Mooney (bass) and Chris Hughes (drums). Original Ants Matthew Ashman (guitar; died of diabetes on 11/21/1995, age 35), Lee Gorman (bass) and Dave Barbarossa (drums) left to join **Bow Wow Wow** in 1980. Ant went solo in 1982. Acted in several movies and TV shows.

3/28/81	ℝ	15	6	1 Dog Eat Dog	—	Kings Of The Wild Frontier	Epic 37033
4/25/81	ℝ	14	12	2 Antmusic	—	↓	
4/25/81	ℝ	19	1	3 Physical (You're So)	—	↓	
				ADAM AND THE ANTS (above 3)			
12/4/82	ℝ	7	9	4 Goody Two Shoes	12	Friend Or Foe	Epic 38370
3/10/90	ⓜ	17	7	5 Room At The Top	17	Manners & Physique	MCA 6315
2/25/95	ⓜ	7	17	6 Wonderful	39	Wonderful	Capitol 30335

ANTHRAX
Hard-rock band formed in Queens, New York: John Bush (vocals), Scott Ian (guitar), Dan Spitz (guitar), Frank Bello (bass) and Charlie Benante (drums). Bello joined **Helmet** in 2004.

5/22/93	ℝ	26	9	1 Only	—	Sound Of White Noise	Elektra 61430
10/9/93	ℝ	38	3	2 Black Lodge	—	↓	

ANTI-FLAG
Punk-rock band from Pittsburgh, Pennsylvania: Justin Sane (vocals, guitar), Chris Head (guitar), Chris "#2" Barker (bass) and Pat Thetic (drums).

5/20/06	ⓜ	37	5	The Press Corpse	—	For Blood And Empire	RCA 76836

Billboard				ARTIST	Hot		
Debut	Cht	Peak	Wks	Track Title	Pos	Album Title	Album Label & Number

APARO, Angie
Born James Angelo Aparo in Atlanta, Georgia. Male singer/songwriter/guitarist.

4/8/00	Ⓜ	35	3	Spaceship	—	*The American*	*Melisma 60000*

APARTMENT 26
Hard-rock band from Leamington, Warwickshire, England: Terence "Biff" Butler (vocals), Jon Greasley (guitar), Andy Huckvale (keyboards), Louis Cruden (bass) and Kevin Temple (drums). Band name inspired by David Lynch's 1977 movie *Eraserhead.*

6/3/00	ℝ	33	6	1 Basic Breakdown	—	*Hallucinating*	*Hollywood 62248*
3/6/04	ℝ	39	2	2 Give Me More	—	*Music For The Massive*	*Atlantic 83669*

APOCALYPTICA
Hard-rock band from Helsinki, Finland: Eicca Toppinen, Paavo Lotjonen, Pertta Kivilaasko and Mikko Siren. All are classically trained cellists.

2/23/08	ℝ	11↑	6↑	I'm Not Jesus	—	*Worlds Collide*	*Jive 21580*
3/1/08	Ⓜ	21↑	5↑	APOCALYPTICA Featuring Corey Taylor			

APOLLO FOUR FORTY
Techno-rock trio from England: brothers Trevor Gray and Howard Gray (vocals, keyboards), with Norman "Noko" Fisher-Jones (guitar).

1/22/00	Ⓜ	21	10	Stop The Rock	—	*Gettin' High On Your Own Supply*	*550 Music 62238*

APPLE, Fiona
Born Fiona Apple Maggart on 9/13/1977 in Manhattan, New York. Female singer/songwriter/pianist. Daughter of singer Diane McAfee and actor Brandon Maggart.

11/30/96	Ⓜ	34	6	1 Shadowboxer	—	*Tidal*	*Clean Slate 67439*
3/22/97	Ⓜ	28	13	2 Sleep To Dream	—	↓	
7/26/97	Ⓜ	4	26	3 Criminal	21	↓	
				Grammy: Rock Female Vocal			
11/6/99	Ⓜ	20	12	4 Fast As You Can	—	*When The Pawn*	*Clean Slate 69195*

APRIL WINE
Rock band fomed in Halifax, Nova Scotia, Canada: Myles Goodwyn (vocals, guitar), Brian Greenway (guitar), Gary Moffet (guitar), Steve Lang (bass) and Jerry Mercer (drums). Lang, Moffet and Mercer replaced by Daniel Barbe (keyboards), Jean Pellerin (bass) and Marty Simon (drums) in 1985. Also see **Classic Rock Tracks** section.

3/21/81	ℝ	11	10	1 Just Between You And Me	21	*The Nature Of The Beast*	*Capitol 12125*
3/21/81	ℝ	19	4	2 Sign Of The Gypsy Queen	57	↓	
3/21/81	ℝ	29	5	3 All Over Town	—	↓	
6/26/82	ℝ	9	12	4 Enough Is Enough	50	*Power Play*	*Capitol 12218*
7/10/82	ℝ	26	3	5 If You See Kay	—	↓	
2/18/84	ℝ	23	10	6 This Could Be The Right One	58	*Animal Grace*	*Capitol 12311*
11/6/93	ℝ	35	7	7 That's Love	—	*Attitude*	*F.R.E. 104*

ARCADE
Hard-rock band formed in Los Angeles, California: Stephen Pearcy (vocals), Frank Wilsex (guitar), Donny Syracuse (guitar), Michael Andrews (bass) and Fred Coury (drums). Pearcy was a member of **Ratt**. Coury was a member of **Cinderella**.

4/17/93	ℝ	29	6	1 Nothin' To Lose	—	*Arcade*	*Epic 53012*
7/31/93	ℝ	27	6	2 Cry No More	—	↓	

ARCADE FIRE
Alternative-rock band from Montreal, Quebec, Canada: husband-and-wife Win Butler and Régine Chassagne, William Butler (Win's brother), Richard Parry and Tim Kingsbury. All members play several different instruments.

4/14/07	Ⓜ	32	6	Keep The Car Running	—	*Neon Bible*	*Merge 285*

ARC ANGELS
Rock band formed in Austin, Texas: **Charlie Sexton** (vocals, guitar), **Doyle Bramhall II** (guitar), Tommy Shanon (bass) and Chris Layton (drums). Shannon, Layton and Bramhall's father were members of **Stevie Ray Vaughan**'s band. Layton and Shannon were also members of **Storyville**. ARC: Austin Rehearsal Complex.

5/2/92	ℝ	6	20	1 Living In A Dream	—	*Arc Angels*	*DGC 24465*
8/15/92	ℝ	6	16	2 Sent By Angels	—	↓	
11/14/92+	ℝ	2³	19	3 Too Many Ways To Fall	—	↓	
3/20/93	ℝ	13	10	4 Shape I'm In	—	↓	

ARCHER, Tasmin
Born on 8/3/1963 in Bradford, Yorkshire, England (of Jamaican parentage). Black female singer.

2/27/93	Ⓜ	12	11	Sleeping Satellite	32	*Great Expectations*	*SBK 80134*

ARCTIC MONKEYS
Punk-pop band from Sheffield, Yorkshire, England: Alex Turner (vocals, guitar), Jamie Cook (guitar), Andy Nicholson (bass) and Matt Helders (drums).

3/18/06	Ⓜ	7	20	I Bet You Look Good On The Dancefloor	118	*Whatever People Say I Am, That's What I'm Not*	*Domino 086*

ARMATRADING, Joan

Born on 12/9/1950 in Basseterre, St. Kitts, West Indies; raised in Birmingham, England. Black female eclectic-rock singer/songwriter/guitarist.

Debut	Cht	Peak	Wks	#	Track Title	Hot Pos	Album Title	Album Label & Number
5/21/83	®	33	10	1	Drop The Pilot	78	The Key	A&M 4912
7/12/86	®	37	5	2	Kind Words	—	Sleight Of Hand	A&M 5130
9/10/88	Ⓜ	30	1	3	Living For You	—	The Shouting Stage	A&M 5211

ARMSTRONG, Tim

Born on 11/25/1966 in Berkeley, California. Hard-rock singer/songwriter/guitarist. Member of **Rancid** and the **Transplants**. Married to Brody Dalle of **The Distillers** from 1997-2003.

Debut	Cht	Peak	Wks	Track Title	Hot Pos	Album Title	Album Label & Number
6/16/07	Ⓜ	39	2	Into Action	—	A Poet's Life	Hellcat 80491

ARMY OF ANYONE

Rock band formed in Los Angeles, California: Richard Patrick (vocals), brothers Dean DeLeo (guitar) and Robert DeLeo (bass), with Ray Luzier (drums). Patrick was lead singer of **Filter**. The DeLeo brothers were members of **Stone Temple Pilots** and **Talk Show**.

Debut	Cht	Peak	Wks	#	Track Title	Hot Pos	Album Title	Album Label & Number
9/9/06	®	3[1]	25	1	Goodbye	—	Army Of Anyone	Firm 60010
10/21/06+	Ⓜ	21	19					
3/24/07	®	31	7	2	Father Figure	↓		

ARTIFICIAL JOY CLUB

Rock band from Ottawa, Ontario, Canada: Louise "Sal" Reny (vocals), Leslie Howe (guitar), Michael Goyette (guitar), Tim Dupont (bass) and Andrew Lamarche (drums).

Debut	Cht	Peak	Wks	Track Title	Hot Pos	Album Title	Album Label & Number
6/28/97	Ⓜ	17	14	Sick & Beautiful	—	Melt	Crunchy 90125

ART IN AMERICA

Pop-rock trio from Detroit, Michigan: brothers Chris Flynn (vocals, guitar) and Dan Flynn (drums), with sister Shishonee Flynn (vocals, harp).

Debut	Cht	Peak	Wks	#	Track Title	Hot Pos	Album Title	Album Label & Number
2/26/83	®	23	10	1	Art In America	—	Art In America	Pavillion 38517
3/5/83	®	33	3	2	Undercover Lover	—	↓	

ARTISTS UNITED AGAINST APARTHEID

Benefit group of 49 superstar artists formed to protest the South African apartheid government; proceeds went to political prisoners in South Africa. Organized by **Little Steven** and Arthur Baker. Featuring **Pat Benatar**, Bono (of **U2**), **Jackson Browne**, Bob Dylan, Peter Gabriel, Bonnie Raitt, Lou Reed, Bruce Springsteen and many others.

Debut	Cht	Peak	Wks	Track Title	Hot Pos	Album Title	Album Label & Number
11/23/85	®	41	5	Sun City	38	Sun City	Manhattan 53019

ART OF NOISE, The

Techno-pop trio from England: Anne Dudley (keyboards), J.J. Jeczalik (keyboards, programmer) and Gary Langan (engineer).

Debut	Cht	Peak	Wks	Track Title	Hot Pos	Album Title	Album Label & Number
12/10/88	Ⓜ	14	6	Kiss	31	The Best Of The Art Of Noise	China 837367

THE ART OF NOISE Featuring Tom Jones
#1 Pop hit for **Prince** in 1986

A's, The

Pop-rock band from Philadelphia, Pennsylvania: Richard Bush (vocals), Rick DiFonzo (guitar), Rocco Notte (keyboards), Terry Bortman (bass) and Mike Snyder (drums).

Debut	Cht	Peak	Wks	Track Title	Hot Pos	Album Title	Album Label & Number
6/20/81	®	18	11	A Woman's Got The Power	106	A Woman's Got The Power	Arista 9554

ASH, Daniel

Born on 7/31/1957 in Northampton, England. Alternative-rock singer/songwriter/guitarist. Former member of **Love And Rockets**.

Debut	Cht	Peak	Wks	#	Track Title	Hot Pos	Album Title	Album Label & Number
1/19/91	Ⓜ	2[3]	13	1	This Love	—	Coming Down	Beggars Banquet 3014
11/14/92+	Ⓜ	3[1]	13	2	Get Out Of Control	—	Foolish Thing Desire	Beggars Banquet 53179

ASHES DIVIDE

Born William Howerdel on 5/18/1970 in West Milford, New Jersey. Eclectic-rock singer/songwriter/musician. One-half of **A Perfect Circle**.

Debut	Cht	Peak	Wks	Track Title	Hot Pos	Album Title	Album Label & Number
2/2/08	®	7↑	9↑	The Stone	—	Keep Telling Myself It's Alright	Island 077002
2/9/08	Ⓜ	16↑	8↑				

ASIA

® 1980s: #38 / All-Time: #88

Progressive-rock band formed in England: John Wetton (vocals, bass; born on 6/12/1949), Steve Howe (guitar; born on 4/8/1947), Geoff Downes (keyboards; born on 8/25/1952) and Carl Palmer (drums; born on 3/20/1950). Howe replaced by Mandy Meyer (of **Krokus**) in 1985. Meyer replaced by Pat Thrall (of **Hughes/Thrall**) in 1990. Wetton had been a member of **King Crimson** and **Uriah Heep**. Howe had been a member of **Yes** and later formed **GTR**. Downes had been a member of Yes and The Buggles. Palmer was also a member of **Emerson, Lake & Palmer**.

TOP HITS: Heat Of The Moment 2)Don't Cry 3)Days Like These

Debut	Cht	Peak	Wks	#	Track Title	Hot Pos	Album Title	Album Label & Number
4/3/82	®	❶[6]	22	1	Heat Of The Moment	4	Asia	Geffen 2008
4/3/82	®	10	19	2	Sole Survivor	—	↓	
4/10/82	®	28	16	3	Wildest Dreams	—	↓	
5/1/82	®	8	22	4	Only Time Will Tell	17	↓	

Debit	Cht	Peak	Wks	ARTIST / Track Title	Hot Pos	Album Title	Album Label & Number
				ASIA — cont'd			
7/3/82	℞	40	1	5 Here Comes The Feeling	—	↓	
7/31/82	℞	43	1	6 Time Again	—	↓	
8/6/83	℞	❶[1]	14	7 Don't Cry	10	Alpha	Geffen 4008
8/20/83	℞	5	12	8 The Heat Goes On	—	↓	
8/20/83	℞	20	11	9 True Colors	—	↓	
10/29/83	℞	25	12	10 The Smile Has Left Your Eyes	34	↓	
8/27/83	℞	24	3	11 Daylight	—	(single only)	Geffen 29571
11/9/85	℞	7	13	12 Go	46	Astra	Geffen 24072
1/11/86	℞	30	5	13 Too Late	—	↓	
8/18/90	℞	2[3]	11	14 Days Like These	64	Then & Now	Geffen 24298

ASS PONYS
Rock band from Los Angeles, California: Chuck Cleaver (vocals, guitar), John Erhardt (guitar), Randy Cheek (bass) and David Morrison (drums).

2/11/95	Ⓜ	26	7	Little Bastard	—	Electric Rock Music	A&M 540270

ASTLEY, Jon
Born in Manchester, England. Rock singer/songwriter/producer. His sister, Karen Astley, was married to **Pete Townshend** from 1968-2000.

7/11/87	℞	7	11	1 Jane's Getting Serious	77	Everyone Loves The Pilot (Except The Crew)	Atlantic 81740
9/24/88	Ⓜ	3[2]	11	2 Put This Love To The Test	74	The Compleat Angler	Atlantic 81881

ATARIS, The
Punk-rock band formed in Anderson, Indiana; later based in Santa Barbara, California: Kris Roe (vocals, guitar), John Collura (guitar), Mike Davenport (bass) and Chris Knapp (drums).

3/1/03	Ⓜ	11	15	1 In This Diary	—	So Long, Astoria	Columbia 86184
6/14/03	Ⓜ	2[1]	22	2 The Boys Of Summer	20	↓	
8/30/03	℞	36	5				
11/1/03	Ⓜ	27	7	3 The Saddest Song	—	↓	

ATHENAEUM
Alternative-rock band from Greensboro, North Carolina: Mark Kano (vocals), Grey Brewster (guitar), Alex McKinney (bass) and Nic Brown (drums).

4/25/98	Ⓜ	14	17	What I Didn't Know	58	Radiance	Atlantic 83071

ATLANTA RHYTHM SECTION
Southern-rock band formed in Doraville, Georgia: Ronnie Hammond (vocals), Barry Bailey (guitar), J.R. Cobb (guitar), Dean Daughtry (keyboards), Paul Goddard (bass) and Roy Yeager (drums). Also see **Classic Rock Tracks** section.

9/5/81	℞	18	13	Alien	29	Quinella	Columbia 37550

ATOMSHIP
Hard-rock trio from Mississippi: Joey Culver (vocals), Nathan Slade (guitar) and Chad Kent (drums).

6/12/04	℞	38	6	Pencil Fight	—	The Crash Of '47	Wind-Up 13086

ATREYU
Hard-rock band from Anaheim, California: Alex Varkatzas (vocals), Dan Jacobs (guitar), Travis Miguel (guitar), Marc McKnight (bass) and Brandon Saller (drums). Band name taken from a character in the 1984 movie *The NeverEnding Story*.

3/25/06	℞	24	20	1 Ex's And Oh's	—	A Death-Grip On Yesterday	Victory 267
8/4/07	℞	5	30	2 Becoming The Bull	—	Lead Sails Paper Anchor	Hollywood 000386
9/1/07+	Ⓜ	11	25				
2/9/08	Ⓜ	9↑	8↑	3 Falling Down	—	↓	
2/16/08	℞	9↑	7↑				

AT THE DRIVE-IN
Alternative-rock band from El Paso, Texas: Cedric Bixler (vocals), Omar Rodriguez (guitar), Jim Ward (guitar), Paul Hinojos (bass) and Tony Hajjar (drums). Ward, Hinojos and Hajjar are also members of **Sparta**.

12/30/00+	Ⓜ	26	13	One Armed Scissor	—	Relationship Of Command	Grand Royal 49999

AUDIOSLAVE   ® 2000s: #7 / All-Time: #46 ★ ⓜ 2000s: #8 / All-Time: #29

Hard-rock band formed in Los Angeles, California: **Chris Cornell** (vocals), Tom Morello (guitar), Tim Cummerford (bass) and Brad Wilk (drums). Cornell was lead singer of **Soundgarden**; the latter three were members of **Rage Against The Machine**.

TOP HITS: 1)Like A Stone 2)Be Yourself 3)Cochise

Debut	Cht	Peak	Wks	Track Title	Hot Pos	Album Title	Label & Number
10/12/02	®	2^2	26	1 Cochise	69	*Audioslave*..................................Interscope 86968
10/12/02	ⓜ	9	22			
2/1/03	®	❶^{12}	39	2 **Like A Stone**	31	↓
2/1/03	ⓜ	❶^2	33			
6/14/03	®	2^1	38	3 Show Me How To Live............................	67	↓
6/28/03	ⓜ	4	26			
10/4/03+	®	2^2	32	4 I Am The Highway	66	↓
10/18/03+	ⓜ	3^3	27			
3/27/04	®	8	20	5 What You Are......................................	125	↓
3/27/04	ⓜ	17	15			
2/5/05	®	40	1	6 We Got The Whip.................................	—	*(download only)*............................Interscope
3/26/05	®	❶^7	26	7 **Be Yourself**	32	*Out Of Exile* ....Epic 004603
3/26/05	ⓜ	❶^4	26			
5/14/05	®	12	12	8 Your Time Has Come	113	↓
5/21/05	ⓜ	12	9			
7/16/05	®	2^1	24	9 Doesn't Remind Me	68	↓
7/16/05	ⓜ	3^2	23			
12/3/05+	®	9	20	10 Out Of Exile.....................................	—	↓
12/3/05+	ⓜ	14	19			
7/29/06	ⓜ	3^2	13	11 Original Fire	79	*Revelations*..........................Interscope 97728
7/29/06	®	4	20			
10/21/06+	®	6	20	12 Revelations	—	↓
11/18/06	ⓜ	38	5			

AUDIOVENT

Rock band from Calabasas, California: Jason Boyd (vocals), Ben Einziger (guitar), Paul Fried (bass) and Jamin Wilcox (drums).

Debut	Cht	Peak	Wks	Track Title	Hot Pos	Album	Label & Number
5/18/02	®	9	19	1 The Energy...................................	—	*Dirty Sexy Knights In Paris* ....Atlantic 83544
6/1/02	ⓜ	17	15			
11/2/02	®	29	9	2 Looking Down..............................	—	↓

AUF DER MAUR

Born Melissa Auf Der Maur on 3/17/1972 in Montreal, Quebec, Canada. Rock singer/bassist. Former member of **Hole**.

| 5/22/04 | ⓜ | 32 | 8 | Followed The Waves .... | — | *Auf Der Maur* ....Capitol 82537 |

AUTHORITY ZERO

Punk-rock band from Mesa, Arizona: Jason DeVore (vocals), Bill Marcks (guitar), Jeremy Wood (bass) and Jim Wilcox (drums).

| 11/9/02 | ⓜ | 30 | 8 | One More Minute .... | — | *A Passage In Time* ....Lava 83578 |

AUTOGRAPH

Hard-rock band from Los Angeles, California: Steve Plunkett (vocals, guitar), Steve Lynch (guitar), Steven Isham (keyboards), Randy Rand (bass) and Keni Richards (drums).

| 11/17/84+ | ® | 17 | 20 | 1 Turn Up The Radio .... | 29 | *Sign In Please*...............................RCA 8040 |
| 10/26/85 | ® | 38 | 5 | 2 Blondes In Black Cars .... | — | *That's The Stuff*..............................RCA 7009 |

AVALON, Mickey

Born Yeshe Perl on 12/3/1975 in Los Angeles, California. White male rapper.

| 2/17/07 | ⓜ | 36 | 5 | Jane Fonda .... | — | *Mickey Avalon*...........................MySpace 7853 |

Billboard				ARTIST		Hot		
Debut	Cht	Peak	Wks	Track Title	ℝ=Mainstream Rock ⓜ=Modern Rock	Pos	Album Title	Album Label & Number

AVENGED SEVENFOLD

Hard-rock band from Huntington Beach, California: Matt "M. Shadows" Sanders (vocals), Brian "Synyster Gates" Haner (guitar), Zach "Zacky Vengeance" Baker (guitar), John "Johnny Christ" Seward (bass) and Jimmy "The Rev" Sullivan (drums).

Debut	Cht	Peak	Wks	Track Title	Hot Pos	Album Title	Album Label & Number
9/3/05+	ℝ	2[1]	35	1 Bat Country	60	City Of Evil	Hopeless 48613
9/10/05+	ⓜ	6	30				
3/11/06	ℝ	19	17	2 Beast And The Harlot	—	↓	
4/29/06	ⓜ	40	1				
7/22/06	ℝ	17	20	3 Seize The Day	—	↓	
10/6/07+	ℝ	3[7]	26↑	4 Almost Easy	106	Avenged Sevenfold	Hopeless 303804
10/20/07+	ⓜ	6	24↑				
3/22/08	ℝ	27↑	2↑	5 Afterlife	—	↓	

AXE

Rock band from Gainesville, Florida: Bobby Barth (vocals, guitar), Michael Osborne (guitar), Edgar Riley (keyboards), Wayne Haner (bass) and Ted Mueller (drums). Osborne died in a car crash on 7/21/1984 (age 34).

Debut	Cht	Peak	Wks	Track Title	Hot Pos	Album Title	Album Label & Number
6/19/82	ℝ	23	9	1 Rock 'N' Roll Party In The Streets	109	Offering	Atco 148
11/26/83	ℝ	36	7	2 I Think You'll Remember Tonight	94	Nemesis	Atco 90099

AZTEC CAMERA

Pop-rock band formed in Glasgow, Scotland: Roddy Frame (vocals, guitar), Gary Sanctuary (keyboards), Paul Powell (bass) and Frank Tontoh (drums).

Debut	Cht	Peak	Wks	Track Title	Hot Pos	Album Title	Album Label & Number
7/14/90	ⓜ	3[3]	11	1 The Crying Scene	—	Stray	Sire 26211
9/29/90	ⓜ	12	6	2 Good Morning Britain	—	↓	

B

BABES IN TOYLAND

Female rock trio from Minneapolis, Minnesota: Kat Bjelland (vocals, guitar), Maureen Herman (bass) and Lori Barbero (drums).

Debut	Cht	Peak	Wks	Track Title	Hot Pos	Album Title	Album Label & Number
7/29/95	ⓜ	37	2	Sweet '69	—	Nemesisters	Reprise 45868

BABY ANIMALS

Rock band from Sydney, Australia: Suze DeMarchi (vocals), Dave Leslie (guitar), Eddie Parise (bass) and Frank Celenza (drums).

Debut	Cht	Peak	Wks	Track Title	Hot Pos	Album Title	Album Label & Number
1/4/92	ℝ	29	11	1 Painless	—	Baby Animals	Imago 21002
3/28/92	ℝ	46	3	2 One Word	—	↓	

BAD COMPANY

ℝ 1990s: #28 / All-Time: #47

Rock band formed in England: **Paul Rodgers** (vocals), Mick Ralphs (guitar), Raymond "Boz" Burrell (bass) and Simon Kirke (drums). Rodgers and Kirke from Free; Ralphs from Mott The Hoople; and Burrell from **King Crimson**. Rodgers, who left group in late 1982, was a member of **The Firm** (1984-86) and **The Law** (in 1991). Vocalist Brian Howe joined in 1986. Burrell left in 1987. Dave "Bucket" Colwell (guitar) and Rick Wills (of **Foreigner**; bass) joined in late 1992. Howe left in early 1995; replaced by Robert Hart. Rodgers returned briefly in 1999. Band named after the 1972 Jeff Bridges movie. Burrell died on 9/21/2006 (age 60). Also see **Classic Rock Tracks** section.

TOP HITS: 1)How About That 2)Holy Water 3)If You Needed Somebody

Debut	Cht	Peak	Wks	Track Title	Hot Pos	Album Title	Album Label & Number
9/4/82	ℝ	2[2]	13	1 Electricland	74	Rough Diamonds	Swan Song 90001
9/25/82	ℝ	39	7	2 Racetrack	—	↓	
10/4/86	ℝ	12	7	3 This Love	85		
11/22/86	ℝ	37	4	4 Fame And Fortune	—	Fame And Fortune	Atlantic 81684
8/20/88	ℝ	4	14	5 No Smoke Without A Fire	—	↓	
11/5/88+	ℝ	9	14	6 One Night	—	Dangerous Age	Atlantic 81884
2/11/89	ℝ	9	11	7 Shake It Up	82	↓	
4/29/89	ℝ	20	7	8 Bad Man	—	↓	
6/2/90	ℝ	❶[2]	15	9 Holy Water	89	Holy Water	Atco 91371
8/11/90	ℝ	3[2]	12	10 Boys Cry Tough	—	↓	
10/27/90+	ℝ	2[2]	20	11 If You Needed Somebody	16	↓	
2/16/91	ℝ	9	13	12 Stranger Stranger	—	↓	
8/24/91	ℝ	14	12	13 Walk Through Fire	28	↓	
8/22/92	ℝ	❶[6]	17	14 How About That	38	Here Comes Trouble	Atco 91759
11/28/92	ℝ	21	8	15 This Could Be The One	87	↓	
2/13/93	ℝ	28	5	16 Here Comes Trouble	—	↓	
6/3/95	ℝ	17	9	17 Down And Dirty	—	Company Of Strangers	EastWest 61808
3/13/99	ℝ	15	15	18 Hey, Hey	—	The 'Original' Bad Co. Anthology	Elektra 62349
6/12/99	ℝ	23	11	19 Hammer Of Love	—	↓	

Billboard				ARTIST	R=Mainstream Rock	Hot		
Debut	Cht	Peak	Wks	Track Title	M=Modern Rock	Pos	Album Title	Album Label & Number

BAD ENGLISH
Pop-rock band formed in Los Angeles, California: **John Waite** (vocals), **Neal Schon** (guitar), Jonathan Cain (keyboards), Ricky Phillips (bass) and Deen Castronovo (drums). Waite, Cain and Phillips were members of The Babys. Schon and Cain were members of **Journey**. Schon and Castronovo with **Hardline** in 1992.

Debut	Cht	Peak	Wks	Track Title	Hot Pos	Album Title	Album Label & Number
6/24/89	Ⓡ	2[1]	13	1 Forget Me Not	45	Bad English	Epic 45083
9/23/89	Ⓡ	10	12	2 When I See You Smile	❶[2]	↓	
12/23/89+	Ⓡ	9	12	3 Best Of What I Got	—	↓	
1/27/90	Ⓡ	30	8	4 Price Of Love	5	↓	
4/14/90	Ⓡ	12	8	5 Heaven Is A 4 Letter Word	66	↓	
8/31/91	Ⓡ	9	9	6 Straight To Your Heart	42	Backlash	Epic 46935

BADFINGER
Rock band formed in Swansea, Wales; later based in London, England: Joey Molland (vocals, guitar), Tom Evans (vocals, bass), Glenn Sherba (guitar), Tony Kaye (keyboards) and Richard Bryans (drums). Kaye was a member of **Yes**. Evans committed suicide on 11/19/1983 (age 36). Also see **Classic Rock Tracks** section.

3/28/81	Ⓡ	42	2	Hold On	56	Say No More	Radio 16030

BADLANDS
Hard-rock band from England: Ray Gillen (vocals), Jake E. Lee (guitar), Greg Chaisson (bass) and Eric Singer (drums). Singer was a member of **Black Sabbath** and **Kiss**. Gillen died of cancer on 12/1/1993 (age 33).

7/22/89	Ⓡ	38	5	Dreams In The Dark	—	Badlands	Atlantic 81966

BADLEES, The
Rock band from Philadelphia, Pennsylvania: Pete Palladino (vocals), Bret Alexander (guitar), Jeff Feltenberger (guitar), Paul Smith (bass) and Ron Simasek (drums).

12/9/95+	Ⓡ	31	9	1 Fear Of Falling	—	River Songs	Atlas 529266
4/27/96	Ⓡ	20	9	2 Angeline Is Coming Home	67	↓	

BAD RELIGION
Punk-rock band from Woodland Hills, California: Greg Graffin (vocals), Brett Gurewitz (guitar), Greg Hetson (guitar), Jay Bentley (bass) and Bobby Schayer (drums). Brian Baker replaced Gurewitz in 1995. Gurewitz owns the Epitaph record label.

9/10/94	Ⓜ	29	5	1 Stranger Than Fiction	—	Stranger Than Fiction	Atlantic 82658
11/19/94	Ⓜ	11	13	2 21st Century (Digital Boy)	—	↓	
2/25/95	Ⓜ	27	8	3 Infected	—	↓	
3/25/95	Ⓡ	33	6				
3/9/96	Ⓜ	34	5	4 A Walk	—	The Gray Race	Atlantic 82870
4/6/96	Ⓡ	38	3				
1/26/02	Ⓜ	35	8	5 Sorrow	—	The Process Of Belief	Epitaph 86635
7/17/04	Ⓜ	40	1	6 Los Angeles Is Burning	—	The Empire Strikes First	Epitaph 86694

BAERWALD, David
Born on 7/11/1960 in Oxford, Ohio. Pop-rock singer/songwriter. Half of the **David & David** duo.

5/26/90	Ⓡ	22	10	1 All For You	—	Bedtime Stories	A&M 5289
9/15/90	Ⓡ	42	4	2 Dance	—	↓	

BAILEY, Philip
Born on 5/8/1951 in Denver, Colorado. R&B singer/songwriter. Falsetto vocalist of Earth, Wind & Fire.

12/1/84+	Ⓡ	5	14	Easy Lover	2[2]	Chinese Wall	Columbia 39542
				PHILIP BAILEY (with Phil Collins)			

BAIRD, Dan
Born on 12/12/1953 in San Diego, California; raised in Atlanta, Georgia. Lead singer of the **Georgia Satellites**.

10/10/92	Ⓡ	5	13	1 I Love You Period.	26	Love Songs For The Hearing Impaired	Def American 26999
1/23/93	Ⓡ	13	8	2 The One I Am	—	↓	

BALAAM & THE ANGEL
Gothic-rock trio formed in Cannock, Staffordshire, England: brothers Mark Morris (vocals), Jim Morris (guitar) and Des Morris (drums). All three were born in Scotland. Band named after a 1836 Gustav Jaeger painting.

3/12/88	Ⓡ	13	12	I Love The Things You Do To Me	—	Live Free Or Die	Virgin 90869

BALIN, Marty
Born Martyn Buchwald on 1/30/1942 in Cincinnati, Ohio. Pop-rock singer/songwriter. Member of **Jefferson Airplane/Starship** and **KBC Band**.

6/13/81	Ⓡ	20	10	Hearts	8	Balin	EMI America 17054

Debut	Cht	Peak	Wks	ARTIST / Track Title	Hot Pos	Album Title	Album Label & Number

® = Mainstream Rock
Ⓜ = Modern Rock

BALLARD, Russ
Born on 10/31/1945 in Waltham Cross, Hertfordshire, England. Pop-rock singer/songwriter/producer.

| 5/12/84 | ® | 15 | 13 | 1 Voices | 110 | Russ Ballard | EMI America 17108 |
| 6/29/85 | ® | 15 | 9 | 2 The Fire Still Burns | 105 | The Fire Still Burns | EMI America 17162 |

BANANARAMA
Female vocal trio from London, England: Sarah Dallin, Keren Woodward and Siobhan Fahey. Group name is a combination of the children's TV show *The Banana Splits* and the **Roxy Music** song "Pyjamarama." Fahey was married to David A. Stewart (of **Eurythmics**) from 1987-96. Fahey later formed the duo **Shakespear's Sister**.

| 4/30/83 | ® | 26 | 3 | Na Na Hey Hey Kiss Him Goodbye
#1 Pop hit for Steam in 1969 | 101 | Deep Sea Skiving | London 810102 |

BAND AID
A benefit recording to assist famine relief in Ethiopia. Organized by **Bob Geldof** of The Boomtown Rats. All-star group also included **Bananarama, Phil Collins, Culture Club, Duran Duran, Frankie Goes To Hollywood, Heaven 17, Paul McCartney, Spandau Ballet, Sting, The Style Council, Ultravox, U2** and **Paul Young**.

| 12/22/84+ | ® | 32 | 5 | Do They Know It's Christmas? [X] | 13 | (single only) | Columbia 04749 |

BAND OF HORSES
Alternative-rock trio formed in Seattle, Washington; later based in Charleston, South Carolina: Ben Bridwell (vocals, guitar), Rob Hampon (bass) and Creighton Barrett (drums).

| 1/26/08 | Ⓜ | 34 | 3 | Is There A Ghost | — | Cease To Begin | Sub Pop 745 |

BANGLES
Female pop-rock band from Los Angeles, California: Susanna Hoffs (guitar), Michael Steele (bass), sisters Vicki Peterson (guitar) and Debbi Peterson (drums). All share vocals. Originally named The Bangs. Steele was previously in The Runaways. Vicki Peterson married John Cowsill (of The Cowsills) on 10/25/2003.

8/11/84	®	59	3	1 Hero Takes A Fall	—	All Over The Place	Columbia 39220
3/8/86	®	43	5	2 Manic Monday written by **Prince** under the pseudonym "Christopher"	2¹	Different Light	Columbia 40039
11/28/87	®	41	8	3 Hazy Shade Of Winter #13 Pop hit for Simon & Garfunkel in 1966	2¹	St: Less Than Zero	Def Jam 44042
10/29/88	Ⓜ	5	13	4 In Your Room	5	Everything	Columbia 44056

BANTON, Pato
Born Patrick Murray in Birmingham, England. Reggae singer.

| 9/10/94 | Ⓜ | 39 | 3 | Baby Come Back
Robin & Ali Campbell (of **UB40**; guest vocals); written by **Eddy Grant**; #32 Pop hit for The Equals in 1968 | | Collections | I.R.S. 27055 |

BARBUSTERS, The — see JETT, Joan

BARDENS, Pete
Born on 6/19/1945 in London, England. Died of cancer on 1/22/2002 (age 56). Rock keyboardist. Former member of Them and Camel.

| 8/29/87 | ® | 41 | 6 | 1 In Dreams | — | Seen One Earth | Cinema 12555 |
| 8/27/88 | ® | 49 | 1 | 2 Gold
Neil Lockwood (vocals, above 2) | — | Speed of Light | Cinema 48967 |

BAREFOOT SERVANTS
Rock band from Boston, Massachusetts: **Jon Butcher** (vocals, guitar), Ben Schultz (guitar), Leland Sklar (bass) and Ray Brinker (drums).

| 2/5/94 | ® | 13 | 9 | Box Of Miracles | — | Barefoot Servants | Epic 57503 |

BARE JR.
Rock band from Nashville, Tennessee: Bobby Bare Jr. (vocals), Michael Grimes (guitar), Tracy Hackney (harmonica), Dean Tomasek (bass) and Keith Brogdon (drums). Bare is the son of veteran country singer Bobby Bare.

| 1/30/99 | ® | 12 | 14 | You Blew Me Off | — | Boo-Tay | Immortal 69353 |
| 3/6/99 | Ⓜ | 40 | 2 | | | | |

BARENAKED LADIES
Pop-rock band from Toronto, Ontario, Canada: Steven Page (vocals, guitar), Ed Robertson (vocals, guitar), brothers Andrew Creeggan (keyboards) and Jim Creeggan (bass) and Tyler Stewart (drums). Kevin Hearn replaced Andrew Creeggan in 1996.

1/24/98	Ⓜ	23	14	1 Brian Wilson	68	Rock Spectacle	Reprise 46393
6/20/98	Ⓜ	❶⁵	26	2 One Week	❶¹	Stunt	Reprise 46963
11/7/98	Ⓜ	15	15	3 It's All Been Done	44	↓	
3/6/99	Ⓜ	33	4	4 Alcohol	—	↓	
9/2/00	Ⓜ	30	16	5 Pinch Me	15	Maroon	Reprise 47814

BARNES, Jimmy
Born on 4/28/1956 in Glasgow, Scotland; raised in Australia. Rock singer/songwriter. Lead singer of **Cold Chisel**.

3/8/86	®	41	3	1 No Second Prize	—	*Jimmy Barnes*	Geffen 24089
4/5/86	®	22	7	2 Working Class Man	74	↓	
6/20/87	®	3¹	12	3 Good Times	47	*St: The Lost Boys*	Atlantic 81767
				INXS AND JIMMY BARNES			
5/14/88	®	3¹	11	4 Too Much Ain't Enough Love	91	*Freight Train Heart*	Geffen 24146
8/13/88	®	38	4	5 Driving Wheels	—	↓	

BASEMENT JAXX
Electro-dance/rock production duo from England: Simon Ratcliffe and Felix Buxton.

2/16/02	ⓜ	39	3	Where's Your Head At	—	*Rooty*	Astralwerks 10423
				samples "This Wreckage" and "M.E.", both by Gary Numan			

BATON ROUGE
Hard-rock band from New Orleans, Louisiana: Kelly Keeling (vocals, guitar), Lance Bulen (guitar), David Cremin (keyboards), Scott Bender (bass) and Corky McClellan (drums).

4/14/90	®	22	13	Walks Like A Woman	—	*Shake Your Soul*	Atlantic 82073

BBM
All-star rock trio: Ginger Baker (drums), Jack Bruce (vocals, bass) and **Gary Moore** (vocals, guitar). Baker and Bruce were members of Cream. Moore a member of **Thin Lizzy**.

9/10/94	®	30	6	Waiting In The Wings	—	*Around The Next Dream*	Virgin 39728

BEASTIE BOYS ⓜ All-Time: #73
White rap-punk trio from Brooklyn, New York: Adam "King Ad-Rock" Horovitz (born on 10/31/1966), Adam "MCA" Yauch (born on 8/15/1967) and Michael "Mike D" Diamond (born on 11/20/1965). Horovitz was married to actress Ione Skye (daughter of **Donovan**) from 1991-99. Group ran own Grand Royal record label from 1993-2001.

8/26/89	ⓜ	18	4	1 Hey Ladies	36	*Paul's Boutique*	Capitol 91743
7/4/92	ⓜ	22	6	2 So What 'Cha Want	93	*Check Your Head*	Capitol 98938
6/18/94	ⓜ	18	11	3 Sabotage	115	*Ill Communication*	Grand Royal 28599
				RS500 #475			
6/13/98	ⓜ	4	26	4 Intergalactic	28	*Hello Nasty*	Grand Royal 37716
				Grammy: Rap Group			
				samples "Prelude C# Minor" by Les Baxter and elements of the album *Powerhouse* by The Jazz Crusaders			
11/14/98	ⓜ	15	16	5 Body Movin'	—	↓	
5/29/99	ⓜ	29	6	6 The Negotiation Limerick File	—	↓	
10/30/99	ⓜ	11	15	7 Alive	—	*Beastie Boys Anthology: The Sounds Of Science*	Grand Royal 22940
5/15/04	ⓜ	❶²	17	8 Ch-Check It Out	68	*To The 5 Boroughs*	Capitol 84571
7/31/04	ⓜ	11	11	9 Triple Trouble	—	↓	

BEAT FARMERS, The
Alternative-rock band from Los Angeles, California: Joey Harris (vocals, guitar), Jerry Raney (guitar), Rollie Love (bass) and Country Dick Montana (drums). Montana died of a heart attack on 11/8/1995 (age 40).

8/8/87	®	27	7	Dark Light	—	*The Pursuit Of Happiness*	MCA/Curb 5993

BEATLES, The
Rock band from Liverpool, England: **John Lennon** (rhythm guitar, keyboards), **Paul McCartney** (bass), **George Harrison** (lead guitar) and **Ringo Starr** (drums). All shared vocals. Group starred in the movies *A Hard Day's Night*, *Help*, *Magical Mystery Tour* and *Let It Be*; contributed soundtrack to the animated movie *Yellow Submarine*. Own Apple label in 1968. McCartney publicly announced the group's dissolution on 4/10/1970. Lennon was shot to death on 12/8/1980 (age 40). Harrison died of cancer on 11/29/2001 (age 58). Widely considered to be the #1 rock band of all-time. Also see **Classic Rock Tracks** section.

AWARDS: R&R Hall of Fame: 1988 ★ Grammys: Best New Artist 1964 / Trustees Award 1972

12/9/95	®	8	6	Free As A Bird	6	*Anthology 1*	Apple 34445
				original demo recorded by **John Lennon** in 1977, with new vocals and instrumentation by the other Beatles; produced by **Jeff Lynne**			

BEAUTIFUL CREATURES
Hard-rock band from Los Angeles, California: Joe Leste (vocals), Darren Jay "DJ" Ashba (guitar), Anthony Fox (guitar), Kenny Kweens (bass) and Glen Sobel (drums). Ashba later joined **Sixx: A.M.**

9/15/01	®	37	3	Wasted	—	*Beautiful Creatures*	Warner 47952

BEAUTIFUL SOUTH, The
Pop band formed in Hull, England: Paul Heaton (vocals), Dave Hemmingway (vocals), David Rotheray (guitar), Sean Welch (bass) and David Stead (drums). Female singer Briana Corrigan joined in 1991.

3/24/90	ⓜ	19	6	1 You Keep It All In	—	*Welcome To The Beautiful South*	Elektra 60917
5/2/92	ⓜ	10	10	2 We Are Each Other	—	*0898 Beautiful South*	Elektra 61308

BECK

Ⓜ **1990s: #27 / All-Time: #22**

Born Beck David Campbell (later changed his last name to his mother's maiden name of Hansen) on 7/8/1970 in Los Angeles, California. Alternative-rock singer/songwriter/guitarist. Married actress Marissa Ribisi on 4/3/2004.

TOP HITS: 1)Loser 2)E-Pro 3)Where It's At

Debut	Cht	Peak	Wks			Hot Pos	Album Title	Label & Number
12/25/93+	Ⓜ	❶⁵	21	1	**Loser**	10	*Mellow Gold*	DGC 24634
4/9/94	®	39	2		R&R Hall of Fame ★ RS500 #200 samples "I Walk On Guilded Splinters" by Dr. John			
7/16/94	Ⓜ	27	2	2	**Beercan**	—	↓	
6/15/96	Ⓜ	5	20	3	**Where It's At**	61	*Odelay*	DGC 24823
					Grammy: Rock Male Vocal samples "Get Up And Dance" by Mantronix			
9/28/96	Ⓜ	23	13	4	**Devils Haircut**	94	↓	
					samples "Out Of Sight" by Them and "Soul Drums" by Pretty Purdie			
2/22/97	Ⓜ	9	20	5	**The New Pollution**	78	↓	
8/2/97	Ⓜ	15	15	6	**Jack-Ass**	73	↓	
					samples "It's All Over Now Baby Blue" by Them			
11/8/97+	Ⓜ	16	17	7	**Deadweight**	—	*St: A Life Less Ordinary*	Innerstate 540809
10/24/98	Ⓜ	21	10	8	**Tropicalia**	—	*Mutations*	DGC 25309
10/23/99	Ⓜ	21	15	9	**Sexx Laws**	—	*Midnite Vultures*	DGC 490485
3/4/00	Ⓜ	36	5	10	**Mixed Bizness**	—	↓	
3/15/03	Ⓜ	36	2	11	**Lost Cause**	—	*Sea Change*	DGC 493393
2/19/05	Ⓜ	❶¹	26	12	**E-Pro**	65	*Guero*	Interscope 003481
4/16/05	®	31	11					
6/18/05	Ⓜ	8	18	13	**Girl**	100	↓	
9/9/06	Ⓜ	13	13	14	**Nausea**	—	*The Information*	Interscope 007576
12/23/06+	Ⓜ	22	16	15	**Think I'm In Love**	—	↓	
9/15/07	Ⓜ	29	8	16	**Timebomb**	103	*(download only)*	Interscope

BECK, Jeff

Born on 6/24/1944 in Wallington, Surrey, England. Prolific rock guitarist. With The Yardbirds from 1964-66. **Rod Stewart** and **Ronnie Wood** were members of the Jeff Beck Group from 1967-69. Member of **The Honeydrippers**.

6/15/85	®	5	13	1	**People Get Ready**	48	*Flash*	Epic 39483
					JEFF BECK & ROD STEWART #14 Pop hit for The Impressions in 1965			
8/10/85	®	20	7	2	**Gets Us All In The End**	—	↓	
					Jimmy Hall (of Wet Willie; vocal)			
5/17/86	®	14	7	3	**I Been Down So Long** .... [L]	—	*VA: Live! For Life*	I.R.S. 5731
					STING & JEFF BECK recorded at The Greek Theatre in Los Angeles, California			
10/28/89	®	35	7	4	**Stand On It** .... [I]	—	*Jeff Beck's Guitar Shop*	Epic 44313
					JEFF BECK WITH TERRY BOZZIO & TONY HYMAS			
12/25/93+	®	10	11	5	**Manic Depression**	—	*VA: Stone Free: A Tribute To Jimi Hendrix* ..	Reprise 45438
					SEAL & JEFF BECK first recorded by Jimi Hendrix in 1967			

BEGGARS & THIEVES

Rock band formed in New York: Louie Merlino (vocals), Ronnie Mancuso (guitar), Phil Soussan (bass) and Bobby Borg (drums).

2/2/91	®	38	3		**Beggars & Thieves**	—	*Beggars & Thieves*	Atlantic 82113

BELEW, Adrian

Born Robert Steven Belew on 12/23/1949 in Covington, Kentucky. Rock singer/songwriter/guitarist. Member of **King Crimson** from 1981-84.

5/27/89	Ⓜ	5	12	1	**Oh Daddy**	58	*Mr. Music Head*	Atlantic 81959
					features vocals by his daughter Audie Belew			
5/19/90	Ⓜ	2¹	10	2	**Pretty Pink Rose**	—	*Young Lions*	Atlantic 82099
5/19/90	®	24	7		ADRIAN BELEW & DAVID BOWIE			
8/4/90	Ⓜ	17	4	3	**Men In Helicopters**	—	↓	

BELLY

Alternative-rock band from Newport, Rhode Island: Tanya Donelly (vocals, guitar) with brothers Thomas Gorman (guitar) and Chris Gorman (drums). Gail Greenwood (bass) joined by mid-1993. Donelly was a member of **Throwing Muses** and **The Breeders**.

Debut	Cht	Peak	Wks	#	Track Title	Hot Pos	Album Title	Album Label & Number
1/30/93	Ⓜ	❶³	15	1	**Feed The Tree**	95	Star	Sire 45187
5/15/93	Ⓜ	17	6	2	Slow Dog	—	↓	
10/30/93	Ⓜ	8	9	3	Gepetto	113	↓	
2/11/95	Ⓜ	17	11	4	Now They'll Sleep	103	King	Sire 45833
6/10/95	Ⓜ	35	3	5	Super-Connected	—	↓	

BELOVED, The

Pop-rock duo from England: Jon Marsh (vocals, keyboards) and Steve Waddington (guitars).

Debut	Cht	Peak	Wks	#	Track Title	Hot Pos	Album Title	Album Label & Number
2/10/90	Ⓜ	6	12	1	Hello	—	Happiness	Atlantic 82047
4/10/93	Ⓜ	23	7	2	Sweet Harmony	114	Conscience	Atlantic 82457

BENATAR, Pat

ℝ 1980s: #14 / All-Time: #43

Born Patricia Andrzejewski on 1/10/1953 in Brooklyn, New York; raised in Lindenhurst, Long Island, New York. Rock singer/songwriter. Married to Dennis Benatar from 1971-79 (took his last name). Married her producer/guitarist Neil Giraldo on 2/20/1982. Played "Jeanette Florescu" in the 1980 movie *Union City*. Also see **Classic Rock Tracks** section.

TOP HITS: 1)Love Is A Battlefield 2)Fire And Ice 3)All Fired Up 4)Shadows Of The Night 5)We Belong

Debut	Cht	Peak	Wks	#	Track Title	Hot Pos	Album Title	Album Label & Number
3/21/81	ℝ	31	2	1	**Treat Me Right**	18	Crimes Of Passion	Chrysalis 1275
7/18/81	ℝ	2⁴	21	2	Fire And Ice	17	Precious Time	Chrysalis 1346
					Grammy: Rock Female Vocal			
7/18/81	ℝ	15	19	3	Just Like Me	—	↓	
					#11 Pop hit for Paul Revere & The Raiders in 1966			
7/25/81	ℝ	16	21	4	Promises In The Dark	38	↓	
7/25/81	ℝ	32	10	5	Take It Anyway You Want It	—	↓	
10/16/82	ℝ	3⁴	19	6	Shadows Of The Night	13	Get Nervous	Chrysalis 1396
					Grammy: Rock Female Vocal			
12/11/82+	ℝ	4	17	7	Looking For A Stranger	39	↓	
12/18/82	ℝ	23	4	8	The Victim	—	↓	
3/5/83	ℝ	38	8	9	Little Too Late	20	↓	
10/1/83	ℝ	❶⁴	17	10	**Love Is A Battlefield**	5	Live From Earth	Chrysalis 41444
					Grammy: Rock Female Vocal			
10/27/84	ℝ	3¹	15	11	We Belong	5	Tropico	Chrysalis 41471
12/8/84	ℝ	20	10	12	Diamond Field	—	↓	
1/19/85	ℝ	22	7	13	Ooh Ooh Song	36	↓	
6/29/85	ℝ	4	14	14	Invincible	10	Seven The Hard Way	Chrysalis 41507
					theme from the movie *The Legend of Billie Jean*			
11/23/85	ℝ	5	11	15	Sex As A Weapon	28	↓	
1/25/86	ℝ	19	8	16	Le Bel Age	54	↓	
7/2/88	ℝ	2¹	12	17	All Fired Up	19	Wide Awake In Dreamland	Chrysalis 41628
9/24/88	ℝ	44	5	18	Don't Walk Away	—	↓	
4/6/91	ℝ	17	9	19	Payin' The Cost To Be The Boss	—	True Love	Chrysalis 21805
					#39 Pop hit for **B.B. King** in 1968			
5/29/93	ℝ	3¹	11	20	Everybody Lay Down	—	Gravity's Rainbow	Chrysalis 21982

BERLIN

Electro-pop band from Los Angeles, California: Terri Nunn (vocals), Rick Olsen (guitar), Matt Reid and David Diamond (keyboards), John Crawford (bass) and Rob Brill (drums).

Debut	Cht	Peak	Wks	#	Track Title	Hot Pos	Album Title	Album Label & Number
3/12/83	ℝ	10	7	1	Sex (I'm A...)	62	Pleasure Victim	Geffen 2036
3/31/84	ℝ	25	11	2	No More Words	23	Love Life	Geffen 4025

BEST KISSERS IN THE WORLD

Rock band from Seattle, Washington: Gerald Collier (vocals), Jeff Stone (guitar), Dave Swafford (bass) and Tim Arnold (drums).

Debut	Cht	Peak	Wks	Track Title	Hot Pos	Album Title	Album Label & Number
11/6/93	Ⓜ	22	6	Miss Teen U.S.A.	—	Been There	MCA 10757

BETTER THAN EZRA

Ⓜ 1990s: #36 / All-Time: #69

Rock trio from New Orleans, Louisiana: Kevin Griffin (vocals, guitar), Tom Drummond (bass) and Cary Bonnecaze (drums). Travis McNabb replaced Bonnecaze by 1996.

Debut	Cht	Peak	Wks	#	Track Title	Hot Pos	Album Title	Album Label & Number
3/4/95	Ⓜ	❶[5]	26	1	Good	30	Deluxe	Elektra 61784
4/15/95	ℝ	3[2]	26					
6/24/95	Ⓜ	4	26	2	In The Blood	48[A]	↓	
7/29/95	ℝ	6	19					
11/11/95	Ⓜ	24	11	3	Rosealia	71	↓	
8/3/96	Ⓜ	5	17	4	King Of New Orleans	62[A]	Friction, Baby	Elektra 61944
8/10/96	ℝ	7	15					
11/30/96+	ℝ	10	22	5	Desperately Wanting	48	↓	
11/23/96+	Ⓜ	11	26					
9/12/98	Ⓜ	32	6	6	One More Murder	—	How Does Your Garden Grow?	Elektra 62247
11/21/98+	Ⓜ	17	17	7	At The Stars	78	↓	
7/21/01	Ⓜ	35	7	8	Extra Ordinary	116	Closer	Beyond 78137

BETTS, Dickey, Band

Born on 12/12/1943 in Sarasota, Florida. Southern-rock singer/songwriter/guitarist. Member of **The Allman Brothers Band**. His band: Warren Haynes (guitar), Johnny Neel (piano), Marty Privette (bass) and Matt Abts (drums). Haynes and Neel were also with The Allman Brothers Band. Hayes later formed **Gov't. Mule**.

Debut	Cht	Peak	Wks	Track Title	Hot Pos	Album Title	Album Label & Number
10/8/88	ℝ	11	8	Rock Bottom		Pattern Disruptive	Epic 44289

B-52's, The

Ⓜ 1990s: #30 / All-Time: #70

New-wave dance band from Athens, Georgia: Fred Schneider (vocals, keyboards; born on 7/1/1951), Kate Pierson (vocals, organ; born on 4/27/1948), Cindy Wilson (vocals, guitar; born on 2/28/1957) and Keith Strickland (guitar; born on 10/26/1953). Wilson left in 1991. Also see **Classic Rock Tracks** section.

Debut	Cht	Peak	Wks	#	Track Title	Hot Pos	Album Title	Album Label & Number
6/3/89	Ⓜ	7	8	1	Cosmic Thing	—	Cosmic Thing	Reprise 25854
7/15/89	Ⓜ	❶[3]	8	2	Channel Z	—	↓	
9/2/89	Ⓜ	❶[4]	12	3	Love Shack	3[2]	↓	
					RS500 #243			
12/2/89+	Ⓜ	6	14	4	Roam	3[2]	↓	
6/20/92	Ⓜ	❶[4]	9	5	Good Stuff	28	Good Stuff	Reprise 26943
8/22/92	Ⓜ	13	9	6	Tell It Like It T-I-Is	—	↓	
5/30/98	Ⓜ	35	5	7	Debbie	—	Time Capsule - Songs For A Future Generation	Reprise 46920
					inspired by **Debbie Harry**			

BIBLE, The

Pop-rock band formed in Cambridge, England: Boo Hewerdine (vocals, guitar), Neill MacColl (guitar), Tony Shepherd (keyboards) and Dave Larcombe (drums).

Debut	Cht	Peak	Wks	Track Title	Hot Pos	Album Title	Album Label & Number
9/10/88	Ⓜ	26	1	Crystal Palace	—	Eureka	Ensign 41613

BIG AUDIO DYNAMITE

Ⓜ 1990s: #33 / All-Time: #74

Alternative-rock band from England: Mick Jones (vocals, guitar; **The Clash**), Don Letts and Dan Donovan (keyboards), Leo Williams (bass) and Greg Roberts (drums). Disbanded in 1989. Jones formed **Big Audio Dynamite II** in 1990 with Nick Hawkins (guitar), Gary Stonadge (bass) and Chris Kavanagh (drums). By 1994, group simply known as **Big Audio**.

Debut	Cht	Peak	Wks	#	Track Title	Hot Pos	Album Title	Album Label & Number
9/10/88	Ⓜ	❶[1]	8	1	Just Play Music!	—	Tighten Up Vol. '88	Columbia 44074
9/17/88	Ⓜ	13	8	2	Other 99	—	↓	
9/2/89	Ⓜ	2[2]	10	3	James Brown	—	Megatop Phoenix	Columbia 45212
10/28/89	Ⓜ	6	12	4	Contact	—	↓	
7/6/91	Ⓜ	❶[4]	15	5	Rush	32	The Globe	Columbia 46147
9/28/91	ℝ	40	7		samples "Baba O'Riley" by **The Who**			
10/5/91	Ⓜ	3[2]	10	6	The Globe	72	↓	
					BIG AUDIO DYNAMITE II (above 2)			
11/19/94	Ⓜ	24	7	7	Looking For A Song	—	Higher Power	Columbia 53827
					BIG AUDIO			

BIG BAD VOODOO DADDY

Eclectic-jazz band from Ventura, California: Scotty Morris (vocals, guitar), Joshua Levy (piano), Jeff Harvis, Karl Hunter, Glen Marhevka and Andy Rowley (horns), Dirk Shumaker (bass) and Kurt Sodergen (drums). Group appeared as the band in the 1996 movie *Swingers*.

Debut	Cht	Peak	Wks	Track Title	Hot Pos	Album Title	Album Label & Number
6/27/98	Ⓜ	31	7	You & Me & The Bottle Makes Three Tonight (Baby)	104	Big Bad Voodoo Daddy	Coolsville 93338

BIG BAM BOO

Pop-rock duo: Simon Scardanelli (from England) and David Shark Shaw (from Canada).

Debut	Cht	Peak	Wks	Track Title	Hot Pos	Album Title	Album Label & Number
4/8/89	ℝ	21	7	Shooting From My Heart	—	Fun, Faith, & Fairplay	Uni 8

Billboard				ARTIST		Hot		
Debut	Cht	Peak	Wks	Track Title	®=Mainstream Rock Ⓜ=Modern Rock	Pos	Album Title	Album Label & Number

BIG BIG SUN
Rock band from England: Robin Boult (vocals, guitar), John Jolliffe (keyboards), David Levy (bass) and Gary Ferguson (drums).

5/27/89	®	50	2	Stop The World	—		*Stop The World* .... Atlantic 81964

BIG COUNTRY
Pop-rock band from Dunfermline, Scotland: Stuart Adamson (vocals, guitar), Bruce Watson (guitar), Tony Butler (bass) and Mark Brzezicki (drums). Adamson committed suicide on 12/16/2001 (age 43).

9/10/83	®	3¹	22	1 In A Big Country	17	*The Crossing* .... Mercury 812870
5/19/84	®	48	3	2 Wonderland	86	*Wonderland* .... Mercury 818835
6/21/86	®	5	12	3 Look Away	—	*The Seer* .... Mercury 826844
9/17/88	Ⓜ	11	9	4 King Of Emotion	—	*Peace In Our Time* .... Reprise 25787
9/10/88	®	20	8			
9/4/93	Ⓜ	17	6	5 The One I Love	—	*The Buffalo Skinners* .... Fox 66294
8/28/93	®	34	6			

BIG DIPPER
Rock band from Boston, Massachusetts: Bill Goffrier (vocals, guitar), Gary Waleik (guitar), Steve Michener (bass) and Jeff Oliphant (drums).

5/12/90	Ⓜ	19	6	Love Barge	—	*Slam* .... Epic 46063

BIG HEAD TODD AND THE MONSTERS
Rock trio from Boulder, Colorado: Todd Park Mohr (guitar, keyboards), Rob Squires (bass) and Brian Nevin (drums). All share vocals.

3/20/93	®	9	19	1 Broken Hearted Savior	—	*Sister Sweetly* .... Giant 24486
8/7/93	®	21	9	2 Circle	—	↓
11/20/93	®	14	13	3 Bittersweet	104	↓
2/8/97	®	13	13	4 Resignation Superman	—	*Beautiful World* .... Revolution 24661
3/1/97	Ⓜ	38	5			
4/11/98	®	29	8	5 Boom Boom	—	↓

BIG HEAD TODD & THE MONSTERS WITH JOHN LEE HOOKER
#60 Pop hit for John Lee Hooker in 1962

BIG WRECK
Rock band from Boston, Massachusetts: Ian Thornley (vocals), Brian Doherty (guitar), Dave Henning (bass) and Forrest Williams (drums).

11/29/97+	®	9	19	1 The Oaf	—	*In Loving Memory Of...* .... Atlantic 83032
2/7/98	Ⓜ	24	9			
5/23/98	®	32	9	2 That Song	—	↓

BILLY & THE BEATERS — see VERA, Billy

BILLY SATELLITE
Rock band from Oakland, California: Monty Byrom (vocals), Danny Chauncey (guitar), Ira Walker (bass) and Tom Falletti (drums). Chauncey later joined **38 Special**.

6/23/84	®	30	10	Satisfy Me	64	*Billy Satellite* .... Capitol 12340

BILLY TALENT
Punk-rock band from Streetsville, Ontario, Canada: Ben Kowalewicz (vocals), Ian D'Sa (guitar), Jon Gallant (bass) and Aaron Solowoniuk (drums).

8/16/03	Ⓜ	24	11	Try Honesty	—	*Billy Talent* .... Atlantic 83614

BIRDLAND
Punk-rock band from Birmingham, England: brothers Robert Vincent (vocals) and Lee Vincent (guitar), Sid Rogers (bass) and Gene Kale (drums).

5/11/91	Ⓜ	12	8	Shoot You Down	—	*Birdland* .... Radioactive 10214

BJÖRK
Born Björk Gudmundsdottir on 11/21/1965 in Reykjavik, Iceland. Female singer/actress. Lead singer of **The Sugarcubes**. Played "Selma Jazkova" in the 2000 movie *Dancer In The Dark*.

7/17/93	Ⓜ	2¹	13	1 Human Behaviour	109	*Debut* .... Elektra 61468
1/1/94	Ⓜ	5	14	2 Big Time Sensuality	88	↓
4/15/95	Ⓜ	21	9	3 Army Of Me	—	*St: Tank Girl* .... Elektra 61760

BLACK, Frank
Born Charles Thompson on 4/6/1965 in Long Beach, California. Alternative-rock singer/guitarist. Former leader of the **Pixies**.

3/27/93	Ⓜ	6	8	1 Los Angeles	—	*Frank Black* .... 4 A D 61467
5/22/93	Ⓜ	8	9	2 Hang On To Your Ego	—	↓
				first recorded by The Beach Boys in 1966		
7/9/94	Ⓜ	10	11	3 Headache	—	*Teenager Of The Year* .... 4 A D 61618

BLACK CROWES, The
® 1990s: #4 / All-Time: #18

Rock and roll band from Atlanta, Georgia: brothers Chris Robinson (vocals; born on 12/20/1966) and Rich Robinson (guitar; born on 5/24/1969), Jeff Cease (guitar), Johnny Colt (bass) and Steve Gorman (drums). Marc Ford replaced Cease in late 1991. Eddie Harsch (keyboards) joined in late 1992. Ford left in August 1997. Audley Freed replaced Colt in 1998; Colt later joined **Train**. Chris Robinson was married to actress Kate Hudson (daughter of Goldie Hawn) from 2000-07.

TOP HITS: 1)Remedy 2)Hotel Illness 3)Thorn In My Pride 4)Hard To Handle 5)Sting Me

Debut	Cht	Peak	Wks	Track Title	Hot Pos	Album Title	Album Label & Number
2/24/90	®	5	23	1 Jealous Again	75	Shake Your Money Maker	Def American 24278
6/30/90	®	11	17	2 Twice As Hard	—	↓	
10/6/90	®	❶²	21	3 Hard To Handle	26	↓	
				#51 Pop hit for Otis Redding in 1968			
1/19/91	®	❶¹	20	4 She Talks To Angels	30	↓	
5/11/91	®	2¹	16	5 Seeing Things	—	↓	
4/25/92	®	❶¹¹	20	6 Remedy	48	The Southern Harmony And Musical Companion	Def American 26916
5/30/92	®	❶⁴	23	7 Thorn In My Pride	80	↓	
5/30/92	®	❶²	15	8 Sting Me	—	↓	
10/10/92	®	❶⁶	20	9 Hotel Illness	—	↓	
1/23/93	®	7	10	10 Sometimes Salvation	—	↓	
5/1/93	®	40	2	11 Bad Luck Blue Eyes Goodbye	—	↓	
10/29/94	®	5	13	12 A Conspiracy	—	Amorica	American 43000
11/12/94	ⓜ	23	8				
1/28/95	®	8	12	13 High Head Blues	—	↓	
5/6/95	®	7	16	14 Wiser Time	—	↓	
7/13/96	®	3⁴	14	15 Good Friday	—	Three Snakes And One Charm	American 43082
9/28/96	®	6	11	16 Blackberry	—	↓	
11/21/98	®	3¹⁰	20	17 Kicking My Heart Around	118	By Your Side	American 69361
2/27/99	®	7	14	18 Only A Fool	—	↓	
6/12/99	®	24	9	19 Go Faster	—	↓	
3/18/00	®	13	13	20 What Is And What Should Never Be [L]	—	Live At The Greek	TVT 2140
				first recorded by **Led Zeppelin** in 1969			
8/5/00	®	33	7	21 Ten Years Gone [L]	—	↓	
				JIMMY PAGE & THE BLACK CROWES (above 2) first recorded by **Led Zeppelin** in 1975			
4/21/01	®	9	10	22 Lickin'	—	Lions	V2 27091
6/30/01	®	12	16	23 Soul Singing	—	↓	
3/15/08	®	33↑	3↑	24 Goodbye Daughters Of The Revolution	—	Warpaint	Silver Arrow 61127

BLACKEYED SUSAN

Hard-rock band from Philadelphia, Pennsylvania: Dean Davidson (vocals), Rick Criniti (guitar), Tony Santoro (guitar), Erik Levy (bass) and Chris Branco (drums). Davidson was a member of **Britny Fox**.

Debut	Cht	Peak	Wks	Track Title	Hot Pos	Album Title	Album Label & Number
6/1/91	®	44	3	None Of It Matters	—	Electric Rattlebone	Mercury 848575

BLACKFOOT

Southern-rock band from Jacksonville, Florida: Rickey Medlocke (vocals, guitar), Charlie Hargrett (guitar), Greg Walker (bass) and Jakson Spires (drums). Medlocke and Walker were original members of **Lynyrd Skynyrd** (Medlocke rejoined Lynyrd Skynyrd in 1995). Hargrett left in 1983. Ken Hensley (keyboards; **Uriah Heep**) joined in early 1984. Spires died of a brain hemorrhage on 3/16/2005 (age 53). Also see **Classic Rock Tracks** section.

Debut	Cht	Peak	Wks	Track Title	Hot Pos	Album Title	Album Label & Number
7/11/81	®	9	9	1 Fly Away	42	Marauder	Atco 107
10/6/84	®	55	2	2 Morning Dew	—	Vertical Smiles	Atco 90218
				first recorded by the **Grateful Dead** in 1967			

BLACK 47

Rock band formed in the Bronx, New York: Larry Kirwan (vocals, guitar), Geoffrey Blythe (sax), Chris Byrne (pipes), Fred Parcells (trombone), David Conrad (bass) and Thomas Hamlin (drums). All are originally from Ireland. Group name stands for the blackest year of the Irish potato famine (1847).

Debut	Cht	Peak	Wks	Track Title	Hot Pos	Album Title	Album Label & Number
1/23/93	ⓜ	27	3	Funky Ceili (Bridie's Song)	—	Black 47	SBK 80971

BLACK GRAPE

Dance-rock band formed in England: Shaun Ryder (vocals), Paul Wagstaff (guitar), Mark Berry (keyboards), Paul Leveridge (bass) and Ged Lynch (drums). Ryder and Berry were members of **Happy Mondays**.

Debut	Cht	Peak	Wks	Track Title	Hot Pos	Album Title	Album Label & Number
12/2/95	ⓜ	31	6	In The Name Of The Father	—	It's Great When You're Straight...Yeah	Radioactive 11224

BLACK LAB
Rock band from Berkeley, California: Paul Durham (vocals), Michael Belfer (guitar), Geoff Stanfield (bass) and Bryan Head (drums).

Debut	Cht	Peak	Wks	Track Title		Hot Pos	Album Title	Album Label & Number
11/1/97+	®	6	22	1 Wash It Away		—	*Your Body Above Me*	DGC 25127
12/27/97+	◍	13	17					
4/25/98	®	26	8	2 Time Ago		75[A] ↓		
4/25/98	◍	28	10					

BLACK LABEL SOCIETY
Hard-rock duo from Jersey City, New Jersey: **Zakk Wylde** (vocals, guitar, bass) and Craig Nunenmacher (drums). Wylde was lead guitarist for **Ozzy Osbourne** and his own group, **Pride & Glory**.

4/12/03	®	12	26	1 Stillborn	—	*The Blessed Hellride*	Spitfire 15091
5/8/04	®	33	9	2 House Of Doom	—	*Hangover Music Vol. VI*	Spitfire 15081
2/12/05	®	24	14	3 Suicide Messiah	—	*Mafia*	Artemis 51610
6/11/05	®	35	5	4 Fire It Up	—	↓	
9/17/05	®	32	12	5 In This River	—	↓	
8/12/06	®	29	12	6 Concrete Jungle	—	*Shot To Hell*	Roadrunner 618048
1/6/07	®	31	12	7 Blood Is Thicker Than Water	—	↓	

BLACK LIGHT BURNS
Hard-rock band formed in Los Angeles, California: Wes Borland (vocals, bass), Danny Lohner (guitar), John Freese (keyboards) and Josh Eustis (drums). Borland was a member of **Limp Bizkit**.

4/21/07	®	23	20	Lie	—	*Cruel Melody*	I Am: Wolfpack 40079

BLACK 'N BLUE
Hard-rock band from Portland, Oregon: Jaime St. James (vocals), Tom Thayer (guitar), Jeff Warner (guitar), Patrick Young (bass) and Pete Holmes (drums).

9/8/84	®	50	4	Hold On To 18	—	*Black 'N Blue*	Geffen 24041

BLACK SABBATH
Heavy-metal rock band from Birmingham, England: **Ozzy Osbourne** (vocals), Tony **Iommi** (guitar), Terry "Geezer" Butler (bass) and William Ward (drums). Lineup in 1981: Iommi, Butler, Ronnie James **Dio** (vocals; **Rainbow**) and Vinnie Appice (drums). Original lineup reunited in 1997. Also see **Classic Rock Tracks** section.

AWARD: R&R Hall of Fame: 2006

12/5/81+	®	24	11	1 Turn Up The Night	—	*Mob Rules*	Warner 3605
12/19/81+	®	46	6	2 Voodoo	—	↓	
10/17/98	®	3[1]	21	3 Psycho Man	—	*Reunion*	Epic 69115
1/30/99	®	17	8	4 Selling My Soul	—	↓	
3/24/07	®	37	6	5 The Devil Cried	—	*The Dio Years*	Warner 116668

BLACK STONE CHERRY
Southern-rock band from Edmonton, Kentucky: Chris Robertson (vocals, guitar), Ben Wells (guitar), Jon Lawhon (bass) and John Fred Young (drums). Young is the son of Richard Young and the nephew of Fred Young, both of The Kentucky Headhunters.

5/20/06	®	14	20	1 Lonely Train	—	*Black Stone Cherry*	In De Goot 618086
11/11/06+	®	30	16	2 Hell And High Water	—	↓	
3/31/07	®	29	11	3 Rain Wizard	—	↓	

BLACK TIDE
Hard-rock band from Miami, Florida: Gabriel Garcia (vocals, guitar), Alex Nunez (guitar), Zachary Sandler (bass) and Steven Spence (drums).

3/1/08	®	28↑	5↑	Shockwave	—	*Light From Above*	Interscope 010565

BLANK THEORY, The
Rock band from Chicago, Illinois: brothers Nathan Leone (vocals, guitar) and Matthew Leone (bass), Michael Foderaro (guitar), Shawn Currie (keyboards) and James Knight (drums).

1/25/03	®	36	5	Middle Of Nowhere	—	*Beyond The Calm Of The Corridor*	Scratchie 39021

BLAQK AUDIO
Electronic-rock duo from San Francisco, California: Davey "Havok" Marchand (vocals) and Jade Puget (instruments). Both are also members of **AFI**.

7/28/07	◍	20	13	Stiff Kittens	—	*Cexcells*	Tiny Evil 009512

BLIND MELON

Male rock band formed in Los Angeles, California: Shannon Hoon (vocals), Rogers Stevens (guitar), Christopher Thorn (guitar), Brad Smith (bass) and Glen Graham (drums). Hoon died of a drug overdose on 10/21/1995 (age 28).

Debut	Cht	Peak	Wks	#	Track Title	Hot Pos	Album Title	Album Label & Number
12/11/93+	®	10	12	1	Tones Of Home	—	Blind Melon	Capitol 96585
10/31/92	Ⓜ	20	14					
7/24/93	Ⓜ	❶³	16	2	No Rain	20	↓	
8/7/93	®	❶²	20					
8/12/95	Ⓜ	8	11	3	Galaxie	54ᴬ	Soup	Capitol 28732
8/19/95	®	25	8					

BLINDSIDE

Rock band from Stockholm, Sweden: Christian Lindskog (vocals), Simon Grenehed (guitar), Tomas Naslund (bass) and Marcus Dahlstrom (drums).

Debut	Cht	Peak	Wks	#	Track Title	Hot Pos	Album Title	Album Label & Number
8/24/02	®	18	17	1	Pitiful	—	Silence	Elektra 62765
10/26/02	Ⓜ	36	4					
2/22/03	®	31	9	2	Sleepwalking	—	↓	

BLINK-182

Ⓜ 2000s: #9 / All-Time: #11

Punk-rock trio from San Diego, California: Tom DeLonge (vocals, guitar), Mark Hoppus (vocals, bass) and Scott Raynor (drums). Travis Barker replaced Raynor in late 1998. DeLonge and Barker also formed **Box Car Racer**. DeLonge also formed **Angels And Airwaves**. Barker is also a member of the **Transplants**. Hoppus and Barker also formed **(+44)**.

TOP HITS: 1)All The Small Things 2)I Miss You 3)What's My Age Again?

Debut	Cht	Peak	Wks	#	Track Title	Hot Pos	Album Title	Album Label & Number
10/11/97+	Ⓜ	11	28	1	Dammit (Growing Up)	61ᴬ	Dude Ranch	MCA 11624
1/24/98	®	26	9					
5/8/99	Ⓜ	2¹¹	30	2	What's My Age Again?	58	Enema Of The State	MCA 11950
5/29/99	®	19	19					
10/16/99	Ⓜ	❶⁸	27	3	All The Small Things	6	↓	
3/18/00	Ⓜ	2⁷	26	4	Adam's Song	101	↓	
9/30/00	Ⓜ	2²	22	5	Man Overboard	117	The Mark, Tom, And Travis Show (The Enema Strikes Back!)	MCA 112379
5/19/01	Ⓜ	2⁴	26	6	The Rock Show	71	Take Off Your Pants And Jacket	MCA 112627
9/22/01	Ⓜ	7	26	7	Stay Together For The Kids	116	↓	
2/2/02	Ⓜ	6	25	8	First Date	106	↓	
10/18/03	Ⓜ	2³	26	9	Feeling This	102	Blink-182	Geffen 001336
1/17/04	Ⓜ	❶²	26	10	I Miss You	42	↓	
5/29/04	Ⓜ	10	14	11	Down	—	↓	
1/1/05	Ⓜ	39	3	12	Always	—	Greatest Hits	Geffen 005607
11/5/05	Ⓜ	18	11	13	Not Now	—	↓	

BLOC PARTY

Alternative-rock band from London, England: Kele Okereke (vocals, guitar), Russell Lissack (guitar), Gordon Moakes (bass) and Matt Tong (drums).

Debut	Cht	Peak	Wks	#	Track Title	Hot Pos	Album Title	Album Label & Number
6/4/05	Ⓜ	34	8	1	Banquet	—	Silent Alarm	Vice 93815
2/3/07	Ⓜ	24	13	2	I Still Remember	119	A Weekend In The City	Vice 94598

BLONDIE

New-wave rock band formed in New York: **Debbie Harry** (vocals), Chris Stein (guitar), Frank Infante (guitar), Jimmy Destri (keyboards), Nigel Harrison (bass) and Clem Burke (drums). Disbanded in 1982; reunited in 1999.

AWARD: R&R Hall of Fame: 2006

Debut	Cht	Peak	Wks		Track Title	Hot Pos	Album Title	Album Label & Number
3/21/81	®	35	2		Rapture	❶²	Autoamerican	Chrysalis 1290

BLOODHOUND GANG

Electro-rock band from Trappe, Pennsylvania: James "Jimmy Pop Ali" Franks (vocals), Matt "Lupus Thunder" Stigliano (guitar), Harry "Q-Ball" Dean (DJ), Jared "Evil Jared Hasselhoff" Hennegan (bass) and Michael "Spanky G" Guthier (drums). Willie "The New Guy" Brehony replaced Guthier in 1999.

Debut	Cht	Peak	Wks	#	Track Title	Hot Pos	Album Title	Album Label & Number
12/14/96+	Ⓜ	18	10	1	Fire Water Burn	—	One Fierce Beer Coaster	Geffen 25124
1/4/97	®	28	6					
3/4/00	Ⓜ	6	15	2	The Bad Touch	52	Hooray For Boobies	Republic 490455

BLOODLINE

Rock band from Florida: Berry Oakley Jr. (vocals), Joe Bonamassa (guitar), Waylon Krieger (guitar), Lou Segreti (keyboards) and Erin Davis (drums). Oakley is the son of the late Berry Oakley of **The Allman Brothers Band**. Davis is the son of the late jazz great Miles Davis. Krieger is the son of **Doors** guitarist Robby Krieger.

10/1/94	R	32	7	Stone Cold Hearted		—	Bloodline	EMI 30060

BLOODSIMPLE

Hard-rock band formed in Long Island, New York: Tim Williams (vocals), Mike Kennedy (guitar), Nick Rowe (guitar), Kyle Sanders (bass) and Chris Hamilton (drums).

2/18/06	R	38	1	1 What If I Lost It		—	A Cruel World	Reprise 49002
4/1/06	R	39	2	2 Sell Me Out		—	↓	
12/22/07+	R	30	15↑	3 Out To Get You		—	Red Harvest	Reprise 21468

BLUE AEROPLANES, The

Pop-rock band formed in Bristol, England: brothers Gerard Langley (vocals) and John Langley (drums), Rodney Allen (guitar), Alex Lee (guitar), Angelo Bruschini (guitar) and Andy McCreeth (bass).

10/5/91	M	13	7	Yr Own World		—	Beatsongs	Ensign 21856

BLUE MURDER

Rock trio formed in New York: John Sykes (vocals, guitar; of **Whitesnake**), Tony Franklin (bass; of **The Firm**) and Carmine Appice (drums; of Vanilla Fudge). Sykes fronted a new lineup in 1994: Nik Green (keyboards), Marco Mendoza (bass) and Tommy O'Steen (drums).

7/22/89	R	15	9	1 Jelly Roll		—	Blue Murder	Geffen 24212
3/26/94	R	35	4	2 We All Fall Down		—	Nothin' But Trouble	Geffen 24419

BLUE NILE, The

Melodic-pop trio from Glasgow, Scotland: Paul Buchanan (vocals, guitar), Robert Bell (bass) and Paul Moore (keyboards).

2/3/90	M	10	11	The Downtown Lights		—	Hats	A&M 5284

BLUE OCTOBER

Rock band from Houston, Texas: brothers Justin Furstenfeld (vocals, guitar) and Jeremy Furstenfeld (drums), with C.B. Hudson (guitar), Ryan Delahoussaye (keyboards) and Matt Noveskey (bass).

2/11/06	M	2⁴	29	1 Hate Me		31	Foiled	Universal Motown 006262
4/22/06	R	21	20					
8/19/06	M	20	20	2 Into The Ocean		53	↓	

BLUE ÖYSTER CULT

Hard-rock band from Long Island, New York: Eric Bloom (vocals), Donald "Buck Dharma" Roeser (guitar), Allen Lanier (keyboards), and brothers Joe Bouchard (bass) and Albert Bouchard (drums). Rick Downey replaced Albert Bouchard in 1982. Downey left in 1984. Tommy Zvoncheck (keyboards) and Jimmy Wilcox (drums) joined in 1985. Original lineup reunited in 1988. Bloom is a cousin of DJ Howard Stern. Also see **Classic Rock Tracks** section.

7/4/81	R	❶²	23	1 Burnin' For You		40	Fire Of Unknown Origin	Columbia 37389
8/8/81	R	49	6	2 Joan Crawford		—	↓	
5/1/82	R	24	4	3 Roadhouse Blues [L]		—	Extraterrestrial Live	Columbia 37946

Robby Krieger (guitar; member of **The Doors** on original version in 1970); recorded on 12/15/1981 at The Country Club in Reseda, California.

11/26/83	R	11	15	4 Take Me Away		—	The Revolution By Night	Columbia 38947
12/3/83	R	16	12	5 Shooting Shark		83	↓	
2/15/86	R	9	10	6 Dancin' In The Ruins		—	Club Ninja	Columbia 39979
7/30/88	R	12	9	7 Astronomy		—	Imaginos	Columbia 40618

BLUE RODEO

Folk-rock band from Toronto, Ontario, Canada: Jim Cuddy (vocals, guitar), Greg Keelor (guitar), Bob Wiseman (keyboards), Bazil Donovan (bass) and Cleave Anderson (drums). Group appeared as Meryl Streep's backing band in the 1990 movie *Postcards From The Edge*.

2/16/91	M	19	5	Til I Am Myself Again		—	Casino	EastWest 91601
2/9/91	R	37	6					

BLUES TRAVELER

Blues-rock band from New York: John Popper (vocals, harmonica), Chan Kinchla (guitar), Bobby Sheehan (bass) and Brendan Hill (drums). Sheehan died of a drug overdose on 8/20/1999 (age 31).

5/29/93	R	34	4	1 Conquer Me		—	Save His Soul	A&M 540080
4/22/95	R	13	26	2 Run-Around		8	four	A&M 540265
4/1/95	M	14	26					

Grammy: Rock Vocal Group

10/7/95	M	13	20	3 Hook		23	↓	
9/30/95	R	15	22					
7/13/96	M	17	13	4 But Anyway [L]		36ᴬ	Live From The Fall	A&M 540515
7/20/96	R	19	11					

BLUES TRAVELER — cont'd

Debut	Cht	Peak	Wks	Track Title	Hot Pos	Album Title	Album Label & Number
6/14/97	®	4	19	5 Carolina Blues	—		
6/21/97	ⓜ	30	6			Straight On Till Morning	A&M 540750
8/30/97	ⓜ	25	10	6 Most Precarious	74ᴬ	↓	
10/4/97	®	27	6				

BLUR

Pop-rock band from London, England: Damon Albarn (vocals), Graham Coxon (guitar), Alex James (bass) and Dave Rowntree (drums). Albarn later formed the animated hip-hop band **Gorillaz**.

Debut	Cht	Peak	Wks	Track Title	Hot Pos	Album Title	Album Label & Number
9/14/91	ⓜ	5	19	1 There's No Other Way	82	Leisure	Food 97880
12/11/93	ⓜ	27	6	2 Chemical World	—	Modern Life Is Rubbish	Food 89442
6/4/94	ⓜ	4	13	3 Girls & Boys	59	Parklife	Food 29194
4/12/97	ⓜ	6	26	4 Song 2	55ᴬ	Blur	Food 42876
5/31/97	®	25	10				
3/29/03	ⓜ	22	9	5 Crazy Beat	—	Think Tank	Food 84242

BOBBY & THE MIDNITES

Rock band formed in San Francisco, California: Bob Weir (vocals, guitar), Brent Mydland (keyboards), Bobby Cochran (guitar), Matthew Kelly (harmonica), Alphonso Johnson (bass) and Billy Cobham (drums). Weir and Mydland were both members of the **Grateful Dead**. Mydland died of a drug overdose on 7/26/1990 (age 37).

Debut	Cht	Peak	Wks	Track Title	Hot Pos	Album Title	Album Label & Number
12/19/81+	®	48	6	Too Many Losers	—	Bobby & The Midnites	Arista 9568

BoDEANS

Rock and roll band from Waukesha, Wisconsin: Kurt Neumann (vocals, guitar), Sam Llanas (vocals, guitar), Bob Griffin (bass) and Guy Hoffman (drums). In 1989, Hoffman left; Michael Ramos (keyboards) and Danny Gayol (drums) joined.

Debut	Cht	Peak	Wks	Track Title	Hot Pos	Album Title	Album Label & Number
10/3/87	®	16	11	1 Only Love	—	Outside Looking In	Slash 25629
2/13/88	®	32	7	2 Dreams	—	↓	
7/15/89	ⓜ	15	7	3 You Don't Get Much	—	home.	Slash 25876
7/1/89	®	20	10				
10/21/89	®	50	2	4 Good Work	—	↓	
4/13/91	®	34	6	5 Black, White And Blood Red	—	Black And White	Slash 26487
12/25/93+	®	34	5	6 Feed The Fire	—	Go Slow Down	Slash 45455

BOLTON, Michael

Born Michael Bolotin on 2/26/1954 in New Haven, Connecticut. Adult Contemporary singer/songwriter. First recorded for Epic in 1968. Lead singer of Blackjack in the late 1970s. Began recording as Michael Bolton in 1983.

Debut	Cht	Peak	Wks	Track Title	Hot Pos	Album Title	Album Label & Number
4/23/83	®	27	8	1 Fools Game	82	Michael Bolton	Columbia 38537
3/16/85	®	38	7	2 Everybody's Crazy	—	Everybody's Crazy	Columbia 39328
12/19/87+	®	12	13	3 (Sittin' On) The Dock Of The Bay	11	The Hunger	Columbia 40473
				#1 Pop hit for Otis Redding in 1968			
5/14/88	®	40	4	4 Wait On Love	79	↓	

BONDS, Gary U.S.

Born Gary Anderson on 6/6/1939 in Jacksonville, Florida; raised in Norfolk, Virginia. Black rock and roll singer/songwriter.

Debut	Cht	Peak	Wks	Track Title	Hot Pos	Album Title	Album Label & Number
5/2/81	®	5	14	1 This Little Girl	11	Dedication	EMI America 17051
5/9/81	®	29	12	2 Jolé Blon	65	↓	
				#1 Country hit for Red Foley in 1947			
6/19/82	®	10	9	3 Out Of Work	21	On The Line	EMI America 17068
				Clarence Clemons (saxophone, above 3); above 3 written (except #2) and produced by **Bruce Springsteen**			

BONHAM

Hard-rock band formed in England: Jason Bonham (drums; born on 7/15/1966; son of **Led Zeppelin**'s John Bonham), Daniel MacMaster (vocals), Ian Hatton (guitar) and John Smithson (keyboards, bass). Charles West and Tony Catania replaced MacMaster and Hatton by 1997. MacMaster died on 3/16/2008 (age 39).

Debut	Cht	Peak	Wks	Track Title	Hot Pos	Album Title	Album Label & Number
9/9/89	®	9	22	1 Wait For You	55	The Disregard Of Timekeeping	WTG 45009
1/6/90	®	29	7	2 Guilty	—	↓	
4/28/90	®	47	1	3 Bringing Me Down	—	↓	
8/1/92	®	32	5	4 Change Of A Season	—	Mad Hatter	WTG 46856
11/8/97	®	33	5	5 Drown In Me	—	When You See The Sun	MJJ Music 68182
				THE JASON BONHAM BAND			

BONHAM, Tracy

Born on 3/16/1967 in Eugene, Oregon. Female singer/songwriter/guitarist.

Debut	Cht	Peak	Wks	Track Title	Hot Pos	Album Title	Album Label & Number
4/6/96	ⓜ	❶³	21	1 Mother Mother	32ᴬ	The Burdens Of Being Upright	Island 524187
4/27/96	®	18	12				
8/17/96	ⓜ	23	9	2 The One	—	↓	

BON JOVI
® 1980s: #37 / All-Time: #41

Rock band from Sayreville, New Jersey: Jon Bon Jovi (vocals; born on 3/2/1962), Richie Sambora (guitar; born on 7/11/1959), Dave Bryan (keyboards; born on 2/7/1962), Alec John Such (bass; born on 11/14/1956) and Tico Torres (drums; born on 10/7/1953). Jon acted in the movies *Moonlight and Valentino*, *The Leading Man*, *No Looking Back*, *U-571* and *Pay It Forward*. Sambora was married to actress Heather Locklear from 1994-2007.

TOP HITS: 1)Livin' On A Prayer 2)Blaze Of Glory 3)Keep The Faith 4)Bad Medicine 5)I'll Be There For You

Debut	Cht	Peak	Wks	Track Title	Pos	Album Title	Label
2/11/84	®	5	13	1 Runaway	39	Bon Jovi	Mercury 814982
5/5/84	®	44	7	2 She Don't Know Me	48	↓	
5/4/85	®	28	7	3 Only Lonely	54	7800° Fahrenheit	Mercury 824509
7/6/85	®	37	7	4 In And Out Of Love	69	↓	
12/28/85+	®	24	8	5 Silent Night	—	↓	
8/23/86	®	9	15	6 You Give Love A Bad Name	❶¹	Slippery When Wet	Mercury 830264
11/1/86	®	13	17	7 Wanted Dead Or Alive	7	↓	
12/13/86+	®	❶²	15	8 Livin' On A Prayer	❶⁴	↓	
3/14/87	®	11	10	9 Never Say Goodbye	28ᴬ	↓	
9/24/88	®	3¹	9	10 Bad Medicine	❶²	New Jersey	Mercury 836345
10/8/88	®	7	17	11 Born To Be My Baby	3¹	↓	
1/28/89	®	5	13	12 I'll Be There For You	❶¹	↓	
5/27/89	®	20	9	13 Lay Your Hands On Me	7	↓	
10/21/89	®	37	6	14 Living In Sin	9	↓	
12/16/89	®	48	4	15 The Boys Are Back In Town [L]	—	VA: Make A Difference Foundation: Stairway To Heaven/Highway To Hell	Mercury 842093
				recorded on 8/12/1989 at the Moscow Music Peace Festival; #12 Pop hit for **Thin Lizzy** in 1976			
7/21/90	®	❶¹	12	16 Blaze Of Glory	❶¹	Blaze Of Glory/Young Guns II	Mercury 846473
10/6/90	®	20	8	17 Miracle	12	↓	
1/4/92	®	27	8	18 Levon	64ᴬ	VA: Two Rooms - Celebrating The Songs Of Elton John & Bernie Taupin	Polydor 845750
				JON BON JOVI (above 3) #24 Pop hit for **Elton John** in 1972			
10/24/92	®	❶¹	14	19 Keep The Faith	29	Keep The Faith	Jambco 514045
1/30/93	®	25	7	20 Bed Of Roses	10	↓	
4/17/93	®	32	6	21 In These Arms	27	↓	
7/10/93	®	29	6	22 I'll Sleep When I'm Dead	97	↓	
9/28/02	®	31	6	23 Everyday	118	Bounce	Island 063055
3/1/03	®	39	1	24 Bounce	—	↓	
9/24/05	®	38	3	25 Have A Nice Day	53	Have A Nice Day	Island 005371

BOOK OF LOVE
Electro-dance/pop band from New York: Susan Ottaviano (vocals), Ted Ottaviano and Lauren Roselli (keyboards), and Jade Lee (percussion). The Ottavianos are not related.

2/16/91	Ⓜ	21	5	Alice Everyday	—	Candy Carol	Sire 26389

BOOM CRASH OPERA
Pop-rock band from Melbourne, Australia: Dale Ryder (vocals), Pete Farnan (guitar), Greg O'Connor (keyboards), Richard Pleasance (bass) and Peter Maslin (drums).

6/23/90	Ⓜ	8	9	Onion Skin	—	These Here Are Crazy Times	Giant 26160

BOO RADLEYS, The
Rock band from Liverpool, England: Simon "Sice" Rowbottom (vocals), Martin Carr (guitar), Tim Brown (bass) and Rob Cieka (drums). Group named after a character in Harper Lee's novel *To Kill A Mockingbird*.

10/2/93	Ⓜ	30	2	1 Lazarus	—	Giant Steps	Creation 53794
1/22/94	Ⓜ	30	1	2 Barney (...And Me)	—	↓	

BOSTON
Rock band from Boston, Massachusetts: Brad Delp (vocals), Tom Scholz (guitar, keyboards), Barry Goudreau (guitar), Fran Sheehan (bass) and Sib Hashian (drums). Goudreau formed **Orion The Hunter** in 1982. By 1986, reduced to a duo of Scholz and Delp. Delp and Goudreau formed **RTZ**. Scholz's 1994 Boston lineup: Fran Cosmo and Tommy Funderburk (vocals), Gary Pihl (guitar), David Sikes (bass) and Doug Huffman (drums). Scholz is an avid inventor with several patented inventions. Delp committed suicide on 3/9/2007 (age 55). Also see **Classic Rock Tracks** section.

9/27/86	®	❶³	9	1 Amanda	❶²	Third Stage	MCA 6188
10/11/86	®	2¹	17	2 We're Ready	9	↓	
10/18/86	®	4	19	3 Cool The Engines	—	↓	
1/31/87	®	7	10	4 Can'tcha Say (You Believe In Me)/Still In Love	20	↓	

BOSTON — cont'd

Debut	Cht	Peak	Wks	Track Title	Hot Pos	Album Title	Label & Number
6/4/94	®	4	9	5 I Need Your Love	51	Walk On	MCA 10973
7/30/94	®	14	8	6 Walk On Medley	—	↓	
				Walkin' At Night/Walk On/Get Organ-Ized/Walk On (some more)			

BOTTLE ROCKETS, The
Rock band from Festus, Missouri: Brian Henneman (vocals, guitar), Tom Parr (guitar), Tom Ray (bass) and Mark Ortmann (drums).

| 11/4/95 | ® | 27 | 11 | Radar Gun | — | The Brooklyn Side | Atlantic 92601 |

BOURGEOIS TAGG
Rock band from Los Angeles, California: Brent Bourgeois (vocals, keyboards), Larry Tagg (vocals, bass), Lyle Workman (guitar), Scott Moon (keyboards) and Michael Urbano (drums).

| 10/17/87 | ® | 8 | 14 | I Don't Mind At All | 38 | YoYo | Island 90638 |
| | | | | produced by Todd Rundgren | | | |

BOWIE, David ® 1980s: #16 / All-Time: #58
Born David Jones on 1/8/1947 in Brixton, London, England. Pop-rock singer/actor. Joined Lindsay Kemp Mime Troupe in 1967. Adopted new personas (Ziggy Stardust, Alladin Sane, Thin White Duke) to accompany several of his musical phases. Married to Angie Barnett, the subject of **The Rolling Stones'** song "Angie," from 1970-80. Acted in several movies. Starred in *The Elephant Man* on Broadway. Formed **Tin Machine** in 1988. Married Somalian actress/supermodel Iman on 4/24/1992. Also see **Classic Rock Tracks** section.

AWARDS: Grammy: Lifetime Achievement 2006 ★ R&R Hall of Fame: 1996

TOP HITS: 1)Blue Jean 2)Pretty Pink Rose 3)Dancing In The Street 4)China Girl 5)Day-In Day-Out

Debut	Cht	Peak	Wks	Track Title	Hot Pos	Album Title	Label & Number
11/7/81	®	7	18	1 Under Pressure	29	Greatest Hits	Elektra 564
				QUEEN & DAVID BOWIE			
3/27/82	®	9	13	2 Cat People (Putting Out Fire)	67	St: Cat People	Backstreet 1759
				also see #4 below			
3/26/83	®	8	16	3 Let's Dance	❶¹	Let's Dance	EMI America 17093
4/9/83	®	11	7	4 Cat People (Putting Out Fire) [R]	—	↓	
				new version of #2 above			
5/7/83	®	6	32	5 Modern Love	14	↓	
5/28/83	®	3¹	17	6 China Girl	10	↓	
				first recorded by Iggy Pop in 1977			
8/20/83	®	31	5	7 Criminal World	—	↓	
				Stevie Ray Vaughan (guitar, above 5)			
9/15/84	®	2²	12	8 Blue Jean	8	Tonight	EMI America 17138
10/13/84	®	40	5	9 Neighborhood Threat	—	↓	
12/8/84	®	32	6	10 Tonight	53	↓	
				Tina Turner (backing vocal)			
2/9/85	®	7	11	11 This Is Not America	32	St: The Falcon And The Snowman	EMI America 17150
				DAVID BOWIE & THE PAT METHENY GROUP			
8/31/85	®	3²	9	12 Dancing In The Street	7	(single only)	EMI America 8288
				MICK JAGGER & DAVID BOWIE			
				#2 Pop hit for Martha & The Vandellas in 1964			
3/29/86	®	9	9	13 Absolute Beginners	53	St: Absolute Beginners	EMI America 17182
6/7/86	®	18	8	14 Underground	—	St: Labyrinth	EMI America 17206
4/4/87	®	3¹	10	15 Day-In Day-Out	21	Never Let Me Down	EMI America 17267
5/2/87	®	7	13	16 Time Will Crawl	—	↓	
5/23/87	®	38	11	17 Bang Bang	—	↓	
8/8/87	®	15	9	18 Never Let Me Down	27	↓	
5/19/90	Ⓜ	2¹	10	19 Pretty Pink Rose	—	Young Lions	Atlantic 82099
5/19/90	®	24	7				
				ADRIAN BELEW & DAVID BOWIE			
8/1/92	Ⓜ	11	6	20 Real Cool World	—	St: Cool World	Warner 45009
4/3/93	Ⓜ	4	8	21 Jump They Say	—	Black Tie White Noise	Savage 50212
9/16/95	Ⓜ	20	7	22 The Hearts Filthy Lesson	92	Outside	Virgin 40711
12/13/97+	Ⓜ	29	8	23 I'm Afraid Of Americans	66	Earthling	Virgin 42627

BOWLING FOR SOUP
Punk-rock band from Wichita Falls, Texas: Jaret Reddick (vocals, guitar), Chris Burney (guitar), Erik Chandler (bass) and Gary Wiseman (drums).

| 9/21/02 | Ⓜ | 38 | 6 | Girl All The Bad Guys Want | 64 | Drunk Enough To Dance | Silvertone 41819 |

BOW WOW WOW
New-wave band assembled in London, England: Annabella Lwin (vocals), Matthew Ashman (guitar), Leroy Gorman (bass) and Dave Barbarossa (drums). Ashman died of diabetes on 11/21/1995 (age 35).

| 5/15/82 | ® | 22 | 12 | I Want Candy | 62 | The Last Of The Mohicans | RCA 13231 |
| | | | | #11 Pop hit for The Strangeloves in 1965 | | | |

BOX, The
Rock band from Montreal, Quebec, Canada: Jean Marc (vocals), Claude Thibault (guitar), Guido Pisapia (keyboards), Jean-Pierre Brie (bass) and Philippe Bernard (drums).

3/2/91	®	49	1	Temptation	—	*The Pleasure And The Pain*	Capitol 94953

BOX CAR RACER
Punk-rock band from San Diego, California: Tom DeLonge (vocals, guitar), David Kennedy (guitar), Anthony Celestino (bass) and Travis Barker (drums). DeLonge and Barker are also members of **Blink-182**. DeLonge is also a member of **Angels And Airwaves**. Barker is also a member of the **Transplants**.

5/18/02	ⓜ	8	16	1 I Feel So....................................	120	*Box Car Racer*	MCA 112894
10/26/02	ⓜ	32	7	2 There Is....................................	—	↓	

BOX OF FROGS
Rock band from England: John Fiddler (vocals), Chris Dreja (guitar), Paul Samwell-Smith (bass) and Jim McCarty (drums). The latter three were members of The Yardbirds. McCarty also with Renaissance and Illusion.

6/30/84	®	14	13	Back Where I Started	—	*Box Of Frogs*	Epic 39327
				Jeff Beck (guitar)			

BOY GEORGE
Born George O'Dowd on 6/14/1961 in Bexleyheath, England. Former lead singer of **Culture Club**.

3/13/93	ⓜ	13	7	The Crying Game...........................	15	*St: The Crying Game*	SBK 89024
				produced by the **Pet Shop Boys**; #87 Pop hit for Brenda Lee in 1965			

BOZZIO, Terry — see BECK, Jeff

BRAGG, Billy
Born Steven William Bragg on 12/20/1957 in Barking, Essex, England. Rock singer/songwriter.

10/22/88	ⓜ	20	1	1 Waiting For The Great Leap Forwards	—	*Workers Playtime*...................	Elektra 60824
11/26/88	ⓜ	16	2	2 She's Got A New Spell	—	↓	
9/7/91	ⓜ	2²	11	3 Sexuality	—	*Don't Try This At Home*	Elektra 61121
11/16/91	ⓜ	16	9	4 You Woke Up My Neighbourhood	—	↓	

BRAMHALL, Doyle II and Smokestack
Born on 12/24/1968 in Austin, Texas. Blues-rock singer/guitarist. Son of songwriter Doyle Bramhall (collaborated with **Stevie Ray Vaughan**). His group Smokestack: Susannah Melvoin (vocals), Chris Bruce (guitar), J.J. Johnson (drums). Melvoin is the sister of Wendy Melvoin (of **Prince**'s Revolution) and the late Jonathan Melvoin (of **The Smashing Pumpkins**).

6/9/01	®	33	9	Green Light Girl	—	*Welcome*	RCA 69360

BRAND NEW
Punk-rock band from Merrick, New York: Jesse Lacey (vocals), Vincent Accardi (guitar), Garrett Tierney (bass) and Brian Lane (drums).

9/6/03	ⓜ	37	6	1 The Quiet Things That No One Ever Knows	—	*Deja Entendu*	Triple Crown 82896
5/5/07	ⓜ	30	10	2 Jesus	—	*The Devil And God Are Raging Inside Me*...........................	Interscope 008034

BRANDOS, The
Rock band from New York: Dave Kincaid (vocals), Ed Rupprecht (guitar), Ernie Mendillo (bass) and Larry Mason (drums).

9/19/87	®	34	6	Gettysburg	—	*Honor Among Thieves*	Relativity 8192

BRANNEN, John
Born in Savannah, Georgia; raised in Charleston, South Carolina. Country-rock singer.

2/6/88	®	21	10	Desolation Angel	—	*Mystery Street*........................	Apache 71650

BRAVERY, The
Alternative-rock band from New York: Sam Endicott (vocals, guitar), Michael Zakarin (guitar), John Conway (keyboards), Mike Hindirt (bass) and Anthony Burulcich (drums).

3/12/05	ⓜ	12	26	1 An Honest Mistake	97	*The Bravery*	Island 004163
10/8/05	ⓜ	34	6	2 Unconditional	—	↓	
3/31/07	ⓜ	10	20	3 Time Won't Let Me Go	124	*The Sun And The Moon*............	Island 008283
10/20/07+	ⓜ	7↑	24↑	4 Believe	—	↓	

BREAKING BENJAMIN ® 2000s: #19 / All-Time: #95 ★ ⓜ 2000s: #33 / All-Time: #66
Hard-rock band from Wilkes-Barre, Pennsylvania: Ben Burnley (vocals, guitar), Aaron Fink (guitar), Mark Klepaski (bass) and Jeremy Hummel (drums). Chad Szeliga replaced Hummel in late 2005.

7/27/02	®	19	17	1 Polyamorous..............................	—	*Saturate*..................................	Hollywood 62356
11/30/02	ⓜ	31	9				
3/8/03	®	24	14	2 Skin	—	↓	
4/12/03	ⓜ	37	4				
5/15/04	®	2³	62	3 So Cold	76	*We Are Not Alone*...................	Hollywood 162428
5/29/04	ⓜ	3³	41				

BREAKING BENJAMIN — cont'd

Debut	Cht	Peak	Wks	Track Title	Hot Pos	Album Title	Album Label & Number
1/15/05	®	2[1]	26	4 Sooner Or Later	99	↓	
1/22/05	ⓜ	7	24				
7/9/05	®	23	10	5 Rain (2005)	—	↓	
7/30/05	ⓜ	39	3				
6/17/06	®	2[3]	36	6 The Diary Of Jane	50	Phobia	Hollywood 162607
6/24/06	ⓜ	4	37				
1/20/07	®	❶[7]	31	7 Breath	84	↓	
1/27/07	ⓜ	3[5]	39				
10/27/07+	®	6	23↑	8 Until The End	122	↓	
12/22/07+	ⓜ	21	15↑				

BREAKING POINT
Rock band from Memphis, Tennessee: Brett Erickson (vocals, guitar), Justin Rimer (guitar), Greg Edmondson (bass) and Jody Abbott (drums). Aaron "Zeke" Dauner replaced Abbott in 2004.

Debut	Cht	Peak	Wks	Track Title	Hot Pos	Album Title	Album Label & Number
5/11/02	®	38	3	1 One Of A Kind	—	Coming Of Age	Wind-Up 642
5/21/05	®	25	12	2 Show Me A Sign	—	Beautiful Disorder	Wind-Up 13108

BREAKS, The
Pop-rock band from Memphis, Tennessee: Susanne Jerome Taylor (vocals), Pat Taylor (guitar), Tom Ward (keyboards), Rob Caudill (bass) and Russ Caudill (drums).

Debut	Cht	Peak	Wks	Track Title	Hot Pos	Album Title	Album Label & Number
10/1/83	®	39	2	She Wants You	—	The Breaks	RCA 4675

BREEDERS, The
Rock band from Dayton, Ohio: twin sisters/guitarists/vocalists Kim and Kelley Deal, bassist Josephine Wiggs (native of Bedfordshire, England) and drummer Jim MacPherson. Kim was a member of the **Pixies**. Tanya Donelly (of **Throwing Muses** and **Belly**) was an early member.

Debut	Cht	Peak	Wks	Track Title	Hot Pos	Album Title	Album Label & Number
9/11/93	ⓜ	2[2]	29	1 Cannonball	44	Last Splash	4 A D 61508
2/5/94	®	32	5				
12/4/93	ⓜ	28	4	2 Divine Hammer	104	↓	
7/9/94	ⓜ	12	8	3 Saints	109	↓	

BRICKELL, Edie, & New Bohemians
Born on 3/10/1966 in Oak Cliff, Texas. Female singer/songwriter. New Bohemians consisted of Kenny Withrow (guitar), Brad Houser (bass) and John Bush (drums). Joining the band by 1990 were Wes Burt-Martin (guitar) and Matt Chamberlain (drums). Brickell married **Paul Simon** on 5/30/1992.

Debut	Cht	Peak	Wks	Track Title	Hot Pos	Album Title	Album Label & Number
9/10/88	ⓜ	4	21	1 What I Am	7	Shooting Rubberbands At The Stars	Geffen 24192
10/15/88	®	9	18				
1/21/89	ⓜ	14	9	2 Little Miss S.	—	↓	
2/4/89	®	38	6				
4/1/89	®	32	8	3 Circle	48	↓	
2/10/90	ⓜ	21	4	4 A Hard Rain's A Gonna Fall	—	St: Born On The Fourth Of July	MCA 6340
1/27/90	®	28	6	first recorded by **Bob Dylan** in 1963			
11/10/90	ⓜ	17	10	5 Mama Help Me	—	Ghost Of A Dog	Geffen 24304
11/17/90	®	26	9				

BRILEY, Martin
Born on 8/17/1949 in London, England. Rock singer/songwriter/guitarist.

Debut	Cht	Peak	Wks	Track Title	Hot Pos	Album Title	Album Label & Number
4/30/83	®	15	14	1 The Salt In My Tears	36	One Night With A Stranger	Mercury 810332
1/26/85	®	31	6	2 Dangerous Moments	—	Dangerous Moments	Mercury 822423

BRITNY FOX
Hard-rock band from Philadelphia, Pennsylvania: "Dizzy" Dean Davidson (vocals), Michael Kelly Smith (guitar), Billy Childs (bass) and Johnny Dee (drums). Davidson later formed **Blackeyed Susan**.

Debut	Cht	Peak	Wks	Track Title	Hot Pos	Album Title	Album Label & Number
7/16/88	®	33	7	1 Long Way To Love	100	Britny Fox	Columbia 44140
2/10/90	®	34	9	2 Dream On	—	Boys In Heat	Columbia 45300

BROADCASTERS, The
Rock band from New York: brothers Billy Roues (vocals, guitar) and Steve Roues (guitar), Blackie Pagano (bass) and Ed Steinberg (drums).

Debut	Cht	Peak	Wks	Track Title	Hot Pos	Album Title	Album Label & Number
1/23/88	®	48	3	Down In The Trenches	—	13 Ghosts	Enigma 73315

BROOKS, Meredith
Born on 6/12/1966 in Oregon City, Oregon. Female rock singer/guitarist.

Debut	Cht	Peak	Wks	Track Title	Hot Pos	Album Title	Album Label & Number
4/12/97	ⓜ	4	21	Bitch	2[4]	Blurring The Edges	Capitol 36919

BROTHER CANE

R 1990s: #38

Rock band from Birmingham, Alabama: Damon Johnson (vocals, guitar), Roman Glick (guitar), Glenn Maxey (bass) and Scott Collier (drums). David Anderson replaced Maxey by 1995. Johnson later joined country band Whiskey Falls.

Debut	Cht	Peak	Wks	Track Title	Hot Pos	Album Title	Album Label & Number
6/5/93	R	2¹	22	1 Got No Shame	—	Brother Cane	Virgin 87797
10/23/93	R	6	18	2 That Don't Satisfy Me	—	↓	
2/26/94	R	12	14	3 Hard Act To Follow	—	↓	
7/1/95	R	❶⁶	26	4 And Fools Shine On	—	Seeds	Virgin 40564
10/28/95	R	25	9	5 Breadmaker	—	↓	
2/17/96	R	30	7	6 Voice Of Eujena	—	↓	
3/28/98	R	❶⁴	26	7 I Lie In The Bed I Make	—	Wishpool	Virgin 45561
8/8/98	R	12	14	8 Machete	—	↓	

BROWN, Danny Joe, And The Danny Joe Brown Band

Born on 8/24/1951 in Jacksonville, Florida. Died of diabetes complications on 3/10/2005 (age 53). Lead singer of **Molly Hatchet**. His band included: Bobby Ingram, Steve Wheeler and Kenny McVay (guitars), John Galvin (keyboards), Buzzy Meekins (bass) and Jimmy Glenn (drums).

| 6/27/81 | R | 12 | 13 | Edge Of Sundown | — | Danny Joe Brown And The Danny Joe Brown Band | Epic 37385 |

BROWNE, Jackson

Born Clyde Jackson Browne on 10/9/1948 in Heidelberg, Germany (U.S. Army base); raised in Los Angeles, California. Pop-rock singer/songwriter/guitarist/pianist. Worked with the **Eagles** and **Warren Zevon**. His wife, Phyllis Majors, committed suicide on 3/25/1976 (age 30). Longtime relationship with actress Daryl Hannah (never married). A prominent activist against nuclear power. Also see **Classic Rock Tracks** section.

AWARD: R&R Hall of Fame: 2004

TOP HITS: 1)For America 2)Lawyers In Love 3)World In Motion

8/7/82	R	4	13	1 Somebody's Baby	7	St: Fast Times At Ridgemont High	Full Moon 60158
7/9/83	R	4	17	2 Lawyers In Love	13	Lawyers In Love	Asylum 60268
8/27/83	R	7	12	3 For A Rocker	45	↓	
9/3/83	R	37	9	4 Cut It Away	—	↓	
10/29/83	R	18	8	5 Tender Is The Night	25	↓	
11/2/85	R	16	11	6 You're A Friend Of Mine	18	Hero	Columbia 40010
				CLARENCE CLEMONS & JACKSON BROWNE			
				includes vocals by actress Daryl Hannah (Browne's then-girlfriend)			
3/1/86	R	3¹	11	7 For America	30	Lives In The Balance	Asylum 60457
3/29/86	R	33	9	8 Lives In The Balance	—	↓	
5/17/86	R	15	10	9 In The Shape Of A Heart	70	↓	
6/3/89	R	4	9	10 World In Motion	—	World In Motion	Elektra 60830
				Bonnie Raitt (harmony vocal)			
7/22/89	R	9	10	11 Chasing You Into The Light	—	↓	
10/30/93	R	18	10	12 I'm Alive	118	I'm Alive	Elektra 61524

BRUCE, Jack

Born John Asher on 5/14/1943 in Glasgow, Scotland. Rock singer/bassist. Member of Cream.

| 4/4/81 | R | 43 | 1 | Won't Let You Down | — | B.L.T. | Chrysalis 1324 |
| | | | | JACK BRUCE / BILL LORDAN / ROBIN TROWER | | | |

BT

Born Brian Transeau on 10/4/1970 in Washington DC. Electronic keyboardist/producer.

| 7/15/00 | M | 16 | 11 | Never Gonna Come Back Down | — | Movement In Still Life | Nettwerk 30154 |

BUCKCHERRY

Hard-rock band from Los Angeles, California: Joshua Todd (vocals), Keith Nelson (guitar), Yugomir "Yogi" Lonich (guitar), Jon Brightman (bass) and Devon Glenn (drums). Disbanded in 2002. Todd and Nelson re-formed the band in 2005 with Steve Dacanay (guitar), Jimmy Ashhurst (bass) and Xavier Muriel (drums).

3/27/99	R	❶³	28	1 Lit Up	—	Buckcherry	DreamWorks 50044
5/15/99	M	33	5				
8/7/99	M	24	12	2 For The Movies	—	↓	
8/21/99	R	25	10				
12/4/99	R	38	3	3 Dead Again	—	↓	
2/19/00	R	29	6	4 Check Your Head	—	↓	
2/24/01	R	9	15	5 Ridin'	—	Time Bomb	DreamWorks 450287
3/4/06	R	3¹	33	6 Crazy Bitch	59	15	Eleven Seven 001
4/29/06	M	13	20				
8/26/06	R	18	20	7 Next 2 You	—	↓	

Billboard Debut	Cht	Peak	Wks	ARTIST / Track Title **ℝ**=Mainstream Rock **Ⓜ**=Modern Rock	Hot Pos	Album Title	Album Label & Number
				BUCKCHERRY — cont'd			
1/27/07	ℝ	6	22	8 Everything	117	↓	
2/10/07	Ⓜ	23	18				
7/28/07	ℝ	28	10	9 Broken Glass	—	↓	
2/16/08	Ⓜ	31	7↑	10 Sorry	9	↓	
3/8/08	ℝ	32↑	4↑				
				BUCKINGHAM, Lindsey Born on 10/3/1949 in Palo Alto, California. Rock singer/songwriter/guitarist. Formed Buckingham-Nicks duo with then-girlfriend, **Stevie Nicks**. Both joined **Fleetwood Mac** in 1975.			
10/24/81	ℝ	12	18	1 Trouble	9	*Law And Order* ....Asylum 561	
7/28/84	ℝ	4	14	2 Go Insane	23	*Go Insane* ....Elektra 60363	
7/4/92	ℝ	23	7	3 Wrong	—	*Out Of The Cradle* ....Reprise 26182	
10/3/92	ℝ	38	2	4 Countdown	—	↓	
				BUCKLEY, Jeff Born on 11/17/1966 in Anaheim, California. Drowned on 5/29/1997 (age 30). Singer/songwriter/guitarist. Son of folk music legend Tim Buckley.			
3/25/95	Ⓜ	19	13	Last Goodbye		*Grace* ....Columbia 57528	
				BUCK-O-NINE Ska-rock band from San Diego, California: Jon Pebsworth (vocals), Jonas Kleiner (guitar), Anthony Curry (trumpet), Dan Albert (trombone), Craig Yarnold (sax), Scott Kennerly (bass) and Steve Bauer (drums).			
8/9/97	Ⓜ	32	8	My Town	—	*Twenty-Eight Teeth* ....TVT 5760	
				BUCK PETS, The Rock band from Dallas, Texas: Andy Thompson (vocals), Chris Savage (guitar), Ian Beach (bass) and Tony Alba (drums).			
2/9/91	Ⓜ	25	2	Libertine	—	*Mercurotones* ....Island 846867	
				BUFFALO TOM Rock trio from Boston, Massachusetts: Bill Janovitz (vocals, guitar), Chris Colbourn (bass) and Tom Maginnis (drums).			
9/18/93	Ⓜ	7	10	Sodajerk	—	*[big red letter day]* ....Beggars Banquet 92292	
				BUFFETT, Jimmy Born on 12/25/1946 in Pascagoula, Mississippi; raised in Mobile, Alabama. Eclectic singer/songwriter/guitarist. Settled in Key West in 1971. Author of several books. Appeared in the 1978 movie *FM*. Faithful fans known as "Parrotheads." Also see **Classic Rock Tracks** section.			
3/21/81	ℝ	51	5	1 It's My Job	57	*Coconut Telegraph* ....MCA 5169	
1/30/82	ℝ	32	8	2 It's Midnight And I'm Not Famous Yet	—	*Somewhere Over China* ....MCA 5285	
				BULLETBOYS Hard-rock band from Los Angeles, California: Marq Torien (vocals), Mick Sweda (guitar), Lonnie Vencent (bass) and Jimmy D'Anda (drums).			
2/11/89	ℝ	30	9	1 For The Love Of Money .... #9 Pop hit for The O'Jays in 1974	78	*BulletBoys* ....Warner 25782	
6/17/89	ℝ	23	9	2 Smooth Up	71	↓	
5/25/91	ℝ	22	9	3 Hang On St. Christopher	—	*Freakshow* ....Warner 26168	
				BULLET FOR MY VALENTINE Hard-rock band from Bridgend, South Wales: Matthew Tuck (vocals, guitar), Michael Paget (guitar), Jason James (bass) and Michael Thomas (drums).			
7/1/06	ℝ	24	20	1 Tears Don't Fall	—	*The Poison* ....Trustkill 74	
8/19/06	Ⓜ	32	14				
1/27/07	ℝ	13	20	2 All These Things I Hate (Revolve Around Me)	—	↓	
3/3/07	Ⓜ	30	11				
12/29/07+	ℝ	16	14↑	3 Scream Aim Fire	—	*Scream Aim Fire* ....Jive 721393	
2/2/08	Ⓜ	26	9↑				
				BUNBURYS, The All-star rock band: **Eric Clapton**, The Bee Gees, **Elton John** and **George Harrison**.			
9/17/88	ℝ	8	8	Fight (No Matter How Long)	—	*VA: 1988 Summer Olympics Album/* *One Moment In Time* ....Arista 8551	
				BURDEN BROTHERS, The Rock band formed in Fort Worth, Texas: Todd Lewis (vocals), Corey Rozzoni (guitar), Casey Orr (bass) and Taz Bentley (drums). Lewis was lead singer of the **Toadies**.			
4/3/04	ℝ	33	11	1 Beautiful Night	—	*Buried In Your Black Heart* ....Trauma 74077	
12/23/06	ℝ	36	5	2 Everybody Is Easy (We Sink/We Swim)	—	*Mercy* ....Kirtland 32	

BURNING BRIDES
Hard-rock trio from Philadelphia, Pennsylvania: Dimitri Coats (vocals, guitar), Melanie Campbell (bass) and Mike Ambs (drums).

Debut	Cht	Peak	Wks	Track Title	Hot Pos	Album Title	Album Label & Number
3/1/03	ⓜ	31	6	1 Arctic Snow	—	*Fall Of The Plastic Empire*	File 13 35
7/3/04	ⓜ	32	9	2 Heart Full Of Black	—	*Leave No Ashes*	V2 27181
8/7/04	®	38	2				

BURTNICK, Glen
Born on 4/8/1955 in New Brunswick, New Jersey. Pop-rock singer/guitarist. Member of **Styx** from 1990-2004.

Debut	Cht	Peak	Wks	Track Title	Hot Pos	Album Title	Album Label & Number
3/29/86	®	40	4	1 Little Red House	—	*Talking In Code*	A&M 5114
8/22/87	®	23	9	2 Follow You	65	*Heroes & Zeros*	A&M 5166

BUSH   ® 1990s: #23 / All-Time: #66 ★ ⓜ 1990s: #8 / All-Time: #12
Rock band from London, England: **Gavin Rossdale** (vocals, guitar; born on 10/30/1967), Nigel Pulsford (guitar; born on 4/11/1963), Dave Parsons (bass; born on 7/2/1965) and Robin Goodridge (drums; born on 9/10/1966). Disbanded in 2002. Rossdale married **Gwen Stefani** (lead singer of **No Doubt**) on 9/14/2002. Rossdale went on to form **Institute**.

TOP HITS: 1)Swallowed 2)The Chemicals Between Us 3)Glycerine

Debut	Cht	Peak	Wks	Track Title	Hot Pos	Album Title	Album Label & Number
12/10/94+	ⓜ	2[2]	26	1 Everything Zen	40[A]	*Sixteen Stone*	Trauma 92531
2/11/95	®	5	26				
4/8/95	ⓜ	4	23	2 Little Things	46[A]	↓	
5/6/95	®	6	26				
7/22/95	ⓜ	❶[2]	26	3 Comedown	30	↓	
8/12/95	®	2[1]	26				
11/11/95	ⓜ	❶[2]	23	4 Glycerine	28	↓	
11/25/95+	®	4	26				
2/24/96	ⓜ	4	26	5 Machinehead	43	↓	
2/24/96	®	4	26				
11/2/96	ⓜ	❶[7]	20	6 Swallowed	27[A]	*Razorblade Suitcase*	Trauma 90091
11/2/96	®	2[2]	19				
12/28/96+	ⓜ	3[1]	26	7 Greedy Fly	41[A]	↓	
12/28/96+	®	5	25				
4/19/97	®	18	9	8 Cold Contagious	—	↓	
4/26/97	ⓜ	23	10				
10/25/97	ⓜ	5	23	9 Mouth	63[A]	*St: An American Werewolf In Paris*	Hollywood 62131
11/29/97+	®	28	13				
9/25/99	ⓜ	❶[5]	26	10 The Chemicals Between Us	67	*The Science Of Things*	Trauma 490483
9/25/99	®	3[3]	31				
1/22/00	ⓜ	4	17	11 Letting The Cables Sleep	113	↓	
1/29/00	®	26	9				
5/13/00	®	16	11	12 Warm Machine	—	↓	
6/17/00	ⓜ	38	2				
9/15/01	®	10	14	13 The People That We Love	114	*Golden State*	Atlantic 83488
9/15/01	ⓜ	11	13	originally titled "Speed Kills" (changed due to the 9/11 terrorist attacks)			
12/15/01	®	34	7	14 Headful Of Ghosts	—	↓	
1/5/02	ⓜ	38	3				

BUSH, Kate
Born on 7/30/1958 in Bexleyheath, Kent, England. Eclectic singer/songwriter.

Debut	Cht	Peak	Wks	Track Title	Hot Pos	Album Title	Album Label & Number
11/16/85	®	34	5	1 Running Up That Hill	30	*Hounds Of Love*	EMI America 17171
10/28/89	ⓜ	❶[4]	15	2 Love And Anger	—	*The Sensual World*	Columbia 44164
1/20/90	ⓜ	6	8	3 The Sensual World	—	↓	
11/9/91	ⓜ	11	10	4 Rocket Man (I Think It's Going To Be A Long, Long Time)	—	*VA: Two Rooms - Celebrating The Songs Of Elton John & Bernie Taupin*	Polydor 845750
				#6 Pop hit for **Elton John** in 1972			
10/2/93	ⓜ	10	7	5 Eat The Music	—	*The Red Shoes*	Columbia 53737
11/20/93	ⓜ	7	11	6 Rubberband Girl	88	↓	

BUTCHER, Jon, Axis

Born in Boston, Massachusetts. Black rock singer/guitarist. The Axis included Chris Martin (bass) and Derek Blevins (drums). Martin left in early 1985. Thom Gimbel (keyboards) and Jimmy Johnson (bass) joined in 1985. Butcher went solo in early 1987. Butcher also formed **Barefoot Servants**.

Debut	Cht	Peak	Wks	#	Track Title	Hot Pos	Album Title	Album Label & Number
4/23/83	R	26	5	1	Life Takes A Life	—	Jon Butcher Axis	Polydor 810059
3/10/84	R	24	5	2	Don't Say Goodnight	—	Stare At The Sun	Polydor 817493
9/21/85	R	31	6	3	Stop	—	Along The Axis	Capitol 12425
					JON BUTCHER:			
3/7/87	R	7	12	4	Goodbye Saving Grace	—	Wishes	Capitol 12542
5/30/87	R	25	5	5	Holy War	—	↓	
8/15/87	R	42	5	6	Wishes	—	↓	
1/21/89	R	7	11	7	Send Me Somebody	—	Pictures From The Front	Capitol 90238
4/8/89	R	38	4	8	Might As Well Be Free	—	↓	

BUTTHOLE SURFERS

Rock band from San Antonio, Texas: Gibby Haynes (vocals), Paul Leary (guitar), Jeff Pinkus (bass) and Jeff "King" Coffey (drums).

Debut	Cht	Peak	Wks	#	Track Title	Hot Pos	Album Title	Album Label & Number
5/22/93	M	24	2	1	Who Was In My Room Last Night?	—	Independent Worm Saloon	Capitol 98798
5/18/96	M	●[3]	26	2	Pepper	26[A]	Electriclarryland	Capitol 29842
6/29/96	R	19	13					
8/18/01	M	24	10	3	The Shame Of Life	—	Weird Revolution	Surfdog 162269

BYRDS, The

Folk-rock band formed in Los Angeles, California: **Roger McGuinn** and **David Crosby** (guitars), Gene Clark (tambourine, guitar), Chris Hillman (bass) and Mike Clarke (drums). All shared vocals. Group had several hits from 1965-67. Numerous personnel changes. McGuinn, Crosby and Hillman reunited in 1990. Gene Clark died on 5/24/1991 (age 46). Mike Clarke died on 12/19/1993 (age 47). Also see **Classic Rock Tracks** section.

AWARD: R&R Hall of Fame: 1991

Debut	Cht	Peak	Wks	Track Title	Hot Pos	Album Title	Album Label & Number
11/3/90	R	14	11	Love That Never Dies	—	The Byrds	Columbia 46773

BYRNE, David

Born on 5/14/1952 in Dumbarton, Scotland; raised in Baltimore, Maryland. Lead singer of the **Talking Heads**. Composed scores for several movies and plays. Formed own Luaka Bop record label.

Debut	Cht	Peak	Wks	#	Track Title	Hot Pos	Album Title	Album Label & Number
10/21/89	M	11	7	1	Make Believe Mambo	—	Rei Momo	Luaka Bop 25990
12/9/89	M	8	6	2	Dirty Old Town	—	↓	
3/7/92	M	3[2]	11	3	She's Mad	—	Uh-Oh	Luaka Bop 26799
6/4/94	M	24	4	4	Angels	—	David Byrne	Luaka Bop 45558

C

CADELL, Meryn

Born in New York; raised in Waterloo, Ontario, Canada. Female singer/songwriter. Underwent a sex change operation in the mid-1990s to become a male.

Debut	Cht	Peak	Wks	Track Title	Hot Pos	Album Title	Album Label & Number
5/30/92	M	24	3	The Sweater	—	Angel Food For Thought	Sire 26877

CAESARS

Alternative-rock band from Borlänge, Sweden: Joakim Ahlund (vocals, guitar), Cesar Vidal (guitar), David Lindquist (bass) and Nino Keller (drums).

Debut	Cht	Peak	Wks	Track Title	Hot Pos	Album Title	Album Label & Number
4/30/05	M	40	2	Jerk It Out	70	Paper Tigers	Astralwerks 60828

CAFFERTY, John, And The Beaver Brown Band

Rock band from Narragansett, Rhode Island: John Cafferty (vocals, guitar), Gary Gramolini (guitar), Robert Cotoia (keyboards), Michael Antunes (sax), Pat Lupo (bass) and Ken Silva (drums). Wrote and recorded the music for the soundtrack *Eddie And The Cruisers*. Cotoia died on 9/3/2004 (age 51).

Debut	Cht	Peak	Wks	#	Track Title	Hot Pos	Album Title	Album Label & Number
9/1/84	R	●[5]	11	1	On The Dark Side	7	Eddie And The Cruisers	Scotti Brothers 38929
11/3/84	R	10	14	2	Tender Years	31	↓	
5/11/85	R	●[2]	13	3	Tough All Over	22	Tough All Over	Scotti Brothers 39405
7/20/85	R	9	11	4	C-I-T-Y	18	↓	
6/4/88	R	47	1	5	Song & Dance	—	Roadhouse	Scotti Brothers 40980

CAKE
ⓜ All-Time: #75

Rock band from Sacramento, California: John McCrea (vocals, guitar), Greg Brown (guitar), Vince DiFiore (trumpet), Victor Damiani (bass) and Todd Roper (drums). Xan McCurdy replaced Brown in 1997. Gabriel Nelson replaced Damiani in early 1998.

Debut	Cht	Peak	Wks	Track Title		Hot Pos	Album Title	Label & Number
4/22/95	ⓜ	31	7	1 Rock 'N' Roll Lifestyle		—	Motorcade Of Generosity	Capricorn 42035
10/5/96	ⓜ	4	25	2 The Distance		35[A]	Fashion Nugget	Capricorn 532867
12/14/96	®	38	5					
2/15/97	ⓜ	28	8	3 I Will Survive		—	↓	
				#1 Pop hit for Gloria Gaynor in 1979				
9/26/98	ⓜ	❶³	33	4 Never There		78	Prolonging The Magic	Capricorn 538092
2/6/99	®	40	1					
2/20/99	ⓜ	16	14	5 Sheep Go To Heaven		—	↓	
7/17/99	ⓜ	28	10	6 Let Me Go		—	↓	
6/30/01	ⓜ	7	20	7 Short Skirt/Long Jacket		119	Comfort Eagle	Columbia 62132
9/11/04	ⓜ	13	15	8 No Phone		—	Pressure Chief	Columbia 92629

CALE, John
Born on 3/9/1940 in Crynant, West Glamorgan, Wales. Eclectic-rock singer/songwriter/producer. Member of the Velvet Underground.

5/12/90	ⓜ	13	7	1 Nobody But You		—	Songs For Drella	Sire 26140
				LOU REED & JOHN CALE				
10/27/90	ⓜ	11	10	2 Been There Done That		—	Wrong Way Up	Opal 26421
				BRIAN ENO & JOHN CALE				

CALL, The
Rock band from San Francisco, California: Michael Been (vocals, guitar), Tom Ferrier (guitar), Greg Freeman (bass) and Scott Musick (drums). Jim Goodwin (keyboards) replaced Freeman in 1984.

4/23/83	®	17	6	1 The Walls Came Down		74	Modern Romans	Mercury 810307
3/1/86	®	17	13	2 I Still Believe (Great Design)		—	Reconciled	Elektra 60440
6/28/86	®	38	7	3 Everywhere I Go		—	↓	
				Peter Gabriel and Jim Kerr (of Simple Minds; backing vocals)				
8/1/87	®	38	3	4 I Don't Wanna		—	Into The Woods	Elektra 60739
6/10/89	®	❶¹	19	5 Let The Day Begin		51	Let The Day Begin	MCA 6303
6/24/89	ⓜ	5	12					
10/14/89	®	29	8	6 You Run		—	↓	
10/13/90	ⓜ	25	4	7 What's Happened To You		—	Red Moon	MCA 10033
10/13/90	®	39	4	Bono (of U2; backing vocal)				

CALLING, The
Rock band from Los Angeles, California: Alex Band (vocals), Aaron Kamin (guitar), Sean Woolstenhulme (guitar), Billy Mohler (bass) and Nate Wood (drums).

6/23/01	ⓜ	14	14	Wherever You Will Go		5	Camino Palmero	RCA 67585
7/14/01	®	37	8					

CAMOUFLAGE
Dance trio from Germany: Marcus Meyn (vocals), Heiko Maile (keyboards) and Oliver Kreyssig (backing vocals; left in 1990).

10/22/88	ⓜ	3²	15	1 The Great Commandment		59	Voices & Images	Atlantic 81886
2/11/89	ⓜ	26	5	2 That Smiling Face		—	↓	
10/14/89	ⓜ	23	3	3 Love Is A Shield		—	Methods Of Silence	Atlantic 82002
6/1/91	ⓜ	18	5	4 Heaven (I Want You)		—	Meanwhile	Atlantic 82212

CAMPER VAN BEETHOVEN
Rock band from Santa Cruz, California: David Lowery (vocals, guitar), Greg Lisher (guitar), Morgan Fichter (violin), Victor Krummenacher (bass) and Chris Pedersen (drums). Lowery later formed **Cracker**.

9/16/89	ⓜ	❶³	12	Pictures Of Matchstick Men		—	Key Lime Pie	Virgin 91289
				#12 Pop hit for Status Quo in 1968				

CANDLEBOX
Rock band from Seattle, Washington: Kevin Martin (vocals), Peter Klett (guitar), Bardi Martin (bass) and Scott Mercado (drums). Dave Krusen replaced Mercado in 1997.

8/14/93	®	18	16	1 Change		—	Candlebox	Maverick 45313
12/4/93+	®	6	26	2 You		78	↓	
4/23/94	®	4	35	3 Far Behind		18	↓	
7/23/94	ⓜ	7	25					
11/5/94	®	8	18	4 Cover Me		—	↓	
11/19/94	ⓜ	23	8					

Debug	Cht	Peak	Wks	ARTIST / Track Title	Hot Pos	Album Title	Album Label & Number

Billboard — ARTIST / Track Title — ℝ=Mainstream Rock ℳ=Modern Rock — Hot Pos — Album Title — Album Label & Number

CANDLEBOX — cont'd

Debut	Cht	Peak	Wks	Track Title	Hot Pos	Album Title	Album Label & Number
9/16/95	ℝ	5	12	5 Simple Lessons	60[A]	Lucy	Maverick 45962
9/16/95	ℳ	12	8				
11/25/95	ℝ	19	11	6 Understanding	—	↓	
6/27/98	ℝ	2[6]	18	7 It's Alright	—		
8/22/98	ℳ	32	4			Happy Pills	Maverick 46975
10/17/98	ℝ	13	15	8 10,000 Horses	—	↓	
2/13/99	ℝ	17	10	9 Happy Pills	—	↓	

CANDYFLIP

Dance-pop duo from England: Danny Spencer (vocals) and Ric Peet (keyboards).

Debut	Cht	Peak	Wks	Track Title	Hot Pos	Album Title	Album Label & Number
8/4/90	ℳ	11	6	1 Strawberry Fields Forever	—	Madstock...	Atlantic 82264
				#8 Pop hit for **The Beatles** in 1967			
8/3/91	ℳ	19	6	2 Redhills Road	—	↓	

CANDY SKINS, The

Psychedelic-pop band formed in Oxford, England: brothers Nick Cope (vocals) and Mark Cope (guitar), Nick Burton (guitar) and John Halliday (drums). Karl Shale (bass) joined in 1992. The Cope brothers are the sons of TV actor/comedian Kenneth Cope.

Debut	Cht	Peak	Wks	Track Title	Hot Pos	Album Title	Album Label & Number
6/29/91	ℳ	9	10	1 Submarine Song	—	Space I'm In	DGC 24370
2/13/93	ℳ	12	8	2 Wembley	—	Fun?	DGC 24494

CANTRELL, Jerry

Born on 3/18/1966 in Tacoma, Washington. Rock singer/songwriter/guitarist. Member of **Alice In Chains**.

Debut	Cht	Peak	Wks	Track Title	Hot Pos	Album Title	Album Label & Number
5/25/96	ℝ	14	13	1 Leave Me Alone	—	St: The Cable Guy	Work 67654
2/28/98	ℝ	5	23	2 Cut You In	—	Boggy Depot	Columbia 68147
3/7/98	ℳ	15	15				
5/30/98	ℝ	6	21	3 My Song	—	↓	
12/12/98	ℝ	36	2	4 Dickeye	—	↓	
4/27/02	ℝ	10	18	5 Anger Rising	—	Degradation Trip	Roadrunner 618451

CAPALDI, Jim

Born on 8/24/1944 in Evesham, Worcestershire, England. Died of cancer on 1/28/2005 (age 60). Rock drummer/singer/songwriter. Member of **Traffic**.

Debut	Cht	Peak	Wks	Track Title	Hot Pos	Album Title	Album Label & Number
10/6/84	ℝ	58	2	1 I'll Keep Holding On	106	One Man Mission	Atlantic 80182
10/29/88	ℝ	4	14	2 Something So Strong	—	Some Come Running	Island 91024
				Steve Winwood (guitar, keyboards)			

CARAMEL

Rock band from Toronto, Ontario, Canada: Andy Curran (vocals, bass), Simon Brierley (guitar), Virginia Storey (guitar), and Eddie Zeeman (drums).

Debut	Cht	Peak	Wks	Track Title	Hot Pos	Album Title	Album Label & Number
5/23/98	ℝ	35	7	Lucy	—	Caramel	Geffen 25228

CARDIGANS, The

Pop-rock band from Jönköping, Sweden: Nina Persson (vocals), Peter Svensson (guitar), Lars-Olof Johansson (keyboards), Magnus Sveningsson (bass) and Bengt Lagersburg (drums).

Debut	Cht	Peak	Wks	Track Title	Hot Pos	Album Title	Album Label & Number
12/28/96+	ℳ	9	17	1 Lovefool	2[8A]	First Band On The Moon	Stockholm 533117
11/28/98+	ℳ	16	26	2 My Favourite Game	—	Gran Turismo	Stockholm 559081

CAREY, Tony

Born on 10/16/1952 in Watsonville, California. Rock singer/songwriter/keyboardist. Former member of **Rainbow** and **Planet P**.

Debut	Cht	Peak	Wks	Track Title	Hot Pos	Album Title	Album Label & Number
2/19/83	ℝ	8	16	1 I Won't Be Home Tonight	79	Tony Carey [I Won't Be Home Tonight]	Rocshire 0001
3/10/84	ℝ	❶[1]	12	2 A Fine Fine Day	22	Some Tough City	MCA 5464
6/16/84	ℝ	21	8	3 The First Day Of Summer	33	↓	

CARNES, Kim

Born on 7/20/1945 in Los Angeles, California. Pop singer/songwriter/pianist.

Debut	Cht	Peak	Wks	Track Title	Hot Pos	Album Title	Album Label & Number
5/2/81	ℝ	5	12	1 Bette Davis Eyes	❶[9]	Mistaken Identity	EMI America 17052
				Grammys: Record & Song of the Year			
6/27/81	ℝ	46	3	2 Break The Rules Tonite (Out Of School)	—	↓	

CAROLINE'S SPINE

Rock band from Tulsa, Oklahoma: Jimmy Newquist (vocals), Mark Haugh (guitar), Scott Jones (bass) and Jason Gilardi (drums). Gilardi is the son of actress/singer Annette Funicello.

Debut	Cht	Peak	Wks	Track Title	Hot Pos	Album Title	Album Label & Number
12/27/97+	ℝ	23	11	1 Sullivan	—	Monsoon	Hollywood 62087
8/28/99	ℝ	30	8	2 Attention Please	—	Attention Please	Hollywood 62133
4/1/00	ℝ	23	10	3 Nothing To Prove	—	↓	

CARRACK, Paul

Born on 4/22/1951 in Sheffield, Yorkshire, England. Pop-rock singer/guitarist/keyboardist. Lead singer of Ace, **Squeeze** and **Mike + The Mechanics**.

Debut	Cht	Peak	Wks	# Track Title	Hot Pos	Album Title	Label & Number
10/16/82	Ⓡ	33	3	1 Lesson In Love	—	Suburban Voodoo	Epic 38161
10/23/82	Ⓡ	22	4	2 I Need You	37	↓	
10/24/87+	Ⓡ	5	18	3 Don't Shed A Tear	9	One Good Reason	Chrysalis 41578
3/12/88	Ⓡ	20	9	4 One Good Reason	28	↓	
11/17/90	Ⓡ	37	3	5 Hey You ...... [L]	—	VA: The Wall - Live In Berlin	Mercury 846611

recorded at the Berlin Wall on 7/21/1990; first recorded by **Pink Floyd** in 1979

CARROLL, Jim, Band

Born on 8/1/1950 in Brooklyn, New York. Poet/rock singer. His band included Brian Linsley and Terrell Winn (guitars), Steve Linsley (bass) and Wayne Woods (drums). The 1995 movie *The Basketball Diaries* was based on Carroll's autobiographical book.

Debut	Cht	Peak	Wks	Track Title	Hot Pos	Album Title	Label & Number
3/21/81	Ⓡ	50	3	People Who Died	103	Catholic Boy	Atco 7314

CARS, The

Ⓡ 1980s: #15 / All-Time: #61

Rock and roll band from Boston, Massachusetts: **Ric Ocasek** (vocals, guitar; born on 3/23/1949), **Benjamin Orr** (bass, vocals; born on 8/9/1947; died of cancer on 10/3/2000, age 53), **Elliot Easton** (guitar; born on 12/18/1953), Greg Hawkes (keyboards; born on 3/15/1950) and David Robinson (drums; born on 4/2/1953). Also see **Classic Rock Tracks** section.

TOP HITS: 1)Tonight She Comes 2)You Might Think 3)Magic

Debut	Cht	Peak	Wks	# Track Title	Hot Pos	Album Title	Label & Number
11/28/81+	Ⓡ	2²	21	1 Shake It Up	4	Shake It Up	Elektra 567
12/26/81+	Ⓡ	37	13	2 Cruiser	—	↓	
2/27/82	Ⓡ	39	2	3 Victim Of Love	—	↓	
4/3/82	Ⓡ	24	4	4 Since You're Gone	41	↓	
3/10/84	Ⓡ	❶³	14	5 You Might Think	7	Heartbeat City	Elektra 60296
3/31/84	Ⓡ	❶¹	20	6 Magic	12	↓	
3/31/84	Ⓡ	22	24	7 Hello Again	20	↓	
6/2/84	Ⓡ	3³	21	8 Drive	3³	↓	
6/9/84	Ⓡ	31	16	9 It's Not The Night	—	↓	
1/26/85	Ⓡ	11	14	10 Why Can't I Have You	33	↓	
2/9/85	Ⓡ	19	8	11 Breakaway	—	(single only)	Elektra 69657
11/2/85	Ⓡ	❶³	14	12 Tonight She Comes	7	The Cars Greatest Hits	Elektra 60464
2/22/86	Ⓡ	29	5	13 I'm Not The One	32	↓	
8/29/87	Ⓡ	2³	8	14 You Are The Girl	17	Door To Door	Elektra 60747
9/12/87	Ⓡ	4	11	15 Strap Me In	85	↓	
11/28/87	Ⓡ	42	3	16 Double Trouble	—	↓	

CARTER U.S.M.

Alternative-pop duo from England: Jim "Jim Bob" Morrison (vocals) and Les "Fruit Bat" Carter (guitar). U.S.M.: Unstoppable Sex Machine.

Debut	Cht	Peak	Wks	# Track Title	Hot Pos	Album Title	Label & Number
9/14/91	Ⓜ	29	1	1 Sheriff Fatman	—	101 Damnations	Chrysalis 21881
8/29/92	Ⓜ	26	2	2 The Only Living Boy In New Cross	—	1992 The Love Album	Chrysalis 21946

CARTER

CASE, Peter

Born on 4/5/1954 in Buffalo, New York. Rock singer/songwriter. Lead singer of **The Plimsouls**.

Debut	Cht	Peak	Wks	Track Title	Hot Pos	Album Title	Label & Number
4/4/92	Ⓜ	16	8	Dream About You	—	Six-Pack Of Love	Geffen 24466

CASH, Johnny

Born J.R. Cash on 2/26/1932 in Kingsland, Arkansas; raised in Dyess, Arkansas. Died of diabetes on 9/12/2003 (age 71). Legendary country singer/songwriter/guitarist.

AWARDS: Grammys: Legend 1991 / Lifetime Achievement Award 1999 ★ R&R Hall of Fame: 1992

Debut	Cht	Peak	Wks	Track Title	Hot Pos	Album Title	Label & Number
3/15/03	Ⓜ	33	2	Hurt	—	American IV: The Man Comes Around	American 063339

CATERWAUL

Rock band formed in Los Angeles, California: Betsy Martin (vocals), Mark Schafer (guitar), Fred Cross (bass) and Kevin Pinnt (drums).

Debut	Cht	Peak	Wks	Track Title	Hot Pos	Album Title	Label & Number
4/29/89	Ⓜ	25	8	The Sheep's A Wolf	—	Pin And Web	I.R.S. 42281

CATHERINE WHEEL
Rock band from England: Rob Dickinson (vocals), Brian Futter (guitar), Dave Hawes (bass) and Neil Sims (drums). Ben Ellis replaced Hawes in 1999. Dickinson is the cousin of **Bruce Dickinson** (of **Iron Maiden**).

Debut	Cht	Peak	Wks	Track Title	Hot Pos	Album Title	Album Label & Number
6/6/92	Ⓜ	9	11	1 Black Metallic	—	Ferment	Fontana 512510
9/5/92	Ⓜ	20	5	2 I Want To Touch You	—	↓	
8/7/93	Ⓜ	5	13	3 Crank	—	Chrome	Fontana 518039
5/27/95	Ⓜ	15	10	4 Waydown	—	Happy Days	Mercury 526850
6/17/95	Ⓡ	24	8				
8/19/95	Ⓜ	22	8	5 Judy Staring At The Sun	—	↓	
5/20/00	Ⓜ	37	3	6 Sparks Are Gonna Fly	—	Wishville	Columbia 69515

CAUSE & EFFECT
Pop duo formed in California: Sean Rowley (keyboards) and Robert Rowe (vocals, guitar). Rowley died of asthma-related cardiac arrest on 11/12/1992 (age 23).

Debut	Cht	Peak	Wks	Track Title	Hot Pos	Album Title	Album Label & Number
6/18/94	Ⓜ	12	8	It's Over Now (It's Alright)	67	Trip	Zoo 11056

CAVEDOGS, The
Rock trio from Boston, Massachusetts: Todd Spahr (vocals, guitar), Brian Stevens (bass) and Mark Rivers (drums).

Debut	Cht	Peak	Wks	Track Title	Hot Pos	Album Title	Album Label & Number
8/25/90	Ⓜ	17	8	Leave Me Alone	—	Joyrides For Shut-Ins	Enigma 73571

CAVE IN
Rock band from Boston, Massachusetts: Stephen Brodsky (vocals, guitar), Adam McGrath (guitar), Caleb Scofield (bass) and John-Robert Conners (drums).

Debut	Cht	Peak	Wks	Track Title	Hot Pos	Album Title	Album Label & Number
5/10/03	Ⓜ	34	4	Anchor	—	Antenna	RCA 68131
6/7/03	Ⓡ	37	1				

CAVIAR
Rock band from Chicago, Illinois: Blake Smith (vocals, guitar), Dave Suh (guitar), Mike Willison (bass) and Jason Batchko (drums).

Debut	Cht	Peak	Wks	Track Title	Hot Pos	Album Title	Album Label & Number
9/30/00	Ⓜ	28	7	Tangerine Speedo	—	Caviar	Island 542917

CERVENKA, Exene
Born Christine Cervenka on 2/1/1956 in Chicago, Illinois. Female singer. Lead singer of **X** (with former husband **John Doe**).

Debut	Cht	Peak	Wks	Track Title	Hot Pos	Album Title	Album Label & Number
9/16/89	Ⓜ	17	6	He's Got A She	—	Old Wives' Tales	Rhino 70913

CETERA, Peter
Born on 9/13/1944 in Chicago, Illinois. Pop singer/songwriter/bassist. Member of **Chicago** from 1967-85.

Debut	Cht	Peak	Wks	Track Title	Hot Pos	Album Title	Album Label & Number
12/19/81+	Ⓡ	6	16	1 Livin' In The Limelight	—	Peter Cetera	Full Moon 3624
9/10/88	Ⓡ	32	6	2 You Never Listen To Me	—	One More Story	Full Moon 25704

CHALK FARM
Rock band from Los Angeles, California: Michael Duff (vocals, guitar), Trace Ritter (guitar), Orlando Sims (bass) and Toby Scarbrough (drums).

Debut	Cht	Peak	Wks	Track Title	Hot Pos	Album Title	Album Label & Number
9/21/96	Ⓡ	13	15	1 Lie On Lie	—	Notwithstanding	Columbia 67613
10/26/96	Ⓜ	36	5				
4/26/97	Ⓡ	35	4	2 Live Tomorrow	—	↓	

CHAPMAN, Tracy
Born on 3/30/1964 in Cleveland, Ohio. Black female singer/songwriter/guitarist.
AWARD: Grammy: Best New Artist 1988

Debut	Cht	Peak	Wks	Track Title	Hot Pos	Album Title	Album Label & Number
5/21/88	Ⓡ	19	13	1 Fast Car	6	Tracy Chapman	Elektra 60774
				Grammy: Pop Female Vocal ★ RS500 #165			
7/30/88	Ⓡ	22	10	2 Talkin' 'Bout A Revolution	75	↓	
9/10/88	Ⓜ	24	1				
10/14/89	Ⓜ	7	9	3 Crossroads	90	Crossroads	Elektra 60888
10/7/89	Ⓡ	26	7				

CHAPTERHOUSE
Rock band formed in England: Andrew Sheriff (vocals, guitar), Stephen Patman (vocals, guitar), Simon Rowe (guitar), Russell Barrett (bass) and Ashley Bates (drums).

Debut	Cht	Peak	Wks	Track Title	Hot Pos	Album Title	Album Label & Number
6/29/91	Ⓜ	7	9	1 Pearl	—	Whirlpool	Dedicated 3006
1/11/92	Ⓜ	21	4	2 Mesmerise	—	↓	
2/26/94	Ⓜ	29	1	3 We Are The Beautiful	—	Blood Music	Arista 18742

CHARLATANS UK, The

Rock band from Northwich, Cheshire, England: Tim Burgess (vocals), Jon Baker (guitar), Rob Collins (organ), Martin Blunt (bass) and Jon Brookes (drums). Mark Collins (guitar) replaced Baker in 1993. Simply known as **The Charlatans** by 1994. Rob Collins died in a car crash on 7/23/1996 (age 32).

8/18/90	Ⓜ	5	11	1 The Only One I Know	—		Some Friendly	Beggars Banquet 2411
12/15/90+	Ⓡ	37	7					
10/27/90	Ⓜ	4	16	2 Then	—		↓	
2/2/91	Ⓜ	18	2	3 White Shirt	—		↓	
2/23/91	Ⓜ	25	3	4 Sproston Green	—		↓	
3/21/92	Ⓜ	❶¹	16	5 Weirdo	—		Between 10th & 11th	Beggars Banquet 61108
6/20/92	Ⓜ	13	8	6 I Don't Want To See The Sights	—		↓	
3/19/94	Ⓜ	6	9	7 Can't Get Out Of Bed	—		Up To Our Hips	Beggars Banquet 92352
				THE CHARLATANS				

CHARLIE

Rock band from England: Terry Slesser (vocals), Terry Thomas (guitar), Julian Colbeck (guitar), John Anderson (bass) and Steve Gadd (drums).

8/20/83	Ⓡ	13	6	It's Inevitable	38		Charlie	Mirage 90098

CHEAP TRICK

Rock band from Rockford, Illinois: **Robin Zander** (vocals; born on 1/23/1953), Rick Nielsen (guitar; born on 12/22/1946), Tom Petersson (bass; born on 5/9/1950) and Brad "Bun E. Carlos" Carlson (drums; born on 6/12/1951). Petersson replaced by Jon Brant in 1980; returned in 1988, replacing Brant.

TOP HITS: 1)The Flame 2)Can't Stop Fallin' Into Love 3)Tonight It's You

5/29/82	Ⓡ	11	10	1 If You Want My Love	45		One On One	Epic 38021
3/31/84	Ⓡ	36	2	2 Up The Creek	—		St: Up The Creek	Pasha 39333
8/3/85	Ⓡ	8	13	3 Tonight It's You	44		Standing On The Edge	Epic 39592
4/9/88	Ⓡ	3⁴	14	4 The Flame	❶²		Lap Of Luxury	Epic 40922
6/25/88	Ⓡ	35	6	5 Let Go	—		↓	
8/6/88	Ⓡ	8	9	6 Don't Be Cruel	4		↓	
				#1 Pop hit for Elvis Presley in 1956				
11/26/88	Ⓡ	32	7	7 Ghost Town	33		↓	
3/18/89	Ⓡ	45	2	8 Never Had A Lot To Lose	75		↓	
7/21/90	Ⓡ	4	10	9 Can't Stop Fallin' Into Love	12		Busted	Epic 46013
9/29/90	Ⓡ	32	5	10 Back 'N Blue	—		↓	
4/2/94	Ⓡ	16	6	11 Woke Up With A Monster	—		Woke Up With A Monster	Warner 45425
4/26/97	Ⓡ	39	2	12 Say Goodbye	119		Cheap Trick	Red Ant 002

CHECKER, Chubby

Born Ernest Evans on 10/3/1941 in Andrews, South Carolina; raised in Philadelphia, Pennsylvania. Black male singer. Best known for popularizing "The Twist" craze in the early 1960s.

5/15/82	Ⓡ	33	5	Harder Than Diamond	104		The Change Has Come	MCA 5291

CHEECH & CHONG

Duo of comedians Richard "Cheech" Marin (born on 7/13/1946 in Watts, California) and Thomas Chong (born on 5/24/1938 in Edmonton, Alberta, Canada). Top selling comedy duo of the 1970s. Starred in several movies. Also see **Classic Rock Tracks** section.

1/10/98	Ⓡ	38	1	Santa Claus And His Old Lady [X-C]	—		VA: Billboard Rock 'N' Roll Christmas	Rhino 71789
				recorded in 1971				

CHEMICAL BROTHERS, The

Techno-dance DJ duo from England: Tom Rowlands and Ed Simons.

6/21/97	Ⓜ	40	1	1 Block Rockin' Beats [I]	105		Dig Your Own Hole	Astralwerks 6180
				Grammy: Rock Instrumental				
				samples "Gucci Again" by Schooly D				
6/12/99	Ⓜ	29	8	2 Let Forever Be [I]	—		Surrender	Freestyle Dust 47610

CHEQUERED PAST

Hard-rock band formed in Los Angeles, California: Michael Des Barres (vocals), Tony Sales (guitar), Steve Jones (guitar), Nigel Harrison (bass) and Clem Burke (drums). Sales was a member of **Utopia** and **Tin Machine**. Jones was a founding member of the Sex Pistols. Harrison and Burke were members of **Blondie**.

8/18/84	Ⓡ	50	4	How Much Is Too Much?	—		Chequered Past	EMI America 17123

CHERRY, Eagle-Eye

Born on 5/7/1969 in Stockholm, Sweden; raised in Brooklyn, New York. Son of jazz trumpeter Don Cherry. Half-brother of **Neneh Cherry**.

7/25/98	Ⓜ	8	26	Save Tonight	5		Desireless	Work 69434

CHERRY, Neneh

Born on 3/10/1964 in Stockholm, Sweden; raised in Brooklyn, New York. Female R&B singer. Stepdaughter of jazz trumpeter Don Cherry. Half-sister of **Eagle-Eye Cherry**.

11/7/92+	M	2¹	14	Trout	—	Homebrew ....Virgin 86516

NENEH CHERRY Featuring Michael Stipe

CHERRY POPPIN' DADDIES

Retro-swing band from Eugene, Oregon: Steve Perry (vocals, guitar), Jason Moss (guitar), Dana Heitman, Sean Falnnery and Ian Early (horns), Darren Cassidy (bass) and Tim Donahue (drums).

3/7/98	M	15	25	Zoot Suit Riot	41ᴬ	Zoot Suit Riot ....Mojo 53081

CHEVELLE   R 2000s: #18 / All-Time: #93 ★ M 2000s: #24 / All-Time: #50

Rock trio from Chicago, Illinois: brothers Pete Loeffler (vocals, guitar), Joe Loeffler (bass) and Sam Loeffler (drums). Dean Bernardini replaced Joe Loeffler in late 2005.

2/26/00	R	40	1	1 Point #1	—	Point #1 ....Squint 5930
7/20/02+	R	3²	43	2 The Red	56	Wonder What's Next ....Epic 86157
7/27/02	M	4	39			
2/8/03	R	❶⁴	35	3 Send The Pain Below	65	↓
2/15/03	M	❶¹	36			
10/11/03+	M	11	22	4 Closure	120	↓
9/20/03+	R	17	23			
8/21/04	R	❶²	26	5 Vitamin R (Leading Us Along)	68	This Type Of Thinking (Could Do Us In) ....Epic 86908
8/21/04	M	3²	26			
1/22/05	R	3²	27	6 The Clincher..	108	↓
2/5/05	M	8	26			
8/6/05	R	26	13	7 Panic Prone	—	↓
2/17/07	R	4	20	8 Well Enough Alone	119	Vena Sera ....Epic 02698
2/17/07	M	9	19			
8/4/07+	M	4	35↑	9 I Get It	118	↓
6/30/07	R	5	24			
2/2/08	R	13	9↑	10 The Fad	—	↓
3/22/08	M	40↑	2↑			

CHICAGO

Jazz-oriented rock band from Chicago, Illinois. Lineup in 1984: **Peter Cetera** (vocals, bass), Chris Pinnick (guitar), Robert Lamm and Bill Champlin (keyboards), James Pankow (trombone), Lee Loughnane (trumpet), Walt Parazaider (reeds) and Danny Seraphine (drums). Band had numerous personnel changes. Also see **Classic Rock Tracks** section.

5/19/84	R	7	12	1 Stay The Night	16	Chicago 17..Full Moon 25060
3/9/85	R	10	10	2 Along Comes A Woman	14	↓

CHILDS, Toni

Born on 7/20/1960 in Orange, California. Female rock singer.

9/10/88	M	17	4	Don't Walk Away	72	Union ....A&M 5175

CHILLIWACK

Rock band from Vancouver, British Columbia, Canada: Bill Henderson (vocals, guitar), Brian MacLeod (guitar), Ab Bryant (bass) and Rick Taylor (drums). Bryant and MacLeod later joined Headpins. Bryant was also with **Prism**. MacLeod died of brain cancer on 4/25/1992 (age 41).

9/26/81	R	16	17	1 My Girl (Gone, Gone, Gone)	22	Wanna Be A Star................................Millennium 7759
10/30/82	R	29	2	2 Whatcha Gonna Do	41	Opus X ....Millennium 7766
12/25/82+	R	48	4	3 Don't It Make You Feel Good...................	—	↓

CHILLS, The

Rock band formed in Dunedin, New Zealand: Martin Phillipps (vocals, guitar), Andrew Todd (keyboards), Justin Harwood (bass) and James Stephenson (drums).

4/14/90	M	17	7	Heavenly Pop Hit	—	Submarine Bells ....Slash 26130

CHOIRBOYS

Rock band from Sydney, Australia: Mark Gable (vocals), Brett Williams (guitar), Ian Hulme (bass) and Lindsay Tebbutt (drums).

3/18/89	R	33	6	Run To Paradise	80	Big Bad Noise ....WTG 45112

CHRISTMAS
Rock trio from Boston, Massachusetts: brothers Michael Cudahy (vocals, guitar) and Nicholas Cudahy (bass), with Elizabeth Cox (vocals, drums).

| 2/25/89 | ⓜ | 26 | 3 | Stupid Kids .... | | — | Ultraprophets Of Thee Psykick Revolution..I.R.S. 42273 |

CHRONIC FUTURE
Rock band from Phoenix, Arizona: Mike Busse (vocals), Ben Collins (guitar), Brandon Lee (bass) and Barry Collins (drums).

| 9/4/04 | ⓜ | 40 | 1 | Time And Time Again... | | — | Lines In My Face ....Interscope 002823 |

CHUMBAWAMBA
Post-punk rock band from Leeds, England: Alice Nutter, Lou Watts, Danbert Nubacon, Paul Greco, Jude Abbott, Dunstan Bruce, Neil Ferguson and Harry Hamer.

| 9/20/97 | ⓜ | ❶⁷ | 25 | Tubthumping | | 6 | Tubthumper...Republic 53099 |

CHURCH, The
Alternative pop-rock band from Canberra, Australia: Steve Kilbey (vocals, bass), Peter Koppes (guitar), Marty Willson-Piper (guitar) and Richard Ploog (drums).

3/5/88	®	2[1]	17	1 Under The Milky Way		24	Starfish..Arista 8521
7/16/88	®	27	7	2 Reptile		—	↓
3/3/90	ⓜ	❶[1]	15	3 Metropolis		—	Gold Afternoon Fix ....Arista 8579
3/17/90	®	11	11				
6/30/90	ⓜ	27	2	4 You're Still Beautiful		—	↓
2/29/92	ⓜ	3[1]	10	5 Ripple		—	Priest = Aura ....Arista 18683

CINDER
Rock band from Fort Myers, Florida: Roger Young (vocals), Kenny Craig (guitar), Pat McGuire (bass) and Brian Colbert (drums).

| 11/23/02 | ® | 26 | 14 | Soul Creation .... | | — | Break Your Silence...................................Geffen 493580 |

CINDERELLA
Hard-rock band from Philadelphia, Pennsylvania: Tom Keifer (vocals, guitar; born on 1/26/1961), Jeff LaBar (guitar; born on 3/18/1963), Eric Brittingham (bass; born on 5/8/1960) and Fred Coury (drums; born on 10/20/1966). Coury was also a member of **Arcade**.

TOP HITS: 1)Shelter Me 2)Heartbreak Station 3)Don't Know What You Got (Till It's Gone)

8/9/86	®	41	7	1 Shake Me		—	Night Songs ....Mercury 830076
1/10/87	®	25	10	2 Nobody's Fool		13	↓
3/21/87	®	37	5	3 Somebody Save Me...		66	↓
7/9/88	®	20	9	4 Gypsy Road		51	Long Cold Winter ....Mercury 834612
9/3/88	®	10	12	5 Don't Know What You Got (Till It's Gone)		12	↓
1/28/89	®	18	8	6 The Last Mile		36	↓
4/1/89	®	13	13	7 Coming Home		20	↓
11/17/90	®	5	15	8 Shelter Me		36	Heartbreak Station...................................Mercury 848018
2/16/91	®	10	16	9 Heartbreak Station		44	↓
6/8/91	®	41	6	10 The More Things Change		—	↓
3/14/92	®	45	2	11 Hot And Bothered...		—	St: Wayne's World ....Reprise 26805
11/26/94	®	37	4	12 Bad Attitude Shuffle		—	Still Climbing ....Mercury 522947

CINDER ROAD
Rock band from Lutherville, Maryland: Mike Ruocco (vocals), Chris Shucosky (guitar), Pat Patrick (guitar), Nat Doegen (bass) and Mac Calvaresi (drums).

| 7/7/07 | ® | 31 | 17 | Get In Get Out .... | | — | Superhuman ....Caroline 94301 |

CITIZEN KING
Rock band from Milwaukee, Wisconsin: Matt Sims (vocals, bass), Kristian Riley (guitar), Malcolm Michiles (DJ), Dave Cooley (keyboards) and DJ Brooks (drums).

| 3/6/99 | ⓜ | 3[1] | 26 | Better Days (And The Bottom Drops Out) .... | | 25 | Mobile Estates ....Warner 47023 |

CIV
Punk-rock band from New York: Anthony Civocelli (vocals), Charlie Garriga (guitar), Arthur Smilios (bass) and Sam Sigeler (drums).

| 9/23/95 | ⓜ | 21 | 8 | Can't Wait One Minute More.................................... | | — | Set Your Goals ....Lava 92603 |

CKY
Punk-rock band from West Chester, Pennsylvania: Deron Miller (vocals, guitar), Chad Ginsburg (guitar), Vern Zaborowski (bass) and Jess Margera (drums; brother of Bam Margera of MTV's *Jackass*). Matt Dies replaced Zaborowski in 2004. CKY: Camp Kill Yourself.

| 12/21/02+ | ® | 38 | 4 | 1 Flesh Into Gear .... | | — | Infiltrate-Destroy-Rebuild ....Island 063100 |
| 6/25/05 | ® | 32 | 11 | 2 Familiar Realm .... | | — | An Answer Can Be Found ....Island 004837 |

CLAIL, Gary, & The On-U Sound System

Born in Ireland; raised In Bristol, England. Techno-rave artist. The On-U Sound System consisted of over 30 musicians.

8/10/91	Ⓜ	10	9	**Human Nature (On The Mix)**	—	*The Emotional Hooligan* .... Perfecto 61007

CLAPTON, Eric

ℝ **1980s: #22 / 1990s: #17 / All-Time: #13**

Born Eric Clapp on 3/30/1945 in Ripley, England. Legendary rock-blues singer/songwriter/guitarist. Member of The Yardbirds, John Mayall's Bluesbreakers, Cream and Blind Faith. Nicknamed "Slowhand" in 1964 while with The Yardbirds. Also see **The Bunburys** and **Classic Rock Tracks** section.

AWARD: R&R Hall of Fame: 2000

TOP HITS: 1)Pretending 2)Bad Love 3)Forever Man 4)I Can't Stand It 5)It's In The Way That You Use It

Debut	Cht	Peak	Wks	Track Title	Hot Pos	Album Title	Album Label & Number
3/21/81	ℝ	❶²	12	1 **I Can't Stand It**	10	*Another Ticket* .... RSO 3095
3/21/81	ℝ	18	11	2 **Rita Mae**	—	↓
3/21/81	ℝ	23	8	3 **Catch Me If You Can**	—	↓
4/11/81	ℝ	24	1	4 **Blow Wind Blow**	—	↓
				ERIC CLAPTON AND HIS BAND (above 4)		
2/5/83	ℝ	24	15	5 **I've Got A Rock N' Roll Heart**	18	*Money And Cigarettes* .... Duck 23773
3/12/83	ℝ	32	2	6 **Ain't Going Down**	—	↓
3/9/85	ℝ	❶²	12	7 **Forever Man**	26	*Behind The Sun* .... Duck 25166
3/30/85	ℝ	11	11	8 **She's Waiting**	—	↓
				Phil Collins (drums, producer)		
5/11/85	ℝ	20	12	9 **See What Love Can Do**	89	↓
11/8/86+	ℝ	❶¹	15	10 **It's In The Way That You Use It**	—	*St: The Color Of Money* .... MCA 6189
12/13/86+	ℝ	5	15	11 **Tearing Us Apart**	—	*August* .... Duck 25476
				Tina Turner (female vocal)		
1/24/87	ℝ	9	13	12 **Miss You**	—	↓
4/11/87	ℝ	21	8	13 **Run**	—	↓
				above 3 produced by Phil Collins		
4/30/88	ℝ	4	9	14 **After Midnight**	—	*Crossroads* .... Polydor 835261
				new version of his #18 Pop hit in 1970		
11/11/89	ℝ	❶⁶	14	15 **Pretending**	55	*Journeyman* .... Duck 26074
				Chaka Khan (backing vocal)		
11/25/89+	ℝ	❶³	21	16 **Bad Love**	88	↓
				Grammy: Rock Male Vocal		
				Phil Collins (drums, backing vocal)		
2/24/90	ℝ	4	16	17 **No Alibis**	—	↓
				Daryl Hall (harmony vocal)		
5/5/90	ℝ	9	16	18 **Before You Accuse Me**	—	↓
				Robert Cray (guitar); first recorded by Bo Diddley in 1959		
8/11/90	ℝ	40	4	19 **Run So Far**	—	↓
				George Harrison (guitar, harmony vocal)		
10/19/91	ℝ	21	12	20 **Watch Yourself** .... [L]	—	*24 Nights* .... Duck 26420
				Robert Cray (guitar); recorded at The Royal Albert Hall in London		
1/11/92	ℝ	9	18	21 **Tears In Heaven**	2⁴	*St: Rush* .... Reprise 26794
				Grammys: Record & Song of the Year / Pop Male Vocal ★ RS500 #RS500 #353		
				Clapton wrote this for his son, Conor, who fell to his death on 3/20/1991 (age 4) from a New York City apartment window		
2/8/92	ℝ	6	20	22 **Help Me Up**	—	↓
6/13/92	ℝ	20	5	23 **It's Probably Me**	—	*St: Lethal Weapon 3* .... Reprise 26989
				STING & ERIC CLAPTON		
8/15/92	ℝ	10	7	24 **Runaway Train**	—	↓
				ELTON JOHN & ERIC CLAPTON		
9/5/92	ℝ	9	17	25 **Layla** .... [L]	12	*Unplugged* .... Duck 45024
				Grammy: Rock Song		
				live version of his #10 Pop hit in 1972 (as Derek And The Dominos)		
3/6/93	ℝ	15	13	26 **Running On Faith** .... [L]	—	↓
11/13/93	ℝ	4	13	27 **Stone Free**	—	*VA: Stone Free: A Tribute To Jimi Hendrix* .. Reprise 45438
				first recorded by Jimi Hendrix in 1969		
9/10/94	ℝ	5	13	28 **I'm Tore Down**	—	*From The Cradle* .... Duck 45735
				#5 R&B hit for Freddy King in 1961		
12/3/94	ℝ	23	10	29 **Motherless Child**	114	↓
				blues version of the traditional spiritual		
2/21/98	ℝ	26	6	30 **My Father's Eyes**	16ᴬ	*Pilgrim* .... Duck 46577
4/4/98	ℝ	19	15	31 **She's Gone**	—	↓
6/17/00	ℝ	26	11	32 **Riding With The King**	—	*Riding With The King* .... Reprise 47612
				B.B. KING & ERIC CLAPTON		
				first recorded by John Hiatt in 1983		
3/3/01	ℝ	21	11	33 **Superman Inside**	—	*Reptile* .... Duck 47966

Billboard				ARTIST		Hot		
Debut	Cht	Peak	Wks	Track Title	ℝ=Mainstream Rock ⓂϺ=Modern Rock	Pos	Album Title	Album Label & Number

CLARKE, Gilby
Born on 8/17/1962 in Cleveland, Ohio. Rock singer/guitarist. Member of **Guns N' Roses** from 1991-95.

8/6/94	ℝ	15	14	1 Cure Me...Or Kill Me...	—	Pawnshop Guitars	Virgin 39567
12/17/94+	ℝ	28	8	2 Tijuana Jail	↓		
				Slash (lead guitar, above 2)			

CLASH, The
Punk-rock band from London, England: John "Joe Strummer" Mellor (vocals), Mick Jones (guitar), Paul Simonon (bass) and Nicky "Topper" Headon (drums). Political activists who wrote songs protesting racism and oppression. Headon left in May 1983; replaced by Peter Howard. Jones (not to be confused with Mick Jones of Foreigner) left band in 1984 to form **Big Audio Dynamite**. Strummer disbanded The Clash in early 1986, and appeared in the 1987 movie *Straight To Hell*. Simonon formed **Havana 3 A.M.** in 1990. Strummer died of heart failure on 12/22/2002 (age 50). Also see **Classic Rock Tracks** section.

AWARD: R&R Hall of Fame: 2003

3/21/81	ℝ	21	4	1 Police On My Back	—	Sandinista!	Epic 37037
4/18/81	ℝ	53	3	2 Hitsville U.K.	—	↓	
12/19/81+	ℝ	45	5	3 This Is Radio Clash	—	(single only)	CBS 1797
				available only as a British import single			
6/5/82	ℝ	13	20	4 Should I Stay Or Should I Go	45	Combat Rock	Epic 37689
				RS500 #228			
7/24/82	ℝ	6	22	5 Rock The Casbah	8	↓	

CLASS OF '99
All-star rock band: Layne Staley (vocals; of **Alice In Chains**), Tom Morello (guitar; of **Rage Against The Machine**), Martyn LeNoble (bass; of **Porno For Pyros**) and Stephen Perkins (drums; of Porno For Pyros).

| 12/26/98+ | ℝ | 18 | 9 | Another Brick In The Wall (Part 2) | — | St: The Faculty | Columbia 69762 |
| 1/2/99 | ⓂϺ | 34 | 5 | #1 Pop hit for **Pink Floyd** in 1980 | | | |

CLEGG, Johnny, & Savuka
Born on 7/13/1953 in Rochdale, Lancashire, England; raised in South Africa. Singer/guitarist/dancer. Savuka: Steve Mavuso (keyboards), Keith Hutchinson (sax), Solly Letwaba (bass) and Dundu Zulu and Derek De Beer (drums).

| 5/12/90 | ⓂϺ | 27 | 3 | Cruel, Crazy, Beautiful World | — | Cruel, Crazy, Beautiful World | Capitol 93446 |

CLEMONS, Clarence
Born on 1/11/1942 in Norfolk, Virginia. R&B saxophonist. Member of **Bruce Springsteen**'s E Street Band. Known as the "Big Man."

| 11/2/85 | ℝ | 16 | 11 | You're A Friend Of Mine | 18 | Hero | Columbia 40010 |
| | | | | **CLARENCE CLEMONS & JACKSON BROWNE** includes vocals by actress Daryl Hannah (Browne's then-girlfriend) | | | |

CLIFFS OF DOONEEN
Rock band from Boston, Massachusetts: Eric Sean Murphy (vocals), Martin Crotty (guitars), Ira Nulton (bass) and Lex Lianos (drums).

| 1/4/92 | ⓂϺ | 10 | 7 | Through An Open Window | — | The Dog Went East, And God Went West | Critique 15404 |

CLOCKS
Rock band from Wichita, Kansas: Jerry Sumner (vocals, bass), Lance Threet (guitar), Gerald Graves (keyboards) and Steve Swaim (drums). Swaim died of liver failure on 3/18/2006 (age 51).

| 8/7/82 | ℝ | 47 | 1 | She Looks A Lot Like You | 67 | Clocks | Boulevard 37981 |

CLUTCH
Rock band from Germantown, Maryland: Neil Fallon (vocals), Tim Sult (guitar), Dan Maines (bass) and Jean Paul Gaster (drums).

6/23/01	ℝ	24	12	1 Careful With That Mic...	—	Pure Rock Fury	Atlantic 83433
6/5/04	ℝ	39	2	2 The Mob Goes Wild	—	Blast Tyrant	DRT 410
4/21/07	ℝ	38	1	3 Electric Worry	—	From Beale Street To Oblivion	Issachar 00449

COAL CHAMBER
Hard-rock band from Los Angeles, California: Brad Fafara (vocals), Miquel Rascon (guitar), Rayna Rose (bass) and Mike Cox (drums). Fafara is the nephew of actor Stanley Fafara (played "Whitey Whitney" on TV's *Leave It To Beaver*).

| 10/16/99 | ℝ | 26 | 7 | Shock The Monkey | — | Chamber Music | Roadrunner 8659 |
| | | | | **COAL CHAMBER Featuring Ozzy Osbourne** | | | |

COBRA STARSHIP
Rock band formed in New Jersey: Gabe Saporta (vocals), Alex Suarez (guitar), Victoria Asher (keyboards), Ryland Blackinton (bass) and Nate Navarro (drums). Saporta was the singer/bassist for the band **Midtown**.

| 8/12/06 | ⓂϺ | 32 | 5 | Snakes On A Plane (Bring It) | — | While The City Sleeps, We Rule The Streets | Decaydance 089 |

COC — see CORROSION OF CONFORMITY

Billboard				ARTIST		Hot		
Debut	Cht	Peak	Wks	Track Title	ⓡ=Mainstream Rock ⓜ=Modern Rock	Pos	Album Title	Album Label & Number

COCHRANE, Tom / RED RIDER

Born on 5/13/1953 in Lynn Lake, Manitoba, Canada. Rock singer/songwriter/guitarist. His band Red Rider: Ken Greer (guitar), Peter Boynton (keyboards), Jeff Jones (bass) and Rob Baker (drums). Steve Sexton replaced Boynton in 1982; left in early 1984. Cochrane went solo in 1989.

TOP HITS: 1)Life Is A Highway 2)No Regrets 3)Big League

RED RIDER:

Debut	Cht	Peak	Wks	#	Track Title	Hot Pos	Album Title	Label & Number
9/12/81	ⓡ	11	26	1	Lunatic Fringe	—	*As Far As Siam*	Capitol 12145
1/29/83	ⓡ	13	8	2	Power (Strength In Numbers)	—	*Neruda*	Capitol 12226
2/12/83	ⓡ	11	15	3	Human Race	—	↓	
2/19/83	ⓡ	39	3	4	Crack The Sky (Breakaway)	—	↓	
5/19/84	ⓡ	13	11	5	Young Thing, Wild Dreams (Rock Me)	71	*Breaking Curfew*	Capitol 12317

TOM COCHRANE AND RED RIDER:

Debut	Cht	Peak	Wks	#	Track Title	Hot Pos	Album Title	Label & Number
6/28/86	ⓡ	17	11	6	Boy Inside The Man	—	*Tom Cochrane And Red Rider*	Capitol 12484
10/4/86	ⓡ	48	2	7	The Untouchable One	—	↓	
10/8/88	ⓡ	9	10	8	Big League	—	*Victory Day*	RCA 8532
1/14/89	ⓡ	42	4	9	Calling America	—	↓	

TOM COCHRANE:

Debut	Cht	Peak	Wks	#	Track Title	Hot Pos	Album Title	Label & Number
2/29/92	ⓡ	6	26	10	Life Is A Highway	6	*Mad Mad World*	Capitol 97723
7/25/92	ⓡ	7	8	11	No Regrets	—	↓	

COCKBURN, Bruce

Born on 5/27/1945 in Ottawa, Canada. Pop-rock singer/songwriter. Name pronounced: coe-burn.

Debut	Cht	Peak	Wks	#	Track Title	Hot Pos	Album Title	Label & Number
9/1/84	ⓡ	56	3	1	Lovers In A Dangerous Time	—	*Stealing Fire*	Gold Mountain 80012
12/22/84+	ⓡ	16	9	2	If I Had A Rocket Launcher	88	↓	
2/11/89	ⓜ	20	8	3	If A Tree Falls	—	*Big Circumstance*	Gold Castle 71320
11/23/91	ⓜ	22	6	4	A Dream Like Mine	—	*Nothing But A Burning Light*	Columbia 47983

COCKER, Joe

Born John Cocker on 5/20/1944 in Sheffield, Yorkshire, England. Pop-rock singer. Notable spastic stage antics were based on Ray Charles's movements at the piano. Also see **Classic Rock Tracks** section.

Debut	Cht	Peak	Wks	#	Track Title	Hot Pos	Album Title	Label & Number
3/8/86	ⓡ	11	9	1	Shelter Me	91	*Cocker*	Capitol 12394
5/31/86	ⓡ	35	4	2	You Can Leave Your Hat On	—	↓	
					first recorded by **Randy Newman** in 1972			
10/17/87	ⓡ	11	13	3	Unchain My Heart	—	*Unchain My Heart*	Capitol 48285
					Clarence Clemons (sax solo)			
1/16/88	ⓡ	11	10	4	Two Wrongs	—	↓	
8/12/89	ⓡ	6	16	5	When The Night Comes	11	*One Night Of Sin*	Capitol 92861
					co-written by **Bryan Adams**			
6/2/90	ⓡ	44	6	6	What Are You Doing With A Fool Like Me	96	*Joe Cocker Live*	Capitol 93416
6/27/92	ⓡ	7	10	7	Love Is Alive	—	*Night Calls*	Capitol 97801
					#2 Pop hit for **Gary Wright** in 1976			

COCK ROBIN

Pop band from Los Angeles, California: Peter Kingsbery (vocals, bass), Anna LaCazio (vocals, keyboards), Clive Wright (guitars) and Louis Molino (drums).

Debut	Cht	Peak	Wks	#	Track Title	Hot Pos	Album Title	Label & Number
8/24/85	ⓡ	28	5		When Your Heart Is Weak	35	*Cock Robin*	Columbia 39582

COCTEAU TWINS

Pop trio from Grangemouth, Scotland: Elizabeth Fraser (vocals), Robin Guthrie (guitar) and Simon Raymonde (bass).

Debut	Cht	Peak	Wks	#	Track Title	Hot Pos	Album Title	Label & Number
10/8/88	ⓜ	2²	11	1	Carolyn's Fingers	—	*Blue Bell Knoll*	Capitol 90892
9/15/90	ⓜ	4	11	2	Iceblink Luck	—	*Heaven or Las Vegas*	Capitol 93669
11/24/90+	ⓜ	9	11	3	Heaven Or Las Vegas	—	↓	

COHEED AND CAMBRIA

Hard-rock band from Nyack, New York: Claudio Sanchez (vocals, guitar), Travis Stever (guitar), Mic Todd (bass) and Josh Eppard (drums). Chris Pennie replaced Eppard in late 2006.

Debut	Cht	Peak	Wks	#	Track Title	Hot Pos	Album Title	Label & Number
7/24/04	ⓜ	13	15	1	A Favor House Atlantic	—	*In Keeping Secrets Of Silent Earth: 3*	Equal Vision 87
8/28/04	ⓡ	40	4					
12/11/04+	ⓜ	29	9	2	Blood Red Summer	—	↓	
10/8/05	ⓜ	16	18	3	The Suffering	110	*Good Apollo I'm Burning Star IV*	Equal Vision 97683
12/3/05	ⓡ	29	9					
3/4/06	ⓡ	24	14	4	Welcome Home	—	↓	
4/22/06	ⓜ	36	5					
10/13/07	ⓜ	19	19	5	The Running Free	—	*No World For Tomorrow*	Columbia 16454
11/17/07+	ⓡ	31	12					

| ARTIST / Track Title | | Hot Pos | Album Title | Album Label & Number |

🅡=Mainstream Rock 🅜=Modern Rock

COHN, Marc

Born on 7/5/1959 in Cleveland, Ohio. Pop-rock singer/songwriter/pianist. Married ABC-TV news anchor Elizabeth Vargas on 7/20/2002. Shot in the head during an attempted car jacking on 8/7/2005 (fully recovered).

AWARD: Grammy: Best New Artist 1991

Debut	Cht	Peak	Wks	#	Track Title	Hot Pos	Album Title	Label & Number
4/6/91	🅡	7	16	1	Walking In Memphis	13	Marc Cohn	Atlantic 82178
7/6/91	🅡	22	9	2	Silver Thunderbird	63	↓	

COLD

Hard-rock band from Jacksonville, Florida: Ronald "Scooter" Ward (vocals, guitar), Stephen "Kelly" Hayes (guitar), Terry Balsamo (guitar), Jeremy Marshall (bass) and Sam McCandless (drums). Zachary Gilbert replaced Blasamo in late 2003. Matt Loughran replaced Hayes in 2004. Disbanded in early 2006.

Debut	Cht	Peak	Wks	#	Track Title	Hot Pos	Album Title	Label & Number
9/9/00	🅡	25	12	1	Just Got Wicked	—	13 Ways To Bleed On Stage	Geffen 490726
2/24/01	🅜	13	17	2	No One		↓	
2/24/01	🅡	17	17					
7/7/01	🅡	24	9	3	End Of The World	—	↓	
4/27/02	🅡	28	8	4	Gone Away	—	VA: WWF: Tough Enough 2	Geffen 493314
3/15/03	🅡	4	28	5	Stupid Girl	87	Year Of The Spider	Flip 000006
3/29/03	🅜	6	26					
9/6/03	🅡	17	16	6	Suffocate	—	↓	
9/20/03	🅜	21	12					
7/9/05	🅡	21	18	7	Happens All The Time	—	A Different Kind Of Pain	Flip 94107
8/13/05	🅜	29	8					
12/31/05+	🅡	35	11	8	A Different Kind Of Pain	—	↓	
1/21/06	🅜	38	2					

COLD CHISEL

Rock band from Adelaide, Australia: **Jimmy Barnes** (vocals), Ian Moss (guitar), Don Walker (keyboards), Phil Small (bass) and Steven Prestwich (drums).

Debut	Cht	Peak	Wks	Track Title	Hot Pos	Album Title	Label & Number
5/23/81	🅡	32	7	My Baby	—	East	Elektra 336

COLDPLAY

🅜 2000s: #29 / All-Time: #58

Alternative-rock band formed in London, England: Chris Martin (vocals; born on 3/2/1977), Jon Buckland (guitar; born on 9/11/1977), Guy Berryman (bass; born on 4/12/1978) and Will Champion (drums; born on 7/31/1978). Martin married actress Gwyneth Paltrow on 12/5/2003.

TOP HITS: 1)Speed Of Sound 2)Talk 3)Yellow

Debut	Cht	Peak	Wks	#	Track Title	Hot Pos	Album Title	Label & Number
12/2/00+	🅜	6	26	1	Yellow	48	Parachutes	Nettwerk 30162
5/19/01	🅜	26	8	2	Shiver	—	↓	
10/27/01	🅜	28	17	3	Trouble	115	↓	
7/20/02	🅜	17	15	4	In My Place	117	A Rush Of Blood To The Head	Capitol 40504
					Grammy: Rock Vocal Group			
11/30/02+	🅜	9	26	5	Clocks	29	↓	
4/26/03	🅜	18	12	6	The Scientist	—	↓	
11/8/03	🅜	24	12	7	Moses [L]	—	Coldplay Live 2003	Capitol 99014
5/7/05	🅜	5	23	8	Speed Of Sound	8	X&Y	Capitol 74786
8/27/05	🅜	18	10	9	Fix You	59	↓	
11/19/05+	🅜	5	20	10	Talk	86	↓	

COLD WAR KIDS

Rock band from Fullerton, California: Nathan Willett (vocals, piano), Jonnie Russell (guitar), Matt Maust (bass) and Matt Aveiro (drums).

Debut	Cht	Peak	Wks	Track Title	Hot Pos	Album Title	Label & Number
3/3/07	🅜	26	14	Hang Me Up To Dry	122	Robbers & Cowards	Downtown 70009

COLE, Jude

Born on 6/18/1960 in Carbon Cliff, Illinois; raised in East Moline, Illinois. Male singer/guitarist.

Debut	Cht	Peak	Wks	#	Track Title	Hot Pos	Album Title	Label & Number
3/24/90	🅡	3[1]	17	1	Baby, It's Tonight	16	A View From 3rd Street	Reprise 26164
7/21/90	🅡	33	6	2	Time For Letting Go	32	↓	
9/5/92	🅡	6	12	3	Start The Car	71	Start The Car	Reprise 26898
12/19/92+	🅡	19	9	4	It Comes Around	—	↓	

COLE, Lloyd

Born on 1/31/1961 in Buxton, Derbyshire, England; raised in Glasgow, Scotland. His band The Commotions: Neil Clark (guitar), Blair Cowan (keyboards), Lawrence Donegan (bass) and Steven Irvine (drums).

Debut	Cht	Peak	Wks	Track Title	Hot Pos	Album Title	Album Label & Number
10/8/88	⑩	13	9	1 My Bag	—		
				LLOYD COLE & THE COMMOTIONS		Mainstream	Capitol 90893
4/21/90	⑩	5	11	2 Downtown	—	Lloyd Cole	Capitol 92751
9/7/91	⑩	7	11	3 She's A Girl And I'm A Man	—	Don't Get Weird On Me, Babe	Capitol 96077
12/14/91+	⑩	6	9	4 Tell Your Sister	↓		

COLE, Paula

Born on 4/5/1968 in Rockport, Massachusetts. Female singer/songwriter.

AWARD: Grammy: Best New Artist 1997

Debut	Cht	Peak	Wks	Track Title	Hot Pos	Album Title	Album Label & Number
4/19/97	⑩	32	7	Where Have All The Cowboys Gone?	8	This Fire	Imago 46424

COLLAPSIS

Rock band from Chapel Hill, North Carolina: Ryan Pickett (vocals, guitar), Mike Garrigan (guitar), Chris Holloway (bass) and Scott Carle (drums).

Debut	Cht	Peak	Wks	Track Title	Hot Pos	Album Title	Album Label & Number
4/1/00	⑩	28	5	Automatic	—	Dirty Wake	Cherry 153792

COLLECTIVE SOUL   ® 1990s: #5 / All-Time: #19 ★ ⑩ 1990s: #26 / All-Time: #53

Rock band from Stockbridge, Georgia: brothers Ed Roland (vocals; born on 8/3/1963) and Dean Roland (guitar; born on 10/10/1972), with Ross Childress (guitar; born on 9/8/1970), Will Turpin (bass; born on 2/8/1971) and Shane Evans (drums; born on 4/26/1970). Joel Kosche replaced Childress in 2001. Ryan Hoyle replaced Evans in 2005.

TOP HITS: 1)Heavy 2)December 3)Shine 4)Listen 5)The World I Know

Debut	Cht	Peak	Wks	Track Title	Hot Pos	Album Title	Album Label & Number
3/26/94	®	❶[8]	26	1 Shine	11	Hints Allegations And Things Left Unsaid	Atlantic 82596
5/7/94	⑩	4	18				
8/6/94	®	12	13	2 Breathe	—	↓	
1/28/95	®	2[4]	26	3 Gel	49[A]	St: The Jerky Boys	Select 82708
2/4/95	⑩	14	11				
4/22/95	®	❶[9]	26	4 December	20	Collective Soul	Atlantic 82745
4/29/95	⑩	2[1]	24				
8/19/95	®	8	13	5 Smashing Young Man	—	↓	
11/11/95+	®	❶[4]	26	6 The World I Know	19	↓	
11/18/95+	⑩	6	24				
3/23/96	®	❶[2]	26	7 Where The River Flows	—	↓	
2/15/97	®	❶[4]	26	8 Precious Declaration	65	Disciplined Breakdown	Atlantic 82984
2/15/97	⑩	6	15				
5/24/97	®	❶[5]	26	9 Listen	72	↓	
5/31/97	⑩	17	16				
9/27/97	®	11	11	10 Blame	—	↓	
1/3/98	®	16	12	11 She Said	—	St: Scream 2	Capitol 21911
2/7/98	⑩	39	1				
1/23/99	®	❶[15]	33	12 Heavy	73	Dosage	Atlantic 83162
1/23/99	⑩	5	26				
4/3/99	⑩	36	3	13 Run	76	↓	
6/19/99	®	10	14	14 No More, No Less	123	↓	
7/10/99	⑩	32	7				
10/9/99	®	35	5	15 Tremble For My Beloved	—	↓	
9/30/00	®	2[7]	26	16 Why Pt. 2	111	Blender	Atlantic 83400
9/30/00	⑩	19	17				
2/10/01	®	34	5	17 Vent	—	↓	
11/3/01	®	39	3	18 Next Homecoming	—	7even Year Itch: Greatest Hits 1994-2001	Atlantic 83510
10/9/04	®	8	21	19 Counting The Days	—	Youth	El 60001
2/26/05	®	35	7	20 Better Now	117	Home	El 90601

COLLINS, Edwyn

Born on 8/23/1959 in Edinburgh, Scotland. Pop-rock singer/songwriter.

Debut	Cht	Peak	Wks	Track Title	Hot Pos	Album Title	Album Label & Number
8/26/95	⑩	7	16	A Girl Like You	32	St: Empire Records	A&M 540384

COLLINS, Phil
ℝ 1980s: #25 / All-Time: #54

Born on 1/30/1951 in Chiswick, London, England. Pop singer/songwriter/drummer. Stage actor as a young child; played the "Artful Dodger" in the London production of *Oliver*. With group Flaming Youth in 1969. Joined **Genesis** in 1970, became lead singer in 1975. Also with jazz-rock group Brand X. Starred in the 1988 movie *Buster*. Left Genesis in April 1996; rejoined in November 2006.

TOP HITS: 1)Against All Odds (Take A Look At Me Now) 2)In The Air Tonight 3)I Don't Care Anymore 4)One More Night 5)Easy Lover

Debut		Peak	Wks	#	Track Title	Hot Pos	Album Title	Label & Number
3/21/81	ℝ	2²	24	1	In The Air Tonight	19	*Face Value*	Atlantic 16029
3/21/81	ℝ	8	14	2	I Missed Again	19	↓	
4/4/81	ℝ	58	1	3	Behind The Lines	—	↓	
11/6/82	ℝ	41	1	4	Do You Know, Do You Care?	—	*Hello, I Must Be Going!*	Atlantic 80035
11/13/82	ℝ	24	14	5	You Can't Hurry Love	10	↓	
					#1 Pop hit for The Supremes in 1966			
12/4/82	ℝ	3¹	13	6	I Don't Care Anymore	39	↓	
12/4/82	ℝ	17	11	7	Like China	—	↓	
3/19/83	ℝ	34	7	8	Thru These Walls	—	↓	
2/25/84	ℝ	❶¹	14	9	Against All Odds (Take A Look At Me Now)	❶³	*St: Against All Odds*	Atlantic 80152
					Grammy: Pop Male Vocal			
12/1/84+	ℝ	5	14	10	Easy Lover	2²	*Chinese Wall*	Columbia 39542
					PHILIP BAILEY (with Phil Collins)			
2/23/85	ℝ	38	4	11	The Man With The Horn	—	*(single only)*	Atlantic 89588
2/9/85	ℝ	4	13	12	One More Night	❶²	*No Jacket Required*	Atlantic 81240
3/30/85	ℝ	9	16	13	Inside Out	—	↓	
4/6/85	ℝ	33	8	14	Don't Lose My Number	4	↓	
4/13/85	ℝ	42	3	15	I Don't Wanna Know	—	↓	
5/4/85	ℝ	10	12	16	Sussudio	❶¹	↓	
3/15/86	ℝ	12	10	17	Take Me Home	7	↓	
					Peter Gabriel and Sting (backing vocals)			
11/4/89	ℝ	7	12	18	Another Day In Paradise	❶⁴	*...But Seriously*	Atlantic 82050
					Grammy: Record of the Year David Crosby (backing vocal)			
1/6/90	ℝ	5	14	19	I Wish It Would Rain Down	3¹	↓	
					Eric Clapton (guitar)			
5/19/90	ℝ	49	1	20	Do You Remember?	4	↓	
8/11/90	ℝ	34	7	21	Something Happened On The Way To Heaven	4	↓	
11/6/93	ℝ	24	5	22	Both Sides Of The Story	25	*Both Sides*	Atlantic 82550

COLOR RED, The
Rock band from California: brothers Jon Zamora (vocals) and Marc Zamora (bass), with Billy Meyer (guitar), Adrian Verloop (guitar) and Dave Schartoff (drums).

8/24/02	ℝ	34	7		Sore Throat	—	*Clear*	Dirty Martini 68080

COLOUR, The
Rock band from Anaheim, California: Wyatt Hull (vocals), Luke MacMaster (guitar), Derek Van Heule (bass) and Nathan Warkentin (drums).

11/25/06+	ℝ	26	14		Devil's Got A Holda Me	—	*Between Earth & Sky*	Rethink 52812

COLVIN, Shawn
Born Shanna Colvin on 1/10/1956 in Vermillion, South Dakota. Female contemporary folk singer/songwriter/guitarist.

1/20/90	Ⓜ	23	3	1	Steady On	—	*Steady On*	Columbia 45209
12/5/92+	Ⓜ	25	7	2	Round Of Blues	—	*Fat City*	Columbia 47122

COMPANY OF WOLVES
Hard-rock band from New Jersey: Kyf Brewer (vocals), Steve Conte (guitar), John Conte (bass) and Frankie Larocka (drums). Brewer was keyboardist of **The Ravyns**.

2/10/90	ℝ	26	7	1	Call Of The Wild	—	*Company Of Wolves*	Mercury 842184
6/9/90	ℝ	49	1	2	The Distance	—	↓	
8/18/90	ℝ	26	8	3	Hangin' By A Thread	—	↓	

COMPULSION
Rock band from Ireland: Joseph Mary (vocals), Garret Lee (guitar), Sid Rainey (bass) and Jan Alkema (drums).

11/19/94	Ⓜ	37	2		Delivery	—	*Comforter*	Interscope 92456

CONCRETE BLONDE　Ⓜ All-Time: #96

Rock band from Los Angeles, California: Johnette Napolitano (vocals, bass), James Andrew Mankey (guitar) and Harry Rushakoff (drums). Paul Thompson replaced Rushakoff in early 1990; Rushakoff returned in late 1991, replacing Thompson.

Debut	Cht	Peak	Wks	Track Title	Hot Pos	Album Title	Album Label & Number
2/28/87	®	42	6	1 True	—	Concrete Blonde	I.R.S. 5835
5/13/89	Ⓜ	15	9	2 God Is A Bullet	—	Free	I.R.S. 82001
6/17/89	®	49	1				
6/9/90	Ⓜ	❶⁴	14	3 Joey	19	Bloodletting	I.R.S. 82037
6/23/90	®	20	14				
11/24/90	Ⓜ	23	4	4 Caroline	—	↓	
9/22/90	®	20	4	5 Everybody Knows	—	St: Pump Up The Volume	MCA 8039
2/22/92	Ⓜ	2¹	9	6 Ghost Of Texas Ladies' Man	—	Walking In London	I.R.S. 13137
4/18/92	Ⓜ	8	11	7 Someday?	—	↓	
10/30/93	Ⓜ	16	8	8 Heal It Up	—	Mexican Moon	Capitol 81129

CONEY HATCH

Rock band from Toronto, Ontario, Canada: Carl Dixon (vocals), Steve Shelski (guitar), Andy Curran (bass) and Dave Ketchum (drums).

Debut	Cht	Peak	Wks	Track Title	Hot Pos	Album Title	Album Label & Number
10/23/82	®	44	2	1 Devil's Deck	—	Coney Hatch	Mercury 4056
9/17/83	®	38	3	2 First Time For Everything	—	Outa Hand	Mercury 812869

CONNELLS, The

Rock band from Raleigh, North Carolina: brothers Mike Connell (guitar) and David Connell (bass), with Doug MacMillan (vocals), George Huntley (guitar) and Peele Wimberley (drums). Steve Potak (keyboards) joined by 1993.

Debut	Cht	Peak	Wks	Track Title	Hot Pos	Album Title	Album Label & Number
4/8/89	Ⓜ	7	9	1 Something to Say	—	Fun & Games	TVT 2550
11/10/90	Ⓜ	3²	12	2 Stone Cold Yesterday	—	One Simple Word	TVT 2580
2/9/91	Ⓜ	24	2	3 Get A Gun	—	↓	
10/2/93	Ⓜ	9	10	4 Slackjawed	—	Ring	TVT 2590

CONTRABAND

Hard-rock band formed in Los Angeles, California: Richard Black (vocals), Tracii Guns (guitar; of **L.A. Guns**), Michael Schenker (guitar; of **McAuley Schenker Group**), Share Pedersen (bass; of **Vixen**) and Bobby Blotzer (drums; of **Ratt**).

Debut	Cht	Peak	Wks	Track Title	Hot Pos	Album Title	Album Label & Number
4/27/91	®	12	11	All The Way From Memphis	—	Contraband	Impact 10247

CONWELL, Tommy, And The Young Rumblers

Born in Philadelphia, Pennsylvania. Rock singer/guitarist. The Young Rumblers: Chris Day (guitar), Rob Miller (keyboards; **Hooters**), Paul Slivka (bass) and Jim Hannum (drums).

Debut	Cht	Peak	Wks	Track Title	Hot Pos	Album Title	Album Label & Number
8/6/88	®	❶¹	14	1 I'm Not Your Man	74	Rumble	Columbia 44186
11/5/88+	®	9	15	2 If We Never Meet Again	48	↓	
9/22/90	®	15	9	3 I'm Seventeen	—	Guitar Trouble	Columbia 46235
12/8/90+	®	21	9	4 Let Me Love You Too	—	↓	

COOL FOR AUGUST

Rock band from Los Angeles, California: Gordon Vaughn (vocals), Trevor Kustiak (guitar), Andrew Shives (bass) and Shane Hills (drums).

Debut	Cht	Peak	Wks	Track Title	Hot Pos	Album Title	Album Label & Number
4/26/97	®	15	13	1 Don't Wanna Be Here	—	Grand World	Warner 46105
9/27/97	®	24	8	2 Trials	—	↓	
2/7/98	®	16	12	3 Walk Away	—	↓	

COOPER, Alice

Born Vincent Furnier on 2/4/1948 in Detroit, Michigan; raised in Phoenix, Arizona. Rock singer/songwriter. Formed own band in Phoenix in 1965; adopted his stage name in 1966 from a 16th-century witch. To Los Angeles in 1968, then to Detroit in 1969. Known primarily for his bizarre stage antics. Appeared in the movies *Prince Of Darkness* and *Wayne's World*. Hosts own nightly syndicated radio show. Also see **Classic Rock Tracks** section.

Debut	Cht	Peak	Wks	Track Title	Hot Pos	Album Title	Album Label & Number
8/12/89	®	15	13	1 Poison	7	Trash	Epic 45137
1/13/90	®	39	7	2 House Of Fire	56	↓	
				co-written by **Joan Jett**			
3/31/90	®	19	8	3 Only My Heart Talkin'	89	↓	
6/29/91	®	13	8	4 Hey Stoopid	78	Hey Stoopid	Epic 46786
				Ozzy Osbourne (backing vocal); **Slash** (guitar)			
10/12/91	®	31	6	5 Love's A Loaded Gun	—	↓	

COPE, Julian
Born on 10/21/1957 in Deri, South Wales; raised in Tamworth, England. Male singer/songwriter/bassist.

Debut	Cht	Peak	Wks	Track Title	Hot Pos	Album Title	Album Label & Number
2/7/87	R	22	7	1 World Shut Your Mouth	84	Julian Cope	Island 90560
11/12/88+	M	❶¹	14	2 Charlotte Anne	—	My Nation Underground	Island 91025
1/28/89	M	10	8	3 5 O'Clock World	—	↓	
				#4 Pop hit for The Vogues in 1966			
5/4/91	M	4	8	4 Beautiful Love	—	Peggy Suicide	Island 848388
7/6/91	M	25	4	5 East Easy Rider	—	↓	

CORNELL, Chris
Born Christopher Boyle on 7/20/1964 in Seattle, Washington. Hard-rock singer/songwriter/guitarist. Lead singer of **Soundgarden** and **Audioslave**.

Debut	Cht	Peak	Wks	Track Title	Hot Pos	Album Title	Album Label & Number
1/24/98	R	8	17	1 Sunshower	—	St: Great Expectations	Atlantic 83058
1/31/98	M	12	14				
8/28/99	R	5	15	2 Can't Change Me	102	Euphoria Morning	A&M 490412
8/28/99	M	7	17				
4/14/07	R	33	5	3 No Such Thing	—	Carry On	Suretone 008742

CORNERSHOP
Rock band formed in London, England: Tjinder Singh (vocals), Ben Ayers (guitar), Anthony Saffrey (sitar), Peter Bengry (percussion) and Nick Simms (drums).

Debut	Cht	Peak	Wks	Track Title	Hot Pos	Album Title	Album Label & Number
11/15/97+	M	16	21	Brimful Of Asha	—	When I Was Born For The 7th Time	Luaka Bop 46576

CORNWELL, Hugh
Born on 8/28/1949 in London, England. Male singer/songwriter/guitarist. Member of **The Stranglers**.

Debut	Cht	Peak	Wks	Track Title	Hot Pos	Album Title	Album Label & Number
9/17/88	M	11	11	Another Kind Of Love	—	Wolf	Virgin 90947

CORROSION OF CONFORMITY
Hard-rock band from Raleigh, North Carolina: Pepper Keenan (vocals, guitar), Woody Weatherman (guitar), Mike Dean (bass) and Reed Mullin (drums). Keenan was also a member of **Down**.

Debut	Cht	Peak	Wks	Track Title	Hot Pos	Album Title	Album Label & Number
11/19/94+	R	19	14	1 Albatross	—	Deliverance	Columbia 66208
2/25/95	R	19	14	2 Clean My Wounds	—	↓	
11/16/96	R	27	10	3 Drowning In A Daydream	—	Wiseblood	Columbia 67583
11/4/00	R	24	14	4 Congratulations Song	—	America's Volume Dealer	Sanctuary 84500

COSTELLO, Elvis
Born Declan McManus on 8/25/1954 in Paddington, London, England. Eclectic rock singer/songwriter/guitarist. Changed name to Elvis Costello in 1976 (Costello is his mother's maiden name). In 1977, formed backing band The Attractions: Steve "Nieve" Nason (keyboards), Bruce Thomas (bass) and Peter Thomas (drums). Married to Cait O'Riordan (former bassist with **The Pogues**) from 1986-2002. Appeared in the 1987 movie *Straight To Hell*. Married singer Diana Krall on 12/6/2003. Also see **Classic Rock Tracks** section.
AWARD: R&R Hall of Fame: 2003

ELVIS COSTELLO AND THE ATTRACTIONS:

Debut	Cht	Peak	Wks	Track Title	Hot Pos	Album Title	Album Label & Number
3/21/81	R	46	1	1 From A Whisper To A Scream	—	Trust	Columbia 37051
9/17/83	R	33	4	2 Everyday I Write The Book	36	Punch The Clock	Columbia 38897
7/28/84	R	44	6	3 The Only Flame In Town	56	Goodbye Cruel World	Columbia 39429
				Daryl Hall (backing vocal)			

ELVIS COSTELLO:

Debut	Cht	Peak	Wks	Track Title	Hot Pos	Album Title	Album Label & Number
3/29/86	R	38	4	4 Don't Let Me Be Misunderstood	—	King Of America	Columbia 40173
				#15 Pop hit for **The Animals** in 1965			
2/11/89	M	❶²	12	5 Veronica	19	Spike	Warner 25848
2/4/89	R	10	15	Paul McCartney (co-writer, bass guitar)			
4/8/89	M	4	13	6 ...This Town...	—	↓	
5/6/89	R	41	5	Roger McGuinn (guitar); Paul McCartney (bass guitar)			
5/11/91	M	❶⁴	10	7 The Other Side Of Summer	—	Mighty Like A Rose	Warner 26575
5/25/91	R	40	4				
3/5/94	M	6	9	8 13 Steps Lead Down	115	Brutal Youth	Warner 45535

COTTON, Josie
Born Kathleen Josey on 5/15/1951 in Dallas, Texas. Pop-rock singer/actress. Appeared in the 1983 movie *Valley Girl*.

Debut	Cht	Peak	Wks	Track Title	Hot Pos	Album Title	Album Label & Number
8/21/82	R	34	5	He Could Be The One	74	Convertible Music	Elektra 60140

COUGAR, John — see MELLENCAMP

Billboard				ARTIST		Hot		
Debut	Cht	Peak	Wks	Track Title	®=Mainstream Rock Ⓜ=Modern Rock	Pos	Album Title	Album Label & Number

COUNTING CROWS
Ⓜ **1990s: #28 / All-Time: #64**

Rock band from San Francisco, California: Adam Duritz (vocals; born on 8/1/1964), David Bryson (guitar; born on 11/5/1961), Charlie Gillingham (piano; born on 1/26/1960), Matt Malley (bass; born on 7/4/1963) and Steve Bowman (drums; born on 1/14/1967). Ben Mize replaced Bowman in 1994. Dan Vickrey (guitar) joined in 1996.

TOP HITS: 1)Einstein On The Beach (For An Eggman) 2)Mr. Jones 3)Angels Of The Silences

11/27/93+	Ⓜ	2³	23	1 Mr. Jones...		5ᴬ	August And Everything After......................DGC 24528	
1/1/94	®	2²	26					
4/16/94	Ⓜ	7	14	2 Round Here		31ᴬ	↓	
5/7/94	®	11	17					
7/16/94	®	4	17	3 Rain King		66ᴬ	↓	
11/19/94+	®	17	14	4 A Murder Of One...		—	↓	
7/23/94	Ⓜ	❶¹	19	5 Einstein On The Beach (For An Eggman)		45ᴬ	VA: DGC Rarities Vol. 1...............................DGC 24704	
10/12/96	Ⓜ	3¹	13	6 Angels Of The Silences		45ᴬ	Recovering The Satellites ....DGC 24975	
10/12/96	®	4	16					
12/21/96+	Ⓜ	5	19	7 A Long December...		6ᴬ	↓	
12/28/96+	®	9	18					
5/3/97	®	24	11	8 Daylight Fading		51ᴬ	↓	
5/3/97	Ⓜ	26	9					
8/30/97	Ⓜ	34	6	9 Have You Seen Me Lately?...................................		—	↓	
9/6/97	®	34	4					
10/16/99	Ⓜ	17	19	10 Hanginaround		28	This Desert Life ....DGC 490415	
11/13/99	®	37	6					

COURSE OF NATURE
Rock trio from Enterprise, Alabama: Mark Wilkerson (vocals, guitar), John Milldrum (bass) and Rickey Shelton (drums).

1/5/02	®	9	20	1 Caught In The Sun..	—	Superkala ....Lava 83526	
2/2/02	Ⓜ	22	12				
6/8/02	®	37	4	2 Wall Of Shame	—	↓	
12/15/07+	®	35	10	3 Anger Cage	—	Damaged ....Silent Majority 395900	

COVERDALE, David
Born on 9/21/1951 in Saltburn, North Yorkshire, England. Hard-rock singer/songwriter. Lead singer of **Deep Purple** and **Whitesnake**. Formed brief duo **Coverdale•Page** with **Jimmy Page** of **Led Zeppelin**.

2/27/93	®	❶⁶	15	1 Pride And Joy	—	Coverdale•Page ....Geffen 24487	
3/27/93	®	3²	17	2 Shake My Tree	—	↓	
6/19/93	®	15	9	3 Take Me For A Little While......................................	115	↓	
8/28/93	®	24	6	4 Over Now..	—	↓	
				COVERDALE•PAGE (above 4)			
12/9/00	®	33	9	5 Slave	—	Into The Light................................Dragonshead 112251	

COWBOY JUNKIES
Alternative-rock band from Toronto, Ontario, Canada: siblings Margo Timmins (vocals), Michael Timmins (guitar) and Peter Timmins (drums), with Alan Anton (bass).

12/17/88+	Ⓜ	5	17	1 Sweet Jane	—	The Trinity Session ....RCA 8568	
4/1/89	®	50	1	*first recorded by* **Lou Reed** *in 1974; also see #5 below*			
3/17/90	Ⓜ	11	9	2 Sun Comes Up, It's Tuesday Morning	—	The Caution Horses....................................RCA 2058	
3/7/92	Ⓜ	25	6	3 Murder, Tonight, In The Trailer Park......................	—	Black Eyed Man ....RCA 61049	
12/25/93	Ⓜ	28	6	4 Anniversary Song...	—	Pale Sun, Crescent Moon ....RCA 66344	
10/8/94	Ⓜ	9	17	5 Sweet Jane .... [R]	52ᴬ	St: Natural Born Killers.............................Nothing 92460	
				edited version of #1 above, with dialog dubbed in from the movie Natural Born Killers *starring Woody Harrelson and Juliette Lewis*			
3/23/96	Ⓜ	20	12	6 A Common Disaster	75ᴬ	Lay It Down ....Geffen 24952	

COWBOY MOUTH
Rock band from New Orleans, Louisiana: John Thomas Griffith (vocals), Paul Sanchez (guitar), Rob Savoy (bass) and Fred LeBlanc (drums).

4/26/97	®	26	7	1 Jenny Says..	—	Are You With Me? ....MCA 11447	
5/17/97	Ⓜ	33	8				
10/24/98	Ⓜ	35	4	2 Whatcha Gonna Do?	—	Mercyland..MCA 11847	
10/31/98	®	39	2				

CRACKER
M **All-Time: #98**

Rock trio from Redlands, California: David Lowery (vocals; of **Camper Van Beethoven**), John Hickman (guitar) and Dave Faragher (bass). Faragher left in 1995. Bob Rupe (bass) and Charlie Quintana (drums) joined in 1996. Quintana was also a member of **Izzy Stradlin And The Ju Ju Hounds** and **Social Distortion**.

Debut	Cht	Peak	Wks	Track Title	Pos	Album Title	Label & Number
3/21/92	M	❶²	14	1 Teen Angst (What The World Needs Now)	—	Cracker	Virgin 91816
5/23/92	R	27	9				
6/13/92	M	13	8	2 Happy Birthday To Me	—	↓	
9/11/93	M	3²	20	3 Low	64	Kerosene Hat	Virgin 39012
11/27/93+	R	5	28				
1/22/94	M	6	14	4 Get Off This	102	↓	
5/7/94	R	18	16				
9/3/94	M	25	9	5 Euro-Trash Girl	—	↓	
3/30/96	M	13	7	6 I Hate My Generation	67ᴬ	The Golden Age	Virgin 41498
4/6/96	R	24	6				
6/29/96	M	32	5	7 Nothing To Believe In		↓	
7/27/96	R	40	2				
10/26/96	R	33	6	8 Sweet Thistle Pie	—	↓	

CRACK THE SKY

Rock band from Steubenville, Ohio: John Palumbo (vocals), Rick Witkowski (guitar), Vince DePaul (keyboards) and Joe D'Amico (drums).

Debut	Cht	Peak	Wks	Track Title	Pos	Album Title	Label & Number
5/27/89	R	49	1	From The Greenhouse	—	From The Greenhouse	Grudge 4500

CRAMPS, The

Punk-rock band formed in New York: Erick "Lux Interior" Purkhiser (vocals), Christine "Poison Ivy" Wallace (guitar), Candy Del Marr (bass) and Nicholas "Nick Knox" Stephanoff (drums).

Debut	Cht	Peak	Wks	Track Title	Pos	Album Title	Label & Number
3/10/90	M	10	8	Bikini Girls With Machine Guns		Stay Sick!	Enigma 73543

CRANBERRIES, The
M **1990s: #22 / All-Time: #52**

Pop-rock band from Limerick, Ireland: Dolores O'Riordan (vocals; born on 9/6/1971), brothers Noel Hogan (guitar; born on 12/25/1971) and Mike Hogan (bass; born on 4/29/1973), and Fergal Lawler (drums; born on 3/4/1971).

Debut	Cht	Peak	Wks	Track Title	Pos	Album Title	Label & Number
5/29/93	M	15	25	1 Dreams	42	Everybody Else Is Doing It, So Why Can't We?	Island 514156
9/4/93	M	4	26	2 Linger	8		
10/1/94	M	❶⁶	23	3 Zombie	22ᴬ	No Need To Argue	Island 524050
12/31/94+	R	32	7				
1/7/95	M	11	19	4 Ode To My Family	39ᴬ	↓	
5/20/95	M	14	12	5 Ridiculous Thoughts	—		
4/13/96	M	❶⁴	14	6 Salvation	21ᴬ	To The Faithful Departed	Island 524234
5/4/96	R	25	8				
7/6/96	M	8	14	7 Free To Decide	48	↓	
3/27/99	M	12	10	8 Promises	—	Bury The Hatchet	Island 524611

CRASH TEST DUMMIES

Pop-rock band from Winnipeg, Manitoba, Canada: brothers Brad Roberts (vocals) and Dan Roberts (bass), with Ellen Reid (keyboards), Benjamin Darvill (harmonica) and Mitch Dorge (drums).

Debut	Cht	Peak	Wks	Track Title	Pos	Album Title	Label & Number
1/22/94	M	❶¹	17	1 Mmm Mmm Mmm Mmm	4	God Shuffled His Feet	Arista 16531
4/2/94	R	25	7				
6/11/94	M	13	9	2 Afternoons & Coffeespoons	66	↓	

CRAVING THEO

Rock band from Portland, Oregon: Calvin Baty (vocals, guitar), Bob Capka (guitar), Brian McMillen (bass) and Jason Dunn (drums).

Debut	Cht	Peak	Wks	Track Title	Pos	Album Title	Label & Number
9/8/01	R	39	2	Stomp	—	Craving Theo	Valley 15146

CRAVIN' MELON

Rock band from Clemson, South Carolina: Doug Jones (vocals), Jim Chapman (guitar), JJ Bowers (bass) and Rick Reames (drums).

Debut	Cht	Peak	Wks	Track Title	Pos	Album Title	Label & Number
3/29/97	R	37	2	Come Undone	—	Red Clay Harvest	Mercury 534305

CRAY, Robert, Band

Born on 8/1/1953 in Columbus, Georgia. Blues-rock singer/guitarist. Played bass with fictional band Otis Day & The Knights in the movie *Animal House*. Band formed in 1974 as backing tour group for Albert Collins. Lineup from 1986-89: Richard Cousins (bass), Peter Boe (keyboards) and David Olson (drums). Lineup in 1990: Cousins, Tim Kaihatsu (guitar), Jim Pugh (keyboards) and Kevin Hayes (drums). Karl Sevareid (bass) joined in 1992.

Debut	Cht	Peak	Wks	Track Title	Pos	Album Title	Label & Number
11/29/86+	R	2¹	19	1 Smoking Gun	22	Strong Persuader	Mercury 830568
3/28/87	R	28	6	2 I Guess I Showed Her	—	↓	

CRAY, Robert, Band — cont'd

Debut	Cht	Peak	Wks	Track Title	Hot Pos	Album Title	Album Label & Number
5/9/87	®	27	6	3 Right Next Door (Because Of Me)	80	↓	
7/30/88	®	4	10	4 Don't Be Afraid Of The Dark	74		
10/22/88	®	49	3	5 Night Patrol	—	Don't Be Afraid Of The Dark	Mercury 834923
12/24/88+	®	24	10	6 Acting This Way	—	↓	
9/15/90	®	11	10	7 The Forecast (Calls For Pain)	—	↓	
12/8/90+	®	32	9	8 Consequences	—	Midnight Stroll	Mercury 846652
9/26/92	®	33	5	9 Just A Loser	—	I Was Warned	Mercury 512721

CRAZY TOWN

White rock-rap band from Los Angeles, California: Seth "Shifty Shellshock" Binzer (vocals), Bret "Epic" Mazur (vocals), DJ AM (DJ), Craig Tyler (guitar), Anthony Valli (guitar), Doug Miller (bass) and James Bradley (drums).

Debut	Cht	Peak	Wks	Track Title	Hot Pos	Album Title	Album Label & Number
11/18/00+	ⓜ	❶²	26	1 Butterfly	❶²	The Gift Of Game	Columbia 63654
1/27/01	®	21	14	samples "Pretty Little Ditty" by the Red Hot Chili Peppers			
11/9/02	®	24	12	2 Drowning	—	Darkhorse	Columbia 85647
11/16/02	ⓜ	24	10				

CREATURES, The

Duo from England: Siouxsie Sioux (vocals) and her husband, Peter "Budgie" Clark (percussion). Both are members of **Siouxsie And The Banshees**.

Debut	Cht	Peak	Wks	Track Title	Hot Pos	Album Title	Album Label & Number
11/25/89+	ⓜ	4	14	1 Standing There	—	Boomerang	Geffen 24275
3/3/90	ⓜ	12	7	2 Fury Eyes	—	↓	

CREED

® 1990s: #20 / 2000s: #20 / All-Time: #24 ★ ⓜ All-Time: #32

Christian rock band formed in Tallahassee, Florida: **Scott Stapp** (vocals; born on 8/8/1973), Mark Tremonti (guitar; born on 4/18/1974), Brian Marshall (bass; born on 4/24/1974) and Scott Phillips (drums; born on 2/22/1973). Marshall left in late 2000. Group disbanded in June 2004. Tremonti, Marshall and Phillips formed **Alter Bridge**.

TOP HITS: 1)Higher 2)My Sacrifice 3)What's This Life For

Debut	Cht	Peak	Wks	Track Title	Hot Pos	Album Title	Album Label & Number
8/30/97	®	2¹⁰	44	1 My Own Prison	54ᴬ	My Own Prison	Wind-Up 13049
11/29/97+	ⓜ	7	28				
2/21/98	®	3⁵	28	2 Torn	—	↓	
6/20/98	®	❶⁶	39	3 What's This Life For	—	↓	
6/27/98	ⓜ	10	26				
12/19/98+	®	2⁷	38	4 One	70	↓	
12/26/98+	ⓜ	2²	31				
9/11/99	®	❶¹⁷	51	5 Higher	7	Human Clay	Wind-Up 13053
9/11/99	ⓜ	❶³	27				
1/8/00	®	3¹	26	6 What If	102	↓	
1/22/00	ⓜ	15	16				
4/22/00	®	❶⁴	31	7 With Arms Wide Open	❶¹	↓	
4/8/00	ⓜ	2⁴	26	Grammy: Rock Song			
9/9/00	®	4	28	8 Are You Ready?	125	↓	
10/14/00	ⓜ	37	4				
12/16/00+	®	28	13	9 Riders On The Storm	—	VA: Stoned Immaculate - The Music Of The Doors	Elektra 62475
				#14 Pop hit for **The Doors** in 1971			
10/27/01	®	❶⁹	28	10 My Sacrifice	4	Weathered	Wind-Up 13075
10/27/01+	ⓜ	2¹	26				
2/2/02	®	11	12	11 Bullets	—	↓	
2/9/02	ⓜ	27	7				
4/27/02	®	5	26	12 One Last Breath	6	↓	
5/11/02	ⓜ	17	24				
11/23/02+	®	7	26	13 Weathered	—	↓	
12/7/02	ⓜ	30	10				

CRENSHAW, Marshall

Born on 11/11/1953 in Detroit, Michigan. Rockabilly singer/guitarist. Played **John Lennon** in the road show of *Beatlemania* in 1976. Appeared in the 1986 movie *Peggy Sue Got Married* and portrayed Buddy Holly in the 1987 movie *La Bamba*.

6/12/82	R	25	1	1 Someday, Someway	36	Marshall Crenshaw	Warner 3673
				#76 Pop hit for Robert Gordon in 1981			
6/11/83	R	23	10	2 Whenever You're On My Mind	103	Field Day	Warner 23873
6/15/91	M	17	5	3 Better Back Off	—	Life's Too Short	Paradox 10223

CROSBY, David

Born on 8/14/1941 in Los Angeles, California. Folk-rock singer/songwriter/guitarist. Member of **The Byrds** from 1964-68 and later **Crosby, Stills & Nash**. Son of cinematographer Floyd Crosby (*High Noon*). Frequent troubles with the law due to drug charges. Movie cameos in *Backdraft*, *Hook* and *Thunderheart*; appeared on TV's *Roseanne*. Underwent a successful liver transplant on 11/19/1994. In early 2000, it was announced that he was the biological father (via artificial insemination) of two children for the couple of **Melissa Etheridge** and Julie Cypher.

2/4/89	R	3[1]	9	Drive My Car	—	Oh Yes I Can	A&M 5232

CROSBY, STILLS & NASH

Folk-rock trio formed in Laurel Canyon, California: **David Crosby** (guitar), **Stephen Stills** (guitar, keyboards, bass) and **Graham Nash** (guitar). All shared vocals. Crosby had been in **The Byrds**, Stills had been in The Buffalo Springfield, and Nash was with The Hollies. **Neil Young** (guitar), formerly with Buffalo Springfield, joined group in 1970, left in 1974. Reunions in 1988 and 1999. Also see **Classic Rock Tracks** section.

AWARDS: R&R Hall of Fame: 1997 ★ Grammy: Best New Artist 1969

TOP HITS: 1)Got It Made 2)American Dream 3)Live It Up

7/3/82	R	9	13	1 Wasted On The Way	9	Daylight Again	Atlantic 19360
7/10/82	R	39	1	2 Southern Cross	18	↓	
7/31/82	R	46	1	3 Too Much Love To Hide	69	↓	
6/25/83	R	13	8	4 War Games	45	Allies	Atlantic 80075
11/12/88	R	4	10	5 American Dream	—	American Dream	Atlantic 81888
11/26/88+	R	❶[2]	15	6 Got It Made	69	↓	
11/26/88	R	39	7	7 Nighttime For Generals	—	↓	
12/3/88+	R	25	12	8 That Girl	—	↓	
				CROSBY, STILLS, NASH & YOUNG (above 4)			
6/9/90	R	7	9	9 Live It Up	—	Live It Up	Atlantic 82107
8/25/90	R	44	2	10 If Anybody Had A Heart	—	↓	
10/30/99	R	34	8	11 No Tears Left	—	Looking Forward	Reprise 47436
				CROSBY, STILLS, NASH & YOUNG			

CROSS, Christopher

Born Christopher Geppert on 5/3/1951 in San Antonio, Texas. Male singer/songwriter/guitarist. Also see **Classic Rock Tracks** section.

AWARD: Grammy: Best New Artist 1980

9/26/81	R	13	10	Arthur's Theme (Best That You Can Do)	❶[3]	St. Arthur	Warner 3582

CROSSFADE

Rock band from Columbia, South Carolina: Ed Sloan (vocals, guitar), Tony Byroads (DJ, backing vocals), Mitch James (bass) and Brian Geiger (drums). James Branham replaced Geiger in 2005. Byroads left in 2005; Les Hall (guitar) joined.

7/10/04+	M	2[3]	46	1 Cold	81	Crossfade	Columbia 87148
3/6/04	R	3[4]	56				
11/6/04+	R	4	26	2 So Far Away	—	↓	
2/12/05	M	14	16				
5/21/05	R	6	26	3 Colors	—	↓	
6/18/05	M	18	12				
7/15/06	R	18	13	4 Invincible	—	Falling Away	Columbia 84238
10/14/06+	R	21	19	5 Drown You Out	—	↓	

CROW, Sheryl

M All-Time: #92

Born on 2/11/1962 in Kennett, Missouri. Female singer/songwriter/guitarist. After attending the University of Missouri, worked as a grade school music teacher, until moving to Los Angeles in 1986. Worked as backing singer for **Michael Jackson**, **Don Henley**, **George Harrison** and others.

AWARD: Grammy: Best New Artist 1994

2/12/94	M	8	13	1 Leaving Las Vegas	60	Tuesday Night Music Club	A&M 540126
7/23/94	M	4	19	2 All I Wanna Do	2[6]	↓	
				Grammys: Record of the Year / Pop Female Vocal			
10/8/94	R	35	6				
1/21/95	M	10	14	3 Strong Enough	5	↓	
7/15/95	M	38	3	4 Can't Cry Anymore	36	↓	

CROW, Sheryl — cont'd

Debut	Cht	Peak	Wks	Track Title	Hot Pos	Album Title	Album Label & Number
8/31/96	ⓜ	6	22	5 If It Makes You Happy	10	Sheryl Crow	A&M 540587
10/19/96	®	37	2	Grammy: Rock Female Vocal			
1/4/97	ⓜ	17	16	6 Everyday Is A Winding Road	11	↓	
2/15/97	®	31	6				
6/7/97	ⓜ	25	9	7 A Change Would Do You Good	19ᴬ	↓	
9/12/98	ⓜ	26	11	8 My Favorite Mistake	9ᴬ	The Globe Sessions	A&M 540959

CROWDED HOUSE

Pop-rock band formed in Melbourne, Australia: Neil Finn (vocals, guitar, piano), Nick Seymour (bass) and Paul Hester (drums). Finn and Hester were members of **Split Enz**. Neil's brother, Tim Finn (also of Split Enz), joined band in 1991; left in 1993, replaced by Mark Hart. Hester left band in April 1994. Group disbanded in June 1996. Hester committed suicide on 3/26/2005 (age 46).

Debut	Cht	Peak	Wks	Track Title	Hot Pos	Album Title	Album Label & Number
2/14/87	®	11	12	1 Don't Dream It's Over	2¹	Crowded House	Capitol 12485
5/2/87	®	10	12	2 Something So Strong	7	↓	
8/15/87	®	45	3	3 World Where You Live	65	↓	
7/2/88	®	18	10	4 Better Be Home Soon	42	Temple Of Low Men	Capitol 48763
9/10/88	ⓜ	29	1				
10/8/88	®	45	2	5 Never Be The Same	—	↓	
6/15/91	ⓜ	2¹	11	6 Chocolate Cake	—	Woodface	Capitol 93559
8/17/91	ⓜ	5	10	7 It's Only Natural	—	↓	
12/25/93+	ⓜ	8	13	8 Locked Out	120	Together Alone	Capitol 27048
4/16/94	ⓜ	26	3	9 Distant Sun	113	↓	

CRUEL STORY OF YOUTH

Rock band from New York: John Are (vocals), Michael Gross (guitar), David Penick (bass) and Bobby Siems (drums).

Debut	Cht	Peak	Wks	Track Title	Hot Pos	Album Title	Album Label & Number
3/25/89	®	29	7	You're What You Want To Be	—	Cruel Story Of Youth	Columbia 44206

CRUISE, Julee

Born on 12/1/1956 in Creston, Iowa. Eclectic-pop singer/actress. Appeared in the TV series *Twin Peaks*.

Debut	Cht	Peak	Wks	Track Title	Hot Pos	Album Title	Album Label & Number
6/2/90	ⓜ	11	7	Falling	—	Floating Into The Night	Warner 25859

CRUSH

Rock band formed in New York: Fred Schreck (vocals), John Valentine Carruthers (guitar), John Micco (bass) and Paul Ferguson (drums).

Debut	Cht	Peak	Wks	Track Title	Hot Pos	Album Title	Album Label & Number
5/15/93	ⓜ	26	2	The Rain	—	Crush	EastWest 4992

CRUZADOS

Rock band from Los Angeles, California: Tito Larriva (vocals), Steven Hufsteter (guitar), Tony Marsico (bass) and Chalo Quintana (drums). Marshall Rohner replaced Hufsteter in early 1987. Disbanded in 1988.

Debut	Cht	Peak	Wks	Track Title	Hot Pos	Album Title	Album Label & Number
10/5/85	®	15	10	1 Motorcycle Girl	—	Cruzados	Arista 8383
6/27/87	®	4	12	2 Bed Of Lies	—	After Dark	Arista 8439
9/26/87	®	39	3	3 Small Town Love	—	↓	

CRY OF LOVE

Rock band from Raleigh, North Carolina: Kelly Holland (vocals), Audley Freed (guitar), Robert Kearns (bass) and Jason Patterson (drums).

Debut	Cht	Peak	Wks	Track Title	Hot Pos	Album Title	Album Label & Number
7/10/93	®	❶⁴	20	1 Peace Pipe	—	Brother	Columbia 53404
10/30/93+	®	2³	26	2 Bad Thing	—	↓	
2/26/94	®	13	11	3 Too Cold In The Winter	—	↓	
8/16/97	®	22	9	4 Sugarcane	—	Diamonds & Debris	Columbia 66881

CRYSTAL METHOD, The

Electronic-dance duo from Los Angeles, California: Ken Jordan and Scott Kirkland.

Debut	Cht	Peak	Wks	Track Title	Hot Pos	Album Title	Album Label & Number
8/16/97	ⓜ	29	10	1 (Can't You) Trip Like I Do FILTER & THE CRYSTAL METHOD	—	St: Spawn	Immortal 68494
7/14/01	ⓜ	22	10	2 Name Of The Game	—	Tweekend	Geffen 493063
12/20/03+	ⓜ	26	11	3 Born Too Slow	—	Legion Of Boom	V2 27176

CRY WOLF

Rock band from San Francisco, California: Tim Hall (vocals), Steve McKnight (guitar), Phil Deckard (bass) and Paul Cancilla (drums).

Debut	Cht	Peak	Wks	Track Title	Hot Pos	Album Title	Album Label & Number
2/23/91	®	46	2	Pretender	—	Crunch	I.R.S. 13050

CULT, The

Rock band formed in England: Ian Astbury (vocals; born on 5/14/1962), Billy Duffy (guitar; born on 5/12/1961), Jamie Stewart (bass) and Les Warner (drums). Numerous personnel changes with Astbury and Duffy the only constants.

TOP HITS: 1)Fire Woman 2)Rise 3)Wild Hearted Son

Debut	Cht	Peak	Wks	#	Track Title	Hot Pos	Album Title	Album Label & Number
3/28/87	ℝ	15	11	1	Love Removal Machine	—	Electric	Sire 25555
6/20/87	ℝ	34	5	2	Lil' Devil	—	↓	
9/5/87	ℝ	39	3	3	Wild Flower	—	↓	
4/15/89	Ⓜ	2¹	12	4	Fire Woman	46	Sonic Temple	Sire 25871
4/8/89	ℝ	4	16					
6/24/89	ℝ	18	8	5	Sun King	—	↓	
7/15/89	Ⓜ	21	2					
9/2/89	ℝ	17	9	6	Edie (Ciao Baby)	93	↓	
1/20/90	ℝ	14	10	7	Sweet Soul Sister	—	↓	
9/21/91	Ⓜ	4	8	8	Wild Hearted Son	—	Ceremony	Sire 26673
9/21/91	ℝ	12	12					
11/23/91	Ⓜ	21	3	9	Heart Of Soul	—	↓	
1/25/92	ℝ	41	3					
10/8/94	ℝ	13	8	10	Coming Down (Drug Tongue)	—	The Cult	Sire 45673
10/8/94	Ⓜ	26	8					
7/8/00	ℝ	26	8	11	Painted On My Heart	—	St: Gone In 60 Seconds	Island 542793
5/12/01	ℝ	3⁶	22	12	Rise	125	Beyond Good And Evil	Lava 83440
5/19/01	Ⓜ	19	9					
9/1/07	ℝ	38	3	13	Dirty Little Rockstar	—	Born Into This	New Wilderness 617971

CULTURE CLUB

Pop band formed in London, England: George "Boy George" O'Dowd (vocals), Roy Hay (guitar, keyboards), Michael Craig (bass) and Jon Moss (drums).

AWARD: Grammy: Best New Artist 1983

Debut	Cht	Peak	Wks	#	Track Title	Hot Pos	Album Title	Album Label & Number
12/25/82+	ℝ	21	9	1	Do You Really Want To Hurt Me	2³	Kissing To Be Clever	Epic 38398
5/21/83	ℝ	17	21	2	Church Of The Poison Mind	10	Colour By Numbers	Epic 39107

CURE, The

Ⓜ 1990s: #7 / All-Time: #16

Techno-rock band from England: Robert Smith (vocals, guitar; born on 4/21/1959), Porl Thompson (guitar), Laurence "Lol" Tolhurst (keyboards), Simon Gallup (bass) and Boris Williams (drums). Numerous personnel changes with Smith the only constant.

TOP HITS: 1)Fascination Street 2)Friday I'm In Love 3)High

Debut	Cht	Peak	Wks	#	Track Title	Hot Pos	Album Title	Album Label & Number
4/22/89	Ⓜ	❶⁷	16	1	Fascination Street	46	Disintegration	Elektra 60855
5/6/89	ℝ	24	11					
7/1/89	Ⓜ	2³	17	2	Love Song	2¹	↓	
8/19/89	ℝ	30	10					
11/18/89	Ⓜ	23	8	3	Lullaby	74	↓	
4/21/90	Ⓜ	19	7	4	Pictures Of You	71	↓	
					RS500 #278			
9/22/90	Ⓜ	❶³	17	5	Never Enough	72	Mixed Up	Elektra 60978
9/29/90	ℝ	33	7					
10/20/90	Ⓜ	6	9	6	Hello I Love You	—	VA: Rubaiyat - Elektra's 40th Anniversary	Elektra 60940
					#1 Pop hit for The Doors in 1968			
3/28/92	Ⓜ	❶⁴	11	7	High	42	Wish	Fiction 61309
5/2/92	ℝ	42	4					
5/9/92	Ⓜ	❶⁴	14	8	Friday I'm In Love	18	↓	
6/6/92	ℝ	21	10					
8/8/92	Ⓜ	2¹	10	9	A Letter To Elise	—	↓	
11/27/93+	Ⓜ	2¹	16	10	Purple Haze	66ᴬ	VA: Stone Free: A Tribute To Jimi Hendrix	Reprise 45438
					#65 Pop hit for Jimi Hendrix in 1967			
4/20/96	Ⓜ	15	6	11	The 13th	44	Wild Mood Swings	Fiction 61744
6/1/96	Ⓜ	14	12	12	Mint Car	58	↓	

				CURE, The — cont'd				
10/18/97	ⓜ	8	16	13 Wrong Number		64ᴬ	*Galore - The Singles 1987-1997*	Fiction 62117
2/5/00	ⓜ	10	11	14 Maybe Someday		—	*Bloodflowers*	Fiction 62236
5/29/04	ⓜ	19	11	15 The End Of The World		—	*The Cure*	I Am 002870
				CURFMAN, Shannon				
				Born on 7/31/1985 in Fargo, North Dakota; later based in Minneapolis, Minnesota. Female blues-rock singer/guitarist.				
11/13/99	®	27	13	1 True Friends		—	*Loud Guitars, Big Suspicions*	Arista 14614
4/8/00	®	37	6	2 Playing With Fire		—	↓	
				CURRY, Mark				
				Born in Sacramento, California. Male singer/songwriter/guitarist.				
10/3/92	ⓜ	20	4	Sorry About The Weather		—	*It's Only Time*	Virgin 86290
				CURVE				
				Pop-rock band from England: Toni Halliday (vocals), Debbie Smith (guitar), Alex Mitchell (guitar), Dean Garcia (bass) and Monti (drums).				
11/9/91	ⓜ	12	8	1 Coast Is Clear		—	*Frozen*	Charisma 96293
3/28/92	ⓜ	17	6	2 Fait Accompli		—	*Doppelganger*	Anxious 92108
5/30/92	ⓜ	23	5	3 Horror Head		—	↓	
				CUSTOM				
				Born Duane Lavold in Calgary, Alberta, Canada. Male singer/songwriter.				
12/29/01+	ⓜ	20	17	Hey Mister		—	*Fast*	Artist Direct 1016
1/5/02	®	28	12					
				CUTTING CREW				
				Pop-rock band formed in England: Nick Van Eede (vocals), Kevin MacMichael (guitar), Colin Farley (bass) and Martin Beedle (drums). MacMichael died of cancer on 12/31/2002 (age 51).				
2/28/87	®	4	14	1 (I Just) Died In Your Arms		❶²	*Broadcast*	Virgin 90573
6/13/87	®	29	6	2 One For The Mockingbird		38	↓	
9/19/87	®	50	1	3 I've Been In Love Before		9	↓	
5/20/89	®	41	3	4 (Between A) Rock And A Hard Place		77	*The Scattering*	Virgin 91239
				CYPRESS HILL				
				Latin rap trio from Los Angeles, California: Senen "Sen Dog" Reyes, Louis "B-Real" Freeze and Lawrence "DJ Muggs" Muggerud. Group appeared in the 1993 movie *The Meteor Man*.				
4/8/00	ⓜ	18	24	1 (Rock) Superstar		—	*Skull & Bones*	Columbia 69990
3/6/04	ⓜ	23	10	2 What's Your Number?		—	*Till Death Do Us Part*	Columbia 90781

D

				D.A.D.				
				Hard-rock band from Copenhagen, Denmark: brothers Jesper Binzer (vocals) and Jacob Binzer (guitar), with Stig Pedersen (bass) and Peter Jensen (drums). D.A.D.: Disneyland After Dark.				
9/9/89	®	23	10	Sleeping My Day Away		—	*No Fuel Left For The Pilgrims*	Warner 25999
				dada				
				Rock trio from Los Angeles, California: Joie Calio (vocals, bass), Michael Gurley (guitar) and Phil Leavitt (drums).				
11/7/92	ⓜ	5	12	1 Dizz Knee Land		102	*Puzzle*	I.R.S. 13141
11/28/92	®	27	5					
3/20/93	ⓜ	24	4	2 Dim		—	↓	
9/24/94	ⓜ	27	8	3 All I Am		—	*American Highway Flower*	I.R.S. 27986
				DALTREY, Roger				
				Born on 3/1/1944 in Hammersmith, London, England. Rock singer. Lead singer of **The Who**. Starred in the movies *Tommy*, *Lisztomania*, *The Legacy* and *McVicar*.				
4/17/82	®	38	2	1 Martyrs And Madmen		—	*Best Bits*	MCA 5301
5/1/82	®	41	3	2 Say It Ain't So, Joe		—	↓	
				above 2 recorded in 1977				
3/3/84	®	4	7	3 Walking In My Sleep		62	*Parting Should Be Painless*	Atlantic 80128
9/14/85	®	3²	11	4 After The Fire		48	*Under A Raging Moon*	Atlantic 81269
				written by **Pete Townshend**				
10/5/85	®	10	12	5 Under A Raging Moon		—	↓	
12/7/85+	®	11	13	6 Let Me Down Easy		86	↓	
				co-written by **Bryan Adams**				
2/1/86	®	11	8	7 Quicksilver Lightning		—	*St: Quicksilver*	Atlantic 81631

DALTREY, Roger — cont'd

Debut	Cht	Peak	Wks	Track Title	Hot Pos	Album Title	Album Label & Number
6/27/87	R	46	3	8 Take Me Home	—	*Can't Wait To See The Movie*	Atlantic 81759
7/11/92	R	6	9	9 Days Of Light	—	*Rocks In The Head*	Atlantic 82359

DAMAGEPLAN

Hard-rock band formed in Texas: Pat Lachman (vocals), "Dimebag" Darrell Abbott (guitar), Bob "Zilla" Kakaha (bass) and Vinnie Paul Abbott (drums). Brothers Darrell and Vinnie were members of **Pantera**. Darrell was shot to death on stage on 12/8/2004 (age 38). Kakaha and Vinnie Paul Abbott later joined **HellYeah**.

1/31/04	R	16	18	1 Save Me	—	*New Found Power*	Elektra 62939
9/4/04	R	30	10	2 Pride	—	↓	

DAMBUILDERS, The

Pop-rock band from Boston, Massachusetts: Eric Masunaga (vocals, guitar), Joan Wasser (violin), Dave Derby (bass) and Kevin March (drums).

7/30/94	M	13	10	Shrine	—	*Encendedor*	EastWest 92356

DAMNED, The

Punk-rock band from England: David Vanian (vocals), Roman Jugg (guitar), Bryn Merrick (bass) and Chris "Rat Scabies" Miller (drums).

4/25/87	R	50	2	Alone Again Or	—	*Anything*	MCA 5966

#99 Pop hit for Love in 1970

DAMN YANKEES

All-star rock band: **Ted Nugent** (guitar, vocals), **Tommy Shaw** (guitar, vocals), Jack Blades (bass, vocals) and Michael Cartellone (drums). Nugent was with the Amboy Dukes. Shaw was with **Styx**. Blades was with **Night Ranger**.

3/17/90	R	❶[1]	15	1 Coming Of Age	60	*Damn Yankees*	Warner 26159
6/2/90	R	5	16	2 Come Again	50	↓	
9/8/90	R	2[1]	22	3 High Enough	3[2]	↓	
12/8/90+	R	9	13	4 Runaway	—	↓	
3/2/91	R	31	7	5 Bad Reputation	—	↓	
8/1/92	R	3[1]	9	6 Don't Tread On Me	—	*Don't Tread*	Warner 45025
9/26/92	R	6	18	7 Where You Goin' Now	20	↓	
12/19/92+	R	3[2]	18	8 Mister Please	—	↓	
3/27/93	R	20	8	9 Silence Is Broken	62	↓	

DAMONE

Pop-rock band from Waltham, Massachusetts: Noelle Leblanc (vocals, guitar), Mike Woods (guitar), Mike Vazquez (bass) and Dustin Hengst (drums).

5/20/06	M	32	10	Out Here All Night	—	*Out Here All Night*	Island 006483

DANDELION

Rock band from Philadelphia, Pennsylvania: brothers Kevin Morpurgo (vocals, guitar) and Mike Morpurgo (bass), with Carl Hinds (guitar) and Dante Cimino (drums).

8/5/95	M	14	9	Weird-Out	74[A]	*Dyslexicon*	Ruffhouse 64194
8/26/95	R	36	4				

DANDY WARHOLS, The

Rock band from Portland, Oregon: Courtney Taylor (vocals), Peter Holmstrom (guitar), Zia McCabe (bass) and Eric Hedford (drums).

8/16/97	M	31	7	1 Not If You Were The Last Junkie On Earth	—	*...The Dandy Warhols Come Down*	Capitol 36505
8/19/00	M	28	6	2 Bohemian Like You	—	*Thirteen Tales From Urban Bohemia*	Capitol 57787

DANGER, Harvey — see HARVEY DANGER

DANGER DANGER

Hard-rock band from Queens, New York: Ted Poley (vocals), Andy Timmons (guitar), Kasey Smith (keyboards), Bruno Ravel (bass) and Steve West (drums).

6/16/90	R	39	3	Bang Bang	49	*Danger Danger*	Epic 44342

DANGERMAN

Rock duo from New York: Chris Scianni (vocals, guitar, bass) and Dave Borla (drums).

3/20/99	M	20	10	Let's Make A Deal	—	*Dangerman*	550 Music 69774

DANGEROUS TOYS

Hard-rock band from Austin, Texas: Jason McMaster (vocals), Scott Dalhover (guitar), Danny Aaron (guitar), Mike Watson (bass) and Mark Geary (drums).

11/11/89	R	46	2	Scared	—	*Dangerous Toys*	Columbia 45031

DANIELS, Charlie, Band
Born on 10/28/1936 in Wilmington, North Carolina. Country-rock singer/fiddle player. Also see **Classic Rock Tracks** section.

7/25/81	®	52	3	1 Sweet Home Alabama .... [L]		110	*VA: Volunteer Jam VII*	Epic 37178
				recorded on 1/17/1981 at the Nashville Municipal Auditorium; #8 Pop hit for **Lynyrd Skynyrd** in 1974				
3/27/82	®	2¹	11	2 Still In Saigon		22	*Windows*	Epic 37694
7/18/87	®	22	7	3 Bogged Down In Love With You		—	*Powder Keg*	Epic 40760

DANZIG
Born Glenn Anzalone on 6/23/1959 in Lodi, New Jersey. Hard-rock singer/songwriter. His band: John Christ (guitar), Eerie Von (bass) and Chuck Biscuits (drums).

11/20/93+	®	17	26	1 Mother		43	*(single only)*	American 18256
				remix of song from Danzig's self-titled 1988 debut album				
2/18/95	M	40	1	2 Cantspeak		—	*Danzig 4*	American 45647

D'ARBY, Terence Trent
Born on 3/15/1962 in Brooklyn, New York; later based in London, England. R&B singer/songwriter/producer. Last name originally spelled Darby. Was a member of the U.S. boxing team.

5/8/93	M	5	12	She Kissed Me			*Terence Trent D'Arby's Symphony Or Damn*	Columbia 53616

DARKNESS, The
Rock band from London, England: brothers Justin Hawkins (vocals) and Dan Hawkins (guitar), with Frankie Poullain (bass) and Ed Graham (drums). Richie Edwards replaced Poullain in early 2005.

12/13/03+	M	9	21	1 I Believe In A Thing Called Love		119	*Permission To Land*	Atlantic 60817
12/27/03+	®	23	17					
5/15/04	M	31	7	2 Growing On Me		—	↓	
6/12/04	®	40	1					

DARK NEW DAY
Hard-rock band formed in Orlando, Florida: brothers Clint Lowery (guitar; of **Sevendust**) and Corey Lowery (bass; of **Stereomud**), Brett Hestla (vocals), Troy McLawhorn (guitar) and Will Hunt (drums).

5/7/05	®	7	26	1 Brother		—	*Twelve Year Silence*	Warner 49318
8/20/05	M	38	2					
11/26/05	®	28	14	2 Pieces		—	↓	

DARLAHOOD
Rock trio from New York: Luke Janklow (vocals, guitar), David Sellar (bass) and Joe Magistra (drums). Band named after the child actress who was a regular in the *Our Gang* movie series.

10/26/96	®	16	16	Grow Your Own		—	*Big Fine Thing*	Reprise 46214

DARLING BUDS, The
Pop band from Caerlon, Wales: Andrea Lewis (vocals), Harley Farr (guitar), Chris McDonagh (bass) and Bloss (drums). Jimmy Hughes replaced Bloss in early 1992.

7/15/89	M	27	4	1 Let's Go Round There		—	*Pop Said...*	Columbia 45208
9/29/90	M	5	10	2 Crystal Clear		—	*Crawdaddy*	Columbia 46816
12/22/90+	M	13	8	3 It Makes No Difference		—	↓	
10/10/92	M	22	6	4 Please Yourself		—	*Erotica*	Chaos 52913

DASHBOARD CONFESSIONAL
Rock band from Boca Raton, Florida: Christopher Carraba (vocals, guitar), John Lefler (guitar), Scott Shoenbeck (bass) and Mike Marsh (drums).

4/6/02	M	22	11	1 Screaming Infidelities		—	*The Places You Have Come To Fear The Most*	Vagrant 354
7/26/03	M	8	21	2 Hands Down		—	*A Mark, A Mission, A Brand, A Scar*	Vagrant 0385
1/31/04	M	37	3	3 Rapid Hope Loss		—	↓	
6/5/04	M	2¹	26	4 Vindicated		103	*St: Spider-Man 2*	Columbia 92628
6/10/06	M	17	12	5 Don't Wait		80	*Dusk And Summer*	Vagrant 006061

DAUGHTRY
Rock band formed in North Carolina: Chris Daughtry (born on 12/26/1979 in Roanoke Rapids, North Carolina; finalist on the 2006 season of TV's *American Idol*), Josh Steeley (guitar), Jeremy Brady (guitar), Josh Paul (bass) and Joey Barnes (drums).

12/16/06+	®	5	23	1 It's Not Over		4	*Daughtry*	RCA 88860
1/6/07	M	17	20					
5/12/07	®	6	20	2 What I Want		—	↓	
				DAUGHTRY Featuring Slash				
10/6/07	®	24	18	3 Crashed		—	↓	

Debut	Cht	Peak	Wks	ARTIST / Track Title	Hot Pos	Album Title	Album Label & Number
				DAVID & DAVID			
				Pop-rock duo from Los Angeles, California: **David Baerwald** and David Ricketts.			
8/16/86	Ⓡ	8	14	1 Welcome To The Boomtown	37	Boomtown	A&M 5134
10/25/86	Ⓡ	14	13	2 Swallowed By The Cracks	—	↓	
1/10/87	Ⓡ	17	10	3 Ain't So Easy	51	↓	
				DAVID J			
				Born David John Haskins on 4/24/1957 in Northampton, England. Rock singer/bassist. Member of **Love And Rockets**.			
7/14/90	Ⓜ	❶[1]	11	I'll Be Your Chauffeur	—	Songs From Another Season	Beggars Banquet 2261
				DAVIS, Jimmy, & Junction			
				Born in Memphis, Tennessee. Rock singer/guitarist. His band Junction: Tommy Burroughs (guitar), John Scott (piano) and Chuck Reynolds (drums).			
10/10/87	Ⓡ	32	8	Kick The Wall	67	Kick The Wall	MCA 42015
				DAVIS, Martha			
				Born on 1/15/1951 in Berkeley, California. Female singer. Lead singer of **The Motels**.			
11/7/87	Ⓡ	47	4	Just Like You	—	Policy	Capitol 48054
				DAX, Danielle			
				Born Danielle Gardner on 9/23/1958 in Southend, Essex, England. Eclectic female singer/songwriter.			
12/10/88+	Ⓜ	19	8	1 Cat-House	—	Dark Adapted Eye	Sire 25818
12/8/90+	Ⓜ	5	10	2 Tomorrow Never Knows	—	Blast The Human Flower	Sire 26126
				DAY OF FIRE			
				Christian rock band from Jackson, Tennessee: Joshua Brown (vocals), brothers Joe Pangallo (guitar) and Chris Pangallo (bass), Gregg Hionis (guitar) and Zach Simms (drums).			
6/4/05	Ⓡ	27	12	Fade Away	—	Day Of Fire	Essential 10738
				DAYS OF THE NEW Ⓡ 1990s: #34			
				Rock band from Louisville, Kentucky: Travis Meeks (vocals), Todd Whitener (guitar), Jesse Vest (bass) and Matt Taul (drums). Whitener, Vest and Taul left in 1999 to form **Tantric**; Meeks continued group name as a solo project.			
7/26/97	Ⓡ	❶[16]	46	1 Touch, Peel And Stand	57[A]	Days Of The New	Outpost 30004
9/27/97+	Ⓜ	6	28				
1/3/98	Ⓡ	3[5]	26	2 Shelf In The Room	—	↓	
2/28/98	Ⓜ	22	16				
6/6/98	Ⓡ	❶[10]	27	3 The Down Town	—	↓	
7/18/98	Ⓜ	19	15				
8/7/99	Ⓡ	2[4]	26	4 Enemy	110	Days Of The New	Outpost 30037
8/14/99	Ⓜ	10	13				
1/29/00	Ⓡ	10	12	5 Weapon & The Wound	—	↓	
8/25/01	Ⓡ	18	11	6 Hang On To This	—	Days Of The New	Outpost 490767
				DEACON BLUE			
				Pop band from Glasgow, Scotland: Ricky Ross (male vocals) Lorraine McIntosh (female vocals), Graeme Kelling (guitar), James Prime (keyboards), Ewen Vernal (bass) and Douglas Vipond (drums). Band name taken from **Steely Dan**'s 1978 pop hit "Deacon Blues." Kelling died of cancer on 6/10/2004 (age 47).			
4/2/88	Ⓡ	22	9	1 Dignity	—	Raintown	Columbia 40915
7/17/93	Ⓜ	27	3	2 Your Town	—	Whatever You Say, Say Nothing	Chaos 53755
				DEAD CAN DANCE			
				Alternative-pop duo formed in Australia: Lisa Gerard (vocals) and Brendan Perry (guitar).			
11/13/93	Ⓜ	8	11	The Ubiquitous Mr Lovegrove	—	Into The Labyrinth	4 A D 45384
				DEAD MILKMEN, The			
				Punk-rock band from Philadelphia, Pennsylvania: Rodney "Anonymous" Linderman (vocals), Anthony "Jasper Thread" Genaro (guitar), David "Lord Maniac" Schulthise (bass) and Dean "Clean" Sabatino (drums). Schulthise committed suicide on 3/10/2004 (age 47).			
1/7/89	Ⓜ	11	10	Punk Rock Girl	—	Beelzebubba	Enigma 73351
				DEAN, Paul			
				Born on 2/19/1946 in Calgary, Alberta, Canada. Rock singer/guitarist. Member of **Loverboy**.			
1/28/89	Ⓡ	27	7	Sword And Stone	—	Hard Core	Columbia 44462
				DEAR ENEMY			
				Rock band from Melbourne, Australia: Ron Martini (vocals), Les Barker (guitar), Chris Langford (guitar), Martin Fisher (keyboards), Peter Lesley (bass) and Ian Morrison (drums).			
3/10/84	Ⓡ	59	1	Computer One	—	Ransom Note	Capitol 12295

Billboard				ARTIST			
Debut	Cht	Peak	Wks	Track Title	Hot Pos	Album Title	Album Label & Number

ℝ=Mainstream Rock
Ⓜ=Modern Rock

DEATH CAB FOR CUTIE

Pop-rock band from Bellingham, Washington: Benjamin Gibbard (vocals, guitar), Chris Walla (keyboards), Nick Harmer (bass) and Jason McGerr (drums). Gibbard is also one-half of the duo The Postal Service.

Debut	Cht	Peak	Wks	Track Title	Hot Pos	Album Title	Album Label & Number
9/3/05	Ⓜ	5	26	1 Soul Meets Body	60	Plans	Barsuk 83834
2/4/06	Ⓜ	10	19	2 Crooked Teeth	—	↓	
7/15/06	Ⓜ	28	14	3 I Will Follow You Into The Dark	—	↓	

DeBURGH, Chris

Born Christopher Davidson on 10/15/1948 in Buenos Aires, Argentina (of Irish parentage). Pop-rock singer/songwriter.

Debut	Cht	Peak	Wks	Track Title	Hot Pos	Album Title	Album Label & Number
3/26/83	ℝ	29	11	1 Don't Pay The Ferryman	34	The Getaway	A&M 4929
6/2/84	ℝ	3[1]	14	2 High On Emotion	44	Man On The Line	A&M 5002

DEEP BLUE SOMETHING

Pop-rock band from Dallas, Texas: brothers Todd Pipes (vocals, bass) and Toby Pipes (guitar), with Kirk Tatom (guitar) and John Kirtland (drums).

Debut	Cht	Peak	Wks	Track Title	Hot Pos	Album Title	Album Label & Number
9/23/95	Ⓜ	30	12	Breakfast At Tiffany's	5	Home	RainMaker 92608

DEEP FOREST

Experimental keyboard duo from France: Michel Sanchez and Eric Mouquet.

Debut	Cht	Peak	Wks	Track Title	Hot Pos	Album Title	Album Label & Number
7/17/93	Ⓜ	14	9	Sweet Lullaby	78	Deep Forest	Epic 53747

DEEP PURPLE

Hard-rock band from England: Ian Gillan (vocals), Ritchie Blackmore (guitar), Jon Lord (keyboards), Roger Glover (bass) and Ian Paice (drums). Blackmore also formed **Rainbow**. Gillan left in 1989; replaced by **Joe Lynn Turner**, then returned to replace Turner in 1992. Also see **Classic Rock Tracks** section.

Debut	Cht	Peak	Wks	Track Title	Hot Pos	Album Title	Album Label & Number
11/17/84+	ℝ	7	19	1 Knocking At Your Back Door	61	Perfect Strangers	Mercury 824003
11/17/84	ℝ	12	17	2 Perfect Strangers	—	↓	
2/23/85	ℝ	20	9	3 Nobody's Home	—	↓	
1/17/87	ℝ	14	8	4 Bad Attitude	—	The House Of Blue Light	Mercury 831318
2/21/87	ℝ	14	10	5 Call Of The Wild	—	↓	
7/9/88	ℝ	44	4	6 Hush	—	Nobody's Perfect	Mercury 835897
				new version of their #4 Pop hit in 1968			
10/13/90	ℝ	6	12	7 King Of Dreams	—	Slaves And Masters	RCA 2421
1/5/91	ℝ	20	7	8 Fire In The Basement	—	↓	
8/14/93	ℝ	22	6	9 The Battle Rages On	—	The Battle Rages On...	Giant 24517

DEFAULT

Rock band from Vancouver, British Columbia, Canada: Dallas Smith (vocals), Jeremy Hora (guitar), Dave Benedict (bass) and Danny Craig (drums).

Debut	Cht	Peak	Wks	Track Title	Hot Pos	Album Title	Album Label & Number
9/22/01+	ℝ	2[7]	44	1 Wasting My Time	13	The Fallout	TVT 2310
9/29/01+	Ⓜ	3[1]	37				
4/13/02	ℝ	7	26	2 Deny	—	↓	
5/11/02	Ⓜ	14	22				
11/9/02	ℝ	31	9	3 Live A Lie	—	↓	
11/1/03	ℝ	25	15	4 (Taking My) Life Away	—	Elocation	TVT 6000
4/24/04	ℝ	30	7	5 Throw It All Away	—	↓	
8/6/05	ℝ	22	20	6 Count On Me	—	One Thing Remains	TVT 6060
10/29/05	Ⓜ	39	2				

DEF LEPPARD

ℝ 1980s: #21 / 1990s: #24 / All-Time: #17

Hard-rock band from Sheffield, Yorkshire, England: Joe Elliott (vocals; born on 8/1/1959), Steve Clark (guitar; born on 4/23/1960; died of alcohol-related respiratory failure on 1/8/1991, age 30), Pete Willis (guitar; born on 2/16/1960), Rick Savage (bass; born on 12/2/1960) and Rick Allen (drums; born on 11/1/1963). Phil Collen (born on 12/8/1957) replaced Willis in late 1982. Allen lost his left arm in a car crash on 12/31/1984. Vivian Campbell (guitar; born on 8/25/1962) joined in April 1992. Campbell had been with **Dio**, **Whitesnake**, **Riverdogs** and **Shadow King**.

TOP HITS: 1)Photograph 2)Stand Up (Kick Love Into Motion) 3)Promises 4)Rock Of Ages 5)Let's Get Rocked

Debut	Cht	Peak	Wks	Track Title	Hot Pos	Album Title	Album Label & Number
8/22/81	ℝ	34	6	1 Let It Go	—	High 'n' Dry	Mercury 4021
2/12/83	ℝ	❶[6]	26	2 Photograph	12	Pyromania	Mercury 810308
4/23/83	ℝ	❶[1]	24	3 Rock Of Ages	16	↓	
5/21/83	ℝ	9	15	4 Too Late For Love	—	↓	
7/9/83	ℝ	9	23	5 Foolin'	28	↓	
9/17/83	ℝ	24	7	6 Comin' Under Fire	—	↓	
10/15/83	ℝ	33	4	7 Billy's Got A Gun	—	↓	

				ARTIST		Hot		
Debut	Cht	Peak	Wks	Track Title	®=Mainstream Rock ⓜ=Modern Rock	Pos	Album Title	Album Label & Number

DEF LEPPARD — cont'd

Debut	Cht	Peak	Wks	#	Track Title	Hot Pos	Album Title	Album Label & Number
10/15/83	®	42	2	8	Action! Not Words	—	↓	
8/1/87	®	7	7	9	Women	80	Hysteria	Mercury 830675
8/15/87	®	5	13	10	Animal	19	↓	
9/12/87+	®	9	25	11	Hysteria	10	↓	
1/30/88	®	25	11	12	Pour Some Sugar On Me	2¹	↓	
8/13/88	®	3¹	13	13	Love Bites	❶¹	↓	
11/5/88	®	3⁴	15	14	Armageddon It	3²	↓	
2/25/89	®	5	10	15	Rocket	12	↓	
4/4/92	®	❶¹	13	16	Let's Get Rocked	15	Adrenalize	Mercury 512185
4/18/92+	®	❶⁵	20	17	Stand Up (Kick Love Into Motion)	34	↓	
5/23/92	®	3¹	12	18	Make Love Like A Man	36	↓	
8/22/92	®	7	15	19	Have You Ever Needed Someone So Bad	12	↓	
3/13/93	®	13	12	20	Tonight	62	↓	
11/7/92	®	22	2	21	Elected [L]	—	(single only)	Mercury 864136
					#26 Pop hit for **Alice Cooper** in 1972			
7/24/93	®	15	14	22	Two Steps Behind	12	St: Last Action Hero	Columbia 57127
10/23/93	®	12	7	23	Desert Song	—	Retro Active	Mercury 518305
5/11/96	®	6	12	24	Work It Out	—	Slang	Mercury 532486
6/5/99	®	❶³	19	25	Promises	102	Euphoria	Mercury 546212
9/11/99	®	11	17	26	Paper Sun	—	↓	
2/5/00	®	22	9	27	Day After Day	—	↓	
8/3/02	®	26	11	28	Now	—	X	Island 063121
12/21/02+	®	30	11	29	Four Letter Word	—	↓	

DEFTONES

Alternative-rock band from Sacramento, California: Chino Moreno (vocals), Stephen Carpenter (guitar), Frank Delgado (keyboards), Chi Cheng (bass) and Abe Cunningham (drums).

Debut	Cht	Peak	Wks	#	Track Title	Hot Pos	Album Title	Album Label & Number
5/9/98	®	29	7	1	Be Quiet And Drive (Far Away)	—	Around The Fur	Maverick 46810
5/27/00	ⓜ	3⁴	26	2	Change (In The House Of Flies)	105	White Pony	Maverick 47667
6/3/00	®	9	24					
11/4/00	ⓜ	27	8	3	Back To School	—	↓	
11/11/00	®	35	5					
1/27/01	ⓜ	16	11	4	Digital Bath	—	↓	
2/17/01	®	38	4					
5/3/03	ⓜ	9	15	5	Minerva	120	Deftones	Maverick 48350
5/10/03	®	16	14					
9/16/06	ⓜ	18	19	6	Hole In The Earth	—	Saturday Night Wrist	Maverick 43239
9/16/06	®	19	20					
4/21/07	®	40	1	7	Mein	—	↓	

DEL AMITRI

Pop-rock band from Glasgow, Scotland: Justin Currie (vocals, bass), David Cummings (guitar), Iain Harvie (guitar) and Brian McDermott (drums).

Debut	Cht	Peak	Wks	#	Track Title	Hot Pos	Album Title	Album Label & Number
3/10/90	ⓜ	13	10	1	Kiss This Thing Goodbye	35	Waking Hours	A&M 5287
3/24/90	®	17	16					
6/27/92	ⓜ	11	9	2	Always The Last To Know	30	Change Everything	A&M 5385
6/27/92	®	18	18					

DE LA SOUL

Alternative-rap trio from Amityville, Long Island, New York: Kelvin "Posdnous" Mercer, David "Trugoy the Dove" Jolicoeur and Vincent "Pasemaster Mase" Mason.

Debut	Cht	Peak	Wks		Track Title	Hot Pos	Album Title	Album Label & Number
4/30/05	ⓜ	❶⁸	42		Feel Good Inc	14	Demon Days	Parlophone 73838
					GORILLAZ & DE LA SOUL			

DEL FUEGOS, The

Rock band from Boston, Massachusetts: brothers Dan Zanes (vocals, guitar) and Warren Zanes (guitar), with Tom Lloyd (bass) and Woody Giessmann (drums). Warren Zanes and Giessmann left in 1988; replaced by Adam Roth and Joe Donnelly.

Debut	Cht	Peak	Wks	#	Track Title	Hot Pos	Album Title	Album Label & Number
11/23/85	®	46	4	1	Don't Run Wild	—	Boston, Mass.	Slash 25339
3/1/86	®	33	7	2	I Still Want You	87	↓	
5/16/87	®	43	2	3	Name Names	—	Stand Up	Slash 25540
11/18/89	ⓜ	22	3	4	Move With Me Sister	—	Smoking In The Fields	RCA 9860
10/21/89	®	32	8					

DEPECHE MODE

Ⓜ **1990s: #12 / All-Time: #20**

All-synthesized electro-pop band formed in Basildon, Essex, England: singer Dave Gahan and synthesizer players **Martin L. Gore**, Vince Clarke and Andy Fletcher. Clarke left in 1982 (formed Yaz, then **Erasure**), replaced by Alan Wilder (left in 1995).

TOP HITS: 1)I Feel You 2)Enjoy The Silence 3)Policy Of Truth

Debut	Cht	Peak	Wks	Track Title	Hot Pos	Album Title	Label & Number
4/15/89	Ⓜ	13	9	1 Everything Counts .... [L]	—	*101* .... Sire 25853
				recorded on 6/18/1988 at the Rose Bowl in Pasadena, California			
1/13/90	Ⓜ	13	6	2 Dangerous	—	*(single only)* .... Sire 19941
10/7/89	Ⓜ	3³	13	3 Personal Jesus	28	*Violator* .... Sire 26081
				RS500 #368			
3/10/90	Ⓜ	❶³	12	4 Enjoy The Silence	8	↓
4/28/90	Ⓜ	❶¹	16	5 Policy Of Truth	15	↓
8/11/90	Ⓜ	21	3	6 Halo	—	↓
9/22/90	Ⓜ	17	4	7 World In My Eyes	52	↓
2/27/93	Ⓜ	❶⁵	11	8 I Feel You	37	*Songs Of Faith And Devotion* .... Sire 45243
4/24/93	Ⓜ	❶¹	15	9 Walking In My Shoes	69	↓
8/28/93	Ⓜ	23	5	10 Condemnation	—	↓
1/18/97	Ⓜ	11	9	11 Barrel Of A Gun	47	*Ultra* .... Mute 46522
4/12/97	Ⓜ	4	22	12 It's No Good	38	↓
10/3/98	Ⓜ	36	4	13 Only When I Lose Myself	61	*The Singles 86-98* .... Mute 47110
4/14/01	Ⓜ	12	17	14 Dream On	85	*Exciter* .... Mute 47960
10/8/05+	Ⓜ	23	19	15 Precious	71	*Playing The Angel* .... Sire 49348
3/18/06	Ⓜ	38	3	16 Suffer Well	—	↓

DEVO

Robotic-rock band from Akron, Ohio: brothers Mark Mothersbaugh (synthesizers) and Bob Mothersbaugh (vocals, guitar), brothers Jerry Casale (bass) and Bob Casale (guitar), and Alan Myers (drums). Also see **Classic Rock Tracks** section.

8/8/81	®	53	7	1 Working In The Coal Mine	43	*St: Heavy Metal* .... Asylum 90004
				#8 Pop hit for Lee Dorsey in 1966			
7/21/90	Ⓜ	7	9	2 Post Post-Modern Man	—	*smoothnoodlemaps* .... Enigma 73526

DEXTER FREEBISH

Rock band from Austin, Texas: Rob Kyle (vocals), Scott Romig (guitar), Charles Martin (guitar), Chris Lowe (bass) and Rob Schilz (drums).

| 8/26/00 | Ⓜ | 25 | 19 | Leaving Town .... | 111 | *A Life Of Saturdays* .... Capitol 20464 |

DEXYS MIDNIGHT RUNNERS

Pop-rock band from Birmingham, England: Kevin Rowland (vocals), Billy Adams (guitar), Brian Maurice (sax), Paul Speare (flute), Jimmy Patterson (trombone), Micky Billingham (piano), Giorgio Kilkenny (bass) and Seb Shelton (drums). Billingham was later with **General Public**.

| 12/18/82+ | ® | 6 | 19 | Come On Eileen .... | ❶¹ | *Too-Rye-Ay* .... Mercury 4069 |

DeYOUNG, Dennis

Born on 2/18/1947 in Chicago, Illinois. Pop-rock singer/songwriter/keyboardist. Former member of **Styx**.

| 9/8/84 | ® | 31 | 8 | Desert Moon .... | 10 | *Desert Moon* .... A&M 5006 |

D4, The

Punk-rock band from Auckland, New Zealand: Jimmy Christmas (vocals, guitar), Dion Palmer (vocals, guitar), Vaughan (bass) and Beaver (drums).

| 4/5/03 | Ⓜ | 39 | 1 | Get Loose .... | — | *6twenty* .... Flying Nun 162388 |

DFX2

Rock band from San Diego, California: brothers David Farage (vocals, guitar) and Douglas Farage (guitar), with Eric Gotthelf (bass) and Frank Hailey (drums).

| 8/13/83 | ® | 22 | 6 | Emotion .... | — | *Emotion* .... MCA 36000 |

DICKINSON, Bruce

Born Paul Bruce Dickinson on 8/7/1958 in Worksop, Nottinghamshire, England; raised in Sheffield, Yorkshire, England. Hard-rock singer. Lead singer of **Iron Maiden** from 1981-1993.

| 7/7/90 | ® | 42 | 5 | 1 Tattooed Millionaire .... | — | *Tattooed Millionaire* .... Columbia 46139 |
| 9/10/94 | ® | 36 | 4 | 2 Tears Of The Dragon .... | — | *Balls To Picasso* .... Mercury 522491 |

DIESEL
Rock band from the Netherlands: Rob Vunderink (vocals, guitar), Mark Boon (guitar), Frank Papendrecht (bass) and Pim Koopman (drums).

7/18/81	®	27	19	Sausalito Summernight	25	Watts In A Tank	Regency 19315

DIE TRYING
Rock band from Sacramento, California: Jassen Jenson (vocals), Jack Sinamian (guitar), Steve Avery (bass) and Matt Conley (drums).

| 6/21/03 | Ⓜ | 29 | 6 | Oxygen's Gone | — | Die Trying | Island 000099 |
| 6/7/03 | ® | 35 | 8 | | | | |

DIFFUSER
Rock band from Long Island, New York: Tom Costanza (vocals, guitar), Tony Cangelosi (guitar), Larry Sullivan (bass) and Billy Alemaghides (drums).

| 12/2/00+ | ® | 20 | 14 | Karma | — | Injury Loves Melody | Hollywood 162246 |
| 12/30/00+ | Ⓜ | 26 | 11 | | | | |

DIG
Rock band from San Diego, California: Scott Hackwith (vocals, guitar), Jon Morris (guitar), Johnny Cornwell (guitar), Phil Friedmann (bass) and Anthony Smedile (drums).

| 2/5/94 | Ⓜ | 19 | 8 | Believe | — | Dig | Radioactive 10916 |
| 2/19/94 | ® | 34 | 9 | | | | |

DILLINGER
Rock band from Kansas: Chris Post (vocals), Blake Bachman (guitar), Buck Bowhall (bass) and Greg Tobin (drums).

| 10/5/91 | ® | 45 | 4 | Home For Better Days | — | Horses & Hawgs | JRS 35800 |

DINK
Rock band from Akron, Ohio: Rob Lightbody (vocals), Sean Carlin (guitar), Jer Herring (guitar), Jeff Finn (bass) and Jan Eddy Van Der Kuil (drums).

| 1/7/95 | Ⓜ | 35 | 6 | Green Mind | 118 | Dink | Capitol 7243 |

DINOSAUR JR.
Rock trio from Amherst, Massachusetts: Joseph Mascis (vocals, guitar), Mike Johnson (guitar) and Patrick Murphy (drums). George Berz replaced Murphy in late 1993.

4/6/91	Ⓜ	22	6	1 The Wagon	—	Green Mind	Sire 26479
2/6/93	Ⓜ	3³	14	2 Start Choppin	—	Where You Been	Sire 45108
8/27/94	Ⓜ	4	20	3 Feel The Pain	62^A	Without A Sound	Sire 45719

DIO
Born Ronald Padavona on 7/10/1949 in Portsmouth, New Hampshire. Stage name: Ronnie James Dio. Hard-rock singer. Former lead singer of **Black Sabbath** and **Rainbow**. His band: Vivian Campbell (guitar), Jimmy Bain (bass) and Vinnie Appice (drums). Claude Schnell (keyboards) joined in 1984. Campbell left in 1986, replaced by Craig Goldie. Campbell also with **Whitesnake**, **Riverdogs**, **Shadow King** and **Def Leppard**.

8/27/83	®	14	16	1 Rainbow In The Dark	—	Holy Diver	Warner 23836
10/8/83	®	40	2	2 Holy Diver	—	↓	
8/4/84	®	10	9	3 The Last In Line	—	The Last In Line	Warner 25100
9/1/84	®	20	9	4 Mystery	—	↓	
3/2/85	®	30	6	5 Hungry For Heaven	—	Sacred Heart	Warner 25292
8/31/85	®	26	8	6 Rock 'N' Roll Children	—	↓	
8/1/87	®	33	5	7 I Could Have Been A Dreamer	—	Dream Evil	Warner 25612

DIRE STRAITS   ® All-Time: #98
Rock band formed in London, England: brothers Mark Knopfler (vocals, guitar) and David Knopfler (guitar), with John Illsley (bass) and Pick Withers (drums). David left in mid-1980; replaced by Hal Lindes (left in 1985). Added keyboardist Alan Clark in 1982. Terry Williams replaced Withers in 1983. Guitarist Guy Fletcher added in 1984. Mark and Guy were also members of **The Notting Hillbillies** in 1990. Lineup in 1991: Knopfler, Illsley, Fletcher and Clark, with Chris White (sax), Paul Franklin (pedal steel), Danny Cummings (percussion), Phil Palmer (guitar) and Chris Whitten (drums). Also see **Classic Rock Tracks** section.

TOP HITS: 1)Money For Nothing   2)Heavy Fuel   3)Calling Elvis

3/21/81	®	39	5	1 Expresso Love	—	Making Movies	Warner 3480
4/4/81	®	31	1	2 Skateaway	58	↓	
4/4/81	®	56	1	3 Solid Rock	—	↓	
10/30/82	®	9	18	4 Industrial Disease	75	Love Over Gold	Warner 23728
2/12/83	®	12	10	5 Twisting By The Pool	105	Twisting By The Pool	Warner 29800
6/1/85	®	❶³	20	6 Money For Nothing	❶³	Brothers In Arms	Warner 25264
				Grammy: Rock Vocal Group **Sting** (backing vocal, co-writer)			
6/1/85	®	6	28	7 Walk Of Life	7	↓	
8/17/85	®	29	13	8 So Far Away	19	↓	

DIRE STRAITS — cont'd

Debut	Cht	Peak	Wks	Track Title	Hot Pos	Album Title	Album Label & Number
8/24/85	®	8	14	9 One World	—	↓	
1/11/86	®	21	10	10 Ride Across The River	—	↓	
9/7/91	®	3[1]	8	11 Calling Elvis	—	On Every Street	Warner 26680
9/28/91	ⓜ	25	3				
9/21/91	®	❶[1]	34	12 Heavy Fuel	—	↓	
12/7/91	ⓜ	22	2				
1/11/92	®	8	12	13 The Bug	—	↓	

#16 Country hit for Mary-Chapin Carpenter in 1993

DISHWALLA

Pop-rock band from Santa Barbara, California: J.R. Richards (vocals), Rodney Cravens (guitar), Scott Alexander (bass) and George Pendergast (drums). Jim Wood (keyboards) added in 1997.

Debut	Cht	Peak	Wks	Track Title	Hot Pos	Album Title	Album Label & Number
4/6/96	ⓜ	❶[1]	26	1 Counting Blue Cars	15	Pet Your Friends	A&M 540319
3/23/96	®	2[4]	30				
10/12/96	®	24	11	2 Charlie Brown's Parents	—	↓	
8/8/98	®	17	10	3 Once In A While	—	And You Think You Know What	
8/1/98	ⓜ	20	11			Life's About	A&M 540948

DISTILLERS, The

Punk-rock band from Australia: Brody Dalle (female vocals, guitar), Tony Bradley (male vocals, guitar), Ryan Sinn (bass) and Andy Granelli (drums). Dalle was formerly married to **Tim Armstrong**. Sinn is also a member of **Angels And Airwaves**.

Debut	Cht	Peak	Wks	Track Title	Hot Pos	Album Title	Album Label & Number
11/22/03	ⓜ	28	10	Drain The Blood	—	Coral Fang	Hellcat 48586

DISTURBED

® 2000s: #9 / All-Time: #53 ★ ⓜ 2000s: #21 / All-Time: #45

Hard-rock formed in Chicago, Illinois: **David Draiman** (vocals; born on 3/13/1973), Dan Donegan (guitar; born on 8/1/1968), Steve "Fuzz" Kmak (bass; born in 1970) and Mike Wengren (drums). John Moyer (of **The Union Underground**; born on 11/30/1973) replaced Kmak in early 2003.

TOP HITS: 1)Land Of Confusion 2)Stricken 3)Prayer

Debut	Cht	Peak	Wks	Track Title	Hot Pos	Album Title	Album Label & Number
6/24/00	ⓜ	10	26	1 Stupify	112	The Sickness	Giant 24738
5/20/00	®	12	32				
12/16/00+	®	16	26	2 Voices	—	↓	
12/23/00+	ⓜ	18	24				
6/16/01	®	5	46	3 Down With The Sickness	104	↓	
6/23/01	ⓜ	8	28				
2/2/02	®	34	7	4 The Game	—	↓	
8/17/02	®	3[5]	36	5 Prayer	58	Believe	Reprise 48320
8/17/02	ⓜ	3[2]	26				
12/28/02+	®	6	30	6 Remember	110	↓	
1/4/03	ⓜ	22	25				
6/21/03	®	4	27	7 Liberate	121	↓	
7/12/03	ⓜ	22	21				
7/9/05	®	7	21	8 Guarded	117	Ten Thousand Fists	Reprise 49433
7/16/05	ⓜ	28	6				
8/6/05	®	2[4]	35	9 Stricken	95	↓	
8/13/05	ⓜ	13	26				
12/31/05+	®	4	30	10 Just Stop	—	↓	
2/25/06	ⓜ	24	20				
7/15/06	®	❶[3]	37	11 Land Of Confusion	105	↓	
7/22/06	ⓜ	18	20				
12/23/06+	®	7	24	12 Ten Thousand Fists	—	↓	
2/17/07	ⓜ	37	8				

DIVING FOR PEARLS

Pop-rock band from New York: Danny Malone (vocals), Yul Vazquez (guitar), Jack Moran (keyboards), David Weeks (bass) and Peter Clemente (drums).

Debut	Cht	Peak	Wks	Track Title	Hot Pos	Album Title	Album Label & Number
12/9/89+	®	21	13	Gimme Your Good Lovin'	84	Diving For Pearls	Epic 45130

Billboard				ARTIST / Track Title	Hot Pos	Album Title	Album Label & Number
Debut	Cht	Peak	Wks				

Ⓡ=Mainstream Rock Ⓜ=Modern Rock

DIVINYLS
Rock band from Australia: Christina Amphlett (vocals), Mark McEntee (guitar), Bjarne Olin (keyboards), Richard Grossman (bass) and J.J. Harris (drums). Grossman joined the **Hoodoo Gurus** in 1989. By 1991, group reduced to a duo of Amphlett and McEntee.

Debut	Cht	Peak	Wks	Track Title	Hot Pos	Album Title	Album Label & Number
11/16/85	Ⓡ	12	13	1 Pleasure And Pain	76	What A Life!	Chrysalis 41511
2/9/91	Ⓜ	2²	11	2 I Touch Myself	4	Divinyls	Virgin 91397
3/23/91	Ⓡ	35	7				
4/27/91	Ⓜ	19	9	3 Make Out Alright	—	↓	

DIXIE DREGS — see DREGS, The

DLR BAND — see ROTH, David Lee

D.N.A.
Remix duo from Bristol, England: Neal Slateford and Nick Bett.

Debut	Cht	Peak	Wks	Track Title	Hot Pos	Album Title	Album Label & Number
9/1/90	Ⓜ	7	10	Tom's Diner	5	(single only)	A&M 1529

D.N.A. Featuring Suzanne Vega
special mix of Vega's original acapella recording which appeared on her 1987 *Solitude Standing* album

DR. ALBAN
Born Alban Nwapa on 8/26/1957 in Nigeria; later based in Stockholm, Sweden. Dance DJ.

Debut	Cht	Peak	Wks	Track Title	Hot Pos	Album Title	Album Label & Number
5/1/93	Ⓜ	28	1	It's My Life	88	It's My Life	Arista 18720

DOE, John
Born John Nommensen on 2/25/1953 in Decatur, Illinois. Founded the band **X** with his former wife **Exene Cervenka**. Appeared in several movies. Took name from the 1941 movie *Meet John Doe*.

Debut	Cht	Peak	Wks	Track Title	Hot Pos	Album Title	Album Label & Number
6/16/90	Ⓜ	19	7	Let's Be Mad	—	Meet John Doe	DGC 24291

DOG'S EYE VIEW
Rock band from Manhattan, New York: Peter Stuart (vocals, guitar), Oren Bloedow (guitar), John Abbey (bass) and Alan Bezozi (drums).

Debut	Cht	Peak	Wks	Track Title	Hot Pos	Album Title	Album Label & Number
2/10/96	Ⓡ	18	15	Everything Falls Apart	14ᴬ	Happy Nowhere	Columbia 66882
2/17/96	Ⓜ	19	14				

DOKKEN
Hard-rock band from Los Angeles, California: Don Dokken (vocals; born on 6/29/1953), George Lynch (guitar), Juan Croucier (bass) and Mick Brown (drums). Jeff Pilson replaced Croucier in late 1983. Disbanded in 1988. Lynch and Brown formed **Lynch Mob** in 1990. Dokken, Lynch, Pilson and Brown reunited as Dokken in early 1995.

TOP HITS: 1)Alone Again 2)Burning Like A Flame 3)Into The Fire

Debut	Cht	Peak	Wks	Track Title	Hot Pos	Album Title	Album Label & Number
10/15/83	Ⓡ	32	13	1 Breaking The Chains	—	Breaking The Chains	Elektra 60290
9/22/84	Ⓡ	21	11	2 Into The Fire	—	Tooth And Nail	Elektra 60376
1/5/85	Ⓡ	27	7	3 Just Got Lucky	105	↓	
4/27/85	Ⓡ	20	14	4 Alone Again	64	↓	
12/21/85+	Ⓡ	25	9	5 The Hunter	—	Under Lock And Key	Elektra 60458
3/1/86	Ⓡ	24	7	6 In My Dreams	77	↓	
3/14/87	Ⓡ	22	7	7 Dream Warriors	—	Back For The Attack	Elektra 60735
11/7/87	Ⓡ	20	13	8 Burning Like A Flame	72	↓	
2/13/88	Ⓡ	37	5	9 Prisoner	—	↓	
2/4/89	Ⓡ	48	3	10 Walk Away	—	Beast From The East	Elektra 60823
9/1/90	Ⓡ	26	8	11 Mirror Mirror	—	Up From The Ashes	Geffen 24301

DON DOKKEN

Debut	Cht	Peak	Wks	Track Title	Hot Pos	Album Title	Album Label & Number
6/3/95	Ⓡ	29	8	12 Too High To Fly	—	Dysfunctional	Columbia 67075

DOLBY, Thomas
Born Thomas Robertson on 10/14/1958 in London, England. New-wave singer/songwriter/keyboardist.

Debut	Cht	Peak	Wks	Track Title	Hot Pos	Album Title	Album Label & Number
9/11/82	Ⓡ	37	2	1 Europa And The Pirate Twins	67	The Golden Age Of Wireless	Capitol 12271
2/19/83	Ⓡ	17	16	2 One Of Our Submarines	—	↓	
3/5/83	Ⓡ	6	12	3 She Blinded Me With Science	5	↓	

features brief spoken-word interludes by British scientist/TV personality Magnus Pyke (died on 10/19/1992, age 83)

Debut	Cht	Peak	Wks	Track Title	Hot Pos	Album Title	Album Label & Number
3/10/84	Ⓡ	39	5	4 Hyperactive	62	The Flat Earth	Capitol 12309
11/21/92+	Ⓜ	9	12	5 Eastern Bloc	—	Astronauts & Heretics	Giant 24478

DONNAS, The
Female punk-rock band from Palo Alto, California: Brett "Donna A." Anderson (vocals), Allison "Donna R." Robertson (guitar), Maya "Donna F." Ford (bass) and Torry "Donna C." Castellano (drums).

Debut	Cht	Peak	Wks	Track Title	Hot Pos	Album Title	Album Label & Number
12/21/02+	Ⓜ	17	15	1 Take It Off	—	Spend The Night	Atlantic 83567
1/4/03	Ⓡ	31	10				
10/16/04	Ⓜ	29	7	2 Fall Behind Me	—	Gold Medal	Atlantic 83758

DOOBIE BROTHERS, The

Rock band formed in San Jose, California. Original lineup: **Tom Johnston** (vocals, guitar), **Patrick Simmons** (vocals, guitar), Dave Shogren (bass) and John Hartman (drums). **Michael McDonald** joined as lead singer in 1975. Numerous personnel changes. 1989-91 lineup: Johnston and Simmons (vocals, guitars), Tiran Porter (bass), Hartman and Michael Hossack (drums), and Bobby LaKind (percussion). LaKind left in 1990 due to illness; died of cancer on 12/24/1992 (age 47). Also see **Classic Rock Tracks** section.

5/20/89	ℝ	❶³	9	1 **The Doctor**		9	Cycles	Capitol 90371
6/3/89	ℝ	3¹	15	2 **Need A Little Taste Of Love**		45	↓	
				first recorded by The Isley Brothers in 1974				
6/10/89	ℝ	30	8	3 **South Of The Border**		—	↓	
4/13/91	ℝ	2³	11	4 **Dangerous**		—	Brotherhood	Capitol 94623
7/6/91	ℝ	12	9	5 **Rollin' On**		—	↓	

DOORS, The

Rock band formed in Los Angeles, California: Jim Morrison (vocals), Robby Krieger (guitar), Ray Manzarek (keyboards) and John Densmore (drums). Morrison left band on 12/12/1970; died of heart failure in Paris on 7/3/1971 (age 27). Group disbanded in 1973. The 1991 movie based on group's career, *The Doors*, starred Val Kilmer as Morrison. Also see **Classic Rock Tracks** section.

AWARD: R&R Hall of Fame: 1993

11/5/83	ℝ	18	12	**Gloria** [L]		71	Alive, She Cried	Elektra 60269
				recorded as a "soundcheck" in 1969; written by **Van Morrison**; #10 Pop hit for The Shadows Of Knight in 1966				

DOPE

Hard-rock band from Brooklyn, New York: brothers Brian "Edsel Dope" Ebejer (vocals) and "Simon Dope" Ebejer (keyboards), with Acey Slade (guitar), Virus (guitar), Sloane Jentry (bass) and Racci "Sketchy" Shay (drums).

8/26/00	ℝ	37	3	1 **You Spin Me 'Round (Like A Record)**		—	Felons And Revolutionaries	Flip 61383
				#11 Pop hit for Dead Or Alive in 1985				
10/27/01	ℝ	28	12	2 **Now Or Never**		—	Life	Flip 85644
3/16/02	ℝ	29	5	3 **Slipping Away**		—	↓	
9/17/05	ℝ	38	1	4 **Always**		—	American Apathy	3Sixty 51568

DOUBLEDRIVE

Rock band from Atlanta, Georgia: Donnie Hamby (vocals), Troy McLawhorn (guitar), Joshua Sattler (bass) and Mike Froedge (drums).

9/4/99	ℝ	32	8	1 **Tattooed Bruise**		—	1000 Yard Stare	MCA 11965
4/5/03	ℝ	22	19	2 **Imprint**		—	Blue In The Face	Roadrunner 618441

DOVETAIL JOINT

Rock band from Chicago, Illinois: Chuck Gladfelter (vocals), Robert Byrne (guitar), Jon Kooker (bass) and Joe Dapier (drums).

2/20/99	Ⓜ	17	13	**Level On The Inside**		—	001	Columbia 69451
4/17/99	ℝ	38	3					

DOWN

Hard-rock band formed in New Orleans, Louisiana: Philip Anselmo (vocals), Pepper Keenan (guitar), Kirk Windstein (guitar), Todd Strange (bass), and Jimmy Bower (drums). Anselmo is the lead singer of **Pantera**. Keenan is also a member of **Corrosion Of Conformity**.

11/18/95	ℝ	40	2	**Stone The Crow**		—	Nola	EastWest 61830

DRAGONFORCE

Hard-rock band formed in London, England: ZP "Zippy" Theart (vocals), Herman Li (guitar), Sam Totman (guitar), Vadim Pruzhanov (keyboards), Frederic Leclercq (bass) and Dave Mackintosh (drums).

3/15/08	ℝ	34↑	3↑	**Through The Fire And Flames**		86	Inhuman Rampage	Roadrunner 618034

DRAIMAN, David

Born on 3/13/1973 in Brooklyn, New York; later based in Chicago, Illinois. Hard-rock singer/songwriter. Lead singer of **Disturbed**.

3/2/02	ℝ	25	10	**Forsaken**		—	St: Queen Of The Damned	Warner Sunset 48285

DRAIN S.T.H.

Female hard-rock band from Stockholm, Sweden: Maria Sjoholm (vocals), Flavia Canel (guitar), Anna Kjellberg (bass) and Martina Axen (drums).

4/19/97	ℝ	33	6	1 **I Don't Mind**		—	Horror Wrestling	Enclave 558459
7/11/98	ℝ	25	10	2 **Crack The Liar's Smile**		—	↓	
7/24/99	ℝ	34	4	3 **Enter My Mind**		—	Freaks Of Nature	Enclave 546262
11/6/99	ℝ	24	12	4 **Simon Says**		—	↓	

DRAMARAMA

Alternative-rock band formed in Wayne, New Jersey: John Easdale (vocals), Peter Wood (guitar), Mark "Mr. E Boy" Englert (guitar), Chris Carter (bass) and Jesse Farbman (drums).

Debut	Cht	Peak	Wks	#	Track Title	Hot Pos	Album Title	Album Label & Number
11/18/89	ⓜ	13	11	1	Last Cigarette	—	Stuck In Wonderamaland	Chameleon 74822
10/12/91+	ⓜ	6	15	2	Haven't Got A Clue	—	Vinyl	Chameleon 61242
1/25/92	ⓜ	10	8	3	What Are We Gonna Do?	—	↓	
7/3/93	ⓜ	10	8	4	Work For Food	—	Hi-Fi Sci-Fi	Chameleon 61489

DREAM ACADEMY, The

Pop-rock trio from England: Nick Laird-Clowes (guitar, vocals), Gilbert Gabriel (keyboards) and Kate St. John (vocals).

Debut	Cht	Peak	Wks	#	Track Title	Hot Pos	Album Title	Album Label & Number
11/30/85+	®	7	13	1	Life In A Northern Town	7	The Dream Academy	Warner 25265
3/8/86	®	37	5	2	The Edge Of Forever	—	↓	

DREAMS SO REAL

Rock trio from Athens, Georgia: Barry Marler (vocals, guitar), Trent Allen (bass) and Drew Worsham (drums).

Debut	Cht	Peak	Wks	Track Title	Hot Pos	Album Title	Album Label & Number
11/26/88+	®	28	10	Rough Night In Jericho	—	Rough Night In Jericho	Arista 8555

DREAM THEATER

Hard-rock band from Los Angeles, California: James LaBrie (vocals), John Petrucci (guitar), Kevin Moore (keyboards), John Myung (bass) and Mike Portnoy (drums). Derek Sherinian replaced Moore in September 1994. Jordan Rudess replaced Sherinian in 1999.

Debut	Cht	Peak	Wks	#	Track Title	Hot Pos	Album Title	Album Label & Number
12/12/92+	®	10	20	1	Pull Me Under	—	Images And Words	Atco 92148
3/27/93	®	29	5	2	Take The Time	—	↓	
6/19/93	®	22	6	3	Another Day	—	↓	
10/8/94	®	38	3	4	Lie	—	Awake	EastWest 90126
10/25/97	®	33	6	5	Burning My Soul	—	Falling Into Infinity	EastWest 62060
2/7/98	®	40	2	6	You Not Me	—	↓	

DREAM WARRIORS

Hip-hop duo from Toronto, Ontario, Canada: "King Lou" Robinson (born in Jamaica) and Frank "Capitol Q" Alert (born in Trinidad).

Debut	Cht	Peak	Wks	Track Title	Hot Pos	Album Title	Album Label & Number
5/11/91	ⓜ	24	5	My Definition Of A Boombastic Jazz Style	—	And Now The Legacy Begins	4th & Broadway 444037

DREGS, The

Instrumental rock band formed in Miami, Florida: Steve Morse (guitar), T Lavitz (piano), Allen Sloan (violin), Andy West (bass) and Rod Morgenstein (drums). Mark O'Connor (violin) replaced Sloan in late 1981. Morse joined **Kansas** in 1986. Morgenstein later joined **Winger**. Group first known as the Dixie Dregs.

Debut	Cht	Peak	Wks	#	Track Title	Hot Pos	Album Title	Album Label & Number
5/9/81	®	46	7	1	Cruise Control [I]	—	Unsung Heroes	Arista 9548
4/3/82	®	18	11	2	Crank It Up	110	Industry Standard	Arista 9588
					Alex Ligertwood (of **Santana**; vocal)			

DREW, David

Born in Manhattan, New York. Rock singer/songwriter/guitarist.

Debut	Cht	Peak	Wks	Track Title	Hot Pos	Album Title	Album Label & Number
7/23/88	®	29	6	Green-Eyed Lady	—	Safety Love	MCA 42171
				#3 Pop hit for Sugarloaf in 1970			

DRIVIN' N' CRYIN'

Rock band from Atlanta, Georgia: Kevn Kinney (vocals), Buren Fowler (guitar), Tim Nielsen (bass) and Jeff Sullivan (drums).

Debut	Cht	Peak	Wks	#	Track Title	Hot Pos	Album Title	Album Label & Number
2/2/91	ⓜ	15	7	1	Fly Me Courageous	—	Fly Me Courageous	Island 848000
2/9/91	®	19	14					
6/8/91	®	15	13	2	Build A Fire	—	↓	
10/19/91	®	30	12	3	The Innocent	—	↓	
2/20/93	®	11	8	4	Turn It Up Or Turn It Off	—	Smoke	Island 514319
5/1/93	®	23	7	5	Smoke	—	↓	

DROGE, Pete

Born on 3/11/1969 in Portland, Oregon. Rock singer/songwriter/guitarist.

Debut	Cht	Peak	Wks	Track Title	Hot Pos	Album Title	Album Label & Number
12/24/94+	®	28	8	If You Don't Love Me (I'll Kill Myself)	119	Necktie Second	American 45620
12/17/94	ⓜ	40	1				

DROPBOX

Hard-rock band formed in Boston, Massachusetts: John Kosco (vocals), Lee Richards (guitar), Joe Wilkinson (guitar), Jim Preziosa (bass) and Bob Jenkins (drums). Richards also joined **Another Animal**.

Debut	Cht	Peak	Wks	#	Track Title	Hot Pos	Album Title	Album Label & Number
3/6/04	®	23	22	1	Wishbone	—	Dropbox	Republic 002057
7/31/04	®	7	26	2	Touché	—	The Other Side	Republic 001539
8/14/04	ⓜ	33	6		GODSMACK Featuring Dropbox			

DROPPING DAYLIGHT
Rock band from Minneapolis, Minnesota: brothers Sebastian Davin (vocals) and Seth Davin (guitar), with Rob Burke (bass) and Allen Maier (drums).

12/30/06+	®	30	15	Tell Me		—	Brace Yourself	Octone 50010

DROWNING POOL
Hard-rock band from Dallas, Texas: Dave Williams (vocals), C.J. Pierce (guitar), Stevie Benton (bass) and Mike Luce (drums). Williams died of a rare heart ailment (cardiomyopathy) on 8/13/2002 (age 30). Jason "Gong" Jones joined as lead singer in 2003. Ryan McCombs (of **Soil**) replaced Jones in 2006.

® **2000s: #38**

5/26/01	®	6	26	1 Bodies	119	Sinner	Wind-Up 13065
7/28/01	Ⓜ	12	16				
12/1/01	®	28	10	2 Sinner	—	↓	
12/15/01+	Ⓜ	36	6				
3/9/02	®	18	19	3 Tear Away	—	↓	
4/20/02	Ⓜ	37	4				
2/21/04	®	7	26	4 Step Up	—	Desensitized	Wind-Up 13080
9/11/04	®	21	22	5 Love And War	—	↓	
3/5/05	®	28	10	6 Killin' Me	—	↓	
7/7/07	®	20	20	7 Soldiers	—	Full Circle	Eleven Seven 140
12/29/07+	®	24↑	14↑	8 Enemy	—	↓	

DUARTE, Chris, Group
Born on 2/16/1963 in San Antonio, Texas. Singer/songwriter/guitarist. His group: Reese Wynans (keyboards), John Jordan (bass) and Eric Tatuaka (drums). Wynans was a member of **Stevie Ray Vaughan**'s Double Trouble.

10/11/97	®	40	2	Cleopatra		—	Tailspin Headwhack	Silvertone 41611

DUDEK, Les
Born on 8/2/1957 in Rhode Island. Prolific session guitarist.

6/27/81	®	52	3	Deja Vu (Da Voodoo's In You)		—	Gypsy Ride	Columbia 36798

DUKE JUPITER
Rock band from Rochester, New York: Marshall James Styler (vocals, keyboards), Greg Walker (guitar), George Barajas (bass) and David Corcoran (drums). Barajas died on 8/17/1982 (age 33). Rickey Ellis (bass) joined in 1983.

3/27/82	®	16	10	1 I'll Drink To You	58	Duke Jupiter 1	Coast To Coast 37912
4/28/84	®	12	13	2 Little Lady	68	White Knuckle Ride	Morocco 6097

DUNNERY, Francis
Born on 12/25/1962 in England. Male rock singer/guitarist.

6/25/94	®	38	2	American Life In The Summertime		—	Fearless	Atlantic 82582

DUPREE, Jesse James
Born in Atlanta, Georgia. Hard-rock singer/songwriter. Former lead singer of **Jackyl**.

6/17/00	®	34	6	Mainline		—	Foot Fetish	V2 27072

DURAN DURAN
Synth-pop-dance band from Birmingham, England: Simon LeBon (vocals), **Andy Taylor** (guitar), Nick Rhodes (keyboards), John Taylor (bass) and Roger Taylor (drums). None of the Taylors are related. Group named after a villain in the 1968 movie *Barbarella*. In 1984, Andy and Roger left the group. In 1985, Andy and John recorded with supergroup **The Power Station**; Simon, Nick and Roger recorded as Arcadia.

TOP HITS: 1)Hungry Like The Wolf 2)Union Of The Snake 3)Ordinary World

8/14/82+	®	❶³	26	1 Hungry Like The Wolf **R&R Hall of Fame**	3³	Rio	Harvest 12211
2/12/83	®	5	14	2 Rio	14	↓	
4/9/83	®	19	13	3 Girls On Film	—	Duran Duran	Capitol 12158
5/14/83	®	3¹	15	4 Is There Something I Should Know	4	↓	
11/5/83+	®	2¹	14	5 Union Of The Snake	3³	Seven And The Ragged Tiger	Capitol 12310
1/21/84	®	4	10	6 New Moon On Monday	10	↓	
5/5/84	®	35	7	7 The Reflex	❶²		
11/17/84	®	42	4	8 The Wild Boys	2⁴	Arena	Capitol 12374
6/22/85	®	42	3	9 A View To A Kill	❶²	St: A View To A Kill	Capitol 12413
10/29/88	Ⓜ	13	7	10 I Don't Want Your Love	4	Big Thing	Capitol 90958
1/28/89	Ⓜ	24	6	11 All She Wants Is	22	↓	
8/25/90	Ⓜ	13	6	12 Violence Of Summer (Love's Taking Over)	64	Liberty	Capitol 94292
12/26/92+	Ⓜ	2¹	13	13 Ordinary World	3³	Duran Duran	Capitol 98876
3/27/93	Ⓜ	12	10	14 Come Undone	7	↓	
6/5/93	Ⓜ	30	1	15 Too Much Information	45	↓	

Billboard				ARTIST Track Title	R=Mainstream Rock M=Modern Rock	Hot Pos	Album Title	Album Label & Number
Debut	Cht	Peak	Wks					

DURST, Fred
Born William Frederick Durst on 8/20/1970 in Gastonia, North Carolina; raised in Jacksonville, Florida. Hard-rock singer/songwriter. Leader of **Limp Bizkit**.

12/16/00+	R	❶²	26	Outside [L]		56	*VA: The Family Values Tour 1999*........Flawless 490641	
11/25/00+	M	2⁶	25	**AARON LEWIS with Fred Durst**				

DUST FOR LIFE
Rock band from Memphis, Tennessee: Chris Gavin (vocals, guitar), Jason Hughes (guitar), David Rhea (bass) and Rick Shelton (drums).

10/28/00+	R	16	18	1 Step Into The Light..............		—	*Dust For Life*.........................Wind-Up 13060	
11/11/00+	M	22	14					
4/28/01	R	39	1	2 Seed..............		—	↓	

DYLAN, Bob
Born Robert Zimmerman on 5/24/1941 in Duluth, Minnesota; raised in Hibbing, Minnesota. Highly influential singer/songwriter/guitarist/harmonica player. Innovator of folk-rock style. Took stage name from poet Dylan Thomas. To New York City in December 1960. Worked Greenwich Village folk clubs. Signed to Columbia Records in October 1961. Motorcycle crash on 7/29/1966 led to short retirement. Subject of documentaries *Don't Look Back* (1965), *Eat The Document* (1969) and *No Direction Home* (2005). Acted in movies *Pat Garrett And Billy The Kid* (1973), *Renaldo And Clara* (1978) and *Hearts Of Fire* (1987). Member of the supergroup **Traveling Wilburys**. His son Jakob is the lead singer of **The Wallflowers**. Also see **Classic Rock Tracks** section.

AWARDS: R&R Hall of Fame: 1988 ★ Grammy: Lifetime Achievement Award 1991

TOP HITS: 1)Silvio 2)Everything Is Broken 3)Slow Train

8/29/81	R	38	6	1 Shot Of Love..............		—	*Shot Of Love*.........................Columbia 37496	
12/17/83+	R	37	7	2 Neighborhood Bully..............		—	*Infidels*.........................Columbia 38819	
6/15/85	R	19	9	3 Tight Connection To My Heart (Has Anybody Seen My Love)..............		103	*Empire Burlesque*.........................Columbia 40110	
4/19/86	R	28	6	4 Band Of The Hand (Hell Time, Man!).............. **BOB DYLAN with The Heartbreakers** produced by Tom Petty		—	*St: Band Of The Hand*.........................MCA 6167	
8/2/86	R	23	7	5 Got My Mind Made Up.............. Tom Petty (guitar)		—	*Knocked Out Loaded*.........................Columbia 40439	
11/7/87	R	25	6	6 The Usual.............. Eric Clapton (guitar)		—	*St: Hearts Of Fire*.........................Columbia 40870	
6/11/88	R	5	8	7 Silvio..............		—	*Down In The Groove*.........................Columbia 40957	
2/4/89	R	8	6	8 Slow Train.............. [L] **BOB DYLAN & GRATEFUL DEAD**		—	*Dylan & The Dead*.........................Columbia 45056	
9/30/89	R	8	8	9 Everything Is Broken..............		—	*Oh Mercy*.........................Columbia 45281	
9/29/90	R	21	6	10 Unbelievable..............		—	*Under The Red Sky*.........................Columbia 46794	
8/21/93	R	26	7	11 My Back Pages.............. [L] **BOB DYLAN & FRIENDS** (Roger McGuinn, Tom Petty, Neil Young, Eric Clapton & George Harrison) recorded on 10/16/1992 at Madison Square Garden in New York City; #30 Pop hit for **The Byrds** in 1967		—	*VA: Bob Dylan - The 30th Anniversary Concert*.........................Columbia 53230	

DYLANS, The
Rock band formed in Sheffield, Yorkshire, England: Colin Gregory (vocals), Jim Rodger (guitar), Quentin Jennings (keyboards), Garry Jones (bass) and Andy Cook (drums).

11/23/91	M	10	11	Planet Love..............		—	*The Dylans*.........................Beggars Banquet 61054	

DYNAMITE HACK
Rock band from Austin, Texas: Mark Morris (vocals, guitar), Mike Vlahakis (guitar), Chad Robinson (bass) and Chase Scott (drums). Group name taken from a line in the 1980 movie *Caddyshack*.

5/6/00	M	12	16	Boyz-N-The-Hood..............		—	*Superfast*.........................Woppitzer 157884	

E

E
Born Mark Everett on 4/9/1963 in Richmond, Virginia. Eclectic singer/songwriter. Later formed the **Eels**.

3/21/92	M	8	10	Hello Cruel World..............		—	*A Man Called (E)*.........................Polydor 511570	

EAGLES
Rock-country band formed in Los Angeles, California. Original lineup: **Glenn Frey** (vocals, guitar), Bernie Leadon (guitar), **Randy Meisner** (bass) and **Don Henley** (drums). **Don Felder** (guitar) joined in 1975. Leadon replaced by **Joe Walsh** in 1975. Meisner replaced by **Timothy B. Schmit** in 1977. Group disbanded in 1982. Henley, Frey, Felder, Walsh and Schmit reunited in 1994. Also see **Classic Rock Tracks** section.

AWARD: R&R Hall of Fame: 1998

10/22/94	R	4	14	1 Get Over It..............		31	*Hell Freezes Over*.........................Geffen 24725	
1/21/95	R	33	7	2 Learn To Be Still..............		61ᴬ	↓	

EARLE, Steve
Born on 1/17/1955 in Fort Monroe, Virginia; raised in Schertz, Texas. Country-rock singer/songwriter/guitarist.

Debut	Cht	Peak	Wks		Hot Pos	Album Title	Album Label & Number
6/27/87	®	26	8	1 I Ain't Ever Satisfied	—	Exit O .... MCA 5998	
				STEVE EARLE AND THE DUKES			
10/29/88	®	10	13	2 Copperhead Road	—	Copperhead Road .... Uni 7	
2/4/89	®	20	8	3 Back To The Wall	—	↓	
7/14/90	®	37	5	4 The Other Kind	—	The Hard Way .... MCA 6430	
				STEVE EARLE AND THE DUKES			

EARSHOT
Hard-rock band from Los Angeles, California: Wil Martin (vocals), Mike Callahan (guitar), Scott Kohler (guitar), Guy Couturier (bass) and Dieter Hartmann (drums). John Sprague replaced Couturier in 2003.

Debut	Cht	Peak	Wks		Hot Pos	Album Title	Album Label & Number
3/16/02	®	6	28	1 Get Away	—	Letting Go .... Warner 47961	
4/6/02	ⓜ	20	23				
9/21/02	®	24	10	2 Not Afraid	—	↓	
5/29/04	®	13	22	3 Wait	—	Two .... Warner 48694	
6/26/04	ⓜ	33	8				
11/6/04+	®	27	16	4 Someone	—	↓	

EARTH TO ANDY
Rock band from New York: Andy Waldeck (vocals, guitar), Tony Lopacinski (guitar), Chris Reardon (bass) and Kevin Murphy (drums).

Debut	Cht	Peak	Wks		Hot Pos	Album Title	Album Label & Number
1/8/00	®	39	2	Still After You	—	Chronicle Kings .... Giant 24727	

EASTERHOUSE
Rock duo from Manchester, England: brothers Andy Perry (vocals) and Ivor Perry (guitar).

Debut	Cht	Peak	Wks		Hot Pos	Album Title	Album Label & Number
2/11/89	ⓜ	7	11	Come Out Fighting	82	Waiting For The Redbird .... Columbia 44467	
2/11/89	®	17	10				

EASTON, Elliot
Born Elliot Shapiro on 12/18/1953 in Brooklyn, New York. Rock singer/guitarist. Member of **The Cars**.

Debut	Cht	Peak	Wks		Hot Pos	Album Title	Album Label & Number
2/23/85	®	36	6	(Wearing Down) Like A Wheel	—	Change No Change .... Elektra 60393	

ECHO & THE BUNNYMEN
Post-punk band from Liverpool, England: **Ian McCulloch** (vocals), Will Sergent (guitar), Les Pattinson (bass) and Pete DeFreitas (drums). DeFreitas died in a motorcycle accident on 6/14/1989 (age 27). McCulloch went solo in 1988, replaced by Noel Burke. Lineup in 1990: Burke (vocals), Sergeant (guitar), Jake Brockman (mellotron), Pattinson (bass) and Damon Reece (drums). McCulloch and Sergeant also collaborated in **Electrafixion**.

Debut	Cht	Peak	Wks		Hot Pos	Album Title	Album Label & Number
12/1/90+	ⓜ	8	10	1 Enlighten Me	—	Reverberation .... Sire 26388	
2/16/91	ⓜ	23	3	2 Gone, Gone, Gone	—	↓	
6/21/97	ⓜ	26	10	3 I Want To Be There (When You Come)	—	Evergreen .... London 828905	

ECONOLINE CRUSH
Rock band formed in Winnipeg, Manitoba, Canada: Trevor Hurst (vocals), Robbie Morfitt (guitar), Ziggy Sigmund (guitar), Don Binns (bass) and Nico Quintal (drums).

Debut	Cht	Peak	Wks		Hot Pos	Album Title	Album Label & Number
5/23/98	®	35	4	1 Home	—	The Devil You Know .... Restless 72960	
10/3/98	®	18	19	2 Surefire (Never Enough)	—	↓	
3/27/99	®	18	13	3 All That You Are (X3)	—	↓	
5/22/99	ⓜ	28	11				
4/14/01	®	21	11	4 Make It Right	—	Brand New History .... Restless 773727	
7/21/01	®	29	6	5 You Don't Know What It's Like	—	↓	

EDDIE, John
Born in 1959 in Richmond, Virginia; raised in New Jersey. Pop-rock singer/songwriter.

Debut	Cht	Peak	Wks		Hot Pos	Album Title	Album Label & Number
5/24/86	®	17	10	Jungle Boy	52	John Eddie .... Columbia 40181	

EDDIE AND THE TIDE
Rock band from Berkeley, California: Eddie Rice (vocals), Johnny Perri (guitar), Cazz McCaslin (keyboards), George Diebold (bass) and Scott Mason (drums).

Debut	Cht	Peak	Wks		Hot Pos	Album Title	Album Label & Number
8/24/85	®	22	7	One In A Million	85	Go Out And Get It .... Atco 90289	

EDELWEISS
Trio of remixers from Austria: Martin Gletschermayer, Walter Werzowa and Matthias Schweger.

Debut	Cht	Peak	Wks		Hot Pos	Album Title	Album Label & Number
5/20/89	ⓜ	24	5	Bring Me Edelweiss	—	(single only) .... Atlantic 88911	
				Maria Mathis (vocal); same melody as "SOS" by Abba (#15 Pop hit in 1975)			

EDGE CITY OUTLAWS
Hard-rock duo from Toronto, Ontario, Canada: Luke Metcalf (vocals) and Griffin (guitar).

Debut	Cht	Peak	Wks		Hot Pos	Album Title	Album Label & Number
4/15/06	®	39	1	Women & Wine	—	(download only) .... Universal	

Debug	Cht	Peak	Wks	ARTIST / Track Title	Hot Pos	Album Title	Album Label & Number

EDMUNDS, Dave
Born on 4/15/1944 in Cardiff, Wales. Rock and roll singer/songwriter/guitarist/producer. Formed Love Sculpture in 1967. Formed rockabilly band **Rockpile** in 1976. Produced for Shakin' Stevens, Brinsley Schwarz and **Stray Cats**. Also see **Classic Rock Tracks** section.

5/2/81	®	18	11	1 Almost Saturday Night	54	Twangin	Swan Song 16034
				#78 Pop hit for **John Fogerty** in 1975			
5/1/82	®	28	7	2 From Small Things (Big Things One Day Come)	—	D.E. 7th	Columbia 37930
				written by **Bruce Springsteen**			
5/8/82	®	47	3	3 Me And The Boys	—	↓	
5/28/83	®	7	13	4 Slipping Away	39	Information	Columbia 38651
				written and produced by **Jeff Lynne**			
9/15/84	®	16	7	5 Something About You	—	Riff Raff	Columbia 39273
				#19 Pop hit for the Four Tops in 1965			
1/31/87	®	35	7	6 The Wanderer [L]	—	I Hear You Rockin'	Columbia 40603
				THE DAVE EDMUNDS BAND #2 Pop hit for Dion in 1962			
3/10/90	®	38	5	7 Closer To The Flame	—	Closer To The Flame	Capitol 90372

EELS
Alternative-rock trio formed in Los Angeles, California: Mark Everett (vocals, guitar), Tommy Walter (bass) and Butch Norton (drums). Everett later recorded solo as **E**. Walker later recorded solo as **Abandoned Pools**.

| 8/17/96 | ⓜ | ❶² | 25 | 1 Novocaine For The Soul | 39ᴬ | Beautiful Freak | DreamWorks 50001 |
| 11/14/98 | ⓜ | 40 | 4 | 2 Last Stop: This Town | — | Electro-Shock Blues | DreamWorks 50052 |

EGYPT CENTRAL
Rock band from Memphis, Tennessee: John Falls (vocals), Heath Hindman (guitar), Jeff James (guitar), Joey Chicago (bass) and Blake Allison (drums).

| 12/22/07+ | ® | 22↑ | 15↑ | You Make Me Sick | — | Egypt Central | Fat Lady 95255 |

EIGHTEEN VISIONS
Alternative-rock band from Anaheim, California: James Hart (vocals), Keith Barney (guitar), Mick Morris (bass) and Ken Floyd (drums).

5/27/06	®	38	2	1 Tonightless	—	Eighteen Visions	Trustkill 74632
7/1/06	®	15	20	2 Victim	—	↓	
1/6/07	®	38	3	3 Broken Hearted	—	↓	

805
Rock band from New York: Dave Porter (vocals, guitar), Ed Vivenzio (keyboards), Greg Liss (bass) and Frank Briggs (drums).

| 8/14/82 | ® | 37 | 4 | Young Boys | — | Stand In Line | RCA 8013 |

808 STATE
Techno-dance band from England: Martin Price (vocals), Graham Massey (programmer), and Darren Partington & Andy Barker (DJs). Formed at Price's Manchester record shop, Eastern Bloc. 808 refers to the Roland 808 Drum Machine.

1/23/93	ⓜ	13	9	1 One In Ten	—	Gorgeous	Tommy Boy 1067
				UB40 (guest vocals)			
3/13/93	ⓜ	21	6	2 Moses	—	↓	

8STOPS7
Rock band from Los Angeles, California: Evan Sula-Goff (vocals, guitar), Seth Watson (guitar), Adam Powell (bass) and Alex Viveros (drums).

3/11/00	®	26	14	1 Satisfied	—	In Moderation	Reprise 47387
4/22/00	ⓜ	35	7				
7/29/00	®	16	11	2 Question Everything	—	↓	
7/22/00	ⓜ	25	9				

ELASTICA
Alternative-rock band from London, England: Justine Frischmann (vocals), Donna Matthews (guitar), Annie Holland (bass) and Justin Welch (drums).

3/4/95	ⓜ	2³	25	1 Connection	53	Elastica	DGC 24728
6/24/95	®	40	1				
7/8/95	ⓜ	10	13	2 Stutter	67	↓	
12/9/95	ⓜ	33	3	3 Car Song	—	↓	

ELECTRAFIXION
Alternative-rock trio formed in England: **Ian McCulloch**, Johnny Marr and Will Sergeant. McCulloch and Sergeant were with **Echo & The Bunnymen**. Marr was also with **Electronic**.

| 2/18/95 | ⓜ | 38 | 1 | Zephyr | — | (single only) | Spacejunk 61793 |

Debut	Cht	Peak	Wks	Artist / Track Title	Hot Pos	Album Title	Album Label & Number
				ELECTRIC BOYS			
				Male rock band from Sweden: Conny Bloom (vocals), Franco Santunione (guitar), Andy Christell (bass) and Niclas Sigevall (drums).			
5/5/90	ℝ	16	13	1 All Lips N' Hips	76	Funk-O-Metal Carpet Ride	Atco 91337
6/6/92	ℝ	29	6	2 Mary In The Mystery World	—	Groovus Maximus	Atco 92143
				ELECTRIC LIGHT ORCHESTRA			
				Orchestral rock band formed in Birmingham, England. Core members: **Jeff Lynne** (vocals, guitar), Richard Tandy (keyboards), Kelly Groucutt (bass) and Bev Bevan (drums). Lynne was also a prolific producer and a member of the supergroup **Traveling Wilburys**. Also see **Classic Rock Tracks** section.			
8/15/81	ℝ	2[1]	16	1 Hold On Tight	10	Time	Jet 37371
7/9/83	ℝ	19	9	2 Rock 'N' Roll Is King	19	Secret Messages	Jet 38490
				ELO (above 2)			
2/8/86	ℝ	22	9	3 Calling America	18	Balance Of Power	CBS Associated 40048
				ELECTRONIC			
				Dance duo from Manchester, England: Bernard Sumner (of **New Order**) and Johnny Marr (of **Electrafixion**).			
1/20/90	ⓜ	4	11	1 Getting Away With It	38	Electronic	Warner 26387
4/27/91	ⓜ	❶[2]	16	2 Get The Message	—	↓	
7/13/91	ⓜ	6	10	3 Tighten Up	—	↓	
9/28/91	ⓜ	27	2	4 Feel Every Beat	—	↓	
7/25/92	ⓜ	9	9	5 Disappointed	—	St: Cool World	Warner 45009
				ELEMENT EIGHTY			
				Hard-rock band from Tyler, Texas: Dave Galloway (vocals), Matt Woods (guitar), Roon (bass) and Ryan Carroll (drums).			
11/29/03	ℝ	36	9	Broken Promises	—	Element Eighty	Republic 128402
				ELEVEN			
				Rock trio from Los Angeles, California: Alain Johannes (guitar, vocals), Natasha Shneider (clavinet, bass, vocals) and Jack Irons (drums). Irons was also a member of **Red Hot Chili Peppers** and **Pearl Jam**.			
5/28/94	ℝ	40	1	Reach Out		Eleven	Third Rail 61516
				ELEVENTH DREAM DAY			
				Pop-rock band from Chicago, Illinois: husband-and-wife Rick Rizzo (guitar) and Janet Bean (drums), with Baird Figi (guitar) and Doug McCombs (bass).			
1/20/90	ⓜ	26	2	1 Testify	—	Beet	Atlantic 82053
3/23/91	ⓜ	27	3	2 Rose Of Jericho	—	Lived To Tell	Atlantic 82179
				ELWOOD			
				Eclectic hip-hop/pop duo formed in New York: Prince Elwood Strickland (vocals) and Brian Boland (producer).			
6/24/00	ⓜ	33	6	Sundown	—	The Parlance Of Our Time	Palm 2047
				#1 Pop hit for Gordon Lightfoot in 1974			
				ELY, Joe			
				Born on 2/9/1947 in Amarillo, Texas; raised in Lubbock, Texas. Country-rock singer/songwriter/guitarist.			
4/4/81	ℝ	40	3	Musta Notta Gotta Lotta	—	Musta Notta Gotta Lotta	SouthCoast 5183
				EMERSON, LAKE & PALMER			
				Progressive rock trio from England: Keith Emerson (keyboards), **Greg Lake** (vocals, guitar, bass) and Carl Palmer (drums). Group split up in 1979, with Palmer joining **Asia**. Emerson and Lake re-grouped in 1986 with new drummer Cozy Powell (of **Whitesnake**). Palmer returned in 1987, replacing Powell who joined **Black Sabbath** in 1990. Powell died in a car crash on 4/5/1998 (age 50). Also see **3** and **Classic Rock Tracks** section.			
5/24/86	ℝ	2[2]	13	1 Touch & Go	60	Emerson, Lake & Powell	Polydor 829297
				EMERSON, LAKE & POWELL			
6/20/92	ℝ	44	1	2 Black Moon	—	Black Moon	Victory 480003
				EMF			
				Dance-techno-funk band from Forest of Dean, Gloucestershire, England: James Atkin (vocals), Ian Dench (guitar), Derry Brownson (keyboards, percussion), Zac Foley (bass) and Mark Decloedt (drums). Foley died of a drug overdose on 1/3/2002 (age 31).			
2/16/91	ⓜ	3[2]	12	1 Unbelievable	❶[1]	Schubert Dip	EMI 96238
				contains brief audio samples of comedian Andrew Dice Clay			
4/27/91	ⓜ	10	9	2 I Believe	—	↓	
7/27/91	ⓜ	26	2	3 Children	—	↓	
9/14/91	ⓜ	27	2	4 Lies	18	↓	
12/12/92	ⓜ	27	2	5 They're Here	—	Stigma	EMI 80348

Debug	Cht	Peak	Wks	ARTIST / Track Title	Hot Pos	Album Title	Album Label & Number

EMINEM

Born Marshall Mathers III on 10/17/1972 in Kansas City, Missouri; raised in Detroit, Michigan. White male rapper/actor. Protege of rapper/producer Dr. Dre. First recorded with the rap group Soul Intent in 1995. Created his alter ego, Slim Shady, for his 1999 album *The Slim Shady LP*. Starred in the 2002 movie *8 Mile*.

3/20/99	ⓜ	37	4	1 My Name Is	36	The Slim Shady LP	Aftermath 90287
				Grammy: Rap Solo			
6/3/00	ⓜ	19	9	2 The Real Slim Shady	4	The Marshall Mathers LP	Aftermath 490629
				Grammy: Rap Solo			
6/1/02	ⓜ	15	12	3 Without Me	2⁵	The Eminem Show	Aftermath 493290
10/19/02	ⓜ	14	18	4 Lose Yourself	❶¹²	St: 8 Mile	Shady 493508
				Grammys: Rap Song / Rap Male Solo ★ RS500 #166 ★ Oscar: Best Song			

EMMETT, Rik

Born on 7/10/1953 in Toronto, Ontario, Canada. Rock singer/guitarist. Leader of **Triumph** from 1975-88.

| 12/15/90+ | ® | 22 | 9 | 1 Big Lie | — | Absolutely | Charisma 91606 |
| 2/23/91 | ® | 16 | 15 | 2 Saved By Love | — | ↓ | |

EMOTIONAL FISH, An

Rock band formed in Dublin, Ireland: Gerard Whelan (vocals), David Frew (guitar), Enda Wyatt (bass) and Martin Murphy (drums).

10/13/90	ⓜ	4	16	1 Celebrate	—	An Emotional Fish	Atlantic 82150
2/2/91	ⓜ	18	8	2 Grey Matter	—	↓	
6/19/93	ⓜ	15	7	3 Rain	—	Junk Puppets	Atlantic 82473

ENDEVERAFTER

Rock band from Sacramento, California: Michael Grant (vocals, guitar), Kristian Mallory (guitar), Tommi Andrews (bass) and Eric Humbert (drums).

| 11/24/07+ | ® | 25 | 19↑ | I Wanna Be Your Man | — | Kiss Or Kill | Razor & Tie 82985 |

ENIGMA

Born Michael Cretu on 5/18/1957 in Bucharest, Romania; later based in Germany. Electronic musician/producer. Worked with **Vangelis** and **The Art Of Noise**. Featured vocalist is Cretu's wife, Sandra.

| 2/9/91 | ⓜ | 6 | 9 | 1 Sadeness Part 1 | [F] 5 | MCMXC A.D. | Charisma 91642 |
| 2/26/94 | ⓜ | 2⁵ | 15 | 2 Return To Innocence | 4 | Enigma 2: The Cross of Changes | Charisma 39236 |

ENO, Brian

Born on 5/15/1948 in Woodbridge, Suffolk, England. Rock producer/keyboardist. Founding member of **Roxy Music**. Production work for **David Bowie**, **Devo**, **Ultravox** and **Talking Heads**.

| 10/27/90 | ⓜ | 11 | 10 | Been There Done That | — | Wrong Way Up | Opal 26421 |
| | | | | BRIAN ENO & JOHN CALE | | | |

ENTWISTLE, John

Born on 10/9/1944 in Chiswick, London, England. Died of a heart attack on 6/27/2002 (age 57). Rock singer/bassist. Member of **The Who**.

| 12/12/81+ | ® | 41 | 6 | Talk Dirty | — | Too Late The Hero | Atco 142 |
| | | | | Joe Walsh (guitar) | | | |

ENUFF Z'NUFF

Rock band from Chicago, Illinois: Chip Z'Nuff (bass), Donnie Vie (vocals), Derek Frigo (guitar) and Vikki Foxx (drums). Frigo died on 5/28/2004 (age 36).

9/2/89	®	35	9	1 New Thing	67	Enuff Z'nuff	Atco 91262
1/20/90	®	27	10	2 Fly High Michelle	47	↓	
4/27/91	®	17	10	3 Mother's Eyes	—	Strength	Atco 91638

ENYA

Born Eithne Ni Brennan on 5/17/1961 in Gweedore, County Donegal, Ireland. Female singer.

| 1/7/89 | ⓜ | 6 | 12 | 1 Orinoco Flow (Sail Away) | 24 | Watermark | Geffen 24233 |
| 12/7/91+ | ⓜ | 3⁴ | 14 | 2 Caribbean Blue | 79 | Shepherd Moons | Reprise 26775 |

EPIDEMIC

Hard-rock band from San Diego, California: Boris Bouma (vocals), Bruce Allan (guitar), Jim McDaniel (bass) and Tim Ganard (drums).

| 7/27/02 | ® | 34 | 5 | Walk Away | — | Epidemic | Elektra 62769 |

ERASURE

Techno-rock-dance duo formed in London, England: Andy Bell (vocals; born on 4/25/1964) and Vince Clarke (instruments; born on 7/3/1960). Clarke was a member of **Depeche Mode** and **Yaz**.

9/10/88	ⓜ	22	2	1 Chains Of Love	12	The Innocents	Sire 25730
11/26/88+	ⓜ	15	10	2 A Little Respect	14	↓	
3/4/89	ⓜ	19	9	3 Stop!	97	Crackers International	Sire 25904
10/14/89	ⓜ	11	9	4 Drama!	—	Wild!	Sire 26026

Debit	Cht	Peak	Wks	ARTIST / Track Title	Hot Pos	Album Title	Album Label & Number

Billboard

ARTIST
Track Title
®=Mainstream Rock
◍=Modern Rock

ERASURE — cont'd

Debut	Cht	Peak	Wks	Track Title	Hot Pos	Album Title	Album Label & Number
7/13/91	◍	4	12	5 Chorus (Fishes In The Sea)	83	Chorus	Sire 26668
10/19/91	◍	6	12	6 Love To Hate You	—	↓	
4/30/94	◍	8	11	7 Always	20	I Say I Say I Say	Mute 61633

ESCAPE CLUB, The

Pop-rock band formed in London, England: Trevor Steel (vocals), John Holliday (guitar), Johnnie Christo (bass) and Milan Zekavica (drums).

Debut	Cht	Peak	Wks	Track Title	Hot Pos	Album Title	Album Label & Number
9/10/88	◍	3[2]	6	Wild, Wild West	❶[1]	Wild Wild West	Atlantic 81871
9/10/88	®	45	5				

ETHERIDGE, Melissa

Born on 5/29/1961 in Leavenworth, Kansas. Pop-rock singer/songwriter/guitarist. In early 2000, it was announced that **David Crosby** was the biological father (via artificial insemination) of two children for the couple of Etheridge and Julie Cypher (couple later split). Diagnosed with breast cancer in October 2004 (fully recovered in 2005).

TOP HITS: 1)Your Little Secret 2)Similar Features 3)No Souvenirs

Debut	Cht	Peak	Wks	Track Title	Hot Pos	Album Title	Album Label & Number
7/23/88	®	10	13	1 Bring Me Some Water	—	Melissa Etheridge	Island 90875
10/29/88	®	28	12	2 Like The Way I Do	42	↓	
2/18/89	®	6	13	3 Similar Features	94	↓	
5/13/89	®	22	7	4 Chrome Plated Heart	—	↓	
9/9/89	®	9	12	5 No Souvenirs	95	Brave And Crazy	Island 91285
9/30/89	◍	18	4				
11/18/89	®	13	12	6 Let Me Go	—	↓	
3/3/90	®	34	7	7 The Angels	—	↓	
3/14/92	®	10	10	8 Ain't It Heavy	—	Never Enough	Island 512120
				Grammy: Rock Female Vocal			
9/18/93	®	10	14	9 I'm The Only One	8	Yes I Am	Island 848660
1/1/94	®	22	12	10 Come To My Window	25	↓	
				Grammy: Rock Female Vocal			
4/16/94	®	24	8	11 All American Girl	—	↓	
10/28/95	®	4	14	12 Your Little Secret	47[A]	Your Little Secret	Island 524154
10/28/95	◍	32	6				
2/3/96	®	22	10	13 I Want To Come Over	22	↓	

EUROGLIDERS

Pop-rock band from Perth, Australia: Grace Knight (vocals), Crispin Akerman (guitar), Amanda Vincent and Bernie Lynch (keyboards), Ron Francois (bass) and John Bennetts (drums).

Debut	Cht	Peak	Wks	Track Title	Hot Pos	Album Title	Album Label & Number
11/3/84	®	21	11	Heaven (Must Be There)	65	This Island	Columbia 39588

EUROPE

Hard-rock band from Stockholm, Sweden: Joey Tempest (vocals), Kee Marcello (guitar), John Leven (bass), Mic Michaeli (keyboards) and Ian Haugland (drums). Founding guitarist **John Norum** went solo in 1987.

Debut	Cht	Peak	Wks	Track Title	Hot Pos	Album Title	Album Label & Number
12/27/86+	®	18	13	1 The Final Countdown	8	The Final Countdown	Epic 40241
4/4/87	®	22	8	2 Rock The Night	30	↓	
8/1/87	®	35	8	3 Carrie	3[2]	↓	
8/6/88	®	9	11	4 Superstitious	31	Out Of This World	Epic 44185

EURYTHMICS

New-wave pop-rock duo: **Annie Lennox** (vocals, keyboards; born on 12/25/1954 in Aberdeen, Scotland) and David A. Stewart (guitar; born on 9/9/1952 in Sunderland, England). Both had been in The Tourists from 1977-80. Stewart was married to Siobhan Fahey of **Bananarama** from 1987-96.

Debut	Cht	Peak	Wks	Track Title	Hot Pos	Album Title	Album Label & Number
6/11/83	®	16	15	1 Sweet Dreams (Are Made of This)	❶[1]	Sweet Dreams (Are Made Of This)	RCA 4681
				R&R Hall of Fame ★ RS500 #356			
1/21/84	®	8	15	2 Here Comes The Rain Again	4	Touch	RCA 4917
4/27/85	®	2[1]	14	3 Would I Lie To You?	5	Be Yourself Tonight	RCA 5429
7/13/85	®	36	5	4 I Love You Like A Ball And Chain	—	↓	
7/5/86	®	❶[1]	14	5 Missionary Man	14	Revenge	RCA 5847
				Grammy: Rock Vocal Duo			
12/19/87+	®	32	8	6 I Need A Man	46	Savage	RCA 6794
11/11/89	◍	12	8	7 Don't Ask Me Why	40	We Too Are One	Arista 8606

EVANESCENCE
Rock band from Little Rock, Arkansas: **Amy Lee** (vocals), Ben Moody (guitar), Josh LeCompt (bass) and Rocky Gray (drums).

Debut	Cht	Peak	Wks	Track Title	Hot Pos	Album Title	Label
1/25/03	⑩	❶²	26	1 Bring Me To Life	5	Fallen	Wind-Up 13063

Grammy: Hard Rock Performance
Paul McCoy (of **12 Stones**; guest vocal); featured in the movie *Daredevil* starring Ben Affleck

Debut	Cht	Peak	Wks	Track Title	Hot Pos	Album Title	Label
3/15/03	®	11	26				
6/28/03	⑩	5	25	2 Going Under	104	↓	
8/2/03	®	26	15				
4/10/04	⑩	36	8	3 Everybody's Fool	—	Anywhere But Here	Wind-Up 13106
8/19/06	⑩	4	23	4 Call Me When You're Sober	10	The Open Door	Wind-Up 13120
8/19/06	®	5	25				
2/10/07	⑩	37	3	5 Lithium	124	↓	
2/10/07	®	39	4				
3/31/07	®	24	15	6 Sweet Sacrifice	—	↓	

EVANS BLUE
Rock band from Toronto, Ontario, Canada: Kevin Matisyn (vocals), Parker Lauzon (guitar), Vlad Tanaskovic (guitar), Joe Pitter (bass) and Darryl Brown (drums).

Debut	Cht	Peak	Wks	Track Title	Hot Pos	Album Title	Label
12/31/05+	®	8	25	1 Cold (But I'm Still Here)	—	The Melody And The Energetic Nature Of Volume	The Pocket 162585
1/28/06	⑩	28	20				
8/5/06	®	28	12	2 Over	—	↓	
6/9/07	®	17	20	3 The Pursuit	—	The Pursuit Begins When This Portrayal Of Life Ends	The Pocket 000304
7/14/07	⑩	32	12				

EVERCLEAR
⑩ 1990s: #31 / All-Time: #39

Rock trio formed in Portland, Oregon: Art Alexakis (vocals, guitar; born on 4/12/1962), Craig Montoya (bass; born on 9/14/1970) and Greg Eklund (drums; born on 4/18/1970).

TOP HITS: 1)Santa Monica (Watch The World Die) 2)Everything To Everyone 3)I Will Buy You A New Life

Debut	Cht	Peak	Wks	Track Title	Hot Pos	Album Title	Label
6/24/95	⑩	34	5	1 Heroin Girl	—	Sparkle And Fade	Capitol 30929
12/23/95+	®	❶³	31	2 Santa Monica (Watch The World Die)	29ᴬ	↓	
11/11/95+	⑩	5	29				
5/4/96	⑩	13	10	3 Heartspark Dollarsign	85	↓	
5/25/96	®	29	8				
9/13/97	⑩	❶¹	29	4 Everything To Everyone	43ᴬ	So Much For The Afterglow	Capitol 36503
9/27/97	®	15	19				
2/7/98	⑩	3⁴	27	5 I Will Buy You A New Life	33ᴬ	↓	
2/14/98	®	20	13				
7/25/98	⑩	4	27	6 Father Of Mine	46ᴬ	↓	
8/22/98	®	29	8				
1/23/99	⑩	12	13	7 One Hit Wonder	—	↓	
8/21/99	®	40	2	8 The Boys Are Back In Town	—	St: Detroit Rock City	Mercury 546389

#12 Pop hit for **Thin Lizzy** in 1976

Debut	Cht	Peak	Wks	Track Title	Hot Pos	Album Title	Label
6/3/00	⑩	3²	20	9 Wonderful	11	Songs From An American Movie Vol. One: Learning How To Smile	Capitol 97061
6/17/00	®	28	10				
9/16/00	⑩	15	9	10 AM Radio	101	↓	
11/18/00+	®	10	13	11 When It All Goes Wrong Again	121	Songs From An American Movie, Vol. Two: Good Time For A Bad Attitude	Capitol 95873
11/18/00	⑩	12	13				
3/24/01	⑩	34	5	12 Out Of My Depth	—	↓	
2/1/03	⑩	30	6	13 Volvo Driving Soccer Mom	—	Slow Motion Daydream	Capitol 38270

Debut	Cht	Peak	Wks	ARTIST / Track Title	Hot Pos	Album Title	Album Label & Number

Ⓡ=Mainstream Rock Ⓜ=Modern Rock

EVERLAST
Ⓜ All-Time: #99
Born Erik Schrody on 8/18/1969 in Valley Stream, New York. Singer/songwriter/guitarist/actor. Former member of rap group House Of Pain. Played "Rhodes" in the 1993 movie *Judgment Night*.

Debut	Cht	Peak	Wks	Track Title	Hot Pos	Album Title	Album Label & Number
10/10/98	Ⓜ	❶⁹	34	1 What It's Like	13	*Whitey Ford Sings The Blues*	Tommy Boy 1236
11/21/98+	Ⓡ	❶¹	30				
4/3/99	Ⓜ	7	21	2 Ends	109	↓	
4/10/99	Ⓡ	13	16				
9/25/99	Ⓡ	8	27	3 Put Your Lights On	118	*Supernatural*	Arista 19080
10/2/99	Ⓜ	17	21	SANTANA Featuring Everlast Grammy: Rock Vocal Duo			
9/23/00	Ⓜ	15	15	4 Black Jesus	—	*Eat At Whitey's*	Tommy Boy 1411
9/30/00	Ⓡ	30	12				
1/13/01	Ⓜ	24	9	5 I Can't Move	—	↓	

EVERY MOTHER'S NIGHTMARE
Hard-rock band formed in Nashville, Tennessee: Rick Ruhl (vocals), Steve Malone (guitar), Mark McMurtry (bass) and Jim Phipps (drums).

Debut	Cht	Peak	Wks	Track Title	Hot Pos	Album Title	Album Label & Number
10/27/90	Ⓡ	22	11	Love Can Make You Blind	—	*Every Mother's Nightmare*	Arista 8633

EVERYTHING
Ska-rock band from Sperryville, Virginia: Craig Honeycutt (vocals, guitar), Rich Bradley, Wolfe Quinn and Steve Van Dam (horns), David Slankard (bass) and Nate Brown (drums).

Debut	Cht	Peak	Wks	Track Title	Hot Pos	Album Title	Album Label & Number
7/4/98	Ⓜ	12	15	Hooch	34ᴬ	*Super Natural*	Blackbird 38003

EVERYTHING BUT THE GIRL
Pop duo formed in London, England: Tracey Thorn (vocals) and Ben Watt (instruments). Group name taken from a furniture store on England's Hull University campus.

Debut	Cht	Peak	Wks	Track Title	Hot Pos	Album Title	Album Label & Number
3/24/90	Ⓜ	26	4	Driving	—	*The Language Of Life*	Atlantic 82057

EVE 6
Ⓜ All-Time: #78
Rock trio from Los Angeles, Claifornia: Max Collins (vocals, bass), Jon Siebels (guitar) and Tony Fagenson (drums).

Debut	Cht	Peak	Wks	Track Title	Hot Pos	Album Title	Album Label & Number
5/2/98	Ⓜ	❶⁴	41	1 Inside Out	28	*Eve 6*	RCA 67617
8/1/98	Ⓡ	5	29				
12/12/98+	Ⓜ	6	21	2 Leech	—	↓	
12/19/98+	Ⓡ	10	17				
5/8/99	Ⓜ	23	9	3 Open Road Song	—	↓	
6/17/00	Ⓜ	3¹	20	4 Promise	108	*Horrorscope*	RCA 67713
7/15/00	Ⓡ	25	9				
11/11/00	Ⓜ	19	13	5 On The Roof Again	—	↓	
3/31/01	Ⓜ	33	10	6 Here's To The Night	30	↓	
6/14/03	Ⓜ	9	17	7 Think Twice	—	*It's All In Your Head*	RCA 52346

EVE'S PLUM
Rock band from New York: Colleen Fitzpatrick (vocals), brothers Michael (guitar) and Ben (drums) Kotch, and Theo Mack (bass). Fitzpatrick later recorded as Vitamin C. Group's name derived from actress Eve Plumb ("Jan" on TV's *The Brady Bunch*).

Debut	Cht	Peak	Wks	Track Title	Hot Pos	Album Title	Album Label & Number
4/2/94	Ⓜ	30	1	I Want It All	—	*Envy*	550 Music 53070

EXIES, The
Alternative-rock band from Los Angeles, California: Scott Stevens (vocals, guitar), David Walsh (guitar), Freddy Herrera (bass) and Dennis Wolfe (drums).

Debut	Cht	Peak	Wks	Track Title	Hot Pos	Album Title	Album Label & Number
11/2/02	Ⓡ	20	19	1 My Goddess	—	*Inertia*	Melisma 13309
12/14/02+	Ⓜ	26	14				
11/13/04+	Ⓡ	11	26	2 Ugly	—	*Head For The Door*	Melisma 91822
12/4/04+	Ⓜ	13	26				
7/30/05	Ⓡ	40	3	3 What You Deserve	—	↓	
3/17/07	Ⓡ	27	18	4 Different Than You	—	*A Modern Way Of Living With The Truth*	Eleven Seven 130

EXPANDING MAN
Rock band from New York: Aaron Lippert (vocals), Dave Wanamaker (guitar), Bill Guerra (guitar), Pete Armata (bass) and Chris Hancock (drums).

Debut	Cht	Peak	Wks	Track Title	Hot Pos	Album Title	Album Label & Number
9/14/96	Ⓡ	22	10	Download (I Will)	—	*Head To The Ground*	QDivision 67601

Debut	Cht	Peak	Wks	ARTIST — Track Title	Hot Pos	Album Title	Album Label & Number
				®=Mainstream Rock ⓜ=Modern Rock			
				EXPLOSION, The			
				Punk-rock band from Boston, Massachusetts: Matt Hock (vocals), Dave Walsh (guitar), Sam Cave (guitar), Damian Genaurdi (bass) and Dan Colby (drums).			
10/23/04	ⓜ	39	3	Here I Am	—	Black Tape	Tarantula 81723
				EXTREME			
				Pop-rock band from Boston, Massachusetts: Gary Cherone (vocals), Nuno Bettencourt (guitar), Pat Badger (bass) and Paul Geary (drums). Geary replaced by Mike Mangini by 1995. Cherone became lead singer of **Van Halen** in September 1996 (for one album). Bettencourt later joined **Satellite Party**.			
4/8/89	®	39	6	1 Kid Ego	—	Extreme	A&M 5238
9/1/90	®	45	2	2 Decadence Dance	—	Pornograffitti	A&M 5313
3/2/91	®	12	17	3 More Than Words	❶¹	↓	
6/22/91	®	2⁴	18	4 Hole Hearted	4	↓	
10/26/91	®	34	7	5 Get The Funk Out	—	↓	
9/12/92	®	❶²	20	6 Rest In Peace	96	III Sides To Every Story	A&M 540006
12/26/92+	®	9	11	7 Stop The World	95	↓	
4/10/93	®	10	13	8 Am I Ever Gonna Change	—	↓	
2/4/95	®	26	7	9 Hip Today	—	Waiting For The Punchline	A&M 540327

F

Debut	Cht	Peak	Wks	ARTIST — Track Title	Hot Pos	Album Title	Album Label & Number
				FABULON			
				Born Kevin MacBeth in Miami, Florida. Rock singer/keyboardist.			
8/21/93	ⓜ	24	3	In A Mood	—	All Girls Are Pretty Volume I	Chrysalis 21999
				FABULOUS THUNDERBIRDS, The			
				Male blues-rock band from Austin, Texas: Kim Wilson (vocals, harmonica), Jimmie Vaughan (guitar; older brother of **Stevie Ray Vaughan**), Keith Ferguson (bass) and Fran Christina (drums). Preston Hubbard replaced Ferguson in late 1981. Vaughan appeared in the 1989 movie *Great Balls Of Fire* and recorded in **The Vaughan Brothers** in 1990. Disbanded in June 1990. Reorganized in 1991 with Wilson, Hubbard, Christina and guitarists Duke Robillard and Kid Bangham. Ferguson died of liver failure on 4/29/1997 (age 49).			
				TOP HITS: 1)Powerful Stuff 2)Tuff Enuff 3)Twist Of The Knife			
4/11/81	®	44	1	1 Tip On In	—	Butt Rockin'	Chrysalis 1319
				#37 R&B hit for Slim Harpo in 1967			
4/18/81	®	41	2	2 One's Too Many	—	↓	
2/22/86	®	4	16	3 Tuff Enuff	10	Tuff Enuff	CBS Associated 40304
5/24/86	®	8	11	4 Wrap It Up	50	↓	
				#93 Pop hit for Archie Bell & The Drells in 1970			
8/30/86	®	20	8	5 Look At That, Look At That	—	↓	
6/27/87	®	8	8	6 Stand Back	76	Hot Number	CBS Associated 40818
8/15/87	®	22	8	7 How Do You Spell Love	—	↓	
				above 5 produced by **Dave Edmunds**			
7/16/88	®	3¹	12	8 Powerful Stuff	65	St: Cocktail	Elektra 60806
4/22/89	®	10	8	9 Rock This Place	—	Powerful Stuff	CBS Associated 45094
7/27/91	®	7	10	10 Twist Of The Knife	—	Walk That Walk, Talk That Talk	Epic/Associated 47878
				FACE TO FACE			
				Rock band from Boston, Massachusetts: Laurie Sargent (vocals), brothers Angelo Kimball (guitar) and Stuart Kimball (guitar), John Ryder (bass) and William Beard (drums).			
6/9/84	®	55	2	Out Of My Hands	—	Face To Face	Epic 38857
				FACE TO FACE			
				Punk-rock band from Los Angeles, California: Trevor Keith (vocals), Chad Yaro (guitar), Scott Shiflett (bass) and Rob Kurth (drums).			
3/18/95	ⓜ	39	2	Disconnected	—	Big Choice	Victory 38348
				FAGEN, Donald			
				Born on 1/10/1948 in Passaic, New Jersey. Pop-rock singer/songwriter/keyboardist. Member of **Steely Dan**.			
10/23/82	®	17	12	1 I.G.Y. (What A Beautiful World)	26	The Nightfly	Warner 23696
				I.G.Y.: International Geophysical Year (July 1957-December 1958)			
3/26/88	®	12	8	2 Century's End	83	St: Bright Lights, Big City	Warner 25688
11/2/91	®	17	12	3 Pretzel Logic	[L] —	VA: The New York Rock And Soul Revue	Giant 24423
				DONALD FAGEN & MICHAEL McDONALD recorded at the Beacon Theatre in New York City; #57 Pop hit for **Steely Dan** in 1974			
6/5/93	®	20	8	4 Tomorrow's Girls	121	Kamakiriad	Reprise 45230

Billboard				ARTIST		Hot		
Debut	Cht	Peak	Wks	Track Title	®=Mainstream Rock ⑩=Modern Rock	Pos	Album Title	Album Label & Number

FAILURE
Rock band from Los Angeles, California: Ken Andrews (vocals), Troy Van Leeuwen (guitar), Greg Edwards (bass) and Kellii Scott (drums).

12/7/96+	⑩	23	9	Stuck On You	—	*Fantastic Planet*	Slash 46269
12/14/96+	®	31	9				

FAIRGROUND ATTRACTION
Pop band from England: Eddi Reader (female vocals), Mark Nevin (guitar), Simon Edwards (bass) and Roy Dodds (drums).

12/3/88	⑩	23	6	Perfect	80	*The First Of A Million Kisses*	RCA 8596

FAIR TO MIDLAND
Eclectic-rock band from Sulpher Springs, Texas: Darroh Sudderth (vocals), Cliff Campbell (guitar), Matt Langley (keyboards), Jon Dicken (bass) and Brett Stowers (drums).

4/7/07	®	19	21	1 Dance Of The Manatee	—	*Fables From A Mayfly: What I Tell You Three Times Is True*	Serjical Strike 008996
11/17/07	®	38	1	2 Tall Tales Taste Like Sour Grapes	—	↓	

FAITH NO MORE
Rock band from San Francisco, California: Michael Patton (vocals), Jim Martin (guitar), Roddy Bottum (keyboards), Billy Gould (bass) and Mike Bordin (drums). Martin left in 1994; replaced by Dean Menta. Menta left by 1995. Patton later recorded solo as **Peeping Tom**.

7/14/90	®	25	11	1 Epic	9	*The Real Thing*	Slash 25878
10/13/90	®	40	5	2 Falling To Pieces	92	↓	
6/13/92	⑩	❶¹	12	3 MidLife Crisis	—	*Angel Dust*	Slash 26785
7/25/92	®	32	5				
8/29/92	⑩	11	10	4 A Small Victory	—	↓	
6/21/97	®	14	21	5 Last Cup Of Sorrow	—	*Album Of The Year*	Slash 46629
11/15/97+	®	23	12	6 Ashes To Ashes	—	↓	

FAKTION
Hard-rock band from Denton, Texas: Ryan Gibbs (vocals), Marshall Dutton (guitar), Josh Franklin (guitar), Jeremy Coan (bass) and Jeremy Moore (drums).

2/25/06	®	29	12	Take It All Away	—	*Faktion*	Roadrunner 618200

FALCO
Born Johann Holzel on 2/19/1957 in Vienna, Austria. Died in a car crash on 2/6/1998 (age 40). Male singer/songwriter.

3/19/83	®	22	12	Der Kommissar [F]		*Einzelhaft*	A&M 4951

original German language version; also see English version by **After The Fire**

FALCON, Billy
Born on 7/13/1956 in Valley Stream, New York. Rock singer/songwriter/guitarist.

7/20/91	®	19	12	Power Windows	35	*Pretty Blue World*	Jambco 848800

co-produced by **Jon Bon Jovi**

FALL OUT BOY
Punk-pop band from Wilmette, Illinois: Patrick Stump (vocals, guitar), Joe Trohman (guitar), Pete Wentz (bass) and Andy Hurley (drums).

6/4/05	⑩	3¹	31	1 Sugar, We're Goin' Down	8	*From Under The Cork Tree*	Island 004140
11/5/05	®	36	3				
11/19/05+	⑩	2³	25	2 Dance, Dance	9	↓	
4/29/06	⑩	38	2	3 A Little Less Sixteen Candles, A Little More Touch Me	65	↓	
12/9/06+	⑩	8	20	4 This Ain't A Scene, It's An Arms Race	2²	*Infinity On High*	Fueled By Ramen 008109
4/14/07	⑩	19	20	5 Thnks Fr Th Mmrs	11	↓	

FAMILIAR 48
Rock band from Philadelphia, Pennsylvania: Jay Mannon (vocals), Kevin Hug (guitar), Scott Stanley (bass) and Nick DeNofa (drums).

3/23/02	®	30	8	The Question	—	*Wonderful Nothing*	Refugee 112852

FARM, The
Pop-rock-dance band from Liverpool, England: Peter Hooton (vocals), Steve Grimes (guitar), Keith Mullin (guitar), Ben Leach (keyboards), Carl Hunter (bass) and Roy Boulter (drums).

4/27/91	⑩	7	9	1 All Together Now	—	*Spartacus*	Sire 26600
6/29/91	⑩	15	10	2 Groovy Train	41	↓	
1/9/93	⑩	30	2	3 Love See No Colour	—	*Love See No Colour*	Sire 26959
7/2/94	⑩	30	1	4 Messiah	—	*Hullabaloo*	Sire 45588

FARRENHEIT
Rock trio from Boston, Massachusetts: Charlie Farren (vocals, guitar), David Heit (bass) and Muzz (drums). Farren was lead singer of the **Joe Perry Project**.

4/25/87	®	42	4	Fool In Love		—	*Farrenheit*	Warner 25564

FASTBALL
Rock trio from Austin, Texas: Miles Zuniga (vocals, guitar), Tony Scalzo (vocals, bass) and Joey Shuffield (drums).

2/21/98	ⓜ	❶⁷	26	1 The Way		5ᴬ	*All The Pain Money Can Buy*	Hollywood 62130
5/9/98	®	25	16					
8/15/98	ⓜ	13	15	2 Fire Escape		86	↓	
9/5/98	®	25	13					

FASTER PUSSYCAT
Hard-rock band from Los Angeles, California: Taime Downe (vocals), Greg Steele (guitar), Brent Muscat (guitar), Eric Stacy (bass) and Mark Michals (drums). Brett Bradshaw replaced Michals in early 1992. Band name taken from the 1965 movie *Faster Pussycat! Kill! Kill!*

3/31/90	®	23	10	1 House Of Pain		28	*Wake Me When It's Over*	Elektra 60883
9/12/92	®	35	2	2 Nonstop To Nowhere		—	*Whipped!*	Elektra 61124

FASTWAY
Hard-rock band from England: David King (vocals), Fast Eddie Clarke (guitar), Charlie McCracken (bass) and Jerry Shirley (drums). Clarke was with Motorhead. Shirley was with **Humble Pie**.

5/28/83	®	32	6	1 Easy Livin'		—	*Fastway*	Columbia 38662
6/11/83	®	14	11	2 Say What You Will		—	↓	
7/7/84	®	27	9	3 Tell Me		—	*All Fired Up*	Columbia 39373

FATBOY SLIM
Born Norman Cook on 7/31/1963 in Brighton, Sussex, England. Techno-house instrumentalist.

1/17/98	ⓜ	28	7	1 Going Out Of My Head		—	*Better Living Through Chemistry*	Astralwerks 6203
8/29/98	ⓜ	39	2	2 The Rockafeller Skank		76	*You've Come A Long Way, Baby*	Skint 66247
				samples "Beat Girl" by John Barry				
1/30/99	ⓜ	2⁷	26	3 Praise You		36	↓	
				samples "Take Yo Praise" by Camille Yarborough				
6/2/01	ⓜ	33	5	4 Weapon Of Choice		—	*Halfway Between The Gutter And The Stars*	Skint 50460

FAT LADY SINGS, The
Rock band from Dublin, Ireland: Nick Kelly (vocals), Tim Bradshaw (guitar), Dermot Lynch (bass) and Robert Hamilton (drums).

7/20/91	ⓜ	20	6	Man Scared		—	*Twist*	Atlantic 82211

FEAR FACTORY
Hard-rock band from Los Angeles, California: Burton Bell (vocals), Dino Cazares (guitar), Christian Olde Wolbers (bass) and Raymond Herrera (drums).

4/3/99	®	38	2	1 Descent		—	*Obsolete*	Roadrunner 8752
5/22/99	®	16	11	2 Cars		—	↓	
6/5/99	ⓜ	38	7	#9 Pop hit for Gary Numan in 1980				
6/9/01	®	31	7	3 Linchpin		—	*Digimortal*	Roadrunner 8487

FEEDER
Rock trio formed in Newport, South Wales: Grant Nicholas (vocals), Taka Hirose (bass) and Jon Lee (drums). Lee committed suicide on 1/7/2002 (age 33).

3/21/98	®	31	5	1 Cement		—	*Polythene*	Echo/Elektra 62085
6/27/98	ⓜ	24	12	2 High		—	↓	
7/18/98	®	36	4					

FEELIES, The
Rock band from Hoboken, New Jersey: Glenn Mercer (vocals), Bill Million (guitar), Dave Weckerman (percussion), Brenda Sauter (bass) and Stanley Demeski (drums).

10/15/88	ⓜ	6	10	1 Away		—	*Only Life*	A&M 5214
4/6/91	ⓜ	13	7	2 Sooner Or Later		—	*Time For A Witness*	A&M 5344

FEIST
Born Leslie Feist on 2/13/1976 in Amherst, Nova Scotia, Canada. Female singer/songwriter.

10/27/07	ⓜ	34	7	1234		8	*The Reminder*	Cherrytree 008819

FELDER, Don
Born on 9/21/1947 in Gainesville, Florida. Singer/songwriter/guitarist. Former member of the **Eagles**.

8/1/81	®	5	17	1 Heavy Metal (Takin' A Ride)		43	*St: Heavy Metal*	Asylum 90004
12/10/83	®	34	8	2 Bad Girls		104	*Airborne*	Elektra 60295

Debit	Cht	Peak	Wks	ARTIST / Track Title	Hot Pos	Album Title	Album Label & Number

FENIX*TX
Punk-rock band from Houston, Texas: Willie Salazar (vocals, guitar), Damon De La Paz (guitar), Adam Lewis (bass) and Donnie Vomit (drums).

| 4/29/00 | Ⓜ | 21 | 14 | All My Fault | — | Fenix*TX | MCA 12013 |

FENN, Rick
Born in England. Rock singer/guitarist.

| 8/3/85 | Ⓡ | 21 | 7 | Lie For A Lie
NICK MASON & RICK FENN | — | Profiles | Columbia 40142 |

FERGUSON, Jay
Born John Ferguson on 5/10/1947 in Burbank, California. Pop-rock singer/songwriter. Member of **Spirit**.

| 3/13/82 | Ⓡ | 34 | 8 | White Noise
Joe Walsh (guitar) | — | White Noise | Capitol 12196 |

FERRY, Bryan
Born on 9/26/1945 in County Durham, England. Pop-rock singer/songwriter. Lead singer of **Roxy Music**.

6/29/85	Ⓡ	19	9	1 Slave To Love	109	Boys And Girls	Warner 25082
2/27/88	Ⓡ	40	5	2 Kiss And Tell	31	Bete Noire	Reprise 25598
10/29/94	Ⓜ	37	3	3 Mamouna	—	Mamouna	Virgin 39838

FETCHIN BONES
Rock band from Los Angeles, California: Hope Nicholls (vocals), Aaron Pitkin (guitar), Errol Stewart (guitar), Danna Pentes (bass) and Clay Richardson (drums).

| 8/12/89 | Ⓜ | 19 | 5 | Love Crushing | — | Monster | Capitol 90661 |

FIALKA, Karel
Born in Bengal, India (Czech father/Scottish mother); raised in England. Male singer/songwriter.

| 2/11/89 | Ⓜ | 29 | 2 | Hey Matthew | — | Human Animal | I.R.S. 42252 |

FIGHT
Hard-rock band formed in England: Rob Halford (vocals), Russ Parrish (guitar), Brian Tilse (guitar), Jay Jay (bass) and Scott Travis (drums). Halford was lead singer of **Judas Priest**.

| 11/27/93+ | Ⓡ | 21 | 12 | Little Crazy | — | War Of Words | Epic 57372 |

FIGHTING INSTINCT
Christian rock band from Winston-Salem, North Carolina: TJ Harris (vocals, guitar), Derek Drye (guitar), Jason Weekly (bass) and Chris Burrow (drums).

| 4/22/06 | Ⓡ | 31 | 8 | I Found Forever | — | Fighting Instinct | Gotee 38740 |

FIGURES ON A BEACH
Techno-rock band from Boston, Massachusetts: Anthony Kaczynski (vocals), John Rolski (guitar), Christopher Ewen (keyboards), Percy Tell (bass) and Michael Smith (drums).

| 8/19/89 | Ⓜ | 14 | 6 | Accidentally 4th St. (Gloria) | — | Figures On A Beach | Sire 25804 |

FILTER
Industrial rock duo from Cleveland, Ohio: Richard Patrick (vocals, guitar, bass) and Brian Liesegang (keyboards, drums). Both worked with Trent Reznor in **Nine Inch Nails**. Patrick later formed **Army Of Anyone**.

4/29/95	Ⓜ	10	20	1 Hey Man Nice Shot	76	Short Bus	Reprise 45864
5/13/95	Ⓡ	19	18				
8/16/97	Ⓜ	29	10	2 (Can't You) Trip Like I Do FILTER & THE CRYSTAL METHOD	—	St: Spawn	Immortal 68494
7/31/99	Ⓡ	8	14	3 Welcome To The Fold	—	Title Of Record	Reprise 47388
7/31/99	Ⓜ	17	13				
10/16/99+	Ⓜ	3[2]	26	4 Take A Picture	12	↓	
11/6/99+	Ⓡ	4	25				
4/1/00	Ⓜ	18	10	5 The Best Things	—	↓	
4/15/00	Ⓡ	31	7				
7/13/02	Ⓜ	11	10	6 Where Do We Go From Here	94	theAmalgamut	Reprise 47963
7/13/02	Ⓡ	12	10				
10/19/02	Ⓡ	40	1	7 American Cliche	—	↓	

FINCH
Rock band from Los Angeles, California: Nate Barcalow (vocals), Randy Strohmeyer (guitar), Alex Linares (guitars), Derek Doherty (bass) and Alex Pappas (drums).

| 2/22/03 | Ⓜ | 15 | 16 | What It Is To Burn | — | What It Is To Burn | Drive-Thru 860991 |
| 3/1/03 | Ⓡ | 35 | 10 | | | | |

Billboard				ARTIST		Hot		
Debut	Cht	Peak	Wks	Track Title	®=Mainstream Rock ⓂModern Rock	Pos	Album Title	Album Label & Number

FINE YOUNG CANNIBALS

Pop-rock trio formed in Birmingham, England: Roland Gift (vocals), Andy Cox (guitar) and David Steele (bass). Cox and Steele were with English Beat. Group name taken from the 1960 movie *All The Fine Young Cannibals*. Group appeared in the 1987 movie *Tin Men*. Gift acted in the movies *Sammy And Rosie Get Laid* and *Scandal*.

1/28/89	Ⓜ	5	15	1 She Drives Me Crazy	❶¹	The Raw & The Cooked	I.R.S. 6273
3/25/89	Ⓜ	2¹	19	2 Good Thing	❶¹	↓
6/3/89	®	39	4			
8/12/89	Ⓜ	9	7	3 Don't Look Back	11	↓
8/19/89	®	38	8			

FINGER ELEVEN

Rock band from Burlington, Ontario, Canada: brothers Scott Anderson (vocals) and Sean Anderson (bass), with Rick Jackett (guitar), James Black (guitar) and Rob Gommerman (drums).

9/26/98	®	28	10	1 Quicksand	—	Tip	Wind-Up 13052
4/17/99	®	34	7	2 Above	—	↓
11/29/03+	Ⓜ	5	26	3 One Thing	16	Finger Eleven	Wind-Up 13058
10/4/03	®	38	8			
2/3/07	®	❶¹	52	4 Paralyzer	6	Them Vs. You Vs. Me	Wind-Up 13112
3/3/07	Ⓜ	❶¹	52			
9/8/07	®	25	20	5 Falling On	—	↓
12/8/07+	Ⓜ	31	9			

FINGERTIGHT

Rock band from San Francisco, California: Scott Rose (vocals), Sergio Renoso (guitar), Jesse Del Rio (bass) and Kirk Shelton (drums).

| 9/13/03 | ® | 34 | 6 | Guilt (Hold Down) | — | In The Name Of Progress | Columbia 86377 |

FIONA

Born Fiona Flanagan on 9/13/1961 in Manhattan, New York. Female rock singer/actress. Played "Molly McGuire" in the 1987 movie *Hearts Of Fire*.

3/23/85	®	12	12	1 Talk To Me	64	Fiona	Atlantic 81242
10/28/89	®	22	10	2 Everything You Do (You're Sexing Me)	52	Heart Like A Gun	Atlantic 81903
				FIONA with Kip Winger		

FIREHOSE

Rock trio formed in San Pedro, California: Ed Crawford (vocals, guitar), **Mike Watt** (bass) and George Hurley (drums).

| 4/15/89 | Ⓜ | 26 | 2 | Time With You | — | "fROMOHIO" | SST 235 |

FIREHOUSE

Pop-rock band from Charlotte, North Carolina: C.J. Snare (vocals), Bill Leverty (guitar), Perry Richardson (bass) and Michael Foster (drums).

1/19/91	®	16	18	1 Don't Treat Me Bad	19	Firehouse	Epic 46186
11/16/91+	®	25	10	2 All She Wrote	58	↓
6/20/92	®	27	10	3 Reach For The Sky	83	Hold Your Fire	Epic 48615

FIRE TOWN

Rock trio from Madison, Wisconsin: Doug Erickson (vocals, guitar), Phil Davis (vocals, guitar) and Butch Vig (drums). Vig and Erickson later formed **Garbage**.

| 3/18/89 | Ⓜ | 18 | 6 | The Good Life | — | The Good Life | Atlantic 81945 |

FIRM, The

All-star rock band formed in England: **Paul Rodgers** (vocals), **Jimmy Page** (guitar), Tony Franklin (bass) and Chris Slade (drums). Rodgers was with **Bad Company**. Page was with **Led Zeppelin**. Disbanded in 1986. Franklin joined **Blue Murder** in 1989. Slade joined **AC/DC** in 1990. Rodgers joined **The Law** in 1991.

2/2/85	®	❶¹	15	1 Radioactive	28	The Firm	Atlantic 81239
3/9/85	®	19	10	2 Closer	—	↓
3/16/85	®	4	15	3 Satisfaction Guaranteed	73	↓
2/1/86	®	❶⁴	12	4 All The Kings Horses	61	Mean Business	Atlantic 81628
3/1/86	®	21	11	5 Live In Peace	—	↓

FISHBONE

Funk-rock band from Los Angeles, California: Angelo Moore (vocals, sax), Kendall Jones (guitar), Charlie Down (guitar), Christopher Dowd (keyboards), Walter Kirby (trumpet), John Fisher (bass) and Phillip Fisher (drums).

| 4/13/91 | Ⓜ | 7 | 10 | 1 Sunless Saturday | — | The Reality Of My Surroundings | Columbia 46142 |
| 6/22/91 | Ⓜ | 14 | 6 | 2 Everyday Sunshine | — | ↓ |

Billboard				ARTIST		Hot	
Debut	Cht	Peak	Wks	Track Title	℞=Mainstream Rock ℳ=Modern Rock	Pos	Album Title	Album Label & Number

FIVE FINGER DEATH PUNCH

Hard-rock band formed in Los Angeles, California: Ivan Moody (vocals), Zoltan Bathory (guitar), Darrell Roberts (guitar), Matt Snell (bass) and Jeremy Spencer (drums). Moody was also lead singer of **Motograter**.

Debut	Cht	Peak	Wks	Track Title	Hot Pos	Album Title	Album Label & Number
8/11/07+	℞	9	33↑	The Bleeding	—	The Way Of The Fist	Firm 70116

FIVESPEED

Rock band from Peoria, Arizona: Jared Woosley (vocals), Jesse Lacross (guitar), Brad Cole (guitar), Matt Turner (bass) and Shane Addington (drums).

| 12/3/05 | ℞ | 29 | 13 | The Mess | — | Morning Over Midnight | Equal Vision 80921 |

FIVE THIRTY

Rock trio from London, England: Paul Bassett (vocals, guitar), Tara Milton (bass) and Phil Hopper (drums).

| 10/12/91 | ℳ | 14 | 7 | 13th Disciple | — | Bed | Atco 91757 |

FIXX, The   ℞ 1980s: #27 / All-Time: #72

Techno-pop band formed in London, England: Cy Curnin (vocals), Jamie West-Oram (guitar), Rupert Greenall (keyboards), Dan Brown (bass) and Adam Woods (drums).

TOP HITS: 1)Driven Out 2)Secret Separation 3)Are We Ourselves?

Debut	Cht	Peak	Wks	#	Track Title	Hot Pos	Album Title	Album Label & Number
9/18/82	℞	7	21	1	Stand Or Fall	76	Shuttered Room	MCA 5345
2/19/83	℞	13	11	2	Red Skies	101	↓	
5/28/83	℞	9	18	3	Saved By Zero	20	Reach The Beach	MCA 39001
6/4/83	℞	2¹	26	4	One Thing Leads To Another	4	↓	
1/21/84	℞	20	4	5	The Sign Of Fire	32	↓	
5/12/84	℞	3²	14	6	Deeper And Deeper	—	St: Streets Of Fire	MCA 5492
8/18/84	℞	❶²	13	7	Are We Ourselves?	15	Phantoms	MCA 5507
9/8/84	℞	37	13	8	Sunshine In The Shade	69	↓	
5/17/86	℞	❶²	15	9	Secret Separation	19	Walkabout	MCA 5705
7/5/86	℞	13	14	10	Built For The Future	—	↓	
7/4/87	℞	32	5	11	Don't Be Scared	—	React	MCA 42008
1/21/89	℞	❶⁴	14	12	Driven Out	55	Calm Animals	RCA 8566
1/28/89	ℳ	11	11					
4/29/89	℞	23	7	13	Precious Stone	—	↓	
2/23/91	ℳ	10	7	14	How Much Is Enough	35	Ink	MCA 10205
2/16/91	℞	11	9					

FLAMING LIPS, The

Rock band from Oklahoma City, Oklahoma: Wayne Coyne (vocals), Ron Jones (guitar), Michael Ivins (bass) and Steven Drozd (drums).

| 12/10/94+ | ℳ | 9 | 14 | She Don't Use Jelly | 55 | Transmissions From The Satellite Heart | Warner 45334 |

FLAW

Rock band from Louisville, Kentucky: Chris Volz (vocals), Lance Arny (guitar), Jason Daunt (keyboards), Ryan Jurhs (bass) and Chris Ballinger (drums).

Debut	Cht	Peak	Wks	#	Track Title	Hot Pos	Album Title	Album Label & Number
11/10/01	℞	33	7	1	Payback	—	Through The Eyes	Republic 014891
6/1/02	℞	38	2	2	Whole	—	↓	
5/22/04	℞	25	10	3	Recognize	—	Endangered Species	Republic 002396

FLEETWOOD, Mick

Born on 6/24/1942 in Redruth, Cornwall, England. Blues-rock drummer. Co-founder of **Fleetwood Mac**; also formed **The Zoo**. Played "Mic" in the 1987 movie *The Running Man*.

| 7/18/81 | ℞ | 30 | 6 | Rattlesnake Shake | — | The Visitor | RCA 4080 |

FLEETWOOD MAC   ℞ All-Time: #85

Pop-rock band formed in England by **Mick Fleetwood** (drums) and John McVie (bass). Group went through several personnel changes. **Bob Welch** was a member from 1971-74. **Christine McVie** (vocals, keyboards) joined in August 1970 (married to John from 1968-77). Americans **Lindsey Buckingham** (guitar, vocals) and **Stevie Nicks** (vocals) joined in January 1975. Buckingham left in July 1987; replaced by Billy Burnette and Rick Vito. The classic lineup of Fleetwood, John and Christine McVie, Buckingham and Nicks reuinted in May 1997. Also see **Classic Rock Tracks** section.

AWARD: R&R Hall of Fame: 1998

TOP HITS: 1)Big Love 2)Seven Wonders 3)Hold Me

Debut	Cht	Peak	Wks	#	Track Title	Hot Pos	Album Title	Album Label & Number
4/11/81	℞	59	1	1	Fireflies	60	Fleetwood Mac Live	Warner 3500
6/19/82	℞	3³	16	2	Hold Me	4	Mirage	Warner 23607
7/24/82	℞	4	17	3	Gypsy	12	↓	
7/31/82	℞	36	2	4	Straight Back	—	↓	
3/28/87	℞	2³	10	5	Big Love	5	Tango In The Night	Warner 25471
4/25/87	℞	2¹	16	6	Seven Wonders	19	↓	
5/2/87	℞	14	17	7	Isn't It Midnight	—	↓	

FLEETWOOD MAC — cont'd

Debut	Cht	Peak	Wks	#	Track Title	Hot Pos	Album Title	Album Label & Number
5/2/87	R	28	9	8	Tango In The Night	—	↓	
8/22/87	R	14	11	9	Little Lies	4	↓	
12/5/87+	R	22	11	10	Everywhere	14	↓	
11/26/88+	R	15	12	11	As Long As You Follow	43	Greatest Hits	Warner 25801
12/24/88+	R	37	7	12	No Questions Asked	—	↓	
4/7/90	R	3[2]	9	13	Save Me	33	Behind The Mask	Warner 26111
4/28/90	R	7	11	14	Love Is Dangerous	—	↓	
7/28/90	R	40	4	15	Skies The Limit	—	↓	
12/12/92	R	26	4	16	Paper Doll	108	25 Years-The Chain	Warner 45129
10/25/97	R	30	6	17	The Chain [L]	—	The Dance	Reprise 46702

studio version first released on their 1977 album *Rumours*

FLESH FOR LULU

Punk-rock band from England: Nick Marsh (vocals), Rocco Barker (guitar), Derek Greening (keyboards), Mike Steed (bass) and Hans Perrson (drums).

Debut	Cht	Peak	Wks	#	Track Title	Hot Pos	Album Title	Album Label & Number
9/23/89	M	15	6	1	Decline And Fall	—	Plastic Fantastic	Beggars Banquet 90232
11/11/89	M	9	10	2	Time And Space	—	↓	

FLICKERSTICK

Rock band from Dallas, Texas: brothers Brandin Lea (vocals, guitar) and Fletcher Lea (bass), with Rex James Ewing (guitar), Cory Kreig (keyboards) and Dominic Weir (drums).

Debut	Cht	Peak	Wks	#	Track Title	Hot Pos	Album Title	Album Label & Number
11/3/01	M	27	8		Beautiful	—	Welcoming Home The Astronauts	Epic 86132

FLIES ON FIRE

Rock band from Los Angeles, California: Tim Paruszkiewicz (vocals), Howard Drossin (guitar), Mess Messal (bass) and Richard D'Albis (drums).

Debut	Cht	Peak	Wks	#	Track Title	Hot Pos	Album Title	Album Label & Number
8/17/91	R	38	4		Cry To Myself	—	Outside Looking Inside	Atco 91675

FLOCK OF SEAGULLS, A

New-wave band from Liverpool, England: brothers Mike Score (vocals, keyboards) and Ali Score (drums), with Paul Reynolds (guitar) and Frank Maudsley (bass).

Debut	Cht	Peak	Wks	#	Track Title	Hot Pos	Album Title	Album Label & Number
5/15/82	R	3[1]	29	1	I Ran (So Far Away)	9	A Flock Of Seagulls	Jive 66000
6/19/82	R	59	2	2	Space Age Love Song	30	↓	
5/14/83	R	3[1]	14	3	Wishing (If I Had A Photograph Of You)	26	Listen	Jive 8013
8/4/84	R	10	10	4	The More You Live, The More You Love	56	The Story Of A Young Heart	Jive 8250

FLYLEAF

Christian rock band formed in Belton, Texas: Lacey Mosley (vocals), Sameer Bhattacharya (guitar), Jared Hartmann (guitar), Pat Seals (bass) and James Culpepper (drums).

Debut	Cht	Peak	Wks	#	Track Title	Hot Pos	Album Title	Album Label & Number
12/17/05+	R	12	20	1	I'm So Sick	—	Flyleaf	Octone 50005
1/7/06	M	27	20					
6/24/06	R	13	26	2	Fully Alive	125	↓	
9/2/06+	M	31	17					
6/23/07	M	6	26	3	All Around Me	93	↓	
5/12/07	R	20	20					
1/26/08	R	36	5	4	Breathe Today	—	↓	

FLYS, The

Rock band from Los Angeles, California: brothers Adam and Joshua Paskowitz (vocals), Peter Perdichizzi (guitar), James Book (bass) and Nick Lucero (drums).

Debut	Cht	Peak	Wks	#	Track Title	Hot Pos	Album Title	Album Label & Number
8/22/98	M	5	29	1	Got You (Where I Want You)	104	St: Disturbing Behavior	Trauma 74007
9/12/98+	R	8	30					
4/3/99	M	32	5	2	She's So Huge	—	Holiday Man	Delicious Vinyl 74006

FOGELBERG, Dan

Born on 8/13/1951 in Peoria, Illinois. Died of prostate cancer on 12/16/2007 (age 56). Singer/songwriter/guitarist. Also see **Classic Rock Tracks** section.

Debut	Cht	Peak	Wks	#	Track Title	Hot Pos	Album Title	Album Label & Number
9/5/81	R	14	14	1	Hard To Say Glenn Frey (harmony vocal)	7	The Innocent Age	Full Moon 37393
9/19/81	R	45	9	2	Lost In The Sun	—	↓	
12/11/82	R	30	2	3	Missing You	23	Dan Fogelberg/Greatest Hits	Full Moon 38308
2/25/84	R	8	10	4	The Language Of Love	13	Windows And Walls	Full Moon 39004
4/7/84	R	31	2	5	Gone Too Far Timothy B. Schmit (harmony vocal, above 2)	—	↓	
5/23/87	R	13	8	6	She Don't Look Back	84	Exiles	Full Moon 40271

FOGERTY, John

Born on 5/28/1945 in Berkeley, California. Singer/songwriter/multi-instrumentalist. Leader of Creedence Clearwater Revival. Also see **Classic Rock Tracks** section.

Debut	Cht	Peak	Wks	#	Track Title	Hot Pos	Album Title	Label & Number
12/22/84+	®	❶³	14	1	The Old Man Down The Road	10	Centerfield...................................Warner 25203	
1/19/85	®	5	18	2	Rock And Roll Girls....................	20	↓	
3/30/85	®	4	13	3	Centerfield...............................	44	↓	
8/30/86	®	3²	9	4	Eye Of The Zombie......................	81	Eye Of The Zombie...................Warner 25449	
9/27/86	®	3¹	13	5	Change In The Weather	—	↓	
10/4/86	®	27	6	6	Headlines	—	↓	
6/21/97	®	14	12	7	Walking In A Hurricane	—	Blue Moon Swamp.....................Warner 45426	
10/4/97	®	32	6	8	Blueboy....................................	—	↓	
6/6/98	®	19	13	9	Premonition.......................... [L]	—	Premonition ....Reprise 46908	

recorded at The Burbank Studio

FOGHAT

Rock band formed in England: "Lonesome" Dave Peverett (vocals, guitar), Erik Cartwright (guitar), Craig MacGregor (bass) and Roger Earl (drums). Nick Jameson replaced MacGregor in early 1982. Peverett died of pneumonia on 2/7/2000 (age 57). Price died of head trauma on 3/22/2005 (age 57). Also see **Classic Rock Tracks** section.

Debut	Cht	Peak	Wks	#	Track Title	Hot Pos	Album Title	Label & Number
7/18/81	®	15	10	1	Live Now-Pay Later	102	Girls To Chat & Boys To Bounce............Bearsville 3578	
11/20/82	®	12	8	2	Slipped, Tripped, Fell In Love	—	In The Mood For Something Rude ....Bearsville 23747	

FOLDS, Ben, Five

Born on 9/12/1966 in Winston-Salem, North Carolina. Singer/songwriter/pianist. His trio included Robert Sledge (bass) and Darren Jessee (drums).

Debut	Cht	Peak	Wks	#	Track Title	Hot Pos	Album Title	Label & Number
3/29/97	Ⓜ	22	12	1	Battle Of Who Could Care Less	—	Whatever And Ever Amen...................550 Music 67762	
11/22/97+	Ⓜ	6	26	2	Brick	19ᴬ	↓	
5/9/98	Ⓜ	23	9	3	Song For The Dumped.................	—	↓	
4/24/99	Ⓜ	17	11	4	Army	—	The Unauthorized Biography Of Reinhold Messner ....550 Music 69808	
8/11/01	Ⓜ	28	11	5	Rockin' The Suburbs.................... **BEN FOLDS**	—	Rockin' The Suburbs ....Epic 61610	

FOLK IMPLOSION

Rock duo from San Francisco, California: Lou Barlow (vocals, bass) and John Davis (guitar, drums).

Debut	Cht	Peak	Wks		Track Title	Hot Pos	Album Title	Label & Number
10/21/95	Ⓜ	4	26		Natural One	29	Kids ....London 828640	
1/27/96	®	20	10				St:	

FOO FIGHTERS   ® 2000s: #13 / All-Time: #26 ★ Ⓜ 1990s: #18 / 2000s: #3 / All-Time: #4

Rock band formed in Seattle, Washington: **Dave Grohl** (vocals, guitar; born on 1/14/1969), Pat Smear (guitar; born on 8/5/1959), Nate Mendel (bass; born on 12/2/1968) and William Goldsmith (drums; born on 7/4/1972). Taylor Hawkins (born on 2/10/1968) replaced Goldsmith in 1997. Franz Stahl (born on 10/30/1961) replaced Smear in 1998. Chris Shiflett (born on 5/6/1971) replaced Stahl in 2000. Grohl was the drummer for **Nirvana**. Group name taken from the fiery UFO-like apparitions seen by U.S. pilots during World War II.

TOP HITS: 1)The Pretender 2)All My Life 3)Best Of You 4)DOA 5)Long Road To Ruin

Debut	Cht	Peak	Wks	#	Track Title	Hot Pos	Album Title	Label & Number
7/8/95	Ⓜ	2²	15	1	This Is A Call................................	35ᴬ	Foo Fighters...........................Roswell 34027	
7/8/95	®	6	16					
9/23/95	Ⓜ	8	22	2	I'll Stick Around	51ᴬ	↓	
10/7/95	®	12	17					
1/27/96	Ⓜ	3⁵	23	3	Big Me..	13ᴬ	↓	
3/2/96	®	18	11					
5/10/97	®	9	20	4	Monkey Wrench.............................	58ᴬ	The Colour And The Shape ....Roswell 55832	
5/3/97	Ⓜ	9	15					
8/2/97	Ⓜ	3⁹	28	5	Everlong	42ᴬ	↓	
8/23/97	®	4	28					
1/17/98	Ⓜ	6	26	6	My Hero	59ᴬ	↓	
1/31/98	®	8	26					
6/6/98	Ⓜ	12	15	7	Walking After You	—	↓	
4/18/98	®	34	5	8	Baker Street	—	VA: Essential Interpretations ....EMI-Capitol 93335	
					#2 Pop hit for Gerry Rafferty in 1978			
10/2/99	Ⓜ	❶¹	26	9	Learn To Fly	19	There Is Nothing Left To Lose.................Roswell 67892	
10/2/99	®	2⁴	30					

Debut	Cht	Peak	Wks	Track Title	Hot Pos	Album Title	Album Label & Number
				FOO FIGHTERS — cont'd			
2/12/00	®	9	13	10 Stacked Actors	—	↓	
2/12/00	ℳ	25	7				
4/1/00	ℳ	8	18	11 Breakout	—	↓	
5/13/00	®	11	12				
9/9/00	ℳ	17	10	12 Next Year	—	↓	
12/22/01+	ℳ	14	13	13 The One	121	St: Orange County	Columbia 85933
12/29/01+	®	20	11				
9/14/02	ℳ	❶¹⁰	35	14 **All My Life**	43	One By One	Roswell 68008
9/21/02	®	3¹	32	Grammy: Hard Rock Performance			
1/25/03	ℳ	5	28	15 Times Like These	65	↓	
2/1/03	®	5	26				
7/19/03	ℳ	15	11	16 Low	—	↓	
7/26/03	®	23	10				
11/29/03+	ℳ	15	26	17 Darling Nikki	—	(single only)	Roswell 56370
				first recorded by **Prince** in 1984; only available as an Australian import single			
5/7/05	ℳ	❶⁷	29	18 **Best Of You**	18	In Your Honor	Roswell 68038
5/7/05	®	❶⁴	33				
9/10/05	ℳ	❶⁶	26	19 **DOA**	68	↓	
9/10/05	®	5	24				
2/11/06	ℳ	2²	20	20 No Way Back	—	↓	
2/18/06	®	6	20				
8/18/07	ℳ	❶¹⁸	33↑	21 **The Pretender**	37	Echoes, Silence, Patience & Grace	Roswell 11516
8/18/07	®	❶⁶	32				
11/10/07+	ℳ	❶⁵↑	21↑	22 **Long Road To Ruin**	—	↓	
12/15/07+	®	2⁴↑	16↑				
				FORBERT, Steve			
				Born on 12/15/1954 in Meridian, Mississippi. Singer/songwriter/guitarist. Also see **Classic Rock Tracks** section.			
7/31/82	®	54	1	Ya Ya (Next To Me)	—	Steve Forbert	Nemperor 37434
				FORD, Lita			
				Born Carmelita Ford on 9/19/1958 in London, England; raised in Los Angeles, California. Rock singer/guitarist. Member of The Runaways from 1975-79.			
8/4/84	®	51	5	1 Gotta Let Go	—	Dancin' On The Edge	Mercury 818864
2/27/88	®	40	5	2 Kiss Me Deadly	12	Lita	RCA 6397
7/30/88	®	22	8	3 Back To The Cave	—	↓	
4/29/89	®	25	9	4 Close My Eyes Forever	8	↓	
				LITA FORD (with Ozzy Osbourne)			
7/22/89	®	37	5	5 Falling In And Out Of Love	—	↓	
5/26/90	®	14	9	6 Hungry	98	Stiletto	RCA 2090
11/2/91	®	21	10	7 Shot Of Poison	45	Dangerous Curves	RCA 61025
				FOREIGNER ® 1980s: #28 / All-Time: #56			
				British-American rock band formed in New York. Lineup by 1981: **Lou Gramm** (vocals), **Mick Jones** (guitar), Rick Wills (bass) and Dennis Elliott (drums). Gramm was also a member of **Shadow King**. Wills was also a member of **Roxy Music** and **Bad Company**. Jones not to be confused with Mick Jones of The Clash and Big Audio Dynamite. Also see **Classic Rock Tracks** section.			
				TOP HITS: 1)Urgent 2)Say You Will 3)I Want To Know What Love Is			
7/18/81	®	❶⁴	30	1 **Urgent**	4	4	Atlantic 3831
				Jr. Walker (sax solo)			
7/25/81	®	3²	34	2 Juke Box Hero	26	4	Atlantic 16999
8/1/81	®	14	16	3 Night Life	—	↓	
11/21/81	®	❶¹	11	4 **Waiting For A Girl Like You**	2¹⁰	↓	
12/8/84+	®	❶¹	14	5 **I Want To Know What Love Is**	❶²	Agent Provocateur	Atlantic 81999
				RS500 #476 New Jersey Mass Choir and Jennifer Holliday (backing vocals)			
1/5/85	®	47	2	6 Tooth And Nail	—	↓	
1/19/85	®	4	19	7 That Was Yesterday	12	↓	
2/2/85	®	44	1	8 Reaction To Action	54	↓	
12/5/87	®	❶⁴	11	9 **Say You Will**	6	Inside Information	Atlantic 81808
12/19/87+	®	7	14	10 Heart Turns To Stone	56	↓	

Debit	Cht	Peak	Wks	ARTIST / Track Title	Hot Pos	Album Title	Album Label & Number

FOREIGNER — cont'd

2/13/88	ℝ	18	12	11 Can't Wait	—	↓	
3/26/88	ℝ	18	9	12 I Don't Want To Live Without You	5	↓	
6/22/91	ℝ	4	9	13 Lowdown And Dirty	—	Unusual Heat	Atlantic 82299
8/24/91	ℝ	42	4	14 I'll Fight For You	—	↓	
9/26/92	ℝ	5	7	15 Soul Doctor Robin Zander (backing vocal)	—	The Very Best...And Beyond	Atlantic 89999
2/25/95	ℝ	28	6	16 Under The Gun	—	Mr. Moonlight	Generama 53961

FOREST FOR THE TREES
Born Carl Stephenson in Los Angeles, California. Eclectic singer/songwriter/multi-instrumentalist.

| 8/30/97 | Ⓜ | 18 | 11 | Dream | 72 | Forest For The Trees | DreamWorks 50002 |

FOR SQUIRRELS
Rock band from Gainesville, Florida: John Francis Vigliatura (vocals), Travis Michael Tooke (guitar), William Richard White (bass) and Thomas Jacob Griego (drums). Vigliatura (age 20) and White (age 22) were killed in a car crash on 9/8/1995. Tooke and Griego went on to form Subrosa.

| 12/9/95+ | Ⓜ | 15 | 14 | Mighty K.C. K.C.: Kurt Cobain (of **Nirvana**) | 70A | Example | 550 Music 67150 |

40 BELOW SUMMER
Hard-rock band formed in New Jersey: Max Illidge (vocals), Joe D'Amico (guitar), Jordan Plingos (guitar), Hector Graziani (bass) and Carlos Aguilar (drums).

| 12/27/03+ | ℝ | 39 | 3 | Self Medicate | — | The Mourning After | Razor & Tie 82898 |

FOUNTAINS OF WAYNE
Pop-rock duo from New York: Chris Collingwood (vocals, guitar) and Adam Schlesinger (keyboards, drums).

11/30/96+	Ⓜ	14	13	1 Radiation Vibe	71A	Fountains Of Wayne	Atlantic 92725
5/8/99	Ⓜ	34	4	2 Denise	—	Utopia Parkway	Scratchie 83177
9/13/03	Ⓜ	31	7	3 Stacy's Mom	21	Welcome Interstate Managers	S-Curve 90875

FOUR HORSEMEN, The
Hard-rock band from Los Angeles, California: Frank Starr (vocals), Dave Lizmi (guitar), Stephen Harris (guitar), Ben Pape (bass) and Ken Montgomery (drums).

8/3/91	ℝ	16	12	1 Nobody Said It Was Easy	—	Nobody Said It Was Easy	Def Amer. 26561
11/16/91+	ℝ	38	9	2 Rockin' Is Ma' Business	—	↓	
2/29/92	ℝ	27	10	3 Tired Wings	—	↓	

4 NON BLONDES
Pop-rock band from San Francisco, California: Linda Perry (vocals), Roger Rocha (guitar), Christa Hillhouse (bass) and Dawn Richardson (drums).

4/10/93	ℝ	16	14	1 What's Up	14	Bigger, Better, Faster, More!	Interscope 92112
3/13/93	Ⓜ	29	1				
10/9/93	ℝ	39	4	2 Spaceman	117	↓	

4 OF US, The
Rock band from Newry, Ireland: brothers Brendan Murphy (vocals), Paul Murphy (keyboards) and Declan Murphy (drums), with John McCandless (bass).

| 5/5/90 | Ⓜ | 22 | 4 | Drag My Bad Name Down | 77 | Songs For The Tempted | Columbia 46025 |

FOXBORO HOT TUBS — see GREEN DAY

FRAMPTON, Peter
Born on 4/22/1950 in Beckenham, Kent, England. Rock singer/songwriter/guitarist. Former member of **Humble Pie**. Played "Billy Shears" in the 1978 movie *Sgt. Pepper's Lonely Hearts Club Band*. Also see **Classic Rock Tracks** section.

6/13/81	ℝ	12	11	1 Breaking All The Rules	—	Breaking All The Rules	A&M 3722
1/25/86	ℝ	4	12	2 Lying	74	Premonition	Atlantic 81290
9/30/89	ℝ	27	6	3 Holding On To You	—	When All The Pieces Fit	Atlantic 82030
1/29/94	ℝ	9	16	4 Day In The Sun	—	Peter Frampton	Relativity 1192

FRANKE & THE KNOCKOUTS
Soft-rock band from New Brunswick, New Jersey: Franke Previte (vocals), Billy Elworthy (guitar), Blake Levinsohn (keyboards), Leigh Foxx (bass) and Claude LeHenaff (drums).

4/4/81	ℝ	27	11	1 Sweetheart	10	Franke & The Knockouts	Millennium 7755
4/11/81	ℝ	45	1	2 Come Back	—	↓	
4/10/82	ℝ	38	7	3 Never Had It Better	—	Below The Belt	Millennium 7763

FRANKIE GOES TO HOLLYWOOD

Dance-rock band from Liverpool, England: William "Holly" Johnson and Paul Rutherford (vocals), Brian Nash (guitar), Mark O'Toole (bass) and Peter Gill (drums). Group's name inspired by publicity recounting Frank Sinatra's move into the movie industry.

10/27/84	®	27	9	Two Tribes	43	Welcome To The Pleasuredome ....Island 90232

FRANKLIN, Aretha

Born on 3/25/1942 in Memphis, Tennessee; raised in Detroit, Michigan. Legendary R&B singer/songwriter/pianist. Known as "The Queen of Soul."
AWARDS: R&R Hall of Fame: 1987 ★ Grammy: Lifetime Achievement Award 1994

10/4/86	®	36	4	Jumpin' Jack Flash	21	Aretha ....Arista 8442

Keith Richards (guitar, producer); #3 Pop hit for **The Rolling Stones** in 1968

FRANZ FERDINAND

Punk-rock band from Glasgow, Scotland: Alex Kapranos (vocals, guitar), Nick McCarthy (guitar), Bob Hardy (bass) and Paul Thomson (drums). Group named after the Austrian archduke whose murder helped spark World War I.

5/22/04	ⓜ	3^3	26	1 Take Me Out	66	Franz Ferdinand ....Domino 27
10/30/04	ⓜ	17	16	2 This Fire	—	↓
9/3/05	ⓜ	9	20	3 Do You Want To	76	You Could Have It So Much Better ....Domino 94800
2/25/06	ⓜ	39	1	4 The Fallen	—	↓

FRASER, Andy

Born on 8/7/1952 in London, England. Rock singer/bassist. Formerly with John Mayall's Bluesbreakers and Free.

6/23/84	®	43	7	Fine, Fine Line	101	Fine Fine Line ....Island 90153

FRATELLIS, The

Alternative-rock trio from Glasgow, Scotland: John Lawler (vocals, guitar), Barry Wallace (bass) and Gordon McRory (drums).

4/14/07	ⓜ	33	8	Flathead	73	Costello Music ....Cherrytree 008561

FRAY, The

Alternative pop-rock band from Denver, Colorado: Isaac Slade (vocals, piano), Joe King (guitar), Dave Welsh (bass) and Ben Wysocki (drums).

10/8/05	ⓜ	37	3	1 Over My Head (Cable Car)	8	How To Save A Life ....Epic 93931
7/1/06	ⓜ	31	10	2 How To Save A Life	3^1	↓

FRAZIER CHORUS

Pop trio from Brighton, Sussex, England: Tim Freeman (vocals), Kate Holmes (woodwinds) and Chris Taplin (bass).

3/30/91	ⓜ	17	6	Cloud 8	—	Ray ....Charisma 91641

FREDDY JONES BAND, The

Rock band formed in Chicago, Illinois: Marty Lloyd (vocals, guitar), Wayne Healy (vocals, guitar), brothers Rob Bonaccorsi (guitar) and Jim Bonaccorsi (bass), and Simon Horrocks (drums).

9/3/94	®	37	1	In A Daydream	—	The Freddy Jones Band ....Capricorn 42029

FREHLEY, Ace

Born Paul Frehley on 4/27/1951 in the Bronx, New York. Rock guitarist. Member of **Kiss**. Also see **Classic Rock Tracks** section.

5/30/87	®	27	7	Into The Night	—	Frehley's Comet ....Megaforce 81749

FRENTE!

Pop-rock band from Melbourne, Australia: Angie Hart (vocals), Simon Austin (guitar), Tim O'Connor (bass) and Mark Picton (drums). Band name is Spanish for "Front."

4/9/94	ⓜ	10	10	1 Bizarre Love Triangle	49	Marvin The Album ....Mammoth 92390
7/2/94	ⓜ	9	9	2 Labour Of Love	106	↓

FREY, Glenn

Born on 11/6/1948 in Detroit, Michigan. Singer/songwriter/guitarist. Founding member of the **Eagles**. Played "Cody McMahon" on the 1993 TV series *South of Sunset*.

6/19/82	®	5	15	1 Partytown	—	No Fun Aloud ....Asylum 60129
7/17/82	®	57	2	2 I Found Somebody	31	↓
10/9/82	®	25	2	3 Don't Give Up	—	↓
7/28/84+	®	13	19	4 Smuggler's Blues	12	The Allnighter ....MCA 5501
1/5/85	®	4	12	5 The Heat Is On	2^1	St: Beverly Hills Cop ....MCA 5547
9/21/85	®	❶^3	11	6 You Belong To The City	2^2	St: Miami Vice ....MCA 6150
8/20/88	®	15	8	7 True Love	13	Soul Searchin' ....MCA 6239
4/27/91	®	9	9	8 Part Of You, Part Of Me	55	St: Thelma & Louise ....MCA 10239

Billboard				ARTIST			
Debut	**Cht**	**Peak**	**Wks**	**Track Title**	ℝ=Mainstream Rock ⓂM=Modern Rock	**Hot Pos**	**Album Title**	**Album Label & Number**

FRIDA
Born Anni-Frid Lyngstad on 11/15/1945 in Narvik, Norway. Female singer. Member of Abba.

| 10/16/82+ | ℝ | 17 | 17 | I Know There's Something Going On .... | 13 | Something's Going On.............................Atlantic 80018 |
| | | | | Phil Collins (drums, producer) | | |

FROM ZERO
Hard-rock band from Chicago, Illinois: Paul "Jett" Weiner (vocals), Joe Pettinato (guitar), Peter Capizzi (guitar), Rob Ruccia (bass) and John "Kid" Dinu (drums).

| 6/9/01 | ℝ | 37 | 1 | Check Ya .... | — | One Nation Under ....Arista 14670 |

FRONT, The
Hard-rock band from Kansas City, Missouri: brothers Michael Franano (vocals) and Bobby Franano (keyboards), with Mike Greene (guitar), Randy Jordan (bass) and Shane Miller (drums).

| 3/3/90 | ℝ | 44 | 3 | 1 Fire.. | — | The Front ....Columbia 45260 |
| 5/5/90 | ℝ | 41 | 4 | 2 Le Motion .... | — | ↓ |

FRONT 242
Industrial dance band from Brussels, Belgium: vocalists Jean-Luc De Meyer and Richard Jonckheere with instrumentalists Daniel Bressanutti and Patrick Codenys.

| 12/8/90 | Ⓜ | 18 | 9 | Tragedy For You.. | — | Tyranny For You ....Epic 46998 |

FROZEN GHOST
Pop-rock duo from Canada: Arnold Lanni (vocals, guitar, keyboards) and Wolf Hassel (bass). Both were members of the group Sheriff.

| 3/14/87 | ℝ | 4 | 14 | 1 Should I See... | 69 | Frozen Ghost..Atlantic 81736 |
| 9/3/88 | ℝ | 44 | 5 | 2 Round And Round.. | — | Nice Place To Visit....................................Atlantic 81875 |

FUEL ℝ 2000s: #34 ★ Ⓜ 2000s: #37 / All-Time: #43
Rock band from Harrisburg, Pennsylvania: Brett Scallions (vocals; born on 12/21/1971), Carl Bell (guitar; born on 1/9/1968), Jeff Abercrombie (bass; born on 1/8/1969) and Kevin Miller (drums; born on 9/6/1970). Tommy Stewart (of **Godsmack**) replaced Miller in 2005. Toryn Green replaced Scallions in April 2007. Miller joined **Tantric** in late 2007.

TOP HITS: 1)Hemorrhage (In My Hands) 2)Shimmer 3)Innocent

3/14/98	Ⓜ	2[1]	31	1 Shimmer	42	Sunburn...550 Music 68554
4/11/98	ℝ	11	26			
10/10/98+	ℝ	15	22	2 Bittersweet	—	↓
10/3/98	Ⓜ	17	23			
5/15/99	ℝ	24	9	3 Jesus Or A Gun	—	↓
5/15/99	Ⓜ	26	9			
11/20/99	Ⓜ	31	9	4 Sunburn..	—	↓
8/26/00	Ⓜ	❶[12]	40	5 Hemorrhage (In My Hands)	30	Something Like Human ....550 Music 69436
8/26/00	ℝ	2[3]	56			
2/3/01	Ⓜ	4	20	6 Innocent	113	↓
2/10/01	ℝ	10	16			
6/16/01	Ⓜ	12	18	7 Bad Day	64	↓
6/16/01	ℝ	14	18			
11/17/01	ℝ	21	12	8 Last Time..	—	↓
11/24/01	Ⓜ	25	10			
1/4/03	ℝ	22	11	9 Won't Back Down	—	St: Daredevil ....Wind-Up 13079
2/8/03	Ⓜ	37	3			
8/9/03	ℝ	9	26	10 Falls On Me	52	Natural Selection...Epic 86392
8/9/03	Ⓜ	11	17			
1/3/04	ℝ	16	15	11 Million Miles	—	↓
1/31/04	Ⓜ	33	4			
7/7/07	ℝ	24	14	12 Wasted Time	—	Angels & Devils ....Epic 00952

FULL DEVIL JACKET
Rock band from Jackson, Tennessee: Josh Brown (vocals), Mike Reaves (guitar), Jon Montoya (guitar), Kevin Bebout (bass) and Keith Foster (drums).

| 4/1/00 | ℝ | 23 | 14 | 1 Now You Know .... | — | Full Devil Jacket ....The Enclave 546809 |
| 9/2/00 | ℝ | 19 | 12 | 2 Where Did You Go?..................................... | — | ↓ |

Debut	Cht	Peak	Wks	ARTIST / Track Title	Hot Pos	Album Title	Album Label & Number

R=Mainstream Rock **M**=Modern Rock

FU MANCHU
Rock band from Los Angeles, California: Scott Hill (vocals, guitar), Bob Balch (guitar), Brad Davis (bass) and Brant Bjork (drums).

| 2/9/02 | R | 23 | 9 | Squash That Fly | — | California Crossing | Mammoth 165515 |

FUN LOVIN' CRIMINALS
Eclectic hip-hop trio from Syracuse, New York: Huey Morgan (vocals, guitar), Brian Leiser (bass, keyboards) and Steve Borgovini (drums).

| 9/7/96 | M | 14 | 17 | Scooby Snacks | 73[A] | Come Find Yourself | EMI 35703 |

samples "Moment Of Fear" by Tones on Tail

FURY IN THE SLAUGHTERHOUSE
Pop-rock band from Hannover, Germany: Kai Uwe Wingenfelder (vocals), Thorsten Wingenfelder (guitar), Christof Stein (guitar), Gero Drenk (keyboards), Hannes Schafer (bass) and Rainer Schumann (drums).

| 2/19/94 | M | 13 | 10 | Every Generation Got Its Own Disease | — | Mono | RCA 66352 |
| 4/2/94 | R | 21 | 9 | | | | |

FUTURE LEADERS OF THE WORLD
Rock band from Buffalo, New York: Phil Tayler (vocals), Jake Stutevoss (guitar), Bill Hershey (bass) and Carl Messina (drums).

7/3/04	R	6	29	1 Let Me Out	—	LVL IV	Epic 89192
8/28/04	M	32	19				
2/12/05	R	30	10	2 Everyday	—	↓	

FUZZBOX
Female rock band from Birmingham, England: sisters Jo Dunne (guitar) and Maggie Dunne (bass), with Vickie Perks (vocals) and Tina O'Neill (drums).

| 9/30/89 | M | 16 | 7 | Self! | — | Big Bang! | Geffen 24185 |

G

GABRIEL, Peter
Born on 2/13/1950 in Woking, Surrey, England. Pop-rock singer/songwriter. Lead singer of **Genesis** from 1966-75. Also see **Classic Rock Tracks** section.

R All-Time: #77

TOP HITS: 1)Steam 2)Digging In The Dirt 3)Sledgehammer

10/2/82	R	❶[2]	12	1 Shock The Monkey	29	Peter Gabriel (Security)	Geffen 2011
10/30/82	R	34	1	2 Kiss Of Life	—	↓	
12/25/82	R	46	4	3 I Have The Touch	—	↓	
8/6/83	R	38	4	4 I Go Swimming [L]	—	Peter Gabriel/Plays Live	Geffen 4012
5/3/86	R	❶[2]	15	5 Sledgehammer	❶[1]	So	Geffen 24088
6/14/86	R	3[3]	14	6 Red Rain	—	↓	

also see #15 below

6/21/86	R	❶[1]	20	7 In Your Eyes	26	↓	
10/18/86	R	14	8	8 That Voice Again	—	↓	
11/29/86+	R	3[2]	15	9 Big Time	8	↓	
9/12/92	M	❶[2]	14	10 Digging In The Dirt	52	Us	Geffen 24473
9/12/92	R	❶[1]	15				
11/7/92	M	❶[5]	16	11 Steam	32	↓	
11/7/92	R	2[4]	20				
3/6/93	R	18	9	12 Kiss That Frog	—	↓	
2/6/93	M	18	8				
7/17/93	R	34	4	13 Secret World	—	↓	
1/29/94	M	22	8	14 Lovetown	—	St: Philadelphia	Epic Soundtrax 57624
10/1/94	R	33	3	15 Red Rain [L-R]	—	Secret World Live	Geffen 24722

live version of #6 above; recorded on 11/16/1993 in Modena, Italy

GALES, Eric, Band
Blues-rock trio from Memphis, Tennessee: brothers Eric Gales (guitar) and Eugene Gales (vocals, bass), with Hubert Crawford (drums).

| 7/13/91 | R | 9 | 11 | 1 Sign Of The Storm | — | The Eric Gales Band | Elektra 61083 |
| 8/21/93 | R | 31 | 5 | 2 Paralyzed | — | Picture Of A Thousand Faces | Elektra 61466 |

GAMMA
Rock band formed in San Francisco, California: Davey Pattison (vocals), Ronnie Montrose (guitar), Mitchell Froom (keyboards), Glenn Letsch (bass) and Denny Carmassi (drums). Carmassi later joined **Heart**. Froom, also a producer, married **Suzanne Vega** on 3/17/1995.

| 3/6/82 | R | 10 | 14 | Right The First Time | 77 | Gamma 3 | Elektra 60034 |

GANG OF FOUR
Punk-rock band from Leeds, England: Jon King (vocals), Andy Gill (guitar), Dave Allen (bass) and Hugo Burnham (drums).

5/18/91	Ⓜ	14	7	Don't Fix What Ain't Broke	—	Mall	Polydor 849124

GARBAGE
Ⓜ 1990s: #20 / All-Time: #42

Alternative-rock band formed in Madison, Wisconsin: Shirley Manson (vocals, guitar; born on 8/26/1966 in Edinburgh, Scotland), Doug Erikson (guitar, bass, keyboards; born on 1/15/1953), Steve Marker (guitar, samples; born on 3/16/1959) and Bryan "Butch" Vigorsin (drums; born on 8/2/1955). Vig was also a prolific record producer.

TOP HITS: 1)#1 Crush 2)Stupid Girl 3)Push It

6/17/95	Ⓜ	26	9	1 Vow	97	Garbage	Almo Sounds 80004
9/23/95	Ⓜ	12	15	2 Queer	57ᴬ	↓	
1/27/96	Ⓜ	16	19	3 Only Happy When It Rains	55	↓	
6/8/96	Ⓜ	2¹	25	4 Stupid Girl	24	↓	
8/24/96	ℝ	39	2				
11/30/96+	Ⓜ	❶⁴	22	5 #1 Crush	29ᴬ	St: Romeo & Juliet	Capitol 37715
4/11/98	Ⓜ	5	21	6 Push It	52	Version 2.0	Almo Sounds 80018
7/18/98	Ⓜ	6	26	7 I Think I'm Paranoid	70ᴬ	↓	
10/31/98+	Ⓜ	11	26	8 Special	52	↓	
5/1/99	Ⓜ	23	15	9 When I Grow Up	—	↓	
3/5/05	Ⓜ	8	11	10 Why Do You Love Me	94	Bleed Like Me	Almo Sounds 004195
5/28/05	Ⓜ	27	9	11 Bleed Like Me	—	↓	

GARY O'
Born Gary O'Connor in Toronto, Ontario, Canada. Rock singer/songwriter.

3/2/85	ℝ	23	8	Shades Of '45	—	Strange Behavior	RCA 5304

GEGGY TAH
Rock trio from Los Angeles, California: singers/multi-instrumentalists Tommy Jordan and Greg Kurstin, with drummer Daren Hahn.

8/31/96	Ⓜ	16	14	Whoever You Are	67ᴬ	Sacred Cow	Luaka Bop 46113

GEILS, J., Band
Rock band from Boston, Massachusetts: Jerome Geils (guitar), **Peter Wolf** (vocals), Magic Dick Salwitz (harmonica), Seth Justman (keyboards, vocals), Danny Klein (bass) and Stephen Jo Bladd (drums). Wolf left for a solo career in the fall of 1983. Also see **Classic Rock Tracks** section.

11/14/81+	ℝ	❶³	25	1 Centerfold	❶⁶	Freeze-Frame	EMI America 17062
11/21/81+	ℝ	8	26	2 Freeze-Frame	4	↓	
2/20/82	ℝ	30	4	3 Flamethrower	—	↓	
11/20/82	ℝ	5	15	4 I Do	[L] 24	Showtime!	EMI America 17087
				#37 Pop hit for The Marvelows in 1965			
11/3/84	ℝ	26	9	5 Concealed Weapons	63	You're Gettin' Even While I'm Gettin' Odd	EMI America 17137

GELDOF, Bob
Born on 10/5/1951 in Dublin, Ireland. Rock singer. Leader of The Boomtown Rats. Played "Pink" in the 1982 **Pink Floyd** movie *The Wall*. Organized British superstar benefit group **Band Aid** and earned a Nobel Peace Prize nomination.

11/15/86	ℝ	23	10	1 This Is The World Calling	82	Deep In The Heart Of Nowhere	Atlantic 81687
9/15/90	Ⓜ	24	6	2 Love Or Something	—	The Vegetarians Of Love	Atlantic 82041

GENE LOVES JEZEBEL
Techno-rock band formed in England: Jay Aston (vocals), James Stevenson (guitar), Peter Rizzo (bass) and Chris Bell (drums).

6/30/90	Ⓜ	❶²	12	1 Jealous	68	Kiss Of Life	Geffen 24260
7/14/90	ℝ	12	15				
11/28/92	Ⓜ	18	9	2 Josephina	—	Heavenly Bodies	Savage 50210

GENERAL PUBLIC
Pop band from Birmingham, England: Dave Wakeling (vocals, guitar), **Ranking Roger** (vocals, keyboards), Micky Billingham (keyboards), Kevin White (guitar), Horace Panter (bass) and Stoker (drums). Wakeling and Roger had been in English Beat. Billingham was with **Dexys Midnight Runners**.

1/19/85	ℝ	39	4	1 Tenderness	27	...All The Rage	I.R.S. 70046
4/2/94	Ⓜ	6	10	2 I'll Take You There	22	St: Threesome	Epic Soundtrax 57881
				#1 Pop hit for The Staple Singers in 1972			
4/29/95	Ⓜ	40	1	3 Rainy Days	93	Rub It Better	Epic 64270

GENESIS

® 1980s: #9 / All-Time: #25

Pop-rock trio formed in England: **Phil Collins** (vocals, drums), **Mike Rutherford** (guitar, bass) and Tony Banks (keyboards). **Peter Gabriel** was lead singer from 1967-75. Steve Hackett (of **GTR**) was lead guitarist from 1970-77. Regular touring members included Americans Daryl Stuermer (guitar) and Chester Anderson (drums). Collins announced his departure from the group in April 1996; Ray Wilson (of **Stiltskin**) joined as lead singer in June 1997. Collins returned to replace Wilson in November 2006. Also see **Classic Rock Tracks** section.

TOP HITS: 1)Throwing It All Away 2)Invisible Touch 3)I Can't Dance 4)No Reply At All 5)That's All!

Debut	Cht	Peak	Wks	Track Title	Hot Pos	Album Title	Album Label & Number
9/26/81	®	2²	17	1 No Reply At All	29	Abacab ....Atlantic 19313	
				features the Earth, Wind & Fire horn section			
10/17/81	®	4	26	2 Abacab	26	↓	
3/27/82	®	14	8	3 Man On The Corner	40	↓	
6/12/82	®	2¹	16	4 Paperlate	32	Three Sides Live ....Atlantic 2000	
7/3/82	®	40	7	5 You Might Recall	—	↓	
9/17/83	®	5	12	6 Mama	73	Genesis ....Atlantic 80116	
10/8/83	®	16	25	7 It's Gonna Get Better............	—	↓	
10/29/83	®	10	19	8 Just A Job To Do	—	↓	
11/5/83+	®	2¹	17	9 That's All!	6	↓	
11/5/83+	®	21	16	10 Illegal Alien	44	↓	
11/5/83+	®	24	10	11 Home By The Sea	—	↓	
2/25/84	®	41	5	12 Taking It All Too Hard	50	↓	
5/31/86	®	❶³	11	13 Invisible Touch	❶¹	Invisible Touch........................Atlantic 81641	
6/21/86	®	❶³	18	14 Throwing It All Away	4	↓	
6/21/86	®	29	10	15 The Last Domino	—	↓	
6/28/86	®	11	30	16 Land Of Confusion	4	↓	
6/28/86	®	40	4	17 Anything She Does	—	↓	
7/5/86	®	34	12	18 In Too Deep............................	3¹	↓	
7/26/86	®	45	5	19 Tonight, Tonight, Tonight	3¹	↓	
11/2/91	®	3⁵	14	20 No Son Of Mine......................	12	We Can't Dance.................Atlantic 82344	
12/7/91+	®	2³	29	21 I Can't Dance	7	↓	
12/21/91+	®	24	19	22 Jesus He Knows Me	23	↓	
6/13/92	®	25	8	23 Driving The Last Spike	—	↓	
8/23/97	®	25	7	24 Congo	—	Calling All Stations.................Atlantic 83037	

GEORGE, Robin

Born in Wolverhampton, West Midlands, England. Rock singer/guitarist.

Debut	Cht	Peak	Wks	Track Title	Hot Pos	Album Title	Album Label & Number
2/16/85	®	40	9	Heartline	92	Dangerous Music ....Bronze 90244	

GEORGIA SATELLITES

Rock band from Atlanta, Georgia: **Dan Baird** (vocals, guitar), Rick Richards (guitar), Rich Price (bass) and Mauro Magellan (drums). Richards later joined **Izzy Stradlin & The Ju Ju Hounds**.

Debut	Cht	Peak	Wks	Track Title	Hot Pos	Album Title	Album Label & Number
10/18/86	®	2²	18	1 Keep Your Hands To Yourself	2¹	Georgia Satellites ....Elektra 60496	
1/24/87	®	11	12	2 Battleship Chains	86	↓	
4/18/87	®	34	4	3 Railroad Steel	—	↓	
6/11/88	®	6	9	4 Open All Night	—	Open All Night.......................Elektra 60793	
9/3/88	®	33	5	5 Don't Pass Me By	—	↓	
10/22/88	®	13	7	6 Hippy Hippy Shake.................	45	St: Cocktail.........................Elektra 60806	
				#24 Pop hit for The Swinging Blue Jeans in 1964			
10/21/89	®	47	2	7 Another Chance.......................	—	In The Land Of Salvation And Sin ......Elektra 60887	
12/16/89+	®	17	14	8 All Over But The Cryin'	—	↓	

GHOST OF AN AMERICAN AIRMAN

Rock band from Belfast, Ireland: Andrew "Dodge" McKay (vocals), Ben Trowell (guitar), Allan Galbraith (bass) and Matt Matthews (drums). Band named for legend of an American pilot shot down over Ireland.

Debut	Cht	Peak	Wks	Track Title	Hot Pos	Album Title	Album Label & Number
11/6/93	®	38	1	King Of Nothing......................	—	Skin ....Hollywood 61408	

GIANT

Rock band formed in Nashville, Tennessee: brothers Dan Huff (vocals, guitar) and David Huff (drums), with Alan Pasqua (keyboards) and Mike Brignardello (bass).

Debut	Cht	Peak	Wks	Track Title	Hot Pos	Album Title	Album Label & Number
9/9/89	®	13	14	1 I'm A Believer.........................	56	Last Of The Runaways ....A&M 5272	
12/16/89+	®	11	11	2 Innocent Days	—	↓	
3/31/90	®	7	16	3 I'll See You In My Dreams	20	↓	
4/4/92	®	16	10	4 Chained	—	Time To Burn ....Epic 48509	

GILLAN, Ian

Born on 8/19/1945 in Hounslow, Middlesex, England. Rock singer. Lead singer of **Deep Purple**. Portrayed Jesus in the rock opera *Jesus Christ Superstar*. Joined **Black Sabbath** for *Born Again* album.

10/8/88	®	15	7	Telephone Box	—	*Accidentally On Purpose*	Virgin 90953

IAN GILLAN & ROGER GLOVER

GILLIS, Brad

Born on 6/15/1957 in San Francisco, California. Rock guitarist. Member of **Night Ranger**.

5/1/93	®	20	8	Honest To God	—	*Gilrock Ranch*	Guitar 99203

Gregg Allman (vocal)

GILMOUR, David

Born on 3/6/1944 in Cambridge, England. Rock singer/songwriter/guitarist. Member of **Pink Floyd**.

3/17/84	®	10	6	1 All Lovers Are Deranged	—	*About Face*	Columbia 39296
3/31/84	®	13	12	2 Murder	—	↓	
4/14/84	®	35	4	3 Blue Light	62	↓	
2/18/06	®	29	10	4 On An Island	—	*On An Island*	Columbia 80280

GIN BLOSSOMS

Pop-rock band from Tempe, Arizona: Robin Wilson (vocals), Jesse Valenzuela (guitar), Scott Johnson (guitar), Bill Leen (bass) and Phillip Rhodes (drums). Early guitarist Doug Hopkins died of a self-inflicted gunshot wound on 12/5/1993 (age 32).

4/3/93	®	36	2	1 Mrs. Rita	—	*New Miserable Experience*	A&M 5403
7/10/93	®	4	20	2 Hey Jealousy	25	↓	
10/30/93+	Ⓜ	❶[1]	23	3 Found Out About You	25	↓	
11/6/93+	®	5	26				
4/30/94	Ⓜ	13	14	4 Until I Fall Away	21[A]	↓	
6/18/94	®	40	1				
9/17/94	®	20	10	5 Allison Road	24[A]	↓	
10/8/94	Ⓜ	39	1				
8/12/95	®	4	16	6 Til I Hear It From You	11	*St: Empire Records*	A&M 540384
8/5/95	Ⓜ	5	14				
2/10/96	®	6	13	7 Follow You Down	9	*Congratulations I'm Sorry*	A&M 540469
2/10/96	Ⓜ	8	12				
5/18/96	Ⓜ	21	7	8 Day Job	—	↓	
6/1/96	®	29	9				

GIRLS AGAINST BOYS

Rock band from Washington DC: Eli Janney (vocals), Scott McCloud (guitar), Johnny Temple (bass) and Alexis Fleisig (drums).

6/20/98	®	28	10	Park Avenue	—	*Freak*On*Ica*	DGC 25156

GIUFFRIA

Rock band from California: Gregg Giuffria (keyboards), David Glen Eisley (vocals), Craig Goldy (guitar), Chuck Wright (bass) and Alan Krigger (drums). Lanny Cordola and David Sikes replaced Goldy and Wright in late 1985. Giuffria, Wright and Cordola joined **House Of Lords** in 1988.

11/17/84+	®	3[2]	16	1 Call To The Heart	15	*Giuffria*	MCA 5524
2/16/85	®	41	4	2 Do Me Right	—	↓	
4/20/85	®	43	3	3 Lonely In Love	57	↓	
5/10/86	®	28	7	4 I Must Be Dreaming	52	*Silk + Steel*	MCA 5742

GLAMOUR CAMP

Pop-rock band formed in New York: Christopher Otcasek (vocals), Eddie Martinez (guitar), Sid McGinnis (guitar), Mark Egan (bass), Will Lee (bass), Alexander Lasarenko (keyboards) and Andy Newmark (drums). Otcasek is the son of **Ric Ocasek** of **The Cars**. McGinnis and Lee were members of David Letterman's *Late Show* band.

3/18/89	®	42	6	She Did It	—	*Glamour Camp*	EMI 48685

GLASS TIGER

Pop-rock band from Newmarket, Ontario, Canada: Alan Frew (vocals), Al Connelly (guitar), Sam Reid (keyboards), Wayne Parker (bass) and Michael Hanson (drums).

8/2/86	®	17	9	1 Don't Forget Me (When I'm Gone)	2[1]	*The Thin Red Line*	Manhattan 53032

Bryan Adams (response vocal)

3/21/87	®	21	6	2 I Will Be There	34	↓	
4/16/88	®	12	9	3 I'm Still Searching	31	*Diamond Sun*	EMI-Man. 48684

GLOVER, Roger

Born on 11/30/1945 in Brecon, Powys, Wales. Rock singer/bassist. Member of **Deep Purple** and **Rainbow**.

6/2/84	®	20	8	1 The Mask	102	*Mask*	21 Records 9009
10/8/88	®	15	7	2 Telephone Box	—	*Accidentally On Purpose*	Virgin 90953

IAN GILLAN & ROGER GLOVER

Debut	Cht	Peak	Wks	ARTIST / Track Title	Hot Pos	Album Title	Album Label & Number
				GNARLS BARKLEY Collaboration between R&B producer Brian "Danger Mouse" Burton and singer Thomas "Cee-Lo" Callaway (of Goodie Mob).			
5/13/06	Ⓜ	7	20	1 Crazy	2⁷	St. Elsewhere	Downtown 70003
9/30/06	Ⓜ	26	13	2 Gone Daddy Gone	—	↓	
3/8/08	Ⓜ	35	4↑	3 Run (I'm A Natural Disaster)	—	The Odd Couple	Downtown 460236
				GOANNA Rock band from Australia: Shane Howard (vocals), Warrick Harwood (guitar), Graham Davidge (guitar), Peter Coughlan (bass) and Robert Ross (drums).			
6/11/83	Ⓡ	31	9	Solid Rock	71	Spirit Of Place	Atco 90081
				GO-BETWEENS, The Rock band from Australia: Robert Forster (vocals), Grant McLennan (guitar), Amanda Brown (violin), John Willsteed (bass) and Lindy Morrison (drums). McLennan died on 5/6/2006 (age 48).			
12/24/88+	Ⓜ	16	7	Was There Anything I Could Do?	—	16 Lovers Lane	Beggars Banquet 91230
				GODFATHERS, The Rock band formed in London, England: brothers Peter Coyne (vocals) and Chris Coyne (bass), with Mike Gibson (guitar), Kris Dollimore (guitar) and George Mazur (drums).			
2/6/88	Ⓡ	38	10	1 Birth, School, Work, Death	—	Birth, School, Work, Death	Epic 40946
5/13/89	Ⓜ	8	8	2 She Gives Me Love	—	More Songs About Love & Hate	Epic 45023
3/9/91	Ⓜ	6	9	3 Unreal World	—	Unreal World	Epic 46026
				GODLEY & CREME Pop-rock duo from Manchester, England: Kevin Godley (born on 10/7/1945) and Lol Creme (born on 9/19/1947). Both were members of 10cc.			
7/27/85	Ⓡ	6	10	Cry	16	The History Mix Volume 1	Polydor 825981
				GOD LIVES UNDERWATER Techno-rock duo from Los Angeles, California: David Reilly and Jeff Turzo.			
3/14/98	Ⓜ	17	15	From Your Mouth	—	Life In The So-Called Space Age	A&M 540871
				GODS CHILD Rock band from New York: Chris Seefried (vocals, guitar), Gary DeRosa (keyboards), Craig Ruda (bass) and Alex Alexander (drums).			
8/27/94	Ⓡ	18	10	Everybodys 1	—	Everybody	Qwest 45632
9/10/94	Ⓜ	25	3				
				GODSMACK Ⓡ 2000s: #2 / All-Time: #22 ★ Ⓜ 2000s: #17 / All-Time: #28 Hard-rock band formed in Boston, Massachusetts: Salvatore "Sully" Erna (vocals; born on 2/7/1968), Tony Rombola (guitar; born on 11/24/1964), Robbie Merrill (bass; born on 6/13/1963) and Tommy Stewart (drums; born on 5/26/1966). Shannon Larkin (born on 4/24/1967) replaced Stewart in late 2002. Stewart joined **Fuel** in 2005. Rombola, Merrill and Larkin later formed **Another Animal**. *TOP HITS: 1)Speak 2)I Stand Alone 3)Straight Out Of Line*			
10/24/98+	Ⓡ	7	44	1 Whatever	116	Godsmack	Republic 53190
4/10/99	Ⓜ	19	26				
5/8/99	Ⓡ	5	48	2 Keep Away	—	↓	
10/23/99	Ⓜ	31	12				
11/20/99+	Ⓡ	5	37	3 Voodoo	102	↓	
2/19/00	Ⓜ	6	26				
6/17/00	Ⓡ	8	26	4 Bad Religion	—	↓	
8/5/00	Ⓜ	32	6				
10/14/00+	Ⓡ	❶¹	53	5 Awake	101	Awake	Republic 159688
10/21/00+	Ⓜ	12	28				
3/24/01	Ⓡ	3²	32	6 Greed	123	↓	
4/14/01	Ⓜ	28	23				
9/15/01	Ⓡ	12	13	7 Bad Magick	—	↓	
9/29/01	Ⓜ	28	8				
2/16/02	Ⓡ	❶⁴	43	8 I Stand Alone	102	St: The Scorpion King	Universal 017115
2/16/02	Ⓜ	20	26				
2/15/03	Ⓡ	❶²	29	9 Straight Out Of Line	73	Faceless	Republic 067854
2/15/03	Ⓜ	9	25				

Billboard				ARTIST		Hot Pos	Album Title	Album Label & Number
Debut	Cht	Peak	Wks	Track Title	®=Mainstream Rock ⓜ=Modern Rock			

Billboard	Cht	Peak	Wks	ARTIST / Track Title	Hot Pos	Album Title	Album Label & Number
Debut				R=Mainstream Rock M=Modern Rock			

GOOD CHARLOTTE — cont'd

Debut	Cht	Peak	Wks	Track Title	Hot Pos	Album Title	Album Label & Number
9/11/04	Ⓜ	28	9	5 Predictable	106	The Chronicles Of Life And Death	Daylight 92425
4/28/07	Ⓜ	38	3	6 The River	39	Good Morning Revival	Daylight 76940

GOO GOO DOLLS   Ⓡ 1990s: #33 ★ Ⓜ 1990s: #15 / All-Time: #31

Rock trio from Buffalo, New York: Johnny Rzeznik (vocals, guitar; born on 12/5/1965), Robby Takac (bass; born on 9/30/1964) and George Tutuska (drums). Mike Malinin (born on 10/10/1967) replaced Tutuska in 1995.

TOP HITS: 1)Iris 2)Name 3)Slide

Debut	Cht	Peak	Wks	Track Title	Hot Pos	Album Title	Album Label & Number
1/12/91	Ⓜ	24	3	1 There You Are	—	Hold Me Up	Metal Blade 26259
3/6/93	Ⓜ	5	10	2 We Are The Normal	—	Superstar Car Wash	Metal Blade 45206
4/8/95	Ⓡ	21	11	3 Only One	—	A Boy Named Goo	Warner 45750
4/15/95	Ⓜ	36	3				
8/5/95	Ⓡ	38	3	4 Flat Top	— ↓		
9/9/95	Ⓡ	❶⁵	26	5 Name	5 ↓		
8/12/95	Ⓜ	❶⁴	26				
1/27/96	Ⓡ	8	15	6 Naked	47ᴬ ↓		
12/30/95+	Ⓜ	9	17				
6/1/96	Ⓡ	7	17	7 Long Way Down	— ↓		
6/29/96	Ⓜ	25	9				
7/26/97	Ⓡ	9	14	8 Lazy Eye	—	St: Batman & Robin	Warner Sunset 46620
7/26/97	Ⓜ	20	10				
4/11/98	Ⓜ	❶⁵	26	9 Iris	❶¹⁸ᴬ	St: City Of Angels	Warner Sunset 46867
5/2/98	Ⓡ	8	26				
9/19/98	Ⓜ	❶²	26	10 Slide	8	Dizzy Up The Girl	Warner 47058
9/26/98	Ⓡ	4	26				
3/6/99	Ⓜ	9	14	11 Dizzy	108 ↓		
3/6/99	Ⓡ	13	14				
6/26/99	Ⓜ	13	16	12 Black Balloon	16 ↓		
7/17/99	Ⓡ	28	9				
5/13/00	Ⓜ	38	6	13 Broadway	24 ↓		
3/30/02	Ⓜ	21	10	14 Here Is Gone	18	Gutterflower	Warner 48206
4/6/02	Ⓡ	29	9				

GORE, Martin L.

Born Martin Lee Gore on 7/23/1961 in Basildon, Essex, England. Member of **Depeche Mode**.

Debut	Cht	Peak	Wks	Track Title	Hot Pos	Album Title	Album Label & Number
8/19/89	Ⓜ	18	7	Compulsion	—	Counterfeit e.p.	Sire 25980

GORILLAZ

Animated hip-hop band created by Jamie Hewlett and Damon Albarn (of **Blur**): 2-D (vocals, keyboards), Noodle (guitar), Murdoc (bass) and Russel (drums).

Debut	Cht	Peak	Wks	Track Title	Hot Pos	Album Title	Album Label & Number
7/7/01	Ⓜ	3¹	26	1 Clint Eastwood	57	Gorillaz	Parlophone 33748
11/17/01	Ⓜ	23	12	2 19-2000	— ↓		
4/30/05	Ⓜ	❶⁸	42	3 Feel Good Inc	14	Demon Days	Parlophone 73838
				GORILLAZ & DE LA SOUL			
11/12/05+	Ⓜ	8	23	4 Dare	87 ↓		

GORKY PARK

Rock band from Russia: Nikolai Noskov (vocals), Alexei Belov and Jan Ianenkov (guitars), "Big" Sasha Minkov (bass) and "Little" Sasha Lvov (drums). Group named after a famous park in Moscow.

Debut	Cht	Peak	Wks	Track Title	Hot Pos	Album Title	Album Label & Number
9/23/89	Ⓡ	41	4	Bang	—	Gorky Park	Mercury 838628

GOV'T MULE

Southern-rock trio from Macon, Georgia: Warren Haynes (vocals, guitar), Allen Woody (bass) and Matt Abts (drums). Haynes and Woody were both members of **The Allman Brothers Band**. Woody died of a heart attack on 8/26/2000 (age 44).

Debut	Cht	Peak	Wks	Track Title	Hot Pos	Album Title	Album Label & Number
4/15/00	Ⓡ	40	1	1 Bad Little Doggie	—	Life Before Insanity	Capricorn 546489
11/30/02+	Ⓡ	33	11	2 Drivin' Rain	—	The Deep End Volume 2	ATO 21507

Billboard				ARTIST		Hot		
Debut	Cht	Peak	Wks	Track Title	ⓡ=Mainstream Rock ⓜ=Modern Rock	Pos	Album Title	Album Label & Number

GRAMM, Lou
Born Lou Grammatico on 5/2/1950 in Rochester, New York. Lead singer of **Foreigner** and **Shadow King**.

1/31/87	ⓡ	❶⁵	14	1 Midnight Blue		5	Ready Or Not	Atlantic 81728
2/28/87	ⓡ	7	16	2 Ready Or Not		54	↓	
6/13/87	ⓡ	47	2	3 Heartache		—	↓	
10/28/89	ⓡ	4	15	4 Just Between You And Me		6	Long Hard Look	Atlantic 81915
2/10/90	ⓡ	23	9	5 True Blue Love		40	↓	
5/19/90	ⓡ	42	4	6 Angel With A Dirty Face		—	↓	

GRAND PRIX
Rock band from England: Robin McAuley (vocals), Mick O'Donoghue (guitar), Phil Lanzon (keyboards), Ralph Hood (bass) and Andy Bierne (drums). McAuley later formed the **McAuley Schenker Group**.

10/29/83	ⓡ	43	3	Shout		—	Samurai	Chrysalis 41430

GRANT, Eddy
Born Edmond Grant on 3/5/1948 in Plaisance, Guyana; raised in London, England. Rock-reggae singer. Member of The Equals.

4/30/83	ⓡ	12	14	1 Electric Avenue		2⁵	Killer On The Rampage	Portrait 38554
5/26/84	ⓡ	39	9	2 Romancing The Stone		26	Going For Broke	Portrait 39261

GRANT LEE BUFFALO
Rock trio from Los Angeles, California: Grant Lee Phillips (vocals, guitar), Paul Kimble (bass) and Joey Peters (drums).

9/17/94	ⓜ	14	10	1 Mockingbirds		—	Mighty Joe Moon	Slash 45714
6/13/98	ⓜ	11	13	2 Truly, Truly		—	Jubilee	Slash 46879

GRAPES OF WRATH, The
Folk-rock band from Kelowna, British Columbia, Canada: brothers Tom Hooper (bass) and Chris Hooper (drums), with Kevin Kane (vocals, guitar) and Vincent Jones (piano).

10/5/91	ⓜ	27	3	I Am Here		—	These Days	Capitol 96431

GRATEFUL DEAD
Legendary rock band formed in San Francisco, California: Jerry Garcia (vocals, guitar), Bob Weir (vocals, guitar), Brent Mydland (keyboards), Phil Lesh (bass) and Mickey Hart & Bill Kreutzmann (drums). Weir also formed **Bobby & The Midnites**. Mydland died of a drug overdose on 7/26/1990 (age 37); **Bruce Hornsby** then took over keyboards on tour until **Tubes** keyboardist Vince Welnick joined band. Garcia died of a heart attack on 8/9/1995 (age 53). Welnick died of a heart attack on 6/2/2006 (age 55). Incessant touring band with faithful followers known as "Deadheads." Weir, Lesh, Hart and Hornsby formed The Other Ones. Also see **Classic Rock Tracks** section.

AWARD: R&R Hall of Fame: 1994

TOP HITS: 1)Touch Of Grey 2)Hell In A Bucket 3)Foolish Heart

4/18/81	ⓡ	50	2	1 Ripple	[L]	—	Reckoning	Arista 8604
5/2/81	ⓡ	37	4	2 Dire Wolf	[L]	—	↓	
7/4/87	ⓡ	❶³	12	3 Touch Of Grey		9	In The Dark	Arista 8452
7/25/87	ⓡ	3¹	13	4 Hell In A Bucket		—	↓	
8/8/87	ⓡ	40	4	5 West L.A. Fadeaway		—	↓	
8/15/87	ⓡ	45	5	6 When Push Comes To Shove		—	↓	
12/5/87+	ⓡ	15	10	7 Throwing Stones		—	↓	
2/4/89	ⓡ	8	6	8 Slow Train	[L]	—	Dylan & The Dead	Columbia 45056
				BOB DYLAN & GRATEFUL DEAD				
10/28/89	ⓡ	8	10	9 Foolish Heart		—	Built To Last	Arista 8575
1/13/90	ⓡ	41	5	10 Just A Little Light		—	↓	

GRAVITY KILLS
Techno-rock band from Jefferson City, Missouri: Jeff Scheel (vocals), Matt Dudenhoeffer (guitar), Douglas Firley (keyboards) and Kurt Kerns (bass, drums).

3/2/96	ⓜ	24	24	1 Guilty		86	Gravity Kills	TVT 5910
6/8/96	ⓡ	39	3					
6/27/98	ⓡ	35	6	2 Falling		—	Perversion	TVT 5920
2/23/02	ⓡ	24	10	3 One Thing		—	Superstarved	Sanctuary 84539

GRAY, David
Born on 6/13/1968 in Manchester, England; raised in Solva, Wales. Rock singer/songwriter/guitarist.

12/2/00+	ⓜ	25	13	Babylon		57	White Ladder	ATO 69351

GREAT BUILDINGS
Pop-rock band formed in Los Angeles, California: **Danny Wilde** (vocals), Phil Solem (guitar), Ian Ainsworth (bass) and Richard Sandford (drums). Wilde and Solem later recorded as **The Rembrandts**.

4/18/81	ⓡ	48	3	Maybe It's You		—	Apart From The Crowd	Columbia 36920

GREAT WHITE

Hard-rock band formed in Los Angeles, California: Jack Russell (vocals), Mark Kendall (guitar), Lorne Black (bass) and Gary Holland (drums). Audie Desbrow replaced Holland in 1986. Michael Lardie (keyboards) joined in 1987. Tony Montana replaced Black in 1987. Many personnel changes since 1991. The band's pyrotechnic show during a Rhode Island club set off a fire that killed nearly 100 people on 2/21/2003, including the band's guitarist, Ty Longley.

TOP HITS: 1)Call It Rock N' Roll 2)Once Bitten Twice Shy 3)House Of Broken Love

Debut	Cht	Peak	Wks	Track Title	Hot Pos	Album Title	Label & Number
4/7/84	®	56	1	1 Stick It....................	—	Great White.....................EMI America 17111	
7/4/87	®	9	13	2 Rock Me....................	60	Once Bitten.....................Capitol 12565	
10/31/87	®	47	2	3 Lady Red Light	—	↓	
12/19/87+	®	9	15	4 Save Your Love	57	↓	
4/1/89	®	6	21	5 Once Bitten Twice Shy....................	5	...Twice Shy.....................Capitol 90640	
				first recorded by **Ian Hunter** in 1975			
7/1/89	®	27	9	6 Mista Bone	—	↓	
9/9/89	®	18	12	7 The Angel Song	30	↓	
1/6/90	®	7	16	8 House Of Broken Love....................	83	↓	
2/23/91	®	4	11	9 Call It Rock N' Roll	53	Hooked.....................Capitol 95330	
5/11/91	®	16	9	10 Desert Moon....................	—	↓	
9/19/92	®	20	8	11 Big Goodbye	—	Psycho City ....Capitol 98835	
12/19/92+	®	23	10	12 Old Rose Motel	—	↓	
6/11/94	®	9	16	13 Sail Away....................	—	Sail Away.....................Zoo 11080	
7/10/99	®	8	15	14 Rollin' Stoned	—	Can't Get There From Here.....................Portrait 69547	

GREBENSHIKOV, Boris

Born on 11/27/1953 in Leningrad, Russia. Rock singer/songwriter/guitarist.

Debut	Cht	Peak	Wks	Track Title	Hot Pos	Album Title	Label & Number
7/8/89	Ⓜ	7	10	Radio Silence....................	—	Radio Silence.....................Columbia 44364	
8/5/89	®	44	4	produced by Dave Stewart (of **Eurythmics**)			

GREEN DAY ® 1990s: #37 / 2000s: #23 / All-Time: #35 ★ Ⓜ 1990s: #6 / 2000s: #6 / All-Time: #3

Punk-rock trio formed in Berkeley, California: Billie Joe Armstrong (vocals, guitar; born on 2/17/1972), Mike "Dirnt" Pritchard (bass; born on 5/4/1972) and Frank "Tre Cool" Wright (drums; born on 12/9/1972). Also recorded as **Foxboro Hot Tubs**.

TOP HITS: 1)Boulevard Of Broken Dreams 2)When I Come Around 3)American Idiot 4)Basket Case 5)Minority

Debut	Cht	Peak	Wks	Track Title	Hot Pos	Album Title	Label & Number
3/19/94	Ⓜ	❶[1]	22	1 Long View	36[A]	Dookie ....Reprise 45529	
5/21/94	®	13	18				
7/16/94	Ⓜ	❶[5]	23	2 Basket Case	26[A]	↓	
8/27/94	®	9	22				
9/24/94	Ⓜ	7	18	3 Welcome To Paradise	56[A]	↓	
12/3/94+	Ⓜ	❶[7]	26	4 When I Come Around	6[A]	↓	
12/10/94+	®	2[2]	26				
4/15/95	Ⓜ	5	17	5 She....................	41[A]	↓	
5/20/95	®	18	14				
7/29/95	Ⓜ	❶[1]	12	6 J.A.R. (Jason Andrew Relva)	22[A]	St: Angus.....................Reprise 45960	
8/12/95	®	17	8				
10/7/95	Ⓜ	3[3]	12	7 Geek Stink Breath	27[A]	Insomniac ....Reprise 46046	
10/7/95	®	9	12				
12/23/95+	Ⓜ	3[1]	25	8 Brain Stew/Jaded	35[A]	↓	
12/30/95+	®	8	26				
6/15/96	Ⓜ	21	9	9 Walking Contradiction	70[A]	↓	
6/22/96	®	25	7				
9/13/97	Ⓜ	5	24	10 Hitchin' A Ride	59[A]	Nimrod ....Reprise 46794	
9/20/97	®	9	15				
11/29/97+	Ⓜ	2[13]	26	11 Good Riddance (Time Of Your Life)	11[A]	↓	
12/13/97+	®	7	22				
4/25/98	Ⓜ	16	13	12 Redundant....................	—	↓	
10/17/98	Ⓜ	31	6	13 Nice Guys Finish Last	—	↓	

GREEN DAY — cont'd

Debut	Cht	Peak	Wks	#	Track Title	Hot Pos	Album Title	Album Label & Number
9/9/00	⬤	❶⁵	23	14	**Minority**	101	*Warning:* ....Reprise 47613	
9/16/00	®	15	11					
12/2/00+	⬤	3¹	19	15	Warning	114	↓	
12/30/00+	®	24	10					
3/31/01	⬤	26	8	16	Waiting	—	↓	
8/21/04	⬤	❶⁶	26	17	American Idiot	61	*American Idiot*.....................................Reprise 48777	
8/21/04	®	5	26					
10/16/04	⬤	❶¹⁶	32	18	**Boulevard Of Broken Dreams**	2⁵	↓	
11/20/04+	®	❶¹⁴	38					
2/5/05	⬤	❶³	29	19	**Holiday**	19	↓	
4/2/05	®	❶³	26					
7/2/05	⬤	2²	22	20	Wake Me Up When September Ends	6	↓	
7/30/05	®	12	20					
12/10/05+	⬤	27	10	21	Jesus Of Suburbia...................................	—	*Bullet In A Bible* ....Reprise 49466	
10/14/06	⬤	22	7	22	The Saints Are Coming .... [L]	51	*(download only)* ....Island	
10/28/06	®	33	7		**U2 & GREEN DAY** first recorded by punk-rock band The Skids in 1978; recorded on 9/25/2006 at the re-opening of the Louisiana Superdome (home of the New Orleans Saints)			
5/19/07	⬤	10	12	23	Working Class Hero	53	*VA: Working Class Hero - A Tribute*	
5/19/07	®	18	11		written and first recorded by **John Lennon** in 1970		*To John Lennon*..........................Hollywood 62015	
2/2/08	⬤	16	9↑	24	Mother Mary .... **FOXBORO HOT TUBS**	—	*(download only)*................................Foxboro Hot Tubs	

GREENWHEEL

Rock band from St. Louis, Missouri: Ryan Jordan (vocals), Andrew Dwiggins (guitar), Marc Wanninger (guitar), Brandon Armstrong (bass) and Douglas Randall (drums).

| 9/21/02 | ⬤ | 37 | 3 | Breathe .... | — | *Soma Holiday* ....10 Inch 586661 |

GREN

Rock trio from Culver City, California: Brett White (vocals, guitar), Marcus (guitar) and Possum (drums).

| 1/27/96 | ® | 39 | 2 | She Shines .... | — | *Camp Grenada*...I.R.S. 31722 |

GROHL, Dave

Born on 1/14/1969 in Warren, Ohio; raised in Springfield, Virginia. Rock singer/songwriter/guitarist/drummer. Member of **Nirvana**. Leader of **Foo Fighters**.

| 10/7/00 | ® | 10 | 18 | Goodbye Lament ....
IOMMI Featuring Dave Grohl | — | *Iommi*...Divine 57857 |

GTR

Rock band formed in England: Max Bacon (vocals), Steve Hackett (guitar), Steve Howe (guitar), Phil Spalding (bass) and Jonathan Mover (drums). Hackett was with **Genesis**. Howe was with **Yes** and **Asia**. Band name is short for guitar.

| 4/26/86 | ® | 3¹ | 14 | 1 | When The Heart Rules The Mind .... | 14 | *GTR* ....Arista 8400 |
| 7/12/86 | ® | 14 | 10 | 2 | The Hunter .... | 85 | ↓ |

GUADALCANAL DIARY

Rock band formed in Marietta, Georgia: Murray Attaway (vocals), Jeff Walls (guitar), Rhett Crowe (bass) and John Poe (drums). Group named after the 1943 movie starring Anthony Quinn.

| 3/11/89 | ⬤ | 7 | 10 | Always Saturday.. | — | *Flip-Flop*...Elektra 60848 |

GUANO APES

Rock band from Gottingen, Germany: Sandra Nasic (vocals), Henning Ruemenapp (guitar), Stefan Ude (bass) and Dennis Poschwatta (drums).

| 12/11/99+ | ® | 24 | 15 | Open Your Eyes.. | — | *Proud Like A God*..RCA 67858 |

GUN

Rock band from Glasgow, Scotland: Mark Rankin (vocals), Giuliano Gizzi (guitar), Baby Stafford (guitar), Dante Gizzi (bass) and Scott Shields (drums).

| 2/17/90 | ® | 19 | 12 | Better Days .... | — | *Taking On The World*.................................A&M 5285 |

Billboard				ARTIST	®=Mainstream Rock	Hot		Album Title	Album Label & Number
Debut	Cht	Peak	Wks	Track Title	ⓜ=Modern Rock	Pos			

GUNS N' ROSES
® 1990s: #30 / All-Time: #67

Hard-rock band formed in Los Angeles, California: William "Axl Rose" Bailey (vocals), Saul "Slash" Hudson (guitar), Jeffrey "**Izzy Stradlin'**" Isbell (guitar), Michael "Duff" McKagen (bass) and Steven Adler (drums). Rose married Erin Everly (daughter of Don Everly of The Everly Brothers) briefly in 1990. Matt Sorum replaced Adler in 1990. Keyboardist Dizzy Reed joined in 1990. **Gilby Clarke** replaced Stradlin' in late 1991. Slash married model Renee Surran in November 1992. Clarke left band in January 1995. Slash, Sorum and Clarke recorded in 1995 in **Slash's Snakepit**.

TOP HITS: 1)Don't Cry 2)You Could Be Mine 3)Civil War

Debut	Cht	Peak	Wks	#	Track Title	Hot Pos	Album Title	Album Label & Number
4/2/88	®	37	11	1	Welcome To The Jungle	7	Appetite For Destruction	Geffen 24148
					R&R Hall of Fame ★ RS500 #467			
6/11/88	®	7	19	2	Sweet Child O' Mine	❶^2	↓	
					RS500 #196			
1/21/89	®	14	11	3	Paradise City	5	↓	
					RS500 #453			
7/29/89	®	26	5	4	Nightrain	93	↓	
12/24/88+	®	7	21	5	Patience	4	G N' R Lies	Geffen 24198
7/21/90	®	18	9	6	Knockin' On Heaven's Door	—	St: Days Of Thunder	DGC 24294
					#12 Pop hit for **Bob Dylan** in 1973			
8/4/90	®	4	11	7	Civil War	—	VA: Nobody's Child - Romanian Angel Appeal	Warner 26280
9/21/91	®	3^2	26	8	Don't Cry	10	Use Your Illusion I	Geffen 24415
9/28/91+	®	15	26	9	November Rain	3^2	↓	
9/28/91	®	20	12	10	Live And Let Die	33	↓	
					#2 Pop hit for **Paul McCartney** & Wings in 1973			
6/29/91	®	3^1	10	11	You Could Be Mine	29	Use Your Illusion II	Geffen 24420
3/21/92	®	35	8	12	Pretty Tied Up	—	↓	
10/17/92	®	13	14	13	Yesterdays	72	↓	
12/11/93+	®	16	10	14	Estranged	—	↓	
11/13/93	®	8	7	15	Ain't It Fun	—	The Spaghetti Incident?	Geffen 24617
					first recorded by The Dead Boys in 1978			
12/11/93+	®	11	13	16	Hair Of The Dog	—	↓	
					first recorded by **Nazareth** in 1975			
11/19/94	®	10	8	17	Sympathy For The Devil	55	St: Interview With The Vampire	Geffen 24719
					first recorded by **The Rolling Stones** in 1968			
10/30/99	®	26	5	18	Oh My God	—	St: End Of Days	Geffen 490508

GUSTER
Rock trio from Boston, Massachusetts: Adam Gardner (vocals, guitar), Ryan Miller (guitar) and Brian Rosenworcel (drums).

6/20/98	ⓜ	35	5		Airport Song	—	Goldfly	Hybrid 20006

H

HAGAR, Sammy
® 1980s: #33 / All-Time: #28

Born on 10/13/1947 in Monterey, California. Rock singer/songwriter/guitarist. Nicknamed "The Red Rocker." Lead singer of Montrose (1973-75) and **Van Halen** (1985-96). The Waboritas: Victor Johnson (guitar), Jesse Harms (keyboards), Mona (bass) and David Lauser (drums). Harms was a member of **REO Speedwagon**. Also see **Hager, Schon, Aaronson, Shrieve**.

TOP HITS: 1)Little White Lie 2)Give To Live 3)Mas Tequila 4)I'll Fall In Love Again 5)Winner Takes It All

Debut	Cht	Peak	Wks	#	Track Title	Hot Pos	Album Title	Album Label & Number
1/16/82	®	2^3	17	1	I'll Fall In Love Again	43	Standing Hampton	Geffen 2006
3/13/82	®	31	6	2	There's Only One Way To Rock	—	↓	
4/3/82	®	35	4	3	Baby's On Fire	—	↓	
5/1/82	®	49	2	4	Can't Get Loose	—	↓	
8/21/82	®	21	10	5	Fast Times At Ridgemont High	—	St: Fast Times At Ridgemont High	Full Moon 60158
12/18/82+	®	3^1	16	6	Your Love Is Driving Me Crazy	13	Three Lock Box	Geffen 2021
1/15/83	®	6	10	7	Remember The Heroes	—	↓	
					Mike Reno (of **Loverboy**; guest vocal)			
3/5/83	®	24	7	8	I Don't Need Love	—	↓	
7/14/84	®	5	13	9	Two Sides Of Love	38	VOA	Geffen 24043
8/11/84	®	9	16	10	I Can't Drive 55	26	↓	
2/7/87	®	3^2	12	11	Winner Takes It All	54	St: Over The Top	Columbia 40655
6/13/87	®	❶^3	11	12	Give To Live	23	Sammy Hagar (I Never Said Goodbye)	Capitol 24144
7/25/87	®	15	7	13	Boys' Night Out	—	↓	
8/29/87	®	20	7	14	Returning Home	—	↓	
10/10/87	®	22	8	15	Eagles Fly	82	↓	

HAGAR, Sammy — cont'd

Debut	Cht	Peak	Wks	Track Title	Hot Pos	Album Title	Album Label & Number
3/19/94	®	4	16	16 High Hopes	—	Unboxed	Geffen 24702
7/2/94	®	36	4	17 Buying My Way Into Heaven	—	↓	
5/10/97	®	❶5	16	18 Little White Lie	—	Marching To Mars	MCA 11627
8/9/97	®	3¹	13	19 Marching To Mars	—	↓	
10/25/97	®	11	20	20 Both Sides Now	—	↓	

SAMMY HAGAR AND THE WABORITAS:

3/13/99	®	2⁶	21	21 Mas Tequila	116	Red Voodoo	MCA 11872
6/26/99	®	22	9	22 Shag	—	↓	
9/30/00	®	10	12	23 Serious JuJu	—	Ten 13	Cabo Wabo 78110
12/16/00+	®	16	13	24 Let Sally Drive (Ride Sally Ride)	—	↓	
10/26/02	®	35	13	25 Things've Changed	—	Not 4 Sale	33rd Street 3315

HAGAR, SCHON, AARONSON, SHRIEVE

All-star rock band formed in Los Angeles, California: **Sammy Hagar** (vocals), **Neal Schon** (guitar), Kenny Aaronson (bass) and Michael Shrieve (drums).

3/31/84	®	15	6	1 Top Of The Rock	—	Through The Fire	Geffen 4023
4/14/84	®	37	6	2 Missing You	—	↓	
4/28/84	®	30	6	3 Whiter Shade Of Pale	94	↓	

#5 Pop hit for **Procol Harum** in 1967

HAIRCUT ONE HUNDRED

Pop-rock band from Beckenham, Kent, England: **Nick Heyward** (vocals), Graham Jones (guitar), Phil Smith (sax), Mark Fox (percussion), Les Nemes (bass) and Blair Cunningham (drums).

5/8/82	®	18	9	1 Love Plus One	37	Pelican West	Arista 6600
8/21/82	®	50	7	2 Favourite Shirts (Boy Meets Girl)	101	↓	

HALL, Daryl

Born Daryl Hohl on 10/11/1948 in Philadelphia, Pennsylvania. "Blue-eyed soul" singer/songwriter/keyboardist. One-half of **Hall & Oates** duo.

8/2/86	®	11	10	Dreamtime	5	Three Hearts In The Happy Ending Machine	RCA 7196

HALL, Daryl, & John Oates

"Blue-eyed soul" pop duo: **Daryl Hall** (see previous entry) and John Oates (guitar, vocals; born on 4/7/1949 in Brooklyn, New York. Met while students at Temple University in 1967. Hall played with The Electric Indian and sang backup for many top soul groups before teaming up with Oates in 1972.

TOP HITS: 1)Maneater 2)Out Of Touch 3)Say It Isn't So

4/11/81	®	54	3	1 Kiss On My List	❶3	Voices	RCA Victor 3646
7/18/81	®	35	3	2 You Make My Dreams	5	↓	
10/17/81	®	33	8	3 Private Eyes	❶2	Private Eyes	RCA Victor 4028
11/28/81+	®	28	11	4 I Can't Go For That (No Can Do)	❶1	↓	
10/30/82	®	18	16	5 Maneater	❶4	H2O	RCA Victor 4383
11/19/83	®	18	13	6 Say It Isn't So	2⁴	Rock 'N Soul, Part 1	RCA Victor 4858
2/18/84	®	23	9	7 Adult Education	8	↓	
10/6/84	®	18	11	8 Out Of Touch	❶2	Big Bam Boom	RCA Victor 5309
2/2/85	®	42	3	9 Method Of Modern Love	5	↓	
8/31/85	®	43	3	10 The Way You Do The Things You Do/My Girl . [L]	20	Live At The Apollo	RCA Victor 7035

DARYL HALL & JOHN OATES with David Ruffin & Eddie Kendrick recorded at the reopening of New York's Apollo Theatre on 5/23/1985; medley of #11/#1 Pop hits for The Temptations in 1964/1965

HALL, John, Band

Born on 10/25/1948 in Baltimore, Maryland. Rock singer/guitarist. Leader of Orleans. Band includes Bob Leinbach (keyboards), John Troy (bass) and Eric Parker (drums). Hall was elected to the U.S. House of Representatives (in New York) in 2006.

11/14/81+	®	13	21	1 Crazy (Keep On Falling)	42	All Of The Above	EMI America 17058
2/19/83	®	41	3	2 Love Me Again	64	Searchparty	EMI America 17082

HAMM, Stuart

Born on 2/8/1960 in Los Angeles, California. Rock singer/bassist. Member of **Joe Satriani**'s touring band.

8/17/91	®	39	4	Lone Star [I]	—	The Urge	Relativity 1052

HAMMER, Jan

Born on 4/17/1948 in Prague, Czechoslovakia. Male jazz-rock keyboardist.

2/19/83	®	42	1	1 No More Lies	—	Here To Stay	Columbia 38428

NEAL SCHON & JAN HAMMER

9/28/85	®	29	7	2 Miami Vice Theme [I]	❶1	St: Miami Vice	MCA 6150

HANDSOME DEVIL
Punk-rock band from Orange County, California: Danny Walker (vocals, guitar), Billie Stevens (guitar), Darren Roberts (bass) and Keith Morgan (drums).

| 9/1/01 | M | 22 | 9 | Makin' Money .... | — | Love And Kisses From The Underground.....RCA 68055 |

HAPPYHEAD
Pop-rock trio formed in London, England: Carl Marsh (vocals, guitar), Steve Gretham (bass) and Jim Kimberly (drums).

| 3/14/92 | M | 7 | 9 | Fabulous .... | — | Give Happyhead ....EastWest 92114 |

HAPPY MONDAYS
Dance-rock band formed in Manchester, England: brothers Shaun Ryder (vocals) and Paul Ryder (bass), Mark Day (guitar), Paul Davis (keyboards), Mark Berry (percussion) and Gary Whelan (drums). Shaun Ryder and Berry later formed **Black Grape**.

7/14/90	M	9	11	1 Step On	—	Pills 'N' Thrills And Bellyaches...................Elektra 60986
12/1/90+	M	❶[1]	12	2 Kinky Afro	—	↓
3/23/91	M	23	3	3 Bob's Yer Uncle	—	↓
9/19/92	M	21	7	4 Stinkin Thinkin	—	Yes, Please! ....Elektra 61391

HARD-FI
Rock band from Staines, Surrey, England: Richard Archer (vocals), Ross Phillips (guitar), Kai Stephens (bass) and Steven Kemp (drums).

| 1/7/06 | M | 15 | 15 | 1 Cash Machine .... | — | Stars Of CCTV...................Necessary 78691 |
| 5/27/06 | M | 34 | 7 | 2 Hard To Beat .... | — | ↓ |

HARDING, John Wesley
Born Wesley Harding Stace on 10/22/1965 in Hastings, England. Male singer/songwriter. Adopted stage name from the 1968 **Bob Dylan** album.

2/10/90	M	17	10	1 The Devil In Me	—	Here Comes The Groom ....Sire 26087
3/16/91	M	8	7	2 The Person You Are	—	The Name Above The Title...................Sire 26481
5/11/91	M	29	2	3 The People's Drug	—	↓

HARDLINE
Rock band formed in San Francisco, California: **Neal Schon** (guitar; of **Journey**), brothers Johnny Gioeli (vocals) and Joey Gioeli (guitar), Todd Jensen (bass) and Deen Castronovo (drums; of **Bad English**).

| 6/13/92 | R | 37 | 4 | 1 Takin' Me Down .... | — | Double Eclipse ....MCA 10586 |
| 9/12/92 | R | 25 | 14 | 2 Hot Cherie .... | — | ↓ |

HARRISON, George
Born on 2/24/1943 in Wavertree, Liverpool, England. Died of cancer on 11/29/2001 (age 58). Singer/songwriter/guitarist. Member of **The Beatles** and the **Traveling Wilburys**. Also see **The Bunburys** and **Classic Rock Tracks** section.
AWARDS: R&R Hall of Fame: 2004 ★ Billboard: Century Award 1992

6/13/81	R	6	7	1 All Those Years Ago	2[3]	Somewhere In England...................Dark Horse 3492
				tribute to **John Lennon**		
7/4/81	R	51	3	2 Teardrops	102	↓
10/24/87	R	4	11	3 Got My Mind Set On You	❶[1]	Cloud Nine...................Dark Horse 25643
				first recorded by James Ray in 1962		
11/14/87+	R	2[1]	18	4 When We Was Fab	23	↓
11/14/87	R	4	13	5 Devil's Radio	—	↓
11/21/87+	R	9	10	6 Cloud 9	—	↓
4/16/88	R	17	7	7 This Is Love	—	↓
8/5/89	R	7	8	8 Cheer Down	—	St: Lethal Weapon 2 ....Warner 25985
10/28/89	R	21	7	9 Poor Little Girl	—	Best Of Dark Horse 1976-1989 ....Dark Horse 25726

HARRISON, Jerry: Casual Gods
Born on 2/21/1949 in Milwaukee, Wisconsin. Rock keyboardist/producer. Member of **Talking Heads**. The Casual Gods are 13 backing musicians.

2/6/88	R	7	16	1 Rev It Up	—	Casual Gods...................Sire 25663
5/19/90	M	13	8	2 Flying Under Radar	—	Walk On Water ....Sire 25943
6/2/90	R	42	4			

HARRY, Deborah
Born on 7/1/1945 in Miami, Florida; raised in Hawthorne, New Jersey. Lead singer of **Blondie**. Acted in several movies.

9/10/88	M	14	4	1 Liar, Liar	—	St: Married To The Mob...................Reprise 25763
				DEBBIE HARRY		
				#12 Pop hit for the Castaways in 1965		
9/30/89	M	2[2]	11	2 I Want That Man	—	Def, Dumb & Blonde ....Sire 25938
12/16/89+	M	12	6	3 Kiss It Better	—	↓

				Billboard	ARTIST			
Debut	**Cht**	**Peak**	**Wks**		**Track Title**	®=Mainstream Rock ⓜ=Modern Rock	**Hot Pos**	**Album Title**	**Album Label & Number**

HART, Corey
Born on 5/31/1962 in Montreal, Quebec, Canada; raised in Malaga, Spain and Mexico City. Male singer/songwriter/keyboardist.

6/23/84	®	15	13	1 Sunglasses At Night	7	First Offense	EMI America 17117
10/27/84	®	36	7	2 It Ain't Enough	17	↓	
6/29/85	®	8	12	3 Never Surrender	3²	Boy In The Box	EMI America 17161

HARVEY, PJ
Born Polly Jean Harvey on 10/9/1969 in Yeovil, England. Female singer/guitarist. Had own trio, also named PJ Harvey, which included bassist Stephen Vaughan and drummer Rob Ellis.

7/25/92	ⓜ	9	10	1 Sheela-Na-Gig	—	Dry	Indigo 555001
2/25/95	ⓜ	2³	14	2 Down By The Water	48ᴬ	To Bring You My Love	Island 524085
9/26/98	ⓜ	33	3	3 A Perfect Day Elise		Is This Desire?	Island 524563

HARVEY DANGER
Rock band from Seattle, Washington: Sean Nelson (vocals), Jeff Lin (guitar), Aaron Huffman (bass) and Evan Sult (drums).

4/11/98	ⓜ	3⁵	28	1 Flagpole Sitta	38ᴬ	Where Have All The Merrymakers Gone?	Slash 556000
8/22/98	®	33	5				
3/20/99	ⓜ	29	5	2 Save It For Later	—	St: 200 Cigarettes	Mercury 538738
9/2/00	ⓜ	27	9	3 Sad Sweetheart Of Rodeo	—	King James Version	London 31143

HATFIELD, Juliana, Three
Born on 7/2/1967 in Wiscasset, Maine. Female rock singer/guitarist. Group also included bassist Dean Fisher and drummer Todd Philips.

8/7/93	ⓜ	❶¹	12	1 My Sister	112	Become What You Are	Atlantic 92278
3/25/95	ⓜ	5	12	2 Universal Heart-Beat JULIANA HATFIELD	84	Only Everything	Mammoth 92540

HAVANA BLACK
Hard-rock band from Helsinki, Finland: Hannu Leiden (vocals), Markku Heiskanen (guitar), Risto Hankala (bass) and Jussi Tegelman (drums). Group name taken from a box of Cuban cigars.

2/3/90	®	17	9	Lone Wolf	—	Indian Warrior	Capitol 90567

HAVANA 3 A.M.
Rock band formed in England: Nigel Dixon (vocals, guitar), Gary Myrick (guitar), Paul Simonon (bass) and Travis Williams (drums). Simonon was a member of **The Clash**.

2/16/91	ⓜ	6	11	Reach The Rock	—	Havana 3 A.M.	I.R.S. 13069

HAWKS
Rock band from Otho, Iowa: Dave Hearn (vocals), Kirk Kaufman (guitar), Dave Steen (guitar), Frank Wiewel (bass) and Larry Adams (drums).

4/18/81	®	32	7	It's All Right, It's O.K.	—	Hawks	Columbia 36922

HAWTHORNE HEIGHTS
Alternative-rock band from Dayton, Ohio: JT Woodruff (vocals, guitar), Casey Calvert (guitar), Micah Carli (guitar), Matt Ridenour (bass) and Eron Bucciarelli (drums). Calvert died of a drug overdose on 11/24/2007 (age 26).

8/20/05	ⓜ	34	8	1 Ohio Is For Lovers	—	The Silence In Black And White	Victory 220
12/24/05	ⓜ	40	1	2 Niki FM	—	↓	
2/11/06	ⓜ	7	19	3 Saying Sorry	—	If Only You Were Lonely	Victory 265

HAY, Colin James
Born on 6/29/1953 in Kilwinning, North Ayrshire, Scotland; rasied in Melbourne, Australia. Lead singer/guitarist of **Men At Work**.

2/14/87	®	41	6	Hold Me	99	Looking For Jack	Columbia 40611

HAZA, Ofra
Born on 11/19/1957 in Tel Aviv, Israel. Died of AIDS on 2/23/2000 (age 42). Female singer/songwriter/actress.

12/3/88	ⓜ	18	9	Im Nin'alu	—	Shaday	Sire 25816

HAZIES, The
Rock band from Los Angeles, California: Ken Logan (vocals), Greg Zink (guitar), Wes Eubanks (keyboards), Dave Walker (bass) and Steven Tanner (drums).

6/8/96	®	13	14	1 Skin & Bones	—	Vinnie Smokin' In The Big Room	EMI 37369
12/7/96+	®	21	10	2 Trip Free Life	—	↓	

HEADSTRONG
Rock band from London, Ontario, Canada: Matt Kinna (vocals), Joel Krass (guitar), Jon Cohen (bass) and Brian Mathews (drums).

2/9/02	®	15	15	Adriana	—	Headstrong	RCA 68004

HEALEY, Jeff, Band

Born Norman Jeffrey Healey on 3/25/1966 in Toronto, Ontario, Canada. Died of cancer on 3/2/2008 (age 41). Blues-rock singer/guitarist. Blind since age one. Formed own group with Joe Rockman (bass) and Tom Stephen (drums). Band appeared in the 1989 movie *Road House*.

TOP HITS: 1)Cruel Little Number 2)I Think I Love You Too Much 3)While My Guitar Gently Weeps

Debut	Cht	Peak	Wks	Track Title	Hot Pos	Album Title	Album Label & Number
10/1/88	®	11	12	1 Confidence Man	—	See The Light	Arista 8553
1/14/89	®	33	6	2 See The Light	—	↓	
4/15/89	®	24	7	3 Angel Eyes	5	↓	
5/27/89	®	29	6	4 Roadhouse Blues	—	St: Road House	Arista 8576
				first recorded by **The Doors** in 1970			
5/26/90	®	5	15	5 I Think I Love You Too Much	—	Hell To Pay	Arista 8632
				Mark Knopfler (of **Dire Straits**; writer, guitar, backing vocal)			
8/11/90	®	7	17	6 While My Guitar Gently Weeps	—	↓	
				George Harrison (writer, guitar, backing vocal); first recorded by **The Beatles** in 1968			
11/17/90	®	16	11	7 Full Circle	—	↓	
2/16/91	®	34	4	8 How Long Can A Man Be Strong	—	↓	
11/7/92	®	2[1]	13	9 Cruel Little Number	—	Feel This	Arista 18706
2/6/93	®	20	7	10 Heart Of An Angel	—	↓	
8/26/95	®	39	4	11 Stuck In The Middle With You	—	Cover To Cover	Arista 18770
				#6 Pop hit for Stealers Wheel in 1973			

HEAR 'N AID

Collection of 40 hard-rock artists formed to raise money for famine relief efforts in Africa and around the world.

Debut	Cht	Peak	Wks	Track Title	Hot Pos	Album Title	Album Label & Number
5/10/86	®	39	4	Stars	—	Hear 'N Aid	Mercury 826044
				co-written, produced and arranged by Ronnie James **Dio**			

HEART

® 1980s: #36 / All-Time: #45

Rock band formed in Seattle, Washington: sisters Ann Wilson (vocals) and Nancy Wilson (guitar), Howard Leese (guitar), Mark Andes (bass; of **Spirit**) and Denny Carmassi (drums; of **Gamma**). Andes left by 1993. Carmassi left in 1994 to join **Whitesnake**. Nancy married movie director Cameron Crowe on 7/27/1986. Also see **Classic Rock Tracks** section.

TOP HITS: 1)How Can I Refuse 2)Who Will You Run To 3)These Dreams

Debut	Cht	Peak	Wks	Track Title	Hot Pos	Album Title	Album Label & Number
5/22/82	®	16	7	1 This Man Is Mine	33	Private Audition	Epic 38049
6/5/82	®	15	7	2 City's Burning	—	↓	
8/13/83	®	❶[1]	16	3 How Can I Refuse	44	Passionworks	Epic 38800
10/8/83	®	43	6	4 Sleep Alone	—	↓	
4/21/84	®	40	4	5 The Heat	—	St: Up The Creek	Pasha 39333
6/1/85	®	3[2]	16	6 What About Love?	10	Heart	Capitol 12410
9/7/85	®	2[2]	18	7 Never	4	↓	
1/25/86	®	2[3]	12	8 These Dreams	❶[1]	↓	
4/26/86	®	6	10	9 Nothin' At All	10	↓	
5/16/87	®	3[1]	11	10 Alone	❶[3]	Bad Animals	Capitol 12546
6/6/87	®	2[3]	16	11 Who Will You Run To	7	↓	
11/21/87+	®	16	12	12 There's The Girl	12	↓	
3/31/90	®	2[1]	8	13 All I Wanna Do Is Make Love To You	2[2]	Brigade	Capitol 91820
4/14/90	®	3[2]	16	14 Wild Child	—	↓	
4/28/90	®	24	8	15 Tall, Dark Handsome Stranger	—	↓	
6/30/90	®	13	9	16 I Didn't Want To Need You	23	↓	
10/20/90	®	25	8	17 Stranded	13	↓	
10/12/91	®	20	7	18 You're The Voice [L]	—	Rock The House Live!	Capitol 95797
				recorded on 11/28/1990 at The Centrum in Worcester, Massachusetts; #82 Pop hit for John Farnham in 1990			
10/30/93	®	4	8	19 Black On Black II	—	Desire Walks On	Capitol 99627
				first recorded by Dalbello in 1986			

HEART THROBS, The

Rock band from Reading, England: sisters Rose Carlotti (vocals) and Rachel Carlotti (bass), Alan Barclay (guitar), Stephen Ward (keyboards) and Mark Side (drums).

Debut	Cht	Peak	Wks	Track Title	Hot Pos	Album Title	Album Label & Number
8/11/90	Ⓜ	2[3]	11	1 Dreamtime	—	Cleopatra Grip	Elektra 60961
10/27/90	Ⓜ	21	4	2 She's In A Trance	—	↓	

HEAVEN 17

Electro-pop trio from England: Glenn Gregory (vocals), Martyn Ware and Ian Craig Marsh (synthesizers). Ware and Marsh were founding members of **Human League**.

4/23/83	®	32	3	Let Me Go	74	Heaven 17 ....Arista 6606

(HED)PLANET EARTH

Rap-rock band from Huntington Beach, California: Paolo "Jahred Shane" Gomes (vocals), Doug "DJ Product" Boyce (DJ), Wes "Wesstyle" Geer (guitar), Chad "Chizad" Benekos (guitar), Mark "Mawk" Young (bass) and Ben "B.C." Vaught (drums).

8/26/00	®	23	14	1 Bartender (I Just Want Your Company)	—	Broke ....Volcano 41710
9/16/00	Ⓜ	27	11			
2/15/03	®	21	15	2 Blackout	—	Blackout ....Volcano 41817
3/22/03	Ⓜ	32	8			
8/16/03	®	40	1	3 Other Side	↓	

HELIX

Hard-rock band from Waterloo, Ontario, Canada: Brian Vollmer (vocals), Brent Doerner (guitar), Paul Hackman (guitar), Mike Uzelac (bass) and Greg "Fritz" Hinz (drums). Daryl Gray replaced Uzelac in 1984. Hackman was killed in a bus crash on 7/5/1992 (age 39).

9/17/83	®	23	17	1 Heavy Metal Love	—	No Rest For The Wicked ....Capitol 12281
8/4/84	®	32	8	2 Rock You...	101	Walkin' The Razor's Edge ....Capitol 12362
6/22/85	®	20	9	3 Deep Cuts The Knife	—	Long Way To Heaven...............................Capitol 12411

HELLYEAH

All-star rock band: Chad Gray (vocals), Greg Tribbett (guitar), Tom Maxwell (guitar), Bob "Zilla" Kakaha (bass) and Vinnie Paul Abbott (drums). Gray and Tribbett were with **Mudvayne**. Maxwell was with **Nothingface**. Kakaha and Abbott were with **Damageplan**. Abbott was also with **Pantera**.

3/3/07	®	5	25	1 You Wouldn't Know..	—	HellYeah..Epic 07408
6/9/07	Ⓜ	35	9			
7/28/07	®	7	21	2 Alcohaulin' Ass...	↓	
1/12/08	®	37	6	3 Thank You	↓	

HELMET

Rock band from New York: Page Hamilton (vocals, guitar), Peter Mengede (guitar), Henry Bogdan (bass) and John Stanier (drums). Rob Echeverria replaced Mengede in 1993; left by 1997. Lineup in 2004: Hamilton, Chris Traynor (guitar), Frank Bello (bass; of **Anthrax**) and John Tempesta (drums; of **Testament** and **White Zombie**). Traynor later joined **Institute**.

10/10/92	Ⓜ	29	1	1 Unsung	—	Meantime...Interscope 92162
11/14/92	®	32	4			
7/16/94	®	39	2	2 Milquetoast	—	Betty..Interscope 92404
3/29/97	®	19	9	3 Exactly What You Wanted	—	Aftertaste ....Interscope 90073
9/4/04	®	29	9	4 See You Dead	—	Size Matters..Interscope 002968

HENLEY, Don

® **1980s: #19 / All-Time: #31**

Born on 7/22/1947 in Gilmer, Texas. Rock singer/songwriter/drummer. Member of the **Eagles**. Married model Sharon Summerall on 5/20/1995. Later became an environmental activist; founded the Walden Woods Project in 1990.

TOP HITS: 1)The Boys Of Summer   2)The End Of The Innocence   3)Dirty Laundry   4)All She Wants To Do Is Dance   5)The Heart Of The Matter

11/28/81+	®	26	12	1 Leather And Lace	6	Bella Donna ....Modern 139
				STEVIE NICKS with Don Henley		
8/21/82	®	29	3	2 Johnny Can't Read..	42	I Can't Stand Still ....Asylum 60048
				Andrew Gold (keyboards)		
9/11/82	®	❶³	21	3 Dirty Laundry	3³ ↓	
				Joe Walsh and Steve Lukather (Toto) (guitar solos)		
10/2/82	®	44	3	4 You Better Hang Up	— ↓	
				Timothy B. Schmit and J.D. Souther (harmony vocals)		
11/10/84	®	❶⁵	17	5 The Boys Of Summer	5	Building The Perfect Beast ....Geffen 24026
				Grammy: Rock Male Vocal ★ RS500 #416		
12/15/84+	®	7	15	6 Sunset Grill	22 ↓	
				Patty Smyth (harmony vocal)		
1/26/85	®	❶²	18	7 All She Wants To Do Is Dance	9 ↓	
				Martha Davis and Patty Smyth (harmony vocals)		
4/13/85	®	9	10	8 Drivin' With Your Eyes Closed	— ↓	
6/8/85	®	17	9	9 Not Enough Love In The World	34 ↓	
11/1/86	®	3¹	13	10 Who Owns This Place	—	St: The Color Of Money ....MCA 6189
6/24/89	®	❶⁴	12	11 The End Of The Innocence	8	The End Of The Innocence......................Geffen 24217
				co-written and produced by Bruce Hornsby (also on piano)		

HENLEY, Don — cont'd

Debut	Cht	Peak	Wks	Track Title	Hot Pos	Album Title	Album Label & Number
7/8/89	R	2[1]	16	12 I Will Not Go Quietly	—	↓	
				Axl Rose (of Guns N' Roses; harmony vocal)			
8/12/89+	R	8	14	13 If Dirt Were Dollars	—	↓	
				Sheryl Crow and J.D. Souther (backing vocals)			
9/16/89	R	4	17	14 The Last Worthless Evening	21	↓	
2/17/90	R	2[2]	15	15 The Heart Of The Matter	21	↓	
6/30/90	R	8	11	16 How Bad Do You Want It?	48	↓	
11/3/90	R	24	11	17 New York Minute	48	↓	
11/25/95+	R	16	12	18 The Garden Of Allah	—	Actual Miles - Henley's Greatest Hits	Geffen 24834
2/24/96	R	22	10	19 You Don't Know Me At All	—	↓	
1/25/97	R	33	4	20 Through Your Hands	—	St: Michael	Revolution 24666
4/8/00	R	21	11	21 Workin' It	—	Inside Job	Warner 47083

HEYWARD, Nick
Born on 5/20/1961 in Beckenham, Kent, England. Pop-rock singer/guitarist. Member of **Haircut One Hundred** (1981-83).

Debut	Cht	Peak	Wks	Track Title	Hot Pos	Album Title	Album Label & Number
12/4/93+	M	4	16	Kite	107	From Monday To Sunday	Epic 57755

HIATT, John
Born on 8/20/1952 in Indianapolis, Indiana. Singer/songwriter/guitarist. Member of **Little Village**.

Debut	Cht	Peak	Wks	Track Title	Hot Pos	Album Title	Album Label & Number
6/20/87	R	27	8	1 Thank You Girl	—	Bring The Family	A&M 5158
9/10/88	R	8	13	2 Slow Turning	—	Slow Turning	A&M 5206
10/1/88	M	22	4				
12/3/88+	R	18	12	3 Paper Thin	—	↓	
6/23/90	R	17	13	4 Child Of The Wild Blue Yonder	—	Stolen Moments	A&M 5310
7/7/90	M	24	5				
9/25/93	R	16	9	5 Perfectly Good Guitar	—	Perfectly Good Guitar	A&M 540135
1/1/94	R	31	7	6 Something Wild	—	↓	

HIGH, The
Rock band from Manchester, England: John Matthews (vocals), Andy Couzens (guitar), Simon Davies (bass) and Chris Goodwin (drums).

Debut	Cht	Peak	Wks	Track Title	Hot Pos	Album Title	Album Label & Number
12/22/90+	M	19	7	Up & Down	—	Somewhere Soon	London 828224

HILL, Rocky
Born on 2/1/1946 in Dallas, Texas. Blues-rock singer/guitarist. Brother of Dusty Hill (of **ZZ Top**).

Debut	Cht	Peak	Wks	Track Title	Hot Pos	Album Title	Album Label & Number
4/23/88	R	31	5	I Won't Be Your Fool	—	Rocky Hill	Virgin 90862

HIM
Goth-rock band from Finland: Ville Valo (vocals), Mikko "Linde" Lindström (guitar), Emerson Burton (keyboards), Migé Amour (bass) and Gas Lipstick (drums). HIM: His Infernal Majesty.

Debut	Cht	Peak	Wks	Track Title	Hot Pos	Album Title	Album Label & Number
11/26/05+	M	19	23	Wings Of A Butterfly	87	Dark Light	Sire 49284
10/22/05+	R	20	20				

HIMMELMAN, Peter
Born in 1962 in St. Louis Park, Minnesota. Male singer/songwriter.

Debut	Cht	Peak	Wks	Track Title	Hot Pos	Album Title	Album Label & Number
12/26/87+	R	41	6	1 Waning Moon	—	Gematria	Island 90663
6/1/91	M	18	6	2 Woman With The Strength Of 10,000 Men	—	From Strength To Strength	Epic 47073

HINDER
Alternative-rock band from Oklahoma City, Oklahoma: Austin Winkler (vocals), Joe Garvey (guitar), Mark King (guitar), Mike Rodden (bass) and Cody Hanson (drums).

Debut	Cht	Peak	Wks	Track Title	Hot Pos	Album Title	Album Label & Number
8/13/05+	R	4	39	1 Get Stoned	103	Extreme Behavior	Universal 005390
1/21/06	M	37	3				
4/22/06	R	3[1]	35	2 Lips Of An Angel	3[4]	↓	
8/5/06	M	8	20				
10/28/06+	R	6	20	3 How Long	—	↓	
2/24/07	R	16	20	4 Better Than Me	31	↓	
3/24/07	M	37	5				
7/14/07	R	16	14	5 Homecoming Queen	—	↓	

HINDU LOVE GODS
All-star rock band: **Warren Zevon** (vocals) with **R.E.M.** members: Peter Buck (guitar), Mike Mills (bass) and Bill Berry (drums). Zevon died of cancer on 9/7/2003 (age 56).

Debut	Cht	Peak	Wks	Track Title	Hot Pos	Album Title	Album Label & Number
10/27/90	M	23	7	Raspberry Beret	—	Hindu Love Gods	Giant 24406

Debut	Cht	Peak	Wks	Track Title	Hot Pos	Album Title	Album Label & Number

HITCHCOCK, Robyn, & The Egyptians
Born on 3/3/1952 in London, England. Male rock singer/guitarist. The Egyptians: Andy Metcalfe (bass) and Morris Windsor (drums).

3/18/89	Ⓜ	2³	11	1 Madonna Of The Wasps	—	Queen Elvis	A&M 5241
8/24/91	Ⓜ	❶⁵	11	2 So You Think You're In Love	—	Perspex Island	A&M 5368
11/23/91	Ⓜ	29	2	3 Oceanside	↓		
				Peter Buck (of R.E.M.; guitar, above 2)			
1/25/92	Ⓜ	23	2	4 Ultra Unbelievable Love	—	↓	
3/13/93	Ⓜ	19	7	5 Driving Aloud (Radio Storm)	—	Respect	A&M 540064

HIVES, The
Rock band from Fagersta, Sweden: brothers Pelle Almqvist (vocals) and Niklas Almqvist (guitar), with Mikael "Vigilante Carlstroem" Astrom (guitar), Mattias "Dr. Matt Destruction" Bernvall (bass) and Christian "Chris Dangerous" Grahn (drums).

5/25/02	Ⓜ	6	25	1 Hate To Say I Told You So	86	Veni Vidi Vicious	Epitaph 48327
8/17/02	®	35	2				
7/3/04	Ⓜ	19	12	2 Walk Idiot Walk	—	Tyrannosaurus Hives	Interscope 002756
8/14/04	®	36	3				
10/27/07	Ⓜ	36	6	3 Tick Tick Boom	—	The Black And White Album	A&M 010030

HODGSON, Roger
Born on 5/21/1950 in London, England. Pop-rock singer/songwriter/guitarist/pianist. Lead singer of Supertramp.

10/13/84	®	5	17	1 Had A Dream (Sleeping With The Enemy)	48	In The Eye Of The Storm	A&M 5004
1/19/85	®	30	6	2 In Jeopardy	↓		
10/10/87	®	38	4	3 You Make Me Love You	—	Hai Hai	A&M 5112

HOEY, Gary
Born on 8/23/1960 in Lowell, Massachusetts. Rock guitarist.

8/28/93	®	5	20	1 Hocus Pocus [I]	—	Animal Instinct	Reprise 45350
				#9 Pop hit for Focus in 1973			
7/2/94	®	15	11	2 Low Rider [I]	—	St: The Endless Summer II	Reprise 45615
				#7 Pop hit for War in 1975			

HOG
Rock trio from Los Angeles, California: Kirk Miller (vocals, guitar), Dillinger (bass) and Matt Gillis (drums).

| 3/30/96 | ® | 34 | 4 | Get A Job | — | Nothing Sacred | DGC 24958 |

HOLE
Rock band formed in Los Angeles, California: Courtney Love (vocals, guitar), Eric Erlandson (guitar), Kristen Pfaff (bass) and Patty Schemel (drums). Love acted in several movies; married to Kurt Cobain (of Nirvana) from 2/24/1992 until his death on 4/8/1994. Pfaff was found dead in her bathtub on 6/16/1994 (age 27); replaced by Melissa Auf Der Maur.   Ⓜ 1990s: #29 / All-Time: #68

4/23/94	Ⓜ	13	10	1 Miss World	—	Live Through This	DGC 24631
10/15/94	Ⓜ	4	17	2 Doll Parts	58	↓	
2/11/95	Ⓜ	29	10	3 Violet	—	↓	
2/11/95	Ⓜ	36	4	4 Asking For It	—	↓	
8/19/95	Ⓜ	32	5	5 Softer, Softest	—	↓	
7/27/96	Ⓜ	31	9	6 Gold Dust Woman	—	St: The Crow - City Of Angels	Miramax 20476
				first recorded by Fleetwood Mac in 1977			
9/5/98	Ⓜ	❶⁴	26	7 Celebrity Skin	56ᴬ	Celebrity Skin	DGC 25164
9/12/98	®	4	26				
12/12/98+	Ⓜ	3³	20	8 Malibu	81	↓	
2/13/99	®	16	9				
4/17/99	Ⓜ	13	14	9 Awful	—	↓	

HOLLOW MEN, The
Rock band formed in Manchester, England: David Ashmore (vocals), Brian Roberts (guitar), Choque (guitar), Howard Taylor (bass) and Johnny Cragg (drums).

| 2/16/91 | Ⓜ | 16 | 7 | November Comes | — | Cresta | Arista 8666 |

HONEYDRIPPERS, The
All-star rock band: Robert Plant (vocals), Jimmy Page (guitar), Jeff Beck (guitar), and Nile Rodgers (bass). Plant and Page are from Led Zeppelin and Rodgers is from Chic.

10/13/84	®	8	18	1 Rockin' At Midnight	25	Volume One	Es Paranza 90220
				#2 R&B hit for Roy Brown in 1949			
10/27/84	®	11	12	2 Sea Of Love	3¹	↓	
				#2 Pop hit for Phil Phillips in 1959			

Billboard				ARTIST	Ⓡ=Mainstream Rock Ⓜ=Modern Rock	Hot Pos	Album Title	Album Label & Number
Debut	Cht	Peak	Wks	Track Title				

HONEYMOON SUITE
Rock band from Toronto, Ontario, Canada: Johnnie Dee (vocals), Dermot Grehan (guitar), Ray Coburn (keyboards), Garry Lalonde (bass) and Dave Betts (drums). Coburn left in 1987; replaced by Rob Preuss.

Debut	Cht	Peak	Wks	Track Title	Hot Pos	Album Title	Label & Number
7/28/84	Ⓡ	7	15	1 New Girl Now	57	Honeymoon Suite	Warner 25098
10/20/84	Ⓡ	47	6	2 Burning In Love	—	↓	
2/22/86	Ⓡ	8	16	3 Feel It Again	34	The Big Prize	Warner 25293
5/10/86	Ⓡ	22	8	4 Bad Attitude	—	↓	
7/19/86	Ⓡ	38	6	5 What Does It Take	52	↓	
4/9/88	Ⓡ	13	11	6 Love Changes Everything	91	Racing After Midnight	Warner 25652

HONKY TOAST
Rock band from New York: Eric Toast (vocals), Richard Croissant (guitar), E.Z. Bake (bass) and Frank Butter (drums).

Debut	Cht	Peak	Wks	Track Title	Hot Pos	Album Title	Label & Number
3/20/99	Ⓡ	29	9	Shakin' And A Bakin'	—	Whatcha Gonna Do Honky?	550 Music 69360

HOOBASTANK   Ⓡ 2000s: #36 ★ Ⓜ 2000s: #26 / All-Time: #54
Hard-rock band from Agoura Hills, California: Doug Robb (vocals; born 1/12/1975), Dan Estrin (guitar; born on 7/9/1976), Markku Lappalainen (bass) and Chris Hesse (drums). Josh Moreau replaced Lappalainen in 2005.

TOP HITS: 1)The Reason   2)Running Away   3)Crawling In The Dark

Debut	Cht	Peak	Wks	Track Title	Hot Pos	Album Title	Label & Number
10/27/01+	Ⓜ	3[1]	36	1 Crawling In The Dark	68	Hoobastank	Island 586435
11/10/01+	Ⓡ	7	27				
4/27/02	Ⓜ	2[5]	28	2 Running Away	44	↓	
5/4/02	Ⓡ	9	26				
10/12/02	Ⓜ	23	12	3 Remember Me	—	↓	
10/12/02	Ⓡ	28	10				
11/1/03	Ⓜ	9	17	4 Out Of Control	—	The Reason	Island 001488
10/25/03+	Ⓡ	16	19				
2/14/04	Ⓜ	❶[1]	26	5 The Reason	2[1]	↓	
2/28/04	Ⓡ	4	26				
7/31/04	Ⓜ	14	12	6 Same Direction	—	↓	
7/3/04	Ⓡ	20	14				
11/20/04	Ⓜ	24	10	7 Disappear	101	↓	
3/4/06	Ⓜ	23	8	8 If I Were You	117	Every Man For Himself	Island 006162
5/13/06	Ⓡ	27	13	9 Inside Of You	—	↓	
6/3/06	Ⓜ	27	11				
11/4/06	Ⓡ	25	14	10 Born To Lead	—	↓	

HOODOO GURUS
Pop-rock band from Sydney, Australia: Dave Faulkner (vocals), Brad Shepherd (guitar), Rick Grossman (bass) and Mark Kingsmill (drums).

Debut	Cht	Peak	Wks	Track Title	Hot Pos	Album Title	Label & Number
7/22/89	Ⓜ	❶[3]	13	1 Come Anytime	—	Magnum Cum Louder	RCA 9781
4/6/91	Ⓜ	3[2]	9	2 Miss Freelove '69	—	Kinky	RCA 3009

HOOKER, John Lee
Born on 8/22/1917 in Clarksdale, Mississippi. Died on 6/21/2001 (age 83). Legendary blues singer/guitarist.

AWARDS: AWARDS: Grammy: Lifetime Achievement 2000 ★ R&R Hall of Fame: 1991

Debut	Cht	Peak	Wks	Track Title	Hot Pos	Album Title	Label & Number
4/11/98	Ⓡ	29	8	Boom Boom	—	Beautiful World	Revolution 24661

BIG HEAD TODD & THE MONSTERS with John Lee Hooker
#60 Pop hit for Hooker in 1962

HOOTERS
Pop-rock band from Philadelphia, Pennsylvania: Eric Bazilian (vocals, guitar), Rob Hyman (vocals, keyboards), John Lilley (guitar), Andy King (bass) and David Uosikkinen (drums). Fran Smith replaced King in early 1989.

Debut	Cht	Peak	Wks	Track Title	Hot Pos	Album Title	Label & Number
5/11/85	Ⓡ	11	13	1 All You Zombies	58	Nervous Night	Columbia 39912
8/3/85	Ⓡ	3[1]	17	2 And We Danced	21	↓	
12/21/85+	Ⓡ	3[1]	12	3 Day By Day	18	↓	
4/19/86	Ⓡ	34	7	4 Where Do The Children Go	38	↓	
				Patty Smyth (backing vocal)			
7/11/87	Ⓡ	3[3]	10	5 Johnny B	61	One Way Home	Columbia 40659
8/22/87	Ⓡ	13	11	6 Satellite	61	↓	
12/26/87+	Ⓡ	47	3	7 Karla With A K	—	↓	
11/11/89	Ⓡ	20	10	8 500 Miles	97	Zig Zag	Columbia 45058
				Peter, Paul & Mary (harmony vocals)			
1/27/90	Ⓡ	37	5	9 Brother, Don't You Walk Away	—	↓	

Debug	Cht	Peak	Wks	ARTIST / Track Title	®=Mainstream Rock Ⓜ=Modern Rock	Hot Pos	Album Title	Album Label & Number

HOOTIE & THE BLOWFISH

Pop-rock band formed in South Carolina: Darius Rucker (vocals; born on 5/13/1966), Mark Bryan (guitar; born on 5/6/1967), Dean Felber (bass; born on 6/9/1967) and Jim Sonefeld (drums; born on 10/20/1964).

AWARD: Grammy: Best New Artist 1995

Debut	Cht	Peak	Wks	Track	Hot Pos	Album	Label
7/30/94	®	4	26	1 Hold My Hand	10	Cracked Rear View	Atlantic 82613
12/24/94+	®	9	26	2 Let Her Cry	9	↓	
5/6/95	Ⓜ	34	6				
6/10/95	®	2²	23	3 Only Wanna Be With You	6	↓	
7/1/95	Ⓜ	22	11				
10/14/95	®	21	8	4 Drowning	—	↓	
1/13/96	®	26	9	5 Time	14	↓	
4/8/95	®	15	12	6 Hey Hey What Can I Do	—	VA: Encomium: A Tribute To Led Zeppelin	Atlantic 82731
				first recorded by **Led Zeppelin** in 1970			
4/20/96	®	6	11	7 Old Man & Me (When I Get To Heaven)	13	Fairweather Johnson	Atlantic 82886
4/27/96	Ⓜ	33	2				
7/20/96	®	29	8	8 Tucker's Town	38	↓	

HORNSBY, Bruce, And The Range

Born on 11/23/1954 in Williamsburg, Virginia. Pop-rock singer/songwriter/pianist. The Range: George Marinelli (guitar), David Mansfield (guitar), Joe Puerta (bass) and John Molo (drums). Puerta was a member of **Ambrosia**. Hornsby later toured as a member of the **Grateful Dead** and The Other Ones.

AWARD: Grammy: Best New Artist 1986

TOP HITS: 1)The Valley Road 2)Across The River 3)Mandolin Rain

Debut	Cht	Peak	Wks	Track	Hot Pos	Album	Label
6/21/86	®	18	11	1 Every Little Kiss	72	The Way It Is	RCA Victor 5904
9/13/86	®	3¹	15	2 The Way It Is	❶¹	↓	
11/29/86+	®	6	13	3 On The Western Skyline	—	↓	
1/24/87	®	2²	11	4 Mandolin Rain	4	↓	
4/30/88	®	❶³	11	5 The Valley Road	5	scenes from the southside	RCA 6686
5/21/88	®	5	17	6 Look Out Any Window	35	↓	
5/28/88	®	11	10	7 Defenders Of The Flag	—	↓	
				Huey Lewis (harmonica)			
6/16/90	®	❶¹	14	8 Across The River	18	A Night On The Town	RCA 2041
				Jerry Garcia (of the **Grateful Dead**; guitar)			
8/4/90	®	4	13	9 A Night On The Town	—	↓	
10/27/90	®	50	1	10 Fire On The Cross	—	↓	
6/1/91	®	33	6	11 Set Me In Motion	—	St: Backdraft	RCA 3141
4/17/93	®	38	5	12 Harbor Lights	—	Harbor Lights	RCA 66114
				BRUCE HORNSBY			

HOT ACTION COP

Hard-rock/hip-hop band formed in Nashville, Tennessee: Rob Werthner (vocals), Tim Flaherty (guitar), Luis Espaillat (bass) and Kory Knipp (drums).

Debut	Cht	Peak	Wks	Track	Hot Pos	Album	Label
4/12/03	Ⓜ	38	1	Fever For The Flava	—	Hot Action Cop	Lava 83554

HOT HOT HEAT

Rock band from Victoria, British Columbia, Canada: Steve Bays (vocals, keyboards), Dante DeCaro (guitar), Dustin Hawthorne (bass) and Paul Hawley (drums).

Debut	Cht	Peak	Wks	Track	Hot Pos	Album	Label
5/10/03	Ⓜ	19	19	1 Bandages	—	Make Up The Breakdown	Sub Pop 70599
10/18/03	Ⓜ	33	5	2 Talk To Me, Dance With Me	—	↓	
3/19/05	Ⓜ	27	11	3 Goodnight Goodnight	102	Elevator	Sire 48988
6/25/05	Ⓜ	23	17	4 Middle Of Nowhere	—	↓	

HOTHOUSE FLOWERS

Folk-rock band from Dublin, Ireland: Liam O'Maonlai (vocals), Fiachna O'Braonain (guitar), Peter O'Toole (bass) and Jerry Fehily (drums).

Debut	Cht	Peak	Wks	Track	Hot Pos	Album	Label
9/10/88	Ⓜ	7	9	1 Don't Go	—	people	London 828101
8/27/88	®	16	10				
10/22/88	Ⓜ	12	13	2 I'm Sorry	—	↓	
11/19/88+	®	23	11				
6/2/90	Ⓜ	2¹	14	3 Give It Up	—	Home	London 828197
6/30/90	®	29	8				
3/20/93	Ⓜ	14	7	4 Thing Of Beauty	—	Songs From The Rain	London 828350
3/27/93	®	32	6				

Debut	Cht	Peak	Wks	ARTIST / Track Title	Hot Pos	Album Title	Album Label & Number

Billboard

ⓡ=Mainstream Rock   ⓜ=Modern Rock

HOTWIRE
Hard-rock band from Newbury Park, California: Russ Martin (vocals, guitar), Gabe Garcia (guitar), Chris Strauser (bass) and Brian Borg (drums).

| 9/13/03 | ⓡ | 40 | 1 | Not Today | — | *The Routine* | RCA 50669 |

HOUSE, A
Rock band from Dublin, Ireland: David Couse (vocals), Fergal Bunbury (guitar), Martin Healy (bass) and Dermot Wylie (drums).

| 12/10/88+ | ⓜ | 9 | 10 | Call Me Blue | — | *On Our Big Fat Merry-Go-Round* | Sire 25821 |

HOUSE OF FREAKS
Rock duo from Richmond, Virginia: singer/guitarist Bryan Harvey and drummer Johnny Hott. Harvey (age 49) and his wife and two daughters were brutally murdered on 1/1/2006.

4/29/89	ⓜ	23	6	1 Sun Gone Down	—	*Tantilla*	Rhino 70846
7/15/89	ⓜ	27	4	2 When The Hammer Came Down	—	↓	
9/28/91	ⓜ	11	8	3 Rocking Chair	—	*Cakewalk*	Giant 24417

HOUSE OF LORDS
Hard-rock band formed in Los Angeles, California: James Christian (vocals), Lanny Cordola (guitar), Gregg Giuffria (keyboards), Chuck Wright (bass) and Ken Mary (drums). Cordola was with **Ozzy Osbourne**. Giuffria and Wright were both with **Giuffria**; Wright was also with **Quiet Riot**. Mary was with **Alice Cooper**. Michael Guy replaced Cordola in 1990.

12/17/88+	ⓡ	43	5	1 I Wanna Be Loved	58	*House Of Lords*	RCA 8530
4/29/89	ⓡ	50	1	2 Love Don't Lie	—	↓	
9/8/90	ⓡ	10	19	3 Can't Find My Way Home	—	*Sahara*	RCA 2170
				written by **Steve Winwood**; first recorded by Blind Faith in 1969			
12/15/90+	ⓡ	20	12	4 Remember My Name	72	↓	

HOUSE OF LOVE, The
Pop-rock band formed in Camberwall, London, England: Guy Chadwick (vocals, guitar), Simon Walker (guitar), Chris Groothuizen (bass) and Pete Evans (drums).

9/10/88	ⓜ	8	10	1 Christine	—	*The House Of Love*	Relativity 8245
3/3/90	ⓜ	2¹	14	2 I Don't Know Why I Love You	—	*The House Of Love*	Fontana 842293
6/29/91	ⓜ	5	11	3 Marble	—	*A Spy In The House Of Love*	Fontana 848671
8/29/92	ⓜ	9	12	4 You Don't Understand	—	*Babe Rainbow*	Fontana 512549

HOWLIN' MAGGIE
Rock band from Columbus, Ohio: Harold "Happy" Chichester (vocals), Andy Harrison (guitar), James Rico (bass) and Jerome Dillon (drums).

| 4/27/96 | ⓡ | 25 | 7 | Alcohol | — | *Honeysuckle Strange* | Columbia 67421 |
| 5/25/96 | ⓜ | 37 | 2 | | | | |

HUFFAMOOSE
Rock band from Philadelphia, Pennsylvania: Craig Elkins (vocals), Kevin Hanson (guitar), Jim Stager (bass) and Erik Johnson (drums).

| 2/14/98 | ⓜ | 34 | 6 | Wait | — | *We've Been Had Again* | Interscope 90076 |

HUGHES/THRALL
Rock duo formed in Los Angeles, California: Glenn Hughes (vocals, bass; of **Deep Purple**) and Pat Thrall (guitar; of **Asia**).

| 11/13/82 | ⓡ | 28 | 2 | The Look In Your Eye | — | *Hughes/Thrall* | Boulevard 38116 |

HUM
Rock band from Champaign, Illinois: Matt Talbott (vocals), Tim Lash (guitar), Jeff Dimpsey (bass) and Bryan St. Pere (drums).

6/3/95	ⓜ	11	16	1 Stars	72ᴬ	*You'd Prefer An Astronaut*	RCA 66577
7/29/95	ⓡ	28	7				
2/14/98	ⓜ	37	3	2 Comin' Home	—	*Downward Is Heavenward*	RCA 67446

HUMAN LEAGUE, The
Electro-pop trio from Sheffield, Yorkshire, England: lead singer/synthesist Philip Oakey, with female vocalists Joanne Catherall and Susanne Sulley. Early members Martyn Ware and Ian Craig Marsh left to form **Heaven 17**.

4/3/82	ⓡ	4	16	1 Don't You Want Me	❶³	*Dare*	A&M 12045
				R&R Hall of Fame			
1/22/83	ⓡ	22	9	2 Mirror Man	30	*Fascination!*	A&M 2501
5/28/83	ⓡ	14	7	3 (Keep Feeling) Fascination	8	↓	
9/29/90	ⓜ	17	7	4 Heart Like A Wheel	32	*Romantic?*	Virgin 5316

HUMAN RADIO
Rock band from Memphis, Tennessee: Ross Rice (vocals), Kye Kennedy (guitar), Peter Hyrka (mandolin), Steve Arnold (bass) and Steve Ebe (drums).

| 6/23/90 | ⓡ | 32 | 7 | Me & Elvis | — | *Human Radio* | Columbia 45432 |

Billboard				ARTIST		Hot		
Debut	Cht	Peak	Wks	Track Title	®=Mainstream Rock ⓜ=Modern Rock	Pos	Album Title	Album Label & Number

HUMBLE PIE
Rock band from England: Steve Marriott (vocals, guitar), Bobby Tench (guitar), Anthony Jones (bass) and Jerry Shirley (drums). **Peter Frampton** was lead vocalist until October 1971. Shirley later joined **Fastway**. Marriott died on 4/20/1991 (age 44). Also see **Classic Rock Tracks** section.

| 5/23/81 | ® | 58 | 2 | Tin Soldier .... | — | | Go For The Throat ....Atco 131 |

HUNGER, The
Industrial-rock band from Houston, Texas: brothers Jeff Wilson (vocals) and Thomas Wilson (keyboards), Stephen Bogle (guitar), Brian Albritton (bass) and Max Schuldberg (drums).

| 5/18/96 | ® | 10 | 26 | Vanishing Cream .... | — | | Devil Thumbs A Ride ....Universal 53000 |

HUNTER, Ian
Born on 6/3/1946 in Shrewsbury, England. Rock singer/songwriter/guitarist. Leader of Mott The Hoople from 1969-74.

9/12/81	®	47	10	1 I Need Your Love	—		Short Back N' Sides ....Chrysalis 1326
7/16/83	®	25	8	2 All Of The Good Ones Are Taken	—		All Of The Good Ones Are Taken ....Columbia 38628
10/7/89	®	24	7	3 American Music	—		Y U I ORTA ....Mercury 838973
				IAN HUNTER & MICK RONSON			

HUNTERS & COLLECTORS
Rock band from Melbourne, Australia: Mark Seymour (vocals, guitar), Barry Palmer (guitar), Jeremy Smith, Michael Waters and Jack Howard (horns), John Archer (bass) and Doug Falconer (drums).

| 9/10/88 | ⓜ | 6 | 12 | 1 Back On The Breadline .... | — | | Fate ....I.R.S. 42110 |
| 5/5/90 | ⓜ | 5 | 11 | 2 When The River Runs Dry .... | — | | Ghost Nation ....Atlantic 82096 |

HURRICANE
Hard-rock band from Los Angeles, California: Kelly Hansen (vocals), Robert Sarzo (guitar), Tony Cavazo (bass) and Jay Schellen (drums). Sarzo is the brother of **Whitesnake**'s Rudy Sarzo. Cavazo is the brother of **Quiet Riot**'s Carlos Cavazo.

| 6/18/88 | ® | 33 | 9 | I'm On To You .... | — | | Over The Edge ....Enigma 73320 |

HURT
Alternative-rock band from Culpepper, Virginia: J. Loren Wince (vocals, guitar), Paul Spatola (guitar), Josh Ansley (bass) and Evan Johns (drums).

2/4/06	®	17	20	1 Rapture	—		Vol. 1 ....Capitol 41137
8/19/06	®	16	20	2 Falls Apart	—		↓
9/1/07+	®	6	31↑	3 Ten Ton Brick	—		Vol. II ....Capitol 94656
11/17/07+	ⓜ	28	13↑				

HYDE, Paul, And The Payola$
Pop-rock band from Canada: Paul Hyde (vocals), Bob Rock (guitar), Lawrence Wilkins (bass) and Chris Taylor (drums). Alex Boynton replaced Wilkins in 1984. Hyde and Rock later recorded as the duo **Rock And Hyde**.

9/11/82	®	22	15	1 Eyes Of A Stranger	—		No Stranger To Danger ....A&M 4908
				PAYOLA$			
6/1/85	®	37	4	2 You're The Only Love	84		Here's The World For Ya ....A&M 5025

HYMAS, Tony — see BECK, Jeff

HYNDE, Chrissie
Born on 9/7/1951 in Akron, Ohio. Female singer/songwriter/guitarist. Moved to England in 1973 and eventually began writing for music magazine *New Musical Express*. Formed **The Pretenders** in 1978. Married to Jim Kerr of **Simple Minds** from 1984-90.

8/17/85	®	40	5	1 I Got You Babe	28		Little Baggariddim ....A&M 5090
				#1 Pop hit for Sonny & Cher in 1965			
9/10/88	ⓜ	4	8	2 Breakfast In Bed	—		UB40 ....A&M 5213
				UB40 with Chrissie Hynde (above 2)			

HYTS
Rock band from San Francisco, California: Pat Little (vocals, guitar), Tommy Thompson (keyboards), Stan Miller (bass) and Roy Garcia (drums).

| 2/11/84 | ® | 48 | 1 | Backstabber .... | — | | Hyts ....Gold Mountain 80002 |

I

ICEHOUSE
Rock band formed in Sydney, Australia: Iva Davies (vocals, guitar), Anthony Smith (keyboards), Keith Welsh (bass) and John Lloyd (drums). Numerous personnel changes through the 1980s, with Davies the only constant. Group name is Australian slang for an insane asylum.

7/11/81	®	51	3	1 We Can Get Together	62		Icehouse ....Chrysalis 1350
8/1/81	®	28	11	2 Icehouse	—		↓
10/16/82	®	31	1	3 Hey' Little Girl	—		Primitive Man ....Chrysalis 1390
5/17/86	®	9	13	4 No Promises	79		Measure For Measure ....Chrysalis 41527
8/30/86	®	19	7	5 Cross The Border	—		↓

Billboard				ARTIST / Track Title	Hot Pos	Album Title	Album Label & Number
Debut	Cht	Peak	Wks	ℝ=Mainstream Rock Ⓜ=Modern Rock			

ICEHOUSE — cont'd

9/26/87	ℝ	10	17	6 Crazy..	14	*Man of Colours* ....Chrysalis 41592	
1/23/88	ℝ	10	14	7 Electric Blue...	7	↓	
				John Oates (of **Hall & Oates**; co-writer, backing vocal)			

ICICLE WORKS
Rock trio from Liverpool, England: Robert Ian McNabb (vocals, guitar), Chris Layhe (bass) and Chris Sharrock (drums).

3/31/84	ℝ	18	12	1 Whisper To A Scream (Birds Fly)	37	*Icicle Works*...................................Arista 8202	
9/10/88	Ⓜ	13	2	2 High Time	—	*Blind* ....Beggars Banquet 8424	

IDOL, Billy   ℝ **All-Time: #86**
Born William Broad on 11/30/1955 in Stanmore, Middlesex, England. Rock singer. Leader of punk group Generation X from 1977-81. Appeared as himself in the 1998 movie *The Wedding Singer*.

TOP HITS: 1)Cradle Of Love 2)To Be A Lover 3)White Wedding

8/28/82	ℝ	31	1	1 Hot In The City	23	*Billy Idol*..................................Chrysalis 41377	
4/2/83	ℝ	4	15	2 White Wedding	36	↓	
11/26/83+	ℝ	9	15	3 Rebel Yell	46	*Rebel Yell*..................................Chrysalis 41450	
5/12/84	ℝ	5	13	4 Eyes Without A Face	4	↓	
8/18/84	ℝ	8	11	5 Flesh For Fantasy	29	↓	
11/24/84	ℝ	24	8	6 Catch My Fall	50	↓	
10/4/86	ℝ	2⁴	14	7 To Be A Lover	6	*Whiplash Smile*.............................Chrysalis 41514	
				#45 Pop hit for William Bell in 1969			
11/15/86+	ℝ	10	16	8 Don't Need A Gun	37	↓	
3/28/87	ℝ	26	8	9 Sweet Sixteen	20	↓	
9/5/87	ℝ	27	7	10 Mony Mony "Live" .... [L]	❶¹	*(single only)* ....Chrysalis 43161	
				#3 Pop hit for Tommy James & The Shondells in 1968			
5/5/90	ℝ	❶²	14	11 Cradle Of Love	2¹	*Charmed Life* ....Chrysalis 21735	
5/5/90	Ⓜ	7	10				
7/28/90	ℝ	18	10	12 L.A. Woman..	52	↓	
				first recorded by **The Doors** in 1971			
11/24/90+	ℝ	35	9	13 Prodigal Blues	—	↓	
6/19/93	ℝ	7	8	14 Shock To The System	105	*Cyberpunk*..................................Chrysalis 26000	
6/19/93	Ⓜ	23	5				
7/23/94	ℝ	38	2	15 Speed..	—	*St: Speed* ....Arista 11018	
2/12/05	ℝ	26	13	16 Scream	—	*Devil's Playground*..........................CS 84735	

ILL NIÑO
Rock band from New Jersey: Cristian Machado (vocals), Arhue Luster (guitar), Jardel Paisante (guitar), Danny Couto (percussion), Lazaro Pina (bass) and Dave Chavarri (drums).

12/29/01+	ℝ	28	10	1 What Comes Around...	—	*Revolution Revolución*.......................Roadrunner 8497	
8/30/03	ℝ	26	16	2 How Can I Live	—	*St: Freddy vs. Jason* ....Roadrunner 618347	
2/14/04	ℝ	36	6	3 This Time's For Real	—	*Confession*...............................Roadrunner 618391	
9/24/05	ℝ	33	9	4 What You Deserve	—	*One Nation Underground* ....Roadrunner 61817	

IMBRUGLIA, Natalie
Born on 2/4/1975 in Sydney, Australia. Female singer/songwriter/actress. Played "Beth Brennan" on the popular Australian TV soap *Neighbours* from 1992-94. Married to Daniel Johns (lead singer of **Silverchair**) from 2003-08.

2/14/98	Ⓜ	12	22	1 Torn	❶¹¹ᴬ	*Left Of The Middle* ....RCA 67634	
7/4/98	Ⓜ	26	8	2 Wishing I Was There	25ᴬ	↓	

I MOTHER EARTH
Rock band from Toronto, Ontario, Canada: Edwin (vocals), Jagori Tanna (guitar), Bruce Gordon (bass) and Christian Tanna (drums).

8/3/96	ℝ	19	10	One More Astronaut	—	*Scenery And Fish* ....Capitol 32919	

IMPERIAL DRAG
Rock band from San Francisco, California: Eric Dover (vocals, guitar; of **Slash's Snakepit**), Roger Manning (keyboards; of **Jellyfish**), Joseph Karnes (bass) and Eric Skadis (drums).

5/25/96	Ⓜ	30	5	Boy Or A Girl...	—	*Imperial Drag* ....Work 67378	

INCUBUS
ℝ 2000s: #15 / All-Time: #89 ★ Ⓜ 2000s: #4 / All-Time: #10

Hard-rock band from Calabasas, California: Brandon Boyd (vocals; born on 2/15/1976), Mike Einziger (guitar; born on 6/21/1976), Chris Kilmore (DJ; born on 1/21/1973), Alex "Dirk Lance" Katunich (bass; born on 8/18/1976) and Jose Pasillas (drums; born on 4/26/1976). Ben Kenny (born on 3/12/1977) replaced Katunich in 2003.

TOP HITS: 1)Drive 2)Megalomaniac 3)Anna-Molly

Debut	Cht	Peak	Wks	Track Title	Hot Pos	Album Title	Album Label & Number
11/13/99+	Ⓜ	3³	42	1 Pardon Me	102	*Make Yourself*	Immortal 63652
12/4/99+	ℝ	7	32				
7/1/00	Ⓜ	2¹	26	2 Stellar	107	↓	
7/15/00	ℝ	17	16				
12/2/00+	Ⓜ	❶⁸	39	3 Drive	9	↓	
12/9/00+	ℝ	8	26				
8/25/01	Ⓜ	2⁶	37	4 Wish You Were Here	60	*Morning View*	Immortal 85227
9/1/01	ℝ	4	28				
12/22/01+	ℝ	9	26	5 Nice To Know You	105	↓	
12/22/01+	Ⓜ	9	23				
5/4/02	Ⓜ	3²	26	6 Warning	104	↓	
5/4/02	ℝ	27	13				
9/7/02	ℝ	31	6	7 Circles	—	↓	
1/3/04	Ⓜ	❶⁶	26	8 Megalomaniac	55	*A Crow Left Of The Murder*...	Immortal 90890
1/3/04	ℝ	2⁶	26				
4/17/04	Ⓜ	3³	26	9 Talk Shows On Mute	116	↓	
5/15/04	ℝ	18	13				
6/11/05	Ⓜ	17	9	10 Make A Move	—	*St: Stealth*	Epic 94475
6/11/05	ℝ	19	9				
10/21/06	Ⓜ	❶⁵	24	11 Anna-Molly	66	*Light Grenades*	Immortal 83852
10/21/06+	ℝ	4	20				
1/27/07	Ⓜ	4	28	12 Dig	94	↓	
2/17/07	ℝ	17	20				
6/30/07	Ⓜ	8	20	13 Oil And Water	—	↓	
7/28/07	ℝ	38	3				

INDIA.ARIE
Born India Arie Simpson on 10/3/1976 in Denver, Colorado; raised in Atlanta, Georgia. Female R&B singer/songwriter/guitarist.

Debut	Cht	Peak	Wks	Track Title	Hot Pos	Album Title	Album Label & Number
10/6/01	ℝ	38	3	Peaceful World	104	*Cuttin' Heads*	Columbia 85098
				JOHN MELLENCAMP Featuring India.Arie			

INDIGENOUS
Native American blues-rock band from Marty, South Dakota: siblings Mato Nanji (vocals, guitar), Horse Nanji (percussion), Pte Nanji (bass) and Wanbdi Nanji (drums).

Debut	Cht	Peak	Wks	Track Title	Hot Pos	Album Title	Album Label & Number
1/2/99	ℝ	22	12	Now That You're Gone	—	*Things We Do*	Pachyderm 0001

INDIGO GIRLS
Folk-rock duo from Decatur, Georgia: singers/songwriters/guitarists Amy Ray (born on 4/12/1964) and Emily Sailers (born on 7/22/1963).

Debut	Cht	Peak	Wks	Track Title	Hot Pos	Album Title	Album Label & Number
6/17/89	Ⓜ	26	1	1 Closer To Fine	52	*Indigo Girls*	Epic 45044
8/5/89	ℝ	48	1				
10/20/90	Ⓜ	12	5	2 Hammer And A Nail	—	*Nomads-Indians-Saints*	Epic 46820
				Mary-Chapin Carpenter (backing vocal)			
5/16/92	Ⓜ	10	10	3 Galileo	89	*Rites Of Passage*	Epic 48865
				Jackson Browne and **David Crosby** (backing vocals)			
9/3/94	Ⓜ	28	5	4 Least Complicated	—	*Swamp Ophelia*	Epic 57621

INDIO
Born Gordon Peterson in Toronto, Ontario, Canada. Singer/songwriter/guitarist.

Debut	Cht	Peak	Wks	Track Title	Hot Pos	Album Title	Album Label & Number
7/8/89	Ⓜ	10	11	Hard Sun	—	*Big Harvest*	A&M 5257
7/29/89	ℝ	34	7				

Debut	Cht	Peak	Wks	ARTIST / Track Title	Hot Pos	Album Title	Album Label & Number

INFORMATION SOCIETY
Techno-dance band formed in Minneapolis, Minnesota: Kurt Harland (vocals), Paul Robb (guitar), Amanda Kramer (keyboards) and James Cassidy (bass). Reduced to a trio in 1990 with departure of Kramer.

Debut	Cht	Peak	Wks	Track Title	Hot Pos	Album Title	Album Label & Number
9/10/88	ⓜ	10	3	1 What's On Your Mind (Pure Energy)	3[1]	Information Society	Tommy Boy 25691
12/17/88	ⓜ	15	8	2 Walking Away	9	↓	

INJECTED
Rock band from Atlanta, Georgia: Danny Grady (vocals, guitar), Jade Lemmons (guitar), Steve Slovisky (bass) and Chris Wojtal (drums).

Debut	Cht	Peak	Wks	Track Title	Hot Pos	Album Title	Album Label & Number
2/2/02	®	19	15	1 Faithless	—	Burn It Black	Island 548878
2/2/02	ⓜ	22	11				
8/3/02	®	32	9	2 Bullet (What Did You Sell Your Soul For?)	—	↓	

INNOCENCE MISSION, The
Rock band from Lancaster, Pennsylvania: Karen Peris (vocals), her husband Don Peris (guitar), with Mike Bitts (bass) and Steve Brown (drums).

Debut	Cht	Peak	Wks	Track Title	Hot Pos	Album Title	Album Label & Number
10/14/89	ⓜ	22	5	1 Black Sheep Wall	—	The Innocence Mission	A&M 5274
9/9/95	ⓜ	33	4	2 Bright As Yellow	117	St: Empire Records	A&M 540384

INSIDERS
Rock band from Chicago, Illinois: John Siegle (vocals), Jay O'Rourke (guitar), Gary Yerkins (guitar), Jim DeMonte (bass) and Ed Breckenfeld (drums).

Debut	Cht	Peak	Wks	Track Title	Hot Pos	Album Title	Album Label & Number
8/15/87	®	8	10	Ghost On The Beach	—	Ghost On The Beach	Epic 40630

INSPIRAL CARPETS
Post-punk band from Manchester, England: Tom Hingley (vocals), Graham Lambert (guitar), Clint Boon (keyboards), Martyn Walsh (bass) and Craig Gill (drums).

Debut	Cht	Peak	Wks	Track Title	Hot Pos	Album Title	Album Label & Number
11/17/90	ⓜ	27	4	1 Commercial Rain	—	Life	Mute 60987
2/2/91	ⓜ	22	4	2 This Is How It Feels	—	↓	
5/25/91	ⓜ	15	7	3 Caravan	—	The Beast Inside	Mute 61089
12/5/92+	ⓜ	8	13	4 Two Worlds Collide	—	Revenge Of The Goldfish	Mute 61397

INSTITUTE
Band is actually a project by former **Bush** lead singer **Gavin Rossdale**. Includes guitarist Chris Traynor (of **Helmet**) and bassist Cache Tolman.

Debut	Cht	Peak	Wks	Track Title	Hot Pos	Album Title	Album Label & Number
8/27/05	®	26	14	Bullet-Proof Skin	—	Distort Yourself	Interscope 004968
8/27/05	ⓜ	26	11				

INSTRUCTION
Hard-rock band from New York: Arty Shepherd (vocals), Tom Capone (guitar), Adam Marino (bass) and Ti Krek (drums).

Debut	Cht	Peak	Wks	Track Title	Hot Pos	Album Title	Album Label & Number
10/9/04	®	34	12	Breakdown	—	God Doesn't Care	Geffen 002948

INTANGIBLE
Rock band from Los Angeles, California: Justin Wright (vocals), Bruce Watson (guitar), Kevin McCormick (bass) and Sergio Gonzalez (drums).

Debut	Cht	Peak	Wks	Track Title	Hot Pos	Album Title	Album Label & Number
6/4/05	®	37	5	Those Around You	—	Elevate	Larkio 23752

INTERPOL
Rock band from Manhattan, New York: Dan Kessler (vocals, guitar), Paul Banks (guitar), Carlos Dengler (bass) and Sam Fogarino (drums).

Debut	Cht	Peak	Wks	Track Title	Hot Pos	Album Title	Album Label & Number
9/25/04	ⓜ	15	17	1 Slow Hands	—	Antics	Matador 616
2/5/05	ⓜ	24	15	2 Evil	—	↓	
5/26/07	ⓜ	11	19	3 The Heinrich Maneuver	118	Our Love To Admire	Capitol 76538

INTO ANOTHER
Rock band from New York: Richie Birkenhead (vocals), Peter Moses (guitar), Tony Bono (bass) and Drew Thomas (drums).

Debut	Cht	Peak	Wks	Track Title	Hot Pos	Album Title	Album Label & Number
4/20/96	®	39	2	T.A.I.L.	—	Seemless	Hollywood 62008

IN TUA NUA
Rock band from Dublin, Ireland: Leslie Dowdall (vocals), Martin Clancy (guitar), Jack Dublin (guitar), Lovely Previn (violin), Brian O'Briain (sax), Matt Spalding (bass) and Paul Byrne (drums).

Debut	Cht	Peak	Wks	Track Title	Hot Pos	Album Title	Album Label & Number
9/10/88	ⓜ	17	4	All I Wanted	—	The Long Acre	Virgin 90948

Debut	Cht	Peak	Wks	ARTIST / Track Title	Hot Pos	Album Title	Album Label & Number

R=Mainstream Rock M=Modern Rock

INXS

R 1980s: #31 / All-Time: #38 ★ M 1990s: #17 / All-Time: #44

Rock band from Sydney, Australia: Michael Hutchence (vocals; born on 1/22/1960; committed suicide on 11/22/1997, age 37), Kirk Pengilly (guitar, saxophone; born on 7/4/1958), Garry Beers (bass, born on 6/22/1957) and brothers Tim Farris (guitar; born on 8/16/1957), Andy Farris (keyboards, guitar; born on 3/27/1959) and Jon Farris (drums; born on 8/10/1961). Hutchence starred in the movies *Dogs In Space* and *Frankenstein Unbound*; formed the group **Max Q**. Jon Farriss married actress Leslie Bega (TV's *Head Of The Class*) on 2/14/1992. Canadian Jason Dean "J.D. Fortune" Bennison became new lead singer in 2005 after winning the reality TV series *Rock Star: INXS*.

TOP HITS: 1)Suicide Blonde 2)Not Enough Time 3)The One Thing 4)Devil Inside 5)Heaven Sent

Debut	Cht	Peak	Wks	Track Title	Hot Pos	Album Title	Album Label & Number
3/19/83	R	2¹	20	1 The One Thing	30	Shabooh Shoobah	Atco 90072
6/11/83	R	17	12	2 Don't Change	80	↓	
3/31/84	R	43	10	3 Original Sin	58	The Swing	Atco 90160
				Daryl Hall (backing vocal)			
7/28/84	R	41	6	4 I Send A Message	77	↓	
10/19/85	R	11	14	5 This Time	81	Listen Like Thieves	Atlantic 81277
1/25/86	R	3³	15	6 What You Need	5	↓	
4/26/86	R	12	11	7 Listen Like Thieves	54	↓	
8/16/86	R	24	7	8 Kiss The Dirt (Falling Down The Mountain)	—	↓	
6/20/87	R	3¹	12	9 Good Times	47	St: The Lost Boys	Atlantic 81767
				INXS AND JIMMY BARNES			
10/24/87	R	12	15	10 Need You Tonight	❶¹	Kick	Atlantic 81796
12/26/87+	R	2¹	17	11 Devil Inside	2²	↓	
3/19/88	R	8	14	12 New Sensation	3¹	↓	
6/18/88	R	33	6	13 Kick	—	↓	
8/13/88	R	5	14	14 Never Tear Us Apart	7	↓	
9/10/88	M	28	1				
12/17/88+	R	17	13	15 Mystify	—	↓	
9/8/90	R	❶⁴	10	16 Suicide Blonde	9	X	Atlantic 82140
9/8/90	M	❶¹	10				
11/3/90+	R	6	17	17 Disappear	8	↓	
11/3/90	M	10	14				
2/2/91	R	4	15	18 Bitter Tears	46	↓	
2/2/91	M	6	9				
11/9/91	M	4	10	19 Shining Star	—	Live Baby Live	Atlantic 82294
11/9/91	R	14	6				
7/11/92	M	2¹	6	20 Heaven Sent	—	Welcome To Wherever You Are	Atlantic 82394
7/11/92	R	4	8				
8/15/92	M	2⁵	12	21 Not Enough Time	28	↓	
8/22/92	R	13	11				
11/7/92	M	5	10	22 Taste It	101	↓	
1/16/93	M	10	10	23 Beautiful Girl	46	↓	
10/16/93	M	6	7	24 The Gift	—	Full Moon, Dirty Hearts	Atlantic 82541
12/11/93	M	25	2	25 Time	—	↓	
3/29/97	M	13	12	26 Elegantly Wasted	27[A]	Elegantly Wasted	Mercury 534531
4/19/97	R	37	3				

IOMMI

Born Tony Iommi on 2/19/1948 in Birmingham, England. Hard-rock guitarist. Member of **Black Sabbath**.

Debut	Cht	Peak	Wks	Track Title	Hot Pos	Album Title	Album Label & Number
10/7/00	R	10	18	Goodbye Lament	—	Iommi	Divine 57857
				IOMMI Featuring Dave Grohl			

IRIS, Donnie

Born Dominic Ierace on 2/28/1943 in Beaver Falls, Pennsylvania. Rock singer/songwriter/guitarist. Former member of The Jaggerz.

Debut	Cht	Peak	Wks	Track Title	Hot Pos	Album Title	Album Label & Number
3/21/81	R	19	6	1 Ah! Leah!	29	Back On The Streets	MCA 3272
4/4/81	R	47	1	2 I Can't Hear You	—	↓	
9/19/81	R	31	13	3 Sweet Merilee	80	King Cool	MCA 5237
12/12/81+	R	9	18	4 Love Is Like A Rock	37	↓	
10/23/82	R	39	5	5 The High And The Mighty	—	The High And The Mighty	MCA 5358
11/6/82	R	26	6	6 Tough World	57	↓	
7/9/83	R	20	10	7 Do You Compute?	64	Fortune 410	MCA 5427
2/9/85	R	28	9	8 Injured In The Game Of Love	91	No Muss...No Fuss	HME 39949

Billboard				ARTIST	R=Mainstream Rock M=Modern Rock	Hot Pos	Album Title	Album Label & Number
Debut	Cht	Peak	Wks	Track Title				

IRON MAIDEN
Hard-rock band formed in London, England: Paul Di'anno (vocals), Dave Murray (guitar), Adrian Smith (guitar), Steve Harris (bass) and Clive Burr (drums). **Bruce Dickinson** replaced Di'anno in early 1982. Nick McBrain replaced Burr in early 1983. Blaze Bayley replaced Dickinson in September 1993. Janick Gers replaced Smith in 1994. Dickinson returned to replace Bayley in 1999; Adrian Smith returned that same year.

Debut	Cht	Peak	Wks	Track Title	Hot Pos	Album Title	Album Label & Number
7/18/81	R	31	5	1 Wrathchild	—	Killers	Harvest 12141
4/17/82	R	50	2	2 Hallowed Be Thy Name	—	The Number Of The Beast	Harvest 12202
6/18/83	R	8	12	3 Flight Of Icarus	—	Piece Of Mind	Capitol 12274
7/30/83	R	28	6	4 The Trooper	—	↓	
9/22/84	R	25	6	5 2 Minutes To Midnight	—	Powerslave	Capitol 12321
5/14/88	R	47	3	6 Can I Play With Madness	—	Seventh Son Of A Seventh Son	Capitol 90258
6/10/00	R	19	13	7 The Wicker Man	—	Brave New World	Portrait 62208

ISAAK, Chris
Born on 6/26/1956 in Stockton, California. Singer/songwriter/guitarist/actor. Acted in several movies; starred in own TV show.

Debut	Cht	Peak	Wks	Track Title	Hot Pos	Album Title	Album Label & Number
7/8/89	M	18	7	1 Don't Make Me Dream About You	—	Heart Shaped World	Reprise 25837
4/20/91	R	39	6				
1/5/91	M	2[1]	11	2 Wicked Game	6	↓	
1/26/91	R	10	12				
4/24/93	M	7	8	3 Can't Do A Thing (To Stop Me)	105	San Francisco Days	Reprise 45116
7/22/95	M	34	2	4 Somebody's Crying	45	Forever Blue	Reprise 45845
12/23/95+	M	32	6	5 Go Walking Down There	102	↓	

ISLE OF Q
Rock band from Philadelphia, Pennsylvania: David Ringler (vocals), Doug Kennedy (guitar), Beau Bodine (bass) and Josh Cedar (drums).

Debut	Cht	Peak	Wks	Track Title	Hot Pos	Album Title	Album Label & Number
8/5/00	R	29	8	1 Little Scene	—	Isle Of Q	Universal 157885
12/9/00+	R	29	10	2 Bag Of Tricks	—	↓	

ISLEY, Ernie
Born on 3/7/1952 in Cincinnati, Ohio. R&B singer/guitarist. Member of The Isley Brothers and Isley, Jasper, Isley.

Debut	Cht	Peak	Wks	Track Title	Hot Pos	Album Title	Album Label & Number
6/9/90	R	31	6	Back To Square One	—	High Wire	Elektra 60902

J

JACK RUBIES, The
Pop band from London, England: Ian Wright (vocals), SD Ineson (guitar), Steve Brockway (bass), Lawrence Giltnane (percussion) and Peter Maxted (drums). Named after the man who shot Lee Harvey Oswald, the assassin of President John F. Kennedy.

Debut	Cht	Peak	Wks	Track Title	Hot Pos	Album Title	Album Label & Number
11/26/88	M	18	8	Be With You	—	Fascinatin' Vacation	TVT 2560

JACKSON, Joe
Born on 8/11/1955 in Burton-on-Trent, England. Eclectic pop-rock singer/songwriter/pianist. Also see **Classic Rock Tracks** section.

Debut	Cht	Peak	Wks	Track Title	Hot Pos	Album Title	Album Label & Number
9/25/82	R	7	18	1 Steppin' Out	6	Night And Day	A&M 17201
3/31/84	R	12	14	2 You Can't Get What You Want (Till You Know What You Want)	15	Body And Soul	A&M 5000
4/12/86	R	11	11	3 Right And Wrong [L]	—	Big World	A&M 6021
4/29/89	M	4	9	4 Nineteen Forever	—	Blaze Of Glory	A&M 5249
4/22/89	R	16	8				
5/4/91	M	2[3]	10	5 Obvious Song	—	Laughter & Lust	Virgin 91628
5/4/91	R	28	6				
7/13/91	M	20	2	6 Oh Well	—	↓	
6/15/91	R	25	7	#55 Pop hit for **Fleetwood Mac** in 1970			

JACKSON, Michael
Born on 8/29/1958 in Gary, Indiana. R&B-pop singer/songwriter/dancer. Lead singer of **The Jacksons**. Played "The Scarecrow" in the 1978 movie musical The Wiz. Married to Elvis Presley's daughter, Lisa Marie, from 1994-96.
AWARDS: Grammy: Legend 1993 ★ R&R Hall of Fame: 2001

Debut	Cht	Peak	Wks	Track Title	Hot Pos	Album Title	Album Label & Number
4/30/83	R	14	5	1 Beat It	❶[3]	Thriller	Epic 38112
				Grammys: Record of the Year / Rock Male Vocal ★ R&R Hall of Fame ★ RS500 #337 Eddie **Van Halen** (lead guitar)			
2/4/84	R	42	2	2 Thriller	4	↓	
				Vincent Price (rap)			
10/29/83	R	24	12	3 Say Say Say	❶[6]	Pipes Of Peace	Columbia 39149
				PAUL McCARTNEY AND MICHAEL JACKSON			

Debug	Cht	Peak	Wks	ARTIST / Track Title	Hot Pos	Album Title	Album Label & Number

JACKSONS, The
R&B group of brothers from Gary, Indiana: Jackie, Tito, Jermaine, Marlon, Randy and lead singer **Michael Jackson**. Known as The Jackson 5 from 1968-75.

AWARD: R&R Hall of Fame: 1997

Debut	Cht	Peak	Wks	Track	Hot Pos	Album	Label
7/14/84	ℝ	42	2	State Of Shock .... Mick Jagger (guest vocal)	3³	Victory	Epic 38946

JACKYL
Hard-rock band from Atlanta, Georgia: **Jesse James Dupree** (vocals), Jimmy Stiff (guitar), Jeff Worley (guitar), Tom Bettini (bass) and Chris Worley (drums). Stiff left in 2001. Roman Glick replaced Bettini in 2001.

TOP HITS: Push Comes To Shove 2)Down On Me 3)When Will It Rain

Debut	Cht	Peak	Wks	# Track	Hot Pos	Album	Label
9/19/92	ℝ	32	3	1 I Stand Alone	—	Jackyl	Geffen 24489
11/14/92	ℝ	24	11	2 The Lumberjack	—	↓	
2/13/93	ℝ	10	20	3 Down On Me	—	↓	
5/29/93	ℝ	11	18	4 When Will It Rain	—	↓	
9/4/93	ℝ	35	5	5 Dirty Little Mind	—	↓	
7/30/94	ℝ	7	14	6 Push Comes To Shove		Push Comes To Shove	Geffen 24710
11/12/94	ℝ	35	4	7 Headed For Destruction	—	↓	
7/19/97	ℝ	15	11	8 Locked & Loaded	—	Cut The Crap	Epic 67948
10/10/98	ℝ	31	7	9 We're An American Band	—	Choice Cuts	Geffen 25302
				#1 Pop hit for Grand Funk in 1973			
11/16/02	ℝ	39	5	10 Kill The Sunshine	—	Relentless	Humidity 136

JAGGER, Mick
Born Michael Jagger on 7/26/1943 in Dartford, Kent, England. Lead singer of **The Rolling Stones**. Appeared in the movies *Ned Kelly* and *Freejack*. Married to model Bianca Jagger from 1971-80. Married to actress/model Jerry Hall from 1990-99. Also see "State Of Shock" by **The Jacksons**.

TOP HITS: 1)Just Another Night 2)Don't Tear Me Up 3)Dancing In The Street

Debut	Cht	Peak	Wks	# Track	Hot Pos	Album	Label
2/9/85	ℝ	❶²	13	1 Just Another Night	12	She's The Boss	Columbia 39940
3/9/85	ℝ	9	12	2 Lonely At The Top .... Pete Townshend (guitar)	—	↓	
4/27/85	ℝ	5	12	3 Lucky In Love .... Jeff Beck (guitar, above 3)	38	↓	
8/31/85	ℝ	3²	9	4 Dancing In The Street .... MICK JAGGER & DAVID BOWIE #2 Pop hit for Martha & The Vandellas in 1964	7	(single only)	EMI America 8288
6/28/86	ℝ	14	10	5 Ruthless People	51	St: Ruthless People	Epic 40398
9/12/87	ℝ	7	6	6 Let's Work	39	Primitive Cool	Columbia 40919
9/26/87	ℝ	7	11	7 Throwaway	67	↓	
12/5/87	ℝ	39	1	8 Say You Will	—	↓	
1/30/93	ℝ	❶¹	18	9 Don't Tear Me Up	—	Wandering Spirit	Atlantic 82436
1/30/93	ℝ	34	2	10 Sweet Thing	84	↓	
3/13/93	ℝ	3¹	15	11 Wired All Night	—	↓	
10/27/01	ℝ	24	16	12 God Gave Me Everything	—	Goddess In The Doorway	Virgin 11288

JAM, The
Punk-rock trio from England: **Paul Weller** (vocals, bass), Bruce Foxton (guitar) and Rick Buckler (drums). Disbanded in 1982. Weller formed **The Style Council**.

Debut	Cht	Peak	Wks	Track	Hot Pos	Album	Label
4/24/82	ℝ	31	9	Town Called Malice	—	The Gift	Polydor 6349

JAMES
Rock band from Manchester, England: Tim Booth (vocals), James Gott (guitar), Mark Hunter (keyboards), Saul Davies (violin), Andy Diagram (trumpet), Jim Glennie (bass) and David Baynton-Power (drums).

Debut	Cht	Peak	Wks	# Track	Hot Pos	Album	Label
8/3/91	Ⓜ	9	9	1 Sit Down	—	James	Fontana 848658
3/7/92	Ⓜ	5	15	2 Born Of Frustration	—	Seven	Fontana 510932
10/16/93	Ⓜ	3³	28	3 Laid	61	Laid	Fontana 514943
5/21/94	Ⓜ	19	10	4 Say Something	105	↓	

JAMES, Colin
Born Colin Munn on 8/17/1964 in Regina, Saskatchewan, Canada. Singer/songwriter/guitarist.

Debut	Cht	Peak	Wks	# Track	Hot Pos	Album	Label
9/3/88	ℝ	30	7	1 Voodoo Thing	—	Colin James	Virgin 90931
6/30/90	ℝ	7	14	2 Just Came Back	—	Sudden Stop	Virgin 91376
10/20/90	ℝ	21	11	3 Keep On Loving Me Baby	—	↓	

JAMES, Melvin
Born in Des Moines, Iowa. Rock singer/songwriter/guitarist.

Debut	Cht	Peak	Wks	Track	Hot Pos	Album	Label
8/29/87	ℝ	17	10	Why Won't You Stay (Come In, Come Out Of The Rain)	—	The Passenger	MCA 5663

				ARTIST			
Billboard	Cht	Peak	Wks	Track Title	ℝ=Mainstream Rock ⓂModern Rock	Hot Pos	Album Title	Album Label & Number
Debut							

JAMES, Vinnie
Born in Newark, New Jersey. Black rock singer/songwriter/guitarist.

| 4/27/91 | ℝ | 13 | 10 | Black Money .... | — | *All American Boy* ....RCA 2387 |

JAMIROQUAI
Interracial alternative-dance band led by singer/songwriter Jason Kay (born on 12/30/1969 in Stretford, Manchester, England).

| 5/10/97 | Ⓜ | 38 | 4 | Virtual Insanity .... | — | *Traveling Without Moving* ....Work 67903 |

JANE'S ADDICTION   Ⓜ All-Time: #59
Alternative-rock band from Los Angeles, California: **Perry Farrell** (vocals), **Dave Navarro** (guitar), Eric Avery (bass) and Stephen Perkins (drums). Farrell and Perkins later formed **Porno For Pyros**. Navarro later joined **Red Hot Chili Peppers**; married to actress Carmen Electra from 2003-07. Farrell formed **Satellite Party** in 2007.

10/8/88	Ⓜ	6	7	1 Jane Says	—	*Nothing's Shocking* ....Warner 25727
				also see #7 below		
8/11/90	Ⓜ	❶²	9	2 Stop!	—	*Ritual de lo Habitual* ....Warner 25993
9/29/90	Ⓜ	❶⁴	17	3 Been Caught Stealing	—	↓
10/20/90	ℝ	29	17	R&R Hall of Fame		
1/26/91	Ⓜ	15	6	4 Classic Girl	—	↓
5/25/91	Ⓜ	13	6	5 Ripple	—	*VA: Deadicated* ....Arista 8669
				first recorded by the **Grateful Dead** in 1970		
11/8/97	Ⓜ	22	6	6 So What!	—	*Kettle Whistle* ....Warner 46752
12/6/97	ℝ	37	1			
12/13/97+	Ⓜ	25	18	7 Jane Says .... [L-R]	—	↓
1/24/98	ℝ	37	2	live version of #1 above		
6/14/03	Ⓜ	❶¹	19	8 Just Because	72	*Strays* ....Capitol 90186
6/14/03	ℝ	4	19			
10/18/03	Ⓜ	30	5	9 True Nature	—	↓
10/18/03	ℝ	35	5			

JANUS STARK
Rock trio from England: Graham "Gizz" Butt (vocals, guitar), Swapan "Shop" Nandi (bass) and Andrew "Pinch" Pinching (drums).

| 12/5/98 | ℝ | 32 | 8 | Every Little Thing Counts .... | — | *Great Adventure Cigar* ....Trauma 74008 |

JARS OF CLAY
Christian alternative-pop band formed in Illinois: Dan Haseltine (vocals), Steve Mason (guitar), Matt Odmark (guitar) and Charlie Lowell (keyboards).

3/2/96	Ⓜ	12	17	1 Flood	37	*Jars Of Clay* ....Essential 5573
5/11/96	ℝ	16	14			
10/25/97	Ⓜ	38	2	2 Crazy Times	—	*Much Afraid* ....Essential 41612

JASON & THE SCORCHERS
Rock band from Nashville, Tennessee: Jason Ringenberg (vocals), Warner Hodges (guitar), Jeff Johnson (bass) and Perry Baggs (drums).

| 4/20/85 | ℝ | 34 | 4 | 1 White Lies .... | — | *Lost & Found* ....EMI America 17153 |
| 11/29/86+ | ℝ | 16 | 11 | 2 Golden Ball And Chain .... | — | *Still Standing* ....EMI America 17219 |

JAYHAWKS, The
Rock band from Minneapolis, Minnesota: Mark Olson (vocals), Gary Louris (guitar), Marc Perlman (bass) and Ken Callahan (drums).

| 1/9/93 | ℝ | 20 | 10 | Waiting For The Sun .... | — | *Hollywood Town Hall* ....Def American 26829 |
| 12/19/92 | Ⓜ | 29 | 3 | | | |

JEFFERSON AIRPLANE / STARSHIP   ℝ 1980s: #26 / All-Time: #78
Rock band formed as **Jefferson Airplane** in San Francisco, California: **Grace Slick** (female vocals), **Marty Balin** (male vocals, piano), Paul Kantner (vocals, guitar), Jorma Kaukonen (guitar), Jack Casady (bass) and Spencer Dryden (drums). Numerous personnel changes. Group name changed to **Jefferson Starship** in 1974. Lineup in 1981: **Mickey Thomas** (male vocals), Slick (female vocals), Kantner (guitar, vocals), Craig Chaquico (guitar), David Freiberg (keyboards), Pete Sears (bass) and Aynsley Dunbar (drums). Dunbar was replaced by Don Baldwin in August 1982. Kantner (**KBC Band**) and Freiberg left in 1984. Due to legal difficulties, band name shortened to **Starship**. Sears left in late 1986. Slick left in early 1988; Mark Morgan (keyboards) and Brett Bloomfield (bass) joined. In 1989, the original 1966 lineup reunited as Jefferson Airplane with Kenny Aronoff (from **John Cougar Mellencamp**'s band) replacing Dryden. Also see **Classic Rock Tracks** section.

AWARD: R&R Hall of Fame: 1996

TOP HITS: 1)No Way Out 2)We Built This City 3)Find Your Way Back

JEFFERSON STARSHIP:

4/11/81	ℝ	3³	15	1 Find Your Way Back	29	*Modern Times* ....Grunt 3848
5/2/81	ℝ	17	18	2 Stranger	48	↓
6/27/81	ℝ	49	7	3 Save Your Love	104	↓

JEFFERSON AIRPLANE / STARSHIP — cont'd

Debut	Cht	Peak	Wks	#	Track Title	Hot Pos	Album Title	Album Label & Number
10/30/82	®	16	15	4	Can't Find Love	—	Winds Of Change	Grunt 4372
11/6/82	®	18	15	5	Winds Of Change	38	↓	
11/6/82	®	33	4	6	Be My Lady	28	↓	
5/12/84	®	❶[1]	14	7	No Way Out	23	Nuclear Furniture	Grunt 4921
6/16/84	®	6	17	8	Layin' It On The Line	66	↓	
9/1/84	®	50	3	9	Sorry Me, Sorry You	—	↓	

STARSHIP:

Debut	Cht	Peak	Wks	#	Track Title	Hot Pos	Album Title	Album Label & Number
9/7/85	®	❶[1]	13	10	We Built This City	❶[2]	Knee Deep In The Hoopla	Grunt 5488
12/14/85+	®	12	13	11	Sara	❶[1]	↓	
4/26/86	®	25	7	12	Tomorrow Doesn't Matter Tonight	26	↓	
2/7/87	®	16	8	13	Nothing's Gonna Stop Us Now	❶[2]	No Protection	Grunt 6413
6/27/87	®	9	9	14	It's Not Over ('Til It's Over)	9	↓	
12/17/88+	®	30	7	15	Wild Again	73	St: Cocktail	Elektra 60806
8/5/89	®	10	11	16	It's Not Enough	12	Love Among The Cannibals	RCA 9693

JEFFERSON AIRPLANE:

Debut	Cht	Peak	Wks	#	Track Title	Hot Pos	Album Title	Album Label & Number
9/2/89	®	24	6	17	Planes	—	Jefferson Airplane	Epic 45271

JEFFREYS, Garland
Born on 6/29/1943 in Brooklyn, New York. Black rock singer.

Debut	Cht	Peak	Wks	#	Track Title	Hot Pos	Album Title	Album Label & Number
3/21/81	®	5	10	1	96 Tears	66	Escape Artist	Epic 36983
					#1 Pop hit for ? (Question Mark) & The Mysterians in 1966			
3/28/81	®	25	9	2	R.O.C.K.	—	↓	

JELLYFISH
Rock band from San Francisco, California: Andy Sturmer (vocals, drums), Jason Falkner (guitar), and brothers Chris Manning (bass) and Roger Manning (keyboards). Falkner and Chris Manning left by 1993; bassist Tim Smith joined. Roger Manning joined **Imperial Drag**.

Debut	Cht	Peak	Wks	#	Track Title	Hot Pos	Album Title	Album Label & Number
9/1/90	ⓜ	19	7	1	The King Is Half-Undressed	—	Bellybutton	Charisma 91400
12/22/90+	ⓜ	11	10	2	That Is Why	—	↓	
2/20/93	ⓜ	9	9	3	The Ghost At Number One	—	Spilt Milk	Charisma 86459

JEREMIAH FREED
Rock band from Portland, Maine: Joe Smith (vocals), Nick Goodale (guitar), Jake Roche (guitar), Matt Cosby (bass) and Kerry Ryan (drums).

Debut	Cht	Peak	Wks	#	Track Title	Hot Pos	Album Title	Album Label & Number
3/30/02	®	36	6		Again	—	Jeremiah Freed	Republic 017057

JESUS & MARY CHAIN, The
ⓜ **All-Time: #94**

Alternative pop-rock band from Glasgow, Scotland: brothers William Reid and Jim Reid (vocals, guitars), with Douglas Hart (bass) and Murray Dalglish (drums). Numerous personnel changes with the Reid brothers the only constants.

Debut	Cht	Peak	Wks	#	Track Title	Hot Pos	Album Title	Album Label & Number
11/11/89+	ⓜ	❶[2]	11	1	Blues From A Gun	—	Automatic	Warner 26015
1/20/90	ⓜ	2[4]	14	2	Head On	—	↓	
3/10/90	®	45	4					
2/22/92	ⓜ	22	2	3	Sugar Ray	—	St: Freejack	Morgan Creek 20008
4/25/92	ⓜ	3[2]	15	4	Far Gone And Out	—	Honey's Dead	Def American 26830
8/8/92	ⓜ	13	6	5	Almost Gold	—	↓	
8/13/94	ⓜ	4	16	6	Sometimes Always	96	Stoned & Dethroned	American 45573
					Hope Sandoval of **Mazzy Star** (female vocal)			

JESUS JONES
Alternative pop-rock band formed in London, England: Mike Edwards (vocals, guitar), Jerry DeBorg (guitar), Iain Baker (keyboards), Al Jaworski (bass) and Simon Matthews (drums).

Debut	Cht	Peak	Wks	#	Track Title	Hot Pos	Album Title	Album Label & Number
1/19/91	ⓜ	❶[5]	14	1	Right Here, Right Now	2[1]	Doubt	Food 95715
4/6/91	®	7	20					
3/23/91	ⓜ	6	13	2	International Bright Young Thing	—	↓	
8/3/91	ⓜ	26	3	3	Real, Real, Real	4	↓	
1/16/93	ⓜ	❶[6]	11	4	The Devil You Know	—	Perverse	Food 80647
3/27/93	ⓜ	12	8	5	The Right Decision	—	↓	

JET

® 2000s: #39 ★ ◎ 2000s: #39 / All-Time: #83

Hard-rock band from Melbourne, Australia: brothers Nick Cester (guitar) and Chris Cester (drums), with Cameron Muncey (vocals, guitar) and Mark Wilson (bass).

Debut	Cht	Peak	Wks	Track Title	Hot Pos	Album Title	Album Label & Number
9/13/03+	◎	3³	30	1 Are You Gonna Be My Girl	29	Get Born	Elektra 62892
9/27/03+	®	7	28				
2/14/04	®	❶⁸	33	2 **Cold Hard Bitch**	55	↓	
2/21/04	◎	❶³	26				
7/17/04	®	14	12	3 Rollover D.J.	—	↓	
7/17/04	◎	14	11				
10/23/04+	◎	3²	23	4 Look What You've Done	37	↓	
11/6/04	®	33	9				
8/26/06	◎	7	15	5 Put Your Money Where Your Mouth Is	109	Shine On	Atlantic 83806
8/26/06	®	14	17				
12/9/06+	◎	30	10	6 Shine On	—	↓	
12/23/06+	®	22	17	7 Stand Up	—	↓	

JETHRO TULL

Progressive-rock band formed in Blackpool, Lancashire, England: Ian Anderson (vocals, flute), Martin Barre (guitar), Peter Vettese (keyboards), David Pegg (bass) and Gerry Conway (drums). Conway left in 1983. Vettese left in 1986. Doane Perry (drums) joined in 1989. Group named after 18th-century agriculturist/inventor of seed drill.
Also see **Classic Rock Tracks** section.

Debut	Cht	Peak	Wks	Track Title	Hot Pos	Album Title	Album Label & Number
5/8/82	®	20	7	1 Fallen On Hard Times	108	The Broadsword And The Beast	Chrysalis 1380
5/15/82	®	50	4	2 Beastie	—	↓	
10/13/84	®	30	6	3 Lap Of Luxury	—	Under Wraps	Chrysalis 41461
9/26/87	®	10	8	4 Steel Monkey	—	Crest Of A Knave	Chrysalis 41590
10/10/87	®	7	16	5 Farm On The Freeway	—	↓	
12/26/87+	®	12	10	6 Jump Start	—	↓	
6/11/88	®	10	10	7 Part Of The Machine	—	20 Years Of Jethro Tull	Chrysalis 41653
9/9/89	®	6	10	8 **Kissing Willie**	—	Rock Island	Chrysalis 21708
8/31/91	®	14	7	9 This Is Not Love		Catfish Rising	Chrysalis 21863

JETT, Joan, & The Blackhearts

Born Joan Larkin on 9/22/1958 in Philadelphia, Pennsylvania. Rock singer/guitarist. Member of The Runaways from 1975-78. The Blackhearts: Ricky Byrd (guitar), Gary Ryan (bass) and Lee Crystal (drums). Kasim Sulton and Thommy Price replaced Ryan and Crystal in 1987. Jett played "Patti Rasnick" in the 1987 movie *Light Of Day* as the leader of a rock band called **The Barbusters** (see #9 below).

TOP HITS: 1)*I Love Rock 'N Roll* 2)*Crimson And Clover* 3)*Backlash*

Debut	Cht	Peak	Wks	Track Title	Hot Pos	Album Title	Album Label & Number
3/21/81+	®	21	9	1 Do You Wanna Touch Me (Oh Yeah)	20	Bad Reputation	Boardwalk 37065
				first recorded by Gary Glitter in 1972			
4/4/81	®	48	1	2 Bad Reputation	—	↓	
12/12/81+	®	❶⁵	26	3 **I Love Rock 'N Roll**	❶⁷	I Love Rock-N-Roll	Boardwalk 33243
				R&R Hall of Fame ★ RS500 #484			
2/6/82	®	6	23	4 Crimson And Clover	7	↓	
				#1 Pop hit for Tommy James & The Shondells in 1969			
7/17/82	®	24	9	5 Summertime Blues	—	↓	
				#8 Pop hit for Eddie Cochran in 1958			
7/9/83	®	18	10	6 Fake Friends	35	Album	Blackheart 5437
8/6/83	®	30	8	7 The French Song	—		
1/17/87	®	46	4	8 Roadrunner	—	Good Music	Blackheart 40544
2/21/87	®	13	8	9 Light Of Day	33	St: Light Of Day	Blackheart 40654
				THE BARBUSTERS / written by Bruce Springsteen			
5/7/88	®	20	11	10 I Hate Myself For Loving You	8	Up Your Alley	Blackheart 44146
11/5/88	®	13	14	11 Little Liar	19	↓	
1/20/90	®	23	7	12 Dirty Deeds	36	The Hit List	Blackheart 45473
				JOAN JETT			
8/24/91	◎	7	8	13 Backlash	—	Notorious	Blackheart 47488
9/21/91	®	40	4				

JEWEL

Born Jewel Kilcher on 5/23/1974 in Payson, Utah; raised in Homer, Alaska. Singer/songwriter/guitarist. Wrote own book of poetry. Played "Sue Lee Shelley" in the 1999 movie *Ride With The Devil*.

Debut	Cht	Peak	Wks	Track Title	Hot Pos	Album Title	Album Label & Number
5/4/96	◎	14	21	1 Who Will Save Your Soul	11	Pieces Of You	Atlantic 82700
3/15/97	◎	26	10	2 You Were Meant For Me	2²	↓	

JIMMIE'S CHICKEN SHACK

Rock band from Bowie, Maryland: James Davies (vocals), David Dowling (guitar), Che Lemon (bass) and Mike Sipple (drums).

8/23/97	®	20	15	1 High	—		
3/28/98	®	33	8	2 Dropping Anchor	—	Pushing The Salmanilla Envelope	Rocket 540724
9/4/99	ⓜ	12	21	3 Do Right	—	↓ Bring Your Own Stereo	Rocket 546382

JIMMY EAT WORLD

ⓜ 2000s: #18 / All-Time: #41

Rock band from Mesa, Arizona: Jim Adkins (vocals; born on 11/10/1975), Tom Linton (guitar; born on 8/8/1975), Rick Burch (bass; born on 2/4/1975) and Zach Lind (drums; born on 3/19/1976).

7/14/01	ⓜ	18	15	1 Bleed American	—		
11/10/01+	ⓜ	❶4	36	2 The Middle	5	Bleed American	DreamWorks 450334
4/13/02	®	39	3			↓	
6/1/02	ⓜ	2³	26	3 Sweetness	75	↓	
10/26/02+	ⓜ	16	20	4 A Praise Chorus	—	↓	
9/11/04	ⓜ	❶1	29	5 Pain	93		
12/25/04+	ⓜ	6	21	6 Work	110	Futures	Interscope 003358
6/4/05	ⓜ	27	9	7 Futures	—	↓	
9/15/07	ⓜ	3⁴	20	8 Big Casino	122	Chase This Light	Tiny Evil 009924
12/29/07+	ⓜ	14	14↑	9 Always Be	—	↓	

JOEL, Billy

Born William Martin Joel on 5/9/1949 in the Bronx, New York; raised in Hicksville, Long Island, New York. Member of The Hassles in the late 1960s. Involved in a serious motorcycle accident in Long Island in 1982. Married to supermodel Christie Brinkley from 1985-94. Toured and recorded in Russia in 1987. Also see **Classic Rock Tracks** section.

AWARDS: Grammy: Legend 1991 ★ R&R Hall of Fame: 1999 ★ Billboard: Century Award 1994

TOP HITS: 1)We Didn't Start The Fire 2)Pressure 3)I Go To Extremes

10/3/81	®	11	10	1 Say Goodbye To Hollywood [L] recorded at the Milwaukee Arena	17	Songs In The Attic	Columbia 37461
10/2/82	®	8	18	2 Pressure	20		
10/9/82	®	38	2	3 Scandinavian Skies	—	The Nylon Curtain	Columbia 38200
11/13/82	®	27	5	4 A Room Of Our Own	—	↓	
12/18/82	®	28	15	5 Allentown	17	↓	
8/6/83	®	17	13	6 Tell Her About It	❶1	An Innocent Man	Columbia 38837
10/1/83	®	22	8	7 Uptown Girl	3⁵	↓	
7/27/85	®	26	7	8 You're Only Human (Second Wind)	9	Greatest Hits, Volume I & Volume II	Columbia 40121
6/14/86	®	34	5	9 Modern Woman	10	St: Ruthless People	Epic 40398
8/16/86	®	14	12	10 A Matter Of Trust	10	The Bridge	Columbia 40402
12/13/86+	®	32	7	11 This Is The Time	18	↓	
10/31/87	®	45	2	12 Back In The U.S.S.R. [L] recorded in Leningrad, Russia; first recorded by **The Beatles** in 1968	—	Kohu,ept	Columbia 40996
10/14/89	®	6	8	13 We Didn't Start The Fire	❶2	Storm Front	Columbia 44366
12/2/89+	®	18	10	14 That's Not Her Style	77	↓	
1/20/90	®	10	10	15 I Go To Extremes	6	↓	
4/14/90	®	33	8	16 The Downeaster "Alexa"	57	↓	
8/7/93	®	18	6	17 No Man's Land	—	River Of Dreams	Columbia 53003

JOHANSEN, David

Born on 1/9/1950 in Staten Island, New York. Rock singer/actor. Leader of the New York Dolls from 1971-75. Recorded jazz-pop as Buster Poindexter. Acted in several movies.

7/3/82	®	28	12	We Gotta Get Out Of This Place/Don't Bring Me Down/It's My Life [L] medley of hits by **The Animals**: #13 Pop hit in 1965/#12 in 1966/#23 in 1966	—	Live It Up	Blue Sky 38004

Billboard

| | Cht | Peak | Wks | ARTIST / Track Title | ®=Mainstream Rock ⓂModern Rock | Hot Pos | Album Title | Album Label & Number |

Debut	Cht	Peak	Wks	ARTIST / Track Title		Hot Pos	Album Title	Album Label & Number

JOHN, Elton

Born Reginald Kenneth Dwight on 3/25/1947 in Pinner, Middlesex, England. Pop-rock singer/songwriter/pianist. Formed his first group Bluesology. Took the name of Elton John from the first names of Bluesology members Elton Dean and Long John Baldry. Teamed up with lyricist Bernie Taupin beginning in 1969. Formed Rocket Records in 1973. Played the "Pinball Wizard" in the movie version of *Tommy*. Also see **The Bunburys** and **Classic Rock Tracks** section.

AWARDS: Grammy: Legend 1999 ★ R&R Hall of Fame: 1994

TOP HITS: 1)Runaway Train 2)I Don't Wanna Go On With You Like That 3)Ball & Chain

Debut	Cht	Peak	Wks	Track	Hot Pos	Album Title	Label
6/20/81	®	36	4	1 Breaking Down Barriers	—	*The Fox*	Geffen 2002
5/22/82	®	14	4	2 Ball & Chain	—	*Jump Up!*	Geffen 2013
6/4/83	®	34	7	3 I'm Still Standing	12	*Too Low For Zero*	Geffen 4006
1/28/84	®	22	3	4 I Guess That's Why They Call It The Blues	4	↓	
				Stevie Wonder (harmonica solo)			
6/16/84	®	24	9	5 Sad Songs (Say So Much)	5	*Breaking Hearts*	Geffen 24031
7/28/84	®	16	8	6 Restless	—	↓	
9/15/84	®	18	8	7 Who Wears These Shoes?	16	↓	
6/18/88	®	13	11	8 I Don't Wanna Go On With You Like That	2[1]	*Reg Strikes Back*	MCA 6240
8/20/88	®	22	7	9 Goodbye Marlon Brando	—	↓	
10/22/88	®	42	3	10 A Word In Spanish	19	↓	
8/26/89	®	23	8	11 Healing Hands	13	*Sleeping With The Past*	MCA 6321
8/15/92	®	10	7	12 Runaway Train	—	*St: Lethal Weapon 3*	Reprise 26989
				ELTON JOHN & ERIC CLAPTON			

JOHNNY & THE DISTRACTIONS

Rock band from Portland, Oregon: Johnny Koonce (vocals), Mark Spangler (guitar), Gregg Perry (keyboards), Laure Todd (bass) and Kevin Jarvis (drums).

Debut	Cht	Peak	Wks	Track	Hot Pos	Album Title	Label
2/20/82	®	42	4	1 Shoulder Of The Road	—	*Let It Rock*	A&M 4884
3/13/82	®	25	7	2 Complicated Now	—	↓	

JOHNS, Huck

Born in Detroit, Michigan. Male rock singer/songwriter/guitarist.

Debut	Cht	Peak	Wks	Track	Hot Pos	Album Title	Label
3/18/06	®	36	8	Oh Yeah	—	*Huck*	Hideout 48091

JOHNSON, Don

Born on 12/15/1949 in Flatt Creek, Missouri. Actor/singer. Played "Sonny Crockett" on TV's *Miami Vice* and title role on TV's *Nash Bridges*. Starred in several movies. Twice married to and divorced from actress Melanie Griffith.

Debut	Cht	Peak	Wks	Track	Hot Pos	Album Title	Label
8/23/86	®	26	8	Heartbeat	5	*Heartbeat*	Epic 40366

JOHNSON, Eric

Born on 8/17/1954 in Austin, Texas. Rock guitarist.

Debut	Cht	Peak	Wks	Track	Hot Pos	Album Title	Label
4/21/90	®	31	8	1 High Landrons	—	*Ah Via Musicom*	Capitol 90517
8/4/90	®	5	24	2 Cliffs Of Dover [I]	—	↓	
				Grammy: Rock Instrumental			
11/24/90+	®	8	23	3 Righteous [I]	—	↓	
3/16/91	®	7	15	4 Trademark [I]	—	↓	
9/7/96	®	33	7	5 Pavilion	—	*Venus Isle*	Capitol 98331

JOHNSON, Jack

Born on 5/18/1975 in Oahu, Hawaii. Male singer/songwriter/guitarist. Former professional surfer.

Debut	Cht	Peak	Wks	Track	Hot Pos	Album Title	Label
3/9/02	Ⓜ	22	26	1 Flake	73	*Brushfire Fairytales*	Enjoy 860994
11/16/02	Ⓜ	39	4	2 Bubbletoes	—	↓	
4/12/03	Ⓜ	31	10	3 The Horizon Has Been Defeated	—	*On And On*	Moonshine Conspiracy 075012
2/5/05	Ⓜ	25	20	4 Sitting, Waiting, Wishing	66	*In Between Dreams*	Jack Johnson 004149
8/13/05	Ⓜ	29	18	5 Good People	—	↓	
1/14/06	Ⓜ	40	1	6 Breakdown	—	↓	
3/4/06	Ⓜ	25	15	7 Upside Down	—	*St: Curious George*	Brushfire 006116
12/22/07+	Ⓜ	7	15↑	8 If I Had Eyes	47	*Sleep Through The Static*	Brushfire 010580

JOHNSTON, Freedy

Born on 3/7/1961 in Kinsley, Kansas; later based in New York. Male singer/songwriter.

Debut	Cht	Peak	Wks	Track	Hot Pos	Album Title	Label
9/24/94	Ⓜ	28	9	Bad Reputation	54	*This Perfect World*	Elektra 61655

JOHNSTON, Tom

Born on 8/15/1948 in Visalia, California. Lead singer/guitarist of **The Doobie Brothers**. Also see **Classic Rock Tracks** section.

Debut	Cht	Peak	Wks	Track	Hot Pos	Album Title	Label
6/13/81	®	54	4	Madman	—	*Still Feels Good*	Warner 3527

Debut	Cht	Peak	Wks	ARTIST / Track Title	Hot Pos	Album Title	Album Label & Number

🅡=Mainstream Rock 🅜=Modern Rock

JON & VANGELIS
Duo of **Jon Anderson** (lead singer of **Yes**; born on 10/25/1944 in Lancashire, England) and **Vangelis** (born on 3/29/1943 in Valos, Greece).

| 8/22/81 | 🅡 | 33 | 11 | The Friends Of Mr. Cairo | — | The Friends Of Mr. Cairo | Polydor 6326 |

JONES, Danko
Hard-rock trio from Toronto, Ontario, Canada: Danko Jones (vocals, guitar), John Calabrese (bass) and Dan Cornelius (drums).

| 7/2/05 | 🅡 | 36 | 9 | 1 Lovercall | — | We Sweat Blood | Razor & Tie 82928 |
| 5/20/06 | 🅡 | 34 | 6 | 2 First Date | — | Sleep Is The Enemy | Razor & Tie 82955 |

JONES, Freddy, Band — see FREDDY

JONES, Howard
Born John Howard Jones on 2/23/1955 in Southampton, Hampshire, England. Pop singer/songwriter/keyboardist.

3/31/84	🅡	20	14	1 What Is Love?	33	Human's Lib	Elektra 60346
3/31/84	🅡	58	1	2 New Song	27	↓	
4/6/85	🅡	21	13	3 Things Can Only Get Better	5	Dream Into Action	Elektra 60390
7/13/85	🅡	36	8	4 Life In One Day	19	↓	
4/26/86	🅡	20	10	5 No One Is To Blame	4	Action Replay	Elektra 60466
				Phil Collins (drums, backing vocal)			
11/8/86	🅡	46	5	6 You Know I Love You...Don't You?	17	One To One	Elektra 60499
4/1/89	🅜	19	7	7 Everlasting Love	12	Cross That Line	Elektra 60794
4/29/89	🅡	49	1				
7/29/89	🅜	24	5	8 The Prisoner	30	↓	

JONES, Jesus — see JESUS

JONES, Mick
Born on 12/27/1944 in London, England. Rock guitarist. Member of **Foreigner**. Not to be confused with Mick Jones of The Clash.

| 8/12/89 | 🅡 | 16 | 8 | Just Wanna Hold | — | Mick Jones | Atlantic 81991 |
| | | | | written by Jones, **Ian Hunter** and **Mick Jagger** | | | |

JONES, Rickie Lee
Born on 11/8/1954 in Chicago, Illinois. Female singer/songwriter. Also see **Classic Rock Tracks** section.
AWARD: Grammy: Best New Artist 1979

8/8/81	🅡	31	11	1 Woody And Dutch On The Slow Train To Peking	—	Pirates	Warner 3432
8/22/81	🅡	40	8	2 Pirates (So Long Lonely Avenue)	—	↓	
10/21/89	🅜	23	5	3 Satellites	—	Flying Cowboys	Geffen 24246

JONES, Tom
Born Thomas Jones Woodward on 6/7/1940 in Pontypridd, Glamorgan, Wales. Pop singer. Host of own TV musical variety series from 1969-71. Knighted by Queen Elizabeth in 2006.
AWARD: Grammy: Best New Artist 1965

12/10/88	🅜	14	6	Kiss	31	The Best Of The Art Of Noise	China 837367
				THE ART OF NOISE Featuring **Tom Jones**			
				#1 Pop hit for **Prince** in 1986			

JOPLIN, Janis
Born on 1/19/1943 in Port Arthur, Texas. Died of a heroin overdose on 10/4/1970 (age 27). White blues-rock singer. Nicknamed "Pearl." Moved to San Francisco in 1966, joined Big Brother & The Holding Company. Left band to go solo in 1968. Also see **Classic Rock Tracks** section.
AWARDS: Grammy: Lifetime Achievement 2005 ★ R&R Hall of Fame: 1995

| 1/30/82 | 🅡 | 35 | 9 | One Night Stand | — | Farewell Song | Columbia 37569 |
| | | | | recorded on 3/28/1970 | | | |

JOPLIN, Josh, Group
Born in Lancaster, Pennsylvania. Singer/songwriter/guitarist. His group: Deb Davis (guitar), Allen Broyles (keyboards), Geoff Melkonian (bass) and Eric Taylor (drums).

| 2/10/01 | 🅜 | 40 | 2 | Camera One | — | Useful Music | Artemis 751058 |

JORDAN, Sass
Born on 12/23/1962 in Birmingham, England; raised in Montreal, Quebec, Canada. Female rock singer. One of the judges on the TV talent show *Canadian Idol*.

4/25/92	🅡	11	16	1 Make You A Believer	—	Racine	Impact 10524
8/1/92	🅡	12	12	2 You Don't Have To Remind Me	—	↓	
11/21/92	🅡	17	11	3 If You're Gonna Love Me	—	↓	
2/19/94	🅡	6	11	4 High Road Easy	—	Rats	Impact/MCA 10980

Debug	Cht	Peak	Wks	ARTIST / Track Title	R=Mainstream Rock / M=Modern Rock	Hot Pos	Album Title	Album Label & Number

JOURNEY   **R 1980s: #17 / All-Time: #51**

Rock band formed in San Francisco, California: **Steve Perry** (vocals), **Neal Schon** (guitar), Jonathan Cain (keyboards), Ross Valory (bass) and Steve Smith (drums). Schon had been in **Santana**. Cain was with The Babys. In 1986 group pared down to a three-man core: Perry, Schon and Cain. The latter two hooked up with **Bad English** in 1989. Smith, Valory and Rolie joined **The Storm** in 1991. Schon with **Hardline** in 1992. Reunion in 1996 of Perry, Schon, Cain, Valory and Smith. Steve Augeri (of **Tall Stories**) replaced Perry in 1998. Also see **Classic Rock Tracks** section.

TOP HITS: 1)Separate Ways (Worlds Apart) 2)Be Good To Yourself 3)The Party's Over (Hopelessly In Love)
4)Only The Young 5)Ask The Lonely

Debut		Peak	Wks			Hot Pos		
3/21/81	R	2¹	10	1	The Party's Over (Hopelessly In Love)	34	*Captured*	Columbia 37016
3/21/81	R	30	1	2	Dixie Highway .... [L]	—	↓	
8/1/81	R	4	20	3	Who's Crying Now	4	*Escape*	Columbia 37408
8/1/81	R	13	20	4	Stone In Love	—	↓	
8/15/81	R	8	26	5	Don't Stop Believin'	9	↓	
1/16/82	R	35	10	6	Open Arms	2⁶	↓	
7/3/82	R	47	2	7	Still They Ride	19	↓	
8/14/82	R	22	5	8	Only Solutions	—	*St: Tron*	CBS 37782
2/5/83	R	❶⁴	25	9	Separate Ways (Worlds Apart)	8	*Frontiers*	Columbia 38504
2/26/83	R	30	4	10	After The Fall	23	↓	
12/3/83+	R	3¹	12	11	Ask The Lonely	—	*St: Two Of A Kind*	MCA 6127
1/26/85	R	3³	12	12	Only The Young	9	*St: Vision Quest*	Geffen 24063
4/12/86	R	2²	10	13	Be Good To Yourself	9	*Raised On Radio*	Columbia 39936
5/10/86	R	9	18	14	Girl Can't Help It	17	↓	
5/10/86	R	27	5	15	Raised On Radio	—	↓	
6/14/86	R	11	9	16	Suzanne	17	↓	
1/10/87	R	26	6	17	I'll Be Alright Without You	14	↓	
1/2/93	R	32	5	18	Natural Thing	—	*Time3*	Columbia 48937
					recorded in 1979			
10/5/96	R	18	12	19	Message Of Love	—	*Trial By Fire*	Columbia 67514
2/8/97	R	33	5	20	Can't Tame The Lion	—	↓	

JOYDROP

Rock band from Toronto, Ontario, Canada: Tara Slone (vocals), Thomas Payne (guitar), Tom McKay (bass) and Tony Rabalao (drums).

| 7/24/99 | M | 20 | 12 | | Beautiful | — | *Metasexual* | Tommy Boy 1237 |

JUDAS PRIEST

Heavy metal band formed in Birmingham, England: Rob Halford (vocals), K.K. Downing (guitar), Glenn Tipton (guitar), Ian Hill (bass) and Dave Holland (drums). Scott Travis replaced Holland in 1990. Halford later formed **Fight** and **Two**. Tim "Ripper" Owens was lead singer from 1996-2004. Original lineup reunited in 2005. Also see **Classic Rock Tracks** section.

4/18/81	R	10	9	1	Heading Out To The Highway	—	*Point Of Entry*	Columbia 37052
7/31/82	R	4	37	2	You've Got Another Thing Comin'	67	*Screaming For Vengeance*	Columbia 38160
11/13/82	R	38	2	3	Electric Eye	—	↓	
3/3/84	R	42	5	4	Some Heads Are Gonna Roll	—	*Defenders Of The Faith*	Columbia 39219
3/29/86	R	25	9	5	Locked In	—	*Turbo*	Columbia 40158
6/7/86	R	44	4	6	Turbo Lover	—	↓	
4/23/88	R	47	1	7	Johnny B. Goode	—	*St: Johnny Be Good*	Atlantic 81837
					#8 Pop hit for Chuck Berry in 1958			
11/10/90	R	29	8	8	A Touch Of Evil	—	*Painkiller*	Columbia 46891
1/22/05	R	23	10	9	Revolution	—	*Angel Of Retribution*	Epic 93966

JUDE

Born Michael Jude Christodal on 10/16/1967 in Boston, Massachusetts. Male singer/songwriter.

| 3/20/99 | M | 28 | 7 | | Rick James | — | *No One Is Really Beautiful* | Maverick 47087 |

JUDYBATS, The

Rock band formed in Knoxville, Tennessee: Jeff Heiskell (vocals), Johnny Sughrue (guitar), Ed Winters (guitar), Peggy Hambright (keyboards; left in late 1992), Timothy Stutz (bass) and Terry Casper (drums; left in late 1991). Paul Noe replaced Stutz and Dave Jenkins joined in early 1993.

2/23/91	M	9	11	1	Native Son	—	*Native Son*	Sire 26459
2/29/92	M	21	5	2	Saturday	—	*Down In The Shacks Where The Satellite Dishes Grow*	Sire 26801
4/3/93	M	7	9	3	Being Simple	—	*Pain Makes You Beautiful*	Sire 45155

JULES, Gary

Born Gary Jules Aguirre in 1969 in San Diego, California. Alternative-pop singer/songwriter.

2/28/04	M	30	9		Mad World	—	*St: Donnie Darko*	Universal 71802
					MICHAEL ANDREWS Featuring Gary Jules			
					first recorded by **Tears For Fears** *in 1983*			

JUNGKLAS, Rob
Born in Boston, Massachusetts. Rock singer/songwriter/guitarist.

| 5/31/86 | ® | 41 | 4 | 1 Boystown | — | Closer To The Flame...........................Manhattan 53017 |
| 1/31/87 | ® | 41 | 5 | 2 Make It Mean Something | 86 | ↓ |

JUNKYARD
Hard-rock band formed in Los Angeles, California: David Roach (vocals), Chris Gates and Brian Baker (guitars), Clay Anthony (bass) and Pat Muzingo (drums).

| 12/16/89 | ® | 47 | 4 | 1 Simple Man | — | Junkyard ....Geffen 24227 |
| 6/8/91 | ® | 24 | 9 | 2 All The Time In The World | — | Sixes, Sevens & Nines.............................Geffen 24372 |

K

KAISER CHIEFS
Punk-rock band from Leeds, England: Ricky Wilson (vocals), Andrew White (guitar), Nick Baines (keyboards), Simon Rix (bass) and Nick Hodgson (drums).

| 3/19/05 | ⓜ | 34 | 9 | 1 I Predict A Riot | — | Employment ....B-Unique 004215 |
| 2/17/07 | ⓜ | 14 | 16 | 2 Ruby | — | Yours Truly, Angry Mob......................B-Unique 008588 |

KAJAGOOGOO
Pop-synth band formed in Leighton Buzzard, Hertfordshire, England: Christopher "Limahl" Hamill (vocals), Steve Askew (guitar), Stuart Neale (keyboards), Nick Beggs (bass) and Jez Strode (drums).

| 6/4/83 | ® | 23 | 5 | Too Shy | 5 | White Feathers..................................EMI America 17094 |

KANSAS
Pop-rock band from Topeka, Kansas: Steve Walsh (vocals, keyboards), Kerry Livgren (guitar, keyboards), Rich Williams (guitar), Robby Steinhart (violin), Dave Hope (bass) and Phil Ehart (drums). John Elefante replaced Walsh in 1981. Revised lineup in 1986: Walsh, Ehart, Williams, Steve Morse (guitar; of **The Dregs**) and Billy Greer (bass).
Also see **Classic Rock Tracks** section.

5/8/82	®	4	18	1 Play The Game Tonight	17	Vinyl Confessions...............................Kirshner 38002
6/19/82	®	54	2	2 Chasing Shadows	—	↓
7/10/82	®	33	6	3 Right Away	73	↓
8/13/83	®	3[1]	13	4 Fight Fire With Fire	58	Drastic Measures ....CBS Associated 38733
10/22/83	®	34	3	5 Everybody's My Friend	—	↓
9/1/84	®	54	2	6 Perfect Lover	—	The Best Of Kansas ....CBS Associated 39283
11/8/86	®	10	12	7 All I Wanted	19	Power ....MCA 5838
1/24/87	®	38	7	8 Power	84	↓
10/8/88	®	13	8	9 Stand Beside Me	—	In The Spirit Of Things ....MCA 6254

KASABIAN
Rock band from Leicester, England: Tom Meighan (vocals), Sergio Pizzorno (guitar), Chris Edwards (bass) and Chris Karloff (drums). Band named after Manson Family member Linda Kasabian.

| 1/8/05 | ⓜ | 27 | 11 | 1 Club Foot | — | Kasabian ....RCA 66428 |
| 7/9/05 | ⓜ | 32 | 5 | 2 L.S.F. (Lost Souls Forever) | — | ↓ |

KATRINA AND THE WAVES
Pop-rock band formed in London, England: Katrina Leskanich (vocals; born in Topeka, Kansas), Kimberley Rew (guitar), Vince Dela Cruz (bass) and Alex Cooper (drums).

| 4/20/85 | ® | 21 | 9 | Walking On Sunshine | 9 | Katrina And The Waves ....Capitol 12400 |

KATYDIDS
Pop band formed in San Diego, California: Susie Hug (vocals), Adam Seymour (guitar), Dan James (guitar), Dave Hunter (bass) and Shane Young (drums).

| 7/14/90 | ⓜ | 17 | 8 | Heavy Weather Traffic | — | Katydids...Reprise 26146 |

KAY, John — see STEPPENWOLF

KBC BAND
Rock trio of former **Jefferson Airplane** bandmates: Paul Kantner (guitar), **Marty Balin** (vocals) and Jack Casady (bass).

| 10/11/86 | ® | 6 | 13 | 1 It's Not You, It's Not Me | 89 | KBC Band..Arista 8440 |
| 12/13/86+ | ® | 8 | 13 | 2 America | — | ↓ |

KEANE
Alternative-rock trio from Battle, East Sussex, England: Tom Chaplin (vocals), Tim Rice-Oxley (piano) and Richard Hughes (drums).

| 10/23/04 | ⓜ | 32 | 14 | 1 Somewhere Only We Know | 50 | Hopes And Fears............................Interscope 002507 |
| 7/1/06 | ⓜ | 18 | 17 | 2 Is It Any Wonder? | 78 | Under The Iron Sea ....Interscope 006855 |

Billboard Debut	Cht	Peak	Wks	ARTIST / Track Title	Hot Pos	Album Title	Album Label & Number
				KELLY, Paul, and The Messengers Born on 1/12/1955 in Adelaide, Australia. Rock singer/songwriter/guitarist. The Messengers: Steve Connolly (guitar), Peter Bull (keyboards), Jon Schofield (bass) and Michael Barclay (drums).			
8/8/87	Ⓡ	19	8	1 Darling It Hurts	—	*Gossip*..A&M 5157
9/10/88	Ⓜ	16	1	2 Dumb Things	—	*Under The Sun* ....A&M 5207
8/13/88	Ⓡ	49	3			
				KENDRICK, Eddie — see HALL & OATES			
				KERSHAW, Nik Born on 3/1/1958 in Bristol, Somerset, England. Pop-rock singer/songwriter/guitarist.			
5/26/84	Ⓡ	58	4	Wouldn't It Be Good	46	*Human Racing*............................MCA 39020
				KHALEEL Born Robert Khaleel on 6/7/1965 in the Bronx, New York. Male singer/songwriter.			
1/16/99	Ⓜ	36	2	No Mercy	123	*People Watching* ....Hollywood 62110
				KID ROCK Ⓡ **2000s: #29 / All-Time: #100** Born Robert Ritchie on 1/17/1971 in Romeo, Michigan. White hip-hop/rock singer. Married to actress Pamela Anderson from 2006-07. Acted in the movies *Joe Dirt* (2001) and *Biker Boyz* (2003). *TOP HITS: 1)So Hott 2)Cowboy 3)Only God Knows Why*			
12/5/98+	Ⓡ	31	10	1 I Am The Bullgod	—	*Devil Without A Cause*................Lava 83119
4/10/99	Ⓜ	10	26	2 Bawitdaba	104	↓
4/3/99	Ⓡ	11	26			
8/28/99	Ⓜ	5	24	3 Cowboy	82	↓
8/28/99	Ⓡ	10	18			
12/25/99+	Ⓡ	5	26	4 Only God Knows Why	19	↓
12/25/99+	Ⓜ	13	19			
9/2/00	Ⓡ	35	4	5 Wasting Time	—	↓
5/13/00	Ⓡ	20	13	6 American Bad Ass	—	*The History Of Rock* ....Lava 83314
5/20/00	Ⓜ	33	9			
11/3/01	Ⓡ	18	13	7 Forever	—	*Cocky*..Lava 83482
11/10/01	Ⓜ	21	7			
2/2/02	Ⓡ	15	12	8 Lonely Road Of Faith	—	↓
5/25/02	Ⓡ	32	7	9 You Never Met A Motherfucker Quite Like Me......	—	↓
11/8/03	Ⓡ	33	12	10 Feel Like Makin Love	—	*Kid Rock*..Top Dog 83685
				#10 Pop hit for **Bad Company** in 1975			
2/14/04	Ⓡ	14	17	11 Jackson, Mississippi..............................	—	↓
6/26/04	Ⓡ	28	11	12 I Am...	—	↓
8/25/07	Ⓡ	2³	20	13 So Hott	—	*Rock N Roll Jesus* ....Top Dog 290556
9/1/07	Ⓜ	13	14			
12/1/07+	Ⓡ	11	17	14 Amen	—	↓
12/15/07+	Ⓜ	27	10			
				KIHN, Greg, Band Born on 7/10/1950 in Baltimore, Maryland. White pop-rock singer/songwriter/guitarist. His band consisted of Dave Carpender (guitar), Gary Phillips (keyboards), Steve Wright (bass) and Larry Lynch (drums). Greg Douglass replaced Carpender in late 1982. Kihn went solo in late 1984.			
4/11/81	Ⓡ	39	4	1 Sheila...	102	*Rockihnroll*....................................Beserkley 10069
				#1 Pop hit for Tommy Roe in 1962			
4/11/81	Ⓡ	57	1	2 The Girl Most Likely	104	↓
5/2/81	Ⓡ	5	21	3 The Breakup Song (They Don't Write 'Em)........	15	↓
4/10/82	Ⓡ	5	13	4 Testify...	—	*Kihntinued*....................................Beserkley 60101
5/15/82	Ⓡ	30	5	5 Happy Man	62	↓
2/5/83	Ⓡ	5	16	6 Jeopardy	2¹	*Kihnspiracy*..................................Beserkley 60224
5/19/84	Ⓡ	9	10	7 Reunited	101	*Kihntagious*..................................Beserkley 60354
				GREG KIHN:			
3/2/85	Ⓡ	24	7	8 Lucky	30	*Citizen Kihn*..................................EMI America 17152
4/19/86	Ⓡ	50	2	9 Love And Rock And Roll	92	*Love And Rock And Roll* ....EMI America 17180
				Joe Satriani (lead guitar)			
				KIK TRACEE Hard-rock band formed in Los Angeles, California: Stephen Shareaux (vocals), Mike Marquis (guitar), Gregory Hex (guitar), Rob Grad (bass) and Johnny Douglas (drums).			
9/28/91	Ⓡ	47	1	You're So Strange	—	*No Rules* ....RCA 2189

KILLERS, The
Ⓜ 2000s: #25 / All-Time: #51

Alternative-rock band from Las Vegas, Nevada: Brandon Flowers (vocals, keyboards), David Keuning (guitar), Mark Stoermer (bass) and Ronnie Vannucci (drums).

Debut	Cht	Peak	Wks	Track Title	Hot Pos	Album Title · Label
5/29/04	Ⓜ	3²	30	1 Somebody Told Me	51	Hot Fuss .... Island 002468
10/16/04+	Ⓜ	3³	40	2 Mr. Brightside	10	↓
4/2/05	Ⓜ	15	17	3 Smile Like You Mean It	—	↓
7/23/05	Ⓜ	10	20	4 All These Things That I've Done	74	↓
7/29/06	Ⓜ	❶²	29	5 When You Were Young	14	Sam's Town .... Island 007026
9/2/06	Ⓡ	30	16			
11/25/06	Ⓜ	21	9	6 Bones	—	↓
1/20/07	Ⓜ	8	20	7 Read My Mind	62	↓
11/3/07+	Ⓜ	19	20	8 Shadowplay	68	Sawdust .... Island 010226

KILL HANNAH
Rock band from Chicago, Illinois: Mat Devine (vocals), Jonathan Radtke (guitar), Dan Wiese (guitar), Greg Corner (bass) and Elias Mallin (drums).

Debut	Cht	Peak	Wks	Track Title	Hot Pos	Album Title · Label
10/7/06	Ⓜ	35	5	Lips Like Morphine	—	Until There's Nothing Left Of Us .... Atlantic 83972

KILLSWITCH ENGAGE
Hard-rock band from New York: Jesse Leach (vocals), Joel Stroetzel (guitar), Mike D'Antonio (bass) and Adam Dutkiewitz (drums).

Debut	Cht	Peak	Wks	Track Title	Hot Pos	Album Title · Label
9/11/04	Ⓡ	31	25	1 The End Of Heartache	—	The End Of Heartache .... Roadrunner 618373
11/25/06+	Ⓡ	21	20	2 My Curse	—	As Daylight Dies .... Roadrunner 618058
6/30/07	Ⓡ	30	10	3 The Arms Of Sorrow	—	↓
9/22/07	Ⓡ	12	23	4 Holy Diver	—	↓

KILZER, John
Born on 4/10/1963 in Jackson, Tennessee; raised in Memphis, Tennessee. Rock singer/songwriter/guitarist.

Debut	Cht	Peak	Wks	Track Title	Hot Pos	Album Title · Label
5/7/88	Ⓡ	12	12	1 Red Blue Jeans	—	Memory In The Making .... Geffen 24190
8/20/88	Ⓡ	36	5	2 Green, Yellow And Red	—	↓

KIMMEL, Tom
Born Thomas Hobbs in 1953 in Memphis, Tennessee. Rock singer/songwriter.

Debut	Cht	Peak	Wks	Track Title	Hot Pos	Album Title · Label
6/20/87	Ⓡ	17	8	That's Freedom	64	5 To 1 .... Mercury 832248

KIND, The
Rock band from Chicago, Illinois: Frank Capek (vocals, guitar), Frank Jalovec (guitar), Mike Gardner (bass) and Frank Sberno (drums).

Debut	Cht	Peak	Wks	Track Title	Hot Pos	Album Title · Label
2/25/84	Ⓡ	43	3	I've Got You	—	Pain And Pleasure .... Three-Sixty 334

KING, B.B.
Born Riley King on 9/16/1925 in Itta Bena, Mississippi. Legendary blues singer/guitarist. His guitar named "Lucille."

AWARDS: Grammy: Lifetime Achievement 1994 ★ R&R Hall of Fame: 1987

Debut	Cht	Peak	Wks	Track Title	Hot Pos	Album Title · Label
10/22/88+	Ⓡ	2¹	20	1 When Love Comes To Town	68	Rattle And Hum .... Island 91003
11/19/88	Ⓜ	10	13	U2 with B.B. King		
6/17/00	Ⓡ	26	11	2 Riding With The King	—	Riding With The King .... Reprise 47612
				B.B. KING & ERIC CLAPTON first recorded by John Hiatt in 1983		

KING CRIMSON
Progressive-rock band formed in England: Adrian Belew (vocals, guitar), Robert Fripp (guitar), Tony Levin (bass) and Bill Bruford (drums; of Yes). Also see Classic Rock Tracks section.

Debut	Cht	Peak	Wks	Track Title	Hot Pos	Album Title · Label
7/31/82	Ⓡ	57	1	1 Heartbeat	—	Beat .... Warner 23692
4/14/84	Ⓡ	51	3	2 Sleepless	—	Three of a Perfect Pair .... Warner 25071

KINGDOM COME
Hard-rock band formed in Los Angeles, California: Lenny Wolf (vocals; from Hamburg, Germany), Danny Stag (guitar), Rick Steier (guitar), Johnny Frank (bass) and James Kottak (drums). In 1984, Wolf formed and fronted Stone Fury.

Debut	Cht	Peak	Wks	Track Title	Hot Pos	Album Title · Label
2/13/88	Ⓡ	4	12	1 Get It On	69	Kingdom Come .... Polydor 835368
4/9/88	Ⓡ	27	7	2 Living Out Of Touch	—	↓
6/4/88	Ⓡ	26	8	3 What Love Can Be	—	↓
4/22/89	Ⓡ	21	7	4 Do You Like It	—	In Your Face .... Polydor 839192
7/8/89	Ⓡ	37	4	5 Who Do You Love	—	↓

KING MISSILE
Rock band formed in New York: John Hall (vocals), Dave Rick (guitar), Chris Xefos (bass) and Roger Murdock (drums).

Debut	Cht	Peak	Wks	Track Title	Hot Pos	Album Title · Label
1/30/93	Ⓜ	25	5	Detachable Penis	—	Happy Hour .... Atlantic 82459

Billboard

| Debut | Cht | Peak | Wks | ARTIST / Track Title | ⓡ=Mainstream Rock ⓜ=Modern Rock | Hot Pos | Album Title | Album Label & Number |

KINGOFTHEHILL
Rock-funk band from St. Louis, Missouri: Frankie Muriel (vocals), Jimmy Griffin (guitar), George Potsos (bass) and Vito Bono (drums).

Debut	Cht	Peak	Wks	Track	Title	Hot Pos	Album	Label
3/2/91	ⓡ	39	8	1	I Do U	—	Kingofthehill	SBK 95827
8/3/91	ⓡ	37	4	2	If I Say	63	↓	

KINGS OF LEON
Rock band from Nashville, Tennessee: brothers Caleb Followill (vocals, guitar), Jared Followill (bass) and Nathan Followill (drums), with their cousin Matthew Followill (guitar).

3/12/05	ⓜ	23	9		The Bucket	—	Aha Shake Heartbreak	RCA 64544

KINGS OF THE SUN
Hard-rock band from Sydney, Australia: brothers Jeffrey Hoad (vocals) and Clifford Hoad (drums), Glen Morris (guitar) and Anthony Ragg (bass).

4/9/88	ⓡ	19	9	1	Serpentine	—	Kings Of The Sun	RCA 6826
5/5/90	ⓡ	30	10	2	Drop The Gun	—	Full Frontal Attack	RCA 9889

KING SWAMP
Rock band formed in London, England: Walter Wray (vocals), Steve Halliwell (guitar), Dominic Miller (guitar), Dave Allen (bass) and Martin Barker (drums).

5/6/89	ⓡ	21	12		Is This Love?	—	King Swamp	Virgin 91069

KING'S X
Rock trio from Houston, Texas: Douglas Pinnick (vocals, bass), Ty Tabor (guitar) and Jerry Gaskill (drums).

11/10/90+	ⓡ	6	18	1	Its Love	—	Faith Hope Love By King's X	Megaforce 82145
							King's X	Atlantic 82372
3/28/92	ⓡ	17	11	2	Black Flag	—		
1/29/94	ⓡ	20	9	3	Dogman	—	Dogman	Atlantic 82558

KINISON, Sam
Born on 12/8/1953 in Peoria, Illinois. Died in a car crash on 4/10/1992 (age 38). Shock comedian/actor. Acted in the 1986 movie *Back To School* and the TV show *Charlie Hoover*.

11/19/88	ⓡ	18	8		Wild Thing	—	Have You Seen Me Lately?	Warner 25748

#1 Pop hit for The Troggs in 1966

KINKS, The
Rock band formed in London, England: brothers Ray Davies (vocals, guitar) and Dave Davies (guitar, vocals), Ian Gibbons (keyboards), Jim Rodford (bass) and Mick Avory (drums). Also see **Classic Rock Tracks** section.

AWARD: R&R Hall of Fame: 1990

TOP HITS: 1)Destroyer 2)Do It Again 3)Better Things

8/22/81	ⓡ	12	17	1	Better Things	92	Give The People What They Want	Arista 9567
10/3/81	ⓡ	3[1]	16	2	Destroyer	85	↓	
1/15/83	ⓡ	17	17	3	Come Dancing	6	State Of Confusion	Arista 8018
7/9/83	ⓡ	26	10	4	State Of Confusion	—	↓	
10/1/83	ⓡ	16	5	5	Don't Forget To Dance	29	↓	
11/17/84	ⓡ	4	14	6	Do It Again	41	Word Of Mouth	Arista 8264
2/9/85	ⓡ	24	9	7	Living On A Thin Line	—	↓	
12/6/86	ⓡ	37	6	8	Rock 'N' Roll Cities	—	Think Visual	MCA 5822
12/20/86+	ⓡ	16	10	9	Working At The Factory	—	↓	
2/28/87	ⓡ	37	5	10	Lost And Found	—	↓	
1/16/88	ⓡ	14	7	11	The Road	—	The Road	MCA 42107
11/4/89	ⓡ	21	7	12	How Do I Get Close	—	UK Jive	MCA 6337
12/21/91	ⓡ	48	2	13	Did Ya	—	Did Ya	Columbia 74050
4/24/93	ⓡ	19	7	14	Hatred (A Duet)	—	Phobia	Columbia 48724

KISS
Hard-rock band formed in New York: Paul Stanley (vocals, guitar), Gene Simmons (vocals, bass), **Ace Frehley** (guitar) and Peter Criss (drums). Noted for elaborate makeup and highly theatrical stage shows; Simmons was made up as "The Bat Lizard," Stanley as "Star Child," Frehley as "Space Man" and Criss as "The Cat." Criss replaced by Eric Carr in 1981. Frehley replaced by Vinnie Vincent in 1984. Group appeared without makeup for the first time in 1983 on *Lick It Up* album cover. Mark St. John replaced Vincent in 1984. Bruce Kulick replaced St. John in 1985. Carr died of cancer on 11/25/1991 (age 41); replaced by Eric Singer. The original group reunited in 1996. Also see **Classic Rock Tracks** section.

TOP HITS: 1)Psycho Circus 2)Jungle 3)Heaven's On Fire

10/22/83	ⓡ	19	15	1	Lick It Up	66	Lick It Up	Mercury 814297
9/22/84	ⓡ	11	11	2	Heaven's On Fire	49	Animalize	Mercury 822495
9/28/85	ⓡ	20	9	3	Tears Are Falling	51	Asylum	Mercury 826099
9/19/87	ⓡ	37	6	4	Crazy Crazy Nights	65	Crazy Nights	Mercury 832626
11/28/87	ⓡ	34	10	5	Reason To Live	64	↓	
11/4/89	ⓡ	22	11	6	Hide Your Heart	66	Hot In The Shade	Mercury 838913

Debut	Cht	Peak	Wks	ARTIST / Track Title	Hot Pos	Album Title	Album Label & Number
				KISS — cont'd			
2/10/90	®	17	11	7 Forever	8	↓	
6/16/90	®	40	4	8 Rise To It	81	↓	
8/3/91	®	21	8	9 God Gave Rock And Roll To You II	—	St: Bill & Ted's Bogus Journey	Interscope 91725
6/20/92	®	34	5	10 I Just Wanna	—	Revenge	Mercury 848037
8/29/92	®	26	8	11 Domino	—	↓	
5/29/93	®	22	6	12 I Love It Loud [L]	—	Alive III	Mercury 514777
				studio version was a #102 Pop hit in 1983			
3/30/96	®	13	10	13 Rock And Roll All Nite [L]	—	MTV Unplugged	Mercury 528950
				previous live version was a #12 Pop hit in 1976			
10/18/97	®	8	14	14 Jungle	—	Carnival Of Souls - The Final Sessions	Mercury 536323
9/5/98	®	❶¹	21	15 Psycho Circus	—	Psycho Circus	Mercury 558992
12/19/98+	®	22	8	16 You Wanted The Best	—	↓	

KITCHENS OF DISTINCTION
Pop-rock trio formed in London, England: Patrick Fitzgerald (vocals, bass), Julian Swales (guitar) and Dan Goodwin (drums).

Debut	Cht	Peak	Wks	Track Title	Hot Pos	Album Title	Album Label & Number
2/9/91	Ⓜ	12	11	1 Drive That Fast	—	Strange Free World	A&M 5340
4/13/91	Ⓜ	18	5	2 Quick As Rainbows	—	↓	
8/22/92	Ⓜ	15	8	3 Smiling	—	The Death Of Cool	A&M 5402
10/24/92	Ⓜ	28	2	4 4 Men	—	↓	

KITTIE
Female rock band from London, Ontario, Canada: sisters Morgan Lander (vocals, guitar) and Mercedes Lander (drums), with Tara McLeod (guitar) and Trish Doan (bass).

Debut	Cht	Peak	Wks	Track Title	Hot Pos	Album Title	Album Label & Number
4/14/07	®	40	1	Funeral For Yesterday	—	Funeral For Yesterday	X Of Infamy 0001

KIX
Hard-rock band from Hagerstown, Maryland: Steve Whiteman (vocals), Ronnie Younkins (guitar), Brian Forsythe (guitar), Donnie Purnell (bass) and Jimmy Chalfant (drums).

Debut	Cht	Peak	Wks	Track Title	Hot Pos	Album Title	Album Label & Number
10/14/89	®	16	12	1 Don't Close Your Eyes	11	Blow My Fuse	Atlantic 81877
7/20/91	®	26	8	2 Girl Money	—	Hot Wire	EastWest 91714
2/22/92	®	42	5	3 Tear Down The Walls	—	↓	

KLF, The
Dance duo formed in England: Bill Drummond and Jim Cauty. KLF: Kopyright Liberation Front. Previously recorded as **The Timelords**.

Debut	Cht	Peak	Wks	Track Title	Hot Pos	Album Title	Album Label & Number
10/1/88	Ⓜ	17	6	1 Doctorin' The Tardis	66	(single only)	TVT 4025
				THE TIMELORDS			
2/8/92	Ⓜ	21	3	2 Justified & Ancient	11	The White Room	Arista 8657
				THE KLF Featuring Tammy Wynette			

KNACK, The
Rock band formed in Los Angeles, California: Doug Fieger (vocals, guitar), Berton Averre (guitar), Prescott Niles (bass) and Billy Ward (drums). Also see **Classic Rock Tracks** section.

Debut	Cht	Peak	Wks	Track Title	Hot Pos	Album Title	Album Label & Number
1/26/91	®	9	10	Rocket O' Love	—	Serious Fun	Charisma 91607

KOOKS, The
Rock band from Brighton, East Sussex, England: Luke Pritchard (vocals, guitar), Hugh Harris (guitar), Max Rafferty (bass) and Paul Garred (drums).

Debut	Cht	Peak	Wks	Track Title	Hot Pos	Album Title	Album Label & Number
1/27/07	Ⓜ	22	14	1 Naive	—	Inside In / Inside Out	Virgin 50723
8/11/07	Ⓜ	39	1	2 She Moves In Her Own Way	—	↓	

KORN
® **2000s: #6 / All-Time: #34 ★ Ⓜ 2000s: #13 / All-Time: #21**

Hard-rock band formed in Bakersfield, California: Jonathan Davis (vocals; born on 1/18/1971), Brian "Head" Welch (guitar; born on 6/19/1970), James "Munky" Shaffer (guitar; born on 6/6/1970), Reggie "Fieldy" Arvizu (bass; born on 11/2/1969) and David Silveria (drums; born on 9/21/1972). Davis is the half brother of Mark Chavez (of **Adema**). Welch left in 2005. Silveria left in 2006; Davis took over on drums.

TOP HITS: 1)Twisted Transistor 2)Here To Stay 3)Coming Undone 4)Evolution 5)Freak On A Leash

Debut	Cht	Peak	Wks	Track Title	Hot Pos	Album Title	Album Label & Number
8/22/98	®	15	26	1 Got The Life	—	Follow The Leader	Immortal 69001
8/22/98	Ⓜ	17	26				
2/20/99	Ⓜ	6	27	2 Freak On A Leash	106	↓	
2/20/99	®	10	26	also see #18 below			
11/13/99+	Ⓜ	7	24	3 Falling Away From Me	108	Issues	Immortal 63710
11/13/99+	®	7	26				

KORN — cont'd

Debut	Cht	Peak	Wks	Track Title	Hot Pos	Album Title & Label & Number
2/19/00	M	7	26	4 Make Me Bad	114	↓
2/19/00	R	9	26			
7/29/00	R	23	9	5 Somebody Someone	—	↓
7/22/00	M	23	8			
3/30/02	M	4	22	6 Here To Stay	72	Untouchables ....Immortal 61488
3/30/02	R	4	26	Grammy: Metal Performance		
6/29/02	R	6	26	7 Thoughtless	108	↓
7/6/02	M	11	21			
11/9/02	R	19	14	8 Alone I Break	—	↓
11/30/02	M	34	4			
7/12/03	R	12	19	9 Did My Time	38	Take A Look In The Mirror.....................Immortal 90335
7/12/03	M	17	14	featured in the movie Lara Croft Tomb Raider: The Cradle Of Life starring Angelina Jolie		
10/18/03	R	11	19	10 Right Now	119	↓
10/25/03	M	13	16			
1/24/04	R	23	11	11 Y'all Want A Single	—	↓
5/8/04	R	30	7	12 Everything I've Known	—	↓
9/4/04	R	16	12	13 Word Up	123	Greatest Hits Vol. I ....Immortal 92700
9/4/04	M	17	13	#6 Hot 100 hit for Cameo in 1986		
11/13/04	R	12	24	14 Another Brick In The Wall	—	↓
12/25/04	M	37	7	#1 Hot 100 hit for Pink Floyd in 1980		
10/1/05+	R	3³	26	15 Twisted Transistor	64	See You On The Other Side ....Virgin 45889
10/8/05	M	9	24			
3/4/06	R	4	36	16 Coming Undone	79	↓
3/25/06	M	14	22			
9/9/06+	R	18	20	17 Politics	—	↓
2/17/07	R	22	9	18 Freak On A Leash (Unplugged) .... [L]	89	MTV Unplugged...Virgin 86027
2/24/07	M	29	7	KORN Featuring Amy Lee / new version of #2 above		
6/9/07	R	4	20	19 Evolution	107	Untitled...Virgin 03878
6/9/07	M	20	20			
10/13/07+	R	9	23	20 Hold On	—	↓
12/29/07+	M	35	9			

KOTTONMOUTH KINGS

Rap-rock band from Los Angeles, California: Brad "Daddy X" Xavier, Dustin "D-Loc" Miller, Timothy "Johnny Richter" McNutt, Robert "Bobby B" Adams, Lou Dog and Pakelika.

Debut	Cht	Peak	Wks	Track Title	Hot Pos	Album Title & Label & Number
8/21/99	M	28	9	1 Bump	—	Royal Highness ....Capitol 23857
7/8/00	M	37	5	2 Peace Not Greed	—	High Society.................................Suburban Noize 21480

KRAVITZ, Lenny   R 1990s: #29 / All-Time: #82 ★ M 1990s: #25 / All-Time: #40

Born on 5/26/1964 in Brooklyn, New York; raised in Los Angeles, California. Pop-rock singer/songwriter/guitarist. Married to actress Lisa Bonet from 1987-93. Son of actress Roxie Roker (played "Helen Willis" on TV's The Jeffersons).

TOP HITS: 1)Fly Away 2)Are You Gonna Go My Way 3)American Woman

Debut	Cht	Peak	Wks	Track Title	Hot Pos	Album Title & Label & Number
10/28/89	M	5	15	1 Let Love Rule	89	Let Love Rule...Virgin 91290
11/25/89+	R	23	13			
2/24/90	M	25	4	2 I Build This Garden For Us	—	↓
5/12/90	R	50	1	3 Mr. Cab Driver	—	↓
4/6/91	M	8	8	4 Always On The Run	—	Mama Said...Virgin 91610
5/4/91	R	40	4			
3/20/93	R	❶²	28	5 Are You Gonna Go My Way	—	Are You Gonna Go My Way ....Virgin 86984
3/20/93	M	2²	15			
6/5/93	M	10	18	6 Believe	60	↓
7/3/93	R	15	11			
10/9/93	R	19	9	7 Is There Any Love In Your Heart	—	↓

Debut	Cht	Peak	Wks	ARTIST / Track Title	Hot Pos	Album Title	Album Label & Number
				KRAVITZ, Lenny — cont'd			
2/19/94	Ⓡ	37	4	8 Spinning Around Over You	flip	St: Reality Bites	RCA 66364
6/25/94	Ⓡ	15	8	9 Deuce	—	VA: Kiss My Ass: Classic Kiss Regrooved	Mercury 522123
				Stevie Wonder (harmonica); first recorded by **Kiss** in 1974			
9/2/95	Ⓡ	4	10	10 Rock And Roll Is Dead	75	Circus	Virgin 40696
9/2/95	Ⓜ	10	8				
5/16/98	Ⓜ	39	4	11 If You Can't Say No	—	5	Virgin 45605
7/18/98	Ⓡ	❶³	47	12 **Fly Away**	12	↓	
9/5/98	Ⓜ	❶²	32	Grammy: Rock Male Vocal			
5/22/99	Ⓡ	3⁸	26	13 American Woman	49	St: Austin Powers - The Spy Who Shagged Me	Maverick 47348
5/29/99	Ⓜ	7	24	Grammy: Rock Male Vocal #1 Pop hit for The Guess Who in 1970			
10/21/00+	Ⓜ	23	26	14 **Again**	4	Greatest Hits	Virgin 50316
				Grammy: Rock Male Vocal			
9/29/01	Ⓡ	11	19	15 Dig In	31	Lenny	Virgin 11233
9/22/01	Ⓜ	13	13	Grammy: Rock Male Vocal			
3/2/02	Ⓜ	38	2	16 Stillness Of Heart	118	↓	
4/24/04	Ⓡ	30	11	17 Where Are We Runnin'?	69	Baptism	Virgin 84145
5/15/04	Ⓜ	40	3				
11/24/07	Ⓡ	25	13	18 Bring It On	—	It Is Time For A Love Revolution	Virgin 63786
				KROEGER, Chad Born on 11/15/1974 in Hanna, Alberta, Canada. Lead singer of **Nickelback**.			
5/4/02	Ⓜ	❶³	21	**Hero**	3²	St: Spider-Man	Columbia 86402
5/4/02	Ⓡ	❶²	24	CHAD KROEGER Featuring Josey Scott			
				KROKUS Hard-rock band from Zurich, Switzerland: Marc Storace (vocals), Fernando Von Arb and Tommy Kiefer (guitars), Chris Von Rohr (bass) and Freddy Steady (drums). Kiefer was replaced by Mark Kohler in late 1981. Steady was replaced by Steve Pace in late 1982. Pace was replaced by Jeff Klaven in 1984. Von Rohr left in 1984.			
4/4/81	Ⓡ	46	1	1 Burning Bones	—	Hardware	Ariola 1508
4/11/81	Ⓡ	26	6	2 Winning Man	—	↓	
5/1/82	Ⓡ	22	5	3 Long Stick Goes Boom	—	One Vice At A Time	Arista 9591
5/29/82	Ⓡ	53	2	4 American Woman	—	↓	
				#1 Pop hit for The Guess Who in 1970			
5/28/83	Ⓡ	33	1	5 Eat The Rich	—	Headhunter	Arista 9623
6/4/83	Ⓡ	21	12	6 Screaming In The Night	—	↓	
11/19/83	Ⓡ	31	9	7 Stayed Awake All Night	—	↓	
8/18/84	Ⓡ	10	12	8 **Midnite Maniac**	71	The Blitz	Arista 8243
11/17/84+	Ⓡ	22	11	9 Our Love	—	↓	
				K'S CHOICE Rock band from Belgium: Sarah Bettens (vocals), her brother Gert Bettens (vocals, keyboards), Jan Van Sichem (guitar) and Bart Van Der Zeeuw (drums).			
3/29/97	Ⓜ	5	26	1 Not An Addict	56ᴬ	Paradise In Me	550 Music 67720
8/15/98	Ⓜ	28	6	2 Everything For Free	—	Cocoon Crash	550 Music 69366
				KULA SHAKER Rock band from London, England: Crispian Mills (vocals, guitar), Jay Darlington (keyboards), Alonza Bevan (bass) and Paul Winter-Hart (drums). Mills is the son of actress/singer Hayley Mills.			
11/2/96	Ⓜ	10	14	1 Tattva	63ᴬ	K	Columbia 67822
3/1/97	Ⓜ	25	7	2 Hey Dude	—	↓	
10/18/97	Ⓡ	19	14	3 Hush	—	St: I Know What You Did Last Summer	Columbia 68696
				KWELLER, Ben Born on 6/16/1981 in Greenville, Texas. Male singer/songwriter/guitarist.			
7/27/02	Ⓜ	29	7	**Wasted & Ready**	—	Sha Sha	ATO 68114

141

Billboard				ARTIST	Ⓡ=Mainstream Rock	Hot		
Debut	Cht	Peak	Wks	Track Title	Ⓜ=Modern Rock	Pos	Album Title	Album Label & Number

L

LACUNA COIL
Goth-rock band from Milan, Italy: Cristina Scabbia (female vocals), Andrea Ferro (male vocals), Cristiano Migliore (guitar), Marco Zelati (bass) and Cristiano Mozzati (drums).

4/8/06	Ⓡ	36	5	Our Truth	—	*Karma Code* ....Century Media 8360

L.A. GUNS
Hard-rock band from Los Angeles, California: Philip Lewis (vocals), Tracii Guns (guitar), Mick Cripps (guitar), Kelly Nickels (bass), and Steve Riley (drums). Guns was also a member of **Contraband** in 1991.

10/21/89	Ⓡ	47	3	1 Rip And Tear	—	*Cocked & Loaded*......................................Vertigo 838592
4/14/90	Ⓡ	25	12	2 The Ballad Of Jayne	33	↓
7/6/91	Ⓡ	16	11	3 Kiss My Love Goodbye	—	*Hollywood Vampires*...............................Polydor 849485
11/30/91	Ⓡ	48	1	4 Some Lie 4 Love	—	↓
2/22/92	Ⓡ	25	10	5 It's Over Now	62	↓

LAING, Shona
Born in 1955 in New Zealand. Female singer/songwriter/guitarist.

9/10/88	Ⓜ	14	8	(Glad I'm) Not A Kennedy	—	*South* ....TVT 2470

LAJON
Born Lajon Witherspoon on 10/3/1972 in Nashville, Tennessee; raised in Atlanta, Georgia. Black hard-rock singer. Member of **Sevendust**.

11/25/00+	Ⓡ	11	18	Angel's Son	—	*VA: Strait Up* ....Immortal 50365
12/9/00+	Ⓜ	15	13			

LAKE, Greg
Born on 11/10/1948 in Bournemouth, Dorset, England. Rock singer/guitarist. Member of **King Crimson** and **Emerson, Lake & Palmer**.

12/5/81+	Ⓡ	34	8	Nuclear Attack	—	*Greg Lake* ....Chrysalis 1357

LANE, Robin, & The Chartbusters
Born in 1947 in Los Angeles, California; later based in in Boston, Massachusetts. Female rock singer. Daughter of Dean Martin's pianist, Ken Lane. The Chartbusters: Asa Brebner (guitar), Leroy Radcliffe (keyboards), Scott Baerenwald (bass) and Tim Jackson (drums).

5/9/81	Ⓡ	53	1	Send Me An Angel	—	*Imitation Life* ....Warner 3537

LANG, Jonny
Born Jon Langseth on 1/29/1981 in Fargo, North Dakota. White blues-rock singer/guitarist. Nicknamed "Kid."

3/8/97	Ⓡ	12	22	1 Lie To Me	—	*Lie To Me* ....A&M 540640
8/30/97	Ⓡ	28	7	2 Hit The Ground Running	—	↓
10/3/98	Ⓡ	8	26	3 Still Rainin'	—	*Wander This World* ....A&M 540984
3/13/99	Ⓡ	23	12	4 Wander This World	—	↓

LA'S, The
Rock band from Liverpool, England: brothers Lee Mavers (vocals) and Neil Mavers (drums), with Peter Camell (guitar) and John Power (bass). Band name is slang for lads.

4/13/91	Ⓜ	2[1]	13	1 There She Goes	49	*The La's*..London 828202
7/13/91	Ⓜ	12	8	2 Timeless Melody	—	↓

LAUPER, Cyndi
Born on 6/22/1953 in Queens, New York. Pop-rock singer. In the movies *Vibes* and *Life With Mikey*. Married actor David Thornton on 11/24/1991.

AWARD: Grammy: Best New Artist 1984

12/17/83+	Ⓡ	10	18	1 Time After Time	❶[2]	*She's So Unusual* ....Portrait 38930
1/21/84	Ⓡ	16	10	2 Girls Just Want To Have Fun	2[2]	↓
				R&R Hall of Fame		
8/4/84	Ⓡ	27	9	3 She Bop	3[3]	↓
10/20/84	Ⓡ	38	6	4 All Through The Night	5	↓
1/5/85	Ⓡ	37	5	5 Money Changes Everything	27	↓

LAW, The
Rock duo from England: vocalist **Paul Rodgers** (of **Bad Company**) and drummer Kenney Jones (of **The Who**).

3/16/91	Ⓡ	2[1]	16	1 Laying Down The Law	—	*The Law*..Atlantic 82195
6/8/91	Ⓡ	38	7	2 Miss You In A Heartbeat	—	↓
				#39 Pop hit for **Def Leppard** in 1994		

LED ZEPPELIN

Hard-rock band formed in England: **Robert Plant** (vocals; born on 8/20/1948), **Jimmy Page** (guitar; born on 1/9/1944), John Paul Jones (bass, keyboards; born John Baldwin on 1/3/1946) and John "Bonzo" Bonham (drums; born on 5/31/1948; died of asphyxiation on 9/25/1980, age 32). Group formed own Swan Song label in 1974. In concert movie *The Song Remains The Same* in 1976. Group disbanded in December 1980. Plant and Page formed **The Honeydrippers** in 1984. Page also with **The Firm** (1984-86). "**Bonham**" is the name of group formed by Jason Bonham, John's son, in 1989. Also see **Classic Rock Tracks** section.

AWARDS: Grammy: Lifetime Achievement 2005 ★ R&R Hall of Fame: 1995

Debut	Cht	Peak	Wks	Track Title	Hot Pos	Album Title	Album Label & Number
12/11/82	®	4	11	1 Darlene recorded on 11/16/1978	—	Coda	Swan Song 90051
12/11/82	®	14	11	2 Ozone Baby recorded on 11/14/1978	—	↓	
12/18/82	®	18	7	3 Poor Tom recorded on 6/5/1970	—	↓	
10/20/90	®	7	8	4 Travelling Riverside Blues [L] recorded on 6/23/1969	—	Led Zeppelin (Boxed Set)	Atlantic 82144
9/25/93	®	4	7	5 Baby Come On Home recorded on 10/10/1968	—	Boxed Set 2	Atlantic 82477
11/15/97	®	4	22	6 The Girl I Love She Got Long Black Wavy Hair... [L] recorded on 6/16/1969	—	BBC Sessions	Atlantic 83061

LEE, Alvin

Born on 12/19/1944 in Nottingham, England. Rock singer/guitarist. Leader of **Ten Years After**.

Debut	Cht	Peak	Wks	Track Title	Hot Pos	Album Title	Album Label & Number
7/26/86	®	24	8	Detroit Diesel	—	Detroit Diesel	21 Records 90517

LEE, Amy

Born on 12/13/1981 in Riverside, California; raised in Little Rock, Arkansas. Lead singer of **Evanescence**.

Debut	Cht	Peak	Wks	Track Title	Hot Pos	Album Title	Album Label & Number
5/1/04	®	4	26	1 Broken	20	Disclaimer II	Wind-Up 13100
4/24/04	®	9	26	SEETHER Featuring Amy Lee			
2/17/07	®	22	9	2 Freak On A Leash (Unplugged) [L]	89	MTV Unplugged	Virgin 86027
2/24/07	®	29	7	KORN Featuring Amy Lee			

LEE, Geddy

Born Gary Lee Weinrib on 7/29/1953 in Toronto, Ontario, Canada. Lead singer/bassist of **Rush**.

Debut	Cht	Peak	Wks	Track Title	Hot Pos	Album Title	Album Label & Number
11/4/00	®	20	12	1 My Favorite Headache	—	My Favorite Headache	Anthem 83384
2/3/01	®	28	6	2 Grace To Grace	—	↓	

LEE, Tommy

Born Thomas Lee Bass on 10/3/1962 in Athens, Greece; raised in West Covina, California. Rock singer/drummer. Former member of **Mötley Crüe**. Married to actress Heather Locklear from 1986-93. Married to actress Pamela Anderson from 1995-98.

Debut	Cht	Peak	Wks	Track Title	Hot Pos	Album Title	Album Label & Number
3/30/02	®	5	26	1 Hold Me Down	—	Never A Dull Moment	MCA 112856
6/25/05	®	26	10	2 Tryin To Be Me	—	Tommyland: The Ride	TL Edu. 90005

LEISUREWORLD

Rock band from Toronto, Ontario, Canada: Cade Lakeshore (vocals), Patricia Melia (guitar), Patrick Worthington (bass) and Brent Empress (drums).

Debut	Cht	Peak	Wks	Track Title	Hot Pos	Album Title	Album Label & Number
3/1/03	®	37	2	I'm Dead	—	Double Wide Double High	Artist Direct 1122

LEMONHEADS, The

Pop-rock trio from Boston, Massachusetts: Evan Dando (vocals, guitar), Nic Dalton (bass) and David Ryan (drums).

Debut	Cht	Peak	Wks	Track Title	Hot Pos	Album Title	Album Label & Number
6/20/92	Ⓜ	5	11	1 It's A Shame About Ray	—	It's A Shame About Ray	Atlantic 82460
11/14/92	Ⓜ	8	13	2 Mrs. Robinson #1 Pop hit for Simon & Garfunkel in 1968	118	↓	
10/23/93	Ⓜ	❶⁹	16	3 Into Your Arms	67	Come On Feel The Lemonheads	Atlantic 82537
1/29/94	Ⓜ	15	9	4 The Great Big NO	—	↓	
10/12/96	Ⓜ	15	12	5 If I Could Talk I'd Tell You	—	Car Button Cloth	Atlantic 92726

LEN

Alternative-rock band from Toronto, Ontario, Canada: Marc Costanzo (vocals), his sister Sharon Costanzo, D. Rock, DJ Moves, Planet Pea and Drunkness Monster.

Debut	Cht	Peak	Wks	Track Title	Hot Pos	Album Title	Album Label & Number
5/29/99	Ⓜ	5	25	Steal My Sunshine samples "More More More" by the Andrea True Connection	9	You Can't Stop The Bum Rush	Work 69528

Billboard				ARTIST	R=Mainstream Rock	Hot		
Debut	Cht	Peak	Wks	Track Title	M=Modern Rock	Pos	Album Title	Album Label & Number

LENNON, John

Born on 10/9/1940 in Woolton, Liverpool, England. Shot to death on 12/8/1980 in Manhattan, New York (age 40). Founding member of **The Beatles**. Married to Cynthia Powell (1962-68); their son is **Julian Lennon**. Met Yoko Ono in 1966; married her on 3/20/1969. Formed Plastic Ono Band in 1969. To New York City in 1971. Fought deportation from the U.S., 1972-76, until he was granted a permanent visa. Also see **Classic Rock Tracks** section.

AWARDS: Grammy: Lifetime Achievement Award 1991 ★ R&R Hall of Fame: 1994

3/21/81	R	26	3	1 Woman	2^3	Double Fantasy	Geffen 2001
3/21/81	R	54	3	2 I'm Losing You	—	↓	
3/28/81	R	25	9	3 Watching The Wheels	10	↓	
1/21/84	R	2¹	10	4 Nobody Told Me	5	Milk And Honey	Polydor 817160
2/11/84	R	34	7	5 I'm Stepping Out	55	↓	
9/29/84	R	52	3	6 Every Man Has A Woman Who Loves Him	—	VA: Every Man Has A Woman	Polydor 823490

first recorded by Yoko Ono in 1980; all of above recorded in 1980 (shortly before Lennon's death)

2/8/86	R	25	7	7 Come Together ... [L]	—	Live In New York City	Capitol 12451

#1 Pop hit for **The Beatles** in 1969

2/15/86	R	20	6	8 Imagine	—	↓	

studio version was a #3 Pop hit in 1971; above 2 recorded on 8/30/1972 at Madison Square Garden

10/8/88	R	12	6	9 Jealous Guy	80	Imagine: John Lennon	Capitol 90803

JOHN LENNON AND THE PLASTIC ONO BAND (with The Flux Fiddlers)
first released on the 1971 album *Imagine*

LENNON, Julian

Born on 4/8/1963 in Liverpool, England. Singer/songwriter/keyboardist. Son of Cynthia and **John Lennon**.

10/20/84	R	2¹	14	1 Valotte	9	Valotte	Atlantic 80184
12/8/84+	R	11	18	2 Too Late For Goodbyes	5	↓	
4/20/85	R	3²	10	3 Say You're Wrong	21	↓	
3/22/86	R	❶³	13	4 Stick Around	32	The Secret Value of DayDreaming	Atlantic 81640
3/18/89	R	❶¹	10	5 Now You're In Heaven	93	Mr. Jordan	Atlantic 81928
5/6/89	M	27	2				
8/24/91	R	31	6	6 Listen	—	Help Yourself	Atlantic 82280

LENNOX, Annie

Born on 12/25/1954 in Aberdeen, Scotland. Female singer/songwriter. One-half of the **Eurythmics** duo.

AWARD: Billboard: Century Award 2002

5/9/92	M	12	11	1 Why	34	Diva	Arista 18704
8/15/92	M	7	7	2 Walking On Broken Glass	14	↓	
12/26/92+	M	24	5	3 Love Song For A Vampire	—	St: Bram Stoker's Dracula	Columbia 53165

LE ROUX

Rock band from Baton Rouge, Louisiana: Jeff Pollard (vocals), Tony Haselden (guitar), Rod Roddy (keyboards), Bobby Campo (horns), Leon Medica (bass) and David Peters (drums).

2/13/82	R	7	11	Addicted	—	Last Safe Place	RCA Victor 4195

LESS THAN JAKE

Rock trio from Gainesville, Florida: Chris DeMakes (vocals, guitar), Roger Manganelli (bass) and Vinnie Fiorello (drums).

12/26/98	M	39	2	1 History Of A Boring Town	—	Hello Rockview	Capitol 57663
8/9/03	M	36	5	2 The Science Of Selling Yourself Short	—	Anthem	Sire 48459

LET'S ACTIVE

Pop-rock trio formed in North Carolina: Mitch Easter (vocals, guitar), Faye Hunter (bass) and Sara Romweber (drums).

9/24/88	M	17	5	Every Dog Has His Day	—	Every Dog Has His Day	I.R.S. 42151

LETTERS TO CLEO

Pop-rock band from Boston, Massachusetts: Kay Hanley (vocals), Michael Eisenstein and Greg McKenna (guitars), Scott Riebling (bass) and Stacy Jones (drums). Jones later became lead singer with **American Hi-Fi**.

1/21/95	M	10	19	1 Here & Now	56	Aurora Gory Alice	Giant 24598
8/5/95	M	17	11	2 Awake	88	Wholesale Meats And Fish	Giant 24613

LEVEL 42

Pop-rock band formed in Manchester, England: Mark King (vocals, bass), brothers Boon Gould (guitar) and Phil Gould (drums), and Mike Lindup (keyboards).

4/12/86	R	45	4	Something About You	7	World Machine	Polydor 827487

LEVELLERS

Post-punk band formed in Brighton, England: Mark Chadwick (vocals), Simon Friend (guitar), Jon Sevink (violin), Jeremy Cunningham (bass) and Charlie Heather (drums).

6/13/92	M	11	8	One Way	—	Levelling The Land	China 61325

LEWIS, Aaron
Born on 4/13/1972 in Boston, Massachusetts. Lead singer of **Staind**.

Debut	Cht	Peak	Wks	Track Title	Hot Pos	Album Title	Album Label & Number
12/16/00+	ℝ	❶²	26	**Outside** [L]	56		
11/25/00+	Ⓜ	2⁶	25	**AARON LEWIS** with Fred Durst		VA: The Family Values Tour 1999........Flawless 490641

LEWIS, Huey, and The News
ℝ **1980s: #11 / All-Time: #36**

Born Hugh Cregg III on 7/5/1950 in New York; raised in Danville, California. Pop-rock singer/songwriter. Formed the News in San Francisco, California: Chris Hayes (guitar), Sean Hopper (keyboards), Johnny Colla (sax), Mario Cipollina (bass) and Bill Gibson (drums). Lewis acted in the movies *Back To The Future* and *Short Cuts*.

TOP HITS: 1)The Power Of Love 2)Heart And Soul 3)Hip To Be Square 4)Stuck With You 5)Back In Time

Debut	Cht	Peak	Wks	#	Track Title	Hot Pos	Album Title	Album Label & Number
2/27/82	ℝ	12	10	1	Do You Believe In Love	7	Picture This	Chrysalis 1340
3/20/82	ℝ	20	13	2	Workin' For A Livin'	41	↓	
10/8/83	ℝ	❶¹	17	3	Heart And Soul	8	Sports	Chrysalis 41412
10/22/83	ℝ	7	23	4	I Want A New Drug	6	↓	
2/18/84	ℝ	16	15	5	Walking On A Thin Line	18	↓	
3/17/84	ℝ	5	19	6	The Heart Of Rock & Roll	6	↓	
7/28/84	ℝ	3¹	12	7	If This Is It	6	↓	
9/15/84	ℝ	41	5	8	Finally Found A Home	—	↓	
4/20/85	ℝ	11	10	9	Trouble In Paradise [L]	—	We Are The World (USA For Africa)......Columbia 40043
					recorded on 2/21/1985 in San Francisco, California			
6/29/85	ℝ	❶²	14	10	The Power Of Love	❶²	St: Back To The Future	MCA 6144
7/27/85	ℝ	3²	14	11	Back In Time	—	↓	
8/2/86	ℝ	2²	8	12	Stuck With You	❶³	Fore!	Chrysalis 41534
9/6/86	ℝ	❶¹	13	13	Hip To Be Square	3²	↓	
9/6/86	ℝ	10	23	14	Jacob's Ladder	❶¹	↓	
					co-written by **Bruce Hornsby**			
9/6/86	ℝ	25	10	15	I Know What I Like	9	↓	
9/13/86	ℝ	38	6	16	Whole Lotta Lovin'	—	↓	
7/16/88	ℝ	5	8	17	Perfect World	3²	Small World	Chrysalis 41622
8/20/88	ℝ	47	3	18	Walking With The Kid	—	↓	
8/27/88	ℝ	28	8	19	Small World	25	↓	
4/27/91	ℝ	3¹	10	20	Couple Days Off	11	Hard At Play	EMI 93355
7/6/91	ℝ	27	7	21	Build Me Up	—	↓	

LIFEHOUSE
Rock trio from Malibu, California: Jason Wade (vocals, guitar), Sergio Andrade (bass) and Rick Woolstenhulme (drums).

Debut	Cht	Peak	Wks	#	Track Title	Hot Pos	Album Title	Album Label & Number
10/28/00+	Ⓜ	❶³	35	1	Hanging By A Moment	2⁴	No Name Face	DreamWorks 50231
11/25/00+	ℝ	7	28					
5/26/01	Ⓜ	21	12	2	Sick Cycle Carousel	—	↓	
6/30/01	ℝ	38	1					
8/10/02	Ⓜ	25	9	3	Spin	71	Stanley Climbfall	DreamWorks 50377
8/17/02	ℝ	34	4					

LIFE OF AGONY
Rock band from Brooklyn, New York: Keith **Caputo** (vocals), "Joey Z" Zampella (guitar), Alan Robert (bass) and Sal Abruscato (drums). Dan Richardson replaced Abruscato in 1997. Joey Z and Richardson later joined **Stereomud**.

Debut	Cht	Peak	Wks	#	Track Title	Hot Pos	Album Title	Album Label & Number
11/8/97	ℝ	27	13	1	Weeds	—	Soul Searching Sun	Roadrunner 8816
4/11/98	ℝ	37	3	2	Tangerine	—	↓	
5/7/05	ℝ	25	12	3	Love To Let You Down	—	Broken Valley	Epic 93515
7/28/07	ℝ	33	8	4	What Have You Done	—	The Heart Of Everything	Roadrunner 618021
					WITHIN TEMPTATION Featuring Keith Caputo			

LIGHTNING SEEDS, The
Born Ian Broudie on 8/4/1958 in Liverpool, England. Alternative-rock singer/producer.

Debut	Cht	Peak	Wks	#	Track Title	Hot Pos	Album Title	Album Label & Number
4/7/90	Ⓜ	8	10	1	Pure	31	Cloudcuckooland	MCA 6404
6/9/90	Ⓜ	9	11	2	All I Want	—	↓	
2/1/92	Ⓜ	2¹	12	3	The Life Of Riley	98	Sense	MCA 10388
4/18/92	Ⓜ	19	4	4	Blowing Bubbles	—	↓	
9/24/94	Ⓜ	38	3	5	Lucky You	—	Jollification	Trauma 71008

LILAC TIME, The

Rock band formed in Herefordshire, West Midlands, England: brothers Stephen Duffy (vocals) and Nick Duffy (guitar), with Michael Giri (bass) and Micky Harris (drums).

Debut	Cht	Peak	Wks	Track Title	Hot Pos	Album Title	Album Label & Number
2/24/90	ⓜ	28	2	1 **American Eyes**	—	*Lilac Time*	Fontana 836744
10/6/90	ⓜ	22	6	2 **All For Love And Love For All**	—	*& Love For All*	Fontana 846190

LIMP BIZKIT
® 2000s: #35 ★ ⓜ 2000s: #35 / All-Time: #38

Alternative-metal band from Jacksonville, Florida: **Fred Durst** (vocals; born on 8/20/1970), Wes Borland (guitar; born on 2/7/1975), Sam Rivers (bass; born in 1979) and John Otto (drums; born on 3/22/1977). Borland left band in October 2001, replaced by Mike Smith. Borland returned in August 2004, replacing Smith. Borland also formed **Black Light Burns**.

TOP HITS: 1)Re-Arranged 2)Nookie 3)My Way

Debut	Cht	Peak	Wks	Track Title	Hot Pos	Album Title	Album Label & Number
1/23/99	ⓜ	28	12	1 **Faith**	—	*Three Dollar Bill, Y'all$*	Flip 90124
1/2/99	®	33	11	#1 Pop hit for George Michael in 1987			
6/12/99	ⓜ	3⁴	26	2 **Nookie**	80	*Significant Other*	Flip 90335
6/19/99	®	6	26				
10/9/99	ⓜ	❶¹	29	3 **Re-Arranged**	88	↓	
10/16/99	®	8	26				
3/11/00	ⓜ	14	26	4 **Break Stuff**	123	↓	
3/4/00	®	19	26				
4/29/00	ⓜ	8	22	5 **Take A Look Around**	115	*St: Mission: Impossible 2*	Hollywood 62244
5/27/00	®	15	17				
9/23/00	ⓜ	4	26	6 **Rollin'** (Urban Assault Vehicle)	65	*Chocolate Starfish And The Hot Dog Flavored Water*	Flip 490759
9/23/00	®	10	26				
9/23/00	ⓜ	18	9	7 **My Generation**	—	↓	
9/23/00	®	33	7				
2/24/01	ⓜ	3⁴	26	8 **My Way**	75	↓	
3/3/01	®	4	26				
7/28/01	®	30	8	9 **Boiler**	—	↓	
1/8/00	ⓜ	31	7	10 **Crushed**	—	*St: End Of Days*	Geffen 490508
8/23/03	®	16	10	11 **Eat You Alive**	—	*Results May Vary*	Flip 001235
8/23/03	ⓜ	20	8				
10/25/03+	®	11	26	12 **Behind Blue Eyes**	71	↓	
12/20/03+	ⓜ	18	19	#34 Pop hit for **The Who** in 1971			
6/26/04	®	33	5	13 **Almost Over**	—	↓	

LINDLEY, David

Born on 1/1/1944 in San Marino, California. Rock session guitarist.

Debut	Cht	Peak	Wks	Track Title	Hot Pos	Album Title	Album Label & Number
5/9/81	®	34	13	**Mercury Blues**	—	*El Rayo-X*	Asylum 524
				#2 Country hit for Alan Jackson in 1993			

LINKIN PARK
® 2000s: #5 / All-Time: #32 ★ ⓜ 2000s: #1 / All-Time: #7

Alternative hard-rock band from Los Angeles, California: Chester Bennington (vocals; born on 3/20/1976), Mike Shinoda (rap vocals; born on 2/11/1977), Joseph Hahn (DJ; born on 3/15/1977), Brad Delson (guitar; born on 12/1/1977), David "Phoenix" Farrell (bass; born on 2/8/1977) and Rob Bourdon (drums; born on 1/20/1979). Shinoda also recorded solo side project Fort Minor. Also see **Mötley Crüe**.

TOP HITS: 1)What I've Done 2)Numb 3)Faint

Debut	Cht	Peak	Wks	Track Title	Hot Pos	Album Title	Album Label & Number
9/16/00+	®	4	42	1 **One Step Closer**	75	*Hybrid Theory*	Warner 47755
10/7/00+	ⓜ	5	33				
4/21/01	®	3⁴	34	2 **Crawling**	79	↓	
3/31/01	ⓜ	5	34	Grammy: Hard Rock Performance			
8/25/01	ⓜ	❶⁵	44	3 **In The End**	2¹	↓	
9/22/01	®	3⁴	41				
3/16/02	ⓜ	32	18	4 **Papercut**	—	↓	

Debut	Cht	Peak	Wks	ARTIST / Track Title	Hot Pos	Album Title	Album Label & Number

Ⓡ=Mainstream Rock Ⓜ=Modern Rock

LINKIN PARK — cont'd

Debut	Cht	Peak	Wks	Track Title	Hot Pos	Album Title	Album Label & Number
5/25/02	Ⓡ	37	9	5 Runaway	—	↓	
7/6/02	Ⓜ	40	1				
8/10/02	Ⓜ	29	10	6 Points Of Authority	—	*Reanimation*.........Warner 48326	
3/15/03	Ⓜ	❶^5	26	7 Somewhere I Belong	32	*Meteora*.........Warner 48186	
3/15/03	Ⓡ	❶^1	26				
5/17/03	Ⓜ	❶^6	37	8 Faint	48	↓	
6/21/03	Ⓡ	2^2	28				
10/4/03	Ⓜ	❶^{12}	30	9 Numb	11	↓	
10/11/03+	Ⓡ	❶^3	30				
2/28/04	Ⓜ	❶^3	26	10 Lying From You	58	↓	
2/28/04	Ⓡ	2^5	26				
6/26/04	Ⓜ	❶^4	26	11 Breaking The Habit	20	↓	
6/26/04	Ⓡ	❶^3	26				
4/21/07	Ⓜ	❶^{15}	31	12 What I've Done	7	*Minutes To Midnight*.........Machine Shop 44477	
4/21/07	Ⓡ	❶^8	27				
6/30/07	Ⓜ	2^9	36	13 Bleed It Out	52	↓	
7/14/07	Ⓡ	3^1	24				
10/20/07+	Ⓜ	2^4	24↑	14 Shadow Of The Day	15	↓	
11/3/07+	Ⓡ	6	20				
3/15/08	Ⓡ	23↑	3↑	15 Given Up	99	↓	
3/22/08	Ⓜ	27↑	2↑				

LIT   Ⓜ **All-Time: #71**

Rock band from Anaheim, California: brothers A. Jay Popoff (vocals) and Jeremy Popoff (guitar), Kevin Blades (bass) and Allen Shellenberger (drums).

Debut	Cht	Peak	Wks	Track Title	Hot Pos	Album Title	Album Label & Number
2/13/99	Ⓜ	❶^{11}	36	1 My Own Worst Enemy	51	*A Place In The Sun*.........RCA 67775	
3/27/99	Ⓡ	6	26				
8/14/99	Ⓜ	11	15	2 Zip-Lock	—	↓	
9/25/99	Ⓡ	34	6				
12/18/99+	Ⓜ	3^3	26	3 Miserable	117	↓	
3/4/00	Ⓡ	29	10				
6/17/00	Ⓜ	22	9	4 Over My Head	—	*St: Titan A.E.*.........Java 25275	
9/8/01	Ⓜ	10	12	5 Lipstick And Bruises	—	*Atomic*.........RCA 68086	
9/15/01	Ⓡ	28	9				
12/22/01+	Ⓜ	23	9	6 Addicted	—	↓	
7/10/04	Ⓜ	34	6	7 Looks Like They Were Right	—	*Lit*.........Dirty Martini 00413	

LITTLE AMERICA

Rock band formed in Los Angeles, California: Mike Magrisi (vocals, bass), Andy Logan (guitar), John Hussey (guitar) and Kurt Custer (drums). Custer was a member of **Lynyrd Skynyrd** from 1991-94.

Debut	Cht	Peak	Wks	Track Title	Hot Pos	Album Title	Album Label & Number
4/11/87	Ⓡ	10	12	1 Walk On Fire	—	*Little America*.........Geffen 24113	
2/18/89	Ⓡ	17	11	2 Where Were You	—	*Fairgrounds*.........Geffen 24200	

LITTLE CAESAR

Hard-rock band formed in Los Angeles, California: Ron Young (vocals), Apache (guitar), Louren Molinare (guitar), Fidel Paniagua (bass), and Tom Morris (drums). Band named after the 1931 gangster movie starring Edward G. Robinson.

Debut	Cht	Peak	Wks	Track Title	Hot Pos	Album Title	Album Label & Number
5/19/90	Ⓡ	17	10	1 Chain Of Fools	88	*Little Caesar*.........DGC 24288	
				#2 Pop hit for **Aretha Franklin** in 1968			
2/23/91	Ⓡ	35	7	2 In Your Arms	79	↓	

LITTLE FEAT

Eclectic rock band formed in Los Angeles, California: Lowell George (vocals), Paul Barrere (guitar), Bill Payne (keyboards), Kenny Gradney (bass), Sam Clayton (percussion) and Richard Hayward (drums). Disbanded in April 1979. George died of drug-related heart failure on 6/29/1979 (age 34). Regrouped in 1988, adding Craig Fuller (vocals, guitar) and Fred Tackett (guitar).

Debut	Cht	Peak	Wks	Track Title	Hot Pos	Album Title	Album Label & Number
8/22/81	Ⓡ	34	10	1 Rock And Roll Doctor	—	*Hoy-Hoy!*.........Warner 3538	
				recorded in 1976			
7/30/88	Ⓡ	❶^4	11	2 Hate To Lose Your Lovin'	—	*Let It Roll*.........Warner 25750	
8/20/88	Ⓡ	3^1	13	3 Let It Roll	—	↓	
10/29/88	Ⓡ	19	11	4 Long Time Till I Get Over You	—	↓	
1/21/89	Ⓡ	10	11	5 One Clear Moment	—	↓	

LITTLE FEAT — cont'd

Debut	Cht	Peak	Wks	Track Title	Hot Pos	Album Title	Album Label & Number
7/22/89	R	23	7	6 Rad Gumbo	—	*St: Road House*	Arista 8576
4/7/90	R	❶¹	12	7 Texas Twister	—	*Representing The Mambo*	Warner 26163
6/23/90	R	21	8	8 Woman In Love	—	↓	
9/7/91	R	14	10	9 Shake Me Up	—	*Shake Me Up*	Morgan Creek 20005

LITTLE RIVER BAND

Pop-rock band formed in Melbourne, Australia: Glenn Shorrock (vocals), Graham Goble (guitar), Beeb Birtles (guitar), David Briggs (guitar), Wayne Nelson (bass), and Derek Pellici (drums). Lineup in 1985: John Farnham (vocals), Goble (guitar), Stephen Housden (guitar), David Hirschfelder (keyboards), Nelson (bass) and Steven Prestwich (drums).

Debut	Cht	Peak	Wks	Track Title	Hot Pos	Album Title	Album Label & Number
9/5/81	R	9	16	1 The Night Owls	6	*Time Exposure*	Capitol 12163
1/26/85	R	15	11	2 Playing To Win	60	*Playing To Win*	Capitol 12365
				LRB			

LITTLE STEVEN AND THE DISCIPLES OF SOUL

Born Steven Lento (later adopted his stepfather's last name) on 11/22/1950 in Winthrop, Massachusetts; raised in Middletown, New Jersey. Rock singer/guitarist/actor. Formed **Southside Johnny & The Jukes** with co-lead singer Johnny Lyon in 1974. Joined **Bruce Springsteen**'s E Street Band in 1975. Organized **Artists United Against Apartheid**. Played "Silvio Dante" on TV's *The Sopranos*. Hosts own syndicated radio show *Little Steven's Underground Garage*.

Debut	Cht	Peak	Wks	Track Title	Hot Pos	Album Title	Album Label & Number
11/6/82	R	30	5	1 Lyin' In A Bed Of Fire	—	*Men Without Women*	EMI America 17086
1/29/83	R	39	3	2 Forever	63	↓	
6/9/84	R	27	8	3 Los Desaparecidos (The Disappeared Ones)	—	*Voice Of America*	EMI America 17120
5/16/87	R	29	6	4 Trail Of Broken Treaties	—	*Freedom No Compromise*	Manhattan 53048
3/4/00	R	40	2	5 Salvation	—	*Born Again Savage*	Renegade Nation 6
				LITTLE STEVEN			

LITTLE VILLAGE

All-star band formed in Los Angeles, California: **John Hiatt** (vocals), Ry Cooder (guitar), **Nick Lowe** (bass) and Jim Keltner (drums).

Debut	Cht	Peak	Wks	Track Title	Hot Pos	Album Title	Album Label & Number
2/29/92	R	17	9	1 She Runs Hot	—	*Little Village*	Reprise 26713
5/16/92	R	35	7	2 Solar Sex Panel	—	↓	

LIVE R 1990s: #16 / All-Time: #50 ★ M 1990s: #9 / All-Time: #15

Alternative-rock band formed in York, Pennsylvania: Ed Kowalczyk (vocals; born on 7/16/1971), Chad Taylor (guitar; born on 11/24/1970), Pat Dahlheimer (bass; born on 5/30/1971) and Chad Gracey (drums; born on 7/23/1971). Also see **Tricky**.

TOP HITS: 1)Lightning Crashes 2)Selling The Drama 3)Lakini's Juice

Debut	Cht	Peak	Wks	Track Title	Hot Pos	Album Title	Album Label & Number
1/25/92	M	9	9	1 Operation Spirit (The Tyranny Of Tradition)	—	*Mental Jewelry*	Radioactive 10346
5/2/92	M	24	6	2 Pain Lies On The Riverside	—	↓	
4/9/94	M	❶³	19	3 Selling The Drama	43	*Throwing Copper*	Radioactive 10997
6/4/94	R	4	25				
8/20/94	M	6	26	4 I Alone	38ᴬ	↓	
9/24/94	R	6	26				
2/11/95	R	❶¹⁰	26	5 Lightning Crashes	12ᴬ	↓	
1/28/95	M	❶⁹	25				
6/3/95	R	2¹	26	6 All Over You	33ᴬ	↓	
5/6/95	M	4	26				
8/5/95	R	12	12	7 White, Discussion	71ᴬ	↓	
7/29/95	M	15	12				
2/1/97	M	❶¹	18	8 Lakini's Juice	35ᴬ	*Secret Samadhi*	Radioactive 11590
2/1/97	R	2⁴	26				
4/26/97	R	5	14	9 Freaks	73ᴬ	↓	
4/26/97	M	13	9				
6/14/97	M	3³	21	10 Turn My Head	45ᴬ	↓	
7/12/97	R	3³	15				
10/25/97	R	15	14	11 Rattlesnake	—	↓	
10/25/97	M	18	12				
9/4/99	R	2⁶	26	12 The Dolphin's Cry	78	*The Distance To Here*	Radioactive 11966
9/4/99	M	3⁴	26				

Debug				ARTIST					

LIVE — cont'd

Debut	Cht	Peak	Wks	Track Title	Hot Pos	Album Title	Album Label & Number
2/12/00	Ⓜ	14	11	13 **Run To The Water**..	—	↓	
2/12/00	®	17	12				
8/5/00	®	24	8	14 **They Stood Up For Love**..............................	—	↓	
8/12/00	Ⓜ	31	4				
8/11/01	®	11	11	15 **Simple Creed**	—	V...Radioactive 12485	
8/11/01	Ⓜ	18	9	LIVE Featuring Tricky			
10/13/01	Ⓜ	30	4	16 **Overcome**	—	↓	
5/3/03	Ⓜ	33	6	17 **Heaven**..	59	*Birds Of Pray*.........................Radioactive 000374	
5/10/03	®	33	7				

LIVING COLOUR

Black rock band from Brooklyn, New York: Corey Glover (vocals), Vernon Reid (guitar), Muzz Skillings (bass) and William Calhoun (drums). Doug Wimbish replaced Skillings in early 1992. Glover played "Francis" in the movie *Platoon*.

TOP HITS: 1)Type 2)Leave It Alone 3)Love Rears Its Ugly Head

Debut	Cht	Peak	Wks	Track Title	Hot Pos	Album Title	Album Label & Number
12/17/88+	®	9	20	1 **Cult Of Personality**	13	*Vivid* ....Epic 44099	
				Grammy: Hard Rock Performance			
4/15/89	®	11	10	2 **Open Letter** (To A Landlord)	82	↓	
9/23/89	®	26	7	3 **Glamour Boys**..	31	↓	
				Mick Jagger (producer, backing vocal)			
9/8/90	Ⓜ	3[1]	11	4 **Type**	—	*Time's Up* ....Epic 46202	
9/8/90	®	5	9				
11/24/90	®	42	4	5 **Pride**	—	↓	
12/1/90	Ⓜ	25	2	6 **Elvis Is Dead**	—	↓	
2/2/91	Ⓜ	8	9	7 **Love Rears Its Ugly Head**	—	↓	
2/2/91	®	28	10				
7/27/91	Ⓜ	12	7	8 **Talkin' Loud And Sayin' Nothing**	—	*Biscuits*...Epic 47988	
				#27 Pop hit for James Brown in 1972			
2/27/93	Ⓜ	4	11	9 **Leave It Alone**	—	*Stain* ....Epic 52780	
3/6/93	®	14	10				
5/15/93	Ⓜ	17	8	10 **Nothingness**	—	↓	

LIVING END, The

Rock trio from Melbourne, Australia: Chris Cheney (vocals, guitar), Scott Owen (bass) and Travis Demsey (drums). Andy Strachan replaced Demsey in 2003.

Debut	Cht	Peak	Wks	Track Title	Hot Pos	Album Title	Album Label & Number
2/6/99	Ⓜ	23	13	1 **Prisoner Of Society**	—	*The Living End*..Reprise 47128	
4/14/01	Ⓜ	33	4	2 **Roll On**...	—	*Roll On*...Reprise 48063	
2/21/04	Ⓜ	26	12	3 **Who's Gonna Save Us?**	—	*Modern Artillery* ....Reprise 48519	

LIVING THINGS

Rock band from St. Louis, Missouri: brothers Jason "Lillian Berlin" Rothman (vocals), Justin "Eve Berlin" Rothman (bass) and Josh "Bosh Berlin" Rothman (drums), with Cory Becker (guitar).

Debut	Cht	Peak	Wks	Track Title	Hot Pos	Album Title	Album Label & Number
11/5/05	Ⓜ	21	17	**Bom Bom Bom**	—	*Ahead Of The Lions*....................................Jive 71460	
2/25/06	®	37	3				

LOCAL H

Rock duo from Zion, Illinois: Scott Lucas (vocals, guitar, bass) and Joe Daniels (drums).

Debut	Cht	Peak	Wks	Track Title	Hot Pos	Album Title	Album Label & Number
9/28/96	Ⓜ	5	26	1 **Bound For The Floor**	46[A]	*As Good As Dead* ....Island 524202	
9/28/96	®	10	26				
4/5/97	®	36	3	2 **Fritz's Corner**	—	↓	
7/19/97	Ⓜ	38	2	3 **Eddie Vedder**	—	↓	
8/29/98	®	19	12	4 **All The Kids Are Right**	—	*Pack Up The Cats*....................................Island 524549	
8/29/98	Ⓜ	20	13				
3/23/02	®	40	1	5 **Half Life**	—	*Here Comes The Zoo* ....Palm 2072	

LOEB, Lisa, & Nine Stories

Born on 3/11/1968 in Bethesda, Maryland; raised in Dallas, Texas. Female singer/songwriter/guitarist. Nine Stories consisted of Tim Bright (guitar), Joe Quigley (bass) and Jonathan Feinberg (drums).

Debut	Cht	Peak	Wks	Track Title	Hot Pos	Album Title	Album Label & Number
6/18/94	Ⓜ	7	14	1 **Stay (I Missed You)**......................................	❶[3]	*St: Reality Bites*..RCA 66364	
9/16/95	Ⓜ	20	11	2 **Do You Sleep?**	18	*Tails* ....Geffen 24734	

Debut	Cht	Peak	Wks	Track Title	Hot Pos	Album Title	Album Label & Number

LOFGREN, Nils
Born on 6/21/1951 in Chicago, Illinois; raised in Maryland. Pop-rock singer/guitarist/pianist. Member of **Bruce Springsteen**'s E Street Band from 1984-85.

| 3/2/91 | ® | 37 | 8 | Valentine .... Bruce Springsteen (harmony vocal) | — | Silver Lining ....Rykodisc 10170 |

LO FIDELITY ALLSTARS
Electronica-dance/rock band from Brighton, Sussex, England: Dave Randall (vocals), Martin Whiteman (keyboards), Andy Dickinson (bass) and Johnny Machin (drums).

| 4/17/99 | ⓜ | 6 | 26 | Battle Flag .... LO FIDELITY ALLSTARS Featuring Pigeonhead | 117 | How To Operate With A Blown Mind............Skint 69654 |

LOGGINS, Kenny
Born on 1/7/1948 in Everett, Washington. Pop-rock singer/songwriter/guitarist.

9/4/82	®	4	16	1 **Don't Fight It** .... KENNY LOGGINS with Steve Perry	17	High Adventure ....Columbia 38127
2/4/84	®	2²	14	2 **Footloose**	❶³	St: Footloose...Columbia 39242
5/5/84	®	42	9	3 **I'm Free** (Heaven Helps The Man)	22	↓
3/30/85	®	18	8	4 **Vox Humana**	29	Vox Humana ....Columbia 39174
5/24/86	®	7	11	5 **Danger Zone**	2¹	St: Top Gun ....Columbia 40323
7/23/88	®	30	6	6 **Nobody's Fool**	8	St: Caddyshack II....................................Columbia 44317

LONDON QUIREBOYS, The
Hard-rock band formed in London, England: Jonathan "Spike" Gray (vocals), Guy Bailey (guitar), Guy Griffin (guitar), Chris Johnstone (keyboards), Nigel Mogg (bass) and Ian Wallace (drums).

| 3/24/90 | ® | 15 | 13 | 7 O'Clock... | — | A Bit Of What You Fancy ....Capitol 93177 |

LONE JUSTICE
Country-rock band from Los Angeles, California: Maria McKee (vocals), Ryan Hedgecock (guitar), Marvin Etzioni (bass) and Don Heffington (drums). Etzioni and Heffington left in early 1986; Shane Fontayne (guitar), Bruce Brody (keyboards), Gregg Sutton (bass) and Rudy Richman (drums) joined.

| 5/18/85 | ® | 29 | 7 | 1 **Ways To Be Wicked** .... co-written by **Tom Petty** | 71 | Lone Justice...Geffen 24060 |
| 11/15/86 | ® | 26 | 10 | 2 **Shelter** .... | 47 | Shelter...Geffen 24122 |

LONG BEACH DUB ALLSTARS
Rock-reggae band from Long Beach, California: Opie Ortiz (vocals), Richard "Ras-1" Smith (guitar), Jack Maness (keyboards), Marshall Goodman (percussion), Tim Wu (sax), Eric Wilson (bass) and Bud Gaugh (drums). Wilson and Gaugh were members of **Sublime**.

| 8/18/01 | ⓜ | 28 | 6 | Sunny Hours .... | — | Wonders Of The World ....DreamWorks 450295 |

LONGPIGS
Rock band from Sheffield, Yorkshire, England: Crispin Hunt (vocals, guitar), Richard Hawley (guitar), Simon Stafford (bass) and Dee Boyle (drums).

| 10/11/97 | ⓜ | 17 | 12 | On And On .... | 106 | The Sun Is Often Out ....Mother 531542 |

LO-PRO
Rock band formed in Los Angeles, California: Pete Murray (vocals), Neil Godfrey (guitar), Pete Ricci (guitar), John Fahnestock (bass) and Tommy Stewart (drums).

| 1/31/04 | ® | 20 | 16 | Sunday .... | — | Lo-Pro ....Geffen 001056 |
| 2/14/04 | ⓜ | 27 | 10 | | | |

LORDAN, Bill
Born on 5/22/1947 in Minneapolis, Minnesota. Rock drummer.

| 4/4/81 | ® | 43 | 1 | Won't Let You Down.. JACK BRUCE / BILL LORDAN / ROBIN TROWER | — | B.L.T. ....Chrysalis 1324 |

LORDS OF THE NEW CHURCH, The
Rock band formed in England: Steven "Stiv Bators" Bator (vocals; born in Youngstown, Ohio), Brian James (guitar), Dave Tregunna (bass) and Nicky Turner (drums). Bator died after being struck by a car on 6/4/1990 (age 40).

| 7/31/82 | ® | 27 | 7 | Open Your Eyes... | — | The Lords Of The New Church ...................I.R.S. 70029 |

LORD TRACY
Rock band from Texas: Terrence Lee Glaze (vocals), Jimmy Rusidoff (guitar), Kinley Wolfe (bass) and Chris Craig (drums).

| 12/9/89+ | ® | 40 | 6 | Out With The Boys .... | — | Deaf Gods Of Babylon ....Uni 606 |

LOS LOBOS
Latin rock band formed in Los Angeles, California: David Hildago (vocals; born on 10/6/1954), Cesar Rosas (guitar; born on 9/26/1954), Steve Berlin (sax; born on 9/14/1955), Conrad Lozano (bass; born on 3/21/1951) and Louie Perez (drums; born on 1/29/1953).

12/8/84+	®	28	9	1 **Don't Worry Baby**	—	How Will The Wolf Survive?.......................Slash 25177
3/16/85	®	26	7	2 **Will The Wolf Survive?**............................	78	↓
1/17/87	®	4	13	3 **Shakin' Shakin' Shakes**	—	By The Light Of The Moon ....Slash 25523

Debut	Cht	Peak	Wks	ARTIST / Track Title	Hot Pos	Album Title	Album Label & Number
				LOS LOBOS — cont'd			
4/4/87	R	21	8	4 **Set Me Free (Rosa Lee)**	—	↓	
7/11/87	R	11	9	5 **La Bamba** [F] #22 Pop hit for Ritchie Valens in 1959	❶[3]	*St: La Bamba*	Slash 25605
9/12/87	R	33	7	6 **Come On, Let's Go** #42 Pop hit for Ritchie Valens in 1958	21	↓	
9/1/90	M	16	9	7 **Down On The Riverbed**	—	*The Neighborhood*	Slash 26131
9/15/90	R	33	6				
6/8/91	M	24	2	8 **Bertha** first recorded by the **Grateful Dead** in 1971	—	*VA: Deadicated*	Arista 8669
5/18/91	R	37	5				
7/4/92	M	24	4	9 **Reva's House**	—	*Kiko*	Slash 26786
				LOSTPROPHETS Rock band formed in Pontypridd, Glamorgan, Wales: Ian Watkins (vocals), Lee Gaze (guitar), Mike Lewis (guitar), Stuart Richardson (bass) and Mike Chiplin (drums). Ilan Rubin replaced Chiplin in early 2006.			
3/9/02	M	33	6	1 **Shinobi vs. Dragon Ninja**	—	*The Fake Sound Of Progress*	Columbia 85955
12/27/03+	M	❶[1]	26	2 **Last Train Home**	75	*Start Something*	Columbia 86554
12/27/03+	R	10	26				
6/26/04	M	9	25	3 **Wake Up (Make A Move)**	—	↓	
6/26/04	R	16	19				
11/20/04+	M	11	16	4 **I Don't Know**	—	↓	
12/11/04+	R	24	12				
6/3/06	M	15	19	5 **Rooftops (A Liberation Broadcast)**	114	*Liberation Transmission*	Columbia 96531
6/3/06	R	22	16				
				LOUD LUCY Rock trio from Chicago, Illinois: Christian Lane (vocals, guitar), Tom Furar (bass) and Mark Doyle (drums).			
12/30/95+	M	31	8	**Ticking**	—	*Breathe*	DGC 24733
2/10/96	R	38	2				
				LOUDMOUTH Rock band from Chicago, Illinois: Bob Feddersen (vocals), Tony McQuaid (guitar), Mike Flaherty (bass) and John Sullivan (drums).			
3/20/99	R	11	18	**Fly**	—	*Loudmouth*	Hollywood 62181
				LOUIS XIV Punk-rock band from San Diego, California: Jason Hill (vocals, guitar), Brian Karscig (guitar), Jimmy Armbrust (bass) and Mark Maigaard (drums). Band named after the French monarch who reigned from 1643-1715.			
2/5/05	M	28	12	**Finding Out True Love Is Blind**	—	*The Best Little Secrets Are Kept*	Pineapple 93825
				LOVE, Courtney Born on 7/9/1964 in San Francisco, California. Rock singer/songwriter/guitarist/actress. Lead singer of **Hole**. Acted in several movies. Married to Kurt Cobain (lead singer of **Nirvana**) from 1992-94 (his death).			
1/24/04	M	18	9	1 **Mono**	—	*America's Sweetheart*	Virgin 91459
5/1/04	M	39	2	2 **Hold On To Me**	—	↓	
				LOVE, G. Born Garrett Sutton on 10/3/1972 in Philadelphia, Pennsylvania. Blues singer/guitarist. Special Sauce: Jim Prescott (bass) and Jeff Clemens (drums).			
11/22/97	M	30	9	1 **Stepping Stones**	—	*Yeah, It's That Easy*	Okeh 67784
8/28/99	M	39	3	2 **Rodeo Clowns** **G. LOVE & SPECIAL SAUCE** (above 2)	—	*Philadelphonic*	Okeh 69746
8/14/04	M	37	3	3 **Astronaut**	—	*The Hustle*	Brushfire 003092
				LOVE AND ROCKETS Pop-rock trio formed in England: **Daniel Ash** (vocals, guitar), **David J** (bass) and Kevin Haskins (drums).			
1/17/87	R	49	4	1 **All In My Mind**	—	*Express*	Big Time 6011
12/5/87+	R	18	13	2 **No New Tale To Tell**	—	*Earth.Sun.Moon*	Big Time 6058
2/25/89	M	20	8	3 **Motorcycle**	—	*Love And Rockets*	Beggars Banquet 9715
5/6/89	M	❶[5]	16	4 **So Alive**	3[1]	↓	
5/13/89	R	9	16				
9/2/89	M	29	1	5 **Rock And Roll Babylon**	—	↓	
9/16/89	M	19	5	6 **No Big Deal**	82	↓	
3/16/96	M	10	10	7 **Sweet Lover Hangover**	66[A]	*Sweet F.A.*	American 43058

Cht: R = Mainstream Rock; M = Modern Rock

LOVE/HATE
Rock band from Los Angeles, California: Jim "Jizzy Pearl" Wilkinson (vocal), Jon Love (guitar), Chris "Skid" Rose (bass) and Joey Gold (drums).

Debut	Cht	Peak	Wks	Track Title	Pos	Album Title	Label
9/22/90	R	46	4	Why Do You Think They Call It Dope?	—	Blackout In The Red Room .... Columbia 45263

LOVERBOY
R 1980s: #39 / All-Time: #96

Rock band formed in Calgary, Alberta, Canada: Mike Reno (vocals; born on 6/8/1955), **Paul Dean** (guitar; born on 2/19/1946), Doug Johnson (keyboards; born on 12/19/1957), Scott Smith (bass; born on 2/13/1955; drowned on 11/30/2000, age 45) and Matt Frenette (drums; born on 3/7/1954).

TOP HITS: 1)Hot Girls In Love 2)Working For The Weekend 3)Lovin' Every Minute Of It

Debut	Cht	Peak	Wks		Track Title	Pos	Album Title	Label
3/21/81	R	6	15	1	Turn Me Loose	35	Loverboy .... Columbia 36762
6/6/81	R	42	8	2	The Kid Is Hot Tonite	55	↓
11/21/81+	R	2¹	22	3	Working For The Weekend	29	Get Lucky .... Columbia 37638
1/23/82	R	21	22	4	When It's Over	26	↓
					Nancy Nash (backing vocal)		
2/20/82	R	36	9	5	Lucky Ones	—	↓
4/10/82	R	23	10	6	Take Me To The Top	—	↓
6/11/83	R	2³	14	7	Hot Girls In Love	11	Keep It Up .... Columbia 38703
7/16/83	R	23	14	8	Strike Zone	—	↓
7/30/83	R	11	15	9	Queen Of The Broken Hearts	34	↓
8/24/85	R	3²	13	10	Lovin' Every Minute Of It	9	Lovin' Every Minute Of It .... Columbia 39953
11/16/85	R	23	10	11	Dangerous	65	↓
2/1/86	R	9	9	12	This Could Be The Night	10	↓
8/22/87	R	8	7	13	Notorious	38	Wildside .... Columbia 40893
					co-written by Jon Bon Jovi		
12/2/89+	R	27	8	14	Too Hot	84	Big Ones .... Columbia 45411

LOVE SPIT LOVE
Rock band formed in England: brothers Richard Butler (vocals) and Tim Butler (bass), with Richard Fortus (guitar) and Frank Ferrer (drums). The Butler brothers were also members of the **Psychedelic Furs**.

Debut	Cht	Peak	Wks		Track Title	Pos	Album Title	Label
7/30/94	M	3³	15	1	Am I Wrong	83	Love Spit Love .... Imago 21030
12/3/94	M	31	5	2	Change In The Weather	—	↓
9/13/97	M	33	6	3	Long Long Time	—	Trysome Eatone .... Maverick 46560
12/20/97	M	39	2	4	Fall On Tears	—	↓

LOVETT, Lyle
Born on 11/1/1957 in Klein, Texas. Country singer/songwriter/guitarist. Acted in several movies. Married to actress Julia Roberts from 1993-95.

Debut	Cht	Peak	Wks	Track Title	Pos	Album Title	Label
9/19/92	R	36	2	You've Been So Good Up To Now	—	Joshua Judges Ruth .... Curb 10475

LOVICH, Lene
Born Lili Marlene Premilovich on 3/30/1949 in Detroit, Michigan; raised in Hull, Yorkshire, England. Singer/actress. Acted in the movies *Cha-Cha* and *Mata Hari*.

Debut	Cht	Peak	Wks	Track Title	Pos	Album Title	Label
12/25/82	R	51	4	It's You, Only You (Mein Schmerz)	—	No-Man's-Land .... Stiff 38399

LOWE, Nick
Born on 3/25/1949 in Walton, Surrey, England. Pop-rock singer/songwriter/guitarist. Member of **Rockpile** and **Little Village**. Married to country singer Carlene Carter from 1979-90. Also see **Classic Rock Tracks** section.

Debut	Cht	Peak	Wks		Track Title	Pos	Album Title	Label
3/6/82	R	43	8	1	Stick It Where The Sun Don't Shine	—	Nick The Knife .... Columbia 37932
9/14/85	R	27	9	2	I Knew The Bride (When She Use To Rock And Roll) ...	77	The Rose Of England .... Columbia 39958
					NICK LOWE AND HIS COWBOY OUTFIT		
					produced by **Huey Lewis**		

LRB — see LITTLE RIVER BAND

L7
Female punk-rock band from Los Angeles, California: Suzi Gardner (guitar, vocals), Donita Sparks (guitar, vocals), Jennifer Finch (bass, vocals) and Dee Plakas (drums).

Debut	Cht	Peak	Wks		Track Title	Pos	Album Title	Label
5/23/92	M	8	13	1	Pretend We're Dead	—	Bricks Are Heavy .... Slash 26784
8/13/94	M	20	6	2	Andres	—	Hungry For Stink .... Slash 45624

LUCAS
Born Lucas Secon in 1970 in Copenhagen, Denmark. Male rapper/producer.

Debut	Cht	Peak	Wks	Track Title	Pos	Album Title	Label
10/1/94	M	22	7	Lucas With The Lid Off	29	Lucacentric .... Big Beat 92467
				Junior Dangerous (ragga vocal)		

LUCKY BOYS CONFUSION
Ska-rock band from Chicago, Illinois: Kaustubh Pandav (vocals), Adam Krier (guitar), Joe Sell (guitar), Jason Shultejann (bass) and Ryan Fergus (drums).

Debut	Cht	Peak	Wks	Track Title	Pos	Album Title	Label
4/21/01	M	34	8	Fred Astaire	—	Throwing The Game .... Elektra 62641

LUSCIOUS JACKSON

Female pop-rock band from Manhattan, New York: Jill Cunniff (vocals, bass), Gabrielle Glaser (vocals, guitar), Vivian Trimble (keyboards) and Kate Schellenbach (drums). Trimble left in 1998. Group named after former NBA player Lucious Jackson (played for the Philadelphia 76ers from 1964-72).

11/5/94	ℳ	39	1	1 Citysong	—	Natural Ingredients	Grand Royal 28356
				samples "On And On" by Gladys Knight & The Pips			
11/2/96+	ℳ	18	26	2 Naked Eye	36	Fever In Fever Out	Grand Royal 35534
6/19/99	ℳ	28	10	3 Ladyfingers	—	Electric Honey	Grand Royal 96084

LUSH

Rock band from London, England: Miki Berenyi (vocals, guitar), Emma Anderson (guitar), Steve Ribbon (bass) and Chris Acland (drums). Philip King replaced Ribbon in 1991. Acland committed suicide on 10/17/1996 (age 30).

12/15/90+	ℳ	4	9	1 Sweetness And Light	—	Gala	4 A D 26463
3/2/91	ℳ	14	8	2 De-Luxe	—	↓	
12/21/91+	ℳ	22	7	3 Nothing Natural	—	Spooky	4 A D 26798
2/8/92	ℳ	9	12	4 For Love	—	↓	
4/20/96	ℳ	18	9	5 Ladykillers	—	Lovelife	4 A D 46170

LYNCH, Liam

Born on 9/5/1970 in Akron, Ohio; raised in Hudson, Ohio. Eclectic singer/songwriter/guitarist. Co-creator of the short-lived MTV sock-puppet comedy series *The Sifl & Olly Show*.

3/29/03	ℳ	34	6	United States Of Whatever	—	Fake Songs	S-Curve 83743

LYNCH MOB

Hard-rock band formed in Los Angeles, California: George Lynch (guitar; born on 9/28/1954), Oni Logan (vocals), Anthony Esposito (bass) and Mick Brown (drums). Lynch and Brown were members of **Dokken**. Esposito was a member of **Beggars & Thieves**.

11/17/90	ℝ	31	9	1 Wicked Sensation	—	Wicked Sensation	Elektra 60954
2/2/91	ℝ	19	9	2 River Of Love	—	↓	
5/9/92	ℝ	13	13	3 Tangled In The Web	—	Lynch Mob	Elektra 61322
8/29/92	ℝ	23	11	4 Dream Until Tomorrow	—	↓	

LYNNE, Jeff

Born on 12/30/1947 in Birmingham, England. Singer/songwriter/prolific producer. Leader of **Electric Light Orchestra**. Member of the **Traveling Wilburys**.

6/2/90	ℝ	9	10	Every Little Thing	—	Armchair Theatre	Reprise 26184
				George Harrison (guitar, backing vocal)			

LYNYRD SKYNYRD

Southern-rock band formed in Jacksonville, Florida: Ronnie Van Zant (vocals), Gary Rossington (guitar), Allen Collins (guitar), Steve Gaines (guitar), Billy Powell (keyboards), Leon Wilkeson (bass) and Artimus Pyle (drums). Plane crash on 10/20/1977 in Gillsburg, Mississippi, killed Ronnie Van Zant and Steve Gaines. Gary and Allen formed the **Rossington Collins Band**. Rossington and vocalist **Johnny Van Zant** (the younger brother of Ronnie and **38 Special** lead singer Donnie Van Zant) regrouped with old and new band members for the 1987 Lynyrd Skynyrd Tribute Tour. Collins (paralyzed in a car accident in 1986) died of pneumonia on 1/23/1990 (age 37). Surviving members regrouped in 1991. Original drummer Ricky Medlocke (of **Blackfoot**) joined as a guitarist in 1995. Guitarist Hughie Thomasson (of **The Outlaws**) joined in 1996. Wilkeson died on 7/27/2001 (age 49). Kurt Custer (drums; of **Little America**) was a member from 1991-94. Also see **Classic Rock Tracks** section.

AWARD: R&R Hall of Fame: 2006

TOP HITS: 1)*Smokestack Lightning* 2)*Good Lovin's Hard To Find* 3)*Keeping The Faith*

9/26/87	ℝ	12	7	1 Truck Drivin' Man ... [L]	—	Legend	MCA 42084
				previously unreleased song (vocals by Ronnie Van Zant)			
3/26/88	ℝ	16	7	2 Swamp Music ... [L]	—	Southern By The Grace Of God/Lynyrd Skynyrd	
				recorded on 10/23/1987 at the Starwood Ampitheatre in Nashville, Tennessee		Tribute Tour - 1987	MCA 8027
6/8/91	ℝ	2¹	12	3 Smokestack Lightning	—	Lynyrd Skynyrd 1991	Atlantic 82258
8/10/91	ℝ	10	9	4 Keeping The Faith	—	↓	
2/27/93	ℝ	6	9	5 Good Lovin's Hard To Find	—	The Last Rebel	Atlantic 82447
5/22/93	ℝ	37	2	6 Born To Run	—	↓	
5/10/97	ℝ	22	8	7 Travelin' Man	—	Twenty	CMC International 86211
8/16/97	ℝ	33	5	8 Bring It On	—	↓	
7/31/99	ℝ	13	15	9 Workin'	—	Edge Of Forever	CMC International 86272
11/27/99	ℝ	26	12	10 Preacher Man	—	↓	
4/26/03	ℝ	27	16	11 Red White & Blue	—	Vicious Cycle	Sanctuary 84607

M

MacCOLL, Kirsty
Born on 10/10/1959 in Croydon, Surrey, England. Died in a boating accident in Mexico on 12/18/2000 (age 41). Singer/songwriter/guitarist. Married to noted record producer Steve Lillywhite from 1984-94.

7/6/91	Ⓜ	4	12	1 Walking Down Madison		—	Electric Landlady	Charisma 91688
10/23/93	Ⓜ	20	7	2 Can't Stop Killing You		—	Titanic Days	I.R.S. 27214
2/5/94	Ⓜ	26	3	3 Angel		—	↓	

MACHINES OF LOVING GRACE
Rock band from New York: Scott Benzel (vocals), Stuart Kupers (guitar, bass), Mike Fisher (keyboards) and Brad Kemp (drums). Band named after a poem by Richard Brautigan.

10/9/93	Ⓜ	13	15	Butterfly Wings	—	Concentration	Mammoth 92282

MAD AT GRAVITY
Rock band from Anaheim, California: J. Lynn Johnston (vocals), James Lee Barlow (guitar), Anthony Boscarini (guitar), Ben Froehlich (bass) and Jake Fowler (drums).

9/14/02	ℝ	38	2	Walk Away	—	Resonance	Artist Direct 1034

MADINA LAKE
Hard-rock band from Chicago, Illinois: twin brothers Nathan Leone (vocals) and Matthew Leone (bass), with Mateo Camargo (guitar) and Dan Torelli (drums).

5/12/07	Ⓜ	38	1	House Of Cards	—	From Them, Through Us, To You	Roadrunner 18085

MADNESS
Ska-rock band formed in London, England: Graham McPherson (vocals), Chris Foreman (guitar), Mike Barson (keyboards), Carl Smyth (trumpet), Lee Thompson (sax), Mark Bedford (bass) and Dan Woodgate (drums; later with **Voice Of The Beehive**).

5/14/83	ℝ	9	17	Our House	7	Madness	Geffen 4003

MAD SEASON
All-star rock band formed in Seattle, Washington: Layne Staley (vocals, guitar; of **Alice In Chains**), Mike McCready (guitar; of **Pearl Jam**), John Baker Saunders (bass) and Barrett Martin (drums; of **Screaming Trees**). Band name is an English term for the time of year when psilocybin mushrooms are in full bloom. Staley died of a drug overdose on 4/5/2002 (age 34).

4/1/95	ℝ	2[1]	24	1 River Of Deceit	—	Above	Columbia 67057
4/1/95	Ⓜ	9	18				
7/29/95	ℝ	20	8	2 I Don't Know Anything	—	↓	

MAGNA-FI
Rock band formed in Cleveland, Ohio: brothers Mike Szuter (vocals) and C.J. Szuter (guitar), with Rob Kley (bass) and Charlie Smaldino (drums).

10/9/04	ℝ	40	1	Down In It	—	Burn Out The Stars	Aezra 51004

MAGNAPOP
Rock band from Athens, Georgia: Linda Hopper (vocals), Ruthie Morris (guitar), Shannon Mulvaney (bass) and David McNair (drums).

9/10/94	Ⓜ	25	7	1 Slowly, Slowly	—	Hot Boxing	Priority 53909
6/22/96	Ⓜ	28	9	2 Open The Door	—	Rubbing Doesn't Help	Priority 53992

MAGNIFICENT BASTARDS, The
All-star rock band formed in Los Angeles, California: **Scott Weiland** (vocals; of **Stone Temple Pilots**), Zander Schloss (guitar; of **Thelonious Monster** and **Red Hot Chili Peppers**), Jeff Nolan (guitar), and Bob Thomson (bass).

4/29/95	Ⓜ	12	10	Mockingbird Girl	66[A]	St: Tank Girl	Elektra 61760
6/10/95	ℝ	27	6				

MAIDS OF GRAVITY
Rock trio from Los Angeles, California: Ed Ruscha (vocals, bass), Jim Putnam (guitar, piano) and Craig "Irwin" Levitz (drums).

8/26/95	ℝ	40	1	Only Dreaming	—	Maids Of Gravity	Vernon Yard 40178

MALLOY, Mitch
Born in Dickinson, North Dakota. Rock singer/songwriter.

3/21/92	ℝ	43	6	Anything At All	49	Mitch Malloy	RCA 61044

MALMSTEEN('S), Yngwie J., Rising Force
Born on 6/30/1963 in Stockholm, Sweden. Rock guitarist. Rising Force: **Joe Lynn Turner** (vocals), Jens Johansson (keyboards) and Anders Johansson (drums).

4/16/88	ℝ	19	11	Heaven Tonight	—	Odyssey	Polydor 835451

MANBREAK
Rock band from Liverpool, England: Steve Swindelli (vocals), Snaykee (guitar), Mr. Blonde (guitar), Roy Van Der Kerkoff (bass) and Stu Boy Stu (drums).

7/12/97	ℝ	37	2	Ready Or Not	—	Come And See	Almo Sounds 80013

Billboard				ARTIST			
Debut	Cht	Peak	Wks	Track Title	®=Mainstream Rock ⓜ=Modern Rock	Hot Pos	Album Title	Album Label & Number

MANFRED MANN'S EARTH BAND

Born Manfred Lubowitz on 10/21/1940 in Johannesburg, South Africa. Formed pop-rock band in England: Mann (keyboards), Chris Thompson (vocals, guitar), Steve Waller (guitar), Matt Irving (bass) and Geoff Britton (drums). Also see **Classic Rock Tracks** section.

Debut	Cht	Peak	Wks	Track	Hot Pos	Album	Label & Number
3/21/81	®	15	5	1 For You................... *first recorded by* **Bruce Springsteen** *in 1973*	106	*Chance*	Warner 3498
2/4/84	®	3³	13	2 Runner...................	22	*Somewhere In Afrika*	Arista 8194
5/19/84	®	34	5	3 Rebel...................	—	↓	

MANITOBA'S WILD KINGDOM

Hard-rock band from New York: Richard "Dick Manitoba" Blum (vocals), Ross Funicello (guitar), Adny Shernoff (bass) and J.P. Patterson (drums).

6/16/90	®	48	1	The Party Starts Now!!..........	—	*...And You?*	MCA 6367

MANMADE GOD

Rock band from San Francisco, California: Pann (vocals), Craig Locicero (guitar), James Walker (bass) and Steve Jacobs (drums).

6/21/03	®	36	8	Safe Passage..........	—	*Manmade God*	American 014102

MANN, Aimee

Born on 9/8/1960 in Richmond, Virginia. Female singer/songwriter/guitarist. Lead singer of '**Til Tuesday**. Married **Michael Penn** on 12/29/1997.

5/29/93	ⓜ	16	8	1 I Should've Known..........	—	*Whatever*	Imago 21017
11/5/94+	ⓜ	24	13	2 That's Just What You Are..........	93	*St: Melrose Place*	Giant 24577

MANSON, Marilyn   ⓜ All-Time: #87

Born Brian Warner on 1/5/1969 in Canton, Ohio. Hard-rock singer/songwriter. Noted for his controversial stage performances. His band includes: Scott "Daisy Berkowitz" Putesky (guitar), Steve "Madonna Wayne Gacy" Bier (keyboards), Jeordi "Twiggy Ramirez" White (bass) and Ken "Ginger Fish" Wilson (drums).

TOP HITS: 1)The Dope Show 2)Personal Jesus 3)mOBSCENE

5/4/96	ⓜ	26	7	1 Sweet Dreams (Are Made Of This)..........	—	*Smells Like Children*	Nothing 92641
4/27/96	®	31	7				
10/5/96	ⓜ	26	16	2 The Beautiful People..........	—	*Antichrist Superstar*	Nothing 90086
10/12/96	®	29	15				
2/8/97	®	30	7	3 Tourniquet..........	—	↓	
8/29/98	®	12	21	4 The Dope Show	122	*Mechanical Animals*	Nothing 90273
8/29/98	ⓜ	15	21				
1/16/99	®	25	10	5 I Don't Like The Drugs (But The Drugs Like Me)..........	—	↓	
1/30/99	ⓜ	36	5				
4/10/99	®	28	7	6 Rock Is Dead..........	—	↓	
4/17/99	ⓜ	30	7				
11/4/00	®	22	9	7 Disposable Teens..........	—	*Holy Wood (In The Shadow Of The Valley Of Death)*	Nothing 490790
11/4/00	ⓜ	24	11				
12/8/01+	®	30	8	8 Tainted Love..........	—	*St: Not Another Teen Movie*	Maverick 48250
12/8/01+	ⓜ	33	8				
5/3/03	®	18	13	9 mOBSCENE..........	—	*The Golden Age Of Grotesque*	Nothing 000370
5/3/03	ⓜ	26	10				
10/2/04	ⓜ	12	20	10 Personal Jesus..........	124	*Lest We Forget: The Best Of*	Nothing 003478
9/18/04	®	20	21				
5/12/07	ⓜ	24	12	11 Heart Shaped Glasses (When The Heart Guides The Hand)..........	—	*Eat Me, Drink Me*	Interscope 009054
5/19/07	®	31	10				

MANSUN

Rock band from Manchester, England: Paul Draper (vocals), Dominic Chad (guitar), Stove King (bass) and Andie Rathbone (drums).

7/5/97	ⓜ	25	9	Wide Open Space..........	—	*Attack Of The Grey Lantern*	Epic 67935

MARCHELLO

Hard-rock band from Long Island, New York: Gene Marchello (vocals, guitar), Gary Bivona (keyboards), Nick DiMichino (bass) and John Miceli (drums).

4/15/89	®	46	3	First Love..........	—	*Destiny*	CBS Associated 45096

MARCY PLAYGROUND
Rock trio from Manhattan, New York: John Wozniak (vocals, guitar), Dylan Keefe (bass) and Dan Reiser (drums).

11/1/97	Ⓜ	❶¹⁵	34	1 Sex And Candy	8	Marcy Playground	Capitol 53569
12/20/97+	Ⓡ	4	27				
5/9/98	Ⓜ	8	21	2 Saint Joe On The School Bus	—	↓	
6/27/98	Ⓡ	30	8				
10/30/99	Ⓜ	25	9	3 It's Saturday	—	Shapeshifter	Capitol 23142

MARILLION
Rock band from Aylesbury, England: Derek "Fish" Dick (vocals), Steve Rothery (guitar), Mark Kelly (keyboards), Pete Trewavas (bass) and Mick Pointer (drums). Ian Mosley replaced Pointer in 1984. Steve Hogarth replaced Fish in late 1988.

6/11/83	Ⓡ	21	4	1 He Knows, You Know	—	Script For A Jester's Tear	Capitol 12269
8/17/85	Ⓡ	14	14	2 Kayleigh	74	Misplaced Childhood	Capitol 12431
3/29/86	Ⓡ	30	4	3 Lady Nina	—	Brief Encounter	Capitol 15023
7/4/87	Ⓡ	24	6	4 Incommunicado	—	Clutching At Straws	Capitol 12539
11/18/89	Ⓡ	49	2	5 Hooks In You	—	Seasons End	Capitol 12877

MARINO, Frank
Born on 8/22/1954 in Montreal, Quebec, Canada. Rock singer/guitarist. Leader of Mahogany Rush.

12/18/82+	Ⓡ	9	18	Strange Dreams	—	Juggernaut	Columbia 38023

MARLEY, Bob, & The Wailers
Born on 2/6/1945 in Rhoden Hall, Jamaica. Died of cancer on 5/11/1981 (age 36). The most popular reggae singer/songwriter of all-time. Father of **Ziggy Marley & The Melody Makers**.

11/21/92	Ⓜ	11	9	Iron Lion Zion	—	Songs Of Freedom	Tuff Gong 512280
				previously unreleased recording			

MARLEY, Ziggy, And The Melody Makers
Family reggae band from Kingston, Jamaica: David "Ziggy" Marley (vocals, guitar; born on 10/17/1968), Stephen Marley, Sharon Marley and Cedella Marley. Children of **Bob Marley**.

5/7/88	Ⓡ	16	9	1 Tomorrow People	39	Conscious Party	Virgin 90878
9/10/88	Ⓜ	5	4	2 Tumblin' Down	—	↓	
8/13/88	Ⓡ	43	4				
8/5/89	Ⓜ	2¹	10	3 Look Who's Dancing	—	One Bright Day	Virgin 91256
6/22/91	Ⓜ	6	7	4 Kozmik	—	Jahmekya	Virgin 91626
7/3/93	Ⓜ	16	9	5 Brothers And Sisters	—	Joy And Blues	Virgin 87961

MAROON 5
Alternative pop-rock band from Los Angeles, California: Adam Levine (vocals, guitar), James Valentine (guitar), Jesse Carmichael (keyboards), Mickey Madden (bass) and Ryan Dusick (drums).

1/18/03	Ⓜ	31	9	Harder To Breathe	18	Songs About Jane	Octone 50001

MARS, Chris
Born on 4/26/1961 in Minneapolis, Minnesota. Rock singer/drummer. Member of **The Replacements** from 1980-90.

5/16/92	Ⓜ	9	8	Popular Creeps	—	Horseshoes And Hand Grenades	Smash 513198

MARSHALL TUCKER BAND, The
Southern-rock band from Spartanburg, South Carolina: Doug Gray (vocals), Toy Caldwell (guitar), George McCorkle (guitar), Jerry Eubanks (sax, flute) and Paul Riddle (drums). Caldwell died of respiratory failure on 2/25/1993 (age 45). McCorkle died on 6/29/2007 (age 60). Marshall Tucker was the owner of the band's rehearsal hall. Also see **Classic Rock Tracks** section.

6/27/81	Ⓡ	60	1	Silverado	—	Dedicated	Warner 3525

MARS VOLTA, The
Progressive-rock band from El Paso, Texas: Cedric Bixler-Zavala (vocals), Omar Rodriguez-Lopez (guitar), Isaiah "Ikey" Owens (keyboards), Marcel Rodriguez (percussion), Juan Alderete (bass) and Jon Theodore (drums).

1/22/05	Ⓜ	7	16	The Widow	95	Frances The Mule	Strummer 004129
3/5/05	Ⓡ	25	14				

MARTIN, Eric, Band
Born on 10/10/1960 in San Francisco, California. His band: John Nyman (guitar), Mark Ross (guitar), David Jacobson (keyboards), Tom Duke (bass) and Troy Luccketta (drums). Martin formed **Mr. Big** in 1988. Luccketta joined **Tesla**.

10/1/83	Ⓡ	42	2	Sucker For A Pretty Face	—	Sucker For A Pretty Face	Elektra 60238

MARTIN, Marilyn
Born on 5/4/1954 in Louisville, Kentucky. Adult Contemporary singer/songwriter. Former session singer.

2/8/86	Ⓡ	18	9	Night Moves	28	Marilyn Martin	Atlantic 81292

MARVELOUS 3

Rock trio from Atlanta, Georgia: Butch Walker (vocals, guitar), Jayce Fincher (bass) and Doug "Slug" Mitchell (drums).

Debut	Cht	Peak	Wks	Track Title	Hot Pos	Album Title	Album Label & Number
1/9/99	ℳ	5	20	Freak Of The Week	112	Hey! Album	HiFi 62375
2/27/99	®	23	11				

MARX, Richard

Born on 9/16/1963 in Chicago, Illinois. Pop-rock singer/songwriter. Professional jingle singer since age five. Backing singer for **Lionel Richie**. Married Cynthia Rhodes (of Animotion) on 1/8/1989.

Debut	Cht	Peak	Wks	Track Title	Hot Pos	Album Title	Album Label & Number
5/23/87	®	❶¹	14	1 Don't Mean Nothing	3¹	Richard Marx	EMI-Manhattan 53049
8/8/87	®	7	10	2 Should've Known Better	3¹	↓	
11/14/87	®	17	11	3 Have Mercy	—	↓	
2/13/88	®	41	4	4 Endless Summer Nights	2²	↓	
5/6/89	®	5	11	5 Satisfied	❶¹	Repeat Offender	EMI 90380
7/22/89	®	12	9	6 Nothin' You Can Do About It	—	↓	
1/20/90	®	17	8	7 Too Late To Say Goodbye	12	↓	

MARY'S DANISH

Pop-rock band from Los Angeles, California: Gretchen Seager (vocals), Julie Ritter (vocals), David King (guitar), Louis Gutierrez (guitar), Chris Wagner (bass) and James Bradley (drums).

Debut	Cht	Peak	Wks	Track Title	Hot Pos	Album Title	Album Label & Number
7/22/89	ℳ	7	10	1 Don't Crash The Car Tonight	—	There Goes The Wondertruck	Chameleon 74803
8/10/91	ℳ	14	9	2 Julie's Blanket (pigsheadsnakeface)	—	Circa	Morgan Creek 20003
9/26/92	ℳ	20	8	3 Leave It Alone	—	American Standard	Morgan Creek 20016

MASON, Dave

Born on 5/10/1946 in Worcester, West Midlands, England. Rock singer/songwriter/guitarist. Original member of **Traffic**. Brief member of **Fleetwood Mac** in 1993. Also see **Classic Rock Tracks** section.

Debut	Cht	Peak	Wks	Track Title	Hot Pos	Album Title	Album Label & Number
11/7/87	®	24	6	Something In The Heart Steve Winwood (synthesizer)	—	Two Hearts	MCA 42086

MASON, Nick

Born on 1/27/1945 in Birmingham, England. Rock drummer. Member of **Pink Floyd**.

Debut	Cht	Peak	Wks	Track Title	Hot Pos	Album Title	Album Label & Number
8/3/85	®	21	7	Lie For A Lie NICK MASON & RICK FENN	—	Profiles	Columbia 40142

MASSIVE ATTACK

Electronica-dance band from Bristol, England: Robert "3-D" Del Naja, Andy "Mushroom" Vowles and Grant "Daddy G" Marshall.

Debut	Cht	Peak	Wks	Track Title	Hot Pos	Album Title	Album Label & Number
9/14/91	ℳ	28	2	Safe From Harm		Blue Lines	Virgin 91685

MASTERS OF REALITY

Rock trio formed in Syracuse, New York: Chris Goss (vocals), Googe (bass) and Ginger Baker (drums). Baker was with Cream and **BBM**. Band name derived from the 1971 album by **Black Sabbath**.

Debut	Cht	Peak	Wks	Track Title	Hot Pos	Album Title	Album Label & Number
2/20/93	®	8	12	She Got Me (When She Got Her Dress On)	—	Sunrise On The Sufferbus	Chrysalis 21976

MASTODON

Hard-rock band from Atlanta, Georgia: Brent Hinds (vocals, guitar), Bill Kelliher (guitar), Troy Sanders (bass) and Brann Dailor (drums).

Debut	Cht	Peak	Wks	Track Title	Hot Pos	Album Title	Album Label & Number
1/13/07	®	33	12	Colony Of Birchmen	—	Blood Mountain	Relapse 44364

MATCHBOX 20

Pop-rock band from Orlando, Florida: **Rob Thomas** (vocals; born on 2/14/1972), Kyle Cook (guitar; born on 8/29/1975), Adam Gaynor (guitar; born on 11/26/1963), Brian Yale (bass; born on 10/24/1968) and Paul Doucette (drums; born on 8/22/1972).

Debut	Cht	Peak	Wks	Track Title	Hot Pos	Album Title	Album Label & Number
10/19/96+	®	8	22	1 Long Day	—	Yourself Or Someone Like You	Lava 92721
5/3/97	ℳ	❶¹	26	2 Push	5ᴬ	↓	
3/15/97	®	4	35				
11/1/97+	®	2²	26	3 3 AM	3⁸ᴬ	↓	
10/18/97	ℳ	3¹	26				
4/4/98	ℳ	13	25	4 Real World	9ᴬ	↓	
4/11/98	®	17	21				
4/29/00	ℳ	16	18	5 Bent	❶¹	Mad Season	Lava 83339
5/6/00	®	24	11	MATCHBOX TWENTY			

MATERIAL ISSUE

Pop trio from Chicago, Illinois: Jim Ellison (vocals, guitar), Ted Ansani (bass) and Mike Zelenko (drums). Ellison committed suicide on 6/20/1996 (age 31).

Debut	Cht	Peak	Wks	Track Title	Hot Pos	Album Title	Album Label & Number
2/16/91	ℳ	3¹	11	1 Valerie Loves Me	—	International Pop Overthrow	Mercury 848155
4/27/91	ℳ	6	11	2 Diane	—	↓	
5/23/92	ℳ	6	11	3 What Girls Want	—	Destination Universe	Mercury 512333
4/9/94	ℳ	20	7	4 Kim The Waitress	—	Freak City Soundtrack	Mercury 518894

Debut	Cht	Peak	Wks	ARTIST / Track Title	Hot Pos	Album Title	Album Label & Number

MATISYAHU
Born Matthew Miller on 6/30/1979 in West Chester, Pennsylvania; raised in White Plains, New York. Hasidic reggae rapper/singer. Name is Hebrew for "Gift of God." Wears traditional Hasidic clothing and raps in English, Hebrew and Yiddish.

| 11/19/05+ | Ⓜ | 7 | 20 | 1 King Without A Crown | 28 | Youth | Or 81239 |
| 3/25/06 | Ⓜ | 19 | 13 | 2 Youth | 121 | ↓ | |

MATTHEWS, Dave, Band
Ⓜ **1990s: #23 / All-Time: #25**

Born on 1/9/1967 in Johannesburg, South Africa; raised in Westchester County, New York. Alternative-rock singer/songwriter/guitarist. Formed his band in Charlottesville, Virginia: Leroi Moore (sax; born on 9/7/1961), Boyd Tinsley (violin; born on 5/16/1964), Stefan Lessard (bass; born on 6/4/1974) and Carter Beauford (drums; born on 11/2/1957). Popular touring band.

TOP HITS: 1)Don't Drink The Water 2)I Did It 3)Too Much

2/25/95	®	5	26	1 What Would You Say	22[A]	Under The Table And Dreaming	RCA 66449
2/18/95	Ⓜ	11	23				
7/1/95	Ⓜ	18	19	2 Ants Marching	21[A]	↓	
7/22/95	®	18	17				
12/16/95+	Ⓜ	18	12	3 Satellite	55[A]	↓	
1/20/96	®	36	4				
4/13/96	Ⓜ	5	15	4 Too Much	39[A]	Crash	RCA 66904
4/13/96	®	9	16				
7/20/96	Ⓜ	19	14	5 So Much To Say	48[A]	↓	
8/3/96	®	20	10	Grammy: Rock Vocal Group			
11/30/96+	Ⓜ	7	26	6 Crash Into Me	19[A]	↓	
5/31/97	Ⓜ	18	15	7 Tripping Billies	—	↓	
4/11/98	Ⓜ	4	16	8 Don't Drink The Water	50[A]	Before These Crowded Streets	RCA 67660
4/18/98	®	19	13				
7/11/98	Ⓜ	8	16	9 Stay (Wasting Time)	44[A]	↓	
8/15/98	®	35	5				
10/31/98+	Ⓜ	11	29	10 Crush	75	↓	
1/20/01	Ⓜ	5	14	11 I Did It	71	Everyday	RCA 67988
1/27/01	®	23	13				
4/21/01	Ⓜ	10	25	12 The Space Between	22	↓	
11/17/01	Ⓜ	38	4	13 Everyday	101	↓	
6/1/02	Ⓜ	20	17	14 Where Are You Going	39	Busted Stuff	RCA 68117
12/14/02	Ⓜ	33	6	15 Grey Street	119	↓	
9/13/03	Ⓜ	35	5	16 Gravedigger	—	Some Devil	RCA 55167
				DAVE MATTHEWS			
				Grammy: Rock Male Vocal			

MAX Q
Rock duo formed in Melbourne, Australia: Michael Hutchence (of **INXS**) and Ian Olsen. Max Q is the name of Olsen's dog. Hutchence committed suicide on 11/22/1997 (age 37).

| 9/2/89 | Ⓜ | 6 | 10 | Way Of The World | — | Max Q | Atlantic 82014 |

MAY, Brian
Born on 7/19/1947 in Twickenham, Middlesex, England. Lead guitarist of **Queen**.

| 2/27/93 | ® | 9 | 9 | Driven By You | — | Back To The Light | Hollywood 61404 |

MAYFIELD FOUR, The
Rock band from Spokane, Washington: Myles Kennedy (vocals), Craig Johnson (guitar), Marty Meisner (bass) and Zia Uddin (drums).

| 7/7/01 | ® | 37 | 4 | Eden (Turn The Page) | — | Second Skin | Epic 61080 |

MAZZY STAR
Alternative-rock duo from California: songwriter/guitarist David Roback and vocalist Hope Sandoval. Also see **The Jesus & Mary Chain.**

8/11/90	Ⓜ	29	3	1 Blue Flower	—	She Hangs Brightly	Rough Trade 80077
8/13/94	Ⓜ	3[1]	18	2 Fade Into You	44	So Tonight That I Might See	Capitol 98253
12/3/94+	Ⓜ	19	12	3 Halah	—	She Hangs Brightly	Capitol 96508

Billboard				ARTIST	Hot		
Debut	Cht	Peak	Wks	Track Title ®=Mainstream Rock ⓜ=Modern Rock	Pos	Album Title	Album Label & Number

MC 900 FT. JESUS
Experimental electronic artist Mark Griffin (born in Dallas, Texas). Name refers to a vision by evangelist Oral Roberts.

7/23/94	ⓜ	25	8	If I Only Had A Brain..	—	One Step Ahead Of The Spider............American 45560

McAULEY SCHENKER GROUP
Hard-rock band led by Irish vocalist Robin McAuley (former member of **Grand Prix**) and West German-born guitarist Michael Schenker (brother Rudolf is a member of **Scorpions**). Schenker was also a member of **Contraband**.

3/17/84	®	55	2	1 Rock My Nights Away	—	Built To Destroy....................................Chrysalis 41441
				THE MICHAEL SCHENKER GROUP		
10/24/87	®	40	7	2 Gimme Your Love...	—	Perfect Timing ....Capitol 46985
1/23/88	®	49	2	3 Love Is Not A Game	—	↓
12/2/89+	®	5	17	4 Anytime	69	Save Yourself ....Capitol 92752
3/7/92	®	16	11	5 When I'm Gone	—	MSG ....Impact 10385
				SCHENKER/McAULEY		

McCAIN, Edwin
Born on 1/20/1970 in Greenville, South Carolina. Singer/songwriter/guitarist.

9/9/95	®	25	11	Solitude	72	Honor Among Thieves ....Lava 92597

McCARTNEY, Paul
Born James Paul McCartney on 6/18/1942 in Liverpool, England. Founding member/bass guitarist of **The Beatles**. Married Linda Eastman on 3/12/1969 (she died of cancer on 4/17/1998, age 55). Formed group Wings in 1971; disbanded in 1981. Starred in own movie *Give My Regards To Broad Street*. Knighted by Queen Elizabeth II in 1997. Also see **Classic Rock Tracks** section.

AWARDS: Grammy: Lifetime Achievement Award 1990 ★ R&R Hall of Fame: 1999

TOP HITS: 1)Figure Of Eight   2)My Brave Face   3)No More Lonely Nights

4/24/82	®	34	2	1 Ebony And Ivory..	❶⁷	Tug Of War ....Columbia 37462
				PAUL McCARTNEY with Stevie Wonder		
5/15/82	®	22	8	2 Ballroom Dancing..	—	↓
5/22/82	®	39	7	3 Take It Away...	10	↓
5/29/82	®	44	5	4 The Pound Is Sinking	—	↓
6/12/82	®	46	1	5 Here Today	—	↓
10/29/83	®	24	12	6 Say Say Say	❶⁶	Pipes Of Peace ....Columbia 39149
				PAUL McCARTNEY AND MICHAEL JACKSON		
10/20/84	®	16	9	7 No More Lonely Nights	6	Give My Regards To Broad Street.........Columbia 39613
11/30/85	®	31	8	8 Spies Like Us	7	St: Spies Like Us...................................Capitol 5537
9/13/86	®	44	3	9 Angry	—	Press To Play ....Capitol 12475
5/27/89	®	12	8	10 My Brave Face	25	Flowers In The Dirt ....Capitol 91653
				co-written by **Elvis Costello**		
12/16/89+	®	8	11	11 Figure Of Eight	92	↓
3/17/90	®	43	3	12 We Got Married	—	↓
8/25/90	®	41	3	13 Hey Jude .... [L]	—	VA: Knebworth - The Album....................Polydor 84702
				#1 Pop hit for **The Beatles** in 1968		
10/27/90	®	35	7	14 Birthday .... [L]	—	Tripping The Live Fantastic ....Capitol 94778
				first recorded by **The Beatles** in 1968		
5/24/97	®	23	12	15 The World Tonight..	64	Flaming Pie ....Capitol

McCLINTON, Delbert
Born on 11/4/1940 in Lubbock, Texas. Rock singer/harmonica player. Also see **Classic Rock Tracks** section.

5/16/92	®	13	14	Every Time I Roll The Dice	—	Never Been Rocked Enough ....Curb 77521
				Melissa Etheridge (backing vocal); **Bonnie Raitt** (guitar)		

McCULLOCH, Ian
Born on 5/5/1959 in Liverpool, England. Lead singer of **Echo & The Bunnymen** and **Electrafixion**.

10/28/89	ⓜ	❶⁴	15	1 Proud To Fall	—	Candleland ....Sire 26012
2/3/90	ⓜ	10	7	2 Faith And Healing...	—	↓
12/7/91+	ⓜ	13	8	3 Hey That's No Way To Say Goodbye..........................	—	VA: I'm Your Fan: The Songs Of Leonard Cohen...Atlantic 82349
				first recorded by Leonard Cohen in 1968		
2/22/92	ⓜ	6	10	4 Honeydrip..	—	Mysterio ....Sire 26684
4/25/92	ⓜ	9	9	5 Lover Lover Lover	—	↓

McDERMOTT, Michael
Born in Chicago, Illinois. Rock singer/songwriter/guitarist.

8/3/91	®	34	7	A Wall I Must Climb	—	620 W. Surf ....Giant 24416

Billboard				ARTIST		Hot		
Debut	Cht	Peak	Wks	Track Title	®=Mainstream Rock ⓜ=Modern Rock	Pos	Album Title	Album Label & Number

McDONALD, Michael
Born on 2/12/1952 in St. Louis, Missouri. Pop-rock singer/songwriter/keyboardist. Former lead singer of **The Doobie Brothers**.

8/3/85	®	4	11	1 No Lookin' Back	34	No Lookin' Back ....Warner 25291
9/21/85	®	38	6	2 Bad Times	—	↓
				Joe Walsh (guitar)		
11/2/91	®	17	12	3 Pretzel Logic .... [L]	—	VA: The New York Rock And Soul Revue ...Giant 24423
				DONALD FAGEN & MICHAEL McDONALD		
				recorded at the Beacon Theatre in New York City; #57 Pop hit for **Steely Dan** in 1974		

McGUINN, Roger
Born James McGuinn on 7/13/1942 in Chicago, Illinois. Lead singer/guitarist of **The Byrds**. Changed name to Roger in 1968.

1/19/91	®	2²	13	1 King Of The Hill	—	Back From Rio ....Arista 8648
				Tom Petty (co-writer, guest vocal)		
3/30/91	®	12	10	2 Someone To Love	—	↓

McKEE, Maria
Born on 8/17/1964 in Los Angeles, California. Former lead singer of **Lone Justice**.

8/12/89	ⓜ	29	1	I've Forgotten What It Was In You (That Put The Need In Me)	—	Maria McKee ....Geffen 24229

McKENNITT, Loreena
Born on 2/17/1957 in Morden, Manitoba, Canada. Female singer/songwriter/harpist.

12/27/97+	ⓜ	17	15	The Mummers' Dance	18	The Book Of Secrets.................................Warner 46719

McKENZIE, Bob & Doug
Comedy duo from Canada: Rick "Bob" Moranis (born on 4/18/1953) and Dave "Doug" Thomas (born on 5/20/1949). Characters created for brief segments of *SCTV* television show. Both starred (as the McKenzie brothers) in the movie *Strange Brew*. Moranis later acted in several movies. Thomas, the brother of singer Ian Thomas, hosted own CBS-TV series in 1990 and was a cast member of TV's *Grace Under Fire*.

1/23/82	®	7	11	Take Off .... [N]	16	Great White North ....Mercury 4034
				Geddy Lee (of **Rush**; vocal)		

McLACHLAN, Sarah
Born on 1/28/1968 in Halifax, Nova Scotia, Canada. Female singer/songwriter/guitarist/pianist. Founded the all-female *Lilith Fair* concert tour in 1997.

2/15/92	ⓜ	4	15	1 Into The Fire...	—	Solace ....Arista 18631
3/26/94	ⓜ	4	15	2 Possession	73	Fumbling Towards Ecstasy ....Arista 18725
9/10/94	ⓜ	16	14	3 Good Enough..	77	↓
2/4/95	ⓜ	29	11	4 Hold On	—	↓
7/5/97	ⓜ	3¹	26	5 Building A Mystery	13	Surfacing ....Arista 18970
11/8/97	ⓜ	14	20	6 Sweet Surrender	28	↓

McMURTRY, James
Born on 3/18/1962 in Fort Worth, Texas. Folk-rock guitarist. Son of novelist Larry McMurtry.

9/2/89	®	33	7	Painting By Numbers	—	Too Long In The Wasteland ....Columbia 45229

McQUEEN STREET
Hard-rock band from Montgomery, Alabama: brothers Derek Welsh (vocals) and Chris Welsh (drums), with Michael Powers (guitar) and Richard Hatcher (bass).

11/23/91+	®	32	7	In Heaven	—	McQueen Street ....SBK 96428

McVIE, Christine
Born Christine Perfect on 7/12/1943 in Birmingham, England. Singer/keyboardist with **Fleetwood Mac** since 1970. Married to Fleetwood Mac bassist John McVie (1968-77).

2/4/84	®	❶²	11	1 Got A Hold On Me	10	Christine McVie...Warner 25059
2/25/84	®	27	5	2 One In A Million	—	↓
4/7/84	®	24	10	3 Love Will Show Us How....................................	30	↓

MEAT LOAF
Born Marvin Lee Aday on 9/27/1947 in Dallas, Texas. Pop-rock singer. Sang lead vocals on **Ted Nugent**'s 1976 *Free-For-All* album. Played "Eddie" in the Los Angeles production and movie of *The Rocky Horror Picture Show*. Appeared several other movies. Also see **Classic Rock Tracks** section.

5/18/85	®	41	3	1 Modern Girl	—	Bad Attitude ....RCA Victor 5451
9/11/93	®	10	12	2 I'd Do Anything For Love (But I Won't Do That)	❶⁵	Bat Out Of Hell II: Back Into Hell ....MCA 10699
				Grammy: Rock Vocal Performance		
12/11/93	®	17	7	3 Life Is A Lemon And I Want My Money Back........	—	↓
2/5/94	®	25	7	4 Rock And Roll Dreams Come Through	13	↓

MEAT PUPPETS

Rock trio from Phoenix, Arizona: brothers Curt Kirkwood (vocals, guitar) and Cris Kirkwood (bass), with Derrick Bostrom (drums).

Debut	Cht	Peak	Wks	#	Track Title	Hot Pos	Album Title	Label & Number
8/10/91	Ⓜ	13	8	1	Sam	—	Forbidden Places	London 828254
3/5/94	®	2³	26	2	Backwater	47	Too High To Die	London 828484
2/19/94	Ⓜ	11	24					
8/13/94	®	28	7	3	We Don't Exist	—	↓	
9/30/95	®	20	7	4	Scum	—	No Joke!	London 828665
9/30/95	Ⓜ	23	6					

MEGADETH

® 1990s: #36 / All-Time: #84

Thrash-metal band formed in Los Angeles, California: Dave Mustaine (vocals, guitar), Marty Friedman (guitar), Dave Ellefson (bass) and Nick Menza (drums). Jimmy DeGrasso replaced Menza in 1998. Al Pitrelli replaced Friedman in 2000. Mustaine was an early guitarist with **Metallica**.

TOP HITS: 1)Trust 2)Breadline 3)Crush 'Em

Debut	Cht	Peak	Wks	#	Track Title	Hot Pos	Album Title	Label & Number
9/5/92	®	29	7	1	Symphony Of Destruction	71	Countdown To Extinction	Capitol 98531
12/5/92	®	30	8	2	Foreclosure Of A Dream	—	↓	
2/27/93	®	27	9	3	Sweating Bullets	—	↓	
6/26/93	®	18	9	4	Angry Again	—	St: Last Action Hero	Columbia 57127
11/27/93	®	23	10	5	99 Ways To Die	—	VA: The Beavis & Butt-head Experience	Geffen 24613
11/26/94	®	29	11	6	Train Of Consequences	—	Youthanasia	Capitol 29004
3/18/95	®	31	7	7	A Tout Le Monde	—	↓	
5/31/97	®	5	26	8	Trust	—	Cryptic Writings	Capitol 38262
10/11/97	®	8	26	9	Almost Honest	—	↓	
2/21/98	®	15	20	10	Use The Man	—	↓	
7/11/98	®	19	12	11	A Secret Place	—	↓	
7/10/99	®	6	12	12	Crush 'Em	—	Risk	Capitol 99134
9/25/99	®	26	8	13	Insomnia	—	↓	
12/4/99+	®	6	17	14	Breadline	—	↓	
9/30/00	®	21	11	15	Kill The King	—	Capitol Punishment	Capitol 25916
4/21/01	®	22	11	16	Moto Psycho	—	The World Needs A Hero	Sanctuary 684503
8/21/04	®	21	17	17	Die Dead Enough	—	The System Has Failed	Sanctuary 84708
2/5/05	®	39	1	18	Of Mice And Men	—	↓	

MEISNER, Randy

Born on 3/8/1946 in Scottsbluff, Nebraska. Pop-rock singer/bassist. Member of **Poco** (1968-69), Rick Nelson's Stone Canyon Band (1969-71) and the **Eagles** (1971-77). Also see **Classic Rock Tracks** section.

Debut	Cht	Peak	Wks	#	Track Title	Hot Pos	Album Title	Label & Number
3/21/81	®	14	3		Hearts On Fire	19	One More Song	Epic 36748

MELLENCAMP, John Cougar

® 1980s: #1 / 1990s: #14 / All-Time: #5

Born on 10/7/1951 in Seymour, Indiana. Rock singer/songwriter/guitarist. Given name Johnny Cougar by **David Bowie**'s manager, Tony DeFries. First recorded for MCA in 1976. Directed and starred as "Bud Parks" in the 1992 movie *Falling From Grace*. Married model Elaine Irwin on 9/5/1992. Also see **Classic Rock Tracks** section.

AWARDS: R&R Hall of Fame: 2008 ★ Billboard: Century Award 2001

TOP HITS: 1)Lonely Ol' Night 2)Paper In Fire 3)Get A Leg Up 4)Again Tonight 5)What If I Came Knocking

JOHN COUGAR:

Debut	Cht	Peak	Wks	#	Track Title	Hot Pos	Album Title	Label & Number
3/21/81	®	44	2	1	Ain't Even Done With The Night	17	Nothin' Matters And What If It Did	Riva 7403
5/1/82	®	❶¹	26	2	Hurts So Good	2⁴	American Fool	Riva 7501
					Grammy: Rock Male Vocal			
6/26/82	®	3²	10	3	Jack & Diane	❶⁴	↓	
9/25/82	®	36	7	4	Thundering Hearts	—	↓	

JOHN COUGAR MELLENCAMP:

Debut	Cht	Peak	Wks	#	Track Title	Hot Pos	Album Title	Label & Number
10/15/83	®	2¹	19	5	Crumblin' Down	9	Uh-Huh	Riva 7504
10/29/83+	®	3²	19	6	Pink Houses	8	↓	
					RS500 #439			
1/28/84	®	34	4	7	Serious Business	—	↓	
2/4/84	®	28	5	8	Play Guitar	—	↓	
2/18/84	®	15	11	9	Authority Song	15	↓	
					R&R Hall of Fame			
8/17/85	®	❶⁵	14	10	Lonely Ol' Night	6	Scarecrow	Riva 824865
9/14/85	®	2²	20	11	Small Town	6	↓	
9/14/85	®	6	22	12	R.O.C.K. In The U.S.A. (A Salute To 60's Rock)	2¹	↓	
9/21/85+	®	16	27	13	Rain On The Scarecrow	21	↓	

				ARTIST / Track Title	Hot Pos	Album Title	Album Label & Number

R=Mainstream Rock
M=Modern Rock

MELLENCAMP, John Cougar — cont'd

Debut	Cht	Peak	Wks	Track Title	Hot Pos	Album Title	Album Label & Number
11/30/85+	R	28	13	14 Justice And Independence '85	—	↓	
1/18/86	R	14	11	15 Minutes To Memories	—	↓	
7/5/86	R	4	10	16 Rumbleseat	28	↓	
2/15/86	R	19	8	17 Under The Boardwalk	—	(single only)	Riva 884455
				#4 Pop hit for The Drifters in 1964			
8/15/87	R	❶⁵	11	18 Paper In Fire	9	The Lonesome Jubilee	Mercury 832465
9/5/87	R	❶¹	20	19 Cherry Bomb	8	↓	
9/5/87	R	10	13	20 Hard Times For An Honest Man	—	↓	
9/12/87+	R	3²	11	21 The Real Life	—	↓	
2/6/88	R	3³	12	22 Check It Out	14	↓	
5/7/88	R	7	9	23 Rooty Toot Toot	61	↓	
9/10/88	R	17	7	24 Rave On	—	St: Cocktail	Elektra 60806
				#37 Pop hit for Buddy Holly in 1958			
4/29/89	R	2³	8	25 Pop Singer	15	Big Daddy	Mercury 838220
5/20/89	R	8	11	26 Martha Say	—	↓	
6/3/89	R	42	8	27 Let It All Hang Out	—	↓	
				#12 Pop hit for the Hombres in 1967			
7/8/89	R	20	8	28 Jackie Brown	48	↓	

JOHN MELLENCAMP:

Debut	Cht	Peak	Wks	Track Title	Hot Pos	Album Title	Album Label & Number
10/5/91	R	❶³	25	29 Get A Leg Up	14	Whenever We Wanted	Mercury 510151
11/2/91+	R	5	21	30 Love And Happiness	—	↓	
1/25/92	R	❶²	20	31 Again Tonight	36	↓	
4/4/92	R	3¹	20	32 Now More Than Ever	—	↓	
7/4/92	R	12	11	33 Last Chance	—	↓	
7/24/93	R	❶²	14	34 What If I Came Knocking	—	Human Wheels	Mercury 518088
9/18/93	R	2¹	20	35 Human Wheels	48	↓	
12/18/93	R	35	4	36 When Jesus Left Birmingham	—	↓	
2/5/94	R	35	4	37 Junior	—	↓	
5/28/94	R	17	20	38 Wild Night	3²	Dance Naked	Mercury 522428
				JOHN MELLENCAMP & ME'SHELL NDEGEOCELLO			
				#28 Pop hit for Van Morrison in 1971			
10/15/94	R	21	9	39 Dance Naked	41	↓	
8/17/96	R	10	14	40 Key West Intermezzo (I Saw You First)	14	Mr. Happy Go Lucky	Mercury 532896
11/30/96+	R	13	22	41 Just Another Day	46	↓	
11/29/97+	R	25	13	42 Without Expression	—	The Best That I Could Do 1978-1988	Mercury 536738
9/19/98	R	15	14	43 Your Life Is Now	62ᴬ	John Mellencamp	Columbia 69602
2/13/99	R	37	4	44 I'm Not Running Anymore	—	↓	
10/6/01	R	38	3	45 Peaceful World	104	Cuttin' Heads	Columbia 85098
				JOHN MELLENCAMP Featuring India.Arie			

MEMBERS, The

Pop-rock band from Surrey, England: Nicky Tesco (vocals), Jean-Marie Carroll (guitar), Nigel Bennett (guitar), Simon Lloyd and Steve Thompson (horns), Chris Payne (bass) and Adrian Lillywhite (drums).

Debut	Cht	Peak	Wks	Track Title	Hot Pos	Album Title	Album Label & Number
3/5/83	R	34	2	Working Girl	—	Uprhythm, Downbeat	Arista 6605

MEMENTO

Rock band formed in Australia: Justin Cotta (vocals), Jason "Space" Smith (guitar), Leighton "Lats" Kearns (bass) and Steve Clark (drums).

Debut	Cht	Peak	Wks	Track Title	Hot Pos	Album Title	Album Label & Number
5/24/03	R	28	10	1 Nothing Sacred	—	Beginnings	Columbia 86631
11/15/03	R	35	6	2 Saviour	—	↓	

MEN, The

Rock band from Santa Monica, California: Jef Scott (vocals, guitar), sisters Lore Wilhelm (guitar) and Nancy Hathorn (bass), and David Botkin (drums).

Debut	Cht	Peak	Wks	Track Title	Hot Pos	Album Title	Album Label & Number
5/16/92	R	8	16	Church Of Logic, Sin, & Love	—	The Men	Polydor 511987

MEN AT WORK

Pop-rock band from Melbourne, Australia: **Colin James Hay** (vocals, guitar), Ron Strykert (guitar), Greg Ham (sax, keyboards), John Rees (bass) and Jerry Speiser (drums). Speiser and Rees left in 1984.

AWARD: Grammy: Best New Artist 1982

Debut	Cht	Peak	Wks	Track Title	Hot Pos	Album Title	Album Label & Number
7/10/82	R	46	1	1 Who Can It Be Now?	❶¹	Business As Usual	Columbia 37978
10/23/82	R	❶⁵	17	2 Down Under	❶⁴	↓	
1/22/83	R	3²	9	3 Be Good Johnny	—	↓	
3/5/83	R	20	4	4 Underground	—	↓	
4/9/83	R	3⁵	14	5 Overkill	3¹	Cargo	Columbia 38660

Billboard Debut	Cht	Peak	Wks	ARTIST / Track Title	Hot Pos	Album Title	Album Label & Number

ℝ=Mainstream Rock 𝕄=Modern Rock

MEN AT WORK — cont'd

Debut	Cht	Peak	Wks	Track Title	Hot Pos	Album Title	Album Label & Number
4/30/83	ℝ	12	13	6 Dr. Heckyll & Mr. Jive	28	↓	
5/28/83	ℝ	23	8	7 High Wire	—	↓	
6/11/83	ℝ	27	11	8 It's A Mistake	6	↓	
6/15/85	ℝ	28	6	9 Everything I Need	47	Two Hearts	Columbia 40078

MEN WITHOUT HATS

Techno-rock band from Montreal, Quebec, Canada: brothers Ivan Doroschuk (vocals), Stefan Doroschuk (guitar) and Colin Doroschuk (keyboards), with Allan McCarthy (drums; died of AIDS on 8/11/1995, age 38).

| 8/27/83 | ℝ | 21 | 8 | The Safety Dance | 3⁴ | Rhythm Of Youth | Backstreet 39002 |

MERCHANT, Natalie

Born on 10/26/1963 in Jamestown, New York. Female singer/songwriter. Lead singer of **10,000 Maniacs** from 1981-93.

11/13/93	𝕄	9	14	1 Photograph	—	VA: Born To Choose	Rykodisc 10256
				R.E.M. with Natalie Merchant			
6/17/95	𝕄	12	23	2 Carnival	10	Tigerlily	Elektra 61745
10/21/95	𝕄	16	20	3 Wonder	20	↓	
5/16/98	𝕄	32	9	4 Kind & Generous	18ᴬ	Ophelia	Elektra 62196

MERCY FALL

Rock band from Flagstaff, Arizona: Nate Stone (vocals), Jeff Lusby (guitar), Kieran Smiley (bass) and Ethan Rea (drums).

| 5/6/06 | ℝ | 36 | 8 | I Got Life | — | For The Taken | Atlantic 83942 |

MESH STL

Rock band from St. Louis, Missouri: Scott Gertken (vocals), Matt Arana (guitar), Scott Davis (guitar), Rich Criebaum (bass) and Brian Pearia (drums).

| 9/29/01 | ℝ | 26 | 15 | 1 Maybe Tomorrow | — | Lowercase | The Label 45030 |
| 3/23/02 | ℝ | 39 | 1 | 2 Believe Me | — | ↓ | |

MESSIAH

Techno-dance duo from England: Ali Ghani and Mark Davies.

| 11/28/92 | 𝕄 | 17 | 10 | Temple Of Dreams | 117 | 21st Century Jesus | Def American 18697 |

METALLICA

ℝ 1990s: #7 / 2000s: #28 / All-Time: #11

Heavy metal band formed in Los Angeles, California: James Hetfield (vocals, guitar; born on 8/3/1963), Kirk Hammett (guitar; born on 11/18/1962), Cliff Burton (bass; born on 2/10/1962) and Lars Ulrich (drums; born on 12/26/1963). Original guitarist Dave Mustaine left in 1982 to form **Megadeth**. Burton was killed in a bus crash on 9/27/1986 (age 24); replaced by Jason Newsted (born on 3/4/1963). Newsted left in 2001; replaced by Robert Trujillo (of **Suicidal Tendencies**) in 2003. Group's life from 2001-03 was chronicled in the 2004 documentary movie *Some Kind Of Monster*.

TOP HITS: 1)Turn The Page 2)Until It Sleeps 3)I Disappear 4)No Leaf Clover 5)Hero Of The Day

3/11/89	ℝ	46	3	1 One	35	...And Justice For All	Elektra 60812
				Grammy: Metal Performance			
8/17/91	ℝ	10	20	2 Enter Sandman	16	Metallica	Elektra 61113
				R&R Hall of Fame ★ RS500 #399			
11/2/91+	ℝ	10	34	3 The Unforgiven	35	↓	
3/14/92	ℝ	11	20	4 Nothing Else Matters	34	↓	
7/11/92	ℝ	25	16	5 Wherever I May Roam	82	↓	
12/5/92+	ℝ	15	19	6 Sad But True	98	↓	
6/1/96	ℝ	❶⁸	26	7 Until It Sleeps	10	Load	Elektra 61923
6/8/96	𝕄	27	7				
7/6/96	ℝ	15	18	8 Ain't My Bitch	—	↓	
9/21/96	ℝ	❶³	33	9 Hero Of The Day	60	↓	
1/18/97	ℝ	6	27	10 King Nothing	90	↓	
6/14/97	ℝ	6	24	11 Bleeding Me	—	↓	
11/22/97	ℝ	3¹	22	12 The Memory Remains	28	Reload	Elektra 62126
				Marianne Faithull (female vocal)			
12/6/97+	ℝ	2³	26	13 The Unforgiven II	59	↓	
12/20/97+	ℝ	6	26	14 Fuel	—	↓	
8/1/98	ℝ	7	17	15 Better Than You	—	↓	
				Grammy: Metal Performance			
11/21/98	ℝ	❶¹¹	26	16 Turn The Page	102	Garage Inc.	Elektra 62299
1/2/99	𝕄	39	2	first recorded by Bob Seger in 1973			
1/23/99	ℝ	4	26	17 Whiskey In The Jar	124	↓	
				Grammy: Hard Rock Performance			
				first recorded by Thin Lizzy in 1972			

METALLICA — cont'd

Debut	Cht	Peak	Wks	Track Title	Hot Pos	Album Title	Album Label & Number
6/5/99	R	26	12	18 Die, Die My Darling	—	↓	
				first recorded by The Misfits in 1984			
12/4/99+	R	❶⁷	34	19 No Leaf Clover	[L] 74	S&M	Elektra 62504
12/11/99+	M	18	20	*with the San Francisco Symphony Orchestra; recorded on 4/21/1999 at the Berkeley Community Theater*			
5/6/00	R	❶⁷	43	20 I Disappear	76	St: Mission: Impossible 2 ....Hollywood 62244	
5/6/00	M	11	24				
6/14/03	R	2²	11	21 St. Anger	107	St. Anger ....Elektra 62853	
6/14/03	M	17	8	*Grammy: Metal Performance*			
8/9/03	R	21	10	22 Frantic	—	↓	
12/20/03+	R	28	11	23 The Unnamed Feeling	—	↓	
7/17/04	R	19	11	24 Some Kind Of Monster	—	Some Kind Of Monster ....Elektra 48835	
3/3/07	R	21	11	25 The Ecstasy Of Gold	—	VA: We All Love Ennio Morricone ..Sony Classical 706590	
				tune written and recorded for the 1968 movie The Good, The Bad & The Ugly starring Clint Eastwood			

METHENY, Pat, Group

Born on 8/12/1955 in Kansas City, Missouri. Male jazz guitarist.

Debut	Cht	Peak	Wks	Track Title	Hot Pos	Album Title	Album Label & Number
2/9/85	R	7	11	This Is Not America	32	St: The Falcon And The Snowman ...EMI America 17150	
				DAVID BOWIE & THE PAT METHENY GROUP			

MGMT

Electronic-rock duo from Brooklyn, New York: Ben Goldwasser and Andrew VanWyngarden.

Debut	Cht	Peak	Wks	Track Title	Hot Pos	Album Title	Album Label & Number
2/23/08	M	35↑	4↑	Time To Pretend	—	Oracular Spectacular ....Columbia 19512	

MIDNIGHT OIL   **M 1990s: #32 / All-Time: #72**

Rock band formed in Sydney, Australia: Peter Garrett (vocals), Martin Rotsey (guitar), James Moginie (keyboards), Dwayne Hillman (bass) and Rob Hirst (drums). Garrett later became involved in politics and was named Australian Arts and Environment Minister in November 2007.

TOP HITS: 1)Forgotten Years   2)Blue Sky Mine   3)King Of The Mountain

Debut	Cht	Peak	Wks	Track Title	Hot Pos	Album Title	Album Label & Number
2/20/88	R	6	19	1 Beds Are Burning	17	Diesel And Dust ....Columbia 40967	
				R&R Hall of Fame			
6/4/88	R	11	14	2 The Dead Heart	53	↓	
10/29/88	M	16	3	3 Dreamworld	—	↓	
10/15/88	R	37	4				
2/17/90	R	❶¹	14	4 Blue Sky Mine	47	Blue Sky Mining ....Columbia 45398	
2/17/90	M	❶¹	11				
3/31/90	M	❶¹	13	5 Forgotten Years	—	↓	
4/21/90	R	11	12				
6/30/90	M	3¹	10	6 King Of The Mountain	—	↓	
7/21/90	R	20	8				
5/30/92	M	20	5	7 Sometimes	[L] —	Scream In Blue Live ....Columbia 52731	
4/3/93	M	10	7	8 Drums Of Heaven	—	Earth And Sun And Moon ....Columbia 53793	
4/17/93	M	4	13	9 Truganini	—	↓	
4/24/93	R	10	11				
7/24/93	M	9	11	10 Outbreak Of Love	108	↓	

MIDTOWN

Punk-rock band formed in New Jersey: Heath Saraceno (guitar), Tyler Rann (guitar), Gabe Saporta (bass) and Rob Hitt (drums). All share vocals. Saporta later formed **Cobra Starship**.

Debut	Cht	Peak	Wks	Track Title	Hot Pos	Album Title	Album Label & Number
6/26/04	M	32	6	Give It Up	—	Forget What You Know ....Columbia 92584	

MIGHTY JOE PLUM

Rock band from Tampa, Florida: Brett Williams (vocals), Marlin Clark (guitar), Davey Mason (bass) and Mark Mercado (drums).

Debut	Cht	Peak	Wks	Track Title	Hot Pos	Album Title	Album Label & Number
7/26/97	R	6	26	Live Through This (Fifteen Stories)	—	The Happiest Dogs ....Atlantic 83023	

MIGHTY LEMON DROPS, The

Pop band from Wolverhampton, England: Paul Marsh (vocals), David Newton (guitar), Marcus Williams (bass) and Keith Rowley (drums).

Debut	Cht	Peak	Wks	Track Title	Hot Pos	Album Title	Album Label & Number
10/7/89	M	5	11	1 Into The Heart Of Love	—	Laughter ....Sire 26017	
1/6/90	M	8	9	2 Where Do We Go From Heaven?	—	↓	
6/8/91	M	28	3	3 Unkind	—	Sound...Goodbye To Your Standards ....Sire 26512	

MIGHTY MIGHTY BOSSTONES, The

Ska-rock band from Boston, Massachusetts: Dickey Barrett (vocals), Nate Albert (guitar), Ben Carr (dancer), Kevin Lenear, Tim Burton and Dennis Brockenborough (horns), Joe Gittleman (bass) and Joe Sirois (drums). Lawrence Katz replaced Albert and Roman Fleysher replaced Lenear in 1999.

Debut	Cht	Peak	Wks	#	Track Title	Hot Pos	Album Title	Album Label & Number
7/24/93	ⓜ	19	5	1	Someday I Suppose	—	Don't Know How To Party	Mercury 514836
3/8/97	ⓜ	❶¹	29	2	The Impression That I Get	23ᴬ	Let's Face It	Mercury 534472
8/9/97	ⓜ	7	20	3	The Rascal King	68ᴬ	↓	
12/13/97+	ⓜ	22	11	4	Royal Oil	—	↓	
4/8/00	ⓜ	11	13	5	So Sad To Say	—	Pay Attention	Big Rig 542451

MIKE + THE MECHANICS

Rock band formed in England: Mike Rutherford (bass; of Genesis), Paul Carrack and Paul Young (vocals), Adrian Lee (keyboards) and Peter Van Hooke (drums). Young, not to be confused with the same-named solo singer, died of a heart attack on 7/17/2000 (age 53).

Debut	Cht	Peak	Wks	#	Track Title	Hot Pos	Album Title	Album Label & Number
11/9/85	®	❶⁵	17	1	Silent Running (On Dangerous Ground)	6	Mike + The Mechanics	Atlantic 81287
2/1/86	®	6	14	2	All I Need Is A Miracle	5	↓	
11/5/88	®	3²	11	3	Nobody's Perfect	63	Living Years	Atlantic 81923
1/21/89	®	5	11	4	The Living Years	❶¹	↓	
4/8/89	®	18	8	5	Seeing Is Believing	62	↓	
3/30/91	®	30	5	6	Word Of Mouth	78	Word Of Mouth	Atlantic 82233

MILLA

Born Milla Jovovich on 12/17/1975 in Kiev, Ukraine; raised in Sacramento, California. Female actress/model. Starred in several movies.

Debut	Cht	Peak	Wks	Track Title	Hot Pos	Album Title	Album Label & Number
4/30/94	ⓜ	21	7	Gentleman Who Fell	—	The Divine Comedy	SBK 27984

MILLER, Steve, Band

Born on 10/5/1943 in Milwaukee, Wisconsin; raised in Dallas, Texas. Pop-rock singer/songwriter/guitarist. Formed band in high school, The Marksmen, which included Boz Scaggs. Moved to San Francisco in 1966; formed the Steve Miller Band, which featured a fluctuating lineup, including long-term members Lonnie Turner (bass) and Gary Mallaber (drums). Also see Classic Rock Tracks section.

Debut	Cht	Peak	Wks	#	Track Title	Hot Pos	Album Title	Album Label & Number
11/14/81	®	17	12	1	Heart Like A Wheel	24	Circle Of Love	Capitol 12121
6/5/82	®	4	17	2	Abracadabra	❶²	Abracadabra	Capitol 12216
11/1/86	®	❶⁶	14	3	I Want To Make The World Turn Around	97	Living In The 20th Century	Capitol 12445
					Kenny G (sax solo)			
12/27/86+	®	9	12	4	Nobody But You Baby	—	↓	
9/10/88	®	10	6	5	Ya Ya	—	Born 2B Blue	Capitol 48303
					STEVE MILLER #7 Pop hit for Lee Dorsey in 1961			
6/19/93	®	7	10	6	Wide River	64	Wide River	Polydor 519441
9/18/93	®	39	2	7	Blue Eyes	—	↓	
7/9/94	®	24	7	8	Rock It	—	Steve Miller Band Box Set	Capitol 12263

MILLTOWN BROTHERS

Pop-rock band from Colne, Lancashire, England: Matt Nelson (vocals), Simon Nelson (guitar), Barney James (keyboards), James Fraser (bass) and Nian Brindle (drums).

Debut	Cht	Peak	Wks	Track Title	Hot Pos	Album Title	Album Label & Number
6/15/91	ⓜ	10	9	Which Way Should I Jump?	—	Slinky	A&M 5346

MINISTRY

An assemblage of musicians spearheaded by Chicago-based producers/performers Alain Jourgensen and Paul Barker. Formed by Jourgensen in 1981. Barker joined Ministry in 1986. Varying personnel are members of The Tribe, an affiliation of musicians from various groups.

Debut	Cht	Peak	Wks	#	Track Title	Hot Pos	Album Title	Album Label & Number
12/16/89+	ⓜ	23	9	1	Burning Inside	—	The Mind Is A Terrible Thing To Taste	Sire 26004
11/30/91+	ⓜ	19	7	2	Jesus Built My Hotrod	—	Psalm 69	Sire 26727
8/8/92	ⓜ	11	8	3	N.W.O.	—	↓	
					N.W.O.: New World Order			

MIRACLE LEGION

Pop-rock band from Connecticut: Mark Mulcahey (vocals), Ray Neal (guitar), Dave McCaffrey (bass) and Scott Boutier (drums).

Debut	Cht	Peak	Wks	Track Title	Hot Pos	Album Title	Album Label & Number
3/28/92	ⓜ	28	3	Snacks and Candy	—	Drenched	Morgan Creek 20006

MI-SEX

Rock band from New Zealand: Steve Gilpin (vocals), Kevin Stanton (guitar), Colin Bayley (guitar), Murray Burns (keyboards), Don Martin (bass) and Paul Dunningham (drums). Gilpin died in a car crash on 11/25/1992 (age 41).

Debut	Cht	Peak	Wks	Track Title	Hot Pos	Album Title	Album Label & Number
3/31/84	®	31	4	Castaway	—	Where Do They Go?	Epic 39263

Debut	Cht	Peak	Wks	ARTIST / Track Title	®=Mainstream Rock ⓂＭ=Modern Rock	Hot Pos	Album Title	Album Label & Number

MISSING PERSONS
New-wave band formed in Los Angeles, California: Dale Bozzio (vocals), her then-husband Terry Bozzio (drums), Warren Cuccurullo (guitar), Patrick O'Hearn (bass, synthesizer) and Chuck Wild (keyboards). All but Wild were with **Frank Zappa**'s band. Disbanded in 1986. Terry Bozzio worked with **Jeff Beck** in 1989. Cuccurullo joined **Duran Duran** in 1990.

Debut	Cht	Peak	Wks	Track Title	Hot Pos	Album Title	Album Label & Number
6/26/82	®	60	1	1 Words	42	Missing Persons	Capitol 15001
11/6/82	®	24	14	2 Destination Unknown	42	Spring Session M	Capitol 12228
11/13/82+	®	12	23	3 Walking In L.A.	70	↓	
2/5/83	®	22	5	4 Windows	63	↓	
3/31/84	®	29	5	5 Give	67	Rhyme & Reason	Capitol 12315

MISSION U.K., The
Rock band formed in Leeds, England: Wayne Hussey (vocals, guitar), Simon Hinkler (guitar), Craig Adams (bass) and Mick Brown (drums). Hussey and Adams were members of **The Sisters Of Mercy**.

2/10/90	Ⓜ	6	14	1 Deliverance	—	Carved In Sand	Mercury 842251
4/7/90	®	27	8				
4/28/90	Ⓜ	23	5	2 Butterfly On A Wheel	—	↓	
12/15/90+	Ⓜ	7	9	3 Hands Across The Ocean	—	Grains Of Sand	Mercury 846937

MR. BIG
Rock band from San Francisco, California: Eric Martin (vocals), Paul Gilbert (guitar), Billy Sheehan (bass) and Pat Torpey (drums).

7/29/89	®	39	6	1 Addicted To That Rush	—	Mr. Big	Atlantic 81990
4/20/91	®	33	7	2 Green-Tinted Sixties Mind	—	Lean Into It	Atlantic 82209
10/12/91	®	19	26	3 To Be With You	❶³	↓	
4/25/92	®	18	9	4 Just Take My Heart	16	↓	
10/9/93	®	33	4	5 Wild World	27	Bump Ahead	Atlantic 82495

#11 Pop hit for Cat Stevens in 1971

MR. MIRAINGA
Rock-salsa band formed in California: Craig Poturalski (vocals), Steve Garcia (guitar), Steve "Hedge" Gunderson (bass) and Greg "Drt" Jones (drums).

| 11/25/95 | Ⓜ | 25 | 9 | Burnin' Rubber | 122 | St: Ace Ventura: When Nature Calls | MCA Soundtrax 11374 |

MR. MISTER
Pop-rock band formed in Los Angeles, California: Richard Page (vocals, bass), Steve Farris (guitar), Steve George (keyboards) and Pat Mastelotto (drums).

4/7/84	®	36	3	1 Hunters Of The Night	57	I Wear The Face	RCA Victor 4864
8/24/85	®	4	17	2 Broken Wings	❶²	Welcome To The Real World	RCA Victor 8045
12/14/85+	®	❶¹	13	3 Kyrie	❶²	↓	
3/22/86	®	17	11	4 Is It Love	8	↓	
8/22/87	®	27	8	5 Something Real (Inside Me/Inside You)	29	Go On...	RCA Victor 6276

MITCHELL, Joni
Born Roberta Joan Anderson on 11/7/1943 in Fort McLeod, Alberta, Canada; raised in Saskatoon, Saskatchewan. Singer/songwriter/guitarist/pianist. Married to her producer/bassist, Larry Klein, from 1982-94. Also see **Classic Rock Tracks** section.
AWARDS: R&R Hall of Fame: 1997 ★ Grammy: Lifetime Achievement Award 2002 ★ Billboard: Century Award 1995

11/23/85	®	28	8	1 Good Friends	85	Dog Eat Dog	Geffen 24074
				Michael McDonald (harmony vocal)			
3/19/88	®	32	8	2 Snakes And Ladders	—	Chalk Mark In A Rain Storm	Geffen 24172
				Don Henley (harmony vocal)			

MITCHELL, Kim
Born Joseph Kim Mitchell on 7/10/1952 in Sarnia, Ontario, Canada. Male rock singer/guitarist.

| 5/4/85 | ® | 12 | 12 | 1 Go For Soda | 86 | Akimbo Alogo | Bronze 90257 |
| 7/26/86 | ® | 36 | 6 | 2 Patio Lanterns | — | Shakin' Like A Human Being | Atlantic 81664 |

MOBY
Born Richard Melville Hall on 9/11/1965 in Harlem, New York; raised in Darien, Connecticut. Techno-dance singer/musician/producer/remixer.

7/24/99	Ⓜ	26	11	1 Bodyrock	—	Play	V2 27049
1/22/00	Ⓜ	24	11	2 Natural Blues	—	↓	
				samples "Trouble So Hard" by Vera Hall			
5/13/00	Ⓜ	18	16	3 Porcelain	—	↓	
11/4/00+	Ⓜ	3³	31	4 South Side	14	↓	
				MOBY Featuring Gwen Stefani			
4/20/02	Ⓜ	22	8	5 We Are All Made Of Stars	—	18	V2 27127

Debug	Billboard Cht	Peak	Wks	ARTIST Track Title	®=Mainstream Rock Ⓜ=Modern Rock	Hot Pos	Album Title	Album Label & Number

MOCK TURTLES, The
Rock band from Manchester, England: Martin Coogan (vocals, guitar), Martin Glyn Murray (guitar), Joanne Gent (keyboards), Andrew Stewardson (bass) and Steve Cowen (drums).

| 8/31/91 | Ⓜ | 19 | 4 | Can You Dig It?... | — | *Turtle Soup*..Relativity 1058 |

MODELS
Pop-rock band formed in Melbourne, Australia: Sean Kelly (vocals, guitar), Roger Mason (keyboards), James Valentine (sax), James Freud (bass) and Barton Price (drums).

| 4/26/86 | ® | 22 | 9 | 1 Out Of Mind Out Of Sight.. | 37 | *Out Of Mind Out Of Sight*..........................Geffen 24100 |
| 7/19/86 | ® | 29 | 6 | 2 Cold Fever .... | — | ↓ |

MODERN ENGLISH
New-wave band formed in Colchester, England: Robbie Grey (vocals), Gary McDowell (guitar), Stephen Walker (keyboards), Michael Conroy (bass) and Richard Brown (drums).

| 3/26/83 | ® | 7 | 11 | 1 I Melt With You.. | 78 | *After The Snow*...................................Sire 23821 |
| 3/31/84 | ® | 47 | 5 | 2 Hands Across The Sea .... | 91 | *Ricochet Days* ....Sire 25066 |

MODEST MOUSE
Alternative-rock trio from Isaaquah, Washington: Isaac Brock (vocals, guitar), Eric Judy (bass) and Jeremiah Green (drums).

4/3/04	Ⓜ	❶[1]	28	1 Float On	68	*Good News For People Who Love Bad*
9/11/04	Ⓜ	6	26	2 Ocean Breathes Salty	—	*News* ....Epic 87125
1/20/07	Ⓜ	5	20	3 Dashboard..	61	*We Were Dead Before The Ship Even Sank* Epic 86139
6/9/07	Ⓜ	24	14	4 Missed The Boat	—	↓

MOIST
Rock band from Vancouver, British Columbia, Canada: David Usher (vocals), Mark Makowy (guitar), Kevin Young (keyboards), Jeff Pearce (bass) and Paul Wilcox (drums).

| 11/26/94 | ® | 37 | 4 | Push... | — | *Silver*...Chrysalis/EMI 29608 |

MOLLY HATCHET
Southern-rock band formed in Jacksonville, Florida: **Danny Joe Brown** (vocals), Dave Hlubek, Duane Roland and Steve Holland (guitars), Banner Thomas (bass) and Bruce Crump (drums). Jimmy Farrar replaced Brown in 1980; Brown returned and replaced Farrar in 1983. Holland and Thomas left in 1983; John Galvin (keyboards) and Riff West (bass) joined. Bobby Ingram replaced Hlubek in 1988. Brown died of diabetes complications on 3/10/2005 (age 53). Roland died on 6/19/2006 (age 53). Also see **Classic Rock Tracks** section.

12/5/81+	®	31	9	1 Bloody Reunion	—	*Take No Prisoners*...............................Epic 37480
12/19/81+	®	46	5	2 Lady Luck	—	↓
10/13/84	®	13	12	3 Satisfied Man	81	*The Deed Is Done* ....Epic 39621
12/15/84+	®	26	9	4 Stone In Your Heart	—	↓
9/16/89	®	26	6	5 There Goes The Neighborhood.............................	—	*Lightning Strikes Twice*.......................Capitol 92114

MONACO
Rock duo from England: Peter Hook (of **New Order**) and David Potts.

| 7/12/97 | Ⓜ | 24 | 10 | What Do You Want From Me? .... | 61[A] | *Music For Pleasure*.................................Polydor 537629 |

MONDO ROCK
Rock band formed in Australia: Ross Wilson (vocals), Eric McCusker (guitar), Duncan Veall (keyboards), Andrew Ross (sax), James Gillard (bass) and J.J. Hackett (drums).

| 5/9/87 | ® | 31 | 6 | Primitive Love Rites .... | 71 | *Boom Baby Boom* ....Columbia 40470 |

MONEY, Eddie
® **1980s: #32 / All-Time: #57**

Born Edward Mahoney on 3/2/1949 in Brooklyn, New York. Rock singer/songwriter. Discovered and subsequently managed by the late West Coast promoter Bill Graham. Formerly an officer with the New York City Police Department. Also see **Classic Rock Tracks** section.

TOP HITS: 1)Think I'm In Love 2)Take Me Home Tonight 3)The Love In Your Eyes

7/3/82	®	❶[3]	14	1 Think I'm In Love	16	*No Control*..Columbia 37960
7/24/82	®	9	27	2 Shakin'	63	↓
8/7/82	®	60	1	3 No Control...	—	↓
11/26/83	®	17	11	4 The Big Crash	54	*Where's The Party?* ....Columbia 38862
9/29/84	®	25	7	5 I'm Moving On..	—	*VA: Every Man Has A Woman* ....Polydor 823490
				first recorded by Yoko Ono in 1980		
8/9/86	®	❶[2]	15	6 Take Me Home Tonight	4	*Can't Hold Back* ....Columbia 40096
				Ronnie Spector (female vocal)		
10/25/86	®	18	12	7 We Should Be Sleeping	90	↓
12/20/86+	®	3[1]	15	8 I Wanna Go Back	14	↓
3/21/87	®	10	11	9 Endless Nights	21	↓
10/1/88	®	2[5]	12	10 Walk On Water	9	*Nothing To Lose* ....Columbia 44302

MONEY, Eddie — cont'd

Debut	Cht	Peak	Wks		Track Title	Hot Pos	Album Title	Album Label & Number
12/10/88+	ℝ	❶¹	15	11	The Love In Your Eyes	24	↓	
2/18/89	ℝ	36	5	12	Forget About Love	—	↓	
4/29/89	ℝ	30	5	13	Let Me In	60	↓	
12/2/89+	ℝ	2²	11	14	Peace In Our Time	11	Greatest Hits Sound Of Money	Columbia 45381
9/14/91	ℝ	6	8	15	Heaven In The Back Seat	58	Right Here	Columbia 46756
11/16/91+	ℝ	5	12	16	She Takes My Breath Away	—	↓	

MONO
Dance duo from England: Siobahn DeMare (female vocals) and Martin Virgo (instruments).

Debut	Cht	Peak	Wks		Track Title	Hot Pos	Album Title	Album Label & Number
2/28/98	ⓜ	28	9		Life In Mono	70	Formica Blues	Echo 536676

MONROES, The
Pop-rock band from San Diego, California: Jesus Ortiz (vocals), Rusty Jones (guitar), Eric Denton (keyboards), Bob "Monroe" Davis (bass) and Jonnie Gilstrap (drums).

Debut	Cht	Peak	Wks		Track Title	Hot Pos	Album Title	Album Label & Number
6/5/82	ℝ	20	6		What Do All The People Know	59	The Monroes	Alfa 15015

MONSTER MAGNET
Hard-rock band from Red Bank, New Jersey: David Wyndorf (vocals), Ed Mundell (guitar), Joe Calandra (bass) and Joe Kleiman (drums). Phil Caivano (guitar) joined in 2000.

Debut	Cht	Peak	Wks		Track Title	Hot Pos	Album Title	Album Label & Number
4/29/95	ℝ	19	15	1	Negasonic Teenage Warhead	—	Dopes To Infinity	A&M 540315
5/20/95	ⓜ	26	7					
5/30/98	ℝ	3⁵	27	2	Space Lord	—	Powertrip	A&M 540908
8/8/98	ⓜ	29	12					
10/31/98	ℝ	20	24	3	Powertrip	—	↓	
4/3/99	ℝ	25	12	4	Temple Of Your Dreams	—	↓	
4/1/00	ℝ	15	14	5	Silver Future	—	St: Heavy Metal 2000	Restless 73717
3/17/01	ℝ	26	11	6	Heads Explode	—	God Says No	A&M 490749
7/10/04	ℝ	31	8	7	Unbroken (Hotel Baby)	—	Monolithic Baby!	Steamhammer 6943

MOODSWINGS
Techno-dance duo from London, England: J.F.T. "Fred" Hood and Grant Showbiz.

Debut	Cht	Peak	Wks		Track Title	Hot Pos	Album Title	Album Label & Number
9/12/92	ⓜ	6	12		Spiritual High (State Of Independence) Part II Chrissie Hynde (guest vocal)	—	Moodfood	Arista 18619

MOODY BLUES, The
Rock band formed in Birmingham, England: Justin Hayward (vocals, guitar), John Lodge (vocals, bass), Patrick Moraz (keyboards) and Graeme Edge (drums). Moraz was a former member of **Yes**. Also see **Classic Rock Tracks** section.

TOP HITS: 1)The Voice 2)I Know You're Out There Somewhere 3)Your Wildest Dreams

Debut	Cht	Peak	Wks		Track Title	Hot Pos	Album Title	Album Label & Number
6/6/81	ℝ	❶⁴	27	1	The Voice	15	Long Distance Voyager	Threshold 2901
6/6/81	ℝ	13	13	2	Gemini Dream	12	↓	
7/4/81	ℝ	38	6	3	22,000 Days	—	↓	
8/22/81	ℝ	11	15	4	Meanwhile	—	↓	
9/3/83	ℝ	3¹	14	5	Sitting At The Wheel	27	The Present	Threshold 2902
10/22/83	ℝ	32	7	6	Blue World	62	↓	
4/19/86	ℝ	2¹	15	7	Your Wildest Dreams	9	The Other Side Of Life	Threshold 829179
6/7/86	ℝ	11	16	8	The Other Side Of Life	58	↓	
6/4/88	ℝ	2²	10	9	I Know You're Out There Somewhere	30	Sur La Mer	Polydor 835756
9/3/88	ℝ	50	1	10	Here Comes The Weekend	—	↓	
6/22/91	ℝ	22	8	11	Say It With Love	—	Keys Of The Kingdom	Polydor 849433

MOON DOG MANE
Rock band formed in California: Broadie Stewart (vocals), Frank Hannon (guitar; of **Tesla**), Kevin Hampton (guitar), Chris Martinez (keyboards), Joel Krueger (bass) and Cortney Daugustine (drums).

Debut	Cht	Peak	Wks		Track Title	Hot Pos	Album Title	Album Label & Number
12/26/98+	ℝ	36	3	1	Turn It Up	—	Turn It Up	Eureka 02262
5/1/99	ℝ	38	2	2	I Believe	—	↓	

MOORE, Abra
Born on 6/8/1969 in San Diego, California; raised in Puni, Hawaii. Female singer/songwriter/guitarist/actress.

Debut	Cht	Peak	Wks		Track Title	Hot Pos	Album Title	Album Label & Number
5/24/97	ⓜ	27	10		Four Leaf Clover	63	Strangest Places	Arista Austin 18839

Ⓡ=Mainstream Rock
Ⓜ=Modern Rock

MOORE, Gary
Born on 4/4/1952 in Belfast, Ireland. Rock singer/guitarist. Member of **Thin Lizzy** (1974, 1978-79) and **BBM**.

Debut	Cht	Peak	Wks	Track Title	Hot Pos	Album Title	Album Label & Number
5/28/83	Ⓡ	31	2	1 Don't Take Me For A Loser	—	Corridors Of Power	Mirage 90077
4/25/87	Ⓡ	24	7	2 Over The Hills And Far Away	—	Wild Frontier	Virgin 90588
3/4/89	Ⓡ	13	11	3 Ready For Love	—	After The War	Virgin 91066
6/2/90	Ⓡ	15	12	4 Oh Pretty Woman	—	Still Got The Blues	Charisma 91369
9/15/90	Ⓡ	9	22	5 Still Got The Blues	97	↓	
2/16/91	Ⓡ	30	6	6 Moving On	—	↓	
3/7/92	Ⓡ	22	11	7 Cold Day In Hell	—	After Hours	Charisma 91825
7/4/92	Ⓡ	37	1	8 Story Of The Blues	—	↓	

MOORE, Ian
Born on 8/8/1968 in Berkeley, California; raised in Austin, Texas. White blues singer/guitarist.

Debut	Cht	Peak	Wks	Track Title	Hot Pos	Album Title	Album Label & Number
8/21/93	Ⓡ	15	12	1 How Does It Feel	—	Ian Moore	Capricorn 42018
12/18/93+	Ⓡ	23	10	2 Nothing	—	↓	
7/8/95	Ⓡ	18	12	3 Muddy Jesus	—	Modernday Folklore	Capricorn 42038

MOORE, Mae
Born in Brandon, Manitoba, Canada. Female singer/songwriter/guitarist.

Debut	Cht	Peak	Wks	Track Title	Hot Pos	Album Title	Album Label & Number
12/11/93+	Ⓜ	25	10	Bohemia	—	Bohemia	Tristar 57373

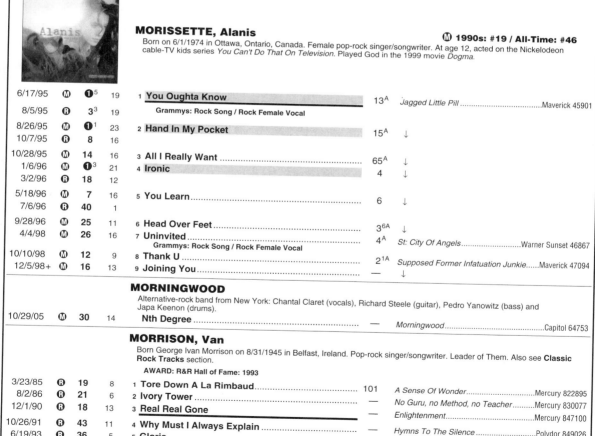

MORISSETTE, Alanis
Ⓜ 1990s: #19 / All-Time: #46

Born on 6/1/1974 in Ottawa, Ontario, Canada. Female pop-rock singer/songwriter. At age 12, acted on the Nickelodeon cable-TV kids series *You Can't Do That On Television*. Played God in the 1999 movie *Dogma*.

Debut	Cht	Peak	Wks	Track Title	Hot Pos	Album Title	Album Label & Number
6/17/95	Ⓜ	❶[5]	19	1 You Oughta Know	13[A]	Jagged Little Pill	Maverick 45901
				Grammys: Rock Song / Rock Female Vocal			
8/5/95	Ⓡ	3[3]	19				
8/26/95	Ⓜ	❶[1]	23	2 Hand In My Pocket	15[A]	↓	
10/7/95	Ⓡ	8	16				
10/28/95	Ⓜ	14	16	3 All I Really Want	65[A]	↓	
1/6/96	Ⓜ	❶[3]	21	4 Ironic	4	↓	
3/2/96	Ⓡ	18	12				
5/18/96	Ⓜ	7	16	5 You Learn	6	↓	
7/6/96	Ⓡ	40	1				
9/28/96	Ⓜ	25	11	6 Head Over Feet	3[6A]	↓	
4/4/98	Ⓜ	26	16	7 Uninvited	4[A]	St: City Of Angels	Warner Sunset 46867
				Grammys: Rock Song / Rock Female Vocal			
10/10/98	Ⓜ	12	9	8 Thank U	2[1A]	Supposed Former Infatuation Junkie	Maverick 47094
12/5/98+	Ⓜ	16	13	9 Joining You	—	↓	

MORNINGWOOD
Alternative-rock band from New York: Chantal Claret (vocals), Richard Steele (guitar), Pedro Yanowitz (bass) and Japa Keenon (drums).

Debut	Cht	Peak	Wks	Track Title	Hot Pos	Album Title	Album Label & Number
10/29/05	Ⓜ	30	14	Nth Degree	—	Morningwood	Capitol 64753

MORRISON, Van
Born George Ivan Morrison on 8/31/1945 in Belfast, Ireland. Pop-rock singer/songwriter. Leader of Them. Also see **Classic Rock Tracks** section.

AWARD: R&R Hall of Fame: 1993

Debut	Cht	Peak	Wks	Track Title	Hot Pos	Album Title	Album Label & Number
3/23/85	Ⓡ	19	8	1 Tore Down A La Rimbaud	101	A Sense Of Wonder	Mercury 822895
8/2/86	Ⓡ	21	6	2 Ivory Tower	—	No Guru, no Method, no Teacher	Mercury 830077
12/1/90	Ⓡ	18	13	3 Real Real Gone	—	Enlightenment	Mercury 847100
10/26/91	Ⓡ	43	11	4 Why Must I Always Explain	—	Hymns To The Silence	Polydor 849026
6/19/93	Ⓡ	36	5	5 Gloria	—	Too Long In Exile	Polydor 519219

John Lee Hooker (additional vocal); #10 Pop hit for The Shadows Of Knight in 1966

MORRISSEY

℗ 1990s: #11 / All-Time: #26

Born Stephen Morrissey on 5/22/1959 in Davyhulme, Lancashire, England. Eclectic singer/songwriter. Former lead singer/songwriter of The Smiths.

TOP HITS: 1)The More You Ignore Me, The Closer I Get   2)Tomorrow   3)Piccadilly Palare

Debut	Cht	Peak	Wks	#	Track Title	Hot Pos	Album Title	Label & Number
3/18/89	Ⓜ	3¹	9	1	The Last Of The Famous International Playboys ..	—	Bona Drag	Sire 26221
7/1/89	Ⓜ	11	7	2	Interesting Drug	—	↓	
12/23/89+	Ⓜ	2¹	9	3	Ouija Board, Ouija Board	—	↓	
5/19/90	Ⓜ	6	9	4	November Spawned A Monster	—	↓	
11/24/90+	Ⓜ	2²	10	5	Piccadilly Palare	—	↓	
3/16/91	Ⓜ	2²	9	6	Our Frank	—	Kill Uncle	Sire 26514
5/18/91	Ⓜ	10	9	7	Sing Your Life	—	↓	
5/30/92	Ⓜ	2²	9	8	We Hate It When Our Friends Become Successful	—	Your Arsenal	Sire 26994
7/25/92	Ⓜ	❶⁶	14	9	Tomorrow	—	↓	
10/3/92	Ⓜ	13	8	10	Glamorous Glue	—	↓	
3/19/94	Ⓜ	❶⁷	12	11	The More You Ignore Me, The Closer I Get	46	Vauxhall And I	Sire 45451
5/29/04	Ⓜ	36	6	12	Irish Blood, English Heart	—	You Are The Quarry	Attack 86001

MOTELS, The

Pop-rock band formed in Los Angeles, California: **Martha Davis** (vocals), Guy Perry (guitar), Marty Jourard (keyboards), Michael Goodroe (bass) and Brian Glascock (drums). Scott Thurston (guitar) joined in 1983. Disbanded in 1987.

Debut	Cht	Peak	Wks	#	Track Title	Hot Pos	Album Title	Label & Number
5/1/82	®	6	22	1	Only The Lonely	9	All Four One	Capitol 12177
5/1/82	®	36	4	2	Take The L	52	↓	
5/29/82	®	23	15	3	Mission Of Mercy	—	↓	
9/10/83	®	❶²	19	4	Suddenly Last Summer	9	Little Robbers	Capitol 12288
10/22/83	®	18	13	5	Little Robbers	—	↓	
1/21/84	®	12	5	6	Remember The Nights	36	↓	
7/27/85	®	10	11	7	Shame	21	Shock	Capitol 12378

MOTHER STATION, The

Blues-rock band from Memphis, Tennessee: Susan Marshall (vocals), Gwin Spencer (guitar), Paul Brown (keyboards), Michael Jaques (bass) and Rick Shelton (drums).

Debut	Cht	Peak	Wks	Track Title	Hot Pos	Album Title	Label & Number
6/11/94	®	34	6	Put The Blame On Me	—	Brand New Bag	EastWest 92366

MÖTLEY CRÜE

® All-Time: #64

Hard-rock band formed in Los Angeles, California: **Vince Neil** (vocals; born Vince Wharton on 2/8/1961), Mick Mars (guitar; born Bob Deal on 4/3/1956), Nikki Sixx (bass; born Frank Ferranna on 12/11/1958) and **Tommy Lee** (drums; born Thomas Bass on 10/3/1962). John Corabi replaced Neil for one album (songs #14 & #15 below) in 1994. Sixx was married to actress Donna D'Errico from 1996-2007. Lee was married to actress Heather Locklear from 1986-93 and to actress Pamela Anderson from 1995-98. Lee left group in April 1999. Drummer Randy Castillo joined in early 2000. Castillo died of cancer on 3/26/2002 (age 51). Sixx later formed **Sixx: A.M.**

TOP HITS: 1)If I Die Tomorrow   2)Smokin' In The Boys Room   3)Dr. Feelgood   4)Afraid   5)Hooligan's Holiday

Debut	Cht	Peak	Wks	#	Track Title	Hot Pos	Album Title	Label & Number
11/12/83+	®	12	17	1	Looks That Kill	54	Shout At The Devil	Elektra 60289
11/12/83	®	30	3	2	Shout At The Devil	—	↓	
5/12/84	®	17	12	3	Too Young To Fall In Love	90	↓	
7/6/85	®	7	13	4	Smokin' In The Boys Room	16	Theatre Of Pain	Elektra 60418
					#3 Pop hit for Brownsville Station in 1974			
10/5/85	®	38	6	5	Home Sweet Home	89	↓	
					also see #13 & 23 below			
5/30/87	®	20	9	6	Girls, Girls, Girls	12	Girls, Girls, Girls	Elektra 60725
9/2/89	®	7	10	7	Dr. Feelgood	6	Dr. Feelgood	Elektra 60829
11/4/89	®	18	15	8	Kickstart My Heart	27	↓	
2/17/90	®	11	11	9	Without You	8	↓	
5/12/90	®	13	14	10	Don't Go Away Mad (Just Go Away)	19	↓	
8/18/90	®	34	8	11	Same Ol' Situation (S.O.S.)	78	↓	
9/7/91	®	21	10	12	Primal Scream	63	Decade Of Decadence - '81-'91	Elektra 61204
12/14/91+	®	41	8	13	Home Sweet Home '91 [R]	37	↓	
					remix of #5 above			
2/26/94	®	10	10	14	Hooligan's Holiday	—	Mötley Crüe	Elektra 61534
5/7/94	®	24	7	15	Misunderstood	—	↓	
5/31/97	®	10	12	16	Afraid	—	Generation Swine	Elektra 61901
9/20/97	®	37	3	17	Beauty	—	↓	

Debug	Cht	Peak	Wks	ARTIST / Track Title	Hot Pos	Album Title	Album Label & Number

Billboard

®=Mainstream Rock
ⓜ=Modern Rock

MÖTLEY CRÜE — cont'd

Debut	Cht	Peak	Wks	Track	Hot Pos	Album	Label
10/17/98	®	22	10	18 Bitter Pill	—	Greatest Hits	Beyond 78002
8/14/99	®	35	4	19 Teaser	—	Supersonic And Demonic Relics	Mötley 78031
7/1/00	®	13	12	20 Hell On High Heels	—	New Tattoo	Mötley 78120
12/25/04+	®	4	19	21 If I Die Tomorrow	—	Red, White & Crüe	Hip-O 003908
4/16/05	®	22	10	22 Sick Love Song	—	↓	
11/5/05	®	39	2	23 Home Sweet Home ... [R]	—	↓	

MÖTLEY CRÜE Featuring Chester Bennington
new version of #5 above

MOTOGRATER

Hard-rock band formed in Los Angeles, California: Ivan "Ghost" Moody (vocals), Matt "Nuke" Nunes (guitar), Joey "Smur" Krzywonski (bass) and Chris "Crispy" Binns (drums). Moody later joined **Five Finger Death Punch**.

| 8/16/03 | ® | 29 | 12 | Down | — | Motograter | Elektra 62837 |

MOULD, Bob

Born on 10/12/1960 in Malone, New York; later based in Minneapolis, Minnesota. Singer/songwriter/guitarist. Member of Hüsker Dü and Sugar.

| 5/20/89 | ⓜ | 4 | 13 | 1 See A Little Light | — | Workbook | Virgin 91240 |
| 8/25/90 | ⓜ | 10 | 10 | 2 It's Too Late | — | Black Sheets Of Rain | Virgin 91395 |

MOYET, Alison

Born Genevieve Alison-Jane Moyet on 6/18/1961 in Basildon, Essex, England. Female singer.

| 12/14/91 | ⓜ | 29 | 3 | It Won't Be Long | — | Hoodoo | Columbia 47841 |

MUDHONEY

Rock band formed in Seattle, Washington: Mark Arm (vocals), Steve Turner (guitar), Matt Lukin (bass) and Dan Peters (drums).

| 11/7/92 | ⓜ | 23 | 6 | Suck You Dry | — | Piece Of Cake | Reprise 45090 |

MUDVAYNE   ® 2000s: #31

Hard-rock band from Peoria, Illinois: Chad Gray (vocals), Greg Tribbett (guitar), Ryan Martinie (bass) and Matt McDonough (drums). Gray and Tribbett later formed **HellYeah**.

4/21/01	®	33	9	1 Dig	—	L.D. 50	No Name 63821
7/28/01	®	32	8	2 Death Blooms	—	↓	
10/26/02+	®	11	31	3 Not Falling	—	The End Of All Things To Come	Epic 86487
12/28/02+	ⓜ	28	18				
5/31/03	®	16	26	4 World So Cold	—	↓	
2/19/05	®	❶[1]	33	5 Happy?	89	Lost And Found	Epic 90784
2/26/05	ⓜ	8	26				
7/23/05	®	8	27	6 Forget To Remember	—	↓	
1/7/06	®	4	31	7 Fall Into Sleep	—	↓	
10/27/07	®	17	20	8 Dull Boy	—	By The People, For The People	Epic 19023

MULLINS, Shawn

Born on 3/8/1968 in Atlanta, Georgia. Male singer/songwriter/guitarist.

| 9/5/98 | ⓜ | 9 | 22 | Lullaby | 7 | Soul's Core | Columbia 69637 |

MUNDY

Born Edmund Enright in 1976 in Birr, Offaly, Ireland. Male singer/songwriter/guitarist.

| 3/1/97 | ⓜ | 37 | 2 | To You I Bestow | — | Jelly Legs | Epic 67894 |

MURMURS, The

Female rock duo from Manhattan, New York: singers/guitarists Heather Grody and Leisha Hailey.

| 11/26/94 | ⓜ | 23 | 9 | You Suck | 89 | The Murmurs | MCA 11086 |

MURPHY, Peter

Born on 7/11/1957 in Northampton, England. Male singer/songwriter.

11/4/89	ⓜ	18	5	1 The Line Between The Devil's Teeth (And That Which Cannot Be Repeat)	—	Deep	Beggars Banquet 9877
1/20/90	ⓜ	❶[7]	18	2 Cuts You Up	55	↓	
2/17/90	®	10	13				
7/7/90	ⓜ	21	5	3 A Strange Kind Of Love	—	↓	
4/11/92	ⓜ	2[1]	12	4 The Sweetest Drop	—	Holy Smoke	Beggars Banquet 66007
6/27/92	ⓜ	18	5	5 You're So Close	—	↓	

MUSE
Rock trio from Teignmouth, Devon, England: Matthew Bellamy (vocals, guitar), Chris Wolstenhome (bass) and Dominic Howard (drums).

◍ All-Time: #88

Debut	Cht	Peak	Wks	#	Track Title	Hot Pos	Album Title	Album Label & Number
4/10/04	◍	9	21	1	Time Is Running Out	—	Absolution	Warner 48733
9/11/04+	◍	9	28	2	Hysteria (I Want It Now)	118	↓	
5/21/05	◍	31	6	3	Stockholm Syndrome	—	↓	
7/1/06	◍	10	20	4	Knights Of Cydonia	—	Black Holes And Revelations	Warner 44284
11/11/06+	◍	2³	26	5	Starlight	101	↓	
5/19/07	◍	6	24	6	Supermassive Black Hole	—	↓	

MUSHROOMHEAD
Hard-rock band from Cleveland, Ohio: Jeff "Jeffrey Nothing" Hatrix (lead vocals), Jason "J Mann" Popson (vocals), Marko "Bronson" Vukcevich (guitar), Dave "Gravy" Felton (guitar), Rick "Stitch" Thomas (samples), Tom "Shmotz" Schmitz (keyboards), Jack "Pig Benis" Kilcoyne (bass) and Steve "Skinny" Felton (drums).

Debut	Cht	Peak	Wks	Track Title	Hot Pos	Album Title	Album Label & Number
10/7/06	®	39	3	Simple Survival	—	Savior Sorrow	Filthy Hands 902

MUSIC, The
Rock band from Kippax, Leeds, England: Robert Harvey (vocals), Adam Nutter (guitar), Stuart Coleman (bass) and Phil Jordan (drums).

Debut	Cht	Peak	Wks	#	Track Title	Hot Pos	Album Title	Album Label & Number
10/9/04	®	39	1	1	Freedom Fighters	—	Welcome To The North	Capitol 78516
11/6/04+	◍	20	13	2	Breakin'	—	↓	

MUST
Rock trio formed in London, England: Dave Ireland (vocals, guitar), Kai Lemke (bass) and Reuben Alexander (drums).

Debut	Cht	Peak	Wks	Track Title	Hot Pos	Album Title	Album Label & Number
8/24/02	®	38	4	Freechild	—	Androgynous Jesus	Wind-Up 13070

MUTE MATH
Rock band formed in New Orleans, Louisiana: Paul Meany (vocals), Greg Hill (guitar), Roy Mitchell-Cardenas (bass) and Darren King (drums).

Debut	Cht	Peak	Wks	Track Title	Hot Pos	Album Title	Album Label & Number
8/4/07	◍	33	14	Typical	—	Mute Math	Warner 44462

MXPX
Christian punk-rock trio from Bremerton, Washington: Mike Herrera (vocals, bass), Tom Wisniewski (guitar) and Yuri Ruley (drums).

Debut	Cht	Peak	Wks	Track Title	Hot Pos	Album Title	Album Label & Number
7/15/00	◍	24	8	Responsibility	—	The Ever Passing Moment	A&M 490656

MY BLOODY VALENTINE
Rock band from Dublin, Ireland: Bilinda Butcher (vocals, guitar), Kevin Shields (vocals, guitar), Debbie Googe (bass) and Colm O'Ciosoig (drums). Group named after a 1981 horror movie.

Debut	Cht	Peak	Wks	Track Title	Hot Pos	Album Title	Album Label & Number
2/1/92	◍	27	2	Only Shallow	—	Loveless	Sire 26759

MY CHEMICAL ROMANCE
Rock band formed in Jersey City, New Jersey: brothers Gerard Way (vocals) and Mikey Way (bass), with Ray Toro (guitar), Frank Iero (guitar) and Matt Pelissier (drums). Bob Bryar replaced Pelissier in late 2004.

◍ 2000s: #31 / All-Time: #62

Debut	Cht	Peak	Wks	#	Track Title	Hot Pos	Album Title	Album Label & Number
10/23/04+	◍	4	25	1	I'm Not Okay (I Promise)	86	Three Cheers For Sweet Revenge	Reprise 48615
3/26/05	◍	11	26	2	Helena (So Long & Goodnight)	33	↓	
5/21/05	◍	28	6	3	Under Pressure	41	In Love And Death	Reprise 48789
					THE USED & MY CHEMICAL ROMANCE			
10/22/05	◍	9	20	4	The Ghost Of You	84	Life On The Murder Scene	Reprise 49476
12/24/05	®	38	4					
9/23/06	◍	❶⁷	29	5	Welcome To The Black Parade	9	The Black Parade	Reprise 44427
10/21/06	®	24	20					
12/23/06+	◍	4	20	6	Famous Last Words	88	↓	
2/17/07	®	23	13					
6/2/07	◍	13	20	7	Teenagers	67	↓	

MY FRIEND STEVE
Rock band from Orlando, Florida: Steven Burry (vocals), Eric Steinberg (guitar), Patrick Koch (keyboards), David McMahon (bass) and Eric Gardner (drums).

Debut	Cht	Peak	Wks	Track Title	Hot Pos	Album Title	Album Label & Number
4/24/99	◍	38	3	Charmed	—	Hope & Wait	Mammoth 980191

MYLES, Alannah
Born on 12/25/1955 in Toronto, Ontario, Canada; raised in Buckhorn, Ontario, Canada. Female singer.

Debut	Cht	Peak	Wks	#	Track Title	Hot Pos	Album Title	Album Label & Number
12/9/89+	®	❶²	18	1	Black Velvet	❶²	Alannah Myles	Atlantic 81956
					Grammy: Rock Female Vocal			
5/12/90	®	19	7	2	Love Is	36	↓	

Billboard				ARTIST	R=Mainstream Rock	Hot		
Debut	Cht	Peak	Wks	Track Title	M=Modern Rock	Pos	Album Title	Album Label & Number

MY LIFE WITH THE THRILL KILL KULT
Rock band from Chicago, Illinois. Assembled by Mr. Groovie Mann (vocals) and Mr. Buzz McCoy (keyboards).

7/13/91+	Ⓜ	17	11	Sex On Wheelz		—	*Sexplosion!*	Wax Trax! 7163

N

NADA SURF
Rock trio from Los Angeles, California: Matthew Caws (vocals, guitar), Daniel Lorca (bass) and Ira Elliot (drums).

7/6/96	Ⓜ	11	13	Popular	51[A]	*High/Low*	Elektra 61913

NAKED
Rock band from New Jersey: Jonathan Sheldon (vocals, guitar), Jeremy Ireland (guitar), Damon Martin (bass) and Petur Smith (drums).

4/5/97	Ⓡ	13	14	Mann's Chinese	—	*Naked*	Gasoline Alley 005

NAKED EYES
Pop duo from England: Pete Byrne (vocals) and Rob Fisher (keyboards, synthesizer). Fisher later formed Climie Fisher. Fisher died on 8/25/1999 (age 39).

4/16/83	Ⓡ	20	10	Always Something There To Remind Me	8	*Naked Eyes*	EMI America 17089
				#27 Pop hit for R.B. Greaves in 1970			

NASH, Graham
Born on 2/2/1942 in Blackpool, Lancashire, England. Singer/songwriter/guitarist. Former member of The Hollies. Formed **Crosby, Stills & Nash** in 1968. Also see **Classic Rock Tracks** section.

4/5/86	Ⓡ	14	7	Innocent Eyes	84	*Innocent Eyes*	Atlantic 81633
				Kenny Loggins (backing vocal)			

NAVARRO, Dave
Born on 6/7/1967 in Santa Monica, California. Rock singer/guitarist. Former member of **Jane's Addiction** and **Red Hot Chili Peppers**. Married to actress Carmen Electra from 2003-07.

6/2/01	Ⓡ	9	12	1 Rexall	—	*Trust No One*	Capitol 32802
6/9/01	Ⓜ	12	11				
9/29/01	Ⓜ	24	7	2 Hungry	—	↓	
10/20/01	Ⓡ	38	3				

NAZARETH
Hard-rock band formed in Dunfermline, Fife, Scotland: Dan McCafferty (vocals), **Billy Rankin** (guitar), Manny Charlton (guitar), John Locke (keyboards), Pete Agnew (bass) and Darrell Sweet (drums). Sweet died of a heart attack on 4/30/1999 (age 51). Also see **Classic Rock Tracks** section.

7/17/82	Ⓡ	19	12	Love Leads To Madness	105	*2XS*	A&M 4901

NDEGÉOCELLO, Me'Shell
Born Michelle Johnson on 8/29/1969 in Berlin, Maryland; raised in Oxon Hill, Maryland. Black female R&B-dance singer/bassist. Last name (pronounced: Nuh-DAY-gay-O-CHEL-lo) means "free like a bird" in Swahili.

5/28/94	Ⓡ	17	20	Wild Night	3[2]	*Dance Naked*	Mercury 522428
				JOHN MELLENCAMP & ME'SHELL NDEGEOCELLO			
				#28 Pop hit for **Van Morrison** in 1971			

N'DOUR, Youssou
Born on 10/1/1959 in Dakar, Senegal, Africa. Popular singer in his native language of Wolof.

8/19/89	Ⓜ	9	6	Shakin' The Tree	—	*The Lion*	Virgin 91253
				Peter Gabriel (co-lead vocal)			

NED'S ATOMIC DUSTBIN
Rock band from Stourbridge, West Midlands, England: Jonathan Penney (vocals), Garath Pring (guitar), Alexander Griffin (bass), Matthew Cheslin (bass) and Daniel Worton (drums).

7/20/91	Ⓜ	11	11	1 Happy	—	*God Fodder*	Columbia 47929
10/19/91	Ⓜ	24	6	2 Grey Cell Green	—	↓	
10/24/92+	Ⓜ	❶[1]	17	3 Not Sleeping Around	—	*Are You Normal?*	Columbia 53154
1/30/93	Ⓜ	13	8	4 Walking Through Syrup	—	↓	
7/31/93	Ⓜ	26	1	5 Saturday Night	—	*St: So I Married An Axe Murderer*	Chaos 57303
				#1 Pop hit for the Bay City Rollers in 1976			

NEIL, Vince
Born Vincent Neil Wharton on 2/8/1961 in Hollywood, California. Lead singer of **Mötley Crüe**.

5/23/92	Ⓡ	17	9	1 You're Invited But Your Friend Can't Come	—	*St: Encino Man*	Hollywood 61330
5/1/93	Ⓡ	12	10	2 Sister Of Pain	—	*Exposed*	Warner 45260
7/24/93	Ⓡ	34	4	3 Can't Have Your Cake	—	↓	

Billboard				ARTIST		Hot		
Debut	Cht	Peak	Wks	Track Title	®=Mainstream Rock Ⓜ=Modern Rock	Pos	Album Title	Album Label & Number

NELSON
Rock duo from Los Angeles, California: Gunnar Nelson (vocals, bass) and Matthew Nelson (vocals, guitar). The identical twin sons (born on 9/20/1967) of Ricky Nelson.

7/21/90	®	20	13	1 (Can't Live Without Your) **Love And Affection**.............		❶¹	*After The Rain*...DGC 24290	
11/24/90	®	39	8	2 **After The Rain**...		6	↓	
4/6/91	®	44	3	3 **More Than Ever**		14	↓	

NENA
Rock band formed in Berlin, Germany: Gabriele "Nena" Kerner (vocals), Carlo Karges (guitar), Uwe Fahrenkrog-Petersen (keyboards), Jurgen Demel (bass) and Rolf Brendel (drums). Karges died of liver failure on 1/30/2002 (age 50).

1/28/84	®	23	9	**99 Luftballons** .... [F]		2¹	*99 Luftballons*...................................Epic 39294	
				nuclear protest song				

N*E*R*D
Male rap/production trio from Virginia Beach, Virginia: Shay, Chad Hugo and Pharrell Williams.

8/3/02	Ⓜ	36	5	**Rock Star**..		—	*In Search Of*..Virgin 11521	

NERF HERDER
Rock trio from Santa Barbara, California: Parry Gripp (vocals, guitar), Charlie Dennis (bass) and Steve Sherlock (drums). Group named after a line in the 1980 movie *The Empire Strikes Back*.

1/4/97	Ⓜ	34	4	**Van Halen**		—	*Nerf Herder* ....Arista 18954	

NESS, Mike
Born on 4/3/1962 in Stoneham, Massachusetts. Lead singer of **Social Distortion**.

5/8/99	Ⓜ	28	8	**Don't Think Twice**		—	*Cheating At Solitaire* ....Time Bomb 43524	

NEUROSONIC
Hard-rock band from Vancouver, British Columbia, Canada: Jason Darr (vocals, guitar), Troy Healy (guitar), Jacen Ekstrom (bass) and Shane Smith (drums).

11/3/07+	®	30	14	**So Many People**		—	*Drama Queen* ....Bodog 1004	

NEUROTIC OUTSIDERS
All-star rock band: Steve Jones (vocals, guitar), John Taylor (vocals, bass), Duff McKagan (guitar) and Matt Sorum (drums). Jones was with the Sex Pistols. Taylor was with **Duran Duran**. McKagen and Sorum were with **Guns N' Roses**.

8/31/96	®	31	6	**Jerk**		—	*Neurotic Outsiders*..................................Maverick 46290	

NEVE
Rock band from Los Angeles, California: John Stephens (vocals), Mike Raphael (guitar), Tommy Gruber (bass) and Brian Burwell (drums).

3/13/99	Ⓜ	30	5	**It's Over Now**		—	*St: The Faculty*....................................Columbia 69762	

NEVERLAND
Rock band formed in Los Angeles, California: Dean Ortega (vocals), Patrick Sugg (guitar), Gary Lee (bass) and Scott Garrett (drums).

7/27/91	®	41	4	**Drinking Again**		—	*Neverland*...Interscope 91713	

NEVILLE, Ivan
Born on 7/23/1965 in New Orleans, Louisiana. Rock singer/bassist. Son of Aaron Neville.

10/22/88	®	6	15	**Not Just Another Girl**		26	*If My Ancestors Could See Me Now*.......Polydor 834896	

NEW AMERICAN SHAME
Rock band from Seattle, Washington: Johnny Reidt (vocals), Jimmy Paulson (guitar), Terry Bratsch (guitar), Kelly Wheeler (bass) and Geoff Reading (drums).

7/3/99	®	35	5	**Under It All**		—	*New American Shame* ....Will 83204	

NEW FAST AUTOMATIC DAFFODILS
Pop-rock band from Manchester, England: Andy Spearpont (vocals), Dolan Hewison (guitar), Icarus Wilson-Wright (percussion), Justin Crawford (bass) and Perry Saunders (drums).

2/20/93	Ⓜ	30	4	**Stockholm**		—	*Body Exit Mind*..................................Mute/Elektra 61398	

NEW FOUND GLORY
Punk-rock band from Coral Springs, Florida: Jordan Pundik (vocals), Chad Gilbert (guitar), Steve Klein (guitar), Ian Grushka (bass) and Cyrus Bolooki (drums).

2/17/01	Ⓜ	15	16	1 **Hit Or Miss**		—	*New Found Glory* ....Drive-Thru 112338	
6/22/02	Ⓜ	5	26	2 **My Friends Over You**		85	*Sticks And Stones* ....Drive-Thru 112916	
11/16/02	Ⓜ	28	11	3 **Head On Collision**		—	↓	
5/1/04	Ⓜ	11	13	4 **All Downhill From Here**		—	*Catalyst* ....Drive-Thru 002383	

NEWMAN, Randy

Born on 11/28/1943 in New Orleans, Louisiana. Singer/songwriter/pianist. Nephew of composers Alfred, Emil and Lionel Newman. Scored several movies. Also see **Classic Rock Tracks** section.

AWARD: Billboard: Century Award 2000

Debut	Cht	Peak	Wks	Track Title	Hot Pos	Album Title	Label & Number
10/1/88	R	❶²	12	**It's Money That Matters** Mark Knopfler (of **Dire Straits**; guitar)	60	*Land Of Dreams* ....Reprise 25773

NEW ORDER

Techno-dance band formed in Manchester, England: Bernard Sumner (vocals, guitar), Gillian Gilbert (keyboards), Peter Hook (bass) and Stephen Morris (drums). Sumner was also a member of **Electronic**. Hook was also a member of **Monaco** and **Revenge**. Morris and Gilbert also recorded as **The Other Two**.   **M All-Time: #97**

Debut	Cht	Peak	Wks	Track Title	Hot Pos	Album Title	Label & Number
1/7/89	M	3¹	13	1 Fine Time	—	*Technique* ....Qwest 25845
3/18/89	M	6	13	2 Round & Round	64	↓
7/7/90	M	5	8	3 World In Motion	—	*(single only)* ....Qwest 21582
4/17/93	M	❶⁶	18	4 Regret	28	*Republic* ....Qwest 45250
7/17/93	M	30	1	5 Ruined In A Day	—	↓
7/31/93	M	5	10	6 World (The Price Of Love)	92	↓

NEW RADICALS

Born Gregg Alexander on 5/4/1970 in Grosse Point, Michigan. New Radicals is his band project of revolving musicians.

Debut	Cht	Peak	Wks	Track Title	Hot Pos	Album Title	Label & Number
10/31/98+	M	8	23	**You Get What You Give**	36	*Maybe You've Been Brainwashed Too* ....MCA 11858

NEWTON, Juice

Born Judy Kay Cohen on 2/18/1952 in Lakehurst, New Jersey. Pop-country singer/guitarist.

Debut	Cht	Peak	Wks	Track Title	Hot Pos	Album Title	Label & Number
3/21/81	R	57	1	**Angel Of The Morning** .... #7 Pop hit for Merrilee Rush in 1968	4	*Juice* ....Capitol 12136

NICKELBACK

R 2000s: #1 / All-Time: #20 ★ M 2000s: #10 / All-Time: #30

Hard-rock band formed in Vancouver, British Columbia, Canada: brothers **Chad Kroeger** (vocals; born on 11/15/1974) and Mike Kroeger (bass; born on 6/25/1972), with Ryan Peake (guitar; born on 3/1/1973) and Ryan Vikedal (drums; born on 5/9/1975). Daniel Adair (of **3 Doors Down**) replaced Vikedal in January 2005.

TOP HITS: 1)How You Remind Me   2)Figured You Out   3)Photograph

Debut	Cht	Peak	Wks	Track Title	Hot Pos	Album Title	Label & Number
3/4/00	R	8	25	1 Leader Of Men	—	*The State* ....Roadrunner 8586
7/1/00	M	21	16			
8/12/00	R	10	17	2 Breathe	—	↓
11/25/00+	M	21	15			
12/23/00+	R	24	10	3 Old Enough	—	↓
7/28/01	R	❶¹³	48	4 How You Remind Me	❶⁴	*Silver Side Up* ....Roadrunner 618485
8/4/01	M	❶¹³	38			
12/15/01+	R	❶³	32	5 Too Bad	42	↓
12/15/01+	M	6	27			
7/20/02	R	❶³	27	6 Never Again	124	↓
8/3/02	M	24	13			
8/16/03	R	2⁸	26	7 Someday	7	*The Long Road* ....Roadrunner 618400
8/16/03	M	4	26			
11/15/03+	R	❶¹³	39	8 Figured You Out	65	↓
12/6/03+	M	4	26			
5/15/04	R	3⁴	26	9 Feelin' Way Too Damn Good	48	↓
6/5/04	M	23	13			
9/25/04	R	7	24	10 Because Of You	—	↓
8/20/05	R	❶⁷	24	11 Photograph	2¹	*All The Right Reasons* ....Roadrunner 618300
8/27/05	M	3¹	20			
11/26/05+	R	❶⁶	34	12 Animals	97	↓
12/10/05+	M	16	20			
3/11/06	R	11	20	13 Savin' Me	19	↓
4/22/06	M	29	14			

| Billboard | | | | ARTIST | ℝ=Mainstream Rock Ⓜ=Modern Rock | Hot Pos | Album Title | Album Label & Number |
| Debut | Cht | Peak | Wks | Track Title | | | | |

Debut	Cht	Peak	Wks	Track Title	Hot Pos	Album Title	Album Label & Number
				NICKELBACK — cont'd			
7/29/06	ℝ	4	28	14 Rockstar	6	↓	
9/16/06	Ⓜ	37	6				
3/17/07	ℝ	7	20	15 Side Of A Bullet	—	↓	
3/24/07	ℝ	37	2	16 If Everyone Cared	17	↓	

NICKS, Stevie   ℝ 1980s: #18 / All-Time: #55

Born Stephanie Nicks on 5/26/1948 in Phoenix, Arizona; raised in San Francisco, California. Pop-rock singer/songwriter. Teamed up with **Lindsey Buckingham** in 1973. Both joined **Fleetwood Mac** in 1975.

TOP HITS: 1)Talk To Me 2)Rooms On Fire 3)Stand Back

Debut	Cht	Peak	Wks	Track Title	Hot Pos	Album Title	Album Label & Number
8/1/81	ℝ	2^1	24	1 Stop Draggin' My Heart Around **STEVIE NICKS with Tom Petty and The Heartbreakers**	3^6	*Bella Donna*	Modern 139
8/8/81	ℝ	4	25	2 Edge Of Seventeen (Just Like The White Winged Dove) also see #4 below	11	↓	
11/28/81+	ℝ	26	12	3 Leather And Lace **STEVIE NICKS with Don Henley**	6	↓	
2/27/82	ℝ	26	9	4 Edge Of Seventeen (Just Like The White Winged Dove) [L-R] new version of #2 above	—	*(single only)*	Modern 7401
6/4/83	ℝ	2^3	18	5 Stand Back	5	*The Wild Heart*	Modern 90084
7/16/83	ℝ	12	12	6 Enchanted	—	↓	
7/23/83	ℝ	35	4	7 I Will Run To You **STEVIE NICKS with Tom Petty and The Heartbreakers**	—	↓	
7/30/83	ℝ	19	9	8 Nothing Ever Changes	—	↓	
9/24/83	ℝ	8	11	9 If Anyone Falls	14	↓	
2/11/84	ℝ	32	2	10 Nightbird **STEVIE NICKS with Sandy Stewart**	33	↓	
3/31/84	ℝ	19	8	11 Violet And Blue	—	*St: Against All Odds*	Atlantic 80152
11/16/85	ℝ	❶^2	13	12 Talk To Me	4	*Rock A Little*	Modern 90479
11/30/85+	ℝ	6	18	13 I Can't Wait	16	↓	
12/28/85+	ℝ	17	11	14 Needles And Pins [L] **TOM PETTY AND THE HEARTBREAKERS with Stevie Nicks** #13 Pop hit for The Searchers in 1964; recorded at the Wiltern Theater in Los Angeles, California	37	*Pack Up The Plantation - Live!*	MCA 8021
5/6/89	ℝ	❶^1	14	15 Rooms On Fire	16	*The Other Side Of The Mirror*	Modern 91245
7/1/89	ℝ	11	12	16 Long Way To Go	—	↓	
8/31/91	ℝ	7	9	17 Sometimes It's A Bitch written by **Billy Falcon** and **Jon Bon Jovi** (also on guitar)	56	*TimeSpace - The Best Of Stevie Nicks*	Modern 91711
6/25/94	ℝ	36	3	18 Maybe Love Will Change Your Mind	57	*Street Angel*	Modern 92246

NIGHT RANGER

Rock band formed in San Francisco, California: Jack Blades (vocals, bass; born on 4/24/1954), Kelly Keagy (vocals, drums; born on 9/15/1952), Jeff Watson (guitar; born on 11/4/1956), **Brad Gillis** (guitar; born on 6/15/1957), and Alan Fitzgerald (keyboards; born on 7/16/1949). Blades later joined **Damn Yankees** and formed duo with **Tommy Shaw**.

TOP HITS: 1)Sister Christian 2)Sentimental Street 3)Don't Tell Me You Love Me

Debut	Cht	Peak	Wks	Track Title	Hot Pos	Album Title	Album Label & Number
12/11/82+	ℝ	4	18	1 Don't Tell Me You Love Me	40	*Dawn Patrol*	Boardwalk 33259
3/19/83	ℝ	39	2	2 Sing Me Away	54	↓	
11/19/83	ℝ	15	19	3 (You Can Still) Rock In America	51	*Midnight Madness*	MCA/Camel 5456
2/25/84	ℝ	26	5	4 Rumours In The Air	—	↓	
3/31/84	ℝ	2^1	14	5 Sister Christian	5	↓	
7/7/84	ℝ	7	15	6 When You Close Your Eyes	14	↓	
5/25/85	ℝ	3^2	13	7 Sentimental Street	8	*7 Wishes*	MCA/Camel 5593
8/17/85	ℝ	13	12	8 Four In The Morning (I Can't Take Any More)	19	↓	
11/30/85+	ℝ	16	12	9 Goodbye	17	↓	
3/21/87	ℝ	12	10	10 The Secret Of My Success	64	*St: The Secret Of My Success*	MCA 6205
9/24/88	ℝ	16	8	11 I Did It For Love	75	*Man In Motion*	MCA/Camel 6238
1/14/89	ℝ	48	1	12 Reason To Be	—	↓	

NILE, Willie

Born Robert Noonan in 1949 in Buffalo, New York. Rock singer/songwriter.

Debut	Cht	Peak	Wks	Track Title	Hot Pos	Album Title	Album Label & Number
5/9/81	ℝ	55	2	1 Golden Down	—	*Golden Down*	Arista 4284
4/13/91	ℝ	16	12	2 Heaven Help The Lonely	—	*Places I Have Never Been*	Columbia 44434

NINEDAYS
Rock band from New York: John Hampson (vocals, guitar), Brian Desveaux (vocals, guitar), Jeremy Dean (keyboards), Nick Dimichino (bass) and Vincent Tattanelli (drums).

Debut	Cht	Peak	Wks	Track Title	Hot Pos	Album Title	Album Label & Number
4/15/00	M	10	19	**Absolutely (Story Of A Girl)**	6	The Madding Crowd	550 Music 63634

NINE INCH NAILS
M 1990s: #39 / 2000s: #19 / All-Time: #17

Born Trent Reznor on 5/17/1965 in Mercer, Pennsylvania; later based in Cleveland, Ohio. Formed and fronted Nine Inch Nails as an industrial-rock project with revolving musicians, including Richard Patrick and Brian Liesegang of **Filter**.

TOP HITS: 1)Only 2)The Hand That Feeds 3)Every Day Is Exactly The Same

Debut	Cht	Peak	Wks	Track Title	Hot Pos	Album Title	Album Label & Number
12/16/89+	M	16	12	1 **Down In It**	—	Pretty Hate Machine	TVT 2610
3/31/90	M	28	1	2 **Head Like A Hole**	109	↓	
10/3/92	M	13	9	3 **Happiness In Slavery**	—	Broken	Nothing 92213
				Grammy: Metal Performance			
2/20/93	M	25	1	4 **Wish**	—	↓	
				Grammy: Metal Performance			
5/7/94	M	11	25	5 **Closer**	41	The Downward Spiral	Nothing 92346
9/24/94	R	35	4				
12/24/94+	M	20	9	6 **Piggy**	—	↓	
4/22/95	M	8	14	7 **Hurt**	54^A	↓	
2/1/97	M	11	14	8 **The Perfect Drug**	46	St: Lost Highway	Nothing 90090
2/8/97	R	21	10				
8/7/99	M	39	3	9 **Starfuckers, Inc.**	—	The Fragile	Nothing 490473
9/18/99	M	11	14	10 **We're In This Together**	—	↓	
9/18/99	R	21	13				
12/4/99+	M	11	18	11 **Into The Void**	—	↓	
1/1/00	R	27	9				
5/26/01	M	18	9	12 **Deep**	—	St: Lara Croft: Tomb Raider	Elektra 62665
6/23/01	R	37	4				
4/2/05	M	❶⁵	27	13 **The Hand That Feeds**	31	With Teeth	Nothing 004553
4/2/05	R	2²	32				
8/6/05	M	❶⁷	29	14 **Only**	90	↓	
9/10/05	R	22	20				
12/31/05+	M	❶⁴	20	15 **Every Day Is Exactly The Same**	56	↓	
1/7/06	R	12	20				
3/3/07	M	❶¹	13	16 **Survivalism**	68	Y34RZ3R0R3MIX3D	Nothing 010331
3/10/07	R	14	12				
5/12/07	M	6	18	17 **Capital G**	—	↓	
5/26/07	R	25	14				

NIRVANA
R 1990s: #31 / All-Time: #90 ★ M 1990s: #16 / All-Time: #27

Grunge-rock trio from Aberdeen, Washington: Kurt Cobain (vocals, guitar; born on 2/20/1967), Krist Novoselic (bass; born on 5/16/1965) and **Dave Grohl** (drums; born on 1/14/1969). Cobain married **Courtney Love** (lead singer of **Hole**) on 2/24/1992. Cobain died of a self-inflicted gunshot wound on 4/8/1994 (age 27). Grohl formed **Foo Fighters** in 1995.

TOP HITS: 1)You Know You're Right 2)Heart-Shaped Box 3)All Apologies

Debut	Cht	Peak	Wks	Track Title	Hot Pos	Album Title	Album Label & Number
9/21/91	M	❶¹	20	1 **Smells Like Teen Spirit**	6	Nevermind	DGC 24425
11/2/91+	R	7	24	R&R Hall of Fame ★ RS500 #9			
1/25/92	R	3⁴	25	2 **Come As You Are**	32	↓	
1/18/92	M	3¹	18	RS500 #455			
1/18/92	M	25	2	3 **On A Plain**	—	↓	
6/20/92	R	16	16	4 **Lithium**	64	↓	
2/8/92	M	25	3				
12/26/92+	R	5	17	5 **In Bloom**	—	↓	
				RS500 #407			

Billboard				ARTIST	R=Mainstream Rock M=Modern Rock	Hot Pos	Album Title	Album Label & Number
Debut	Cht	Peak	Wks	Track Title				

NIRVANA — cont'd

Debut	Cht	Peak	Wks			Hot Pos		
1/23/93	Ⓜ	19	4	6 Sliver		—	*Incesticide*	DGC 24504
9/18/93	Ⓜ	❶³	14	7 Heart-Shaped Box		—	*In Utero*	DGC 24607
9/18/93	Ⓡ	4	21					
12/4/93+	Ⓜ	❶²	21	8 All Apologies		45ᴬ	↓	
12/18/93+	Ⓡ	4	26	RS500 #455				
10/15/94	Ⓜ	❶¹	19	9 About A Girl	[L]	22ᴬ	*MTV Unplugged In New York*	DGC 24727
10/15/94	Ⓡ	3³	26	studio version on their 1989 album *Bleach*				
1/7/95	Ⓜ	6	21	10 The Man Who Sold The World	[L]	39ᴬ	↓	
1/28/95	Ⓡ	12	12	first recorded by **David Bowie** in 1970				
5/27/95	Ⓡ	22	9	11 Lake Of Fire	[L]	—	↓	
				above 3 recorded on 11/18/1993				
9/28/96	Ⓡ	11	9	12 Aneurysm	[L]	63ᴬ	*From The Muddy Banks Of The Wishkah*	DGC 25105
9/28/96	Ⓜ	13	12	recorded on 12/28/1991 at Del Mar Fairgrounds in California				
10/12/02	Ⓜ	❶⁴	26	13 You Know You're Right		45	*Nirvana*	DGC 493507
10/12/02	Ⓡ	❶⁴	26	recorded on 1/30/1994				

NITZER EBB

Industrial-rock duo from Chelmford, Essex, England: Douglas McCarthy and Bon Harris.

Debut	Cht	Peak	Wks			Hot Pos		
2/25/89	Ⓜ	25	2	1 Control Im Here		—	*Belief*	Geffen 24213
4/28/90	Ⓜ	28	2	2 Lightning Man		—	*Showtime*	Geffen 24284
9/7/91	Ⓜ	21	5	3 Family Man		—	*Ebbhead*	Geffen 24456
11/30/91	Ⓜ	27	2	4 I Give To You		—	↓	

NIXON, Mojo, & Skid Roper

Novelty-rock duo. Nixon (vocals, guitar) was born Neill Kirby McMillan on 8/2/1957 in Chapel Hill, North Carolina. Roper (washboard, bass) was born Richard Banke on 10/19/1954 in National City, California. Split in early 1990. Nixon appeared in the 1989 movie *Great Balls Of Fire*.

Debut	Cht	Peak	Wks			Hot Pos		
5/6/89	Ⓜ	16	4	1 Debbie Gibson Is Pregnant With My Two Headed Love Child	[N]	—	*Root Hog Or Die*	Enigma 73335
9/29/90	Ⓜ	20	4	2 Don Henley Must Die	[N]	—	*Otis*	Enigma 73529
				MOJO NIXON				

NIXONS, The

Rock band from Dallas, Texas: Zac Maloy (vocals, guitar), Jesse Davis (guitar), Ricky Brooks (bass) and John Humphrey (drums).

Debut	Cht	Peak	Wks			Hot Pos		
1/20/96	Ⓡ	6	26	1 Sister		48ᴬ	*Foma*	MCA 11209
3/16/96	Ⓜ	11	20					
7/20/96	Ⓡ	27	9	2 Wire		—	↓	
6/7/97	Ⓡ	9	17	3 Baton Rouge		—	*The Nixons*	MCA 11644
9/20/97	Ⓡ	22	8	4 The Fall		—	↓	
5/27/00	Ⓡ	32	6	5 First Trip To The Moon		—	*Latest Thing*	Koch 8085

NO ADDRESS

Rock band from Tallahassee, Florida: Ben Lauren (vocals), Justin Long (guitar), Phil Moreton (guitar), Bill Donaldson (bass) and Randy Lane (drums).

Debut	Cht	Peak	Wks			Hot Pos		
3/19/05	Ⓡ	12	19	When I'm Gone (Sadie)		—	*Time Doesn't Notice*	Atlantic 83774
3/26/05	Ⓜ	21	15					

NO DOUBT Ⓜ **All-Time: #61**

Ska-rock band from Orange County, California: **Gwen Stefani** (vocals; born on 10/3/1969), Tom Dumont (guitar; born on 1/11/1968), Tony Kanal (bass; born on 8/27/1970) and Adrian Young (drums; born on 8/26/1969). Stefani married **Gavin Rossdale** (lead singer of **Bush**) on 9/14/2002.

Debut	Cht	Peak	Wks			Hot Pos		
11/18/95+	Ⓜ	10	26	1 Just A Girl		23	*Tragic Kingdom*	Trauma 92580
4/27/96	Ⓜ	5	26	2 Spiderwebs		18ᴬ	↓	
10/19/96	Ⓜ	2⁵	23	3 Don't Speak		❶¹⁶ᴬ	↓	
2/8/97	Ⓜ	17	10	4 Excuse Me Mr.		—	↓	
3/13/99	Ⓜ	7	22	5 New		123	*St: Go*	Work 69851
2/5/00	Ⓜ	2³	18	6 Ex-Girlfriend		111	*Return Of Saturn*	Trauma 490441
5/13/00	Ⓜ	14	14	7 Simple Kind Of Life		38	↓	
1/10/04	Ⓜ	32	6	8 It's My Life		10	*The Singles 1992-2003*	Interscope 001495

Billboard				ARTIST		Hot		
Debut	Cht	Peak	Wks	Track Title	®=Mainstream Rock ⓜ=Modern Rock	Pos	Album Title	Album Label & Number

NOISE THERAPY
Rock band from Vancouver, British Columbia, Canada: Dave Ottoson (vocals), Kai Markus (guitar), James F. (Keyboards), Rob Thiessen (bass) and Bobby James (drums).

12/28/02+	®	34	9	Get Up		—	*Tension*	Redline 70007

NONPOINT
Rock band from Miami, Florida: Elias Soriano (vocals), Andrew Goldman (guitar), Ken "KB" Charman (bass) and Robb Rivera (drums).

3/3/01	®	24	15	1 What A Day	—	*Statement*	MCA 112364
6/29/02	®	36	7	2 Your Signs	—	*Development*	MCA 112920
7/10/04	®	22	15	3 The Truth	—	*Recoil*	Lava 93303
12/25/04+	®	34	6	4 In The Air Tonight	103	↓	
11/26/05+	®	22	20	5 Bullet With A Name	—	*To The Pain*	Bieler Bros. 70007
5/27/06	®	36	11	6 Alive And Kicking	—	↓	
11/17/07+	®	28	18	7 March Of War	—	*Vengeance*	Bieler Bros. 70021

NORTHERN PIKES, The
Rock band from Saskatoon, Saskatchewan, Canada: Jay Semko (vocals, bass), Merl Bryck (vocals, guitar), Bryan Potvin (guitar) and Don Schmid (drums).

10/10/87	®	37	6	Things I Do For Money	—	*Big Blue Sky*	Virgin 90635

NORTHSIDE
Rock band from Manchester, England: Warren Dermody (vocals), Tim Walsh (guitar), Cliff Ogier (bass) and Paul Walsh (drums).

8/31/91	ⓜ	5	11	Take 5	—	*Chicken Rhythms*	Geffen 24412

NORUM, John
Born on 2/23/1964 in Vardo, Norway; raised in Stockholm, Sweden. Lead guitarist of **Europe** from 1982-87.

7/9/88	®	34	6	Back On The Streets	—	*Total Control*	Epic 44220

NOTHINGFACE
Hard-rock band from Washington DC: Matt Holt (vocals), Tom Maxwell (guitar), Bill Gaal (bass) and Chris Houck (drums). Maxwell later joined **HellYeah**.

2/10/01	®	32	9	Bleeder	—	*Violence*	TVT 5880

NOTTING HILLBILLIES, The
Gorup of rock guitarists: Mark Knopfler and Guy Fletcher (both of **Dire Straits**), with Brendan Croker and Steve Phillips. Recorded at Knopfler's studio in London's Notting Hill Gate.

3/10/90	®	20	8	Your Own Sweet Way	—	*Missing...Presumed Having A Good Time*	Warner 26147

NOVA, Aldo
Born Aldo Scarporuscio on 11/13/1956 in Montreal, Quebec, Canada. Rock singer/songwriter/guitarist.

2/13/82	®	3[1]	22	1 Fantasy	23	*Aldo Nova*	Portrait 37498
10/8/83	®	12	16	2 Monkey On Your Back	—	*Subject: Aldo Nova*	Portrait 38721
5/18/91	®	14	9	3 Blood On The Bricks	—	*Blood On The Bricks*	Jambco 848513
8/24/91	®	43	4	4 Medicine Man	—	↓	
				Jon Bon Jovi (backing vocal, above 2)			

NOVA, Heather
Born on 7/6/1968 on an island in the Bermuda Sound. Raised on a 40-foot sailboat in the Caribbean. Later settled in London, England. Female singer/songwriter.

9/2/95	ⓜ	13	14	Walk This World	63[A]	*Oyster*	Big Cat 67113

NOVO COMBO
Rock band formed in New York: Pete Hewlett (vocals), Jack Griffith (guitar), Stephen Dees (bass) and Michael Shrieve (drums; of **Santana**).

10/17/81+	®	43	13	1 Up Periscope	—	*Novo Combo*	Polydor 6331
2/20/82	®	42	8	2 Tattoo	103	↓	

NUGENT, Ted
Born on 12/13/1948 in Detroit, Michigan. Hard-rock singer/guitarist. Leader of The Amboy Dukes. Later joined **Damn Yankees**. An avid game hunter and an active supporter of the National Rifle Association. Nicknamed "The Motor City Madman." Had own *Surviving Nugent* reality TV show. Also see **Classic Rock Tracks** section.

3/21/81	®	36	3	1 The Flying Lip Lock	[L]	—	*Intensities In 10 Cities*	Epic 37084
3/21/81	®	56	1	2 Jailbait	[L]	—	↓	
3/28/81	®	47	1	3 Land Of A Thousand Dances	[L]	—	↓	
				#6 Pop hit for Wilson Pickett in 1966				
3/3/84	®	41	2	4 Tied Up In Love		107	*Penetrator*	Atlantic 80125
3/15/86	®	22	9	5 Little Miss Dangerous		—	*Little Miss Dangerous*	Atlantic 81632

O

O.A.R.

Pop-rock band from Columbus, Ohio: Marc Roberage (vocals, guitar), Richard On (guitar), Jerry DePizzo (sax), Benj Gershman (bass) and Chris Culos (drums). O.A.R.: Of A Revolution.

Debut	Cht	Peak	Wks	Track Title	Hot Pos	Album Title	Label & Number
10/22/05	ⓜ	30	12	**Love And Memories**	116	*Stories Of A Stranger* ....Everfine 94109

OASIS

ⓜ **1990s: #14 / All-Time: #24**

Rock band from Manchester, England: brothers Liam Gallagher (vocals; born on 9/21/1972) and Noel Gallagher (guitar; born on 5/29/1967), with Paul Arthurs (guitar; born on 6/23/1965), Paul McGuigan (bass; born on 5/9/1971) and Tony McCarroll (drums). Alan White (of **Starclub**; born on 5/26/1972) replaced McCarroll in 1995. Zak Starkey (son of **Ringo Starr**) replaced White in 2004.

TOP HITS: 1)Wonderwall 2)Champagne Supernova 3)Live Forever

Debut	Cht	Peak	Wks	Track Title	Hot Pos	Album Title	Label & Number
10/1/94	ⓜ	11	16	1 **Supersonic**	—	*Definitely Maybe* ....Epic 66431
12/24/94	®	38	2			
1/7/95	ⓜ	2²	24	2 **Live Forever**	39ᴬ ↓	
2/25/95	®	10	14			
6/3/95	ⓜ	36	4	3 **Rock 'N' Roll Star**	— ↓	
10/7/95	ⓜ	24	6	4 **Morning Glory**	—	*(What's The Story) Morning Glory?* ....Epic 67351
11/25/95	ⓜ	❶¹⁰	25	5 **Wonderwall**	8 ↓	
12/30/95+	®	9	17			
2/24/96	ⓜ	❶⁵	19	6 **Champagne Supernova**	20ᴬ ↓	
4/13/96	®	8	15			
6/22/96	ⓜ	10	14	7 **Don't Look Back In Anger**	55 ↓	
7/19/97	ⓜ	4	16	8 **D' You Know What I Mean?**	49ᴬ	*Be Here Now* ....Epic 68530
8/16/97	®	36	5			
9/27/97	ⓜ	5	18	9 **Don't Go Away**	35ᴬ ↓	
11/15/97	®	36	4			
1/24/98	ⓜ	15	9	10 **All Around The World**	— ↓	
10/31/98	ⓜ	24	9	11 **Acquiesce**	—	*The Masterplan* ....Epic 69647
1/29/00	ⓜ	14	11	12 **Go Let It Out**	—	*Standing On The Shoulder Of Giants* ....Epic 63586
4/30/05	ⓜ	19	10	13 **Lyla**	108	*Don't Believe The Truth* ....Epic 94493

OCASEK, Ric

Born Richard Otcasek on 3/23/1949 in Baltimore. Lead singer/guitarist/songwriter of **The Cars**. Appeared in the 1987 movie *Made In Heaven*. Married supermodel/actress Paulina Porizkova on 8/23/1989. His son Christopher Otcasek is leader of **Glamour Camp**.

Debut	Cht	Peak	Wks	Track Title	Hot Pos	Album Title	Label & Number
1/29/83	®	5	17	1 **Something To Grab For**	47	*Beatitude* ....Geffen 2022
2/5/83	®	25	1	2 **Jimmy Jimmy**	— ↓	
9/6/86	®	❶¹	12	3 **Emotion In Motion**	15	*This Side Of Paradise* ....Geffen 24098
10/11/86	®	9	17	4 **True To You**	75 ↓	
6/29/91	®	11	8	5 **Rockaway**	—	*Fireball Zone* ....Reprise 26552
7/6/91	ⓜ	19	5			

OCEAN BLUE, The

Pop-rock band formed in Hershey, Pennsylvania: Dave Schelzel (vocals, guitar), Steve Lau (keyboards), Bobby Mittan (bass) and Rob Minnig (drums).

Debut	Cht	Peak	Wks	Track Title	Hot Pos	Album Title	Label & Number
8/19/89	ⓜ	2³	13	1 **Between Something And Nothing**	—	*The Ocean Blue* ....Sire 25906
12/2/89	ⓜ	10	10	2 **Drifting, Falling**	— ↓	
9/28/91	ⓜ	16	6	3 **Cerulean**	—	*Cerulean* ....Sire 26550
11/16/91+	ⓜ	3²	13	4 **Ballerina Out Of Control**	— ↓	
2/15/92	ⓜ	27	2	5 **Mercury**	— ↓	
8/28/93	ⓜ	3¹	12	6 **Sublime**	121	*Beneath The Rhythm And Sound* ....Sire 45369

O'CONNOR, Sinéad

Born on 12/8/1966 in Dublin, Ireland. Female singer/songwriter.

Debut	Cht	Peak	Wks	Track Title	Hot Pos	Album Title	Label & Number
9/17/88	ⓜ	17	3	1 **Jump In The River**	—	*St: Married To The Mob* ....Reprise 25763
2/10/90	ⓜ	❶¹	13	2 **Nothing Compares 2 U**	❶⁴	*I Do Not Want What I Haven't Got* ....Ensign 21759
3/31/90	®	23	7	RS500 #162 written by **Prince**		

O'CONNOR, Sinéad — cont'd

Debut	Cht	Peak	Wks	Track Title	Hot Pos	Album Title	Album Label & Number
4/7/90	Ⓜ	❶[1]	15	3 The Emperor's New Clothes	60	↓	
5/26/90	Ⓡ	40	3				
9/12/92	Ⓜ	20	6	4 Success Has Made A Failure Of Our Home	—	*Am I Not Your Girl?*	Ensign 21952
4/2/94	Ⓜ	24	2	5 You Made Me The Thief Of Your Heart	—	*St: In The Name Of The Father*	Island 518841

OFFSPRING, The

Ⓡ 1990s: #27 / 2000s: #40 / All-Time: #44 ★
Ⓜ 1990s: #13 / 2000s: #34 / All-Time: #9

Punk-rock band from Garden Grove, California: Bryan "Dexter" Holland (vocals; born on 12/29/1966), Kevin "Noodles" Wasserman (guitar; born on 2/4/1963), Greg Kriesel (bass; born on 1/20/1965) and Ron Welty (drums; born on 2/1/1971). Adam "Atom" Willard replaced Welty in early 2003. Willard is also a member of **Angels And Airwaves**.

TOP HITS: 1)Gone Away 2)Come Out And Play 3)Hit That 4)Original Prankster 5)Pretty Fly (For A White Guy)

Debut	Cht	Peak	Wks	Track Title	Hot Pos	Album Title	Album Label & Number
5/28/94	Ⓜ	❶[2]	26	1 Come Out And Play	38[A]	*Smash*	Epitaph 86432
7/16/94	Ⓡ	10	26				
8/13/94	Ⓜ	4	25	2 Self Esteem	45[A]	↓	
10/1/94	Ⓡ	7	26				
11/26/94+	Ⓜ	6	20	3 Gotta Get Away	58[A]	↓	
1/28/95	Ⓡ	15	23				
4/15/95	Ⓜ	22	10	4 Kick Him When He's Down	—	*Ignition*	Epitaph 86424
6/17/95	Ⓜ	16	10	5 Smash It Up	47[A]	*St: Batman Forever*	Atlantic 82759
1/18/97	Ⓜ	13	8	6 All I Want	65[A]	*Ixnay On The Hombre*	Columbia 67810
1/18/97	Ⓡ	18	7				
3/1/97	Ⓡ	❶[2]	34	7 Gone Away	50[A]	↓	
3/8/97	Ⓜ	4	24				
8/2/97	Ⓡ	5	22	8 I Choose	—	↓	
10/4/97	Ⓜ	24	10				
10/17/98	Ⓜ	3[2]	26	9 Pretty Fly (For A White Guy)	53	*Americana*	Columbia 69661
10/17/98+	Ⓡ	5	25	*intro samples "Rock Of Ages" by* **Def Leppard**			
1/30/99	Ⓜ	4	26	10 Why Don't You Get A Job?	74	↓	
2/13/99	Ⓡ	10	20				
5/29/99	Ⓜ	6	26	11 The Kids Aren't Alright	105	↓	
6/12/99	Ⓡ	11	26				
10/23/99	Ⓜ	11	15	12 She's Got Issues	—	↓	
10/23/99	Ⓡ	19	16				
5/13/00	Ⓜ	27	9	13 Totalimmortal	—	*St: Me, Myself & Irene*	Elektra 62512
6/10/00	Ⓡ	36	1				
10/21/00	Ⓜ	2[2]	17	14 Original Prankster	70	*Conspiracy Of One*	Columbia 61419
10/21/00+	Ⓡ	7	18				
1/6/01	Ⓜ	10	16	15 Want You Bad	—	↓	
2/10/01	Ⓡ	23	10				
12/8/01+	Ⓡ	8	21	16 Defy You	77	*St: Orange County*	Columbia 85933
12/1/01+	Ⓜ	8	18				
11/15/03+	Ⓜ	❶[1]	24	17 Hit That	64	*Splinter*	Columbia 89026
11/15/03+	Ⓡ	6	26				
3/13/04	Ⓜ	6	20	18 (Can't Get My) Head Around You	120	↓	
3/13/04	Ⓡ	16	18				
5/21/05	Ⓜ	9	15	19 Can't Repeat	110	*Greatest Hits*	Columbia 93459
5/21/05	Ⓡ	10	15				
10/15/05	Ⓡ	29	7	20 Next To You	—	↓	
10/29/05	Ⓜ	37	3				

	Billboard			ARTIST	ℝ=Mainstream Rock	Hot		
Debut	Cht	Peak	Wks	Track Title	Ⓜ=Modern Rock	Pos	Album Title	Album Label & Number

OINGO BOINGO
New-wave rock band formed in Los Angeles, California: Danny Elfman (vocals), Steve Bartek (guitar), John Avila (bass) and Johnny Hernandez (drums). Band appeared in the 1986 movie *Back To School*. Elfman also scored several movies; married actress Bridget Fonda on 11/29/2003.

10/22/88	Ⓜ	14	6	1 Winning Side		—	*Boingo Alive*	MCA 8030
3/3/90	Ⓜ	15	6	2 When The Lights Go Out		—	*Dark At The End Of The Tunnel*	MCA 6365
6/11/94	Ⓜ	23	6	3 Hey!		—	*Boingo*	Giant 24555
				BOINGO				

OK GO
Pop-rock band from Chicago, Illinois: Damian Kulash (vocals), Andrew Duncan (guitar), Tim Nordwind (bass) and Dan Konopka (drums).

9/7/02	Ⓜ	20	17	1 Get Over It		—	*Ok Go*	Capitol 33724
9/16/06	Ⓜ	17	20	2 Here It Goes Again		38	*Oh No*	Capitol 78800

OLDFIELD, Mike
Born on 5/15/1953 in Reading, England. Classical-rock, multi-instrumentalist/composer.

1/30/88	ℝ	10	9	Magic Touch		—	*Islands*	Virgin 90645
				Max Bacon (of **GTR**; vocal)				

OLEANDER
Pop-rock band from Sacramento, California: Thomas Flowers (vocals), Ric Ivanisevich (guitar), Doug Eldridge (bass) and Fred Nelson (drums). Scott Devours replaced Nelson in late 1999.

2/20/99	ℝ	3²	33	1 Why I'm Here		107	*February Son*	Republic 53242
5/29/99	Ⓜ	13	25					
9/11/99	ℝ	24	11	2 I Walk Alone		—	↓	
12/4/99	Ⓜ	37	4					
2/17/01	ℝ	6	17	3 Are You There?		—	*Unwind*	Republic 013377
2/17/01	Ⓜ	19	12					
2/15/03	ℝ	25	10	4 Hands Off The Wheel		—	*Joyride*	Sanctuary 84593

OMAR & THE HOWLERS
Blues-rock band from Austin, Texas: Kent "Omar" Dykes (vocals, guitar), Bruce Jones (bass) and Gene Brandon (drums). Eric Scortia (keyboards) joined in late 1987.

6/6/87	ℝ	19	10	1 Hard Times In The Land Of Plenty		—	*Hard Times In The Land Of Plenty*	Columbia 40815
9/24/88	ℝ	36	5	2 Rattlesnake Shake		—	*Wall Of Pride*	Columbia 44102

ONE DOVE
Dance trio from Glasgow, Scotland: Dorothy Allison, Ian Carmichael and Jim McKinven.

12/18/93+	Ⓜ	14	10	White Love		—	*Morning Dove White*	FFRR 351042

ONE MINUTE SILENCE
Rock band from England: Brian Barry (vocals), Massimo Fiocco (guitar), Glen Diani (bass) and Eddie Stratton (drums).

5/27/00	ℝ	39	1	Holy Man		—	*Buy Now...Saved Later*	V2 27069

ONE WAY RIDE
Rock band from Los Angeles, California: Leldon (vocals, guitar), Chris Scott (guitar), Tim Lunsford (bass) and Brian Carhart (drums).

7/15/00	ℝ	16	11	Painted Perfect		—	*Straight Up!*	Refuge 112347

OPEN SKYZ
Rock band from New York: Hugo (vocals), Adam Holland (guitar), Craig Pullman (keyboards) and Gerard Zappa (bass).

1/8/94	ℝ	25	7	Every Day Of My Life		—	*Open Skyz*	Zito 66343

OPERATOR
Hard-rock band formed in Los Angeles, California: Johnny Strong (vocals), Wade Carpenter (guitar), Ricki Lixx (guitar), Paul Phillips (bass) and Dorman Pantfoeder (drums). Phillips was also guitarist of **Puddle Of Mudd**. Strong is also an actor who appeared in several action movies.

5/5/07	ℝ	8	22	1 Soulcrusher		—	*Soulcrusher*	Atlantic 229180
6/30/07	Ⓜ	29	10					
10/20/07+	ℝ	23	19	2 Nothing To Lose		—	↓	

OPM
Rock trio from Los Angeles, California: Matthew Lo (vocals, guitar), John Necro (bass) and Geoff Turney (drums).

8/5/00	Ⓜ	18	9	Heaven Is A Halfpipe (If I Die)		—	*Menace To Sobriety*	Atlantic 83369

O-POSITIVE
Rock band from Boston, Massachusetts: Dave Herlihy (vocal), Dave Martin (guitar), Alan Petitti (keyboards), David Ingham (bass) and Alex Lob (drums).

6/2/90	Ⓜ	22	4	Back Of My Mind		—	*Toy Boat*	Epic 46018

Debut	Cht	Peak	Wks	ARTIST / Track Title (ℝ=Mainstream Rock, Ⓜ=Modern Rock)	Hot Pos	Album Title	Album Label & Number
				OPUS III			
				Pop-rock band from England: vocalist Kirsty Hawkshaw with trio of producers/musicians Kevin Dodds, Ian Munro and Nigel Walton.			
8/15/92	Ⓜ	30	2	It's A Fine Day	—	*Mind Fruit* ....EastWest 92160
				ORBISON, Roy			
				Born on 4/23/1936 in Vernon, Texas. Died of a heart attack on 12/6/1988 (age 52). Pop-rock singer/songwriter/guitarist. Member of the **Traveling Wilburys**.			
				AWARDS: R&R Hall of Fame: 1987 ★ Grammy: Lifetime Achievement Award 1998			
1/21/89	ℝ	2²	13	1 You Got It .... written by Orbison, **Jeff Lynne** and **Tom Petty**	9	*Mystery Girl*..Virgin 91058
3/11/89	ℝ	26	9	2 She's A Mystery To Me .... written by Bono and The Edge (both of **U2**)	—	↓
				ORBIT			
				Rock trio from Boston, Massachusetts: Jeff Lowe Robbins (vocals, guitar), Wally Gagel (bass) and Paul Buckley (drums).			
4/19/97	ℝ	29	4	Medicine	—	*Libido Speedway*...A&M 540652
4/19/97	Ⓜ	32	6				
				ORCHESTRAL MANOEUVRES IN THE DARK			
				Electro-pop band formed in England: keyboardist/vocalists Andrew McCluskey and Paul Humphreys, multi-instrumentalist Martin Cooper and drummer Malcolm Holmes. Humphreys left in 1989.			
3/26/83	ℝ	32	8	1 Telegraph	—	*Dazzle Ships* ....Epic 38543
4/2/83	ℝ	32	9	2 Genetic Engineering	—	↓
8/3/91	Ⓜ	19	5	3 Pandora's Box (It's A Long, Long Way)	—	*Sugar Tax* ....Virgin 91715
6/12/93	Ⓜ	5	10	4 Stand Above Me	75ᴬ	*Liberator*...Virgin 88225
				ORGY			
				Electronic rock band from Los Angeles, California: Jay Gordon (vocals), Ryan Shuck (guitar), Amir Derakh (keyboards), Paige Haley (bass) and Bobby Hewitt (drums).			
12/5/98+	Ⓜ	4	31	1 Blue Monday	56	*Candyass*...Elementree 46923
1/23/99	ℝ	18	24				
7/3/99	Ⓜ	18	13	2 Stitches	—	↓
7/24/99	ℝ	38	4				
9/9/00	Ⓜ	6	21	3 Fiction (Dreams In Digital)	—	*Vapor Transmission*...........................Elementree 47832
9/16/00	ℝ	38	4				
3/3/01	Ⓜ	26	6	4 Opticon	—	↓
				ORIGIN, The			
				Pop-rock band from La Jolla, California: Michael Andrews (vocals), Daniel Silverman (keyboards), Topper Rimel (bass) and Rony Abada (drums).			
6/9/90	Ⓜ	19	9	1 Growing Old..	—	*The Origin* ....Virgin 91353
2/15/92	Ⓜ	17	9	2 Bonfires Burning	—	*Bend* ....Virgin 91740
				ORION THE HUNTER			
				Rock band formed in Boston, Massachusetts: Fran Cosmo (vocals), Barry Goudreau (guitar), Bruce Smith (bass) and Michael DeRosier (drums). Goudreau was a member of **Boston** and **RTZ**. Cosmo joined **Boston** in 1994.			
4/21/84	ℝ	7	12	So You Ran	58	*Orion The Hunter*.....................................Portrait 39239
				ORR, Benjamin			
				Born Benjamin Orzechowski on 8/9/1947 in Cleveland, Ohio. Died of cancer on 10/3/2000 (age 53). Bassist/vocalist of **The Cars**.			
10/25/86	ℝ	6	14	1 Stay The Night	24	*The Lace*..Elektra 60460
1/31/87	ℝ	25	8	2 Too Hot To Stop	—	↓
				ORTON, Beth			
				Born on 12/14/1970 in Norwich, Norfolk, England. Female singer/songwriter.			
4/24/99	Ⓜ	32	7	Stolen Car	—	*Central Reservation*............................Heavenly 19038
				OSBORNE, Joan			
				Born on 7/8/1962 in Anchorage, Kentucky. Female singer/songwriter/guitarist.			
9/30/95	Ⓜ	7	24	One Of Us..	4	*Relish* ....Blue Gorilla 526699
11/11/95+	ℝ	26	10				

OSBOURNE, Ozzy

® 1990s: #22 / 2000s: #24 / All-Time: #15

Born John Osbourne on 12/3/1948 in Birmingham, England. Hard-rock singer/songwriter. Lead singer of **Black Sabbath**. Controversial in his concert antics. Married his manager Sharon Arden on 7/4/1982. Appeared in the 1986 movie *Trick Or Treat*. *The Osbournes*, a reality show based on his family's home life, ran on MTV from 2002-05.

TOP HITS: 1)*I Don't Wanna Stop* 2)*Gets Me Through* 3)*Mama, I'm Coming Home* 4)*N.I.B.* 5)*Flying High Again*

Debut	Cht	Peak	Wks	#	Track Title	Hot Pos	Album Title	Label & Number
4/18/81	®	9	21	1	Crazy Train	106	Blizzard Of Ozz	Jet 36812
11/14/81+	®	2[1]	25	2	Flying High Again	—	Diary Of A Madman	Jet 37492
1/23/82	®	41	13	3	You Can't Kill Rock And Roll	—	↓	
2/6/82	®	38	8	4	Over The Mountain	—	↓	
12/25/82+	®	25	7	5	Paranoid [L]	—	Speak Of The Devil	Jet 38350
					#61 Pop hit for **Black Sabbath** in 1970			
12/25/82+	®	32	8	6	Iron Man/Children Of The Grave [L]	—		
					medley of **Black Sabbath** tunes; "Iron Man" was a #52 Pop hit in 1972; "Children Of The Grave" first recorded on their 1971 album *Master Of Reality*; above 2 recorded on 9/26/1982 at The Ritz in New York City			
12/10/83+	®	12	13	7	Bark At The Moon	109	Bark At The Moon	CBS Associated 38987
2/11/84	®	40	4	8	Rock 'N' Roll Rebel	—	↓	
2/8/86	®	10	13	9	Shot In The Dark	68	The Ultimate Sin	CBS Associated 40026
4/29/89	®	25	9	10	Close My Eyes Forever	8	Lita	RCA 6397
					LITA FORD with Ozzy Osbourne			
9/21/91	®	10	24	11	No More Tears	71	No More Tears	Epic/Associated 46795
12/14/91+	®	2[3]	29	12	Mama, I'm Coming Home	28	↓	
5/9/92	®	3[3]	20	13	Road To Nowhere	—	↓	
9/19/92	®	34	3	14	Mr. Tinkertrain	—	↓	
10/10/92	®	6	19	15	Time After Time	—	↓	
6/5/93	®	9	12	16	Changes [L]	—	Live & Loud	Epic/Associated 48973
					first recorded by **Black Sabbath** in 1972			
10/14/95	®	3[2]	23	17	Perry Mason	—	Ozzmosis	Epic 67091
12/23/95+	®	5	19	18	See You On The Other Side	—	↓	
5/18/96	®	24	7	19	I Just Want You	—	↓	
11/23/96	®	28	8	20	Walk On Water	—	St: Beavis And Butt-Head Do America	Geffen 25002
11/1/97	®	3[5]	26	21	Back On Earth	—	The Ozzman Cometh	Epic 67980
10/16/99	®	26	7	22	Shock The Monkey	—	Chamber Music	Roadrunner 8659
					COAL CHAMBER Featuring Ozzy Osbourne			
7/15/00	®	2[2]	41	23	N.I.B.	—	VA: Nativity In Black II: A Tribute To Black Sabbath	Divine 26095
					PRIMUS with Ozzy Osbourne first recorded by **Black Sabbath** in 1970			
9/15/01	®	2[6]	26	24	Gets Me Through	118	Down To Earth	Epic 63580
12/8/01+	®	10	23	25	Dreamer	—	↓	
3/12/05	®	10	12	26	Mississippi Queen	—	Under Cover	Epic 97750
					#21 Pop hit for Mountain in 1970			
4/28/07	®	❶[5]	27	27	I Don't Wanna Stop	61	Black Rain	Epic 05334
8/4/07	®	14	20	28	Not Going Away	—	↓	
12/8/07+	®	19	14	29	Black Rain	—	↓	

OTHER ONES, The

Pop-rock band consisting of Australian siblings Jayney (vocals), Alf (vocals) and Johnny (bass) Klimek, and Germans Andreas Schwarz-Ruszczynski (guitar), Stephen Gottwald (keyboards) and Uwe Hoffmann (drums).

5/9/87	®	38	4		We Are What We Are	53	The Other Ones	Virgin 90576

OTHER TWO, The

Duo from England: **New Order** members Gillian Gilbert (vocals, keyboards, guitar) and Stephen Morris (programs, percussion).

2/12/94	Ⓜ	30	2		Selfish	—	The Other Two And You	Qwest 45140

OUR LADY PEACE
Rock band from Toronto, Ontario, Canada: Raine Maida (vocals), Mike Turner (guitar), Chris Eacrett (bass) and Jeremy Taggart (drums). Duncan Coutts replaced Eacrett in 1996. Steve Mazur replaced Turner in 2002.

ⓜ **All-Time: #63**

TOP HITS: 1)Clumsy 2)Starseed 3)Somewhere Out There

Debut	Cht	Peak	Wks			Hot Pos	Album Title	Album Label & Number
3/25/95	ℝ	7	16	1	Starseed	—	Naveed	Relativity 1507
3/18/95	ⓜ	10	14					
8/2/97	ⓜ	11	20	2	Superman's Dead	74[A]	Clumsy	Columbia 67940
6/28/97	ℝ	14	19					
12/6/97+	ⓜ	5	26	3	Clumsy	59[A]	↓	
12/13/97+	ℝ	13	20					
5/23/98	ⓜ	31	11	4	4 AM	—	↓	
7/4/98	ℝ	38	2					
8/28/99	ⓜ	13	14	5	One Man Army	—	Happiness...Is Not A Fish That You Can Catch	Columbia 63707
9/18/99	ℝ	16	11					
2/5/00	ⓜ	20	14	6	Is Anybody Home?	—	↓	
2/12/00	ℝ	27	9					
2/10/01	ⓜ	27	12	7	Life	—	Spiritual Machines	Columbia 85368
4/20/02	ⓜ	7	22	8	Somewhere Out There	44	Gravity	Columbia 86585
5/11/02	ℝ	26	14					
9/7/02	ⓜ	20	12	9	Innocent	—	↓	
10/19/02	ℝ	35	5					
8/13/05	ⓜ	28	9	10	Where Are You	—	Healthy In Paranoid Times	Columbia 94777

OURS
Born James Gnecco in Ridgefield Park, New Jersey. Male singer/songwriter/guitarist.

5/26/01	ⓜ	31	5		Sometimes	—	Distorted Lullabies	DreamWorks 50036

OUTFIELD, The
Pop-rock trio formed in London, England: Tony Lewis (vocals, bass), John Spinks (guitar) and Alan Jackman (drums). Jackman left by 1990; Lewis and Spinks continued as a duo.

TOP HITS: 1)Voices Of Babylon 2)Your Love 3)Since You've Been Gone

8/31/85	ℝ	18	13	1	Say It Isn't So	—	Play Deep	Columbia 40027
1/18/86	ℝ	7	15	2	Your Love	6	↓	
5/24/86	ℝ	14	11	3	All The Love In The World	19	↓	
9/27/86	ℝ	20	8	4	Everytime You Cry	66	↓	
6/6/87	ℝ	11	12	5	Since You've Been Gone	31	Bangin'	Columbia 40619
9/19/87	ℝ	40	3	6	Bangin' On My Heart	—	↓	
3/25/89	ℝ	2[2]	12	7	Voices Of Babylon	25	Voices Of Babylon	Columbia 44449
6/17/89	ℝ	34	6	8	My Paradise	72	↓	
11/3/90	ℝ	13	13	9	For You	21	Diamond Days	MCA 10111
6/6/92	ℝ	46	1	10	Closer To Me	43	Rockeye	MCA 10476

OUTHOUSE
Rock trio from Kansas City, Missouri: Bill Latas (vocals, guitar), Brad Gaddy (bass) and Shawn Poores (drums).

4/12/97	ℝ	30	9		Welcome	—	Welcome	Mercury 534399

OUTKAST
Male hip-hop duo from Atlanta, Georgia: Andre "Dre" Benjamin and Antoine "Big Boi" Patton.

10/18/03	ⓜ	16	18		Hey Ya!	❶[9]	Speakerboxxx/The Love Below	Arista 50133

Grammy: Alternative R&B Group ★ RS500 #180

OUTLAWS
Southern-rock band formed in Tampa, Florida: Henry Paul (vocals, guitar), Hughie Thomasson (guitar), Billy Jones (guitar), Frank O'Keefe (bass) and Monte Yoho (drums). By 1981, Freddie Salem, Rick Cua and David Dix had replaced Paul, O'Keefe and Yoho. Thomasson joined Lynyrd Skynyrd in 1996. Jones died on 2/7/1995 (age 45). O'Keefe died of a drug overdose on 2/26/1995 (age 44). Thomasson died of a heart attack on 9/9/2007 (age 55). Also see Classic Rock Tracks section.

3/21/81	ℝ	15	4		(Ghost) Riders In The Sky	31	Ghost Riders	Arista 9542

#1 Pop hit for Vaughn Monroe in 1949

OUTSPOKEN
Rock band from Louisville, Kentucky: David Frazier (vocals), Kevin McCreery (guitar), Shaun Kennedy (guitar), Frank Green (bass) and Donnie Highland (drums).

1/25/03	ℝ	22	10		Farther	—	Bitter Shovel	Lava 83589

P

PABLO CRUISE
Pop-rock band from San Francisco, California: Dave Jenkins (vocals, guitar), Angelo Rossi (guitar), Cory Lerios (keyboards), John Pierce (bass) and Stephen Price (drums).

Debut	Cht	Peak	Wks	Track Title	Hot Pos	Album Title	Label
7/25/81	Ⓡ	23	16	Cool Love	13	Reflector	A&M 3726

PACIFIER
Rock band from New Zealand: Jon Toogood (vocals, guitar), Phil Knight (guitar), Karl Kippenberger (bass) and Tom Larkin (drums).

12/7/02+	Ⓡ	27	16	Bullitproof	—	Pacifier	Arista 14794
2/15/03	Ⓜ	37	5				

PAGE, Jimmy
Ⓡ 1990s: #40 / All-Time: #87

Born on 1/9/1944 in Heston, Middlesex, England. Rock guitarist. Member of The Yardbirds (1966-68). In October 1968, formed The New Yardbirds, which evolved into **Led Zeppelin**. Page produced all of the group's music. Joined **The Honeydrippers** in 1984, also co-founded **The Firm** with vocalist **Paul Rodgers**.

TOP HITS: 1)Pride And Joy 2)Most High 3)Gallows Pole

Debut	Cht	Peak	Wks	#	Track Title	Hot Pos	Album Title	Label
6/25/88	Ⓡ	4	8	1	Wasting My Time	—	Outrider	Geffen 24188
					John Miles (vocal)			
7/2/88	Ⓡ	13	10	2	The Only One	—	↓	
					Robert Plant (vocal)			
9/10/88	Ⓡ	26	8	3	Prison Blues	—	↓	
					Chris Farlow (vocal)			
2/27/93	Ⓡ	❶⁶	15	4	Pride And Joy	—	Coverdale•Page	Geffen 24487
3/27/93	Ⓡ	3²	17	5	Shake My Tree	—	↓	
6/19/93	Ⓡ	15	9	6	Take Me For A Little While	115	↓	
8/28/93	Ⓡ	24	6	7	Over Now	—	↓	
					COVERDALE•PAGE (above 4)			
10/22/94	Ⓡ	2³	14	8	Gallows Pole	—	No Quarter	Atlantic 82706
					first recorded by Led Zeppelin in 1970			
12/17/94+	Ⓡ	8	14	9	Thank You	—	↓	
					first recorded by Led Zeppelin in 1969			
4/18/98	Ⓡ	❶²	13	10	Most High	—	Walking Into Clarksdale	Atlantic 83092
					Grammy: Hard Rock Performance			
5/30/98	Ⓡ	6	18	11	Shining In The Light	—	↓	
					JIMMY PAGE & ROBERT PLANT (above 4)			
3/18/00	Ⓡ	13	13	12	What Is And What Should Never Be [L]	—	Live At The Greek	TVT 2140
8/5/00	Ⓡ	33	7	13	Ten Years Gone [L]	—	↓	
					JIMMY PAGE & THE BLACK CROWES (above 2)			

PALMER, Robert
Born Alan Palmer on 1/19/1949 in Batley, Yorkshire, England; raised on the Mediterranean island of Malta. Died of a heart attack on 9/26/2003 (age 54). Pop-rock singer. Lead singer of **The Power Station**. Also see **Classic Rock Tracks** section.

TOP HITS: 1)Simply Irresistible 2)Addicted To Love 3)You're Amazing

Debut	Cht	Peak	Wks	#	Track Title	Hot Pos	Album Title	Label
5/22/82	Ⓡ	59	2	1	Some Guys Have All The Luck	—	Maybe It's Live	Island 9665
					#39 Pop hit for The Persuaders in 1973			
6/18/83	Ⓡ	33	4	2	You Are In My System	78	Pride	Island 99866
					#64 Pop hit for The System in 1983			
2/15/86	Ⓡ	❶²	14	3	Addicted To Love	❶¹	Riptide	Island 90471
					Grammy: Rock Male Vocal			
5/3/86	Ⓡ	21	11	4	Hyperactive	33	↓	
9/27/86	Ⓡ	41	4	5	I Didn't Mean To Turn You On	2¹	↓	
					#79 Pop hit for Cherrelle in 1984			
7/2/88	Ⓡ	❶³	12	6	Simply Irresistible	2²	Heavy Nova	EMI-Manhattan 48057
					Grammy: Rock Male Vocal			
9/3/88	Ⓡ	40	7	7	Early In The Morning	19	↓	
					#24 Pop hit for The Gap Band in 1982			
3/10/90	Ⓡ	7	9	8	Life In Detail	—	St: Pretty Woman	EMI 93492
3/17/90	Ⓜ	14	8					
11/17/90	Ⓡ	5	10	9	You're Amazing	28	Don't Explain	EMI 93935
1/26/91	Ⓜ	24	2	10	I'll Be Your Baby Tonight	—	↓	
					first recorded by Bob Dylan in 1968			

PANIC AT THE DISCO

Punk-rock band from Las Vegas, Nevada: Brendan Urie (vocals, guitar), Ryan Ross (guitar), Brent Wilson (bass) and Spencer Smith (drums).

2/18/06	Ⓜ	5	20	1 The Only Difference Between Martyrdom And Suicide Is Press Coverage		77	A Fever You Can't Sweat Out...............Decaydance 077	
6/3/06	Ⓜ	12	20	2 I Write Sins Not Tragedies..		7	↓	
11/4/06	Ⓜ	28	12	3 Lying Is The Most Fun A Girl Can Have Without Taking Her Clothes Off		104	↓	
2/16/08	Ⓜ	12↑	7↑	4 Nine In The Afternoon		—	Pretty. Odd ....Decaydance 430524	

PANIC CHANNEL, The

Punk-rock band from Japan: Meguru (vocals), Kana (guitar), Mayo (guitar), Kiri (bass) and Kyo-Ya (drums).

7/8/06	Ⓜ	33	5	Why Cry...		—	(ONe)..Capitol 35318	
8/12/06	ℝ	39	1					

PANTERA

Heavy-metal band formed in Arlington, Texas: Philip Anselmo (vocals), "Dimebag" Darrell Abbott (guitar), Rex Brown (bass) and Vinnie Paul Abbott (drums). Darrell and Paul are brothers. Group name is Spanish for Panther. Anselmo also with **Down** in 1995. Brown, Darrell and Vinnie also formed **Rebel Meets Rebel**. Darrell was shot to death on stage on 12/8/2004 (age 38). Vinnie was also with **Damageplan** and **HellYeah**.

9/3/94	ℝ	21	12	1 Planet Caravan		—	Far Beyond Driven ....EastWest 92302	
				first recorded by **Black Sabbath** in 1971				
9/18/99	ℝ	40	1	2 Cat Scratch Fever		—	St: Detroit Rock City ....Mercury 546389	
				#30 Pop hit for **Ted Nugent** in 1977				
3/25/00	ℝ	28	11	3 Revolution Is My Name		—	Reinventing The Steel............................EastWest 62451	

PAPA ROACH   ℝ 2000s: #14 / All-Time: #74 ★ Ⓜ 2000s: #7 / All-Time: #23

Hard-rock band from Vacaville, California: Jacoby Shaddix (vocals; born on 7/28/1976), Jerry Horton (guitar; born on 3/10/1975), Tobin Esperance (bass; born on 11/14/1979) and Dave Buckner (drums; born on 5/29/1976). Buckner was married to Mia Tyler (daughter of **Steven Tyler**) from 2003-05. Tony Palermo replaced Buckner in early 2008.

TOP HITS: 1)Last Resort 2)Forever 3)Getting Away With Murder

4/22/00	Ⓜ	❶⁷	37	1 Last Resort		57	Infest...DreamWorks 50223	
5/6/00	ℝ	4	44					
10/7/00	Ⓜ	9	20	2 Broken Home		—	↓	
9/30/00	ℝ	18	20					
3/3/01	Ⓜ	16	15	3 Between Angels And Insects		—	↓	
3/3/01	ℝ	27	8					
5/18/02	ℝ	3³	25	4 She Loves Me Not		76	Lovehatetragedy................................DreamWorks 50381	
5/25/02	Ⓜ	5	22					
10/5/02	ℝ	26	9	5 Time And Time Again..		—	↓	
10/19/02	Ⓜ	33	5					
7/24/04	ℝ	2⁷	38	6 Getting Away With Murder		69	Getting Away With Murder ....El Tonal 003142	
7/31/04	Ⓜ	4	26					
11/20/04+	Ⓜ	2⁶	26	7 Scars...		15	↓	
11/20/04+	ℝ	4	26					
4/30/05	ℝ	11	18	8 Take Me		—	↓	
5/7/05	Ⓜ	23	11					
8/12/06	ℝ	8	24	9 To Be Loved		116	The Paramour Sessions.........................El Tonal 007486	
8/19/06	Ⓜ	14	20					
2/3/07	Ⓜ	2⁹	36	10 Forever		55	↓	
1/27/07	ℝ	2⁶	46					
8/11/07	ℝ	15	17	11 Time Is Running Out		—	↓	
8/18/07	Ⓜ	17	19					
1/26/08	ℝ	40	1	12 Reckless..		—	↓	

PAPA VEGAS

Rock band from Grand Rapids, Michigan: Joel Ferguson (vocals), Pete Dunning (guitar), Mick Force (bass) and Scott Stefanski (drums).

4/24/99	Ⓜ	20	9	Bombshell		—	Hello Vertigo ....RCA 67644	

Billboard				ARTIST	R=Mainstream Rock	Hot		
Debut	Cht	Peak	Wks	Track Title	M=Modern Rock	Pos	Album Title	Album Label & Number

PARAMORE
Pop-rock band formed in Franklin, Tennessee: Hayley Williams (vocals), brothers Josh Farro (guitar) and Zac Farro (drums), with Jeremy Davis (bass).

7/21/07	Ⓜ	3²	29	1 Misery Business		26	Riot!	Fueled By Ramen 159612
12/1/07+	Ⓜ	4	18↑	2 Crushcrushcrush		54	↓	

PARKER, Graham
Born on 11/18/1950 in London, England. Pop-rock singer/songwriter/guitarist.

4/17/82	Ⓡ	52	3	1 Temporary Beauty	—	Another Grey Area	Arista 9589
5/1/82	Ⓡ	42	4	2 You Hit The Spot	—	↓	
5/11/85	Ⓡ	19	10	3 Wake Up (Next To You)	39	Steady Nerves	Elektra 60388
				GRAHAM PARKER AND THE SHOT			
5/28/88	Ⓡ	23	10	4 Get Started, Start A Fire	—	The Mona Lisa's Sister	RCA 8316
9/10/88	Ⓜ	27	1	5 Don't Let It Break You Down	—	↓	
11/11/89	Ⓜ	18	9	6 Big Man On Paper	—	Human Soul	RCA 9876

PARKER, Ray Jr.
Born on 5/1/1954 in Detroit, Michigan. R&B singer/songwriter/guitarist. Leader of band Raydio from 1977-82.

7/14/84	Ⓡ	38	5	Ghostbusters	❶³	St: Ghostbusters	Arista 8246

PARR, John
Born on 11/18/1954 in Nottingham, Nottinghamshire, England. Pop-rock singer/songwriter.

11/10/84+	Ⓡ	6	19	1 Naughty Naughty	23	John Parr	Atlantic 80180
3/16/85	Ⓡ	28	6	2 Magical	73	↓	
6/29/85	Ⓡ	2³	13	3 St. Elmo's Fire (Man In Motion)	❶²	St: St. Elmo's Fire	Atlantic 81261

PARSONS, Alan, Project
Born on 12/20/1949 in London, England. Guitarist/keyboardist/producer. Engineered *Abbey Road* by **The Beatles** and *Dark Side Of The Moon* by **Pink Floyd**. Project features various musicians and vocalists. Eric Woolfson (vocals, keyboards) contributes most of the lyrics. Also see **Classic Rock Tracks** section.

TOP HITS: 1)Standing On Higher Ground 2)Prime Time 3)Stereotomy

3/21/81	Ⓡ	47	1	1 Snake Eyes	67	The Turn Of A Friendly Card	Arista 9518
				Chris Rainbow (vocal)			
6/26/82	Ⓡ	22	11	2 You're Gonna Get Your Fingers Burned	—	Eye In The Sky	Arista 9599
				Lenny Zakatek (vocal)			
7/10/82	Ⓡ	54	2	3 Psychobabble	57	↓	
				Elmer Gantry (vocal)			
7/17/82	Ⓡ	11	14	4 Eye In The Sky	3³	↓	
				Eric Woolfson (vocal)			
12/3/83	Ⓡ	12	17	5 You Don't Believe	54	The Best Of The Alan Parsons Project	Arista 8193
				Lenny Zakatek (vocal)			
3/31/84	Ⓡ	3¹	7	6 Prime Time	34	Ammonia Avenue	Arista 8204
3/31/84	Ⓡ	15	8	7 Don't Answer Me	15	↓	
				Eric Woolfson (vocal, above 2)			
2/9/85	Ⓡ	10	11	8 Let's Talk About Me	56	Vulture Culture	Arista 8263
				David Paton (vocal)			
4/27/85	Ⓡ	30	7	9 Days Are Numbers (The Traveller)	71	↓	
				Chris Rainbow (vocal)			
1/18/86	Ⓡ	5	11	10 Stereotomy	82	Stereotomy	Arista 8384
				John Miles (vocal)			
1/24/87	Ⓡ	3²	12	11 Standing On Higher Ground	—	Gaudi	Arista 8448
				Geoff Barradale (vocal)			

PAUL, Henry, Band
Born on 8/25/1949 in Kingston, New York. Rock singer/guitarist. Member of **The Outlaws**. His band: Dave Fiester (guitar), Billy Crain (guitar), Wally Dentz (bass) and Bill Hoffman (drums).

12/5/81+	Ⓡ	23	12	Keeping Our Love Alive	50	Anytime	Atlantic 19325

PAVEMENT
Rock band formed in Stockton, California: Stephen Malkmus (vocals, guitar), Scott Kannberg (guitar), Bob Nastanovich (percussion), Mark Ibold (bass) and Steve West (drums).

3/26/94	Ⓜ	10	12	Cut Your Hair	—	Crooked Rain, Crooked Rain	Matador/Atl. 92343

PEACE TOGETHER
Group formed to benefit youths in Northern Ireland. Formed by Robert Hamilton (from Dublin) and Alistair McMordie (from Belfast). Main vocals by **Peter Gabriel**, **Sinéad O'Connor** and Feargal Sharkey.

8/28/93	Ⓜ	28	2	Be Still	—	VA: Peace Together	Island 518063

Billboard				ARTIST	Hot		
Debut	Cht	Peak	Wks	Track Title	ℝ=Mainstream Rock ⓂM=Modern Rock	Pos	Album Title	Album Label & Number

PEARL JAM
ℝ 1990s: #1 / All-Time: #7 ★ Ⓜ 1990s: #3 / All-Time: #5

Rock band formed in Seattle, Washington: **Eddie Vedder** (vocals; born on 12/23/1964), Mike McCready (guitar; born on 7/20/1966), Stone Gossard (guitar; born on 4/5/1966), Jeff Ament (bass; born on 3/10/1963) and Dave Krusen (drums; born on 3/10/1966). Dave Abbruzzese (born on 5/17/1968) replaced Krusen in 1993. Gossard and Ament were members of Mother Love Bone. All except Krusen recorded with **Temple Of The Dog**. Band acted in the 1992 movie *Singles* as Matt Dillon's band, Citizen Dick. Abbruzzese left band in August 1994. Drummer Jack Irons (of the **Red Hot Chili Peppers**; born on 7/18/1962) joined in late 1994. McCready also put together **Mad Season** in 1994. Matt Cameron (of **Soundgarden**; born on 11/28/1962) replaced Irons in 1999.

TOP HITS: 1)Better Man 2)Daughter 3)Given To Fly 4)World Wide Suicide 5)Who You Are

Debut	Cht	Peak	Wks	Track Title	Hot Pos	Album Title	Album Label & Number
1/4/92	ℝ	16	25	1 **Alive**	107	Ten	Epic/Associated 47857
1/25/92	Ⓜ	18	8				
5/2/92	ℝ	3³	24	2 **Even Flow**	108	↓	
5/16/92	Ⓜ	21	6				
8/22/92	ℝ	5	20	3 **Jeremy**	70ᴬ	↓	
8/15/92	Ⓜ	5	11	R&R Hall of Fame			
12/26/92+	ℝ	3²	25	4 **Black**	—	↓	
12/26/92+	Ⓜ	20	9				
8/7/93	Ⓜ	8	10	5 **Crazy Mary**	—	VA: Sweet Relief: A Benefit For Victoria Williams	Thirsty Ear 57134
9/18/93	ℝ	26	5				
10/16/93	ℝ	3¹	8	6 **Go**	—	Vs.	Epic/Associated 53136
10/16/93	Ⓜ	8	7				
10/30/93	ℝ	❶⁸	26	7 **Daughter**	33ᴬ	↓	
10/30/93+	Ⓜ	❶¹	19				
10/30/93+	ℝ	21	13	8 **Animal**	—	↓	
2/26/94	Ⓜ	17	9	9 **Elderly Woman Behind The Counter In A Small Town**	—	↓	
6/11/94	ℝ	23	12	also see #29 below			
3/12/94	ℝ	3¹	23	10 **Dissident**	118	↓	
7/2/94	ℝ	39	1	11 **Glorified G**	—	↓	
9/3/94	ℝ	21	19	12 **Yellow Ledbetter**	flip	(single only)	Epic 77935
7/9/94	Ⓜ	26	3				
11/19/94	Ⓜ	11	3	13 **Spin The Black Circle**	58	Vitalogy	Epic 66900
11/19/94	ℝ	16	3	Grammy: Hard Rock Performance			
11/19/94	ℝ	16	6	14 **Tremor Christ**	18	↓	
11/19/94	Ⓜ	16	4				
12/10/94+	ℝ	❶⁸	26	15 **Better Man**	13ᴬ	↓	
12/3/94+	Ⓜ	2⁴	26				
12/10/94+	Ⓜ	13	26	16 **Corduroy**	53ᴬ	↓	
1/21/95	ℝ	22	22				
4/1/95	ℝ	12	11	17 **Not For You**	102	↓	
4/8/95	Ⓜ	38	3				
7/8/95	ℝ	10	17	18 **Immortality**	102	↓	
7/8/95	Ⓜ	31	6				
12/9/95+	ℝ	2⁴	26	19 **I Got ID**	7	(single only)	Epic 78199
12/9/95	Ⓜ	3²	20				
3/9/96	ℝ	24	7	20 **Leaving Here**	—	VA: Home Alive - The Art Of Self Defense	Epic 67486
3/9/96	Ⓜ	31	4	#76 Pop hit for Eddie Holland in 1964			
8/10/96	Ⓜ	❶¹	11	21 **Who You Are**	31	No Code	Epic 67500
8/10/96	ℝ	5	10				
9/14/96	ℝ	9	16	22 **Hail, Hail**	69ᴬ	↓	
10/5/96	Ⓜ	9	16				
9/14/96	ℝ	37	4	23 **Red Mosquito**	—	↓	
1/4/97	Ⓜ	31	6	24 **Off He Goes**	—	↓	
1/25/97	ℝ	34	2				
1/3/98	ℝ	❶⁶	23	25 **Given To Fly**	21	Yield	Epic 68164
1/3/98	Ⓜ	3¹⁰	25				

PEARL JAM — cont'd

Debut	Cht	Peak	Wks	Track Title	Hot Pos	Album Title	Album Label & Number
8/1/98	Ⓜ	13	11	26 In Hiding	—	↓	
2/21/98	Ⓡ	14	22				
2/28/98	Ⓜ	6	26	27 Wishlist	47	↓	
4/25/98	Ⓡ	6	16				
10/10/98	Ⓜ	33	4	28 Do The Evolution	—	↓	
10/10/98	Ⓡ	40	2				
11/28/98	Ⓡ	21	11	29 Elderly Woman Behind The Counter In A Small Town [L-R]	—	Live On Two Legs	Epic 69752
11/28/98	Ⓜ	26	10	new version of #9 above			
5/1/99	Ⓜ	2³	22	30 Last Kiss	2¹	VA: No Boundaries - A Benefit For The Kosovar Refugees	Epic 63653
5/29/99	Ⓡ	5	18	#2 Pop hit for J. Frank Wilson and The Cavaliers in 1964			
4/29/00	Ⓡ	3¹	11	31 Nothing As It Seems	49	Binaural	Epic 63665
4/29/00	Ⓜ	10	9				
7/1/00	Ⓡ	17	9	32 Light Years	—	↓	
7/8/00	Ⓜ	26	7				
10/5/02	Ⓜ	6	12	33 I Am Mine	43	Riot Act	Epic 86825
10/5/02	Ⓡ	7	17				
12/28/02+	Ⓡ	23	9	34 Save You	—	↓	
1/4/03	Ⓜ	29	6				
3/25/06	Ⓜ	❶³	19	35 World Wide Suicide	41	Pearl Jam	J Records 71467
3/25/06	Ⓡ	2¹	20				
6/10/06	Ⓜ	10	11	36 Life Wasted	—	↓	
6/10/06	Ⓡ	13	13				
9/30/06	Ⓜ	40	1	37 Gone	—	↓	
9/30/06				38 Love Reign O'er Me	108	(download only)	Ten Club
4/7/07	Ⓡ	32	6	featured in the movie *Reign O'er Me* starring **Adam Sandler** and Don Cheadle; #76 Pop hit for **The Who** in 1973			

PEEPING TOM
Born Michael Patton on 1/27/1968 in Eureka, California. Hard-rock singer. Leader of **Faith No More**.

| 9/9/06 | Ⓜ | 40 | 1 | Mojo | — | Peeping Tom | Ipecac 77 |

PENN, Michael
Born on 8/1/1958 in Manhattan, New York. Pop-rock singer/songwriter. Brother of actors Sean and Christopher Penn.
Son of actor/director Leo Penn and actress Eileen Ryan. Married **Aimee Mann** on 12/29/1997.

11/18/89+	Ⓜ	4	17	1 No Myth	13	March	RCA 9692
12/16/89+	Ⓡ	5	16				
3/10/90	Ⓜ	10	13	2 This & That	53	↓	
3/31/90	Ⓡ	16	12				
8/4/90	Ⓜ	20	5	3 Brave New World	—	↓	
7/28/90	Ⓡ	26	8				
9/5/92	Ⓜ	5	13	4 Seen The Doctor	—	Free-For-All	RCA 61113
10/31/92	Ⓡ	33	4				
12/19/92+	Ⓜ	14	10	5 Long Way Down (Look What The Cat Drug In)	—	↓	

PENNYWISE
Hard-rock band from Hermosa Beach, California: Jim Lindberg (vocals), Fletcher Dragge (guitar), Randy Bradbury (bass) and
Byron McMackin (drums). Band named after a character in Stephen King's 1986 novel *It*.

7/31/99	Ⓜ	36	4	1 Alien	—	Straight Ahead	Epitaph 86553
8/4/01	Ⓜ	38	2	2 F**k Authority	—	Land Of The Free?	Epitaph 86600
3/22/08	Ⓜ	34↑	2↑	3 The Western World	—	Reason To Believe	MySpace 10013

PEOPLE IN PLANES
Rock band from Cardiff, Wales: Gareth Jones (vocals, keyboards), Pete Roberts (guitar), Kris Blight (bass) and John Maloney
(drums).

| 3/18/06 | Ⓜ | 33 | 11 | If You Talk Too Much (My Head Will Explode) | — | As Far As The Eye Can See | Wind-Up 13117 |

PEPPER
Ska-rock trio from Hawaii; later based in California: Kaleco Wassman (vocals, guitar), Bret Bollinger (bass) and Yesod Williams
(drums).

| 5/21/05 | Ⓜ | 34 | 4 | 1 Give It Up | — | (download only) | Volcom |
| 10/14/06+ | Ⓜ | 19 | 18 | 2 No Control | — | No Shame | Volcom 94536 |

Debug	Cht	Peak	Wks	ARTIST / Track Title	Hot Pos	Album Title	Album Label & Number

R=Mainstream Rock **M**=Modern Rock

PERE UBU
Rock band from Cleveland, Ohio: David Thomas (vocals), Jim Jones (guitar), Allen Ravenstine (keyboards), Scott Krause (percussion), Tony Maimone (bass) and Chris Cutler (drums).

| 6/17/89 | **M** | 6 | 9 | Waiting For Mary | — | Cloudland | Fontana 838237 |

PERFECT CIRCLE, A
R 2000s: #30 ★ **M** 2000s: #32 / All-Time: #65
Hard-rock duo from Hollywood, California: Maynard James Keenan (vocals) and Billy Howerdel (guitar). Keenan also formed **Tool** and **Puscifer**. Howerdel also recorded as **Ashes Divide**.

4/29/00	**R**	4	27	1 Judith	105	Mer De Noms	Virgin 49253
4/29/00	**M**	5	26				
9/16/00	**M**	12	26	2 3 Libras	—	↓	
9/16/00	**R**	12	23				
2/17/01	**R**	14	14	3 The Hollow	—	↓	
2/17/01	**M**	17	14				
8/16/03	**R**	**❶**²	26	4 Weak And Powerless	61	Thirteenth Step	Virgin 80918
8/16/03	**M**	**❶**²	26				
12/20/03+	**R**	3¹	27	5 The Outsider	79	↓	
12/13/03+	**M**	5	28				
8/14/04	**R**	19	12	6 Blue	—	↓	
8/14/04	**M**	21	10				
10/16/04	**R**	26	13	7 Imagine	—	eMOTIVe	Virgin 66687
10/23/04	**M**	26	10	#3 Pop hit for **John Lennon** in 1971			
1/29/05	**M**	14	13	8 Passive	—	↓	
1/29/05	**R**	14	16				

PERRY, Joe, Project
Born on 9/10/1950 in Lawrence, Massachusetts. Lead guitarist of **Aerosmith**. The Project included Charlie Farren (vocals, guitar; of **Farrenheit**), David Hull (bass) and Ronnie Stewart (drums).

| 7/11/81 | **R** | 48 | 3 | Listen To The Rock | — | I've Got The Rock 'N' Rolls Again | Columbia 37364 |

PERRY, Steve
Born on 1/22/1949 in Hanford, California. Lead singer of **Journey**.

9/4/82	**R**	4	16	1 Don't Fight It	17	High Adventure	Columbia 38127
				KENNY LOGGINS with Steve Perry			
4/7/84	**R**	**❶**²	13	2 Oh Sherrie	3¹	Street Talk	Columbia 39334
5/5/84	**R**	43	1	3 I Believe	—	↓	
5/12/84	**R**	15	16	4 She's Mine	21	↓	
9/22/84	**R**	17	8	5 Strung Out	40	↓	
7/16/94	**R**	6	11	6 You Better Wait	29	For The Love Of Strange Medicine	Columbia 44287

PETE.
Rock band from Newark, New Jersey: David Terrana (vocals), Rich Andruska (guitar), Lars Alverson (bass) and Scott Anderson (drums).

| 6/30/01 | **R** | 17 | 13 | Sweet Daze | — | Pete. | Warner 47939 |

PETER, BJORN AND JOHN
Rock trio from Stockholm, Sweden: Peter Moren (vocals, guitar), Bjorn Yttling (bass) and John Eriksson (drums).

| 4/28/07 | **M** | 22 | 18 | Young Folks | 110 | Writer's Block | Almost Gold 002 |

PET SHOP BOYS
Pop duo formed in England: Neil Tennant (vocals) and Chris Lowe (keyboards).

4/12/86	**R**	37	5	1 West End Girls	**❶**¹	Please	EMI America 17193
10/22/88	**M**	22	5	2 Domino Dancing	18	Introspective	EMI-Manhattan 90868
9/22/90	**M**	17	7	3 So Hard	62	Behavior.	EMI 94310
8/21/93	**M**	10	9	4 Can You Forgive Her?	109	Very	EMI 89721

Billboard	Debut	Cht	Peak	Wks	ARTIST / Track Title	Hot Pos	Album Title	Album Label & Number

ⓡ=Mainstream Rock ⓜ=Modern Rock

PETTY, Tom, And The Heartbreakers
ⓡ **1980s: #2 / 1990s: #6 / All-Time: #2**

Born on 10/20/1950 in Gainesville, Florida. Rock singer/songwriter/guitarist. Formed The Heartbreakers in Los Angeles: Mike Campbell (guitar; born on 2/1/1954), Benmont Tench (keyboards; born on 9/7/1954), Ron Blair (bass; born on 9/16/1952) and Stan Lynch (drums; born on 5/21/1955). Howie Epstein (born on 7/21/1955; died of a drug overdose on 2/23/2003, age 47) replaced Blair in 1982; Blair returned in 2002, replacing Epstein. Steve Ferrone replaced Lynch in 1995. Petty appeared in the movies *FM* and *Made In Heaven*. Member of the **Traveling Wilburys**. Also see **Classic Rock Tracks** section.

AWARDS: R&R Hall of Fame: 2002 ★ Billboard: Century Award 2005

TOP HITS: 1)The Waiting 2)Learning To Fly 3)I Won't Back Down 4)Jammin' Me 5)You Got Lucky

Debut	Cht	Peak	Wks	Track Title	Hot Pos	Album Title	Label & Number
5/2/81	ⓡ	❶⁶	23	1 The Waiting	19	*Hard Promises*	Backstreet 5160
5/16/81	ⓡ	5	26	2 A Woman In Love (It's Not Me)	79	↓	
5/23/81	ⓡ	21	22	3 Nightwatchman	—	↓	
8/1/81	ⓡ	2¹	24	4 Stop Draggin' My Heart Around	3⁶	*Bella Donna*	Modern 139
				STEVIE NICKS with Tom Petty and The Heartbreakers			
11/13/82	ⓡ	❶³	16	5 You Got Lucky	20	*Long After Dark*	Backstreet 5360
11/27/82+	ⓡ	10	13	6 Change Of Heart	21	↓	
11/27/82	ⓡ	37	2	7 We Stand A Chance	—	↓	
12/4/82	ⓡ	15	10	8 One Story Town	—	↓	
12/4/82	ⓡ	35	1	9 Between Two Worlds	—	↓	
7/23/83	ⓡ	35	4	10 I Will Run To You	—	*The Wild Heart*	Modern 90084
				STEVIE NICKS with Tom Petty and The Heartbreakers			
3/16/85	ⓡ	2⁴	13	11 Don't Come Around Here No More	13	*Southern Accents*	MCA 5486
4/6/85	ⓡ	5	14	12 Rebels	74	↓	
6/8/85	ⓡ	12	10	13 Make It Better (Forget About Me)	54	↓	
12/21/85+	ⓡ	9	11	14 So You Want To Be A Rock & Roll Star [L]	—	*Pack Up The Plantation - Live!*	MCA 8021
				#29 Pop hit for **The Byrds** in 1967			
12/28/85+	ⓡ	17	11	15 Needles And Pins [L]	37	↓	
				TOM PETTY AND THE HEARTBREAKERS with Stevie Nicks			
				#13 Pop hit for The Searchers in 1964; above 2 recorded at the Wiltern Theater in Los Angeles, California			
4/19/86	ⓡ	28	6	16 Band Of The Hand (Hell Time, Man!)	—	*St: Band Of The Hand*	MCA 6167
				BOB DYLAN with The Heartbreakers / produced by Petty			
4/18/87	ⓡ	❶⁴	12	17 Jammin' Me	18	*Let Me Up (I've Had Enough)*	MCA 5836
				co-written by Bob Dylan			
5/9/87	ⓡ	6	13	18 Runaway Trains	—	↓	
5/9/87	ⓡ	36	9	19 Think About Me	—	↓	
8/1/87	ⓡ	19	6	20 All Mixed Up	—	↓	
				TOM PETTY:			
4/15/89	ⓡ	❶⁵	14	21 I Won't Back Down	12	*Full Moon Fever*	MCA 6253
5/13/89	ⓜ	29	2	George Harrison (guitar, backing vocal)			
5/6/89	ⓡ	❶¹	33	22 Free Fallin'	7	↓	
				RS500 #177			
5/6/89	ⓡ	❶¹	23	23 Runnin' Down A Dream	23	↓	
5/6/89	ⓡ	18	7	24 Feel A Whole Lot Better	—	↓	
				first recorded by **The Byrds** in 1965			
9/23/89	ⓡ	7	20	25 Love Is A Long Road	—	↓	
1/27/90	ⓡ	5	15	26 A Face In The Crowd	46	↓	
4/21/90	ⓡ	5	13	27 Yer So Bad	—	↓	
				TOM PETTY AND THE HEARTBREAKERS:			
6/22/91	ⓡ	❶⁶	15	28 Learning To Fly	28	*Into The Great Wide Open*	MCA 10317
7/13/91	ⓡ	❶²	21	29 Out In The Cold	—	↓	
9/21/91	ⓡ	4	22	30 Into The Great Wide Open	92	↓	
12/21/91+	ⓡ	4	15	31 Kings Highway	—	↓	
3/21/92	ⓡ	30	7	32 Makin' Some Noise	—	↓	
11/6/93	ⓡ	❶²	26	33 Mary Jane's Last Dance	14	*Greatest Hits*	MCA 10813
2/5/94	ⓡ	19	8	34 Something In The Air	—	↓	
				TOM PETTY:			
11/5/94	ⓡ	❶¹	23	35 You Don't Know How It Feels	13	*Wildflowers*	Warner 45759
				Grammy: Rock Male Vocal			
12/10/94+	ⓡ	2¹	26	36 You Wreck Me	—	↓	
4/8/95	ⓡ	6	16	37 It's Good To Be King	68	↓	
7/22/95	ⓡ	12	12	38 A Higher Place	—	↓	
11/11/95	ⓡ	29	6	39 Cabin Down Below	—	↓	

Debut	Cht	Peak	Wks	ARTIST / Track Title	Hot Pos	Album Title	Album Label & Number

Billboard

| Debut | Cht | Peak | Wks | ARTIST — ®=Mainstream Rock / Track Title — ⓜ=Modern Rock | Hot Pos | Album Title | Album Label & Number |

TOM PETTY & THE HEARTBREAKERS:

Debut	Cht	Peak	Wks	Track Title	Hot Pos	Album Title	Album Label & Number
12/9/95+	®	6	15	40 Waiting For Tonight	—	Playback	MCA 11375
7/27/96	®	6	13	41 Walls (Circus)	69	St: She's The One	Warner 46285
10/12/96	®	6	17	42 Climb That Hill	—	↓	
1/4/97	®	20	12	43 Change The Locks	—	↓	
3/13/99	®	5	14	44 Free Girl Now	120	Echo	Warner 47294
4/24/99	®	19	12	45 Room At The Top	—	↓	
7/31/99	®	17	11	46 Swingin'	—	↓	
9/28/02	®	22	13	47 The Last DJ	—	The Last DJ	Warner 47955
7/8/06	®	26	20	48 Saving Grace	100	Highway Companion	American 44285

PHAIR, Liz
Born on 4/17/1967 in New Haven, Connecticut. Pop-rock singer/songwriter.

Debut	Cht	Peak	Wks	Track Title	Hot Pos	Album Title	Album Label & Number
9/17/94	ⓜ	6	19	1 Supernova	78	Whip-Smart	Matador 92429
1/28/95	ⓜ	24	7	2 Whip-Smart	—	↓	

PHANTOM PLANET
Rock band from Los Angeles, California: Alex Greenwald (vocals), Jacques Brautbaur (guitar), Darren Robinson (guitar), Sam Farrar (bass) and Jason Schwartzman (drums). Farrar is the son of prolific songwriter John Farrar. Schwartzman is the son of actress Talia Shire; he starred in the 1998 movie *Rushmore*.

Debut	Cht	Peak	Wks	Track Title	Hot Pos	Album Title	Album Label & Number
3/30/02	ⓜ	35	5	1 California	—	The Guest	Daylight 62066
2/14/04	ⓜ	20	11	2 Big Brat	—	Phantom Planet	Daylight 86964

PHANTOM, ROCKER & SLICK
Rock trio formed in New York: Slim Jim Phantom (drums), Lee Rocker (vocals, bass), and Earl Slick (guitar). Phantom and Rocker were members of the **Stray Cats** and Slick was a member of **Silver Condor**.

Debut	Cht	Peak	Wks	Track Title	Hot Pos	Album Title	Album Label & Number
10/12/85	®	7	11	1 Men Without Shame	—	Phantom, Rocker & Slick	EMI America 17172
1/25/86	®	33	4	2 My Mistake	—	↓	

Keith Richards (guitar)

PHILLIPS, Sam
Born Leslie Phillips on 1/28/1962 in Glendale, California. Female singer/songwriter/actress. Married to record producer T-Bone Burnett from 1989-2004. Played "Katya" in the 1995 movie *Die Hard With A Vengeance*.

Debut	Cht	Peak	Wks	Track Title	Hot Pos	Album Title	Album Label & Number
4/22/89	ⓜ	22	1	Holding On To The Earth	—	The Indescribable Wow	Virgin 90919

PHISH
Alternative-rock band from Burlington, Vermont: Trey Anastasio (guitar), Page McConnell (keyboards), Mike Gordon (bass) and Jon Fishman (drums). All share vocals. Popular "jam band" with several concert appearances.

Debut	Cht	Peak	Wks	Track Title	Hot Pos	Album Title	Album Label & Number
5/14/94	®	33	4	1 Down With Disease	—	(Hoist)	Elektra 61628
10/19/96	®	11	14	2 Free	—	Billy Breathes	Elektra 61971
11/2/96	ⓜ	24	11		—		

PHUNK JUNKEEZ
Punk-funk band from Arizona: Soulman and K-Tel Disco (vocals), Jeff O'Rourke (guitar), Jumbo Jim (bass) and Disko Danny Dynomite (drums).

Debut	Cht	Peak	Wks	Track Title	Hot Pos	Album Title	Album Label & Number
4/29/95	ⓜ	38	1	I Love It Loud	—	Injected	Trauma 92556

PILLAR
Christian hard-rock band from Hays, Kansas: Rob Beckley (vocals), Noah Hanson (guitar), Michael "Kalel" Wittig (bass) and Brad Noone (drums).

Debut	Cht	Peak	Wks	Track Title	Hot Pos	Album Title	Album Label & Number
6/28/03	®	37	6	1 Fireproof	—	Fireproof	Flicker 2617
7/31/04	®	26	12	2 Bring Me Down	—	Where Do We Go From Here	Flicker 82631

PINK FLOYD ® All-Time: #48
Progressive-rock band formed in England: **David Gilmour** (vocals, guitar; born on 3/6/1944), **Roger Waters** (vocals, bass; born on 9/6/1944), Rick Wright (keyboards; born on 7/28/1945) and **Nick Mason** (drums; born on 1/27/1945). Wright left in early 1982. Waters left in 1984. Band inactive from 1984-86. Gilmour, Mason and Wright regrouped in 1987. Group name taken from Georgia bluesmen Pink Anderson and Floyd Council. Also see **Classic Rock Tracks** section.

AWARD: R&R Hall of Fame: 1996

TOP HITS: 1)Keep Talking 2)Learning To Fly 3)On The Turning Away 4)Take It Back 5)One Slip

Debut	Cht	Peak	Wks	Track Title	Hot Pos	Album Title	Album Label & Number
12/12/81+	®	37	8	1 Money	—	A Collection Of Great Dance Songs	Columbia 37680
				new version of their #13 Pop hit from 1973			
4/2/83	®	7	18	2 Not Now John	—	The Final Cut	Columbia 38243
4/2/83	®	8	10	3 Your Possible Pasts	—	↓	
4/30/83	®	31	10	4 The Hero's Return	—	↓	
9/5/87	®	❶³	12	5 Learning To Fly	70	A Momentary Lapse Of Reason	Columbia 40599
				also see #13 below			
9/26/87+	®	❶¹	24	6 On The Turning Away	—	↓	

Debit	Cht	Peak	Wks	ARTIST / Track Title	Hot Pos	Album Title	Album Label & Number

PINK FLOYD — cont'd

Debut	Cht	Peak	Wks	Track Title	Hot Pos	Album Title	Album Label & Number
9/26/87	Ⓡ	5	17	7 One Slip	—	↓	
9/26/87+	Ⓡ	30	11	8 The Dogs Of War	—	↓	
3/5/88	Ⓡ	36	6	9 Sorrow	—	↓	
12/3/88	Ⓡ	24	7	10 Comfortably Numb .... [L] studio version on their 1979 album *The Wall*	—	*Delicate Sound Of Thunder* ....Columbia 44484	
12/10/88	Ⓡ	34	6	11 Time .... [L] studio version on their 1973 album *The Dark Side Of The Moon*	—	↓	
12/10/88	Ⓡ	42	5	12 Another Brick In The Wall Part II .... [L] studio version was a #1 Pop hit in 1980	—	↓	
12/17/88	Ⓡ	45	4	13 Learning To Fly .... [L-R] live version of #5 above	—	↓	
4/2/94	Ⓡ	❶⁶	26	14 Keep Talking	—	*The Division Bell* ....Columbia 64200	
4/16/94	Ⓡ	4	21	15 Take It Back	73	↓	
4/16/94	Ⓡ	16	20	16 What Do You Want From Me .... also see #19 below	—	↓	
8/27/94	Ⓡ	7	13	17 High Hopes	—	↓	
12/3/94+	Ⓡ	21	10	18 Lost For Words	—	↓	
6/17/95	Ⓡ	13	8	19 What Do You Want From Me .... [L-R] live version of #16 above	—	*Pulse* ....Columbia 67065	
4/8/00	Ⓡ	15	7	20 Young Lust .... [L] studio version on their 1979 album *The Wall*	—	*Is There Anybody Out There? - The Wall Live 1980-81* ....Columbia 62055	

PIXIES

Alternative punk-rock band formed in Boston, Massachusetts: **Frank Black** (vocals), Joey Santiago (guitar), Kim Deal (bass) and David Lovering (drums). Deal was also a member of **The Breeders**.

Debut	Cht	Peak	Wks	Track Title	Hot Pos	Album Title	Album Label & Number
4/22/89	Ⓜ	5	11	1 Monkey Gone To Heaven .... RS500 #410	—	*Doolittle* ....Elektra 60856	
6/24/89	Ⓜ	3⁴	14	2 Here Comes Your Man	—	↓	
8/11/90	Ⓜ	4	9	3 Velouria	—	*Bossanova* ....Elektra 60963	
10/20/90	Ⓜ	11	14	4 Dig For Fire	—	↓	
10/19/91	Ⓜ	6	9	5 Letter To Memphis	—	*Trompe Le Monde* ....Elektra 61118	
1/4/92	Ⓜ	6	6	6 Head On	—	↓	

PLACEBO

Punk-pop trio from England: Brian Molko (vocals, guitar), Stefan Olsdal (bass) and Steve Hewitt (drums).

Debut	Cht	Peak	Wks	Track Title	Hot Pos	Album Title	Album Label & Number
10/31/98	Ⓜ	19	19	1 Pure Morning	—	*Without You I'm Nothing* ....Hut 46531	
2/13/99	Ⓡ	40	2				
7/15/06	Ⓜ	35	6	2 Infra-Red	—	*Meds* ....Elevator 53035	

PLAIN WHITE T'S

Rock band from Villa Park, Illinois: Tom Higgenson (vocals), Dave Tirio (guitar), Tim Lopez (guitar), Mike Retondo (bass) and De'Mar Hamilton (drums).

Debut	Cht	Peak	Wks	Track Title	Hot Pos	Album Title	Album Label & Number
9/16/06	Ⓜ	25	18	1 Hate (I Really Don't Like You)	68	*Every Second Counts* ....Fearless 162637	
3/17/07	Ⓜ	3⁴	28	2 Hey There Delilah	❶²	↓	
10/27/07	Ⓜ	29	14	3 Our Time Now	90	↓	

PLAN B

Techno-rock band from Berlin, Germany: Johnny Haeussler (vocals, guitar), Hans Hackenberger (guitar, vocals), Fritz (bass) and Andreas Perzborn (drums, samples).

Debut	Cht	Peak	Wks	Track Title	Hot Pos	Album Title	Album Label & Number
9/4/93	Ⓜ	28	4	Life's A Beat	—	*Cyber Chords And Sushi Stories* ....Imago 21031	

PLANET P

Studio band assembled by German producer Peter Hauke. **Tony Carey** was lead singer.

Debut	Cht	Peak	Wks	Track Title	Hot Pos	Album Title	Album Label & Number
4/2/83	Ⓡ	4	15	1 Why Me?	64	*Planet P* ....Geffen 4000	
6/4/83	Ⓡ	24	5	2 Static	—	↓	
12/1/84	Ⓡ	25	8	3 What I See .... PLANET P PROJECT	—	*Pink World* ....MCA 8019	

Billboard				ARTIST			
Debut	Cht	Peak	Wks	Track Title	Hot Pos	Album Title	Album Label & Number

Ⓡ=Mainstream Rock Ⓜ=Modern Rock

PLANT, Robert

Ⓡ 1980s: #8 / 1990s: #19 / All-Time: #10

Born on 8/20/1948 in West Bromwich, England. Hard-rock singer/songwriter. Member of **Led Zeppelin** and **The Honeydrippers**. Studied accounting before becoming lead singer of such British blues groups as Black Snake Moan, The Banned and The Crawling King Snakes. Also with the groups Listen and Band Of Joy. Fully recovered from a serious auto accident in Greece on 8/4/1975. Regular musicians in the 1980s included Robbie Blunt (guitar) and Paul Martinez (bass). The Strange Sensation (see #33 below): Justin Adams (guitar), Skin Tyson (guitar), John Baggot (keyboards), Billy Fuller (bass) and Clive Dreamer (drums).

TOP HITS: 1)Hurting Kind (I've Got My Eyes On You) 2)Heaven Knows 3)Tall Cool One 4)Most High 5)Little By Little

Debut	Cht	Peak	Wks	#	Track Title	Hot Pos	Album Title	Album Label & Number
4/18/81	Ⓡ	8	8	1	Little Sister .... [L]	—	VA: Concerts For The People Of	
					ROCKPILE with Robert Plant #5 Pop hit for Elvis Presley in 1961		Kampuchea	Atlantic 7005
7/10/82	Ⓡ	3²	24	2	Burning Down One Side	64	Pictures At Eleven	Swan Song 8512
7/10/82	Ⓡ	10	16	3	Worse Than Detroit	—	↓	
7/17/82	Ⓡ	11	14	4	Pledge Pin	74	↓	
7/17/82	Ⓡ	19	4	5	Slow Dancer	—	↓	
10/30/82+	Ⓡ	12	18	6	Far Post	—	(single only)	Swan Song 19429
7/23/83	Ⓡ	❶¹	21	7	Other Arms	—	The Principle Of Moments	Es Paranza 90101
7/23/83	Ⓡ	6	23	8	Big Log	20	↓	
7/30/83	Ⓡ	4	23	9	In The Mood	39	↓	
10/15/83	Ⓡ	44	1	10	Horizontal Departure	—	↓	
5/18/85	Ⓡ	❶²	14	11	Little By Little	36	Shaken 'N' Stirred	Es Paranza 90265
6/8/85	Ⓡ	18	13	12	Sixes And Sevens	—	↓	
2/13/88	Ⓡ	❶⁶	12	13	Heaven Knows	—	Now And Zen	Es Paranza 90863
3/5/88	Ⓡ	❶⁴	16	14	Tall Cool One	25	↓	
					features brief guitar riffs from **Led Zeppelin**'s "Whole Lotta Love," "Dazed And Confused," "Custard Pie," "Black Dog" and "The Ocean"; **Jimmy Page** (guitar, above 2)			
3/5/88	Ⓡ	3¹	23	15	Ship Of Fools	84	↓	
6/25/88	Ⓡ	10	13	16	Dance On My Own	—	↓	
11/12/88	Ⓡ	46	3	17	The Way I Feel	—	↓	
12/24/88+	Ⓡ	39	5	18	Walking Towards Paradise	—	↓	
3/17/90	Ⓡ	❶⁶	13	19	Hurting Kind (I've Got My Eyes On You)	46	Manic Nirvana	Es Paranza 91336
3/31/90	Ⓡ	6	16	20	Tie Dye On The Highway	—	↓	
4/7/90	Ⓡ	35	4	21	Big Love	—	↓	
4/7/90	Ⓡ	39	6	22	I Cried	—	↓	
6/9/90	Ⓡ	8	13	23	Your Ma Said You Cried In Your Sleep Last Night..	—	↓	
					#24 Pop hit for Kenny Dino in 1961			
8/18/90	Ⓡ	47	3	24	S S S & Q	—	↓	
5/15/93	Ⓡ	3⁴	10	25	Calling To You	—	Fate Of Nations	Es Paranza 92264
6/26/93	Ⓡ	4	20	26	29 Palms	111	↓	
10/9/93	Ⓡ	9	9	27	I Believe	—	↓	
10/22/94	Ⓡ	2³	14	28	Gallows Pole	—	No Quarter	Atlantic 82706
12/17/94+	Ⓡ	8	14	29	Thank You	—	↓	
4/18/98	Ⓡ	❶²	13	30	Most High	—	Walking Into Clarksdale	Atlantic 83092
					Grammy: Hard Rock Performance			
5/30/98	Ⓡ	6	18	31	Shining In The Light	—	↓	
					JIMMY PAGE & ROBERT PLANT (above 4)			
6/22/02	Ⓡ	27	11	32	Darkness, Darkness	—	Dreamland	Universal 586962
3/26/05	Ⓡ	18	20	33	Shine It All Around	—	Mighty Rearranger	Es Paranza 84747
					ROBERT PLANT AND THE STRANGE SENSATION			

PLIMSOULS, The

Rock band from Los Angeles, California: **Peter Case** (vocals), Eddie Munoz (guitar), Dave Pahoa (bass) and Lou Ramirez (drums).

Debut	Cht	Peak	Wks	Track Title	Hot Pos	Album Title	Album Label & Number
5/1/82	Ⓡ	11	7	A Million Miles Away	82	(single only)	Shaky City 134

(+44)

Pop-punk band formed in Los Angeles, California: **Blink-182** members Mark Hoppus (vocals, bass) and Travis Barker (drums), with guitarists Shane Gallagher and Craig Fairbaugh.

Debut	Cht	Peak	Wks	Track Title	Hot Pos	Album Title	Album Label & Number
10/14/06	Ⓜ	14	19	When Your Heart Stops Beating	89	When Your Heart Stops Beating	Interscope 007754

P.M. DAWN

Hip-hop duo from Jersey City, New Jersey: brothers Attrell "Prince Be" Cordes (born on 5/15/1970) and Jarrett "DJ Minutemix" Cordes (born on 7/17/1971).

Debut	Cht	Peak	Wks	Track Title	Hot Pos	Album Title	Album Label & Number
9/16/95	Ⓜ	39	3	Downtown Venus	48	Jesus Wept	Gee Street 524147
				samples "Hush" by **Deep Purple**			

POCO

Country-rock band formed in Los Angeles, California. Numerous personnel changes. Lineup from 1981-84: Rusty Young (vocals), Paul Cotton (guitar), Kim Bullard (keyboards), Charlie Harrison (bass; replaced by Neil Stubenhaus in 1983) and Steve Chapman (drums). Disbanded in 1984. In 1989, original members Young (pedal steel guitar), Richie Furay (rhythm guitar), Jim Messina (lead guitar), **Randy Meisner** (bass) and George Grantham (drums) reunited. Also see **Classic Rock Tracks** section.

Debut	Cht	Peak	Wks	Track Title	Hot Pos	Album Title	Album Label & Number
7/25/81	®	33	13	1 Widowmaker	—	Blue And Gray	MCA 5227
5/26/84	®	58	3	2 Days Gone By	80	Inamorata	Atlantic 80148
8/26/89	®	3²	12	3 Call It Love	18	Legacy	RCA 9694
3/3/90	®	30	6	4 The Nature Of Love	—	↓	

P.O.D.
® 2000s: #26 ★ ⓜ 2000s: #28 / All-Time: #56

Christian hard-rock band from San Diego, California: Paul "Sonny" Sandoval (vocals; born on 5/16/1974), Marcos Curiel (guitar; born on 9/9/1974), Mark "Traa" Daniels (bass; born on 12/30/1970) and Noah "Wuv" Bernardo (drums; born on 2/24/1974). Jason Truby replaced Curiel in early 2003; Curiel returned to replace Truby in 2006. P.O.D.: Payable On Death.

TOP HITS: 1)Youth Of The Nation 2)Alive 3)Will You

Debut	Cht	Peak	Wks	Track Title	Hot Pos	Album Title	Album Label & Number
3/18/00	ⓜ	28	8	1 Southtown	—	The Fundamental Elements Of	
2/5/00	®	31	12			Southtown	Atlantic 83216
8/5/00	®	25	8	2 Rock The Party (Off The Hook)	—	↓	
8/19/00	ⓜ	27	6				
12/16/00	ⓜ	38	3	3 School Of Hard Knocks	—	St: Little Nicky	Maverick 47856
9/8/01	ⓜ	2⁴	26	4 Alive	41	Satellite	Atlantic 83475
8/25/01	®	4	31				
12/15/01+	ⓜ	❶²	26	5 Youth Of The Nation	28	↓	
12/22/01+	®	6	26				
4/27/02	ⓜ	13	17	6 Boom	123	↓	
5/4/02	®	21	16				
8/31/02	®	15	10	7 Satellite	—	↓	
8/31/02	ⓜ	21	7				
5/3/03	ⓜ	14	9	8 Sleeping Awake	—	St: The Matrix Reloaded	Warner Sunset 48411
5/3/03	®	20	9				
10/11/03	®	12	18	9 Will You	117	Payable On Death	Atlantic 83676
10/11/03	ⓜ	12	16				
2/21/04	®	32	6	10 Change The World	—	↓	
3/6/04	ⓜ	38	4				
11/26/05+	®	17	17	11 Goodbye For Now	48	Testify	Atlantic 83857
12/3/05+	ⓜ	25	13				
5/6/06	®	30	8	12 Lights Out	—	↓	
12/2/06	®	35	8	13 Going In Blind	—	Greatest Hits: The Atlantic Years	Atlantic 74790
3/29/08	®	40↑	1↑	14 Addicted	—	When Angels And Serpents Dance	Ino 709255

POE

Born Annie Danielewski on 3/3/1968 in Manhattan, New York. Female singer/songwriter.

Debut	Cht	Peak	Wks	Track Title	Hot Pos	Album Title	Album Label & Number
12/16/95	ⓜ	27	9	1 Trigger Happy Jack	106	Hello	Modern 92605
7/20/96	ⓜ	7	17	2 Angry Johnny	60ᴬ	↓	
11/30/96+	ⓜ	13	14	3 Hello	65ᴬ	↓	
3/17/01	ⓜ	13	16	4 Hey Pretty	—	Haunted	FEI 83362

POGUES, The

Punk-folk band formed in London, England: Shane MacGowan (vocals), Philip Chevron (guitar), Terry Woods (mandolin), Spider Stacy (tin whistle), James Fearnley (accordion), Jem Finer (banjo), Darryl Hunt (bass) and Andrew Ranken (drums). Original bassist Cait O'Riordan was married to **Elvis Costello** from 1986-2002. MacGowan left band in mid-1991. Joe Strummer (formerly with **The Clash**) joined as lead singer from late 1991-93, then Stacy took over lead vocals.

Debut	Cht	Peak	Wks	Track Title	Hot Pos	Album Title	Album Label & Number
2/18/89	ⓜ	17	7	1 Yeah Yeah Yeah Yeah Yeah	—	St: Lost Angels	A&M 3926
1/5/91	ⓜ	23	5	2 The Sunny Side Of The Street	—	Hell's Ditch	Island 422846
11/6/93	ⓜ	11	12	3 Tuesday Morning	—	Waiting For Herb	Chameleon 61598

POINT BLANK

Southern-rock band from Irving, Texas: Bubba Keith (vocals), Rusty Burns (guitar), Kim Davis (guitar), Mike Hamilton (keyboards), Bill Randolph (bass) and Buzzy Gruen (drums). Randolph died of a heart attack on 6/19/2001 (age 50).

Debut	Cht	Peak	Wks	Track Title	Hot Pos	Album Title	Album Label & Number
4/18/81	®	38	7	1 Let Me Stay With You Tonight	107	American Exce$$	MCA 5189
6/20/81	®	20	21	2 Nicole	39	↓	
4/24/82	®	27	4	3 On A Roll	—	On A Roll	MCA 5312
5/15/82	®	34	2	4 Great White Line	—	↓	

Billboard				ARTIST			
Debut	Cht	Peak	Wks	Track Title	ℝ=Mainstream Rock / ⓜ=Modern Rock	Hot Pos	Album Title — Album Label & Number

POISON

Glam-metal band formed in Harrisburg, Pennsylvania: Bret Michaels (vocals; born on 3/15/1963), C.C. DeVille (guitar; born on 5/14/1962), Bobby Dall (bass; born on 11/2/1958) and Rikki Rockett (drums; born on 8/8/1961). Richie Kotzen (born on 3/5/1960) replaced DeVille from 1992-97.

Debut	Cht	Peak	Wks	Track Title	Hot Pos	Album Title — Label & Number
5/7/88	ℝ	19	11	1 Nothin' But A Good Time	6	Open Up and Say...Ahh!.............Enigma 48493
8/20/88	ℝ	32	7	2 Fallen Angel	12	↓
11/12/88	ℝ	11	12	3 Every Rose Has Its Thorn	❶³	↓
3/4/89	ℝ	39	4	4 Your Mama Don't Dance	10	↓
				#4 Pop hit for **Kenny Loggins** & Jim Messina in 1973		
7/7/90	ℝ	5	13	5 Unskinny Bop	3¹	Flesh & Blood ....Capitol 918132
10/6/90	ℝ	5	15	6 Something To Believe In	4	↓
2/9/91	ℝ	25	9	7 Ride The Wind	38	↓
1/30/93	ℝ	15	7	8 Stand	50	Native Tongue ....Capitol 98961

POLICE, The

ℝ **1980s: #29 / All-Time: #80**

Reggae-inflected rock trio formed in England: Gordon "Sting" Sumner (vocals, bass; born on 10/2/1951), Andy Summers (guitar; born on 12/31/1942) and Stewart Copeland (drums; born on 7/16/1952). Sting went on to a highly successful solo career. Copeland formed Animal Logic in 1989. Group reunited in 2007. Also see **Classic Rock Tracks** section.

AWARD: R&R Hall of Fame: 2003

TOP HITS: 1)Every Breath You Take 2)King Of Pain 3)Every Little Thing She Does Is Magic

Debut	Cht	Peak	Wks	Track Title	Hot Pos	Album Title — Label & Number
3/21/81	ℝ	11	7	1 Don't Stand So Close To Me	10	Zenyatta Mondatta ....A&M 4831
				Grammy: Rock Vocal Group / also see #11 below		
3/28/81	ℝ	35	2	2 Driven To Tears	—	↓
9/26/81	ℝ	❶²	28	3 Every Little Thing She Does Is Magic	3²	Ghost In The Machine ....A&M 3730
12/5/81+	ℝ	7	21	4 Spirits In The Material World	11	↓
2/6/82	ℝ	29	16	5 Secret Journey	46	↓
12/4/82	ℝ	27	9	6 I Burn For You	—	St: Brimstone & Treacle ....A&M 4915
6/4/83	ℝ	❶⁹	21	7 Every Breath You Take	❶⁸	Synchronicity ....A&M 3735
				Grammys: Song of the Year / Pop Vocal Group ★ R&R Hall of Fame ★ RS500 #84		
7/9/83	ℝ	❶⁵	31	8 King Of Pain	3²	↓
7/9/83	ℝ	9	27	9 Wrapped Around Your Finger	8	↓
7/16/83	ℝ	9	31	10 Synchronicity II	16	↓
10/25/86	ℝ	10	7	11 Don't Stand So Close To Me '86 [R]	46	Every Breath You Take - The Singles ....A&M 3902
				new version of #1 above		

POOR, The

Rock band from England: Skenie (vocals), Jullan Grynglas (guitar), Matt Whitby (bass) and James Young (drums).

Debut	Cht	Peak	Wks	Track Title	Hot Pos	Album Title — Label & Number
4/23/94	ℝ	30	5	More Wine Waiter Please	—	Who Cares ....550 Music 57552

POORBOYS

Rock band from Claremont, California: Dennis Hill (vocals, guitar), Rik Sanchez (guitar), Joey Phillipy (bass) and Andre Bonter (drums).

Debut	Cht	Peak	Wks	Track Title	Hot Pos	Album Title — Label & Number
9/19/92	ℝ	24	4	1 Brand New Amerika	—	Pardon Me..............Hollywood 60997
12/19/92+	ℝ	16	16	2 Guilty	122	↓

POP, Iggy

Born James Jewel Osterberg on 4/21/1947 in Muskegon, Michigan. Punk-rock pioneer. Leader of The Stooges from 1969-74. Acted in the movies *Cry Baby*, *Hardware* and *The Crow: City Of Angels*. Adopted nickname "Iggy" from his first band, The Iguanas.

Debut	Cht	Peak	Wks	Track Title	Hot Pos	Album Title — Label & Number
10/11/86	ℝ	34	7	1 Cry For Love	—	Blah-Blah-Blah ....A&M 5145
12/27/86+	ℝ	27	12	2 Real Wild Child (Wild One)	—	↓
				#68 Pop hit for Ivan in 1958		
7/23/88	ℝ	37	5	3 Cold Metal	—	Instinct ....A&M 5198
11/25/89	ⓜ	16	4	4 Livin' On The Edge Of The Night	—	St: Black Rain ....Virgin 91292
7/21/90	ⓜ	2¹	10	5 Home	—	Brick By Brick ....Virgin 91381
8/4/90	ℝ	46	5			
9/22/90	ⓜ	5	17	6 Candy	28	↓
10/20/90+	ℝ	30	16	Kate Pierson (of **The B-52's**; female vocal)		
10/9/93	ⓜ	25	3	7 Wild America	—	American Caesar ....Virgin 39002
12/6/03	ⓜ	35	8	8 Little Know It All	—	Skull Ring...........Virgin 80774

POPINJAYS, The

Pop-rock trio from London, England: Wendy Robinson (vocals), Polly Hancock (guitar) and Ben Kesteven (bass).

Debut	Cht	Peak	Wks	Track Title	Hot Pos	Album Title — Label & Number
5/25/91	ⓜ	17	5	Vote Elvis	—	Vote Elvis...........Alpha International 73021

Debut	Cht	Peak	Wks	ARTIST / Track Title	Hot Pos	Album Title	Album Label & Number

®=Mainstream Rock Ⓜ=Modern Rock

POP WILL EAT ITSELF
Psychedelic-rap-rock band from Stourbridge, England: Clint Mansell and Graham Crabb (vocals), Adam Mole (guitar) and Richard March (bass).

| 9/24/88 | Ⓜ | 30 | 1 | 1 Def Con One | — | Def Con One | Chapter 22 12001 |
| 2/9/91 | Ⓜ | 11 | 11 | 2 X Y & Zee | — | Cure For Sanity | RCA 2485 |

PORCUPINE TREE
Progressive-rock band from Hempstead, Hertfordshire, England: Steven Wilson (vocals, guitar), Richard Barbieri (keyboards), Colin Edwin (bass) and Gavin Harrison (drums).

| 4/16/05 | ® | 26 | 11 | Shallow | — | Deadwing | Lava 93812 |

PORNO FOR PYROS
Alternative-rock band formed in Los Angeles, California: Perry Farrell (vocals), Peter DiStefano (guitar), Martyn LeNoble (bass) and Stephen Perkins (drums). Farrell and Perkins were with **Jane's Addiction**. LeNoble and Perkins also recorded with **Class Of '99**. Farrell later formed **Satellite Party**.

4/10/93	Ⓜ	3²	10	1 Cursed Female	—	Porno For Pyros	Warner 45228
5/22/93	Ⓜ	❶⁵	14	2 Pets	67	↓	
7/10/93	®	25	6				
5/25/96	Ⓜ	8	19	3 Tahitian Moon	46ᴬ	Good God's Urge	Warner 46126
2/22/97	Ⓜ	23	7	4 Hard Charger	—	St: Private Parts	Warner 46477

PORTISHEAD
Alternative pop-rock duo from Bristol, England: multi-instrumentalist Geoff Barrow and vocalist Beth Gibbons. Duo named after a coastal shipping town near Bristol.

| 12/17/94+ | Ⓜ | 5 | 17 | Sour Times (Nobody Loves Me) | 53 | Dummy | London 828553 |

POSIES, The
Rock band from Seattle, Washington: Jon Auer (vocals, guitar), Ken Stringfellow (vocals, guitar), Rick Roberts (bass) and Mike Musburger (drums).

10/20/90	Ⓜ	17	7	1 Golden Blunders	—	Dear 23	DGC 24305
5/22/93	Ⓜ	4	14	2 Dream All Day	—	Frosting On the Beater	DGC 24522
7/3/93	®	17	10				

POSSUM DIXON
Rock band from Los Angeles, California: Rob Zabrecky (vocals, bass), Celso Chavez (guitar), Robert O'Sullivan (keyboards) and Richard Treuel (drums). Group named after a fugitive seen on TV's *America's Most Wanted*.

| 1/29/94 | Ⓜ | 9 | 11 | Watch The Girl Destroy Me | 110 | Possum Dixon | Interscope 92291 |
| 4/30/94 | ® | 37 | 3 | | | | |

POUND
Rock band from New York: brothers Jason Terwilliger (vocals) and Jerry Terwilliger (drums), with Pat Gasperini (guitar) and Sandy Nardone (bass).

| 4/24/99 | ® | 16 | 11 | Upside Down | — | Same Old Life | Island 524641 |

POWDERFINGER
Rock band from Brisbane, Australia: Bernard Fanning (vocals), Darren Middleton (guitar), Ian Haug (guitar), John Collins (bass) and Jon Coghill (drums).

| 3/10/01 | Ⓜ | 23 | 10 | My Happiness | — | Odyssey Number Five | Republic 549092 |

POWERMAN 5000
Hard-rock band formed in Boston, Massachusetts: Michael "Spider One" Cummings (vocals; younger brother of **Rob Zombie**), Adam Williams (guitar), Mike Tempesta (guitar), Dorian Heartsong (bass) and Al Pahanish (drums). Heartsong and Pahanish left in 2002, replaced by Siggy Siursen (bass) and Adrian Ost (drums).

7/10/99	®	16	26	1 When Worlds Collide	—	Tonight The Stars Revolt!	DreamWorks 50107
7/17/99	Ⓜ	18	22				
12/18/99+	®	18	16	2 Nobody's Real	—	↓	
12/18/99+	Ⓜ	23	13				
12/23/00	®	38	5	3 Ultra Mega	—	St: Dracula 2000	Columbia 61585
7/28/01	®	26	7	4 Bombshell	—	Anyone For Doomsday?	DreamWorks 50296
4/5/03	®	10	25	5 Free	—	Transform	DreamWorks 450433
5/31/03	Ⓜ	38	2				
9/6/03	®	27	9	6 Action	—	↓	

POWER STATION, The

All-star rock band: **Robert Palmer** (vocals), **Andy Taylor** (guitar), John Taylor (bass) and Tony Thompson (drums). The Taylors were members of **Duran Duran**. Thompson was a member of Chic. Palmer died of a heart attack on 9/26/2003 (age 54). Thompson died of cancer on 11/12/2003 (age 48).

Debut	Cht	Peak	Wks	Track	Hot Pos	Album Title	Label & Number
5/4/85	ℝ	19	16	1 **Get It On**	9	*The Power Station*	Capitol 12380
				#10 Pop hit for T. Rex in 1972			
5/4/85	ℝ	34	5	2 **Some Like It Hot**	6	↓	

PREFAB SPROUT

Pop band from England: brothers Paddy McAloon (male vocals, guitar) and Martin McAloon (bass), with Wendy Smith (female vocals) and Neil Conti (drums).

10/26/85	ℝ	42	2	**When Love Breaks Down**	—	*Two Wheels Good*	Epic 40100

PRESENCE

Rock band from Tallahassee, Florida: Jay Slim (vocals), Dave Fulmer (guitar), D.J. Stange (bass) and Nick Wells (drums).

4/26/03	ℝ	31	7	**Tonz Of Fun**	—	*Rise*	Curb 78766

PRESIDENTS OF THE UNITED STATES OF AMERICA, The

Rock trio from Seattle, Washington: Chris Ballew (vocals), Dave Dederer (guitar) and Jason Finn (drums).

8/19/95	Ⓜ	❶[1]	26	1 **Lump**	21[A]	*The Presidents Of The United States Of America*	Columbia 67291
9/16/95	ℝ	7	20				
11/25/95	Ⓜ	13	10	2 **Kitty**	67[A]	↓	
2/3/96	Ⓜ	8	12	3 **Peaches**	29	↓	
2/24/96	ℝ	24	8				
11/9/96	Ⓜ	11	11	4 **Mach 5**	68[A]	*II*	Columbia 67577
11/23/96	ℝ	24	10				

PRESSURE 4-5

Rock band from Santa Barbara, California: Adam Rich (vocals), brothers Joe Schmidt (guitar) and Tom Schmidt (drums), Mark Barry (guitar) and Lyle McKeany (bass).

11/24/01	ℝ	39	2	**Beat The World**	—	*Burning The Process*	DreamWorks 450325

PRETENDERS, The

ℝ 1980s: #35 / All-Time: #76

New-wave rock band formed in England: **Chrissie Hynde** (vocals, guitar; born on 9/7/1951 in Akron, Ohio), James Honeyman-Scott (guitar), Pete Farndon (bass) and Martin Chambers (drums). Honeyman-Scott died of a drug overdose on 6/16/1982 (age 24); replaced by Robbie McIntosh. Farndon died of a drug overdose on 4/14/1983 (age 30); replaced by Malcolm Foster. Hynde was married to Jim Kerr (of **Simple Minds**) from 1984-90. Lineup in 1994: Hynde, Chambers, Adam Seymour (guitar) and Andy Hobson (bass). Also see **Classic Rock Tracks** section.

AWARD: R&R Hall of Fame: 2005

TOP HITS: 1)Don't Get Me Wrong 2)My Baby 3)Middle Of The Road

3/21/81	ℝ	5	16	1 **Message Of Love**	—	*Extended Play*	Sire 3563
8/22/81	ℝ	12	16	2 **The Adultress**	—	*Pretenders II*	Sire 3572
10/16/82+	ℝ	4	31	3 **Back On The Chain Gang**	5	*St: The King Of Comedy*	Warner 23765
10/23/82+	ℝ	11	16	4 **My City Was Gone**	—	*(single only)*	Sire 29840
				song later used as the intro theme for radio's *Rush Limbaugh Show*			
12/24/83+	ℝ	2[4]	15	5 **Middle Of The Road**	19	*Learning To Crawl*	Sire 23980
2/4/84	ℝ	6	14	6 **Time The Avenger**	—	↓	
2/18/84	ℝ	8	15	7 **Show Me**	28	↓	
2/25/84	ℝ	57	1	8 **Thumbelina**	—	↓	
10/11/86	ℝ	❶[3]	13	9 **Don't Get Me Wrong**	10	*Get Close*	Sire 25488
11/8/86+	ℝ	❶[2]	19	10 **My Baby**	64	↓	
11/29/86+	ℝ	28	11	11 **Room Full Of Mirrors**	—	↓	
8/15/87	ℝ	26	4	12 **Where Has Every Body Gone**	—	*St: The Living Daylights*	Warner 25616
11/12/88	Ⓜ	21	2	13 **1969**	—	*(single only)*	Polydor 887816
5/19/90	Ⓜ	4	11	14 **Never Do That**	—	*packed!*	Sire 26219
5/19/90	ℝ	5	11				
7/21/90	Ⓜ	18	5	15 **Hold A Candle To This**	—	↓	
9/1/90	Ⓜ	23	3	16 **Sense Of Purpose**	—	↓	
4/30/94	Ⓜ	2[2]	13	17 **Night In My Veins**	71	*Last Of The Independents*	Warner 45572
4/30/94	ℝ	13	11				
8/13/94	Ⓜ	21	7	18 **I'll Stand By You**	16	↓	

PRE-THING

Rock trio from Los Angeles, California: Rust Epique (vocals, guitar), Jon Troy Winquist (bass) and Dino Licious (drums).

4/17/04	ℝ	38	1	**Faded Love**	—	*22nd Century Lifestyle*	V2 27157

Debut	Cht	Peak	Wks	ARTIST / Track Title (ⓡ=Mainstream Rock, ⓜ=Modern Rock)	Hot Pos	Album Title	Album Label & Number
				PREVIEW			
				Rock band from New York: Jon Fiore (vocals), Danny Gold (guitar), Ernie Gold (keyboards), Skip Parker (bass) and Ed Bettinelli (drums).			
2/18/84	ⓡ	39	1	Red Lights	—	Preview ....Geffen 2015	
				PRIDE & GLORY			
				Rock trio formed in New York: Zakk Wylde (vocals, guitar), James LoMenzo (bass) and Brian Tichy (drums). Wylde formerly with **Ozzy Osbourne**'s band; later formed **Black Label Society**.			
6/11/94	ⓡ	14	15	Losin' Your Mind	—	Pride & Glory...Geffen 24703	
				PRIESTESS			
				Hard-rock band from Canada: Mike Heppner (vocals, guitar), Dan Watchorn (guitar), Mike Dyball (bass) and Vince Nudo (drums).			
12/16/06+	ⓡ	33	9	Talk To Her	—	Hello Master..RCA 84465	
				PRIMAL SCREAM			
				Rock-funk band from Glasgow, Scotland: Bobby Gillespie (vocals), Andrew Innes (guitar), Robert Young (guitar), Henry Raycock (bass) and Toby Toman (drums).			
11/10/90	ⓜ	19	4	1 Loaded...	—	Come Together...Sire 26384	
12/22/90+	ⓜ	13	9	2 Come Together	—	↓	
10/12/91	ⓜ	2[1]	16	3 Movin' On Up	—	Screamadelica...Sire 26714	
10/19/91	ⓡ	28	13				
4/9/94	ⓜ	16	7	4 Rocks..	107	Give Out But Don't Give Up..........................Sire 45538	
4/30/94	ⓡ	29	6				
				PRIMER 55			
				Rock band from Memphis, Tennessee: Jason Luttrell (vocals), Bobby Burns (guitar), Kobie Jackson (bass) and Preston Nash (drums).			
10/20/01	ⓡ	37	1	This Life..	—	(The) New Release...................................Island 586183	
				PRIME STH			
				Rock band from Stockholm, Sweden: Noa Moden (vocals), Martin Pahlsson (guitar), Jesper Eksjoo (bass) and Kasper Lindgren (drums).			
6/2/01	ⓡ	27	13	I'm Stupid (Don't Worry 'Bout Me)...............................	—	Underneath The Surface ....Giant 24774	
6/9/01	ⓜ	27	11				
				PRIMITIVE RADIO GODS			
				Born Christopher O'Connor on 5/7/1965 in Santa Barbara, California. Rock singer/songwriter/guitarist. His touring band includes Luke McAuliffe (guitar), Jeff Sparks (bass) and Tim Lauteiro (drums).			
6/8/96	ⓜ	❶[6]	21	Standing Outside A Broken Phone Booth With Money In My Hand	10[A]	Rocket ....Ergo 67600	
7/20/96	ⓡ	32	9	samples "How Blue Can You Get" by **B.B. King**			
				PRIMITIVES, The			
				Pop-rock band from Coventry, West Midlands, England: Tracy Tracey (vocals), Paul Court (guitar), Steve Dullaghan (bass) and Tig Williams (drums).			
9/10/88	ⓜ	3[1]	6	1 Crash	—	Lovely ....RCA 8443	
				also see #5 below			
11/19/88	ⓜ	8	10	2 Way Behind Me	—	↓	
9/23/89	ⓜ	9	10	3 Sick Of It	—	Pure ....RCA 9934	
12/2/89	ⓜ	12	9	4 Secrets	—	↓	
2/18/95	ⓜ	33	6	5 Crash - The '95 Mix... [R]	—	St: Dumb And Dumber.................................RCA 66523	
				remix of #1 above			
				PRIMUS			
				Thrash-jazz-rock trio from San Francisco, California: Les Claypool (vocals, bass), Larry LaLonde (guitar) and Tim Alexander (drums).			
7/13/91	ⓜ	23	3	1 Jerry Was A Race Car Driver..................................	—	Sailing The Seas Of Cheese ....Interscope 91659	
2/15/92	ⓜ	30	1	2 Making Plans For Nigel..	—	Miscellaneous Debris ....Interscope 96208	
				first recorded by **XTC** in 1980			
5/1/93	ⓜ	9	10	3 My Name Is Mud	—	Pork Soda...Interscope 92257	
6/10/95	ⓜ	12	12	4 Wynona's Big Brown Beaver...................................	62[A]	Tales From The Punchbowl...................Interscope 92553	
7/15/95	ⓡ	23	9				
7/15/00	ⓡ	2[2]	41	5 N.I.B.	—	VA: Nativity In Black II: A Tribute To Black Sabbath.......................................Divine 26095	
				PRIMUS with Ozzy Osbourne first recorded by **Black Sabbath** in 1970			

Debug	Cht	Peak	Wks	ARTIST Track Title	Hot Pos	Album Title	Album Label & Number

ℝ=Mainstream Rock
𝕄=Modern Rock

PRINCE

Born Prince Roger Nelson on 6/7/1958 in Minneapolis, Minnesota. R&B singer/songwriter/multi-instrumentalist. Starred in the movies *Purple Rain*, *Under The Cherry Moon*, *Sign 'O' The Times* and *Graffiti Bridge*. The Revolution: Wendy Melvoin (guitar), Lisa Coleman and Matt Fink (keyboards), Eric Leeds (sax), Brownmark (bass) and Bobby Z (drums).

AWARD: R&R Hall of Fame: 2004

Debut	Cht	Peak	Wks	#	Track Title	Hot Pos	Album Title	Label & Number
4/30/83	ℝ	17	5	1	Little Red Corvette	6	*1999*	Warner 23720
					R&R Hall of Fame ★ RS500 #108			
6/16/84	ℝ	31	13	2	When Doves Cry	❶⁵	*St: Purple Rain*	Warner 25110
					R&R Hall of Fame ★ RS500 #52			
8/11/84	ℝ	19	11	3	Let's Go Crazy	❶²	↓	
9/22/84	ℝ	18	8	4	Purple Rain	2²	↓	
					RS500 #147			
5/18/85	ℝ	40	6	5	Raspberry Beret	2¹	*Around The World In A Day*	Paisley Park 25286
					PRINCE and The Revolution (above 3)			
7/1/89	𝕄	18	7	6	Batdance	❶¹	*St: Batman*	Warner 25936

PRISM

Rock band formed in Vancouver, British Columbia, Canada: Henry Small (vocals), Lindsay Mitchell (guitar), Tom Lavin (guitar), John Hall (keyboards), Allen Harlow (bass) and Rocket Norton (drums).

1/23/82	ℝ	❶¹	17	1	Don't Let Him Know	39	*Small Change*	Capitol 12184
					co-written by Bryan Adams			
6/26/82	ℝ	55	2	2	Hole In Paradise	—	↓	
9/17/83	ℝ	37	1	3	Is He Better Than Me?	—	*Beat Street*	Capitol 12266

PROCLAIMERS, The

Pop duo from Edinburgh, Scotland: identical twin brothers Craig Reid and Charlie Reid (born on 3/5/1962).

3/18/89	𝕄	21	6	1	I'm Gonna Be (500 Miles)	—	*Sunshine On Leith*	Chrysalis 41668
6/12/93	𝕄	8	15	2	I'm Gonna Be (500 Miles) [R]	3¹	*St: Benny & Joon*	Milan 35644
					above 2 are the same version			

PROCOL HARUM

Rock band formed in England: Gary Brooker (vocals, piano), **Robin Trower** (guitar), Matthew Fisher (organ), Dave Bronze (bass) and Mark Brzezicki (drums). Also see **Classic Rock Tracks** section.

8/10/91	ℝ	29	6		All Our Dreams Are Sold	—	*The Prodigal Stranger*	Zoo 11011

PRODIGY

Techno-dance band from England: Maxim Reality and Keith Flint (vocals), Liam Howlett (instruments) and Leeroy Thronhill (dancer).

2/8/97	𝕄	24	9	1	Firestarter	30	*The Fat Of The Land*	Maverick 46606
					samples "SOS" by **The Breeders** and "Close (To The Edit)" by **Art Of Noise**			
7/12/97	𝕄	18	23	2	Breathe	—	↓	

PRODUCERS, The

Pop-rock band from Atlanta, Georgia: Van Temple (vocals, guitar), Wayne Famous (keyboards), Kyle Henderson (bass) and Bryan Holmes (drums).

10/2/82	ℝ	48	2		She Sheila	—	*You Make The Heat*	Portrait 38060

PROJECT 86

Christian rock band from Anaheim, California: Andrew Schwab (vocals), Randy Torres (guitar), Steven Dail (bass) and Alex Albert (drums).

3/8/03	ℝ	35	5		Hollow Again	—	*Truthless Heros*	Atlantic 83568

PROM KINGS, The

Rock band from Los Angeles, California: Chris Carney (vocals), Fred Ramberg (guitar), Renato Lopez (guitar), Mauricio Jacome (bass) and Josh Heffernan (drums).

2/19/05	ℝ	24	20		Alone	—	*The Prom Kings*	Three Kings 513902

PSEUDO ECHO

Pop-rock band from Melbourne, Australia: Brian Canham (vocals, guitar), James Leigh (keyboards), Pierre Gigliotti (bass) and Vince Leigh (drums).

3/14/87	ℝ	44	2		Living In A Dream	57	*Love An Adventure*	RCA Victor 5730

PSYCHEDELIC FURS

𝕄 **All-Time: #95**

Techno-rock band formed in England: brothers Richard Butler (vocals) and Tim Butler (bass), John Ashton (guitar) and Vince Ely (drums). Phillip Calvert replaced Ely in 1983. The Butler brothers formed **Love Spit Love** in 1994.

10/9/82	ℝ	30	3	1	Love My Way	44	*Forever Now*	Columbia 38261
5/5/84	ℝ	25	12	2	The Ghost In You	59	*Mirror Moves*	Columbia 39278
2/21/87	ℝ	11	14	3	Heartbreak Beat	26	*Midnight To Midnight*	Columbia 40466
9/10/88	𝕄	❶³	9	4	All That Money Wants	—	*All Of This And Nothing*	Columbia 44377
11/4/89	𝕄	8	9	5	Should God Forget	—	*Book Of Days*	Columbia 45412
12/2/89+	𝕄	❶³	13	6	House	—	↓	

Debut	Cht	Peak	Wks	Track Title		Hot Pos	Album Title	Album Label & Number
				PSYCHEDELIC FURS — cont'd				
7/20/91	Ⓜ	❶²	13	7 Until She Comes		—	World Outside ....Columbia 47303	
10/19/91	Ⓜ	13	6	8 Don't Be A Girl		—	↓	

PUBLIC IMAGE LTD.
Punk-rock band formed by lead singer Johnny "Rotten" Lydon (of the Sex Pistols). Featured an ever-changing lineup with Lydon the only constant.

Debut	Cht	Peak	Wks	Track Title	Hot Pos	Album Title	Album Label & Number
4/22/89	Ⓜ	16	5	1 Warrior.. **PIL**	—	St: Slaves Of New York ....Virgin 91229	
6/3/89	Ⓜ	❶¹	13	2 Disappointed	—	9...Virgin 91062	
9/9/89	Ⓜ	15	5	3 Happy	—	↓	
10/20/90	Ⓜ	2²	14	4 Don't Ask Me..	—	The Greatest Hits So Far.............................Virgin 91581	
2/29/92	Ⓜ	11	9	5 Covered	—	That What Is Not..Virgin 91815	
5/9/92	Ⓜ	29	2	6 Acid Drops .... **PIL** (above 2)	—	↓	

PUDDLE OF MUDD   Ⓡ 2000s: #8 / All-Time: #49 ★ Ⓜ 2000s: #14 / All-Time: #35
Hard-rock band formed in Los Angeles, California: Wes Scantlin (vocals, guitar; born on 6/9/1972), Paul Phillips (guitar; born on 6/26/1975), Doug Ardito (bass; born on 3/10/1971) and Greg Upchurch (drums; born on 12/1/1971). Christian Stone replaced Phillips in 2005; Phillips joined **Operator**. Ryan Yerdon replaced Upchurch in 2005; Upchurch joined **3 Doors Down**.

Debut	Cht	Peak	Wks	Track Title	Hot Pos	Album Title	Album Label & Number
7/7/01	Ⓡ	3⁵	40	1 Control..	68	Come Clean..Flawless 493074	
7/7/01	Ⓜ	3¹	29				
11/3/01+	Ⓡ	❶¹⁰	42	2 Blurry	5	↓	
11/3/01+	Ⓜ	❶⁹	34				
4/20/02	Ⓡ	❶⁶	29	3 Drift & Die	61	↓	
4/13/02	Ⓜ	3⁴	26				
8/10/02	Ⓡ	❶¹	27	4 She Hates Me	13	↓	
8/17/02	Ⓜ	2³	26				
10/25/03	Ⓡ	❶³	26	5 Away From Me	72	Life On Display ....Flawless 001080	
10/25/03	Ⓜ	5	20				
2/21/04	Ⓡ	6	19	6 Heel Over Head	116	↓	
2/21/04	Ⓜ	10	14				
6/19/04	Ⓡ	16	12	7 Spin You Around	—	↓	
7/10/04	Ⓜ	38	5				
6/2/07	Ⓡ	2⁵	24	8 Famous..	118	Famous...Flawless 009377	
6/16/07	Ⓜ	20	20				
10/20/07+	Ⓡ	❶⁶↑	24↑	9 Psycho	—	↓	
11/17/07+	Ⓜ	2¹↑	20↑				

PURE
Pop-rock band from Vancouver, British Columbia, Canada: Jordy Birch (vocals), Todd Simko (guitar), Mark Henning (keyboards), Dave Hadley (bass) and Leigh Grant (drums).

Debut	Cht	Peak	Wks	Track Title	Hot Pos	Album Title	Album Label & Number
2/27/93	Ⓜ	22	6	Blast...	—	Pureafunalia ....Reprise 45038	

PURSUIT OF HAPPINESS, The
Rock band from Toronto, Ontario, Canada: Moe Berg (vocals, guitar), Leslie Stanwyck (vocals), Kris Abbott (guitar), John Sinclair (bass) and Dave Gilby (drums).

Debut	Cht	Peak	Wks	Track Title	Hot Pos	Album Title	Album Label & Number
11/19/88+	Ⓜ	6	14	I'm An Adult Now..	—	Love Junk...Chrysalis 41675	
11/12/88	Ⓡ	22	11				

PUSCIFER
Solo project of Maynard James Keenan (of **Tool** and **A Perfect Circle**). Includes a revolving set of singers and musicians.

Debut	Cht	Peak	Wks	Track Title	Hot Pos	Album Title	Album Label & Number
11/3/07	Ⓜ	26	9	Queen B...	—	V Is For Vagina ....Puscifer 88800	

PUSHMONKEY
Rock band from Austin, Texas: Tony Park (vocals), Will Hoffman (guitar), Howie Behrens (guitar), Pat Fogarty (bass) and Darwin Keys (drums).

Debut	Cht	Peak	Wks	Track Title	Hot Pos	Album Title	Album Label & Number
11/7/98	Ⓡ	26	9	Handslide	—	Pushmonkey ....Arista 19008	

Q

QUARASHI
Rap-rock band from Reykjavik, Iceland: Sölvi Blondal, Hössi Olafsson, Steini Fjelsted and Omar Swarez.

3/30/02	ⓜ	27	11	Stick 'Em Up	—	Jinx .... Time Bomb 86179

QUARTERFLASH
Pop-rock band from Portland, Oregon: husband-and-wife Marv Ross (guitar) and Rindy Ross (vocals, sax), with Jack Charles (guitar), Rick DiGiallonardo (keyboards), Rich Gooch (bass) and Brian David Willis (drums). Charles and DiGiallonardo left in 1984. Group originally known as Seafood Mama.

10/31/81	ℝ	❶³	24	1 Harden My Heart	3²	Quarterflash .... Geffen 2003
11/21/81+	ℝ	12	22	2 Find Another Fool	16	↓
7/9/83	ℝ	6	12	3 Take Me To Heart	14	Take Another Picture .... Geffen 4011
9/21/85	ℝ	41	7	4 Talk To Me	83	Back Into Blue .... Geffen 24078

QUAYE, Finley
Born on 3/25/1974 in Edinburgh, Scotland. Male singer/songwriter.

2/7/98	ⓜ	26	11	Sunday Shining	—	Maverick A Strike .... 550 Music 68506

QUEEN
Rock band formed in England: Freddie Mercury (vocals; born Farrokh Bulsara on 9/5/1946 in Zanzibar, Tanzania; died of AIDS on 11/24/1991, age 45), **Brian May** (guitar; born on 7/19/1947), John Deacon (bass; born on 8/19/1951) and Roger Taylor (drums; born on 7/26/1949). Wrote soundtrack for the movie *Flash Gordon* in 1980. **Paul Rodgers** joined group for 2005 album and concert tour. Also see **Classic Rock Tracks** section.

AWARD: R&R Hall of Fame: 2001

TOP HITS: 1)*I Want It All* 2)*Headlong* 3)*Under Pressure*

11/7/81	ℝ	7	18	1 Under Pressure	29	Greatest Hits .... Elektra 564
				QUEEN & DAVID BOWIE		
5/8/82	ℝ	19	7	2 Body Language	11	Hot Space .... Elektra 60128
5/29/82	ℝ	15	7	3 Put Out The Fire	—	↓
5/29/82	ℝ	40	8	4 Calling All Girls	60	↓
6/19/82	ℝ	57	2	5 Life Is Real (Song For Lennon)	—	↓
				tribute to **John Lennon**		
2/25/84	ℝ	22	8	6 Radio Ga-Ga	16	The Works .... Capitol 12322
3/31/84	ℝ	52	1	7 Tear It Up	—	↓
4/7/84	ℝ	57	1	8 Hammer To Fall	—	↓
				also see #16 below		
12/14/85	ℝ	19	11	9 One Vision	61	St: Iron Eagle .... Capitol 12499
5/13/89	ℝ	3²	11	10 I Want It All	50	The Miracle .... Capitol 92357
1/26/91	ℝ	3¹	10	11 Headlong	—	Innuendo .... Hollywood 61020
3/16/91	ℝ	17	9	12 Innuendo	—	↓
6/8/91	ℝ	28	6	13 I Can't Live With You	—	↓
1/11/92	ℝ	40	3	14 The Show Must Go On	—	↓
4/4/92	ℝ	16	10	15 Bohemian Rhapsody	2¹	St: Wayne's World .... Reprise 26805
				R&R Hall of Fame ★ RS500: 163		
				#9 Pop hit in 1976		
5/16/92	ℝ	35	6	16 Hammer To Fall .... [R]	—	Classic Queen .... Hollywood 61311
				same version as #8 above		

QUEENS OF THE STONE AGE
ⓜ **2000s: #36 / All-Time: #76**

Hard-rock duo formed in Palm Desert, California: Josh Homme (vocals, guitar; born on 5/17/1973) and Nick Oliveri (bass; born on 10/21/1971). Touring band includes several different musicians. Oliveri left in early 2004; Homme continued with more musicians.

6/24/00	ℝ	21	11	1 The Lost Art Of Keeping A Secret	—	Rated R .... Interscope 490683
9/2/00	ⓜ	36	6			
10/12/02+	ⓜ	❶⁴	36	2 No One Knows	51	Songs For The Deaf .... Interscope 493425
10/19/02+	ℝ	5	28			
4/12/03	ⓜ	7	25	3 Go With The Flow	116	↓
5/3/03	ℝ	24	11			
1/29/05	ⓜ	2²	26	4 Little Sister	88	Lullabies To Paralyze .... Rekords 004186
2/5/05	ℝ	13	19			
6/11/05	ⓜ	32	8	5 In My Head	—	↓
7/2/05	ℝ	39	1			
12/3/05	ⓜ	40	1	6 Burn The Witch	—	↓

QUEENS OF THE STONE AGE — cont'd

Debut	Cht	Peak	Wks	Track Title	Hot Pos	Album Title	Album Label & Number
5/26/07	Ⓜ	23	11	7 Sick, Sick, Sick	—	Era Vulgaris	Rekords 009039
7/14/07	Ⓡ	40	2				
10/6/07	Ⓜ	25	16	8 3's & 7's	—	↓	

QUEENSRŸCHE   Ⓡ 1990s: #21 / All-Time: #79

Heavy-metal band from Bellevue, Washington: Geoff Tate (vocals; born on 1/14/1959), Michael Wilton (guitar; born on 2/23/1962), Chris DeGarmo (guitar; born on 6/14/1963), Eddie Jackson (bass; born on 1/29/1961) and Scott Rockenfield (drums; born on 6/15/1963). Mike Stone (born on 11/30/1969) replaced DeGarmo in 1998. Rockenfield is also a member of **Slave to The System.**

TOP HITS: 1)*Silent Lucidity* 2)*Sign Of The Times* 3)*Real World*

Debut	Cht	Peak	Wks	Track Title	Hot Pos	Album Title	Album Label & Number
5/13/89	Ⓡ	35	5	1 Eyes Of A Stranger	—	Operation:mindcrime	EMI-Manhattan 48640
8/5/89	Ⓡ	41	5	2 I Don't Believe In Love	—	↓	
7/14/90	Ⓡ	27	8	3 Last Time In Paris	—	St: The Adventures Of Ford Fairlane	Elektra 60952
9/22/90	Ⓡ	22	10	4 Empire	—	Empire	EMI 92806
12/8/90+	Ⓡ	28	9	5 Best I Can	—	↓	
1/26/91	Ⓡ	❶[1]	21	6 Silent Lucidity	9	↓	
5/25/91	Ⓡ	6	19	7 Jet City Woman	—	↓	
10/5/91+	Ⓡ	7	29	8 Another Rainy Night (Without You)	—	↓	
2/15/92	Ⓡ	16	17	9 Anybody Listening?	—	↓	
6/12/93	Ⓡ	3[1]	14	10 Real World	111	St: Last Action Hero	Columbia 57127
10/22/94	Ⓡ	8	9	11 I Am I	—	Promised Land	EMI 30711
12/17/94+	Ⓡ	6	18	12 Bridge	—	↓	
5/6/95	Ⓡ	32	4	13 Disconnected	—	↓	
3/22/97	Ⓡ	3[2]	21	14 Sign Of The Times	—	Hear In The Now Frontier	EMI 56141
7/5/97	Ⓡ	11	11	15 You	—	↓	
9/11/99	Ⓡ	27	7	16 Breakdown	—	Q2K	Atlantic 83225
8/2/03	Ⓡ	38	1	17 Open	—	Tribe	Sanctuary 84578

QUIET RIOT

Hard-rock band formed in Los Angeles, California: Kevin DuBrow (vocals), Carlos Cavazo (guitar), Rudy Sarzo (bass) and Frankie Banali (drums). DuBrow died of a drug overdose on 11/25/2007 (age 52).

Debut	Cht	Peak	Wks	Track Title	Hot Pos	Album Title	Album Label & Number
4/23/83	Ⓡ	7	26	1 Cum On Feel The Noize	5	Metal Health	Pasha 38443
				#98 Pop hit for **Slade** in 1973			
5/7/83	Ⓡ	37	9	2 Bang Your Head (Metal Health)	31	↓	
9/10/83	Ⓡ	32	7	3 Slick Black Cadillac	—	↓	
2/11/84	Ⓡ	22	7	4 Don't Wanna Let You Go	—	↓	
6/16/84	Ⓡ	13	11	5 Mama Weer All Crazee Now	51	Condition Critical	Pasha 39516
				#76 Pop hit for **Slade** in 1973			
8/4/84	Ⓡ	28	7	6 Sign Of The Times	—	↓	

R

RA

Rock band from Brooklyn, New York: Sahaj Ticotin (vocals, guitar), Ben Carroll (guitar), Sean Corcoran (bass) and Skoota Warner (drums). By 2005, P.J. Farley replaced Corcoran and Andy Ryan replaced Warner.

Debut	Cht	Peak	Wks	Track Title	Hot Pos	Album Title	Album Label & Number
10/26/02+	Ⓡ	14	26	1 Do You Call My Name	—	From One	Republic 066093
5/24/03	Ⓡ	30	8	2 Rectifier	—	↓	
6/4/05	Ⓡ	29	15	3 Fallen Angels	—	Duality	Republic 004836
10/7/06	Ⓡ	36	4	4 Don't Turn Away	—	Raw	Cement Shoes 1002

RABIN, Trevor

Born Trevor Rabinowitz on 1/13/1954 in Johannesburg, South Africa. Rock singer/songwriter/guitarist. Joined member of **Yes** from 1983-95.

Debut	Cht	Peak	Wks	Track Title	Hot Pos	Album Title	Album Label & Number
8/5/89	Ⓡ	3[3]	12	Something To Hold On To	—	Can't Look Away	Elektra 60781

RACONTEURS, The

Rock band formed in Detroit, Michigan: Jack White (vocals, guitar; of **The White Stripes**), Brandon Benson (vocals, guitar), Jack Lawrence (bass) and Patrick Keeler (drums).

Debut	Cht	Peak	Wks	Track Title	Hot Pos	Album Title	Album Label & Number
4/8/06	Ⓜ	❶[1]	28	1 Steady, As She Goes	54	Broken Boy Soldiers	Third Man 27306
6/10/06	Ⓡ	30	17				
9/23/06+	Ⓜ	7	20	2 Level	—	↓	

Billboard				ARTIST			
Debut	Cht	Peak	Wks	Track Title	Hot Pos	Album Title	Album Label & Number

®=Mainstream Rock Ⓜ=Modern Rock

RADFORD
Rock band from Los Angeles, California: Jonny Mead (vocals, guitar), Chris Hower (guitar), Bobby Stefano (bass) and Kane McGee (drums).

Debut	Cht	Peak	Wks	Track Title	Hot Pos	Album Title	Album Label & Number
4/15/00	Ⓜ	32	4	Don't Stop	—	Radford ....RCA 67776

RADIATORS, The
Rock band from New Orleans, Louisiana: Dave Malone (vocals), Camile Baudoin (guitar), Ed Volker (keyboards), Glenn Sears (percussion), Reggie Scanlan (bass) and Frank Bua (drums).

10/17/87	®	23	9	1 Like Dreamers Do	—	Law Of The Fish ....Epic 40888
1/16/88	®	20	8	2 Doctor Doctor	—	↓
3/4/89	®	8	10	3 Confidential...	—	Zigzagging Through Ghostland....................Epic 44343

RADIOHEAD   Ⓜ All-Time: #55
Alternative-rock band from Oxford, England: Thom Yorke (vocals, guitar; born on 10/7/1968), born on 11/5/1971) and Colin Greenwood (bass; born on 6/26/1969), brothers Jon Greenwood (guitar; born on 11/5/1971) and Colin Greenwood (bass; born on 6/26/1969), Ed O'Brien (guitar; born on 4/15/1968), and Phil Selway (drums; born on 5/23/1967).

TOP HITS: 1)Creep 2)Bodysnatchers 3)Optimistic

4/17/93	Ⓜ	2¹	17	1 Creep	34	Pablo Honey ....Capitol 81409
8/14/93	®	20	9			
10/16/93	Ⓜ	23	3	2 Stop Whispering	—	↓
5/6/95	Ⓜ	11	11	3 Fake Plastic Trees	65ᴬ	The Bends ....Capitol 29626
				RS500 #376		
11/4/95	Ⓜ	37	3	4 Just	—	↓
12/23/95+	Ⓜ	18	13	5 High And Dry	78	↓
8/16/97	Ⓜ	29	8	6 Let Down	—	OK Computer ....Capitol 55229
11/15/97+	Ⓜ	14	26	7 Karma Police	69ᴬ	↓
10/7/00	Ⓜ	10	18	8 Optimistic	—	Kid A ....Capitol 27753
5/19/01	Ⓜ	27	8	9 I Might Be Wrong	—	Amnesiac ....Capitol 27642
5/10/03	Ⓜ	14	15	10 There There	—	Hail To The Thief......................................Capitol 84543
9/13/03	Ⓜ	32	5	11 Go To Sleep	—	↓
11/10/07+	Ⓜ	8	21↑	12 Bodysnatchers	—	In Rainbows ....TBD 21622

RAGE AGAINST THE MACHINE   Ⓜ All-Time: #93
Hard-rock band formed in Los Angeles, California: Zack de la Rocha (vocals; born on 1/12/1970), Tom Morello (guitar; born on 5/30/1964), Tim Commerford (bass; born on 2/26/1968) and Brad Wilk (drums; born on 9/5/1968). Morello, Commerford and Wilk later formed **Audioslave**. Morello also recorded with **Class Of '99**.

4/20/96	Ⓜ	11	16	1 Bulls On Parade...............................	62ᴬ	Evil Empire ....Epic 57523
5/25/96	®	36	5			
12/20/97+	Ⓜ	34	7	2 The Ghost Of Tom Joad	—	(single only)...Epic 3455
12/13/97+	®	35	9	first recorded by **Bruce Springsteen** in 1995		
6/27/98	®	30	7	3 No Shelter	—	St: Godzilla ....Epic 69338
6/27/98	Ⓜ	33	10			
10/16/99+	Ⓜ	6	26	4 Guerrilla Radio	69	The Battle Of Los Angeles ....Epic 69630
10/16/99+	®	11	26	**Grammy: Hard Rock Performance**		
2/26/00	Ⓜ	8	24	5 Sleep Now In The Fire	112	↓
2/26/00	®	16	18			
8/12/00	Ⓜ	16	16	6 Testify..	—	↓
8/12/00	®	22	11			
11/25/00	Ⓜ	9	26	7 Renegades Of Funk..........................	109	Renegades ....Epic 85289
12/2/00+	®	19	18			
3/31/01	Ⓜ	37	2	8 How I Could Just Kill A Man	—	↓
3/31/01	®	39	1	#77 Pop hit for **Cypress Hill** in 1992		

RAGING SLAB
Hard-rock band from New York: Greg Strempka (vocals), Mark Middleton (guitar), Elyse Steinman (guitar), Alec Morton (bass) and Bob Pantella (drums).

5/15/93	®	18	8	1 Anywhere But Here	—	Dynamite Monster Boogie Concert...........Warner 45244
9/25/93	®	27	6	2 Take A Hold	—	↓

RAILWAY CHILDREN, The
Pop-rock band from Manchester, England: Gary Newby (vocals), Brian Bateman (guitar), Stephen Hull (bass) and Guy Keegan (drums).

7/21/90	Ⓜ	❶¹	10	Every Beat Of The Heart	—	Native Place..Virgin 91385

Billboard			ARTIST	R=Mainstream Rock	Hot		
Debut	Cht	Peak	Wks	Track Title	M=Modern Rock	Pos	Album Title	Album Label & Number

RAINBOW

Hard-rock band formed in England by former **Deep Purple** members Ritchie Blackmore (guitar) and **Roger Glover** (bass). Numerous personnel changes. Lineup from 1981-84: **Joe Lynn Turner** (vocals), Blackmore (guitar), Don Airey (keyboards), Glover (bass) and Bobby Rondinelli (drums). David Rosenthal replaced Airey in early 1982. Earlier members included Ronnie James **Dio**, **Tony Carey** and Cozy Powell (of **Emerson, Lake & Powell**). Also see **Classic Rock Tracks** section.

3/28/81	Ⓡ	19	7	1 I Surrender		105	Difficult To Cure ....Polydor 6316
11/14/81	Ⓡ	13	15	2 Jealous Lover		—	Jealous Lover ....Polydor 502
4/10/82	Ⓡ	❶¹	15	3 Stone Cold		40	Straight Between The Eyes...................Mercury 4041
5/22/82	Ⓡ	35	3	4 Power		—	↓
9/24/83	Ⓡ	2¹	18	5 Street Of Dreams		60	Bent Out Of Shape ....Mercury 815305
3/10/84	Ⓡ	53	3	6 Desperate Heart		—	↓

RAINDOGS

Rock band from Boston, Massachusetts: Mark Cutler (vocals), Emerson Torrey (guitar), Johnny Cunningham (fiddle), Darren Hill (bass) and James Reilly (drums).

2/24/90	Ⓜ	23	5	I'm Not Scared		—	Lost Souls ....Atco 91297
4/14/90	Ⓡ	44	3				

RAINMAKERS, The

Rock band from Kansas City, Missouri: Bob Walkenhorst (vocals), Steve Phillips (guitar), Rich Ruth (bass) and Pat Tomek (drums).

11/14/87	Ⓡ	31	9	Snakedance		—	Tornado ....Mercury 832795

RAITT, Bonnie

Born on 11/8/1949 in Burbank, California. Blues-rock singer/guitarist. Daughter of Broadway actor/singer John Raitt. Married to actor Michael O'Keefe from 1991-99.

AWARD: R&R Hall of Fame: 2000

3/20/82	Ⓡ	39	8	1 Keep This Heart In Mind		104	Green Light...Warner 3630
				Jackson Browne (backing vocal)			
8/16/86	Ⓡ	15	9	2 No Way To Treat A Lady		—	Nine Lives ....Warner 25486
				co-written by Bryan Adams			
3/18/89	Ⓡ	11	10	3 Thing Called Love		—	Nick Of Time...Capitol 91268
				first recorded by John Hiatt in 1987			
6/24/89	Ⓡ	49	2	4 Love Letter		—	↓
6/22/91	Ⓡ	12	16	5 Something To Talk About		5	Luck Of The Draw....................................Capitol 96111
				Grammy: Pop Female Vocal ★ R&R Hall of Fame			
10/5/91	Ⓡ	28	10	6 Slow Ride		—	↓
3/26/94	Ⓡ	25	9	7 Love Sneakin' Up On You		19	Longing In Their Hearts...........................Capitol 81427

RAMMSTEIN

Hard-rock band from Berlin, Germany: Till Lindemann (vocals), Richard Kruspe (guitar), Paul Landers (guitar), Flake Lorenz (keyboards), Oliver Riedel (bass) and Christoph Schneider (drums).

6/27/98	Ⓡ	20	17	Du Hast [F]		—	Sehnsucht...Slash 539901

RAMONES

Highly influential punk-rock band formed in Brooklyn, New York. Jeffrey "Joey Ramone" Hyman (vocals; born on 5/19/1951; died on 4/15/2001, age 49), John "Johnny Ramone" Cummings (guitar; born on 10/8/1948; died of cancer on 9/15/2004, age 55), Douglas "Dee Dee Ramone" Colvin (bass; born on 9/18/1952; died of a drug overdose on 6/5/2002, age 49) and Tom "Tommy Ramone" Erdelyi (drums; born on 1/29/1952). Tommy became the band's co-producer in 1978; replaced by Marc "Marky Ramone" Bell (born on 7/15/1956). Richard "Richie Ramone" Reinhardt (born on 8/11/1957) replaced Marky from 1983-87. Dee Dee left band in 1989 and Chris "C.J. Ramone" Ward (born on 10/8/1965) was added. Band appeared in the 1979 movie Rock 'n' Roll High School. Also see **Classic Rock Tracks** section.

AWARD: R&R Hall of Fame: 2002

5/13/89	Ⓜ	4	10	1 Pet Sematary		—	Brain Drain..Sire 25905
9/5/92	Ⓜ	6	12	2 Poison Heart		—	Mondo Bizarro...................................Radioactive 10615
7/15/95	Ⓜ	30	6	3 I Don't Want To Grow Up		—	Adios Amigos....................................Radioactive 11273
				first recorded by Tom Waits in 1992			

RANCID

Punk-rock band from Berkeley, California: **Tim Armstrong** (vocals, guitar), Lars Frederiksen (vocals, guitar), Matt Freeman (bass) and Brett Reed (drums). Armstrong was also a member of the **Transplants**. Armstrong was formerly married to Brody Dalle of **The Distillers**.

9/17/94+	Ⓜ	21	15	1 Salvation		—	Let's Go ....Epitaph 86434
12/24/94+	Ⓜ	27	8	2 Roots Radical		—	↓
8/26/95	Ⓜ	8	17	3 Time Bomb		48ᴬ	...And Out Come The Wolves...................Epitaph 86444
12/16/95+	Ⓜ	13	15	4 Ruby Soho		63ᴬ	↓
8/2/03	Ⓜ	13	11	5 Fall Back Down		—	Indestructible ....Hellcat 48529

RANKIN, Billy

Born on 4/25/1959 in Glasgow, Scotland. Rock singer/guitarist. Member of **Nazareth** from 1981-82.

3/31/84	Ⓡ	22	6	Baby Come Back		52	Growin' Up Too Fast.....................................A&M 4977

RANKING ROGER
Born Roger Charley on 2/21/1961 in Birmingham, England. Black rock singer. Member of English Beat and **General Public**.

| 9/10/88 | Ⓜ | 23 | 1 | So Excited .... | — | | *Radical Departure* .... I.R.S. 42197 |

RATCAT
Rock trio from Sydney, Australia: Simon Day (vocals, guitar), Amr Zaid (bass) and Andrew Polin (drums).

| 10/26/91 | Ⓜ | 27 | 3 | That Ain't Bad .... | — | | *Tingles* .... Roo-Art 868573 |

RATT
Hard-rock band formed in Los Angeles, California: Stephen Pearcy (vocals), Warren DeMartini (guitar), Robbin Crosby (guitar), Juan Croucier (bass) and Bobby Blotzer (drums). Pearcy joined **Arcade**. Blotzer joined **Contraband**. Pearcy, DeMartini and Blotzer reunited in 1998 with Robbie Crane (bass). Crosby died of AIDS on 6/6/2002 (age 42).

TOP HITS: 1)*Round And Round* 2)*Lay It Down* 3)*Way Cool Jr.*

4/28/84	Ⓡ	4	21	1 Round And Round	12	*Out Of The Cellar* .... Atlantic 80143
7/28/84	Ⓡ	27	10	2 Back For More	—	↓
10/6/84	Ⓡ	38	3	3 Wanted Man	87	↓
6/15/85	Ⓡ	11	13	4 Lay It Down	40	*Invasion Of Your Privacy* .... Atlantic 81257
9/7/85	Ⓡ	34	6	5 You're In Love	89	↓
10/25/86	Ⓡ	36	5	6 Dance	59	*Dancing Undercover* .... Atlantic 81683
11/19/88+	Ⓡ	16	14	7 Way Cool Jr.	75	*Reach For The Sky* .... Atlantic 81929
8/25/90	Ⓡ	18	9	8 Lovin' You's A Dirty Job	—	*Detonator* .... Atlantic 82127
1/5/91	Ⓡ	39	6	9 Givin' Yourself Away	—	↓
8/28/99	Ⓡ	36	3	10 Over The Edge	—	*Ratt* .... Portrait 69586

RAVE-UPS, The
Rock band formed in Los Angeles, California: Jimmer Podrasky (vocals, guitar), Terry Wilson (guitar), Tom Blatnik (bass) and Tim Jimenez (drums). Group appeared in the 1986 movie *Pretty In Pink*.

| 2/3/90 | Ⓜ | 12 | 11 | Respectfully King Of Rain .... | — | *Chance* .... Epic 45255 |

RAVYNS, The
Rock band from Baltimore, Maryland: Rob Fahey (vocals, guitar), David Bell (guitar), Kyf Brewer (keyboards), Lee Townsend (bass) and Tim Steele (drums). Brewer later became lead singer for **Company Of Wolves**.

| 4/7/84 | Ⓡ | 49 | 1 | Don't Leave Me This Way .... | — | *The Ravyns* .... RDM 39015 |

REA, Chris
Born on 3/4/1951 in Middlesborough, Cleveland, England. Pop-rock singer/songwriter.

| 1/21/89 | Ⓡ | ❶[1] | 15 | 1 Working On It .... | 73 | *New Light Through Old Windows* .... Geffen 24232 |
| 2/10/90 | Ⓡ | 11 | 10 | 2 The Road To Hell .... | — | *The Road To Hell* .... Geffen 24276 |

REACHAROUND
Rock band from Los Angeles, California: Matt Caisley (vocals), Ted Hutt (guitar), Jeff Peters (bass) and Scott Capizzano (drums).

| 8/3/96 | Ⓜ | 28 | 9 | Big Chair .... | — | *Who's Tommy Cooper?* .... Trauma 90067 |
| 8/10/96 | Ⓡ | 33 | 6 | | | |

REAL LIFE
Pop-rock band from Melbourne, Australia: David Sterry (vocals, guitar), Richard Zatorski (keyboards), Allan Johnson (bass) and Danny Simcic (drums).

1/14/84	Ⓡ	18	8	1 Send Me An Angel	29	*Heart Land* .... Curb 5459
4/14/84	Ⓡ	46	2	2 Catch Me I'm Falling	40	↓
7/21/90	Ⓜ	15	9	3 God Tonight	—	*Lifetime* .... Curb 77271

REAL PEOPLE, The
Pop band from Liverpool, England: brothers Tony Griffiths (vocals, bass) and Chris Griffiths (vocals, guitar), with Sean Simpson (guitar) and Tony Elson (drums).

| 2/1/92 | Ⓜ | 11 | 8 | Window Pane .... | — | *The Real People* .... Relativity 1080 |

REBEL MEETS REBEL
Hard-rock band formed by former **Pantera** members/brothers "Dimebag" Darrell Abbott (guitar) and Vinnie Paul Abbott (drums), with fellow Pantera member Rex Brown (bass) and country singer David Allan Coe (vocals). Darrell was shot to death on stage on 12/8/2004 (age 38).

| 5/13/06 | Ⓡ | 32 | 7 | Get Outta My Life .... | — | *Rebel Meets Rebel* .... Big Vin 0001 |

RED
Christian heavy-metal band from Nashville, Tennessee: Michael Barnes (vocals, keyboards), identical twin brothers Anthony Armstrong (guitar) and Randy Armstrong (bass), Jasen Rauch (guitar) and Hayden Lamb (drums).

3/10/07	Ⓡ	15	21	1 Breathe Into Me	—	*End Of Silence* .... Essential 10807
10/13/07+	Ⓡ	21	20	2 Let Go	—	↓
3/22/08	Ⓡ	29↑	2↑	3 Already Over	—	↓

REDD KROSS

Pop-rock trio from Los Angeles, California: brothers Jeff McDonald (vocals, guitar) and Steve McDonald (bass), with Robert Hecker (guitar).

11/10/90	ⓜ	16	6	Annie's Gone		—	Third Eye ....Atlantic 82148

RED HOT CHILI PEPPERS

® 1990s: #26 / 2000s: #11 / All-Time: #21 ★
ⓜ 1990s: #5 / 2000s: #2 / All-Time: #1

Rock band formed in Los Angeles, California: Anthony Kiedis (vocals; born on 11/1/1962), Hillel Slovak (guitar; born on 4/13/1962; died of a drug overdose on 6/25/1988, age 26), Michael "Flea" Balzary (bass; born on 10/16/1962) and Jack Irons (drums; born on 7/18/1962). Slovak was replaced by John Frusciante (born on 3/5/1970). Irons left in 1988 and later joined **Eleven**, then **Pearl Jam**; replaced by Chad Smith (born on 10/25/1962). Frusciante left in May 1992; replaced by Zander Schloss (of **Thelonious Monster** and **The Magnificent Bastards**), then by Arik Marshall, then by Jesse Tobias and finally by **Dave Navarro** (of **Jane's Addiction**) in September 1993. Frusciante returned in 1998, replacing Navarro. Kiedis appeared in the 1991 movie *Point Break*. Flea and Kiedis appeared in the 1994 movie *The Chase*. Navarro was married to actress Carmen Electra from 2003-07.

TOP HITS: 1)Scar Tissue 2)By The Way 3)Dani California 4)Otherside 5)Snow ((Hey Oh))

9/2/89	ⓜ	6	10	1 Knock Me Down...	—	Mother's Milk...EMI 92152
10/28/89	ⓜ	11	14	2 Higher Ground	—	↓
12/2/89+	®	26	10	#4 Pop hit for **Stevie Wonder** in 1973		
4/7/90	ⓜ	10	8	3 Show Me Your Soul..	—	St: Pretty Woman ....EMI 93492
9/21/91	ⓜ	❶²	17	4 Give It Away	73	Blood Sugar Sex Magik ....Warner 26681
				Grammy: Hard Rock Performance ★ R&R Hall of Fame		
12/14/91+	ⓜ	15	9	5 Suck My Kiss	—	↓
4/4/92	®	2⁸	20	6 Under The Bridge	2¹	↓
2/15/92	ⓜ	6	17			
8/8/92	®	15	13	7 Breaking The Girl	—	↓
8/8/92	ⓜ	19	9			
11/21/92	ⓜ	7	10	8 Behind The Sun	124	What Hits!? ....EMI 94762
8/7/93	ⓜ	❶⁵	13	9 Soul To Squeeze	22	St: Coneheads ....Warner 45345
8/21/93	®	7	20			
9/2/95	ⓜ	7	9	10 Warped	41ᴬ	One Hot Minute...Warner 45733
9/2/95	®	13	12			
10/7/95	®	❶⁴	26	11 My Friends	27ᴬ	↓
9/30/95	ⓜ	❶⁴	23			
1/27/96	ⓜ	8	17	12 Aeroplane	49ᴬ	↓
2/3/96	®	12	16			
11/16/96	ⓜ	14	14	13 Love Rollercoaster	40ᴬ	St: Beavis & Butt-Head Do America...........Geffen 25002
				#1 Pop hit for the Ohio Players in 1976		
6/5/99	ⓜ	❶¹⁶	26	14 Scar Tissue	9	Californication ....Warner 47386
6/5/99	®	❶¹⁰	29			
				Grammy: Rock Song		
9/25/99	ⓜ	7	23	15 Around The World	108	↓
10/23/99	®	16	14			
1/1/00	ⓜ	❶¹³	27	16 Otherside	14	↓
1/29/00	®	2⁵	27			
7/1/00	®	❶²	26	17 Californication	69	↓
6/17/00	ⓜ	❶¹	26			
3/24/01	ⓜ	37	2	18 Parallel Universe	—	↓
6/15/02	ⓜ	❶¹⁴	26	19 By The Way	34	By The Way ....Warner 48140
6/15/02	®	❶⁷	26			
8/24/02	ⓜ	6	23	20 The Zephyr Song	49	↓
10/12/02	®	14	12			
12/28/02+	ⓜ	❶³	27	21 Can't Stop	57	↓
1/4/03	®	15	26			
5/31/03	ⓜ	13	14	22 Dosed	—	↓
11/22/03	ⓜ	8	15	23 Fortune Faded	112	Greatest Hits...Warner 48545
11/22/03	®	22	13			
4/22/06	ⓜ	❶¹⁴	23	24 Dani California	6	Stadium Arcadium...................................Warner 49996
4/22/06	®	❶¹²	25	Grammys: Rock Song / Rock Vocal Group		

Billboard				ARTIST		Hot Pos	Album Title	Album Label & Number
Debut	Cht	Peak	Wks	Track Title	®=Mainstream Rock ⓜ=Modern Rock			

RED HOT CHILI PEPPERS — cont'd

Debut	Cht	Peak	Wks	Track Title	Hot Pos	Album Title	Album Label & Number
7/8/06	ⓜ	❶⁴	24	25 Tell Me Baby	50	↓	
8/12/06	®	8	20				
11/11/06+	®	❶⁵	25	26 Snow ((Hey Oh))	22	↓	
11/18/06+	®	3⁴	21				
4/21/07	ⓜ	8	12	27 Hump De Bump	—	↓	
4/14/07	®	27	12				

RED HOUSE, The
Rock band from New Jersey: Bruce Tunkel (vocals, keyboards), Tony Stives (guitar), Ron Baumann (bass) and Bob Nicol (drums).

8/11/90	®	30	7	I Said A Prayer	—	The Red House .... SBK 94476

RED JUMPSUIT APPARATUS, The
Pop-punk band from Middleburg, Florida: Ronnie Winter (vocals), Elias Reidy (guitar), Duke Kitchens (guitar), Joey Westwood (bass) and John Wilkes (drums).

8/5/06+	ⓜ	3¹	52	1 Face Down	24	Don't You Fake It .... Virgin 62829
3/17/07	®	38	2			
5/19/07	ⓜ	39	4	2 False Pretense	—	↓

RED RIDER — see COCHRANE, Tom

RED ROCKERS
Rock band from Algiers, Louisiana: John Griffith (vocals), James Singletary (guitar), Darren Hill (bass) and Jim Reilly (drums). Shawn Paddock replaced Singletary in early 1984.

5/28/83	®	19	9	1 China	53	Good As Gold .... Columbia 38629
10/6/84	®	54	2	2 Eve Of Destruction	—	Schizophrenic Circus .... Columbia 39281
				#1 Pop hit for Barry McGuire in 1965		

RED SIREN
Rock band from New York: Kristin Massey (vocals), Robert Haas (guitar), Jon Brant (bass) and Gregg Potter (drums).

2/18/89	®	10	13	1 All Is Forgiven	—	All Is Forgiven .... Mercury 836776
6/17/89	®	39	5	2 One Good Lover	—	↓

REED, Lou
Born on 3/2/1942 in Freeport, Long Island, New York. Lead singer/songwriter of the New York seminal rock band Velvet Underground. Regarded as the godfather of punk rock. Appeared in the 1980 movie *One Trick Pony*. Also see **Classic Rock Tracks** section.

8/4/84	®	28	11	1 I Love You, Suzanne	—	New Sensations .... RCA Victor 4998
5/17/86	®	19	10	2 No Money Down	—	Mistrial .... RCA Victor 7190
1/21/89	ⓜ	❶⁴	13	3 Dirty Blvd.	—	New York .... Sire 25829
1/28/89	®	18	13			
4/29/89	ⓜ	11	5	4 Busload Of Faith	—	↓
4/29/89	®	47	3			
5/12/90	ⓜ	13	7	5 Nobody But You	—	Songs For Drella .... Sire 26140
				LOU REED & JOHN CALE		
1/18/92	ⓜ	❶³	10	6 What's Good	—	Magic And Loss .... Sire 26662

REEF
Rock band from Butleigh, Somerset, England: Gary Stringer (vocals), Kenwyn House (guitar), Jack Bessant (bass) and Domenic Greensmith (drums).

8/9/97	®	29	6	Place Your Hands	—	Glow .... Epic 67971

REEL BIG FISH
Ska-punk band from Huntington Beach, California: Aaron Barrett (vocals, guitar), Scott Klopfenstein (vocals, trumpet), Tavis Werts (trumpet), Grant Barry and Dan Regan (trombones), Matt Wong (bass) and Andrew Gonzales (drums).

5/24/97	ⓜ	10	26	Sell Out	69ᴬ	Turn The Radio Off .... Mojo 53013

RE-FLEX
Techno-rock/dance band formed in London, England: Baxter (vocals, guitar), Paul Fishman (keyboards), Nigel Ross-Scott (bass) and Roland Kerridge (drums).

1/14/84	®	19	7	The Politics Of Dancing	24	The Politics Of Dancing .... Capitol 12314

REFRESHMENTS, The
Rock band from Tempe, Arizona: Roger Clyne (vocals, guitar), Brian Blush (guitar), Buddy Edwards (bass) and P.H. Naffah (drums).

5/11/96	®	11	18	1 Banditos	71ᴬ	Fizzy Fuzzy Big & Buzzy .... Mercury 528999
4/27/96	ⓜ	14	21			
9/28/96	ⓜ	38	1	2 Down Together	—	↓

REHAB
Hip-hop duo from Atlanta, Georgia: James "Brooks" Buford and Danny "Boone" Alexander.

4/14/01	Ⓜ	20	13	It Don't Matter	—	Southern Discomfort...................................Epic 63648

R.E.M.
Ⓡ 1980s: #34 / 1990s: #12 ★ All-Time: #14 ★ Ⓜ 1990s: #2 / All-Time: #6

Alternative-rock band formed in Athens, Georgia: **Michael Stipe** (vocals; born on 1/4/1960), Peter Buck (guitar; born on 12/6/1956), Mike Mills (bass; born on 12/17/1958) and Bill Berry (drums; born on 7/31/1958). Developed huge following with college audiences in the early 1980s as one of the first "alternative-rock" bands. Buck, Mills and Berry also recorded with **Warren Zevon** as the **Hindu Love Gods**. Berry retired from the group in 1997.

AWARD: R&R Hall of Fame: 2007

TOP HITS: 1)*Losing My Religion* 2)*Orange Crush* 3)*What's The Frequency, Kenneth?* 4)*Drive* 5)*Bang And Blame*

Debut	Cht	Peak	Wks	Track Title	Hot Pos	Album Title	Album Label & Number
5/21/83	Ⓡ	25	4	1 Radio Free Europe	78	Murmur..I.R.S. 70604
				R&R Hall of Fame ★ RS500 #379		
5/26/84	Ⓡ	43	11	2 so. Central Rain (I'm Sorry)......................	85	Reckoning ....I.R.S. 70044
9/8/84	Ⓡ	44	1	3 Pretty Persuasion	—	↓
7/6/85	Ⓡ	14	11	4 Can't Get There From Here........................	110	Fables Of The Reconstruction .......................I.R.S. 5592
9/7/85	Ⓡ	22	11	5 Driver 8	—	↓
8/9/86	Ⓡ	5	12	6 Fall On Me	94	Lifes Rich Pageant ...................................I.R.S. 5783
11/1/86	Ⓡ	17	10	7 Superman	—	
5/9/87	Ⓡ	39	5	8 Ages Of You	—	Dead Letter Office ...................................I.R.S. 70054
9/5/87	Ⓡ	2⁴	16	9 The One I Love......................................	9	R.E.M. No. 5: Document ............................I.R.S. 42059
11/21/87	Ⓡ	16	11	10 Its The End Of The World As We Know It	69	↓
				(And I Feel Fine)		↓
2/6/88	Ⓡ	28	11	11 Finest Worksong	—	↓
11/19/88	Ⓜ	❶⁸	12	12 Orange Crush	—	Green ....Warner 25795
11/12/88	Ⓡ	❶²	12			
12/10/88+	Ⓜ	❶²	17	13 Stand	6	↓
12/3/88+	Ⓡ	❶¹	19	by 1990 became the theme song for TV's *Get A Life* starring Chris Elliott		
5/6/89	Ⓡ	14	9	14 Pop Song 89..	86	↓
12/3/88	Ⓜ	16	8			
3/11/89	Ⓡ	7	11	15 Turn You Inside-Out	—	↓
3/18/89	Ⓡ	10	8			
3/9/91	Ⓜ	❶⁸	11	16 Losing My Religion	4	Out Of Time ....Warner 26496
3/9/91	Ⓡ	❶³	17	Grammy: Pop Vocal Group ★ R&R Hall of Fame ★ RS500 #169		
5/18/91	Ⓜ	4	8	17 Texarkana..	—	↓
5/18/91	Ⓡ	7	13			
6/29/91	Ⓜ	3¹	12	18 Shiny Happy People...............................	10	↓
7/13/91	Ⓡ	8	11	Kate Pierson of **The B-52's** (backing vocal)		
10/12/91	Ⓡ	43	6	19 Radio Song	—	↓
1/18/92	Ⓜ	11	4	20 First We Take Manhattan......................	—	VA: I'm Your Fan: The Songs Of
				first recorded by Jennifer Warnes in 1987		Leonard Cohen...............................Atlantic 82349
10/3/92	Ⓜ	❶⁵	11	21 Drive	28	Automatic For The People ....Warner 45138
10/3/92	Ⓡ	2²	20			
11/28/92+	Ⓡ	4	13	22 Ignoreland	—	↓
11/21/92	Ⓜ	5	9			
1/16/93	Ⓜ	2¹	11	23 Man On The Moon	30	↓
1/30/93	Ⓡ	4	16	tribute to comedian Andy Kaufman (died on 5/6/1984, age 35)		
5/1/93	Ⓜ	24	3	24 The Sidewinder Sleeps Tonite	—	↓
5/8/93	Ⓡ	28	5			
10/16/93	Ⓜ	21	2	25 Everybody Hurts......................................	29	↓
11/13/93	Ⓜ	9	14	26 Photograph	—	VA: Born To Choose ....Rykodisc 10256
				R.E.M. with Natalie Merchant		
9/24/94	Ⓜ	❶⁵	19	27 What's The Frequency, Kenneth?	21	Monster..Warner 45740
9/24/94	Ⓡ	2⁵	26			
11/26/94	Ⓜ	❶³	15	28 Bang And Blame	19	↓
12/3/94+	Ⓡ	3²	18			

Billboard				ARTIST		Hot		
Debut	Cht	Peak	Wks	Track Title	®=Mainstream Rock M=Modern Rock	Pos	Album Title	Album Label & Number

R.E.M. — cont'd

Debut	Cht	Peak	Wks	Track Title	Hot Pos	Album Title	Album Label & Number
2/18/95	M	8	10	29 Star 69	74^A ↓		
3/11/95	®	15	10				
5/20/95	®	8	13	30 Strange Currencies	47 ↓		
4/29/95	M	14	11				
8/12/95	®	20	9	31 Crush With Eyeliner	113 ↓		
8/12/95	M	33	5				
8/31/96	M	2¹	9	32 E-Bow The Letter	49	New Adventures In Hi-Fi ....Warner 46320	
8/31/96	®	15	7	Patti Smith (female vocal)			
10/12/96	M	6	16	33 Bittersweet Me	46 ↓		
10/12/96	®	7	17				
1/25/97	®	30	5	34 The Wake-Up Bomb	— ↓		
10/17/98	M	18	10	35 Daysleeper	57	Up ....Warner 47112	
10/24/98	®	30	7				
2/6/99	M	31	6	36 Lotus	— ↓		
2/6/99	®	31	8				
11/20/99+	M	11	17	37 The Great Beyond	57	St: Man On The Moon ....Warner 47483	
12/25/99+	®	33	8				
4/28/01	M	22	9	38 Imitation Of Life	83	Reveal ....Warner 47946	
3/1/08	M	22↑	5↑	39 Supernatural Superserious	—	Accelerate ....Warner 418620	
3/22/08	®	39↑	2↑				

REMBRANDTS, The
Pop-rock duo from Los Angeles, California: **Danny Wilde** and Phil Solem. Both were members of **Great Buildings**.

Debut	Cht	Peak	Wks	Track Title	Hot Pos	Album Title	Album Label & Number
11/10/90+	®	13	15	1 Just The Way It Is, Baby	14	The Rembrandts ....Atco 91412	
2/16/91	®	36	10	2 Burning Timber	— ↓		
10/10/92	M	17	6	3 Johnny Have You Seen Her? ...	54	Untitled ....Atco 92200	
9/26/92	®	24	10				
6/10/95	M	23	5	4 I'll Be There For You	17	St: Friends ....Reprise 46008	

REMY ZERO
Rock band formed in Birmingham, Alabama: brothers Cinjun Tate (vocals) and Shelby Tate (guitar), with Jeff Cain (guitar), Cedric LeMoyne (bass) and Greg Slay (drums).

Debut	Cht	Peak	Wks	Track Title	Hot Pos	Album Title	Album Label & Number
12/26/98+	®	25	10	1 Prophecy	—	Villa Elaine ....DGC 25300	
11/28/98+	M	27	12				
10/20/01	M	27	12	2 Save Me	—	The Golden Hum ....Elektra 62678	

RENEGADE SOUNDWAVE
Techno-dance trio from England: Karl Bonnie (vocals), Gary Asqwith and Danny Briochett.

Debut	Cht	Peak	Wks	Track Title	Hot Pos	Album Title	Album Label & Number
2/17/90	M	11	8	Biting My Nails	—	Soundclash ....Enigma/Mute 75422	

RENTALS, The
Pop-rock band from Los Angeles, California: Matt Sharp (vocals, bass), Cherielynn Westrich (vocals), Petra Haden (violin), Rod Cervera (guitar), Tom Gaimley (synthesizer) and Pat Wilson (drums). Sharp and Wilson are also members of **Weezer**.

Debut	Cht	Peak	Wks	Track Title	Hot Pos	Album Title	Album Label & Number
10/21/95	M	7	12	Friends Of P.	82	Return Of The Rentals ....Maverick 46093	

REO SPEEDWAGON   ® All-Time: #99
Rock band from Champaign, Illinois: Kevin Cronin (vocals, guitar; born on 10/6/1951), Gary Richrath (guitar; born on 10/18/1949), Neal Doughty (keyboards; born on 7/29/1946), Bruce Hall (bass; born on 5/3/1953) and Alan Gratzer (drums; born on 11/9/1948). Graham Lear replaced Gratzer in 1988. Lineup in 1990: Cronin, Doughty and Hall, joined by new members Dave Amato (guitar), Jesse Harms (keyboards) and Bryan Hitt (drums). Harms later joined **Sammy Hagar**'s Waboritas. Band appeared in the 1978 movie *FM*. Also see **Classic Rock Tracks** section.

TOP HITS: 1)Keep The Fire Burnin' 2)That Ain't Love 3)I Do'wanna Know

Debut	Cht	Peak	Wks	Track Title	Hot Pos	Album Title	Album Label & Number
3/21/81	®	6	13	1 Take It On The Run	5	Hi Infidelity ....Epic 36844	
3/21/81	®	9	12	2 Keep On Loving You	❶¹ ↓		
3/21/81	®	11	26	3 Don't Let Him Go	24 ↓		
3/21/81	®	25	3	4 Tough Guys	— ↓		
3/28/81	®	59	1	5 Out Of Season	— ↓		
6/19/82	®	2¹	16	6 Keep The Fire Burnin'	7	Good Trouble ....Epic 38100	
7/10/82	®	19	10	7 Stillness Of The Night	— ↓		
8/7/82	®	51	2	8 Good Trouble	— ↓		
8/14/82	®	34	3	9 The Key	— ↓		
10/27/84	®	5	13	10 I Do'wanna Know	29	Wheels Are Turnin' ....Epic 39593	

Billboard				ARTIST	R=Mainstream Rock	Hot		
Debut	Cht	Peak	Wks	Track Title	M=Modern Rock	Pos	Album Title	Album Label & Number

REO SPEEDWAGON — cont'd

12/8/84+	R	5	17	11 Can't Fight This Feeling....................................		❶³	↓	
4/13/85	R	17	8	12 One Lonely Night...		19	↓	
1/31/87	R	5	11	13 That Ain't Love...		16	Life As We Know It.......................................Epic 40444	
4/18/87	R	28	8	14 Variety Tonight..		60	↓	
8/11/90	R	6	9	15 Live It Up		—	The Earth, A Small Man, His Dog And A Chicken......................................Epic 45246	
10/13/90	R	31	5	16 Love Is A Rock..		65	↓	

REPLACEMENTS, The   **Ⓜ All-Time: #91**

Alternative-rock band from Minneapolis, Minnesota: Paul Westerberg (vocals, guitar, piano), Slim Dunlap (guitar), Tommy Stinson (bass) and Chris Mars (drums). Steve Foley replaced Mars in early 1990.

11/26/88+	M	11	8	1 Cruella De Ville	—	VA: Stay Awake: Various Interpretations Of Music From Vintage Disney Films ....A&M 3918
2/4/89	R	❶³	15	2 I'll Be You	51	Don't Tell A Soul ....Sire 25831
2/4/89	M	❶¹	14			
6/10/89	M	28	1	3 Back To Back	—	↓
5/20/89	R	43	5			
8/19/89	M	22	4	4 Achin' To Be	—	↓
8/5/89	R	37	5			
9/29/90	M	❶⁴	10	5 Merry Go Round	—	All Shook Down ....Sire 26298
12/15/90+	M	15	7	6 Someone Take The Wheel	—	↓
1/26/91	M	4	10	7 When It Began	—	↓

REPUBLICA

Rock band from London, England: Samantha "Saffron" Sprackling (vocals), Johnny Male (guitar), Tim Dorney (keyboards), Andy Todd (keyboards) and Dave Barbarossa (drums).

7/27/96	M	7	21	1 Ready To Go	56	Republica.......................................Deconstruction 66899
2/1/97	M	39	1	2 Drop Dead Gorgeous	93	↓

REVEILLE

Rock band from Harvard, Massachusetts: Drew Simollardes (vocals), Steve Miloszewski (guitar), Greg Sullivan (guitar), Carl Randolph (bass) and Justin Wilson (drums).

3/16/02	R	28	9	Inside Out (Can You Feel Me Now)............................	—	Bleed The Sky ....Elektra 62770

REVELATION THEORY

Rock band formed in Massachusetts: Rich Luzzi (vocals), Julien Jorgensen (guitar), Matt McCluskey (bass) and Dave Agoglia (drums).

12/10/05+	R	27	19	Slowburn	—	Truth Is Currency ....Century Media 90030

REVENGE

Rock trio from Manchester, England: Peter Hook (vocals, bass; New Order), Dave Hicks (guitar) and Chris Jones (keyboards).

6/2/90	M	8	11	Pineapple Face	—	One True Passion ....Capitol 94053

REVEREND HORTON HEAT

Rock trio from Corpus Christi, Texas: Jim "Reverend" Horton Heath (vocals, guitar), Jimbo Wallace (bass) and Scott Churilla (drums).

10/8/94	M	40	1	One Time For Me	—	Liquor In The Front................................Sub Pop 92364

REVIS

Rock band from Carbondale, Illinois: Justin Holman (vocals), Robert Davis (guitar), Nathaniel Cox (guitars), Bob Thiemann (bass) and David Piribauer (drums).

3/8/03	R	8	26	1 Caught In The Rain.......................................	—	Places For Breathing..................................Epic 86514
3/22/03	M	20	16			
10/11/03	R	29	10	2 Seven	—	↓

RHYTHM CORPS

Rock band from Detroit, Michigan: Michael Persh (vocals), Greg Apro (guitar), Davey Holmbo (bass) and Richie Lovsin (drums).

6/18/88	R	9	17	Common Ground...	—	Common Ground......................................Pasha 44159

RICHARDS, Keith

Born on 12/18/1943 in Dartford, Kent, England. Lead guitarist of The Rolling Stones. Married model Patti Hansen on 12/18/1983.

10/15/88	R	3²	9	1 Take It So Hard	—	Talk Is Cheap...Virgin 90973
11/19/88+	R	18	13	2 You Don't Move Me	—	↓
2/25/89	R	47	4	3 Struggle	—	↓
10/31/92+	R	3¹	18	4 Wicked As It Seems	—	Main Offender ....Virgin 86499
1/30/93	R	17	8	5 Eileen	—	↓

Billboard				ARTIST		Hot		
Debut	Cht	Peak	Wks	Track Title	®=Mainstream Rock ⓜ=Modern Rock	Pos	Album Title	Album Label & Number

RICHIE, Lionel
Born on 6/20/1949 in Tuskegee, Alabama. R&B singer/songwriter/pianist. Former lead singer of the Commodores. His adopted daughter, Nicole Richie, starred with Paris Hilton on the reality TV series *The Simple Life*.

2/18/84	®	49	1	Running With The Night		7	*Can't Slow Down*	Motown 6059

RIDDLIN' KIDS
Punk-rock band from Austin, Texas: Clint Baker (vocals, guitar), Dustin Stroud (guitar), Mark Johnson (bass) and Dave Keel (drums).

6/29/02	ⓜ	35	6	I Feel Fine		—	*Hurry Up And Wait*	Aware 85118

RIDE
Rock band formed in Oxford, England: Mark Gardener (vocals), Andrew Bell (guitar), Steve Queralt (bass) and Loz Colbert (drums).

2/9/91	ⓜ	24	5	1 Taste		—	*Nowhere*	Sire 26462
3/14/92	ⓜ	20	7	2 Leave Them All Behind		—	*Going Blank Again*	Sire 26836
5/16/92	ⓜ	12	8	3 Twisterella		—	↓	

RIDGWAY, Stan
Born on 4/5/1954 in Los Angeles, California. Lead singer of **Wall Of Voodoo** from 1977-83.

5/13/89	ⓜ	8	9	1 Goin' Southbound		—	*Mosquitos*	Geffen 24216
8/12/89	ⓜ	13	3	2 Calling Out To Carol		—	↓	
6/22/91	ⓜ	13	6	3 I Wanna Be A Boss		—	*Partyball*	Geffen 24385

RIGHT SAID FRED (R*S*F)
Pop-dance-novelty trio from England: brothers Richard Fairbrass (vocals) and Fred Fairbrass (guitar), with Rob Manzoli (guitar).

1/11/92	ⓜ	28	2	I'm Too Sexy		❶³	*Up*	Charisma 92107

RINOCEROSE
Experimental-rock duo from France: Jean-Philippe Freu and Patrice Carrie.

5/27/06	ⓜ	40	1	Cubicle		—	*Schizophonia*	V2 34512

RIOT
Hard-rock band formed in New York: Rhett Forrester (vocals), Mark Reale (guitar), Rick Ventura (guitar), Kip Leming (bass) and Sandy Slavin (drums). Forrester was shot to death on 1/22/1994 (age 37).

9/25/82	®	35	3	1 Showdown		—	*Restless Breed*	Elektra 60134
12/17/83	®	44	4	2 Born In America		—	*Born In America*	Quality 1008

RISE AGAINST
Punk-rock band from Chicago, Illinois: Tim McLlrath (vocals, guitar), Chris Chasse (guitar), Joe Principe (bass) and Brandon Barnes (drums).

1/1/05	ⓜ	37	2	1 Give It All		—	*Siren Song Of The Counter Culture*	Geffen 002967
5/28/05	ⓜ	12	25	2 Swing Life Away		117	↓	
12/24/05+	ⓜ	33	9	3 Life Less Frightening		—	↓	
6/24/06	ⓜ	13	20	4 Ready To Fall		—	*The Sufferer & The Witness*	Geffen 006976
12/16/06+	ⓜ	7	25	5 Prayer Of The Refugee		—	↓	
7/14/07+	ⓜ	6	38↑	6 The Good Left Undone		—	↓	

RIVERDOGS
Rock band formed in Los Angeles, California: Rob Lamothe (vocals), Vivian Campbell (guitar), Nick Brophy (bass) and Marc Danzeisen (drums). Campbell, formerly with **Dio** and **Whitesnake**, later joined **Def Leppard**.

6/16/90	®	26	9	1 Toy Soldier		—	*Riverdogs*	Epic/Associated 46021
9/22/90	®	50	1	2 I Believe		—	↓	

RIVERSIDE
Pop-rock band from Philadelphia, Pennsylvania: brothers Keith Kochan (vocals, guitar) and Glenn Kochan (bass, vocals), with Ken Dai (guitar) and John Liney (drums).

10/31/92	ⓜ	26	6	Waterfall		—	*One*	Sire 45012

ROADRUNNER UNITED
Hard-rock project which unites over 50 artists from the Roadrunner record label.

11/12/05	®	40	2	The End		—	*The All-Star Session*	Roadrunner 618157

ROBERTSON, Robbie
Born Jaime Robbie Robertson on 7/5/1944 in Toronto, Ontario, Canada. Rock singer/songwriter/guitarist. Member of The Band.

10/17/87	®	2¹	15	1 Showdown At Big Sky		—	*Robbie Robertson*	Geffen 24160
				BoDeans (backing vocals)				
11/7/87+	®	7	15	2 Sweet Fire Of Love		—	↓	
				U2 (backing band)				
2/13/88	®	21	7	3 American Roulette		—	↓	
				BoDeans and **Maria McKee** (backing vocals)				

Billboard				ARTIST	R=Mainstream Rock	Hot	Album Title	Album Label & Number
Debut	Cht	Peak	Wks	Track Title	M=Modern Rock	Pos		

ROBERTSON, Robbie — cont'd

4/23/88	R	24	8	4 Somewhere Down The Crazy River	—	↓		
10/5/91	R	15	10	5 What About Now..............................	—	*Storyville* ....Geffen 24303		
10/19/91	M	28	5					
2/8/92	R	32	5	6 Go Back To Your Woods	—	↓		
				Bruce Hornsby (piano, backing vocal)				

ROB RULE
Rock band formed in Los Angeles, California: Edward Anisko (vocals), David King (guitar), Robbie Allen (guitar, piano), Steven Ossana (bass) and James Bradley (drums).

5/28/94	R	28	8	She Gets Too High	—	*Rob Rule*...................................Mercury 522119		

ROCK AND HYDE
Pop-rock duo from Vancouver, British Columbia, Canada: Paul Hyde (vocals) and Bob Rock (guitar, keyboards). Both formerly with **Paul Hyde & The Payolas**.

4/11/87	R	6	10	Dirty Water	61	*Under The Volcano* ....Capitol 12569		

ROCK CITY ANGELS
Rock band from Memphis, Tennessee: Bobby Durango (vocals), Mike Barnes (guitar), Doug Banx (guitar), Andy Panik (bass) and Jackie Jukes (drums).

10/22/88	R	49	1	Deep Inside My Heart	—	*Young Man's Blues* ....Geffen 24193		

ROCKETS, The
Rock band from Detroit, Michigan: David Gilbert (vocals), Jim McCarty (guitar), Dennis Robbins (guitar), Donnie Backus (keyboards), Bobby Neil Haralson (bass) and John Badanjek (drums). McCarty and Badanjek were members of Mitch Ryder & The Detroit Wheels. Gilbert died of cancer on 8/1/2001 (age 49). Also see **Classic Rock Tracks** section.

8/22/81	R	42	3	I Can't Get Satisfied............................	—	*Back Talk* ....Elektra 351		

ROCK KILLS KID
Alternative-rock band from Los Angeles, California: Jeff Tucker (vocals, guitar), Sean Stopnik (guitar), Reed Calhoun (keyboards), Shawn Dailey (bass) and Mike Balboa (drums).

4/8/06	M	12	18	Paralyzed	—	*Are You Nervous?* ....Reprise 44236		

ROCKPILE
Pop-rock band formed in London, England: **Dave Edmunds** (vocals, guitar), **Nick Lowe** (vocals, bass), Billy Bremner (guitar) and Terry Williams (drums).

4/18/81	R	8	8	Little Sister .... [L]	—	*VA: Concerts For The People Of Kampuchea*......................Atlantic 7005		
				ROCKPILE with Robert Plant #5 Pop hit for Elvis Presley in 1961				

ROCKWELL
Born Kennedy Gordy on 3/15/1964 in Detroit, Michigan. R&B singer. Son of Motown chairman Berry Gordy.

2/25/84	R	31	5	Somebody's Watching Me	2[3]	*Somebody's Watching Me*.............Motown 6052		
				Michael Jackson (backing vocal)				

RODGERS, Paul
Born on 12/17/1949 in Middlesbrough, Cleveland, England. Lead singer of **Free** (1969-73), **Bad Company** (1974-82), **The Firm** (1984-86) and **The Law** (1991). Joined **Queen** for a 2005 album and concert tour.

11/26/83+	R	15	10	1 Cut Loose................................	102	*Cut Loose* ....Atlantic 80121		
4/24/93	R	6	10	2 The Hunter	—	*Muddy Water Blues - A Tribute To Muddy Waters* ....Victory 480013		
				Slash (of Guns N' Roses; lead guitar)				
7/19/97	R	15	14	3 Soul Of Love	—	*Now*.....................................Velvel 79790		
6/24/00	R	33	5	4 Drifters..................................	—	*Electric* ....CMC International 86294		

ROGUE WAVE
Alternative-rock band from Oakland, California: Zach Schwartz (vocals, guitar), Gram LeBron (guitar), Patrick Abernathy (bass) and Pat Spurgeon (drums).

12/22/07+	M	29	12	Lake Michigan................................	—	*Asleep At Heaven's Gate* ....Brushfire 009805		

ROLLING STONES, The

R 1980s: #6 / 1990s: #18 / All-Time: #8

Blues-influenced rock band formed in London, England: **Mick Jagger** (vocals; born on 7/26/1943), Brian Jones (guitar; born on 2/28/1942; drowned on 7/3/1969, age 27), **Keith Richards** (guitar; born on 12/18/1943), Bill Wyman (bass; born on 10/24/1936) and Charlie Watts (drums; born on 6/2/1941). Band took name from a Muddy Waters song. Promoted as the bad boys in contrast to **The Beatles**. Mick Taylor (born on 1/17/1964) replaced Jones in 1969. **Ronnie Wood** (born on 6/1/1947) replaced Taylor in 1975. Movie *Gimme Shelter* is a documentary of the group's performance at the 1969 Altamont concert. Wyman and Watts also formed **Willie And The Poor Boys**. Wyman left in late 1992. Bassist Darryl Jones (born on 12/11/1961; billed as a "side musician") joined in 1994. Considered by many as the world's all-time greatest rock and roll band. Also see **Classic Rock Tracks** section.

AWARDS: R&R Hall of Fame: 1989 ★ Grammy: Lifetime Achievement Award 1986

TOP HITS: 1)Start Me Up 2)Rock And A Hard Place 3)Mixed Emotions 4)Highwire 5)Almost Hear You Sigh

Debut		Peak	Wks		Track Title	Hot Pos	Album Title	Album Label & Number
4/18/81	R	26	4	1	If I Was A Dancer (Dance Pt. 2)	—	*Sucking In The Seventies*	Rolling Stones 16028
8/22/81	R	❶¹³	32	2	**Start Me Up**	2³	*Tattoo You*	Rolling Stones 16052
9/26/81	R	2³	17	3	**Hang Fire**	20	↓	
10/10/81	R	5	16	4	**Little T & A**	—	↓	
11/28/81+	R	8	14	5	**Waiting On A Friend**	13	↓	
6/12/82	R	5	12	6	**Going To A Go-Go** [L]	25	*"Still Life" (American Concert 1981)*	Rolling Stones 39113
					#11 Pop hit for The Miracles in 1966			
11/12/83	R	2¹	14	7	**Undercover Of The Night**	9	*Undercover*	Rolling Stones 90120
11/19/83+	R	4	19	8	**She Was Hot**	44	↓	
11/19/83	R	14	12	9	**Too Tough**	—	↓	
12/17/83	R	38	11	10	**Too Much Blood**	—	↓	
3/3/84	R	50	2	11	**Think I'm Going Mad**	—	*(single only)*	Rolling Stones 99788
3/15/86	R	2³	10	12	**Harlem Shuffle**	5	*Dirty Work*	Rolling Stones 40250
					#44 Pop hit for Bob & Earl in 1964			
4/5/86	R	3⁵	16	13	**One Hit (To The Body)**	28	↓	
4/12/86	R	10	13	14	**Winning Ugly**	—	↓	
9/2/89	R	❶⁵	9	15	**Mixed Emotions**	5	*Steel Wheels*	Rolling Stones 45333
9/16/89	M	22	5					
9/9/89	R	❶⁵	19	16	**Rock And A Hard Place**	23	↓	
9/9/89	R	14	10	17	**Sad Sad Sad**	—	↓	
9/23/89+	R	8	15	18	**Terrifying**	—	↓	
1/20/90	R	❶¹	13	19	**Almost Hear You Sigh**	50	↓	
3/9/91	R	❶³	11	20	**Highwire**	57	*Flashpoint*	Rolling Stones 47456
3/23/91	M	28	1					
5/25/91	R	40	3	21	**Sex Drive**	—	↓	
7/9/94	R	2⁵	17	22	**Love Is Strong**	91	*Voodoo Lounge*	Virgin 39782
7/23/94	R	2¹	19	23	**You Got Me Rocking**	113	↓	
10/29/94	R	14	14	24	**Out Of Tears**	60	↓	
1/7/95	R	30	8	25	**Sparks Will Fly**	—	↓	
4/1/95	R	20	9	26	**I Go Wild**	—	↓	
11/18/95	R	16	8	27	**Like A Rolling Stone**	109	*Stripped*	Virgin 41040
					#2 Pop hit for **Bob Dylan** in 1965			
9/20/97	R	3⁶	16	28	**Anybody Seen My Baby?**	—	*Bridges To Babylon*	Virgin 44712
11/22/97+	R	13	18	29	**Saint Of Me**	94	↓	
11/22/97	R	14	13	30	**Flip The Switch**	—	↓	
11/28/98	R	29	8	31	**Gimme Shelter** [L]	—	*No Security*	Virgin 46740
					first recorded on their 1969 album *Let It Bleed*			
9/14/02	R	21	16	32	**Don't Stop**	—	*Forty Licks*	Abkco 13378
8/13/05	R	25	15	33	**Rough Justice**	—	*A Bigger Bang*	Virgin 30067
11/19/05	R	34	6	34	**Oh No, Not You Again**	—	↓	

ROLLINS BAND

Born Henry Garfield on 2/13/1961 in Washington DC. Hard-rock singer/poet/actor. Acted in several movies. His band: Chris Haskett (guitar), Melvin Gibbs (bass) and Sim Cain (drums).

3/28/92	M	25	4	1	**Low Self Opinion**	—	*The End Of Silence*	Imago 21006
5/7/94	M	26	4	2	**Liar**	109	*Weight*	Imago 21034
6/25/94	R	40	1					

ROMANTICS, The

Pop-rock band from Detroit, Michigan: Wally Palmar (vocals, guitar), Coz Canler (guitar), Mike Skill (bass) and Jimmy Marinos (drums). David Petratos replaced Marinos in early 1985. Also see **Classic Rock Tracks** section.

10/15/83	R	2³	17	1	**Talking In Your Sleep**	3³	*In Heat*	Nemperor 38880
10/22/83	R	49	5	2	**Rock You Up**	—	↓	
3/31/84	R	22	6	3	**One In A Million**	37	↓	
9/21/85	R	44	3	4	**Test Of Time**	71	*Rhythm Romance*	Nemperor 40106

ROMEO VOID

Pop-rock band from San Francisco, California: Debora Iyall (vocals), Peter Woods (guitar), Ben Bossi (sax), Frank Zincavage (bass) and Aaron Smith (drums).

10/16/82	®	27	7	1 Never Say Never		—	Benefactor	Columbia 38182
8/11/84	®	17	12	2 A Girl In Trouble (Is A Temporary Thing)		35	Instincts	Columbia 39155

RONSON, Mick

Born on 5/26/1946 in Hull, Yorkshire, England. Died of cancer on 4/29/1993 (age 46). Rock singer/guitarist. Member of **David Bowie**'s band from 1969-73 and Mott The Hoople in late 1974.

10/7/89	®	24	7	American Music IAN HUNTER & MICK RONSON		—	Y U I ORTA	Mercury 838973

RONSTADT, Linda

Born on 7/15/1946 in Tucson, Arizona. Pop-rock-country singer. Also see **Classic Rock Tracks** section.

10/16/82	®	34	7	Get Closer		29	Get Closer	Asylum 60185

ROSSDALE, Gavin

Born on 10/30/1967 in London, England. Lead singer of **Bush**. Married **Gwen Stefani** (of **No Doubt**) on 9/14/2002.

8/24/02	ⓜ	20	7	Adrenaline		—	St: XXX	Universal 156259
8/31/02	®	24	7					

ROSSINGTON COLLINS BAND

Southern-rock band formed in Jacksonville, Florida: Dale Krantz (vocals), Gary Rossington, Allen Collins and Barry Harwood (guitars), Billy Powell (keyboards), Leon Wilkeson (bass) and Derek Hess (drums). Rossington, Collins, Powell and Wilkeson were members of **Lynyrd Skynyrd**. Disbanded in 1982. Rossington and wife Dale, Jay Johnson (guitar), Ronnie Eades (sax), Tim Sharpton (keyboards), Tim Lindsey (bass) and Mitch Rigel (drums) recorded as **The Rossington Band** in 1988. Collins died of pneumonia on 1/23/1990 (age 37). Wilkeson died on 7/27/2001 (age 49).

11/7/81	®	50	3	1 Gotta Get It Straight		—	This Is The Way	MCA 5207
5/28/88	®	9	11	2 Welcome Me Home THE ROSSINGTON BAND		—	Love Your Man	MCA 42166

ROTH, David Lee   ® All-Time: #83

Born on 10/10/1954 in Bloomington, Indiana; raised in Pasadena, California. Lead singer of **Van Halen** from 1973-1985 (with brief reunions in 1996, 2000 and 2007). Began hosting own short-lived syndicated morning radio show in January 2006. Nicknamed "Diamond Dave."

TOP HITS: 1)Just Like Paradise 2)Damn Good 3)A Lil' Ain't Enough

1/19/85	®	3[1]	10	1 California Girls #3 Pop hit for The Beach Boys in 1965		3[1]	Crazy From The Heat	Warner 25222
2/16/85	®	14	9	2 Easy Street #83 Pop hit for the Edgar Winter Group in 1974		—	↓	
4/6/85	®	25	7	3 Just A Gigolo/I Ain't Got Nobody #1 Pop hit for Ted Lewis in 1931/#3 Pop hit for Marion Harris in 1921		12	↓	
7/5/86	®	10	9	4 Yankee Rose		16	Eat 'Em And Smile	Warner 25470
7/19/86	®	10	11	5 Tobacco Road #14 Pop hit for the Nashville Teens in 1964		—	↓	
8/30/86	®	12	10	6 Goin' Crazy!		66	↓	
1/16/88	®	❶[4]	10	7 Just Like Paradise		6	Skyscraper	Warner 25671
2/6/88	®	5	16	8 Stand Up		64	↓	
2/6/88	®	45	7	9 Knucklebones		—	↓	
2/13/88	®	2[1]	12	10 Damn Good		—	↓	
1/19/91	®	3[3]	10	11 A Lil' Ain't Enough		—	A Little Ain't Enough	Warner 26477
3/9/91	®	6	14	12 Sensible Shoes		—	↓	
6/15/91	®	39	5	13 Tell The Truth		—	↓	
3/5/94	®	12	8	14 She's My Machine		—	Your Filthy Little Mouth	Reprise 45391
4/25/98	®	11	15	15 Slam Dunk DLR BAND		—	DLR Band	Wawazat 1217

ROTHBERG, Patti

Born on 5/4/1972 in Scarsdale, New York. Female singer/songwriter/guitarist/pianist.

5/25/96	ⓜ	25	16	Inside		71[A]	Between The 1 And The 9	EMI 36834

ROXY BLUE

Hard-rock band from Memphis, Tennessee: Todd Poole (vocals), Sid Fletcher (guitar), Josh Weil (bass) and Scott Trammell (drums).

8/15/92	®	38	1	Luv On Me		—	Want Some?	Geffen 24464

ROXY MUSIC

Art-rock band formed in London, England: **Bryan Ferry** (vocals, keyboards), Phil Manzanera (guitar), Andy MacKay (horns) and Paul Thompson (drums). Also see **Classic Rock Tracks** section.

Debut	Cht	Peak	Wks	Track Title	Hot Pos	Album Title	Album Label & Number
7/3/82	®	58	1	1 More Than This	102	Avalon	Warner 23686
7/24/82	®	59	5	2 Avalon	—	↓	
5/21/83	®	24	5	3 Like A Hurricane [L]	—	Musique/The High Road	Warner 23808

recorded at the Apollo Theatre in Glasgow, Scotland; first recorded by **Neil Young** in 1977

ROYAL CRESCENT MOB

Pop-rock band from Columbus, Ohio: David Ellison (vocals), Brian "B" Emch (guitar), Harold Chichester (bass) and Carlton Smith (drums).

6/17/89	ⓜ	27	3	Hungry	—	Spin The World	Sire 25914

ROYAL JELLY

Rock band from Los Angeles, California: John Edwards (vocals), Dan Steigerwald (guitar), David Seaton (bass) and Jeff Klaven (drums).

11/5/94	®	29	7	Ceiling	—	Royal Jelly	Island 524015

RTZ

Rock band formed in Boston, Massachusetts: Brad Delp (vocals), Barry Goudreau (guitar), Brian Maes (keyboards), Tim Archibald (bass) and David Stefanelli (drums). Delp and Goudreau were members of **Boston**. Goudreau was also with **Orion The Hunter**. Delp committed suicide on 3/9/2007 (age 55). RTZ: Return To Zero.

7/27/91	®	5	10	1 Face The Music	49	Return To Zero	Giant 24422
10/5/91	®	19	13	2 There's Another Side	—	↓	
2/8/92	®	38	7	3 Until Your Love Comes Back Around	26	↓	

RUBY

Pop-rock duo: vocalist Lesley Rankine (from England) and producer Mark Walk (from Seattle).

2/10/96	ⓜ	22	10	Tiny Meat	—	Salt Peter	Creation 67458

RUFFIN, David — see HALL & OATES

RUFFNER, Mason

Born in Fort Worth, Texas. Rock singer/songwriter/guitarist.

5/16/87	®	11	10	1 Gypsy Blood	—	Gypsy Blood	CBS Associated 40601
8/8/87	®	42	3	2 Dancin' On Top Of The World	—	↓	

above 2 produced by **Dave Edmunds**

RUNDGREN, Todd

Born on 6/22/1948 in Upper Darby, Pennsylvania. Pop-rock singer/songwriter/multi-instrumentalist. Leader of Nazz and **Utopia**. Also see **Classic Rock Tracks** section.

3/21/81	®	18	2	1 Time Heals	107	Healing	Bearsville 3522
3/21/81	®	48	1	2 Compassion	—	↓	
5/28/83	®	29	3	3 Bang The Drum All Day	63	The Ever Popular Tortured Artist Effect	Bearsville 23732
5/27/89	®	15	10	4 The Want Of A Nail	—	Nearly Human	Warner 25881

RUSH

® 1980s: #12 / 1990s: #11 / All-Time: #6

Hard-rock trio formed in Toronto, Ontario, Canada: **Geddy Lee** (vocals, bass; born on 7/29/1953), Alex Lifeson (guitar; born on 8/27/1953) and Neil Peart (drums; born on 9/12/1952). Peart writes most of the group's lyrics. Also see **Bob & Doug McKenzie**, **Victor** and **Classic Rock Tracks** section.

TOP HITS: 1)Dreamline 2)Stick It Out 3)Test For Echo 4)New World Man 5)Show Don't Tell

3/21/81	®	4	15	1 Limelight	55	Moving Pictures	Mercury 4013
3/21/81	®	8	21	2 Tom Sawyer	44	↓	
				also see #4 below			
11/21/81+	®	21	15	3 Closer To The Heart [L]	69	Exit...Stage Left	Mercury 7001
				live version of their #76 Pop hit in 1977			
12/12/81+	®	42	6	4 Tom Sawyer [L-R]	—	↓	
				live version of #2 above			
9/11/82	®	❶²	21	5 New World Man	21	Signals	Mercury 4063
9/25/82	®	8	29	6 Subdivisions	105	↓	
9/25/82	®	19	7	7 The Analog Kid	—	↓	
4/28/84	®	3¹	14	8 Distant Early Warning	—	Grace Under Pressure	Mercury 818476
5/5/84	®	23	13	9 Body Electric	105	↓	
5/5/84	®	39	3	10 Between The Wheels	—	↓	
5/12/84	®	21	11	11 Red Sector A	—	↓	
10/12/85	®	4	14	12 The Big Money	45	Power Windows	Mercury 826098

Billboard				ARTIST	R=Mainstream Rock M=Modern Rock	Hot Pos	Album Title	Album Label & Number
Debut	Cht	Peak	Wks	Track Title				
				RUSH — cont'd				
11/16/85	R	30	13	13 Territories		—	↓	
11/23/85+	R	10	14	14 Manhattan Project		—	↓	
3/8/86	R	21	6	15 Mystic Rhythms		—	↓	
9/5/87	R	3¹	9	16 Force Ten		—	Hold Your Fire ....Mercury 832464	
9/19/87	R	3²	14	17 Time Stand Still		—	↓	
12/12/87+	R	16	10	18 Lock And Key		—	↓	
1/14/89	R	6	8	19 Marathon	[L]	—	A Show Of Hands ....Mercury 836346	
3/11/89	R	33	5	20 Mission	[L]	—	↓	
11/18/89+	R	❶¹	12	21 Show Don't Tell		—	Presto ....Atlantic 82040	
1/6/90	R	14	12	22 Presto		—	↓	
3/3/90	R	15	11	23 The Pass		—	↓	
5/19/90	R	37	6	24 Superconductor		—	↓	
9/7/91	R	❶⁴	20	25 Dreamline		—	Roll The Bones ....Atlantic 82293	
10/19/91+	R	9	22	26 Roll The Bones		—	↓	
11/30/91+	R	2¹	27	27 Ghost Of A Chance		—	↓	
3/28/92	R	13	10	28 Bravado		—	↓	
10/23/93	R	❶⁴	12	29 Stick It Out		—	Counterparts ....Atlantic 82528	
11/20/93+	R	2¹	22	30 Cold Fire		—	↓	
2/26/94	R	9	11	31 Nobody's Hero		—	↓	
5/21/94	R	35	3	32 Animate		—	↓	
9/7/96	R	❶³	13	33 Test For Echo		—	Test For Echo ....Atlantic 82925	
11/16/96+	R	6	16	34 Half The World		—	↓	
3/22/97	R	20	8	35 Driven		—	↓	
11/7/98	R	27	8	36 The Spirit Of Radio	[L]		Different Stages - Live ....Atlantic 83122	
				live version of their #51 Pop hit in 1980				
4/20/02	R	10	13	37 One Little Victory		—	Vapor Trails ....Anthem 83531	
7/6/02	R	25	9	38 Secret Touch		—	↓	
6/19/04	R	30	10	39 Summertime Blues		—	Feedback ....Anthem 83728	
				#8 Hot 100 hit for Eddie Cochran in 1958				
3/31/07	R	22	20	40 Far Cry		—	Snakes & Arrows ....Anthem 135484	
				RUSSELL, Leon Born Claude Russell Bridges on 4/2/1942 in Lawton, Oklahoma. Rock singer/songwriter/multi-instrumentalist. Prolific session musician. Also see **Classic Rock Tracks** section.				
5/16/92	R	47	1	No Man's Land		—	Anything Can Happen ....Virgin 91821	
				RUST Rock band from San Diego, California: John Brinton (vocals), Michael Suzick (guitar), Tim Blankenship (bass) and Pat Hogan (drums).				
3/2/96	R	33	5	Not Today		—	Bar Chord Ritual ....Atlantic 82822	
				RUSTY Rock band from Canada: Ken MacNeil (vocals), Scott McCullough (guitar), Jim Moore (bass) and Mitch Perkins (drums).				
8/5/95	M	26	6	Wake Me		—	Fluke ....Tag 92573	
				RUTHERFORD, Mike Born on 10/2/1950 in Guildford, Surrey, England. Bassist of **Genesis** and leader of **Mike + The Mechanics**.				
10/2/82	R	37	2	Maxine		—	Acting Very Strange ....Atlantic 80015	
				RUTH RUTH Punk-rock trio from New York: Chris Kennedy (vocals, bass), Mike Lustig (guitar) and Dave Snyder (drums).				
12/2/95+	R	24	11	Uninvited		—	Laughing Gallery ....Ventrue 43039	
10/21/95	M	24	8					

S

				SAGA Rock band formed in Toronto, Ontario, Canada: Michael Sadler (vocals), brothers Ian Crichton (guitar) and Jim Crichton (bass), Jim Gilmour (keyboards) and Steve Negus (drums).				
10/9/82	R	3²	26	1 On The Loose	26	Worlds Apart ....Portrait 38246	
12/25/82+	R	24	21	2 Wind Him Up	64	↓	
11/5/83	R	19	11	3 The Flyer	79	Heads Or Tales ....Portrait 38999	
8/31/85	R	24	8	4 What Do I Know?	—	Behaviour ....Portrait 40145	

SAIGON KICK
Hard-rock band formed in Miami, Florida: Matt Kramer (vocals), Jason Bieler (guitar), Tom DeFile (bass) and Phil Varone (drums).

Debut	Cht	Peak	Wks	Track Title	Hot Pos	Album Title	Album Label & Number
8/8/92	®	8	20	1 Love Is On The Way	12		
11/28/92+	®	15	14	2 All I Want	111	*The Lizard*	Third Stone 92158
					↓		

ST. ETIENNE
Dance trio formed in London, England: Moira Lambert (vocals), Bob Stanley and Peter Wiggs.

1/18/92	ⓜ	11	9	Only Love Can Break Your Heart	97	*Foxbase Alpha*	Warner 26793
				#33 Pop hit for **Neil Young** in 1970			

SAINTS, The
Punk-rock trio from Brisbane, Australia: Chris Bailey (vocals, guitar), Kym Bradshaw (bass) and Ivor Hay (drums).

1/7/89	ⓜ	11	7	1 Grain Of Sand	—	*Prodigal Son*	TVT 2121
2/4/89	ⓜ	19	5	2 Music Goes Round My Head	—	↓	

SALIVA
® **2000s: #16 / All-Time: #91**
Hard-rock band from Memphis, Tennessee: **Josey Scott** (vocals; born on 5/3/1972), Wayne Swinny (guitar), Chris D'abaldo (guitar), Dave Novotny (bass) and Paul Crosby (drums). Jonathan Montoya replaced D'abaldo in 2005.

TOP HITS: 1)Always 2)Ladies And Gentlemen 3)Your Disease

3/10/01	®	3[1]	32	1 Your Disease	116	*Every Six Seconds*	Island 542959
3/17/01	ⓜ	7	26				
8/18/01	®	15	23	2 Click Click Boom		↓	
9/1/01	ⓜ	25	20				
1/12/02	®	31	8	3 After Me	—	↓	
10/5/02+	ⓜ	❶[1]	27	4 Always	51	*Back Into Your System*	Island 063153
10/5/02+		2[12]	35				
3/15/03	®	11	17	5 Rest In Pieces	93	↓	
3/22/03	ⓜ	20	14				
7/19/03	®	29	8	6 Raise Up	—	↓	
6/26/04	®	6	21	7 Survival Of The Sickest	—	*Survival Of The Sickest*	Island 002957
7/3/04	ⓜ	22	12				
11/6/04	®	17	15	8 Razor's Edge	—	↓	
11/11/06+	®	2[9]	27	9 Ladies And Gentlemen	101	*Blood Stained Love Story*	Island 008107
1/6/07	ⓜ	25	14				
4/28/07	®	8	20	10 Broken Sunday	—	↓	
9/22/07	®	24	11	11 King Of The Stereo	—	↓	

SALT
Rock trio from Stockholm, Sweden: Nina Ramsby (vocals, guitar), Daniel Ewerman (bass) and Jim Tegman (drums).

2/3/96	ⓜ	21	10	Bluster	—	*Auscultate*	Island 524198

SAMBORA, Richie
Born on 7/11/1959 in Woodbridge, New Jersey. Guitarist of **Bon Jovi**. Married to actress Heather Locklear from 1994-2007.

8/31/91	®	13	10	1 Ballad Of Youth	63	*Stranger In This Town*	Mercury 848895
1/11/92	®	38	3	2 Stranger In This Town	—	↓	
4/4/98	®	39	1	3 Hard Times Come Easy	—	*Undiscovered Soul*	Mercury 536972

SANDLER, Adam
Born on 9/9/1966 in Brooklyn, New York. Actor/comedian. Cast member of TV's *Saturday Night Live* (1990-95). Starred in several movies.

1/6/96+	®	20	5	1 The Chanukah Song [X-C-L]	10[A]	*What The Hell Happened To Me?*	Warner 46151
1/6/96+	ⓜ	25	5				
12/13/97+	®	29	3	2 The Thanksgiving Song [C]	67[A]	*They're All Gonna Laugh At You*	Warner 45393

SANTANA
Born Carlos Santana on 7/20/1947 in Autlan de Navarro, Mexico. Latin-rock guitarist. Various band members over the years include Alex Ligertwood (vocals), Gregg Rolie (keyboards), **Neal Schon** (guitar), David Brown (bass) and Michael Shrieve (drums). Schon and Rolie formed **Journey**. Also see **Classic Rock Tracks** section.

TOP HITS: 1)Winning 2)Put Your Lights On 3)Smooth

4/4/81	®	2[2]	18	1 Winning	17	*Zebop!*	Columbia 37158
				written and first recorded by **Russ Ballard** in 1976			
5/9/81	®	26	12	2 Searchin'	—	↓	
7/4/81	®	45	3	3 Changes	—	↓	
				first recorded by Cat Stevens in 1971			
8/28/82	®	13	27	4 Nowhere To Run	66	*Shango*	Columbia 38122

Billboard				ARTIST	R=Mainstream Rock	Hot		
Debut	Cht	Peak	Wks	Track Title	M=Modern Rock	Pos	Album Title	Album Label & Number

SANTANA — cont'd

8/28/82	R	17	11	5 Hold On		15	↓	
				written and first recorded by Ian Thomas in 1981				
9/18/82	R	34	1	6 Night Hunting Time		—	↓	
2/16/85	R	15	11	7 Say It Again		46	Beyond Appearances .... Columbia 39527	
2/14/87	R	21	9	8 Veracruz		—	Freedom .... Columbia 40272	
7/14/90	R	14	9	9 Peace On Earth...Mother Earth...Third Stone From The Sun		—	Spirits Dancing In The Flesh .... Columbia 46065	
				"Third Stone From The Sun" was first recorded by Jimi Hendrix in 1967				
7/10/99	R	10	26	10 Smooth		❶12	Supernatural .... Arista 19080	
11/13/99	M	24	12	**SANTANA Featuring Rob Thomas**				
9/25/99	R	8	27	11 Put Your Lights On.........................		118	↓	
10/2/99	M	17	21	**SANTANA Featuring Everlast** Grammy: Rock Vocal Duo				
12/17/05	R	37	8	12 Just Feel Better		107	All That I Am .... Arista 59773	
				SANTANA Featuring Steven Tyler				

SAOSIN
Alternative-rock band from Newport Beach, California: Cove Reber (vocals), Beau Burchell (guitar), Justin Shekoski (guitar), Chris Sorenson (bass) and Alex Rodriguez (drums).

| 12/30/06+ | M | 25 | 13 | Voices .... | | — | Saosin .... Capitol 73694 | |

SARAYA
Rock band from New Jersey: Sandi Saraya (vocals), Tony Rey (guitar), Gregg Munier (keyboards), Gary Taylor (bass) and Chuck Bonfante (drums). Rey, Munier and Taylor left in 1990; Tony Bruno (guitar) and Barry Dunaway (bass) joined.

4/1/89	R	9	13	1 Love Has Taken Its Toll		64	Saraya .... Polydor 837764	
7/22/89	R	33	4	2 Get U Ready		—	↓	
10/14/89	R	26	7	3 Back To The Bullet		63	↓	
5/25/91	R	41	5	4 Seducer		—	When The Blackbird Sings... .... Polydor 849087	

SATELLITE PARTY
Alternative-rock band formed in Los Angeles, California: Perry Farrell (vocals), Nuno Bettencourt (guitar; of **Extreme**), Carl Restivo (bass) and Kevin Figueiredo (drums). Farrell was also leader of **Jane's Addiction** and **Porno For Pyros**.

| 4/28/07 | M | 26 | 12 | Wish Upon A Dog Star .... | | — | Ultra Payload .... Columbia 87523 | |

SATRIANI, Joe
Born on 7/15/1956 in Westbury, New York. Rock guitarist. Began playing guitar at age 14; later studied music under guitarist Billy Bauer and pianist Lennie Tristano. Moved to California in 1978 and began teaching guitar classes.

TOP HITS: 1)Summer Song 2)The Crush Of Love 3)Friends

2/13/88	R	22	8	1 Satch Boogie	[I]	—	Surfing With The Alien .... Relativity 8193	
4/9/88	R	37	8	2 Surfing With The Alien	[I]	—	↓	
11/12/88+	R	6	16	3 The Crush Of Love	[I]	—	Dreaming #11.................................. Relativity 8265	
4/22/89	R	17	9	4 One Big Rush	[I]	—	St: Say Anything............................... WTG 45140	
10/28/89	R	17	12	5 Big Bad Moon		—	Flying In A Blue Dream .... Relativity 1015	
2/10/90	R	31	7	6 Back To Shalla-Bal	[I]	—	↓	
4/14/90	R	36	7	7 I Believe		—	↓	
7/25/92	R	5	19	8 Summer Song	[I]	—	The Extremist .... Relativity 1053	
11/14/92	R	12	11	9 Friends	[I]	—	↓	
3/27/93	R	24	10	10 Cryin'	[I]	—	↓	
11/13/93	R	21	11	11 All Alone	[I]	—	Time Machine.................................. Relativity 1177	
11/4/95	R	30	12	12 (You're) My World		—	Joe Satriani.................................... Relativity 1500	
3/14/98	R	28	11	13 Ceremony	[I]	—	Crystal Planet.................................. Epic 68018	

SAVATAGE
Hard-rock band from Florida: Zachary Stevens (vocals), Criss Oliva (guitar), Johnny Lee Middleton (bass) and Steve Wacholz (drums). Oliva died in a car crash on 10/17/1993 (age 30).

| 7/24/93 | R | 26 | 8 | Edge Of Thorns .... | | — | Edge Of Thorns .... Atlantic 82488 | |

SAVE FERRIS
Ska-rock band from California: Monique Powell (vocals), Brian Mashburn (vocals, guitar), Eric Zamora, T-Bone Willy and Jose Castellanos (horns), Bill Uechi (bass) and Marc Harismendy (drums).

| 10/4/97 | M | 26 | 7 | 1 Come On Eileen............................. | | 104 | It Means Everything .... Starpool 68183 | |
| 1/24/98 | M | 32 | 8 | 2 Goodbye .... | | — | ↓ | |

SAVING ABEL
Rock band from Corinth, Mississippi: Jared Weeks (vocals), Jason Null (guitar), Scott Bartlett (guitar), Eric Taylor (bass) and Blake Dixon (drums).

| 2/23/08 | R | 17↑ | 6↑ | Addicted .... | | — | Saving Abel...................................... Virgin 15019 | |

Billboard				ARTIST	®=Mainstream Rock	Hot		
Debut	Cht	Peak	Wks	Track Title	ⓂModern Rock	Pos	Album Title	Album Label & Number

SAY ANYTHING
Alternative-rock band from Los Angeles, California: Max Bemis (vocals), Jake Turner (guitar), Jeff Turner (guitar), Parker Case (keyboards), Alex Kent (bass) and Coby Linder (drums).

9/2/06	Ⓜ	28	16	1 Alive With The Glory Of Love	—	...Is A Real Boy	Doghouse 108
12/8/07+	Ⓜ	29	9	2 Baby Girl, I'm A Blur	—	In Defense Of The Genre	Doghouse 18701

SCANDAL
Rock band from New York: **Patty Smyth** (vocals), Zack Smith (guitar), Keith Mack (guitar), Ivan Elias (bass) and Thommy Price (drums).

12/18/82+	®	5	19	1 Goodbye To You	65	Scandal	Columbia 38194
5/7/83	®	28	4	2 Love's Got A Line On You	59	↓	

SCANDAL FEATURING PATTY SMYTH:

6/23/84	®	❶²	18	3 The Warrior	7	Warrior	Columbia 39173
9/15/84	®	10	14	4 Beat Of A Heart	41	↓	
11/3/84	®	21	9	5 Hands Tied	41	↓	

SCAPEGOAT WAX
Born Martin James in California. Trip-hop singer/songwriter.

7/14/01	Ⓜ	38	3	Aisle 10	—	Okeeblow	Grand Royal 10130

SCHILLING, Peter
Born on 1/28/1956 in Stuttgart, Germany. Pop singer/songwriter.

9/24/83	®	8	19	Major Tom (Coming Home) inspired by **David Bowie**'s "Space Oddity"	14	Error In The System	Elektra 60265

SCHMIT, Timothy B.
Born on 10/30/1947 in Sacramento, California. Singer/songwriter/bassist. Member of **Poco** and the **Eagles**.

10/27/84	®	48	2	1 Playin' It Cool	101	Playin' It Cool	Asylum 60359
9/19/87	®	17	8	2 Boys Night Out	25	Timothy B	MCA 42049

SCHON, Neal
Born on 2/27/1954 in San Mateo, California. Rock singer/guitarist. Member of **Santana**, **Journey** and **Bad English**. Also see **Hagar, Schon, Aaronson & Shrieve**.

2/19/83	®	42	1	No More Lies	—	Here To Stay	Columbia 38428

NEAL SCHON & JAN HAMMER

SCHOOL OF FISH
Pop-rock band from Los Angeles, California: Josh Clayton-Felt (vocals, guitar), Michael Ward (guitar, vocals), Dominic Nardini (bass) and Michael "M.P." Petrak (drums). Clayton-Felt died of cancer on 1/19/2000 (age 32).

4/6/91	Ⓜ	6	8	1 3 Strange Days	—	School Of Fish	Capitol 94557
6/8/91	®	12	21				
2/13/93	Ⓜ	5	11	2 Take Me Anywhere	—	Human Cannonball	Capitol 98930

SCHWARTZ, Eddie
Born on 12/22/1949 in Toronto, Ontario, Canada. Pop-rock singer/songwriter/producer.

2/13/82	®	40	6	No Refuge	—	No Refuge	Atco 141

SCORPIONS
® 1990s: #39 / All-Time: #59

Hard-rock band formed in Hanover, Germany: Klaus Meine (vocals; born on 5/25/1948), Rudolf Schenker (guitar; born on 8/31/1948), Matthias Jabs (guitar; born on 10/25/1955), Francis Buchholz (bass; born on 2/19/1954) and Herman Rarebell (drums; born on 11/18/1949). Ralph Rieckermann replaced Buchholz in 1992. Curt Cress replaced Rarebell in 1995. James Kottak replaced Cress in late 1996. Schenker is the brother of Michael Schenker (of **McAuley Schenker Group**).

TOP HITS: 1)*No One Like You* 2)*Wind Of Change* 3)*Rock You Like A Hurricane*

4/3/82	®	❶¹	18	1 No One Like You	65	Blackout	Mercury 4039
6/19/82	®	47	4	2 Can't Live Without You	—	↓	
3/3/84	®	5	19	3 Rock You Like A Hurricane	25	Love At First Sting	Mercury 814981
4/14/84	®	14	10	4 Big City Nights	—	↓	
6/23/84	®	56	3	5 I'm Leaving You	—	↓	
6/30/84	®	36	11	6 Still Loving You	64	↓	
4/16/88	®	6	12	7 Rhythm Of Love	75	Savage Amusement	Mercury 832963
7/2/88	®	12	12	8 Believe In Love	—	↓	
11/18/89+	®	5	17	9 I Can't Explain #93 Pop hit for **The Who** in 1965	—	Best Of Rockers 'N' Ballads	Mercury 842002
11/3/90	®	8	16	10 Tease Me Please Me	—	Crazy World	Mercury 846908
1/19/91	®	13	12	11 Don't Believe Her	—	↓	
4/6/91	®	2³	21	12 Wind Of Change	4	↓	
8/31/91	®	8	20	13 Send Me An Angel	44	↓	
1/25/92	®	24	8	14 Hit Between The Eyes	—	St: Freejack	Morgan Creek 20008

SCORPIONS — cont'd

Debut	Cht	Peak	Wks	#	Track Title	Pos	Album Title	Label & Number
9/11/93	Ⓡ	10	10	15	Alien Nation	—	*Face The Heat*	Mercury 518258
11/27/93	Ⓡ	15	10	16	Woman	—	↓	
1/29/94	Ⓡ	16	9	17	Under The Same Sun	—	↓	
5/25/96	Ⓡ	19	8	18	Wild Child	—	*Pure Instinct*	Atlantic 82913
7/10/99	Ⓡ	26	11	19	Mysterious	—	*Eye II Eye*	Koch 8052

SCOTT, Josey
Born Joseph Sappington on 5/3/1972 in Memphis, Tennessee. Lead singer of **Saliva**.

Debut	Cht	Peak	Wks		Track Title	Pos	Album Title	Label & Number
5/4/02	Ⓜ	❶³	21		Hero	3²	*St: Spider-Man*	Columbia 86402
5/4/02	Ⓡ	❶²	24		**CHAD KROEGER** Featuring Josey Scott			

SCREAM, The
Rock band formed in Los Angeles, California: John Corabi (vocals), Bruce Bouillet (guitar), John Alderete (bass) and Walt Woodward (drums). Corabi was lead singer of **Mötley Crüe** from 1992-96.

Debut	Cht	Peak	Wks		Track Title	Pos	Album Title	Label & Number
8/31/91	Ⓡ	25	10		Man In The Moon	—	*Let It Scream*	Hollywood 60994

SCREAMIN' CHEETAH WHEELIES, The
Rock band formed in Nashville, Tennessee: Mike Farris (vocals), Rick White (guitar), Bob Watkins (guitar), Steve Burgess (bass) and Terry Thomas (drums).

Debut	Cht	Peak	Wks	#	Track Title	Pos	Album Title	Label & Number
10/23/93	Ⓡ	9	15	1	Shakin' The Blues	—	*The Screamin' Cheetah Wheelies*	Atlantic 82507
2/12/94	Ⓡ	20	9	2	Ride The Tide	—	↓	
5/18/96	Ⓡ	25	9	3	Hello From Venus	—	*Magnolia*	Capricorn 534502
5/3/97	Ⓡ	29	7	4	Magnolia	—	↓	
9/5/98	Ⓡ	18	16	5	Boogie King	—	*Big Wheel*	Capricorn 558715

SCREAMING TREES
Hard-rock band from Ellensburg, Washington: brothers Van Conner (bass) and Gary Lee Conner (guitar), with Mark Lanegan (vocals) and Barrett Martin (drums). Martin was also a member of **Mad Season**.

Debut	Cht	Peak	Wks	#	Track Title	Pos	Album Title	Label & Number
2/23/91	Ⓜ	23	7	1	Bed Of Roses	—	*Uncle Anesthesia*	Epic 46800
9/5/92	Ⓜ	5	19	2	Nearly Lost You	—	*Sweet Oblivion*	Epic 48996
12/12/92+	Ⓡ	12	13					
1/9/93	Ⓜ	28	2	3	Dollar Bill	—	↓	
7/3/93	Ⓡ	40	1					
7/6/96	Ⓡ	9	17	4	All I Know	62ᴬ	*Dust*	Epic 64178
6/29/96	Ⓜ	9	13					

SCREAMING TRIBESMEN, The
Pop-rock band from Brisbane, Australia: Mick Medew (vocals, guitar), Chris "Klondike" Masuak (guitar), Bob Wackley (bass) and Warwick Fraser (drums).

Debut	Cht	Peak	Wks		Track Title	Pos	Album Title	Label & Number
9/17/88	Ⓜ	7	12		I've Got A Feeling	—	*Bones & Flowers*	Rykodisc 10077

SCRUFFY THE CAT
Rock band from Boston, Massachusetts: Charlie Chesterman (vocals), Stephen Fredette (guitar), Burns Stanfield (keyboards), Mac Stanfield (bass) and Randall Gibson (drums).

Debut	Cht	Peak	Wks		Track Title	Pos	Album Title	Label & Number
12/10/88+	Ⓜ	23	6		Moons Of Jupiter	—	*Moons Of Jupiter*	Relativity 8237

SEAL
Born Sealhenry Samuel on 2/19/1963 in Paddington, England (Nigerian/Brazilian parents). Male singer. Married model Heidi Klum on 5/10/2005.

Debut	Cht	Peak	Wks	#	Track Title	Pos	Album Title	Label & Number
6/15/91	Ⓜ	5	13	1	Crazy	7	*Seal*	Sire 26627
12/25/93+	Ⓡ	10	11	2	Manic Depression	—	*VA: Stone Free: A Tribute To Jimi Hendrix*	Reprise 45438
					SEAL & JEFF BECK first recorded by Jimi Hendrix in 1967			
6/11/94	Ⓜ	3¹	17	3	Prayer For The Dying	21	*Seal*	ZTT 45415
8/12/95	Ⓜ	35	2	4	Kiss From A Rose	❶¹	*St: Batman Forever*	Atlantic 82759

SEAWEED
Rock band from Tacoma, Washington: Aaron Stauffer (vocals), Wade Neal (guitar), Clint Werner (guitar), John Atkins (bass) and Bob Bulgrien (drums).

Debut	Cht	Peak	Wks		Track Title	Pos	Album Title	Label & Number
10/14/95	Ⓜ	38	1		Start With	—	*Spanaway*	Hollywood 62009

SEBADOH
Rock trio from Boston, Massachusetts: Lou Barlow (vocals, guitar), Jason Lowenstein (bass) and Bob Fay (drums).

Debut	Cht	Peak	Wks		Track Title	Pos	Album Title	Label & Number
9/7/96	Ⓜ	23	8		Ocean	—	*Harmacy*	Sub Pop 370

Billboard				ARTIST			Hot		
Debut	Cht	Peak	Wks	Track Title	®=Mainstream Rock ⓜ=Modern Rock		Pos	Album Title	Album Label & Number

SECOND COMING
Rock band from Seattle, Washington: Travis John Bracht (vocals, guitar), Dudley Taft (guitar), Yanni Bacolas (bass) and James Bergstrom (drums).

9/19/98	®	16	20	1 Soft	—		
2/20/99	®	16	16	2 Vintage Eyes	—	↓	Second Coming ....Capitol 95894

SEERS, The
Rock band from New York: Spider McCallum (vocals), Leigh Wildman (guitar), Kat Day (harmonica), Jason Kidd (bass) and Age Blackmore (drums).

5/4/91	ⓜ	16	7	Psych Out..	—	Psych Out...Cherry Red 1043

SEETHER   ® 2000s: #12 / All-Time: #68 ★ ⓜ 2000s: #23 / All-Time: #48
Hard-rock band from Pretoria, Gauteng, South Africa: Shaun Morgan (vocals, guitar; born on 12/21/1978), Pat Callahan (guitar), Dale Stewart (bass) and Nick Oshiro (drums). John Humphrey replaced Oshiro in 2003; Oshiro joined Static-X. Callahan left in June 2006.

8/3/02+	®	3⁵	48	1 Fine Again	61	Disclaimer..Wind-Up 13068
8/10/02+	ⓜ	6	38			
3/22/03	®	13	26	2 Driven Under	122	↓
3/22/03	ⓜ	13	22			
9/13/03	®	8	26	3 Gasoline	—	↓
10/4/03	ⓜ	37	5			
5/1/04	ⓜ	4	26	4 Broken	20	Disclaimer II...Wind-Up 13100
4/24/04	®	9	26	SEETHER Featuring Amy Lee		
4/23/05	®	❶⁸	52	5 Remedy	70	Karma And Effect....................................Wind-Up 13115
4/30/05	ⓜ	5	27			
9/24/05	®	8	25	6 Truth	123	↓
10/15/05	ⓜ	25	20			
3/11/06	®	8	22	7 The Gift	—	↓
7/1/06	ⓜ	29	10			
9/8/07	®	❶¹⁴	30↑	8 Fake It	56	Finding Beauty In Negative Spaces........Wind-Up 13127
9/15/07+	ⓜ	❶⁸	29↑			
3/8/08	®	10↑	4↑	9 Rise Above This	—	↓
3/8/08	ⓜ	11↑	4↑			

SEGER, Bob, & The Silver Bullet Band   ® 1980s: #23 / All-Time: #40
Born on 5/6/1945 in Dearborn, Michigan; raised in Detroit, Michigan. Rock singer/songwriter/guitarist. Formed own backing group, The Silver Bullet Band, in 1976: Alto Reed (horns), Robyn Robbins (keyboards), Drew Abbott (guitar), Chris Campbell (bass) and Charlie Martin (drums). Various personnel changes since then. Also see Classic Rock Tracks section.

AWARD: R&R HOF: 2004

TOP HITS: 1)Shakedown 2)Like A Rock 3)Tryin' To Live My Life Without You 4)Even Now 5)American Storm

9/12/81	®	2⁴	19	1 Tryin' To Live My Life Without You .... [L]	5	Nine Tonight ....Capitol 12182
				recorded on 10/6/1980 at Boston Garden; #102 Pop hit for Otis Clay in 1973		
12/25/82	®	29	3	2 House Behind A House..................................	—	The Distance ....Capitol 12254
1/15/83	®	2³	19	3 Even Now	12	↓
1/15/83	®	13	13	4 Roll Me Away	27	↓
1/22/83	®	11	12	5 Boomtown Blues..	—	↓
				Glenn Frey (harmony vocal)		
10/13/84	®	5	16	6 Understanding	17	St: Teachers ....Capitol 12371
3/22/86	®	9	8	7 Fortunate Son .... [L]	—	(single only)..Capitol 5532
				recorded on 3/31/1983 at Cobo Hall in Detroit, Michigan; #14 Pop hit for Creedence Clearwater Revival in 1969		
3/15/86	®	2²	10	8 American Storm...	13	Like A Rock ....Capitol 12398
4/19/86	®	❶²	13	9 Like A Rock	12	↓
5/10/86	®	35	6	10 Tightrope	—	↓
6/14/86	®	9	11	11 The Aftermath	—	↓
8/23/86	®	8	9	12 It's You..	52	↓

Billboard	Cht	Peak	Wks	ARTIST / Track Title	Hot Pos	Album Title	Album Label & Number
Debut				ⓇR=Mainstream Rock ⓂM=Modern Rock			

SEGER, Bob, & The Silver Bullet Band — cont'd

11/29/86	Ⓡ	47	3	13 Miami .... Don Henley and Timothy B. Schmit (backing vocals)	70	↓	
5/23/87	Ⓡ	❶⁴	10	14 Shakedown	❶¹	St: Beverly Hills Cop II ....MCA 6207	
6/10/89	Ⓡ	40	4	15 Blue Monday .... BOB SEGER (above 2) #5 Pop hit for Fats Domino in 1957		St: Road House ....Arista 8576	
8/24/91	Ⓡ	4	8	16 The Real Love	24	The Fire Inside ....Capitol 91134	
9/21/91	Ⓡ	6	14	17 The Fire Inside	—	↓	
11/30/91+	Ⓡ	10	15	18 Take A Chance..	—	↓	
11/4/95	Ⓡ	22	11	19 Lock And Load	—	It's A Mystery ....Capitol 99774	
2/17/96	Ⓡ	29	6	20 Hands In The Air	—	↓	
12/24/05+	Ⓡ	32	14	21 Landing In London (All I Think About Is You) .... 3 DOORS DOWN Featuring Bob Seger	—	Seventeen Days...................................Republic 004018	

SEMBELLO, Michael
Born on 4/17/1954 in Philadelphia, Pennsylvania. Pop singer/guitarist. Prolific studio musician.

| 7/30/83 | Ⓡ | 34 | 8 | Maniac .... | ❶² | St: Flashdance...................................Casablanca 811492 | |

SEMISONIC
Rock trio from Minneapolis, Minnesota: Dan Wilson (vocals, guitar), John Munson (bass) and Jacob Slichter (drums).

1/25/97	Ⓡ	30	4	1 F.N.T.	—	Great Divide ....MCA 11414	
3/14/98	Ⓜ	❶⁵	26	2 Closing Time	11ᴬ	Feeling Strangely Fine ....MCA 11733	
3/21/98	Ⓡ	13	26				
9/5/98	Ⓜ	11	13	3 Singing In My Sleep	—	↓	
9/26/98	Ⓡ	31	8				
2/6/99	Ⓜ	21	8	4 Secret Smile	—	↓	
2/10/01	Ⓜ	39	1	5 Chemistry	—	All About Chemistry ....MCA 112355	

SETZER, Brian
Born on 4/10/1959 in Massapequa, Long Island, New York. Lead singer/guitarist of the **Stray Cats**. Played Eddie Cochran in the 1987 movie *La Bamba*. Formed own 16-piece swing orchestra in 1994.

2/22/86	Ⓡ	13	11	1 The Knife Feels Like Justice	—	The Knife Feels Like Justice ....EMI America 17178	
5/7/88	Ⓡ	36	6	2 When The Sky Comes Tumblin' Down	—	Live Nude Guitars..........................EMI-Manhattan 46963	
7/25/98	Ⓜ	15	16	3 Jump Jive An' Wail .... THE BRIAN SETZER ORCHESTRA first recorded by Louis Prima in 1956	23ᴬ	The Dirty Boogie...................................Interscope 90183	

SEVEN CHANNELS
Rock band from Dallas, Texas: Kevin Kirkwood (vocals), Dallas Perry (guitar), Dalton Humphreys (bass) and Ben Holt (drums).

| 8/18/01 | Ⓡ | 31 | 10 | Breathe.. | — | Seven Channels ....Palm 2070 | |

SEVENDUST   Ⓡ **2000s: #27 / All-Time: #94**
Hard-rock band formed in Atlanta, Georgia: **Lajon** Witherspoon (vocals; born on 10/3/1972), Clint Lowery (guitar; born on 12/15/1971), John Connolly (guitar; born on 10/21/1968), Vinnie Hornsby (bass; born on 10/22/1967) and Morgan Rose (drums; born on 12/13/1968). Sonny Mayo (born on 7/16/1971) replaced Lowery in 2004. Clint is the brother of Corey Lowery (of **Stereomud**); the Lowery brothers later formed **Dark New Day**.

TOP HITS: 1)Enemy 2)Driven 3)Ugly

1/10/98	Ⓡ	30	11	1 Black..	—	Sevendust ....TVT 5730	
5/16/98	Ⓡ	39	1	2 Too Close To Hate..................................	—	↓	
12/5/98	Ⓡ	30	9	3 Bitch..	—	↓	
8/14/99	Ⓡ	14	25	4 Denial...	—	Home..TVT 5820	
9/25/99	Ⓜ	26	14				
2/26/00	Ⓡ	23	17	5 Waffle	—	↓	
4/15/00	Ⓜ	33	3				
10/20/01	Ⓡ	15	21	6 Praise	—	Animosity..TVT 5870	
10/27/01	Ⓜ	23	16				
3/9/02	Ⓡ	21	13	7 Live Again	—	↓	
3/30/02	Ⓜ	36	6				
12/28/02	Ⓡ	38	1	8 Xmas Day	—	↓	
9/6/03	Ⓡ	10	26	9 Enemy	—	Seasons ....TVT 5990	
9/20/03	Ⓜ	30	11				
1/31/04	Ⓡ	20	15	10 Broken Down	—	↓	
10/23/04+	Ⓡ	22	20	11 Face To Face..	—	↓	

Debug	Cht	Peak	Wks	Track Title	Hot Pos	Album Title	Album Label & Number

R=Mainstream Rock
M=Modern Rock

SEVENDUST — cont'd

Debut	Cht	Peak	Wks	Track Title	Hot Pos	Album Title	Album Label & Number
8/27/05+	R	12	26	12 Ugly	—	*Next*	Winedark 07
3/25/06	R	28	10	13 Failure	—	↓	
2/3/07	R	10	23	14 Driven	—	*Alpha*	7Bros 100437
8/4/07	R	33	14	15 Beg To Differ	—	↓	
3/8/08	R	26↑	4↑	16 Prodigal Son	—	*Chapter VII: Hope And Sorrow*	7Bros 429692

SEVEN MARY THREE
Rock band formed in Williamsburg, Virginia: Jason Ross (vocals), Jason Pollock (guitar), Casey Daniel (bass) and Giti Khalsa (drums). Thomas Juliano replaced Pollock in 2000.

Debut	Cht	Peak	Wks	Track Title	Hot Pos	Album Title	Album Label & Number
9/16/95+	R	❶⁴	35	1 **Cumbersome**	39	*American Standard*	Mammoth 92633
10/28/95+	M	7	26				
3/2/96	R	7	23	2 Water's Edge	—	↓	
6/1/96	M	37	3				
8/10/96	R	19	10	3 My My	—	↓	
5/10/97	R	17	7	4 Rock Crown	—	*Rock Crown*	Mammoth 83018
9/27/97	M	19	18	5 Lucky	—	↓	
10/25/97	R	35	4				
7/11/98	R	7	14	6 Over Your Shoulder	—	*Orange Ave.*	Mammoth 83114
7/18/98	M	16	12				
5/5/01	R	7	15	7 Wait	—	*The Economy Of Sound*	Mammoth 65516
5/12/01	M	21	10				
9/29/01	R	39	1	8 Sleepwalking	—	↓	

707
Rock band from Detroit, Michigan: Kevin Chalfant (vocals), Kevin Russell (guitar), Tod Howarth (keyboards), Phil Bryant (bass) and Jim McClarty (drums). Chalfant co-founded **The Storm** in 1991.

Debut	Cht	Peak	Wks	Track Title	Hot Pos	Album Title	Album Label & Number
5/29/82	R	12	14	Mega Force	62	*Mega Force*	Boardwalk 33253

SEXTON, Charlie
Born on 8/11/1968 in San Antonio, Texas. Rock singer/guitarist. Lead guitarist for **Joe Ely**'s band. Co-founder of the **Arc Angels**. Appeared in the 1991 movie *Thelma & Louise*. His brother is the leader of **Will & The Kill**.

Debut	Cht	Peak	Wks	Track Title	Hot Pos	Album Title	Album Label & Number
12/21/85+	R	24	13	1 Beat's So Lonely	17	*Pictures For Pleasure*	MCA 5629
2/4/89	R	22	8	2 Don't Look Back	—	*Charlie Sexton*	MCA 6280
5/13/95	R	18	8	3 Everyone Will Crawl	—	*Under The Wishing Tree*	MCA 11208

CHARLIE SEXTON SEXTET

SEYMOUR, Phil
Born on 5/15/1952 in Tulsa, Oklahoma. Died of cancer on 8/17/1993 (age 41). Rock singer/drummer. Formerly with **Dwight Twilley**'s band.

Debut	Cht	Peak	Wks	Track Title	Hot Pos	Album Title	Album Label & Number
4/4/81	R	34	3	Precious To Me	22	*Phil Seymour*	Boardwalk 36996

SHADES APART
Rock trio from Bridgewater, New Jersey: Mark Vecchiarelli (vocals, guitar), Kevin Lynch (bass) and Ed Brown (drums).

Debut	Cht	Peak	Wks	Track Title	Hot Pos	Album Title	Album Label & Number
5/22/99	R	31	8	Valentine	—	*Eyewitness*	Universal 53249

SHADOW KING
Rock band formed in New York: **Lou Gramm** (vocals; of **Foreigner**), Vivian Campbell (guitar), Bruce Turgon (bass) and Kevin Valentine (drums). Campbell later joined **Def Leppard**.

Debut	Cht	Peak	Wks	Track Title	Hot Pos	Album Title	Album Label & Number
10/5/91	R	22	7	I Want You	—	*Shadow King*	Atlantic 82324

SHADOWS FALL
Hard-rock band from Boston, Massachusetts: Brian Fair (vocals), Jonathan Donais (guitar), Matthew Bachand (guitar), Paul Romanko (bass) and Jason Bittner (drums).

Debut	Cht	Peak	Wks	Track Title	Hot Pos	Album Title	Album Label & Number
1/1/05	R	38	5	1 What Drives The Weak	—	*The War Within*	Century Media 8228
6/4/05	R	33	3	2 Inspiration On Demand	—	↓	
4/28/07	R	37	9	3 Redemption	—	*Threads Of Life*	Atlantic 115516
10/27/07	R	40	3	4 Another Hero Lost	—	↓	

SHAGGY
Born Orville Richard Burrell on 10/22/1968 in Kingston, Jamaica. Reggae singer.

Debut	Cht	Peak	Wks	Track Title	Hot Pos	Album Title	Album Label & Number
8/14/93	M	14	6	Oh Carolina	59	*Pure Pleasure*	Virgin 87953

samples "Peter Gunn" by Henry Mancini

Billboard	Cht	Peak	Wks	ARTIST / Track Title	Hot Pos	Album Title	Album Label & Number
Debut				R=Mainstream Rock M=Modern Rock			

SHAKESPEAR'S SISTER
Female vocal duo: Siobhan Fahey and Marcy "Marcella Detroit" Levy. Fahey was a member of **Bananarama**; married to David A. Stewart (of **Eurythmics**) from 1987-96. Levy was a prominent backing vocalist.

2/22/92	Ⓜ	22	3	1 Goodbye Cruel World	—	Hormonally Yours	London 828266
8/22/92	Ⓜ	25	2	2 Stay	4	↓	

SHALAMAR
R&B vocal trio formed in Los Angeles, California: Jody Watley, Howard Hewett and Jeffrey Daniels.

9/24/83	Ⓡ	41	1	Dead Giveaway	22	The Look	Solar 60239

SHAMEN, The
Techno-rave dance band from Aberdeen, Scotland: brothers Derek McKenzie and Keith McKenzie, Richard West, Colin Angus, Will Sinnott and Peter Stephenson. Sinnott drowned on 5/23/1990 (age 31).

10/19/91	Ⓜ	4	14	Move Any Mountain (Progen 91)	38	En-Tact	Epic 48722

SHAW, Tommy
Born on 9/11/1953 in Montgomery, Alabama. Rock singer/songwriter/guitarist. Member of **Styx** and **Damn Yankees**. Formed **Shaw/Blades** duo with Jack Blades (of **Night Ranger**; see #4 below).

9/29/84	Ⓡ	6	10	1 Girls With Guns	33	Girls With Guns	A&M 5020
10/12/85	Ⓡ	18	7	2 Remo's Theme (What If)	81	What If	A&M 5097
10/24/87	Ⓡ	41	5	3 No Such Thing	—	Ambition	Atlantic 81798
3/11/95	Ⓡ	26	8	4 My Hallucination	—	Hallucination	Warner 45835
				SHAW/BLADES			

SHELLEYAN ORPHAN
Pop duo from Bournemouth, England: Jemaur Tayle (vocals, guitar) and Caroline Crawley (vocals, clarinet).

9/30/89	Ⓜ	23	4	Shatter	—	Century Flower	Columbia 45198

SHEPHERD, Kenny Wayne   Ⓡ 1990s: #35 / All-Time: #81
Born Kenny Wayne Brobst Jr. on 6/12/1977 in Shreveport, Louisiana. Blues-rock guitarist. Married Hannah Gibson (daughter of actor Mel Gibson) on 9/16/2006. His band: Noah Hunt (vocals), Robby Emerson (bass) and Sam Bryant (drums). Keith Christopher replaced Emerson in 1998.

TOP HITS: 1)Blue On Black 2)Slow Ride 3)Somehow, Somewhere, Someway

10/28/95	Ⓡ	9	23	1 Deja Voodoo	—	Ledbetter Heights	Giant 24621
3/16/96	Ⓡ	15	11	2 Born With A Broken Heart	—	↓	
6/29/96	Ⓡ	23	9	3 Aberdeen	—	↓	
				KENNY WAYNE SHEPHERD BAND:			
9/27/97	Ⓡ	3²	25	4 Slow Ride	—	Trouble Is	Giant 24689
1/24/98	Ⓡ	❶⁶	42	5 Blue On Black	78	↓	
7/18/98	Ⓡ	3¹	22	6 Somehow, Somewhere, Someway	—	↓	
11/21/98+	Ⓡ	10	16	7 Everything Is Broken	—	↓	
10/16/99	Ⓡ	5	19	8 In 2 Deep	—	Live On	Giant 24729
1/29/00	Ⓡ	9	17	9 Was	—	↓	
7/29/00	Ⓡ	14	14	10 Last Goodbye	—	↓	
9/4/04	Ⓡ	13	21	11 Alive	—	The Place You're In	Reprise 48866
1/15/05	Ⓡ	30	9	12 The Place You're In	—	↓	

SHERBS
Pop-rock band from Sydney, Australia: Daryl Braithwaite (vocals), Harvey James (guitar), Garth Porter (keyboards), Tony Mitchell (bass) and Alan Sandow (drums). Group originally known as Sherbet.

3/21/81	Ⓡ	14	5	1 I Have The Skill	61	The Skill	Atco 137
6/5/82	Ⓡ	26	16	2 We Ride Tonight	—	Defying Gravity	Atco 38146

SHERIFF
Pop-rock band from Toronto, Ontario, Canada: Freddy Curci (vocals), Steve DeMarchi (guitar), Arnold Lanni (keyboards), Wolf Hassel (bass) and Rob Elliott (drums). Disbanded in 1983. Hassel and Lanni formed **Frozen Ghost**. Curci and DeMarchi formed **Alias**.

10/2/82	Ⓡ	33	2	You Remind Me	—	Sheriff	Capitol 12227

SHE WANTS REVENGE
Punk-rock duo formed in Los Angeles, California: Justin Warfield (vocals, guitar) and Adam Bravin (bass, drums).

12/24/05+	Ⓜ	6	21	1 Tear You Apart	122	She Wants Revenge	Flawless 005587
5/13/06	Ⓜ	22	16	2 These Things	—	↓	

Billboard				ARTIST				
Debut	Cht	Peak	Wks	Track Title	ℝ=Mainstream Rock Ⓜ=Modern Rock	Hot Pos	Album Title	Album Label & Number

SHINEDOWN
Ⓡ **2000s: #17 / All-Time: #92**
Rock band from Jacksonville, Florida: Brent Smith (vocals), Jasin Todd (guitar), Brad Stewart (bass) and Barry Kerch (drums).

4/19/03	Ⓡ	5	29	1 Fly From The Inside		—	Leave A Whisper	Atlantic 83566
6/21/03	Ⓜ	34	5					
11/1/03+	Ⓡ	3⁴	42	2 45		—	↓	
4/24/04	Ⓜ	12	26					
6/19/04	Ⓡ	5	24	3 Simple Man		—	↓	
10/2/04	Ⓜ	40	1	first recorded by Lynyrd Skynyrd in 1973				
10/30/04+	Ⓡ	2⁴	30	4 Burning Bright		105	↓	
12/4/04+	Ⓜ	22	21					
8/27/05	Ⓡ	❶¹²	38	5 Save Me		72	Us And Them	Atlantic 83817
9/3/05	Ⓜ	2²	28					
1/28/06	Ⓡ	2¹	27	6 I Dare You		88	↓	
3/4/06	Ⓜ	8	20					
7/15/06	Ⓡ	4	36	7 Heroes		—	↓	
8/12/06	Ⓜ	28	13					

SHINS, The
Pop-rock band from Albuquerque, New Mexico: James Mercer (vocals, guitar), Marty Crandall (keyboards), Dave Hernandez (bass) and Jesse Sandoval (drums).

12/23/06+	Ⓜ	16	20	Phantom Limb		86	Wincing The Night Away	Sub Pop 705

SHINY TOY GUNS
Alternative-rock band from Los Angeles, California: Carah Faye (female vocals), Chad Petree (male vocals, guitar, bass), Jeremy Dawson (keyboards) and Mikey Martin (drums).

10/28/06+	Ⓜ	26	18	1 Le Disko		114	We Are Pilots	Universal Motown 007615
4/28/07	Ⓜ	25	21	2 You Are The One		—	↓	
11/24/07+	Ⓜ	23	15	3 Rainy Monday		—	↓	

SHOCKED, Michelle
Born Michelle Johnston on 2/24/1962 in Dallas, Texas. Folk singer/songwriter.

9/17/88	Ⓜ	16	4	1 Anchorage		66	Short Sharp Shocked	Mercury 834294
10/22/88	Ⓜ	20	6	2 If Love Was A Train		—	↓	
10/15/88	Ⓡ	33	7					
12/23/89+	Ⓜ	19	7	3 On The Greener Side		—	Captain Swing	Mercury 838878

SHOOTING STAR
Rock band from Kansas City, Missouri: Gary West (vocals), Van McLain (guitar, vocals), Bill Guffey (keyboards), Charles Waltz (violin), Ron Verlin (bass) and Steve Thomas (drums).

1/23/82	Ⓡ	52	4	1 Hang On For Your Life		—	Hang On For Your Life	Epic 37407
9/25/82	Ⓡ	37	1	2 Do You Feel Alright		—	III Wishes	Epic 38020
9/17/83	Ⓡ	25	5	3 Straight Ahead		—	Burning	Epic 38683

SHOOTYZ GROOVE
Rap-rock band from the Bronx, New York: Miguel "Sense Live" Rodriguez (vocals), Jose "Season Love" Baez (vocals), "Donny Rock" Radeljic (guitar), "Paul Freaky" Rivera (bass) and Nelson "Dose" Ramirez (drums).

7/31/99	Ⓜ	40	1	L Train		—	High Definition	Kinetic 47359

SHOTGUN MESSIAH
Hard-rock band from Skovde, Sweden: Tim Skold (vocals), Harry Cody (guitar), Bobby Lycon (bass) and Stixx Galore (drums).

4/11/92	Ⓡ	46	2	Heartbreak Blvd		—	Second Coming	Relativity 1060

SHOWOFF
Rock band from Chicago, Illinois: brothers Chris Envy (vocals) and Dave Envy (bass), with Graham Jordan (guitar) and Dan Castady (drums).

8/14/99	Ⓜ	36	4	Falling Star		—	Showoff	Maverick 47380

SHRIEKBACK
Pop-rock trio formed in London, England: Barry Andrews (vocals, bass), Mike Cozzi (guitar) and Martin Barker (drums).

9/10/88	Ⓜ	6	5	1 Intoxication		—	Go Bang!	Island 90949
9/17/88	Ⓜ	19	2	2 Shark Walk		—	↓	

| Billboard | | | | ARTIST | Hot | | |
Debut	Cht	Peak	Wks	Track Title	Pos	Album Title	Album Label & Number

Ⓡ=Mainstream Rock **Ⓜ**=Modern Rock

SICK PUPPIES
Alternative-rock trio from Sydney, Australia: Shimon Moore (vocals, guitar), Emma Anzai (bass) and Mark Goodwin (drums).

3/3/07	Ⓜ	8	32	1 All The Same	—	Dressed Up As Life	RMR 89752
4/21/07	Ⓡ	36	12				
12/15/07+	Ⓜ	20	16↑	2 My World	—	↓	

SIDEWINDERS
Rock band from Tucson, Arizona: Dave Slutes (vocals, guitar), Rich Hopkins (guitar), Mark Perrodin (bass) and Andrea Curtis (drums). Bruce Halper replaced Curtis in early 1990.

| 4/15/89 | Ⓜ | 18 | 6 | 1 Witchdoctor | — | Witchdoctor | Mammoth 9663 |
| 6/2/90 | Ⓜ | 23 | 6 | 2 We Don't Do That Anymore | — | Auntie Ramos' Pool Hall | Mammoth 2068 |

SILENCERS, The
Pop-rock band from Scotland: Jimmie O'Neill (vocals, guitar), Cha Burns (guitar), Joe Donnelly (bass) and Martin Hanlin (drums). Burns died of cancer on 3/26/2007 (age 50).

| 8/1/87 | Ⓡ | 23 | 10 | 1 Painted Moon | 82 | A Letter From St. Paul | RCA Victor 6442 |
| 1/27/90 | Ⓜ | 14 | 8 | 2 Razor Blades Of Love | — | A Blues For Buddha | RCA 9960 |

SILVERCHAIR   Ⓜ All-Time: #82
Alternative-rock trio from Newcastle, Australia: Daniel Johns (vocals, guitar; born on 4/22/1979), Chris Joannou (bass; born on 11/10/1979) and Ben Gillies (drums; born on 10/24/1979). Johns was married to **Natalie Imbruglia** from 2003-08.

6/24/95	Ⓜ	❶³	26	1 **Tomorrow**	28ᴬ	Frogstomp	Epic 67247
7/8/95	Ⓡ	❶³	26				
11/4/95+	Ⓡ	12	16	2 Pure Massacre	72ᴬ	↓	
11/11/95	Ⓜ	17	12				
3/9/96	Ⓡ	39	1	3 Israel's Son	—	↓	
1/25/97	Ⓜ	4	16	4 Abuse Me	44ᴬ	Freak Show	Epic 67905
1/25/97	Ⓡ	4	16				
5/3/97	Ⓡ	25	7	5 Freak	—	↓	
4/26/97	Ⓜ	29	7				
3/13/99	Ⓜ	12	13	6 Anthem For The Year 2000	—	Neon Ballroom	Epic 69816
3/13/99	Ⓡ	15	13				
7/3/99	Ⓜ	12	13	7 Ana's Song (Open Fire)	—	↓	
7/17/99	Ⓡ	28	9				
7/21/07	Ⓜ	12	20	8 Straight Lines	—	Young Modern	Eleven 255548
2/2/08	Ⓜ	36	2	9 The Greatest View	—	Diorama	Atlantic 83559
				recorded in 2002			

SILVER CONDOR
Rock band from New York: Joe Cerisano (vocals), Earl Slick (guitar), John Corey (keyboards), Jay Davis (bass) and Claude Pepper (drums). Slick joined **Phantom, Rocker & Slick** in 1985.

| 6/13/81 | Ⓡ | 49 | 2 | 1 Angel Eyes | — | Silver Condor | Columbia 37163 |
| 7/4/81 | Ⓡ | 26 | 5 | 2 For The Sake Of Survival | — | ↓ | |

SILVERSUN PICKUPS
Alternative-rock band formed in Los Angeles, California: Brian Aubert (vocals, guitar), Joe Lester (keyboards), Nikki Monninger (bass) and Christopher Guanlao (drums).

| 1/27/07 | Ⓜ | 5 | 26 | 1 Lazy Eye | 102 | Carnavas | DangerBird 009 |
| 8/11/07+ | Ⓜ | 9 | 27 | 2 Well Thought Out Twinkles | — | ↓ | |

SILVERTIDE
Rock band from Philadelphia, Pennsylvania: Walt Lafty (vocals), Nick Perri (guitar), Mark Melchiorre (guitar), Brian Weaver (bass) and Kevin Frank (drums).

8/21/04	Ⓡ	6	26	1 Ain't Comin' Home	—	Show & Tell	J Records 78949
3/5/05	Ⓡ	12	20	2 Blue Jeans	—	↓	
11/12/05+	Ⓡ	18	17	3 Devil's Daughter	—	↓	

SIMMONS, Patrick
Born on 1/23/1950 in Aberdeen, Washington; raised in San Jose, California. Rock singer/songwriter/guitarist. Member of **The Doobie Brothers**.

| 5/21/83 | Ⓡ | 18 | 2 | So Wrong | 30 | Arcade | Elektra 60225 |

Debut	Cht	Peak	Wks	ARTIST / Track Title	Hot Pos	Album Title	Album Label & Number

Billboard — ®=Mainstream Rock ⓜ=Modern Rock

SIMON, Paul

Born on 10/13/1941 in Newark, New Jersey; raised in Queens, New York. Singer/songwriter/guitarist. One-half of Simon & Garfunkel duo. Married to actress/author Carrie Fisher from 1983-85. Married **Edie Brickell** on 5/30/1992. In the movies *Annie Hall* and *One-Trick Pony*. Also see **Classic Rock Tracks** section.

AWARD: R&R Hall of Fame: 2001

| 9/13/86 | ® | 42 | 4 | 1 You Can Call Me Al | 23 | *Graceland* | Warner 25447 |
| 11/15/86 | ® | 38 | 5 | 2 Graceland | 81 | ↓ | |

Grammy: Record of the Year ★ R&R Hall of Fame ★ RS500 #485
The Everly Brothers (backing vocals)

2/21/87	®	15	9	3 The Boy In The Bubble	86	↓	
10/13/90	®	21	10	4 The Obvious Child	92	*The Rhythm Of The Saints*	Warner 26098
11/10/90	ⓜ	24	7				

SIMON SAYS

Rock band from Sacramento, California: Matt Franks (vocals), Zac Diebels (guitar), Mike Arrieta (bass) and Mike Johnston (drums).

7/10/99	®	34	7	1 Slider	—	*Jump Start*	Hollywood 162183
12/18/99+	®	23	10	2 Life Jacket	—	↓	
7/14/01	®	31	5	3 Blister	—	*Shut Your Breath*	Hollywood 162283

SIMPLE MINDS

Pop-rock band formed in Glasgow, Scotland: Jim Kerr (vocals; born on 7/9/1959), Charles Burchill (guitar), Michael MacNeil (keyboards), John Giblin (bass) and Mel Gaynor (drums). MacNeil and Giblin left in 1989. Kerr was married to **Chrissie Hynde** (of **The Pretenders**) from 1984-90 and to actress Patsy Kensit from 1992-96.

TOP HITS: 1)Don't You (Forget About Me) 2)See The Lights 3)Alive & Kicking

2/23/85	®	❶³	16	1 Don't You (Forget About Me)	❶¹	*St: The Breakfast Club*	A&M 5045
10/19/85	®	2²	15	2 Alive & Kicking	3²	*Once Upon A Time*	A&M 5092
12/28/85+	®	3²	13	3 Sanctify Yourself	14	↓	
3/22/86	®	9	13	4 All The Things She Said	28	↓	
4/1/89	ⓜ	17	4	5 Mandela Day	—	*Street Fighting Years*	A&M 3927
				tribute to Nelson Mandela			
5/20/89	ⓜ	12	5	6 This Is Your Land	—	↓	
5/13/89	®	37	5	Lou Reed (additional vocal)			
6/24/89	ⓜ	14	6	7 Take A Step Back	—	↓	
3/23/91	ⓜ	❶²	13	8 See The Lights	40	*Real Life*	A&M 5352
3/23/91	®	10	13				
6/22/91	ⓜ	4	5	9 Stand By Love	—	↓	
6/29/91	®	42	5				
1/28/95	®	6	12	10 She's A River	52	*Good News From The Next World*	Virgin 39922
1/21/95	ⓜ	10	12				
5/27/95	®	40	1	11 And The Band Played On	—	↓	

SINCH

Hard-rock band from Brooklyn, New York: Jamie Stern (vocals), Tony Lannutti (guitar), Mike Abramson (bass) and Dan McFarland (drums).

| 7/6/02 | ® | 27 | 10 | Something More | — | *Sinch* | Roadrunner 618478 |

SINOMATIC

Rock band from Youngstown, Ohio: Ken Cooper (vocals), Rick Deak (guitar), Bryan Patrick (guitar), Dave Markasky (bass) and Matt Lawrence (drums).

| 4/28/01 | ® | 32 | 7 | Bloom | — | *Sinomatic* | Atlantic 83424 |

SIOUXSIE AND THE BANSHEES

ⓜ **1990s: #34 / All-Time: #77**

Avant-punk band formed by singer Siouxsie Sioux (Susan Dallion) and bassist Steve Severin (Steve Havoc). Fluctuating personnel around nucleus of group: Sioux, Severin and Peter "Budgie" Clark (drums). Husband-and-wife, Sioux and Budgie, also recorded as **The Creatures**.

9/10/88	ⓜ	❶²	14	1 Peek-A-Boo	53	*Peepshow*	Geffen 24205
10/1/88	ⓜ	2¹	19	2 The Killing Jar	—	↓	
5/25/91	ⓜ	❶⁵	15	3 Kiss Them For Me	23	*Superstition*	Geffen 24387
9/21/91	ⓜ	13	6	4 Shadowtime	—	↓	
1/4/92	ⓜ	12	7	5 Fear (Of The Unknown)	—	↓	
7/11/92	ⓜ	7	7	6 Face To Face	—	*St: Batman Returns*	Warner 26972
2/18/95	ⓜ	21	7	7 O Baby	125	*The Rapture*	Geffen 24630

Billboard				ARTIST		Hot		
Debut	Cht	Peak	Wks	Track Title	ℝ=Mainstream Rock Ⓜ=Modern Rock	Pos	Album Title	Album Label & Number

SISTER HAZEL
Pop-rock band formed in Gainesville, Florida: Ken Block (vocals), Ryan Newell (guitar), Andrew Copeland (guitar), Jeff Beres (bass) and Mark Trojanowski (drums).

10/4/97	Ⓜ	39	3	1 All For You	11	...Somewhere More Familiar ....Universal 53030
12/27/97+	ℝ	31	8	2 Happy	73ᴬ	↓
2/7/98	Ⓜ	37	2			

SISTERS OF MERCY, The
Rock duo formed in Leeds, England: Andrew Taylor (vocals) and Patricia Morrison (bass). Morrison left in early 1990; expanded to a quintet which included Tony James, Tim Bricheno and Andreas Bruhn (guitars), and Doktor Avalanche (drums).

11/17/90	Ⓜ	❶⁵	13	1 More	—	Vision Thing ....Elektra 61017
3/2/91	Ⓜ	17	8	2 Detonation Boulevard		↓

SIXX: A.M.
Rock trio formed in Los Angeles, California: James Michael (vocals, guiar), Nikki Sixx (bass) and Darren Jay "DJ" Ashba (drums). Sixx was a member of **Mötley Crüe**. Ashba was a member of **Beautiful Creatures**.

7/21/07	ℝ	2⁸	37↑	1 Life Is Beautiful	106	The Heroin Diaries Soundtrack ....Eleven Seven 171
2/9/08	Ⓜ	25	8↑			
3/29/08	ℝ	35↑	1↑	2 Pray For Me	—	↓

SKID ROW
Heavy-metal band formed in Toms River, New Jersey: Sebastian Bach (vocals; born on 4/3/1968), Dave Sabo (guitar), Scott Hill (guitar), Rachel Bolan (bass) and Rob Affuso (drums).

2/25/89	ℝ	27	10	1 Youth Gone Wild	99	Skid Row ....Atlantic 81936
6/17/89	ℝ	11	17	2 18 And Life	4	↓
10/7/89+	ℝ	23	21	3 I Remember You	6	↓
6/15/91	ℝ	13	11	4 Monkey Business	—	Slave To The Grind ....Atlantic 82278
12/14/91+	ℝ	30	13	5 Wasted Time	88	↓
4/29/95	ℝ	28	6	6 Into Another	—	Subhuman Race ....Atlantic 82730

SKILLET
Christian rock band from Memphis, Tennessee: brothers John Cooper (vocals, bass) and Korey Cooper (keyboards), with Ben Kasica (guitar) and Lori Peters (drums).

5/22/04	ℝ	26	13	1 Savior	—	Collide ....Ardent 72522
11/25/06	ℝ	34	12	2 Whispers In The Dark	—	Comatose ....Ardent 94537
3/10/07	ℝ	27	11	3 The Older I Get	—	↓

SKINDRED
Punk-rock band from Newport, South Wales: Benji Webbe (vocals), Mikey Dee (guitar), Daniel Pugsley (bass) and Dirty Arya (drums).

8/21/04	ℝ	14	24	1 Nobody	—	Nobody ....Lava 93304
8/28/04	Ⓜ	23	16			
2/12/05	ℝ	30	10	2 Pressure	—	Babylon ....Lava 93304

SKRAPE
Hard-rock band from Orlando, Florida: Billy Keeton (vocals), Mike Lynchard (guitar), Brian Milner (keyboards), Pete Sison (bass) and Will Hunt (drums).

2/24/01	ℝ	29	9	1 Waste	—	New Killer America ....RCA 67935
6/16/01	ℝ	35	4	2 Isolated	—	↓
12/6/03	ℝ	34	10	3 Stand Up (Summer Song)	—	Up The Dose ....RCA 54528

SLADE
Hard-rock band formed in Wolverhampton, England: Neville "Noddy" Holder (vocals), David Hill (guitar), Jim Lea (bass, keyboards) and Don Powell (drums). Band starred in the 1975 movie *Flame*.

2/25/84	ℝ	32	9	1 My Oh My	37	Keep Your Hands Off My Power Supply ....CBS Associated 39336
3/31/84	ℝ	❶²	17	2 Run Runaway	20	↓
4/20/85	ℝ	13	8	3 Little Sheila	86	Rogues Gallery ....CBS Associated 39976

SLASH'S SNAKEPIT
Born Saul Hudson on 7/23/1965 in Staffordshire, England; raised in Los Angeles, California. Lead guitarist of **Guns N' Roses** and **Velvet Revolver**. His band included **Gilby Clarke** (guitar; of Guns N' Roses), Eric Dover (vocals, guitar; of **Imperial Drag**), Mike Inez (bass; of **Alice In Chains**) and Matt Sorum (drums; of Guns N' Roses).

2/18/95	ℝ	21	9	1 Beggars & Hangers-On	—	It's Five O'Clock Somewhere ....Geffen 24630
5/12/07	ℝ	6	20	2 What I Want	—	Daughtry ....RCA 88860
				DAUGHTRY Featuring Slash		

SLAUGHTER

Hard-rock band formed in Las Vegas, Nevada: Mark Slaughter (vocals; born on 7/4/1964), Tim Kelly (guitar), Dana Strum (bass) and Blas Elias (drums). Slaughter and Strum were with the Vinnie Vincent Invasion. Kelly died in a car crash on 2/5/1998 (age 35).

Debut	Cht	Peak	Wks	Track Title	Hot Pos	Album Title	Album Label & Number
3/3/90	®	21	13	1 Up All Night	27	Stick It To Ya	Chrysalis 21702
8/4/90	®	15	13	2 Fly To The Angels	19	↓	
12/1/90+	®	28	11	3 Spend My Life	39	↓	
4/20/91	®	37	7	4 Mad About You	—	↓	
7/20/91	®	40	4	5 Shout It Out	—		
5/2/92	®	28	6	6 The Wild Life	—	St: Bill & Ted's Bogus Journey	Interscope 91725
7/18/92	®	24	8	7 Real Love	69	The Wild Life	Chrysalis 21911
						↓	

SLAVE TO THE SYSTEM

Hard-rock band formed in Washington: Kelly Gray (vocals, guitar), Damon Johnson (guitar), Roman Glick (bass) and Scott Rockenfield (drums; of **Queensrÿche**).

3/4/06	®	33	12	Stigmata	—	Slave To The System	Spitfire 15263

SLEEZE BEEZ

Hard-rock band formed in the Netherlands: Andrew Elt (vocals), Chriz Van Jaarsveld (guitar), Don Van Spall (guitar), Ed Jongsma (bass) and Jan Koster (drums).

4/21/90	®	21	9	Stranger Than Paradise	—	Screwed Blued & Tattooed	Atlantic 82069

SLICK, Grace

Born Grace Wing on 10/30/1939 in Chicago, Illinois. Female lead singer of **Jefferson Airplane/Starship**.

3/21/81	®	33	2	Sea Of Love	—	Welcome To The Wrecking Ball!	RCA Victor 3851

SLIPKNOT

Hard-rock band from Des Moines, Iowa: **Corey Taylor** (vocals), Mick Thomson (guitar), Jim Root (guitar), Sid Wilson (DJ), Craig Jones (samples), Chris Fehn and Shawn Crahan (percussion), Paul Gray (bass) and Joey Jordison (drums). Taylor and Root also formed **Stone Sour**.

1/15/00	®	34	7	1 Wait And Bleed	—	Slipknot	Roadrunner 8655
8/25/01	®	30	10	2 Left Behind	—	Iowa	Roadrunner 8564
5/1/04	®	5	35	3 Duality	106	Vol. 3: (The Subliminal Verses)	Roadrunner 618388
5/8/04	Ⓜ	6	27				
10/23/04+	®	14	26	4 Vermillion	—	↓	
11/6/04+	Ⓜ	17	19				
3/12/05	®	11	28	5 Before I Forget	—	↓	
4/23/05	Ⓜ	32	7	Grammy: Metal Performance			
11/12/05	®	25	16	6 The Nameless	—	↓	

SLOAN

Rock band from Halifax, Nova Scotia, Canada: Jay Ferguson (vocals), Patrick Pentland (guitar), Chris Murphy (bass) and Andrew Scott (drums).

2/27/93	Ⓜ	25	4	Underwhelmed	—	Smeared	DGC 24498

SLOTH

Rock band from Los Angeles, California: Rich Love (vocals), Kristo Panos (guitar), Andy Kovatch (bass) and Adam Figura (drums).

8/16/03	®	25	13	Someday	—	Dead Generation	Hollywood 162374

SMASHING PUMPKINS, The   ® 1990s: #25 / All-Time: #69 ★ Ⓜ 1990s: #4 / All-Time: #8

Alternative-rock band formed in Chicago, Illinois: Billy Corgan (vocals, guitar; born on 3/17/1967), James Iha (guitar; born on 3/26/1968), D'Arcy Wretzky (bass; born on 5/1/1968) and Jimmy Chamberlin (drums; born on 6/10/1964). Touring keyboardist Jonathan Melvoin, brother of Wendy Melvoin (of **Prince**'s Revolution), died of a drug overdose on 7/12/1996 (age 34). Disbanded in 2001. Corgan and Chamberlain formed **Zwan** in 2002. Band reunited in 2006.

TOP HITS: 1)1979 2)Bullet With Butterfly Wings 3)Tarantula 4)Stand Inside Your Love 5)Thirty-Three

11/9/91	Ⓜ	27	3	1 Rhinoceros	—	Gish	Caroline 1705
10/17/92	Ⓜ	24	4	2 Drown	—	St: Singles	Epic 52476
7/24/93	Ⓜ	7	14	3 Cherub Rock	—	Siamese Dream	Virgin 88267
8/28/93	®	23	12				
3/19/94	®	5	22	4 Disarm	48[A]	↓	
9/11/93+	Ⓜ	8	26				

Billboard				ARTIST	Hot		
Debut	Cht	Peak	Wks	Track Title	Pos	Album Title	Album Label & Number

R=Mainstream Rock M=Modern Rock

SMASHING PUMPKINS, The — cont'd

Debut	Cht	Peak	Wks	#	Track Title	Hot Pos	Album Title	Album Label & Number
10/30/93	M	4	23	5	Today	69[A]	↓	
1/22/94	R	28	6					
7/16/94	R	28	7	6	Rocket	—	↓	
10/15/94	M	3³	17	7	Landslide	30[A]	Pisces Iscariot	Virgin 39834
					first recorded by **Fleetwood Mac** in 1975			
10/21/95	M	2⁶	22	8	Bullet With Butterfly Wings	22	Mellon Collie And The Infinite Sadness	Virgin 40861
10/21/95	R	4	25					
					Grammy: Hard Rock Performance			
12/9/95+	R	❶²	26	9	1979	12	↓	
11/25/95+	M	❶¹	26					
2/17/96	M	9	19	10	Zero	49[A]	↓	
3/16/96	R	15	15					
6/15/96	R	4	16	11	Tonight, Tonight	36	↓	
6/1/96	M	5	22					
9/14/96	M	8	17	12	Muzzle	57[A]	↓	
10/5/96	R	10	16					
12/7/96+	M	2¹	21	13	Thirty-Three	39	↓	
2/1/97	R	18	9					
3/22/97	M	8	18	14	Eye	49[A]	St: Lost Highway	Nothing 90090
6/7/97	M	4	12	15	The End Is The Beginning Is The End	50[A]	St: Batman & Robin	Warner Sunset 46620
6/7/97	R	12	10					
					Grammy: Hard Rock Performance			
5/23/98	M	3²	24	16	Ava Adore	42	Adore	Virgin 45879
5/23/98	R	8	15					
6/27/98	M	3⁴	26	17	Perfect	54	↓	
8/29/98	R	33	6					
12/25/99+	M	4	11	18	The Everlasting Gaze	113	Machina/The Machines Of God	Virgin 48936
1/1/00	R	14	9					
2/26/00	M	2³	16	19	Stand Inside Your Love	106	↓	
3/4/00	R	11	12					
6/2/07	M	2⁴	20	20	Tarantula	54	Zeitgeist	Martha's Music 138620
6/9/07	R	6	18					
9/8/07	M	23	12	21	That's The Way (My Love Is)	—	↓	
10/6/07	R	32	6					

SMASH MOUTH
Pop-rock band from San Jose, California: Steve Harwell (vocals), Greg Camp (guitar), Paul DeLisle (bass) and Kevin Coleman (drums).

Debut	Cht	Peak	Wks	#	Track Title	Hot Pos	Album Title	Album Label & Number
7/19/97	M	❶⁵	32	1	Walkin' On The Sun	2¹[A]	Fush Yu Mang	Interscope 90142
9/13/97	R	13	26					
1/31/98	M	28	6	2	Why Can't We Be Friends	—	↓	
					#6 Pop hit for War in 1975			
8/8/98	M	30	7	3	Can't Get Enough Of You Baby	27[A]	St: Can't Hardly Wait	Elektra 62201
					#56 Pop hit for ? & The Mysterians in 1967			
5/8/99	M	2³	26	4	All Star	4	Astro Lounge	Interscope 90316
10/16/99	M	26	18	5	Then The Morning Comes	11	↓	

SMILE EMPTY SOUL
Hard-rock trio from Los Angeles, California: Sean Danielsen (vocals, guitar), Ryan Martin (bass) and Derek Gledhill (drums).

Debut	Cht	Peak	Wks	#	Track Title	Hot Pos	Album Title	Album Label & Number
5/10/03	M	7	26	1	Bottom Of A Bottle	107	Smile Empty Soul	Throback 83639
5/10/03	R	8	27					
11/22/03+	R	26	16	2	Nowhere Kids	—	↓	
12/6/03+	M	27	11					
4/3/04	M	22	14	3	Silhouettes	—	Smile Empty Soul	ThroBack 83639
4/10/04	R	25	13					
9/10/05	R	37	3	4	Don't Need You	—	Anxiety	ThroBack 94102

Billboard				ARTIST		Hot		
Debut	Cht	Peak	Wks	Track Title	®=Mainstream Rock ⓜ=Modern Rock	Pos	Album Title	Album Label & Number

SMITH, Patti
Born on 12/30/1946 in Chicago, Illinois; raised in New Jersey. Highly influential punk-rock singer. Not to be confused with Patty Smyth of Scandal. Also see **Classic Rock Tracks** section.
AWARD: R&R Hall of Fame: 2007

Debut	Cht	Peak	Wks	Track Title	Hot Pos	Album Title	Album Label & Number
6/25/88	®	19	9	1 People Have The Power	—	Dream Of Life	Arista 8453
9/10/88	ⓜ	6	7	2 Up There Down There		↓	

SMITHEREENS, The
Power-pop band formed in Carteret, New Jersey: Pat DiNizio (vocals, guitar; born on 10/12/1955), Jim Babjak (guitar), Mike Mesaros (bass) and Dennis Diken (drums).
TOP HITS: 1)Only A Memory 2)A Girl Like You 3)Top Of The Pops

Debut	Cht	Peak	Wks	Track Title	Hot Pos	Album Title	Album Label & Number
8/30/86	®	14	11	1 Blood And Roses	—	Especially For You	Enigma 73208
12/6/86+	®	23	12	2 Behind The Wall Of Sleep		↓	
3/26/88	®	❶[1]	14	3 Only A Memory	92	Green Thoughts	Capitol 48375
6/18/88	®	14	10	4 House We Used To Live In	—	↓	
9/3/88	®	34	8	5 Drown In My Own Tears	—	↓	
10/21/89	®	2[2]	21	6 A Girl Like You	38	11	Enigma 91194
10/21/89	ⓜ	3[1]	13				
2/10/90	®	7	14	7 Blues Before And After	94	↓	
1/20/90	ⓜ	18	4				
2/3/90	ⓜ	16	8	8 Yesterday Girl	—	↓	
5/26/90	®	20	9				
9/7/91	ⓜ	2[1]	8	9 Top Of The Pops	—	Blow Up	Capitol 94963
9/7/91	®	19	7				
11/2/91	ⓜ	11	13	10 Tell Me When Did Things Go So Wrong	—	↓	
11/16/91+	®	28	10				
4/23/94	®	17	9	11 Miles From Nowhere	—	A Date With The Smithereens	RCA 66391

SMOKING POPES
Rock band from Crystal Lake, Illinois: brothers Josh Caterer (vocals), Eli Caterer (guitar) and Matt Caterer (bass), with Mike Felumlee (drums).

Debut	Cht	Peak	Wks	Track Title	Hot Pos	Album Title	Album Label & Number
7/15/95	ⓜ	35	3	Need You Around	—	Born To Quit	Capitol 33831

SMYTH, Patty
Born on 6/26/1957 in New York. Lead singer of **Scandal**. Married tennis star John McEnroe in April 1997.

Debut	Cht	Peak	Wks	Track Title	Hot Pos	Album Title	Album Label & Number
2/28/87	®	4	10	1 Never Enough	61	Never Enough	Columbia 40182
5/23/87	®	40	4	2 Downtown Train	95	↓	
				first recorded by Tom Waits in 1985			
7/25/87	®	26	6	3 Isn't It Enough	—	↓	

SNAKE RIVER CONSPIRACY
Rock duo from San Francisco, California: Tobey Torres (female vocals) and Jason Slater (instruments).

Debut	Cht	Peak	Wks	Track Title	Hot Pos	Album Title	Album Label & Number
7/8/00	ⓜ	38	5	How Soon Is Now?	—	Sonic Jihad	Reprise 47383

SNEAKER
Pop-rock band formed in Los Angeles, California: Mitch Crane (vocals, guitar), Michael Carey Schneider (vocals, keyboards), Tim Torrance (guitar), Jim King (keyboards), Michael Cottage (bass) and Mike Hughes (drums).

Debut	Cht	Peak	Wks	Track Title	Hot Pos	Album Title	Album Label & Number
12/5/81+	®	25	9	Don't Let Me In	63	Sneaker	Handshake 37631
				written by Walter Becker and **Donald Fagen (Steely Dan)**			

SNEAKER PIMPS
Dance-rock trio from Reading, England: Kelli Drayton (vocals), Chris Comer (guitar) and Liam Howe (keyboards).

Debut	Cht	Peak	Wks	Track Title	Hot Pos	Album Title	Album Label & Number
4/26/97	ⓜ	7	26	6 Underground	45	Becoming X	Virgin 42587

SNIDER, Todd
Born on 10/11/1966 in Portland, Oregon. Male singer/songwriter/guitarist.

Debut	Cht	Peak	Wks	Track Title	Hot Pos	Album Title	Album Label & Number
12/24/94+	®	31	5	Talkin' Seattle Grunge Rock Blues		Songs For The Daily Planet	Margaritaville 11067

SNOW PATROL
Rock band from Dundee, Scotland: Gary Lightbody (vocals, guitar), Nathan Connolly (guitar), Mark McClelland (bass) and John Quinn (drums). Paul Wilson replaced McClelland in 2005. Tom Simpson (keyboards) joined in 2005.

Debut	Cht	Peak	Wks	Track Title	Hot Pos	Album Title	Album Label & Number
6/5/04	ⓜ	39	3	1 Spitting Games	—	Final Straw	Polydor 002271
8/21/04	ⓜ	15	19	2 Run	—	↓	
3/26/05	ⓜ	40	2	3 Chocolate	—	↓	
4/29/06	ⓜ	21	16	4 Hands Open	—	Eyes Open	Polydor 006675

Billboard				ARTIST / Track Title	Hot Pos	Album Title	Album Label & Number
Debut	Cht	Peak	Wks			R=Mainstream Rock M=Modern Rock	

SNOW PATROL — cont'd

Debut	Cht	Peak	Wks	Track	Hot Pos	Album Title	Album Label & Number
8/26/06	Ⓜ	8	23	5 Chasing Cars	5 ↓		
2/24/07	Ⓜ	27	7	6 You're All I Have	— ↓		

SOBULE, Jill
Born on 1/16/1959 in Denver, Colorado. Pop-rock singer/songwriter/guitarist.

| 5/20/95 | Ⓜ | 20 | 8 | I Kissed A Girl | 67 | Jill Sobule | Lava 82741 |

SOCIALBURN
Rock band from Blountstown, Florida: Neil Alday (vocals, guitar), Chris Cobb (guitar), Dusty Price (bass) and Brandon Bittner (drums).

12/7/02+	Ⓡ	9	26	1 Down	123	Where You Are	Elektra 62790
12/14/02+	Ⓜ	17	21				
5/31/03	Ⓡ	23	11	2 Everyone	— ↓		
6/7/03	Ⓜ	27	10				

SOCIAL DISTORTION Ⓜ All-Time: #67
Hard-rock band formed in Los Angeles, California: **Mike Ness** (vocals, guitar), Dennis Danell (guitar), John Maurer (bass) and Christopher Reece (drums). Danell died of a brain aneurysm on 2/29/2000 (age 38); replaced by Jonny "2 Bags" Wickersham. Charlie Quintana (of **Cracker** and **Izzy Stradlin And The Ju Ju Hounds**) replaced Reece in 2000.

TOP HITS: 1)Bad Luck 2)I Was Wrong 3)Cold Feelings

3/24/90	Ⓜ	11	9	1 Let It Be Me	—	Social Distortion	Epic 46055
5/26/90	Ⓜ	13	11	2 Ball And Chain	— ↓		
9/8/90	Ⓜ	25	4	3 Ring Of Fire	— ↓		
				#17 Pop hit for Johnny Cash in 1963			
2/1/92	Ⓜ	2⁴	12	4 Bad Luck	—	Somewhere Between Heaven And Hell	Epic 47978
4/11/92	Ⓡ	44	5				
5/2/92	Ⓜ	11	7	5 Cold Feelings	— ↓		
6/27/92	Ⓜ	14	6	6 When She Begins	— ↓		
9/14/96	Ⓜ	4	22	7 I Was Wrong	54ᴬ	White Light White Heat White Trash	550 Music 64380
9/21/96	Ⓡ	12	19				
2/15/97	Ⓡ	32	6	8 When The Angels Sing	— ↓		
2/1/97	Ⓜ	33	6				
10/2/04	Ⓜ	27	26	9 Reach For The Sky	—	Sex, Love And Rock 'N' Roll	Time Bomb 43547
6/9/07	Ⓜ	19	20	10 Far Behind	—	Greatest Hits	Time Bomb 43548

SOFT CELL
Techno-pop duo from London, England: **Marc Almond** (vocals) and David Ball (synthesizer).

| 1/23/82 | Ⓡ | 12 | 21 | Tainted Love | 8 | Non-Stop Erotic Cabaret | Sire 3647 |
| | | | | first recorded by Gloria Jones in 1964 | | | |

SOHO
Interracial dance trio formed in London, England: identical twin sisters Jackie and Pauline Cuff (vocals), with Tim Brinkhurst (guitar).

| 9/8/90 | Ⓜ | 11 | 9 | Hippychick | 14 | Goddess | Savage 91585 |
| | | | | samples "How Soon Is Now" by The Smiths | | | |

SOIL
Hard-rock band from Chicago, Illinois: Ryan McCombs (vocals), Shaun Glass and Adam Zadel (guitars), Tim King (bass) and Tom Schofield (drums). McCombs joined **Drowning Pool** in 2006.

8/4/01	Ⓡ	22	18	1 Halo	—	Scars	J Records 20022
2/9/02	Ⓡ	31	8	2 Unreal	— ↓		
3/6/04	Ⓡ	11	19	3 Redefine	—	Redefine	J Records 59071

SOLUTION A.D.
Rock band from Pennsylvania: Toby Costa (vocals, guitar), Mike Hoover (guitar), Kevin Leggieri (bass) and M.J. Law (drums).

| 6/8/96 | Ⓜ | 33 | 6 | Fearless | — | Happily Ever After | Atlantic 92708 |

SOMETHING CORPORATE
Rock band from Anaheim, California: Andrew McMahon (vocals, piano), Josh Partington (guitar), Kevin "Clutch" Page (bass) and Brian Ireland (drums).

| 2/23/02 | Ⓜ | 29 | 8 | 1 If You C Jordan | — | Leaving Through The Window | Drive-Thru 112887 |
| 11/8/03 | Ⓜ | 37 | 5 | 2 Space | — | North | Drive-Thru 001190 |

SOMETHING HAPPENS
Pop-rock band from Dublin, Ireland: Tom Dunne (vocals), Ray Harman (guitar), Alan Byrne (bass) and Eamonn Ryan (drums).

| 6/16/90 | Ⓜ | 14 | 9 | Hello, Hello, Hello, Hello, Hello, (Petrol) | — | Stuck Together With God's Glue | Charisma 91365 |

Billboard				ARTIST	Hot		
Debut	Cht	Peak	Wks	Track Title	Pos	Album Title	Album Label & Number

Ⓡ=Mainstream Rock
Ⓜ=Modern Rock

SONIC YOUTH

Post-punk art rock band formed in New York: husband-and-wife Thurston Moore (guitar; born on 7/25/1958) and Kim Gordon (bass; born on 4/28/1953), with Lee Ranaldo (guitar; born on 2/3/1956) and Steve Shelley (drums; born on 6/23/1963). All share vocals. Moore and Gordon married on 6/9/1984.

Debut	Cht	Peak	Wks	Track Title	Hot Pos	Album Title	Label & Number
12/24/88+	Ⓜ	20	9	1 Teen Age Riot	—	Daydream Nation	Enigma 75403
				R&R Hall of Fame			
6/30/90	Ⓜ	7	12	2 Kool Thing	—	Goo	DGC 24297
7/18/92	Ⓜ	4	13	3 100%	—	Dirty	DGC 24493
5/28/94	Ⓜ	13	8	4 Bull In The Heather	—	Experimental Jet Set, Trash And No Star	DGC 24632
9/17/94	Ⓜ	26	7	5 Superstar	—	VA: If I Were A Carpenter	A&M 540258
				#2 Pop hit for the Carpenters in 1971			

SONS OF ANGELS

Hard-rock band from Oslo, Norway: Solli (vocals), Staffan William-Olsson (guitar), Lars K. (keyboards), Torstein (bass) and Geir Digernes (drums).

6/16/90	Ⓡ	35	6	Cowgirl	—	Sons Of Angels	Atlantic 82101

SON VOLT

Rock band formed in New Orleans, Louisiana: Jay Farrar (vocals), brothers Dave Boquist (guitar) and Jim Boquist (bass), and Mike Heidorn (drums).

2/10/96	Ⓡ	10	17	Drown	—	Trace	Warner 46010
1/27/96	Ⓜ	25	10				

SOUL ASYLUM　　　　Ⓜ 1990s: #21 / All-Time: #47

Rock band from Minneapolis, Minnesota: Dave Pirner (vocals, guitar; born on 4/16/1962), Karl Mueller (bass; born on 7/27/1963; died of throat cancer on 6/17/2005, age 41) and Grant Young (drums; born on 1/5/1963). Pirner appeared in the 1994 movie *Reality Bites*. Sterling Campbell (of **Duran Duran**) replaced Young in 1995.

TOP HITS: 1)Misery 2)Somebody To Shove 3)Runaway Train

Debut	Cht	Peak	Wks	Track Title	Hot Pos	Album Title	Label & Number
9/8/90	Ⓜ	15	7	1 Spinnin'	—	And The Horse They Rode In On	A&M 5318
12/8/90	Ⓜ	26	2	2 Easy Street	—	↓	
10/10/92	Ⓜ	❶¹	16	3 Somebody To Shove	—	Grave Dancers Union	Columbia 48898
1/2/93	Ⓡ	9	14				
3/20/93	Ⓡ	4	20	4 Black Gold	—	↓	
1/23/93	Ⓜ	6	11				
6/12/93	Ⓡ	3³	20	5 Runaway Train	5	↓	
5/15/93	Ⓜ	13	17				
				Grammy: Rock Song			
9/25/93	Ⓡ	6	12	6 Without A Trace	—	↓	
10/2/93	Ⓜ	27	4				
7/31/93	Ⓜ	20	7	7 Summer Of Drugs	—	VA: Sweet Relief: A Benefit For Victoria Williams	Thirsty Ear 57134
11/20/93	Ⓜ	10	9	8 Sexual Healing	—	VA: No Alternative	Arista 18737
				#3 Pop hit for Marvin Gaye in 1983			
10/29/94	Ⓜ	16	6	9 Can't Even Tell	—	St: Clerks	Chaos 66660
11/12/94	Ⓡ	24	6				
5/20/95	Ⓜ	❶³	13	10 Misery	20	Let Your Dim Light Shine	Columbia 57616
5/27/95	Ⓡ	2⁴	19				
8/26/95	Ⓡ	11	11	11 Just Like Anyone	—	↓	
9/9/95	Ⓜ	19	7				
1/20/96	Ⓡ	29	6	12 Promises Broken	63	↓	
5/2/98	Ⓡ	23	8	13 I Will Still Be Laughing	—	Candy From A Stranger	Columbia 67618
5/2/98	Ⓜ	24	8				

SOUL COUGHING

Rock band from New York: Mike Doughty (vocals, guitar), Mark Antoni (keyboards), Sebastian Steinberg (bass) and Yuval Gabay (drums).

9/14/96	Ⓜ	37	5	1 Soundtrack To Mary	—	Irresistible Bliss	Slash 46175
12/21/96+	Ⓜ	27	12	2 Super Bon Bon	—	↓	
9/19/98	Ⓜ	8	25	3 Circles	124	El Oso	Slash/Warner 46800

Debit	Cht	Peak	Wks	ARTIST / Track Title	Hot Pos	Album Title	Album Label & Number

SOULHAT
Rock band from Austin, Texas: Kevin McKinney (vocals, guitar), Bill Cassis (guitar, vocals), Brian Walsh (bass), and B.E. "Frosty" Smith (drums).

| 9/17/94 | Ⓡ | 25 | 8 | Bonecrusher .... | — | *Good To Be Gone* ....Epic 57824 |

SOULMOTOR
Rock band from Sacramento, California: Darin Wood (vocals), Tom McClendon (guitar), Brian Wheat (bass) and Mike Vanderhule (drums).

| 5/15/99 | Ⓡ | 39 | 3 | Guardian Angel .... | — | *Soulmotor* ....CMC Int'l. 86273 |

SOUNDGARDEN   Ⓡ 1990s: #15 / All-Time: #73 ★ Ⓜ 1990s: #24 / All-Time: #57
Hard-rock band formed in Seattle, Washington: **Chris Cornell** (vocals; born on 7/20/1964), Kim Thayil (guitar; born on 9/4/1960), Ben Shepherd (bass; born on 9/20/1968) and Matt Cameron (drums; born on 11/28/1962). Cornell and Cameron also recorded with **Temple Of The Dog**. Group disbanded on 4/9/1997. Cameron joined **Pearl Jam** in 1999. Cornell later formed **Audioslave**.

TOP HITS: 1)Black Hole Sun 2)Burden In My Hand 3)Blow Up The Outside World

1/11/92	Ⓡ	45	6	1 Outshined	—	*Badmotorfinger* ....A&M 5374
3/5/94	Ⓡ	3²	26	2 Spoonman	—	*Superunknown* ....A&M 540198
3/12/94	Ⓜ	9	10			
				Grammy: Metal Performance		
5/14/94	Ⓡ	❶⁷	26	3 Black Hole Sun	24ᴬ	↓
4/23/94	Ⓜ	2¹	24			
				Grammy: Hard Rock Performance		
8/27/94	Ⓡ	4	26	4 Fell On Black Days	54ᴬ	↓
8/20/94	Ⓜ	13	26			
11/5/94	Ⓡ	11	19	5 My Wave	—	↓
10/22/94	Ⓜ	18	9			
3/25/95	Ⓡ	13	15	6 The Day I Tried To Live	—	↓
4/1/95	Ⓜ	25	7			
5/11/96	Ⓜ	2¹	16	7 Pretty Noose	37ᴬ	*Down On The Upside* ....A&M 540526
5/4/96	Ⓡ	4	26			
6/15/96	Ⓡ	❶⁵	26	8 Burden In My Hand	40ᴬ	↓
6/29/96	Ⓜ	2²	26			
10/19/96	Ⓡ	❶⁴	26	9 Blow Up The Outside World	53ᴬ	↓
10/26/96	Ⓜ	8	21			
3/29/97	Ⓡ	19	15	10 Rhinosaur	—	↓
11/8/97	Ⓡ	13	11	11 Bleed Together	—	*A-Sides* ....A&M 540833
11/15/97	Ⓜ	32	6			

SOUP DRAGONS, The
Pop-rock band from Glasgow, Scotland: Sean Dickson (vocals), Jim McCulloch (guitar), Sushil Dade (bass) and Paul Quinn (drums).

8/25/90	Ⓜ	2²	14	1 I'm Free	79	*Lovegod* ....Big Life 842985
				first recorded by The Rolling Stones in 1965		
4/25/92	Ⓜ	3³	12	2 Divine Thing	35	*Hotwired* ....Big Life 13178
7/11/92	Ⓜ	14	9	3 Pleasure	69	↓

SOUTHER, J.D.
Born John David Souther on 11/2/1945 in Detroit, Michigan; raised in Amarillo, Texas. Pop-rock singer/songwriter/guitarist.

| 3/21/81 | Ⓡ | 21 | 5 | Her Town Too .... | 11 | *Dad Loves His Work* ....Columbia 37009 |
| | | | | **JAMES TAYLOR & J.D. SOUTHER** | | |

SOUTHSIDE JOHNNY & THE JUKES
Born John Lyon on 12/4/1948 in Neptune, New Jersey. Rock singer/harmonica player. Core members of The Jukes: Billy Rush (guitar), Kevin Kavanaugh (keyboards) and Alan Berger (bass).

8/11/84	Ⓡ	43	7	1 New Romeo	103	*In The Heat* ....Mirage 90186
10/26/91	Ⓡ	22	13	2 It's Been A Long Time	—	*Better Days* ....Impact 10445
				SOUTHSIDE JOHNNY & THE ASBURY JUKES written by **Little Steven**		

SPACE
Rock band from Liverpool, England: Tommy Scott (vocals, bass), Jamie Murphy (guitar), Franny Griffith (keyboards) and Andy Parle (drums).

| 2/8/97 | Ⓜ | 15 | 13 | Female Of The Species .... | 71ᴬ | *Spiders* ....Universal 53028 |

Billboard				ARTIST / Track Title		Hot Pos	Album Title	Album Label & Number
Debut	Cht	Peak	Wks					

SPACEHOG
Rock band from Leeds, Yorkshire, England: brothers Royston Langdon (vocals, bass) and Antony Langdon (guitar), with Richard Steel (guitar) and Jonny Cragg (drums). Royston Langdon married actress Liv Tyler on 3/25/2003.

Debut	Cht	Peak	Wks	Track	Hot Pos	Album	Label
12/16/95+	ⓡ	❶⁴	32	1 In The Meantime	32	Resident Alien	Sire 61834
12/9/95+	Ⓜ	2³	26				
7/6/96	ⓡ	29	5	2 Cruel To Be Kind	—	↓	
3/14/98	ⓡ	19	10	3 Mungo City	—	The Chinese Album	Sire 46851
3/7/98	Ⓜ	21	9				
3/10/01	ⓡ	23	10	4 I Want To Live	—	The Hogyssey	Artemis 751068

SPACE MONKEYS
Rock band from Manchester, England: Richard McNevin-Duff (vocals, guitar), Tony Pipes (keyboards), Dom Morrison (bass) and Chas Morrison (drums).

11/8/97	Ⓜ	20	14	Sugar Cane	58	The Daddy Of Them All	Chingón 90153
				samples "Bring The Noise" by Public Enemy			

SPANDAU BALLET
Pop band formed in London, England: Tony Hadley (vocals), brothers Gary Kemp (guitar) and Martin Kemp (bass), Steve Norman (sax) and John Keeble (drums). The Kemps starred in the 1990 movie *The Krays*. Gary Kemp was married to actress Sadie Frost from 1988-97.

10/15/83	ⓡ	34	4	1 True	4	True	Chrysalis 41403
8/4/84	ⓡ	40	10	2 Only When You Leave	34	Parade	Chrysalis 41473

SPANOS, Danny
Born in Detroit, Michigan. Rock singer/songwriter/guitarist.

8/27/83	ⓡ	15	9	1 Hot Cherie	—	Passion In The Dark	Epic 38805
2/16/85	ⓡ	42	4	2 I'd Lie To You For Your Love	—	Looks Like Trouble	Epic 39459

SPARKLEHORSE
Born Mark Linkous in Bremo Bluff, Virginia. Male singer/songwriter/guitarist.

4/20/96	Ⓜ	35	4	Someday I Will Treat You Good	—	Vivadixiesubmarinetransmissionplot	Capitol 32816

SPARTA
Rock band from El Paso, Texas: Jim Ward (vocals, guitar), Paul Hinojos (guitar), Matt Miller (bass) and Tony Hajjar (drums). Ward, Hinojos and Hajjar are also members of **At The Drive-In**.

1/4/03	ⓡ	35	3	1 Air	—	Wiretap Scars	DreamWorks 450366
11/4/06+	ⓡ	24	18	2 Taking Back Control	—	Threes	Hollywood 162613
12/2/06+	Ⓜ	25	13				

SPECIALS, The
Ska-rock band from Coventry, England: Neville Staple (vocals), Roddy Byers (guitar), Lynval Golding (guitar), Adam Birch and Jonathan Reed (horns), Mark Adams (keyboards), Horace Panter (bass) and Harrington Bembridge (drums).

3/28/98	Ⓜ	29	9	It's You	—	Guilty 'Til Proved Innocent!	Way Cool Music 11735

SPIDERBAIT
Punk-rock trio from Australia: Mark Maher (vocals, drums), Damien Whity (guitar) and Janet English (bass).

10/2/04	ⓡ	32	17	Black Betty	—	Alright Tonight	Interscope 003218
				#18 Pop hit for Ram Jam in 1977			

SPIN DOCTORS
Rock band formed in New York: Christopher Barron (vocals), Eric Schenkman (guitar), Mark White (bass) and Aaron Comess (drums). Anthony Krizan replaced Schenkman in 1993.

6/27/92	ⓡ	2⁴	30	1 Little Miss Can't Be Wrong	17	Pocket Full Of Kryptonite	Epic/Assc. 47461
10/10/92	ⓡ	8	19	2 Jimmy Olsen's Blues	78	↓	
1/23/93	ⓡ	2⁷	21	3 Two Princes	7	↓	
5/22/93	ⓡ	26	6	4 What Time Is It?	—	↓	
8/14/93	ⓡ	28	7	5 How Could You Want Him (When You Know You Could Have Me?)	102	↓	
6/4/94	Ⓜ	22	5	6 Cleopatra's Cat	84	Turn It Upside Down	Epic 52907
6/4/94	ⓡ	22	6				
7/9/94	ⓡ	8	13	7 You Let Your Heart Go Too Fast	42	↓	
7/30/94	Ⓜ	20	7				

SPINESHANK
Hard-rock band from Los Angeles, California: Johnny Santos (vocals), Mike Sarkisyan (guitar), Robert Garcia (bass) and Tom Decker (drums).

3/24/01	ⓡ	33	7	New Disease	—	The Height Of Callousness	Roadrunner 8563

				ARTIST ®=Mainstream Rock	**Hot**		
				Track Title Ⓜ=Modern Rock	**Pos**	**Album Title**	**Album Label & Number**

SPIRIT
Rock band formed in Los Angeles, California: Randy California (vocals), **Jay Ferguson** (guitar, vocals), John Locke (keyboards), Mark Andes (bass; of **Heart**) and Ed Cassidy (drums). California drowned on 1/2/1997 near Molokai, Hawaii (age 45). Locke died on 8/4/2006 (age 62). Also see **Classic Rock Tracks** section.

| 8/18/84 | ® | 54 | 2 | **I Got A Line On You** .... | — | *Spirit Of '84* ....Mercury 818514 |
| | | | | new version of their #25 Pop hit in 1969 | | |

SPLENDER
Interracial rock band formed in New York: Waymon Boone (vocals), Jonathan Svec (guitar), James Cruz (bass) and Mike Slutsky (drums).

| 6/12/99 | Ⓜ | 24 | 18 | **Yeah, Whatever**.. | — | *Halfway Down The Sky* ....Columbia 69144 |

SPLIT ENZ
New-wave pop band formed in Auckland, New Zealand: brothers Tim Finn (vocals) and Neil Finn (guitar, vocals), Eddy Rayner (keyboards), Noel Crombie (percussion), Nigel Griggs (bass) and Malcolm Green (drums). The Finns were later members of **Crowded House**.

| 5/16/81 | ® | 33 | 9 | **History Never Repeats** .... | — | *Waiata* ....A&M 4848 |

SPONGE
Rock band from Detroit, Michigan: Vinnie Dombrowski (vocals), Mike Cross (guitar), Joe Mazzola (guitar), Tim Cross (bass) and Jimmy Paluzzi (drums). Charlie Grover replaced Paluzzi in early 1996.

2/4/95	Ⓜ	5	23	1 Plowed..	41[A]	*Rotting Piñata* ....Work 57800
11/19/94+	®	9	26			
5/13/95	Ⓜ	3[2]	26	2 **Molly (Sixteen Candles)**	55	↓
6/3/95	®	11	14			
10/14/95	®	18	10	3 Rainin'..	—	↓
11/4/95	Ⓜ	34	4			
6/29/96	®	11	13	4 Wax Ecstatic (To Sell Angelina)	64[A]	*Wax Ecstatic* ....Columbia 67578
6/22/96	Ⓜ	15	13			
11/9/96+	®	7	23	5 Have You Seen Mary		↓

SPOON
Alternative-rock band from Austin, Texas: Britt Daniel (vocals, guitar), Eric Harvey (keyboards), Rob Pope (bass) and Jim Eno (drums).

| 10/6/07 | Ⓜ | 26 | 16 | 1 The Underdog .... | — | *Ga Ga Ga Ga Ga* ....Merge 295 |
| 1/26/08 | Ⓜ | 33 | 10↑ | 2 Don't You Evah .... | — | ↓ |

SPRINGFIELD, Rick
Born Richard Springthorpe on 8/23/1949 in Sydney, Australia. Singer/songwriter/guitarist/actor. Played "Dr. Noah Drake" on the TV soap *General Hospital*. Starred in the 1984 movie *Hard To Hold*.

3/21/81	®	10	20	1 Jessie's Girl	❶[2]	*Working Class Dog* ....RCA 3697
				Grammy: Rock Male Vocal		
1/16/82	®	40	9	2 Love Is Alright Tonite	20	↓
3/6/82	®	11	9	3 Don't Talk To Strangers	2[4]	*Success Hasn't Spoiled Me Yet* ....RCA 4125
3/13/82	®	4	12	4 Calling All Girls	—	↓
5/14/83	®	23	8	5 Affair Of The Heart	9	*Living In Oz* ....RCA 4660
8/20/83	®	34	4	6 Human Touch	18	↓
3/31/84	®	13	8	7 Love Somebody	5	*St: Hard To Hold* ....RCA 4935
6/16/84	®	41	6	8 Don't Walk Away	26	↓
2/27/88	®	45	3	9 Rock Of Life	22	*Rock Of Life* ....RCA 6620

SPRINGSTEEN, Bruce — ® 1980s: #3 / All-Time: #9
Born on 9/23/1949 in Freehold, New Jersey. Rock singer/songwriter/guitarist. Nicknamed "The Boss." His E-Street Band: **Little Steven** Van Zant (guitar), **Clarence Clemons** (sax), Roy Bittan (keyboards), Gary Tallent (bass) and Max Weinberg (drums). Married to model/actress Julianne Phillips from 1985-89. Married backing singer Patti Scialfa on 6/8/1991. One of the most popular live concert attractions of all-time. Also see **Classic Rock Tracks** section.

AWARD: R&R Hall of Fame: 1999

TOP HITS: 1)Dancing In The Dark 2)Tunnel Of Love 3)Trapped 4)Human Touch 5)Brilliant Disguise

3/21/81	®	14	2	1 Fade Away..	20	*The River* ....Columbia 36854
3/21/81	®	42	1	2 I'm A Rocker	—	↓
3/28/81	®	48	2	3 Cadillac Ranch...	—	↓
4/4/81	®	20	1	4 Point Blank	—	↓
4/11/81	®	30	1	5 Ramrod	—	↓
3/28/81	®	42	1	6 Be True	—	*(single only)* ....Columbia 11431
10/9/82	®	10	10	7 Atlantic City	—	*Nebraska* ....Columbia 38358

Billboard				ARTIST	Hot Pos	Album Title	Album Label & Number
Debut	Cht	Peak	Wks	Track Title ®=Mainstream Rock ⓜ=Modern Rock			

SPRINGSTEEN, Bruce — cont'd

Debut	Cht	Peak	Wks	Track Title	Hot Pos	Album Title	Album Label & Number
10/9/82	®	22	10	8 Open All Night	—	↓	
10/9/82	®	50	2	9 Johnny 99	—	↓	
6/2/84	®	27	14	10 Pink Cadillac	—	(single only)	Columbia 04463
				#5 Pop hit for Natalie Cole in 1988			
5/26/84	®	❶⁶	17	11 Dancing In The Dark	2⁴	Born In The U.S.A.	Columbia 38653
				Grammy: Rock Male Vocal ★ R&R Hall of Fame			
6/16/84	®	29	16	12 No Surrender	—	↓	
6/23/84	®	2²	21	13 Cover Me	7	↓	
6/23/84	®	8	20	14 Born In The U.S.A.	9	↓	
				RS500 #275			
6/23/84	®	36	9	15 Bobby Jean	—	↓	
2/16/85	®	4	14	16 I'm On Fire	6	↓	
5/25/85	®	3¹	14	17 Glory Days	5	↓	
9/7/85	®	9	9	18 I'm Goin' Down	9	↓	
12/14/85+	®	6	9	19 My Hometown	6	↓	

BRUCE SPRINGSTEEN & THE E STREET BAND:

Debut	Cht	Peak	Wks	Track Title	Hot Pos	Album Title	Album Label & Number
4/13/85	®	❶³	12	20 Trapped [L]	—	We Are The World (USA For Africa)	Columbia 40043
				recorded on 8/6/1984 at the New Jersey Meadowlands			
7/6/85	®	32	8	21 Stand On It	—	(single only)	Columbia 04924
				#12 Country hit for Mel McDaniel in 1985			
11/22/86	®	4	10	22 War [L]	8	Bruce Springsteen & The E Street Band Live/1975-85	Columbia 40558
				recorded on 9/30/1985 at the Los Angeles Coliseum; #1 Pop hit for Edwin Starr in 1970			
11/22/86+	®	14	14	23 Fire [L]	46	↓	
				recorded on 12/16/1978 at Winterland in San Francisco, California; #2 Pop hit for the Pointer Sisters in 1979			
12/6/86+	®	22	9	24 Because The Night [L]	—	↓	
				recorded on 12/28/1980 at the Nassau Coliseum in New York; #13 Pop hit for **Patti Smith** in 1978			
12/20/86	®	44	6	25 Raise Your Hand [L]	—	↓	
				recorded on 7/7/1978 at the Roxy in New York City; #79 Pop hit for Eddie Floyd in 1967			

BRUCE SPRINGSTEEN:

Debut	Cht	Peak	Wks	Track Title	Hot Pos	Album Title	Album Label & Number
10/3/87	®	❶¹	8	26 Brilliant Disguise	5	Tunnel of Love	Columbia 40999
10/17/87	®	❶⁴	17	27 Tunnel Of Love	9	↓	
10/17/87	®	28	13	28 Spare Parts	—	↓	
12/12/87+	®	2¹	17	29 One Step Up	13	↓	
2/27/88	®	5	12	30 All That Heaven Will Allow	—	↓	
4/16/88	®	45	3	31 Roulette	—	(single only)	Columbia 07726
9/17/88	®	16	5	32 Chimes Of Freedom [L]	—	Chimes Of Freedom	Columbia 44445
				recorded on 7/3/1988 in Stockholm, Sweden; first recorded by **Bob Dylan** in 1964			
3/21/92	®	❶³	10	33 Human Touch	16	Human Touch	Columbia 53000
4/11/92	®	6	10	34 57 Channels (And Nothin' On)	68	↓	
4/11/92	®	47	2	35 All Or Nothin' At All	—	↓	
4/25/92	®	6	3	36 Roll Of The Dice	—	↓	
3/21/92	®	2¹	5	37 Better Days	flip	Lucky Town	Columbia 53001
8/29/92	®	28	3	38 Leap Of Faith	—	↓	
2/12/94	®	25	7	39 Streets Of Philadelphia	9	St: Philadelphia	Epic Soundtrax 57624
				Grammys: Song of the Year / Rock Song / Rock Male Vocal ★ Oscar: Best Song			
3/4/95	®	14	8	40 Murder Incorporated	—	Greatest Hits	Columbia 67060
				recorded in 1982			
12/5/98	®	33	3	41 I Wanna Be With You	—	Tracks	Columbia 69475
7/20/02	®	24	12	42 The Rising	52	The Rising	Columbia 86600
				Grammys: Rock Song / Rock Male Vocal			

SPRUNG MONKEY

Rock band from San Diego, California: brothers Steve Summers (vocals), Mike Summers (guitar), with William Riley (guitar), Tony Delocht (bass) and Ernie Longoria (drums).

Debut	Cht	Peak	Wks	Track Title	Hot Pos	Album Title	Album Label & Number
5/30/98	ⓜ	13	19	1 Get 'Em Outta Here	—	Mr. Funny Face	Surfdog 62151
12/12/98+	®	25	10	2 Super Breakdown	—	↓	

SPYS

Rock band from New York: John Blanco (vocals), John DiGaudio (guitar), Al Greenwood (keyboards), Ed Gagliardi (bass) and Billy Milne (drums). Greenwood and Gagliardi were members of **Foreigner**.

Debut	Cht	Peak	Wks	Track Title	Hot Pos	Album Title	Album Label & Number
8/7/82	®	19	10	Don't Run My Life	82	Spys	EMI America 17073

SQUEEZE

Pop-rock band formed in London by vocalists/guitarists Chris Difford and Glenn Tilbrook. Originally known as UK Squeeze due to confusion with American band Tight Squeeze. **Paul Carrack** (of **Mike + The Mechanics**) was keyboardist/vocalist in 1981 of fluctuating lineup; re-joined in 1993.

TOP HITS: 1)Satisfied 2)If It's Love 3)Tempted

Debut	Cht	Peak	Wks	#	Track Title	Hot Pos	Album Title	Album Label & Number
6/6/81	®	39	8	1	In Quintessence	—	East Side Story..	A&M 4854
6/20/81	®	8	22	2	Tempted	49	↓	
5/22/82	®	26	11	3	Black Coffee In Bed	103	Sweets From A Stranger	A&M 4899
2/19/83	®	40	2	4	Annie Get Your Gun	—	Singles-45's And Under	A&M 4922
10/5/85	®	39	7	5	Hits Of The Year	—	Cosi Fan Tutti Frutti	A&M 5085
9/5/87	®	22	11	6	Hourglass	15	Babylon And On	A&M 5161
12/19/87	®	50	3	7	Trust Me To Open My Mouth	—	↓	
1/23/88	®	37	5	8	853-5937	32	↓	
9/30/89	Ⓜ	7	9	9	If It's Love	—	frank.	A&M 5278
8/3/91	Ⓜ	3[4]	11	10	Satisfied	—	Play	Reprise 26644
8/17/91	®	49	1					
10/26/91	Ⓜ	14	6	11	Crying In My Sleep	—	↓	
9/18/93	Ⓜ	9	8	12	Everything In The World	—	Some Fantastic Place	A&M 540140

SQUIER, Billy

® **1980s: #20 / All-Time: #52**

Born on 5/12/1950 in Wellesley Hills, Massachusetts. Hard-rock singer/songwriter/guitarist.

TOP HITS: 1)Everybody Wants You 2)Rock Me Tonite 3)The Stroke 4)Don't Say You Love Me 5)She Goes Down

Debut	Cht	Peak	Wks	#	Track Title	Hot Pos	Album Title	Album Label & Number
5/2/81	®	7	31	1	In The Dark	35	Don't Say No	Capitol 12146
5/16/81	®	3[1]	26	2	The Stroke	17	↓	
6/20/81	®	31	13	3	My Kinda Lover	45	↓	
8/8/81	®	28	19	4	Lonely Is The Night	—	↓	
8/7/82	®	❶[6]	20	5	Everybody Wants You	32	Emotions In Motion	Capitol 12217
8/7/82	®	20	7	6	Emotions In Motion	68	↓	
8/7/82	®	46	1	7	Keep Me Satisfied	—	↓	
10/2/82	®	15	12	8	Learn How To Live	—	↓	
3/12/83	®	44	1	9	She's A Runner	75	↓	
7/7/84	®	❶[2]	15	10	Rock Me Tonite	15	Signs Of Life	Capitol 12361
8/11/84	®	10	13	11	All Night Long	75	↓	
9/29/84	®	51	2	12	Can't Get Next To You	—	↓	
1/5/85	®	29	5	13	Eye On You	80	↓	
9/27/86	®	17	8	14	Love Is The Hero	—	Enough Is Enough	Capitol 12483
11/22/86	®	30	4	15	Shot O' Love	—	↓	
6/3/89	®	4	13	16	Don't Say You Love Me	58	Hear & Now	Capitol 48748
8/19/89	®	20	10	17	Tied Up	—	↓	
11/4/89	®	38	6	18	Don't Let Me Go	—	↓	
3/30/91	®	4	12	19	She Goes Down	—	Creatures Of Habit	Capitol 94303
6/22/91	®	37	6	20	Facts Of Life	—	↓	
4/17/93	®	15	6	21	Angry	—	Tell The Truth	Capitol 98690

SQUIRREL NUT ZIPPERS

Eclectic-jazz band from Chapel Hill, North Carolina: Jim Mathus (vocals, guitar, trombone), Katharine Whalen (vocals, banjo), Ken Mosher (guitar, sax), Tom Maxwell (sax, clarinet), Je Widenhouse (trumpet), Don Raleigh (bass) and Chris Phillips (drums). Group name taken from a brand of candy.

Debut	Cht	Peak	Wks		Track Title	Hot Pos	Album Title	Album Label & Number
4/12/97	Ⓜ	13	19		Hell	72[A]	Hot	Mammoth 0137

SR-71

Rock band from Baltimore, Maryland: Mitch Allan (vocals, guitar), Mark Beauchemin (guitar), Jeff Reid (bass) and Dan Garvin (drums).

Debut	Cht	Peak	Wks	#	Track Title	Hot Pos	Album Title	Album Label & Number
5/27/00	Ⓜ	2[1]	27	1	Right Now	102	Now You See Inside	RCA 67845
9/2/00	®	38	2					
12/2/00+	Ⓜ	22	10	2	Politically Correct	—	↓	
10/12/02	Ⓜ	18	14	3	Tomorrow	—	Tomorrow	RCA 68130

STABBING WESTWARD

Rock band from Chicago, Illinois: Christopher Hall (vocals, guitar), Walter Flakus (keyboards), Jim Sellers (bass) and Andy Kubiszewski (drums).

Debut	Cht	Peak	Wks	Track	Hot Pos	Album	Label
2/10/96	®	7	21	1 What Do I Have To Do?	60[A]	Wither Blister Burn + Peel	Columbia 66152
2/3/96	Ⓜ	11	19				
7/20/96	®	7	26	2 Shame	69[A]	↓	
8/3/96	Ⓜ	14	16				
3/21/98	®	4	26	3 Save Yourself	—	Darkest Days	Columbia 69329
3/28/98	Ⓜ	20	26				
9/12/98	®	20	14	4 Sometimes It Hurts	—	↓	
10/17/98	Ⓜ	39	3				
1/30/99	®	19	11	5 Haunting Me	—	↓	
2/27/99	Ⓜ	34	4				
5/5/01	Ⓜ	21	10	6 So Far Away	—	Stabbing Westward	Koch 8204
4/28/01	®	23	13				

STABILIZERS

Pop-rock duo from Erie, Pennsylvania: Dave Christenson (vocals) and Rich Nevens (keyboards, guitar).

Debut	Cht	Peak	Wks	Track	Hot Pos	Album	Label
10/25/86	®	21	13	One Simple Thing	93	Tyranny	Columbia 40264

STAGE DOLLS

Rock trio from Trondheim, Norway: Torstein Flakne (vocals), Terje Storli (bass) and Steinar Krokstad (drums).

Debut	Cht	Peak	Wks	Track	Hot Pos	Album	Label
7/29/89	®	14	10	1 Love Cries	46	Stage Dolls	Chrysalis 21716
10/21/89	®	37	7	2 Still In Love	—	↓	

STAIND

® 2000s: #4 / All-Time: #27 ★ Ⓜ 2000s: #5 / All-Time: #18

Alternative-rock band from Boston, Massachusetts: **Aaron Lewis** (vocals; born on 4/13/1972), Mike Mushok (guitar; born on 4/10/1970), Johnny April (bass; born on 3/27/1965) and Jon Wysocki (drums; born on 1/17/1971).

TOP HITS: 1)It's Been Awhile 2)So Far Away 3)Right Here

Debut	Cht	Peak	Wks	Track	Hot Pos	Album	Label
4/3/99	®	24	14	1 Just Go	—	Dysfunction	Flip 62356
8/7/99	®	10	28	2 Mudshovel	—	↓	
9/4/99	Ⓜ	14	26				
2/12/00	®	11	26	3 Home	—	↓	
3/4/00	Ⓜ	17	20				
4/7/01	®	❶[20]	42	4 It's Been Awhile	5	Break The Cycle	Flip 62626
4/7/01	Ⓜ	❶[16]	29				
5/19/01	®	11	26	5 Outside	111	↓	
5/12/01	Ⓜ	16	26				
8/25/01	®	3[5]	26	6 Fade	62	↓	
9/1/01	Ⓜ	4	26				
12/22/01+	®	3[4]	40	7 For You	63	↓	
12/29/01+	Ⓜ	3[1]	32				
5/11/02	®	22	14	8 Epiphany	—	↓	
5/25/02	Ⓜ	28	17				
4/19/03	®	2[1]	17	9 Price To Play	66	14 Shades Of Grey	Flip 62882
4/19/03	Ⓜ	6	17				
6/28/03	®	❶[14]	42	10 So Far Away	24	↓	
6/28/03	Ⓜ	❶[7]	30				
11/22/03+	®	10	21	11 How About You	119	↓	
11/29/03+	Ⓜ	10	16				
5/28/05	®	❶[2]	30	12 Right Here	55	Chapter V	Flip 62982
6/4/05	Ⓜ	3[4]	26				

Debut	Cht	Peak	Wks	ARTIST / Track Title	Hot Pos	Album Title	Album Label & Number

STAIND — cont'd

10/22/05+ ®	7	20	13 Falling	—	↓	
11/12/05+ ℳ	19	18				
3/11/06 ®	22	16	14 Everything Changes	—	↓	
4/15/06 ℳ	32	7				
7/15/06 ®	27	12	15 King Of All Excuses	—	↓	

STAKKA BO
Dance-rap duo from Sweden: Johan "Stakka Bo" Renck and Oscar Franzen.

| 5/21/94 ℳ | 20 | 7 | Here We Go .... | 109 | Supermarket .... Polydor 521089 |

STANLEY, Michael, Band
Born Michael Stanley Gee on 3/25/1948 in Cleveland, Ohio. Rock singer/guitarist. His band: Kevin Raleigh (vocals, keyboards), Bob Pelander (keyboards), Gary Markshay (guitar), Rick Bell (sax), Mike Gismondi (bass) and Tom Dobeck (drums). Don Powers replaced Markshay in 1982.

8/1/81 ®	6	18	1 In The Heartland	—	North Coast .... EMI America 17056
9/4/82 ®	24	10	2 In Between The Lines	—	MSB .... EMI America 17071
9/24/83 ®	11	12	3 My Town	39	You Can't Fight Fashion .... EMI America 17100

STAPP, Scott
Born on 8/8/1973 in Orlando, Florida. Rock singer. Former lead singer of **Creed**.

| 10/15/05 ® | 20 | 18 | The Great Divide .... | 110 | The Great Divide .... Wind-Up 13099 |

STARCLUB
Pop-rock band from England: Owen Vyse (vocals, guitar), Steve French (guitar), Julian Taylor (bass) and Alan White (drums). White was a member of **Oasis** from 1995-2004.

| 1/16/93 ℳ | 10 | 8 | Hard To Get .... | 119 | Starclub .... Island 514320 |

STARFIGHTERS
Hard-rock band formed in Birmingham, England: Steve Burton (vocals), Pat Hambly (guitar), Steve Young (guitar), Doug Dennis (bass) and Steve Bailey (drums).

| 1/30/82 ® | 28 | 5 | Alley Cat Blues .... | — | Starfighters .... Arista 9576 |

STARR, Ringo
Born Richard Starkey on 7/7/1940 in Liverpool, England. Drummer of **The Beatles**. Married actress Barbara Bach on 4/27/1981. His son, Zak Starkey, joined **Oasis** in 2004. Also see **Classic Rock Tracks** section.

| 6/13/92 ® | 43 | 1 | Weight Of The World .... | — | Time Takes Time .... Private M. 82097 |

STARSAILOR
Rock band from Chorley, Lancashire, England: James Walsh (vocals, guitar), Barry Westhead (keyboards), James Stelfox (bass) and Ben Byrne (drums).

| 1/26/02 ℳ | 28 | 9 | Good Souls .... | — | Love Is Here .... Capitol 36448 |

STARSHIP — see JEFFERSON AIRPLANE/STARSHIP

STARTING LINE, The
Punk-rock band from Churchville, Pennsylvania: Kenny Vasoli (vocals, bass), Matt Watts (guitar), Mike Golla (guitar), and Tom Gryskiewicz (drums).

| 8/4/07 ℳ | 21 | 20 | Island (Float Away) .... | — | Direction .... Virgin 53613 |

STATIC-X
Alternative-metal rock band formed in Los Angeles, California: Wayne "Static" Wells (vocals, guitar), Koichi Fukuda (guitar, keyboards), Tony Campos (bass) and Ken Jay (drums). Fukuda left in 2000; Static took over keyboards and Tod "Tripp Eisen" Salvador (guitar) joined. Nick Oshiro (of **Seether**) replaced Lacey in early 2003. Salvador was fired in 2005; Fukuda returned.

TOP HITS: 1)Push It 2)I'm The One 3)The Only

6/26/99 ®	36	6	1 Bled For Days	—	Wisconsin Death Trip .... Warner 47271
10/9/99 ®	20	20	2 Push It	—	↓	
11/27/99 ℳ	36	8				
4/15/00 ®	38	2	3 I'm With Stupid (He's A Loser)	—	↓	
6/9/01 ®	36	4	4 This Is Not	—	Machine .... Warner 47948
10/20/01 ®	35	5	5 Black & White	—	↓	
3/2/02 ®	29	8	6 Cold	—	↓	
9/27/03 ®	22	16	7 The Only	—	Shadow Zone .... Warner 48427
4/3/04 ®	37	4	8 So	—	↓	
5/28/05 ®	22	21	9 I'm The One	—	Start A War .... Warner 49373
11/26/05 ®	27	20	10 Dirthouse	—	↓	
3/10/07 ®	23	20	11 Destroyer	—	Cannibal .... Reprise 101710

Billboard				ARTIST		Hot		
Debut	Cht	Peak	Wks	Track Title	®=Mainstream Rock ⑩=Modern Rock	Pos	Album Title	Album Label & Number

STEALIN HORSES
Rock-country band from Lexington, Kentucky: Kiya Heartwood (vocals), Mandy Meyer (guitar), John Durno (bass) and Kopana Terry (drums).

| 6/25/88 | ® | 50 | 1 | Turnaround .... | — | Stealin Horses ....Arista 8520 |

STEEL BREEZE
Pop band from Sacramento, California: Ric Jacobs (vocals), Ken Goorabian and Waylin Carpenter (guitars), Rod Toner (keyboards), Vinnie Pantleoni (bass) and Barry Lowenthal (drums).

| 9/25/82 | ® | 9 | 12 | You Don't Want Me Anymore .... | 16 | Steel Breeze ....RCA 4424 |

STEELHEART
Hard-rock band from Norwalk, Connecticut: Michael Matijevic (vocals), Chris Risola (guitar), Frank Dicostanzo (guitar), Jimmy Ward (bass) and John Fowler (drums). Fowler died on 3/21/2008 (age 42).

| 1/19/91 | ® | 24 | 11 | 1 I'll Never Let You Go (Angel Eyes)............. | 23 | Steelheart..MCA 6368 |
| 5/25/91 | ® | 34 | 6 | 2 Everybody Loves Eileen .... | — | ↓ |

STEELY DAN
Jazz-rock band formed in Los Angeles, California, by **Donald Fagen** (keyboards, vocals; born on 1/10/1948 in Passaic, New York) and Walter Becker (bass, vocals; born on 2/20/1950 in Manhattan, New York). Group, primarily known as a studio unit, featured Fagen and Becker with various studio musicians. Duo split from 1981-92. Also see **Classic Rock Tracks** section.
    AWARD: R&R Hall of Fame: 2001

| 3/21/81 | ® | 13 | 7 | Time Out Of Mind .... | 22 | Gaucho...MCA 6102 |

Mark Knopfler of **Dire Straits** (guitar solo); **Michael McDonald** (backing vocal)

STEFANI, Gwen
Born on 10/3/1969 in Anaheim, California. Lead singer of **No Doubt**. Played Jean Harlow in the 2004 movie *The Aviator*. Married **Gavin Rossdale** (lead singer of **Bush**) on 9/14/2002.

| 11/4/00+ | ⑩ | 3³ | 31 | South Side .... | 14 | Play ....V2 27049 |

MOBY Featuring Gwen Stefani

STEGOSAURUS
Rock trio from Santa Barbara, California: Jesse Rhodes (vocals, guitar), Drew Ross (bass) and David Liker (drums).

| 5/16/98 | ® | 37 | 5 | At The Water .... | — | Stegosaurus ....Reprise 46865 |

STEINMAN, Jim
Born on 11/1/1947 in Brooklyn, New York. Songwriter/pianist/producer.

| 5/30/81 | ® | 14 | 12 | Rock And Roll Dreams Come Through .... | 32 | Bad For Good ....Cleveland Int'l. 36531 |

Rory Dodd (lead vocal)

STEPHENSON, Van
Born on 11/4/1953 in Hamilton, Ohio. Died of cancer on 4/8/2001 (age 47). Male singer/songwriter.

| 5/12/84 | ® | 9 | 11 | Modern Day Delilah .... | 22 | Righteous Anger ....MCA 5482 |

STEPPENWOLF
Hard-rock band formed in Los Angeles, California. Numerous personnel changes. Lineup in 1987: founder John Kay (vocals, guitar), Rocket Ritchotte (guitar), Michael Wilk (bass) and Ron Hurst (drums). Also see **Classic Rock Tracks** section.

| 8/29/87 | ® | 50 | 1 | Hold On (Never Give Up, Never Give In) ...... | — | Rock & Roll Rebels ....Qwil 1560 |

JOHN KAY & STEPPENWOLF

STEREO MC'S
Dance trio from London, England: Rob Birch, Nick Hallam and Owen Rossiter.

| 1/30/93 | ⑩ | 5 | 13 | 1 Connected... | 20 | Connected ....Gee Street 514061 |
| 5/8/93 | ⑩ | 19 | 6 | 2 Step It Up.. | 58 | ↓ |

STEREOMUD
Hard-rock band formed in New York: Eric Rogers (vocals), John Fattoruso (guitar), "Joey Z" Zampella (guitar), Corey Lowery (bass) and Dan Richardson (drums). Joey Z and Richardson were members of **Life Of Agony**. Lowery is the brother of Clint Lowery (of **Sevendust**); the Lowery brothers later formed **Dark New Day**.

4/28/01	®	8	20	1 Pain...	—	Perfect Self ....Loud 85483
6/30/01	⑩	34	5			
10/13/01	®	29	8	2 Steppin' Away	—	↓
1/25/03	®	29	11	3 Breathing..	—	Every Given Moment ....Columbia 86488

STEREOPHONICS
Rock trio from Cwmaman, South Wales: Kelly Jones (vocals, guitar), Richard Jones (bass) and Stuart Cable (drums).

| 7/9/05 | ⑩ | 34 | 6 | Dakota (You Made Me Feel Like The One) .... | — | Language. Sex. Violence. Other? ....V2 27245 |

STEVENS, Corey
Born Mark Womble in Centralia, Illinois. Blues-rock singer/guitarist.

| 6/21/97 | ® | 22 | 10 | One More Time .... | — | Road To Zen ....Eureka 77061 |

STEWART, Rod

® All-Time: #75

Born on 1/10/1945 in Highgate, London, England. Pop-rock singer/songwriter. Member of the **Jeff Beck** Group from 1967-69. With Faces from 1969-75. Married to actress Alana Hamilton from 1979-84. Married to supermodel Rachel Hunter from 1990-2003. Also see **Classic Rock Tracks** section.

AWARDS: R&R Hall of Fame: 1994 ★ Grammy: Living Legends Award 1989

TOP HITS: 1)Downtown Train 2)Lost In You 3)People Get Ready 4)Infatuation 5)Forever Young

Debut		Peak	Wks	#	Track Title	Hot Pos	Album Title	Album Label & Number
4/4/81	®	45	1	1	Gi' Me Wings	—	Foolish Behaviour	Warner 3485
10/31/81+	®	23	16	2	Young Turks	5	Tonight I'm Yours	Warner 3602
12/12/81+	®	38	11	3	Tora, Tora, Tora (Out With The Boys)	—	↓	
1/30/82	®	44	3	4	Jealous	—	↓	
2/20/82	®	29	3	5	Tonight I'm Yours (Don't Hurt Me)	20	↓	
11/13/82	®	21	4	6	Guess I'll Always Love You [L]	—	Absolutely Live	Warner 23743
5/26/84	®	5	15	7	Infatuation	6	Camouflage	Warner 25095
					Jeff Beck (guitar solo)			
9/15/84	®	27	8	8	Some Guys Have All The Luck	10	↓	
					#39 Pop hit for The Persuaders in 1973			
6/15/85	®	5	13	9	People Get Ready	48	Flash	Epic 39483
					JEFF BECK & ROD STEWART			
					#14 Pop hit for The Impressions in 1965			
6/7/86	®	26	8	10	Love Touch	6	Rod Stewart	Warner 25446
					theme from the movie *Legal Eagles* starring Robert Redford			
9/13/86	®	45	3	11	Another Heartache	52	↓	
					co-written by Bryan Adams			
5/7/88	®	3¹	11	12	Lost In You	12	Out Of Order	Warner 25684
5/28/88	®	16	11	13	Dynamite	—	↓	
8/27/88	®	13	11	14	Forever Young	12	↓	
2/11/89	®	50	1	15	My Heart Can't Tell You No	4	↓	
					Andy Taylor (guitar, above 4)			
11/25/89+	®	❶²	12	16	Downtown Train	3³	Storyteller/The Complete Anthology: 1964-1990	Warner 25987
					first recorded by Tom Waits in 1985			
3/16/91	®	13	10	17	Rhythm Of My Heart	5	Vagabond Heart	Warner 26300
5/4/91	®	17	7	18	Rebel Heart	—	↓	
5/15/93	®	16	7	19	Cut Across Shorty [L]	—	Unplugged...And Seated	Warner 45289
					Ronnie Wood (bass); first recorded by Eddie Cochran in 1960 (first recorded by Stewart in 1970)			
5/23/98	®	13	16	20	Cigarettes And Alcohol	—	When We Were The New Boys	Warner 46792
9/19/98	®	31	6	21	Rocks	—	↓	

STEWART, Sandy

Born in Philadelphia, Pennsylvania. Female singer/songwriter.

2/11/84	®	32	2		Nightbird	33	The Wild Heart	Modern 90084
					STEVIE NICKS with Sandy Stewart			

STILLS, Stephen

Born on 1/3/1945 in Dallas, Texas. Rock singer/songwriter/guitarist. Member of Buffalo Springfield and **Crosby, Stills & Nash**. Also see **Classic Rock Tracks** section.

8/11/84	®	12	10		Stranger	61	Right By You	Atlantic 80177
					Graham Nash (backing vocal)			

STILTSKIN

Rock trio from Edinburgh, Scotland: Ray Wilson (vocals), Peter Lawlor (guitar) and Ross McFarlane (drums). Wilson replaced **Phil Collins** as lead singer of **Genesis** in June 1997.

5/6/95	®	37	2		Inside	—	The Mind's Eye	EastWest 61785

STING

® All-Time: #63

Born Gordon Sumner on 10/2/1951 in Wallsend, England. Singer/songwriter/bassist. Lead singer of **The Police**. Acted in such movies as *Quadrophenia, Dune, The Bride* and *Plenty*. Married actress/producer Trudy Styler on 8/20/1992. Nicknamed "Sting" because of a yellow and black jersey he liked to wear.

AWARD: Billboard Century Award 2003

TOP HITS: 1)All This Time 2)If You Love Somebody Set Them Free 3)Fortress Around Your Heart

4/10/82	®	28	5	1	Roxanne [L]	—	VA: The Secret Policeman's Other Ball/ The Music	Island 9698
					#32 Pop hit for The Police in 1979			
6/8/85	®	❶³	13	2	If You Love Somebody Set Them Free	3²	The Dream Of The Blue Turtles	A&M 3750
7/6/85	®	❶²	18	3	Fortress Around Your Heart	8	↓	
10/5/85	®	19	12	4	Love Is The Seventh Wave	17	↓	
1/11/86	®	34	8	5	Russians	16	↓	
					samples "Romance" melody from Russian composer Sergei Prokofiev's *Lieutenant Kije Suite*			
5/17/86	®	14	7	6	I Been Down So Long [L]	—	VA: Live! For Life	I.R.S. 5731
					STING & JEFF BECK			
					recorded at The Greek Theatre in Los Angeles, California			

Billboard				ARTIST			
Debut	Cht	Peak	Wks	Track Title	Hot Pos	Album Title	Album Label & Number

®=Mainstream Rock
Ⓜ=Modern Rock

STING — cont'd

Debut	Cht	Peak	Wks	Track Title	Hot Pos	Album Title	Album Label & Number
10/10/87	®	20	8	7 We'll Be Together	7	...Nothing Like The Sun	A&M 6402
10/24/87	®	11	13	8 Little Wing	—	↓	
				first recorded by Jimi Hendrix in 1968			
11/28/87	®	30	9	9 The Lazarus Heart	—	↓	
1/16/88	®	2²	12	10 Be Still My Beating Heart	15	↓	
3/26/88	®	32	6	11 Englishman In New York	84	↓	
1/19/91	®	❶⁷	13	12 All This Time	5	The Soul Cages	A&M 6405
1/19/91	Ⓜ	❶²	11				
2/9/91	®	7	15	13 The Soul Cages	—	↓	
				Grammy: Rock Song			
3/16/91	Ⓜ	9	8				
5/18/91	®	32	6	14 Why Should I Cry For You?	—	↓	
6/13/92	®	20	5	15 It's Probably Me	—	St: Lethal Weapon 3	Reprise 26989
				STING & ERIC CLAPTON			
2/13/93	Ⓜ	4	14	16 If I Ever Lose My Faith In You	17	Ten Summoner's Tales	A&M 540070
2/13/93	®	5	16				
5/15/93	Ⓜ	12	9	17 Fields Of Gold	23	↓	
6/12/93	®	24	9				

STIPE, Michael
Born on 1/4/1960 in Decatur, Georgia. Lead singer of **R.E.M.**

Debut	Cht	Peak	Wks	Track Title	Hot Pos	Album Title	Album Label & Number
11/7/92+	Ⓜ	2¹	14	Trout	—	Homebrew	Virgin 86516
				NENEH CHERRY Featuring Michael Stipe			

STIR
Rock trio from St. Charles, Missouri: Andy Schmidt (vocals, guitar), Kevin Gagnepain (bass) and Brad Booker (drums).

Debut	Cht	Peak	Wks	Track Title	Hot Pos	Album Title	Album Label & Number
11/9/96+	®	8	19	1 Looking For	—	Stir	Aware 38398
4/5/97	®	21	7	2 Stale	—	↓	
8/23/97	®	23	9	3 One Angel	—	↓	
3/11/00	®	16	14	4 New Beginning	—	Holy Dogs	Capitol 57098
3/18/00	Ⓜ	18	11				
8/19/00	Ⓜ	39	1	5 Climbing The Walls	—	↓	
8/19/00	®	39	1				

STONE FURY
Hard-rock band formed in Los Angeles, California: Lenny Wolf (vocals), Bruce Gowdy (guitar), Rick Wilson (bass) and Jody Cortez (drums). Wolf formed **Kingdom Come** in 1987.

Debut	Cht	Peak	Wks	Track Title	Hot Pos	Album Title	Album Label & Number
11/24/84	®	47	2	Break Down The Wall	—	Burns Like A Star	MCA 5522

STONE ROSES, The
Alternative pop-rock band from Manchester, England: Ian Brown (vocal), John Squire (guitar), Gary Mounfield (bass) and Alan Wren (drums).

Debut	Cht	Peak	Wks	Track Title	Hot Pos	Album Title	Album Label & Number
8/26/89	Ⓜ	9	9	1 She Bangs The Drums	—	The Stone Roses	Silvertone 1184
12/9/89+	Ⓜ	18	11	2 I Wanna Be Adored	—	↓	
3/24/90	Ⓜ	5	14	3 Fools Gold	—	↓	
8/18/90	Ⓜ	9	9	4 One Love	—	(single only)	Silvertone 1399
12/24/94+	Ⓜ	2¹	21	5 Love Spreads	55ᴬ	Second Coming	Geffen 24503
2/11/95	®	4	21				

STONE SOUR   **®** 2000s: #32
Hard-rock band formed in Des Moines, Iowa: **Corey Taylor** (vocals), Jim Root (guitar), Josh Rand (guitar), Sid Wilson (bass) and Joel Ekman (drums). Taylor and Root are also members of **Slipknot**. Roy Mayorga replaced Ekman in 2006.

Debut	Cht	Peak	Wks	Track Title	Hot Pos	Album Title	Album Label & Number
8/31/02	®	2¹	28	1 Bother	56	Stone Sour	Roadrunner 618425
9/7/02	Ⓜ	4	26				
2/22/03	®	18	11	2 Inhale	—	↓	
6/17/06	®	❶⁷	40	3 Through Glass	39	Come What(ever) May	Roadrunner 618073
6/24/06	Ⓜ	2³	38				
12/2/06+	®	2¹	25	4 Sillyworld	—	↓	
2/3/07	Ⓜ	21	12				
5/19/07	®	12	20	5 Made Of Scars	—	↓	
11/10/07+	®	29	14	6 Zzyzx Rd.	—	↓	

STONE TEMPLE PILOTS ® 1990s: #8 ★ All-Time: #16 ★ ⓜ 1990s: #10 / All-Time: #13

Rock band formed in San Diego, California: **Scott Weiland** (vocals; born on 10/27/1967), brothers Dean DeLeo (guitar; born on 8/23/1961) and Robert DeLeo (bass; born on 2/2/1966), and Eric Kretz (drums; born on 6/7/1966). Weiland also formed **The Magnificent Bastards** and **Velvet Revolver**. The DeLeo brothers and Kretz also formed **Talk Show**. The DeLeo brothers also formed **Army Of Anyone**.

TOP HITS: 1)Interstate Love Song 2)Trippin' On A Hole In A Paper Heart 3)Vasoline 4)Plush 5)Lady Picture Show

Debut	Cht	Peak	Wks	Track Title	Hot Pos	Album Title	Album Label & Number
1/2/93	®	23	8	1 **Sex Type Thing**	—	Core	Atlantic 82418
3/20/93	®	❶¹	31	2 **Plush**	39ᴬ	↓	
4/10/93	ⓜ	9	18	Grammy: Hard Rock Performance			
7/31/93	®	11	20	3 **Wicked Garden**	—	↓	
8/14/93	ⓜ	21	9				
11/13/93+	®	2¹	26	4 **Creep**	59ᴬ	↓	
12/25/93+	ⓜ	12	13				
4/23/94	®	3⁵	26	5 **Big Empty**	50ᴬ	St: The Crow	Atlantic 82519
5/28/94	ⓜ	7	13				
6/11/94	®	❶²	26	6 **Vasoline**	38ᴬ	Purple	Atlantic 82607
6/18/94	ⓜ	2²	23				
8/20/94	®	❶¹⁵	33	7 **Interstate Love Song**	18ᴬ	↓	
8/20/94	ⓜ	2²	26				
12/24/94+	®	8	16	8 **Unglued**	—	↓	
12/31/94+	ⓜ	16	11				
3/18/95	®	12	10	9 **Pretty Penny**	—	↓	
3/25/95	®	3³	17	10 **Dancing Days**	63ᴬ	VA: Encomium: A Tribute To Led Zeppelin	Atlantic 82731
4/1/95	ⓜ	11	11	first recorded by **Led Zeppelin** in 1973			
3/23/96	®	❶¹	16	11 **Big Bang Baby**	28ᴬ	Tiny Music...Songs From The Vatican	
3/23/96	ⓜ	2⁴	15			Gift Shop	Atlantic 82871
5/11/96	®	❶⁴	26	12 **Trippin' On A Hole In A Paper Heart**	36ᴬ	↓	
5/18/96	ⓜ	3³	26				
10/26/96+	®	❶¹	26	13 **Lady Picture Show**	53ᴬ	↓	
10/26/96	ⓜ	6	22				
2/15/97	®	9	15	14 **Tumble In The Rough**	—	↓	
3/15/97	ⓜ	36	4				
10/2/99	®	5	20	15 **Down**	107	No.4	Atlantic 83255
10/2/99	ⓜ	9	11				
1/1/00	®	17	10	16 **Heaven & Hot Rods**	—	↓	
1/1/00	ⓜ	30	7				
4/22/00	ⓜ	3²	26	17 **Sour Girl**	78	↓	
4/22/00	®	4	26				
10/21/00	®	17	9	18 **No Way Out**	—	↓	
10/21/00	ⓜ	24	7				
12/23/00	®	35	5	19 **Break On Through**	—	VA: Stoned Immaculate – The Music Of	
				#126 Pop hit for **The Doors** in 1967		The Doors	Elektra 62475
6/16/01	®	4	11	20 **Days Of The Week**	101	Shangri-La Dee Da	Atlantic 83449
6/16/01	ⓜ	5	11				
9/1/01	®	25	8	21 **Hollywood Bitch**	—	↓	
9/8/01	ⓜ	29	6				
11/17/01	®	30	6	22 **Revolution**	—	(single only)	Atlantic 85200
				#12 Pop hit for **The Beatles** in 1968			
11/1/03	®	5	16	23 **All In The Suit That You Wear**	118	Thank You	Atlantic 83586
11/8/03	ⓜ	19	8				

Billboard				ARTIST		Hot		
Debut	Cht	Peak	Wks	Track Title	®=Mainstream Rock ⓜ=Modern Rock	Pos	Album Title	Album Label & Number

STORM, The
Rock band formed in San Francisco, California: Kevin Chalfant (vocals), Greg Rolie (vocals, keyboards), Josh Ramos (guitar), Ross Valory (bass) and Steve Smith (drums). Rolie was a member of **Santana**. Rolie, Valory and Smith were members of **Journey**. Chalfant was a member of **707**.

Debut	Cht	Peak	Wks	Track Title	Hot Pos	Album Title	Album Label & Number
9/28/91	®	6	21	1 I've Got A Lot To Learn About Love	26	The Storm	Interscope 91741
1/25/92	®	22	8	2 Show Me The Way	—	↓	

STORY OF THE YEAR
Rock band from St. Louis, Missouri: Dan Marsala (vocals), Ryan Phillips (guitar), Philip Sneed (guitar), Adam Russell (bass) and Josh Wills (drums).

11/1/03+	ⓜ	12	26	1 Until The Day I Die	—	Page Avenue	Maverick 48438
5/8/04	ⓜ	10	20	2 Anthem Of Our Dying Day	—	↓	
12/4/04	ⓜ	40	1	3 Sidewalks	—	↓	
10/1/05	ⓜ	28	11	4 We Don't Care Anymore	—	In The Wake Of Determination	Maverick 49390
10/22/05	®	38	5				

STORYVILLE
Rock band formed in Austin, Texas: Malford Milligan (vocals), David Holt (guitar), David Grissom (guitar), Chris Layton (bass) and Tommy Shannon (drums). Layton and Shannon were members of **Arc Angels** and **Stevie Ray Vaughan**'s Double Trouble.

7/18/98	®	28	10	Born Without You	—	Dog Years	Atlantic 83111

STRADLIN, Izzy, And The Ju Ju Hounds
Born Jeffrey Isbell on 4/8/1962 in Lafayette, Indiana. Rock singer/guitarist. Former member of **Guns N' Roses**. The Ju Ju Hounds: Rick Richards (guitar), Jimmy Ashhurst (bass) and Charlie Quintana (drums). Richards was a member of the **Georgia Satellites**. Quintana joined **Social Distortion** in 2000.

10/24/92	®	6	16	1 Shuffle It All	—	Izzy Stradlin And The Ju Ju Hounds	Geffen 24490
2/6/93	®	13	8	2 Somebody Knockin'	—	↓	

STRANGLERS, The
Pop-rock band formed in London, England: **Hugh Cornwell** (vocals, guitar), Dave Greenfield (keyboards), Jean-Jacques Burnel (bass) and Jet Black (drums).

4/11/87	®	47	2	1 Always The Sun	—	Dreamtime	Epic 40607
6/16/90	ⓜ	5	10	2 Sweet Smell Of Success	—	10	Epic 46120

STRAW, Syd
Born Susan Straw Harris in Hollywood, California. Female singer/songwriter/actress. Daughter of movie actor Jack Straw.

7/29/89	ⓜ	16	7	Future 40's (String Of Pearls)	—	Surprise	Virgin 91266
				Michael Stipe of **R.E.M.** (co-writer, backing vocal)			

STRAY CATS
Rockabilly trio from Long Island, New York: **Brian Setzer** (vocals, guitar), Lee Rocker (bass) and Slim Jim Phantom (drums). Also see **Phantom, Rocker & Slick**.

7/17/82	®	4	15	1 Rock This Town	9	Built For Speed	EMI America 17070
				R&R Hall of Fame			
8/21/82	®	41	2	2 Stray Cat Strut	3[3]	↓	
8/13/83	®	2[1]	15	3 (She's) Sexy + 17	5	Rant n' Rave with the Stray Cats	EMI America 17102
3/25/89	®	35	5	4 Bring It Back Again	—	Blast Off	EMI 91401

STREETS
Rock band formed in Atlanta, Georgia: Steve Walsh (vocals, keyboards; of **Kansas**), Mike Slamer (guitar), Billy Greer (bass) and Tim Gehrt (drums).

11/19/83+	®	6	12	If Love Should Go	87	1st	Atlantic 80117

STRESS
Black rock trio from London, England: Wayne Binitie (vocals), Mitch Ogugua (bass) and Ian Mussington (drums).

6/15/91	ⓜ	7	7	Flowers In The Rain	—	Stress	Reprise 26519

STROKE 9
Rock band from San Francisco, California: Luke Esterkyn (vocals), John McDermott (guitar), Greg Gueldner (bass) and Eric Stock (drums).

10/9/99+	ⓜ	6	27	1 Little Black Backpack	104	Nasty Little Thoughts	Cherry 53157
4/22/00	ⓜ	27	11	2 Letters	—	↓	
8/4/01	ⓜ	36	6	3 Kick Some Ass	—	Stroke 9	Cherry 53257

STROKES, The   ⓜ 2000s: #40 / All-Time: #84
Rock band from Manhattan, New York: Julian Casablancas (vocals), Albert Hammond Jr. (guitar; son of Albert Hammond), Nick Valensi (guitar), Nikolai Fraiture (bass) and Fabrizio Moretti (drums).

11/10/01+	ⓜ	5	26	1 Last Nite	108	Is This It	RCA 68101
5/11/02	ⓜ	27	11	2 Hard To Explain	—	↓	
9/14/02	ⓜ	17	13	3 Someday	—	↓	

Billboard Debut	Cht	Peak	Wks	ARTIST / Track Title	®=Mainstream Rock ⓜ=Modern Rock	Hot Pos	Album Title	Album Label & Number
				STROKES, The — cont'd				
9/27/03	ⓜ	15	18	4 **12:51**		—	*Room On Fire* ....RCA 55497	
2/7/04	ⓜ	19	15	5 **Reptilia**		—	↓	
8/28/04	ⓜ	35	4	6 **The End Has No End**		—	↓	
10/15/05	ⓜ	9	19	7 **Juicebox**		98	*First Impressions Of Earth* ....RCA 73177	
2/4/06	ⓜ	21	11	8 **Heart In A Cage**		—	↓	
8/26/06	ⓜ	35	5	9 **You Only Live Once**		—	↓	
				STYLE COUNCIL, The Pop duo from England: **Paul Weller** (vocals) and Mick Talbot (keyboards).				
5/26/84	®	52	3	**My Ever Changing Moods**		29	*My Ever Changing Moods*...........Geffen 4029	
				STYX Pop-rock band from Chicago, Illinois: **Dennis DeYoung** (vocals, keyboards), **Tommy Shaw** (guitar), James Young (guitar), and twin brothers Chuck Panozzo (bass) and John Panozzo (drums). Disbanded in 1984. Reunited in 1990 with guitarist **Glen Burtnick** replacing Shaw, who joined **Damn Yankees**. John Panozzo died on 7/16/1996 (age 47). In Greek mythology, Styx is a river of Hades. Todd Sucherman (drums) joined in 1997. Lawrence Gowan replaced DeYoung in 2000. Shaw returned in 2004 to replace Burtnick. Also see **Classic Rock Tracks** section.				
3/21/81	®	2[1]	17	1 **Too Much Time On My Hands**		9	*Paradise Theater* ....A&M 3719	
3/21/81	®	8	13	2 **Rockin' The Paradise**		—	↓	
3/21/81	®	16	9	3 **The Best Of Times**		3[4]	↓	
3/21/81	®	22	13	4 **Snowblind**		—	↓	
2/12/83	®	3[1]	15	5 **Mr. Roboto**		3[2]	*Kilroy Was Here*............................A&M 3734	
9/29/90	®	9	8	6 **Love Is The Ritual**		80	*Edge Of The Century*....................A&M 5327	
3/1/03	®	37	2	7 **Waiting For Our Time**		—	*Cyclorama*............................Sanctuary 86337	
				SUBLIME Ska-rock trio from Long Beach, California: Brad Nowell (vocals, guitar), Eric Wilson (bass) and Bud Gaugh (drums). Nowell died of a drug overdose on 5/25/1996 (age 28).				
8/24/96	ⓜ	❶[3]	27	1 **What I Got**		29[A]	*Sublime* ....Gasoline Alley 11413	
10/26/96	®	11	26					
1/18/97	ⓜ	3[6]	26	2 **Santeria**		43[A]	↓	
6/14/97	ⓜ	3[1]	26	3 **Wrong Way**		47[A]	↓	
10/4/97	ⓜ	28	10	4 **Doin' Time**		87	↓	
				SUBMERSED Rock band from Stephenville, Texas: Donald Carpenter (vocals), Eric Friedman (guitar), TJ Davis (guitar), Kelan Luker (bass) and Garrett Whitlock (drums).				
11/27/04+	®	19	26	1 **Hollow**		—	*In Due Time* ....Wind-Up 13074	
6/11/05	®	31	13	2 **In Due Time**		—	↓	
8/18/07	®	36	9	3 **Better Think Again**		—	*Immortal Verses*....................Wind-Up 13130	
				SUBWAYS, The Alternative-rock trio formed in London, England: Billy Lunn (vocals, guitar), Charlotte Cooper (bass) and Josh Morgan (drums).				
12/17/05+	ⓜ	29	14	**Rock & Roll Queen**		—	*St: The OC: Mix 5*..........Warner Sunset 49443	
				SUEDE Rock band from London, England: Brett Anderson (vocals), Bernard Butler (guitar, piano), Matt Osman (bass) and Simon Gilbert (drums).				
5/1/93	ⓜ	7	11	**Metal Mickey**		—	*Suede* ....Columbia 53792	
				SUGAR Rock band formed in Athens, Georgia: **Bob Mould** (vocals, guitar), David Barbe (bass) and Malcolm Travis (drums).				
8/29/92	ⓜ	5	13	1 **Helpless**		—	*Copper Blue* ....Rykodisc 10239	
9/3/94	ⓜ	14	11	2 **Your Favorite Thing**		120	*File Under: Easy Listening* ....Rykodisc 10300	
				SUGARCUBES, The Alternative-rock band from Reykjavik, Iceland: **Björk** Gudmundsdottir (vocals), Einar Orn Benediktsson (vocals, trumpet), Thor Eldon Jonsson (guitar), Margret Ornolfsdottir (keyboards), Bragi Olafsson (bass) and Siggi Baldursson (drums). Group began as an artist's collective called Kukl (an Icelandic term for witches). Björk and Thor were married for a time. Thor and Margret married in 1989.				
9/10/88	ⓜ	10	10	1 **Motorcrash**		—	*Life's Too Good* ....Elektra 60801	
9/23/89	ⓜ	2[2]	10	2 **Regina**		—	*Here Today, Tomorrow Next Week!*..........Elektra 60860	
2/8/92	ⓜ	❶[5]	14	3 **Hit**		—	*Stick Around For Joy* ....Elektra 61123	
4/18/92	ⓜ	16	7	4 **Walkabout**		—	↓	

Billboard				ARTIST		Hot		
Debut	Cht	Peak	Wks	Track Title	®=Mainstream Rock Ⓜ=Modern Rock	Pos	Album Title	Album Label & Number

SUGARCULT
Rock band from Santa Barbara, California: Tim Pagnotta (vocals, guitar), "Marko 72" DeSantis (guitar), Airin Older (bass) and Ben Davis (drums). Kenny Livingston replaced Davis in 2004.

4/27/02	Ⓜ	40	1	1 Bouncing Off The Walls		—	Start Static	Ultimatum 076673
9/28/02	Ⓜ	30	10	2 Pretty Girl (The Way)		—	↓	
10/28/06	Ⓜ	40	1	3 Do It Alone		—	Lights Out	Fearless 27324

SUGAR RAY
Ⓜ 1990s: #38 / All-Time: #80

Rock band from Los Angeles, California: Mark McGrath (vocals; born on 3/15/1968), Craig Bullock (DJ; born on 12/17/1970), Rodney Sheppard (guitar; born on 11/25/1967), Murphy Karges (bass; born on 6/20/1967) and Stan Frazier (drums; born on 4/23/1968). McGrath became anchor of TV entertainment magazine *Extra* in 2004.

6/28/97	Ⓜ	❶⁸	30	1 Fly	❶⁶ᴬ	Floored	Lava 83006
8/30/97	®	29	9	SUGAR RAY Featuring Super Cat			
12/27/97+	Ⓜ	35	6	2 RPM	—	↓	
12/12/98+	Ⓜ	❶⁶	26	3 Every Morning	3³	14:59	Lava 83151
3/27/99	®	38	4				
4/24/99	Ⓜ	5	12	4 Falls Apart	29	↓	
6/19/99	Ⓜ	7	21	5 Someday	7	↓	

SUGARTOOTH
Rock band from Seattle, Washington: Marc Hutner (vocals, guitar), Timothy Michael Gruse (guitar), Josh Blum (bass) and Joey Castillo (drums). By 1997, Gruse left and Castillo was replaced by Dusty Watson.

4/30/94	®	26	8	1 Sold My Fortune	—	Sugartooth	DGC 24628
6/21/97	®	38	5	2 Booty Street	—	The Sounds Of Solid	DGC 25006

SUICIDAL TENDENCIES
Hard-rock band from Venice, California: Mike Muir (vocals), Rocky George (guitar), Mike Clark (guitar), and Robert Trujillo (bass). Trujillo joined **Metallica** in 2003.

8/1/92	Ⓜ	21	6	1 I Wasn't Made To Feel This/Asleep At The Wheel...	—	The Art Of Rebellion	Epic 48864
10/31/92	®	28	7	2 Nobody Hears	—	↓	
2/20/93	®	34	5	3 I'll Hate You Better	—	↓	

SUICIDE MACHINES, The
Rock band from Detroit, Michigan: Jason Navarro (vocals), Dan Lukacinsky (guitar), Royce Nunley (bass) and Derek Grant (drums). Ryan Vandeberghe replaced Grant in 1999.

1/4/97	Ⓜ	31	7	1 No Face	—	Destruction By Definition	Hollywood 62048
1/29/00	Ⓜ	22	12	2 Sometimes I Don't Mind	—	The Suicide Machines	Hollywood 62189

SUM 41
Ⓜ 2000s: #30 / All-Time: #60

Punk-rock band from Ajax, Ontario, Canada: Deryck Whibley (vocals, guitar; born on 3/21/1980), Jason "Cone" McCaslin (bass; born on 9/3/1980), Dave Baksh (guitar; bone on 7/26/1980) and Steve Jocz (drums; born on 7/23/1981). Whibley married **Avril Lavigne** on 7/15/2006. Baksh left in 2006.

TOP HITS: 1)Fat Lip 2)Still Waiting 3)In Too Deep

8/19/00	Ⓜ	32	5	1 Makes No Difference	—	Half Hour Of Power	Island 542419
4/28/01	Ⓜ	❶¹	28	2 Fat Lip	66	All Killer No Filler	Island 548662
10/13/01	Ⓜ	10	17	3 In Too Deep	—	↓	
2/2/02	Ⓜ	24	8	4 Motivation	—	↓	
11/2/02+	Ⓜ	7	26	5 Still Waiting	—	Does This Look Infected?	Island 063491
3/15/03	Ⓜ	13	15	6 The Hell Song	—	↓	
9/18/04	Ⓜ	10	20	7 We're All To Blame	—	Chuck	Island 003492
10/16/04	®	36	5				
12/4/04+	Ⓜ	14	21	8 Pieces	107	↓	
6/2/07	Ⓜ	34	7	9 Underclass Hero	116	Underclass Hero	Island 008987
8/25/07	Ⓜ	26	11	10 Walking Disaster	—	↓	

SUMMER, Henry Lee
Born on 7/5/1955 in Brazil, Indiana. Rock singer/songwriter/guitarist.

2/13/88	®	❶¹	15	1 I Wish I Had A Girl	20	Henry Lee Summer	CBS Associated 40895
5/7/88	®	9	10	2 Darlin' Danielle Don't	57	↓	
8/13/88	®	28	8	3 Hands On The Radio	85	↓	
5/20/89	®	6	12	4 Hey Baby	18	I've Got Everything	CBS Associated 45124
1/18/92	®	47	1	5 Turn It Up	—	Way Past Midnight	Epic/Associated 47059

Billboard				ARTIST / Track Title	ℝ=Mainstream Rock ℳ=Modern Rock	Hot Pos	Album Title	Album Label & Number
Debut	Cht	Peak	Wks					

SUMMERCAMP
Rock band from Santa Barbara, California: Tim Cullen (vocals), Sean McCue (guitar), Misha Feldmann (bass) and Tony Sevener (drums).

Debut	Cht	Peak	Wks	Track	Hot Pos	Album	Label
5/31/97	ⓜ	21	10	Drawer	—	Pure Juice	Maverick 46528
7/19/97	ⓡ	37	3				

SUNDAYS, The
Pop-rock band from London, England: Harriet Wheeler (vocals), David Gavurin (guitar), Paul Brindley (bass) and Patrick Hannan (drums). Wheeler and Gavurin were eventually married.

Debut	Cht	Peak	Wks	Track	Hot Pos	Album	Label
4/21/90	ⓜ	❶¹	16	1 Here's Where The Story Ends	—	Reading, Writing And Arithmetic	DGC 24277
10/17/92	ⓜ	2²	14	2 Love	—	Blind	DGC 24479
1/23/93	ⓜ	11	7	3 Goodbye	↓		
9/6/97	ⓜ	10	22	4 Summertime	50ᴬ	Static & Silence	DGC 25131

SUNSCREEM
Techno-pop band from Essex, England: Lucia Holm (vocals), Darren Woodford (guitar), Paul Carnell (keyboards), Rob Fricker (bass) and Sean Wright (drums).

Debut	Cht	Peak	Wks	Track	Hot Pos	Album	Label
12/5/92+	ⓜ	3¹	14	Love U More	36	O₃	Columbia 53449

SUN 60
Rock duo from Los Angeles, California: singer/songwriters Joan Jones and David Russo.

Debut	Cht	Peak	Wks	Track	Hot Pos	Album	Label
7/17/93	ⓜ	29	2	Mary Xmess	—	Only	Epic 53447
				Dave Navarro (lead guitar)			

SUPER CAT
Born William Maragh on 6/25/1963 in Kingston, Jamaica (of East Indian heritage). Dance-hall/hip-hop/reggae singer.

Debut	Cht	Peak	Wks	Track	Hot Pos	Album	Label
6/28/97	ⓜ	❶⁸	30	Fly	❶⁶ᴬ	Floored	Lava 83006
8/30/97	ⓡ	29	9	SUGAR RAY Featuring Super Cat			

SUPERDRAG
Rock band from Knoxville, Tennessee: John Davis (vocals), Brandon Fisher (guitar), Tom Pappas (bass) and Don Coffey (drums).

Debut	Cht	Peak	Wks	Track	Hot Pos	Album	Label
7/6/96	ⓜ	17	12	Sucked Out	72ᴬ	Regretfully Yours	Elektra 61900

SUPERGRASS
Rock band from Oxford, England: brothers Gareth "Gaz" Coombes (vocals, guitar) and Rob Coombes (keyboards), with Mick Quinn (bass) and Danny Goffey (drums).

Debut	Cht	Peak	Wks	Track	Hot Pos	Album	Label
6/21/97	ⓜ	35	4	Cheapskate	—	In It For The Money	Capitol 55228

SUPERTRAMP
Pop-rock band formed in England: **Roger Hodgson** (vocals, guitar), Rick Davies (vocals, keyboards), John Helliwell (sax), Dougie Thomson (bass) and Bob Siebenberg (drums). Hodgson left in 1983. Also see **Classic Rock Tracks** section.

Debut	Cht	Peak	Wks	Track	Hot Pos	Album	Label
10/30/82	ⓡ	7	15	1 It's Raining Again	11	...famous last words...	A&M 3732
11/6/82	ⓡ	10	17	2 Crazy	—	↓	
11/6/82	ⓡ	30	10	3 Waiting So Long	—	↓	
12/4/82	ⓡ	32	2	4 Don't Leave Me Now	—	↓	
5/25/85	ⓡ	4	12	5 Cannonball	28	Brother Where You Bound	A&M 5014

SUPREME LOVE GODS
Pop-rock band from England: Thomas Dew (vocals), Tommy Joy (guitar), John Wilson (bass) and Eric Dansby (drums).

Debut	Cht	Peak	Wks	Track	Hot Pos	Album	Label
11/14/92	ⓜ	16	12	Souled Out	—	Supreme Love Gods	Def Amer. 45073

SURVIVOR
Pop-rock band formed in Chicago, Illinois: Dave Bickler (vocals), Frankie Sullivan (guitar), Jim Peterik (keyboards), Stephan Ellis (bass) and Marc Droubay (drums). Jimi Jamison replaced Bickler in 1983. Droubay and Ellis left in early 1988.

Debut	Cht	Peak	Wks	Track	Hot Pos	Album	Label
11/14/81+	ⓡ	19	16	1 Poor Man's Son	33	Premonition	Scotti Brothers 37549
6/12/82	ⓡ	❶⁵	15	2 Eye Of The Tiger	❶⁶	Eye Of The Tiger	Scotti Brothers 02912
				Grammy: Rock Vocal Group from the movie *Rocky III* starring Sylvester Stallone			
10/22/83	ⓡ	16	7	3 Caught In The Game	77	Caught In The Game	Scotti Brothers 38791
9/15/84	ⓡ	❶³	18	4 I Can't Hold Back	13	Vital Signs	Scotti Brothers 39578
12/15/84+	ⓡ	8	18	5 High On You	8	↓	
11/9/85	ⓡ	11	13	6 Burning Heart	2²	St: Rocky IV	Scotti Brothers 40203
11/8/86	ⓡ	27	10	7 Is This Love	9	When Seconds Count	Scotti Brothers 40457
10/22/88	ⓡ	40	4	8 Didn't Know It Was Love	61	Too Hot To Sleep	Scotti Brothers 44282

SWANS, The
Eclectic-rock trio from New York: Jarobe (female vocals), Michael Gira (guitar) and Norman Westberg (bass).

Debut	Cht	Peak	Wks	Track	Hot Pos	Album	Label
6/3/89	ⓜ	28	4	Saved	—	The Burning World	Uni 601

Billboard				ARTIST		Hot		
Debut	Cht	Peak	Wks	Track Title	®=Mainstream Rock ⓜ=Modern Rock	Pos	Album Title	Album Label & Number

SWEET, Matthew
Born on 10/6/1964 in Lincoln, Nebraska. Pop-rock singer/bassist/drummer.

Debut	Cht	Peak	Wks	Track Title	Hot Pos	Album Title	Label
12/21/91+	ⓜ	23	4	1 Divine Intervention	—	*Girlfriend*	*Zoo 11015*
1/18/92	ⓜ	4	10	2 Girlfriend	—	↓	
4/4/92	®	10	20				
7/3/93	ⓜ	3¹	11	3 The Ugly Truth	—	*Altered Beast*	*Zoo 11050*
8/21/93	®	35	4				
3/11/95	ⓜ	2¹	24	4 Sick Of Myself	58	*100% Fun*	*Zoo 11081*
4/8/95	®	13	17				
8/12/95	ⓜ	34	4	5 We're The Same	113	↓	
3/15/97	ⓜ	14	14	6 Where You Get Love	—	*Blue Sky On Mars*	*Volcano 31130*
3/22/97	®	24	9				

SWINGERS
Rock band from New Zealand: Andrew McLennan (vocals), Phil Judd (guitar), Dwayne Hillman (bass) and Ian Gilroy (drums).

Debut	Cht	Peak	Wks	Track Title	Hot Pos	Album Title	Label
9/18/82	®	45	2	Counting The Beat	—	*Counting The Beat*	*Backstreet 5328*

SWITCHED
Hard-rock band from Cleveland, Ohio: brothers Ben Schigel (vocals) and Joe Schigel (guitar), Brad Kochmit (guitar), Jason French (bass) and Chad Szeliga (drums).

Debut	Cht	Peak	Wks	Track Title	Hot Pos	Album Title	Label
5/11/02	®	30	9	Inside	—	*Subject To Change*	*Immortal 10636*

SWITCHFOOT
Christian rock band from San Diego, California: brothers Jon Foreman (vocals, guitar) and Tim Foreman (bass), with Jerome Fontamillas (keyboards) and Chad Butler (drums). Drew Shirley (guitar) joined in early 2005.

Debut	Cht	Peak	Wks	Track Title	Hot Pos	Album Title	Label
8/9/03+	ⓜ	5	33	1 Meant To Live	18	*The Beautiful Letdown*	*Red Ink 71083*
8/14/04	®	36	4				
3/27/04	ⓜ	9	24	2 Dare You To Move	17	↓	
11/13/04	ⓜ	30	7	3 This Is Your Life	—	↓	
7/16/05	ⓜ	16	12	4 Stars	68	*Nothing Is Sound*	*Columbia 94581*
8/13/05	®	39	1				
12/30/06+	ⓜ	36	6	5 Oh! Gravity	111	*Oh! Gravity*	*Columbia 82880*

SYSTEMATIC
Hard-rock band from San Francisco, California: Adam Ruppel (vocals, guitar), Tim Narducci (guiatr), Nick St. Dennis (bass) and Shaun Bannon (drums).

Debut	Cht	Peak	Wks	Track Title	Hot Pos	Album Title	Label
3/31/01	®	22	12	1 Beginning Of The End	—	*Somewhere In Between*	*TMC 62595*
4/26/03	®	39	3	2 Leaving Only Scars	—	*Pleasure To Burn*	*Elektra 62845*

SYSTEM OF A DOWN   ® 2000s: #22 / All-Time: #97 ★ ⓜ 2000s: #16 / All-Time: #37
Alternative-metal rock band from Los Angeles, California: **Serj Tankian** (vocals; born on 8/21/1967), Daron Malakian (guitar; born on 7/18/1975), Shavo Odadjian (bass; born on 4/22/1974) and John Dolmayan (drums; born on 7/15/1973).

TOP HITS: 1)Aerials 2)Hypnotize 3)Toxicity

Debut	Cht	Peak	Wks	Track Title	Hot Pos	Album Title	Label
11/20/99	®	28	11	1 Sugar	—	*System Of A Down*	*American 68924*
11/27/99+	ⓜ	31	9				
4/1/00	®	25	9	2 Spiders	—	↓	
4/15/00	ⓜ	38	1				
8/4/01	ⓜ	7	35	3 Chop Suey	76	*Toxicity*	*American 62240*
8/4/01	®	12	29				
1/26/02	ⓜ	3¹	26	4 Toxicity	70	↓	
2/2/02	®	10	26				
6/15/02	ⓜ	❶³	26	5 Aerials	55	↓	
6/22/02	®	❶¹	33				
11/23/02+	ⓜ	12	16	6 Innervision	107	↓	
11/23/02	®	14	16				

Billboard				ARTIST	**R**=Mainstream Rock	Hot		
Debut	Cht	Peak	Wks	Track Title	**M**=Modern Rock	Pos	Album Title	Album Label & Number

SYSTEM OF A DOWN — cont'd

Debut	Cht	Peak	Wks		Hot Pos	Album Title	Album Label & Number
2/12/05	M	29	8	7 Cigaro	—	*Mezmerize* ....American 90648	
2/19/05	R	34	5				
4/9/05	M	4	26	8 B.Y.O.B.	27	↓	
4/9/05	R	4	28	Grammy: Hard Rock Performance			
7/30/05	R	7	20	9 Question!	102	↓	
8/6/05	M	9	20				
10/22/05+	M	❶¹	25	10 Hypnotize	57	*Hypnotize* ....American 93871	
10/22/05+	R	5	23				
3/4/06	R	10	20	11 Lonely Day	123	↓	
3/4/06	M	10	20				
7/8/06	R	38	5	12 Kill Rock 'N' Roll.......................	—	↓	

T

TAKING BACK SUNDAY
Rock band from Amityville, Long Island, New York: Adam Lazzara (vocals), Eddie Reyes (guitar), Fred Mascherino (guitar), Matt Rubano (bass) and Mark O'Connell (drums).

Debut	Cht	Peak	Wks		Hot Pos	Album Title	Album Label & Number
8/14/04	M	16	15	1 A Decade Under The Influence	—	*Where You Want To Be* ....Victory 228	
4/15/06	M	8	22	2 MakeDamnSure	48	*Louder Now*.................................Warner 49424	
10/28/06+	M	21	20	3 Liar (It Takes One To Know One)...................	112	↓	

TALKING HEADS
New-wave/rock band formed in New York: **David Byrne** (vocals, guitar), **Jerry Harrison** (keyboards, guitar), Tina Weymouth (bass) and Chris Frantz (drums). Weymouth and Frantz married on 6/18/1977; later formed the Tom Tom Club.
Also see **Classic Rock Tracks** section.
  AWARD: R&R Hall of Fame: 2002
  TOP HITS: 1)Sax And Violins 2)Wild Wild Life 3)(Nothing But) Flowers

Debut	Cht	Peak	Wks		Hot Pos	Album Title	Album Label & Number
7/23/83	R	6	19	1 Burning Down The House	9	*Speaking In Tongues*.....................Sire 23883	
6/22/85	R	25	8	2 Road To Nowhere.......................	105	*Little Creatures* ....Sire 25305	
7/20/85	R	11	18	3 And She Was	54	↓	
10/12/85	R	24	10	4 Stay Up Late.......................	—	↓	
8/23/86	R	4	14	5 Wild Wild Life	25	*True Stories* ....Sire 25512	
10/18/86	R	19	10	6 Puzzlin' Evidence	—	↓	
3/19/88	R	5	11	7 (Nothing But) Flowers	—	*Naked* ....Sire 25654	
5/21/88	R	39	4	8 Blind	—	↓	
12/21/91+	M	❶¹	12	9 Sax And Violins	—	*St: Until The End Of The World* ....Warner 26707	
2/8/92	R	49	3				
10/17/92	M	11	8	10 Lifetime Piling Up	—	*Popular Favorites 1976-1992: Sand In The Vasoline* ....Sire 26760	

TALK SHOW
Rock band formed in Los Angeles, California: Dave Coutts (vocals), brothers Dean DeLeo (guitar) and Robert DeLeo (bass), and Eric Kretz (drums). The latter three were members of **Stone Temple Pilots**. The DeLeo brothers later formed **Army Of Anyone**.

Debut	Cht	Peak	Wks		Hot Pos	Album Title	Album Label & Number
9/6/97	R	10	9	Hello Hello	—	*Talk Show*.................................Atlantic 83040	
9/6/97	M	16	8				

TALK TALK
Pop-rock band formed in London, England: Mark Hollis (vocals), Simon Brenner (keyboards), Paul Webb (bass) and Lee Harris (drums). Brenner left in 1983.

Debut	Cht	Peak	Wks		Hot Pos	Album Title	Album Label & Number
9/11/82	R	26	4	1 Talk Talk	75	*The Party's Over* ....EMI America 17083	
4/14/84	R	23	9	2 It's My Life	31	*It's My Life* ....EMI America 17113	
2/22/86	R	26	9	3 Life's What You Make It	90	*The Colour Of Spring* ....EMI America 17179	

TALL STORIES
Rock band from New York: Steve Augeri (vocals), Jack Morer (guitar), Kevin Totoian (bass) and Tom DeFaria (drums). Augeri replaced **Steve Perry** as lead singer of **Journey** in 1998.

Debut	Cht	Peak	Wks		Hot Pos	Album Title	Album Label & Number
11/9/91+	R	22	16	Wild On The Run	—	*Tall Stories* ....Epic 47145	

Billboard				ARTIST		Hot		
Debut	Cht	Peak	Wks	Track Title	®=Mainstream Rock ⓜ=Modern Rock	Pos	Album Title	Album Label & Number

TANGIER
Hard-rock band from Philadelphia, Pennsylvania: Bill Mattson (vocals), Doug Gordon (guitar), Gari Saint (guitar), Garry Nutt (bass) and Bobby Bender (drums).

6/17/89	®	7	12	On The Line	67	Four Winds	Atco 91251

TANKIAN, Serj
Born on 8/21/1967 in Beirut, Lebanon; later based in Los Angeles, California. Lead singer of **System Of A Down**.

9/29/07	ⓜ	3[5]	25	1 Empty Walls	97	Elect The Dead	Serjical Strike 286076
9/29/07	®	4	23				
2/9/08	ⓜ	22	8↑	2 Sky Is Over	—	↓	
2/23/08	®	25↑	6↑				

TANTRIC
Rock band from Louisville, Kentucky: Hugo Ferreira (vocals), Todd Whitener (guitar), Jesse Vest (bass) and Matt Taul (drums). The latter three were members of **Days Of The New**. The latter three then left in late 2007; replaced by Joe Pessia (guitar), Erik Leonhardt (bass) and Kevin Miller (drums; of **Fuel**).

1/6/01	®	❶[1]	27	1 Breakdown	106	Tantric	Maverick 47978
3/10/01	ⓜ	4	26				
6/23/01	®	7	26	2 Astounded	—	↓	
8/25/01	ⓜ	30	8				
10/27/01	®	18	21	3 Mourning	—	↓	
12/1/01+	ⓜ	22	14				
1/3/04	®	8	18	4 Hey Now	—	After We Go	Maverick 48351
5/15/04	®	36	4	5 The Chain	—	↓	
				first recorded by **Fleetwood Mac** in 1977			
7/3/04	®	30	9	6 After We Go	—	↓	
3/15/08	®	31↑	3↑	7 Down And Out	—	The End Begins	Silent Majority 430844

TAPROOT
Hard-rock band from Ann Arbor, Michigan: Steve Richards (vocals), Mike DeWolf (guitar), Phil Lipscomb (bass) and Jarrod Montague (drums).

11/11/00	®	39	4	1 Again And Again	—	Gift	Atlantic 83341
4/7/01	®	34	4	2 I	—	↓	
9/21/02+	®	5	28	3 Poem	106	Welcome	Atlantic 83561
10/12/02+	ⓜ	10	26				
3/29/03	®	23	12	4 Mine	—	↓	
4/5/03	ⓜ	26	10				
7/9/05	®	11	21	5 Calling	—	Blue-Sky Research	Velvet Hammer 83720
7/23/05	ⓜ	23	13				
2/4/06	®	39	4	6 Birthday	—	↓	

TATTOO RODEO
Hard-rock band from Burbank, California: Dennis Churchill-Dries (vocals, bass), Rick Chadock (guitar), Michael Lord (keyboards) and Rich Wright (drums).

5/18/91	®	20	11	Been Your Fool	—	Rode Hard-Put Away Wet	Atlantic 82241

TAXIRIDE
Rock band from Melbourne, Australia: Tim Watson (guitar), Tim Wild (guitar), Dan Hall (bass) and Jason Singh (drums). All share lead vocals.

5/22/99	ⓜ	36	5	Get Set	—	Imaginate	Sire 31056

TAXXI
Rock trio from England: David Cumming (vocals, guitar), Colin Payne (keyboards) and Jeff Nead (drums).

7/24/82	®	39	4	1 I'm Leaving	—	States Of Emergency	Fantasy 9617
10/8/83	®	31	8	2 Maybe Someday	—	Foreign Tongue	Fantasy 9628
8/10/85	®	36	4	3 Still In Love	—	Expose	MCA 5580

TAYLOR, Andy
Born on 2/16/1961 in Dolver-Hampton, England. Lead guitarist of **Duran Duran** and **The Power Station**.

3/7/87	®	17	10	1 I Might Lie	—	Thunder	MCA 5837
6/6/87	®	36	4	2 Don't Let Me Die Young	—	↓	

TAYLOR, B.E., Group
Born William (Bill) Edward Taylor in 1954 in Aliquippa, Pennsylvania. Rock singer/songwriter/guitarist.

8/7/82	®	54	1	Never Hold Back	—	Innermission	MCA 5335

Billboard				ARTIST	R=Mainstream Rock	Hot		
Debut	Cht	Peak	Wks	Track Title	M=Modern Rock	Pos	Album Title	Album Label & Number

TAYLOR, Corey
Born on 12/8/1973 in Des Moines, Iowa. Lead singer of **Slipknot** and **Stone Sour**.

Debut	Cht	Peak	Wks	Track Title		Hot Pos	Album Title	Album Label & Number
2/23/08	Ⓡ	11	6	I'm Not Jesus		—	Worlds Collide	Jive 21580
3/1/08	Ⓜ	21	5	APOCALYPTICA Featuring Corey Taylor				

TAYLOR, James
Born on 3/12/1948 in Boston, Massachusetts. Soft-rock singer/songwriter/guitarist. Married to Carly Simon from 1972-83. Played "The Driver" in the 1971 movie *Two Lane Blacktop*. Also see **Classic Rock Tracks** section.
AWARDS: R&R Hall of Fame: 2000 ★ Billboard: Century Award 1998

3/21/81	Ⓡ	21	9	1 Stand And Fight	—	Dad Loves His Work	Columbia 37009
3/21/81	Ⓡ	21	5	2 Her Town Too	11	↓	
				JAMES TAYLOR & J.D. SOUTHER			

TEARS FOR FEARS
Pop-rock duo from England: Roland Orzabal (vocals, guitar, keyboards) and Curt Smith (vocals, bass). Adopted name from Arthur Janov's book *Prisoners Of Pain*. Assisted by Ian Stanley (keyboards) and Manny Elias (drums). Smith left in 1992.

5/7/83	Ⓡ	22	15	1 Change	73	The Hurting	Mercury 811039
3/23/85	Ⓡ	2²	15	2 Everybody Wants To Rule The World	❶²	Songs From The Big Chair	Mercury 824300
5/25/85	Ⓡ	6	15	3 Shout	❶³	↓	
8/10/85	Ⓡ	7	14	4 Head Over Heels	3¹	↓	
9/2/89	Ⓜ	❶¹	11	5 Sowing The Seeds Of Love	2¹	The Seeds Of Love	Fontana 838730
9/2/89	Ⓡ	4	12				
12/9/89	Ⓡ	27	6	6 Woman In Chains	36	↓	
				Oleta Adams (female vocal); **Phil Collins** (drums)			
2/29/92	Ⓜ	10	9	7 Laid So Low (Tears Roll Down)	—	Tears Roll Down (Greatest Hits 82-92)	Fontana 510939
6/5/93	Ⓜ	❶³	17	8 Break It Down Again	25	Elemental	Mercury 514875

TEDESCHI, Susan
Born on 11/7/1970 in Norwell, Massachusetts. White blues singer/songwriter/guitarist.

6/19/99	Ⓡ	37	3	Rock Me Right	—	Just Won't Burn	Tone-Cool 1164

TEENAGE FANCLUB
Pop-rock band from Glasgow, Scotland: Norman Blake (vocals, guitar), Ray McGinley (guitar), Gerry Love (bass) and Brendan O'Hare (drums).

11/30/91+	Ⓜ	4	13	1 Star Sign	—	Bandwagonesque	DGC 24461
2/15/92	Ⓜ	12	8	2 The Concept	—	↓	
5/9/92	Ⓜ	19	4	3 What You Do To Me	—	↓	
11/27/93	Ⓜ	19	9	4 Hang On	—	Thirteen	DGC 24533

TELEVISION
Punk-rock band from New York: Tom Verlaine (vocals, guitar), Richard Lloyd (guitar), Fred Smith (bass) and Billy Ficca (drums; of **The Waitresses**).

10/31/92	Ⓜ	27	2	Call Mr. Lee	—	Television	Capitol 98396

TEMPLE OF THE DOG
Gathering of Seattle, Washington, musicians in tribute to Andrew Wood, lead singer of Mother Love Bone, who died of a heroin overdose on 3/16/1990 (age 24). Features Stone Gossard, Jeff Ament, **Eddie Vedder** and Mike McCready of **Pearl Jam**, with **Chris Cornell** and Matt Cameron of **Soundgarden**. Gossard and Ament were members of Mother Love Bone.

7/25/92	Ⓡ	4	20	1 Hunger Strike	—	Temple Of The Dog	A&M 5350
7/18/92	Ⓜ	7	12				
11/7/92+	Ⓡ	5	20	2 Say Hello 2 Heaven	—	↓	

10,000 MANIACS Ⓜ **1990s: #40 / All-Time: #85**
Alternative-rock band formed in Jamestown, New York: **Natalie Merchant** (vocals), Robert Buck (guitar), Dennis Drew (keyboards), Steven Gustafson (bass) and Jerome Augustyniak (drums). Merchant left in August of 1993; replaced by Mary Ramsey. Buck died of liver failure on 12/19/2000 (age 42).

4/30/88	Ⓡ	37	7	1 Like The Weather	68	In My Tribe	Elektra 60738
9/10/88	Ⓜ	9	4	2 What's The Matter Here?	80	↓	
5/27/89	Ⓜ	3⁴	11	3 Trouble Me	44	Blind Man's Zoo	Elektra 60815
5/20/89	Ⓡ	20	11				
7/29/89	Ⓜ	12	9	4 Eat For Two	—	↓	
9/26/92	Ⓜ	❶²	15	5 These Are Days	66	Our Time In Eden	Elektra 61385
12/5/92+	Ⓜ	5	19	6 Candy Everybody Wants	67	↓	
2/20/93	Ⓜ	22	3	7 Everyday Is Like Sunday	—	(single only)	Elektra 66342
				first recorded by **Morrissey** in 1988			
10/23/93	Ⓜ	7	15	8 Because The Night [L]	11	MTV Unplugged	Elektra 61569
				#13 Pop hit for **Patti Smith** in 1978			

Billboard				ARTIST		Hot		
Debut	Cht	Peak	Wks	Track Title	®=Mainstream Rock ⓜ=Modern Rock	Pos	Album Title	Album Label & Number

10 YEARS
Hard-rock band from Knoxville, Tennessee: Jesse Hasek (vocals), Ryan "Tater" Johnson (guitar), Matt Wantland (guitar), Lewis "Big Lew" Cosby (bass) and Brian Vodinh (drums).

8/27/05+	ⓜ	❶[1]	45	1 Wasteland	94	The Autumn Effect ....Republic 005018	
6/25/05	®	2[10]	52				
3/18/06	®	20	20	2 Through The Iris	—	↓	
5/20/06	ⓜ	35	6				
9/9/06	®	32	9	3 Waking Up	—	↓	
2/23/08	®	13↑	6↑	4 Beautiful	—	Division ....Universal Republic 010979	
3/1/08	ⓜ	22	5↑				

TEN YEARS AFTER
Blues-rock band from England: **Alvin Lee** (vocals, guitar), Chick Churchill (keyboards), Leo Lyons (bass) and Ric Lee (drums). Also see **Classic Rock Tracks** section.

8/19/89	®	23	8	Let's Shake It Up..	—	About Time ....Chrysalis 21722	

TEPPER, Robert
Born Antoine Roberto Teppardo in Bayonne, New Jersey. Rock singer/songwriter.

2/1/86	®	12	9	No Easy Way Out..	22	St: Rocky IV ....Scotti Brothers 40203	

TESLA
® **1990s: #32 / All-Time: #71**

Hard-rock band formed in Sacramento, California: Jeff Keith (vocals; born on 10/12/1958), Frank Hannon (guitar), Brian Skeoch (bass) and Troy Luccketta (drums). Band named after the inventor of the alternating current generator, Nikola Tesla. Luccketta was a member of the **Eric Martin Band**. Hannon was also a member of **Moon Dog Mane**. Dave Rude replaced Skeoch in 2006.

TOP HITS: 1)Signs 2)Mama's Fool 3)What You Give 4)Love Song 5)The Way It Is

2/21/87	®	35	7	1 Modern Day Cowboy	—	Mechanical Resonance.............................Geffen 24120	
4/25/87	®	22	9	2 Little Suzi	91	↓	
1/9/88	®	46	3	3 Gettin' Better..	—	↓	
1/28/89	®	13	11	4 Heaven's Trail (No Way Out).............................	—	The Great Radio Controversy ....Geffen 24224	
5/20/89	®	34	6	5 Hang Tough	—	↓	
9/30/89+	®	7	23	6 Love Song	10	↓	
2/17/90	®	13	13	7 The Way It Is	55	↓	
11/24/90+	®	2[1]	17	8 Signs [L]	8	Five Man Acoustical Jam ....Geffen 24311	
				#3 Pop hit for Five Man Electrical Band in 1971			
3/16/91	®	28	8	9 Paradise ....[L]	—	↓	
				above 2 recorded on 7/2/1990 at the Trocadero in Philadelphia, Pennsylvania			
9/7/91	®	20	7	10 Edison's Medicine	—	Psychotic Supper ....Geffen 24424	
11/16/91+	®	19	21	11 Call It What You Want	—	↓	
2/15/92	®	7	21	12 What You Give	86	↓	
6/13/92	®	13	14	13 Song & Emotion	—	↓	
10/17/92	®	35	2	14 Stir It Up	—	↓	
8/13/94	®	5	13	15 Mama's Fool	—	Bust A Nut...Geffen 24713	
11/26/94	®	19	10	16 Need Your Lovin'	—	↓	
3/18/95	®	35	8	17 Alot To Lose...	—	↓	
12/23/95+	®	31	6	18 Steppin' Over	—	Time's Makin' Changes: The Best Of Tesla ....Geffen 24833	
2/14/04	®	21	20	19 Caught In A Dream	—	Into The Now..Sanctuary 84637	
7/24/04	®	35	9	20 Words Can't Explain.....................................	—	↓	
7/14/07	®	39	2	21 Thank You	—	Real To Reel.............................Tesla Electric Co. 001	

TESTAMENT
Hard-rock band formed in San Francisco, California: Chuck Billy (vocals), Eric Peterson (guitar), Glen Abelais (guitar), Greg Christian (bass) and John Tempesta (drums). Tempesta later joined **White Zombie** and **Helmet**.

2/6/93	®	24	10	Return To Serenity	—	The Ritual ....Atlantic 82392	

TEXAS
Pop-rock band from Glasgow, Scotland: Sharleen Spiteri (vocals, guitar), Ally McErlaine (guitar), John McElhone (bass) and Stuart Kerr (drums).

8/5/89	ⓜ	11	9	1 I Don't Want A Lover	77	Southside..Mercury 838171	
7/29/89	®	27	8				
11/2/91	ⓜ	14	7	2 In My Heart	—	Mothers Heaven ....Mercury 848578	

THAT DOG
Alternative-rock band from Los Angeles, California: sisters Rachel Haden (bass) and Petra Haden (violin), with Anna Waronker (vocals, guitar) and Tony Maxwell (drums).

5/31/97	ⓜ	27	7	Never Say Never	—	Retreat From The Sun ....DGC 25115	

Debut	Cht	Peak	Wks	ARTIST / Track Title	Hot Pos	Album Title	Album Label & Number

® = Mainstream Rock
Ⓜ = Modern Rock

THAT PETROL EMOTION
Pop-rock band from Ireland: Steve Mack (vocals), Damian O'Neill (guitar), Reamann O'Gormain (guitar), John Marchini (bass) and Ciaran McLaughlin (drums).

| 4/21/90 | Ⓜ | 9 | 10 | Hey Venus .... | — | *Chemicrazy* .... Virgin 91354 |

THE, The
Born Matthew Johnson on 8/15/1961 in London, England. Eclectic-rock singer/songwriter. His band features an ever-changing lineup of musicians.

6/3/89	Ⓜ	13	8	1 The Beat(en) Generation	—	*Mind Bomb* .... Epic 45241
8/12/89	Ⓜ	15	6	2 Gravitate To Me	—	↓
10/7/89	Ⓜ	16	7	3 Kingdom Of Rain	—	↓
2/10/90	Ⓜ	7	7	4 Jealous Of Youth	—	*(single only)* .... Epic 73151
1/23/93	Ⓜ	2³	12	5 Dogs Of Lust	—	*Dusk* .... Epic 53164
4/17/93	Ⓜ	14	8	6 Love Is Stronger Than Death	—	↓
2/4/95	Ⓜ	24	8	7 I Saw The Light	—	*Hanky Panky* .... 550 Music 66908
				written by Hank Williams in 1948		

THELONIOUS MONSTER
Rock band formed in Los Angeles, California: Bob Forrest (vocals), Dix Denney (guitar), Chris Handsome (bass) and Pete Weiss (drums).

| 4/8/89 | Ⓜ | 29 | 1 | So What If I Did .... | — | *Stormy Weather* .... Relativity 88561 |
| | | | | produced by John Doe | | |

THEORY OF A DEADMAN
Rock band from Delta, British Columbia, Canada: Tyler Connolly (vocals, guitar), David Brenner (guitar), Dean Back (bass) and Tim Hart (drums).

8/17/02	®	8	26	1 Nothing Could Come Between Us	—	*Theory Of A Deadman* .... Roadrunner 618421
2/1/03	®	13	19	2 Make Up Your Mind	—	↓
3/22/03	Ⓜ	38	2		—	
2/12/05	®	8	26	3 No Surprise	—	*Gasoline* .... Roadrunner 618323
4/16/05	Ⓜ	24	13		—	
8/13/05	®	30	10	4 Hello Lonely (Walk Away From This)	—	↓
11/19/05	®	22	17	5 Say Goodbye	—	↓
4/15/06	®	27	13	6 Santa Monica	—	↓
2/9/08	®	3²↑	8↑	7 So Happy	—	*Scars & Souvenirs* .... 604 Records 180092
2/16/08	Ⓜ	24	7↑		—	

THERAPY?
Punk-rock trio from Belfast, Ireland: Andy Cairns (vocals, guitar), Michael McKeegan (bass) and Fyfe Ewing (drums).

| 10/9/93 | Ⓜ | 16 | 7 | Screamager .... | — | *Hats Off To The Insane* .... A&M 540139 |

THEY EAT THEIR OWN
Pop-rock band formed in Los Angeles, California: Laura Baricevic (vocals), Kevin Dixon (guitar), Shark Darkwater (guitar), J.D. Dotson (bass) and Juno Brown (drums).

| 1/19/91 | Ⓜ | 10 | 8 | Like A Drug .... | — | *They Eat Their Own* .... Relativity 1042 |

THEY MIGHT BE GIANTS
Alternative-rock duo from Boston, Massachusetts: John Flansburgh (guitar; born on 5/6/1960) and John Linnell (accordian; born on 6/12/1959). Supported by various musicians. Group named after the 1971 movie starring George C. Scott.

11/5/88	Ⓜ	11	9	1 Ana Ng	—	*Lincoln* .... Bar/None 72600
1/27/90	Ⓜ	3²	11	2 Birdhouse In Your Soul	—	*Flood* .... Elektra 60907
4/14/90	Ⓜ	22	7	3 Twisting	—	↓
3/14/92	Ⓜ	24	8	4 The Statue Got Me High	—	*Apollo 18* .... Elektra 61257
9/3/94	Ⓜ	19	8	5 Snail Shell	—	*John Henry* .... Elektra 61654

THIN LIZZY
Rock band from Dublin, Ireland: Phil Lynott (vocals, bass; born on 8/20/1951; died on 1/4/1986, age 34), Scott Gorham (guitar), Snowy White (guitar) and Brian Downey (drums). Numerous personnel changes. **Gary Moore** was a member from 1978-79. Also see **Classic Rock Tracks** section.

2/27/82	®	38	6	1 Angel Of Death	—	*Renegade* .... Warner 3622
3/20/82	®	24	7	2 Hollywood (Down On Your Luck)	—	↓
3/23/91	®	22	6	3 Dedication	—	*Dedication* .... Mercury 848530

THIRD DAY
Christian rock band from Marietta, Georgia: Mac Powell (vocals), Mark Lee (guitar), Brad Avery (guitar), Tai Anderson (bass) and David Carr (drums).

| 3/8/97 | ® | 34 | 5 | Nothing At All .... | — | *Third Day* .... Reunion 41607 |

THIRD EYE BLIND

Ⓜ 1990s: #37 / All-Time: #49

Rock band from San Francisco, California: Stephan Jenkins (vocals; born on 9/27/1964), Kevin Cadogan (guitar; born on 8/14/1970), Arion Salazar (bass; born on 8/9/1970) and Brad Hargreaves (drums; born on 7/30/1971). Tony Fredianelli (born on 4/2/1969) replaced Cadogan in late 2000.

TOP HITS: 1)Semi-Charmed Life 2)Never Let You Go 3)How's It Going To Be

Debut	Cht	Peak	Wks	#	Track Title	Hot Pos	Album Title	Label & Number
3/29/97	Ⓜ	❶⁸	31	1	Semi-Charmed Life	4	Third Eye Blind	Elektra 62012
5/24/97	Ⓡ	26	13					
8/9/97	Ⓜ	14	16	2	Graduate	—	↓	
10/11/97	Ⓡ	26	10					
11/8/97+	Ⓜ	5	26	3	How's It Going To Be	9	↓	
3/21/98	Ⓜ	13	14	4	Losing A Whole Year	—	↓	
5/2/98	Ⓡ	36	3					
7/25/98	Ⓜ	9	26	5	Jumper	5	↓	
11/20/99	Ⓜ	11	8	6	Anything	—	Blue	Elektra 62415
12/18/99	Ⓡ	35	6					
1/1/00	Ⓜ	4	21	7	Never Let You Go	14	↓	
5/6/00	Ⓜ	21	10	8	10 Days Late	—	↓	
8/26/00	Ⓜ	39	2	9	Deep Inside Of You	69	↓	
4/19/03	Ⓜ	35	5	10	Blinded (When I See You)	116	Out Of The Vein	Elektra 62888

3RD STRIKE

Rock band from Los Angeles, California: Jim Karthe (vocals), Todd Deguchi (guitar), Erik Carlsson (guitar), Gabe Hammersmith (bass) and P.J. McMullan (drums).

Debut	Cht	Peak	Wks	#	Track Title	Hot Pos	Album Title	Label & Number
4/6/02	Ⓡ	23	17	1	No Light	—	Lost Angel	Hollywood 62344
6/15/02	Ⓜ	36	4					
9/28/02	Ⓡ	40	1	2	Redemption	—	↓	

38 SPECIAL

Ⓡ 1980s: #13 / All-Time: #39

Southern-rock band formed in Jacksonville, Florida: Donnie **Van Zant** (vocals; born on 6/11/1952), Don Barnes (guitar), Jeff Carlisi (guitar), Larry Junstrom (bass), Steve Brookins (drums) and Jack Grondin (drums). By 1988, Barnes and Brookins replaced by Danny Chauncey (guitar) and Max Carl (keyboards). Van Zant is the brother of **Lynyrd Skynyrd**'s Ronnie Van Zant. Also see **Classic Rock Tracks** section.

TOP HITS: 1)If I'd Been The One 2)Caught Up In You 3)Second Chance 4)The Sound Of Your Voice 5)Hold On Loosely

Debut	Cht	Peak	Wks	#	Track Title	Hot Pos	Album Title	Label & Number
3/21/81	Ⓡ	3¹	14	1	Hold On Loosely	27	Wild-Eyed Southern Boys	A&M 4835
3/21/81	Ⓡ	30	10	2	Fantasy Girl	52	↓	
4/25/81	Ⓡ	35	1	3	Wild-Eyed Southern Boys	—	↓	
5/1/82	Ⓡ	❶¹	15	4	Caught Up In You	10	Special Forces	A&M 4888
6/5/82	Ⓡ	9	22	5	Chain Lightnin'	—	↓	
8/14/82	Ⓡ	56	1	6	Back On The Track	—	↓	
9/11/82	Ⓡ	7	8	7	You Keep Runnin' Away	38	↓	
11/12/83	Ⓡ	❶⁴	15	8	If I'd Been The One	19	Tour De Force	A&M 4971
12/17/83+	Ⓡ	4	17	9	Back Where You Belong	20	↓	
4/7/84	Ⓡ	17	3	10	One Time For Old Times	—	↓	
9/29/84	Ⓡ	4	10	11	Teacher Teacher	25	St: Teachers	Capitol 12371
5/3/86	Ⓡ	4	11	12	Like No Other Night	14	Strength In Numbers	A&M 5115
5/31/86	Ⓡ	6	15	13	Somebody Like You	48	↓	
8/30/86	Ⓡ	30	7	14	Heart's On Fire	—	↓	
6/27/87	Ⓡ	4	11	15	Back To Paradise	41	Flashback	A&M 3910
10/8/88	Ⓡ	5	9	16	Rock & Roll Strategy	67	Rock & Roll Strategy	A&M 5218
11/19/88+	Ⓡ	15	11	17	Little Sheba	—	↓	
2/18/89	Ⓡ	2²	14	18	Second Chance	6	↓	
7/8/89	Ⓡ	43	4	19	Comin' Down Tonight	67	↓	
					THIRTY EIGHT SPECIAL (above 4)			
6/22/91	Ⓡ	2¹	14	20	The Sound Of Your Voice	33	Bone Against Steel	Charisma 91640

Billboard				ARTIST / Track Title	Ⓡ=Mainstream Rock Ⓜ=Modern Rock	Hot Pos	Album Title	Album Label & Number
Debut	Cht	Peak	Wks					

38 SPECIAL — cont'd

| 9/21/91 | Ⓡ | 30 | 9 | 21 Rebel To Rebel .... | — | ↓ | | |
| 8/9/97 | Ⓡ | 33 | 5 | 22 Fade To Blue .... | — | | *Resolution*..Razor & Tie 2829 |

30 SECONDS TO MARS
Rock band formed in Los Angeles, California: brothers Jared Leto (vocals, guitar) and Shannon Leto (drums), with Solon Bixler (guitar) and Matt Wachter (bass). Jared Leto is also a popular actor (played "Jordan Catalano" on TV's *My So-Called Life*). Tomo Milicevic replaced Bixler in 2003. Wachter is also a member of **Angels And Airwaves**.

9/7/02	Ⓡ	31	8	1 **Capricorn (A Brand New Name)**	—		*30 Seconds To Mars* ....Immortal 12424
7/9/05	Ⓜ	22	20	2 Attack	—		*A Beautiful Lie*...Virgin 90992
7/2/05	Ⓡ	38	1					
3/4/06	Ⓜ	3[1]	52	3 **The Kill (Bury Me)**	65	↓		
4/8/06	Ⓡ	14	25					
11/4/06+	Ⓜ	❶[2]	34	4 **From Yesterday**	76	↓		
12/16/06+	Ⓡ	11	20					
8/18/07	Ⓜ	37	8	5 **A Beautiful Lie**	—	↓		

THIS PICTURE
Rock band from Bath, England: Symon Bye (vocals), Austen Rowley (bass), brothers Robert Forrester (guitar) and Duncan Forrester (drums).

| 10/12/91 | Ⓜ | 10 | 13 | 1 Naked Rain.. | — | | *A Violent Impression* ....Dedicated 3010 |
| 2/8/92 | Ⓜ | 24 | 2 | 2 Breathe Deeply Now.................................. | — | | *Breathe Deeply Now* ....Dedicated 62177 |

THOMAS, Mickey
Born on 12/3/1949 in Cairo, Georgia. Lead singer of **Jefferson Starship/Starship** from 1979-90.

| 2/22/86 | Ⓡ | 35 | 4 | Stand In The Fire .... | — | | *St: Youngblood* ....RCA 7172 |

THOMAS, Rob
Born on 2/14/1972 in Landstuhl, Germany (U.S. military base); raised in Daytona, Florida. Pop-rock singer/songwriter. Lead singer of **Matchbox Twenty**.

| 7/10/99 | Ⓡ | 10 | 26 | Smooth .... | ❶[12] | | *Supernatural* ....Arista 19080 |
| 11/13/99 | Ⓜ | 24 | 12 | **SANTANA Featuring Rob Thomas** | | | | |

THOMPSON, Michael, Band
Born in Long Island, New York. Rock guitarist. His band: Moon Calhoun (vocals), John Schreiner (keyboards), Leon Gaer (bass) and John Keane (drums).

| 4/22/89 | Ⓡ | 33 | 6 | Can't Miss... | — | | *How Long* ....Geffen 24225 |

THOMPSON, Richard
Born on 4/3/1949 in London, England. Singer/songwriter/guitarist. Formed Fairport Convention in 1969. Went solo in 1971. Married to singer Linda Peters from 1972-82.

| 11/12/88 | Ⓜ | 30 | 1 | 1 Turning Of The Tide .... | — | | *Amnesia* ....Capitol 48845 |
| 7/6/91 | Ⓜ | 15 | 8 | 2 I Feel So Good .... | — | | *Rumor And Sigh* ....Capitol 95713 |

THOMPSON TWINS
Synth-rock/dance trio from England: Tom Bailey (vocals, synthesizer), Alannah Currie (xylophone, percussion) and Joe Leeway (conga, synthesizer).

4/2/83	Ⓡ	36	3	1 Love On Your Side	45		*Side Kicks* ....Arista 6607
3/10/84	Ⓡ	9	10	2 **Hold Me Now**	3[2]		*Into The Gap*..Arista 8200
5/5/84	Ⓡ	12	13	3 Doctor! Doctor!	11	↓		
9/8/84	Ⓡ	51	4	4 You Take Me Up...	44	↓		
9/28/85	Ⓡ	14	11	5 Lay Your Hands On Me	6		*Here's To Future Days*................................Arista 8276
2/8/86	Ⓡ	35	4	6 King For A Day	8	↓		
9/30/89	Ⓜ	16	6	7 Sugar Daddy	28		*Big Trash*...Warner 25921
9/7/91	Ⓜ	23	5	8 Come Inside	—		*Queer*..Warner 26631

THORNLEY
Rock band formed in Toronto, Ontario, Canada: Ian Thornley (vocals, guitar), Tavis Stanley (guitar), Ken Tizzard (bass) and Sekou Lumumba (drums).

4/10/04	Ⓡ	15	17	1 So Far So Good	—		*Come Again*....................................604 Records 618325
4/17/04	Ⓜ	27	13					
8/28/04	Ⓡ	27	10	2 Easy Comes	—	↓		

THOROGOOD, George, & The Destroyers

Born on 12/31/1952 in Wilmington, Delaware. Blues-rock singer/guitarist. The Destroyers: Steve Chrismar (guitar), Hank Carter (sax), Billy Blough (bass) and Jeff Simon (drums).

TOP HITS: 1)Get A Haircut 2)Born To Be Bad 3)You Talk Too Much

Debut	Cht	Peak	Wks		Hot Pos	Album Title / Label & Number
8/14/82	®	32	5	1 Nobody But Me .... #8 Pop hit for The Human Beinz in 1968	106	*Bad To The Bone* ....EMI America 17076
9/18/82	®	27	6	2 Bad To The Bone	—	↓
1/19/85	®	26	8	3 Gear Jammer	—	
3/16/85	®	13	10	4 I Drink Alone	—	*Maverick* ....EMI America 17145
6/15/85	®	25	10	5 Willie And The Hand Jive .... #9 Pop hit for Johnny Otis in 1958	63	↓
8/9/86	®	11	9	6 Reelin' & Rockin' .... [L] recorded on 5/23/1986 at the Cincinnati Gardens; #27 Pop hit for Chuck Berry in 1973	—	*Live* ....EMI America 17214
1/23/88	®	4	12	7 You Talk Too Much	—	*Born To Be Bad* ....EMI-Manhattan 46973
3/12/88	®	3¹	9	8 Born To Be Bad	—	↓
6/18/88	®	39	3	9 Treat Her Right .... #2 Pop hit for Roy Head in 1965	—	↓
3/2/91	®	5	11	10 If You Don't Start Drinkin' (I'm Gonna Leave)	—	*Boogie People* ....EMI 92514
5/18/91	®	15	8	11 Hello Little Girl... written by Chuck Berry	—	↓
8/22/92	®	18	11	12 I'm A Steady Rollin' Man .... written by blues legend Robert Johnson	—	*The Baddest Of George Thorogood And The Destroyers* ....EMI 97718
7/24/93	®	2²	11	13 Get A Haircut	124	*Haircut* ....EMI 89529
10/2/93	®	12	8	14 Howlin' For My Baby .... written by Willie Dixon and Howlin' Wolf	—	↓
12/25/93+	®	24	6	15 Gone Dead Train .... first recorded by Crazy Horse in 1971	—	↓
4/17/99	®	24	9	16 I Don't Trust Nobody	—	*Half A Boy/Half A Man* ....CMC International 86270

THOUSAND FOOT KRUTCH

Christian rock trio from Peterborough, Ontario, Canada: Trevor McNevan (vocals, guitar), Joel Bruyere (bass) and Steve Augustine (drums).

Debut	Cht	Peak	Wks		Hot Pos	Album Title / Label & Number
3/13/04	®	28	13	1 Rawkfist..	—	*Phenomenon* ....Tooth & Nail 84799
9/17/05+	®	16	24	2 Move	—	*The Art Of Breaking* ....Tooth & Nail 74819
7/22/06	®	34	6	3 Absolute	—	↓
3/29/08	®	38↑	1↑	4 Falls Apart	—	*The Flame In All Of Us* ....Tooth & Nail 88247

THRASHING DOVES

Pop-rock band from London, England: brothers Ken Foreman (vocals) and Brian Foreman (guitar), with Ian Button (bass) and Kevin Sargent (drums).

Debut	Cht	Peak	Wks		Hot Pos	Album Title / Label & Number
3/4/89	ⓜ	14	9	Angel Visit	—	*Trouble In The Home* ....A&M 5235

3

Rock trio formed in England: Robert Barry (vocals, guitar), Keith Emerson (keyboards) and Carl Palmer (drums). Also see **Emerson, Lake & Palmer**.

Debut	Cht	Peak	Wks		Hot Pos	Album Title / Label & Number
2/20/88	®	9	11	Talkin' Bout	—	*To The Power Of Three* ....Geffen 24181

THREE DAYS GRACE   ® 2000s: #10 / All-Time: #60 ★ ⓜ 2000s: #15 / All-Time: #36

Hard-rock band from Norwood, Ontario, Canada: Adam Gontier (vocals; born on 5/21/1978), Barry Stock (guitar; born on 4/24/1974), Brad Walst (bass; born on 2/16/1977) and Neil Sanderson (drums; born on 12/17/1978).

Debut	Cht	Peak	Wks		Hot Pos	Album Title / Label & Number
7/19/03	ⓜ	2²	45	1 (I Hate) Everything About You	55	*Three Days Grace* ....Jive 53479
8/2/03	®	4	46			
4/17/04	®	❶³	36	2 Just Like You	55	↓
4/24/04	ⓜ	❶³	32			
10/23/04+	®	2⁴	31	3 Home	90	↓
10/30/04+	ⓜ	7	26			
4/22/06	®	❶⁷	48	4 Animal I Have Become	60	*One-X* ....Jive 83504
4/22/06	ⓜ	❶²	41			
10/14/06	®	❶¹³	42	5 Pain	44	↓
11/11/06+	ⓜ	❶⁴	30			

Billboard	Cht	Peak	Wks	ARTIST / Track Title	Hot Pos	Album Title	Album Label & Number
Debut				®=Mainstream Rock ⓂModern Rock			

THREE DAYS GRACE — cont'd

Debut	Cht	Peak	Wks	Track Title	Hot Pos	Album Title	Album Label & Number
5/19/07	®	❶⁷	43	6 Never Too Late	71	↓	
6/9/07	Ⓜ	2¹	43↑				
11/10/07+	®	19↑	20↑	7 Riot	—	↓	
1/5/08	Ⓜ	26	13↑				

3 DOORS DOWN ® 2000s: #3 / All-Time: #30 / Ⓜ 2000s: #11 / All-Time: #33

Rock band from Escatawpa, Mississippi: Brad Arnold (vocals; born on 9/27/1978), Matt Roberts (guitar; born on 1/10/1978), Chris Henderson (guitar; born on 4/30/1971), Todd Harrell (bass; born on 2/13/1972) and Daniel Adair (drums; born on 2/19/1975). Adair left in January 2005 to join **Nickelback**; replaced by Greg Upchurch (born on 12/1/1971).

TOP HITS: 1)Loser 2)When I'm Gone 3)Kryptonite

Debut	Cht	Peak	Wks	Track Title	Hot Pos	Album Title	Album Label & Number
3/25/00	Ⓜ	❶¹¹	33	1 Kryptonite	3³	The Better Life.......................................Republic 153920	
2/5/00	®	❶⁹	51				
6/24/00	®	❶²¹	53	2 Loser	55	↓	
8/5/00	Ⓜ	2¹	32				
1/13/01	®	❶³	26	3 Duck And Run	110	↓	
1/27/01	Ⓜ	11	26				
6/16/01	®	10	26	4 Be Like That	24	↓	
6/23/01	Ⓜ	22	12				
10/5/02	®	❶¹⁷	40	5 When I'm Gone	4	Away From The Sun ....Republic 066165	
10/12/02+	Ⓜ	2²	30				
4/5/03	®	8	22	6 The Road I'm On	—	↓	
4/12/03	Ⓜ	24	13				
8/16/03	®	14	26	7 Here Without You	5	↓	
8/30/03	Ⓜ	22	22				
2/7/04	®	20	14	8 Away From The Sun	62	↓	
2/7/04	Ⓜ	33	8				
12/11/04+	®	6	26	9 Let Me Go	14	Seventeen Days....................................Republic 004018	
12/11/04+	Ⓜ	14	24				
4/23/05	®	12	18	10 Behind Those Eyes	—	↓	
4/30/05	Ⓜ	25	12				
8/27/05	®	18	18	11 Live For Today...	—	↓	
9/24/05	Ⓜ	31	5				
12/24/05+	®	32	14	12 Landing In London (All I Think About Is You)	—	↓	
				3 DOORS DOWN Featuring Bob Seger			
3/1/08	®	4↑	5↑	13 It's Not My Time.......................................	—	3 Doors Down ....Universal Republic 011065	
3/8/08	Ⓜ	14↑	4↑				

311 Ⓜ 1990s: #35 / 2000s: #22 / All-Time: #14

Rock-funk band from Omaha, Nebraska: Nick Hexum (vocals, guitar; born on 4/12/1970), Doug "SA" Martinez (vocals, DJ; born on 10/29/1969), Tim Mahoney (guitar; born on 2/17/1970), Aaron "P-Nut" Wills (bass; born on 6/5/1974) and Chad Sexton (drums; born on 9/7/1970). 311 (pronounced: three-eleven) is the police code for indecent exposure. Also see **The Urge**.

TOP HITS: 1)Down 2)Love Song 3)Don't Tread On Me

Debut	Cht	Peak	Wks	Track Title	Hot Pos	Album Title	Album Label & Number
4/10/93	Ⓜ	27	3	1 Do You Right..	—	Music ....Capricorn 42008	
10/28/95	Ⓜ	29	7	2 Don't Stay Home	—	311 ....Capricorn 42041	
2/24/96+	Ⓜ	4	26	3 All Mixed Up...	36ᴬ	↓	
7/6/96	Ⓜ	❶⁴	26	4 Down	37ᴬ	↓	
8/24/96	®	19	12				
7/5/97	Ⓜ	14	10	5 Transistor	—	Transistor...Capricorn 536181	
8/16/97	®	31	3				
9/6/97	Ⓜ	21	10	6 Prisoner..	—	↓	
12/13/97+	Ⓜ	21	23	7 Beautiful Disaster.......................................	—	↓	

Debug	Cht	Peak	Wks	ARTIST / Track Title ⓇMainstream Rock ⓂModern Rock	Hot Pos	Album Title	Album Label & Number
				311 — cont'd			
9/11/99	Ⓜ	6	19	8 Come Original	119	Soundsystem ....Capricorn 546645	
10/9/99	Ⓡ	39	1				
1/29/00	Ⓜ	17	16	9 Flowing	—	↓	
6/16/01	Ⓜ	7	15	10 You Wouldn't Believe	120	From Chaos ....Volcano 32184	
7/7/01	Ⓡ	32	7				
10/6/01	Ⓜ	15	19	11 I'll Be Here Awhile	—	↓	
3/9/02	Ⓜ	13	30	12 Amber	103	↓	
7/12/03	Ⓜ	3[1]	19	13 Creatures (For A While)	118	Evolver ....Volcano 53714	
11/22/03	Ⓜ	39	2	14 Beyond The Gray Sky	—	↓	
2/14/04	Ⓜ	❶[1]	26	15 Love Song	59	St: 50 First Dates ....Maverick 48675	
6/12/04	Ⓜ	14	12	16 First Straw	—	Greatest Hits '93-'03 ....Volcano 60009	
8/6/05	Ⓜ	2[5]	20	17 Don't Tread On Me	107	Don't Tread On Me ....Volcano 69522	
12/17/05+	Ⓜ	22	13	18 Speak Easy		↓	

3 LB. THRILL
Rock band from Basking Ridge, New Jersey: Matt Brown (vocals), Jeff Jensen (guitar), Bill Becker (bass) and Pete McDade (drums).

| 2/17/96 | Ⓜ | 35 | 6 | Diana .... | — | Vulture ....550 Music 67395 | |

THRICE
Punk-rock band from Anaheim, California: Dustin Kensrue (vocals, guitar), brothers Ed Breckenridge (bass) and Riley Breckenridge (drums), and Teppi Teranishi (guitar).

7/26/03	Ⓜ	24	11	1 All That's Left	—	The Artist In The Ambulance ....Island 000295	
9/20/03	Ⓡ	36	4				
1/31/04	Ⓜ	39	1	2 Stare At The Sun	—	↓	
11/19/05+	Ⓡ	24	14	3 Image Of The Invisible	—	Vheissu...Sub City 005428	

THROWING MUSES
Pop-rock band from Boston, Massachusetts: Kristin Hersh (vocals, guitar), Tanya Donelly (vocals, guita), Leslie Langston (bass) and David Narcizo (drums). Langston left by October 1989, replaced by David Abong. By 1992, reduced to a duo of Hersh and Narcizo. Donnelly (an early member of **The Breeders**) later formed **Belly**.

2/18/89	Ⓜ	8	11	1 Dizzy	—	Hunkpapa ....Sire 25855	
3/30/91	Ⓜ	11	8	2 Counting Backwards	—	The Real Ramona ....Sire 26489	
1/7/95	Ⓜ	20	13	3 Bright Yellow Gun	120	University ....Sire 45796	

THUNDER
Hard-rock band from England: Daniel Bowes (vocals), Luke Morley (guitar), Ben Matthews (keyboards), Mark Luckhurst (bass) and Gary James (drums).

4/13/91	Ⓡ	10	15	1 Dirty Love	55	Backstreet Symphony ....Geffen 24384	
8/24/91	Ⓡ	42	6	2 Until My Dying Day	—	↓	
11/30/91+	Ⓡ	31	14	3 Love Walked In	—	↓	

THURSDAY
Hard-rock band from New Brunswick, New Jersey: Geoff Rickly (vocals), Steve Pedulla (guitar), Tom Keeley (guitar), Tim Payne (bass) and Tucker Rule (drums).

| 10/18/03 | Ⓜ | 30 | 7 | Signals Over The Air .... | — | War All The Time ....Victory 000293 | |

TIKARAM, Tanita
Born on 12/8/1969 in Munster, West Germany; raised in Basingstoke, England. Female singer/songwriter.

| 4/1/89 | Ⓜ | 25 | 4 | Twist In My Sobriety .... | — | Ancient Heart ....Reprise 25839 | |
| 3/25/89 | Ⓡ | 47 | 4 | | | | |

'TIL TUESDAY
Pop-rock band formed in Boston, Massachusetts: **Aimee Mann** (vocals, bass), Robert Holmes (guitar), Joey Pesce (keyboards) and Michael Hausman (drums).

5/4/85	Ⓡ	14	13	1 Voices Carry	8	Voices Carry...Epic 39458	
9/27/86	Ⓡ	9	11	2 What About Love	26	Welcome Home...Epic 40314	
1/10/87	Ⓡ	37	8	3 Coming Up Close	59	↓	
12/17/88	Ⓜ	30	3	4 (Believed You Were) Lucky	95	Everything's Different Now ....Epic 44041	

TIMBUK 3
Husband-and-wife duo from Austin, Texas: Patrick MacDonald and Barbara MacDonald.

9/20/86	Ⓡ	14	10	1 The Future's So Bright, I Gotta Wear Shades........	19	Greetings From Timbuk 3 ....I.R.S. 5739	
12/27/86+	Ⓡ	35	7	2 Life Is Hard..	—	↓	
5/14/88	Ⓡ	34	5	3 Rev. Jack & His Roamin' Cadillac Church	—	Eden Alley ....I.R.S. 42124	

TIMELORDS, The — see KLF, The

TIN MACHINE

Rock band formed in Los Angeles, California: **David Bowie** (vocals), Reeves Gabrels (guitar), Tony Sales (bass; of **Utopia** and **Chequered Past**) and Hunt Sales (drums; of Utopia). The Sales brothers are the sons of TV comedian Soupy Sales.

Debut	Cht	Peak	Wks	Track Title	Pos	Album Title	Album Label & Number
6/3/89	Ⓜ	4	9	1 Under The God	—	Tin Machine	EMI 91990
5/27/89	Ⓡ	8	7				
8/5/89	Ⓜ	12	4	2 Heaven's In Here	—	↓	
7/29/89	Ⓡ	47	2				
8/31/91	Ⓜ	3[1]	9	3 One Shot	—	Tin Machine II	Victory 511216
8/31/91	Ⓡ	17	7				
11/2/91	Ⓜ	21	8	4 Baby Universal	—	↓	

TIN STAR

Trip-hop trio from London, England: David Tomlinson (vocals), Tim Bricheno (guitar) and Tim Gordine (bass).

Debut	Cht	Peak	Wks	Track Title	Pos	Album Title	Album Label & Number
2/6/99	Ⓜ	10	13	Head	—	The Thrill Kisser	V2 27039

TOADIES

Rock band from Fort Worth, Texas: Todd Lewis (vocals, guitar), Darrel Herbert (guitar), Lisa Umbarger (bass) and Mark Reznicek (drums). Clark Vogeler replaced Herbert in 2000. Lewis later formed **The Burden Brothers**.

Debut	Cht	Peak	Wks	Track Title	Pos	Album Title	Album Label & Number
9/2/95	Ⓜ	4	26	1 Possum Kingdom	40[A]	Rubberneck	Interscope 92402
6/10/95	Ⓡ	9	35				
2/3/96	Ⓡ	23	11	2 Away	—	↓	
2/3/96	Ⓜ	28	8				
4/7/01	Ⓡ	34	6	3 Push The Hand	—	Hell Below / Stars Above	Interscope 490872

TOAD THE WET SPROCKET   Ⓜ All-Time: #100

Pop-rock band from Santa Barbara, California: Glen Phillips (vocals), Todd Nichols (guitar), Dean Dinning (bass) and Randy Guss (drums). Name taken from a *Monty Python* skit.

Debut	Cht	Peak	Wks	Track Title	Pos	Album Title	Album Label & Number
9/9/89	Ⓜ	24	4	1 One Little Girl	—	Bread And Circus	Columbia 45326
3/31/90	Ⓜ	27	4	2 Come Back Down	—	Pale	Columbia 46060
6/27/92	Ⓡ	22	11	3 All I Want	15	Fear	Columbia 47309
7/11/92	Ⓜ	22	7				
10/24/92	Ⓡ	27	9	4 Walk On The Ocean	18	↓	
5/21/94	Ⓜ	❶[6]	19	5 Fall Down	33	Dulcinea	Columbia 57744
6/4/94	Ⓡ	5	22				
9/10/94	Ⓜ	9	13	6 Something's Always Wrong	41	↓	
10/22/94	Ⓡ	22	9				
10/14/95	Ⓡ	19	9	7 Good Intentions	23[A]	St: Friends	Reprise 46008
10/14/95	Ⓜ	20	11				
5/3/97	Ⓜ	13	13	8 Come Down	51[A]	Coil	Columbia 67862
5/17/97	Ⓡ	17	11				

TOMMY TUTONE

Rock band formed in San Francisco, California: Tommy Heath (vocals), Jim Keller (guitar), Jon Lyons (bass) and Victor Carberry (drums).

Debut	Cht	Peak	Wks	Track Title	Pos	Album Title	Album Label & Number
11/28/81+	Ⓡ	❶[3]	27	867-5309/Jenny	4	Tommy Tutone-2	Columbia 37401

TOM TOM CLUB

Studio project formed by husband-and-wife Chris Frantz and Tina Weymouth. Both were members of **Talking Heads**.

Debut	Cht	Peak	Wks	Track Title	Pos	Album Title	Album Label & Number
4/29/89	Ⓜ	10	11	1 Suboceana	—	Boom Boom Chi Boom Boom	Sire 25888
6/6/92	Ⓜ	15	7	2 Sunshine And Ecstacy	—	Dark Sneak Love Action	Sire 26951

TONIC

Rock band from Los Angeles, California: Emerson Hart (vocals, guitar), Jeff Russo (guitar), Dan Rothchild (bass) and Kevin Shepard (drums). Dan Lavery replaced Rothchild in 1998.

Debut	Cht	Peak	Wks	Track Title	Pos	Album Title	Album Label & Number
7/13/96	Ⓡ	2[3]	29	1 Open Up Your Eyes	68[A]	Lemon Parade	Polydor 531042
10/19/96	Ⓜ	22	22				
2/1/97	Ⓡ	8	12	2 Casual Affair	—	↓	
4/12/97	Ⓡ	❶[5]	37	3 If You Could Only See	11[A]	↓	
3/29/97	Ⓜ	3[5]	26				
7/3/99	Ⓡ	3[2]	19	4 You Wanted More	103	St: American Pie	Universal 53269
7/3/99	Ⓜ	10	20				
11/13/99	Ⓡ	20	13	5 Knock Down Walls	—	Sugar	Universal 542069

TONIO K.

Born Antonio Krikorian on 4/15/1949 in Palm Desert, California. Eclectic singer/songwriter.

3/12/88	®	42	4	Without Love	—	Notes From The Lost Civilization..................What? 763

TOOL

® 2000s: #25 / All-Time: #70 ★ ⓜ All-Time: #79

Hard-rock band from Los Angeles, California: Maynard James Keenan (vocals; born on 4/17/1964, Adam Jones (guitar; born on 1/15/1965), Paul D'Amour (bass; born on 5/12/1967) and Danny Carey (drums; born on 5/10/1961). Justin Chancellor (born on 11/19/1970) replaced D'Amour in 1995. Keenan also formed **A Perfect Circle** and **Puscifer**.

TOP HITS: 1)The Pot 2)Schism 3)Vicarious

10/9/93	®	13	23	1 Sober	—	Undertow ....Zoo 11052
2/26/94	®	32	9	2 Prison Sex	—	↓
9/28/96	®	17	26	3 Stinkfist	—	↓
10/5/96	ⓜ	19	19		—	Aenima ....Volcano 31087
2/22/97	®	23	18	4 H.	—	↓
8/2/97	®	25	22	5 Aenima	—	↓
				Grammy: Metal Performance		
11/15/97	®	22	18	6 Forty Six & 2	—	↓
5/19/01	®	2¹³	33	7 Schism	67	Lateralus ....Volcano 31160
5/19/01	ⓜ	2¹	29			
				Grammy: Metal Performance		
11/17/01+	®	14	22	8 Lateralus	—	↓
11/17/01+	ⓜ	18	18			
4/20/02	®	10	26	9 Parabola	—	↓
4/27/02	ⓜ	31	7			
5/6/06	®	2⁴	21	10 Vicarious	115	10,000 Days ....Tool Dissectional 81991
5/6/06	ⓜ	2³	20			
8/5/06	®	❶⁴	37	11 The Pot	—	↓
7/22/06	ⓜ	5	30			
2/10/07	®	7	20	12 Jambi	—	↓
4/14/07	ⓜ	23	11			

TOO MUCH JOY

Pop-rock band from Scarsdale, New York: Tim Quirk (vocals), Jay Blumenfield (guitar), Sandy Smallens (bass) and Tommy Vinton (drums).

| 4/27/91 | ⓜ | 17 | 7 | 1 Crush Story | — | Cereal Killers..............................Giant 24410 |
| 9/12/92 | ⓜ | 11 | 8 | 2 Donna Everywhere | — | Mutiny ....Giant 24467 |

TOP

Pop-rock trio from England: Paul Cavanagh (vocals, guitar), Alan Wills (bass) and Joe Fearon (drums).

| 11/30/91+ | ⓜ | 17 | 9 | Number One Dominator | — | Emotion Lotion ....Island 510096 |

TORA TORA

Hard-rock band from Memphis, Tennessee: Anthony Corder (vocals), Keith Douglas (guitar), Patrick Francis (bass) and John Patterson (drums).

| 7/1/89 | ® | 25 | 12 | 1 Walkin' Shoes | 86 | Surprise Attack ....A&M 5261 |
| 7/25/92 | ® | 39 | 1 | 2 Amnesia | — | Wild America ....A&M 5371 |

TORONTO

Rock band from Toronto, Ontario, Canada: Holly Woods (vocals), Sheron Alton (guitar), Brian Allen (guitar), and Scott Kreyer (keyboards) and Jim Fox (drums).

| 8/21/82 | ® | 28 | 6 | Your Daddy Don't Know | 77 | Get It On Credit ....Network 60153 |

TOTO

Pop-rock band formed in Los Angeles, California: brothers Steve Porcaro (vocals, keyboards) and Jeff Porcaro (drums; died of a heart attack on 8/5/1992, age 38), Bobby Kimball (vocals), Steve Lukather (guitar), David Paich (vocals, keyboards) and David Hungate (bass). Prominent session musicians. Steve and Jeff's brother, Mike Porcaro, replaced Hungate in 1982. Fergie Fredericksen replaced Kimball in late 1984. Also see **Classic Rock Tracks** section.

3/21/81	®	40	1	1 Live For Today	—	Turn Back ....Columbia 36813
4/17/82	®	8	14	2 Rosanna	2⁵	Toto IV ....Columbia 37728
				Grammy: Record of the Year		
5/22/82	®	28	4	3 Afraid Of Love	—	↓
6/19/82	®	57	3	4 Lovers In The Night	—	↓
11/3/84	®	7	12	5 Stranger In Town	30	Isolation ....Columbia 38962

Billboard				ARTIST Track Title	ℝ=Mainstream Rock ⓜ=Modern Rock	Hot Pos	Album Title	Album Label & Number
Debut	Cht	Peak	Wks					

TOWNSHEND, Pete

Born on 5/19/1945 in London, England. Rock singer/songwriter/guitarist. Member of **The Who**. First solo album *Who Came First*, 1972. Own publishing house, Eel Pie Press, mid-1970s. Currently plagued by a significant hearing loss. Also see **Classic Rock Tracks** section.

TOP HITS: 1)Face The Face 2)A Friend Is A Friend 3)Give Blood

Debut	Cht	Peak	Wks	Track	Hot Pos	Album	Label
5/30/81	ℝ	39	5	1 **Won't Get Fooled Again** .... [L]	—	VA: The Secret Policeman's Ball/The Music ...Island 9630
				PETE TOWNSHEND & JOHN WILLIAMS #15 Pop hit for **The Who** in 1971		
7/3/82	ℝ	15	10	2 **Face Dances Part Two**	105	All The Best Cowboys Have Chinese Eyes......Atco 149
7/10/82	ℝ	41	5	3 **Slit Skirts**...........................	—	↓
7/24/82	ℝ	30	10	4 **Stardom In Action**	—	↓
11/9/85	ℝ	3³	14	5 **Face The Face**	26	White City - A Novel......................Atco 90473
11/30/85+	ℝ	5	15	6 **Give Blood**	—	↓
4/5/86	ℝ	32	6	7 **Secondhand Love**	—	↓
9/20/86	ℝ	26	6	8 **Barefootin'** .... [L]	—	Pete Townshend's Deep End Live!...............Atco 90553
				#7 Pop hit for Robert Parker in 1966		
10/18/86	ℝ	39	4	9 **Life To Life**	—	St: Playing For Keeps ....Atlantic 81678
6/24/89	ℝ	3²	10	10 **A Friend Is A Friend**	—	The Iron Man: The Musical By Pete Townshend......................Atlantic 81996
6/5/93	ℝ	19	6	11 **English Boy**...........................	—	Psychoderelict ....Atlantic 82494

TOY MATINEE

Pop duo formed in Los Angeles, California: Kevin Gilbert (vocals) and Patrick Leonard (instruments). Gilbert died of accidental asphyxiation on 5/18/1996 (age 29).

Debut	Cht	Peak	Wks	Track	Hot Pos	Album	Label
9/22/90	ℝ	23	11	1 **Last Plane Out**	—	Toy Matinee...............Reprise 26235
1/19/91	ℝ	23	8	2 **The Ballad Of Jenny Ledge**	—	↓

TRAFFIC

Rock band formed in England. Original lineup included **Steve Winwood** (vocals, keyboards), **Dave Mason** (guitar) and **Jim Capaldi** (drums). Disbanded in 1974; Winwood and Capaldi reunited in 1994. Capaldi died on 1/28/2005 (age 60). Also see **Classic Rock Tracks** section.

AWARD: R&R Hall of Fame: 2004

Debut	Cht	Peak	Wks	Track	Hot Pos	Album	Label
5/7/94	ℝ	10	8	**Here Comes A Man**...........................	—	Far From Home...............Virgin 39490

TRAGICALLY HIP, The

Rock band from Kingston, Ontario, Canada: Gordon Downie (vocals), Bobby Baker (guitar), Paul Langlois (guitar), Gord Sinclair (bass) and Johnny Fay (drums).

Debut	Cht	Peak	Wks	Track	Hot Pos	Album	Label
3/31/90	ℝ	30	6	1 **New Orleans Is Sinking**...........................	—	Up To Here...............MCA 6310
4/13/91	ℝ	43	4	2 **Three Pistols**...........................	—	Road Apples...............MCA 10173
2/13/93	ⓜ	16	9	3 **Courage (For Hugh MacLennan)**	—	Fully Completely...............MCA 10700
2/20/93	ℝ	16	8			
9/26/98	ℝ	39	1	4 **Poets**...........................	—	Phantom Power...............Sire 31025

TRAIN

Rock band from San Francisco, California: Patrick Monahan (vocals), Rob Hotchkiss (guitar), Jimmy Stafford (guitar), Charlie Colin (bass) and Scott Underwood (drums). In late 2003, Brandon Bush replaced Hotchkiss and Johnny Colt (of **The Black Crowes**) replaced Colin.

Debut	Cht	Peak	Wks	Track	Hot Pos	Album	Label
11/28/98+	ℝ	12	24	1 **Free**	—	Train ....Aware 38052
5/8/99	ℝ	21	14	2 **Meet Virginia**	20	↓
6/5/99	ⓜ	25	16			
3/3/01	ⓜ	11	26	3 **Drops Of Jupiter (Tell Me)**	5	Drops Of Jupiter ....Aware 69888
3/17/01	ℝ	19	26	Grammy: Rock Song		
3/30/02	ℝ	40	1	4 **She's On Fire**	—	↓
6/14/03	ℝ	40	1	5 **Calling All Angels**...........................	19	My Private Nation...............Columbia 86593

TRANSPLANTS

Rock trio formed in Los Angeles, California: Rob Ashton (vocals), **Tim Armstrong** (guitar, bass) and Travis Barker (drums). Armstrong is also a member of **Rancid**. Barker is also a member of **Blink-182**.

Debut	Cht	Peak	Wks	Track	Hot Pos	Album	Label
12/7/02+	ⓜ	19	15	1 **Diamonds And Guns**...........................	—	Transplants...............Hellcat 80448
6/18/05	ⓜ	25	9	2 **Gangsters And Thugs**	—	Haunted Cities...............LaSalle 93814

TRANS-SIBERIAN ORCHESTRA

Studio orchestra assembled by producer Paul O'Neill.

Debut	Cht	Peak	Wks	Track	Hot Pos	Album	Label
1/3/98	ℝ	29	2	**Christmas Eve - Sarajevo 12/24** .... [X-I]	49ᴬ	Christmas Eve And Other Stories...............Lava 92736

Debut	Cht	Peak	Wks	ARTIST / Track Title (ⓡ=Mainstream Rock ⓜ=Modern Rock)	Hot Pos	Album Title	Album Label & Number
				TRANSVISION VAMP			
				Pop-rock band from England: Wendy James (vocals), Nick Sayer (guitar), Tex Axile (keyboards), Dave Parsons (bass) and Pol Burton (drums).			
9/17/88	ⓜ	9	5	1 **Tell That Girl To Shut Up**	87	*Pop Art* ....Uni 5	
				first recorded by Holly & The Italians in 1981			
8/17/91	ⓜ	14	10	2 **(I Just Wanna) B With U**	—	*Little Magnets Versus The Bubble Of Babble* ....MCA 10331	
				TRAPT			
				Hard-rock band from Los Gatos, California: Chris Brown (vocals, guitar), Simon Ormandy (guitar), Peter Charell (bass) and Aaron Montgomery (drums).	ⓡ 2000s: #33 ★ ⓜ All-Time: #90		
12/21/02+	ⓜ	❶⁵	45	1 **Headstrong**	16	*Trapt* ....Warner 48296	
10/26/02+	ⓡ	❶¹	55				
7/12/03	ⓡ	❶¹	36	2 **Still Frame**	69	↓	
7/19/03	ⓜ	3¹	30				
1/31/04	ⓜ	10	18	3 **Echo**..	125	↓	
2/7/04	ⓡ	13	15				
7/30/05	ⓡ	3²	29	4 **Stand Up**..	104	*Someone In Control* ....Warner 49445	
7/30/05	ⓜ	17	20				
2/4/06	ⓡ	20	14	5 **Waiting**	—	↓	
2/11/06	ⓜ	27	8				
5/27/06	ⓡ	24	13	6 **Disconnected (Out Of Touch)**	—	↓	
				TRASH CAN SINATRAS, The			
				Pop-rock band from Irvine, Scotland: brothers John Douglas (guitar) and Stephen Douglas (drums), with Frank Reader (vocals), Paul Livingston (guitar) and George McDaid (bass). David Hughes replaced McDaid in 1992.			
11/17/90	ⓜ	8	11	1 **Only Tongue Can Tell**	—	*Cake* ....Go! Discs 828201	
2/9/91	ⓜ	12	6	2 **Obscurity Knocks**..	—	↓	
5/29/93	ⓜ	11	9	3 **Hayfever**	—	*I've Seen Everything*...........................Go! Discs 828412	
				TRAVELING WILBURYS			
				Supergroup masquerading as a band of brothers. Spearheaded by Nelson (**George Harrison**), with Lucky (**Bob Dylan**), Otis (**Jeff Lynne**), Lefty (**Roy Orbison**) and Charlie (**Tom Petty**) Wilbury. Orbison died on 12/6/1988 (age 52). For their second album, *Vol. 3*, the names have changed to Spike (Harrison), Muddy (Petty), Clayton (Lynne) and Boo (Dylan). Harrison died of cancer on 11/29/2001 (age 58).			
10/22/88	ⓡ	2²	12	1 **Handle With Care**..	45	*Volume One* ....Wilbury 25796	
11/19/88+	ⓡ	5	15	2 **Last Night**..	—	↓	
1/14/89	ⓡ	41	1	3 **Tweeter And The Monkey Man**	—	↓	
2/4/89	ⓡ	2³	12	4 **End Of The Line**..	63	↓	
4/8/89	ⓡ	7	8	5 **Heading For The Light**	—	↓	
10/27/90	ⓡ	2³	13	6 **She's My Baby**	—	*Vol. 3* ....Wilbury 26324	
12/22/90+	ⓡ	16	11	7 **Inside Out**..	—	↓	
3/9/91	ⓡ	46	4	8 **Wilbury Twist**..	—	↓	
				TRAVERS, Pat			
				Born on 4/12/1954 in Toronto, Ontario, Canada. Rock singer/guitarist. Also see **Classic Rock Tracks** section.			
4/11/81	ⓡ	33	3	1 **New Age Music**	—	*Radio Active* ....Polydor 6313	
4/14/84	ⓡ	23	5	2 **Killer**	—	*Hot Shot* ....Polydor 821064	
				TRAVIS			
				Rock band from Glasgow, Scotland: Fran Healy (vocals), Andy Dunlop (guitar), Dougie Payne (bass) and Neil Primrose (drums).			
6/10/00	ⓜ	35	4	1 **Why Does It Always Rain On Me?**	—	*The Man Who*................................Independiente 62151	
6/2/01	ⓜ	37	3	2 **Sing**..	—	*The Invisible Band*.........................Independiente 85788	
				TREAT HER RIGHT			
				Rock band from Boston, Massachusetts: Mark Sandman (vocals, guitar), David Champagne (guitar), Jim Fitting (harmonica) and Billy Conway (drums). Sandman died of a heart attack on 7/4/1999 (age 46).			
4/2/88	ⓡ	15	12	**I Think She Likes Me**	—	*Treat Her Right* ....RCA 6884	
				TRICKY			
				Born Adrian Thaws on 1/27/1968 in Bristol, Avon, England. Male techno-dance artist.			
6/30/01	ⓜ	35	5	1 **Evolution Revolution Love**	—	*Blowback* ....Hollywood 162285	
				TRICKY Featuring Ed Kowalczyk & Hawkman			
8/11/01	ⓡ	11	11	2 **Simple Creed**	—	*V*...Radioactive 12485	
8/11/01	ⓜ	18	9	LIVE Featuring Tricky			

TRIK TURNER

Rock-rap band from Phoenix, Arizona: David Bowers and Doug Moore (vocals), Danny Marquez (DJ), Tracy "Tre" Thorstad (guitar), Steve Faulkner (bass) and Sean Garden (drums).

Debut	Cht	Peak	Wks	#	Track Title	Hot Pos	Album Title	Album Label & Number
1/26/02	Ⓜ	7	18	1	Friends + Family	123	Trik Turner	RCA 68073
7/20/02	Ⓜ	35	3	2	Sacrifice	—	↓	

TRIPPING DAISY

Pop-rock band from Dallas, Texas: Tim DeLaughter (vocals), Wes Berggren (guitar), Mark Pirro (bass) and Bryan Wakeland (drums). Berggren died on 10/27/1999 (age 28).

Debut	Cht	Peak	Wks	#	Track Title	Hot Pos	Album Title	Album Label & Number
10/30/93	Ⓜ	24	2	1	My Umbrella	—	Bill	Island 555002
6/24/95	Ⓜ	6	15	2	I Got A Girl	53ᴬ	I Am An Elastic Firecracker	Island 524112
7/29/95	Ⓡ	33	6					
11/11/95	Ⓜ	32	6	3	Piranha	—	↓	
11/18/95	Ⓡ	35	4					

TRIUMPH

Hard-rock trio formed in Toronto, Ontario, Canada: Rik Emmett (vocals, guitar; born on 7/10/1953), Mike Levine (keyboards, bass) and Gil Moore (drums). Emmett went solo in 1988. Phil Xenidis (guitar) joined by 1992. Also see **Classic Rock Tracks** section.

TOP HITS: 1)All The Way 2)A World Of Fantasy 3)Magic Power

Debut	Cht	Peak	Wks	#	Track Title	Hot Pos	Album Title	Album Label & Number
10/3/81	Ⓡ	8	21	1	Magic Power	51	Allied Forces	RCA 3902
10/24/81	Ⓡ	55	4	2	Allied Forces	—	↓	
11/14/81	Ⓡ	18	20	3	Fight The Good Fight	—	↓	
3/27/82	Ⓡ	50	4	4	Say Goodbye	102	↓	
1/29/83	Ⓡ	3¹	19	5	A World Of Fantasy	—	Never Surrender	RCA 4382
2/5/83	Ⓡ	23	14	6	Never Surrender	—	↓	
7/30/83	Ⓡ	2²	10	7	All The Way	—	↓	
12/1/84+	Ⓡ	10	11	8	Spellbound	—	Thunder Seven	MCA 5537
2/9/85	Ⓡ	13	11	9	Follow Your Heart	88	↓	
12/7/85	Ⓡ	49	2	10	Mind Games	—	Stages	MCA 8020
8/16/86	Ⓡ	9	13	11	Somebody's Out There	27	The Sport Of Kings	MCA 5786
11/1/86	Ⓡ	23	8	12	Tears In The Rain	—	↓	
11/7/87	Ⓡ	28	10	13	Long Time Gone	—	Surveillance	MCA 42083
1/9/93	Ⓡ	30	6	14	Child Of The City	—	Edge Of Excess	Victory 480012

TRIVIUM

Hard-rock band from Orlando, Florida: Matt Heafy (vocals), Corey Beaulieu (guitar), Paolo Gregoletto (bass) and Travis Smith (drums).

Debut	Cht	Peak	Wks	#	Track Title	Hot Pos	Album Title	Album Label & Number
3/3/07	Ⓡ	32	7		The Rising	—	The Crusade	Roadrunner 618059

TRIXTER

Hard-rock band from Paramus, New Jersey: Peter Loran (vocals), Steve Brown (guitar), P.J. Farley (bass) and Mark Scott (drums).

Debut	Cht	Peak	Wks	#	Track Title	Hot Pos	Album Title	Album Label & Number
9/29/90	Ⓡ	26	12	1	Give It To Me Good	65	Trixter	MCA 6389
2/9/91	Ⓡ	33	6	2	One In A Million	75	↓	

TROWER, Robin

Born on 3/9/1945 in London, England. Male rock guitarist/songwriter. Original member of **Procol Harum**. Also see **Classic Rock Tracks** section.

Debut	Cht	Peak	Wks	#	Track Title	Hot Pos	Album Title	Album Label & Number
3/28/81	Ⓡ	18	8	1	Into Money	—	B.L.T.	Chrysalis 1324
4/4/81	Ⓡ	43	1	2	Won't Let You Down	—	↓	
					JACK BRUCE / BILL LORDAN / ROBIN TROWER			
1/24/87	Ⓡ	25	10	3	No Time	—	Passion	GNP Crescendo 2187
5/7/88	Ⓡ	9	10	4	Tear It Up	—	Take What You Need	Atlantic 81838
3/3/90	Ⓡ	38	5	5	Turn The Volume Up	—	In The Line Of Fire	Atlantic 82080

Davey Pattison (lead vocal, above 3)

TRUSTCOMPANY

Rock band from Montgomery, Alabama: Kevin Palmer (vocals, guitar), James Fukai (guitar), Josh Moates (bass) and Jason Singleton (drums).

Debut	Cht	Peak	Wks	#	Track Title	Hot Pos	Album Title	Album Label & Number
6/1/02	Ⓡ	6	26	1	Downfall	91	The Lonely Position Of Neutral	Geffen 493312
6/15/02	Ⓜ	6	26					
11/23/02+	Ⓜ	22	12	2	Running From Me	—	↓	
11/23/02	Ⓜ	24	13					
2/26/05	Ⓜ	20	10	3	Stronger	—	True Parallels	Geffen 004332
2/19/05	Ⓡ	22	13					

Billboard Debut	Cht	Peak	Wks	ARTIST / Track Title ®=Mainstream Rock ⓜ=Modern Rock	Hot Pos	Album Title	Album Label & Number
				TRUTH, The			
				Rock duo from England: Dennis Greaves and Mick Lister.			
4/18/87	®	7	12	Weapons Of Love	65	Weapons Of Love ....I.R.S. 5981	
				TRYNIN, Jennifer			
				Born on 12/27/1963 in New Jersey. Female singer/songwriter/guitarist.			
6/24/95	ⓜ	15	10	Better Than Nothing	74[A]	Cockamamie ....Squint 45931	
7/29/95	®	40	2				
				TSUNAMI			
				Rock band formed in San Francisco, California: Doug Denton (vocals), Tatsuya Miyazaki (guitar), Tomotaka Yamamoto (guitar), Max Load (bass) and Scott Sherman (drums). Tsunami (pronounced: soo-na-mee) is a Japanese term for a large ocean wave caused by an earthquake or volcano.			
2/18/84	®	60	1	The Runaround	—	Tsunami..Enigma 1032	
				TUBES, The			
				Pop-rock band from San Francisco, California: Fee Waybill (vocals), Bill Spooner (guitar), Roger Steen (guitar), Michael Cotton (keyboards), Vince Welnick (keyboards), Rick Anderson (bass) and Charles "Prairie" Prince (drums). Welnick joined the **Grateful Dead** in 1990. Welnick died on 6/2/2006 (age 55).			
5/30/81	®	7	19	1 Talk To Ya Later	101	The Completion Backward Principle..........Capitol 12151	
8/8/81	®	22	12	2 Don't Want To Wait Anymore	35	↓	
4/9/83	®	❶[5]	15	3 She's A Beauty	10	Outside Inside ....Capitol 12260	
5/21/83	®	16	7	4 The Monkey Time	68	↓	
				#8 Pop hit for Major Lance in 1963			
3/9/85	®	25	6	5 Piece By Piece	87	Love Bomb ....Capitol 12381	
				written and produced by **Todd Rundgren**			
				TURNER, Joe Lynn			
				Born on 8/2/1951 in Hackensack, New Jersey. Rock singer/guitarist. Member of **Rainbow** and **Deep Purple**.			
10/19/85	®	19	8	Endlessly	—	Rescue You ....Elektra 60449	
				TURNER, Tina			
				Born Anna Mae Bullock on 11/26/1938 in Brownsville, Tennessee. R&B singer/actress. Half of Ike & Tina Turner duo. Married to Ike from 1958-76. Acted in the movies *Tommy* and *Mad Max-Beyond Thunderdome*. *What's Love Got To Do With It*, was made into a movie in 1993. Her autobiography,			
				AWARD: R&R Hall of Fame: 1991 (w/ Ike Turner)			
8/18/84	®	51	4	1 What's Love Got To Do With It	❶[3]	Private Dancer.......................................Capitol 12330	
				Grammys: Record & Song of the Year / Pop Female Vocal ★ RS500 #309			
9/22/84	®	32	9	2 Better Be Good To Me..	5	↓	
				Grammy: Rock Female Vocal			
11/24/84	®	7	25	3 It's Only Love	15	Reckless ....A&M 5013	
				BRYAN ADAMS & TINA TURNER			
7/20/85	®	29	8	4 We Don't Need Another Hero (Thunderdome)...........	2[1]	St: Mad Max Beyond Thunderdome..........Capitol 12429	
10/4/86	®	18	8	5 Back Where You Started.......................................	—	Break Every Rule....................................Capitol 12530	
				Grammy: Rock Female Vocal **Bryan Adams** (co-writer, backing vocal)			
				TUTONE, Tommy — see TOMMY			
				TV ON THE RADIO			
				Eclectic-rock band from Brooklyn, New York: Kyp Malone (vocals), Tunde Adebimpe (vocals), David Sitek (instruments), Gerard Smith (bass) and Jaleel Bunton (drums).			
3/10/07	ⓜ	37	2	Wolf Like Me	—	Return To Cookie Mountain...............Interscope 007466	
				12 STONES			
				Hard-rock band from Mandeville, Louisiana: Paul McCoy (vocals), Eric Weaver (guitar), Kevin Dorr (bass) and Aaron Gainer (drums). Also see "Bring Me To Life" by **Evanescence**.			
10/2/04	®	38	1	1 Far Away	—	Potter's Field.......................................Wind-Up 13082	
6/30/07	®	24	20	2 Lie To Me..	—	Anthem For The Underdog....................Wind-Up 13126	
3/1/08	®	30↑	5↑	3 Anthem For The Underdog	—	↓	
				25TH OF MAY, The			
				Techno-dance band from Liverpool, England: Steve Swindelli (vocals), Eddie G. (guitar), NC Cope (bass) and Jimmy Jazz (drums).			
9/5/92	ⓜ	28	3	It's All Right..	—	Lenin & McCarthy..................................Arista 18712	
				TWILLEY, Dwight			
				Born on 6/6/1951 in Tulsa, Oklahoma. Rock singer/songwriter/pianist.			
3/20/82	®	14	7	1 Somebody To Love	106	Scuba Divers.....................................EMI America 17064	
2/11/84	®	2[1]	14	2 Girls..	16	Jungle...EMI America 17107	
				Tom Petty (backing vocal)			
5/12/84	®	44	3	3 Little Bit Of Love..	77	↓	

Billboard	Cht	Peak	Wks	ARTIST / Track Title	®=Mainstream Rock ⓜ=Modern Rock	Hot Pos	Album Title	Album Label & Number
Debut								

TWISTED SISTER
Hard-rock band from Long Island, New York: Dee Snider (vocals), Jay French (guitar), Eddie Ojeda (guitar), Mark Mendosa (bass) and A.J. Pero (drums). Joey Franco replaced Pero in 1987.

Debut	Cht	Peak	Wks	Track	Hot Pos	Album Title	Label
6/16/84	®	7	18	1 We're Not Gonna Take It	21	Stay Hungry	Atlantic 80156
10/6/84	®	35	9	2 I Wanna Rock	68	↓	
1/5/85	®	19	8	3 The Price	107	↓	
12/7/85	®	32	8	4 Leader Of The Pack	53	Come Out And Play	Atlantic 81275
				#1 Pop hit for The Shangri-Las in 1964			
7/18/87	®	31	6	5 Hot Love	—	Love Is For Suckers	Atlantic 81772

TWO
Rock band formed in Phoenix, Arizona: Rob Halford (vocals; of **Judas Priest** and **Fight**), John Lowery (guitar), James Woolley (keyboards), Ray Reandeau (bass) and Sid Riggs (drums).

2/21/98	®	22	11	I Am A Pig	—	Voyeurs	Nothing 90155

TYKETTO
Hard-rock band from Long Island, New York: Danny Vaughn (vocals), Brooke St. James (guitar), Jimi Kennedy (bass) and Michael Clayton (drums).

5/11/91	®	39	4	1 Forever Young	—	Don't Come Easy	DGC 24317
8/3/91	®	25	7	2 Seasons	—	↓	

TYLER, Bonnie
Born Gaynor Hopkins on 6/8/1953 in Swansea, Wales. Female singer known for her raspy vocals.

9/10/83	®	23	7	Total Eclipse Of The Heart	❶4	Faster Than The Speed Of Night	Columbia 38710
				written and produced by **Jim Steinman**			

TYLER, Steven
Born Steven Tallarico on 3/26/1948 in Yonkers, New York. Lead singer of **Aerosmith**. Father of actress Liv Tyler.

12/17/05	®	37	8	Just Feel Better	107	All That I Am	Arista 59773
				SANTANA Featuring Steven Tyler			

TYPE O NEGATIVE
Hard-rock band from Brooklyn, New York: Peter Steele (vocals, bass), Kenny Hickey (guitar), Josh Silver (keyboards) and Johnny Kelly (drums).

10/23/99	®	37	4	1 Everything Dies	—	World Coming Down	Roadrunner 8660
7/5/03	®	40	1	2 I Don't Wanna Be Me	—	Life Is Killing Me	Roadrunner 618438

U

UB40
Reggae band formed in Birmingham, England: brothers Ali Campbell (vocals) and Robin Campbell (guitar, vocals), Terence "Astro" Wilson (vocals), Norman Hassan (percussion), Michael Virtue (keyboards), Brian Travers (sax), Earl Falconer (bass) and James Brown (drums). Name taken from a British unemployment form.

2/18/84	®	41	2	1 Red Red Wine	❶1	Labour Of Love	A&M 4980
				#62 Pop hit for Neil Diamond in 1968			
8/17/85	®	40	5	2 I Got You Babe	28	Little Baggariddim	A&M 5090
				#1 Pop hit for Sonny & Cher in 1965			
9/10/88	ⓜ	4	8	3 Breakfast In Bed	—	UB40	A&M 5213
				UB40 with Chrissie Hynde (above 2)			
1/27/90	ⓜ	6	8	4 Here I Am (Come And Take Me)	7	Labour Of Love II	Virgin 91324
				#10 Pop hit for Al Green in 1973			
5/1/93	ⓜ	11	14	5 Can't Help Falling In Love	❶7	St: Sliver	Virgin 88064
				#2 Pop hit for Elvis Presley in 1962			
8/28/93	ⓜ	14	8	6 Higher Ground	45	Promises And Lies	Virgin 88229

UFO
Hard-rock band formed in England: Phil Mogg (vocals), Paul Chapman (guitar), Neil Carter (keyboards), Pete Way (bass) and Andy Parker (drums). In 1986, Mogg fronted new lineup: Atomic Tommy M (guitar), Paul Raymond (keyboards), Paul Gray (bass) and Jim Simpson (drums).

3/6/82	®	23	8	1 The Writer	—	Mechanix	Chrysalis 1360
4/19/86	®	47	2	2 This Time	—	Misdemeanor	Chrysalis 41518

UGLY KID JOE
Rock band from Isla Vista, California: Whitfield Crane (vocals), Klaus Eichstadt (guitar), Dave Fortman (guitar), Cordell Crockett (bass), and Mark Davis (drums). Crane later joined **Another Animal**. Fortman later became a prolific record producer.

2/1/92	®	6	21	1 Everything About You	9	As Ugly As They Want To Be	Stardog 868823
10/10/92	®	29	4	2 Neighbor	—	America's Least Wanted	Stardog 512571
2/6/93	®	3[1]	14	3 Cats In The Cradle	6	↓	
				#1 Pop hit for Harry Chapin in 1974			
5/15/93	®	22	6	4 Busy Bee	—	↓	

				ARTIST		**Hot**		
Debut	**Cht**	**Peak**	**Wks**	**Track Title**	ℝ=Mainstream Rock ⓜ=Modern Rock	**Pos**	**Album Title**	**Album Label & Number**

ULTRA VIVID SCENE
Born Kurt Ralske in 1967 in Brooklyn, New York. Eclectic singer/songwriter/musician.

Debut	Cht	Peak	Wks	Track	Hot Pos	Album Title	Label & Number
6/2/90	ⓜ	25	2	1 Staring At The Sun	—	Joy 1967-1990	4 A D 46227
8/18/90	ⓜ	19	3	2 It Happens Every Time	—	↓	
10/6/90	ⓜ	14	6	3 Special One	—	↓	
2/13/93	ⓜ	27	3	4 Blood And Thunder	—	Rev	4 A D 53133

ULTRAVOX
Electronic-rock band formed in England: **Midge Ure** (vocals, guitar), Billy Currie (keyboards), Chris Cross (bass) and Warren Cann (drums).

3/26/83	ℝ	27	5	1 Reap The Wild Wind	71	Quartet	Chrysalis 1394
5/12/84	ℝ	55	2	2 One Small Day	—	Lament	Chrysalis 41459

UNDERWORLD
Rock band from England: Karl Hyde (vocals, guitar), Alfie Thomas (guitar), Rick Smith (keyboards), Baz Allen (bass) and Pascal Console (drums).

9/2/89	ⓜ	14	6	Stand Up	67	Change The Weather	Sire 25945

UNION
Rock band formed in Canada: Randy Bachman (vocals, guitar), Frank Ludwig (keyboards), Fred Turner (bass) and Chris Leighton (drums). Bachman and Turner were leaders of Bachman-Turner Overdrive.

8/1/81	ℝ	38	6	Mainstreet U.S.A.		On Strike	Portrait 37368

UNION UNDERGROUND, The
Rock band from San Antonio, Texas: Bryan Scott (vocals, guitar), Patrick Kennison (guitar), John Moyer (bass) and Josh Memelo (drums). Moyer joined **Disturbed** in early 2003.

7/8/00	ℝ	11	26	1 Turn Me On "Mr. Deadman"	—	...An Education In Rebellion	Portrait 67778
1/6/01	ℝ	13	15	2 Killing The Fly	—	↓	
5/19/01	ℝ	26	10	3 Revolution Man	—	↓	
5/18/02	ℝ	29	9	4 Across The Nation	—	VA: WWF: Forceable Entry	Columbia 85211

UNLOCO
Hard-rock band from Austin, Texas: Joey Duenas (vocals), Marc Serrano (guitar), Victor Escareno (bass) and Peter Navarette (drums).

3/22/03	ℝ	25	13	Failure	—	Becoming I	Maverick 48352

UNTOUCHABLES, The
Funk band from Los Angeles, California: Jerry Miller and Chuck Askerneese (vocals), Clyde Grimes (guitar), Brewster (keyboards), Derek Breakfield (bass) and Willie McNeil (drums).

3/25/89	ⓜ	28	1	Agent Double O Soul	—	Agent Double O Soul	Restless 72342

#21 Pop hit for Edwin Starr in 1965

UNWRITTEN LAW
Punk-rock band from Poway, California: Scott Russo (vocals), Rob Brewer (guitar), Steve Morris (guitar), Pat Kim (bass) and Wade Youman (drums). Tony Palermo replaced Youman in 2004. Brewer left in 2005.

8/28/99	ⓜ	28	8	1 Cailin	—	Unwritten Law	Interscope 90189
2/2/02	ⓜ	❶⁴	26	2 Seein' Red	105	Elva	Interscope 493139
7/27/02	ⓜ	14	11	3 Up All Night	—	↓	
1/4/03	ⓜ	16	12	4 Rest Of My Life	—	Music In High Places	Lava 83632
12/18/04+	ⓜ	5	18	5 Save Me	108	Here's To The Mourning	Lava 93147
5/14/05	ⓜ	32	5	6 She Says	—	↓	

U.P.O.
Hard-rock band from Los Angeles, California: Shawn Albro (vocals), Chris Weber (guitar), Ben Shirley (bass) and Tommy Holt (drums).

4/22/00	ℝ	6	26	1 Godless	—	No Pleasantries	Epic 69869
11/18/00	ℝ	25	12	2 Feel Alive	—	↓	

URE, Midge
Born James Ure on 10/10/1953 in Glasgow, Scotland. Rock singer/guitarist. Member of **Ultravox**.

1/21/89	ⓜ	4	12	1 Dear God	95	Answers To Nothing	Chrysalis 41649
1/21/89	ℝ	6	13				
4/29/89	ⓜ	26	2	2 Answers To Nothing	—	↓	
1/18/92	ⓜ	12	7	3 Cold, Cold Heart	—	Pure	RCA 61010

URGE, The
Ska-rock band from St. Louis, Missouri: Steve Ewing (vocals), Jerry Jost (guitar), Bill Reiter, Matt Kwiatkowski (horns), Karl Grable (bass) and John Pessoni (drums).

4/11/98	ⓜ	10	19	Jump Right In	—	Master Of Styles	Immortal 69152

THE URGE Featuring Nick Hexum

URGE OVERKILL

Rock trio from Chicago, Illinois: Nash Kato (guitar), "Eddie" King Roeser (bass) and Blackie Onassis (drums). All share vocals.

7/10/93	M	6	15	1 **Sister Havana**..	—	*Saturation*....................................Geffen 24529
7/31/93	R	10	17			
3/26/94	M	23	4	2 **Positive Bleeding**	—	↓
12/25/93	R	40	2			
11/12/94	M	11	11	3 **Girl, You'll Be A Woman Soon**	59	*St: Pulp Fiction* ....MCA 11103
				#10 Pop hit for Neil Diamond in 1967		
10/21/95	R	34	3	4 **The Break**	—	*Exit The Dragon* ....Geffen 24818

URIAH HEEP

Hard-rock band from England. Numerous personnel changes. Lineup in 1982: Peter Goalby (vocals), Mick Box (guitar), John Sinclair (keyboards), Bob Daisley (bass) and Lee Kerslake (drums). Also see **Classic Rock Tracks** section.

| 8/14/82 | R | 25 | 4 | **That's The Way That It Is** .... | 106 | *Abominog* ....Mercury 4057 |

USA FOR AFRICA

USA: United Support of Artists. Collection of top artists formed to help starving people in Africa.

| 3/23/85 | R | 27 | 7 | **We Are The World** .... | **1**⁴ | *We Are The World* ....Columbia 40043 |
| | | | | **Grammys: Record & Song of the Year / Pop Vocal Group** | | |

USED, The

Rock band from Orem, Utah: Bert McCracken (vocals; born on 2/25/1982), Quinn Allman (guitar), Jeph Howard (bass) and Branden Steineckert (drums).

9/28/02	M	19	18	1 **The Taste Of Ink**	—	*The Used*......................................Reprise 48287
2/15/03	M	13	14	2 **Buried Myself Alive**	—	↓
6/14/03	M	23	11	3 **Blue And Yellow**	—	↓
9/18/04	M	13	12	4 **Take It Away**..	—	*In Love And Death*................................Reprise 48789
12/11/04+	M	19	15	5 **All That I've Got**	—	↓
5/21/05	M	28	6	6 **Under Pressure**	41	↓
				THE USED & MY CHEMICAL ROMANCE		
4/7/07	M	9	20	7 **The Bird And The Worm**	107	*Lies For The Liars*................................Reprise 43309
10/13/07	M	37	4	8 **Pretty Handsome Awkward**	—	↓

US3

Jazz-rap collaboration by London producers Mel Simpson (keyboards) and Geoff Wilkinson (samples). Samples of recordings on the Blue Note jazz record label serve as the backdrop for new rap solos and jazz playing by some of Britain's top players.

| 11/13/93 | M | 29 | 4 | **Cantaloop**.. | 9 | *Hand On The Torch*...............................Blue Note 80883 |

UTAH SAINTS

Techno-rave duo from England: Jez Willis and Tim Garbutt.

| 8/8/92 | M | 7 | 9 | **Something Good** .... | 98 | *Something Good*....................................London 869843 |
| | | | | samples "Cloudbusting" by **Kate Bush** | | |

UTOPIA

Pop-rock band formed in New York: **Todd Rundgren** (vocals, guitar), Roger Powell (keyboards), Kasim Sulton (bass) and John Wilcox (drums).

| 10/23/82 | R | 31 | 6 | 1 **Hammer In My Heart**.................................... | — | *Utopia* ....Network 60183 |
| 2/11/84 | R | 30 | 5 | 2 **Crybaby** .... | — | *Oblivion* ....Passport 6029 |

U2   **R** 1980s: #5 / 1990s: #10 / All-Time: #3 ★ **M** 1990s: #1 / 2000s: #27 / All-Time: #2

Rock band formed in Dublin, Ireland: Paul "Bono" Hewson (vocals; born on 5/10/1960), Dave "The Edge" Evans (guitar; born on 8/8/1961), Adam Clayton (bass; born on 3/13/1960) and Larry Mullen Jr. (drums; born on 10/31/1961). Released concert tour documentary movie *Rattle And Hum* in 1988. Bono eventually became a social activist and was nominated for the Nobel Peace Prize in 2003 for his efforts to relieve third world debt and to promote AIDS awareness in Africa; he was also named *Time* magazine's 2005 Person of the Year (along with Bill and Melinda Gates).

AWARD: R&R Hall of Fame: 2005

TOP HITS: 1)Mysterious Ways 2)Angel Of Harlem 3)With Or Without You 4)Desire 5)Vertigo

4/18/81	R	20	11	1 **I Will Follow**..	—	*Boy* ....Island 9646
3/12/83	R	2²	9	2 **New Year's Day**.......................................	53	*War* ....Island 90067
				RS500 #427		
4/16/83	R	7	17	3 **Sunday Bloody Sunday**	—	↓
				R&R Hall of Fame ★ RS500 #268		
6/11/83	R	12	9	4 **Two Hearts Beat As One**...........................	101	↓
7/16/83	R	27	4	5 **Surrender**	—	↓
12/10/83+	R	30	8	6 **11 O'Clock Tick Tock**................................ [L]	—	*Under A Blood Red Sky*.............................Island 90127
				recorded on 5/6/1983 in Boston, Massachusetts		
9/15/84	R	2³	21	7 **Pride (In The Name Of Love)**............................	33	*The Unforgettable Fire*............................Island 90231
				R&R Hall of Fame ★ RS500 #378		
				a tribute to Martin Luther King		

Debut	Cht	Peak	Wks	ARTIST / Track Title	Hot Pos	Album Title	Album Label & Number
				®=Mainstream Rock ⓜ=Modern Rock			
				U2 — cont'd			
12/8/84+	®	31	9	8 Wire	—	↓	
4/13/85	®	45	3	9 A Sort Of Homecoming	—	↓	
6/22/85	®	16	10	10 Three Sunrises	—	*Wide Awake In America*	Island 90279
8/24/85	®	19	12	11 Bad [L]	—	↓	
3/21/87	®	❶⁵	13	12 **With Or Without You** RS500 #131	❶³	*The Joshua Tree*	Island 90581
3/28/87	®	2⁴	19	13 I Still Haven't Found What I'm Looking For R&R Hall of Fame ★ RS500 #93	❶²	↓	
4/4/87	®	11	24	14 Where The Streets Have No Name	13	↓	
4/4/87	®	14	18	15 Bullet The Blue Sky	—	↓	
4/11/87+	®	6	12	16 In God's Country	44	↓	
6/27/87	®	11	10	17 Spanish Eyes	—	(single only)	Island 99430
9/17/88	ⓜ	9	4	18 Jesus Christ written by Woody Guthrie	—	*VA: Folkways: A Vision Shared*	Columbia 44034
9/10/88	®	38	3				
10/1/88	®	❶⁵	11	19 **Desire** Grammy: Rock Vocal Group	3¹	*Rattle And Hum*	Island 91003
10/8/88	ⓜ	❶⁵	11				
10/22/88	®	❶⁶	18	20 **Angel Of Harlem** a tribute to Billie Holiday	14	↓	
11/5/88	ⓜ	3⁴	17				
10/22/88+	®	2¹	20	21 When Love Comes To Town U2 with B.B. King	68	↓	
11/19/88	ⓜ	10	13				
10/22/88+	®	8	20	22 God Part II sequel to John Lennon's 1970 recording "God"	—	↓	
3/11/89	ⓜ	28	3				
7/1/89	®	13	10	23 All I Want Is You	83	↓	
4/15/89	®	14	7	24 Dancing Barefoot	—	(single only)	Island 99225
7/8/89	ⓜ	11	8	25 Everlasting Love #13 Pop hit for Robert Knight in 1967	—	(single only)	Island 96550
8/5/89	®	46	1				
11/10/90	ⓜ	2³	13	26 Night And Day #1 Pop hit for Fred Astaire in 1932	—	*VA: Red Hot + Blue*	Chrysalis 21799
11/10/90	®	34	5				
10/26/91	ⓜ	❶²	12	27 **The Fly**	61	*Achtung Baby*	Island 10347
10/26/91	®	2¹	7				
11/30/91	®	❶¹²	30	28 **Mysterious Ways**	9	↓	
11/23/91	ⓜ	❶⁹	13				
3/14/92	®	❶²	20	29 **One** RS500 #36	10	↓	
1/4/92	ⓜ	❶¹	23				
1/25/92	®	2¹	16	30 Who's Gonna Ride Your Wild Horses	35	↓	
10/24/92	ⓜ	7	9				
2/1/92	ⓜ	4	8	31 Until The End Of The World	—	↓	
2/1/92	®	5	15				
7/4/92	®	❶³	17	32 **Even Better Than The Real Thing**	32	↓	
7/4/92	ⓜ	5	13				
7/10/93	ⓜ	2¹	12	33 Numb	61ᴬ	*Zooropa*	Island 518047
7/10/93	®	18	3				
7/24/93	®	8	10	34 Zooropa	—	↓	
8/7/93	ⓜ	13	8				
7/31/93	®	12	11	35 Stay (Faraway, So Close!)	61	↓	
12/4/93+	ⓜ	15	14				
10/2/93	ⓜ	3¹	9	36 Lemon	71ᴬ	↓	
6/10/95	ⓜ	❶⁴	15	37 **Hold Me, Thrill Me, Kiss Me, Kill Me**	16	*St: Batman Forever*	Atlantic 82759
6/10/95	®	❶¹	19				
1/25/97	ⓜ	❶⁴	10	38 **Discothéque**	10	*Pop*	Island 524334
1/25/97	®	6	9				
3/15/97	ⓜ	❶³	16	39 **Staring At The Sun**	26	↓	
3/15/97	®	2¹	18				
6/28/97	ⓜ	11	10	40 Last Night On Earth	57	↓	
7/5/97	®	18	8				
11/1/97	ⓜ	31	4	41 Please	103	↓	

Billboard				ARTIST		Hot Pos	Album Title	Album Label & Number
Debut	Cht	Peak	Wks	Track Title	Ⓡ=Mainstream Rock Ⓜ=Modern Rock			

U2 — cont'd

Debut	Cht	Peak	Wks	Track Title	Hot Pos	Album Title	Album Label & Number
10/17/98	Ⓜ	9	24	42 Sweetest Thing	63	*The Best Of 1980-1990/The B-Sides*........Island 524612
10/24/98	Ⓡ	31	6	recorded in 1987		
2/26/00	Ⓜ	20	6	43 The Ground Beneath Her Feet	—	*St: The Million Dollar Hotel*.................Interscope 542395
9/23/00	Ⓜ	5	26	44 Beautiful Day	21	*All That You Can't Leave Behind*........Interscope 524653
9/23/00	Ⓡ	14	26	Grammys: Record & Song of the Year / Rock Vocal Group		
1/6/01	Ⓜ	10	15	45 Walk On	118	↓
1/27/01	Ⓡ	19	12			
4/28/01	Ⓜ	8	15	46 Elevation	116	↓
5/5/01	Ⓡ	21	14	Grammy: Rock Vocal Group		
9/22/01	Ⓡ	35	6	47 Stuck In A Moment You Can't Get Out Of	52	↓
9/15/01	Ⓜ	35	8			
9/21/02	Ⓜ	14	6	48 Electrical Storm	77	*The Best Of 1990-2000* ....Interscope 063361
9/28/02	Ⓡ	26	8			
10/9/04	Ⓜ	❶⁴	23	49 Vertigo	31	*How To Dismantle An Atomic Bomb* ..Interscope 003613
10/9/04	Ⓡ	3⁴	26	Grammys: Rock Song / Rock Vocal Group		
12/18/04+	Ⓜ	6	13	50 All Because Of You	101	↓
1/8/05	Ⓡ	20	13			
3/19/05	Ⓜ	29	8	51 Sometimes You Can't Make It On Your Own	97	↓
				Grammys: Song of the Year / Rock Vocal Group		
10/14/06	Ⓜ	22	7	52 The Saints Are Coming .... [L]	51	*(download only)* ....Island
10/28/06	Ⓡ	33	7	**U2 & GREEN DAY** first recorded by punk-rock band The Skids in 1978; recorded live on 9/25/2006 at the re-opening of the Louisiana Superdome (home of the New Orleans Saints)		
12/2/06	Ⓜ	32	8	53 Window In The Skies.................................	—	*U218: Singles* ....Island 008027

V

VAI, Steve

Born on 6/6/1960 in Long Island, New York. Rock guitarist. With **Frank Zappa**'s band (1979-84), **David Lee Roth**'s band (1986-88) and **Whitesnake** (1989). Formed **Vai** in 1992 which featured vocalist Devin Townsend and fluctuating band members.

Debut	Cht	Peak	Wks	Track Title	Hot Pos	Album Title	Album Label & Number
9/1/90	Ⓡ	38	13	1 I Would Love To .... [I]	—	*Passion and Warfare*...............................Relativity 1037
10/9/93	Ⓡ	36	3	2 In My Dreams With You	—	*Sex & Religion*...Relativity 1132
				VAI		

VAMPIRE WEEKEND

Alternative-rock band from New York: Ezra Koenig (vocals, guitar), Rostam Batmanglij (keyboards), Chris Baio (bass) and Chris Tomson (drums).

Debut	Cht	Peak	Wks	Track Title	Hot Pos	Album Title	Album Label & Number
2/23/08	Ⓜ	30↑	5↑	A-Punk..	—	*Vampire Weekend* ....XL 318

VANDENBERG

Born Adrian Vandenberg on 1/31/1954 in the Netherlands. Hard-rock guitarist. His group: Bert Heerink (vocals), Dick Kemper (bass) and Jos Zoomer (drums). Vandenberg later joined **Whitesnake**.

Debut	Cht	Peak	Wks	Track Title	Hot Pos	Album Title	Album Label & Number
1/15/83	Ⓡ	5	21	1 Burning Heart	39	*Vandenberg* ....Atco 90005
12/24/83	Ⓡ	29	6	2 Friday Night	—	*Heading For A Storm* ....Atco 90121

VANGELIS — see JON & VANGELIS

VAN HALEN   Ⓡ **1980s: #4 / 1990s: #3 / All-Time: #1**

Hard-rock band formed in Pasadena, California: **David Lee Roth** (vocals; born on 10/10/1955), Eddie Van Halen (guitar; born on 1/26/1955), Michael Anthony (bass; born on 6/20/1954) and Alex Van Halen (drums; born on 5/8/1953). The Van Halen brothers were born in Nijmegen, Netherlands; moved to Pasadena in 1968. **Sammy Hagar** replaced Roth as lead singer in 1985. Eddie married actress Valerie Bertinelli on 4/11/1981 (filed for divorce in 2005). Hagar left in June 1996. Gary Cherone (**Extreme**) joined as lead singer in September 1996; left after one album. Roth briefly rejoined group in 1997, 2000 and 2007. Also see **Classic Rock Tracks** section.

AWARD: R&R Hall of Fame: 2007

TOP HITS: 1)Jump 2)Me Wise Magic 3)Without You 4)Top Of The World 5)Runaround

Debut	Cht	Peak	Wks	Track Title	Hot Pos	Album Title	Album Label & Number
5/23/81	Ⓡ	12	13	1 Mean Street	—	*Fair Warning*...Warner 3540
5/30/81	Ⓡ	15	11	2 So This Is Love?	110	↓
6/6/81	Ⓡ	13	11	3 Unchained	—	↓
6/13/81	Ⓡ	29	6	4 Push Comes To Shove	—	↓
2/6/82	Ⓡ	❶²	15	5 (Oh) Pretty Woman	12	*Diver Down* ....Warner 3677
				#1 Pop hit for **Roy Orbison** in 1964		

Debut	Cht	Peak	Wks	Track Title	Hot Pos	Album Title	Album Label & Number

ARTIST — ®=Mainstream Rock ⓜ=Modern Rock

VAN HALEN — cont'd

Debut	Cht	Peak	Wks	Track Title	Hot Pos	Album Title	Album Label & Number
5/8/82	®	3³	15	6 Dancing In The Street	38	↓	
				#2 Pop hit for Martha & The Vandellas in 1964			
5/8/82	®	17	12	7 Where Have All The Good Times Gone!	—	↓	
				first recorded by The Kinks in 1966			
5/8/82	®	33	10	8 Little Guitars	—	↓	
6/12/82	®	22	7	9 Secrets	—	↓	
6/12/82	®	42	3	10 The Full Bug	—	↓	
1/14/84	®	❶⁸	13	11 Jump	❶⁵	*1984 (MCMLXXXIV)*	Warner 23985
				R&R Hall of Fame			
1/21/84	®	2¹	31	12 Panama	13	↓	
1/28/84	®	24	14	13 Hot For Teacher	56	↓	
2/4/84	®	2¹	21	14 I'll Wait	13	↓	
3/15/86	®	❶³	13	15 Why Can't This Be Love	3¹	*5150*	Warner 25394
4/5/86	®	6	18	16 Dreams	22	↓	
4/5/86	®	12	14	17 Best Of Both Worlds	—	↓	
4/19/86	®	4	23	18 Love Walks In	22	↓	
7/26/86	®	33	9	19 Summer Nights	—	↓	
5/14/88	®	❶³	10	20 Black And Blue	34	*OU812*	Warner 25732
6/4/88	®	❶¹	16	21 When It's Love	5	↓	
6/4/88	®	6	17	22 Feels So Good	35	↓	
6/4/88	®	50	3	23 Mine All Mine	—	↓	
6/18/88	®	2³	22	24 Finish What Ya Started	13	↓	
12/10/88	®	31	7	25 Cabo Wabo	—	↓	
6/8/91	®	❶²	11	26 Poundcake	—	*For Unlawful Carnal Knowledge*	Warner 26594
6/29/91	®	❶⁴	20	27 Runaround	—	↓	
6/29/91+	®	2⁴	46	28 Right Now	55	↓	
7/6/91	®	❶⁴	51	29 Top Of The World	27	↓	
2/22/92	®	7	17	30 The Dream Is Over	—	↓	
5/30/92	®	21	8	31 Man On A Mission	—	↓	
2/13/93	®	❶¹	9	32 Won't Get Fooled Again [L]	—	*LIVE: Right here, right now.*	Warner 45198
				#15 Pop hit for The Who in 1971			
1/14/95	®	❶³	19	33 Don't Tell Me (What Love Can Do)	—	*Balance*	Warner 45760
2/4/95	®	36	5	34 The Seventh Seal	—	↓	
2/18/95	®	2⁴	23	35 Can't Stop Lovin' You	30	↓	
5/20/95	®	9	11	36 Amsterdam	—	↓	
8/5/95	®	27	9	37 Not Enough	97	↓	
5/4/96	®	❶²	19	38 Humans Being	—	*St: Twister*	Warner Sunset 46254
10/19/96	®	❶⁶	26	39 Me Wise Magic	—	*Best Of Volume 1*	Warner 46332
11/2/96+	®	12	13	40 Can't Get This Stuff No More	—	↓	
3/7/98	®	❶⁶	12	41 Without You	—	*Van Halen III*	Warner 46662
5/2/98	®	6	13	42 Fire In The Hole	—	↓	
8/15/98	®	27	6	43 One I Want	—	↓	
6/12/04	®	6	11	44 It's About Time	—	*The Best Of Both Worlds*	Warner 78961
8/28/04	®	33	6	45 Up For Breakfast	—	↓	

VANNELLI, Gino

Born on 6/16/1952 in Montreal, Quebec, Canada. Pop singer/songwriter.

Debut	Cht	Peak	Wks	Track Title	Hot Pos	Album Title	Album Label & Number
6/1/85	®	34	8	Black Cars	42	*Black Cars*	HME 40077

VAN ZANT, Johnny, Band

Born on 2/27/1959 in Jacksonville, Florida. Southern-rock singer. Brother of Ronnie Van Zant (of **Lynyrd Skynyrd**) and Donnie Van Zant (of **38 Special**). His band: Robbie Gay and Erik Lundgren (guitars), Danny Clausman (bass) and Robbie Morris (drums). Johnny and Donnie also recorded as Van Zant.

Debut	Cht	Peak	Wks	Track Title	Hot Pos	Album Title	Album Label & Number
6/20/81	®	23	7	1 (Who's) Right Or Wrong	—	*Round Two*	Polydor 6322
10/2/82	®	37	5	2 It's You	—	*The Last Of The Wild Ones*	Polydor 6355
3/30/85	®	16	10	3 I'm A Fighter	—	*Van-Zant*	Geffen 24059
6/15/85	®	27	5	4 You've Got To Believe In Love	102	↓	
				VAN-ZANT (above 2)			
7/14/90	®	❶³	12	5 Brickyard Road	—	*Brickyard Road*	Atlantic 82110
10/6/90	®	24	7	6 Hearts Are Gonna Roll	—	↓	
				JOHNNY VANT ZANT (above 2)			

Billboard	Cht	Peak	Wks	ARTIST Track Title	Ⓡ=Mainstream Rock Ⓜ=Modern Rock	Hot Pos	Album Title	Album Label & Number
Debut								

<table>
<tr><td colspan="9">VAN ZANT, Johnny, Band — cont'd</td></tr>
<tr><td>2/28/98</td><td>Ⓡ</td><td>22</td><td>13</td><td>7 Rage</td><td></td><td>—</td><td>Brother To Brother</td><td>CMC International 86236</td></tr>
<tr><td>3/17/01</td><td>Ⓡ</td><td>33</td><td>5</td><td>8 Get What You Got Comin'
VAN ZANT (above 2)</td><td></td><td>—</td><td>Van Zant II</td><td>CMC International 86301</td></tr>
</table>

VAPORS, The
Pop-rock band from Guildford, Surrey, England: David Fenton (vocals), Ed Bazalgette (guitar), Steve Smith (bass) and Howard Smith (drums).

| 5/2/81 | Ⓡ | 39 | 1 | Jimmie Jones | | — | *Magnets* | Liberty 1090 |

VAST
Born Jonathan Crosby on 7/25/1976 in Long Beach, California. Eclectic singer/songwriter/guitarist. VAST: Visual Audio Sensory Theater.

1/9/99	Ⓜ	31	8	1 Touched		—	*Visual Audio Sensory Theater*	Elektra 62173
10/31/98	Ⓡ	38	4					
8/26/00	Ⓜ	12	13	2 Free		—	*Music For People*	Elektra 62511
9/2/00	Ⓡ	18	11					
2/24/01	Ⓜ	34	5	3 I Don't Have Anything		— ↓		

VAUGHAN, Stevie Ray, and Double Trouble   Ⓡ All-Time: #62
Born on 10/3/1954 in Dallas, Texas. Died in a helicopter crash on 8/27/1990 (age 35). White blues-rock singer/guitarist. Brother of Jimmie Vaughan (of **The Fabulous Thunderbirds**. Double Trouble: Reese Wynans (keyboards), Tommy Shannon (bass) and Chris Layton (drums). Recorded with Jimmie as **The Vaughan Brothers**. Shannon and Layton later joined **Arc Angels** and Storyville.

TOP HITS: 1)Crossfire 2)The Sky Is Crying 3)Telephone Song

8/13/83	Ⓡ	20	9	1 Pride And Joy R&R Hall of Fame		—	*Texas Flood*	Epic 38734
6/9/84	Ⓡ	26	8	2 Voodoo Chile (Slight Return) first recorded by Jimi Hendrix in 1968		—	*Couldn't Stand The Weather*	Epic 39304
7/28/84	Ⓡ	29	8	3 Cold Shot		— ↓	*Soul To Soul*	Epic 40036
9/28/85	Ⓡ	17	10	4 Look At Little Sister first recorded by Hank Ballard in 1960		—		
11/23/85	Ⓡ	17	9	5 Change It		— ↓		
11/15/86	Ⓡ	11	10	6 Superstition #1 Pop hit for Stevie Wonder in 1973	[L]	—	*Live Alive*	Epic 40511
2/14/87	Ⓡ	19	8	7 Willie The Wimp	[L]	— ↓		
6/17/89	Ⓡ	❶³	18	8 <u>Crossfire</u>		—	*In Step*	Epic 45024
9/16/89	Ⓡ	14	13	9 Tightrope		— ↓		
12/16/89+	Ⓡ	18	10	10 The House Is Rockin'		— ↓		
4/7/90	Ⓡ	46	3	11 Wall Of Denial		— ↓		
9/29/90	Ⓡ	7	7	12 Tick Tock		65	*Family Style*	Epic 46225
10/27/90+	Ⓡ	3²	19	13 Telephone Song		— ↓		
2/9/91	Ⓡ	18	11	14 Good Texan THE VAUGHAN BROTHERS (above 3)		— ↓		
11/9/91+	Ⓡ	2¹	20	15 The Sky Is Crying recorded in 1985; written by Elmore James		—	*The Sky Is Crying*	Epic 47390
1/25/92	Ⓡ	3¹	22	16 Empty Arms		— ↓		
5/9/92	Ⓡ	26	9	17 Little Wing Grammy: Rock Instrumental first recorded by Jimi Hendrix in 1968; above 2 recorded in 1984	[I]	— ↓		
10/24/92	Ⓡ	19	8	18 Shake For Me recorded on 4/1/1980 in Austin, Texas	[L]	—	*In The Beginning*	Epic 53168
11/18/95	Ⓡ	32	5	19 Taxman first recorded by The Beatles in 1966			*Greatest Hits*	Epic 66217

VAUX
Rock band from Denver, Colorado: Quentin Smith (vocals), Chris Sorensen (guitar), Adam Tymn (guitar), Greg Daniels (bass) and Joe McChan (drums).

| 10/1/05 | Ⓡ | 37 | 6 | Are You With Me | | — | *Beyond Virtue, Beyond Vice* | Outlook 1005 |

VEDDER, Eddie
Born Edward Severson III (although he grew up with his step-father's last name of Mueller) on 12/23/1964 in Evanston, Illinois; raised in San Diego, California. Lead singer of **Pearl Jam**. Legally changed his last name to Vedder (his mother's last name).

1/5/02	Ⓜ	30	10	1 You've Got To Hide Your Love Away first recorded by The Beatles in 1965		117	*St: I Am Sam*	V2 27119
2/23/02	Ⓡ	40	1					
10/27/07	Ⓜ	13	20	2 Hard Sun		—	*St: Into The Wild*	Monkey Wrench 15944

VEGA, Suzanne

Born on 7/11/1959 in Sacramento, California. Folk-pop singer/songwriter/guitarist. Married record producer Mitchell Froom (of **Gamma**) on 3/17/1995.

Debut	Cht	Peak	Wks	Track Title	Hot Pos	Album Title	Album Label & Number
5/23/87	®	15	11	1 Luka	3¹	Solitude Standing	A&M 5136
8/29/87	®	43	1	2 Solitude Standing	94	↓	
4/21/90	Ⓜ	8	9	3 Book Of Dreams	—	days of open Hand	A&M 5293
5/12/90	®	47	2				
9/1/90	Ⓜ	7	10	4 Tom's Diner	5	(single only)	A&M 1529
				D.N.A. Featuring Suzanne Vega special mix of Vega's original acapella recording which appeared on her 1987 Solitude Standing album			
9/5/92	Ⓜ	❶¹	12	5 Blood Makes Noise	—	99.9 F°	A&M 540005
11/28/92+	Ⓜ	13	13	6 99.9 F°	—		

VELVET REVOLVER

® **2000s: #21**

Hard-rock band formed in Los Angeles, California: **Scott Weiland** (vocals; of **Stone Temple Pilots**) and with former **Guns N' Roses** members Saul "Slash" Hudson (guitar; of **Slash's Snakepit**), Michael "Duff" McKagen (bass) and Matt Sorum (drums).

Debut	Cht	Peak	Wks	Track Title	Hot Pos	Album Title	Album Label & Number
7/5/03	®	17	11	1 Set Me Free	—	St: Hulk	Decca 63302
7/12/03	Ⓜ	32	4				
4/24/04	®	❶⁹	33	2 Slither	56	Contraband	RCA 59794
4/24/04	Ⓜ	❶⁴	26	**Grammy: Hard Rock Performance**			
8/7/04	®	❶¹¹	43	3 Fall To Pieces	67	↓	
8/7/04	Ⓜ	2¹	26				
12/25/04+	®	8	25	4 Dirty Little Thing	—	↓	
1/1/05	Ⓜ	18	13				
7/9/05	®	14	10	5 Come On, Come In	—	St: Fantastic 4	Wind-Up 13114
6/2/07	®	2²	20	6 She Builds Quick Machines	104	Libertad	RCA 88859
6/9/07	Ⓜ	14	13				
9/8/07	®	16	12	7 The Last Fight	—	↓	
2/16/08	®	34	5	8 Get Out The Door	—	↓	

VENDETTA RED

Hard-rock band from Seattle, Washington: Zach Davidson (vocals, guitar), Justin Cronk (guitar), Erik Chapman (keyboards), Michael Vermillion (bass) and Joseph Lee Childres (drums).

Debut	Cht	Peak	Wks	Track Title	Hot Pos	Album Title	Album Label & Number
5/24/03	Ⓜ	16	15	Shatterday	—	Between The Never And The Now	Epic 86415

VERA, Billy

Born William McCord on 5/28/1944 in Riverside, California; raised in Westchester County, New York. Pop singer/songwriter.

Debut	Cht	Peak	Wks	Track Title	Hot Pos	Album Title	Album Label & Number
6/6/81	®	53	2	I Can Take Care Of Myself .... [L]	39	Billy & The Beaters	Alfa 10001
				BILLY & THE BEATERS recorded on 1/15/1981 at the Roxy in Hollywood			

VERTICAL HORIZON

Rock band from Boston, Massachusetts: Matt Scannell (vocals), Keith Kane (guitar), Sean Hurley (bass) and Ed Toth (drums).

Debut	Cht	Peak	Wks	Track Title	Hot Pos	Album Title	Album Label & Number
7/10/99	Ⓜ	21	10	1 We Are	—	Everything You Want	RCA 67818
12/4/99+	Ⓜ	5	26	2 Everything You Want	❶¹	↓	
7/8/00	Ⓜ	15	13	3 You're A God	23	↓	

VERUCA SALT

Rock band from Chicago, Illinois: Nina Gordon (vocals, guitar), Louise Post (vocals, guitar), Steven Lack (bass) and Jim Shapiro (drums). Name taken from a character in the 1964 children's book Charlie & The Chocolate Factory.

Debut	Cht	Peak	Wks	Track Title	Hot Pos	Album Title	Album Label & Number
9/10/94	Ⓜ	8	22	1 Seether	53ᴬ	American Thighs	Minty Fresh 7
1/28/95	Ⓜ	20	8	2 Number One Blind	—	↓	
2/8/97	Ⓜ	8	26	3 Volcano Girls	59ᴬ	Eight Arms To Hold You	Outpost 30001
2/22/97	®	9	26				
9/6/97	®	39	3	4 Shutterbug	—	↓	
12/13/97	®	38	1	5 Straight	—	↓	

VERVE, The

Rock band from Wigan, England: Richard Ashcroft (vocals), Nick McCabe (guitar), Simon Jones (bass) and Peter Salisbury (drums).

Debut	Cht	Peak	Wks	Track Title	Hot Pos	Album Title	Album Label & Number
10/11/97+	Ⓜ	4	29	1 Bitter Sweet Symphony	12	Urban Hymns	Virgin 44913
2/7/98	®	22	10	**RS500 #382**			
5/2/98	Ⓜ	16	12	2 Lucky Man	—	↓	

Billboard				ARTIST / Track Title	®=Mainstream Rock ®=Modern Rock	Hot Pos	Album Title	Album Label & Number
Debut	Cht	Peak	Wks					

VERVE PIPE, The
Rock band from East Lansing, Michigan: brothers Brian Vander Ark (vocals) and Brad Vander Ark (bass), with A.J. Dunning (guitar), Doug Corella (keyboards) and Donny Brown (drums).

Debut	Cht	Peak	Wks	Track	Hot Pos	Album	Label
3/30/96	ⓜ	6	18	1 Photograph	53ᴬ	Villains	RCA 66809
4/27/96	®	17	11				
9/21/96	®	35	3	2 Cup Of Tea	—	↓	
2/15/97	ⓜ	❶³	26	3 The Freshmen	5	↓	
2/22/97	®	9	26				
8/9/97	ⓜ	22	9	4 Villains	—	↓	
7/26/97	®	24	9				
7/10/99	ⓜ	17	11	5 Hero	—	The Verve Pipe	RCA 67664
8/14/99	®	38	2				

VIBROLUSH
Rock band from New York: Phil Vassil (vocals, guitar), James Mazler (guitar), B (bass) and Tobias Ralph (drums).

8/12/00	ⓜ	36	6	Touch And Go	—	Touch And Go	V2 27074

VICTOR
Studio project formed by **Rush** guitarist Alex Lifeson. Features various studio musicians/vocalists.

12/30/95+	®	18	9	Promise	—	Victor	Atlantic 82852

VINES, The
Alternative-rock trio from Sydney, Australia: Craig Nicholls (vocals, guitar), Patrick Matthews (bass) and David Oliffe (drums).

6/15/02	ⓜ	7	20	1 Get Free	122	Highly Evolved	Engineroom 37527
7/6/02	®	27	14				
11/2/02	ⓜ	19	14	2 Outtathaway	—	↓	
2/28/04	ⓜ	13	12	3 Ride	—	Winning Days	Capitol 84338

VIOLENT FEMMES
Punk-rock trio from Milwaukee, Wisconsin: Gordon Gano (vocals, guitar), Brian Ritchie (bass) and Victor DeLorenzo (drums). Guy Hoffman replaced DeLorenzo in 1992.

2/4/89	ⓜ	4	13	1 Nightmares	—	3	Slash 25819
4/13/91	ⓜ	2¹	13	2 American Music	—	Why Do Birds Sing?	Slash 26476
5/14/94	ⓜ	12	9	3 Breakin' Up	—	New Times	Elektra 61553

VIRGOS MERLOT
Hard-rock band from Birmingham, Alabama: Brett Hestla (vocals), Ted Ledbetter (guitar), Jason Marchant (guitar), Chris Dickerson (bass) and JD Charlton (drums).

4/17/99	®	40	1	Gain		Signs Of A Vacant Soul	Atlantic 83157

VITALE, Joe
Born in 1949 in Dundalk, Maryland. Rock singer/drummer.

8/1/81	®	47	9	Lady On The Rock	—	Plantation Harbor	Asylum 529
				Joe Walsh and Don Felder (guitars)			

VITO, Rick
Born on 10/13/1949 in Darby, Pennsylvania. Session guitarist. Member of **Fleetwood Mac** from 1987-91.

3/7/92	®	36	5	Desiree	—	King Of Hearts	Modern 91789
				Stevie Nicks (female vocal)			

VIXEN
Female hard-rock band formed in Los Angeles, California: Janet Gardner (vocals, guitar), Jan Kuehnemund (guitar), Share Pedersen (bass) and Roxy Petrucci (drums). Pedersen later joined **Contraband**.

9/24/88	®	24	11	1 Edge Of A Broken Heart	26	Vixen	EMI-Manhattan 46991
1/14/89	®	22	9	2 Cryin'	22	↓	
7/28/90	®	11	12	3 How Much Love	44	Rev It Up	EMI 92923

VOICE OF THE BEEHIVE
Rock band formed in London, England, by California-born sisters Melissa Belland (vocals) and Tracey Belland (vocals, guitar). British personnel included Mike Jones (guitar), Martin Brett (bass) and former **Madness** member Dan Woodgate (drums). The Bellands are the daughters of Bruce Belland, member of 1950s vocal group The Four Preps.

11/5/88	ⓜ	11	10	1 I Say Nothing		Let It Bee	London 828100
8/31/91	ⓜ	8	10	2 Monsters And Angels	74	Honey Lingers	London 828253

VON BONDIES, The
Rock band from Detroit, Michigan: Jason Stollsteimer (vocals, guitar), Marcie Bolen (guitar), Carrie Smith (bass) and Don Blum (drums).

5/1/04	ⓜ	25	10	C'mon C'mon	—	Pawn Shoppe Heart	Sire 48549

Billboard				ARTIST		Hot		
Debut	Cht	Peak	Wks	Track Title	®=Mainstream Rock ⓜ=Modern Rock	Pos	Album Title	Album Label & Number

V SHAPE MIND
Hard-rock band from Decatur, Illinois: Brad Hursh (vocals, guitar), Jeff McElyea (guitar), Vic Zientara (bass) and Scott Parjani (drums).

11/8/03	®	40	2	Monsters	—	Cul-De-Sac..Republic 101002

W

WAILING SOULS
Reggae band led by vocalists Lloyd "Bread" McDonald and Winston "Pipe" Matthews.

11/6/93	ⓜ	28	3	Wild Wild Life..	—	St: Cool Runnings ....Chaos 57553

WAITE, John
Born on 7/4/1955 in Lancashire, England. Lead singer of The Babys and **Bad English**.

6/19/82	®	16	14	1 Change	54	Ignition ....Chrysalis 1376
6/23/84	®	❶²	18	2 **Missing You**	❶¹	No Brakes ....EMI America 17124
8/25/84	®	8	15	3 Tears...	37	↓
2/9/85	®	28	5	4 Restless Heart	59	↓
8/10/85	®	4	10	5 Every Step Of The Way	25	Mask Of Smiles ....EMI America 17164
6/28/86	®	24	6	6 If Anybody Had A Heart .... co-produced by **Don Henley**	76	St: About Last Night... ....EMI America 17210
6/13/87	®	6	11	7 These Times Are Hard For Lovers	53	Rover's Return ....EMI America 17227

WAITRESSES, The
Rock band from Akron, Ohio: Patty Donahue (vocals), Chris Butler (guitar), Dan Klayman (keyboards), Mars Williams (sax), Tracy Wormworth (bass) and Bill Ficca (drums; of **Television**). Donahue died of cancer on 12/9/1996 (age 40).

2/20/82	®	23	6	I Know What Boys Like..	62	Wasn't Tomorrow Wonderful?..................Polydor 6346

WAKELING, Dave
Born on 2/19/1956 in Birmingham, England. Lead singer of English Beat and **General Public**.

4/20/91	ⓜ	12	8	I Want More	—	No Warning ....I.R.S. 13085

WALLFLOWERS, The
ⓜ All-Time: #89
Rock band formed in Los Angeles, California: Jakob Dylan (vocals; born on 12/9/1969), Michael Ward (guitar), Rami Jaffe (keyboards), Greg Richling (bass) and Mario Calire (drums). Dylan is the son of **Bob Dylan**.

8/3/96	ⓜ	8	19	1 6th Avenue Heartache...	33ᴬ	Bringing Down The Horse ....Interscope 90055
6/22/96	®	10	26			
11/23/96+	®	❶⁵	30	2 **One Headlight**	2⁵ᴬ	↓
12/14/96+	ⓜ	❶⁵	26	Grammys: Rock Song / Rock Vocal Group		
5/17/97	®	3⁸	23	3 The Difference	23ᴬ	↓
5/17/97	ⓜ	5	22			
10/11/97	ⓜ	17	12	4 Three Marlenas	51ᴬ	↓
10/11/97	®	21	12			
5/9/98	®	4	15	5 Heroes .... first recorded by **David Bowie** in 1977	27ᴬ	St: Godzilla...Epic 69338
5/9/98	ⓜ	9	12			
9/30/00	®	26	11	6 Sleepwalker...	73	(Breach)..Interscope 490745
9/30/00	ⓜ	31	10			

WALL OF VOODOO
Alternative-rock band formed in Los Angeles, California: **Stan Ridgway** (vocals), Marc Moreland (guitar), Chas T. Gray (bass) and Joe Nanini (drums). Moreland died of kidney failure on 3/13/2002 (age 44).

9/25/82	®	41	18	Mexican Radio	58	Call Of The West..I.R.S. 70026

WALSH, Joe
Born on 11/20/1947 in Wichita, Kansas; raised in Cleveland, Ohio. Rock singer/songwriter/guitarist. Member of The James Gang and the **Eagles**. Played "Ed" on TV's *The Drew Carey Show*. Also see **Classic Rock Tracks** section.

TOP HITS: 1)A Life Of Illusion 2)Ordinary Average Guy 3)The Confessor

5/16/81	®	❶¹	14	1 **A Life Of Illusion**	34	There Goes The Neighborhood ....Asylum 523
5/30/81	®	36	6	2 Things... Timothy B. Schmit (backing vocal)	—	↓
6/6/81	®	35	8	3 Rivers (Of The Hidden Funk)	—	↓
9/11/82	®	20	7	4 Waffle Stomp	—	St: Fast Times At Ridgemont High........Full Moon 60158
7/9/83	®	21	6	5 Space Age Whiz Kids	52	You Bought It-You Name It....................Warner 23884
7/23/83	®	13	11	6 I Can Play That Rock & Roll	—	↓

WALSH, Joe — cont'd

Debut	Cht	Peak	Wks	Track Title	Hot Pos	Album Title	Album Label & Number
5/11/85	®	8	13	7 The Confessor	—	*The Confessor*	Warner 25281
6/20/87	®	8	8	8 The Radio Song	—	*Got Any Gum?*	Warner 25606
7/25/87	®	14	8	9 In My Car co-written by **Ringo Starr**	—	↓	
5/4/91	®	3²	13	10 Ordinary Average Guy	—	*Ordinary Average Guy*	Pyramid 47384
7/20/91	®	13	9	11 All Of A Sudden	—	↓	
8/22/92	®	10	5	12 Vote For Me	—	*Songs For A Dying Planet*	Pyramid 48916

WANDERLUST
Rock band from Philadelphia, Pennsylvania: Scot Sax (vocals), Bob Bonfiglio (guitar), Mark Levin (bass) and Jim Cavanaugh (drums).

Debut	Cht	Peak	Wks	Track Title	Hot Pos	Album Title	Album Label & Number
7/1/95	®	28	10	I Walked	—	*Prize*	RCA 66575

WANG CHUNG
Pop-rock trio from London, England: Jack Hues (vocals, guitar, keyboards), Nick Feldman (bass, keyboards) and Darren Costin (drums). Costin left in 1985.

Debut	Cht	Peak	Wks	Track Title	Hot Pos	Album Title	Album Label & Number
3/10/84	®	49	3	1 Don't Let Go	38	*Points On The Curve*	Geffen 4004
3/17/84	®	24	15	2 Dance Hall Days	16	↓	
11/2/85	®	21	12	3 To Live And Die In L.A.	41	*St: To Live And Die In L.A.*	Geffen 24081
10/11/86	®	25	8	4 Everybody Have Fun Tonight	2²	*Mosaic*	Geffen 24115
6/24/89	Ⓜ	22	4	5 Praying To A New God	63	*The Warmer Side Of Cool*	Geffen 24222
6/3/89	®	31	5				

WARRANT
Male hard-rock band from Los Angeles, California: Jani Lane (vocals), Erik Turner (guitar) and Joey Allen (guitars), Jerry Dixon (bass) and Steven Sweet (drums).

Debut	Cht	Peak	Wks	Track Title	Hot Pos	Album Title	Album Label & Number
2/25/89	®	13	15	1 Down Boys	27	*Dirty Rotten Filthy Stinking Rich*	Columbia 44383
7/1/89	®	3¹	16	2 Heaven	2²	↓	
10/14/89	®	30	7	3 Big Talk	93	↓	
1/20/90	®	11	11	4 Sometimes She Cries	20	↓	
9/8/90	®	19	9	5 Cherry Pie	10	*Cherry Pie*	Columbia 45487
12/1/90+	®	14	13	6 I Saw Red	10	↓	
2/23/91	®	19	13	7 Uncle Tom's Cabin	78	↓	
7/13/91	®	39	5	8 Blind Faith	88	↓	
9/12/92	®	36	1	9 Machine Gun	—	*Dog Eat Dog*	Columbia 52584

WAS (NOT WAS)
Interracial pop-dance-R&B band from Detroit, Michigan. Fronted by composer/bassist Don Fagenson ("Don Was") and lyricist/flutist David Weiss ("David Was"). Includes vocalists Sweet Pea Atkinson and Sir Harry Bowens. Group appeared in the 1990 movie *The Freshman*.

Debut	Cht	Peak	Wks	Track Title	Hot Pos	Album Title	Album Label & Number
11/19/88	Ⓜ	30	1	Walk The Dinosaur	7	*What Up, Dog?*	Chrysalis 41664

WATERBOYS, The
Rock band formed in London, England, by Mike Scott (vocals, guitar; from Scotland) and Anthony Thistlethwaite (mandolin, saxophone). Numerous personnel changes. Keyboardist Karl Wallinger left in 1985 to record as **World Party**.

Debut	Cht	Peak	Wks	Track Title	Hot Pos	Album Title	Album Label & Number
12/10/88+	Ⓜ	3²	14	1 Fisherman's Blues	—	*Fisherman's Blues*	Chrysalis 41589
2/11/89	Ⓜ	19	6	2 World Party	—	↓	
3/4/89	®	48	1				
11/3/90	Ⓜ	15	9	3 A Life Of Sundays	—	*Room To Roam*	Chrysalis 21768
5/22/93	Ⓜ	10	8	4 The Return Of Pan	—	*Dream Harder*	Geffen 24476

WATERS, Roger
Born George Roger Waters on 9/6/1944 in Cambridgeshire, England. Former leader/bassist of **Pink Floyd**. Went solo in 1983.

Debut	Cht	Peak	Wks	Track Title	Hot Pos	Album Title	Album Label & Number
5/5/84	®	17	10	1 5:01AM (The Pros And Cons Of Hitch Hiking)	110	*The Pros And Cons Of Hitch Hiking*	Columbia 39290
6/6/87	®	12	10	2 Radio Waves	—	*Radio K.A.O.S.*	Columbia 40795
7/18/87	®	15	10	3 Sunset Strip	—	↓	
8/29/92	®	4	9	4 What God Wants, Part I	—	*Amused To Death*	Columbia 47127

WATT, Mike
Born on 12/20/1957 in Portsmouth, Virginia. Hard-rock singer/bassist.

Debut	Cht	Peak	Wks	Track Title	Hot Pos	Album Title	Album Label & Number
3/11/95	Ⓜ	21	8	Against The 70's	—	*Ball-Hog Or Tugboat?*	Columbia 67086

WAX
Pop duo formed in Los Angeles, California: Andrew Gold and Graham Gouldman (of 10cc).

Debut	Cht	Peak	Wks	Track Title	Hot Pos	Album Title	Album Label & Number
4/12/86	®	39	3	Right Between The Eyes	43	*Magnetic Heaven*	RCA 9546

WAX

Rock band formed in Los Angeles, California: Joe Sib (vocals), Tom Gardocki (guitar), Dave Georgeff (bass) and Loomis Fall (drums). Sib later started Sideonedummy record label.

3/25/95	Ⓜ	28	8	California	—	13 Unlucky Numbers .... Interscope 92544

WEEN

Rock duo from Lambertville, New Jersey: Mickey Melchiondo ("Dean Ween") and Aaron Freeman ("Gene Ween").

3/20/93	Ⓜ	21	3	1 Push Th' Little Daisies	—	Pure Guava .... Elektra 61428
12/10/94	Ⓜ	32	5	2 Voodoo Lady	—	Chocolate And Cheese .... Elektra 61639

WEEZER

Ⓜ **2000s: #20 / All-Time: #19**

Rock band from Los Angeles, California: Rivers Cuomo (vocals, guitar; born on 6/13/1970), Matt Sharp (bass; born on 9/20/1969) and Patrick Wilson (drums; born on 2/1/1969). Brian Bell (guitar; born on 12/9/1968), Matt Sharp (bass; born on 9/20/1969) and Patrick Wilson (drums; born on 4/20/1971) replaced Sharp in 1998. Scott Shriner (born on 7/11/1965) replaced Welsh in early 2002. Sharp and Wilson also formed **The Rentals**.

TOP HITS: 1)Perfect Situation 2)Beverly Hills 3)Hash Pipe

7/23/94	Ⓜ	6	18	1 Undone-The Sweater Song	57	Weezer .... DGC 24629
10/1/94	®	30	7			
11/5/94	Ⓜ	2[1]	22	2 Buddy Holly	18[A]	↓
2/4/95	®	34	4	RS500 #497		
6/10/95	Ⓜ	7	24	3 Say It Ain't So	51[A]	↓
9/21/96	Ⓜ	19	10	4 El Scorcho	—	Pinkerton .... DGC 25007
1/11/97	Ⓜ	32	6	5 The Good Life	—	↓
4/28/01	Ⓜ	2[8]	26	6 Hash Pipe	106	Weezer .... Geffen 493045
6/16/01	®	24	15			
7/21/01	Ⓜ	11	20	7 Island In The Sun	111	↓
11/10/01	Ⓜ	17	12	8 Photograph	—	↓
3/23/02	Ⓜ	8	15	9 Dope Nose	—	↓
7/13/02	Ⓜ	15	12	10 Keep Fishin'	—	↓
4/9/05	Ⓜ	❶[1]	27	11 Beverly Hills	10	Make Believe .... Geffen 004520
5/14/05	®	26	12			
7/23/05	Ⓜ	10	14	12 We Are All On Drugs	—	↓
9/3/05	®	35	7			
10/22/05+	Ⓜ	❶[4]	27	13 Perfect Situation	51	↓
4/8/06	Ⓜ	31	6	14 This Is Such A Pity	—	↓

WEILAND, Scott

Born on 10/27/1967 in Santa Cruz, California. Lead singer of **Stone Temple Pilots**, **The Magnificent Bastards** and **Velvet Revolver**.

1/10/98	Ⓜ	39	1	1 Lady, Your Roof Brings Me Down	—	St: Great Expectations .... Atlantic 83058
3/28/98	Ⓜ	36	3	2 Barbarella	—	12 Bar Blues .... Atlantic 83084

WELCH, Bob

Born on 7/31/1946 in Los Angeles, California. Pop-rock singer/guitarist. Member of **Fleetwood Mac** (1971-74). Also see **Classic Rock Tracks** section.

1/16/82	®	45	4	It's What Ya Don't Say	—	Bob Welch .... RCA Victor 4107

WELLER, Paul

Born on 5/25/1958 in Woking, Surrey, England. Rock singer/songwriter. Member of **The Jam** and **The Style Council**.

10/17/92	Ⓜ	10	10	Uh Huh Oh Yeh	—	Paul Weller .... Go! Discs 828343

WESTERBERG, Paul

Born on 12/31/1960 in Minneapolis, Minnesota. Rock singer/guitarist. Member of **The Replacements**.

8/1/92	Ⓜ	4	12	1 Dyslexic Heart	—	St: Singles .... Epic 52476
6/19/93	Ⓜ	4	11	2 World Class Fad	—	14 Songs .... Sire 45255
4/27/96	Ⓜ	21	10	3 Love Untold	—	Eventually .... Reprise 46176

WHALE

Grunge/hip-hop trio from Sweden: Henrik Schyffert, Cia Berg and Gordon Cyrus.

5/7/94	Ⓜ	24	4	Hobo Humpin Slobo Babe	102	(single only) .... EastWest 98281

WHEATUS

Rock band from Long Island, New York: brothers Brendan Brown (vocals, guitar) and Peter Brown (drums), with Phil Jimenez (guitar) and Rich Leigey (bass).

7/22/00	ⓜ	7	24	Teenage Dirtbag	124	Wheatus...Columbia 62146

WHISKEYTOWN

Rock duo from Jacksonville, North Carolina: Ryan Adams (male vocals, guitar) and Caitlin Cary (female vocals, fiddle).

3/14/98	®	35	4	Yesterday's News	—	Strangers Almanac ....Outpost 30005

WHITE LION

Hair-metal band formed in Brooklyn, New York: Mike Tramp (vocals), Vito Bratta (guitar), James Lomenzo (bass) and Greg D'Angelo (drums). Lomenzo and D'Angelo left in 1991; replaced by Tommy Caradonna and Jimmy DeGrasso (of **Y&T**).

1/9/88	®	18	19	1 Wait...	8	Pride ....Atlantic 81768
4/23/88	®	25	9	2 Tell Me	58	↓
12/24/88+	®	7	10	3 When The Children Cry	3[1]	↓
6/17/89	®	12	11	4 Little Fighter..	52	Big Game...Atlantic 81969
4/20/91	®	24	9	5 Love Don't Come Easy...	—	Mane Attraction ....Atlantic 82193

WHITESNAKE

Hard-rock band formed in England. Numerous personnel changes. Lineup in 1984: **David Coverdale** (vocals), John Sykes (guitar), Mel Galley (guitar), Neil Murray (bass) and Cozy Powell (drums; of **Emerson Lake & Powell**). Lineup in 1987: Coverdale, Sykes, Murray and Aynsley Dunbar (drums; of **Jefferson Starship**). Sykes left to form **Blue Murder**. Lineup in 1989: Coverdale, **Steve Vai** and Adrian **Vandenberg** (guitars), Rudy Sarzo (bass) and Tommy Aldridge (drums).

TOP HITS: 1)Fool For Your Loving 2)The Deeper The Love 3)Here I Go Again

6/2/84	®	17	16	1 Slow An' Easy	—	Slide It In ....Geffen 4018
8/25/84	®	33	9	2 Love Ain't No Stranger...	—	↓
3/21/87	®	18	14	3 Still Of The Night	79	Whitesnake ....Geffen 24099
5/30/87	®	4	19	4 Here I Go Again	❶[1]	↓
8/29/87	®	13	16	5 Is This Love	2[1]	↓
11/28/87+	®	22	12	6 Give Me All Your Love	48	↓
11/4/89	®	2[4]	13	7 Fool For Your Loving	37	Slip Of The Tongue ....Geffen 24249
11/18/89	®	32	9	8 Judgment Day..	—	↓
1/20/90	®	4	12	9 The Deeper The Love	28	↓
5/5/90	®	15	8	10 Now You're Gone...	96	↓

WHITE STRIPES, The

ⓜ **2000s: #12 / All-Time: #34**

Alternative-rock duo from Detroit, Michigan: Jack White (vocals, guitar; born John Gillis on 7/9/1975) and Meg White (drums; born on 12/10/1974). Married from 1996-2000. Jack played "Georgia" in the movie *Cold Mountain*. Jack also formed The Raconteurs.

TOP HITS: 1)Seven Nation Army 2)Icky Thump 3)The Denial Twist

3/23/02	ⓜ	12	21	1 Fell In Love With A Girl	121	White Blood Cells ....Third Man 27124
8/10/02	ⓜ	19	19	2 Dead Leaves And The Dirty Ground......................	—	↓
3/8/03	ⓜ	❶[3]	38	3 Seven Nation Army	76	Elephant...Third Man 27148
7/12/03	®	12	26	Grammy: Rock Song		
8/9/03	ⓜ	8	23	4 The Hardest Button To Button	—	↓
1/31/04	ⓜ	25	10	5 I Just Don't Know What To Do With Myself	—	↓
				#29 Hot 100 hit for Dionne Warwick in 1966		
5/7/05	ⓜ	7	17	6 Blue Orchid	43	Get Behind Me Satan ....Third Man 27256
5/21/05	®	32	6			
7/30/05	ⓜ	13	18	7 My Doorbell	116	↓
12/17/05+	ⓜ	5	20	8 The Denial Twist	—	↓
5/12/07	ⓜ	❶[3]	29	9 Icky Thump	26	Icky Thump ....Third Man 162940
5/19/07	®	11	20			
9/8/07	ⓜ	9	20	10 You Don't Know What Love Is (You Just Do As		
10/27/07	®	35	9	As You're Told)	—	↓
2/2/08	ⓜ	30	7	11 Conquest..	—	↓

WHITE TOWN

Born Jyoti Mishra on 7/30/1966 in Rourkela, India; raised in England. Male synth-pop singer/multi-instrumentalist.

2/22/97	ⓜ	5	22	Your Woman	23	Women In Technology....................Chrysalis/EMI 56129

Billboard				ARTIST		Hot		
Debut	Cht	Peak	Wks	Track Title	Ⓡ=Mainstream Rock Ⓜ=Modern Rock	Pos	Album Title	Album Label & Number

WHITE TRASH
Hard-rock band from New York: Dave Alvin (vocals), Ethan Collins (guitar), Aaron Collins (bass) and Mike Caldarella (drums).

| 7/6/91 | Ⓡ | 39 | 7 | Apple Pie | — | *White Trash* ....Elektra 61053 |

WHITE ZOMBIE
Hard-rock band formed in New York: **Rob Zombie** (vocals), Jay Yuenger (guitar), Sean Yseult (bass) and John Tempesta (drums; of **Testament**). Group named after the 1932 movie starring Bela Lugosi. Tempesta joined **Helmet** in 2004.

10/2/93	Ⓡ	26	13	1 Thunder Kiss '65	—	*La Sexorcisto: Devil Music Volume One*....Geffen 24460
2/5/94	Ⓡ	39	2	2 Black Sunshine	—	↓
4/22/95	Ⓜ	7	20	3 More Human Than Human	53[A]	*Astro-Creep: 2000*....................................Geffen 24806
4/22/95	Ⓡ	10	26			
9/9/95	Ⓡ	27	8	4 Electric Head Pt. 2 (The Ecstasy)	—	↓
2/10/96	Ⓡ	39	1	5 Super-Charger Heaven	—	↓

WHITLEY, Chris
Born on 8/31/1960 in Houston, Texas; raised in Vermont. Died of cancer on 11/20/2005 (age 45). Male singer/songwriter/ guitarist.

| 7/27/91 | Ⓡ | 28 | 8 | 1 Living With The Law | — | *Living With The Law*...............................Columbia 46966 |
| 10/19/91 | Ⓡ | 36 | 8 | 2 Big Sky Country | — | ↓ |

WHO, The
Rock band formed in London, England: **Roger Daltrey** (vocals), **Pete Townshend** (guitar, vocals), **John Entwistle** (bass) and Keith Moon (drums). Moon died of a drug overdose on 9/7/1978 (age 31), replaced by Kenney Jones. Disbanded in 1982; reunited several times. Jones formed **The Law** with **Paul Rodgers** in 1991. Enwistle died of a heart attack on 6/27/2002 (age 57). Also see **Classic Rock Tracks** section.
AWARDS: R&R Hall of Fame: 1990 ★ Grammy: Lifetime Achievement Award 2001
TOP HITS: 1)You Better You Bet 2)Athena 3)Eminence Front

3/21/81	Ⓡ	❶[5]	15	1 You Better You Bet	18	*Face Dances*................................Warner 3516
4/4/81	Ⓡ	6	16	2 Another Tricky Day	—	↓
4/4/81	Ⓡ	36	1	3 Daily Records	—	↓
4/4/81	Ⓡ	38	1	4 Did You Steal My Money	—	↓
4/4/81	Ⓡ	51	1	5 You	—	↓
4/11/81	Ⓡ	50	1	6 How Can You Do It Alone	—	↓
9/4/82	Ⓡ	3[4]	25	7 Athena	28	*It's Hard*................................Warner 23731
9/18/82	Ⓡ	5	19	8 Eminence Front	68	↓
9/25/82	Ⓡ	34	4	9 Cry If You Want	—	↓
10/2/82	Ⓡ	38	11	10 Dangerous	—	↓
10/2/82	Ⓡ	39	2	11 It's Hard	—	↓
7/8/89	Ⓡ	9	9	12 Dig	—	*The Iron Man: The Musical by Pete Townshend*.......................Atlantic 81996
7/8/89	Ⓡ	44	2	13 Fire	—	↓
				#2 Pop hit for The Crazy World Of Arthur Brown in 1968		
11/2/91	Ⓡ	8	13	14 Saturday Night's Alright For Fighting	—	*VA: Two Rooms - Celebrating The Songs Of Elton John & Bernie Taupin*..........Polydor 845750
				#12 Pop hit for **Elton John** in 1973		
10/7/06	Ⓡ	37	7	15 It's Not Enough	—	*Endless Wire*..........................Universal Republic 007846

WHY STORE, The
Rock band from Indianapolis, Indiana: Chris Shaffer (vocals), Michael David Smith (guitar), Jeff Pedersen (keyboards), Greg Gardner (bass) and Charlie Bushor (drums).

7/13/96	Ⓡ	27	11	1 Lack Of Water	—	*The Why Store*......................................Way Cool 11420
8/24/96	Ⓜ	37	3			
11/23/96	Ⓡ	32	7	2 Father	—	↓

WIDESPREAD PANIC
Eclectic-rock band from Athens, Georgia: John Bell (vocals, guitar), Michael Houser (guitar), John Hermann (keyboards), Domingo Ortiz (percussion), Dave Schools (bass) and Todd Nance (drums). Houser died of cancer on 8/10/2002 (age 40).

| 3/4/95 | Ⓡ | 34 | 4 | 1 Can't Get High | — | *Ain't Life Grand*....................................Capricorn 42027 |
| 2/8/97 | Ⓡ | 13 | 14 | 2 Hope In A Hopeless World | — | *Bombs & Butterflies*..........................Capricorn 534396 |

WILCO
Rock band from Chicago, Illinois: Jeff Tweedy (vocals, guitar), Jay Bennett (guitar), John Stirratt (bass) and Ken Coomer (drums).

| 3/8/97 | Ⓡ | 22 | 8 | Outtasite (Outta Mind) | — | *Being There*................................Reprise 46236 |
| 3/15/97 | Ⓜ | 39 | 1 | | | |

WILDE, Danny
Born on 6/3/1956 in Maine; raised in California. Singer/songwriter/guitarist. Member of **Great Buildings** and **The Rembrandts**.

| 7/12/86 | R | 35 | 6 | 1 Isn't It Enough.. | — | *The Boyfriend* ....Island 90497 |
| 1/30/88 | R | 15 | 11 | 2 Time Runs Wild .... | — | *Any Man's Hunger*......................................Geffen 24179 |

WILDE, Kim
Born Kim Smith on 11/18/1960 in Chiswick, England. Pop-rock-dance singer. Daughter of singer Marty Wilde.

| 4/24/82 | R | 29 | 10 | 1 Kids In America .... | 25 | *Kim Wilde*..EMI America 17065 |
| 5/15/82 | R | 53 | 2 | 2 Water On Glass... | — | ↓ |

WILDER, Webb
Born John Webb Wilder in 1954 in Hattiesburg, Mississippi. Male singer/songwriter/guitarist.

| 1/25/92 | R | 16 | 11 | Tough It Out .... | — | *Doo Dad* ....Praxis 11010 |

WILL AND THE KILL
Rock band from Austin, Texas: Will Sexton (vocals, guitar), David Grissom (guitar), Alex Napier (bass) and Jeff Boaz (drums). Sexton is the younger brother of **Charlie Sexton**.

| 3/19/88 | R | 28 | 8 | Heart Of Steel.. | — | *Will And The Kill* ....MCA 42054 |

WILLIAMS, John
Born on 2/8/1932 in Flushing, Long Island, New York. Composer/conductor. Composed numerous movie scores. Conducted the Boston Pops Orchestra from 1980-93.

5/30/81	R	39	5	Won't Get Fooled Again .... [L]	—	*VA: The Secret Policeman's Ball/*
				PETE TOWNSHEND & JOHN WILLIAMS		*The Music*..Island 9630
				#15 Pop hit for **The Who** in 1971		

WILLIE AND THE POOR BOYS
All-star rock band: Andy Fairweather Low (vocals, guitar), Mickey Gee (guitar), Geraint Watkins (keyboards), Bill Wyman (bass) and Charlie Watts (drums). Wyman and Watts are members of **The Rolling Stones**.

| 5/18/85 | R | 35 | 7 | Baby Please Don't Go .... | — | *Willie And The Poor Boys*........................Passport 6047 |
| | | | | blues standard written and first recorded by Big Joe Williams in 1935 | | |

WILSON, Ann
Born on 6/19/1951 in San Diego, California. Lead singer of **Heart**.

12/6/86+	R	5	11	1 The Best Man In The World	61	*St: The Golden Child* ....Capitol 12544
1/14/89	R	42	1	2 Surrender To Me..	6	*St: Tequila Sunrise* ....Capitol 91185
				ANN WILSON & ROBIN ZANDER		

WILSON, Brian
Born on 6/20/1942 in Hawthorne, California. Leader of The Beach Boys.

| 7/30/88 | R | 40 | 4 | Love And Mercy.. | — | *Brian Wilson* ....Sire 25669 |

WINEHOUSE, Amy
Born on 9/14/1983 in Southgate, London, England. Female R&B singer.
AWARD: Grammy: Best New Artist 2007

| 5/5/07 | M | 32 | 12 | Rehab .... | 9 | *Back To Black* ....Universal Republic 008428 |
| | | | | Grammys: Record & Song of the Year / Female Pop Vocal | | |

WINGER
Hard-rock band formed in New York: **Kip Winger** (vocals, bass; born on 6/21/1961), Reb Beach (guitar), Paul Taylor (keyboards; left in 1992) and Rod Morgenstein (drums). Kip was a member of **Alice Cooper**'s band. Morgenstein was a member of **The Dregs**.

9/24/88	R	27	9	1 Madalaine	—	*Winger* ....Atlantic 81867
1/21/89	R	19	9	2 Seventeen	26	↓
5/20/89	R	8	16	3 Headed For A Heartbreak	19	↓
9/30/89	R	34	5	4 Hungry...	85	↓
10/28/89	R	22	10	5 Everything You Do (You're Sexing Me).....................	52	*Heart Like A Gun* ....Atlantic 81903
				FIONA with Kip Winger		
7/14/90	R	6	15	6 Can't Get Enuff	42	*In The Heart Of The Young* ....Atlantic 82103
10/6/90	R	14	16	7 Miles Away..	12	↓
1/19/91	R	20	12	8 Easy Come Easy Go..	41	↓
5/8/93	R	15	15	9 Down Incognito	—	*Pull*..Atlantic 82485

WINTER, Johnny
Born on 2/23/1944 in Leland, Mississippi. White (albino) blues-rock singer/guitarist. Brother of Edgar Winter.

| 10/29/88 | R | 43 | 3 | 1 Rain.. | — | *The Winter Of '88* ....MCA 42241 |
| 8/17/91 | R | 36 | 6 | 2 Illustrated Man .... | — | *Let Me In* ....Pointblank 91744 |

Billboard				ARTIST		Hot		
Debut	Cht	Peak	Wks	Track Title	®=Mainstream Rock / ⓜ=Modern Rock	Pos	Album Title	Album Label & Number

WINTER HOURS
Rock band from Lyndhurst, New Jersey: Joseph Marques (vocals), Michael Carlucci and Bob Perry (guitars), Bob Messing (bass) and Dave Scheff (drums).

| 8/26/89 | ⓜ | 12 | 7 | Smoke Rings .... | — | Winter Hours ....Chrysalis 21682 |

WINWOOD, Steve   ® 1980s: #10 / All-Time: #33
Born on 5/12/1948 in Handsworth, Birmingham, England. Pop-rock singer/keyboardist/guitarist. Lead singer of Spencer Davis Group, Blind Faith and **Traffic**. His older brother, Mervyn "Muff" Winwood, worked as a record label executive.

TOP HITS: 1)Higher Love 2)Roll With It 3)One And Only Man

3/21/81	®	2²	12	1 While You See A Chance	7	Arc Of A Diver...Island 9576
3/21/81	®	11	11	2 Arc Of A Diver...	48	↓
8/7/82	®	8	25	3 Still In The Game	47	Talking Back To The Night ....Island 9777
9/4/82	®	13	11	4 Valerie..	70	↓
				also see #11 below		
6/14/86	®	❶⁴	14	5 Higher Love	❶¹	Back In The High Life ....Island 25448
				Grammys: Record of the Year / Pop Male Vocal		
				Chaka Khan (backing vocal)		
7/19/86	®	3¹	16	6 Split Decision..	—	↓
				Joe Walsh (guitar)		
8/9/86	®	33	11	7 Take It As It Comes	—	↓
9/6/86	®	4	14	8 Freedom Overspill...	20	↓
				Joe Walsh (slide guitar)		
11/22/86	®	19	10	9 Back In The High Life Again................................	13	↓
				James Taylor (backing vocal)		
2/7/87	®	5	14	10 The Finer Things	8	↓
10/10/87	®	13	11	11 Valerie...[R]	9	Chronicles..Island 25660
				new version of #4 above		
1/16/88	®	17	9	12 Talking Back To The Night	57	↓
6/11/88	®	❶⁴	11	13 Roll With It	❶⁴	Roll With It ....Virgin 90946
7/2/88	®	❶²	17	14 Don't You Know What The Night Can Do?	6	↓
7/2/88	®	2¹	19	15 Holding On	11	↓
7/9/88+	®	22	10	16 Hearts On Fire..	53	↓
10/29/88	®	25	7	17 Put On Your Dancing Shoes	—	↓
11/3/90	®	❶²	14	18 One And Only Man	18	Refugees of the Heart................................Virgin 91405
1/5/91	®	10	11	19 Another Deal Goes Down	—	↓

WIRE
Punk-rock band from London, England: Colin Newman (vocals, guitar), Bruce Gilbert (guitar), Graham Lewis (bass) and Mark Field (drums).

| 5/20/89 | ⓜ | 2¹ | 12 | 1 Eardrum Buzz .... | — | It's Beginning To And Back Again ....Enigma 73516 |
| 8/19/89 | ⓜ | 24 | 2 | 2 In Vivo .... | — | ↓ |

WIRE TRAIN
Rock band formed in San Francisco, California: Kevin Hunter (vocals), Jeff Trott (guitar), Anders Rundblad (bass) and Brian MacLeod (drums).

| 6/6/92 | ⓜ | 23 | 7 | Stone Me .... | — | No Soul No Strain......................................MCA 10604 |

WITHIN TEMPTATION
Hard-rock band formed in the Netherlands: Sharon Adel (vocals), Robert Westerholt (guitar), Ruud Jolie (guitar), Martin Spierenburg (keyboards), Jeron Veen (bass) and Stephen Haestregt (drums).

| 7/28/07 | ® | 33 | 8 | What Have You Done .... | — | The Heart Of Everything...................Roadrunner 618021 |
| | | | | WITHIN TEMPTATION Featuring Keith Caputo | | |

WOBBLE('S), Jah, Invaders Of The Heart
Rock trio formed in England: Jah Wobble (bass, vocals), Justin Adams (guitar) and Mark Ferda (keyboards, drums). Wobble was bassist of **Public Image Ltd.**

3/28/92	ⓜ	10	9	1 Visions Of You..	—	Rising Above Bedlam ....Atlantic 82386
				Sinead O'Connor (backing vocal)		
7/2/94	ⓜ	22	6	2 The Sun Does Rise..	—	Take Me To God.......................................Island 524000
				Dolores O'Riordan of **The Cranberries** (lead vocal)		

WOLF, Peter
Born Peter Blankfield on 3/7/1946 in the Bronx, New York. Lead singer of the **J. Geils Band**. Married to actress Faye Dunaway from 1974-79. Not to be confused with the record producer of the same name.

7/14/84	R	6	11	1 Lights Out	12	Lights Out	EMI America 17121
8/18/84	R	26	8	2 Crazy	—	↓	
10/20/84	R	22	11	3 I Need You Tonight	36	↓	
2/28/87	R	❶¹	12	4 Come As You Are	15	Come As You Are	EMI America 17230
4/18/87	R	16	9	5 Can't Get Started	75	↓	
2/24/90	R	9	7	6 99 Worlds	78	Up To No Good!	MCA 6349

WOLFGANG PRESS, The
Techno-dance trio from England: Mick Allen (vocals), Andrew Gray (guitar) and Mark Cox (keyboards).

7/4/92	M	2¹	9	1 A Girl Like You	—	Queer	4 A D 26908
2/18/95	M	33	6	2 Going South	—	Funky Little Demons	4 A D 45738

WOLFMOTHER
Hard-rock trio from Sydney, Australia: Andrew Stockdale (vocals, guitar), Chris Ross (bass) and Myles Heskett (drums).

4/8/06	R	7	20	1 Woman	112	Wolfmother	Modular 041
4/8/06	M	10	20	**Grammy: Hard Rock Performance**			
9/9/06	R	27	13	2 Joker And The Thief	—	↓	
9/23/06	M	31	10				
12/23/06+	R	29	12	3 The White Unicorn	—	↓	

WONDER, Stevie
Born Steveland Morris on 5/13/1950 in Saginaw, Michigan. Legendary R&B singer/songwriter/keyboardist. Blind since birth.
AWARDS: Grammy: Lifetime Achievement 1996 ★ R&R Hall of Fame: 1989 ★ Billboard Century: 2004

4/24/82	R	34	2	Ebony And Ivory	❶⁷	Tug Of War	Columbia 37462
				PAUL McCARTNEY with Stevie Wonder			

WONDER STUFF, The
Pop-rock band formed in Wolverhampton, West Midlands, England: Miles Hunt (vocals, guitar), Malcolm Treece (guitar, vocals), Rob Jones (bass) and Martin Gilks (drums). Paul Clifford replaced Jones in 1990. Martin Bell (fiddle) joined in early 1991. Jones died of a heroin overdose on 7/30/1993 (age 29). Gilks died in a motorcycle crash on 4/3/2006 (age 41).

3/4/89	M	17	7	1 Give, Give, Give Me More, More, More	—	The Eight-Legged Groove Machine	Polydor 837802
1/6/90	M	11	8	2 Don't Let Me Down, Gently	—	Hup	Polydor 841187
1/6/90	M	26	2	3 Radio Ass Kiss	—	↓	
7/13/91	M	8	11	4 Caught In My Shadow	—	Never Loved Elvis	Polydor 847252
2/22/92	M	27	2	5 Welcome To The Cheap Seats	—	↓	
10/9/93	M	17	8	6 On The Ropes	—	Construction For The Modern Idiot	Polydor 519894

WOOD, Ron
Born on 6/1/1947 in Hillingdon, Middlesex, England. Rock singer/guitarist. Member of the **Jeff Beck** Group and **The Rolling Stones**.

9/5/92	R	30	7	Show Me	—	Slide On This	Continuum 19210

WORLD PARTY
Born Karl Wallinger on 10/19/1957 in Prestatyn, Wales. Rock singer/songwriter/keyboardist. Former member of **The Waterboys**.

12/20/86+	R	5	17	1 Ship Of Fools (Save Me From Tomorrow)	27	Private Revolution	Chrysalis 41552
5/5/90	M	❶⁵	13	2 Way Down Now	—	Goodbye Jumbo	Ensign 21654
5/19/90	R	21	11				
7/28/90	M	8	9	3 Put The Message In The Box	—	↓	
8/4/90	R	33	8				
4/3/93	M	5	13	4 Is It Like Today?	—	Bang!	Ensign 21991
6/5/93	R	38	2				

WORLD TRADE
Rock band from New York: Billy Sherwood (vocals, bass), Bruce Gowdy (guitar), Guy Allison (keyboards) and Mark Williams (drums).

8/26/89	R	33	5	The Revolution Song	—	World Trade	Polydor 839626

WRABIT
Rock band from Ottawa, Ontario, Canada: Lou Nadeau (vocals), David Aplin (guitar), John Albani (guitar), Les Paulhus (keyboards), Chris Brockway (bass) and Scott "Jeff" Steck (drums).

2/13/82	R	17	8	Anyway Anytime	—	Wrabit	MCA 5268

WRIGHT, Gary
Born on 4/26/1943 in Creskill, New Jersey. Singer/songwriter/keyboardist. Also see **Classic Rock Tracks** section.

7/18/81	®	17	17	Really Wanna Know You	16	The Right Place	Warner 3511

WYLDE, Zakk
Born on 1/14/1967 in Jersey City, New Jersey. Singer/guitarist. Former member of **Ozzy Osbourne**'s band and **Pride & Glory**.

7/13/96	®	28	8	Between Heaven And Hell	—	Book Of Shadows	Geffen 24964

WYNETTE, Tammy
Born Virginia Wynette Pugh on 5/5/1942 in Itawamba County, Mississippi. Died of a blood clot on 4/6/1998 (age 55). Legendary country singer.

2/8/92	M	21	3	Justified & Ancient THE KLF Featuring Tammy Wynette	11	The White Room	Arista 8657

WYNN, Steve
Born on 2/21/1960 in Santa Monica, California. Rock singer/songwriter.

5/26/90	M	10	8	1 Tears Won't Help	—	Kerosene Man	Rhino 70969
5/23/92	M	30	2	2 Drag	—	Dazzling Display	RNA 70283

X

X
Punk-rock band formed in Los Angeles, California: **Exene Cervenka** (vocals), Billy Zoom (guitar), **John Doe** (bass) and Don Bonebrake (drums).

8/10/85	®	27	9	1 Burning House Of Love	—	Ain't Love Grand	Elektra 60430
5/15/93	M	15	9	2 Country At War	—	Hey Zeus!	Big Life 519261
8/14/93	M	26	3	3 New Life	↓		

X-ECUTIONERS, The
Rap-DJ production group from Brooklyn, New York: Mista Sinista, Rob Swift, Total Eclipse and Roc Raida.

2/2/02	M	13	16	It's Goin' Down	85	Built From Scratch	Loud 86410
3/16/02	®	29	7				

XTC
Alternative-rock band formed in Wiltshire, England: Andy Partridge (guitar), Dave Gregory (keyboards), Colin Moulding (bass) and Terry Chambers (drums). All share vocals. Chambers left in 1986.

3/21/81	®	28	3	1 Generals And Majors	104	Black Sea	Virgin 13147
4/24/82	®	38	3	2 Senses Working Overtime	—	English Settlement	Epic 37943
4/4/87	®	37	6	3 Dear God	—	Skylarking	Geffen 24117
2/25/89	M	❶⁵	14	4 The Mayor Of Simpleton	72	Oranges & Lemons	Geffen 24218
2/25/89	®	15	13				
5/27/89	M	11	13	5 King For A Day	↓		
7/8/89	®	38	4				
5/2/92	M	❶²	12	6 The Ballad Of Peter Pumpkinhead	—	Nonsuch	Geffen 24474
5/23/92	®	46	1				
7/25/92	M	18	6	7 Dear Madam Barnum	↓		

XYMOX
Pop trio from Amsterdam, Netherlands: Ronny Moorings (vocals, guitar, keyboards), Pieter Nooten (keyboards) and Anka Wolbert (bass, vocals, keyboards).

5/6/89	M	16	10	1 Obsession	—	Twist Of Shadows	Wing 839233
4/13/91	M	16	8	2 Phoenix Of My Heart contains an interpolation of "Wild Thing" by The Troggs	—	Phoenix	Wing 848516

Y

Y&T
Hard-rock band from San Francisco, California: Dave Meniketti (vocals, guitar), Joey Alves (guitar), Philip Kennemore (bass) and Leonard Haze (drums). Jimmy DeGrasso replaced Haze in 1986. Stef Burns replaced Alves in 1989. Y&T: Yesterday & Today.

9/10/83	®	25	5	1 Mean Streak	—	Mean Streak	A&M 4960
8/11/84	®	33	10	2 Don't Stop Runnin'	—	In Rock We Trust	A&M 5007
7/20/85	®	16	10	3 Summertime Girls	55	Open Fire	A&M 5076
11/30/85	®	48	2	4 All American Boy	—	Down For The Count	A&M 5101
6/20/87	®	41	3	5 Contagious	—	Contagious	Geffen 24142
5/26/90	®	31	8	6 Don't Be Afraid Of The Dark	—	Ten	Geffen 24283

YANKOVIC, "Weird Al"

Born on 10/23/1959 in Lynwood, California. Novelty singer/accordionist. Specializes in song parodies. Starred as "George Newman" in the 1989 movie *UHF*.

Debut	Cht	Peak	Wks			Hot Pos	Album Title	Album Label & Number
3/17/84	®	38	2	1 Eat It	[N]	12	*"Weird Al" Yankovic In 3-D*	Rock 'n' Roll 39221
				parody of "Beat It" by **Michael Jackson**				
4/25/92	®	35	2	2 Smells Like Nirvana	[N]	35	*Off The Deep End*	Scotti Brothers 75256
				parody of "Smells Like Teen Spirit" by **Nirvana**				

YEAH YEAH YEAHS

Punk-rock trio from Long Island, New York: Karen Orzolek (vocals), Nick Zinner (guitar) and Brian Chase (drums).

Debut	Cht	Peak	Wks			Hot Pos	Album Title	Album Label & Number
3/13/04	Ⓜ	9	18	1 Maps		87	*Fever To Tell*	Interscope 000349
2/25/06	Ⓜ	14	18	2 Gold Lion		88	*Show Your Bones*	Dress Up 006337

YELLOWCARD

Punk-rock band from Jacksonville, Florida: Ryan Key (vocals, guitar), Sean Mackin (violin, vocals), Benjamin Harper (guitar), Alex Lewis (bass) and Longineu Parsons (drums). By 2006, Ryan Mendez replaced Harper and Peter Mosely replaced Lewis.

Debut	Cht	Peak	Wks			Hot Pos	Album Title	Album Label & Number
9/6/03	Ⓜ	25	12	1 Way Away		—	*Ocean Avenue*	Capitol 39844
1/24/04	Ⓜ	21	26	2 Ocean Avenue		37	↓	
7/17/04	Ⓜ	15	16	3 Only One		122	↓	
12/3/05+	Ⓜ	4	20	4 Lights And Sounds		50	*Lights And Sounds*	Capitol 70960
5/6/06	Ⓜ	27	12	5 Rough Landing, Holly		—	↓	

YES

® **1980s: #30 / All-Time: #37**

Progressive-rock band formed in London, England. Original lineup: **Jon Anderson** (vocals), Peter Banks (guitar), Tony Kaye (keyboards), Chris Squire (bass) and Bill Bruford (drums). Numerous personnel changes. Banks later formed Flash and **After The Fire**. Group disbanded in 1980. Re-formed in 1983 with Anderson, Trevor Rabin (guitar), Kaye, Squire and Alan White (drums). Anderson left in 1988. Anderson, Bruford, Rick Wakeman and Steve Howe formed self-named group in early 1989. Yes reunited in 1991 with Anderson, Bruford, Wakeman, Howe, Kaye, Squire, White and Rabin. Bruford, Wakeman and Howe had left group by 1994. Lineup in 1996: Anderson, Howe, Squire, Wakeman and White. Billy Sherwood replaced Wakeman in 1997. Also see **Classic Rock Tracks** section.

TOP HITS: 1)Lift Me Up 2)Owner Of A Lonely Heart 3)Love Will Find A Way 4)Rhythm Of Love 5)Brother Of Mine

Debut	Cht	Peak	Wks			Hot Pos	Album Title	Album Label & Number
11/12/83	®	❶⁴	20	1 Owner Of A Lonely Heart		❶²	*90125*	Atco 90125
11/12/83	®	32	2	2 Our Song		—	↓	
11/26/83+	®	6	18	3 Changes		—	↓	
12/3/83+	®	5	17	4 It Can Happen		51	↓	
2/11/84	®	3¹	16	5 Leave It		24	↓	
3/17/84	®	43	2	6 Hold On		—	↓	
11/16/85	®	27	8	7 Hold On	[L-R]	—	*9012Live - The Solos*	Atco 90474
				live version of #6 above				
10/3/87	®	❶³	11	8 Love Will Find A Way		30	*Big Generator*	Atco 90522
10/10/87	®	2⁶	20	9 Rhythm Of Love		40	↓	
11/14/87+	®	11	16	10 Shoot High Aim Low		—	↓	
2/20/88	®	20	9	11 Final Eyes		—	↓	
6/3/89	®	2²	12	12 Brother Of Mine		—	*Anderson, Bruford, Wakeman, Howe*	Arista 90126
8/12/89	®	24	7	13 Order Of The Universe		—	↓	
				ANDERSON, BRUFORD, WAKEMAN, HOWE (above 2)				
4/20/91	®	❶⁶	16	14 Lift Me Up		86	*Union*	Arista 8643
6/22/91	®	9	10	15 Saving My Heart		—	↓	
8/24/91	®	49	2	16 I Would Have Waited Forever		—	↓	
8/24/91	®	36	5	17 Make It Easy		—	*Yesyears*	Atco 91644
				recorded in 1981				
3/12/94	®	3⁵	13	18 The Calling		—	*Talk*	Victory 480033
6/11/94	®	24	7	19 Walls		—	↓	
11/22/97	®	33	7	20 Open Your Eyes		—	*Open Your Eyes*	Beyond 3074

YORKE, Thom

Born on 10/7/1968 in Wellingborough, Northamptonshire, England. Alternative-rock singer/songwriter/guitarist. Lead singer of **Radiohead**.

Debut	Cht	Peak	Wks			Hot Pos	Album Title	Album Label & Number
7/29/06	Ⓜ	40	1	Black Swan		—	*Eraser*	XL 200

YORN, Pete

Born on 7/27/1974 in Montville, New Jersey. Male singer/songwriter/guitarist.

Debut	Cht	Peak	Wks			Hot Pos	Album Title	Album Label & Number
10/27/01	Ⓜ	28	8	1 For Nancy ('Cos It Already Is)		—	*Music For The Morning After*	Columbia 62216
3/23/02	Ⓜ	36	3	2 Strange Condition		—	↓	
5/17/03	Ⓜ	32	5	3 Come Back Home		—	*Day I Forgot*	Columbia 86922
12/9/06	Ⓜ	38	2	4 For Us		—	*Nightcrawler*	Columbia 92892

YOUNG, Neil

R All-Time: #65

Born on 11/12/1945 in Toronto, Ontario, Canada. Rock singer/songwriter/guitarist. Member of Buffalo Springfield and **Crosby, Stills, Nash & Young**. Appeared in the 1987 movie *Made In Heaven*. Also see **Classic Rock Tracks** section.

AWARD: R&R Hall of Fame: 1995

TOP HITS: 1)Rockin' In The Free World   2)Mansion On The Hill   3)Ten Men Workin'   4)Downtown   5)War Of Man

Debut	Cht	Peak	Wks	#	Track Title	Hot Pos	Album Title	Label & Number
11/28/81+	R	22	16	1	Southern Pacific	70	Re-ac-tor	Reprise 2304
1/9/82	R	56	2	2	Surfer Joe And Moe The Sleaze	—	↓	
					NEIL YOUNG & CRAZY HORSE (above 2)			
1/22/83	R	12	10	3	Little Thing Called Love	71	Trans	Geffen 2018
2/5/83	R	14	8	4	Mr. Soul	—	↓	
2/12/83	R	42	1	5	We R In Control	—	↓	
7/26/86	R	8	10	6	Touch The Night	—	Landing On Water	Geffen 24109
9/20/86	R	33	6	7	Weight Of The World	—	↓	
6/20/87	R	14	8	8	Long Walk Home	—	Life	Geffen 24154
					NEIL YOUNG & CRAZY HORSE			
4/16/88	R	6	11	9	Ten Men Workin'	—	This Note's For You	Reprise 25719
5/28/88	R	19	12	10	This Note's For You	—	↓	
					NEIL YOUNG & THE BLUENOTES (above 2)			
9/23/89	R	2[1]	17	11	Rockin' In The Free World	—	Freedom	Reprise 25899
					RS500 #214			
12/23/89+	R	7	13	12	No More	—	↓	
3/24/90	R	34	6	13	Crime In The City (Sixty To Zero Part I)	—	↓	
9/15/90	R	3[1]	10	14	Mansion On The Hill	—	Ragged Glory	Reprise 26315
12/8/90+	R	33	9	15	Over And Over	—	↓	
3/23/91	R	49	1	16	Love To Burn	—	↓	
					NEIL YOUNG & CRAZY HORSE (above 3)			
11/14/92	R	7	11	17	War Of Man	—	Harvest Moon	Reprise 45057
3/20/93	R	38	3	18	Unknown Legend	—	↓	
7/3/93	R	34	4	19	Long May You Run [L]	—	Unplugged	Reprise 45310
					recorded on 2/7/1993			
8/27/94	R	18	9	20	Change Your Mind	—	Sleeps With Angels	Reprise 45749
					NEIL YOUNG & CRAZY HORSE			
7/1/95	R	6	13	21	Downtown	—	Mirror Ball	Reprise 45934
9/23/95	R	34	5	22	Peace And Love	—	↓	
7/27/96	R	35	5	23	Big Time	—	Broken Arrow	Reprise 46291
					NEIL YOUNG & CRAZY HORSE			
1/5/02	R	32	10	24	Let's Roll	—	Are You Passionate?	Reprise 48111

YOUNG, Paul

Born on 1/17/1956 in Bedfordshire, England. Pop-rock singer.

Debut	Cht	Peak	Wks	#	Track Title	Hot Pos	Album Title	Label & Number
3/10/84	R	33	7	1	Come Back And Stay	22	No Parlez	Columbia 38976
5/25/85	R	14	11	2	Everytime You Go Away	①[1]	The Secret Of Association	Columbia 39957
					first recorded by **Daryl Hall & John Oates** in 1980			
12/6/86	R	43	6	3	Some People	65	Between Two Fires	Columbia 40543

YOUNG FRESH FELLOWS

Rock band from Seattle, Washington: Scott McCaughey (vocals), Kurt Bloch (guitar), Jim Sangster (bass) and Tad Hutchinson (drums).

Debut	Cht	Peak	Wks	Track Title	Hot Pos	Album Title	Label & Number
1/13/90	M	29	2	Carrot Head	—	This One's For The Ladies	Frontier 1034

Z

ZANDER, Robin

Born on 1/23/1953 in Rockford, Illinois. Lead singer of **Cheap Trick**.

Debut	Cht	Peak	Wks	#	Track Title	Hot Pos	Album Title	Label & Number
1/14/89	R	42	1	1	Surrender To Me	6	St: Tequila Sunrise	Capitol 91185
					ANN WILSON & ROBIN ZANDER			
7/3/93	R	13	9	2	I've Always Got You	—	Robin Zander	Interscope 92204

ZAPPA, Frank

Born on 12/21/1940 in Baltimore, Maryland; raised in California. Died of prostate cancer on 12/4/1993 (age 52). Rock music's leading satirist. Singer/songwriter/guitarist/activist. Formed The Mothers Of Invention in 1965. In the movies *200 Motels* and *Baby Snakes*. Father of Dweezil and Moon Unit Zappa. Also see **Classic Rock Tracks** section.

AWARDS: R&R Hall of Fame: 1995 ★ Grammy: Lifetime Achievement Award 1997

Debut	Cht	Peak	Wks	Track Title	Hot Pos	Album Title	Label & Number
6/19/82	R	12	8	Valley Girl	32	Ship arriving too late to save a drowning witch	Barking Pumpkin 38066
				featuring Zappa's daughter Moon Unit			

ZEBRA
Rock trio from New Orleans, Louisiana: Randy Jackson (vocals, guitar), Felix Hanemann (bass) and Guy Gelso (drums).

Debut	Cht	Peak	Wks	Track Title	Hot Pos	Album Title	Album Label & Number
5/28/83	ℝ	10	20	1 Who's Behind The Door?	61	Zebra	Atlantic 80054
7/16/83	ℝ	29	8	2 Tell Me What You Want	107	↓	
9/22/84	ℝ	15	10	3 Bears	—	No Tellin' Lies	Atlantic 80159

ZEBRAHEAD
Rock-rap band from Los Angeles, California: Justin Mauriello (vocals), Ali Tabatabee (rap vocals), Greg Bergdorf (guitar), Ben Osmundson (bass) and Ed Udhus (drums).

11/28/98+	Ⓜ	32	10	Get Back	—	Waste Of Mind	Columbia 69155

ZEVON, Warren
Born on 1/24/1947 in Chicago, Illinois. Died of cancer on 9/7/2003 (age 56). Rock singer/songwriter/pianist. Also see **Hindu Love Gods** and **Classic Rock Tracks** section.

9/11/82	ℝ	24	5	1 Let Nothing Come Between You	—	The Envoy	Asylum 60159
5/30/87	ℝ	9	9	2 Sentimental Hygiene	—	Sentimental Hygiene	Virgin 90603
8/15/87	ℝ	44	3	3 Detox Mansion	—	↓	
11/11/89	ℝ	30	6	4 Run Straight Down	—	Transverse City	Virgin 91068

ZOMBIE, Rob
Born Robert Cummings on 1/12/1966 in Haverhill, Massachusetts. Founder of **White Zombie**. Wrote and directed the movies *House Of 1000 Corpses* and *The Devil's Rejects*. Older brother of Michael "Spider One" Cummings of **Powerman 5000**.

TOP HITS: 1)Dragula 2)Living Dead Girl 3)Foxy Foxy

8/22/98	ℝ	6	36	1 Dragula	116	Hellbilly Deluxe	Geffen 25212
10/10/98	Ⓜ	27	26				
1/30/99	ℝ	7	26	2 Living Dead Girl	—	↓	
3/6/99	Ⓜ	22	21				
8/7/99	ℝ	26	11	3 Superbeast	—	↓	
7/29/00	ℝ	25	7	4 Scum Of The Earth	—	St: Mission: Impossible 2	Hollywood 62244
10/13/01	ℝ	10	17	5 Feel So Numb	—	The Sinister Urge	Geffen 493147
10/20/01	Ⓜ	18	15				
1/26/02	ℝ	11	26	6 Never Gonna Stop	—	↓	
2/23/02	Ⓜ	23	13				
7/13/02	ℝ	13	15	7 Demon Speeding	—	↓	
11/15/03	ℝ	39	2	8 Two-Lane Blacktop	—	Past, Present & Future	Geffen 001041
2/25/06	ℝ	8	12	9 Foxy Foxy	—	Educated Horses	Geffen 006331
3/11/06	Ⓜ	26	7				
4/29/06	ℝ	12	20	10 American Witch	—	↓	
9/23/06	ℝ	29	9	11 Let It All Bleed Out	—	↓	

ZOO, The
Rock band formed in Los Angeles, California: Billy Thorpe (male vocals), Bekka Bramlett (female vocals), Gregg Wright (guitar), Brett Tuggle (keyboards), Tom Lilly (bass) and **Mick Fleetwood** (drums).

7/4/92	ℝ	19	8	Shakin' The Cage	—	Shakin' The Cage	Capricorn 42004

Z-TRIP
Born Zachary Sciacca in Phoenix, Arizona. Trip-hop DJ/producer.

4/2/05	Ⓜ	17	9	Walking Dead	—	Shifting Gears	Hard Left 162503

ZUTONS, The
Alternative-rock band from Liverpool, England: Dave McCabe (vocals, guitar), Boyan Chowdhury (guitar), Abi Harding (sax), Russ Pritchard (bass) and Sean Payne (drums).

1/29/05	Ⓜ	29	8	Pressure Point	—	Who Killed...The Zutons	Deltasonic 019

ZWAN
Alternative-rock band formed by former **Smashing Pumpkins** members **Billy Corgan** (vocals, guitar) and Jimmy Chamberlain (drums), with Matt Sweeney (guitar) and David Pajo (bass).

12/14/02+	Ⓜ	7	18	Honestly	103	Mary Star Of The Sea	Reprise 48436
12/14/02+	ℝ	21	13				

ZZ TOP

Ⓡ **1980s: #24 / 1990s: #13 / All-Time: #12**

Boogie-rock trio formed in Houston, Texas: Billy Gibbons (vocals, guitar; born on 12/16/1949), Dusty Hill (vocals, bass; born on 5/19/1949) and Frank Beard (drums; born on 6/11/1949). Gibbons and Hill are noted for their long beards. Group appeared in the movie *Back To The Future III*. Dusty is the brother of **Rocky Hill**. Also see **Classic Rock Tracks** section.

AWARD: R&R Hall of Fame: 2004

TOP HITS: 1)My Head's In Mississippi 2)Doubleback 3)Pincushion 4)Concrete And Steel 5)Stages

Debut	Cht	Peak	Wks	Track Title	Hot Pos	Album Title	Album Label & Number
8/8/81	Ⓡ	4	17	1 Tube Snake Boogie	103	El Loco	Warner 3593
8/15/81	Ⓡ	28	12	2 Pearl Necklace	—	↓	
4/16/83	Ⓡ	2³	14	3 Gimme All Your Lovin	37	Eliminator	Warner 23774
4/16/83	Ⓡ	18	15	4 Got Me Under Pressure	—	↓	
7/9/83	Ⓡ	8	14	5 Sharp Dressed Man	56	↓	
12/10/83	Ⓡ	38	7	6 TV Dinners	—	↓	
4/14/84	Ⓡ	3¹	17	7 Legs R&R Hall of Fame	8	↓	
10/19/85	Ⓡ	❶²	15	8 Sleeping Bag	8	Afterburner	Warner 25342
11/9/85	Ⓡ	8	15	9 Can't Stop Rockin'	—	↓	
11/23/85+	Ⓡ	❶²	19	10 Stages	21	↓	
1/18/86	Ⓡ	5	20	11 Rough Boy	22	↓	
2/15/86	Ⓡ	16	9	12 Delirious	—	↓	
5/24/86	Ⓡ	18	6	13 Woke Up With Wood	—	↓	
7/5/86	Ⓡ	15	12	14 Velcro Fly	35	↓	
5/12/90	Ⓡ	❶⁴	13	15 Doubleback	—	Recycler	Warner 26265
10/6/90	Ⓡ	❶⁴	9	16 Concrete And Steel	—	↓	
10/27/90	Ⓡ	❶⁶	17	17 My Head's In Mississippi	—	↓	
12/22/90+	Ⓡ	2⁴	16	18 Give It Up	79	↓	
3/9/91	Ⓡ	14	8	19 Decision Or Collision	—	↓	
4/18/92	Ⓡ	16	3	20 Viva Las Vegas #29 Pop hit for Elvis Presley in 1964	—	Greatest Hits	Warner 26846
5/9/92	Ⓡ	8	7	21 Gun Love	—	↓	
1/22/94	Ⓡ	❶⁴	9	22 Pincushion	124	Antenna	RCA 66317
3/12/94	Ⓡ	7	11	23 Breakaway	—	↓	
5/28/94	Ⓡ	27	7	24 Girl In A T-Shirt	—	↓	
8/13/94	Ⓡ	30	8	25 Fuzzbox Voodoo	—	↓	
2/17/96	Ⓡ	12	11	26 She's Just Killing Me	—	St: From Dusk Till Dawn	Epic Soundtrax 67523
9/14/96	Ⓡ	5	12	27 What's Up With That	—	Rhythmeen	RCA 66956
11/30/96+	Ⓡ	22	12	28 Bang Bang	—	↓	
5/3/97	Ⓡ	35	5	29 Rhythmeen	—	↓	
10/2/99	Ⓡ	13	11	30 Fearless Boogie	—	XXX	RCA 67850
2/5/00	Ⓡ	31	5	31 36-22-36	—	↓	

TITLE SECTION

This section contains an all-inclusive, alphabetical listing of every track title that appears in the combined artist section. The artist's name is listed next to each track title along with the highest position attained and the year the track peaked on the chart. An 'R' shown in front of a peak position indicates a "Mainstream Rock Tracks" hit and an 'M' indicates a "Modern Rock Tracks" hit. For example, 'R-21/89' indicates the track title peaked at position 21 on the "Mainstream Rock Tracks" chart in 1989. If a track by an artist hits both charts, the track is shown once, with the chart information from both charts shown beneath the track in order of highest peak position.

A song with more than one charted version is listed once, with the artists' names listed below in chronological order. Many songs that have the same title, but are different tunes, are listed separately, with the most popular title listed first. This will make it easy to determine which songs are the same composition, the number of charted versions of a particular song, and which of these were the most popular.

Cross references have been used throughout to aid in finding a title.

Please keep the following in mind when searching for titles:

Titles such as "N.W.O." and "S S S & Q" will be found at the beginning of their respective letters; however, titles such as "C-I-T-Y" and "F.I.N.E." which are spellings of words, are listed with their regular spellings.

Two-word titles which have the <u>exact</u> same spelling as one-word titles are listed together alphabetically. ("High Wire" is listed directly before "Highwire.")

Titles which have only a very slight discrepancy are shown together. ("Last Night" appears immediately above "Last Nite" and "It's Alright" appears immediately above "It's All Right.")

A

R-3/84 **Ask The Lonely** *Journey*
M-36/95 **Asking For It** *Hole*
Asleep At The Wheel ..see: I Wasn't Made To Feel This
Astounded *Tantric*
R-7/01 M-30/01
M-37/04 **Astronaut** *G. Love*
R-12/88 **Astronomy** *Blue Öyster Cult*
M-17/99 **At The Stars** *Better Than Ezra*
R-37/98 **At The Water** *Stegosaurus*
R-3/82 **Athena** *Who*
R-10/82 **Atlantic City** *Bruce Springsteen*
Attack *30 Seconds To Mars*
M-22/05 R-38/05
R-30/99 **Attention Please** *Caroline's Spine*
R-15/84 **Authority Song**
John Cougar Mellencamp
M-28/00 **Automatic** *Collapsis*
Ava Adore *Smashing Pumpkins*
M-3/98 R-8/98
R-59/82 **Avalon** *Roxy Music*
Awake *Godsmack*
R-1/01 M-12/01
M-17/95 **Awake** *Letters To Cleo*
M-6/88 **Away** *Feelies*
Away *Toadies*
R-23/96 M-28/96
Away From Me *Puddle Of Mudd*
R-1/03 M-5/03
Away From The Sun
3 Doors Down
R-20/04 M-33/04
M-13/99 **Awful** *Hole*

B

B.Y.O.B. *System Of A Down*
M-4/05 R-4/05
R-22/84 **Baby Come Back** *Billy Rankin*
M-39/94 **Baby Come Back** *Pato Banton*
R-4/93 **Baby Come On Home**
Led Zeppelin
M-29/08 **Baby Girl, I'm A Blur**
Say Anything
R-3/90 **Baby, It's Tonight** *Jude Cole*
Baby Please Don't Go
Willie & The Poor Boys
R-35/85
Aerosmith
R-7/04
M-21/91 **Baby Universal** *Tin Machine*
R-35/82 **Baby's On Fire** *Sammy Hagar*
M-7/90 **Babydoll** *Laurie Anderson*
M-25/01 **Babylon** *David Gray*
R-27/84 **Back For More** *Ratt*
R-51/81 **Back In Black** *AC/DC*
R-19/86 **Back In The High Life Again**
Steve Winwood
R-45/87 **Back In The U.S.S.R.** *Billy Joel*
R-3/85 **Back In Time** *Huey Lewis*
R-32/90 **Back 'N Blue** *Cheap Trick*
M-22/90 **Back Of My Mind** *O-Positive*
R-3/97 **Back On Earth** *Ozzy Osbourne*
M-6/88 **Back On The Breadline**
Hunters & Collectors
R-4/83 **Back On The Chain Gang**
Pretenders
R-34/88 **Back On The Streets**
John Norum
R-56/82 **Back On The Track** *38 Special*
Back To Back *Replacements*
M-28/89 R-43/89

R-4/87 **Back To Paradise** *38 Special*
Back To School *Deftones*
M-27/00 R-35/00
R-31/90 **Back To Shalla-Bal** *Joe Satriani*
R-31/90 **Back To Square One** *Ernie Isley*
R-26/89 **Back To The Bullet** *Saraya*
R-22/88 **Back To The Cave** *Lita Ford*
R-20/89 **Back To The Wall** *Steve Earle*
R-38/98 **Back To You** *Bryan Adams*
R-14/84 **Back Where I Started**
Box Of Frogs
R-29/94 **Back Where It All Begins**
Allman Brothers Band
R-4/84 **Back Where You Belong**
38 Special
R-18/86 **Back Where You Started**
Tina Turner
Backlash *Joan Jett*
M-7/91 R-40/91
R-48/84 **Backstabber** *Hyts*
Backwater *Meat Puppets*
R-2/94 M-11/94
R-19/85 **Bad** *U2*
R-14/87 **Bad Attitude** *Deep Purple*
R-22/86 **Bad Attitude** *Honeymoon Suite*
R-37/94 **Bad Attitude Shuffle** *Cinderella*
Bad Day *Fuel*
M-12/01 R-14/01
R-34/83 **Bad Girls** *Don Felder*
R-40/00 **Bad Little Doggie** *Gov't Mule*
R-1/90 **Bad Love** *Eric Clapton*
Bad Luck *Social Distortion*
M-2/92 R-44/92
R-40/93 **Bad Luck Blue Eyes Goodbye**
Black Crowes
Bad Magick *Godsmack*
R-12/01 M-28/01
R-20/89 **Bad Man** *Bad Company*
R-3/88 **Bad Medicine** *Bon Jovi*
R-42/91 **Bad Rain** *Allman Brothers Band*
Bad Religion *Godsmack*
R-8/00 M-32/00
M-28/94 **Bad Reputation** *Freedy Johnston*
R-31/91 **Bad Reputation** *Damn Yankees*
R-48/81 **Bad Reputation** *Joan Jett*
R-2/94 **Bad Thing** *Cry Of Love*
R-38/85 **Bad Times** *Michael McDonald*
R-27/82 **Bad To The Bone**
George Thorogood
M-6/00 **Bad Touch** *Bloodhound Gang*
R-29/01 **Bag Of Tricks** *Isle Of Q*
R-34/98 **Baker Street** *Foo Fighters*
M-13/90 **Ball And Chain** *Social Distortion*
R-14/82 **Ball & Chain** *Elton John*
R-25/90 **Ballad Of Jayne** *L.A. Guns*
R-23/91 **Ballad Of Jenny Ledge**
Toy Matinee
Ballad Of Peter Pumpkinhead
XTC
M-1/92 R-46/92
R-13/91 **Ballad Of Youth** *Richie Sambora*
R-25/96 **Ballbreaker** *AC/DC*
M-3/92 **Ballerina Out Of Control**
Ocean Blue
R-22/82 **Ballroom Dancing**
Paul McCartney
R-21/84 **Balls To The Wall** *Accept*
R-28/86 **Band Of The Hand (Hell Time, Man!)**
Bob Dylan w/ The Heartbreakers
M-19/03 **Bandages** *Hot Hot Heat*
Banditos *Refreshments*
R-11/96 M-14/96

R-41/89 **Bang** *Gorky Park*
Bang And Blame *R.E.M.*
M-1/94 R-3/95
R-22/97 **Bang Bang** *ZZ Top*
R-38/87 **Bang Bang** *David Bowie*
R-39/90 **Bang Bang** *Danger Danger*
R-29/83 **Bang The Drum All Day**
Todd Rundgren
R-37/83 **Bang Your Head (Metal Health)**
Quiet Riot
R-40/87 **Bangin' On My Heart** *Outfield*
M-34/05 **Banquet** *Bloc Party*
M-36/98 **Barbarella** *Scott Weiland*
R-26/86 **Barefootin'** *Pete Townshend*
R-12/84 **Bark At The Moon**
Ozzy Osbourne
M-30/94 **Barney (...And Me)** *Boo Radleys*
M-11/97 **Barrel Of A Gun** *Depeche Mode*
Bartender (I Just Want Your Company) *(HED)Planet Earth*
R-23/00 M-27/00
R-33/00 **Basic Breakdown** *Apartment 26*
Basket Case *Green Day*
M-1/94 R-9/94
Bat Country *Avenged Sevenfold*
R-2/06 M-6/06
M-18/89 **Batdance** *Prince*
R-9/97 **Baton Rouge** *Nixons*
M-6/99 **Battle Flag** *Lo Fidelity Allstars*
M-22/97 **Battle Of Who Could Care Less**
Ben Folds Five
R-22/93 **Battle Rages On** *Deep Purple*
R-11/87 **Battleship Chains**
Georgia Satellites
Bawitdaba *Kid Rock*
M-10/99 R-11/99
R-3/83 **Be Good Johnny** *Men At Work*
R-2/86 **Be Good To Yourself** *Journey*
Be Like That *3 Doors Down*
R-10/01 M-22/01
R-33/82 **Be My Lady** *Jefferson Starship*
R-29/98 **Be Quiet And Drive (Far Away)**
Deftones
M-28/93 **Be Still** *Peace Together*
R-2/88 **Be Still My Beating Heart** *Sting*
R-42/81 **Be True** *Bruce Springsteen*
M-18/88 **Be With You** *Jack Rubies*
(also see: I Just Wanna)
Be Yourself *Audioslave*
R-1/05 M-1/05
R-15/84 **Bears** *Zebra*
Beast And The Harlot
Avenged Sevenfold
R-19/06 M-40/06
R-50/82 **Beastie** *Jethro Tull*
R-14/83 **Beat It** *Michael Jackson*
(also see: Eat It)
R-10/84 **Beat Of A Heart** *Scandal*
R-39/01 **Beat The World** *Pressure 4-5*
R-24/86 **Beat's So Lonely** *Charlie Sexton*
M-13/89 **Beat(en) Generation** *The*
Beautiful *10 Years*
R-13/08 M-22/08
M-20/99 **Beautiful** *Joydrop*
M-27/01 **Beautiful** *Flickerstick*
Beautiful Day *U2*
M-5/00 R-14/00
M-21/98 **Beautiful Disaster** *311*
M-10/93 **Beautiful Girl** *INXS*
M-37/07 **Beautiful Lie**
30 Seconds To Mars
M-4/91 **Beautiful Love** *Julian Cope*
R-33/04 **Beautiful Night** *Burden Brothers*

Beautiful People *Marilyn Manson*
  M-26/96 R-29/96
R-37/97 Beauty *Mötley Crüe*
M-17/01 Because I Got High *Afroman*
  (Because Of Me) ..see: Right Next Door
R-7/04 Because Of You *Nickelback*
R-22/87 Because The Night
  Bruce Springsteen
M-7/93 Because The Night
  10,000 Maniacs
  Becoming The Bull *Atreyu*
  R-5/07 M-11/08
R-4/87 Bed Of Lies *Cruzados*
M-23/91 Bed Of Roses *Screaming Trees*
R-25/93 Bed Of Roses *Bon Jovi*
R-6/88 Beds Are Burning *Midnight Oil*
  Been Caught Stealing
  Jane's Addiction
  M-1/90 R-29/90
M-11/90 Been There Done That
  Brian Eno/John Cale
R-20/91 Been Your Fool *Tattoo Rodeo*
M-27/94 Beercan *Beck*
  Before I Forget *Slipknot*
  R-11/05 M-32/05
R-9/90 Before You Accuse Me
  Eric Clapton
R-33/07 Beg To Differ *Sevendust*
R-21/95 Beggars & Hangers-On
  Slash's Snakepit
R-38/91 Beggars & Thieves
  Beggars & Thieves
R-22/01 Beginning Of The End
  Systematic
  Behind Blue Eyes *Limp Bizkit*
  R-11/04 M-18/04
R-58/81 Behind The Lines *Phil Collins*
M-7/92 Behind The Sun
  Red Hot Chili Peppers
R-23/87 Behind The Wall Of Sleep
  Smithereens
  Behind Those Eyes
  3 Doors Down
  R-12/05 M-25/05
M-7/93 Being Simple *Judybats*
M-7/08 Believe *Bravery*
  Believe *Lenny Kravitz*
  M-10/93 R-15/93
  Believe *Dig*
  M-19/94 R-34/94
R-12/88 Believe In Love *Scorpions*
R-39/02 Believe Me *Mesh Stl*
M-30/88 (Believed You Were) Lucky
  'Til Tuesday
  Bent *Matchbox Twenty*
  M-16/00 R-24/00
  Bertha *Los Lobos*
  M-24/91 R-37/91
R-28/91 Best I Can *Queensrÿche*
R-5/87 Best Man In The World
  Ann Wilson
R-12/86 Best Of Both Worlds *Van Halen*
R-16/81 Best Of Times *Styx*
R-9/90 Best Of What I Got *Bad English*
  Best Of You *Foo Fighters*
  R-1/05 M-1/05
  (Best That You Can Do) ..see:
  Arthur's Theme
  Best Things *Filter*
  M-18/00 R-31/00
R-5/81 Bette Davis Eyes *Kim Carnes*
M-17/91 Better Back Off
  Marshall Crenshaw

R-32/84 Better Be Good To Me
  Tina Turner
  Better Be Home Soon
  Crowded House
  R-18/88 M-29/88
R-2/92 Better Days *Bruce Springsteen*
R-19/90 Better Days *Gun*
M-3/99 Better Days (And The Bottom
  Drops Out) *Citizen King*
  Better Man *Pearl Jam*
  R-1/95 M-2/95
R-35/05 Better Now *Collective Soul*
  Better Than Me *Hinder*
  R-16/07 M-37/07
  Better Than Nothing
  Jennifer Trynin
  M-15/95 R-40/95
R-7/98 Better Than You *Metallica*
R-12/81 Better Things *Kinks*
R-36/07 Better Think Again *Submersed*
R-41/89 (Between A) Rock And A Hard
  Place *Cutting Crew*
  Between Angels And Insects
  Papa Roach
  M-16/01 R-27/01
R-28/96 Between Heaven And Hell
  Zakk Wylde
M-2/89 Between Something And
  Nothing *Ocean Blue*
R-39/84 Between The Wheels *Rush*
R-35/82 Between Two Worlds *Tom Petty*
  Beverly Hills *Weezer*
  M-1/05 R-26/05
M-39/03 Beyond The Gray Sky *311*
R-17/89 Big Bad Moon *Joe Satriani*
R-26/81 Big Balls *AC/DC*
  Big Bang Baby
  Stone Temple Pilots
  R-1/96 M-2/96
M-20/04 Big Brat *Phantom Planet*
M-3/07 Big Casino *Jimmy Eat World*
  Big Chair *Reacharound*
  M-28/96 R-33/96
R-14/84 Big City Nights *Scorpions*
R-17/83 Big Crash *Eddie Money*
  Big Empty *Stone Temple Pilots*
  R-3/94 M-7/94
R-20/92 Big Goodbye *Great White*
R-1/93 Big Gun *AC/DC*
R-9/88 Big League
  Tom Cochrane & Red Rider
R-22/91 Big Lie *Rik Emmett*
R-6/83 Big Log *Robert Plant*
R-2/87 Big Love *Fleetwood Mac*
R-35/90 Big Love *Robert Plant*
M-18/89 Big Man On Paper
  Graham Parker
  Big Me *Foo Fighters*
  M-3/96 R-18/96
R-4/85 Big Money *Rush*
R-36/91 Big Sky Country *Chris Whitley*
R-30/89 Big Talk *Warrant*
R-3/87 Big Time *Peter Gabriel*
R-35/96 Big Time
  Neil Young & Crazy Horse
M-5/94 Big Time Sensuality *Björk*
M-10/90 Bikini Girls With Machine Guns
  Cramps
R-33/83 Billy's Got A Gun *Def Leppard*
M-9/07 Bird And The Worm *Used*
M-3/90 Birdhouse In Your Soul
  They Might Be Giants

  (Birds Fly) ..see: Whisper To A
  Scream
R-38/88 Birth, School, Work, Death
  Godfathers
R-35/90 Birthday *Paul McCartney*
R-39/06 Birthday *Taproot*
M-4/97 Bitch *Meredith Brooks*
R-30/98 Bitch *Sevendust*
M-11/90 Biting My Nails
  Renegade Soundwave
R-22/98 Bitter Pill *Mötley Crüe*
  Bitter Sweet Symphony *Verve*
  M-4/98 R-22/98
  Bitter Tears *INXS*
  R-4/91 M-6/91
R-14/93 Bittersweet
  Big Head Todd & The Monsters
  Bittersweet *Fuel*
  M-17/98 R-15/99
  Bittersweet Me *R.E.M.*
  M-6/96 R-7/96
M-10/94 Bizarre Love Triangle *Frente!*
  Black *Pearl Jam*
  R-3/93 M-20/93
R-30/98 Black *Sevendust*
R-1/88 Black And Blue *Van Halen*
  (also see: Back 'N Blue)
R-35/01 Black & White *Static-X*
  Black Balloon *Goo Goo Dolls*
  M-13/99 R-28/99
R-32/04 Black Betty *Spiderbait*
R-34/85 Black Cars *Gino Vannelli*
R-26/82 Black Coffee In Bed *Squeeze*
R-17/92 Black Flag *King's X*
  Black Gold *Soul Asylum*
  R-4/93 M-6/93
  Black Hole Sun *Soundgarden*
  R-1/94 M-2/94
  Black Jesus *Everlast*
  M-15/00 R-30/00
R-38/93 Black Lodge *Anthrax*
M-9/92 Black Metallic *Catherine Wheel*
R-13/91 Black Money *Vinnie James*
R-44/92 Black Moon
  Emerson, Lake & Palmer
R-4/93 Black On Black II *Heart*
R-19/08 Black Rain *Ozzy Osbourne*
M-22/89 Black Sheep Wall
  Innocence Mission
R-39/94 Black Sunshine *White Zombie*
M-40/06 Black Swan *Thom Yorke*
R-1/90 Black Velvet *Alannah Myles*
R-34/91 Black, White And Blood Red
  BoDeans
R-6/96 Blackberry *Black Crowes*
  Blackout *(HED)Planet Earth*
  R-21/03 M-32/03
R-11/97 Blame *Collective Soul*
M-22/93 Blast *Pure*
R-1/90 Blaze Of Glory *Jon Bon Jovi*
M-36/99 Bled For Days *Static-X*
M-18/01 Bleed American *Jimmy Eat World*
  Bleed It Out *Linkin Park*
  M-2/07 R-3/07
M-27/05 Bleed Like Me *Garbage*
  Bleed Together *Soundgarden*
  R-13/97 M-32/97
R-32/01 Bleeder *Nothingface*
R-9/08 Bleeding, The
  Five Finger Death Punch
R-6/97 Bleeding Me *Metallica*
R-39/88 Blind *Talking Heads*
R-39/91 Blind Faith *Warrant*

R-3/94	**Blind Man** *Aerosmith*	
M-35/03	**Blinded (When I See You)**	
	Third Eye Blind	
R-31/01	**Blister** *Simon Says*	
M-40/97	**Block Rockin' Beats**	
	Chemical Brothers	
R-38/85	**Blondes In Black Cars**	
	Autograph	
R-14/86	**Blood And Roses** *Smithereens*	
M-27/93	**Blood And Thunder**	
	Ultra Vivid Scene	
R-31/07	**Blood Is Thicker Than Water**	
	Black Label Society	
M-1/92	**Blood Makes Noise**	
	Suzanne Vega	
R-14/91	**Blood On The Bricks** *Aldo Nova*	
M-29/05	**Blood Red Summer**	
	Coheed & Cambria	
R-31/82	**Bloody Reunion** *Molly Hatchet*	
R-32/01	**Bloom** *Sinomatic*	
	Blow Up The Outside World	
	Soundgarden	
	R-1/96 M-8/96	
R-24/81	**Blow Wind Blow** *Eric Clapton*	
M-19/92	**Blowing Bubbles**	
	Lightning Seeds	
	Blue *Perfect Circle*	
	R-19/04 M-21/04	
M-23/03	**Blue And Yellow** *Used*	
R-39/93	**Blue Eyes** *Steve Miller Band*	
M-29/90	**Blue Flower** *Mazzy Star*	
R-2/84	**Blue Jean** *David Bowie*	
R-12/05	**Blue Jeans** *Silvertide*	
R-35/84	**Blue Light** *David Gilmour*	
	Blue Monday *Orgy*	
	M-4/99 R-18/99	
R-40/89	**Blue Monday** *Bob Seger*	
R-1/98	**Blue On Black**	
	Kenny Wayne Shepherd Band	
	Blue Orchid *White Stripes*	
	M-7/05 R-32/05	
	Blue Sky Mine *Midnight Oil*	
	R-1/90 M-1/90	
R-32/83	**Blue World** *Moody Blues*	
R-32/97	**Blueboy** *John Fogerty*	
	Blues Before And After	
	Smithereens	
	R-7/90 M-18/90	
M-1/90	**Blues From A Gun**	
	Jesus & Mary Chain	
	Blurry *Puddle Of Mudd*	
	R-1/02 M-1/02	
M-21/96	**Bluster** *Salt*	
M-23/91	**Bob's Yer Uncle** *Happy Mondays*	
R-36/84	**Bobby Jean** *Bruce Springsteen*	
	Bodies *Drowning Pool*	
	R-6/01 M-12/01	
R-23/84	**Body Electric** *Rush*	
R-19/82	**Body Language** *Queen*	
M-15/98	**Body Movin'** *Beastie Boys*	
M-26/99	**Bodyrock** *Moby*	
M-8/08	**Bodysnatchers** *Radiohead*	
R-22/87	**Bogged Down In Love With You**	
	Charlie Daniels Band	
M-25/94	**Bohemia** *Mae Moore*	
M-28/00	**Bohemian Like You**	
	Dandy Warhols	
R-16/92	**Bohemian Rhapsody** *Queen*	
R-30/01	**Boiler** *Limp Bizkit*	
	Bom Bom Bom *Living Things*	
	M-21/05 R-37/06	
M-20/99	**Bombshell** *Papa Vegas*	
R-26/01	**Bombshell** *Powerman 5000*	

R-25/94	**Bonecrusher** *Soulhat*	
M-21/06	**Bones** *Killers*	
M-17/92	**Bonfires Burning** *Origin*	
R-18/98	**Boogie King**	
	Screamin' Cheetah Wheelies	
	Book Of Dreams *Suzanne Vega*	
	M-8/90 R-47/90	
	Boom *P.O.D.*	
	M-13/02 R-21/02	
R-29/98	**Boom Boom**	
	Big Head Todd & The Monsters	
	w/ John Lee Hooker	
R-11/83	**Boomtown Blues** *Bob Seger*	
R-38/97	**Booty Street** *Sugartooth*	
R-44/83	**Born In America** *Riot*	
R-8/84	**Born In The U.S.A.**	
	Bruce Springsteen	
M-5/92	**Born Of Frustration** *James*	
R-3/88	**Born To Be Bad**	
	George Thorogood	
R-7/88	**Born To Be My Baby** *Bon Jovi*	
R-25/06	**Born To Lead** *Hoobastank*	
R-37/93	**Born To Run** *Lynyrd Skynyrd*	
M-26/04	**Born Too Slow** *Crystal Method*	
R-15/96	**Born With A Broken Heart**	
	Kenny Wayne Shepherd	
R-28/98	**Born Without You** *Storyville*	
R-11/97	**Both Sides Now** *Sammy Hagar*	
R-24/93	**Both Sides Of The Story**	
	Phil Collins	
	Bother *Stone Sour*	
	R-2/02 M-4/02	
	Bottom Of A Bottle	
	Smile Empty Soul	
	M-7/03 R-8/03	
	Boulevard Of Broken Dreams	
	Green Day	
	M-1/04 R-1/05	
R-39/03	**Bounce** *Bon Jovi*	
M-40/02	**Bouncing Off The Walls**	
	Sugarcult	
	Bound For The Floor *Local H*	
	M-5/96 R-10/96	
R-13/94	**Box Of Miracles**	
	Barefoot Servants	
R-15/87	**Boy In The Bubble** *Paul Simon*	
R-17/86	**Boy Inside The Man**	
	Tom Cochrane & Red Rider	
M-30/96	**Boy Or A Girl** *Imperial Drag*	
	Boys Are Back In Town	
	Bon Jovi	
	R-48/89	
	Everclear	
	R-40/99	
R-3/90	**Boys Cry Tough** *Bad Company*	
R-15/87	**Boys' Night Out** *Sammy Hagar*	
R-17/87	**Boys Night Out**	
	Timothy B. Schmit	
	Boys Of Summer	
	Don Henley	
	R-1/84	
	Ataris	
	M-2/03 R-36/03	
R-41/86	**Boystown** *Rob Jungklas*	
M-12/00	**Boyz-N-The-Hood**	
	Dynamite Hack	
	Brain Stew/Jaded *Green Day*	
	M-3/96 R-8/96	
R-24/92	**Brand New Amerika** *Poorboys*	
	(Brand New Name) ..see: Capricorn	
R-13/92	**Bravado** *Rush*	
	Brave New World *Michael Penn*	
	M-20/90 R-26/90	
R-6/00	**Breadline** *Megadeth*	

R-25/95	**Breadmaker** *Brother Cane*	
R-34/95	**Break, The** *Urge Overkill*	
R-47/84	**Break Down The Wall** *Stone Fury*	
M-1/93	**Break It Down Again**	
	Tears For Fears	
R-35/00	**Break On Through**	
	Stone Temple Pilots	
	Break Stuff *Limp Bizkit*	
	M-14/00 R-19/00	
R-46/81	**Break The Rules Tonite (Out Of**	
	School) *Kim Carnes*	
R-7/94	**Breakaway** *ZZ Top*	
R-19/85	**Breakaway** *Cars*	
	(also see: Crack The Sky)	
	Breakdown *Tantric*	
	R-1/01 M-4/01	
R-27/99	**Breakdown** *Queensrÿche*	
R-34/04	**Breakdown** *Instruction*	
M-40/06	**Breakdown** *Jack Johnson*	
M-30/95	**Breakfast At Tiffany's**	
	Deep Blue Something	
M-4/88	**Breakfast In Bed**	
	UB40 w/ Chrissie Hynde	
M-20/05	**Breakin'** *Music*	
M-12/94	**Breakin' Up** *Violent Femmes*	
R-12/81	**Breaking All The Rules**	
	Peter Frampton	
R-36/81	**Breaking Down Barriers**	
	Elton John	
R-32/83	**Breaking The Chains** *Dokken*	
	Breaking The Girl	
	Red Hot Chili Peppers	
	R-15/92 M-19/92	
	Breaking The Habit *Linkin Park*	
	R-1/04 M-1/04	
	Breakout *Foo Fighters*	
	M-8/00 R-11/00	
R-5/81	**Breakup Song (They Don't Write**	
	'Em) *Greg Kihn Band*	
	Breath *Breaking Benjamin*	
	R-1/07 M-3/07	
	Breathe *Nickelback*	
	R-10/00 M-21/01	
R-12/94	**Breathe** *Collective Soul*	
M-18/97	**Breathe** *Prodigy*	
R-31/01	**Breathe** *Seven Channels*	
M-37/02	**Breathe** *Greenwheel*	
M-24/92	**Breathe Deeply Now** *This Picture*	
R-15/07	**Breathe Into Me** *Red*	
R-36/08	**Breathe Today** *Flyleaf*	
R-29/03	**Breathing** *Stereomud*	
M-23/98	**Brian Wilson** *Barenaked Ladies*	
M-6/98	**Brick** *Ben Folds Five*	
R-1/90	**Brickyard Road** *Johnny Van Zant*	
R-6/95	**Bridge** *Queensrÿche*	
	(Bridie's Song) ..see: Funky Ceili	
M-33/95	**Bright As Yellow**	
	Innocence Mission	
M-20/95	**Bright Yellow Gun**	
	Throwing Muses	
R-1/87	**Brilliant Disguise**	
	Bruce Springsteen	
M-16/98	**Brimful Of Asha** *Cornershop*	
R-35/89	**Bring It Back Again** *Stray Cats*	
R-25/07	**Bring It On** *Lenny Kravitz*	
R-33/97	**Bring It On** *Lynyrd Skynyrd*	
R-26/04	**Bring Me Down** *Pillar*	
M-24/89	**Bring Me Edelweiss** *Edelweiss*	
R-10/88	**Bring Me Some Water**	
	Melissa Etheridge	
	Bring Me To Life *Evanescence*	
	M-1/03 R-11/03	
R-47/90	**Bringing Me Down** *Bonham*	
M-38/00	**Broadway** *Goo Goo Dolls*	

	Broken *Seether*
	R-9/04 M-4/04
R-8/08	**Broken Again** *Another Animal*
R-20/04	**Broken Down** *Sevendust*
R-28/07	**Broken Glass** *Buckcherry*
R-38/07	**Broken Hearted** *Eighteen Visions*
R-9/93	**Broken Hearted Savior**
	Big Head Todd & The Monsters
	Broken Home *Papa Roach*
	M-9/00 R-18/00
R-39/88	**Broken Land** *Adventures*
R-36/03	**Broken Promises** *Element Eighty*
R-8/07	**Broken Sunday** *Saliva*
R-4/85	**Broken Wings** *Mr. Mister*
R-29/05	**Broken Wings** *Alter Bridge*
	Brother *Dark New Day*
	R-7/05 M-38/05
R-37/90	**Brother, Don't You Walk Away**
	Hooters
R-2/89	**Brother Of Mine** *Anderson,*
	Bruford, Wakeman, Howe
M-16/93	**Brothers And Sisters**
	Ziggy Marley
M-39/02	**Bubbletoes** *Jack Johnson*
M-23/05	**Bucket, The** *Kings Of Leon*
	Buddy Holly *Weezer*
	M-2/94 R-34/95
R-8/92	**Bug, The** *Dire Straits*
R-15/91	**Build A Fire** *Drivin' N' Cryin'*
R-27/91	**Build Me Up** *Huey Lewis*
M-3/97	**Building A Mystery**
	Sarah McLachlan
R-13/86	**Built For The Future** *Fixx*
M-13/94	**Bull In The Heather** *Sonic Youth*
	Bullet-Proof Skin *Institute*
	R-26/05 M-26/05
R-14/87	**Bullet The Blue Sky** *U2*
R-32/02	**Bullet (What Did You Sell Your**
	Soul For?) *Injected*
R-22/06	**Bullet With A Name** *Nonpoint*
	Bullet With Butterfly Wings
	Smashing Pumpkins
	M-2/95 R-4/95
	Bullets *Creed*
	R-11/02 M-27/02
	Bullitproof *Pacifier*
	R-27/03 M-37/03
	Bulls On Parade
	Rage Against The Machine
	M-11/96 R-36/96
M-28/99	**Bump** *Kottonmouth Kings*
	Burden In My Hand *Soundgarden*
	R-1/96 M-2/96
M-13/03	**Buried Myself Alive** *Used*
M-40/05	**Burn The Witch**
	Queens Of The Stone Age
R-1/81	**Burnin' For You** *Blue Öyster Cult*
M-25/95	**Burnin' Rubber** *Mr. Mirainga*
R-46/81	**Burning Bones** *Krokus*
	Burning Bright *Shinedown*
	R-2/05 M-22/05
R-3/82	**Burning Down One Side**
	Robert Plant
R-6/83	**Burning Down The House**
	Talking Heads
R-5/83	**Burning Heart** *Vandenberg*
R-11/85	**Burning Heart** *Survivor*
R-27/85	**Burning House Of Love** *X*
R-47/84	**Burning In Love**
	Honeymoon Suite
M-23/90	**Burning Inside** *Ministry*
R-20/87	**Burning Like A Flame** *Dokken*
R-33/97	**Burning My Soul** *Dream Theater*

R-36/91	**Burning Timber** *Rembrandts*
	Busload Of Faith *Lou Reed*
	M-11/89 R-47/89
R-22/93	**Busy Bee** *Ugly Kid Joe*
	But Anyway *Blues Traveler*
	M-17/96 R-19/96
	Butterfly *Crazy Town*
	M-1/01 R-21/01
M-23/90	**Butterfly On A Wheel**
	Mission U.K.
M-13/93	**Butterfly Wings**
	Machines Of Loving Grace
R-36/94	**Buying My Way Into Heaven**
	Sammy Hagar
	By The Way
	Red Hot Chili Peppers
	M-1/02 R-1/02

C

R-29/95	**Cabin Down Below** *Tom Petty*
	(Cable Car) ..see: Over My Head
R-31/88	**Cabo Wabo** *Van Halen*
R-48/81	**Cadillac Ranch**
	Bruce Springsteen
R-16/84	**Cage Of Freedom** *Jon Anderson*
M-28/99	**Cailin** *Unwritten Law*
M-28/95	**California** *Wax*
M-35/02	**California** *Phantom Planet*
R-3/85	**California Girls** *David Lee Roth*
	Californication
	Red Hot Chili Peppers
	R-1/00 M-1/00
R-3/89	**Call It Love** *Poco*
R-4/91	**Call It Rock N' Roll** *Great White*
R-19/92	**Call It What You Want** *Tesla*
M-9/89	**Call Me Blue** *House*
	Call Me When You're Sober
	Evanescence
	M-4/06 R-5/06
M-27/92	**Call Mr. Lee** *Television*
R-14/87	**Call Of The Wild** *Deep Purple*
R-26/90	**Call Of The Wild**
	Company Of Wolves
R-3/85	**Call To The Heart** *Giuffria*
R-3/94	**Calling, The** *Yes*
	Calling *Taproot*
	R-11/05 M-23/05
R-40/03	**Calling All Angels** *Train*
R-4/82	**Calling All Girls** *Rick Springfield*
R-40/82	**Calling All Girls** *Queen*
R-22/86	**Calling America**
	Electric Light Orchestra
R-42/89	**Calling America**
	Tom Cochrane & Red Rider
	Calling Elvis *Dire Straits*
	R-3/91 M-25/91
M-13/89	**Calling Out To Carol**
	Stan Ridgway
R-3/93	**Calling To You** *Robert Plant*
M-40/01	**Camera One** *Josh Joplin Group*
R-47/88	**Can I Play With Madness**
	Iron Maiden
M-19/91	**Can You Dig It?** *Mock Turtles*
M-10/93	**Can You Forgive Her?**
	Pet Shop Boys
	Can't Change Me *Chris Cornell*
	R-5/99 M-7/99
M-38/95	**Can't Cry Anymore** *Sheryl Crow*
M-7/93	**Can't Do A Thing (To Stop Me)**
	Chris Isaak

	Can't Even Tell *Soul Asylum*
	M-16/94 R-24/94
R-5/85	**Can't Fight This Feeling**
	REO Speedwagon
R-16/82	**Can't Find Love**
	Jefferson Starship
R-10/90	**Can't Find My Way Home**
	House Of Lords
M-30/98	**Can't Get Enough Of You Baby**
	Smash Mouth
R-6/90	**Can't Get Enuff** *Winger*
R-34/95	**Can't Get High** *Widespread Panic*
R-49/82	**Can't Get Loose** *Sammy Hagar*
	(Can't Get My) Head Around You
	Offspring
	M-6/04 R-16/04
R-51/84	**Can't Get Next To You**
	Billy Squier
M-6/94	**Can't Get Out Of Bed** *Charlatans*
R-3/88	**Can't Get Over You**
	Gregg Allman Band
R-16/87	**Can't Get Started** *Peter Wolf*
R-14/85	**Can't Get There From Here**
	R.E.M.
R-12/97	**Can't Get This Stuff No More**
	Van Halen
R-34/93	**Can't Have Your Cake** *Vince Neil*
M-11/93	**Can't Help Falling In Love** *UB40*
R-25/87	**Can't Keep Running**
	Gregg Allman Band
R-47/82	**Can't Live Without You**
	Scorpions
R-20/90	**(Can't Live Without Your) Love**
	And Affection *Nelson*
R-33/89	**Can't Miss**
	Michael Thompson Band
	Can't Repeat *Offspring*
	M-9/05 R-10/05
	Can't Speak ..see: Cantspeak
	Can't Stop *Red Hot Chili Peppers*
	M-1/03 R-15/03
R-4/90	**Can't Stop Fallin' Into Love**
	Cheap Trick
M-20/93	**Can't Stop Killing You**
	Kirsty MacColl
R-2/95	**Can't Stop Lovin' You** *Van Halen*
R-8/85	**Can't Stop Rockin'** *ZZ Top*
R-2/91	**Can't Stop This Thing We**
	Started *Bryan Adams*
R-33/97	**Can't Tame The Lion** *Journey*
R-18/88	**Can't Wait** *Foreigner*
M-21/95	**Can't Wait One Minute More** *CIV*
M-29/97	**(Can't You) Trip Like I Do**
	Filter & The Crystal Method
R-7/87	**Can'tcha Say (You Believe In**
	Me)/Still In Love *Boston*
	Candy *Iggy Pop*
	M-5/90 R-30/91
M-5/93	**Candy Everybody Wants**
	10,000 Maniacs
	Cannonball *Breeders*
	M-2/93 R-32/94
R-4/85	**Cannonball** *Supertramp*
M-29/93	**Cantaloop** *US3*
M-40/95	**Cantspeak** *Danzig*
	Capital G *Nine Inch Nails*
	M-6/07 R-25/07
R-31/02	**Capricorn (A Brand New Name)**
	30 Seconds To Mars
M-33/95	**Car Song** *Elastica*
M-15/91	**Caravan** *Inspiral Carpets*
R-24/01	**Careful With That Mic...** *Clutch*
M-3/92	**Caribbean Blue** *Enya*
M-12/95	**Carnival** *Natalie Merchant*

Carolina Blues *Blues Traveler*
R-4/97 M-30/97

M-23/90 **Caroline** *Concrete Blonde*

M-2/88 **Carolyn's Fingers** *Cocteau Twins*

R-35/87 **Carrie** *Europe*

M-29/90 **Carrot Head** *Young Fresh Fellows*

Cars *Fear Factory*
R-16/99 M-38/99

M-15/06 **Cash Machine** *Hard-Fi*

R-31/84 **Castaway** *Mi-Sex*

R-8/97 **Casual Affair** *Tonic*

M-19/89 **Cat-House** *Danielle Dax*

Cat People (Putting Out Fire)
David Bowie
R-9/82
R-11/83

R-40/99 **Cat Scratch Fever** *Pantera*

R-46/84 **Catch Me I'm Falling** *Real Life*

R-23/81 **Catch Me If You Can** *Eric Clapton*

R-24/84 **Catch My Fall** *Billy Idol*

R-3/93 **Cats In The Cradle** *Ugly Kid Joe*

M-13/96 **Caught A Lite Sneeze** *Tori Amos*

R-21/04 **Caught In A Dream** *Tesla*

M-8/91 **Caught In My Shadow**
Wonder Stuff

R-16/83 **Caught In The Game** *Survivor*

Caught In The Rain *Revis*
R-8/03 M-20/03

Caught In The Sun
Course Of Nature
R-9/02 M-22/02

R-1/82 **Caught Up In You** *38 Special*

R-29/94 **Ceiling** *Royal Jelly*

M-4/90 **Celebrate** *Emotional Fish*

Celebrity Skin *Hole*
M-1/98 R-4/98

R-31/98 **Cement** *Feeder*

R-4/85 **Centerfield** *John Fogerty*

R-1/82 **Centerfold** *J. Geils Band*

R-12/88 **Century's End** *Donald Fagen*

R-28/98 **Ceremony** *Joe Satriani*

M-16/91 **Cerulean** *Ocean Blue*

M-1/04 **Ch-Check It Out** *Beastie Boys*

Chain, The
Fleetwood Mac
R-30/97
Tantric
R-36/04

R-9/82 **Chain Lightnin'** *38 Special*

R-17/90 **Chain Of Fools** *Little Caesar*

R-16/92 **Chained** *Giant*

M-22/88 **Chains Of Love** *Erasure*

Champagne Supernova *Oasis*
M-1/96 R-8/96

R-16/82 **Change** *John Waite*

R-18/93 **Change** *Candlebox*

R-22/83 **Change** *Tears For Fears*

Change (In The House Of Flies)
Deftones
M-3/00 R-9/00

R-3/86 **Change In The Weather**
John Fogerty

M-31/94 **Change In The Weather**
Love Spit Love

R-17/85 **Change It** *Stevie Ray Vaughan*

R-32/92 **Change Of A Season** *Bonham*

R-10/83 **Change Of Heart** *Tom Petty*

R-20/97 **Change The Locks** *Tom Petty*

Change The World *P.O.D.*
R-32/04 M-38/04

M-25/97 **Change Would Do You Good**
Sheryl Crow

Change Your Mind
Neil Young & Crazy Horse

R-6/84 **Changes** *Yes*

R-9/93 **Changes** *Ozzy Osbourne*

R-45/81 **Changes** *Santana*

M-1/89 **Channel Z** *B-52's*

Chanukah Song *Adam Sandler*
R-20/98 M-25/98

R-24/96 **Charlie Brown's Parents**
Dishwalla

M-1/89 **Charlotte Anne** *Julian Cope*

M-38/99 **Charmed** *My Friend Steve*

M-8/06 **Chasing Cars** *Snow Patrol*

R-54/82 **Chasing Shadows** *Kansas*

R-9/89 **Chasing You Into The Light**
Jackson Browne

M-35/97 **Cheapskate** *Supergrass*

R-3/88 **Check It Out**
John Cougar Mellencamp

R-37/01 **Check Ya** *From Zero*

R-29/00 **Check Your Head** *Buckcherry*

R-7/89 **Cheer Down** *George Harrison*

M-27/93 **Chemical World** *Blur*

Chemicals Between Us *Bush*
M-1/99 R-3/99

M-39/01 **Chemistry** *Semisonic*

R-1/87 **Cherry Bomb**
John Cougar Mellencamp

R-19/90 **Cherry Pie** *Warrant*

Cherub Rock
Smashing Pumpkins
M-7/93 R-23/93

R-30/93 **Child Of The City** *Triumph*

Child Of The Wild Blue Yonder
John Hiatt
R-17/90 M-24/90

M-26/91 **Children** *EMF*

Children Of The Grave ..see: Iron
Man

R-16/88 **Chimes Of Freedom**
Bruce Springsteen

R-19/83 **China** *Red Rockers*

R-3/83 **China Girl** *David Bowie*

R-13/89 **Chip Away The Stone** *Aerosmith*

M-40/05 **Chocolate** *Snow Patrol*

M-2/91 **Chocolate Cake** *Crowded House*

Chop Suey *System Of A Down*
M-7/01 R-12/01

M-4/91 **Chorus (Fishes In The Sea)**
Erasure

M-8/88 **Christine** *House Of Love*

R-29/98 **Christmas Eve - Sarajevo 12/24**
Trans-Siberian Orchestra

R-31/86 **Christmas Time** *Bryan Adams*

R-22/89 **Chrome Plated Heart**
Melissa Etheridge

R-8/92 **Church Of Logic, Sin, & Love**
Men

R-17/83 **Church Of The Poison Mind**
Culture Club

R-13/98 **Cigarettes And Alcohol**
Rod Stewart

Cigaro *System Of A Down*
M-29/05 R-34/05

R-21/93 **Circle**
Big Head Todd & The Monsters

R-32/89 **Circle** *Edie Brickell*

M-8/98 **Circles** *Soul Coughing*

R-31/02 **Circles** *Incubus*

(Circus) ..see: Walls

R-9/85 **C-I-T-Y** *John Cafferty*

R-15/82 **City's Burning** *Heart*

M-39/94 **Citysong** *Luscious Jackson*

R-4/90 **Civil War** *Guns N' Roses*

R-15/91 **Classic Girl** *Jane's Addiction*

R-19/95 **Clean My Wounds**
Corrosion Of Conformity

R-40/97 **Cleopatra** *Chris Duarte Group*

Cleopatra's Cat *Spin Doctors*
M-22/94 R-22/94

Click Click Boom *Saliva*
R-15/01 M-25/01

R-5/90 **Cliffs Of Dover** *Eric Johnson*

R-6/96 **Climb That Hill** *Tom Petty*

Climbing The Walls *Stir*
M-39/00 R-39/00

Clincher, The *Chevelle*
R-3/05 M-8/05

M-3/01 **Clint Eastwood** *Gorillaz*

M-9/03 **Clocks** *Coldplay*

R-25/89 **Close My Eyes Forever**
Lita Ford w/ Ozzy Osbourne

Closer *Nine Inch Nails*
M-11/94 R-35/94

R-19/85 **Closer** *Firm*

Closer To Fine *Indigo Girls*
M-26/89 R-48/89

R-46/92 **Closer To Me** *Outfield*

R-38/90 **Closer To The Flame**
Dave Edmunds

R-21/82 **Closer To The Heart** *Rush*

Closing Time *Semisonic*
M-1/98 R-13/98

Closure *Chevelle*
M-11/04 R-17/04

M-17/91 **Cloud 8** *Frazier Chorus*

R-9/88 **Cloud 9** *George Harrison*

M-27/05 **Club Foot** *Kasabian*

Clumsy *Our Lady Peace*
M-5/98 R-13/98

M-12/91 **Coast Is Clear** *Curve*

Cochise *Audioslave*
R-2/02 M-9/02

Cold *Crossfade*
R-3/04 M-2/05

R-29/02 **Cold** *Static-X*

Cold (But I'm Still Here)
Evans Blue
R-8/06 M-28/06

M-12/92 **Cold, Cold Heart** *Midge Ure*

Cold Contagious *Bush*
R-18/97 M-23/97

R-22/92 **Cold Day In Hell** *Gary Moore*

M-11/92 **Cold Feelings** *Social Distortion*

R-29/86 **Cold Fever** *Models*

R-2/94 **Cold Fire** *Rush*

Cold Hard Bitch *Jet*
M-1/04 R-1/04

R-37/88 **Cold Metal** *Iggy Pop*

R-29/84 **Cold Shot** *Stevie Ray Vaughan*

R-33/07 **Colony Of Birchmen** *Mastodon*

Colors *Crossfade*
R-6/05 M-18/05

R-5/90 **Come Again** *Damn Yankees*

M-1/89 **Come Anytime** *Hoodoo Gurus*

R-1/87 **Come As You Are** *Peter Wolf*

Come As You Are *Nirvana*
M-3/92 R-3/92

R-45/81 **Come Back**
Franke & The Knockouts

R-33/84 **Come Back And Stay**
Paul Young

M-27/90 **Come Back Down**
Toad The Wet Sprocket

M-32/03 **Come Back Home** *Pete Yorn*

R-17/83 **Come Dancing** *Kinks*

D

D' You Know What I Mean?
Oasis
M-4/97   R-36/97
DOA *Foo Fighters*
M-1/05   R-5/05
R-36/81 **Daily Records** *Who*
M-34/05 **Dakota (You Made Me Feel Like The One)** *Stereophonics*
Dammit (Growing Up) *Blink 182*
M-11/98   R-26/98
R-2/88 **Damn Good** *David Lee Roth*
R-36/86 **Dance** *Ratt*
R-42/90 **Dance** *David Baerwald*
(also see: If I Was A Dancer)
M-2/06 **Dance, Dance** *Fall Out Boy*
R-24/84 **Dance Hall Days** *Wang Chung*
R-21/94 **Dance Naked** *John Mellencamp*
R-19/07 **Dance Of The Manatee**
Fair To Midland
R-10/88 **Dance On My Own** *Robert Plant*
R-9/86 **Dancin' In The Ruins**
Blue Öyster Cult
R-42/87 **Dancin' On Top Of The World**
Mason Ruffner
M-14/89 **Dancing Barefoot** *U2*
Dancing Days
Stone Temple Pilots
R-3/95   M-11/95
R-1/84 **Dancing In The Dark**
Bruce Springsteen
Dancing In The Street
Van Halen
R-3/82
Mick Jagger/David Bowie
R-3/85
R-7/86 **Danger Zone** *Kenny Loggins*
R-2/91 **Dangerous** *Doobie Brothers*
M-13/90 **Dangerous** *Depeche Mode*
R-23/85 **Dangerous** *Loverboy*
R-38/82 **Dangerous** *Who*
R-31/85 **Dangerous Moments**
Martin Briley
Dani California
Red Hot Chili Peppers
R-1/06   M-1/06
M-8/06 **Dare** *Gorillaz*
M-9/04 **Dare You To Move** *Switchfoot*
R-27/87 **Dark Light** *Beat Farmers*
R-27/02 **Darkness, Darkness** *Robert Plant*
R-4/82 **Darlene** *Led Zeppelin*
R-9/88 **Darlin' Danielle Don't**
Henry Lee Summer
R-19/87 **Darling It Hurts** *Paul Kelly*
M-15/04 **Darling Nikki** *Foo Fighters*
M-5/07 **Dashboard** *Modest Mouse*
Daughter *Pearl Jam*
R-1/93   M-1/94
R-22/00 **Day After Day** *Def Leppard*
R-3/86 **Day By Day** *Hooters*
Day I Tried To Live *Soundgarden*
R-13/95   M-25/95
R-3/87 **Day-In Day-Out** *David Bowie*
R-9/94 **Day In The Sun** *Peter Frampton*
Day Job *Gin Blossoms*
M-21/96   R-29/96
R-24/83 **Daylight** *Asia*
Daylight Fading *Counting Crows*
R-24/97   M-26/97
R-30/85 **Days Are Numbers (The Traveller)** *Alan Parsons Project*
R-58/84 **Days Gone By** *Poco*

R-2/90 **Days Like These** *Asia*
R-6/92 **Days Of Light** *Roger Daltrey*
Days Of The Week
Stone Temple Pilots
R-4/01   M-5/01
Daysleeper *R.E.M.*
M-18/98   R-30/98
R-38/99 **Dead Again** *Buckcherry*
R-41/83 **Dead Giveaway** *Shalamar*
R-11/88 **Dead Heart** *Midnight Oil*
M-19/02 **Dead Leaves And The Dirty Ground** *White Stripes*
M-16/98 **Deadweight** *Beck*
Dear God
XTC
R-37/87
Midge Ure
M-4/89   R-6/89
M-18/92 **Dear Madam Barnum** *XTC*
R-32/01 **Death Blooms** *Mudvayne*
M-35/98 **Debbie** *B-52's*
M-16/89 **Debbie Gibson Is Pregnant With My Two Headed Love Child**
Mojo Nixon & Skid Roper
M-18/93 **Debonair** *Afghan Wigs*
M-16/04 **Decade Under The Influence**
Taking Back Sunday
R-45/90 **Decadence Dance** *Extreme*
December *Collective Soul*
R-1/95   M-2/95
R-14/91 **Decision Or Collision** *ZZ Top*
M-15/89 **Decline And Fall** *Flesh For Lulu*
R-22/91 **Dedication** *Thin Lizzy*
Deep *Nine Inch Nails*
M-18/01   R-37/01
R-20/85 **Deep Cuts The Knife** *Helix*
R-49/88 **Deep Inside My Heart**
Rock City Angels
M-39/00 **Deep Inside Of You**
Third Eye Blind
R-3/84 **Deeper And Deeper** *Fixx*
R-4/90 **Deeper The Love** *Whitesnake*
M-30/88 **Def Con One** *Pop Will Eat Itself*
R-11/88 **Defenders Of The Flag**
Bruce Hornsby
Defy You *Offspring*
M-8/02   R-8/02
R-9/95 **Deja Voodoo**
Kenny Wayne Shepherd
R-52/81 **Deja Vu (Da Voodoo's In You)**
Les Dudek
R-16/86 **Delirious** *ZZ Top*
Deliverance *Mission U.K.*
M-6/90   R-27/90
M-37/94 **Delivery** *Compulsion*
M-14/91 **De-Luxe** *Lush*
R-13/02 **Demon Speeding** *Rob Zombie*
Denial *Sevendust*
R-14/99   M-26/99
M-5/06 **Denial Twist** *White Stripes*
M-34/99 **Denise** *Fountains Of Wayne*
Deny *Default*
R-7/02   M-14/02
Der Kommissar
After The Fire
R-4/83
Falco
R-22/83
R-38/99 **Descent** *Fear Factory*
R-16/91 **Desert Moon** *Great White*
R-31/84 **Desert Moon** *Dennis DeYoung*
R-12/93 **Desert Song** *Def Leppard*

Desire *U2*
M-1/88   R-1/88
R-36/92 **Desiree** *Rick Vito*
R-21/88 **Desolation Angel** *John Brannen*
R-53/84 **Desperate Heart** *Rainbow*
Desperately Wanting
Better Than Ezra
R-10/97   M-11/97
R-24/82 **Destination Unknown**
Missing Persons
R-3/81 **Destroyer** *Kinks*
R-23/07 **Destroyer** *Static-X*
M-25/93 **Detachable Penis** *King Missile*
M-17/91 **Detonation Boulevard**
Sisters Of Mercy
R-44/87 **Detox Mansion** *Warren Zevon*
R-24/86 **Detroit Diesel** *Alvin Lee*
R-15/94 **Deuce** *Lenny Kravitz*
R-1/94 **Deuces Are Wild** *Aerosmith*
R-37/07 **Devil Cried** *Black Sabbath*
M-17/90 **Devil In Me** *John Wesley Harding*
R-2/88 **Devil Inside** *INXS*
M-1/93 **Devil You Know** *Jesus Jones*
R-18/06 **Devil's Daughter** *Silvertide*
R-44/82 **Devil's Deck** *Coney Hatch*
R-26/07 **Devil's Got A Holda Me** *Colour*
R-15/06 **Devil's Got A New Disguise**
Aerosmith
R-4/87 **Devil's Radio** *George Harrison*
M-23/96 **Devils Haircut** *Beck*
Devolution Workin' Man Blues
Alarm
M-11/89   R-9/90
R-20/84 **Diamond Field** *Pat Benatar*
M-19/03 **Diamonds And Guns** *Transplants*
R-21/85 **Diana** *Bryan Adams*
M-35/96 **Diana** *3 Lb. Thrill*
M-6/91 **Diane** *Material Issue*
Diary Of Jane *Breaking Benjamin*
R-2/06   M-4/06
R-36/98 **Dickeye** *Jerry Cantrell*
Did My Time *Korn*
R-12/03   M-17/03
R-48/91 **Did Ya** *Kinks*
R-38/81 **Did You Steal My Money** *Who*
R-40/88 **Didn't Know It Was Love**
Survivor
R-21/04 **Die Dead Enough** *Megadeth*
R-26/99 **Die, Die My Darling** *Metallica*
Died In Your Arms ..see: (I Just)
Difference, The *Wallflowers*
R-3/97   M-5/97
M-25/05 **Different** *Acceptance*
Different Kind Of Pain *Cold*
R-35/06   M-38/06
R-27/07 **Different Than You** *Exies*
Dig *Incubus*
M-4/07   R-17/07
R-9/89 **Dig** *Who*
R-33/01 **Dig** *Mudvayne*
M-11/90 **Dig For Fire** *Pixies*
Dig In *Lenny Kravitz*
R-11/01   M-13/01
Digging In The Dirt *Peter Gabriel*
R-1/92   M-1/92
Digital Bath *Deftones*
M-16/01   R-38/01
R-22/88 **Dignity** *Deacon Blue*
M-24/93 **Dim** *Dada*
R-37/81 **Dire Wolf** *Grateful Dead*
R-27/05 **Dirthouse** *Static-X*

Dirty Blvd. *Lou Reed*	
M-1/89 R-18/89	
Dirty Deeds Done Dirt Cheap	
AC/DC	
R-4/81	
Joan Jett	
R-23/90	
R-6/97 **Dirty Eyes** *AC/DC*	
R-1/82 **Dirty Laundry** *Don Henley*	
R-35/93 **Dirty Little Mind** *Jackyl*	
R-38/07 **Dirty Little Rockstar** *Cult*	
Dirty Little Thing *Velvet Revolver*	
R-8/05 M-18/05	
R-10/91 **Dirty Love** *Thunder*	
M-8/89 **Dirty Old Town** *David Byrne*	
R-6/87 **Dirty Water** *Rock & Hyde*	
Disappear *INXS*	
M-10/90 R-6/91	
M-24/04 **Disappear** *Hoobastank*	
(Disappeared Ones) ..see: Los	
Desaparecidos	
M-1/89 **Disappointed** *Public Image Ltd.*	
M-9/92 **Disappointed** *Electronic*	
Disarm *Smashing Pumpkins*	
R-5/94 M-8/94	
R-32/95 **Disconnected** *Queensrÿche*	
M-39/95 **Disconnected** *Face To Face*	
R-24/06 **Disconnected (Out Of Touch)**	
Trapt	
Discothéque *U2*	
M-1/97 R-6/97	
Disneyland ..see: Dizz Knee Land	
Disposable Teens	
Marilyn Manson	
R-22/00 M-24/00	
R-3/94 **Dissident** *Pearl Jam*	
Distance, The *Cake*	
M-4/96 R-38/96	
R-49/90 **Distance, The**	
Company Of Wolves	
R-3/84 **Distant Early Warning** *Rush*	
M-26/94 **Distant Sun** *Crowded House*	
M-28/93 **Divine Hammer** *Breeders*	
M-23/92 **Divine Intervention**	
Matthew Sweet	
M-3/92 **Divine Thing** *Soup Dragons*	
R-30/81 **Dixie Highway** *Journey*	
Dizz Knee Land *Dada*	
M-5/92 R-27/92	
M-8/89 **Dizzy** *Throwing Muses*	
Dizzy *Goo Goo Dolls*	
M-9/99 R-13/99	
R-4/84 **Do It Again** *Kinks*	
M-40/04 **Do It Alone** *Sugarcult*	
M-21/06 **Do It For Me Now**	
Angels & Airwaves	
R-41/85 **Do Me Right** *Giuffria*	
M-12/99 **Do Right** *Jimmie's Chicken Shack*	
Do The Evolution *Pearl Jam*	
M-33/98 R-40/98	
R-32/85 **Do They Know It's Christmas?**	
Band Aid	
R-12/82 **Do You Believe In Love**	
Huey Lewis	
R-14/03 **Do You Call My Name** *RA*	
R-20/83 **Do You Compute?** *Donnie Iris*	
R-37/82 **Do You Feel Alright**	
Shooting Star	
R-41/82 **Do You Know, Do You Care?**	
Phil Collins	
R-21/89 **Do You Like It** *Kingdom Come*	
R-21/83 **Do You Really Want To Hurt Me**	
Culture Club	

R-49/90 **Do You Remember?** *Phil Collins*	
M-27/93 **Do You Right** *311*	
M-20/95 **Do You Sleep?**	
Lisa Loeb & Nine Stories	
R-21/82 **Do You Wanna Touch Me (Oh**	
Yeah) *Joan Jett*	
M-9/05 **Do You Want To** *Franz Ferdinand*	
Dock Of The Bay ..see: (Sittin' On)	
R-1/89 **Doctor, The** *Doobie Brothers*	
R-12/84 **Doctor! Doctor!** *Thompson Twins*	
R-20/88 **Doctor Doctor** *Radiators*	
R-7/89 **Dr. Feelgood** *Mötley Crüe*	
R-12/83 **Dr. Heckyll & Mr. Jive**	
Men At Work	
M-17/88 **Doctorin' The Tardis** *Timelords*	
Doesn't Remind Me *Audioslave*	
R-2/05 M-3/05	
R-15/81 **Dog Eat Dog** *Adam & The Ants*	
R-20/94 **Dogman** *King's X*	
M-2/93 **Dogs Of Lust** *The*	
R-30/88 **Dogs Of War** *Pink Floyd*	
M-28/97 **Doin' Time** *Sublime*	
M-4/94 **Doll Parts** *Hole*	
Dollar Bill *Screaming Trees*	
M-28/93 R-40/93	
Dolphin's Cry *Live*	
R-2/99 M-3/99	
R-26/92 **Domino** *Kiss*	
M-22/88 **Domino Dancing** *Pet Shop Boys*	
M-20/90 **Don Henley Must Die** *Mojo Nixon*	
R-15/84 **Don't Answer Me**	
Alan Parsons Project	
M-2/90 **Don't Ask Me** *Public Image Ltd.*	
M-12/89 **Don't Ask Me Why** *Eurythmics*	
M-13/91 **Don't Be A Girl** *Psychedelic Furs*	
R-4/88 **Don't Be Afraid Of The Dark**	
Robert Cray Band	
R-31/90 **Don't Be Afraid Of The Dark** *Y&T*	
R-8/88 **Don't Be Cruel** *Cheap Trick*	
R-32/87 **Don't Be Scared** *Fixx*	
R-13/91 **Don't Believe Her** *Scorpions*	
Don't Bring Me Down ..see: We	
Gotta Get Out Of This Place	
R-17/83 **Don't Change** *INXS*	
R-16/89 **Don't Close Your Eyes** *Kix*	
R-2/85 **Don't Come Around Here No**	
More *Tom Petty*	
M-7/89 **Don't Crash The Car Tonight**	
Mary's Danish	
R-1/83 **Don't Cry** *Asia*	
R-3/91 **Don't Cry** *Guns N' Roses*	
R-11/87 **Don't Dream It's Over**	
Crowded House	
Don't Drink The Water	
Dave Matthews Band	
M-4/98 R-19/98	
R-4/82 **Don't Fight It**	
Kenny Loggins w/ Steve Perry	
M-14/91 **Don't Fix What Ain't Broke**	
Gang Of Four	
R-25/94 **Don't Follow** *Alice In Chains*	
R-17/86 **Don't Forget Me (When I'm**	
Gone) *Glass Tiger*	
R-16/83 **Don't Forget To Dance** *Kinks*	
R-1/86 **Don't Get Me Wrong** *Pretenders*	
R-25/82 **Don't Give Up** *Glenn Frey*	
Don't Go *Hothouse Flowers*	
M-7/88 R-16/88	
Don't Go Away *Oasis*	
M-5/97 R-36/97	
R-13/90 **Don't Go Away Mad (Just Go**	
Away) *Mötley Crüe*	
R-48/83 **Don't It Make You Feel Good**	
Chilliwack	

R-10/88 **Don't Know What You Got (Till**	
It's Gone) *Cinderella*	
R-32/82 **Don't Leave Me Now** *Supertramp*	
R-49/84 **Don't Leave Me This Way**	
Ravyns	
R-49/84 **Don't Let Go** *Wang Chung*	
R-11/81 **Don't Let Him Go**	
REO Speedwagon	
R-1/82 **Don't Let Him Know** *Prism*	
M-27/88 **Don't Let It Break You Down**	
Graham Parker	
R-38/86 **Don't Let Me Be Misunderstood**	
Elvis Costello	
R-36/87 **Don't Let Me Die Young**	
Andy Taylor	
M-11/90 **Don't Let Me Down, Gently**	
Wonder Stuff	
R-38/89 **Don't Let Me Go** *Billy Squier*	
R-25/82 **Don't Let Me In** *Sneaker*	
Don't Look Back	
Fine Young Cannibals	
M-9/89 R-38/89	
R-22/89 **Don't Look Back** *Charlie Sexton*	
M-10/96 **Don't Look Back In Anger** *Oasis*	
R-33/85 **Don't Lose My Number**	
Phil Collins	
Don't Make Me Dream About You	
Chris Isaak	
M-18/89 R-39/91	
R-1/87 **Don't Mean Nothing**	
Richard Marx	
R-10/87 **Don't Need A Gun** *Billy Idol*	
R-37/05 **Don't Need You**	
Smile Empty Soul	
R-33/88 **Don't Pass Me By**	
Georgia Satellites	
R-29/83 **Don't Pay The Ferryman**	
Chris DeBurgh	
R-19/82 **Don't Run My Life** *Spys*	
R-46/85 **Don't Run Wild** *Del Fuegos*	
R-24/84 **Don't Say Goodnight**	
Jon Butcher Axis	
R-4/89 **Don't Say You Love Me**	
Billy Squier	
R-5/88 **Don't Shed A Tear** *Paul Carrack*	
M-2/96 **Don't Speak** *No Doubt*	
Don't Stand So Close To Me	
Police	
R-11/81	
R-10/86 ['86]	
M-29/95 **Don't Stay Home** *311*	
R-21/02 **Don't Stop** *Rolling Stones*	
M-32/00 **Don't Stop** *Radford*	
R-8/81 **Don't Stop Believin'** *Journey*	
R-33/84 **Don't Stop Runnin'** *Y&T*	
R-31/83 **Don't Take Me For A Loser**	
Gary Moore	
R-11/82 **Don't Talk To Strangers**	
Rick Springfield	
R-1/93 **Don't Tear Me Up** *Mick Jagger*	
R-1/95 **Don't Tell Me (What Love Can**	
Do) *Van Halen*	
R-4/83 **Don't Tell Me You Love Me**	
Night Ranger	
M-28/99 **Don't Think Twice** *Mike Ness*	
M-2/05 **Don't Tread On Me** *311*	
R-3/92 **Don't Tread On Me**	
Damn Yankees	
R-16/91 **Don't Treat Me Bad** *Firehouse*	
R-36/06 **Don't Turn Away** *RA*	
M-17/06 **Don't Wait**	
Dashboard Confessional	
M-17/88 **Don't Walk Away** *Toni Childs*	
R-41/84 **Don't Walk Away** *Rick Springfield*	
R-44/88 **Don't Walk Away** *Pat Benatar*	

R-15/97	**Don't Wanna Be Here** *Cool For August*	

R-15/97 **Don't Wanna Be Here**
  Cool For August
R-22/84 **Don't Wanna Let You Go**
  Quiet Riot
R-22/81 **Don't Want To Wait Anymore**
  Tubes
R-28/85 **Don't Worry Baby** *Los Lobos*
M-33/08 **Don't You Evah** *Spoon*
R-1/85 **Don't You (Forget About Me)**
  Simple Minds
R-1/88 **Don't You Know What The Night**
  Can Do? *Steve Winwood*
R-4/82 **Don't You Want Me**
  Human League
M-11/92 **Donna Everywhere**
  Too Much Joy
M-8/02 **Dope Nose** *Weezer*
   Dope Show *Marilyn Manson*
  R-12/98 M-15/98
M-13/03 **Dosed** *Red Hot Chili Peppers*
R-42/87 **Double Trouble** *Cars*
R-1/90 **Doubleback** *ZZ Top*
   Down *311*
  M-1/96 R-19/96
   Down *Stone Temple Pilots*
  R-5/99 M-9/99
   Down *Socialburn*
  R-9/03 M-17/03
M-10/04 **Down** *Blink-182*
R-29/03 **Down** *Motograter*
R-17/95 **Down And Dirty** *Bad Company*
R-31/08 **Down And Out** *Tantric*
R-13/89 **Down Boys** *Warrant*
 M-2/95 **Down By The Water** *PJ Harvey*
R-10/93 **Down In A Hole** *Alice In Chains*
M-16/90 **Down In It** *Nine Inch Nails*
R-40/04 **Down In It** *Magna-Fi*
R-48/88 **Down In The Trenches**
  Broadcasters
R-15/93 **Down Incognito** *Winger*
R-10/93 **Down On Me** *Jackyl*
   Down On The Riverbed
  Los Lobos
  M-16/90 R-33/90
M-38/96 **Down Together** *Refreshments*
   Down Town *Days Of The New*
  R-1/98 M-19/98
 R-1/82 **Down Under** *Men At Work*
R-33/94 **Down With Disease** *Phish*
   Down With The Sickness
  Disturbed
  R-5/01 M-8/01
R-33/90 **Downeaster "Alexa"** *Billy Joel*
   Downfall *TrustCompany*
  R-6/02 M-6/02
R-22/96 **Download (I Will)** *Expanding Man*
M-5/90 **Downtown** *Lloyd Cole*
R-6/95 **Downtown** *Neil Young*
M-10/90 **Downtown Lights** *Blue Nile*
   Downtown Train
  Patty Smyth
  R-40/87
  Rod Stewart
  R-1/90
M-39/95 **Downtown Venus** *P.M. Dawn*
M-30/92 **Drag** *Steve Wynn*
M-22/90 **Drag My Bad Name Down**
  4 Of Us
   Dragula *Rob Zombie*
  R-6/98 M-27/98
M-28/03 **Drain The Blood** *Distillers*
M-11/89 **Drama!** *Erasure*

   Drawer *Summercamp*
  M-21/97 R-37/97
M-18/97 **Dream** *Forest For The Trees*
M-16/92 **Dream About You** *Peter Case*
   Dream All Day *Posies*
  M-4/93 R-17/93
 R-7/92 **Dream Is Over** *Van Halen*
M-22/91 **Dream Like Mine** *Bruce Cockburn*
M-12/01 **Dream On** *Depeche Mode*
R-34/90 **Dream On** *Britny Fox*
R-23/92 **Dream Until Tomorrow**
  Lynch Mob
R-22/87 **Dream Warriors** *Dokken*
R-10/02 **Dreamer** *Ozzy Osbourne*
 R-1/91 **Dreamline** *Rush*
 R-6/86 **Dreams** *Van Halen*
M-15/93 **Dreams** *Cranberries*
R-32/88 **Dreams** *BoDeans*
R-38/89 **Dreams In The Dark** *Badlands*
 M-2/90 **Dreamtime** *Heart Throbs*
R-11/86 **Dreamtime** *Daryl Hall*
   Dreamworld *Midnight Oil*
  M-16/88 R-37/88
   Drift & Die *Puddle Of Mudd*
  R-1/02 M-3/02
R-33/00 **Drifters** *Paul Rodgers*
M-10/89 **Drifting, Falling** *Ocean Blue*
R-41/91 **Drinking Again** *Neverland*
   Drive *R.E.M.*
  M-1/92 R-2/92
   Drive *Incubus*
  M-1/01 R-8/01
 R-3/84 **Drive** *Cars*
 R-3/89 **Drive My Car** *David Crosby*
M-12/91 **Drive That Fast**
  Kitchens Of Distinction
R-10/07 **Driven** *Sevendust*
R-20/97 **Driven** *Rush*
 R-9/93 **Driven By You** *Brian May*
   Driven Out *Fixx*
  R-1/89 M-11/89
R-35/81 **Driven To Tears** *Police*
   Driven Under *Seether*
  M-13/03 R-13/03
R-22/85 **Driver 8** *R.E.M.*
R-33/03 **Drivin' Rain** *Gov't Mule*
 R-9/85 **Drivin' With Your Eyes Closed**
  Don Henley
M-26/90 **Driving** *Everything But The Girl*
M-19/93 **Driving Aloud (Radio Storm)**
  Robyn Hitchcock
R-25/92 **Driving The Last Spike** *Genesis*
R-38/88 **Driving Wheels** *Jimmy Barnes*
M-39/97 **Drop Dead Gorgeous** *Republica*
R-30/90 **Drop The Gun** *Kings Of The Sun*
R-33/83 **Drop The Pilot** *Joan Armatrading*
R-33/98 **Dropping Anchor**
  Jimmie's Chicken Shack
   Drops Of Jupiter (Tell Me) *Train*
  M-11/01 R-19/01
   Drown *Son Volt*
  R-10/96 M-25/96
M-24/92 **Drown** *Smashing Pumpkins*
R-33/97 **Drown In Me**
  Jason Bonham Band
R-34/88 **Drown In My Own Tears**
  Smithereens
R-21/07 **Drown You Out** *Crossfade*
R-21/95 **Drowning** *Hootie & The Blowfish*
   Drowning *Crazy Town*
  M-24/02 R-24/02
R-27/96 **Drowning In A Daydream**
  Corrosion Of Conformity

M-29/96 **Drugs** *Ammonia*
M-10/93 **Drums Of Heaven** *Midnight Oil*
R-20/98 **Du Hast** *Rammstein*
   Duality *Slipknot*
  R-5/04 M-6/04
   Duck And Run *3 Doors Down*
  R-1/01 M-11/01
 R-4/87 **Dude (Looks Like A Lady)**
  Aerosmith
R-17/07 **Dull Boy** *Mudvayne*
   Dumb Things *Paul Kelly*
  M-16/88 R-49/88
R-16/88 **Dynamite** *Rod Stewart*
 M-4/92 **Dyslexic Heart** *Paul Westerberg*

E

   E-Bow The Letter *R.E.M.*
  M-2/96 R-15/96
   E-Pro *Beck*
  M-1/05 R-31/05
R-22/87 **Eagles Fly** *Sammy Hagar*
 M-2/89 **Eardrum Buzz** *Wire*
R-40/88 **Early In The Morning**
  Robert Palmer
M-25/91 **East Easy Rider** *Julian Cope*
 M-9/93 **Eastern Bloc** *Thomas Dolby*
R-20/91 **Easy Come Easy Go** *Winger*
R-27/04 **Easy Comes** *Thornley*
R-32/83 **Easy Livin'** *Fastway*
 R-5/85 **Easy Lover**
  Philip Bailey w/ Phil Collins
R-14/85 **Easy Street** *David Lee Roth*
M-26/90 **Easy Street** *Soul Asylum*
M-12/89 **Eat For Two** *10,000 Maniacs*
R-38/84 **Eat It** *"Weird Al" Yankovic*
M-10/93 **Eat The Music** *Kate Bush*
 R-5/93 **Eat The Rich** *Aerosmith*
R-33/83 **Eat The Rich** *Krokus*
   Eat You Alive *Limp Bizkit*
  R-16/03 M-20/03
R-34/82 **Ebony And Ivory** *Paul McCartney*
  w/ Stevie Wonder
   Echo *Trapt*
  M-10/04 R-13/04
   (Ecstasy, The) .. see: Electric Head
R-21/07 **Ecstasy Of Gold** *Metallica*
M-38/97 **Eddie Vedder** *Local H*
R-37/01 **Eden (Turn The Page)**
  Mayfield Four
R-24/88 **Edge Of A Broken Heart** *Vixen*
R-37/86 **Edge Of Forever**
  Dream Academy
   Edge Of Seventeen (Just Like
  The White Winged Dove)
  Stevie Nicks
  R-4/81
  R-26/82
R-12/81 **Edge Of Sundown**
  Danny Joe Brown
R-26/93 **Edge Of Thorns** *Savatage*
R-17/89 **Edie (Ciao Baby)** *Cult*
R-20/91 **Edison's Medicine** *Tesla*
R-37/88 **853-5937** *Squeeze*
 R-1/82 **867-5309/Jenny** *Tommy Tutone*
R-11/89 **18 And Life** *Skid Row*
R-17/93 **Eileen** *Keith Richards*
 M-1/94 **Einstein On The Beach (For An**
  Eggman) *Counting Crows*
M-19/96 **El Scorcho** *Weezer*

Elderly Woman Behind The Counter In A Small Town *Pearl Jam*
M-17/94   R-23/94
R-21/98   M-26/98

R-22/92 **Elected** *Def Leppard*
R-12/83 **Electric Avenue** *Eddy Grant*
R-10/88 **Electric Blue** *Icehouse*
R-38/82 **Electric Eye** *Judas Priest*
R-27/95 **Electric Head (The Ecstasy)** *White Zombie*
R-38/07 **Electric Worry** *Clutch*
Electrical Storm *U2*
M-14/02   R-26/02
R-2/82 **Electricland** *Bad Company*
Elegantly Wasted *INXS*
M-13/97   R-37/97
Elevation *U2*
M-8/01   R-21/01
R-30/84 **11 O'Clock Tick Tock** *U2*
M-25/90 **Elvis Is Dead** *Living Colour*
R-5/82 **Eminence Front** *Who*
R-22/83 **Emotion** *DFX2*
R-1/86 **Emotion In Motion** *Ric Ocasek*
R-20/82 **Emotions In Motion** *Billy Squier*
Emperor's New Clothes *Sinéad O'Connor*
M-1/90   R-40/90
R-22/90 **Empire** *Queensrÿche*
R-3/92 **Empty Arms** *Stevie Ray Vaughan*
Empty Walls *Serj Tankian*
M-3/07   R-4/07
R-12/83 **Enchanted** *Stevie Nicks*
R-40/05 **End, The** *Roadrunner United*
M-35/04 **End Has No End** *Strokes*
End Is The Beginning Is The End *Smashing Pumpkins*
M-4/97   R-12/97
R-31/04 **End Of Heartache** *Killswitch Engage*
R-1/89 **End Of The Innocence** *Don Henley*
R-2/89 **End Of The Line** *Traveling Wilburys*
R-2/91 **End Of The Line** *Allman Brothers Band*
M-19/04 **End Of The World** *Cure*
R-24/01 **End Of The World** *Cold*
R-10/87 **Endless Nights** *Eddie Money*
R-41/88 **Endless Summer Nights** *Richard Marx*
R-19/85 **Endlessly** *Joe Lynn Turner*
Ends *Everlast*
M-7/99   R-13/99
Enemy *Days Of The New*
R-2/99   M-10/99
R-4/07 **Enemy, The** *Godsmack*
Enemy *Sevendust*
R-10/03   M-30/03
R-24/08 **Enemy** *Drowning Pool*
Energy, The *Audiovent*
R-9/02   M-17/02
R-19/93 **English Boy** *Pete Townshend*
R-32/88 **Englishman In New York** *Sting*
M-1/90 **Enjoy The Silence** *Depeche Mode*
M-8/91 **Enlighten Me** *Echo & The Bunnymen*
R-9/82 **Enough Is Enough** *April Wine*
R-34/99 **Enter My Mind** *Drain STH*
R-10/91 **Enter Sandman** *Metallica*
R-25/90 **Epic** *Faith No More*

Epiphany *Staind*
R-22/02   M-28/02
R-16/94 **Estranged** *Guns N' Roses*
M-25/94 **Euro-Trash Girl** *Cracker*
R-37/82 **Europa And The Pirate Twins** *Thomas Dolby*
R-54/84 **Eve Of Destruction** *Red Rockers*
Even Better Than The Real Thing *U2*
R-1/92   M-5/92
Even Flow *Pearl Jam*
R-3/92   M-21/92
R-2/83 **Even Now** *Bob Seger*
Everlasting Gaze *Smashing Pumpkins*
M-4/00   R-14/00
Everlasting Love *U2*
M-11/89   R-46/89
Everlasting Love *Howard Jones*
M-19/89   R-49/89
Everlong *Foo Fighters*
M-3/97   R-4/97
M-1/90 **Every Beat Of The Heart** *Railway Children*
R-1/83 **Every Breath You Take** *Police*
Every Day Is Exactly The Same *Nine Inch Nails*
M-1/06   R-12/06
R-25/94 **Every Day Of My Life** *Open Skyz*
M-17/88 **Every Dog Has His Day** *Let's Active*
Every Generation Got Its Own Disease *Fury In The Slaughterhouse*
M-13/94   R-21/94
R-18/86 **Every Little Kiss** *Bruce Hornsby*
R-9/90 **Every Little Thing** *Jeff Lynne*
R-32/98 **Every Little Thing Counts** *Janus Stark*
R-1/81 **Every Little Thing She Does Is Magic** *Police*
R-52/84 **Every Man Has A Woman Who Loves Him** *John Lennon*
Every Morning *Sugar Ray*
M-1/99   R-38/99
R-11/88 **Every Rose Has Its Thorn** *Poison*
R-4/85 **Every Step Of The Way** *John Waite*
R-13/92 **Every Time I Roll The Dice** *Delbert McClinton*
R-29/93 **Everybody** *Animal Bag*
R-25/86 **Everybody Have Fun Tonight** *Wang Chung*
M-21/93 **Everybody Hurts** *R.E.M.*
R-36/06 **Everybody Is Easy (We Sink/We Swim)** *Burden Brothers*
M-20/90 **Everybody Knows** *Concrete Blonde*
R-3/93 **Everybody Lay Down** *Pat Benatar*
R-34/91 **Everybody Loves Eileen** *Steelheart*
R-2/85 **Everybody Wants To Rule The World** *Tears For Fears*
R-1/82 **Everybody Wants You** *Billy Squier*
R-38/85 **Everybody's Crazy** *Michael Bolton*
M-36/04 **Everybody's Fool** *Evanescence*
R-34/83 **Everybody's My Friend** *Kansas*
Everybodys 1 *Gods Child*
R-18/94   M-25/94
R-30/05 **Everyday** *Future Leaders Of The World*

R-31/02 **Everyday** *Bon Jovi*
M-38/01 **Everyday** *Dave Matthews Band*
R-33/83 **Everyday I Write The Book** *Elvis Costello*
Everyday Is A Winding Road *Sheryl Crow*
M-17/97   R-31/97
M-22/93 **Everyday Is Like Sunday** *10,000 Maniacs*
M-14/91 **Everyday Sunshine** *Fishbone*
Everyone *Socialburn*
R-23/03   M-27/03
R-18/95 **Everyone Will Crawl** *Charlie Sexton Sextet*
Everything *Buckcherry*
R-6/07   M-23/07
R-6/92 **Everything About You** *Ugly Kid Joe*
(also see: I Hate)
Everything Changes *Staind*
R-22/06   M-32/06
M-13/89 **Everything Counts** *Depeche Mode*
R-37/99 **Everything Dies** *Type O Negative*
Everything Falls Apart *Dog's Eye View*
R-18/96   M-19/96
M-28/98 **Everything For Free** *K's Choice*
R-10/91 **(Everything I Do) I Do It For You** *Bryan Adams*
R-28/85 **Everything I Need** *Men At Work*
R-30/04 **Everything I've Known** *Korn*
M-9/93 **Everything In The World** *Squeeze*
Everything Is Broken *Bob Dylan*
R-8/89
Kenny Wayne Shepherd Band
R-10/99
Everything To Everyone *Everclear*
M-1/97   R-15/97
R-22/89 **Everything You Do (You're Sexing Me)** *Fiona w/ Kip Winger*
M-5/00 **Everything You Want** *Vertical Horizon*
Everything Zen *Bush*
M-2/95   R-5/95
M-11/07 **Everything's Magic** *Angels & Airwaves*
R-20/86 **Everytime You Cry** *Outfield*
R-14/85 **Everytime You Go Away** *Paul Young*
R-22/88 **Everywhere** *Fleetwood Mac*
R-38/86 **Everywhere I Go** *Call*
M-24/05 **Evil** *Interpol*
Evolution *Korn*
R-4/07   M-20/07
M-35/01 **Evolution Revolution Love** *Tricky*
M-2/00 **Ex-Girlfriend** *No Doubt*
R-24/06 **Ex's And Oh's** *Atreyu*
R-19/97 **Exactly What You Wanted** *Helmet*
M-17/97 **Excuse Me Mr.** *No Doubt*
R-39/81 **Expresso Love** *Dire Straits*
M-35/01 **Extra Ordinary** *Better Than Ezra*
M-8/97 **Eye** *Smashing Pumpkins*
R-11/82 **Eye In The Sky** *Alan Parsons Project*
R-1/82 **Eye Of The Tiger** *Survivor*
R-3/86 **Eye Of The Zombie** *John Fogerty*
R-29/85 **Eye On You** *Billy Squier*

R-32/00 **First Trip To The Moon** *Nixons*
M-11/92 **First We Take Manhattan** *R.E.M.*
M-3/89 **Fisherman's Blues** *Waterboys*
(Fishes In The Sea) ..see: Chorus
R-15/82 **Fits Ya Good** *Bryan Adams*
R-20/89 **500 Miles** *Hooters*
(also see: I'm Gonna Be)
M-10/89 **5 O'Clock World** *Julian Cope*
R-17/84 **5.01 AM. (The Pros and Cons of**
Hitch Hiking) *Roger Waters*
M-18/05 **Fix You** *Coldplay*
Flagpole Sitta *Harvey Danger*
M-3/98 R-33/98
M-22/02 **Flake** *Jack Johnson*
R-3/88 **Flame, The** *Cheap Trick*
R-30/82 **Flamethrower** *J. Geils Band*
R-38/95 **Flat Top** *Goo Goo Dolls*
M-33/07 **Flathead** *Fratellis*
M-5/01 **Flavor Of The Weak**
American Hi-Fi
R-8/84 **Flesh For Fantasy** *Billy Idol*
R-38/03 **Flesh Into Gear** *CKY*
R-26/83 **Flick Of The Switch** *AC/DC*
R-8/83 **Flight Of Icarus** *Iron Maiden*
R-14/97 **Flip The Switch** *Rolling Stones*
M-1/04 **Float On** *Modest Mouse*
Flood *Jars Of Clay*
M-12/96 R-16/96
Flowers ..see: (Nothing But)
M-7/91 **Flowers In The Rain** *Stress*
M-17/00 **Flowing** *311*
Fly, The *U2*
M-1/91 R-2/91
Fly *Sugar Ray*
M-1/97 R-29/97
R-11/99 **Fly** *Loudmouth*
Fly Away *Lenny Kravitz*
M-1/98 R-1/98
R-9/81 **Fly Away** *Blackfoot*
Fly From The Inside *Shinedown*
R-5/03 M-34/03
R-27/90 **Fly High Michelle** *Enuff Z'Nuff*
Fly Me Courageous
Drivin' N' Cryin'
M-15/91 R-19/91
R-15/90 **Fly To The Angels** *Slaughter*
R-19/83 **Flyer, The** *Saga*
R-2/82 **Flying High Again**
Ozzy Osbourne
R-36/81 **Flying Lip Lock** *Ted Nugent*
Flying Under Radar
Jerry Harrison
M-13/90 R-42/90
R-23/87 **Follow You** *Glen Burtnick*
Follow You Down *Gin Blossoms*
R-6/96 M-8/96
R-13/85 **Follow Your Heart** *Triumph*
M-32/04 **Followed The Waves**
Auf Der Maur
R-2/89 **Fool For Your Loving**
Whitesnake
R-42/87 **Fool In Love** *Farrenheit*
R-9/83 **Foolin'** *Def Leppard*
R-8/89 **Foolish Heart** *Grateful Dead*
R-27/83 **Fools Game** *Michael Bolton*
M-5/90 **Fools Gold** *Stone Roses*
R-2/84 **Footloose** *Kenny Loggins*
R-7/83 **For A Rocker** *Jackson Browne*
R-3/86 **For America** *Jackson Browne*
M-9/92 **For Love** *Lush*
M-28/01 **For Nancy ('Cos It Already Is)**
Pete Yorn

R-44/82 **For Openers (Welcome Home)**
Ambrosia
R-30/89 **For The Love Of Money**
BulletBoys
For The Movies *Buckcherry*
M-24/99 R-25/99
R-26/81 **For The Sake Of Survival**
Silver Condor
R-4/82 **For Those About To Rock (We**
Salute You) *AC/DC*
M-38/06 **For Us** *Pete Yorn*
For You *Staind*
R-3/02 M-3/02
R-13/90 **For You** *Outfield*
R-15/81 **For You** *Manfred Mann*
R-3/87 **Force Ten** *Rush*
R-11/90 **Forecast (Calls For Pain)**
Robert Cray Band
R-30/92 **Foreclosure Of A Dream**
Megadeth
Forever *Papa Roach*
M-2/07 R-2/07
R-17/90 **Forever** *Kiss*
Forever *Kid Rock*
R-18/01 M-21/01
R-39/83 **Forever** *Little Steven*
R-1/85 **Forever Man** *Eric Clapton*
R-13/88 **Forever Young** *Rod Stewart*
R-39/91 **Forever Young** *Tyketto*
R-36/89 **Forget About Love** *Eddie Money*
R-2/89 **Forget Me Not** *Bad English*
R-8/05 **Forget To Remember** *Mudvayne*
Forgotten Years *Midnight Oil*
M-1/90 R-11/90
R-25/02 **Forsaken** *David Draiman*
R-1/85 **Fortress Around Your Heart**
Sting
R-9/86 **Fortunate Son** *Bob Seger*
Fortune Faded
Red Hot Chili Peppers
M-8/03 R-22/03
45 *Shinedown*
R-3/04 M-12/04
R-22/97 **Forty Six & 2** *Tool*
Found Out About You
Gin Blossoms
M-1/94 R-5/94
4 AM *Our Lady Peace*
M-31/98 R-38/98
R-13/85 **Four In The Morning (I Can't**
Take Any More) *Night Ranger*
M-27/97 **Four Leaf Clover** *Abra Moore*
R-30/03 **Four Letter Word** *Def Leppard*
M-28/92 **4 Men** *Kitchens Of Distinction*
Foxy Foxy *Rob Zombie*
R-8/06 M-26/06
R-21/03 **Frantic** *Metallica*
Freak *Silverchair*
R-25/97 M-29/97
Freak Of The Week *Marvelous 3*
M-5/99 R-23/99
Freak On A Leash *Korn*
M-6/99 R-10/99
M-29/07 R-22/07 [Unplugged]
Freaking Out *Adema*
R-25/02 M-36/02
Freaks *Live*
R-5/97 M-13/97
M-34/01 **Fred Astaire**
Lucky Boys Confusion
Free *Powerman 5000*
R-10/03 M-38/03

Free *Phish*
R-11/96 M-24/96
Free *Vast*
M-12/00 R-18/00
R-12/99 **Free** *Train*
R-8/95 **Free As A Bird** *Beatles*
R-1/89 **Free Fallin'** *Tom Petty*
R-5/99 **Free Girl Now** *Tom Petty*
M-8/96 **Free To Decide** *Cranberries*
R-38/02 **Freechild** *Must*
R-39/04 **Freedom Fighters** *Music*
R-4/86 **Freedom Overspill**
Steve Winwood
R-8/82 **Freeze-Frame** *J. Geils Band*
R-30/83 **French Song** *Joan Jett*
Freshmen, The *Verve Pipe*
M-1/97 R-9/97
Friday I'm In Love *Cure*
M-1/92 R-21/92
R-29/83 **Friday Night** *Vandenberg*
R-3/89 **Friend Is A Friend**
Pete Townshend
R-12/92 **Friends** *Joe Satriani*
M-7/02 **Friends + Family** *Trik Turner*
R-33/81 **Friends Of Mr. Cairo**
Jon & Vangelis
M-7/95 **Friends Of P.** *Rentals*
R-36/97 **Fritz's Corner** *Local H*
R-46/81 **From A Whisper To A Scream**
Elvis Costello
R-28/82 **From Small Things (Big Things**
One Day Come)
Dave Edmunds
R-49/89 **From The Greenhouse**
Crack The Sky
From Yesterday
30 Seconds To Mars
M-1/07 R-11/07
M-17/98 **From Your Mouth**
God Lives Underwater
M-38/01 **F**k Authority** *Pennywise*
R-6/98 **Fuel** *Metallica*
R-42/82 **Full Bug** *Van Halen*
R-16/90 **Full Circle** *Jeff Healey Band*
Fully Alive *Flyleaf*
R-13/06 M-31/07
R-40/07 **Funeral For Yesterday** *Kittie*
M-27/93 **Funky Ceili (Bridie's Song)**
Black 47
M-12/90 **Fury Eyes** *Creatures*
M-16/89 **Future 40's (String Of Pearls)**
Syd Straw
R-14/86 **Future's So Bright, I Gotta Wear**
Shades *Timbuk 3*
M-27/05 **Futures** *Jimmy Eat World*
R-30/94 **Fuzzbox Voodoo** *ZZ Top*

G

R-40/99 **Gain** *Virgos Merlot*
Galaxie *Blind Melon*
M-8/95 R-25/95
M-10/92 **Galileo** *Indigo Girls*
R-2/94 **Gallows Pole**
Jimmy Page & Robert Plant
R-34/02 **Game, The** *Disturbed*
M-25/05 **Gangsters And Thugs**
Transplants
R-16/96 **Garden Of Allah** *Don Henley*
Gasoline *Seether*
R-8/03 M-37/03
R-26/85 **Gear Jammer** *George Thorogood*

Geek Stink Breath *Green Day*
   M-3/95 R-9/95
Gel *Collective Soul*
   R-2/95 M-14/95
R-13/81 Gemini Dream *Moody Blues*
R-28/81 Generals And Majors *XTC*
R-32/83 Genetic Engineering *Orchestral Manoeuvres In The Dark*
M-21/94 Gentleman Who Fell *Milla*
M-8/93 Gepetto *Belly*
M-13/98 Get 'Em Outta Here *Sprung Monkey*
M-24/91 Get A Gun *Connells*
R-2/93 Get A Haircut *George Thorogood*
R-34/96 Get A Job *Hog*
R-1/91 Get A Leg Up *John Mellencamp*
Get Away *Earshot*
   R-6/02 M-20/02
M-32/99 Get Back *Zebrahead*
Get Born Again *Alice In Chains*
   R-4/99 M-12/99
R-34/82 Get Closer *Linda Ronstadt*
Get Free *Vines*
   M-7/02 R-27/02
R-31/07 Get In Get Out *Cinder Road*
R-4/88 Get It On *Kingdom Come*
R-19/85 Get It On *Power Station*
M-39/03 Get Loose *D4*
Get Off This *Cracker*
   M-6/94 R-18/94
M-3/93 Get Out Of Control *Daniel Ash*
R-34/08 Get Out The Door *Velvet Revolver*
R-32/06 Get Outta My Life *Rebel Meets Rebel*
R-4/94 Get Over It *Eagles*
M-20/02 Get Over It *OK Go*
M-36/99 Get Set *Taxiride*
R-23/88 Get Started, Start A Fire *Graham Parker*
Get Stoned *Hinder*
   R-4/06 M-37/06
R-34/91 Get The Funk Out *Extreme*
M-1/91 Get The Message *Electronic*
R-33/89 Get U Ready *Saraya*
R-34/02 Get Up *Noise Therapy*
R-46/82 Get Up And Go *Go-Go's*
R-33/01 Get What You Got Comin' *Van Zant*
R-2/01 Gets Me Through *Ozzy Osbourne*
R-20/85 Gets Us All In The End *Jeff Beck*
R-46/88 Gettin' Better *Tesla*
M-4/90 Getting Away With It *Electronic*
Getting Away With Murder *Papa Roach*
   R-2/04 M-4/04
R-34/87 Gettysburg *Brandos*
M-9/93 Ghost At Number One *Jellyfish*
R-25/84 Ghost In You *Psychedelic Furs*
R-2/92 Ghost Of A Chance *Rush*
M-2/92 Ghost Of Texas Ladies' Man *Concrete Blonde*
Ghost Of Tom Joad *Rage Against The Machine*
   M-34/98 R-35/98
Ghost Of You *My Chemical Romance*
   M-9/05 R-38/05
R-8/87 Ghost On The Beach *Insiders*
R-15/81 (Ghost) Riders In The Sky *Outlaws*
R-32/88 Ghost Town *Cheap Trick*

R-38/84 Ghostbusters *Ray Parker Jr.*
R-45/81 Gi' Me Wings *Rod Stewart*
M-6/93 Gift, The *INXS*
Gift, The *Seether*
   R-8/06 M-29/06
R-2/83 Gimme All Your Lovin *ZZ Top*
R-29/98 Gimme Shelter *Rolling Stones*
R-21/90 Gimme Your Good Lovin' *Diving For Pearls*
R-40/87 Gimme Your Love *McAuley Schenker Group*
M-8/05 Girl *Beck*
M-38/02 Girl All The Bad Guys Want *Bowling For Soup*
R-9/86 Girl Can't Help It *Journey*
R-4/97 Girl I Love She Got Long Black Wavy Hair *Led Zeppelin*
R-27/94 Girl In A T-Shirt *ZZ Top*
R-17/84 Girl In Trouble (Is A Temporary Thing) *Romeo Void*
Girl Like You *Smithereens*
   R-2/89 M-3/89
M-2/92 Girl Like You *Wolfgang Press*
M-7/95 Girl Like You *Edwyn Collins*
R-26/91 Girl Money *Kix*
R-57/81 Girl Most Likely *Greg Kihn Band*
M-11/94 Girl, You'll Be A Woman Soon *Urge Overkill*
Girl's Not Grey *AFI*
   M-7/03 R-33/03
Girlfriend *Matthew Sweet*
   M-4/92 R-10/92
R-2/84 Girls *Dwight Twilley*
M-4/94 Girls & Boys *Blur*
R-20/87 Girls, Girls, Girls *Mötley Crüe*
R-16/84 Girls Just Want To Have Fun *Cyndi Lauper*
R-25/02 Girls Of Summer *Aerosmith*
R-19/83 Girls On Film *Duran Duran*
R-6/84 Girls With Guns *Tommy Shaw*
R-29/84 Give *Missing Persons*
R-5/86 Give Blood *Pete Townshend*
M-17/89 Give, Give, Give Me More, More, More *Wonder Stuff*
M-37/05 Give It All *Rise Against*
M-1/91 Give It Away *Red Hot Chili Peppers*
R-26/90 Give It To Me Good *Trixter*
Give It Up *Hothouse Flowers*
   M-2/90 R-29/90
R-2/91 Give It Up *ZZ Top*
M-32/04 Give It Up *Midtown*
M-34/05 Give It Up *Pepper*
Give Me ..see: Gimme
R-22/88 Give Me All Your Love *Whitesnake*
R-39/04 Give Me More *Apartment 26*
Give Me Wings ..see: Gi' Me Wings
R-1/87 Give To Live *Sammy Hagar*
Given To Fly *Pearl Jam*
   R-1/98 M-3/98
Given Up *Linkin Park*
   R-23/08 M-27/08
R-39/91 Givin' Yourself Away *Ratt*
Giving In *Adema*
   M-14/01 R-16/01
M-14/88 (Glad I'm) Not A Kennedy *Shona Laing*
M-13/92 Glamorous Glue *Morrissey*
R-26/89 Glamour Boys *Living Colour*
M-3/91 Globe, The *Big Audio Dynamite II*

Gloria
   Doors
   R-18/83
   Van Morrison
   R-36/93
   (also see: Accidentally 4th St.)
R-39/94 Glorified G *Pearl Jam*
R-3/85 Glory Days *Bruce Springsteen*
Glycerine *Bush*
   M-1/95 R-4/96
Go *Pearl Jam*
   R-3/93 M-8/93
R-7/85 Go *Asia*
R-32/92 Go Back To Your Woods *Robbie Robertson*
R-24/99 Go Faster *Black Crowes*
R-12/85 Go For Soda *Kim Mitchell*
R-4/84 Go Insane *Lindsey Buckingham*
M-14/00 Go Let It Out *Oasis*
M-32/03 Go To Sleep *Radiohead*
M-32/96 Go Walking Down There *Chris Isaak*
Go With The Flow *Queens Of The Stone Age*
   M-7/03 R-24/03
M-1/94 God *Tori Amos*
God *U2*
   R-8/89 M-28/89
R-24/01 God Gave Me Everything *Mick Jagger*
R-21/91 God Gave Rock And Roll To You II *Kiss*
God Is A Bullet *Concrete Blonde*
   M-15/89 R-49/89
M-15/90 God Tonight *Real Life*
R-6/00 Godless *U.P.O.*
R-12/86 Goin' Crazy! *David Lee Roth*
M-8/89 Goin' Southbound *Stan Ridgway*
R-35/06 Going In Blind *P.O.D.*
M-28/98 Going Out Of My Head *Fatboy Slim*
M-33/95 Going South *Wolfgang Press*
R-5/82 Going To A Go-Go *Rolling Stones*
Going Under *Evanescence*
   M-5/03 R-26/03
R-49/88 Gold *Pete Bardens*
M-31/96 Gold Dust Woman *Hole*
M-14/06 Gold Lion *Yeah Yeah Yeahs*
R-16/87 Golden Ball And Chain *Jason & The Scorchers*
M-17/90 Golden Blunders *Posies*
R-55/81 Golden Down *Willie Nile*
M-40/06 Gone *Pearl Jam*
Gone Away *Offspring*
   R-1/97 M-4/97
R-28/02 Gone Away *Cold*
M-26/06 Gone Daddy Gone *Gnarls Barkley*
R-24/94 Gone Dead Train *George Thorogood*
M-23/91 Gone, Gone, Gone *Echo & The Bunnymen*
   (also see: My Girl)
R-31/84 Gone Too Far *Dan Fogelberg*
Good *Better Than Ezra*
   M-1/95 R-3/95
R-1/90 Good Clean Fun *Allman Brothers Band*
M-16/94 Good Enough *Sarah McLachlan*
R-3/96 Good Friday *Black Crowes*
R-28/85 Good Friends *Joni Mitchell*

R-19/87 **Hard Times In The Land Of Plenty** *Omar & The Howlers*
M-34/06 **Hard To Beat** *Hard-Fi*
M-27/02 **Hard To Explain** *Strokes*
M-10/93 **Hard To Get** *Starclub*
R-1/90 **Hard To Handle** *Black Crowes*
R-14/81 **Hard To Say** *Dan Fogelberg*
R-1/81 **Harden My Heart** *Quarterflash*
R-33/82 **Harder Than Diamond** *Chubby Checker*
M-31/03 **Harder To Breathe** *Maroon 5*
M-8/03 **Hardest Button To Button** *White Stripes*
R-2/86 **Harlem Shuffle** *Rolling Stones*
Hash Pipe *Weezer*
M-2/01 R-24/01
M-25/06 **Hate (I Really Don't Like You)** *Plain White T's*
Hate Me *Blue October*
M-2/06 R-21/06
R-1/88 **Hate To Lose Your Lovin'** *Little Feat*
Hate To Say I Told You So *Hives*
M-6/02 R-35/02
R-19/93 **Hatred (A Duet)** *Kinks*
R-18/90 **Haunted Heart** *Alias*
Haunting Me *Stabbing Westward*
R-19/99 M-34/99
R-38/05 **Have A Nice Day** *Bon Jovi*
R-17/87 **Have Mercy** *Richard Marx*
R-7/92 **Have You Ever Needed Someone So Bad** *Def Leppard*
R-7/97 **Have You Seen Mary** *Sponge*
Have You Seen Me Lately? *Counting Crows*
R-34/97 M-34/97
M-6/92 **Haven't Got A Clue** *Dramarama*
M-11/93 **Hayfever** *Trash Can Sinatras*
R-41/87 **Hazy Shade Of Winter** *Bangles*
R-34/82 **He Could Be The One** *Josie Cotton*
R-21/83 **He Knows, You Know** *Marillion*
M-17/89 **He's Got A She** *Exene Cervenka*
R-46/82 **He's So Strange** *Go-Go's*
M-10/99 **Head** *Tin Star*
M-28/90 **Head Like A Hole** *Nine Inch Nails*
Head On *Jesus & Mary Chain*
M-2/90 R-45/90
M-6/92 **Head On** *Pixies*
M-28/02 **Head On Collision** *New Found Glory*
M-25/96 **Head Over Feet** *Alanis Morissette*
R-7/85 **Head Over Heels** *Tears For Fears*
R-33/84 **Head Over Heels** *Go-Go's*
M-10/94 **Headache** *Frank Black*
R-8/89 **Headed For A Heartbreak** *Winger*
R-35/94 **Headed For Destruction** *Jackyl*
Headful Of Ghosts *Bush*
R-34/01 M-38/02
R-7/89 **Heading For The Light** *Traveling Wilburys*
R-10/81 **Heading Out To The Highway** *Judas Priest*
R-27/86 **Headlines** *John Fogerty*
R-3/91 **Headlong** *Queen*
R-26/01 **Heads Explode** *Monster Magnet*
Headstrong *Trapt*
R-1/03 M-1/03
M-16/93 **Heal It Up** *Concrete Blonde*
R-23/89 **Healing Hands** *Elton John*
R-1/83 **Heart And Soul** *Huey Lewis*

Heart Full Of Black *Burning Brides*
M-32/04 R-38/04
M-21/06 **Heart In A Cage** *Strokes*
R-17/81 **Heart Like A Wheel** *Steve Miller Band*
M-17/90 **Heart Like A Wheel** *Human League*
R-20/93 **Heart Of An Angel** *Jeff Healey Band*
R-5/84 **Heart Of Rock & Roll** *Huey Lewis*
Heart Of Soul *Cult*
M-21/91 R-41/92
R-28/88 **Heart Of Steel** *Will & The Kill*
R-2/90 **Heart Of The Matter** *Don Henley*
Heart-Shaped Box *Nirvana*
M-1/93 R-4/93
Heart Shaped Glasses (When The Heart Guides The Hand) *Marilyn Manson*
M-24/07 R-31/07
R-7/88 **Heart Turns To Stone** *Foreigner*
R-30/86 **Heart's On Fire** *38 Special*
R-47/87 **Heartache** *Lou Gramm*
R-26/86 **Heartbeat** *Don Johnson*
R-57/82 **Heartbeat** *King Crimson*
R-11/87 **Heartbreak Beat** *Psychedelic Furs*
R-46/92 **Heartbreak Blvd** *Shotgun Messiah*
R-10/91 **Heartbreak Station** *Cinderella*
R-40/85 **Heartline** *Robin George*
R-20/81 **Hearts** *Marty Balin*
R-24/90 **Hearts Are Gonna Roll** *Johnny Van Zant*
M-20/95 **Hearts Filthy Lesson** *David Bowie*
R-3/87 **Hearts On Fire** *Bryan Adams*
R-14/81 **Hearts On Fire** *Randy Meisner*
R-22/89 **Hearts On Fire** *Steve Winwood*
Heartspark Dollarsign *Everclear*
M-13/96 R-29/96
R-40/84 **Heat, The** *Heart*
R-5/83 **Heat Goes On** *Asia*
R-4/85 **Heat Is On** *Glenn Frey*
R-1/82 **Heat Of The Moment** *Asia*
R-2/87 **Heat Of The Night** *Bryan Adams*
R-20/88 **Heatseeker** *AC/DC*
R-3/89 **Heaven** *Warrant*
Heaven *Bryan Adams*
R-9/84
R-27/85
Heaven *Live*
M-33/03 R-33/03
Heaven & Hot Rods *Stone Temple Pilots*
R-17/00 M-30/00
Heaven Beside You *Alice In Chains*
R-3/96 M-6/96
R-16/91 **Heaven Help The Lonely** *Willie Nile*
(Heaven Helps The Man) ..see: I'm Free
M-18/91 **Heaven (I Want You)** *Camouflage*
R-6/91 **Heaven In The Back Seat** *Eddie Money*
R-12/90 **Heaven Is A 4 Letter Word** *Bad English*
M-18/00 **Heaven Is A Halfpipe (If I Die)** *OPM*
R-1/88 **Heaven Knows** *Robert Plant*
R-21/84 **Heaven (Must Be There)** *Eurogliders*

M-9/91 **Heaven Or Las Vegas** *Cocteau Twins*
Heaven Sent *INXS*
M-2/92 R-4/92
R-19/88 **Heaven Tonight** *Yngwie J. Malmsteen*
Heaven's In Here *Tin Machine*
M-12/89 R-47/89
R-11/84 **Heaven's On Fire** *Kiss*
R-13/89 **Heaven's Trail (No Way Out)** *Tesla*
M-17/90 **Heavenly Pop Hit** *Chills*
Heavy *Collective Soul*
R-1/99 M-5/99
Heavy Fuel *Dire Straits*
R-1/91 M-22/91
R-23/83 **Heavy Metal Love** *Helix*
R-5/81 **Heavy Metal (Takin' A Ride)** *Don Felder*
M-17/90 **Heavy Weather Traffic** *Katydids*
Heel Over Head *Puddle Of Mudd*
R-6/04 M-10/04
M-11/07 **Heinrich Maneuver** *Interpol*
M-11/05 **Helena (So Long & Goodnight)** *My Chemical Romance*
M-13/97 **Hell** *Squirrel Nut Zippers*
R-30/07 **Hell And High Water** *Black Stone Cherry*
R-3/87 **Hell In A Bucket** *Grateful Dead*
R-13/00 **Hell On High Heels** *Mötley Crüe*
M-13/03 **Hell Song** *Sum 41*
M-6/90 **Hello** *Beloved*
M-13/97 **Hello** *Poe*
R-22/84 **Hello Again** *Cars*
M-8/92 **Hello Cruel World** *E*
R-25/96 **Hello From Venus** *Screamin' Cheetah Wheelies*
Hello Hello *Talk Show*
R-10/97 M-16/97
M-14/90 **Hello, Hello, Hello, Hello, Hello, (Petrol)** *Something Happens*
M-6/90 **Hello I Love You** *Cure*
R-15/91 **Hello Little Girl** *George Thorogood*
R-30/05 **Hello Lonely (Walk Away From This)** *Theory Of A Deadman*
M-34/01 **Hello Time Bomb** *Matthew Good Band*
R-50/81 **Hells Bells** *AC/DC*
R-6/92 **Help Me Up** *Eric Clapton*
M-5/92 **Helpless** *Sugar*
R-21/91 **Helter Skelter** *Aerosmith*
Hemorrhage (In My Hands) *Fuel*
M-1/00 R-2/00
R-21/81 **Her Town Too** *James Taylor & J.D. Souther*
R-1/95 **Here & Now** *Letters To Cleo*
R-10/94 **Here Comes A Man** *Traffic*
R-40/82 **Here Comes The Feeling** *Asia*
R-8/84 **Here Comes The Rain Again** *Eurythmics*
R-50/88 **Here Comes The Weekend** *Moody Blues*
R-28/93 **Here Comes Trouble** *Bad Company*
M-3/89 **Here Comes Your Man** *Pixies*
M-39/04 **Here I Am** *Explosion*
M-6/90 **Here I Am (Come And Take Me)** *UB40*
R-4/87 **Here I Go Again** *Whitesnake*
M-5/96 **Here In Your Bedroom** *Goldfinger*
Here Is Gone *Goo Goo Dolls*
M-21/02 R-29/02

R-53/81 **Here It Comes Again** *Ian Gomm*
M-17/06 **Here It Goes Again** *OK Go*
Here To Stay *Korn*
M-4/02 R-4/02
R-46/82 **Here Today** *Paul McCartney*
M-20/94 **Here We Go** *Stakka Bo*
Here Without You *3 Doors Down*
R-14/03 M-22/03
M-33/01 **Here's To The Night** *Eve 6*
M-1/90 **Here's Where The Story Ends**
Sundays
Hero *Chad Kroeger*
M-1/02 R-1/02
Hero *Verve Pipe*
M-17/99 R-38/99
R-1/96 **Hero Of The Day** *Metallica*
R-59/84 **Hero Takes A Fall** *Bangles*
R-31/83 **Hero's Return** *Pink Floyd*
Heroes *Wallflowers*
R-4/98 M-9/98
Heroes *Shinedown*
R-4/06 M-28/06
M-34/95 **Heroin Girl** *Everclear*
M-23/94 **Hey!** *Boingo*
R-6/89 **Hey Baby** *Henry Lee Summer*
M-25/97 **Hey Dude** *Kula Shaker*
R-15/99 **Hey, Hey** *Bad Company*
R-15/95 **Hey Hey What Can I Do**
Hootie & The Blowfish
R-4/93 **Hey Jealousy** *Gin Blossoms*
R-41/90 **Hey Jude** *Paul McCartney*
M-18/89 **Hey Ladies** *Beastie Boys*
R-31/82 **Hey' Little Girl** *Icehouse*
Hey Man Nice Shot *Filter*
M-10/95 R-19/95
M-29/89 **Hey Matthew** *Karel Fialka*
Hey Mister *Custom*
M-20/02 R-28/02
R-8/04 **Hey Now** *Tantric*
M-13/01 **Hey Pretty** *Poe*
R-13/91 **Hey Stoopid** *Alice Cooper*
M-13/92 **Hey That's No Way To Say
Goodbye** *Ian McCulloch*
M-3/07 **Hey There Delilah** *Plain White T's*
M-9/90 **Hey Venus** *That Petrol Emotion*
M-16/03 **Hey Ya!** *OutKast*
R-37/90 **Hey You** *Paul Carrack*
R-22/89 **Hide Your Heart** *Kiss*
High *Cure*
M-1/92 R-42/92
R-20/97 **High** *Jimmie's Chicken Shack*
High *Feeder*
M-24/98 R-36/98
M-18/96 **High And Dry** *Radiohead*
R-39/82 **High And The Mighty** *Donnie Iris*
R-2/90 **High Enough** *Damn Yankees*
R-8/95 **High Head Blues** *Black Crowes*
R-4/94 **High Hopes** *Sammy Hagar*
R-7/94 **High Hopes** *Pink Floyd*
R-31/90 **High Landrons** *Eric Johnson*
R-3/84 **High On Emotion** *Chris DeBurgh*
R-8/85 **High On You** *Survivor*
R-6/94 **High Road Easy** *Sass Jordan*
M-13/88 **High Time** *Icicle Works*
R-23/83 **High Wire** *Men At Work*
Highwire *Rolling Stones*
R-1/91 M-28/91
Higher *Creed*
M-1/99 R-1/99
Higher Ground
Red Hot Chili Peppers
M-11/89 R-26/90

M-14/93 **Higher Ground** *UB40*
R-1/86 **Higher Love** *Steve Winwood*
R-12/95 **Higher Place** *Tom Petty*
R-29/92 **Highway To Hell** *AC/DC*
R-1/86 **Hip To Be Square** *Huey Lewis*
R-26/95 **Hip Today** *Extreme*
R-13/88 **Hippy Hippy Shake**
Georgia Satellites
M-11/90 **Hippychick** *Soho*
R-33/81 **History Never Repeats** *Split Enz*
M-39/98 **History Of A Boring Town**
Less Than Jake
M-1/92 **Hit** *Sugarcubes*
R-24/92 **Hit Between The Eyes** *Scorpions*
M-15/01 **Hit Or Miss** *New Found Glory*
Hit That *Offspring*
M-1/04 R-6/04
R-28/97 **Hit The Ground Running**
Jonny Lang
Hitchin' A Ride *Green Day*
M-5/97 R-9/97
R-39/85 **Hits Of The Year** *Squeeze*
R-53/81 **Hitsville U.K.** *Clash*
M-24/94 **Hobo Humpin Slobo Babe**
Whale
R-5/93 **Hocus Pocus** *Gary Hoey*
M-18/90 **Hold A Candle To This**
Pretenders
R-3/82 **Hold Me** *Fleetwood Mac*
R-41/87 **Hold Me** *Colin James Hay*
R-5/02 **Hold Me Down** *Tommy Lee*
R-9/84 **Hold Me Now** *Thompson Twins*
**Hold Me, Thrill Me, Kiss Me, Kill
Me** *U2*
M-1/95 R-1/95
R-4/94 **Hold My Hand**
Hootie & The Blowfish
Hold On *Korn*
R-9/08 M-35/08
R-17/82 **Hold On** *Santana*
Hold On *Yes*
R-43/84
R-27/85
M-29/95 **Hold On** *Sarah McLachlan*
R-42/81 **Hold On** *Badfinger*
R-3/81 **Hold On Loosely** *38 Special*
R-50/87 **Hold On (Never Give Up, Never
Give In)**
John Kay & Steppenwolf
R-2/81 **Hold On Tight** *ELO*
R-50/84 **Hold On To 18** *Black 'n Blue*
M-39/04 **Hold On To Me** *Courtney Love*
R-2/88 **Holding On** *Steve Winwood*
M-22/89 **Holding On To The Earth**
Sam Phillips
R-27/89 **Holding On To You**
Peter Frampton
R-2/91 **Hole Hearted** *Extreme*
R-4/97 **Hole In My Soul** *Aerosmith*
R-55/82 **Hole In Paradise** *Prism*
Hole In The Earth *Deftones*
M-18/06 R-19/06
Holiday *Green Day*
M-1/05 R-1/05
Hollow, The *Perfect Circle*
R-14/01 M-17/01
R-19/05 **Hollow** *Submersed*
R-35/03 **Hollow Again** *Project 86*
Hollywood Bitch
Stone Temple Pilots
R-25/01 M-29/01
R-24/82 **Hollywood (Down On Your Luck)**
Thin Lizzy

Holy Diver
Dio
R-40/83
Killswitch Engage
R-12/07
R-39/00 **Holy Man** *One Minute Silence*
R-25/87 **Holy War** *Jon Butcher*
R-1/90 **Holy Water** *Bad Company*
Home *Three Days Grace*
R-2/05 M-7/05
Home *Iggy Pop*
M-2/90 R-46/90
Home *Staind*
R-11/00 M-17/00
R-35/98 **Home** *Econoline Crush*
R-24/84 **Home By The Sea** *Genesis*
R-45/91 **Home For Better Days** *Dillinger*
Home Sweet Home *Mötley Crüe*
R-38/85
R-41/92 ['91]
R-39/05
R-16/07 **Homecoming Queen** *Hinder*
M-12/05 **Honest Mistake** *Bravery*
R-20/93 **Honest To God** *Brad Gillis*
Honestly *Zwan*
M-7/03 R-21/03
M-6/92 **Honeydrip** *Ian McCulloch*
M-29/96 **Honky's Ladder** *Afghan Whigs*
M-12/98 **Hooch** *Everything*
Hook *Blues Traveler*
M-13/95 R-15/95
R-49/89 **Hooks In You** *Marillion*
R-10/94 **Hooligan's Holiday** *Mötley Crüe*
R-13/97 **Hope In A Hopeless World**
Widespread Panic
(Hopelessly In Love) ..see: Party's
Over
M-31/03 **Horizon Has Been Defeated**
Jack Johnson
R-44/83 **Horizontal Departure**
Robert Plant
M-23/92 **Horror Head** *Curve*
R-45/92 **Hot And Bothered** *Cinderella*
Hot Cherie
Danny Spanos
R-15/83
Hardline
R-25/92
R-24/84 **Hot For Teacher** *Van Halen*
R-2/83 **Hot Girls In Love** *Loverboy*
R-31/82 **Hot In The City** *Billy Idol*
R-31/87 **Hot Love** *Twisted Sister*
R-1/92 **Hotel Illness** *Black Crowes*
R-22/87 **Hourglass** *Squeeze*
M-1/90 **House** *Psychedelic Furs*
R-29/82 **House Behind A House**
Bob Seger
R-18/90 **House Is Rockin'**
Stevie Ray Vaughan
R-7/90 **House Of Broken Love**
Great White
M-38/07 **House Of Cards** *Madina Lake*
R-33/04 **House Of Doom**
Black Label Society
R-39/90 **House Of Fire** *Alice Cooper*
R-23/90 **House Of Pain** *Faster Pussycat*
R-14/88 **House We Used To Live In**
Smithereens
R-1/92 **How About That** *Bad Company*
How About You *Staind*
R-10/04 M-10/04
R-8/90 **How Bad Do You Want It?**
Don Henley

R-46/82 **I Have The Touch** *Peter Gabriel*
R-4/87 **(I Just) Died In Your Arms**
Cutting Crew
M-25/04 **I Just Don't Know What To Do With Myself** *White Stripes*
R-34/92 **I Just Wanna** *Kiss*
M-14/91 **(I Just Wanna) B With U**
Transvision Vamp
R-24/96 **I Just Want You** *Ozzy Osbourne*
M-20/95 **I Kissed A Girl** *Jill Sobule*
R-27/85 **I Knew The Bride (When She Use To Rock And Roll)** *Nick Lowe*
R-17/83 **I Know There's Something Going On** *Frida*
R-23/82 **I Know What Boys Like**
Waitresses
R-25/86 **I Know What I Like** *Huey Lewis*
R-2/88 **I Know You're Out There Somewhere** *Moody Blues*
R-1/98 **I Lie In The Bed I Make**
Brother Cane
I Love It Loud
Kiss
R-22/93
Phunk Junkeez
M-38/95
R-1/82 **I Love Rock 'N Roll** *Joan Jett*
R-13/88 **I Love The Things You Do To Me**
Balaam & The Angel
R-36/85 **I Love You Like A Ball And Chain** *Eurythmics*
R-5/92 **I Love You Period.** *Dan Baird*
R-28/84 **I Love You, Suzanne** *Lou Reed*
R-7/83 **I Melt With You** *Modern English*
M-27/01 **I Might Be Wrong** *Radiohead*
R-17/87 **I Might Lie** *Andy Taylor*
M-1/04 **I Miss You** *Blink-182*
R-8/81 **I Missed Again** *Phil Collins*
I Missed You ..see: (Stay)
R-28/86 **I Must Be Dreaming** *Giuffria*
R-32/88 **I Need A Man** *Eurythmics*
R-22/82 **I Need You** *Paul Carrack*
R-22/84 **I Need You Tonight** *Peter Wolf*
R-4/94 **I Need Your Love** *Boston*
R-47/81 **I Need Your Love** *Ian Hunter*
M-34/05 **I Predict A Riot** *Kaiser Chiefs*
R-3/82 **I Ran (So Far Away)**
Flock Of Seagulls
R-23/90 **I Remember You** *Skid Row*
R-30/90 **I Said A Prayer** *Red House*
R-14/91 **I Saw Red** *Warrant*
M-24/95 **I Saw The Light** *The*
M-11/88 **I Say Nothing**
Voice Of The Beehive
R-41/84 **I Send A Message** *INXS*
M-16/93 **I Should've Known** *Aimee Mann*
I Stand Alone *Godsmack*
R-1/02 M-20/02
R-32/92 **I Stand Alone** *Jackyl*
R-10/94 **I Stay Away** *Alice In Chains*
R-17/86 **I Still Believe (Great Design)** *Call*
R-2/87 **I Still Haven't Found What I'm Looking For** *U2*
M-24/07 **I Still Remember** *Bloc Party*
R-33/86 **I Still Want You** *Del Fuegos*
R-19/81 **I Surrender** *Rainbow*
R-5/90 **I Think I Love You Too Much**
Jeff Healey Band
M-6/98 **I Think I'm Paranoid** *Garbage*
R-15/88 **I Think She Likes Me**
Treat Her Right
R-36/83 **I Think You'll Remember Tonight**
Axe

I Touch Myself *Divinyls*
M-2/91 R-35/91
I Walk Alone *Oleander*
R-24/99 M-37/99
R-28/95 **I Walked** *Wanderlust*
M-13/91 **I Wanna Be A Boss**
Stan Ridgway
M-18/90 **I Wanna Be Adored** *Stone Roses*
R-43/89 **I Wanna Be Loved**
House Of Lords
R-33/98 **I Wanna Be With You**
Bruce Springsteen
R-25/08 **I Wanna Be Your Man**
EndEverAfter
R-3/87 **I Wanna Go Back** *Eddie Money*
R-35/84 **I Wanna Rock** *Twisted Sister*
R-7/83 **I Want A New Drug** *Huey Lewis*
R-22/82 **I Want Candy** *Bow Wow Wow*
R-3/89 **I Want It All** *Queen*
M-30/94 **I Want It All** *Eve's Plum*
M-12/91 **I Want More** *Dave Wakeling*
M-2/89 **I Want That Man** *Deborah Harry*
M-26/97 **I Want To Be There (When You Come)** *Echo & The Bunnymen*
R-22/96 **I Want To Come Over**
Melissa Etheridge
R-1/85 **I Want To Know What Love Is**
Foreigner
R-23/01 **I Want To Live** *Spacehog*
R-1/86 **I Want To Make The World Turn Around** *Steve Miller Band*
M-20/92 **I Want To Touch You**
Catherine Wheel
R-22/91 **I Want You** *Shadow King*
(also see: Heaven)
I Was Wrong *Social Distortion*
M-4/96 R-12/96
M-21/92 **I Wasn't Made To Feel This/Asleep At The Wheel**
Suicidal Tendencies
(I Will) ..see: Download
R-21/87 **I Will Be There** *Glass Tiger*
I Will Buy You A New Life
Everclear
M-3/98 R-20/98
R-20/81 **I Will Follow** *U2*
M-28/06 **I Will Follow You Into The Dark**
Death Cab For Cutie
R-2/89 **I Will Not Go Quietly** *Don Henley*
R-35/83 **I Will Run To You**
Stevie Nicks w/ Tom Petty
I Will Still Be Laughing
Soul Asylum
R-23/98 M-24/98
M-28/97 **I Will Survive** *Cake*
R-1/88 **I Wish I Had A Girl**
Henry Lee Summer
R-5/90 **I Wish It Would Rain Down**
Phil Collins
I Won't Back Down *Tom Petty*
R-1/89 M-29/89
R-8/83 **I Won't Be Home Tonight**
Tony Carey
R-31/88 **I Won't Be Your Fool** *Rocky Hill*
R-49/91 **I Would Have Waited Forever**
Yes
R-38/90 **I Would Love To** *Steve Vai*
M-12/06 **I Write Sins Not Tragedies**
Panic At The Disco
R-10/93 **I'd Do Anything For Love (But I Won't Do That)** *Meat Loaf*
R-42/85 **I'd Lie To You For Your Love**
Danny Spanos
R-26/87 **I'll Be Alright Without You**
Journey

M-15/01 **I'll Be Here Awhile** *311*
R-5/89 **I'll Be There For You** *Bon Jovi*
M-23/95 **I'll Be There For You** *Rembrandts*
I'll Be You *Replacements*
M-1/89 R-1/89
M-24/91 **I'll Be Your Baby Tonight**
Robert Palmer
M-1/90 **I'll Be Your Chauffeur** *David J*
R-16/82 **I'll Drink To You** *Duke Jupiter*
R-2/82 **I'll Fall In Love Again**
Sammy Hagar
R-42/91 **I'll Fight For You** *Foreigner*
R-34/93 **I'll Hate You Better**
Suicidal Tendencies
R-58/84 **I'll Keep Holding On** *Jim Capaldi*
R-24/91 **I'll Never Let You Go (Angel Eyes)** *Steelheart*
R-7/90 **I'll See You In My Dreams** *Giant*
R-29/93 **I'll Sleep When I'm Dead**
Bon Jovi
M-21/94 **I'll Stand By You** *Pretenders*
I'll Stick Around *Foo Fighters*
M-8/95 R-12/95
M-6/94 **I'll Take You There**
General Public
R-2/84 **I'll Wait** *Van Halen*
R-13/89 **I'm A Believer** *Giant*
R-16/85 **I'm A Fighter** *Van-Zant*
R-42/81 **I'm A Rocker** *Bruce Springsteen*
R-18/92 **I'm A Steady Rollin' Man**
George Thorogood
M-29/98 **I'm Afraid Of Americans**
David Bowie
R-18/93 **I'm Alive** *Jackson Browne*
I'm An Adult Now
Pursuit Of Happiness
R-22/88 M-6/89
R-37/03 **I'm Dead** *Leisureworld*
M-2/90 **I'm Free** *Soup Dragons*
R-42/84 **I'm Free (Heaven Helps The Man)**
Kenny Loggins
R-9/85 **I'm Goin' Down**
Bruce Springsteen
I'm Gonna Be (500 Miles)
Proclaimers
M-21/89
M-8/93
R-39/82 **I'm Leaving** *Taxxi*
R-56/84 **I'm Leaving You** *Scorpions*
R-54/81 **I'm Losing You** *John Lennon*
R-25/84 **I'm Moving On** *Eddie Money*
R-1/87 **I'm No Angel** *Gregg Allman Band*
I'm Not Jesus
Apocalyptica w/ Corey Taylor
M-21/08 R-11/08
M-4/05 **I'm Not Okay (I Promise)**
My Chemical Romance
R-37/99 **I'm Not Running Anymore**
John Mellencamp
I'm Not Scared *Raindogs*
M-23/90 R-44/90
R-29/86 **I'm Not The One** *Cars*
R-1/88 **I'm Not Your Man**
Tommy Conwell
R-4/85 **I'm On Fire** *Bruce Springsteen*
R-33/88 **I'm On To You** *Hurricane*
R-26/83 **I'm Ready** *Bryan Adams*
R-15/90 **I'm Seventeen** *Tommy Conwell*
I'm So Sick *Flyleaf*
R-12/06 M-27/06
I'm Sorry *Hothouse Flowers*
M-12/88 R-23/89
(also see: so. Central Rain)
R-34/84 **I'm Stepping Out** *John Lennon*

R-8/97 **Jungle** *Kiss*
R-17/86 **Jungle Boy** *John Eddie*
R-35/94 **Junior** *John Mellencamp*
M-37/95 **Just** *Radiohead*
R-25/85 **Just A Gigolo/I Ain't Got Nobody**
    David Lee Roth
M-10/96 **Just A Girl** *No Doubt*
R-10/83 **Just A Job To Do** *Genesis*
R-41/90 **Just A Little Light** *Grateful Dead*
R-33/92 **Just A Loser** *Robert Cray Band*
R-13/97 **Just Another Day**
    John Mellencamp
R-1/85 **Just Another Night** *Mick Jagger*
Just Because *Jane's Addiction*
    M-1/03 R-4/03
R-4/89 **Just Between You And Me**
    Lou Gramm
R-11/81 **Just Between You And Me**
    April Wine
R-7/90 **Just Came Back** *Colin James*
R-37/05 **Just Feel Better**
    Santana w/ Steven Tyler
R-24/99 **Just Go** *Staind*
R-27/85 **Just Got Lucky** *Dokken*
R-25/00 **Just Got Wicked** *Cold*
Just Like Anyone *Soul Asylum*
    R-11/95 M-19/95
R-15/81 **Just Like Me** *Pat Benatar*
R-1/88 **Just Like Paradise**
    David Lee Roth
Just Like You *Three Days Grace*
    R-1/04 M-1/04
R-47/87 **Just Like You** *Martha Davis*
M-1/88 **Just Play Music!**
    Big Audio Dynamite
R-10/01 **Just Push Play** *Aerosmith*
Just Stop *Disturbed*
    R-4/06 M-24/06
R-18/92 **Just Take My Heart** *Mr. Big*
R-13/91 **Just The Way It Is, Baby**
    Rembrandts
R-16/89 **Just Wanna Hold** *Mick Jones*
R-28/86 **Justice And Independence '85**
    John Cougar Mellencamp
M-21/92 **Justified & Ancient**
    KLF w/ Tammy Wynette

K

R-47/88 **Karla With A K** *Hooters*
Karma *Diffuser*
    R-20/01 M-26/01
M-14/98 **Karma Police** *Radiohead*
R-14/85 **Kayleigh** *Marillion*
Keep Away *Godsmack*
    R-5/99 M-31/99
R-14/83 **(Keep Feeling) Fascination**
    Human League
M-15/02 **Keep Fishin'** *Weezer*
R-46/82 **Keep Me Satisfied** *Billy Squier*
R-21/90 **Keep On Loving Me Baby**
    Colin James
R-9/81 **Keep On Loving You**
    REO Speedwagon
R-1/94 **Keep Talking** *Pink Floyd*
M-32/07 **Keep The Car Running**
    Arcade Fire
R-1/92 **Keep The Faith** *Bon Jovi*
R-2/82 **Keep The Fire Burnin'**
    REO Speedwagon
R-39/82 **Keep This Heart In Mind**
    Bonnie Raitt

R-2/86 **Keep Your Hands To Yourself**
    Georgia Satellites
R-23/82 **Keeping Our Love Alive**
    Henry Paul Band
R-10/91 **Keeping The Faith**
    Lynyrd Skynyrd
R-34/82 **Key, The** *REO Speedwagon*
R-10/96 **Key West Intermezzo (I Saw You**
    First) *John Mellencamp*
R-33/88 **Kick** *INXS*
M-22/95 **Kick Him When He's Down**
    Offspring
M-36/01 **Kick Some Ass** *Stroke 9*
R-32/87 **Kick The Wall**
    Jimmy Davis & Junction
R-3/98 **Kicking My Heart Around**
    Black Crowes
R-18/89 **Kickstart My Heart** *Mötley Crüe*
R-39/89 **Kid Ego** *Extreme*
R-42/81 **Kid Is Hot Tonite** *Loverboy*
Kids Aren't Alright *Offspring*
    M-6/99 R-11/99
R-29/82 **Kids In America** *Kim Wilde*
R-42/85 **Kids Wanna Rock** *Bryan Adams*
Kill (Bury Me)
    30 Seconds To Mars
    M-3/06 R-14/06
R-38/06 **Kill Rock 'N' Roll**
    System Of A Down
R-21/00 **Kill The King** *Megadeth*
R-39/02 **Kill The Sunshine** *Jackyl*
R-23/84 **Killer** *Pat Travers*
R-28/05 **Killin' Me** *Drowning Pool*
M-2/88 **Killing Jar**
    Siouxsie & The Banshees
R-13/01 **Killing The Fly**
    Union Underground
M-20/94 **Kim The Waitress** *Material Issue*
M-32/98 **Kind & Generous**
    Natalie Merchant
R-37/86 **Kind Words** *Joan Armatrading*
King For A Day *XTC*
    M-11/89 R-38/89
R-35/86 **King For A Day** *Thompson Twins*
M-19/90 **King Is Half-Undressed** *Jellyfish*
R-6/97 **King Nothing** *Metallica*
R-27/06 **King Of All Excuses** *Staind*
R-6/90 **King Of Dreams** *Deep Purple*
King Of Emotion *Big Country*
    M-11/88 R-20/88
King Of New Orleans
    Better Than Ezra
    M-5/96 R-7/96
R-38/93 **King Of Nothing**
    Ghost Of An American Airman
R-1/83 **King Of Pain** *Police*
R-2/91 **King Of The Hill** *Roger McGuinn*
King Of The Mountain
    Midnight Oil
    M-3/90 R-20/90
R-24/07 **King Of The Stereo** *Saliva*
M-7/06 **King Without A Crown**
    Matisyahu
M-16/89 **Kingdom Of Rain** *The*
R-4/92 **Kings Highway** *Tom Petty*
M-1/91 **Kinky Afro** *Happy Mondays*
M-14/88 **Kiss** *Art Of Noise w/ Tom Jones*
R-40/88 **Kiss And Tell** *Bryan Ferry*
M-35/95 **Kiss From A Rose** *Seal*
Kiss Him Goodbye ..see: Na Na
    Hey Hey
M-12/90 **Kiss It Better** *Deborah Harry*
R-40/88 **Kiss Me Deadly** *Lita Ford*

R-16/91 **Kiss My Love Goodbye**
    L.A. Guns
R-34/82 **Kiss Of Life** *Peter Gabriel*
R-54/81 **Kiss On My List**
    Daryl Hall & John Oates
Kiss That Frog *Peter Gabriel*
    R-18/93 M-18/93
R-24/86 **Kiss The Dirt (Falling Down The**
    Mountain) *INXS*
M-1/91 **Kiss Them For Me**
    Siouxsie & The Banshees
Kiss This Thing Goodbye
    Del Amitri
    M-13/90 R-17/90
R-6/89 **Kissing Willie** *Jethro Tull*
M-4/94 **Kite** *Nick Heyward*
M-13/95 **Kitty** *Presidents Of The United*
    States Of America
R-13/86 **Knife Feels Like Justice**
    Brian Setzer
M-10/06 **Knights Of Cydonia** *Muse*
R-20/99 **Knock Down Walls** *Tonic*
M-6/89 **Knock Me Down**
    Red Hot Chili Peppers
R-18/90 **Knockin' On Heaven's Door**
    Guns N' Roses
R-7/85 **Knocking At Your Back Door**
    Deep Purple
R-45/88 **Knucklebones** *David Lee Roth*
M-7/90 **Kool Thing** *Sonic Youth*
M-6/91 **Kozmik** *Ziggy Marley*
Kryptonite *3 Doors Down*
    M-1/00 R-1/00
R-1/86 **Kyrie** *Mr. Mister*

L

M-40/99 **L Train** *Shootyz Groove*
R-18/90 **L.A. Woman** *Billy Idol*
M-32/05 **L.S.F. (Lost Souls Forever)**
    Kasabian
R-11/87 **La Bamba** *Los Lobos*
M-9/94 **Labour Of Love** *Frente!*
Lack Of Water *Why Store*
    R-27/96 M-37/96
Ladies And Gentlemen *Saliva*
    R-2/07 M-25/07
R-46/82 **Lady Luck** *Molly Hatchet*
R-30/86 **Lady Nina** *Marillion*
R-47/81 **Lady On The Rock** *Joe Vitale*
Lady Picture Show
    Stone Temple Pilots
    M-6/96 R-1/97
R-47/87 **Lady Red Light** *Great White*
M-39/98 **Lady, Your Roof Brings Me**
    Down *Scott Weiland*
M-28/99 **Ladyfingers** *Luscious Jackson*
M-18/96 **Ladykillers** *Lush*
M-3/93 **Laid** *James*
M-10/92 **Laid So Low (Tears Roll Down)**
    Tears For Fears
M-29/08 **Lake Michigan** *Rogue Wave*
R-22/95 **Lake Of Fire** *Nirvana*
Lakini's Juice *Live*
    M-1/97 R-2/97
R-47/81 **Land Of A Thousand Dances**
    Ted Nugent
Land Of Confusion
    Genesis
    R-11/86
    Disturbed
    R-1/06 M-18/06

M-1/89	**Love And Anger** *Kate Bush*
R-5/92	**Love And Happiness**
	John Mellencamp
M-30/05	**Love And Memories** *O.A.R.*
R-40/88	**Love And Mercy** *Brian Wilson*
R-50/86	**Love And Rock And Roll**
	Greg Kihn
R-21/04	**Love And War** *Drowning Pool*
M-19/90	**Love Barge** *Big Dipper*
R-3/88	**Love Bites** *Def Leppard*
R-22/90	**Love Can Make You Blind**
	Every Mother's Nightmare
R-13/88	**Love Changes Everything**
	Honeymoon Suite
R-14/89	**Love Cries** *Stage Dolls*
M-19/89	**Love Crushing** *Fetchin Bones*
R-24/91	**Love Don't Come Easy**
	White Lion
R-33/90	**Love Don't Come Easy** *Alarm*
R-50/89	**Love Don't Lie** *House Of Lords*
R-9/89	**Love Has Taken Its Toll** *Saraya*
R-1/89	**Love In An Elevator** *Aerosmith*
R-1/89	**Love In Your Eyes** *Eddie Money*
R-19/90	**Love Is** *Alannah Myles*
R-1/83	**Love Is A Battlefield** *Pat Benatar*
R-7/89	**Love Is A Long Road** *Tom Petty*
R-31/90	**Love Is A Rock**
	REO Speedwagon
M-23/89	**Love Is A Shield** *Camouflage*
R-7/92	**Love Is Alive** *Joe Cocker*
R-40/82	**Love Is Alright Tonite**
	Rick Springfield
R-7/90	**Love Is Dangerous**
	Fleetwood Mac
R-9/82	**Love Is Like A Rock** *Donnie Iris*
R-49/88	**Love Is Not A Game**
	McAuley Schenker Group
R-8/92	**Love Is On The Way** *Saigon Kick*
R-2/94	**Love Is Strong** *Rolling Stones*
M-14/93	**Love Is Stronger Than Death**
	The
R-17/86	**Love Is The Hero** *Billy Squier*
R-9/90	**Love Is The Ritual** *Styx*
R-19/85	**Love Is The Seventh Wave** *Sting*
R-19/82	**Love Leads To Madness**
	Nazareth
R-49/89	**Love Letter** *Bonnie Raitt*
M-4/06	**Love Like Winter** *AFI*
R-41/83	**Love Me Again** *John Hall Band*
R-27/90	**Love Me Two Times** *Aerosmith*
R-30/82	**Love My Way** *Psychedelic Furs*
	Love On Me ..see: Luv On Me
R-36/83	**Love On Your Side**
	Thompson Twins
M-24/90	**Love Or Something** *Bob Geldof*
R-18/82	**Love Plus One**
	Haircut One Hundred
	Love Rears Its Ugly Head
	Living Colour
	M-8/91 R-28/91
R-32/07	**Love Reign O'er Me** *Pearl Jam*
R-15/87	**Love Removal Machine** *Cult*
M-14/96	**Love Rollercoaster**
	Red Hot Chili Peppers
M-30/93	**Love See No Colour** *Farm*
M-1/89	**Love Shack** *B-52's*
R-25/94	**Love Sneakin' Up On You**
	Bonnie Raitt
R-13/84	**Love Somebody** *Rick Springfield*
	Love Song
	Cure
	M-2/89 R-30/89
	311
	M-1/04

R-7/90	**Love Song** *Tesla*
M-24/93	**Love Song For A Vampire**
	Annie Lennox
	Love Spreads *Stone Roses*
	M-2/95 R-4/95
R-14/90	**Love That Never Dies** *Byrds*
R-49/91	**Love To Burn**
	Neil Young & Crazy Horse
M-6/91	**Love To Hate You** *Erasure*
R-25/05	**Love To Let You Down**
	Life Of Agony
R-26/86	**Love Touch** *Rod Stewart*
M-3/93	**Love U More** *Sunscreem*
M-21/96	**Love Untold** *Paul Westerberg*
R-31/92	**Love Walked In** *Thunder*
R-4/86	**Love Walks In** *Van Halen*
R-1/87	**Love Will Find A Way** *Yes*
R-24/84	**Love Will Show Us How**
	Christine McVie
	Love You ..see: Love U
R-31/91	**Love's A Loaded Gun**
	Alice Cooper
R-28/83	**Love's Got A Line On You**
	Scandal
M-9/97	**Lovefool** *Cardigans*
M-9/92	**Lover Lover Lover** *Ian McCulloch*
R-36/05	**Lovercall** *Danko Jones*
R-56/84	**Lovers In A Dangerous Time**
	Bruce Cockburn
R-57/82	**Lovers In The Night** *Toto*
M-22/94	**Lovetown** *Peter Gabriel*
R-3/85	**Lovin' Every Minute Of It**
	Loverboy
R-18/90	**Lovin' You's A Dirty Job** *Ratt*
	Low *Cracker*
	M-3/93 R-5/94
	Low *Foo Fighters*
	M-15/03 R-23/03
R-15/94	**Low Rider** *Gary Hoey*
M-25/94	**Low Self Opinion** *Rollins Band*
R-4/91	**Lowdown And Dirty** *Foreigner*
M-22/94	**Lucas With The Lid Off** *Lucas*
	Lucky *Seven Mary Three*
	M-19/97 R-35/97
R-24/85	**Lucky** *Greg Kihn*
	(also see: Believed You Were)
R-5/85	**Lucky In Love** *Mick Jagger*
M-16/98	**Lucky Man** *Verve*
R-36/82	**Lucky Ones** *Loverboy*
M-38/94	**Lucky You** *Lightning Seeds*
R-35/98	**Lucy** *Caramel*
R-15/87	**Luka** *Suzanne Vega*
M-9/98	**Lullaby** *Shawn Mullins*
M-23/89	**Lullaby** *Loverboy*
R-24/92	**Lumberjack, The** *Jackyl*
	Lump *Presidents Of The United*
	States Of America
	M-1/95 R-7/95
R-11/81	**Lunatic Fringe** *Red Rider*
R-38/92	**Luv On Me** *Roxy Blue*
R-30/82	**Lyin' In A Bed Of Fire**
	Little Steven
R-4/86	**Lying** *Peter Frampton*
	Lying From You *Linkin Park*
	M-1/04 R-2/04
M-28/06	**Lying Is The Most Fun A Girl Can Have Without Taking Her Clothes Off** *Panic At The Disco*
M-19/05	**Lyla** *Oasis*

M

	Mach 5 *Presidents Of The United States Of America*
	M-11/96 R-24/96
R-12/98	**Machete** *Brother Cane*
R-36/92	**Machine Gun** *Warrant*
	Machinehead *Bush*
	M-4/96 R-4/96
R-37/91	**Mad About You** *Slaughter*
M-30/04	**Mad World**
	Michael Andrews w/ Gary Jules
R-27/88	**Madalaine** *Winger*
R-12/07	**Made Of Scars** *Stone Sour*
R-54/81	**Madman** *Tom Johnston*
M-2/89	**Madonna Of The Wasps**
	Robyn Hitchcock
R-1/84	**Magic** *Cars*
R-8/81	**Magic Power** *Triumph*
R-10/88	**Magic Touch** *Mike Oldfield*
R-42/88	**Magic Touch** *Aerosmith*
R-28/85	**Magical** *John Parr*
R-29/97	**Magnolia**
	Screamin' Cheetah Wheelies
R-34/00	**Mainline** *Jesse James Dupree*
R-38/81	**Mainstreet U.S.A.** *Union*
R-8/83	**Major Tom (Coming Home)**
	Peter Schilling
	Make A Move *Incubus*
	M-17/05 R-19/05
M-11/89	**Make Believe Mambo**
	David Byrne
M-8/06	**MakeDamnSure**
	Taking Back Sunday
R-12/85	**Make It Better (Forget About Me)**
	Tom Petty
R-36/91	**Make It Easy** *Yes*
R-41/87	**Make It Mean Something**
	Rob Jungklas
R-21/01	**Make It Right** *Econoline Crush*
R-3/92	**Make Love Like A Man**
	Def Leppard
	Make Me Bad *Korn*
	M-7/00 R-9/00
M-19/91	**Make Out Alright** *Divinyls*
	Make Up Your Mind
	Theory Of A Deadman
	R-13/03 M-38/03
R-11/92	**Make You A Believer**
	Sass Jordan
M-32/00	**Makes No Difference** *Sum 41*
M-22/01	**Makin' Money** *Handsome Devil*
R-30/92	**Makin' Some Noise** *Tom Petty*
M-30/92	**Making Plans For Nigel** *Primus*
	Malibu *Hole*
	M-3/99 R-16/99
R-5/83	**Mama** *Genesis*
	Mama Help Me *Edie Brickell*
	M-17/90 R-26/90
R-2/92	**Mama, I'm Coming Home**
	Ozzy Osbourne
R-13/84	**Mama Weer All Crazee Now**
	Quiet Riot
R-5/94	**Mama's Fool** *Tesla*
M-37/94	**Mamouna** *Bryan Ferry*
	(Man In Motion) ..see: St. Elmo's Fire
	Man In The Box *Alice In Chains*
	R-18/91
	R-39/00
R-25/91	**Man In The Moon** *Scream*
R-21/92	**Man On A Mission** *Van Halen*
R-14/82	**Man On The Corner** *Genesis*

M-10/88 **Motorcrash** *Sugarcubes*
M-20/89 **Motorcycle** *Love & Rockets*
R-15/85 **Motorcycle Girl** *Cruzados*
Mourning *Tantric*
R-18/01 M-22/02
Mouth *Bush*
M-5/97 R-28/98
R-16/06 **Move** *Thousand Foot Krutch*
M-4/91 **Move Any Mountain (Progen 91)**
Shamen
Move With Me Sister *Del Fuegos*
M-22/89 R-32/89
Movies *Alien Ant Farm*
M-18/01 R-38/02
Movin' On Up *Primal Scream*
M-2/91 R-28/91
R-30/91 **Moving On** *Gary Moore*
M-3/05 **Mr. Brightside** *Killers*
R-50/90 **Mr. Cab Driver** *Lenny Kravitz*
Mr. Jones *Counting Crows*
R-2/94 M-2/94
R-3/93 **Mister Please** *Damn Yankees*
R-3/83 **Mr. Roboto** *Styx*
R-14/83 **Mr. Soul** *Neil Young*
R-34/92 **Mr. Tinkertrain** *Ozzy Osbourne*
R-36/93 **Mrs. Rita** *Gin Blossoms*
M-8/92 **Mrs. Robinson** *Lemonheads*
R-18/95 **Muddy Jesus** *Ian Moore*
Mudshovel *Staind*
R-10/99 M-14/99
M-17/98 **Mummers' Dance**
Loreena McKennitt
Mungo City *Spacehog*
R-19/98 M-21/98
R-13/84 **Murder** *David Gilmour*
R-14/95 **Murder Incorporated**
Bruce Springsteen
R-17/95 **Murder Of One** *Counting Crows*
M-25/92 **Murder, Tonight, In The Trailer
Park** *Cowboy Junkies*
M-19/89 **Music Goes Round My Head**
Saints
R-40/81 **Musta Notta Gotta Lotta** *Joe Ely*
Muzzle *Smashing Pumpkins*
M-8/96 R-10/96
R-1/87 **My Baby** *Pretenders*
R-32/81 **My Baby** *Cold Chisel*
R-26/93 **My Back Pages**
*Bob Dylan/Roger McGuinn/
Tom Petty/Neil Young/
Eric Clapton/George Harrison*
M-13/88 **My Bag** *Lloyd Cole*
R-12/89 **My Brave Face** *Paul McCartney*
R-11/83 **My City Was Gone** *Pretenders*
R-21/07 **My Curse** *Killswitch Engage*
M-24/91 **My Definition Of A Boombastic
Jazz Style** *Dream Warriors*
M-13/05 **My Doorbell** *White Stripes*
R-52/84 **My Ever Changing Moods**
Style Council
R-26/98 **My Father's Eyes** *Eric Clapton*
R-20/00 **My Favorite Headache**
Geddy Lee
M-26/98 **My Favorite Mistake** *Sheryl Crow*
M-16/99 **My Favourite Game** *Cardigans*
My Friends
Red Hot Chili Peppers
M-1/95 R-1/95
M-5/02 **My Friends Over You**
New Found Glory
My Generation *Limp Bizkit*
M-18/00 R-33/00
My Girl ..see: Nite At The Apollo

R-16/81 **My Girl (Gone, Gone, Gone)**
Chilliwack
My Goddess *Exies*
R-20/02 M-26/03
R-26/95 **My Hallucination** *Shaw/Blades*
M-23/01 **My Happiness** *Powderfinger*
R-1/90 **My Head's In Mississippi** *ZZ Top*
R-50/89 **My Heart Can't Tell You No**
Rod Stewart
My Hero *Foo Fighters*
M-6/98 R-8/98
R-6/86 **My Hometown** *Bruce Springsteen*
R-31/81 **My Kinda Lover** *Billy Squier*
R-33/86 **My Mistake**
Phantom, Rocker & Slick
R-19/96 **My My** *Seven Mary Three*
M-37/99 **My Name Is** *Eminem*
M-9/93 **My Name Is Mud** *Primus*
R-32/84 **My Oh My** *Slade*
My Own Prison *Creed*
R-2/97 M-7/98
My Own Worst Enemy *Lit*
M-1/99 R-6/99
R-34/89 **My Paradise** *Outfield*
My Sacrifice *Creed*
R-1/01 M-2/02
M-1/93 **My Sister** *Juliana Hatfield Three*
R-6/98 **My Song** *Jerry Cantrell*
R-11/83 **My Town** *Michael Stanley Band*
M-32/97 **My Town** *Buck-O-Nine*
M-24/93 **My Umbrella** *Tripping Daisy*
My Wave *Soundgarden*
R-11/94 M-18/94
My Way *Limp Bizkit*
M-3/01 R-4/01
M-20/08 **My World** *Sick Puppies*
(also see: You're)
R-26/99 **Mysterious** *Scorpions*
Mysterious Ways *U2*
M-1/91 R-1/91
R-20/84 **Mystery** *Dio*
R-21/86 **Mystic Rhythms** *Rush*
R-17/89 **Mystify** *INXS*

N

R-2/00 **N.I.B.** *Primus w/ Ozzy Osbourne*
M-11/92 **N.W.O.** *Ministry*
R-26/83 **Na Na Hey Hey Kiss Him
Goodbye** *Bananarama*
M-22/07 **Naive** *Kooks*
Naked *Goo Goo Dolls*
R-8/96 M-9/96
M-18/97 **Naked Eye** *Luscious Jackson*
M-10/91 **Naked Rain** *This Picture*
Name *Goo Goo Dolls*
M-1/95 R-1/95
R-43/87 **Name Names** *Del Fuegos*
M-22/01 **Name Of The Game**
Crystal Method
R-25/05 **Nameless, The** *Slipknot*
M-9/91 **Native Son** *Judybats*
M-24/00 **Natural Blues** *Moby*
Natural One *Folk Implosion*
M-4/95 R-20/96
R-32/93 **Natural Thing** *Journey*
R-30/90 **Nature Of Love** *Poco*
R-6/85 **Naughty Naughty** *John Parr*
M-13/06 **Nausea** *Beck*

Nearly Lost You
Screaming Trees
M-5/92 R-12/93
R-3/89 **Need A Little Taste Of Love**
Doobie Brothers
M-35/95 **Need You Around**
Smoking Popes
R-12/87 **Need You Tonight** *INXS*
R-19/94 **Need Your Lovin'** *Tesla*
R-17/86 **Needles And Pins**
Tom Petty w/ Stevie Nicks
Negasonic Teenage Warhead
Monster Magnet
R-19/95 M-26/95
M-29/99 **Negotiation Limerick File**
Beastie Boys
R-29/92 **Neighbor** *Ugly Kid Joe*
R-37/84 **Neighborhood Bully** *Bob Dylan*
R-40/84 **Neighborhood Threat**
David Bowie
R-2/85 **Never** *Heart*
Never Again *Nickelback*
R-1/02 M-24/02
R-45/88 **Never Be The Same**
Crowded House
Never Do That *Pretenders*
M-4/90 R-5/90
Never Enough *Cure*
M-1/90 R-33/90
R-4/87 **Never Enough** *Patty Smyth*
(also see: Surefire)
M-16/00 **Never Gonna Come Back Down**
BT
Never Gonna Stop *Rob Zombie*
R-11/02 M-23/02
R-45/89 **Never Had A Lot To Lose**
Cheap Trick
R-38/82 **Never Had It Better**
Franke & The Knockouts
R-54/82 **Never Hold Back**
B.E. Taylor Group
R-15/87 **Never Let Me Down** *David Bowie*
M-4/00 **Never Let You Go**
Third Eye Blind
R-11/87 **Never Say Goodbye** *Bon Jovi*
R-27/82 **Never Say Never** *Romeo Void*
M-27/97 **Never Say Never** *That Dog*
R-8/85 **Never Surrender** *Corey Hart*
R-23/83 **Never Surrender** *Triumph*
Never Tear Us Apart *INXS*
R-5/88 M-28/88
Never There *Cake*
M-1/98 R-40/99
Never Too Late
Three Days Grace
R-1/07 M-2/07
M-7/99 **New** *No Doubt*
R-33/81 **New Age Music** *Pat Travers*
New Beginning *Stir*
R-16/00 M-18/00
R-33/01 **New Disease** *Spineshank*
R-7/84 **New Girl Now** *Honeymoon Suite*
M-26/93 **New Life** *X*
R-4/84 **New Moon On Monday**
Duran Duran
R-30/90 **New Orleans Is Sinking**
Tragically Hip
M-9/97 **New Pollution** *Beck*
R-43/84 **New Romeo**
Southside Johnny & The Jukes
R-8/88 **New Sensation** *INXS*
R-58/84 **New Song** *Howard Jones*
R-35/89 **New Thing** *Enuff Z'Nuff*
R-1/82 **New World Man** *Rush*

319

R-3/92	**Now More Than Ever** *John Mellencamp*
R-28/01	**Now Or Never** *Dope*
R-22/99	**Now That You're Gone** *Indigenous*
M-17/95	**Now They'll Sleep** *Belly*
R-23/00	**Now You Know** *Full Devil Jacket*
R-15/90	**Now You're Gone** *Whitesnake*
	Now You're In Heaven *Julian Lennon*
	R-1/89 M-27/89
	Nowhere Kids *Smile Empty Soul*
	R-26/04 M-27/04
R-13/82	**Nowhere To Run** *Santana*
M-30/05	**Nth Degree** *Morningwood*
R-34/82	**Nuclear Attack** *Greg Lake*
	Numb *Linkin Park*
	M-1/03 R-1/04
	Numb *U2*
	M-2/93 R-18/93
M-20/95	**Number One Blind** *Veruca Salt*
M-1/97	**#1 Crush** *Garbage*
M-17/92	**Number One Dominator** *Top*

O

M-21/95	**O Baby** *Siouxsie & The Banshees*
	Oaf, The *Big Wreck*
	R-9/98 M-24/98
M-12/91	**Obscurity Knocks** *Trash Can Sinatras*
M-16/89	**Obsession** *Xymox*
	Obvious Child *Paul Simon*
	R-21/90 M-24/90
	Obvious Song *Joe Jackson*
	M-2/91 R-28/91
M-23/96	**Ocean** *Sebadoh*
M-21/04	**Ocean Avenue** *Yellowcard*
M-6/04	**Ocean Breathes Salty** *Modest Mouse*
M-29/91	**Oceanside** *Robyn Hitchcock*
M-11/95	**Ode To My Family** *Cranberries*
R-39/05	**Of Mice And Men** *Megadeth*
	Off He Goes *Pearl Jam*
	M-31/97 R-34/97
M-14/93	**Oh Carolina** *Shaggy*
M-5/89	**Oh Daddy** *Adrian Belew*
M-36/07	**Oh! Gravity** *Switchfoot*
R-26/99	**Oh My God** *Guns N' Roses*
R-34/05	**Oh No, Not You Again** *Rolling Stones*
R-1/82	**(Oh) Pretty Woman** *Van Halen*
R-15/90	**Oh Pretty Woman** *Gary Moore*
R-1/84	**Oh Sherrie** *Steve Perry*
	Oh Well *Joe Jackson*
	M-20/91 R-25/91
R-36/06	**Oh Yeah** *Huck Johns*
M-34/05	**Ohio Is For Lovers** *Hawthorne Heights*
	Oil And Water *Incubus*
	M-8/07 R-38/07
R-24/01	**Old Enough** *Nickelback*
	Old Man & Me (When I Get To Heaven) *Hootie & The Blowfish*
	R-6/96 M-33/96
R-1/85	**Old Man Down The Road** *John Fogerty*
R-23/93	**Old Rose Motel** *Great White*
R-27/07	**Older I Get** *Skillet*
R-59/82	**Olympia** *Jon Anderson*
M-25/92	**On A Plain** *Nirvana*
R-27/82	**On A Roll** *Point Blank*

R-29/06	**On An Island** *David Gilmour*
M-17/97	**On And On** *Longpigs*
R-1/84	**On The Dark Side** *John Cafferty*
M-19/90	**On The Greener Side** *Michelle Shocked*
R-7/89	**On The Line** *Tangier*
R-3/82	**On The Loose** *Saga*
M-19/00	**On The Roof Again** *Eve 6*
M-17/93	**On The Ropes** *Wonder Stuff*
R-1/88	**On The Turning Away** *Pink Floyd*
R-6/87	**On The Western Skyline** *Bruce Hornsby*
R-6/89	**Once Bitten Twice Shy** *Great White*
	Once In A While *Dishwalla*
	R-17/98 M-20/98
	One *U2*
	M-1/92 R-1/92
	One *Creed*
	M-2/99 R-2/99
	One, The *Foo Fighters*
	M-14/02 R-20/02
M-23/96	**One, The** *Tracy Bonham*
R-46/89	**One** *Metallica*
R-1/90	**One And Only Man** *Steve Winwood*
R-23/97	**One Angel** *Stir*
M-26/01	**One Armed Scissor** *At The Drive-In*
R-17/89	**One Big Rush** *Joe Satriani*
R-10/89	**One Clear Moment** *Little Feat*
R-29/87	**One For The Mockingbird** *Cutting Crew*
R-39/89	**One Good Lover** *Red Siren*
R-20/88	**One Good Reason** *Paul Carrack*
	One Headlight *Wallflowers*
	R-1/97 M-1/97
R-3/86	**One Hit (To The Body)** *Rolling Stones*
M-12/99	**One Hit Wonder** *Everclear*
M-4/92	**100%** *Sonic Youth*
R-13/93	**One I Am** *Dan Baird*
R-2/87	**One I Love** *R.E.M.*
	One I Love *Big Country*
	M-17/93 R-34/93
R-27/98	**One I Want** *Van Halen*
R-22/84	**One In A Million** *Romantics*
R-22/85	**One In A Million** *Eddie & The Tide*
R-27/84	**One In A Million** *Christine McVie*
R-33/91	**One In A Million** *Trixter*
M-13/93	**One In Ten** *808 State*
	One Last Breath *Creed*
	R-5/02 M-17/02
M-24/89	**One Little Girl** *Toad The Wet Sprocket*
R-10/02	**One Little Victory** *Rush*
R-17/85	**One Lonely Night** *REO Speedwagon*
M-9/90	**One Love** *Stone Roses*
	One Man Army *Our Lady Peace*
	M-13/99 R-16/99
R-19/96	**One More Astronaut** *I Mother Earth*
M-30/02	**One More Minute** *Authority Zero*
M-32/98	**One More Murder** *Better Than Ezra*
R-4/85	**One More Night** *Phil Collins*
R-22/97	**One More Time** *Corey Stevens*
R-9/89	**One Night** *Bad Company*
R-7/85	**One Night Love Affair** *Bryan Adams*
R-35/82	**One Night Stand** *Janis Joplin*

R-38/02	**One Of A Kind** *Breaking Point*
R-17/83	**One Of Our Submarines** *Thomas Dolby*
	One Of Us *Joan Osborne*
	M-7/95 R-26/96
	One Shot *Tin Machine*
	M-3/91 R-17/91
R-21/86	**One Simple Thing** *Stabilizers*
R-5/87	**One Slip** *Pink Floyd*
R-55/84	**One Small Day** *Ultravox*
	One Step Closer *Linkin Park*
	R-4/01 M-5/01
R-2/88	**One Step Up** *Bruce Springsteen*
R-15/82	**One Story Town** *Tom Petty*
R-2/83	**One Thing** *INXS*
	One Thing *Finger Eleven*
	M-5/04 R-38/03
R-24/02	**One Thing** *Gravity Kills*
R-2/83	**One Thing Leads To Another** *Fixx*
M-40/94	**One Time For Me** *Reverend Horton Heat*
R-17/84	**One Time For Old Times** *38 Special*
M-34/07	**1234** *Feist*
R-19/85	**One Vision** *Queen*
M-11/92	**One Way** *Levellers*
M-1/98	**One Week** *Barenaked Ladies*
R-46/92	**One Word** *Baby Animals*
R-8/85	**One World** *Dire Straits*
R-41/81	**One's Too Many** *Fabulous Thunderbirds*
M-8/90	**Onion Skin** *Boom Crash Opera*
	Only *Nine Inch Nails*
	M-1/05 R-22/05
R-22/03	**Only, The** *Static-X*
R-26/93	**Only** *Anthrax*
R-7/99	**Only A Fool** *Black Crowes*
R-1/88	**Only A Memory** *Smithereens*
M-5/06	**Only Difference Between Martyrdom And Suicide Is Press Coverage** *Panic At The Disco*
R-40/95	**Only Dreaming** *Maids Of Gravity*
R-44/84	**Only Flame In Town** *Elvis Costello*
	Only God Knows Why *Kid Rock*
	R-5/00 M-13/00
M-16/96	**Only Happy When It Rains** *Garbage*
M-26/92	**Only Living Boy In New Cross** *Carter*
R-28/85	**Only Lonely** *Bon Jovi*
R-16/87	**Only Love** *BoDeans*
M-11/92	**Only Love Can Break Your Heart** *Saint Etienne*
R-19/90	**Only My Heart Talkin'** *Alice Cooper*
R-13/88	**Only One** *Jimmy Page*
M-15/04	**Only One** *Yellowcard*
	Only One *Goo Goo Dolls*
	R-21/95 M-36/95
R-44/83	**Only One** *Bryan Adams*
	Only One I Know *Charlatans UK*
	M-5/90 R-37/91
M-27/92	**Only Shallow** *My Bloody Valentine*
R-22/82	**Only Solutions** *Journey*
R-6/82	**Only The Lonely** *Motels*
R-3/85	**Only The Young** *Journey*
R-8/82	**Only Time Will Tell** *Asia*
M-8/90	**Only Tongue Can Tell** *Trash Can Sinatras*

	Rest In Pieces *Saliva* R-11/03 M-20/03		**Ripple** *Grateful Dead* R-50/81	R-37/99	**Rock Me Right** *Susan Tedeschi*
M-16/03	**Rest Of My Life** *Unwritten Law*		*Jane's Addiction*	R-1/84	**Rock Me Tonite** *Billy Squier*
R-16/84	**Restless** *Elton John*		M-13/91	R-55/84	**Rock My Nights Away** *Michael Schenker Group*
R-28/85	**Restless Heart** *John Waite*		**Rise** *Cult* R-3/01 M-19/01	R-26/85	**Rock 'N' Roll Children** *Dio*
M-10/93	**Return Of Pan** *Waterboys*		**Rise Above This** *Seether*	R-37/86	**Rock 'N' Roll Cities** *Kinks*
M-2/94	**Return To Innocence** *Enigma*		R-10/08 M-11/08	R-19/83	**Rock 'N' Roll Is King** *ELO*
R-24/93	**Return To Serenity** *Testament*	R-40/90	**Rise To It** *Kiss*	M-31/95	**Rock 'N' Roll Lifestyle** *Cake*
R-20/87	**Returning Home** *Sammy Hagar*		**Rise Today** *Alter Bridge*	R-23/82	**Rock 'N' Roll Party In The** **Streets** *Axe*
R-9/84	**Reunited** *Greg Kihn Band*		R-3/07 M-32/07	R-40/84	**Rock 'N' Roll Rebel** *Ozzy Osbourne*
R-7/88	**Rev It Up** *Jerry Harrison*	R-24/02	**Rising, The** *Bruce Springsteen*	M-36/95	**Rock 'N' Roll Star** *Oasis*
R-34/88	**Rev. Jack & His Roamin'** **Cadillac Church** *Timbuk 3*	R-32/07	**Rising, The** *Trivium*	R-1/83	**Rock Of Ages** *Def Leppard*
M-24/92	**Reva's House** *Los Lobos*	R-18/81	**Rita Mae** *Eric Clapton*	R-45/88	**Rock Of Life** *Rick Springfield*
	Revelations *Audioslave* M-38/06 R-6/07	M-38/07	**River, The** *Good Charlotte*	M-2/01	**Rock Show** *Blink-182*
R-23/05	**Revolution** *Judas Priest*		**River Of Deceit** *Mad Season* R-2/95 M-9/95	M-36/02	**Rock Star** *N*E*R*D*
R-30/01	**Revolution** *Stone Temple Pilots*	R-19/91	**River Of Love** *Lynch Mob*		**Rockstar** *Nickelback* R-4/06 M-37/06
R-28/00	**Revolution Is My Name** *Pantera*	R-35/81	**Rivers (Of The Hidden Funk)** *Joe Walsh*	M-18/00	**(Rock) Superstar** *Cypress Hill*
R-26/01	**Revolution Man** *Union Underground*		**Road, The** *Alarm* M-7/90 R-16/90	R-6/82	**Rock The Casbah** *Clash*
R-33/89	**Revolution Song** *World Trade*	R-14/88	**Road, The** *Kinks*	R-22/87	**Rock The Night** *Europe*
	Rexall *Dave Navarro* R-9/01 M-12/01		**Road I'm On** *3 Doors Down* R-8/03 M-24/03		**Rock The Party (Off The Hook)** *P.O.D.* R-25/00 M-27/00
M-27/91	**Rhinoceros** *Smashing Pumpkins*	R-11/90	**Road To Hell** *Chris Rea*	R-10/89	**Rock This Place** *Fabulous Thunderbirds*
R-19/97	**Rhinosaur** *Soundgarden*	R-3/92	**Road To Nowhere** *Ozzy Osbourne*	R-4/82	**Rock This Town** *Stray Cats*
R-2/87	**Rhythm Of Love** *Yes*	R-25/85	**Road To Nowhere** *Talking Heads*	R-32/84	**Rock You** *Helix*
R-6/88	**Rhythm Of Love** *Scorpions*		**Roadhouse Blues** *Blue Öyster Cult* R-24/82	R-5/84	**Rock You Like A Hurricane** *Scorpions*
R-13/91	**Rhythm Of My Heart** *Rod Stewart*		*Jeff Healey Band* R-29/89	R-49/83	**Rock You Up** *Romantics*
R-35/97	**Rhythmeen** *ZZ Top*	R-46/87	**Roadrunner** *Joan Jett*	M-39/98	**Rockafeller Skank** *Fatboy Slim*
M-28/99	**Rick James** *Jude*	M-6/90	**Roam** *B-52's*		**Rockaway** *Ric Ocasek* R-11/91 M-19/91
M-13/04	**Ride** *Vines*	R-25/81	**R.O.C.K.** *Garland Jeffreys*	R-5/89	**Rocket** *Def Leppard*
R-21/86	**Ride Across The River** *Dire Straits*	R-1/89	**Rock And A Hard Place** *Rolling Stones* *(also see: Between A)*	R-28/94	**Rocket** *Smashing Pumpkins*
	(Ride Sally Ride) ..see: Let Sally **Drive**		**Rock And Roll ..also see: Rock 'N'** **Roll / Rockin' Roll**	M-11/91	**Rocket Man** *Kate Bush*
R-20/94	**Ride The Tide** *Screamin' Cheetah Wheelies*	R-13/96	**Rock And Roll All Nite** *Kiss*	R-9/91	**Rocket O' Love** *Knack*
R-25/91	**Ride The Wind** *Poison*	M-29/89	**Rock And Roll Babylon** *Love & Rockets*	R-8/84	**Rockin' At Midnight** *Honeydrippers*
	Riders In The Sky ..see: (Ghost)	R-34/81	**Rock And Roll Doctor** *Little Feat*	R-2/89	**Rockin' In The Free World** *Neil Young*
R-28/01	**Riders On The Storm** *Creed*		**Rock And Roll Dreams Come** **Through**	R-38/92	**Rockin' Is Ma' Business** *Four Horsemen*
M-14/95	**Ridiculous Thoughts** *Cranberries*		*Jim Steinman* R-14/81	R-8/81	**Rockin' The Paradise** *Styx*
R-9/01	**Ridin'** *Buckcherry*		*Meat Loaf* R-25/94	M-28/01	**Rockin' The Suburbs** *Ben Folds*
R-26/00	**Riding With The King** *BB. King & Eric Clapton*	R-5/85	**Rock And Roll Girls** *John Fogerty*	M-11/91	**Rocking Chair** *House Of Freaks*
R-11/86	**Right And Wrong** *Joe Jackson*		**Rock And Roll Is Dead** *Lenny Kravitz* R-4/95 M-10/95	R-44/88	**Rocking Pneumonia And The** **Boogie Woogie Flu** *Aerosmith*
R-33/82	**Right Away** *Kansas*	R-34/81	**Rock & Roll Queen** *Subways*		**Rocks** *Primal Scream* M-16/94 R-29/94
R-39/86	**Right Between The Eyes** *Wax*	M-29/06	**Rock & Roll Queen** *Subways*	R-31/98	**Rocks** *Rod Stewart*
M-12/93	**Right Decision** *Jesus Jones*	R-5/88	**Rock & Roll Strategy** *Thirty Eight Special*	M-39/99	**Rodeo Clowns** *G. Love & Special Sauce*
	Right Here *Staind* R-1/05 M-3/05	R-11/88	**Rock Bottom** *Dickey Betts Band*	R-13/83	**Roll Me Away** *Bob Seger*
	Right Here, Right Now *Jesus Jones* M-1/91 R-7/91	R-17/97	**Rock Crown** *Seven Mary Three*	R-6/92	**Roll Of The Dice** *Bruce Springsteen*
R-27/87	**Right Next Door (Because Of** **Me)** *Robert Cray Band*		**Rock In America ..see: (You Can** **Still)**	M-33/01	**Roll On** *Living End*
	Right Now *SR-71* M-2/00 R-38/00	R-6/85	**R.O.C.K. In The U.S.A.** *John Cougar Mellencamp*	R-9/92	**Roll The Bones** *Rush*
R-2/92	**Right Now** *Van Halen*		**Rock Is Dead** *Marilyn Manson* R-28/99 M-30/99	R-1/88	**Roll With It** *Steve Winwood*
	Right Now *Korn* R-11/03 M-13/03	R-24/94	**Rock It** *Steve Miller Band*	R-12/91	**Rollin' On** *Doobie Brothers*
	Right Or Wrong ..see: (Who's)	R-9/87	**Rock Me** *Great White* *(also see: Young Thing, Wild* *Dreams)*	R-8/99	**Rollin' Stoned** *Great White*
R-10/82	**Right The First Time** *Gamma*				**Rollin' (Urban Assault Vehicle)** *Limp Bizkit* M-4/00 R-10/00
R-8/91	**Righteous** *Eric Johnson*				**Rollover D.J.** *Jet* R-14/04 M-14/04
M-25/90	**Ring Of Fire** *Social Distortion*			R-39/84	**Romancing The Stone** *Eddy Grant*
R-5/83	**Rio** *Duran Duran*				**Rooftops (A Liberation** **Broadcast)** *Lostprophets* M-15/06 R-22/06
	Riot *Three Days Grace* R-19/08 M-26/08				
R-47/89	**Rip And Tear** *L.A. Guns*				
M-3/92	**Ripple** *Church*				

M-17/90	**Room At The Top** *Adam Ant*
R-19/99	**Room At The Top** *Tom Petty*
R-28/87	**Room Full Of Mirrors** *Pretenders*
R-27/82	**Room Of Our Own** *Billy Joel*
R-1/89	**Rooms On Fire** *Stevie Nicks*
R-7/93	**Rooster** *Alice In Chains*
M-27/95	**Roots Radical** *Rancid*
R-7/88	**Rooty Toot Toot**
	John Cougar Mellencamp
	(Rosa Lee) ..see: Set Me Free
R-8/82	**Rosanna** *Toto*
M-27/91	**Rose Of Jericho**
	Eleventh Dream Day
M-24/95	**Rosealia** *Better Than Ezra*
R-5/86	**Rough Boy** *ZZ Top*
R-25/05	**Rough Justice** *Rolling Stones*
M-27/06	**Rough Landing, Holly**
	Yellowcard
R-28/89	**Rough Night In Jericho**
	Dreams So Real
R-45/88	**Roulette** *Bruce Springsteen*
R-4/84	**Round And Round** *Ratt*
M-6/89	**Round & Round** *New Order*
R-44/88	**Round And Round** *Frozen Ghost*
	Round Here *Counting Crows*
	M-7/94 R-11/94
M-25/93	**Round Of Blues** *Shawn Colvin*
R-28/82	**Roxanne** *Sting*
M-22/98	**Royal Oil**
	Mighty Mighty Bosstones
M-7/93	**Rubberband Girl** *Kate Bush*
M-14/07	**Ruby** *Kaiser Chiefs*
M-13/96	**Ruby Soho** *Rancid*
M-30/93	**Ruined In A Day** *New Order*
R-4/86	**Rumbleseat**
	John Cougar Mellencamp
R-26/84	**Rumours In The Air**
	Night Ranger
M-15/04	**Run** *Snow Patrol*
R-21/87	**Run** *Eric Clapton*
M-35/08	**Run** *Gnarls Barkley*
M-36/99	**Run** *Collective Soul*
	Run-Around *Blues Traveler*
	R-13/95 M-14/95
R-1/91	**Runaround** *Van Halen*
R-60/84	**Runaround, The** *Tsunami*
R-1/84	**Run Runaway** *Slade*
R-40/90	**Run So Far** *Eric Clapton*
R-30/89	**Run Straight Down**
	Warren Zevon
R-33/89	**Run To Paradise** *Choirboys*
	Run To The Water *Live*
	M-14/00 R-17/00
R-1/84	**Run To You** *Bryan Adams*
R-5/84	**Runaway** *Bon Jovi*
R-9/91	**Runaway** *Damn Yankees*
	Runaway *Linkin Park*
	R-37/02 M-40/02
	Runaway Train *Soul Asylum*
	R-3/93 M-13/93
R-10/92	**Runaway Train**
	Elton John & Eric Clapton
R-6/87	**Runaway Trains** *Tom Petty*
R-3/84	**Runner** *Manfred Mann*
R-1/89	**Runnin' Down A Dream**
	Tom Petty
	Running Away *Hoobastank*
	M-2/02 R-9/02
	Running Blind *Godsmack*
	R-3/04 M-14/04
	Running Free *Coheed & Cambria*
	M-19/07 R-31/08

	Running From Me *TrustCompany*
	R-24/02 M-22/03
R-15/93	**Running On Faith** *Eric Clapton*
R-34/85	**Running Up That Hill** *Kate Bush*
R-49/84	**Running With The Night**
	Lionel Richie
	Rush *Big Audio Dynamite II*
	M-1/91 R-40/91
R-34/86	**Russians** *Sting*
R-14/86	**Ruthless People** *Mick Jagger*

S

R-47/90	**S S S & Q** *Robert Plant*
	(S.O.S.) ..see: Same Ol' Situation
M-18/94	**Sabotage** *Beastie Boys*
M-35/02	**Sacrifice** *Trik Turner*
R-15/93	**Sad But True** *Metallica*
R-14/89	**Sad Sad Sad** *Rolling Stones*
R-24/84	**Sad Songs (Say So Much)**
	Elton John
M-27/00	**Sad Sweetheart Of Rodeo**
	Harvey Danger
M-27/03	**Saddest Song** *Ataris*
M-6/91	**Sadeness** *Enigma*
M-28/91	**Safe From Harm** *Massive Attack*
R-21/01	**Safe In New York City** *AC/DC*
R-36/03	**Safe Passage** *Manmade God*
R-21/83	**Safety Dance** *Men Without Hats*
R-9/94	**Sail Away** *Great White*
	(also see: Orinoco Flow)
	Saint ..also see: St.
	Saint Joe On The School Bus
	Marcy Playground
	M-8/98 R-30/98
R-13/98	**Saint Of Me** *Rolling Stones*
M-12/94	**Saints** *Breeders*
	Saints Are Coming
	U2 & Green Day
	R-33/06 M-22/06
R-15/83	**Salt In My Tears** *Martin Briley*
	Salvation *Cranberries*
	M-1/96 R-25/96
M-21/95	**Salvation** *Rancid*
M-40/00	**Salvation** *Little Steven*
M-13/91	**Sam** *Meat Puppets*
	Same Direction *Hoobastank*
	M-14/04 R-20/04
R-34/90	**Same Ol' Situation (S.O.S.)**
	Mötley Crüe
R-3/86	**Sanctify Yourself** *Simple Minds*
R-38/98	**Santa Claus And His Old Lady**
	Cheech & Chong
R-27/06	**Santa Monica**
	Theory Of A Deadman
	Santa Monica (Watch The World Die) *Everclear*
	R-1/96 M-5/96
M-3/97	**Santeria** *Sublime*
R-12/86	**Sara** *Starship*
R-22/88	**Satch Boogie** *Joe Satriani*
R-13/87	**Satellite** *Hooters*
	Satellite *P.O.D.*
	R-15/02 M-21/02
	Satellite *Dave Matthews Band*
	M-18/96 R-36/96
R-7/00	**Satellite Blues** *AC/DC*
M-23/89	**Satellites** *Rickie Lee Jones*
R-4/85	**Satisfaction Guaranteed** *Firm*
	Satisfied *Squeeze*
	M-3/91 R-49/91
R-5/89	**Satisfied** *Richard Marx*

	Satisfied *8Stops7*
	R-26/00 M-35/00
R-13/84	**Satisfied Man** *Molly Hatchet*
R-30/84	**Satisfy Me** *Billy Satellite*
M-21/92	**Saturday** *Judybats*
M-26/93	**Saturday Night**
	Ned's Atomic Dustbin
R-8/91	**Saturday Night's Alright For Fighting** *Who*
R-27/81	**Sausalito Summernight** *Diesel*
M-29/99	**Save It For Later** *Harvey Danger*
	Save Me *Shinedown*
	R-1/05 M-2/05
R-3/90	**Save Me** *Fleetwood Mac*
M-5/05	**Save Me** *Unwritten Law*
R-16/04	**Save Me** *Damageplan*
M-27/01	**Save Me** *Remy Zero*
M-8/98	**Save Tonight** *Eagle Eye Cherry*
	Save You *Pearl Jam*
	R-23/03 M-29/03
R-9/88	**Save Your Love** *Great White*
R-49/81	**Save Your Love**
	Jefferson Starship
	Save Yourself
	Stabbing Westward
	R-4/98 M-20/98
M-28/89	**Saved** *Swans*
R-16/91	**Saved By Love** *Rik Emmett*
R-9/83	**Saved By Zero** *Fixx*
	Savin' Me *Nickelback*
	R-11/06 M-29/06
R-26/06	**Saving Grace** *Tom Petty*
R-9/91	**Saving My Heart** *Yes*
R-26/04	**Savior** *Skillet*
R-35/03	**Saviour** *Memento*
	Sax And Violins *Talking Heads*
	M-1/92 R-49/92
R-22/05	**Say Goodbye**
	Theory Of A Deadman
R-39/97	**Say Goodbye** *Cheap Trick*
R-50/82	**Say Goodbye** *Triumph*
R-11/81	**Say Goodbye To Hollywood**
	Billy Joel
R-5/93	**Say Hello 2 Heaven**
	Temple Of The Dog
R-15/85	**Say It Again** *Santana*
M-7/95	**Say It Ain't So** *Weezer*
R-41/82	**Say It Ain't So, Joe** *Roger Daltrey*
R-18/83	**Say It Isn't So**
	Daryl Hall & John Oates
R-18/85	**Say It Isn't So** *Outfield*
R-22/91	**Say It With Love** *Moody Blues*
R-24/83	**Say Say Say** *Paul McCartney & Michael Jackson*
M-19/94	**Say Something** *James*
	Say This Sooner (No One Will See Things The Way I Do).
	Almost
	M-7/07 R-35/07
R-14/83	**Say What You Will** *Fastway*
R-1/87	**Say You Will** *Foreigner*
R-39/87	**Say You Will** *Mick Jagger*
R-3/85	**Say You're Wrong** *Julian Lennon*
M-7/06	**Saying Sorry** *Hawthorne Heights*
R-38/82	**Scandinavian Skies** *Billy Joel*
	Scar Tissue
	Red Hot Chili Peppers
	R-1/99 M-1/99
R-46/89	**Scared** *Dangerous Toys*
	Scars *Papa Roach*
	M-2/05 R-4/05
M-2/01	**Schism** *Tool*
	R-2/01 M-2/01

M-38/00 **School Of Hard Knocks** *P.O.D.*
M-36/03 **Science Of Selling Yourself**
Short *Less Than Jake*
M-18/03 **Scientist, The** *Coldplay*
M-14/96 **Scooby Snacks**
Fun Lovin' Criminals
R-26/05 **Scream** *Billy Idol*
Scream Aim Fire
Bullet For My Valentine
R-16/08 M-26/08
M-16/93 **Screamager** *Therapy?*
R-21/83 **Screaming In The Night** *Krokus*
M-22/02 **Screaming Infidelities**
Dashboard Confessional
Scum *Meat Puppets*
R-20/95 M-23/95
R-25/00 **Scum Of The Earth** *Rob Zombie*
R-11/84 **Sea Of Love** *Honeydrippers*
R-33/81 **Sea Of Love** *Grace Slick*
R-27/91 **Sea Of Sorrow** *Alice In Chains*
R-26/81 **Searchin'** *Santana*
R-25/91 **Seasons** *Tyketto*
R-2/89 **Second Chance**
Thirty Eight Special
(Second Wind) ..see: You're Only
Human
R-32/86 **Secondhand Love**
Pete Townshend
R-29/82 **Secret Journey** *Police*
R-12/87 **Secret Of My Success**
Night Ranger
R-19/98 **Secret Place** *Megadeth*
R-1/86 **Secret Separation** *Fixx*
M-21/99 **Secret Smile** *Semisonic*
R-25/02 **Secret Touch** *Rush*
R-34/93 **Secret World** *Peter Gabriel*
M-12/89 **Secrets** *Primitives*
R-22/82 **Secrets** *Van Halen*
R-41/91 **Seducer** *Saraya*
M-4/89 **See A Little Light** *Bob Mould*
R-33/89 **See The Light** *Jeff Healey Band*
See The Lights *Simple Minds*
M-1/91 R-10/91
R-20/85 **See What Love Can Do**
Eric Clapton
R-29/04 **See You Dead** *Helmet*
R-5/96 **See You On The Other Side**
Ozzy Osbourne
R-39/01 **Seed** *Dust For Life*
M-1/02 **Seein' Red** *Unwritten Law*
R-18/89 **Seeing Is Believing**
Mike + The Mechanics
R-2/91 **Seeing Things** *Black Crowes*
Seen The Doctor *Michael Penn*
M-5/92 R-33/92
M-8/94 **Seether** *Veruca Salt*
R-17/06 **Seize The Day**
Avenged Sevenfold
M-16/89 **Self!** *Fuzzbox*
Self Esteem *Offspring*
M-4/94 R-7/94
R-39/04 **Self Medicate** *40 Below Summer*
M-30/94 **Selfish** *Other Two*
R-39/06 **Sell Me Out** *Bloodsimple*
M-10/97 **Sell Out** *Reel Big Fish*
R-17/99 **Selling My Soul** *Black Sabbath*
Selling The Drama *Live*
M-1/94 R-4/94
Semi-Charmed Life
Third Eye Blind
M-1/97 R-26/97
R-8/91 **Send Me An Angel** *Scorpions*
R-18/84 **Send Me An Angel** *Real Life*

R-53/81 **Send Me An Angel** *Robin Lane*
R-7/89 **Send Me Somebody** *Jon Butcher*
Send The Pain Below *Chevelle*
M-1/03 R-1/03
M-23/90 **Sense Of Purpose** *Pretenders*
R-38/82 **Senses Working Overtime** *XTC*
R-6/91 **Sensible Shoes** *David Lee Roth*
M-6/90 **Sensual World** *Kate Bush*
R-6/92 **Sent By Angels** *Arc Angels*
R-9/87 **Sentimental Hygiene**
Warren Zevon
R-3/85 **Sentimental Street** *Night Ranger*
R-1/83 **Separate Ways (Worlds Apart)**
Journey
Serenity *Godsmack*
R-7/03 M-10/03
R-34/84 **Serious Business**
John Cougar Mellencamp
R-10/00 **Serious JuJu** *Sammy Hagar*
R-19/88 **Serpentine** *Kings Of The Sun*
Set Me Free *Velvet Revolver*
R-17/03 M-32/03
R-21/87 **Set Me Free (Rosa Lee)**
Los Lobos
R-33/91 **Set Me In Motion** *Bruce Hornsby*
R-29/03 **Seven** *Revis*
Seven Nation Army *White Stripes*
M-1/03 R-12/03
R-15/90 **7 O'Clock** *London Quireboys*
R-12/90 **Seven Turns**
Allman Brothers Band
R-2/87 **Seven Wonders** *Fleetwood Mac*
R-19/89 **Seventeen** *Winger*
R-36/95 **Seventh Seal** *Van Halen*
Sex And Candy
Marcy Playground
M-1/97 R-4/98
R-5/85 **Sex As A Weapon** *Pat Benatar*
R-40/91 **Sex Drive** *Rolling Stones*
R-10/83 **Sex (I'm A...)** *Berlin*
M-17/92 **Sex On Wheelz**
My Life With The Thrill Kill Kult
R-23/93 **Sex Type Thing**
Stone Temple Pilots
M-10/93 **Sexual Healing** *Soul Asylum*
M-2/91 **Sexuality** *Billy Bragg*
M-21/99 **Sexx Laws** *Beck*
Sexy + 17 ..see: (She's)
R-23/85 **Shades Of '45** *Gary O'*
Shadow Of The Day *Linkin Park*
M-2/08 R-6/08
M-34/96 **Shadowboxer** *Fiona Apple*
M-19/08 **Shadowplay** *Killers*
R-3/82 **Shadows Of The Night**
Pat Benatar
M-13/91 **Shadowtime**
Siouxsie & The Banshees
R-22/99 **Shag** *Sammy Hagar*
R-19/92 **Shake For Me**
Stevie Ray Vaughan
R-2/82 **Shake It Up** *Cars*
R-9/89 **Shake It Up** *Bad Company*
R-41/86 **Shake Me** *Cinderella*
R-14/91 **Shake Me Up** *Little Feat*
R-3/93 **Shake My Tree** *Coverdale•Page*
R-1/87 **Shakedown** *Bob Seger*
R-9/82 **Shakin'** *Eddie Money*
R-29/99 **Shakin' And A Bakin'**
Honky Toast
R-4/87 **Shakin' Shakin' Shakes**
Los Lobos
R-9/93 **Shakin' The Blues**
Screamin' Cheetah Wheelies

R-19/92 **Shakin' The Cage** *Zoo*
M-9/89 **Shakin' The Tree**
Youssou N'Dour
R-26/05 **Shallow** *Porcupine Tree*
Shame *Stabbing Westward*
R-7/96 M-14/96
R-10/85 **Shame** *Motels*
M-24/01 **Shame Of Life** *Butthole Surfers*
R-13/93 **Shape I'm In** *Arc Angels*
M-19/88 **Shark Walk** *Shriekback*
R-8/83 **Sharp Dressed Man** *ZZ Top*
M-23/89 **Shatter** *Shelleyan Orphan*
M-16/03 **Shatterday** *Vendetta Red*
She *Green Day*
M-5/95 R-18/95
M-9/89 **She Bangs The Drums**
Stone Roses
R-6/83 **She Blinded Me With Science**
Thomas Dolby
R-27/83 **She Bop** *Cyndi Lauper*
She Builds Quick Machines
Velvet Revolver
R-2/07 M-14/07
R-42/89 **She Did It** *Glamour Camp*
R-44/84 **She Don't Know Me** *Bon Jovi*
R-13/87 **She Don't Look Back**
Dan Fogelberg
M-9/95 **She Don't Use Jelly** *Flaming Lips*
M-5/89 **She Drives Me Crazy**
Fine Young Cannibals
R-28/94 **She Gets Too High** *Rob Rule*
M-8/89 **She Gives Me Love** *Godfathers*
R-4/91 **She Goes Down** *Billy Squier*
R-8/93 **She Got Me (When She Got Her**
Dress On) *Masters Of Reality*
She Hates Me *Puddle Of Mudd*
R-1/02 M-2/02
M-5/93 **She Kissed Me**
Terence Trent D'Arby
R-47/82 **She Looks A Lot Like You**
Clocks
She Loves Me Not *Papa Roach*
R-3/02 M-5/02
M-39/07 **She Moves In Her Own Way**
Kooks
R-17/92 **She Runs Hot** *Little Village*
She Said *Collective Soul*
R-16/98 M-39/98
M-32/05 **She Says** *Unwritten Law*
R-48/82 **She Sheila** *Producers*
R-39/96 **She Shines** *Gren*
R-5/92 **She Takes My Breath Away**
Eddie Money
R-1/91 **She Talks To Angels**
Black Crowes
R-39/83 **She Wants You** *Breaks*
R-4/84 **She Was Hot** *Rolling Stones*
R-1/83 **She's A Beauty** *Tubes*
M-7/91 **She's A Girl And I'm A Man**
Lloyd Cole
R-26/89 **She's A Mystery To Me**
Roy Orbison
She's A River *Simple Minds*
R-6/95 M-10/95
R-44/83 **She's A Runner** *Billy Squier*
R-19/98 **She's Gone** *Eric Clapton*
M-16/88 **She's Got A New Spell**
Billy Bragg
She's Got Issues *Offspring*
M-11/99 R-19/99
M-21/90 **She's In A Trance** *Heart Throbs*
R-12/96 **She's Just Killing Me** *ZZ Top*
M-3/92 **She's Mad** *David Byrne*

R-15/84 **She's Mine** *Steve Perry*
R-2/90 **She's My Baby**
Traveling Wilburys
R-12/94 **She's My Machine**
David Lee Roth
R-40/02 **She's On Fire** *Train*
R-2/83 **(She's) Sexy + 17** *Stray Cats*
M-32/99 **She's So Huge** *Flys*
R-11/85 **She's Waiting** *Eric Clapton*
M-9/92 **Sheela-Na-Gig** *PJ Harvey*
M-16/99 **Sheep Go To Heaven** *Cake*
M-25/89 **Sheep's A Wolf** *Caterwaul*
R-39/81 **Sheila** *Greg Kihn Band*
R-20/86 **Shela** *Aerosmith*
Shelf In The Room
Days Of The New
R-3/98 M-22/98
R-26/86 **Shelter** *Lone Justice*
R-5/90 **Shelter Me** *Cinderella*
R-11/86 **Shelter Me** *Joe Cocker*
M-29/91 **Sheriff Fatman** *Carter U.S.M.*
Shimmer *Fuel*
M-2/98 R-11/98
Shine *Collective Soul*
R-1/94 M-4/94
Shine Down *Godsmack*
R-4/06 M-31/06
R-18/05 **Shine It All Around** *Robert Plant*
M-30/07 **Shine On** *Jet*
R-6/98 **Shining In The Light**
Jimmy Page & Robert Plant
Shining Star *INXS*
M-4/91 R-14/91
M-33/02 **Shinobi vs. Dragon Ninja**
Lostprophets
Shiny Happy People *R.E.M.*
M-3/91 R-8/91
R-3/88 **Ship Of Fools** *Robert Plant*
R-5/87 **Ship Of Fools (Save Me From**
Tomorrow) *World Party*
M-26/01 **Shiver** *Coldplay*
Shock The Monkey
Peter Gabriel
R-1/82
Coal Chamber w/ Ozzy Osbourne
R-26/99
Shock To The System *Billy Idol*
R-7/93 M-23/93
R-28/08 **Shockwave** *Black Tide*
R-11/88 **Shoot High Aim Low** *Yes*
R-60/81 **Shoot To Thrill** *AC/DC*
M-12/91 **Shoot You Down** *Birdland*
R-21/89 **Shooting From My Heart**
Big Bam Boo
R-16/83 **Shooting Shark** *Blue Öyster Cult*
M-7/01 **Short Skirt/Long Jacket** *Cake*
R-10/86 **Shot In The Dark** *Ozzy Osbourne*
R-30/86 **Shot O' Love** *Billy Squier*
R-38/81 **Shot Of Love** *Bob Dylan*
R-21/91 **Shot Of Poison** *Lita Ford*
M-8/89 **Should God Forget**
Psychedelic Furs
R-4/87 **Should I See** *Frozen Ghost*
R-13/82 **Should I Stay Or Should I Go**
Clash
R-7/87 **Should've Known Better**
Richard Marx
R-42/82 **Shoulder Of The Road**
Johnny & The Distractions
R-6/85 **Shout** *Tears For Fears*
R-43/83 **Shout** *Grand Prix*
R-30/83 **Shout At The Devil** *Mötley Crüe*
R-40/91 **Shout It Out** *Slaughter*

R-1/90 **Show Don't Tell** *Rush*
R-8/84 **Show Me** *Pretenders*
R-30/92 **Show Me** *Ron Wood*
R-25/05 **Show Me A Sign** *Breaking Point*
Show Me How To Live
Audioslave
R-2/03 M-4/03
R-22/92 **Show Me The Way** *Storm*
M-10/90 **Show Me Your Soul**
Red Hot Chili Peppers
R-40/92 **Show Must Go On** *Queen*
R-35/82 **Showdown** *Riot*
R-2/87 **Showdown At Big Sky**
Robbie Robertson
M-13/94 **Shrine** *Dambuilders*
R-6/92 **Shuffle It All** *Izzy Stradlin*
R-39/97 **Shutterbug** *Veruca Salt*
M-17/97 **Sick & Beautiful**
Artificial Joy Club
Sick Cycle Carousel *Lifehouse*
M-21/01 R-38/01
R-22/05 **Sick Love Song** *Mötley Crüe*
M-9/89 **Sick Of It** *Primitives*
Sick Of Myself *Matthew Sweet*
M-2/95 R-13/95
Sick, Sick, Sick
Queens Of The Stone Age
M-23/07 R-40/07
R-7/07 **Side Of A Bullet** *Nickelback*
M-40/04 **Sidewalks** *Story Of The Year*
Sidewinder Sleeps Tonite
R.E.M.
M-24/93 R-28/93
R-20/84 **Sign Of Fire** *Fixx*
R-19/81 **Sign Of The Gypsy Queen**
April Wine
R-9/91 **Sign Of The Storm**
Eric Gales Band
R-3/97 **Sign Of The Times** *Queensrÿche*
R-28/84 **Sign Of The Times** *Quiet Riot*
M-30/03 **Signals Over The Air** *Thursday*
R-2/91 **Signs** *Tesla*
R-20/93 **Silence Is Broken**
Damn Yankees
M-27/92 **Silent All These Years** *Tori Amos*
R-1/91 **Silent Lucidity** *Queensrÿche*
R-24/86 **Silent Night** *Bon Jovi*
R-7/85 **Silent Running (On Dangerous**
Ground) *Mike + The Mechanics*
Silhouettes *Smile Empty Soul*
M-22/04 R-25/04
Sillyworld *Stone Sour*
R-2/07 M-21/07
Silver And Cold *AFI*
M-7/04 R-39/04
R-15/00 **Silver Future** *Monster Magnet*
R-22/91 **Silver Thunderbird** *Marc Cohn*
R-60/81 **Silverado** *Marshall Tucker Band*
R-5/88 **Silvio** *Bob Dylan*
R-6/89 **Similar Features**
Melissa Etheridge
R-24/99 **Simon Says** *Drain S.T.H.*
Simple Creed *Live*
R-11/01 M-18/01
M-14/00 **Simple Kind Of Life** *No Doubt*
Simple Lessons *Candlebox*
R-5/95 M-12/95
Simple Man *Shinedown*
R-5/04 M-40/04
R-47/89 **Simple Man** *Junkyard*
R-39/06 **Simple Survival** *Mushroomhead*
R-1/88 **Simply Irresistible** *Robert Palmer*
R-24/82 **Since You're Gone** *Cars*

R-11/87 **Since You've Been Gone**
Outfield
M-37/01 **Sing** *Travis*
R-39/83 **Sing Me Away** *Night Ranger*
M-10/91 **Sing Your Life** *Morrissey*
Singing In My Sleep *Semisonic*
M-11/98 R-31/98
R-44/85 **Sink The Pink** *AC/DC*
Sinner *Drowning Pool*
R-28/01 M-36/02
Sister *Nixons*
R-6/96 M-11/96
R-2/84 **Sister Christian** *Night Ranger*
Sister Havana *Urge Overkill*
M-6/93 R-10/93
R-12/93 **Sister Of Pain** *Vince Neil*
M-9/91 **Sit Down** *James*
R-12/88 **(Sittin' On) The Dock Of The Bay**
Michael Bolton
R-3/83 **Sitting At The Wheel**
Moody Blues
M-25/05 **Sitting, Waiting, Wishing**
Jack Johnson
M-7/97 **6 Underground** *Sneaker Pimps*
R-18/85 **Sixes And Sevens** *Robert Plant*
(Sixteen Candles) ..see: Molly
6th Avenue Heartache
Wallflowers
M-8/96 R-10/96
R-39/84 **Sixty Eight Guns** *Alarm*
R-31/81 **Skateaway** *Dire Straits*
R-40/90 **Skies The Limit** *Fleetwood Mac*
Skin *Breaking Benjamin*
R-24/03 M-37/03
R-13/96 **Skin & Bones** *Hazies*
R-2/92 **Sky Is Crying**
Stevie Ray Vaughan
Sky Is Over *Serj Tankian*
M-22/08 R-25/08
M-9/93 **Slackjawed** *Connells*
R-11/98 **Slam Dunk** *DLR Band*
R-33/00 **Slave** *David Coverdale*
R-19/85 **Slave To Love** *Bryan Ferry*
R-1/86 **Sledgehammer** *Peter Gabriel*
R-43/83 **Sleep Alone** *Heart*
Sleep Now In The Fire
Rage Against The Machine
M-8/00 R-16/00
M-28/97 **Sleep To Dream** *Fiona Apple*
Sleeping Awake *P.O.D.*
M-14/03 R-20/03
R-1/85 **Sleeping Bag** *ZZ Top*
R-23/89 **Sleeping My Day Away** *D.A.D.*
M-12/93 **Sleeping Satellite** *Tasmin Archer*
(Sleeping With The Enemy) ..see:
Had A Dream
R-51/84 **Sleepless** *King Crimson*
Sleepwalker *Wallflowers*
R-26/00 M-31/00
R-31/03 **Sleepwalking** *Blindside*
R-39/01 **Sleepwalking** *Seven Mary Three*
R-32/83 **Slick Black Cadillac** *Quiet Riot*
Slide *Goo Goo Dolls*
M-1/98 R-4/98
R-34/99 **Slider** *Simon Says*
R-17/88 **Slip Away** *Gregg Allman Band*
R-12/82 **Slipped, Tripped, Fell In Love**
Foghat
R-7/83 **Slipping Away** *Dave Edmunds*
R-29/02 **Slipping Away** *Dope*
R-41/82 **Slit Skirts** *Pete Townshend*

Slither *Velvet Revolver*
R-1/04   M-1/04

M-19/93 **Sliver** *Nirvana*
R-17/84 **Slow An' Easy** *Whitesnake*
R-19/82 **Slow Dancer** *Robert Plant*
M-17/93 **Slow Dog** *Belly*
M-15/04 **Slow Hands** *Interpol*
R-3/97 **Slow Ride**
Kenny Wayne Shepherd Band
R-28/91 **Slow Ride** *Bonnie Raitt*
R-8/89 **Slow Train**
Bob Dylan & Grateful Dead
Slow Turning *John Hiatt*
R-8/88   M-22/88
R-27/06 **Slowburn** *Revelation Theory*
M-25/94 **Slowly, Slowly** *Magnapop*
R-2/85 **Small Town**
John Cougar Mellencamp
R-39/87 **Small Town Love** *Cruzados*
M-11/92 **Small Victory** *Faith No More*
R-28/88 **Small World** *Huey Lewis*
M-16/95 **Smash It Up** *Offspring*
R-8/95 **Smashing Young Man**
Collective Soul
R-35/92 **Smells Like Nirvana**
"Weird Al" Yankovic
Smells Like Teen Spirit *Nirvana*
M-1/91   R-7/92
R-25/83 **Smile Has Left Your Eyes** *Asia*
M-15/05 **Smile Like You Mean It** *Killers*
M-15/92 **Smiling** *Kitchens Of Distinction*
R-23/93 **Smoke** *Drivin' N' Cryin'*
M-12/89 **Smoke Rings** *Winter Hours*
R-2/91 **Smokestack Lightning**
Lynyrd Skynyrd [1991]
R-7/85 **Smokin' In The Boys Room**
Mötley Crüe
R-2/87 **Smoking Gun** *Robert Cray Band*
Smooth *Santana w/ Rob Thomas*
R-10/99   M-24/99
Smooth Criminal *Alien Ant Farm*
M-1/01   R-18/01
R-23/89 **Smooth Up** *BulletBoys*
R-13/85 **Smuggler's Blues** *Glenn Frey*
M-28/92 **Snacks and Candy**
Miracle Legion
M-19/94 **Snail Shell** *They Might Be Giants*
R-47/81 **Snake Eyes** *Alan Parsons Project*
R-31/87 **Snakedance** *Rainmakers*
R-32/88 **Snakes And Ladders**
Joni Mitchell
M-32/06 **Snakes On A Plane (Bring It)**
Cobra Starship
Snow ((Hey Oh))
Red Hot Chili Peppers
M-1/07   R-3/07
R-22/81 **Snowblind** *Styx*
R-37/04 **So** *Static-X*
So Alive *Love & Rockets*
M-1/89   R-9/89
So Cold *Breaking Benjamin*
R-2/04   M-3/04
M-23/88 **So Excited** *Ranking Roger*
So Far Away *Staind*
M-1/03   R-1/03
So Far Away *Crossfade*
R-4/05   M-14/05
So Far Away *Stabbing Westward*
M-21/01   R-23/01
R-29/85 **So Far Away** *Dire Straits*
So Far So Good *Thornley*
R-15/04   M-27/04

So Happy *Theory Of A Deadman*
R-3/08   M-24/08
M-17/90 **So Hard** *Pet Shop Boys*
So Hott *Kid Rock*
R-2/07   M-13/07
R-30/08 **So Many People** *Neurosonic*
So Much To Say
Dave Matthews Band
M-19/96   R-20/96
M-11/00 **So Sad To Say**
Mighty Mighty Bosstones
R-15/81 **So This Is Love?** *Van Halen*
So What! *Jane's Addiction*
M-22/97   R-37/97
M-22/92 **So What 'Cha Want** *Beastie Boys*
M-29/89 **So What If I Did**
Thelonious Monster
R-18/83 **So Wrong** *Patrick Simmons*
R-7/84 **So You Ran** *Orion The Hunter*
M-1/91 **So You Think You're In Love**
Robyn Hitchcock
R-9/86 **So You Want To Be A Rock &**
Roll Star *Tom Petty*
R-13/93 **Sober** *Tool*
M-7/93 **Sodajerk** *Buffalo Tom*
R-16/98 **Soft** *Second Coming*
M-32/95 **Softer, Softest** *Hole*
R-35/92 **Solar Sex Panel** *Little Village*
Sold Me Down The River *Alarm*
R-2/89   M-3/89
R-26/94 **Sold My Fortune** *Sugartooth*
R-20/07 **Soldiers** *Drowning Pool*
R-10/82 **Sole Survivor** *Asia*
R-31/83 **Solid Rock** *Goanna*
R-56/81 **Solid Rock** *Dire Straits*
R-25/95 **Solitude** *Edwin McCain*
R-43/87 **Solitude Standing** *Suzanne Vega*
Some Guys Have All The Luck
Robert Palmer
R-59/82
Rod Stewart
R-27/84
R-42/84 **Some Heads Are Gonna Roll**
Judas Priest
R-19/04 **Some Kind Of Monster** *Metallica*
R-48/91 **Some Lie 4 Love** *L.A. Guns*
R-34/85 **Some Like It Hot** *Power Station*
R-43/86 **Some People** *Paul Young*
R-1/85 **Somebody** *Bryan Adams*
R-13/93 **Somebody Knockin'** *Izzy Stradlin*
R-6/86 **Somebody Like You** *38 Special*
R-37/87 **Somebody Save Me** *Cinderella*
Somebody Someone *Korn*
R-23/00   M-23/00
R-14/82 **Somebody To Love**
Dwight Twilley
Somebody To Shove
Soul Asylum
M-1/92   R-9/93
M-3/04 **Somebody Told Me** *Killers*
R-4/82 **Somebody's Baby**
Jackson Browne
M-34/95 **Somebody's Crying** *Chris Isaak*
R-9/86 **Somebody's Out There** *Triumph*
R-31/84 **Somebody's Watching Me**
Rockwell
Someday *Nickelback*
R-2/03   M-4/03
M-7/99 **Someday** *Sugar Ray*
M-8/92 **Someday?** *Concrete Blonde*
M-17/02 **Someday** *Strokes*
R-25/03 **Someday** *Sloth*

M-19/93 **Someday I Suppose**
Mighty Mighty Bosstones
M-35/96 **Someday I Will Treat You Good**
Sparklehorse
R-25/82 **Someday, Someway**
Marshall Crenshaw
R-3/98 **Somehow, Somewhere,**
Someway
Kenny Wayne Shepherd Band
R-27/05 **Someone** *Earshot*
M-15/91 **Someone Take The Wheel**
Replacements
R-12/91 **Someone To Love**
Roger McGuinn
R-16/84 **Something About You**
Dave Edmunds
R-45/86 **Something About You** *Level 42*
M-7/92 **Something Good** *Utah Saints*
R-34/90 **Something Happened On The**
Way To Heaven *Phil Collins*
R-19/94 **Something In The Air** *Tom Petty*
R-24/87 **Something In The Heart**
Dave Mason
R-27/02 **Something More** *Sinch*
R-27/87 **Something Real (Inside**
Me/Inside You) *Mr. Mister*
R-4/88 **Something So Strong**
Jim Capaldi
R-10/87 **Something So Strong**
Crowded House
R-5/90 **Something To Believe In** *Poison*
R-5/83 **Something To Grab For**
Ric Ocasek
R-3/89 **Something To Hold On To**
Trevor Rabin
M-7/89 **Something to Say** *Connells*
R-12/91 **Something To Talk About**
Bonnie Raitt
R-31/94 **Something Wild** *John Hiatt*
Something's Always Wrong
Toad The Wet Sprocket
M-9/94   R-22/94
M-20/92 **Sometimes** *Midnight Oil*
M-31/01 **Sometimes** *Ours*
M-4/94 **Sometimes Always**
Jesus & Mary Chain
M-22/00 **Sometimes I Don't Mind**
Suicide Machines
Sometimes It Hurts
Stabbing Westward
R-20/98   M-39/98
R-7/91 **Sometimes It's A Bitch**
Stevie Nicks
R-7/93 **Sometimes Salvation**
Black Crowes
R-11/90 **Sometimes She Cries** *Warrant*
M-29/05 **Sometimes You Can't Make It On**
Your Own *U2*
R-24/88 **Somewhere Down The Crazy**
River *Robbie Robertson*
Somewhere I Belong *Linkin Park*
R-1/03   M-1/03
M-32/04 **Somewhere Only We Know**
Keane
Somewhere Out There
Our Lady Peace
M-7/02   R-26/02
R-47/88 **Song & Dance** *John Cafferty*
R-13/92 **Song & Emotion** *Tesla*
(Song For Lennon) ..see: Life Is
Real
M-23/98 **Song For The Dumped**
Ben Folds Five
Song 2 *Blur*
M-6/97   R-25/97

R-33/06 **Stigmata** *Slave To The System*
R-39/00 **Still After You** *Earth To Andy*
Still Frame *Trapt*
   R-1/03   M-3/03
R-9/90 **Still Got The Blues** *Gary Moore*
R-36/85 **Still In Love** *Taxxi*
R-37/89 **Still In Love** *Stage Dolls*
   (also see: Can'tcha Say You Believe In Me)
R-2/82 **Still In Saigon**
   Charlie Daniels Band
R-8/82 **Still In The Game** *Steve Winwood*
R-36/84 **Still Loving You** *Scorpions*
R-18/87 **Still Of The Night** *Whitesnake*
R-8/98 **Still Rainin'** *Jonny Lang*
R-47/82 **Still They Ride** *Journey*
M-7/03 **Still Waiting** *Sum 41*
R-12/03 **Stillborn** *Black Label Society*
M-38/02 **Stillness Of Heart** *Lenny Kravitz*
R-19/82 **Stillness Of The Night**
   REO Speedwagon
R-1/92 **Sting Me** *Black Crowes*
Stinkfist *Tool*
   R-17/96   M-19/96
M-21/92 **Stinkin Thinkin** *Happy Mondays*
R-35/92 **Stir It Up** *Tesla*
Stitches *Orgy*
   M-18/99   R-38/99
M-30/93 **Stockholm**
   New Fast Automatic Daffodils
M-31/05 **Stockholm Syndrome** *Muse*
M-32/99 **Stolen Car** *Beth Orton*
R-39/01 **Stomp** *Craving Theo*
Stone, The *Ashes Divide*
   R-7/08   M-16/08
R-1/82 **Stone Cold** *Rainbow*
R-32/94 **Stone Cold Hearted** *Bloodline*
M-3/90 **Stone Cold Yesterday** *Connells*
R-4/93 **Stone Free** *Eric Clapton*
R-13/81 **Stone In Love** *Journey*
R-26/85 **Stone In Your Heart**
   Molly Hatchet
M-23/92 **Stone Me** *Wire Train*
R-40/95 **Stone The Crow** *Down*
M-1/90 **Stop!** *Jane's Addiction*
M-19/89 **Stop!** *Erasure*
R-31/85 **Stop** *Jon Butcher Axis*
M-31/08 **Stop** *Against Me!*
R-2/81 **Stop Draggin' My Heart Around**
   Stevie Nicks w/ Tom Petty
M-21/00 **Stop The Rock** *Apollo Four Forty*
R-9/93 **Stop The World** *Extreme*
R-50/89 **Stop The World** *Big Big Sun*
M-23/93 **Stop Whispering** *Radiohead*
(Story Of A Girl) ..see: Absolutely
R-37/92 **Story Of The Blues** *Gary Moore*
R-38/97 **Straight** *Veruca Salt*
R-25/83 **Straight Ahead** *Shooting Star*
R-36/82 **Straight Back** *Fleetwood Mac*
R-11/81 **Straight From The Heart**
   Allman Brothers Band
R-32/83 **Straight From The Heart**
   Bryan Adams
M-12/07 **Straight Lines** *Silverchair*
Straight Out Of Line *Godsmack*
   R-1/03   M-9/03
R-9/91 **Straight To Your Heart**
   Bad English
R-25/90 **Stranded** *Heart*
M-36/02 **Strange Condition** *Pete Yorn*
Strange Currencies *R.E.M.*
   R-8/95   M-14/95
R-9/83 **Strange Dreams** *Frank Marino*

M-21/90 **Strange Kind Of Love**
   Peter Murphy
R-12/84 **Stranger** *Stephen Stills*
R-17/81 **Stranger** *Jefferson Starship*
R-38/92 **Stranger In This Town**
   Richie Sambora
R-7/84 **Stranger In Town** *Toto*
R-9/91 **Stranger Stranger** *Bad Company*
M-29/94 **Stranger Than Fiction**
   Bad Religion
R-21/90 **Stranger Than Paradise**
   Sleeze Beez
R-4/87 **Strap Me In** *Cars*
M-11/90 **Strawberry Fields Forever**
   Candy Flip
R-41/82 **Stray Cat Strut** *Stray Cats*
R-2/83 **Street Of Dreams** *Rainbow*
R-25/94 **Streets Of Philadelphia**
   Bruce Springsteen
R-12/86 **Strength** *Alarm*
Stricken *Disturbed*
   R-2/05   M-13/05
R-23/83 **Strike Zone** *Loverboy*
(String Of Pearls) ..see: Future 40's
R-3/81 **Stroke, The** *Billy Squier*
M-10/95 **Strong Enough** *Sheryl Crow*
Stronger *TrustCompany*
   M-20/05   R-22/05
R-47/89 **Struggle** *Keith Richards*
R-17/84 **Strung Out** *Steve Perry*
Stuck In A Moment You Can't Get Out Of *U2*
   R-35/01   M-35/01
R-39/95 **Stuck In The Middle With You**
   Jeff Healey Band
Stuck On You *Failure*
   M-23/97   R-31/97
R-2/86 **Stuck With You** *Huey Lewis*
Stupid Girl *Garbage*
   M-2/96   R-39/96
Stupid Girl *Cold*
   R-4/03   M-6/03
M-26/89 **Stupid Kids** *Christmas*
Stupify *Disturbed*
   M-10/00   R-12/00
M-10/95 **Stutter** *Elastica*
R-8/82 **Subdivisions** *Rush*
M-3/93 **Sublime** *Ocean Blue*
M-9/91 **Submarine Song** *Candy Skins*
M-10/89 **Suboceana** *Tom Tom Club*
M-20/92 **Success Has Made A Failure Of Our Home** *Sinéad O'Connor*
M-15/92 **Suck My Kiss**
   Red Hot Chili Peppers
M-23/92 **Suck You Dry** *Mudhoney*
M-17/96 **Sucked Out** *Superdrag*
R-42/83 **Sucker For A Pretty Face**
   Eric Martin Band
R-1/83 **Suddenly Last Summer** *Motels*
M-38/06 **Suffer Well** *Depeche Mode*
Suffering, The
   Coheed & Cambria
   M-16/05   R-29/05
Suffocate *Cold*
   R-17/03   M-21/03
Sugar *System Of A Down*
   R-28/99   M-31/00
M-20/97 **Sugar Cane** *Space Monkeys*
R-22/97 **Sugarcane** *Cry Of Love*
M-16/89 **Sugar Daddy** *Thompson Twins*
M-22/92 **Sugar Ray** *Jesus & Mary Chain*

Sugar, We're Goin' Down
   Fall Out Boy
   M-3/05   R-36/05
R-24/05 **Suicide Blonde** *INXS*
   M-1/90   R-1/90
R-24/05 **Suicide Messiah**
   Black Label Society
R-23/98 **Sullivan** *Caroline's Spine*
R-33/86 **Summer Nights** *Van Halen*
M-20/93 **Summer Of Drugs** *Soul Asylum*
R-40/84 **Summer Of '69** *Bryan Adams*
R-5/92 **Summer Song** *Joe Satriani*
M-10/97 **Summertime** *Sundays*
Summertime Blues
   Joan Jett
   R-24/82
   Rush
   R-30/04
R-16/85 **Summertime Girls** *Y&T*
R-41/85 **Sun City**
   Artists United Against Apartheid
M-11/90 **Sun Comes Up, It's Tuesday Morning** *Cowboy Junkies*
M-22/94 **Sun Does Rise** *Jah Wobble's Invaders Of The Heart*
M-23/89 **Sun Gone Down**
   House Of Freaks
Sun King *Cult*
   R-18/89   M-21/89
M-31/99 **Sunburn** *Fuel*
Sunday *Lo-Pro*
   R-20/04   M-27/04
R-7/83 **Sunday Bloody Sunday** *U2*
M-26/98 **Sunday Shining** *Finley Quaye*
M-33/00 **Sundown** *Elwood*
R-15/84 **Sunglasses At Night** *Corey Hart*
M-7/91 **Sunless Saturday** *Fishbone*
M-28/01 **Sunny Hours**
   Long Beach Dub Allstars
M-23/91 **Sunny Side Of The Street**
   Pogues
R-7/85 **Sunset Grill** *Don Henley*
R-15/87 **Sunset Strip** *Roger Waters*
R-23/01 **Sunshine** *Aerosmith*
M-15/92 **Sunshine And Ecstasy**
   Tom Tom Club
R-37/84 **Sunshine In The Shade** *Fixx*
M-29/93 **Sunshine Smile** *Adorable*
Sunshower *Chris Cornell*
   R-8/98   M-12/98
R-39/96 **Super Bon Bon** *Soul Coughing*
R-25/99 **Super Breakdown**
   Sprung Monkey
R-39/96 **Super-Charger Heaven**
   White Zombie
M-35/95 **Super-Connected** *Belly*
R-26/99 **Superbeast** *Rob Zombie*
R-37/90 **Superconductor** *Rush*
R-17/86 **Superman** *R.E.M.*
R-21/01 **Superman Inside** *Eric Clapton*
Superman's Dead
   Our Lady Peace
   M-11/97   R-14/97
M-6/07 **Supermassive Black Hole** *Muse*
Supernatural Superserious
   R.E.M.
   M-22/08   R-39/08
M-6/94 **Supernova** *Liz Phair*
Supersonic *Oasis*
   M-11/94   R-38/94
M-26/94 **Superstar** *Sonic Youth*
   (also see: Rock)
R-11/86 **Superstition** *Stevie Ray Vaughan*

R-9/88 **Superstitious** *Europe*
R-18/98 **Surefire (Never Enough)**
Econoline Crush
R-56/82 **Surfer Joe And Moe The Sleaze**
Neil Young & Crazy Horse
R-37/88 **Surfing With The Alien**
Joe Satriani
R-27/83 **Surrender** *U2*
R-42/89 **Surrender To Me**
Ann Wilson & Robin Zander
Survival Of The Sickest *Saliva*
R-6/04 M-22/04
Survivalism *Nine Inch Nails*
M-1/07 R-14/07
R-10/85 **Sussudio** *Phil Collins*
R-11/86 **Suzanne** *Journey*
Swallowed *Bush*
M-1/96 R-2/96
R-14/86 **Swallowed By The Cracks**
David & David
R-16/88 **Swamp Music** *Lynyrd Skynyrd*
M-24/92 **Sweater, The** *Meryn Cadell*
R-27/93 **Sweating Bullets** *Megadeth*
R-7/88 **Sweet Child O' Mine**
Guns N' Roses
R-17/01 **Sweet Daze** *Pete.*
Sweet Dreams (Are Made Of This)
Eurythmics
R-16/83
Marilyn Manson
M-26/96 R-31/96
R-36/91 **Sweet Emotion** *Aerosmith*
R-7/88 **Sweet Fire Of Love**
Robbie Robertson
M-23/93 **Sweet Harmony** *Beloved*
R-52/81 **Sweet Home Alabama**
Charlie Daniels Band
Sweet Jane *Cowboy Junkies*
M-5/89 R-50/89
M-9/94
M-10/96 **Sweet Lover Hangover**
Love & Rockets
M-14/93 **Sweet Lullaby** *Deep Forest*
R-31/81 **Sweet Merilee** *Donnie Iris*
R-24/07 **Sweet Sacrifice** *Evanescence*
R-26/87 **Sweet Sixteen** *Billy Idol*
M-37/95 **Sweet '69** *Babes In Toyland*
M-5/90 **Sweet Smell Of Success**
Stranglers
R-14/90 **Sweet Soul Sister** *Cult*
M-14/97 **Sweet Surrender**
Sarah McLachlan
R-34/93 **Sweet Thing** *Mick Jagger*
R-33/96 **Sweet Thistle Pie** *Cracker*
M-2/92 **Sweetest Drop** *Peter Murphy*
Sweetest Thing *U2*
M-9/98 R-31/98
R-27/81 **Sweetheart**
Franke & The Knockouts
M-2/02 **Sweetness** *Jimmy Eat World*
M-4/91 **Sweetness And Light** *Lush*
M-12/05 **Swing Life Away** *Rise Against*
M-8/03 **Swing, Swing**
All-American Rejects
R-17/99 **Swingin'** *Tom Petty*
R-27/89 **Sword And Stone** *Paul Dean*
R-10/94 **Sympathy For The Devil**
Guns N' Roses
R-29/92 **Symphony Of Destruction**
Megadeth
R-9/83 **Synchronicity II** *Police*

T

R-38/83 **TV Dinners** *ZZ Top*
M-8/96 **Tahitian Moon** *Porno For Pyros*
R-39/96 **T.A.I.L.** *Into Another*
Tainted Love
Soft Cell
R-12/82
Marilyn Manson
R-30/02 M-33/02
R-10/92 **Take A Chance** *Bob Seger*
R-27/93 **Take A Hold** *Raging Slab*
Take A Look Around *Limp Bizkit*
M-8/00 R-15/00
(Take A Look At Me Now) ..see:
Against All Odds
Take A Picture *Filter*
M-3/00 R-4/00
M-14/89 **Take A Step Back** *Simple Minds*
M-5/91 **Take 5** *Northside*
R-29/06 **Take It All Away** *Faktion*
R-32/81 **Take It Anyway You Want It**
Pat Benatar
R-33/86 **Take It As It Comes**
Steve Winwood
M-13/04 **Take It Away** *Used*
R-39/82 **Take It Away** *Paul McCartney*
R-4/94 **Take It Back** *Pink Floyd*
Take It Off *Donnas*
M-17/03 R-31/03
R-6/81 **Take It On The Run**
REO Speedwagon
R-3/88 **Take It So Hard** *Keith Richards*
Take Me *Papa Roach*
R-11/05 M-23/05
M-5/93 **Take Me Anywhere**
School Of Fish
R-11/83 **Take Me Away** *Blue Öyster Cult*
R-21/83 **Take Me Back** *Bryan Adams*
R-15/93 **Take Me For A Little While**
Coverdale•Page
R-12/86 **Take Me Home** *Phil Collins*
R-46/87 **Take Me Home** *Roger Daltrey*
R-1/86 **Take Me Home Tonight**
Eddie Money
M-3/04 **Take Me Out** *Franz Ferdinand*
R-6/83 **Take Me To Heart** *Quarterflash*
R-23/82 **Take Me To The Top** *Loverboy*
R-7/82 **Take Off** *Bob & Doug McKenzie*
R-36/82 **Take The L.** *Motels*
R-29/93 **Take The Time** *Dream Theater*
R-37/92 **Takin' Me Down** *Hardline*
Taking Back Control *Sparta*
R-24/07 M-25/07
R-41/84 **Taking It All Too Hard** *Genesis*
R-25/03 **(Taking My) Life Away** *Default*
M-5/06 **Talk** *Coldplay*
R-41/82 **Talk Dirty** *John Entwistle*
Talk Shows On Mute *Incubus*
M-3/04 R-18/04
R-26/82 **Talk Talk** *Talk Talk*
R-33/07 **Talk To Her** *Priestess*
R-1/85 **Talk To Me** *Stevie Nicks*
R-12/85 **Talk To Me** *Fiona*
R-41/85 **Talk To Me** *Quarterflash*
M-33/03 **Talk To Me, Dance With Me**
Hot Hot Heat
R-7/81 **Talk To Ya Later** *Tubes*
R-9/88 **Talkin' Bout** *3*
Talkin' Bout A Revolution
Tracy Chapman
R-22/88 M-24/88

M-12/91 **Talkin' Loud And Sayin' Nothing**
Living Colour
R-31/95 **Talkin' Seattle Grunge Rock**
Blues *Todd Snider*
R-17/88 **Talking Back To The Night**
Steve Winwood
R-2/83 **Talking In Your Sleep** *Romantics*
R-1/88 **Tall Cool One** *Robert Plant*
R-24/90 **Tall, Dark Handsome Stranger**
Heart
R-38/07 **Tall Tales Taste Like Sour**
Grapes *Fair To Midland*
R-37/98 **Tangerine** *Life Of Agony*
M-28/00 **Tangerine Speedo** *Caviar*
R-13/92 **Tangled In The Web** *Lynch Mob*
R-28/87 **Tango In The Night**
Fleetwood Mac
Tarantula *Smashing Pumpkins*
M-2/07 R-6/07
M-24/91 **Taste** *Ride*
M-5/92 **Taste It** *INXS*
R-3/98 **Taste Of India** *Aerosmith*
M-19/02 **Taste Of Ink** *Used*
R-42/82 **Tattoo** *Novo Combo*
R-32/99 **Tattooed Bruise** *Doubledrive*
R-42/90 **Tattooed Millionaire**
Bruce Dickinson
M-10/96 **Tattva** *Kula Shaker*
R-32/95 **Taxman** *Stevie Ray Vaughan*
R-4/84 **Teacher Teacher** *38 Special*
Tear Away *Drowning Pool*
R-18/02 M-37/02
R-42/92 **Tear Down The Walls** *Kix*
R-9/88 **Tear It Up** *Robin Trower*
R-52/84 **Tear It Up** *Queen*
M-6/06 **Tear You Apart**
She Wants Revenge
R-51/81 **Teardrops** *George Harrison*
R-5/87 **Tearing Us Apart** *Eric Clapton*
R-8/84 **Tears** *John Waite*
R-20/85 **Tears Are Falling** *Kiss*
Tears Don't Fall
Bullet For My Valentine
R-24/06 M-32/06
R-9/92 **Tears In Heaven** *Eric Clapton*
R-23/86 **Tears In The Rain** *Triumph*
R-36/94 **Tears Of The Dragon**
Bruck Dickinson
M-8/89 **Tears Run Rings** *Marc Almond*
M-10/90 **Tears Won't Help** *Steve Wynn*
R-8/90 **Tease Me Please Me** *Scorpions*
R-35/99 **Teaser** *Mötley Crüe*
M-20/89 **Teen Age Riot** *Sonic Youth*
Teen Angst (What The World
Needs Now) *Cracker*
M-1/92 R-27/92
M-7/00 **Teenage Dirtbag** *Wheatus*
M-13/07 **Teenagers**
My Chemical Romance
R-32/83 **Telegraph** *Orchestral*
Manoeuvres In The Dark
R-15/88 **Telephone Box**
Ian Gillan & Roger Glover
R-3/91 **Telephone Song**
Vaughan Brothers
R-17/83 **Tell Her About It** *Billy Joel*
M-13/92 **Tell It Like It T-I-Is** *B-52's*
R-25/88 **Tell Me** *White Lion*
R-27/84 **Tell Me** *Fastway*
R-30/07 **Tell Me** *Dropping Daylight*
(also see: Drops Of Jupiter)
Tell Me Baby
Red Hot Chili Peppers
M-1/06 R-8/06

R-29/83 **Tell Me What You Want** *Zebra*

Tell Me When Did Things Go So Wrong *Smithereens*
M-11/91 R-28/92

M-9/88 **Tell That Girl To Shut Up** *Transvision Vamp*

R-39/91 **Tell The Truth** *David Lee Roth*

M-6/92 **Tell Your Sister** *Lloyd Cole*

M-17/92 **Temple Of Dreams** *Messiah*

R-25/99 **Temple Of Your Dreams** *Monster Magnet*

R-52/82 **Temporary Beauty** *Graham Parker*

R-49/91 **Temptation** *Box*

R-8/81 **Tempted** *Squeeze*

M-21/00 **10 Days Late** *Third Eye Blind*

R-6/88 **Ten Men Workin'** *Neil Young & The Bluenotes*

Ten Thousand Fists *Disturbed*
R-7/07 M-37/07

R-13/98 **10,000 Horses** *Candlebox*

Ten Ton Brick *Hurt*
R-6/08 M-28/08

R-33/00 **Ten Years Gone** *Jimmy Page & The Black Crowes*

R-18/83 **Tender Is The Night** *Jackson Browne*

R-10/84 **Tender Years** *John Cafferty*

R-39/85 **Tenderness** *General Public*

R-8/90 **Terrifying** *Rolling Stones*

R-30/85 **Territories** *Rush*

R-1/96 **Test For Echo** *Rush*

R-44/85 **Test Of Time** *Romantics*

R-5/82 **Testify** *Greg Kihn Band*

Testify *Rage Against The Machine*
M-16/00 R-22/00

M-26/90 **Testify** *Eleventh Dream Day*

Texarkana *R.E.M.*
M-4/91 R-7/91

R-1/90 **Texas Twister** *Little Feat*

M-12/98 **Thank U** *Alanis Morissette*

R-8/95 **Thank You** *Jimmy Page & Robert Plant*

R-37/08 **Thank You** *HellYeah*

R-39/07 **Thank You** *Tesla*

R-27/87 **Thank You Girl** *John Hiatt*

M-19/07 **Thnks Fr Th Mmrs** *Fall Out Boy*

R-29/98 **Thanksgiving Song** *Adam Sandler*

M-27/91 **That Ain't Bad** *Ratcat*

R-5/87 **That Ain't Love** *REO Speedwagon*

R-6/93 **That Don't Satisfy Me** *Brother Cane*

R-25/89 **That Girl** *Crosby, Stills, Nash & Young*

M-11/91 **That Is Why** *Jellyfish*

M-26/89 **That Smiling Face** *Camouflage*

R-32/98 **That Song** *Big Wreck*

R-14/86 **That Voice Again** *Peter Gabriel*

R-35/84 **That Was Then But This Is Now** *ABC*

R-4/85 **That Was Yesterday** *Foreigner*

R-2/84 **That's All!** *Genesis*

R-17/87 **That's Freedom** *Tom Kimmel*

M-24/95 **That's Just What You Are** *Aimee Mann*

R-35/93 **That's Love** *April Wine*

R-18/90 **That's Not Her Style** *Billy Joel*

R-28/88 **That's The Way I Wanna Rock N Roll** *AC/DC*

That's The Way (My Love Is) *Smashing Pumpkins*
M-23/07 R-32/07

R-25/82 **That's The Way That It Is** *Uriah Heep*

Them Bones *Alice In Chains*
R-24/92 M-30/92

M-4/90 **Then** *Charlatans UK*

M-26/99 **Then The Morning Comes** *Smash Mouth*

R-26/89 **There Goes The Neighborhood** *Molly Hatchet*

M-32/02 **There Is** *Box Car Racer*

M-2/91 **There She Goes** *La's*

M-14/03 **There There** *Radiohead*

R-6/92 **There Will Never Be Another Tonight** *Bryan Adams*

M-24/91 **There You Are** *Goo Goo Dolls*

R-19/91 **There's Another Side** *RTZ*

M-5/91 **There's No Other Way** *Blur*

R-31/82 **There's Only One Way To Rock** *Sammy Hagar*

R-16/88 **There's The Girl** *Heart*

M-1/92 **These Are Days** *10,000 Maniacs*

These Days *Alien Ant Farm*
M-29/03 R-38/03

R-2/86 **These Dreams** *Heart*

M-22/06 **These Things** *She Wants Revenge*

R-6/87 **These Times Are Hard For Lovers** *John Waite*

They Stood Up For Love *Live*
R-24/00 M-31/00

M-27/92 **They're Here** *EMF*

R-11/89 **Thing Called Love** *Bonnie Raitt*

Thing Of Beauty *Hothouse Flowers*
M-14/93 R-32/93

R-36/81 **Things** *Joe Walsh*

R-21/85 **Things Can Only Get Better** *Howard Jones*

R-37/87 **Things I Do For Money** *Northern Pikes*

R-35/02 **Things've Changed** *Sammy Hagar*

R-36/87 **Think About Me** *Tom Petty*

R-50/84 **Think I'm Going Mad** *Rolling Stones*

R-1/82 **Think I'm In Love** *Eddie Money*

M-22/07 **Think I'm In Love** *Beck*

M-9/03 **Think Twice** *Eve 6*

Third Stone From The Sun ..see: Peace On Earth

M-6/94 **13 Steps Lead Down** *Elvis Costello*

M-15/96 **13th, The** *Cure*

M-14/91 **13th Disciple** *Five Thirty*

R-31/00 **36-22-36** *ZZ Top*

Thirty-Three *Smashing Pumpkins*
M-2/97 R-18/97

M-8/07 **This Ain't A Scene, It's An Arms Race** *Fall Out Boy*

This & That *Michael Penn*
M-10/90 R-16/90

R-9/86 **This Could Be The Night** *Loverboy*

R-21/92 **This Could Be The One** *Bad Company*

R-23/84 **This Could Be The Right One** *April Wine*

M-17/04 **This Fire** *Franz Ferdinand*

This Is A Call *Foo Fighters*
M-2/95 R-6/95

M-22/91 **This Is How It Feels** *Inspiral Carpets*

R-17/88 **This Is Love** *George Harrison*

R-36/01 **This Is Not** *Static-X*

R-7/85 **This Is Not America** *David Bowie/Pat Metheny Group*

R-14/91 **This Is Not Love** *Jethro Tull*

R-45/82 **This Is Radio Clash** *Clash*

M-31/06 **This Is Such A Pity** *Weezer*

R-32/87 **This Is The Time** *Billy Joel*

R-23/86 **This Is The World Calling** *Bob Geldof*

This Is Your Land *Simple Minds*
M-12/89 R-37/89

M-30/04 **This Is Your Life** *Switchfoot*

R-37/01 **This Life** *Primer 55*

R-5/81 **This Little Girl** *Gary U.S. Bonds*

M-14/97 **This Lonely Place** *Goldfinger*

M-2/91 **This Love** *Daniel Ash*

R-12/86 **This Love** *Bad Company*

R-16/82 **This Man Is Mine** *Heart*

R-19/88 **This Note's For You** *Neil Young & The Bluenotes*

R-11/85 **This Time** *INXS*

R-21/83 **This Time** *Bryan Adams*

R-47/86 **This Time** *Ufo*

R-36/04 **This Time's For Real** *Ill Niño*

...This Town... *Elvis Costello*
M-4/89 R-41/89

R-1/92 **Thorn In My Pride** *Black Crowes*

R-37/05 **Those Around You** *Intangible*

R-14/92 **Thought I'd Died And Gone To Heaven** *Bryan Adams*

Thoughtless *Korn*
R-6/02 M-11/02

M-11/07 **Thrash Unreal** *Against Me!*

3 AM *Matchbox 20*
M-3/97 R-2/98

3 Libras *Perfect Circle*
R-12/00 M-12/00

Three Marlenas *Wallflowers*
M-17/97 R-21/97

R-43/91 **Three Pistols** *Tragically Hip*

3 Strange Days *School Of Fish*
M-6/91 R-12/91

R-16/85 **Three Sunrises** *U2*

M-25/07 **3's & 7's** *Queens Of The Stone Age*

R-42/84 **Thriller** *Michael Jackson*

M-10/92 **Through An Open Window** *Cliffs Of Dooneen*

Through Glass *Stone Sour*
R-1/06 M-2/06

R-34/08 **Through The Fire And Flames** *DragonForce*

Through The Iris *10 Years*
R-20/06 M-35/06

Through These Walls ..see: Thru These Walls

R-33/97 **Through Your Hands** *Don Henley*

R-30/04 **Throw It All Away** *Default*

R-7/87 **Throwaway** *Mick Jagger*

R-1/86 **Throwing It All Away** *Genesis*

R-15/88 **Throwing Stones** *Grateful Dead*

R-34/83 **Thru These Walls** *Phil Collins*

R-57/84 **Thumbelina** *Pretenders*

R-26/93 **Thunder Kiss '65** *White Zombie*

(Thunderdome) ..see: We Don't Need Another Hero

R-36/82 **Thundering Hearts** *John Cougar*

R-5/90 **Thunderstruck** *AC/DC*

M-36/07 **Tick Tick Boom** *Hives*

333

R-7/90	**Tick Tock** *Vaughan Brothers*	
	Ticking *Loud Lucy*	
	M-31/96 R-38/96	
R-6/90	**Tie Dye On The Highway**	
	Robert Plant	
R-20/89	**Tied Up** *Billy Squier*	
R-41/84	**Tied Up In Love** *Ted Nugent*	
R-19/85	**Tight Connection To My Heart**	
	(Has Anybody Seen My Love)	
	Bob Dylan	
M-6/91	**Tighten Up** *Electronic*	
R-14/89	**Tightrope** *Stevie Ray Vaughan*	
R-35/86	**Tightrope** *Bob Seger*	
R-28/95	**Tijuana Jail** *Gilby Clarke*	
	Til I Am Myself Again	
	Blue Rodeo	
	M-19/91 R-37/91	
	Til I Hear It From You	
	Gin Blossoms	
	R-4/95 M-5/95	
M-25/93	**Time** *INXS*	
R-26/96	**Time** *Hootie & The Blowfish*	
R-34/88	**Time** *Pink Floyd*	
R-6/92	**Time After Time** *Ozzy Osbourne*	
R-10/84	**Time After Time** *Cyndi Lauper*	
R-43/82	**Time Again** *Asia*	
	Time Ago *Black Lab*	
	R-26/98 M-28/98	
M-9/89	**Time And Space** *Flesh For Lulu*	
	Time And Time Again	
	Papa Roach	
	R-26/02 M-33/02	
M-40/04	**Time And Time Again**	
	Chronic Future	
M-8/95	**Time Bomb** *Rancid*	
R-33/90	**Time For Letting Go** *Jude Cole*	
R-18/81	**Time Heals** *Todd Rundgren*	
M-9/04	**Time Is Running Out** *Muse*	
	Time Is Running Out	
	Papa Roach	
	R-15/07 M-17/07	
R-13/81	**Time Out Of Mind** *Steely Dan*	
R-15/88	**Time Runs Wild** *Danny Wilde*	
R-3/87	**Time Stand Still** *Rush*	
R-6/84	**Time The Avenger** *Pretenders*	
R-32/99	**Time To Burn** *Jake Andrews*	
M-35/08	**Time To Pretend** *MGMT*	
M-40/05	**Time To Waste** *Alkaline Trio*	
R-7/87	**Time Will Crawl** *David Bowie*	
M-26/89	**Time With You** *Firehose*	
M-10/07	**Time Won't Let Me Go** *Bravery*	
M-29/07	**Timebomb** *Beck*	
M-12/91	**Timeless Melody** *La's*	
	Times Like These *Foo Fighters*	
	M-5/03 R-5/03	
R-58/81	**Tin Soldier** *Humble Pie*	
M-22/96	**Tiny Meat** *Ruby*	
R-44/81	**Tip On In** *Fabulous Thunderbirds*	
R-27/92	**Tired Wings** *Four Horsemen*	
R-2/86	**To Be A Lover** *Billy Idol*	
	To Be Loved *Papa Roach*	
	R-8/06 M-14/06	
R-19/91	**To Be With You** *Mr. Big*	
R-21/85	**To Live And Die In L.A.**	
	Wang Chung	
M-37/97	**To You I Bestow** *Mundy*	
R-10/86	**Tobacco Road** *David Lee Roth*	
	Today *Smashing Pumpkins*	
	M-4/93 R-28/94	
	Tom Sawyer *Rush*	
	R-8/81	
	R-42/82	

M-7/90	**Tom's Diner**	
	D.N.A. Feat. Suzanne Vega	
	Tomorrow *Silverchair*	
	M-1/95 R-1/95	
M-1/92	**Tomorrow** *Morrissey*	
M-18/02	**Tomorrow** *SR-71*	
R-25/86	**Tomorrow Doesn't Matter**	
	Tonight *Starship*	
M-5/91	**Tomorrow Never Knows**	
	Danielle Dax	
R-16/88	**Tomorrow People** *Ziggy Marley*	
R-20/93	**Tomorrow's Girls** *Donald Fagen*	
	Tones Of Home *Blind Melon*	
	M-20/92 R-10/94	
R-13/93	**Tonight** *Def Leppard*	
R-32/84	**Tonight** *David Bowie*	
R-29/82	**Tonight I'm Yours (Don't Hurt**	
	Me) *Rod Stewart*	
R-8/85	**Tonight It's You** *Cheap Trick*	
R-1/85	**Tonight She Comes** *Cars*	
	Tonight, Tonight	
	Smashing Pumpkins	
	R-4/96 M-5/96	
R-45/86	**Tonight, Tonight, Tonight**	
	Genesis	
R-38/06	**Tonightless** *Eighteen Visions*	
R-31/03	**Tonz Of Fun** *Presence*	
	Too Bad *Nickelback*	
	R-1/02 M-6/02	
R-39/98	**Too Close To Hate** *Sevendust*	
R-13/94	**Too Cold In The Winter**	
	Cry Of Love	
R-29/95	**Too High To Fly** *Dokken*	
R-27/90	**Too Hot** *Loverboy*	
R-25/87	**Too Hot To Stop** *Benjamin Orr*	
R-30/86	**Too Late** *Asia*	
R-11/85	**Too Late For Goodbyes**	
	Julian Lennon	
R-9/83	**Too Late For Love** *Def Leppard*	
R-17/90	**Too Late To Say Goodbye**	
	Richard Marx	
R-48/82	**Too Many Losers**	
	Bobby & The Midnites	
R-2/93	**Too Many Ways To Fall**	
	Arc Angels	
	Too Much *Dave Matthews Band*	
	M-5/96 R-9/96	
R-3/88	**Too Much Ain't Enough Love**	
	Jimmy Barnes	
R-38/83	**Too Much Blood** *Rolling Stones*	
M-30/93	**Too Much Information**	
	Duran Duran	
R-46/82	**Too Much Love To Hide**	
	Crosby, Stills & Nash	
R-2/81	**Too Much Time On My Hands**	
	Styx	
R-16/08	**Too Much, Too Young, Too Fast**	
	Airbourne	
R-23/83	**Too Shy** *Kajagoogoo*	
R-14/83	**Too Tough** *Rolling Stones*	
R-17/84	**Too Young To Fall In Love**	
	Mötley Crüe	
R-47/85	**Tooth And Nail** *Foreigner*	
	Top Of The Pops *Smithereens*	
	M-2/91 R-19/91	
R-15/84	**Top Of The Rock** *Hagar, Schon,*	
	Aaronson, Shrieve	
R-1/91	**Top Of The World** *Van Halen*	
R-38/82	**Tora, Tora, Tora (Out With The**	
	Boys) *Rod Stewart*	
R-19/85	**Tore Down A La Rimbaud**	
	Van Morrison	
R-3/98	**Torn** *Creed*	
M-12/98	**Torn** *Natalie Imbruglia*	

R-23/83	**Total Eclipse Of The Heart**	
	Bonnie Tyler	
	Totalimmortal *Offspring*	
	M-27/00 R-36/00	
R-2/86	**Touch & Go**	
	Emerson, Lake & Powell	
M-36/00	**Touch And Go** *Vibrolush*	
R-29/90	**Touch Of Evil** *Judas Priest*	
R-1/87	**Touch Of Grey** *Grateful Dead*	
	Touch, Peel And Stand	
	Days Of The New	
	R-1/97 M-6/98	
R-13/92	**Touch The Hand** *Bryan Adams*	
R-8/86	**Touch The Night** *Neil Young*	
	Touché *Godsmack*	
	R-7/04 M-33/04	
	Touched *Vast*	
	R-38/98 M-31/99	
R-1/85	**Tough All Over** *John Cafferty*	
	Tough Enough ..see: Tuff Enuff	
R-25/81	**Tough Guys** *REO Speedwagon*	
R-16/92	**Tough It Out** *Webb Wilder*	
R-26/82	**Tough World** *Donnie Iris*	
R-30/97	**Tourniquet** *Marilyn Manson*	
R-31/95	**Tout Le Monde** *Megadeth*	
R-31/82	**Town Called Malice** *Jam*	
	Toxicity *System Of A Down*	
	M-3/02 R-10/02	
R-26/90	**Toy Soldier** *Riverdogs*	
R-7/91	**Trademark** *Eric Johnson*	
M-18/90	**Tragedy For You** *Front 242*	
R-29/87	**Trail Of Broken Treaties**	
	Little Steven	
R-29/94	**Train Of Consequences**	
	Megadeth	
	Transistor *311*	
	M-14/97 R-31/97	
R-1/85	**Trapped** *Bruce Springsteen*	
R-22/97	**Travelin' Man** *Lynyrd Skynyrd*	
	(Traveller, The) ..see: Days Are	
	Numbers	
R-7/90	**Travelling Riverside Blues**	
	Led Zeppelin	
R-39/88	**Treat Her Right**	
	George Thorogood	
R-31/81	**Treat Me Right** *Pat Benatar*	
R-35/99	**Tremble For My Beloved**	
	Collective Soul	
	Tremor Christ *Pearl Jam*	
	M-16/94 R-16/94	
R-24/97	**Trials** *Cool For August*	
M-27/95	**Trigger Happy Jack** *Poe*	
R-21/97	**Trip Free Life** *Hazies*	
M-11/04	**Triple Trouble** *Beastie Boys*	
	Trippin' On A Hole In A Paper	
	Heart *Stone Temple Pilots*	
	R-1/96 M-3/96	
M-18/97	**Tripping Billies**	
	Dave Matthews Band	
R-28/83	**Trooper, The** *Iron Maiden*	
M-21/98	**Tropicalia** *Beck*	
R-12/81	**Trouble** *Lindsey Buckingham*	
M-28/01	**Trouble** *Coldplay*	
R-11/85	**Trouble In Paradise** *Huey Lewis*	
	Trouble Me *10,000 Maniacs*	
	M-3/89 R-20/89	
M-2/93	**Trout**	
	Neneh Cherry w/ Michael Stipe	
R-12/87	**Truck Drivin' Man**	
	Lynyrd Skynyrd	
R-34/83	**True** *Spandau Ballet*	
R-42/87	**True** *Concrete Blonde*	
R-23/90	**True Blue Love** *Lou Gramm*	

R-20/83 **True Colors** *Asia*
R-27/99 **True Friends** *Shannon Curfman*
R-15/88 **True Love** *Glenn Frey*
True Nature *Jane's Addiction*
    M-30/03 R-35/03
R-9/86 **True To You** *Ric Ocasek*
Truganini *Midnight Oil*
    M-4/93 R-10/93
M-11/98 **Truly, Truly** *Grant Lee Buffalo*
R-5/97 **Trust** *Megadeth*
R-50/87 **Trust Me To Open My Mouth**
    Squeeze
Truth *Seether*
    R-8/05 M-25/05
R-22/04 **Truth, The** *Nonpoint*
M-24/03 **Try Honesty** *Billy Talent*
R-26/05 **Tryin To Be Me** *Tommy Lee*
R-2/81 **Tryin' To Live My Life Without**
    You *Bob Seger*
R-4/81 **Tube Snake Boogie** *ZZ Top*
M-1/97 **Tubthumping** *Chumbawamba*
R-29/96 **Tucker's Town**
    Hootie & The Blowfish
M-11/93 **Tuesday Morning** *Pogues*
R-4/86 **Tuff Enuff** *Fabulous Thunderbirds*
Tumble In The Rough
    Stone Temple Pilots
    R-9/97 M-36/97
Tumblin' Down *Ziggy Marley*
    M-5/88 R-43/88
R-1/87 **Tunnel Of Love**
    Bruce Springsteen
R-44/86 **Turbo Lover** *Judas Priest*
R-36/99 **Turn It Up** *Moon Dog Mane*
R-47/92 **Turn It Up** *Henry Lee Summer*
R-11/93 **Turn It Up Or Turn It Off**
    Drivin' N' Cryin'
R-6/81 **Turn Me Loose** *Loverboy*
R-11/00 **Turn Me On "Mr. Deadman"**
    Union Underground
Turn My Head *Live*
    M-3/97 R-3/97
Turn The Page *Metallica*
    R-1/98 M-39/99
R-38/90 **Turn The Volume Up**
    Robin Trower
R-24/82 **Turn Up The Night**
    Black Sabbath
R-17/85 **Turn Up The Radio** *Autograph*
Turn You Inside-Out *R.E.M.*
    R-7/89 M-10/89
R-50/88 **Turnaround** *Stealin Horses*
M-30/88 **Turning Of The Tide**
    Richard Thompson
R-41/89 **Tweeter And The Monkey Man**
    Traveling Wilburys
M-15/03 **12:51** *Strokes*
M-11/94 **21st Century (Digital Boy)**
    Bad Religion
R-4/93 **29 Palms** *Robert Plant*
R-38/81 **22,000 Days** *Moody Blues*
R-11/90 **Twice As Hard** *Black Crowes*
R-1/83 **Twilight Zone** *Golden Earring*
Twist In My Sobriety
    Tanita Tikaram
    M-25/89 R-47/89
R-7/91 **Twist Of The Knife**
    Fabulous Thunderbirds
Twisted Transistor *Korn*
    M-9/05 R-3/06
M-12/92 **Twisterella** *Ride*
M-22/90 **Twisting** *They Might Be Giants*
R-12/83 **Twisting By The Pool** *Dire Straits*

R-12/83 **Two Hearts Beat As One** *U2*
R-39/03 **Two-Lane Blacktop** *Rob Zombie*
R-25/84 **2 Minutes To Midnight**
    Iron Maiden
R-2/93 **Two Princes** *Spin Doctors*
R-5/84 **Two Sides Of Love**
    Sammy Hagar
R-15/93 **Two Steps Behind** *Def Leppard*
R-27/84 **Two Tribes**
    Frankie Goes To Hollywood
M-8/93 **Two Worlds Collide**
    Inspiral Carpets
R-11/88 **Two Wrongs** *Joe Cocker*
Type *Living Colour*
    M-3/90 R-5/90
M-33/07 **Typical** *Mute Math*
(Tyranny Of Tradition) ..see:
    Operation Spirit

U

M-8/93 **Ubiquitous Mr Lovegrove**
    Dead Can Dance
Ugly *Exies*
    R-11/05 M-13/05
R-12/06 **Ugly** *Sevendust*
Ugly Truth *Matthew Sweet*
    M-3/93 R-35/93
M-10/92 **Uh Huh Oh Yeh** *Paul Weller*
R-38/00 **Ultra Mega** *Powerman 5000*
M-23/92 **Ultra Unbelievable Love**
    Robyn Hitchcock
M-3/91 **Unbelievable** *EMF*
R-21/90 **Unbelievable** *Bob Dylan*
R-31/04 **Unbroken (Hotel Baby)**
    Monster Magnet
R-11/87 **Unchain My Heart** *Joe Cocker*
R-13/81 **Unchained** *Van Halen*
R-19/91 **Uncle Tom's Cabin** *Warrant*
M-34/05 **Unconditional** *Bravery*
R-10/85 **Under A Raging Moon**
    Roger Daltrey
R-35/99 **Under It All**
    New American Shame
Under Pressure
    Queen & David Bowie
    R-7/81
    Used & My Chemical Romance
    M-28/05
R-19/86 **Under The Boardwalk**
    John Cougar Mellencamp
Under The Bridge
    Red Hot Chili Peppers
    R-2/92 M-6/92
Under The God *Tin Machine*
    M-4/89 R-8/89
R-28/95 **Under The Gun** *Foreigner*
R-2/88 **Under The Milky Way** *Church*
R-16/94 **Under The Same Sun** *Scorpions*
M-34/07 **Underclass Hero** *Sum 41*
R-33/83 **Undercover Lover** *Art In America*
R-2/83 **Undercover Of The Night**
    Rolling Stones
M-26/07 **Underdog, The** *Spoon*
R-18/86 **Underground** *David Bowie*
R-20/83 **Underground** *Men At Work*
R-35/85 **Underground** *Angel City*
R-5/84 **Understanding** *Bob Seger*
R-19/95 **Understanding** *Candlebox*
M-25/93 **Underwhelmed** *Sloan*

Undone-The Sweater Song
    Weezer
    M-6/94 R-30/94
R-10/92 **Unforgiven, The** *Metallica*
R-2/98 **Unforgiven II** *Metallica*
Unglued *Stone Temple Pilots*
    R-8/95 M-16/95
Uninvited *Ruth Ruth*
    M-24/95 R-24/96
M-26/98 **Uninvited** *Alanis Morissette*
R-2/84 **Union Of The Snake**
    Duran Duran
M-34/03 **United States Of Whatever**
    Liam Lynch
M-5/95 **Universal Heart-Beat**
    Juliana Hatfield
M-28/91 **Unkind** *Mighty Lemon Drops*
R-38/93 **Unknown Legend** *Neil Young*
R-28/04 **Unnamed Feeling** *Metallica*
R-31/02 **Unreal** *Soil*
M-6/91 **Unreal World** *Godfathers*
R-5/90 **Unskinny Bop** *Poison*
Unstable *Adema*
    R-25/03 M-37/03
Unsung *Helmet*
    M-29/92 R-32/92
Until ..also see: Til
Until I Fall Away *Gin Blossoms*
    M-13/94 R-40/94
Until It Sleeps *Metallica*
    R-1/96 M-27/96
R-42/91 **Until My Dying Day** *Thunder*
M-1/91 **Until She Comes**
    Psychedelic Furs
M-12/04 **Until The Day I Die**
    Story Of The Year
Until The End *Breaking Benjamin*
    R-6/08 M-21/08
Until The End Of The World *U2*
    M-4/92 R-5/92
R-38/92 **Until Your Love Comes Back**
    Around *RTZ*
R-48/86 **Untouchable One**
    Tom Cochrane & Red Rider
M-14/02 **Up All Night** *Unwritten Law*
R-21/90 **Up All Night** *Slaughter*
M-19/91 **Up & Down** *High*
R-33/04 **Up For Breakfast** *Van Halen*
R-43/82 **Up Periscope** *Novo Combo*
R-36/84 **Up The Creek** *Cheap Trick*
M-6/88 **Up There Down There**
    Patti Smith
R-16/99 **Upside Down** *Pound*
M-25/06 **Upside Down** *Jack Johnson*
R-22/83 **Uptown Girl** *Billy Joel*
R-1/81 **Urgent** *Foreigner*
R-15/98 **Use The Man** *Megadeth*
R-25/87 **Usual, The** *Bob Dylan*

V

R-13/82 **Vacation** *Go-Go's*
R-31/99 **Valentine** *Shades Apart*
R-37/91 **Valentine** *Nils Lofgren*
Valerie *Steve Winwood*
    R-13/82
    R-13/87
M-3/91 **Valerie Loves Me** *Material Issue*
R-12/82 **Valley Girl** *Frank Zappa*
R-1/88 **Valley Road** *Bruce Hornsby*
R-2/84 **Valotte** *Julian Lennon*
M-34/97 **Van Halen** *Nerf Herder*

R-10/96 **Vanishing Cream** *Hunger*
R-28/87 **Variety Tonight**
REO Speedwagon
Vasoline *Stone Temple Pilots*
R-1/94 M-2/94
R-15/86 **Velcro Fly** *ZZ Top*
M-4/90 **Velouria** *Pixies*
R-34/01 **Vent** *Collective Soul*
R-21/87 **Veracruz** *Santana*
Vermillion *Slipknot*
R-14/05 M-17/05
Veronica *Elvis Costello*
M-1/89 R-10/89
Vertigo *U2*
M-1/04 R-3/04
Vicarious *Tool*
R-2/06 M-2/06
R-15/06 **Victim** *Eighteen Visions*
R-23/82 **Victim, The** *Pat Benatar*
R-10/87 **Victim Of Love** *Bryan Adams*
R-39/82 **Victim Of Love** *Cars*
R-42/85 **View To A Kill** *Duran Duran*
Villains *Verve Pipe*
M-22/97 R-24/97
M-2/04 **Vindicated**
Dashboard Confessional
R-16/99 **Vintage Eyes** *Second Coming*
M-13/90 **Violence Of Summer (Love's
Taking Over)** *Duran Duran*
M-29/95 **Violet** *Hole*
R-19/84 **Violet And Blue** *Stevie Nicks*
M-38/97 **Virtual Insanity** *Jamiroquai*
M-10/92 **Visions Of You** *Jah Wobble's
Invaders Of The Heart*
Vitamin R (Leading Us Along)
Chevelle
R-1/04 M-3/04
R-16/92 **Viva Las Vegas** *ZZ Top*
R-1/81 **Voice, The** *Moody Blues*
R-30/96 **Voice Of Eujena** *Brother Cane*
R-15/84 **Voices** *Russ Ballard*
Voices *Disturbed*
R-16/01 M-18/01
M-25/07 **Voices** *Saosin*
R-14/85 **Voices Carry** *'Til Tuesday*
R-2/89 **Voices Of Babylon** *Outfield*
Volcano Girls *Veruca Salt*
M-8/97 R-9/97
M-30/03 **Volvo Driving Soccer Mom**
Everclear
Voodoo *Godsmack*
R-5/00 M-6/00
R-46/82 **Voodoo** *Black Sabbath*
R-26/84 **Voodoo Chile (Slight Return)**
Stevie Ray Vaughan
M-32/94 **Voodoo Lady** *Ween*
R-30/88 **Voodoo Thing** *Colin James*
M-17/91 **Vote Elvis** *Popinjays*
R-10/92 **Vote For Me** *Joe Walsh*
M-26/95 **Vow** *Garbage*
R-18/85 **Vox Humana** *Kenny Loggins*

W

Waffle *Sevendust*
R-23/00 M-33/00
R-20/82 **Waffle Stomp** *Joe Walsh*
M-22/91 **Wagon, The** *Dinosaur Jr.*
Wait *Seven Mary Three*
R-7/01 M-21/01
Wait *Earshot*
R-13/04 M-33/04

R-18/88 **Wait** *White Lion*
M-34/98 **Wait** *Huffamoose*
R-34/00 **Wait And Bleed** *Slipknot*
R-9/89 **Wait For You** *Bonham*
R-40/88 **Wait On Love** *Michael Bolton*
R-1/81 **Waiting, The** *Tom Petty*
Waiting *Trapt*
R-20/06 M-27/06
M-26/01 **Waiting** *Green Day*
R-1/81 **Waiting For A Girl Like You**
Foreigner
M-6/89 **Waiting For Mary** *Pere Ubu*
R-37/03 **Waiting For Our Time** *Styx*
M-20/88 **Waiting For The Great Leap
Forwards** *Billy Bragg*
Waiting For The Sun *Jayhawks*
M-29/92 R-20/93
R-6/96 **Waiting For Tonight** *Tom Petty*
R-30/94 **Waiting In The Wings** *BBM*
R-8/82 **Waiting On A Friend**
Rolling Stones
R-30/82 **Waiting So Long** *Supertramp*
M-26/95 **Wake Me** *Rusty*
**Wake Me Up When September
Ends** *Green Day*
M-2/05 R-12/05
R-30/97 **Wake-Up Bomb** *R.E.M.*
Wake Up (Make A Move)
Lostprophets
M-9/04 R-16/04
R-19/85 **Wake Up (Next To You)**
Graham Parker & The Shot
R-32/06 **Waking Up** *10 Years*
Walk, A *Bad Religion*
M-34/96 R-38/96
R-16/98 **Walk Away** *Cool For August*
R-34/02 **Walk Away** *Epidemic*
R-38/02 **Walk Away** *Mad At Gravity*
R-48/89 **Walk Away** *Dokken*
Walk Idiot Walk *Hives*
M-19/04 R-36/04
R-6/85 **Walk Of Life** *Dire Straits*
Walk On *U2*
M-10/01 R-19/01
R-10/87 **Walk On Fire** *Little America*
R-14/94 **Walk On Medley** *Boston*
R-27/92 **Walk On The Ocean**
Toad The Wet Sprocket
R-2/88 **Walk On Water** *Eddie Money*
R-16/95 **Walk On Water** *Aerosmith*
R-28/96 **Walk On Water** *Ozzy Osbourne*
M-30/88 **Walk The Dinosaur**
Was (Not Was)
M-13/95 **Walk This World** *Heather Nova*
R-14/91 **Walk Through Fire** *Bad Company*
M-16/92 **Walkabout** *Sugarcubes*
Walkin' On The Sun
Smash Mouth
M-1/97 R-13/97
R-25/89 **Walkin' Shoes** *Tora Tora*
M-12/98 **Walking After You** *Foo Fighters*
M-15/88 **Walking Away**
Information Society
Walking Contradiction
Green Day
M-21/96 R-25/96
M-17/05 **Walking Dead** *Z-Trip*
M-26/07 **Walking Disaster** *Sum 41*
M-4/91 **Walking Down Madison**
Kirsty MacColl
R-14/97 **Walking In A Hurricane**
John Fogerty
R-12/83 **Walking In L.A.** *Missing Persons*

R-7/91 **Walking In Memphis** *Marc Cohn*
M-1/93 **Walking In My Shoes**
Depeche Mode
R-4/84 **Walking In My Sleep**
Roger Daltrey
R-16/84 **Walking On A Thin Line**
Huey Lewis
M-7/92 **Walking On Broken Glass**
Annie Lennox
R-21/85 **Walking On Sunshine**
Katrina & The Waves
M-13/93 **Walking Through Syrup**
Ned's Atomic Dustbin
R-39/89 **Walking Towards Paradise**
Robert Plant
R-47/88 **Walking With The Kid**
Huey Lewis
R-22/90 **Walks Like A Woman**
Baton Rouge
R-34/91 **Wall I Must Climb**
Michael McDermott
R-46/90 **Wall Of Denial**
Stevie Ray Vaughan
R-37/02 **Wall Of Shame** *Course Of Nature*
R-24/94 **Walls** *Yes*
R-17/83 **Walls Came Down** *Call*
R-6/96 **Walls (Circus)** *Tom Petty*
R-23/99 **Wander This World** *Jonny Lang*
R-35/87 **Wanderer, The**
Dave Edmunds Band
R-41/88 **Waning Moon** *Peter Himmelman*
R-15/89 **Want Of A Nail** *Todd Rundgren*
Want You Bad *Offspring*
M-10/01 R-23/01
R-13/86 **Wanted Dead Or Alive** *Bon Jovi*
R-38/84 **Wanted Man** *Ratt*
R-4/86 **War** *Bruce Springsteen*
M-19/07 **War, The** *Angels & Airwaves*
R-13/83 **War Games** *Crosby, Stills & Nash*
R-7/92 **War Of Man** *Neil Young*
Warm Machine *Bush*
R-16/00 M-38/00
Warning *Green Day*
M-3/01 R-24/01
Warning *Incubus*
M-3/02 R-27/02
Warped *Red Hot Chili Peppers*
M-7/95 R-13/95
R-1/84 **Warrior, The** *Scandal*
M-16/89 **Warrior** *PIL*
R-9/00 **Was**
Kenny Wayne Shepherd Band
M-16/89 **Was There Anything I Could Do?**
Go-Betweens
Wash It Away *Black Lab*
R-6/98 M-13/98
R-29/01 **Waste** *Skrape*
R-37/01 **Wasted** *Beautiful Creatures*
M-29/02 **Wasted & Ready** *Ben Kweller*
R-9/82 **Wasted On The Way**
Crosby, Stills & Nash
R-24/07 **Wasted Time** *Fuel*
R-30/92 **Wasted Time** *Skid Row*
Wasteland *10 Years*
R-2/05 M-1/06
Wasting My Time *Default*
R-2/02 M-3/02
R-4/88 **Wasting My Time** *Jimmy Page*
R-35/00 **Wasting Time** *Kid Rock*
(also see: Stay)
R-19/08 **Watch Over You** *Alter Bridge*
Watch The Girl Destroy Me
Possum Dixon
M-9/94 R-37/94

Wild Wild Life
Talking Heads
R-4/86
Wailing Souls
M-28/93
Wild, Wild West *Escape Club*
M-3/88 R-45/88
R-33/93 **Wild World** *Mr. Big*
R-28/82 **Wildest Dreams** *Asia*
R-26/85 **Will The Wolf Survive?**
Los Lobos
Will You *P.O.D.*
R-12/03 M-12/03
R-25/85 **Willie And The Hand Jive**
George Thorogood
R-19/87 **Willie The Wimp**
Stevie Ray Vaughan
R-24/83 **Wind Him Up** *Saga*
R-2/91 **Wind Of Change** *Scorpions*
M-32/06 **Window In The Skies** *U2*
M-11/92 **Window Pane** *Real People*
R-22/83 **Windows** *Missing Persons*
R-18/82 **Winds Of Change**
Jefferson Starship
Wings Of A Butterfly *HIM*
M-19/06 R-20/06
R-3/87 **Winner Takes It All**
Sammy Hagar
R-2/81 **Winning** *Santana*
R-26/81 **Winning Man** *Krokus*
M-14/88 **Winning Side** *Oingo Boingo*
R-10/86 **Winning Ugly** *Rolling Stones*
R-27/96 **Wire** *Nixons*
R-31/85 **Wire** *U2*
R-3/93 **Wired All Night** *Mick Jagger*
R-7/95 **Wiser Time** *Black Crowes*
M-25/93 **Wish** *Nine Inch Nails*
M-26/07 **Wish Upon A Dog Star**
Satellite Party
Wish You Were Here *Incubus*
M-2/01 R-4/01
R-23/04 **Wishbone** *Dropbox*
R-42/87 **Wishes** *Jon Butcher*
M-26/98 **Wishing I Was There**
Natalie Imbruglia
R-3/83 **Wishing (If I Had A Photograph Of You)** *Flock Of Seagulls*
Wishlist *Pearl Jam*
M-6/98 R-6/98
M-18/89 **Witchdoctor** *Sidewinders*
With Arms Wide Open *Creed*
R-1/00 M-2/00
R-1/87 **With Or Without You** *U2*
Without A Trace *Soul Asylum*
R-6/93 M-27/93
R-25/98 **Without Expression**
John Mellencamp
R-42/88 **Without Love** *Tonio K.*
M-15/02 **Without Me** *Eminem*
R-1/98 **Without You** *Van Halen*
R-11/90 **Without You** *Mötley Crüe*
(also see: Another Rainy Night)
R-16/94 **Woke Up With A Monster**
Cheap Trick
R-18/86 **Woke Up With Wood** *ZZ Top*
M-37/07 **Wolf Like Me** *TV On The Radio*
Woman *Wolfmother*
R-7/06 M-10/06
R-15/93 **Woman** *Scorpions*
R-26/81 **Woman** *John Lennon*
M-27/89 **Woman In Chains**
Tears For Fears
R-21/90 **Woman In Love** *Little Feat*

R-5/81 **Woman In Love (It's Not Me)**
Tom Petty
M-18/91 **Woman With The Strength Of 10,000 Men** *Peter Himmelman*
R-18/81 **Woman's Got The Power** *A's*
R-7/87 **Women** *Def Leppard*
R-39/06 **Women & Wine**
Edge City Outlaws
Won't Back Down *Fuel*
R-22/03 M-37/03
Won't Get Fooled Again
Pete Townshend & John Williams
R-39/81
Van Halen
R-1/93
R-43/81 **Won't Let You Down** *Jack Bruce/ Bill Lordan/Robin Trower*
M-16/95 **Wonder** *Natalie Merchant*
Wonderful *Everclear*
M-3/00 R-28/00
M-7/95 **Wonderful** *Adam Ant*
R-48/84 **Wonderland** *Big Country*
Wonderwall *Oasis*
M-1/95 R-9/96
R-31/81 **Woody And Dutch On The Slow Train To Peking**
Rickie Lee Jones
R-42/88 **Word In Spanish** *Elton John*
R-30/91 **Word Of Mouth**
Mike + The Mechanics
Word Up *Korn*
R-16/04 M-17/04
R-60/82 **Words** *Missing Persons*
R-35/04 **Words Can't Explain** *Tesla*
M-6/05 **Work** *Jimmy Eat World*
M-10/93 **Work For Food** *Dramarama*
R-6/96 **Work It Out** *Def Leppard*
R-13/99 **Workin'** *Lynyrd Skynyrd*
R-20/82 **Workin' For A Livin'** *Huey Lewis*
R-21/00 **Workin' It** *Don Henley*
R-16/87 **Working At The Factory** *Kinks*
Working Class Hero *Green Day*
M-10/07 R-18/07
R-22/86 **Working Class Man**
Jimmy Barnes
R-2/82 **Working For The Weekend**
Loverboy
R-34/83 **Working Girl** *Members*
R-53/81 **Working In The Coal Mine** *Devo*
R-1/89 **Working On It** *Chris Rea*
M-4/93 **World Class Fad**
Paul Westerberg
World I Know *Collective Soul*
R-1/96 M-6/96
R-4/89 **World In Motion** *Jackson Browne*
M-5/90 **World In Motion** *New Order*
M-17/90 **World In My Eyes** *Depeche Mode*
R-3/83 **World Of Fantasy** *Triumph*
World Party *Waterboys*
M-19/89 R-48/89
R-22/87 **World Shut Your Mouth**
Julian Cope
R-16/03 **World So Cold** *Mudvayne*
M-5/93 **World (The Price Of Love)**
New Order
R-23/97 **World Tonight** *Paul McCartney*
R-45/87 **World Where You Live**
Crowded House
World Wide Suicide *Pearl Jam*
M-1/06 R-2/06
(Worlds Apart) ..see: Separate Ways
R-10/82 **Worse Than Detroit** *Robert Plant*

Would? *Alice In Chains*
R-31/92
R-19/96
R-2/85 **Would I Lie To You?** *Eurythmics*
R-58/84 **Wouldn't It Be Good**
Nik Kershaw
R-8/86 **Wrap It Up**
Fabulous Thunderbirds
R-9/83 **Wrapped Around Your Finger**
Police
R-31/81 **Wrathchild** *Iron Maiden*
R-23/82 **Writer, The** *UFO*
R-23/92 **Wrong** *Lindsey Buckingham*
M-8/97 **Wrong Number** *Cure*
M-3/97 **Wrong Way** *Sublime*
Wynona's Big Brown Beaver
Primus
M-12/95 R-23/95

X

M-11/91 **X Y & Zee** *Pop Will Eat Itself*
R-38/02 **Xmas Day** *Sevendust*

Y

R-23/04 **Y'all Want A Single** *Korn*
R-10/88 **Ya Ya** *Steve Miller*
R-54/82 **Ya Ya (Next To Me)** *Steve Forbert*
R-10/86 **Yankee Rose** *David Lee Roth*
M-24/99 **Yeah, Whatever** *Splender*
M-17/89 **Yeah Yeah Yeah Yeah Yeah**
Pogues
M-6/01 **Yellow** *Coldplay*
Yellow Ledbetter *Pearl Jam*
R-21/94 M-26/94
R-5/90 **Yer So Bad** *Tom Petty*
Yesterday Girl *Smithereens*
M-16/90 R-20/90
R-35/98 **Yesterday's News** *Whiskeytown*
R-13/92 **Yesterdays** *Guns N' Roses*
R-6/94 **You** *Candlebox*
R-11/97 **You** *Queensrÿche*
R-51/81 **You** *Who*
M-31/98 **You & Me & The Bottle Makes Three Tonight (Baby)**
Big Bad Voodoo Daddy
R-33/83 **You Are In My System**
Robert Palmer
R-2/87 **You Are The Girl** *Cars*
M-25/07 **You Are The One**
Shiny Toy Guns
R-1/85 **You Belong To The City**
Glenn Frey
R-44/82 **You Better Hang Up** *Don Henley*
R-6/94 **You Better Wait** *Steve Perry*
R-1/81 **You Better You Bet** *Who*
You Blew Me Off *Bare Jr.*
R-12/99 M-40/99
R-42/86 **You Can Call Me Al** *Paul Simon*
R-35/86 **You Can Leave Your Hat On**
Joe Cocker
R-15/83 **(You Can Still) Rock In America**
Night Ranger
R-12/84 **You Can't Get What You Want (Till You Know What You Want)** *Joe Jackson*
R-24/82 **You Can't Hurry Love** *Phil Collins*
R-41/82 **You Can't Kill Rock And Roll**
Ozzy Osbourne
R-3/91 **You Could Be Mine**
Guns N' Roses

R-12/83 **You Don't Believe**
Alan Parsons Project

You Don't Get Much *BoDeans*
M-15/89 R-20/89

R-12/92 **You Don't Have To Remind Me**
Sass Jordan

R-1/94 **You Don't Know How It Feels**
Tom Petty

R-22/96 **You Don't Know Me At All**
Don Henley

R-29/01 **You Don't Know What It's Like**
Econoline Crush

**You Don't Know What Love Is
(You Just Do As You're Told)**
White Stripes
M-9/07 R-35/07

R-18/89 **You Don't Move Me**
Keith Richards

M-9/92 **You Don't Understand**
House Of Love

R-9/82 **You Don't Want Me Anymore**
Steel Breeze

M-8/99 **You Get What You Give**
New Radicals

R-9/86 **You Give Love A Bad Name**
Bon Jovi

R-2/89 **You Got It** *Roy Orbison*

R-1/82 **You Got Lucky** *Tom Petty*

R-2/94 **You Got Me Rocking**
Rolling Stones

R-42/82 **You Hit The Spot** *Graham Parker*

M-19/90 **You Keep It All In** *Beautiful South*

R-7/82 **You Keep Runnin' Away**
38 Special

R-46/86 **You Know I Love You...Don't
You?** *Howard Jones*

You Know You're Right *Nirvana*
R-1/02 M-1/02

You Learn *Alanis Morissette*
M-7/96 R-40/96

You Let Your Heart Go Too Fast
Spin Doctors
R-8/94 M-20/94

M-24/94 **You Made Me The Thief Of Your
Heart** *Sinéad O'Connor*

R-38/87 **You Make Me Love You**
Roger Hodgson

R-22/08 **You Make Me Sick** *Egypt Central*

R-35/81 **You Make My Dreams**
Daryl Hall & John Oates

R-40/82 **You Might Recall** *Genesis*

R-1/84 **You Might Think** *Cars*

R-32/88 **You Never Listen To Me**
Peter Cetera

R-32/02 **You Never Met A Motherfucker
Quite Like Me** *Kid Rock*

R-40/98 **You Not Me** *Dream Theater*

M-35/06 **You Only Live Once** *Strokes*

You Oughta Know
Alanis Morissette
M-1/95 R-3/95

R-33/82 **You Remind Me** *Sheriff*

R-29/89 **You Run** *Call*

R-37/00 **You Spin Me 'Round (Like A
Record)** *Dope*

M-23/94 **You Suck** *Murmurs*

R-51/84 **You Take Me Up**
Thompson Twins

R-4/88 **You Talk Too Much**
George Thorogood

You Wanted More *Tonic*
R-3/99 M-10/99

R-22/99 **You Wanted The Best** *Kiss*

M-26/97 **You Were Meant For Me** *Jewel*

M-16/91 **You Woke Up My
Neighbourhood** *Billy Bragg*

You Wouldn't Believe *311*
M-7/01 R-32/01

You Wouldn't Know *HellYeah*
R-5/07 M-35/07

R-2/95 **You Wreck Me** *Tom Petty*

R-16/85 **You're A Friend Of Mine**
*ClarenceClemons & Jackson
Browne*

M-15/00 **You're A God** *Vertical Horizon*

M-27/07 **You're All I Have** *Snow Patrol*

R-5/90 **You're Amazing** *Robert Palmer*

R-22/82 **You're Gonna Get Your Fingers
Burned** *Alan Parsons Project*

R-34/85 **You're In Love** *Ratt*

R-17/92 **You're Invited But Your Friend
Can't Come** *Vince Neil*

R-30/95 **(You're) My World** *Joe Satriani*

R-26/85 **You're Only Human (Second
Wind)** *Billy Joel*

M-18/92 **You're So Close** *Peter Murphy*

R-47/91 **You're So Strange** *Kik Tracee*

M-27/90 **You're Still Beautiful** *Church*

R-37/85 **You're The Only Love** *Paul Hyde*

R-20/91 **You're The Voice** *Heart*

R-29/89 **You're What You Want To Be**
Cruel Story Of Youth

R-36/92 **You've Been So Good Up To
Now** *Lyle Lovett*

R-4/82 **You've Got Another Thing
Comin'** *Judas Priest*

R-27/85 **You've Got To Believe In Love**
Van-Zant

**You've Got To Hide Your Love
Away** *Eddie Vedder*
M-30/02 R-40/02

M-28/03 **Young And The Hopeless**
Good Charlotte

R-37/82 **Young Boys** *805*

M-22/07 **Young Folks** *Peter Bjorn & John*

Young Lust
Bryan Adams
R-7/90
Pink Floyd
R-15/00

R-13/84 **Young Thing, Wild Dreams
(Rock Me)** *Red Rider*

R-23/82 **Young Turks** *Rod Stewart*

R-28/82 **Your Daddy Don't Know** *Toronto*

Your Disease *Saliva*
R-3/01 M-7/01

M-14/94 **Your Favorite Thing** *Sugar*

R-15/98 **Your Life Is Now**
John Mellencamp

Your Little Secret
Melissa Etheridge
R-4/95 M-32/95

R-7/86 **Your Love** *Outfield*

R-3/83 **Your Love Is Driving Me Crazy**
Sammy Hagar

R-8/90 **Your Ma Said You Cried In Your
Sleep Last Night** *Robert Plant*

R-39/89 **Your Mama Don't Dance** *Poison*

R-20/90 **Your Own Sweet Way**
Notting Hillbillies

**Your Own World ..see: Yr Own
World**

R-8/83 **Your Possible Pasts** *Pink Floyd*

R-36/02 **Your Signs** *Nonpoint*

Your Time Has Come *Audioslave*
M-12/05 R-12/05

M-27/93 **Your Town** *Deacon Blue*

R-2/86 **Your Wildest Dreams**
Moody Blues

M-5/97 **Your Woman** *White Town*

M-19/06 **Youth** *Matisyahu*
(also see: Ballad Of)

R-27/89 **Youth Gone Wild** *Skid Row*

Youth Of The Nation *P.O.D.*
M-1/02 R-6/02

M-13/91 **Yr Own World** *Blue Aeroplanes*

Z

M-38/95 **Zephyr** *Electrafixion*

Zephyr Song
Red Hot Chili Peppers
M-6/02 R-14/02

Zero *Smashing Pumpkins*
M-9/96 R-15/96

Zip-Lock *Lit*
M-11/99 R-34/99

Zombie *Cranberries*
M-1/94 R-32/95

Zooropa *U2*
R-8/93 M-13/93

M-15/98 **Zoot Suit Riot**
Cherry Poppin' Daddies

R-29/08 **Zzyzx Rd.** *Stone Sour*

MAINSTREAM ROCK TRACKS WRAP-UP

Top 100 Artists In Rank Order

Top 100 Artists In A-Z Order

Top 40 Artists: 1981-89 / 1990-99 / 2000-08

Top Artists Achievements:

Most Charted Tracks
Most Top 10 Tracks
Most #1 Tracks
Most Weeks At The #1 Position

Top Tracks:

All-Time
1981-89 / 1990-99 / 2000-08

Tracks Of Longevity: 1981-89 / 1990-99 / 2000-08

TOP 100 ARTISTS IN RANK ORDER

This section ranks the Top 100 Mainstream Rock Tracks artists from 1981-2008. Each artist's accumulated point total is shown to the right of their name. This ranking includes all titles that <u>peaked</u> from 1981-2008. A picture of each Top 50 artist is shown next to their listing in the artist section of this book.

POINT SYSTEM:

1. Each artist's charted singles are given points based on their highest charted position:

#1	=	60 points for its first week at #1, plus 5 points for each additional week at #1
#2	=	50 points for its first week at #2, plus 3 points for each additional week at #2
#3	=	40 points for its first week at #3, plus 3 points for each additional week at #3
#4-5	=	35 points
#6-10	=	30 points
#11-20	=	25 points
#21-30	=	20 points
#31-40	=	15 points
#41-50	=	10 points
#51-60	=	5 points

2. Total weeks charted are added in.

In the case of a tie, the artist listed first is determined by the following tie-breaker rules:

1) Most charted tracks
2) Most Top 20 tracks
3) Most Top 10 tracks

Special Symbols:

● = **Deceased Solo Artist or Group Member**

— = Artist did not rank in the Top 100 of the previous edition.

+ = Subject to change — still charted as of the 3/29/2008 cut-off date

TOP 100 MAINSTREAM ROCK ARTISTS

Old Rank	New Rank		Points
(1)	1.	**Van Halen**	2,509
(2)	2.	**Tom Petty** (& The Heartbreakers)	2,474
(4)	3.	**U2**	2,295
(3)	4.	**Aerosmith**	2,254
(5)	5.	**John Cougar Mellencamp**	2,148
(6)	6.	**Rush**	1,791
(9)	7.	**Pearl Jam**	1,756
(7)	8.	**The Rolling Stones** ●	1,755
(8)	9.	**Bruce Springsteen**	1,633
(10)	10.	**Robert Plant**	1,618
(14)	11.	**Metallica** ●	1,555
(11)	12.	**ZZ Top**	1,501
(12)	13.	**Eric Clapton**	1,446
(13)	14.	**R.E.M.**	1,437 +
(20)	15.	**Ozzy Osbourne**	1,416
(17)	16.	**Stone Temple Pilots**	1,380
(16)	17.	**Def Leppard** ●	1,369
(15)	18.	**The Black Crowes**	1,361 +
(18)	19.	**Collective Soul**	1,317
(91)	20.	**Nickelback**	1,292
(33)	21.	**Red Hot Chili Peppers** ●	1,270
(67)	22.	**Godsmack**	1,254
(19)	23.	**Bryan Adams**	1,190
(21)	24.	**Creed**	1,172
(22)	25.	**Genesis**	1,106
(80)	26.	**Foo Fighters**	1,090 +
(73)	27.	**Staind**	1,090
(24)	28.	**Sammy Hagar**	1,087
(23)	29.	**AC/DC** ●	1,079
(76)	30.	**3 Doors Down**	1,049 +
(25)	31.	**Don Henley**	1,017
—	32.	**Linkin Park**	984 +
(26)	33.	**Steve Winwood**	980
—	34.	**Korn**	961
(85)	35.	**Green Day**	957
(27)	36.	**Huey Lewis** (& The News)	934
(28)	37.	**Yes**	928
(29)	38.	**INXS** ●	927
(30)	39.	**38 Special**	924
(32)	40.	**Bob Seger** (& The Silver Bullet Band)	917
(35)	41.	**Bon Jovi**	893
(31)	42.	**Alice In Chains** ●	891
(34)	43.	**Pat Benatar**	878
(54)	44.	**The Offspring**	866
(36)	45.	**Heart**	855
—	46.	**Audioslave**	854
(37)	47.	**Bad Company**	853
(38)	48.	**Pink Floyd**	833
—	49.	**Puddle Of Mudd**	817 +
(41)	50.	**Live**	808
(39)	51.	**Journey**	807
(40)	52.	**Billy Squier**	805
—	53.	**Disturbed**	792
(42)	54.	**Phil Collins**	781
(43)	55.	**Stevie Nicks**	780
(44)	56.	**Foreigner**	772
(45)	57.	**Eddie Money**	766
(46)	58.	**David Bowie**	759
(48)	59.	**Scorpions**	757
—	60.	**Three Days Grace**	755 +
(49)	61.	**The Cars** ●	753
(50)	62.	**Stevie Ray Vaughan** ●	750
(51)	63.	**Sting**	748
(63)	64.	**Mötley Crüe**	740
(47)	65.	**Neil Young**	730
(52)	66.	**Bush**	722
(53)	67.	**Guns N' Roses**	709
—	68.	**Seether**	706 +
(64)	69.	**The Smashing Pumpkins**	705
(98)	70.	**Tool**	705
(69)	71.	**Tesla**	700
(55)	72.	**The Fixx**	692
(56)	73.	**Soundgarden**	690
—	74.	**Papa Roach**	685
(57)	75.	**Rod Stewart**	672
(58)	76.	**The Pretenders** ● ●	672
(59)	77.	**Peter Gabriel**	662
(60)	78.	**Jefferson Airplane/Starship**	658
(62)	79.	**Queensrÿche**	656
(61)	80.	**The Police**	645
(79)	81.	**Kenny Wayne Shepherd Band**	636
(75)	82.	**Lenny Kravitz**	635
(65)	83.	**David Lee Roth**	634
(74)	84.	**Megadeth**	632
(66)	85.	**Fleetwood Mac**	628
(71)	86.	**Billy Idol**	628
(68)	87.	**Jimmy Page**	626
(70)	88.	**Asia**	618
—	89.	**Incubus**	613
(72)	90.	**Nirvana** ●	611
—	91.	**Saliva**	604
—	92.	**Shinedown**	604
—	93.	**Chevelle**	602 +
—	94.	**Sevendust**	581 +
—	95.	**Breaking Benjamin**	566 +
(77)	96.	**Loverboy** ●	565
—	97.	**System Of A Down**	565
(78)	98.	**Dire Straits**	564
(81)	99.	**REO Speedwagon**	557
—	100.	**Kid Rock**	557

A–Z — TOP 100 ARTISTS

The following 16 artists were ranked in the Top 100 Artists of our *Rock Tracks (2002 edition)* book but have now dropped out of the Top 100:

Brother Cane
Jackson Browne
Days Of The New
Melissa Etheridge
Goo Goo Dolls
Great White

Bruce Hornsby & The Range
Mick Jagger
Joan Jett & The Blackhearts
Billy Joel
The Kinks

Kiss
The Moody Blues
George Thorogood & The Destroyers
Triumph
The Who

TOP 40 MAINSTREAM ROCK ARTISTS

1981-89

1. John Cougar Mellencamp . 1,355
2. Tom Petty 1,297
3. Bruce Springsteen 1,275
4. Van Halen 1,241
5. U2 1,135
6. The Rolling Stones 984
7. Bryan Adams 916
8. Robert Plant 909
9. Genesis 861
10. Steve Winwood 860
11. Huey Lewis 857
12. Rush 816
13. 38 Special 811
14. Pat Benatar 793
15. The Cars 753
16. David Bowie 732
17. Journey 730
18. Stevie Nicks 723
19. Don Henley 716
20. Billy Squier 706
21. Def Leppard 705
22. Eric Clapton 703
23. Bob Seger 699
24. ZZ Top 683
25. Phil Collins 674
26. Jefferson Airplane/Starship .. 658
27. The Fixx 658
28. Foreigner 646
29. The Police 645
30. Yes 641
31. INXS 617
32. Eddie Money 617
33. Sammy Hagar 600
34. R.E.M. 598
35. The Pretenders 590
36. Heart 573
37. Bon Jovi 557
38. Asia 551
39. Loverboy 537
40. Aerosmith 501

1990-99

1. Pearl Jam 1,466
2. Aerosmith 1,404
3. Van Halen 1,206
4. The Black Crowes 1,202
5. Collective Soul 1,112
6. Tom Petty 1,104
7. Metallica 1,093
8. Stone Temple Pilots 1,079
9. Alice In Chains 874
10. U2 854
11. Rush 833
12. R.E.M. 799
13. ZZ Top 798
14. John Cougar Mellencamp ... 775
15. Soundgarden 690
16. Live 685
17. Eric Clapton 681
18. The Rolling Stones 679
19. Robert Plant 633
20. Creed 622
21. Queensrÿche 605
22. Ozzy Osbourne 594
23. Bush 591
24. Def Leppard 573
25. The Smashing Pumpkins 565
26. Red Hot Chili Peppers 561
27. The Offspring 550
28. Bad Company 548
29. Lenny Kravitz 527
30. Guns N' Roses 522
31. Nirvana 510
32. Tesla 498
33. Goo Goo Dolls 476
34. Days Of The New 476
35. Kenny Wayne Shepherd
      Band 475
36. Megadeth 470
37. Green Day 468
38. Brother Cane 466
39. Scorpions 463
40. Jimmy Page 460

2000-08

1. Nickelback 1,292
2. Godsmack 1,097
3. 3 Doors Down .... 1,049 +
4. Staind 998
5. Linkin Park .... 984 +
6. Korn 854
7. Audioslave 854
8. Puddle Of Mudd .... 817 +
9. Disturbed 792
10. Three Days Grace .... 755 +
11. Red Hot Chili Peppers 709
12. Seether .... 706 +
13. Foo Fighters .... 688 +
14. Papa Roach 685
15. Incubus 613
16. Saliva 604
17. Shinedown 604
18. Chevelle .... 602 +
19. Breaking Benjamin .... 566 +
20. Creed 550
21. Velvet Revolver 542
22. System Of A Down 534
23. Green Day 489
24. Ozzy Osbourne 471
25. Tool 464
26. P.O.D. .... 455 +
27. Sevendust .... 455 +
28. Metallica 449
29. Kid Rock 433
30. A Perfect Circle 418
31. Mudvayne 415
32. Stone Sour 398
33. Trapt 395
34. Fuel 394
35. Limp Bizkit 366
36. Hoobastank 354
37. Aerosmith 349
38. Drowning Pool .... 337 +
39. Jet 326
40. The Offspring 316

MAINSTREAM ROCK ARTIST ACHIEVEMENTS

MOST CHARTED TRACKS

1. Tom Petty (& The Heartbreakers) 48
2. U2 47
3. Van Halen 45
4. John Cougar Mellencamp 45
5. Aerosmith 42
6. Bruce Springsteen...42
7. Rush 40
8. Pearl Jam 37
9. R.E.M. 35
10. The Rolling Stones..34
11. Robert Plant 33
12. Eric Clapton 33
13. ZZ Top 31
14. Bryan Adams 30
15. Ozzy Osbourne 29
16. Def Leppard 29
17. AC/DC 28
18. Metallica 25
19. Sammy Hagar...25
20. Bon Jovi 25

MOST TOP 10 TRACKS

1. Tom Petty (& The Heartbreakers) 28
2. Van Halen 26
3. Aerosmith 24
4. John Cougar Mellencamp.................................. 23
5. U2 21
6. Robert Plant 21
7. Rush 20
8. The Rolling Stones 18
9. Bruce Springsteen 18
10. Pearl Jam 17
11. The Black Crowes 17
12. ZZ Top 16
13. Eric Clapton 16
14. Ozzy Osbourne 16
15. Def Leppard 16
16. Godsmack 16
17. Metallica 15
18. R.E.M. 15
19. Stone Temple Pilots 15
20. Bryan Adams 15

MOST #1 TRACKS

1. Van Halen 13
2. Tom Petty (& The Heartbreakers) 10
3. Aerosmith 9
4. U2 7
5. John Cougar Mellencamp 7
6. Collective Soul...7
7. Robert Plant 6
8. ZZ Top 6
9. Stone Temple Pilots..6
10. The Black Crowes 6
11. Nickelback..6
12. Rush 5
13. The Rolling Stones..5
14. Bruce Springsteen..5
15. Metallica 5
16. Eric Clapton 5
17. Def Leppard 5
18. Red Hot Chili Peppers 5
19. Puddle Of Mudd 5

(9-way tie at 4)

MOST WEEKS AT THE #1 POSITION

1. 3 Doors Down 50
2. Collective Soul 47
3. Van Halen 45
4. Nickelback... 45
5. Aerosmith 38
6. Metallica 36
7. Creed 36
8. Staind.. 36
9. Red Hot Chili Peppers 35
10. U2.. 34
11. Tom Petty (& The Heartbreakers) 31
12. Three Days Grace 30
13. The Rolling Stones... 27
14. The Black Crowes 26
15. Puddle Of Mudd 26
16. Days Of The New 26
17. Stone Temple Pilots 24
18. Pearl Jam 22
19. ZZ Top 22
20. Seether 22

TOP 100 MAINSTREAM ROCK TRACKS 1981-2008

Peak Year	Wks Chr	Wks T20	Wks T10	Wks @ #1	Rank	Title	Artist
00	53	50	35	21	1.	Loser	3 Doors Down
01	42	42	31	20	2.	It's Been Awhile	Staind
99	51	51	34	17	3.	Higher	Creed
02	40	39	33	17	4.	When I'm Gone	3 Doors Down
97	46	44	30	16	5.	Touch, Peel And Stand	Days Of The New
99	33	33	25	15	6.	Heavy	Collective Soul
94	33	31	23	15	7.	Interstate Love Song	Stone Temple Pilots
03	42	40	31	14	8.	So Far Away	Staind
07	30 +	29 +	28 +	14	9.	Fake It	Seether
05	38	36	24	14	10.	Boulevard Of Broken Dreams	Green Day
01	48	46	38	13	11.	How You Remind Me	Nickelback
04	39	37	26	13	12.	Figured You Out	Nickelback
06	42	39	25	13	13.	Pain	Three Days Grace
81	32	24	21	13	14.	Start Me Up	The Rolling Stones
03	39	37	28	12	15.	Like A Stone	Audioslave
05	38	37	26	12	16.	Save Me	Shinedown
06	25	25	20	12	17.	Dani California	Red Hot Chili Peppers
91	30	21	16	12	18.	Mysterious Ways	U2
04	43	41	25	11	19.	Fall To Pieces	Velvet Revolver
98	26	22	18	11	20.	Turn The Page	Metallica
92	20	18	15	11	21.	Remedy	The Black Crowes
02	42	40	28	10	22.	Blurry	Puddle Of Mudd
99	29	28	23	10	23.	Scar Tissue	Red Hot Chili Peppers
98	27	25	19	10	24.	The Down Town	Days Of The New
95	26	24	18	10	25.	Lightning Crashes	Live
00	51	50	40	9	26.	Kryptonite	3 Doors Down
04	33	32	23	9	27.	Slither	Velvet Revolver
01	28	28	22	9	28.	My Sacrifice	Creed
95	26	25	20	9	29.	December	Collective Soul
93	20	19	13	9	30.	Livin' On The Edge	Aerosmith
83	21	11	11	9	31.	Every Breath You Take	The Police
05	52	51	29	8	32.	Remedy	Seether
04	33	29	19	8	33.	Cold Hard Bitch	Jet
07	27	27	19	8	34.	What I've Done	Linkin Park
94	26	22	18	8	35.	Shine	Collective Soul
96	26	21	18	8	36.	Until It Sleeps	Metallica
95	26	24	17	8	37.	Better Man	Pearl Jam
93	26	20	16	8	38.	Daughter	Pearl Jam
84	13	11	10	8	39.	Jump	Van Halen
06	40	39	29	7	40.	Through Glass	Stone Sour
06	48	47	27	7	41.	Animal I Have Become	Three Days Grace
00	43	43	27	7	42.	I Disappear	Metallica
07	43	41	23	7	43.	Never Too Late	Three Days Grace
00	34	34	22	7	44.	No Leaf Clover	Metallica
07	31	30	22	7	45.	Breath	Breaking Benjamin
02	26	24	18	7	46.	By The Way	Red Hot Chili Peppers
94	26	21	17	7	47.	Black Hole Sun	Soundgarden
05	26	20	17	7	48.	Be Yourself	Audioslave
05	24	23	16	7	49.	Photograph	Nickelback
91	13	10	9	7	50.	All This Time	Sting

TOP 100 MAINSTREAM ROCK TRACKS 1981-2008

Peak Year	Wks Chr	Wks T20	Wks T10	Wks @ #1	Rank	Title	Artist
98	42	41	26	6	51.	Blue On Black	Kenny Wayne Shepherd Band
02	29	27	23	6	52.	Drift & Die	Puddle Of Mudd
98	39	37	22	6	53.	What's This Life For	Creed
07	32	31	22	6	54.	The Pretender	Foo Fighters
06	28	28	21	6	55.	Speak	Godsmack
06	34	33	18	6	56.	Animals	Nickelback
08	24 +	20 +	18 +	6 +	57.	Psycho	Puddle Of Mudd
95	26	22	16	6	58.	And Fools Shine On	Brother Cane
98	23	18	14	6	59.	Given To Fly	Pearl Jam
96	26	15	14	6	60.	Me Wise Magic	Van Halen
92	20	17	13	6	61.	Hotel Illness	The Black Crowes
93	20	17	12	6	62.	Cryin'	Aerosmith
83	26	15	12	6	63.	Photograph	Def Leppard
82	20	16	11	6	64.	Everybody Wants You	Billy Squier
88	18	15	11	6	65.	Angel Of Harlem	U2
92	17	14	11	6	66.	How About That	Bad Company
94	26	13	11	6	67.	Keep Talking	Pink Floyd
93	15	13	11	6	68.	Pride And Joy	Coverdale·Page
89	14	11	11	6	69.	Pretending	Eric Clapton
82	22	14	10	6	70.	Heat Of The Moment	Asia
81	23	12	10	6	71.	The Waiting	Tom Petty & The Heartbreakers
84	17	11	10	6	72.	Dancing In The Dark	Bruce Springsteen
91	16	11	10	6	73.	Lift Me Up	Yes
91	15	11	10	6	74.	Learning To Fly	Tom Petty & The Heartbreakers
90	17	12	9	6	75.	My Head's In Mississippi	ZZ Top
86	14	11	9	6	76.	I Want To Make The World Turn Around	Steve Miller Band
90	13	10	9	6	77.	Hurting Kind (I've Got My Eyes On You)	Robert Plant
98	12	10	9	6	78.	Without You	Van Halen
88	12	9	8	6	79.	Heaven Knows	Robert Plant
97	37	36	28	5	80.	If You Could Only See	Tonic
97	30	27	21	5	81.	One Headlight	The Wallflowers
07	27	26	20	5	82.	I Don't Wanna Stop	Ozzy Osbourne
96	26	24	16	5	83.	Burden In My Hand	Soundgarden
95	26	23	15	5	84.	Name	Goo Goo Dolls
97	26	18	13	5	85.	Listen	Collective Soul
83	31	17	13	5	86.	King Of Pain	The Police
01	26	16	13	5	87.	Jaded	Aerosmith
97	26	14	12	5	88.	Falling In Love (Is Hard On The Knees)	Aerosmith
82	26	14	12	5	89.	I Love Rock 'N Roll	Joan Jett & The Blackhearts
85	17	14	12	5	90.	Silent Running (On Dangerous Ground)	Mike + The Mechanics
84	17	13	12	5	91.	The Boys Of Summer	Don Henley
83	15	13	12	5	92.	She's A Beauty	The Tubes
89	19	13	11	5	93.	Rock And A Hard Place	The Rolling Stones
97	16	13	10	5	94.	Little White Lie	Sammy Hagar
82	15	13	10	5	95.	Eye Of The Tiger	Survivor
81	15	12	10	5	96.	You Better You Bet	The Who
87	14	11	9	5	97.	Midnight Blue	Lou Gramm
85	14	11	9	5	98.	Lonely Ol' Night	John Cougar Mellencamp
87	13	10	9	5	99.	With Or Without You	U2
82	17	13	8	5	100.	Down Under	Men At Work

TOP 50 MAINSTREAM ROCK TRACKS 1981-89

Peak Year	Wks Chr	Wks T20	Wks T10	Wks @ #1	Rank	Title	Artist
81	32	24	21	13	1.	Start Me Up	The Rolling Stones
83	21	11	11	9	2.	Every Breath You Take	The Police
84	13	11	10	8	3.	Jump	Van Halen
83	26	15	12	6	4.	Photograph	Def Leppard
82	20	16	11	6	5.	Everybody Wants You	Billy Squier
88	18	15	11	6	6.	Angel Of Harlem	U2
89	14	11	11	6	7.	Pretending	Eric Clapton
82	22	14	10	6	8.	Heat Of The Moment	Asia
81	23	12	10	6	9.	The Waiting	Tom Petty & The Heartbreakers
84	17	11	10	6	10.	Dancing In The Dark	Bruce Springsteen
86	14	11	9	6	11.	I Want To Make The World Turn Around	Steve Miller Band
88	12	9	8	6	12.	Heaven Knows	Robert Plant
83	31	17	13	5	13.	King Of Pain	The Police
82	26	14	12	5	14.	I Love Rock 'N Roll	Joan Jett & The Blackhearts
85	17	14	12	5	15.	Silent Running (On Dangerous Ground)	Mike + The Mechanics
84	17	13	12	5	16.	The Boys Of Summer	Don Henley
83	15	13	12	5	17.	She's A Beauty	The Tubes
89	19	13	11	5	18.	Rock And A Hard Place	The Rolling Stones
82	15	13	10	5	19.	Eye Of The Tiger	Survivor
81	15	12	10	5	20.	You Better You Bet	The Who
87	14	11	9	5	21.	Midnight Blue	Lou Gramm
85	14	11	9	5	22.	Lonely Ol' Night	John Cougar Mellencamp
87	13	10	9	5	23.	With Or Without You	U2
82	17	13	8	5	24.	Down Under	Men At Work
89	14	10	8	5	25.	I Won't Back Down	Tom Petty
88	11	9	8	5	26.	Desire	U2
87	11	8	8	5	27.	Paper In Fire	John Cougar Mellencamp
89	9	8	7	5	28.	Mixed Emotions	The Rolling Stones
84	11	8	6	5	29.	On The Dark Side	John Cafferty & The Beaver Brown Band
81	27	23	17	4	30.	The Voice	The Moody Blues
81	30	19	17	4	31.	Urgent	Foreigner
83	25	18	16	4	32.	Separate Ways (Worlds Apart)	Journey
83	20	13	12	4	33.	Owner Of A Lonely Heart	Yes
87	17	13	12	4	34.	Tunnel Of Love	Bruce Springsteen
83	15	12	12	4	35.	If I'd Been The One	38 Special
84	15	12	10	4	36.	Run To You	Bryan Adams
86	14	11	10	4	37.	Higher Love	Steve Winwood
89	14	11	9	4	38.	Driven Out	The Fixx
88	16	12	8	4	39.	Tall Cool One	Robert Plant
83	17	10	8	4	40.	Love Is A Battlefield	Pat Benatar
86	12	10	8	4	41.	All The Kings Horses	The Firm
87	12	9	8	4	42.	Jammin' Me	Tom Petty & The Heartbreakers
88	11	9	8	4	43.	Roll With It	Steve Winwood
88	11	8	8	4	44.	Hate To Lose Your Lovin'	Little Feat
89	12	9	7	4	45.	The End Of The Innocence	Don Henley
87	11	8	7	4	46.	Say You Will	Foreigner
88	10	8	7	4	47.	Just Like Paradise	David Lee Roth
87	10	8	7	4	48.	Shakedown	Bob Seger
82	25	17	13	3	49.	Centerfold	J. Geils Band
85	20	15	12	3	50.	Money For Nothing	Dire Straits

TOP 50 MAINSTREAM ROCK TRACKS 1990-99

Peak Year	Wks Chr	Wks T20	Wks T10	Wks @ #1	Rank	Title	Artist
99	51	51	34	17	1.	Higher	Creed
97	46	44	30	16	2.	Touch, Peel And Stand	Days Of The New
99	33	33	25	15	3.	Heavy	Collective Soul
94	33	31	23	15	4.	Interstate Love Song	Stone Temple Pilots
91	30	21	16	12	5.	Mysterious Ways	U2
98	26	22	18	11	6.	Turn The Page	Metallica
92	20	18	15	11	7.	Remedy	The Black Crowes
99	29	28	23	10	8.	Scar Tissue	Red Hot Chili Peppers
98	27	25	19	10	9.	The Down Town	Days Of The New
95	26	24	18	10	10.	Lightning Crashes	Live
95	26	25	20	9	11.	December	Collective Soul
93	20	19	13	9	12.	Livin' On The Edge	Aerosmith
94	26	22	18	8	13.	Shine	Collective Soul
96	26	21	18	8	14.	Until It Sleeps	Metallica
95	26	24	17	8	15.	Better Man	Pearl Jam
93	26	20	16	8	16.	Daughter	Pearl Jam
94	26	21	17	7	17.	Black Hole Sun	Soundgarden
91	13	10	9	7	18.	All This Time	Sting
98	42	41	26	6	19.	Blue On Black	Kenny Wayne Shepherd Band
98	39	37	22	6	20.	What's This Life For	Creed
95	26	22	16	6	21.	And Fools Shine On	Brother Cane
98	23	18	14	6	22.	Given To Fly	Pearl Jam
96	26	15	14	6	23.	Me Wise Magic	Van Halen
92	20	17	13	6	24.	Hotel Illness	The Black Crowes
93	20	17	12	6	25.	Cryin'	Aerosmith
92	17	14	11	6	26.	How About That	Bad Company
94	26	13	11	6	27.	Keep Talking	Pink Floyd
93	15	13	11	6	28.	Pride And Joy	Coverdale·Page
91	16	11	10	6	29.	Life Me Up	Yes
91	15	11	10	6	30.	Learning To Fly	Tom Petty & The Heartbreakers
90	17	12	9	6	31.	My Head's In Mississippi	ZZ Top
90	13	10	9	6	32.	Hurting Kind (I've Got My Eyes On You)	Robert Plant
98	12	10	9	6	33.	Without You	Van Halen
97	37	36	28	5	34.	If You Could Only See	Tonic
97	30	27	21	5	35.	One Headlight	The Wallflowers
96	26	24	16	5	36.	Burden In My Hand	Soundgarden
95	26	23	15	5	37.	Name	Goo Goo Dolls
97	26	18	13	5	38.	Listen	Collective Soul
97	26	14	12	5	39.	Falling In Love (Is Hard On The Knees)	Aerosmith
97	16	13	10	5	40.	Little White Lie	Sammy Hagar
93	20	10	8	5	41.	Stand Up (Kick Love Into Motion)	Def Leppard
96	35	31	21	4	42.	Cumbersome	Seven Mary Three
96	26	23	18	4	43.	Trippin' On A Hole In A Paper Heart	Stone Temple Pilots
96	26	24	17	4	44.	The World I Know	Collective Soul
96	26	24	16	4	45.	Blow Up The Outside World	Soundgarden
96	32	29	15	4	46.	In The Meantime	Spacehog
91	51	22	15	4	47.	Top Of The World	Van Halen
97	26	21	15	4	48.	Precious Declaration	Collective Soul
98	26	20	15	4	49.	I Lie In The Bed I Make	Brother Cane
95	26	20	15	4	50.	My Friends	Red Hot Chili Peppers

TOP 50 MAINSTREAM ROCK TRACKS 2000-08

Peak Year	Wks Chr	Wks T20	Wks T10	Wks @ #1	Rank	Title	Artist
00	53	50	35	21	1.	Loser	3 Doors Down
01	42	42	31	20	2.	It's Been Awhile	Staind
02	40	39	33	17	3.	When I'm Gone	3 Doors Down
03	42	40	31	14	4.	So Far Away	Staind
07	30 +	29 +	28 +	14	5.	Fake It	Seether
05	38	36	24	14	6.	Boulevard Of Broken Dreams	Green Day
01	48	46	38	13	7.	How You Remind Me	Nickelback
04	39	37	26	13	8.	Figured You Out	Nickelback
06	42	39	25	13	9.	Pain	Three Days Grace
03	39	37	28	12	10.	Like A Stone	Audioslave
05	38	37	26	12	11.	Save Me	Shinedown
06	25	25	20	12	12.	Dani California	Red Hot Chili Peppers
04	43	41	25	11	13.	Fall To Pieces	Velvet Revolver
02	42	40	28	10	14.	Blurry	Puddle Of Mudd
00	51	50	40	9	15.	Kryptonite	3 Doors Down
04	33	32	23	9	16.	Slither	Velvet Revolver
01	28	28	22	9	17.	My Sacrifice	Creed
05	52	51	29	8	18.	Remedy	Seether
04	33	29	19	8	19.	Cold Hard Bitch	Jet
07	27	27	19	8	20.	What I've Done	Linkin Park
06	40	39	29	7	21.	Through Glass	Stone Sour
06	48	47	27	7	22.	Animal I Have Become	Three Days Grace
00	43	43	27	7	23.	I Disappear	Metallica
07	43	41	23	7	24.	Never Too Late	Three Days Grace
00	34	34	22	7	25.	No Leaf Clover	Metallica
07	31	30	22	7	26.	Breath	Breaking Benjamin
02	26	24	18	7	27.	By The Way	Red Hot Chili Peppers
05	26	20	17	7	28.	Be Yourself	Audioslave
05	24	23	16	7	29.	Photograph	Nickelback
02	29	27	23	6	30.	Drift & Die	Puddle Of Mudd
07	32	31	22	6	31.	The Pretender	Foo Fighters
06	28	28	21	6	32.	Speak	Godsmack
06	34	33	18	6	33.	Animals	Nickelback
08	24 +	20 +	18 +	6 +	34.	Psycho	Puddle Of Mudd
07	27	26	20	5	35.	I Don't Wanna Stop	Ozzy Osbourne
01	26	16	13	5	36.	Jaded	Aerosmith
02	43	42	31	4	37.	I Stand Alone	Godsmack
06	37	32	22	4	38.	The Pot	Tool
05	33	32	22	4	39.	Best Of You	Foo Fighters
03	35	30	22	4	40.	Send The Pain Below	Chevelle
00	31	29	22	4	41.	With Arms Wide Open	Creed
02	26	17	14	4	42.	You Know You're Right	Nirvana
00	23	16	14	4	43.	Stiff Upper Lip	AC/DC
04	36	31	23	3	44.	Just Like You	Three Days Grace
02	32	30	23	3	45.	Too Bad	Nickelback
06	37	36	21	3	46.	Land Of Confusion	Disturbed
01	26	24	21	3	47.	Duck And Run	3 Doors Down
04	30	27	19	3	48.	Numb	Linkin Park
05	26	21	16	3	49.	Holiday	Green Day
02	27	25	14	3	50.	Never Again	Nickelback

TRACKS OF LONGEVITY

1981-89

Peak Year	Peak Pos	Peak Wks	Wks Chr	Rank	Title	Artist
82	4	1	37	1.	You've Got Another Thing Comin'	Judas Priest
81	3	2	34	2.	Juke Box Hero	Foreigner
89	1	1	33	3.	Free Fallin'	Tom Petty
81	1	13	32	4.	Start Me Up	The Rolling Stones
83	6	1	32	5.	Modern Love	David Bowie
81	15	1	32	6.	Our Lips Are Sealed	Go-Go's
83	1	5	31	7.	King Of Pain	The Police
84	2	1	31	8.	Panama	Van Halen
83	4	2	31	9.	Back On The Chain Gang	The Pretenders
81	7	1	31	10.	In The Dark	Billy Squier
83	9	1	31	11.	Synchronicity II	The Police
81	1	4	30	12.	Urgent	Foreigner

1990-99

Peak Year	Peak Pos	Peak Wks	Wks Chr	Rank	Title	Artist
99	1	17	51	1.	Higher	Creed
91	1	4	51	2.	Top Of The World	Van Halen
99	5	2	48	3.	Keep Away	Godsmack
98	1	3	47	4.	Fly Away	Lenny Kravitz
97	1	16	46	5.	Touch, Peel And Stand	Days Of The New
92	2	4	46	6.	Right Now	Van Halen
97	2	10	44	7.	My Own Prison	Creed
99	7	1	44	8.	Whatever	Godsmack
98	1	6	42	9.	Blue On Black	Kenny Wayne Shepherd Band
98	1	6	39	10.	What's This Life For	Creed
99	2	7	38	11.	One	Creed
97	1	5	37	12.	If You Could Only See	Tonic

2000-08

Peak Year	Peak Pos	Peak Wks	Wks Chr	Rank	Title	Artist
04	2	3	62	1.	So Cold	Breaking Benjamin
00	2	3	56	2.	Hemorrhage (In My Hands)	Fuel
04	3	4	56	3.	Cold	Crossfade
03	1	1	55	4.	Headstrong	Trapt
00	1	21	53	5.	Loser	3 Doors Down
01	1	1	53	6.	Awake	Godsmack
05	1	8	52	7.	Remedy	Seether
07	1	1	52	8.	Paralyzer	Finger Eleven
05	2	10	52	9.	Wasteland	10 Years
00	1	9	51	10.	Kryptonite	3 Doors Down
01	1	13	48	11.	How You Remind Me	Nickelback
06	1	7	48	12.	Animal I Have Become	Three Days Grace

#1 TRACKS

This section lists in chronological order, by peak date, all 355 tracks that hit the #1 position on *Billboard's* "Mainstream Rock Tracks" chart from March 21, 1981 through March 29, 2008.

For the years 1981 through 1991, *Billboard* did not publish a year-end issue. *Billboard* considered the charts listed in the last published issue of the year to be "frozen" and all chart positions remained the same for the unpublished week. This frozen chart data is included in our tabulations. Since 1992, *Billboard* has <u>compiled</u> a chart for the last week of the year, even though an issue is <u>not published</u>. This chart is only available through Member Services of Billboard.com or by mail.

DATE: Date track first peaked at the #1 position

WKS: Total weeks track held the #1 position

⬍: Indicates track hit #1, dropped down, and then returned to the #1 spot

---

The <u>top</u> hit of each year is boxed out for quick reference. The top hit is determined by most weeks at the #1 position, followed by total weeks in the Top 10, Top 20, and total weeks charted.

#1 HITS

#1 HITS

1986 (cont'd)

9.	6/14	3	**Invisible Touch** *Genesis*
10.	7/5	2	**Secret Separation** *The Fixx*
11.	7/19	4	**Higher Love** *Steve Winwood*
12.	8/16	1	**Missionary Man** *Eurythmics*
13.	8/23	3	**Throwing It All Away** *Genesis*
14.	9/13	1	**In Your Eyes** *Peter Gabriel*
15.	9/20	2	**Take Me Home Tonight** *Eddie Money*
16.	10/4	1	**Emotion In Motion** *Ric Ocasek*
17.	10/11	3	**Amanda** *Boston*
18.	11/1	1	**Hip To Be Square** *Huey Lewis & The News*
19.	11/8	3	**Don't Get Me Wrong** *The Pretenders*
20.	11/29	6	**I Want To Make The World Turn Around** *Steve Miller Band*

DATE WKS 1987

1.	1/10	1	**It's In The Way That You Use It** *Eric Clapton*
2.	1/17	2	**My Baby** *The Pretenders*
3.	1/31	2	**Livin' On A Prayer** *Bon Jovi*
4.	2/14	5	**Midnight Blue** *Lou Gramm*
5.	3/21	1	**I'm No Angel** *Gregg Allman Band*
6.	3/28	1	**Come As You Are** *Peter Wolf*
7.	4/4	5	**With Or Without You** *U2*
8.	5/9	4	**Jammin' Me** *Tom Petty & The Heartbreakers*
9.	6/6	4	**Shakedown** *Bob Seger*
10.	7/4	1	**Don't Mean Nothing** *Richard Marx*
11.	7/11	3	**Give To Live** *Sammy Hagar*
12.	8/1	3	**Touch Of Grey** *Grateful Dead*
13.	8/22	5	**Paper In Fire** *John Cougar Mellencamp*
14.	9/26	3	**Learning To Fly** *Pink Floyd*
15.	10/17	1	**Brilliant Disguise** *Bruce Springsteen*
16.	10/24	3	**Love Will Find A Way** *Yes*
17.	11/14	1	**Cherry Bomb** *John Cougar Mellencamp*
18.	11/21	4	**Tunnel Of Love** *Bruce Springsteen*
19.	12/19	4	**Say You Will** *Foreigner*

DATE WKS 1988

1.	1/16	1	**On The Turning Away** *Pink Floyd*
2.	1/23	4	**Just Like Paradise** *David Lee Roth*
3.	2/20	6	**Heaven Knows** *Robert Plant*
4.	4/2	1	**I Wish I Had A Girl** *Henry Lee Summer*
5.	4/9	4	**Tall Cool One** *Robert Plant*
6.	5/7	1	**Only A Memory** *The Smithereens*
7.	5/14	3	**The Valley Road** *Bruce Hornsby & The Range*
8.	6/4	3	**Black And Blue** *Van Halen*
9.	6/25	4	**Roll With It** *Steve Winwood*
10.	7/23	1	**When It's Love** *Van Halen*
11.	7/30	1	**Simply Irresistible** *Robert Palmer*
12.	8/20	4	**Hate To Lose Your Lovin'** *Little Feat*
13.	9/17	2	**Don't You Know What The Night Can Do?** *Steve Winwood*
14.	10/1	1	**I'm Not Your Man** *Tommy Conwell & The Young Rumblers*
15.	10/8	5	**Desire** *U2*
16.	11/12	2	**It's Money That Matters** *Randy Newman*
17.	11/26	2	**Orange Crush** *R.E.M.*
18.	12/10	6	**Angel Of Harlem** *U2*

DATE WKS 1989

1.	1/21	2	**Got It Made** *Crosby, Stills, Nash & Young*
2.	2/4	1	**The Love In Your Eyes** *Eddie Money*
3.	2/11	1	**Stand** *R.E.M.*
4.	2/18	4	**Driven Out** *The Fixx*
5.	3/18	1	**Working On It** *Chris Rea*
6.	3/25	3	**I'll Be You** *The Replacements*
7.	4/15	1	**Now You're In Heaven** *Julian Lennon*
8.	4/22	5	**I Won't Back Down** *Tom Petty*
9.	5/27	3	**The Doctor** *The Doobie Brothers*
10.	6/17	1	**Rooms On Fire** *Stevie Nicks*
11.	6/24	1	**Runnin' Down A Dream** *Tom Petty*
12.	7/1	4	**The End Of The Innocence** *Don Henley*
13.	7/29	3	**Crossfire** *Stevie Ray Vaughan & Double Trouble*
14.	8/19	1	**Let The Day Begin** *The Call*
15.	8/26	1	**Free Fallin'** *Tom Petty*
16.	9/2	5	**Mixed Emotions** *The Rolling Stones*
17.	10/7	2	**Love In An Elevator** *Aerosmith*
18.	10/21	5	**Rock And A Hard Place** *The Rolling Stones*
19.	11/25	6	**Pretending** *Eric Clapton*

DATE WKS 1990

1.	1/6	1	**Show Don't Tell** *Rush*
2.	1/13	2	**Downtown Train** *Rod Stewart*
3.	1/27	3	**Bad Love** *Eric Clapton*
4.	2/17	2↕	**Black Velvet** *Alannah Myles*
5.	2/24	1	**What It Takes** *Aerosmith*
6.	3/10	1	**Almost Hear You Sigh** *The Rolling Stones*
7.	3/17	1	**Blue Sky Mine** *Midnight Oil*
8.	3/24	6	**Hurting Kind (I've Got My Eyes On You)** *Robert Plant*
9.	5/5	1	**Coming Of Age** *Damn Yankees*
10.	5/12	1	**Texas Twister** *Little Feat*
11.	5/19	4	**Doubleback** *ZZ Top*
12.	6/23	2	**Cradle Of Love** *Billy Idol*
13.	7/7	2	**Holy Water** *Bad Company*
14.	7/21	1	**Across The River** *Bruce Hornsby & The Range*
15.	7/28	2	**The Other Side** *Aerosmith*
16.	8/11	1	**Good Clean Fun** *Allman Brothers Band*
17.	8/18	3	**Brickyard Road** *Johnny Van Zant*
18.	9/8	1	**Blaze Of Glory** *Jon Bon Jovi*
19.	9/15	4	**Suicide Blonde** *INXS*
20.	10/13	4	**Concrete And Steel** *ZZ Top*
21.	11/10	2	**Hard To Handle** *The Black Crowes*
22.	11/24	2	**One And Only Man** *Steve Winwood*
23.	12/8	6	**My Head's In Mississippi** *ZZ Top*

DATE WKS 1991

1.	1/19	7	**All This Time** *Sting*
2.	3/9	1	**She Talks To Angels** *The Black Crowes*
3.	3/16	3	**Highwire** *The Rolling Stones*
4.	4/6	1	**Silent Lucidity** *Queensrÿche*
5.	4/13	3	**Losing My Religion** *R.E.M.*
6.	5/4	6	**Lift Me Up** *Yes*
7.	6/15	2	**Poundcake** *Van Halen*

#1 HITS

1991 (cont'd)

8.	6/29	6	**Learning To Fly**	
			Tom Petty & The Heartbreakers	
9.	8/10	4	**Runaround** *Van Halen*	
10.	9/7	2	**Out In The Cold**	
			Tom Petty & The Heartbreakers	
11.	9/21	4	**Dreamline** *Rush*	
12.	10/19	3↕	**Get A Leg Up** *John Mellencamp*	
13.	10/26	4↕	**Top Of The World** *Van Halen*	

> **11/23/1991: Billboard begins compiling "Album Rock Tracks"**
> **chart from data provided by Broadcast Data Systems.**

14.	12/7	1	**Heavy Fuel** *Dire Straits*	
15.	12/14	12	**Mysterious Ways** *U2*	

DATE	WKS	1992	
1.	3/7	2	**Again Tonight** *John Mellencamp*
2.	3/21	3	**Human Touch** *Bruce Springsteen*
3.	4/11	1	**Let's Get Rocked** *Def Leppard*
4.	4/18	2	**One** *U2*
5.	5/2	11	**Remedy** *The Black Crowes*
6.	7/18	2	**Sting Me** *The Black Crowes*
7.	8/1	3	**Even Better Than The Real Thing** *U2*
8.	8/22	4	**Thorn In My Pride** *The Black Crowes*
9.	9/19	6	**How About That** *Bad Company*
10.	10/31	1	**Digging In The Dirt** *Peter Gabriel*
11.	11/7	2	**Rest In Peace** *Extreme*
12.	11/21	1	**Keep The Faith** *Bon Jovi*
13.	11/28	6	**Hotel Illness** *The Black Crowes*

DATE	WKS	1993	
1.	1/9	5	**Stand Up (Kick Love Into Motion)**
			Def Leppard
2.	2/13	1	**Don't Tear Me Up** *Mick Jagger*
3.	2/20	1	**Won't Get Fooled Again** *Van Halen*
4.	2/27	6	**Pride And Joy** *Coverdale•Page*
5.	4/10	9	**Livin' On The Edge** *Aerosmith*
6.	6/12	2	**Are You Gonna Go My Way** *Lenny Kravitz*
7.	6/26	1	**Plush** *Stone Temple Pilots*
8.	7/3	2	**Big Gun** *AC/DC*
9.	7/17	6	**Cryin'** *Aerosmith*
10.	8/28	2	**What If I Came Knocking** *John Mellencamp*
11.	9/11	4	**Peace Pipe** *Cry Of Love*
12.	10/9	2	**No Rain** *Blind Melon*
13.	10/23	4	**Stick It Out** *Rush*
14.	11/20	2	**Mary Jane's Last Dance**
			Tom Petty & The Heartbreakers
15.	12/4	8	**Daughter** *Pearl Jam*

DATE	WKS	1994	
1.	1/29	4	**Pincushion** *ZZ Top*
2.	2/26	4	**Deuces Are Wild** *Aerosmith*
3.	3/26	2	**No Excuses** *Alice In Chains*
4.	4/9	6	**Keep Talking** *Pink Floyd*
5.	5/21	8	**Shine** *Collective Soul*
6.	7/16	7	**Black Hole Sun** *Soundgarden*

7.	9/3	2	**Vasoline** *Stone Temple Pilots*	
8.	9/17	15	**Interstate Love Song** *Stone Temple Pilots*	
9.	12/31	1	**You Don't Know How It Feels** *Tom Petty*	

DATE	WKS	1995	
1.	1/7	8↕	**Better Man** *Pearl Jam*
2.	1/21	3	**Don't Tell Me (What Love Can Do)** *Van Halen*
3.	3/25	10	**Lightning Crashes** *Live*
4.	6/3	9	**December** *Collective Soul*
5.	8/5	1	**Hold Me, Thrill Me, Kiss Me, Kill Me** *U2*
6.	8/12	6	**And Fools Shine On** *Brother Cane*
7.	9/23	3	**Tomorrow** *Silverchair*
8.	10/14	3	**Hard As A Rock** *AC/DC*
9.	11/4	5	**Name** *Goo Goo Dolls*
10.	12/9	4	**My Friends** *Red Hot Chili Peppers*

DATE	WKS	1996	
1.	1/6	4	**Cumbersome** *7 Mary 3*
2.	2/3	4	**The World I Know** *Collective Soul*
3.	3/2	2	**1979** *Smashing Pumpkins*
4.	3/16	3	**Santa Monica (Watch The World Die)**
			Everclear
5.	4/6	4	**In The Meantime** *Spacehog*

> **4/13/1996: Billboard changes name of chart from "Album**
> **Rock Tracks" to "Mainstream Rock Tracks"**

6.	5/4	1	**Big Bang Baby** *Stone Temple Pilots*	
7.	5/11	2	**Where The River Flows** *Collective Soul*	
8.	5/25	2	**Humans Being** *Van Halen*	
9.	6/8	8↕	**Until It Sleeps** *Metallica*	
10.	7/27	4↕	**Trippin' On A Hole In A Paper Heart**	
			Stone Temple Pilots	
11.	8/31	5	**Burden In My Hand** *Soundgarden*	
12.	10/5	3	**Test For Echo** *Rush*	
13.	10/26	6	**Me Wise Magic** *Van Halen*	
14.	12/7	3	**Hero Of The Day** *Metallica*	
15.	12/28	4↕	**Blow Up The Outside World** *Soundgarden*	

DATE	WKS	1997	
1.	1/18	1	**Lady Picture Show** *Stone Temple Pilots*
2.	2/1	5	**One Headlight** *The Wallflowers*
3.	3/8	5	**Falling In Love (Is Hard On The Knees)**
			Aerosmith
4.	4/12	4	**Precious Declaration** *Collective Soul*
5.	5/10	2	**Gone Away** *The Offspring*
6.	5/24	5	**Little White Lie** *Sammy Hagar*
7.	6/28	5	**If You Could Only See** *Tonic*
8.	8/2	5	**Listen** *Collective Soul*
9.	9/6	4	**Pink** *Aerosmith*
10.	10/4	16	**Touch, Peel And Stand** *Days Of The New*

DATE	WKS	1998	
1.	1/24	6	**Given To Fly** *Pearl Jam*
2.	3/7	6	**Without You** *Van Halen*
3.	4/18	6↕	**Blue On Black** *Kenny Wayne Shepherd Band*
4.	5/9	2	**Most High** *Jimmy Page & Robert Plant*

#1 HITS

1998 (cont'd)

5.	6/6	4	**I Lie In The Bed I Make** *Brother Cane*
6.	7/11	10	**The Down Town** *Days Of The New*
7.	9/19	6	**What's This Life For** *Creed*
8.	10/31	1	**Psycho Circus** *Kiss*
9.	11/7	3	**Fly Away** *Lenny Kravitz*
10.	11/28	11	**Turn The Page** *Metallica*

MODERN ROCK TRACKS WRAP-UP

Top 100 Artists In Rank Order

Top 100 Artists In A-Z Order

Top 40 Artists: 1988-99 / 2000-08

Top Artists Achievements:
Most Charted Tracks
Most Top 10 Tracks
Most #1 Tracks
Most Weeks At The #1 Position

Top Tracks:
All-Time
1988-99 / 2000-08

Tracks Of Longevity: 1988-99 / 2000-08

TOP 100 ARTISTS IN RANK ORDER

This section ranks the Top 100 Modern Rock Tracks artists from 1988-2008. Each artist's accumulated point total is shown to the right of their name. This ranking includes all titles that <u>peaked</u> from 1988-2008. A picture of each Top 50 artist is shown next to their listing in the artist section of this book.

POINT SYSTEM:

1. Each artist's charted singles are given points based on their highest charted position:

#1	=	60 points for its first week at #1, plus 5 points for each additional week at #1
#2	=	50 points for its first week at #2, plus 3 points for each additional week at #2
#3	=	40 points for its first week at #3, plus 3 points for each additional week at #3
#4-5	=	35 points
#6-10	=	30 points
#11-20	=	25 points
#21-30	=	20 points
#31-40	=	15 points

2. Total weeks charted are added in.

In the case of a tie, the artist listed first is determined by the following tie-breaker rules:

1) Most charted tracks
2) Most Top 20 tracks
3) Most Top 10 tracks

Special Symbols:

● = **Deceased Solo Artist or Group Member**

— = Artist did not rank in the Top 100 of the previous edition.

+ = Subject to change — still charted as of the 3/29/2008 cut-off date

TOP 100 MODERN ROCK ARTISTS

Old Rank	New Rank		Points
(2)	1.	Red Hot Chili Peppers ●	1,913
(1)	2.	U2	1,801
(5)	3.	Green Day	1,630+
(12)	4.	Foo Fighters	1,534+
(4)	5.	Pearl Jam	1,395
(3)	6.	R.E.M.	1,312+
(52)	7.	Linkin Park	1,286+
(6)	8.	The Smashing Pumpkins	1,131
(11)	9.	The Offspring	1,004
(25)	10.	Incubus	956
(14)	11.	Blink-182	921
(7)	12.	Bush	872
(8)	13.	Stone Temple Pilots	871
(21)	14.	311	868
(9)	15.	Live	858
(10)	16.	The Cure	857
(38)	17.	Nine Inch Nails	856
(31)	18.	Staind	834
(27)	19.	Weezer	745
(13)	20.	Depeche Mode	734
(50)	21.	Korn	705
(37)	22.	Beck	681
(76)	23.	Papa Roach	676
(15)	24.	Oasis	674
(19)	25.	Dave Matthews Band	671
(16)	26.	Morrissey	660
(18)	27.	Nirvana ●	650
(56)	28.	Godsmack	647
—	29.	Audioslave	645
(60)	30.	Nickelback	634
(17)	31.	Goo Goo Dolls	631
(20)	32.	Creed	622
(53)	33.	3 Doors Down	619+
—	34.	The White Stripes	602
(51)	35.	Puddle Of Mudd	594+
—	36.	Three Days Grace	593+
(85)	37.	System Of A Down	582
(28)	38.	Limp Bizkit	568
(22)	39.	Everclear	565
(23)	40.	Lenny Kravitz	555
(88)	41.	Jimmy Eat World	555+
(29)	42.	Garbage	553
(33)	43.	Fuel	544
(24)	44.	INXS ●	530
—	45.	Disturbed	503
(26)	46.	Alanis Morissette	499
(30)	47.	Soul Asylum	482
—	48.	Seether	481+
(35)	49.	Third Eye Blind	479
—	50.	Chevelle	478+
—	51.	The Killers	469
(32)	52.	The Cranberries	468
(34)	53.	Collective Soul	462
—	54.	Hoobastank	457
(54)	55.	Radiohead	448+
(62)	56.	P.O.D.	444
(36)	57.	Soundgarden	443
—	58.	Coldplay	434
(58)	59.	Jane's Addiction	433
—	60.	Sum 41	428
(40)	61.	No Doubt	423
—	62.	My Chemical Romance	406
(46)	63.	Our Lady Peace	404
(39)	64.	Counting Crows	403
—	65.	A Perfect Circle	403
—	66.	Breaking Benjamin	400+
(71)	67.	Social Distortion ●	397
(41)	68.	Hole ●	386
(42)	69.	Better Than Ezra	386
(43)	70.	The B-52's ●	385
(48)	71.	Lit	379
(44)	72.	Midnight Oil	378
(87)	73.	Beastie Boys	377
(45)	74.	Big Audio Dynamite	376
(55)	75.	Cake	372
—	76.	Queens Of The Stone Age	372
(47)	77.	Siouxsie & The Banshees	370
(59)	78.	Eve 6	366
—	79.	Tool	360
(49)	80.	Sugar Ray	355
—	81.	AFI	351
(78)	82.	Silverchair	349
—	83.	Jet	349
—	84.	The Strokes	332
(57)	85.	10,000 Maniacs ●	330
(61)	86.	Alice In Chains ●	318
—	87.	Marilyn Manson	317
—	88.	Muse	316
(63)	89.	The Wallflowers	316
—	90.	Trapt	316
(64)	91.	The Replacements	314
(65)	92.	Sheryl Crow	312
(66)	93.	Rage Against The Machine	312
(67)	94.	The Jesus & Mary Chain	311
(68)	95.	Psychedelic Furs	310
(69)	96.	Concrete Blonde	309
(70)	97.	New Order	308
(72)	98.	Cracker	300
(73)	99.	Everlast	300
(74)	100.	Toad The Wet Sprocket	296

A–Z — TOP 100 ARTISTS

The following 21 artists were ranked in the Top 100 Artists of our *Rock Tracks (2002 edition)* book but have now dropped out of the Top 100:

TOP 40 MODERN ROCK ARTISTS

1988-99

1. **U2** 1,346
2. **R.E.M.** 1,216
3. **Pearl Jam** 1,115
4. **The Smashing Pumpkins** 902
5. **Red Hot Chili Peppers** 884
6. **Green Day** 855
7. **The Cure** 780
8. **Bush** 747
9. **Live** 724
10. **Stone Temple Pilots** 643
11. **Morrissey** 639
12. **Depeche Mode** 635
13. **The Offspring** 614
14. **Oasis** 603
15. **Goo Goo Dolls** 580
16. **Nirvana** 549
17. **INXS** 530
18. **Foo Fighters** 514
19. **Alanis Morissette** 499
20. **Garbage** 483
21. **Soul Asylum** 482
22. **The Cranberries** 468
23. **Dave Matthews Band** 465
24. **Soundgarden** 443
25. **Lenny Kravitz** 436
26. **Collective Soul** 420
27. **Beck** 408
28. **Counting Crows** 403
29. **Hole** 386
30. **The B-52's** 385
31. **Everclear** 384
32. **Midnight Oil** 378
33. **Big Audio Dynamite** 376
34. **Siouxsie & The Banshees** 370
35. **311** 369
36. **Better Than Ezra** 364
37. **Third Eye Blind** 356
38. **Sugar Ray** 355
39. **Nine Inch Nails** 337
40. **10,000 Maniacs** 330

2000-08

1. **Linkin Park** ....1,286 +
2. **Red Hot Chili Peppers** 1,029
3. **Foo Fighters** ....1,020 +
4. **Incubus** 956
5. **Staind** 783
6. **Green Day** ....775 +
7. **Papa Roach** 676
8. **Audioslave** 645
9. **Blink-182** 636
10. **Nickelback** 634
11. **3 Doors Down** ....619 +
12. **The White Stripes** 602
13. **Korn** 597
14. **Puddle Of Mudd** ....594 +
15. **Three Days Grace** ....593 +
16. **System Of A Down** 582
17. **Godsmack** 569
18. **Jimmy Eat World** ....555 +
19. **Nine Inch Nails** 519
20. **Weezer** 515
21. **Disturbed** 503
22. **311** 499
23. **Seether** ....481 +
24. **Chevelle** ....478 +
25. **The Killers** 469
26. **Hoobastank** 457
27. **U2** 455
28. **P.O.D.** 444
29. **Coldplay** 434
30. **Sum 41** 428
31. **My Chemical Romance** 406
32. **A Perfect Circle** 403
33. **Breaking Benjamin** ....400 +
34. **The Offspring** 390
35. **Limp Bizkit** 372
36. **Queens Of The Stone Age** 372
37. **Fuel** 362
38. **AFI** 351
39. **Jet** 349
40. **The Strokes** 332

MODERN ROCK ARTIST ACHIEVEMENTS

MOST CHARTED TRACKS

1. U2 35
2. Pearl Jam 33
3. Red Hot Chili Peppers 27
4. R.E.M. 26
5. Green Day 24
6. Foo Fighters 21
7. The Smashing Pumpkins 20
8. The Offspring 20
9. Stone Temple Pilots 19
10. 311 18
11. Live 17
12. Nine Inch Nails 17
13. Korn 17
14. Depeche Mode 16
15. Beck 16
16. Dave Matthews Band........................ 16
17. Godsmack 16
18. Linkin Park 15
19. The Cure 15
20. Bush 14
21. Weezer 14
22. Blink-182 13
23. Staind 13
24. Oasis 13
25. Goo Goo Dolls 13
26. Lenny Kravitz 13

MOST TOP 10 TRACKS

1. U2 22
2. Red Hot Chili Peppers 21
3. Green Day 17
4. The Smashing Pumpkins 17
5. Foo Fighters 15
6. Pearl Jam 15
7. R.E.M. 15
8. The Offspring 13
9. Linkin Park 11
10. Incubus 11
11. Blink-182 10
12. Bush 10
13. Stone Temple Pilots 10
14. The Cure 10
15. Morrissey 9
16. INXS 9
17. Live 8
18. Weezer 8
19. 311 7
20. Staind 7
21. Nirvana 7
22. Audioslave 7
23. Puddle Of Mudd................................ 7
24. System Of A Down 7
25. Lenny Kravitz 7

(11-way tie at 6)

MOST #1 TRACKS

1. Red Hot Chili Peppers 11
2. U2 8
3. Green Day 8
4. Linkin Park 7
5. Foo Fighters 6
6. R.E.M. 6
7. Nirvana 5
8. Bush 4
9. The Cure 4
10. Nine Inch Nails 4
11. Depeche Mode 4
12. Pearl Jam 3
13. Incubus 3
14. Live 3
15. Goo Goo Dolls 3
16. Three Days Grace 3
17. Alanis Morissette 3
18. Jane's Addiction 3
19. The B-52's 3
20. Psychedelic Furs 3

MOST WEEKS AT THE #1 POSITION

1. Red Hot Chili Peppers 81
2. Linkin Park 50
3. Foo Fighters 47
4. Green Day 44
5. U2 32
6. R.E.M. 31
7. Staind 23
8. Incubus 19
9. The Cure 18
10. Nine Inch Nails................................. 17
11. Bush 16
12. Oasis 15
13. Marcy Playground 15
14. Sugar Ray 14
15. Live 13
16. Morrissey 13
17. Nickelback 13
18. Fuel 12

(6-way tie at 11)

TOP 100 MODERN ROCK TRACKS 1988-2008

Peak Year	Wks Chr	Wks T20	Wks T10	Wks @ #1	Rank	Title	Artist
07	33 +	33 +	32 +	18	1.	The Pretender	Foo Fighters
01	29	29	24	16	2.	It's Been Awhile	Staind
04	32	29	22	16	3.	Boulevard Of Broken Dreams	Green Day
99	26	25	21	16	4.	Scar Tissue	Red Hot Chili Peppers
07	31	31	27	15	5.	What I've Done	Linkin Park
97	34	32	24	15	6.	Sex And Candy	Marcy Playground
02	26	24	21	14	7.	By The Way	Red Hot Chili Peppers
06	23	23	21	14	8.	Dani California	Red Hot Chili Peppers
01	38	36	24	13	9.	How You Remind Me	Nickelback
00	27	24	20	13	10.	Otherside	Red Hot Chili Peppers
00	40	39	29	12	11.	Hemorrhage (In My Hands)	Fuel
03	30	27	21	12	12.	Numb	Linkin Park
99	36	34	27	11	13.	My Own Worst Enemy	Lit
00	33	31	24	11	14.	Kryptonite	3 Doors Down
02	35	34	22	10	15.	All My Life	Foo Fighters
95	25	17	14	10	16.	Wonderwall	Oasis
02	34	32	26	9	17.	Blurry	Puddle Of Mudd
98	34	30	24	9	18.	What It's Like	Everlast
95	25	18	15	9	19.	Lightning Crashes	Live
93	16	15	13	9	20.	Into Your Arms	The Lemonheads
91	13	12	12	9	21.	Mysterious Ways	U2
01	39	37	29	8	22.	Drive	Incubus
05	42	37	26	8	23.	Feel Good Inc	Gorillaz/De La Soul
08	29 +	28 +	25 +	8	24.	Fake It	Seether
99	27	25	22	8	25.	All The Small Things	Blink 182
97	31	30	20	8	26.	Semi-Charmed Life	Third Eye Blind
97	30	28	18	8	27.	Fly	Sugar Ray Featuring Super Cat
91	11	11	10	8	28.	Losing My Religion	R.E.M.
88	12	10	10	8	29.	Orange Crush	R.E.M.
00	37	31	23	7	30.	Last Resort	Papa Roach
05	29	29	23	7	31.	Best Of You	Foo Fighters
03	30	28	23	7	32.	So Far Away	Staind
05	29	27	21	7	33.	Only	Nine Inch Nails
06	29	28	20	7	34.	Welcome To The Black Parade	My Chemical Romance
98	26	24	19	7	35.	The Way	Fastball
95	26	21	17	7	36.	When I Come Around	Green Day
97	25	18	14	7	37.	Tubthumping	Chumbawamba
90	18	17	14	7	38.	Cuts You Up	Peter Murphy
96	20	14	13	7	39.	Swallowed	Bush
89	16	15	11	7	40.	Fascination Street	The Cure
94	12	11	11	7	41.	The More You Ignore Me, The Closer I Get	Morrissey
03	37	32	21	6	42.	Faint	Linkin Park
05	26	25	19	6	43.	DOA	Foo Fighters
04	26	22	19	6	44.	Megalomaniac	Incubus
99	26	21	19	6	45.	Every Morning	Sugar Ray
94	23	17	16	6	46.	Zombie	The Cranberries
04	26	21	15	6	47.	American Idiot	Green Day
93	18	16	15	6	48.	Regret	New Order
96	21	15	12	6	49.	Standing Outside A Broken Phone Booth With Money In My Hand	Primitive Radio Gods
94	19	15	12	6	50.	Fall Down	Toad The Wet Sprocket

TOP 100 MODERN ROCK TRACKS 1988-2008

Peak Year	Wks Chr	Wks T20	Wks T10	Wks @ #1	Rank	Title	Artist
93	11	10	10	6	51.	The Devil You Know	Jesus Jones
92	14	12	9	6	52.	Tomorrow	Morrissey
01	44	40	27	5	53.	In The End	Linkin Park
03	45	34	25	5	54.	Headstrong	Trapt
05	27	27	23	5	55.	The Hand That Feeds	Nine Inch Nails
98	26	24	22	5	56.	Closing Time	Semisonic
97	32	31	21	5	57.	Walkin' On The Sun	Smash Mouth
06	26	25	21	5	58.	Miss Murder	AFI
99	26	23	19	5	59.	The Chemicals Between Us	Bush
98	26	22	19	5	60.	Iris	Goo Goo Dolls
06	24	24	18	5	61.	Anna-Molly	Incubus
07	25	23	17	5	62.	Snow ((Hey Oh))	Red Hot Chili Peppers
03	26	22	17	5	63.	Somewhere I Belong	Linkin Park
98	26	19	16	5	64.	One Week	Barenaked Ladies
95	26	18	16	5	65.	Good	Better Than Ezra
97	26	22	14	5	66.	One Headlight	The Wallflowers
08	21 +	16 +	14 +	5 +	67.	Long Road To Ruin	Foo Fighters
89	16	15	14	5	68.	So Alive	Love & Rockets
94	21	16	13	5	69.	Loser	Beck
95	19	15	13	5	70.	You Oughta Know	Alanis Morissette
91	15	14	13	5	71.	Kiss Them For Me	Siouxsie And The Banshees
94	23	16	12	5	72.	Basket Case	Green Day
93	14	14	11	5	73.	Pets	Porno For Pyros
89	14	14	11	5	74.	The Mayor Of Simpleton	XTC
90	13	13	11	5	75.	More	Sisters Of Mercy
93	13	12	11	5	76.	Soul To Squeeze	Red Hot Chili Peppers
00	23	14	10	5	77.	Minority	Green Day
96	19	14	10	5	78.	Champagne Supernova	Oasis
92	16	13	10	5	79.	Steam	Peter Gabriel
91	14	12	10	5	80.	Right Here, Right Now	Jesus Jones
93	11	11	10	5	81.	I Feel You	Depeche Mode
88	11	11	10	5	82.	Desire	U2
92	14	13	9	5	83.	Hit	The Sugarcubes
94	19	12	9	5	84.	What's The Frequency, Kenneth?	R.E.M.
90	13	11	9	5	85.	Way Down Now	World Party
91	11	10	9	5	86.	So You Think You're In Love	Robyn Hitchcock and the Egyptians
92	11	10	9	5	87.	Drive	R.E.M.
98	41	37	25	4	88.	Inside Out	Eve 6
03	36	33	20	4	89.	No One Knows	Queens Of The Stone Age
02	36	31	20	4	90.	The Middle	Jimmy Eat World
06	27	24	18	4	91.	Perfect Situation	Weezer
04	26	24	18	4	92.	Breaking The Habit	Linkin Park
98	26	23	17	4	93.	Celebrity Skin	Hole
02	26	20	17	4	94.	You Know You're Right	Nirvana
07	30	25	16	4	95.	Pain	Three Days Grace
01	27	22	16	4	96.	Smooth Criminal	Alien Ant Farm
04	26	20	16	4	97.	Slither	Velvet Revolver
95	23	17	15	4	98.	My Friends	Red Hot Chili Peppers
06	24	19	14	4	99.	Tell Me Baby	Red Hot Chili Peppers
95	26	19	13	4	100.	Name	Goo Goo Dolls

TOP 50 MODERN ROCK TRACKS 1988-99

Peak Year	Wks Chr	Wks T20	Wks T10	Wks @ #1	Rank	Title	Artist
99	26	25	21	16	1.	Scar Tissue	Red Hot Chili Peppers
97	34	32	24	15	2.	Sex And Candy	Marcy Playground
99	36	34	27	11	3.	My Own Worst Enemy	Lit
95	25	17	14	10	4.	Wonderwall	Oasis
98	34	30	24	9	5.	What It's Like	Everlast
95	25	18	15	9	6.	Lightning Crashes	Live
93	16	15	13	9	7.	Into Your Arms	The Lemonheads
91	13	12	12	9	8.	Mysterious Ways	U2
99	27	25	22	8	9.	All The Small Things	Blink 182
97	31	30	20	8	10.	Semi-Charmed Life	Third Eye Blind
97	30	28	18	8	11.	Fly	Sugar Ray Featuring Super Cat
91	11	11	10	8	12.	Losing My Religion	R.E.M.
88	12	10	10	8	13.	Orange Crush	R.E.M.
98	26	24	19	7	14.	The Way	Fastball
95	26	21	17	7	15.	When I Come Around	Green Day
97	25	18	14	7	16.	Tubthumping	Chumbawamba
90	18	17	14	7	17.	Cuts You Up	Peter Murphy
96	20	14	13	7	18.	Swallowed	Bush
89	16	15	11	7	19.	Fascination Street	The Cure
94	12	11	11	7	20.	The More You Ignore Me, The Closer I Get	Morrissey
99	26	21	19	6	21.	Every Morning	Sugar Ray
94	23	17	16	6	22.	Zombie	The Cranberries
93	18	16	15	6	23.	Regret	New Order
96	21	15	12	6	24.	Standing Outside A Broken Phone Booth With Money In My Hand	Primitive Radio Gods
94	19	15	12	6	25.	Fall Down	Toad The Wet Sprocket
93	11	10	10	6	26.	The Devil You Know	Jesus Jones
92	14	12	9	6	27.	Tomorrow	Morrissey
98	26	24	22	5	28.	Closing Time	Semisonic
97	32	31	21	5	29.	Walkin' On The Sun	Smash Mouth
99	26	23	19	5	30.	The Chemicals Between Us	Bush
98	26	22	19	5	31.	Iris	Goo Goo Dolls
98	26	19	16	5	32.	One Week	Barenaked Ladies
95	26	18	16	5	33.	Good	Better Than Ezra
97	26	22	14	5	34.	One Headlight	The Wallflowers
89	16	15	14	5	35.	So Alive	Love & Rockets
94	21	16	13	5	36.	Loser	Beck
95	19	15	13	5	37.	You Oughta Know	Alanis Morissette
91	15	14	13	5	38.	Kiss Them For Me	Siouxsie And The Banshees
94	23	16	12	5	39.	Basket Case	Green Day
93	14	14	11	5	40.	Pets	Porno For Pyros
89	14	14	11	5	41.	The Mayor Of Simpleton	XTC
90	13	13	11	5	42.	More	Sisters Of Mercy
93	13	12	11	5	43.	Soul To Squeeze	Red Hot Chili Peppers
96	19	14	10	5	44.	Champagne Supernova	Oasis
92	16	13	10	5	45.	Steam	Peter Gabriel
91	14	12	10	5	46.	Right Here, Right Now	Jesus Jones
93	11	11	10	5	47.	I Feel You	Depeche Mode
88	11	11	10	5	48.	Desire	U2
92	14	13	9	5	49.	Hit	The Sugarcubes
94	19	12	9	5	50.	What's The Frequency, Kenneth?	R.E.M.

TOP 50 MODERN ROCK TRACKS 2000-08

Peak Year	Wks Chr	Wks T20	Wks T10	Wks @ #1	Rank	Title	Artist
07	33 +	33 +	32 +	18	1.	The Pretender	Foo Fighters
01	29	29	24	16	2.	It's Been Awhile	Staind
04	32	29	22	16	3.	Boulevard Of Broken Dreams	Green Day
07	31	31	27	15	4.	What I've Done	Linkin Park
02	26	24	21	14	5.	By The Way	Red Hot Chili Peppers
06	23	23	21	14	6.	Dani California	Red Hot Chili Peppers
01	38	36	24	13	7.	How You Remind Me	Nickelback
00	27	24	20	13	8.	Otherside	Red Hot Chili Peppers
00	40	39	29	12	9.	Hemorrhage (In My Hands)	Fuel
03	30	27	21	12	10.	Numb	Linkin Park
00	33	31	24	11	11.	Kryptonite	3 Doors Down
02	35	34	22	10	12.	All My Life	Foo Fighters
02	34	32	26	9	13.	Blurry	Puddle Of Mudd
01	39	37	29	8	14.	Drive	Incubus
05	42	37	26	8	15.	Feel Good Inc	Gorillaz/De La Soul
08	29 +	28 +	25 +	8	16.	Fake It	Seether
00	37	31	23	7	17.	Last Resort	Papa Roach
05	29	29	23	7	18.	Best Of You	Foo Fighters
03	30	28	23	7	19.	So Far Away	Staind
05	29	27	21	7	20.	Only	Nine Inch Nails
06	29	28	20	7	21.	Welcome To The Black Parade	My Chemical Romance
03	37	32	21	6	22.	Faint	Linkin Park
05	26	25	19	6	23.	DOA	Foo Fighters
04	26	22	19	6	24.	Megalomaniac	Incubus
04	26	21	15	6	25.	American Idiot	Green Day
01	44	40	27	5	26.	In The End	Linkin Park
03	45	34	25	5	27.	Headstrong	Trapt
05	27	27	23	5	28.	The Hand That Feeds	Nine Inch Nails
06	26	25	21	5	29.	Miss Murder	AFI
06	24	24	18	5	30.	Anna-Molly	Incubus
07	25	23	17	5	31.	Snow ((Hey Oh))	Red Hot Chili Peppers
03	26	22	17	5	32.	Somewhere I Belong	Linkin Park
08	21 +	16 +	14 +	5 +	33.	Long Road To Ruin	Foo Fighters
00	23	14	10	5	34.	Minority	Green Day
03	36	33	20	4	35.	No One Knows	Queens Of The Stone Age
02	36	31	20	4	36.	The Middle	Jimmy Eat World
06	27	24	18	4	37.	Perfect Situation	Weezer
04	26	24	18	4	38.	Breaking The Habit	Linkin Park
02	26	20	17	4	39.	You Know You're Right	Nirvana
07	30	25	16	4	40.	Pain	Three Days Grace
01	27	22	16	4	41.	Smooth Criminal	Alien Ant Farm
04	26	20	16	4	42.	Slither	Velvet Revolver
06	24	19	14	4	43.	Tell Me Baby	Red Hot Chili Peppers
02	26	20	12	4	44.	Seein' Red	Unwritten Law
05	26	17	12	4	45.	Be Yourself	Audioslave
04	23	15	11	4	46.	Vertigo	U2
06	20	15	11	4	47.	Every Day Is Exactly The Same	Nine Inch Nails
03	38	36	26	3	48.	Seven Nation Army	The White Stripes
01	35	33	26	3	49.	Hanging By A Moment	Lifehouse
07	29	28	23	3	50.	Icky Thump	The White Stripes

TRACKS OF LONGEVITY

1988-99

Peak Year	Peak Pos	Peak Wks	Wks Chr	Rank	Title	Artist
98	1	4	41	1.	Inside Out	Eve 6
99	1	11	36	2.	My Own Worst Enemy	Lit
97	1	15	34	3.	Sex And Candy	Marcy Playground
98	1	9	34	4.	What It's Like	Everlast
98	1	3	33	5.	Never There	Cake
97	1	5	32	6.	Walkin' On The Sun	Smash Mouth
98	1	2	32	7.	Fly Away	Lenny Kravitz
97	1	8	31	8.	Semi-Charmed Life	Third Eye Blind
99	2	2	31	9.	One	Creed
98	2	1	31	10.	Shimmer	Fuel
99	4	1	31	11.	Blue Monday	Orgy
97	1	8	30	12.	Fly	Sugar Ray Featuring Super Cat

2000-08

Peak Year	Peak Pos	Peak Wks	Wks Chr	Rank	Title	Artist
07	1	1	52	1.	Paralyzer	Finger Eleven
06	3	1	52	2.	The Kill (Bury Me)	30 Seconds To Mars
07	3	1	52	3.	Face Down	The Red Jumpsuit Apparatus
05	2	3	46	4.	Cold	Crossfade
03	1	5	45	5.	Headstrong	Trapt
06	1	1	45	6.	Wasteland	10 Years
03	2	2	45	7.	(I Hate) Everything About You	Three Days Grace
01	1	5	44	8.	In The End	Linkin Park
07	2	1	43 +	9.	Never Too Late	Three Days Grace
05	1	8	42	10.	Feel Good Inc	Gorillaz/De La Soul
00	3	3	42	11.	Pardon Me	Incubus
06	1	2	41	12.	Animal I Have Become	Three Days Grace

#1 TRACKS

This section lists in chronological order, by peak date, all 252 tracks that hit the #1 position on *Billboard's* "Modern Rock Tracks" chart from September 10, 1988 through March 29, 2008.

For the years 1988 through 1991, *Billboard* did not publish a year-end issue. *Billboard* considered the charts listed in the last published issue of the year to be "frozen" and all chart positions remained the same for the unpublished week. This frozen chart data is included in our tabulations. Since 1992, *Billboard* has compiled a chart for the last week of the year, even though an issue is not published. This chart is only available through Member Services of Billboard.com or by mail.

> **DATE:** Date track first peaked at the #1 position
> **WKS:** Total weeks track held the #1 position
> ↕: Indicates track hit #1, dropped down, and then returned to the #1 spot

> The top hit of each year is boxed out for quick reference. The top hit is determined by most weeks at the #1 position, followed by total weeks in the Top 10, Top 20, and total weeks charted.

#1 HITS

1988

	DATE	WKS		
1.	9/10	2↕	**Peek-A-Boo**	*Siouxsie & The Banshees*
2.	9/17	1	**Just Play Music!**	*Big Audio Dynamite*
3.	10/1	3	**All That Money Wants**	*Psychedelic Furs*
4.	10/22	5	**Desire**	*U2*
5.	11/26	8	**Orange Crush**	*R.E.M.*

1989

	DATE	WKS		
1.	1/21	1	**Charlotte Anne**	*Julian Cope*
2.	1/28	2	**Stand**	*R.E.M.*
3.	2/11	4	**Dirty Blvd.**	*Lou Reed*
4.	3/11	1	**I'll Be You**	*The Replacements*
5.	3/18	2	**Veronica**	*Elvis Costello*
6.	4/1	5	**The Mayor Of Simpleton**	*XTC*
7.	5/6	7	**Fascination Street**	*The Cure*
8.	6/24	5	**So Alive**	*Love & Rockets*
9.	7/29	1	**Disappointed**	*Public Image Ltd.*
10.	8/5	3	**Channel Z**	*The B-52's*
11.	8/26	3	**Come Anytime**	*Hoodoo Gurus*
12.	9/16	4	**Love Shack**	*The B-52's*
13.	10/14	1	**Sowing The Seeds Of Love**	*Tears For Fears*
14.	10/21	3	**Pictures Of Matchstick Men**	*Camper Van Beethoven*
15.	11/11	4	**Proud To Fall**	*Ian McCulloch*
16.	12/9	4	**Love And Anger**	*Kate Bush*

1990

	DATE	WKS		
1.	1/6	2	**Blues From A Gun**	*The Jesus & Mary Chain*
2.	1/20	3	**House**	*Psychedelic Furs*
3.	2/10	7	**Cuts You Up**	*Peter Murphy*
4.	3/31	1	**Nothing Compares 2 U**	*Sinéad O'Connor*
5.	4/7	1	**Blue Sky Mine**	*Midnight Oil*
6.	4/14	1	**Metropolis**	*The Church*
7.	4/21	3	**Enjoy The Silence**	*Depeche Mode*
8.	5/12	1	**The Emperor's New Clothes**	*Sinéad O'Connor*
9.	5/19	1	**Forgotten Years**	*Midnight Oil*
10.	5/26	1	**Here's Where The Story Ends**	*The Sundays*
11.	6/2	1	**Policy Of Truth**	*Depeche Mode*
12.	6/9	5	**Way Down Now**	*World Party*
13.	7/14	4	**Joey**	*Concrete Blonde*
14.	8/11	2↕	**Jealous**	*Gene Loves Jezebel*
15.	8/18	1	**I'll Be Your Chauffeur**	*David J*
16.	9/1	2↕	**Stop!**	*Jane's Addiction*
17.	9/8	1	**Every Beat Of The Heart**	*The Railway Children*
18.	9/22	1	**Suicide Blonde**	*INXS*
19.	9/29	3↕	**Never Enough**	*The Cure*
20.	10/13	4↕	**Merry Go Round**	*The Replacements*
21.	10/27	4↕	**Been Caught Stealing**	*Jane's Addiction*
22.	12/15	5	**More**	*Sisters Of Mercy*

1991

	DATE	WKS		
1.	1/19	1	**Kinky Afro**	*Happy Mondays*
2.	1/26	2	**All This Time**	*Sting*
3.	2/9	5	**Right Here, Right Now**	*Jesus Jones*
4.	3/16	8	**Losing My Religion**	*R.E.M.*
5.	5/11	2	**See The Lights**	*Simple Minds*
6.	5/25	4	**The Other Side Of Summer**	*Elvis Costello*
7.	6/22	2	**Get The Message**	*Electronic*
8.	7/6	5	**Kiss Them For Me**	*Siouxsie And The Banshees*
9.	8/10	4	**Rush**	*Big Audio Dynamite II*
10.	9/7	2	**Until She Comes**	*The Psychedelic Furs*
11.	9/21	5	**So You Think You're In Love**	*Robyn Hitchcock and the Egyptians*
12.	10/26	2	**Give It Away**	*Red Hot Chili Peppers*
13.	11/9	2	**The Fly**	*U2*
14.	11/23	1	**Smells Like Teen Spirit**	*Nirvana*
15.	11/30	9	**Mysterious Ways**	*U2*

1992

	DATE	WKS		
1.	2/1	1	**Sax And Violins**	*Talking Heads*
2.	2/8	3	**What's Good**	*Lou Reed*
3.	2/29	5	**Hit**	*The Sugarcubes*
4.	4/4	1	**One**	*U2*
5.	4/11	4	**High**	*The Cure*
6.	5/9	2	**Teen Angst (What The World Needs Now)**	*Cracker*
7.	5/23	1	**Weirdo**	*The Charlatans UK*
8.	5/30	2	**The Ballad Of Peter Pumpkinhead**	*XTC*
9.	6/13	4	**Friday I'm In Love**	*The Cure*
10.	7/11	4	**Good Stuff**	*The B-52's*
11.	8/8	1	**MidLife Crisis**	*Faith No More*
12.	8/15	6	**Tomorrow**	*Morrissey*
13.	9/26	2	**Digging In The Dirt**	*Peter Gabriel*
14.	10/10	1	**Blood Makes Noise**	*Suzanne Vega*
15.	10/17	5	**Drive**	*R.E.M.*
16.	11/21	2	**These Are Days**	*10,000 Maniacs*
17.	12/5	1	**Somebody To Shove**	*Soul Asylum*
18.	12/12	5	**Steam**	*Peter Gabriel*

1993

	DATE	WKS		
1.	1/16	1	**Not Sleeping Around**	*Ned's Atomic Dustbin*
2.	1/23	6	**The Devil You Know**	*Jesus Jones*
3.	3/6	3	**Feed The Tree**	*Belly*
4.	3/27	5	**I Feel You**	*Depeche Mode*
5.	5/1	6	**Regret**	*New Order*
6.	5/15	1	**Walking In My Shoes**	*Depeche Mode*

6/12/1993: Billboard begins compiling "Modern Rock Tracks" chart from data provided by Broadcast Data Systems.

	DATE	WKS		
7.	6/19	5	**Pets**	*Porno For Pyros*
8.	7/24	3	**Break It Down Again**	*Tears For Fears*
9.	8/14	5↕	**Soul To Squeeze**	*Red Hot Chili Peppers*
10.	9/11	1	**My Sister**	*The Juliana Hatfield Three*
11.	9/18	3↕	**No Rain**	*Blind Melon*
12.	10/16	3	**Heart-Shaped Box**	*Nirvana*
13.	11/6	9	**Into Your Arms**	*The Lemonheads*

#1 HITS

1994

	DATE	WKS		
1.	1/8	1	**Daughter**	*Pearl Jam*
2.	1/15	1	**Found Out About You**	*Gin Blossoms*
3.	1/22	2	**All Apologies**	*Nirvana*
4.	2/5	5	**Loser**	*Beck*
5.	3/12	1	**Mmm Mmm Mmm Mmm**	
				Crash Test Dummies
6.	3/19	2	**God**	*Tori Amos*
7.	4/2	7	**The More You Ignore Me, The Closer I Get** *Morrissey*	
8.	5/21	3	**Selling The Drama**	*Live*
9.	6/11	1	**Long View**	*Green Day*
10.	6/18	6	**Fall Down**	*Toad The Wet Sprocket*
11.	7/30	2	**Come Out And Play**	*Offspring*
12.	8/13	1	**Einstein On The Beach (For An Eggman)**	
				Counting Crows
13.	8/20	5	**Basket Case**	*Green Day*
14.	9/24	5	**What's The Frequency, Kenneth?**	*R.E.M.*
15.	10/29	6	**Zombie**	*The Cranberries*
16.	12/10	1	**About A Girl**	*Nirvana*
17.	12/17	3	**Bang And Blame**	*R.E.M.*

1995

	DATE	WKS		
1.	1/7	7	**When I Come Around**	*Green Day*
2.	2/25	9	**Lightning Crashes**	*Live*
3.	4/29	5	**Good**	*Better Than Ezra*
4.	6/3	3	**Misery**	*Soul Asylum*
5.	6/24	4	**Hold Me, Thrill Me, Kiss Me, Kill Me**	*U2*
6.	7/22	5	**You Oughta Know**	*Alanis Morissette*
7.	8/26	1	**J.A.R. (Jason Andrew Relva)**	*Green Day*
8.	9/2	3	**Tomorrow**	*Silverchair*
9.	9/23	2	**Comedown**	*Bush*
10.	10/7	4↕	**Name**	*Goo Goo Dolls*
11.	10/14	1	**Hand In My Pocket**	*Alanis Morissette*
12.	10/21	1	**Lump**	
				The Presidents Of The United States Of America
13.	11/18	4	**My Friends**	*Red Hot Chili Peppers*
14.	12/16	2	**Glycerine**	*Bush*
15.	12/30	10↕	**Wonderwall**	*Oasis*

1996

	DATE	WKS		
1.	3/2	1	**1979**	*Smashing Pumpkins*
2.	3/16	3	**Ironic**	*Alanis Morissette*
3.	4/6	5	**Champagne Supernova**	*Oasis*
4.	5/11	4	**Salvation**	*The Cranberries*
5.	6/8	3	**Mother Mother**	*Tracy Bonham*
6.	6/29	1	**Counting Blue Cars**	*Dishwalla*
7.	7/6	3	**Pepper**	*Butthole Surfers*
8.	7/27	6	**Standing Outside A Broken Phone Booth With Money In My Hand**	
				Primitive Radio Gods
9.	9/7	1	**Who You Are**	*Pearl Jam*
10.	9/14	4	**Down**	*311*

11.	10/12	2	**Novocaine For The Soul**	*Eels*
12.	10/26	3	**What I Got**	*Sublime*
13.	11/16	7	**Swallowed**	*Bush*

1997

	DATE	WKS		
1.	1/4	4	**#1 Crush**	*Garbage*
2.	2/1	4	**Discothéque**	*U2*
3.	3/1	1	**Lakini's Juice**	*Live*
4.	3/8	5	**One Headlight**	*The Wallflowers*
5.	4/12	3	**Staring At The Sun**	*U2*
6.	5/3	3	**The Freshmen**	*The Verve Pipe*
7.	5/24	8↕	**Semi-Charmed Life**	*Third Eye Blind*
8.	6/28	1	**The Impression That I Get**	
				The Mighty Mighty Bosstones
9.	7/26	1	**Push**	*Matchbox 20*
10.	8/2	8	**Fly**	*Sugar Ray Featuring Super Cat*
11.	9/27	5	**Walkin' On The Sun**	*Smash Mouth*
12.	11/1	7	**Tubthumping**	*Chumbawamba*
13.	12/20	1	**Everything To Everyone**	*Everclear*
14.	12/27	15	**Sex And Candy**	*Marcy Playground*

1998

	DATE	WKS		
1.	4/11	7	**The Way**	*Fastball*
2.	5/30	5	**Closing Time**	*Semisonic*
3.	7/4	5	**Iris**	*Goo Goo Dolls*
4.	8/8	4↕	**Inside Out**	*Eve 6*
5.	8/22	5↕	**One Week**	*Barenaked Ladies*
6.	10/10	4↕	**Celebrity Skin**	*Hole*
7.	10/31	2↕	**Slide**	*The Goo Goo Dolls*
8.	11/21	2	**Fly Away**	*Lenny Kravitz*
9.	12/5	3	**Never There**	*Cake*
10.	12/26	9↕	**What It's Like**	*Everlast*

1999

	DATE	WKS		
1.	2/20	6↕	**Every Morning**	*Sugar Ray*
2.	4/10	11	**My Own Worst Enemy**	*Lit*
3.	6/26	16	**Scar Tissue**	*Red Hot Chili Peppers*
4.	10/16	3↕	**Higher**	*Creed*
5.	10/23	5↕	**The Chemicals Between Us**	*Bush*
6.	11/6	1	**Learn To Fly**	*Foo Fighters*
7.	12/18	1	**Re-Arranged**	*Limp Bizkit*
8.	12/25	8	**All The Small Things**	*Blink 182*

2000

	DATE	WKS		
1.	2/19	13	**Otherside**	*Red Hot Chili Peppers*
2.	5/20	11	**Kryptonite**	*3 Doors Down*
3.	8/5	7↕	**Last Resort**	*Papa Roach*
4.	8/12	1	**Californication**	*Red Hot Chili Peppers*
5.	9/30	5	**Minority**	*Green Day*
6.	11/4	12	**Hemorrhage (In My Hands)**	*Fuel*

#1 HITS

2001

	DATE	WKS		
1.	1/27	3	**Hanging By A Moment**	*Lifehouse*
2.	2/17	2	**Butterfly**	*Crazy Town*
3.	3/3	8	**Drive**	*Incubus*
4.	4/28	16	**It's Been Awhile**	*Staind*
5.	8/18	1	**Fat Lip**	*Sum 41*
6.	8/25	4	**Smooth Criminal**	*Alien Ant Farm*
7.	9/22	13	**How You Remind Me**	*Nickelback*
8.	12/22	5	**In The End**	*Linkin Park*

2002

	DATE	WKS		
1.	1/26	9	**Blurry**	*Puddle Of Mudd*
2.	3/30	2	**Youth Of The Nation**	*P.O.D.*
3.	4/13	4	**The Middle**	*Jimmy Eat World*
4.	5/11	4	**Seein' Red**	*Unwritten Law*
5.	6/8	3	**Hero**	*Chad Kroeger Featuring Josey Scott*
6.	6/29	14	**By The Way**	*Red Hot Chili Peppers*
7.	10/5	3	**Aerials**	*System Of A Down*
8.	10/26	4	**You Know You're Right**	*Nirvana*
9.	11/23	10	**All My Life**	*Foo Fighters*

2003

	DATE	WKS		
1.	2/1	1	**Always**	*Saliva*
2.	2/8	4	**No One Knows**	*Queens Of The Stone Age*
3.	3/8	3	**Can't Stop**	*Red Hot Chili Peppers*
4.	3/29	2	**Bring Me To Life**	*Evanescence*
5.	4/12	5	**Somewhere I Belong**	*Linkin Park*
6.	5/17	2	**Like A Stone**	*Audioslave*
7.	5/31	5	**Headstrong**	*Trapt*
8.	7/5	1	**Send The Pain Below**	*Chevelle*
9.	7/12	3	**Seven Nation Army**	*The White Stripes*
10.	8/2	1	**Just Because**	*Jane's Addiction*
11.	8/9	6	**Faint**	*Linkin Park*
12.	9/20	7↕	**So Far Away**	*Staind*
13.	11/1	2	**Weak And Powerless**	*A Perfect Circle*
14.	11/22	12	**Numb**	*Linkin Park*

2004

	DATE	WKS		
1.	2/14	1	**Hit That**	*The Offspring*
2.	2/21	6	**Megalomaniac**	*Incubus*
3.	4/3	2	**I Miss You**	*Blink-182*
4.	4/17	1	**The Reason**	*Hoobastank*
5.	4/24	1	**Last Train Home**	*Lostprophets*
6.	5/1	1	**Love Song**	*311*
7.	5/8	3	**Cold Hard Bitch**	*Jet*
8.	5/29	3	**Lying From You**	*Linkin Park*
9.	6/19	2	**Ch-Check It Out**	*Beastie Boys*
10.	7/3	4	**Slither**	*Velvet Revolver*
11.	7/31	1	**Float On**	*Modest Mouse*
12.	8/7	3	**Just Like You**	*Three Days Grace*

13.	8/28	4	**Breaking The Habit**	*Linkin Park*
14.	9/25	6	**American Idiot**	*Green Day*
15.	11/6	4	**Vertigo**	*U2*
16.	12/4	1	**Pain**	*Jimmy Eat World*
17.	12/11	16	**Boulevard Of Broken Dreams**	*Green Day*

2005

	DATE	WKS		
1.	4/2	1	**E-Pro**	*Beck*
2.	4/9	4	**Be Yourself**	*Audioslave*
3.	5/7	3	**Holiday**	*Green Day*
4.	5/28	5	**The Hand That Feeds**	*Nine Inch Nails*
5.	7/2	1	**Beverly Hills**	*Weezer*
6.	7/9	7	**Best Of You**	*Foo Fighters*
7.	8/27	8	**Feel Good Inc**	*Gorillaz/De La Soul*
8.	10/22	7↕	**Only**	*Nine Inch Nails*
9.	11/26	6↕	**DOA**	*Foo Fighters*

2006

	DATE	WKS		
1.	1/21	1	**Hypnotize**	*System Of A Down*
2.	1/28	4	**Perfect Situation**	*Weezer*
3.	2/25	1	**Wasteland**	*10 Years*
4.	3/4	4	**Every Day Is Exactly The Same**	
				Nine Inch Nails
5.	4/1	3	**World Wide Suicide**	*Pearl Jam*
6.	4/22	14	**Dani California**	*Red Hot Chili Peppers*
7.	7/29	1	**Steady, As She Goes**	*The Raconteurs*
8.	8/5	5	**Miss Murder**	*AFI*
9.	9/9	2	**Animal I Have Become**	*Three Days Grace*
10.	9/23	4	**Tell Me Baby**	*Red Hot Chili Peppers*
11.	10/21	2	**When You Were Young**	*The Killers*
12.	11/4	7	**Welcome To The Black Parade**	
				My Chemical Romance
13.	12/23	5	**Anna-Molly**	*Incubus*

2007

	DATE	WKS		
1.	1/27	5	**Snow ((Hey Oh))**	*Red Hot Chili Peppers*
2.	3/3	3	**Pain**	*Three Days Grace*
3.	3/31	2	**From Yesterday**	*30 Seconds To Mars*
4.	4/14	1	**Survivalism**	*Nine Inch Nails*
5.	4/21	15	**What I've Done**	*Linkin Park*
6.	8/4	3	**Icky Thump**	*White Stripes*
7.	8/28	1	**Paralyzer**	*Finger Eleven*
8.	9/1	18	**The Pretender**	*Foo Fighters*

2008

	DATE	WKS		
1.	1/5	8	**Fake It**	*Seether*
2.	3/1	5	**Long Road To Ruin**	*Foo Fighters*

#1 track as of the 3/29/2008 cut-off date
— peak weeks subject to change

CLASSIC ROCK TRACKS

This section features classic rock artists and tracks beginning with The Beatles invasion of 1964 up to the debut of *Billboard's* Rock Tracks chart in 1981. The term "classic" indicates that these songs are still played regularly on today's classic rock stations throughout the U.S. Please do not consider this to be the definitive list of the best rock songs of all time. Obviously opinions vary widely in regards to "classic rock" hits, but we think this is a great overall guide.

This section is organized alphabetically by artist. The album title from which the track was taken is listed below with the debut year of the album in brackets in italics. Each artist's classic tracks (from 1964-1980) are listed below the album title in alphabetical order. In some cases, the title was released as a single before later appearing on an album. These are identified as *(single only)*.

AC/DC
High Voltage [1976]
  T.N.T.
Let There Be Rock [1977]
  Whole Lotta Rosie
Highway To Hell [1979]
  Girls Got Rhythm
  Highway To Hell
Back In Black [1980]
  You Shook Me All Night Long

ACE
Five-A-Side (an Ace album) [1975]
  How Long

AEROSMITH
Aerosmith [1973]
  Dream On
  Mama Kin
Get Your Wings [1974]
  Same Old Song And Dance
  Train Kept A Rollin'
Toys In The Attic [1975]
  Sweet Emotion
  Walk This Way
Rocks [1976]
  Back In The Saddle
  Last Child
Draw The Line [1977]
  Draw The Line
  Kings And Queens
St: Sgt. Pepper's Lonely Hearts Club Band [1978]
  Come Together
Night In The Ruts [1979]
  Remember (Walking In The Sand)

ALLMAN, Gregg
Laid Back [1973]
  Midnight Rider

ALLMAN BROTHERS BAND, The
The Allman Brothers Band [1970]
  Dreams
  Whipping Post
Idlewild South [1970]
  In Memory Of Elizabeth Reed
  Revival (Love Is Everywhere)
At Fillmore East [1971]
  Statesboro Blues
Eat A Peach [1972]
  Ain't Wastin' Time No More
  Blue Sky
  Melissa
  One Way Out
Brothers And Sisters [1973]
  Jessica
  Ramblin Man
Enlightened Rogues [1979]
  Crazy Love

AMBOY DUKES, The
Journey To The Center Of The Mind [1968]
  Journey To The Center Of The Mind

AMERICA
America [1972]
  Horse With No Name
  Sandman
Homecoming [1972]
  Ventura Highway
Holiday [1974]
  Tin Man
Hearts [1975]
  Sister Golden Hair

ANIMALS, The
The Animals [1964]
  House Of The Rising Sun
Animal Tracks [1965]
  Don't Let Me Be Misunderstood
  We Gotta Get Out Of This Place
The Best Of The Animals[1965]
  It's My Life
Animalization [1966]
  Don't Bring Me Down
  See See Rider
Winds Of Change [1967]
  San Franciscan Nights
The Twain Shall Meet [1968]
  Monterey
  Sky Pilot

APRIL WINE
April Wine [1972]
  You Could Have Been A Lady
First Glance [1979]
  Roller
Harder...Faster [1979]
  I Like To Rock

ARGENT
All Together Now [1972]
  Hold Your Head Up

ATLANTA RHYTHM SECTION
Third Annual Pipe Dream [1974]
  Doraville
A Rock And Roll Alternative [1977]
  So In To You
Champagne Jam [1978]
  Champagne Jam
  I'm Not Gonna Let It Bother Me Tonight
  Imaginary Lover
Underdog [1979]
  Spooky

AVERAGE WHITE BAND
AWB [1974]
  Pick Up The Pieces

* * * * * * * * * * * * * * * * * * * *

BABYS, The
Broken Heart [1977]
  Isn't It Time
Head First [1979]
  Every Time I Think Of You
Union Jacks [1980]
  Back On My Feet Again

BACHMAN-TURNER OVERDRIVE

Bachman-Turner Overdrive [1973]
    Blue Collar
Bachman-Turner Overdrive II [1974]
    Let It Ride
    Takin' Care Of Business
Not Fragile [1974]
    Roll On Down The Highway
    You Ain't Seen Nothin' Yet
Four Wheel Drive [1975]
    Hey You

BAD COMPANY

Bad Company [1974]
    Bad Company
    Can't Get Enough
    Movin' On
    Ready For Love
Straight Shooter [1975]
    Feel Like Makin' Love
    Good Lovin' Gone Bad
    Shooting Star
Run With The Pack [1976]
    Run With The Pack
    Silver, Blue & Gold
    Young Blood
Burnin' Sky [1977]
    Burnin' Sky
Desolation Angels [1979]
    Rock 'N' Roll Fantasy

BADFINGER

Magic Christian Music [1970]
    Come And Get It
No Dice [1970]
    No Matter What
Straight Up [1971]
    Baby Blue
    Day After Day

BAND, The

Music From Big Pink [1968]
    Chest Fever
    This Wheel's On Fire
    Weight, The
The Band [1969]
    Night They Drove Old Dixie Down, The
    Rag Mama Rag
    Up On Cripple Creek
Stage Fright [1970]
    Shape I'm In
    Time To Kill
Cahoots [1971]
    Life Is A Carnival
Rock Of Ages [1971]
    Don't Do It
Moondog Matinee [1973]
    Ain't Got No Home
Northern Lights-Southern Cross [1975]
    Ophelia

BEATLES, The

Meet The Beatles! [1964]
    All My Loving
    I Saw Her Standing There
    I Want To Hold Your Hand
Introducing...The Beatles [1964]
    Do You Want To Know A Secret
    Love Me Do
    Please Please Me
    Twist And Shout
Jolly What! The Beatles & Frank Ifield [1964]
    From Me To You
The Beatles' Second Album [1964]
    Roll Over Beethoven
    She Loves You
St: A Hard Day's Night [1964]
    And I Love Her
    Can't Buy Me Love
    Hard Day's Night
    I Should Have Known Better
Beatles '65 [1965]
    I Feel Fine
    I'm A Loser
    No Reply
    Rock And Roll Music
Beatles VI [1965]
    Eight Days A Week
St: Help! [1965]
    Help!
    Ticket To Ride
    You're Going To Lose That Girl
    You've Got To Hide Your Love Away
Rubber Soul [1965]
    In My Life
    Michelle
    Norwegian Wood (This Bird Has Flown)
"Yesterday"...And Today [1966]
    Day Tripper
    Drive My Car
    Nowhere Man
    We Can Work It Out
    Yesterday
Revolver [1966]
    Eleanor Rigby
    Good Day Sunshine
    Got To Get You Into My Life
    Taxman
    Yellow Submarine
St: Magical Mystery Tour [1967]
    All You Need Is Love
    Baby You're A Rich Man
    Fool On The Hill
    Hello Goodbye
    I Am The Walrus
    Magical Mystery Tour
    Penny Lane
    Strawberry Fields Forever

BEATLES, The — cont'd
Sgt. Pepper's Lonely Hearts Club Band [1967]
Day In The Life, A
Lovely Rita
Lucy In The Sky With Diamonds
Sgt. Pepper's Lonely Hearts Club Band/With A Little
Help From My Friends
When I'm Sixty-Four
The Beatles [White Album] [1968]
Back In The U.S.S.R.
Birthday
Blackbird
Dear Prudence
Glass Onion
Helter Skelter
Ob-La-Di, Ob-La-Da
Revolution
Rocky Raccoon
While My Guitar Gently Weeps
Hey Jude [1968]
Ballad Of John And Yoko
Don't Let Me Down
Hey Jude
Lady Madonna
Old Brown Shoe
Paperback Writer
Abbey Road [1969]
Come Together
Golden Slumbers/Carry That Weight/The End/
Her Majesty
Here Comes The Sun
Maxwell's Silver Hammer
Octopus's Garden
Oh! Darling
She Came In Through The Bathroom Window
Something
Let It Be [1970]
Across The Universe
Get Back
Let It Be
Long And Winding Road

BENATAR, Pat
In The Heat Of The Night [1979]
Heartbreaker
I Need A Lover
We Live For Love
Crimes Of Passion [1980]
Hell Is For Children
Hit Me With Your Best Shot
You Better Run

B-52's, The
The B-52's [1979]
Rock Lobster
Wild Planet [1980]
Private Idaho

BIG BROTHER & THE HOLDING COMPANY
Big Brother & The Holding Company [1967]
Down On Me

Cheap Thrills [1968]
Ball And Chain
Piece Of My Heart

BISHOP, Elvin
Struttin' My Stuff [1976]
Fooled Around And Fell In Love

BLACKFOOT
Strikes [1979]
Highway Song
Train, Train

BLACK OAK ARKANSAS
High On The Hog [1973]
Jim Dandy

BLACK SABBATH
Black Sabbath [1970]
Black Sabbath
N.I.B.
Paranoid [1971]
Iron Man
Paranoid
War Pigs
Master Of Reality [1971]
Children Of The Grave

BLIND FAITH
Blind Faith [1969]
Can't Find My Way Home

BLOOD, SWEAT & TEARS
Blood, Sweat & Tears [1969]
And When I Die
Spinning Wheel
You've Made Me So Very Happy
Blood, Sweat & Tears 3 [1970]
Hi-De-Ho
Lucretia Mac Evil
B, S & T; 4 [1971]
Go Down Gamblin'

BLUE CHEER
Vincebus Eruptum [1968]
Summertime Blues

BLUE ÖYSTER CULT
Agents Of Fortune [1976]
(Don't Fear) The Reaper
Spectres [1977]
Godzilla
Mirrors [1979]
In Thee

BLUES BROTHERS
Briefcase Full Of Blues [1978]
Hey Bartender
Rubber Biscuit
Soul Man

BLUES IMAGE
Open [1970]
Ride Captain Ride

BLUES MAGOOS
Psychedelic Lollipop [1966]
(We Ain't Got) Nothin' Yet

BOOMTOWN RATS, The
The Fine Art Of Surfacing [1979]
   I Don't Like Mondays

BOSTON
Boston [1976]
   Hitch A Ride
   Let Me Take You Home Tonight
   Long Time
   More Than A Feeling
   Peace Of Mind
   Rock & Roll Band
   Smokin'
   Something About You
Don't Look Back [1978]
   Don't Look Back
   Feelin' Satisfied
   It's Easy
   Man I'll Never Be

BOWIE, David
Hunky Dory [1972]
   Changes
The Rise And Fall Of Ziggy Stardust And The Spiders From Mars [1972]
   Starman
   Suffragette City
   Ziggy Stardust
Space Oddity [1973]
   Space Oddity
Aladdin Sane [1973]
   Jean Genie
Diamond Dogs [1974]
   Diamond Dogs
   Rebel Rebel
Young Americans [1975]
   Fame
   Young Americans
Station To Station [1976]
   Golden Years
   TVC 15
"Heroes" [1977]
   Heroes
Scary Monsters [1980]
   Ashes To Ashes
   Fashion

BROWNE, Jackson
Jackson Browne [1972]
   Doctor My Eyes
   Rock Me On The Water
For Everyman [1972]
   Redneck Friend
Late For The Sky [1974]
   Late For The Sky
The Pretender [1976]
   Here Come Those Tears Again
   Pretender, The
Running On Empty [1978]
   Load-Out/Stay
   Running On Empty
   You Love The Thunder

Hold Out [1980]
   Boulevard
   Hold On Hold Out
   That Girl Could Sing

BROWNSVILLE STATION
Yeah! [1973]
   Smokin' In The Boy's Room

BUBBLE PUPPY, The
A Gathering Of Promises [1969]
   Hot Smoke & Sasafrass

BUFFALO SPRINGFIELD, The
Buffalo Springfield [1967]
   For What It's Worth (Stop, Hey What's That Sound)
Buffalo Springfield Again [1967]
   Bluebird
   Mr. Soul
   Rock 'N' Roll Woman

BUFFETT, Jimmy
Changes In Latitudes, Changes In Attitudes [1977]
   Margaritaville
Son Of A Son Of A Sailor [1978]
   Cheeseburger In Paradise

BURDON, Eric, & War
Eric Burdon Declares "War" [1970]
   Spill The Wine

BYRDS, The
Mr. Tambourine Man [1965]
   All I Really Want To Do
   Mr. Tambourine Man
Turn! Turn! Turn! [1966]
   Turn! Turn! Turn! (To Everything There Is A Season)
Fifth Dimension [1966]
   Eight Miles High
   Mr. Spaceman
Younger Than Yesterday [1967]
   My Back Pages
   So You Want To Be A Rock 'N' Roll Star

* *

CANNED HEAT
Boogie With Canned Heat [1968]
   On The Road Again
Living The Blues [1968]
   Going Up The Country
Future Blues [1970]
   Let's Work Together

CARS, The
The Cars [1978]
   Bye Bye Love
   Good Times Roll
   Just What I Needed
   Moving In Stereo
   My Best Friend's Girl
   You're All I've Got Tonight
Candy-O [1979]
   Dangerous Type
   It's All I Can Do
   Let's Go

CARS, The — cont'd
Panorama [1980]
Touch And Go

CHAPIN, Harry
Heads & Tales [1972]
Taxi
Verities & Balderdash [1974]
Cat's In The Cradle

CHEAP TRICK
Heaven Tonight [1978]
Surrender
Cheap Trick At Budokan [1978]
Ain't That A Shame
I Want You To Want Me
Dream Police [1979]
Dream Police
Voices

CHEECH & CHONG
Cheech And Chong [1971]
Dave
Big Bambu [1972]
Sister Mary Elephant
Los Cochinos [1973]
Basketball Jones
Cheech & Chong's Wedding Album [1974]
Black Lassie
Earache My Eye
Three Little Pigs

CHICAGO
Chicago Transit Authority [1969]
Beginnings
Does Anybody Really Know What Time It Is?
I'm A Man
Questions 67 & 68
Chicago II [1970]
Make Me Smile
25 Or 6 To 4
Chicago V [1972]
Saturday In The Park
Chicago VII [1974]
(I've Been) Searchin' So Long
Chicago VIII [1975]
Old Days

CLAPTON, Eric
Eric Clapton [1970]
After Midnight
Blues Power
Let It Rain
Layla [1970]
Bell Bottom Blues
Layla
461 Ocean Boulevard [1974]
I Shot The Sheriff
Willie And The Hand Jive
No Reason To Cry [1976]
Hello Old Friend

Slowhand [1977]
Cocaine
Lay Down Sally
Wonderful Tonight
Backless [1978]
Promises
Tulsa Time
Watch Out For Lucy

CLASH, The
London Calling [1980]
Train In Vain (Stand By Me)

CLIMAX BLUES BAND
Gold Plated [1976]
Couldn't Get It Right

COCKER, Joe
With A Little Help From My Friends [1969]
Feeling Alright
With A Little Help From My Friends
Joe Cocker! [1969]
Delta Lady
She Came In Through The Bathroom Window
Mad Dogs & Englishmen [1970]
Cry Me A River
Letter, The
Joe Cocker [1972]
High Time We Went
I Can Stand A Little Rain [1974]
You Are So Beautiful

COMMANDER CODY AND HIS LOST PLANET AIRMEN
Lost In The Ozone [1971]
Hot Rod Lincoln

COOPER, Alice
Love It To Death [1971]
Eighteen
Killer [1971]
Be My Lover
Under My Wheels
School's Out [1972]
School's Out
Billion Dollar Babies [1973]
Billion Dollar Babies
Elected
Hello Hurray
No More Mr. Nice Guy
Welcome To My Nightmare [1975]
Welcome To My Nightmare
Flush The Fashion [1980]
Clones (We're All)

COSTELLO, Elvis
My Aim Is True [1977]
Alison
Watching The Detectives
This Year's Model [1978]
Pump It Up
Radio, Radio

COSTELLO, Elvis — cont'd
Armed Forces [1979]
    Accidents Will Happen
    Oliver's Army
    (What's So Funny 'Bout) Peace, Love And
      Understanding
Get Happy!! [1980]
    I Can't Stand Up For Falling Down

COUNTRY JOE AND THE FISH
Electric Music For The Mind And Body [1967]
    Not So Sweet Martha Lorraine
I-Feel-Like-I'm-Fixin'-To-Die [1967]
    I-Feel-Like-I'm-Fixin'-To-Die-Rag
Together [1968]
    Rock And Soul Music

CREAM
Fresh Cream [1967]
    I Feel Free
Disraeli Gears [1967]
    Strange Brew
    Sunshine Of Your Love
Wheels Of Fire [1968]
    Crossroads
    Spoonful
    White Room
Goodbye [1969]
    Badge

CREEDENCE CLEARWATER REVIVAL
Creedence Clearwater Revival [1968]
    I Put A Spell On You
    Suzie Q.
Bayou Country [1969]
    Born On The Bayou
    Proud Mary
Green River [1969]
    Bad Moon Rising
    Green River
    Lodi
Willy and the Poorboys [1969]
    Down On The Corner
    Fortunate Son
Cosmo's Factory [1970]
    I Heard It Through The Grapevine
    Long As I Can See The Light
    Lookin' Out My Back Door
    Run Through The Jungle
    Travelin' Band
    Up Around The Bend
    Who'll Stop The Rain
Pendulum [1970]
    Have You Ever Seen The Rain
    Hey Tonight
Mardi Gras [1972]
    Someday Never Comes
    Sweet Hitch-Hiker

CROCE, Jim
You Don't Mess Around With Jim [1972]
    You Don't Mess Around With Jim
Life And Times [1973]
    Bad, Bad Leroy Brown

CROSBY, STILLS , NASH & YOUNG
Crosby, Stills & Nash [1969]
    Helplessly Hoping
    Marrakesh Express
    Suite: Judy Blue Eyes
    Wooden Ships
Deja Vu [1970]
    Almost Cut My Hair
    Carry On
    Our House
    Teach Your Children
    Woodstock
(single only) [1970]
    Ohio
CSN [1977]
    Dark Star
    Fair Game
    Just A Song Before I Go

CROSS, Christopher
Christopher Cross [1980]
    Ride Like The Wind

CROW
Crow Music [1969]
    Evil Woman Don't Play Your Games With Me

* *

DANIELS, Charlie, Band
Fire On The Mountain [1974]
    Long Haired Country Boy
    South's Gonna Do It
Million Mile Reflections [1979]
    Devil Went Down To Georgia

DAVIS, Spencer, Group
Gimme Some Lovin' [1967]
    Gimme Some Lovin'
I'm A Man [1967]
    I'm A Man

DEEP PURPLE
Shades Of Deep Purple [1968]
    Hush
The Book Of Taliesyn [1969]
    Kentucky Woman
    River Deep-Mountain High
(single only) [1970]
    Black Night
Fireball [1971]
    Strange Kind Of Woman
Machine Head [1972]
    Highway Star
    Smoke On The Water
    Space Truckin'
Who Do We Think We Are! [1973]
    Woman From Tokyo
Burn [1974]
    Might Just Take Your Life

DELANEY & BONNIE & FRIENDS
Delaney & Bonnie & Friends On Tour with Eric Clapton [1970]
- Comin' Home
- Only You Know And I Know

Motel Shot [1971]
- Never Ending Song Of Love

DERRINGER, Rick
All American Boy [1973]
- Rock And Roll, Hoochie Koo

DEVO
Freedom Of Choice [1980]
- Whip It

DIRE STRAITS
Dire Straits [1979]
- Sultans Of Swing

DR. HOOK & THE MEDICINE SHOW
Sloppy Seconds [1972]
- Cover Of "Rolling Stone", The

DR. JOHN
In The Right Place [1973]
- Right Place Wrong Time

DONOVAN
Sunshine Superman [1966]
- Sunshine Superman

Mellow Yellow [1967]
- Mellow Yellow

The Hurdy Gurdy Man [1968]
- Hurdy Gurdy Man

Barabajagal [1969]
- Atlantis

DOOBIE BROTHERS, The
Toulouse Street [1972]
- Jesus Is Just Alright
- Listen To The Music
- Rockin' Down The Highway

The Captain And Me [1973]
- China Grove
- Long Train Runnin'
- South City Midnight Lady

What Were Once Vices Are Now Habits [1974]
- Another Park, Another Sunday
- Black Water
- Eyes Of Silver

Stampede [1975]
- Sweet Maxine
- Take Me In Your Arms (Rock Me)

Takin' It To The Streets [1976]
- It Keeps You Runnin'
- Takin' It To The Streets

Livin' On The Fault Line [1977]
- You Belong To Me

Minute By Minute [1978]
- Dependin' On You
- Minute By Minute
- What A Fool Believes

One Step Closer [1980]
- One Step Closer
- Real Love

DOORS, The
The Doors [1967]
- Alabama Song (Whiskey Bar)
- Back Door Man
- Break On Through (To The Other Side)
- Crystal Ship
- End, The
- Light My Fire

Strange Days [1967]
- Love Me Two Times
- Moonlight Drive
- People Are Strange
- Strange Days
- When The Music's Over

Waiting For The Sun [1968]
- Five To One
- Hello, I Love You
- Unknown Soldier

The Soft Parade [1969]
- Tell All The People
- Touch Me
- Wishful Sinful

Morrison Hotel/Hard Rock Café [1970]
- Roadhouse Blues

L.A. Woman [1971]
- L.A. Woman
- Love Her Madly
- Riders On The Storm

DYLAN, Bob
The Freewheelin' Bob Dylan [1963]
- Blowin' In The Wind
- Don't Think Twice, It's All Right

The Times They Are A-Changin' [1964]
- Times They Are A-Changin', The

Another Side Of Bob Dylan [1964]
- It Ain't Me Babe
- My Back Pages

Bringing It All Back Home [1965]
- It's All Over Now, Baby Blue
- Maggie's Farm
- Mr. Tambourine Man
- Subterranean Homesick Blues

Highway 61 Revisited [1965]
- Ballad Of A Thin Man
- Like A Rolling Stone

(single only) [1965]
- Positively 4th Street

(single only) [1966]
- Can You Please Crawl Out Your Window?

Blonde On Blonde [1966]
- I Want You
- Just Like A Woman
- Leopard-Skin Pill-Box Hat
- Rainy Day Women #12 & 35

John Wesley Harding [1968]
- All Along The Watchtower

Nashville Skyline [1969]
- I Threw It All Away
- Lay Lady Lay

Bob Dylan's Greatest Hits, Vol. II [1971]
- Watching The River Flow

DYLAN, Bob — cont'd
Dylan[1973]
　Fool Such As I, A
St: Pat Garrity & Billy The Kid [1973]
　Knockin' On Heaven's Door
Planet Waves [1974]
　Forever Young
　On A Night Like This
　You Angel You
Before The Flood [1974]
　Most Likely You Go Your Way (And I'll Go Mine)
Blood On The Tracks [1975]
　Tangled Up In Blue
Desire [1976]
　Hurricane
　Isis
　Mozambique
Slow Train Coming [1979]
　Gotta Serve Somebody

* *

EAGLES
Eagles [1972]
　Peaceful Easy Feeling
　Take It Easy
　Witchy Woman
Desperado [1973]
　Desperado
　Doolin-Dalton
　Outlaw Man
　Tequila Sunrise
On The Border [1974]
　Already Gone
　Best Of My Love
　James Dean
One Of These Nights [1975]
　After The Thrill Is Gone
　Lyin' Eyes
　One Of These Nights
　Take It To The Limit
Hotel California [1976]
　Hotel California
　Life In The Fast Lane
　New Kid In Town
　Victim Of Love
　Wasted Time
(single only) [1978]
　Please Come Home For Christmas
The Long Run [1979]
　Heartache Tonight
　I Can't Tell You Why
　In The City
　Long Run
　Sad Café
　Those Shoes
Eagles Live [1980]
　Seven Bridges Road

EASYBEATS, The
Friday On My Mind [1967]
　Friday On My Mind

EDMUNDS, Dave
Rockpile [1970]
　I Hear You Knocking

ELECTRIC LIGHT ORCHESTRA
Electric Light Orchestra II [1973]
　Roll Over Beethoven
On The Third Day [1973]
　Showdown
Eldorado [1974]
　Can't Get It Out Of My Head
Face The Music [1975]
　Evil Woman
　Fire On High
　Strange Magic
A New World Record [1976]
　Do Ya
　Livin' Thing
　Telephone Line
Out Of The Blue [1977]
　Mr. Blue Sky
　Sweet Talkin' Woman
　Turn To Stone
Discovery [1979]
　Confusion
　Don't Bring Me Down
　Last Train To London
　Shine A Little Love
St: Xanadu [1980]
　All Over The World
　I'm Alive

ELECTRIC PRUNES, The
The Electric Prunes [1967]
　I Had Too Much To Dream (Last Night)

EMERSON, LAKE & PALMER
Emerson, Lake & Palmer [1971]
　Lucky Man
Trilogy [1972]
　From The Beginning
　Hoedown
Brain Salad Surgery [1973]
　Karn Evil 9
Works, Volume 1 [1977]
　Fanfare For The Common Man

ESSEX, David
Rock On [1974]
　Rock On

* *

FACES
*A Nod Is As Good As A Wink...To A Blind
　Horse [1971]*
　Stay With Me

FEVER TREE
Fever Tree [1968]
　San Francisco Girls (Return Of The Native)

FIVE MAN ELECTRICAL BAND
Good-Byes & Butterflies [1971]
　Signs

FLEETWOOD MAC
English Rose [1969]
  Albatross
  Black Magic Woman
Then Play On [1969]
  Oh Well
Mystery To Me [1973]
  Hypnotized
Fleetwood Mac [1975]
  I'm So Afraid
  Landslide
  Monday Morning
  Over My Head
  Rhiannon (Will You Ever Win)
  Say You Love Me
Rumours [1977]
  Chain, The
  Don't Stop
  Dreams
  Go Your Own Way
  Gold Dust Woman
  I Don't Want To Know
  Never Going Back Again
  Second Hand News
  You Make Loving Fun
(single only) [1977]
  Silver Springs
Tusk [1979]
  Sara
  Think About Me
  Tusk

FOCUS
Moving Waves [1973]
  Hocus Pocus

FOGELBERG, Dan
Souvenirs [1974]
  Part Of The Plan

FOGERTY, John
John Fogerty [1975]
  Almost Saturday Night
  Rockin' All Over The World

FOGHAT
Foghat [1972]
  I Just Want To Make Love To You
Fool For The City [1975]
  Fool For The City
  Slow Ride
Night Shift [1976]
  Drivin' Wheel
Stone Blue [1978]
  Stone Blue
Boogie Motel [1979]
  Third Time Lucky (First Time I Was A Fool)

FORBERT, Steve
Jackrabbit Slim [1979]
  Romeo's Tune

FOREIGNER
Foreigner [1977]
  Cold As Ice
  Feels Like The First Time
  Headknocker
  Long, Long Way From Home
Double Vision [1978]
  Blue Morning, Blue Day
  Double Vision
  Hot Blooded
Head Games [1979]
  Dirty White Boy
  Head Games

FRAMPTON, Peter
Frampton Comes Alive! [1976]
  Baby, I Love Your Way
  Do You Feel Like We Do
  Show Me The Way
I'm In You [1977]
  I'm In You
Where I Should Be [1979]
  I Can't Stand It No More

FREE
Fire And Water [1970]
  All Right Now

FREHLEY, Ace
Ace Frehley [1978]
  New York Groove

FRIJID PINK
Frijid Pink [1970]
  House Of The Rising Sun

· ·

GABRIEL, Peter
Peter Gabriel [1977]
  Solsbury Hill
Peter Gabriel [1980]
  Games Without Frontiers

GEILS, J., Band
The Morning After [1971]
  Looking For A Love
Bloodshot [1973]
  Give It To Me
Nightmares...and other tales from the vinyl jungle [1974]
  Must Of Got Lost
Sanctuary [1978]
  One Last Kiss
Love Stinks [1980]
  Come Back
  Love Stinks

GENESIS
The Lamb Lies Down On Broadway [1974]
  Lamb Lies Down On Broadway
And Then There Were Three... [1978]
  Follow You Follow Me
Duke [1980]
  Misunderstanding
  Turn It On Again

GLITTER, Gary
Glitter [1972]
   Rock And Roll Part 2

GOLDEN EARRING
Moontan [1974]
   Radar Love

GRAND FUNK RAILROAD
Closer To Home [1970]
   Closer To Home/I'm Your Captain
E Pluribus Funk [1971]
   Footstompin' Music
Phoenix [1972]
   Rock 'N Roll Soul
We're An American Band [1973]
   Walk Like A Man
   We're An American Band
Shinin' On [1974]
   Loco-Motion, The
   Shinin' On
All The Girls In The World Beware!!! [1974]
   Bad Time
   Some Kind Of Wonderful

GRATEFUL DEAD
Aoxomoxoa [1969]
   St. Stephen
Live/Dead [1969]
   Dark Star
   Turn On Your Love Light
Workingman's Dead [1970]
   Casey Jones
   Uncle John's Band
American Beauty [1970]
   Ripple
   Sugar Magnolia
   Truckin'
Grateful Dead [1971]
   Bertha
   Playing In The Band
Europe '72 [1972]
   One More Saturday Night
Blues For Allah [1975]
   Franklin's Tower
   Music Never Stopped
Terrapin Station [1977]
   Terrapin Station
Shakedown Street [1978]
   Shakedown Street
Go To Heaven [1980]
   Alabama Getaway

GREENBAUM, Norman
Spirit In The Sky [1970]
   Spirit In The Sky

GUESS WHO, The
Wheatfield Soul [1969]
   These Eyes
Canned Wheat Packed by The Guess Who [1969]
   Laughing
   No Time
   Undun

American Woman [1970]
   American Woman
   No Sugar Tonight/New Mother Nature
Share The Land [1970]
   Hand Me Down World
   Share The Land
(single only) [1971]
   Albert Flasher
Road Food [1974]
   Clap For The Wolfman
   Star Baby
Flavours [1975]
   Dancin' Fool

. . . .

HALL, Daryl, & John Oates
Abandoned Luncheonette [1974]
   She's Gone

HARRISON, George
All Things Must Pass [1970]
   Isn't It A Pity
   My Sweet Lord
   What Is Life
(single only [1971]
   Bangla-Desh
Living In The Material World [1973]
   Give Me Love (Give Me Peace On Earth)
Dark Horse [1974]
   Dark Horse
   Ding Dong; Ding Dong
Extra Texture (Read All About It) [1975]
   You
Thirty-Three & 1/3 [1976]
   Crackerbox Palace
   This Song
George Harrison [1979]
   Blow Away

HEAD EAST
Flat As A Pancake [1975]
   Never Been Any Reason
Head East [1978]
   Since You've Been Gone

HEART
Dreamboat Annie [1976]
   Crazy On You
   Dreamboat Annie
   Magic Man
Little Queen [1977]
   Barracuda
   Kick It Out
   Little Queen
Magazine [1978]
   Heartless
Dog & Butterfly [1978]
   Dog & Butterfly
   Straight On *[78]*
Bebe Le Strange [1980]
   Even It Up
Greatest Hits/Live [1980]
   Tell It Like It Is

HENDRIX, Jimi
Are You Experienced? [1967]
Fire
Foxey Lady
Hey Joe
Manic Depression
Purple Haze
Third Stone From The Sun
Wind Cries Mary, The
Axis: Bold As Love [1968]
If 6 Was 9
Little Wing
Up From The Skies
Electric Ladyland [1968]
All Along The Watchtower
Burning Of The Midnight Lamp
Crosstown Traffic
Voodoo Child (Slight Return)
Smash Hits [1969]
Red House
Stone Free
The Cry Of Love [1971]
Freedom
Rainbow Bridge [1971]
Dolly Dagger
Star Spangled Banner

HOLLIES, The
Distant Light [1972]
Long Cool Woman (In A Black Dress)

HUMBLE PIE
Rock On [1971]
Stone Cold Fever
Performance-Rockin' The Fillmore [1971]
I Don't Need No Doctor
Smokin' [1972]
Hot 'N' Nasty
30 Days In The Hole

. . . .

IDES OF MARCH, The
Vehicle [1970]
Vehicle

IRON BUTTERFLY
In-A-Gadda-Da-Vida [1968]
In-A-Gadda-Da-Vida

IT'S A BEAUTIFUL DAY
It's A Beautiful Day [1969]
White Bird

. . . .

JACKSON, Joe
Look Sharp! [1979]
Is She Really Going Out With Him?

JAMES GANG
James Gang Rides Again [1970]
Funk #49
Thirds [1971]
Walk Away

JEFFERSON AIRPLANE/STARSHIP
Surrealistic Pillow [1967]
Plastic Fantastic Lover
Somebody To Love
White Rabbit
Crown Of Creation [1968]
Crown Of Creation
Greasy Heart
Volunteers [1969]
Volunteers
Bark [1971]
Pretty As You Feel
Dragon Fly [1974]
Ride The Tiger
Red Octopus [1975]
Miracles
Play On Love
Spitfire [1976]
With Your Love
Earth [1978]
Count On Me
Runaway
Freedom At Point Zero [1979]
Jane

JETHRO TULL
Stand Up [1969]
Bouree
New Day Yesterday
Benefit [1970]
Teacher
Aqualung [1971]
Aqualung
Cross-Eyed Mary
Hymn 43
Locomotive Breath
Thick As A Brick [1972]
Thick As A Brick
Living In The Past [1972]
Living In The Past
War Child [1974]
Bungle In The Jungle
Skating Away On The Thin Ice Of A New Day
Minstrel In The Gallery [1975]
Minstrel In The Gallery
Too Old To Rock 'N' Roll: Too Young To Die! [1976]
Too Old To Rock 'N' Roll: Too Young To Die

JOEL, Billy
Piano Man [1974]
Ballad Of Billy The Kid
Captain Jack
Piano Man
Streetlife Serenade [1974]
Entertainer, The
Turnstiles [1976]
New York State Of Mind

JOEL, Billy — cont'd
The Stranger [1977]
 Just The Way You Are
 Movin' Out (Anthony's Song)
 Only The Good Die Young
 Scenes From An Italian Restaurant
 She's Always A Woman
 Stranger, The
52nd Street [1978]
 Big Shot
 Honesty
 My Life
 Rosalinda's Eyes
Glass Houses [1980]
 All For Leyna
 Close To The Borderline
 Don't Ask Me Why
 It's Still Rock And Roll To Me
 Sometimes A Fantasy
 You May Be Right

JOHN, Elton
Elton John [1970]
 Border Song
 Take Me To The Pilot
 Your Song
Tumbleweed Connection [1971]
 Burn Down The Mission
Madman Across The Water [1971]
 Levon
 Madman Across The Water
 Tiny Dancer
Honky Chateau [1972]
 Hercules
 Honky Cat
 Mona Lisas And Mad Hatters
 Rocket Man
Don't Shoot Me I'm Only The Piano Player [1973]
 Crocodile Rock
 Daniel
Goodbye Yellow Brick Road [1973]
 Bennie And The Jets
 Candle In The Wind
 Funeral For A Friend/Love Lies Bleeding
 Goodbye Yellow Brick Road
 Grey Seal
 Harmony
 Saturday Night's Alright For Fighting
(single only) [1973]
 Step Into Christmas
Caribou [1974]
 Bitch Is Back
 Don't Let The Sun Go Down On Me
(single only) [1974]
 Lucy In The Sky With Diamonds
Rock Of The Westies [1975]
 Grow Some Funk Of Your Own
 Island Girl
(single only) [1975]
 Philadelphia Freedom
St: Tommy [1975]
 Pinball Wizard

*Captain Fantastic And The Brown Dirt
 Cowboy [1975]*
 Someone Saved My Life Tonight

JOHNSTON, Tom
Everything You've Heard Is True [1979]
 Savannah Nights

JONES, Rickie Lee
Rickie Lee Jones [1979]
 Chuck E.'s In Love

JOPLIN, Janis
I Got Dem Ol' Kozmic Blues Again Mama! [1969]
 Kozmic Blues
 Try (Just A Little Bit Harder)
Pearl [1971]
 Cry Baby
 Get It While You Can
 Me And Bobby McGee
 Mercedes Benz
 Move Over

JOURNEY
Infinity [1978]
 Anytime
 Lights
 Wheel In The Sky
Evolution [1979]
 Just The Same Way
 Lovin', Touchin', Squeezin'
Departure [1980]
 Any Way You Want It
 Walks Like A Lady

JUDAS PRIEST
British Steel [1980]
 Breaking The Law
 Living After Midnight

. . . .

KANSAS
Leftoverture [1976]
 Carry On Wayward Son
 What's On My Mind
Point Of Know Return [1977]
 Dust In The Wind
 Point Of Know Return
 Portrait (He Knew)
Monolith [1979]
 People Of The South Wind
Audio-Visions [1980]
 Hold On

KING, Carole
Tapestry [1971]
 I Feel The Earth Move
 It's Too Late
 So Far Away

KING CRIMSON
*In The Court Of The Crimson King - An Observation
 By King Crimson [1969]*
 Court Of The Crimson King

KINGS, The
The Kings Are Here [1980]
    This Beat Goes On/Switchin' To Glide

KINKS, The
You Really Got Me [1964]
    You Really Got Me
Kinks-Size [1965]
    All Day And All Of The Night
    Tired Of Waiting For You
Kinks Kinkdom [1965]
    Well Respected Man
Face To Face [1967]
    Sunny Afternoon
*Arthur (or the decline and fall of the British
  Empire) [1969]*
    Victoria
*Lola Versus Powerman and The Moneygoround,
  Part One [1970]*
    Apeman
    Lola
Everybody's In Show-Biz [1972]
    Celluloid Heroes
(single only) [1977]
    Father Christmas
Sleepwalker [1977]
    Sleepwalker
Misfits [1978]
    Rock 'N' Roll Fantasy
Low Budget [1979]
    Low Budget
    (Wish I Could Fly Like) Superman

KISS
Kiss [1974]
    Cold Gin
    Deuce
    Nothin' To Lose
    Strutter
Hotter Than Hell [1974]
    Hotter Than Hell
Dressed To Kill [1975]
    Rock And Roll All Nite
Destroyer [1976]
    Beth
    Detroit Rock City
    God Of Thunder
    Shout It Out Loud
Rock And Roll Over [1976]
    Calling Dr. Love
    Hard Luck Woman
Love Gun [1977]
    Christine Sixteen
    Love Gun
    Shock Me
Alive II [1978]
    Rocket Ride
Dynasty [1979]
    I Was Made For Lovin' You
    Sure Know Something

KNACK, The
Get The Knack [1979]
    Frustrated
    Good Girls Don't
    My Sharona
    (She's So) Selfish
But The Little Girls Understand [1980]
    Baby Talks Dirty

. . . .

LED ZEPPELIN
Led Zeppelin [1969]
    Babe I'm Gonna Leave You
    Communication Breakdown
    Dazed And Confused
    Good Times Bad Times
    How Many More Times
    I Can't Quit You Baby
Led Zeppelin II [1969]
    Heartbreaker
    Living Loving Maid (She's Just A Woman)
    Ramble On
    Thank You
    What Is And What Should Never Be
    Whole Lotta Love
Led Zeppelin III [1970]
    Gallows Pole
    Immigrant Song
    Since I've Been Loving You
Led Zeppelin IV (untitled) [1971]
    Black Dog
    Going To California
    Misty Mountain Hop
    Rock And Roll
    Stairway To Heaven
    When The Levee Breaks
Houses Of The Holy [1973]
    Crunge, The
    D'yer Mak'er
    Dancing Days
    Ocean, The
    Over The Hills And Far Away
    Rain Song
    Song Remains The Same
Physical Graffiti [1975]
    Houses Of The Holy
    Kashmir
    Trampled Under Foot
Presence [1976]
    Nobody's Fault But Mine
In Through The Out Door [1979]
    All My Love
    Fool In The Rain
    Hot Dog
    In The Evening

LENNON, John
(single only) [1969]
    Give Peace A Chance
(single only) [1969]
    Cold Turkey
John Lennon/Plastic Ono Band [1970]
    God
    Mother
(single only) [1970]
    Instant Karma (We All Shine On)
(single only) [1971]
    Happy Xmas (War Is Over)
Imagine [1971]
    Imagine
(single only) [1971]
    Power To The People
Some Time In New York City [1972]
    Woman Is The Nigger Of The World
Mind Games [1973]
    Mind Games
Walls And Bridges [1974]
    #9 Dream
    Whatever Gets You Thru The Night
Rock 'N' Roll [1975]
    Stand By Me
Double Fantasy [1980]
    Beautiful Boy (Darling Boy)
    (Just Like) Starting Over

LIGHTFOOT, Gordon
Sit Down Young Stranger [1970]
    If You Could Read My Mind
Sundown [1974]
    Carefree Highway
    Sundown
Summertime Dream [1976]
    Wreck Of The Edmund Fitzgerald

LIGHTHOUSE
One Fine Morning [1971]
    One Fine Morning

LOGGINS & MESSINA
Sittin' In [1972]
    Danny's Song
Loggins And Messina [1972]
    Your Mama Don't Dance
Full Sail [1973]
    My Music

LOVE
Love [1966]
    My Little Red Book
Da Capo [1967]
    7 And 7 Is
Forever Changes [1968]
    Alone Again Or

LOWE, Nick
Labour Of Lust [1979]
    Cruel To Be Kind

LYNYRD SKYNYRD
Lynyrd Skynyrd (pronounced leh-nerd skin-nerd) [1973]
    Free Bird
    Gimme Three Steps
    I Ain't The One
Second Helping [1974]
    Call Me The Breeze
    Don't Ask Me No Questions
    Sweet Home Alabama
    Workin' For MCA
Nuthin' Fancy [1975]
    Saturday Night Special
Gimme Back My Bullets [1976]
    Double Trouble
    Gimme Back My Bullets
Street Survivors [1977]
    That Smell
    What's Your Name
    You Got That Right

* *

MANFRED MANN
the Manfred Mann album [1964]
    Do Wah Diddy Diddy
The Mighty Quinn [1968]
    Mighty Quinn (Quinn The Eskimo)
Nightingales & Bombers [1975]
    Spirit In The Night
The Roaring Silence [1976]
    Blinded By The Light

MARSHALL TUCKER BAND, The
The Marshall Tucker Band [1973]
    Can't You See
Searchin' For A Rainbow [1975]
    Fire On The Mountain
Carolina Dreams [1977]
    Heard It In A Love Song

MASON, Dave
Alone Together [1970]
    Only You Know And I Know
Let It Flow [1977]
    Let It Go, Let It Flow
    So High (Rock Me Baby And Roll Me Away)
    We Just Disagree

MAYALL, John
The Turning Point [1969]
    Room To Move
Empty Rooms [1970]
    Don't Waste My Time

MC5
Kick Out The Jams [1969]
    Kick Out The Jams

McCARTNEY, Paul
McCartney [1970]
Maybe I'm Amazed
(single only) [1971]
Another Day
Ram [1971]
Uncle Albert/Admiral Halsey
Wild Life [1971]
Bip Bop
(single only) [1972]
Hi, Hi, Hi
St: Live And Let Die [1973]
Live And Let Die
Red Rose Speedway [1973]
My Love
Band On The Run [1973]
Band On The Run
Helen Wheels
Jet
Nineteen Hundred And Eighty Five
(single only) [1974]
Junior's Farm
Venus And Mars [1975]
Letting Go
Listen To What The Man Said
Venus And Mars Rock Show
Wings At The Speed Of Sound [1976]
Let 'Em In
Silly Love Songs
London Town [1978]
I've Had Enough
London Town
With A Little Luck
(single only) [1979]
Goodnight Tonight
Back To The Egg [1979]
Arrow Through Me
Getting Closer
(single only) [1980]
Coming Up (Live At Glasgow)

McCLINTON, Delbert
The Jealous Kind [1980]
Giving It Up For Your Love

McGUINN, CLARK & HILLMAN
McGuinn, Clark & Hillman [1979]
Don't You Write Her Off

McLEAN, Don
American Pie [1971]
American Pie

MEAT LOAF
Bat Out Of Hell [1977]
Bat Out Of Hell
Paradise By The Dashboard Light
Two Out Of Three Ain't Bad
You Took The Words Right Out Of My Mouth

MEISNER, Randy
One More Song [1980]
Deep Inside My Heart

MELLENCAMP, John Cougar
John Cougar [1979]
I Need A Lover
Nothin' Matters And What If It Did [1980]
This Time

MICHAELS, Lee
"5th" [1971]
Do You Know What I Mean

MILLER, Steve, Band
Sailor [1968]
Gangster Of Love
Living In The U.S.A.
Brave New World [1969]
Space Cowboy
Number 5 [1970]
Going To The Country
The Joker [1973]
Joker, The
Your Cash Ain't Nothin' But Trash
Fly Like An Eagle [1976]
Dance, Dance, Dance
Fly Like An Eagle
Rock'n Me
Take The Money And Run
Book Of Dreams [1977]
Jet Airliner
Jungle Love
Stake, The
Swingtown
Winter Time

MITCHELL, Joni
Ladies Of The Canyon [1970]
Big Yellow Taxi
Court And Spark [1974]
Free Man In Paris
Help Me

MOBY GRAPE
Moby Grape [1967]
Hey Grandma
Omaha

MOLLY HATCHET
Flirtin' With Disaster [1979]
Flirtin' With Disaster

MONEY, Eddie
Eddie Money [1978]
Baby Hold On
Two Tickets To Paradise
Life For The Taking [1979]
Gimme Some Water
Maybe I'm A Fool

MONKEES, The
More Of The Monkees [1967]
(I'm Not Your) Steppin' Stone
Pisces, Aquarius, Capricorn & Jones Ltd. [1967]
Daily Nightly
Head [1968]
Porpoise Song
The Monkees Present [1969]
Listen To The Band

MOODY BLUES, The
(single only) [1965]
  Go Now!
Days Of Future Passed [1968]
  Nights In White Satin
  Tuesday Afternoon (Forever Afternoon)
In Search Of The Lost Chord [1968]
  Legend Of A Mind
  Ride My See-Saw
On The Threshold Of A Dream [1969]
  Never Comes The Day
To Our Children's Children's Children [1970]
  Eyes Of A Child
A Question Of Balance [1970]
  Question
Every Good Boy Deserves Favour [1971]
  Story In Your Eyes
Seventh Sojourn [1972]
  I'm Just A Singer (In A Rock And Roll Band)
  Isn't Life Strange
Octave [1978]
  Driftwood
  Steppin' In A Slide Zone

MORRISON, Van
Blowin' Your Mind! [1967]
  Brown Eyed Girl
Moondance [1970]
  Come Running
  Crazy Love
  Into The Mystic
  Moondance
His Band And The Street Choir [1970]
  Blue Money
  Call Me Up In Dreamland
  Domino
Tupelo Honey [1971]
  Tupelo Honey
  Wild Night
Saint Dominic's Preview [1972]
  Jackie Wilson Said (I'm In Heaven When You Smile)
  Redwood Tree
Wavelength [1978]
  Wavelength

MOTT THE HOOPLE
All The Young Dudes [1972]
  All The Young Dudes

MOUNTAIN
Mountain Climbing! [1970]
  Mississippi Queen

* *

NASH, Graham
Songs For Beginners [1971]
  Chicago

NAZARETH
Loud 'N' Proud [1974]
  This Flight Tonight
Hair Of The Dog [1975]
  Hair Of The Dog
  Love Hurts

NEWMAN, Randy
Sail Away [1972]
  Political Science
  Sail Away
Little Criminals [1977]
  Short People

NITTY GRITTY DIRT BAND
Uncle Charlie & His Dog Teddy [1970]
  Mr. Bojangles

NUGENT, Ted
Ted Nugent [1975]
  Hey Baby
Free-For-All [1976]
  Dog Eat Dog
  Free-For-All
Cat Scratch Fever [1977]
  Cat Scratch Fever
  Home Bound
  Wang Dang Sweet Poontang
Double Live Gonzo! [1978]
  Yank Me, Crank Me
Weekend Warriors [1978]
  Need You Bad
Scream Dream [1980]
  Wango Tango

* *

ORLEANS
Let There Be Music [1975]
  Dance With Me

OUTLAWS
Outlaws [1975]
  Green Grass & High Tides
  There Goes Another Love Song

OZARK MOUNTAIN DAREDEVILS
The Ozark Mountain Daredevils [1974]
  If You Wanna Get To Heaven
It'll Shine When It Shines [1974]
  Jackie Blue

* *

PALMER, Robert
Double Fun [1978]
  Every Kinda People
Secrets [1979]
  Bad Case Of Loving You (Doctor, Doctor)
  Can We Still Be Friends

PARSONS, Alan, Project
Tales Of Mystery And Imagination - Edgar Allan Poe [1976]
  Raven, The
  (System Of) Doctor Tarr And Professor Fether
I Robot [1977]
  Breakdown
  Don't Let It Show
  I Robot
  I Wouldn't Want To Be Like You
Pyramid [1978]
  What Goes Up

PARSONS, Alan, Project — cont'd
Eve [1979]
   Damned If I Do
The Turn Of A Friendly Card [1980]
   Games People Play

PETTY, Tom, And The Heartbreakers
Tom Petty & The Heartbreakers [1977]
   American Girl
   Breakdown
You're Gonna Get It! [1978]
   I Need To Know
   Listen To Her Heart
Damn The Torpedoes [1979]
   Don't Do Me Like That
   Even The Losers
   Here Comes My Girl
   Refugee

PINK FLOYD
The Piper At The Gates Of Dawn [1967]
   See Emily Play
Meddle [1971]
   One Of These Days
The Dark Side Of The Moon [1973]
   Brain Damage/Eclipse
   Great Gig In The Sky
   Money
   Speak To Me/Breathe
   Time
   Us And Them
Wish You Were Here [1975]
   Have A Cigar
   Shine On You Crazy Diamond
   Welcome To The Machine
   Wish You Were Here
The Wall [1979]
   Another Brick In The Wall
   Comfortably Numb
   Hey You
   Run Like Hell
   Young Lust

POCO
Legend [1978]
   Crazy Love
   Heart Of The Night

POLICE, The
Outlandos d'Amour [1979]
   Roxanne
Reggatta de Blanc [1979]
   Message In A Bottle
Zenyatta Mondatta [1980]
   De Do Do Do, De Da Da Da

PRETENDERS, The
Pretenders [1980]
   Brass In Pocket (I'm Special)
   Stop Your Sobbing

PRINCE
Prince [1979]
   I Wanna Be Your Lover

PROCOL HARUM
Procol Harum [1967]
   Whiter Shade Of Pale
*Procol Harum Live In Concert with the Edmonton
   Symphony Orchestra [1972]*
   Conquistador

PURE PRAIRIE LEAGUE
Bustin' Out [1975]
   Amie

. . . .

QUEEN
Queen [1973]
   Keep Yourself Alive
Sheer Heart Attack [1974]
   Killer Queen
A Night At The Opera [1975]
   Bohemian Rhapsody
   You're My Best Friend
A Day At The Races [1977]
   Good Old-Fashioned Lover Boy
   Somebody To Love
   Tie Your Mother Down
News Of The World [1977]
   We Will Rock You/We Are The Champions
Jazz [1978]
   Bicycle Race
   Don't Stop Me Now
   Fat Bottomed Girls
The Game [1980]
   Another One Bites The Dust
   Crazy Little Thing Called Love
   Don't Try Suicide
   Play The Game

? (QUESTION MARK) & THE MYSTERIANS
96 Tears [1966]
   96 Tears

QUICKSILVER MESSENGER SERVICE
Just For Love [1970]
   Fresh Air

. . . .

RAFFERTY, Gerry
City To City [1978]
   Baker Street
   Home And Dry
   Right Down The Line

RAINBOW
Down To Earth [1979]
   Since You Been Gone

RAM JAM
Ram Jam [1977]
   Black Betty

RAMONES
Leave Home [1977]
   Sheena Is A Punk Rocker
Rocket To Russia [1977]
   Do You Wanna Dance
   Rockaway Beach

RAMONES — cont'd

Road To Ruin [1978]
I Wanna Be Sedated
End Of The Century [1980]
Do You Remember Rock 'N' Roll Radio?
Rock 'N' Roll High School

RARE EARTH

Get Ready [1969]
Get Ready
One World [1971]
I Just Want To Celebrate

RASPBERRIES

Raspberries [1972]
Go All The Way
Fresh [1972]
I Wanna Be With You

REED, Lou

Transformer [1972]
Satellite Of Love
Walk On The Wild Side
Sally Can't Dance [1974]
Sally Can't Dance
Rock N Roll Animal [1974]
Sweet Jane
White Light/White Heat
Coney Island Baby [1976]
Coney Island Baby
Street Hassle [1978]
Street Hassle

REO SPEEDWAGON

Ridin' The Storm Out [1974]
Ridin' The Storm Out
You can Tune a piano, but you can't Tuna fish [1978]
Roll With The Changes
Time For Me To Fly
Nine Lives [1979]
Back On The Road Again

ROCKETS

Rockets [1979]
Oh Well

ROLLING STONES, The

*England's Newest Hit Makers/The Rolling
Stones [1964]*
Not Fade Away
Tell Me (You're Coming Back)
12 x 5 [1964]
It's All Over Now
Time Is On My Side
The Rolling Stones, Now! [1965]
Heart Of Stone
Out Of Our Heads [1965]
(I Can't Get No) Satisfaction
Last Time
December's Children (and everybody's) [1965]
As Tears Go By
Get Off Of My Cloud

(single only) [1966]
19th Nervous Breakdown
Aftermath [1966]
Lady Jane
Paint It, Black
Under My Thumb
(single only) [1966]
Have You Seen Your Mother, Baby, Standing In
The Shadow?
(single only) [1967]
Dandelion
Between The Buttons [1967]
Let's Spend The Night Together
Ruby Tuesday
Flowers [1967]
Mothers Little Helper
(single only) [1968]
Jumpin' Jack Flash
Their Satanic Majesties Request [1967]
She's A Rainbow
Beggars Banquet [1968]
Street Fighting Man
Sympathy For The Devil
Let It Bleed [1969]
Gimme Shelter
You Can't Always Get What You Want
(single only) [1969]
Honky Tonk Women
Sticky Fingers [1971]
Bitch
Brown Sugar
Wild Horses
Exile On Main St. [1972]
Happy
Tumbling Dice
Goats Head Soup [1973]
Angie
Doo Doo Doo Doo Doo (Heartbreaker)
It's Only Rock 'N Roll [1974]
Ain't Too Proud To Beg
It's Only Rock 'N Roll (But I Like It)
Black And Blue [1976]
Fool To Cry
Some Girls [1978]
Beast Of Burden
Far Away Eyes
Miss You
Shattered
Emotional Rescue [1980]
Emotional Rescue
She's So Cold

ROMANTICS, The

The Romantics [1980]
She's Got Everything
What I Like About You
When I Look In Your Eyes

RONSTADT, Linda
Heart Like A Wheel [1974]
You're No Good
Simple Dreams [1977]
Poor Poor Pitiful Me
Tumbling Dice
Mad Love [1980]
How Do I Make You

ROXY MUSIC
Siren [1975]
Love Is The Drug

RUNDGREN, Todd
Runt [1971]
We Gotta Get You A Woman
Something/Anything? [1972]
Hello It's Me
I Saw The Light
Faithful [1976]
Good Vibrations
Hermit Of Mink Hollow [1978]
Can We Still Be Friends

RUSH
Fly By Night [1975]
Fly By Night
A Farewell To Kings [1977]
Closer To The Heart
Permanent Waves [1980]
Freewill
Spirit Of Radio

RUSSELL, Leon
Carney [1972]
Tight Rope

RYDER, Mitch, And The Detroit Wheels
Take A Ride [1966]
Jenny Take A Ride!
Breakout...!!! [1966]
Devil With A Blue Dress On & Good Golly Miss
Molly
Sock It To Me! [1967]
Sock It To Me-Baby!

* *

SANFORD/TOWNSEND BAND, The
The Sanford/Townsend Band [1977]
Smoke From A Distant Fire

SANTANA
Santana [1969]
Evil Ways
Jingo
Abraxas [1970]
Black Magic Woman/Gypsy Queen
Oye Como Va
Santana III [1971]
Everybody's Everything
No One To Depend On
Amigos [1976]
Let It Shine
Moonflower [1977]
She's Not There

Inner Secrets [1978]
One Chain (Don't Make No Prison)
Stormy
Marathon [1979]
You Know That I Love You

SCAGGS, Boz
My Time [1972]
Dinah Flo
Silk Degrees [1976]
Georgia
It's Over
Lido Shuffle
Lowdown
What Can I Say
Middle Man [1980]
Breakdown Dead Ahead
JoJo
Hits! [1980]
Miss Sun

SEALS & CROFTS
Summer Breeze [1972]
Summer Breeze
Diamond Girl [1973]
Diamond Girl

SEEDS, The
The Seeds [1967]
Pushin' Too Hard

SEGER, Bob
Ramblin' Gamblin' Man [1969]
Ramblin' Gamblin' Man
Beautiful Loser [1975]
Beautiful Loser
Katmandu
Travelin' Man
'Live' Bullet [1975]
Get Out Of Denver
Turn The Page
Night Moves [1976]
Fire Down Below
Mainstreet
Night Moves
Rock And Roll Never Forgets
Stranger In Town [1978]
Feel Like A Number
Hollywood Nights
Old Time Rock & Roll
Still The Same
We've Got Tonite
Against The Wind [1980]
Against The Wind
Betty Lou's Gettin' Out Tonight
Fire Lake
Her Strut
Horizontal Bop
You'll Accomp'ny Me

SEX PISTOLS

Never Mind The Bollocks, Here's The Sex Pistols [1977]
- Anarchy In The U.K.
- God Save The Queen
- Pretty Vacant

SHADOWS OF KNIGHT, The

Gloria [1966]
- Gloria

SIMON, Carly

No Secrets [1972]
- You're So Vain

SIMON, Paul

Paul Simon [1972]
- Me And Julio Down By The Schoolyard
- Mother And Child Reunion

There Goes Rhymin' Simon [1973]
- American Tune
- Kodachrome
- Loves Me Like A Rock

Still Crazy After All These Years [1975]
- 50 Ways To Leave Your Lover
- Still Crazy After All These Years

Greatest Hits, Etc. [1977]
- Slip Slidin' Away

One-Trick Pony [1980]
- Late In The Evening

SIMON & GARFUNKEL

(single only) [1966]
- Hazy Shade Of Winter, A

Parsley, Sage, Rosemary and Thyme [1966]
- Homeward Bound

Sounds of Silence [1966]
- I Am A Rock
- Sound Of Silence, The

Bookends [1968]
- America

St: The Graduate [1968]
- Mrs. Robinson

Bridge Over Troubled Water [1970]
- Boxer, The
- Bridge Over Troubled Water
- Cecilia

(single only) [1975]
- My Little Town

SMALL FACES

There Are But Four Small Faces [1968]
- Itchycoo Park

SMITH, Patti, Group

Easter [1978]
- Because The Night

SNIFF 'N' THE TEARS

Fickle Heart [1979]
- Driver's Seat

SPIRIT

The Family That Plays Together [1969]
- I Got A Line On You

Twelve Days Of Dr. Sardonicus [1970]
- Nature's Way

SPRINGSTEEN, Bruce

Greetings From Asbury Park, N.J. [1973]
- Blinded By The Light
- For You
- Spirit In The Night

The Wild, The Innocent & The E Street Shuffle [1973]
- 4th Of July, Asbury Park (Sandy)
- Rosalita (Come Out Tonight)

Born To Run [1975]
- Born To Run
- Jungleland
- Tenth Avenue Freeze-Out
- Thunder Road

Darkness on the Edge of Town [1978]
- Badlands
- Darkness On The Edge Of Town
- Prove It All Night

The River [1980]
- Hungry Heart

STARR, Ringo

(single only) [1971]
- It Don't Come Easy

(single only) [1972]
- Back Off Boogaloo

Ringo [1973]
- Oh My My
- Photograph
- You're Sixteen

Goodnight Vienna [1974]
- No No Song

STATUS QUO, The

(single only) [1968]
- Pictures Of Matchstick Men

STEALERS WHEEL

Stealers Wheel [1973]
- Stuck In The Middle With You

STEELY DAN

Can't Buy A Thrill [1972]
- Dirty Work
- Do It Again
- Reeling In The Years

Countdown To Ecstasy [1973]
- Bodhisattva
- My Old School
- Show Biz Kids

Pretzel Logic [1974]
- Any Major Dude Will Tell You
- Pretzel Logic
- Rikki Don't Lose That Number

Katy Lied [1975]
- Black Friday

The Royal Scam [1976]
- Fez, The
- Kid Charlemagne

STEELY DAN — cont'd
Aja [1977]
   Aja
   Black Cow
   Deacon Blues
   Josie
   Peg
St: FM [1978]
   FM (No Static At All)
Gaucho [1980]
   Babylon Sisters
   Hey Nineteen

STEPPENWOLF
Steppenwolf [1968]
   Born To Be Wild
   Pusher, The
The Second [1968]
   Magic Carpet Ride
At Your Birthday Party [1969]
   Rock Me
Monster [1969]
   Monster
(single only) [1970]
   Hey Lawdy Mama

STEVENS, Cat
Tea For The Tillerman [1971]
   Wild World
Teaser And The Firecat [1971]
   Moon Shadow
   Morning Has Broken
   Peace Train
(single only) [1974]
   Another Saturday Night
Buddha And The Chocolate Box [1974]
   Oh Very Young

STEWART, Al
Year Of The Cat [1976]
   Year Of The Cat

STEWART, John
Bombs Away Dream Babies [1979]
   Gold
   Lost Her In The Sun
   Midnight Wind

STEWART, Rod
The Rod Stewart Album [1969]
   Handbags And Gladrags
Gasoline Alley [1970]
   Cut Across Shorty
Every Picture Tells A Story [1971]
   Every Picture Tells A Story
   (I Know) I'm Losing You
   Maggie May
   Reason To Believe
Never A Dull Moment [1972]
   Angel
   You Wear It Well
Smiler [1974]
   Mine For Me

Atlantic Crossing [1975]
   Sailing
   This Old Heart Of Mine
A Night On The Town [1976]
   First Cut Is The Deepest
   Killing Of Georgie
   Tonight's The Night (Gonna Be Alright)
Foot Loose & Fancy Free [1977]
   Hot Legs
   I Was Only Joking
   You're In My Heart (The Final Acclaim)
Blondes Have More Fun [1978]
   Ain't Love A Bitch
   Da Ya Think I'm Sexy?
Foolish Behaviour [1980]
   Passion

STILLS, Stephen
Stephen Stills [1970]
   Love The One You're With
   Sit Yourself Down
Stephen Stills 2 [1971]
   Change Partners

STRAWBERRY ALARM CLOCK
Incense And Peppermints [1967]
   Incense And Peppermints

STYX
Styx II [1973]
   Lady
Equinox [1975]
   Lorelei
   Suite Madame Blue
Crystal Ball [1976]
   Crystal Ball
   Mademoiselle
The Grand Illusion [1977]
   Come Sail Away
   Fooling Yourself (The Angry Young Man)
   Grand Illusion, The
   Miss America
Pieces Of Eight [1978]
   Blue Collar Man (Long Nights)
   Renegade
   Sing For The Day
Cornerstone [1979]
   Babe
   Borrowed Time
   Why Me

SUGARLOAF
Sugarloaf [1970]
   Green-Eyed Lady

SUPERTRAMP
Crime Of The Century [1974]
   Bloody Well Right
   Dreamer
   Rudy
   School
Even In The Quietest Moments... [1977]
   Give A Little Bit

SUPERTRAMP — cont'd
Breakfast In America [1979]
Breakfast In America
Goodbye Stranger
Logical Song
Take The Long Way Home

SWEET
Desolation Boulevard [1975]
Ballroom Blitz
Fox On The Run

· ·

TALKING HEADS
Talking Heads: 77 [1977]
Psycho Killer
More Songs About Buildings And Food [1978]
Take Me To The River
Fear Of Music [1979]
Life During Wartime
Remain In Light [1980]
Once In A Lifetime

TAYLOR, James
Sweet Baby James [1970]
Fire And Rain
Mud Slide Slim And The Blue Horizon [1971]
You've Got A Friend
Gorilla [1975]
How Sweet It Is (To Be Loved By You)
In The Pocket [1976]
Shower The People
JT [1977]
Handy Man
Your Smiling Face

10cc
The Original Soundtrack [1975]
I'm Not In Love
Deceptive Bends [1977]
Things We Do For Love

TEN YEARS AFTER
A Space In Time [1971]
I'd Love To Change The World

THEM
Them [1965]
Gloria
Here Comes The Night
Mystic Eyes

THIN LIZZY
Jailbreak [1976]
Boys Are Back In Town

38 SPECIAL
Rockin' Into The Night [1980]
Rockin' Into The Night

THREE DOG NIGHT
Three Dog Night [1969]
One
Try A Little Tenderness

Suitable For Framing [1969]
Celebrate
Easy To Be Hard
Eli's Coming
It Ain't Easy [1970]
Mama Told Me (Not To Come)
Naturally [1970]
Joy To The World
Liar
Harmony [1971]
Never Been To Spain
Old Fashioned Love Song
Cyan [1973]
Shambala

THUNDERCLAP NEWMAN
Hollywood Dream [1970]
Something In The Air

TOTO
Toto [1978]
Girl Goodbye
Hold The Line
I'll Supply The Love
Hydra [1979]
99
Turn Back [1981]
Goodbye Elenore

TOWNSHEND, Pete
Empty Glass [1980]
Let My Love Open The Door
Rough Boys

TRAFFIC
Mr. Fantasy [1968]
Dear Mr. Fantasy
Hole In My Shoe
Paper Sun
Traffic [1968]
Feelin' Alright?
Forty Thousand Headmen
You Can All Join In
John Barleycorn Must Die [1970]
Empty Pages
Freedom Rider
John Barleycorn
The Low Spark Of High Heeled Boys [1971]
Low Spark Of High Heeled Boys
Rock & Roll Stew

TRAVERS, Pat, Band
Pat Travers Band Live! Go For What You Know [1979]
Boom Boom (Out Go The Lights)

T. REX
Electric Warrior [1971]
Bang A Gong (Get It Out)

TRIUMPH
Rock & Roll Machine [1978]
   Rock & Roll Machine
Just A Game [1979]
   Hold On
   Lay It On The Line
Progressions Of Power [1980]
   I Can Survive
   I Live For The Weekend

TROGGS, The
Wild Thing [1966]
   Wild Thing

TROWER, Robin
Bridge Of Sighs [1974]
   Bridge Of Sighs
   Day Of The Eagle
   Little Bit Of Sympathy
   Too Rolling Stoned
Long Misty Days [1976]
   Caledonia
Victims Of The Fury [1980]
   Victims Of The Fury

· ·

URIAH HEEP
Demons And Wizards [1972]
   Easy Livin
Sweet Freedom [1973]
   Stealin'

· ·

VAN HALEN
Van Halen [1978]
   Ain't Talkin' ' Bout Love
   Ice Cream Man
   Jamie's Cryin'
   Runnin' With The Devil
   You Really Got Me
Van Halen II [1979]
   Beautiful Girls
   Dance The Night Away
Women And Children First [1980]
   And The Cradle Will Rock...

VANILLA FUDGE
Vanilla Fudge [1967]
   You Keep Me Hangin' On

· ·

WALSH, Joe
The Smoker You Drink, The Player You Get [1973]
   Meadows
   Rocky Mountain Way
But Seriously, Folks... [1978]
   Life's Been Good
St: Urban Cowboy [1980]
   All Night Long

WAR
The World Is A Ghetto [1972]
   Cisco Kid

Why Can't We Be Friends [1975]
   Low Rider

WELCH, Bob
French Kiss [1977]
   Ebony Eyes
   Sentimental Lady [77]
Three Hearts [1979]
   Precious Love

WET WILLIE
Keep On Smilin' [1974]
   Keep On Smilin'

WHO, The
(single only) [1965]
   I Can't Explain
(single only) [1966]
   My Generation
(single only) [1966]
   Substitute
Happy Jack [1967]
   Boris The Spider
   Happy Jack
The Who Sell Out [1968]
   I Can See For Miles
Magic Bus-The Who On Tour [1968]
   Call Me Lightning
   Magic Bus
   Pictures Of Lily
Tommy [1969]
   I'm Free
   Pinball Wizard
   We're Not Gonna Take It
(single only) [1970]
   See Me, Feel Me
(single only) [1970]
   Seeker, The
Live At Leeds [1970]
   Summertime Blues
Who's Next [1971]
   Baba O'Riley
   Bargain
   Behind Blue Eyes
   Goin' Mobile
   My Wife
   Won't Get Fooled Again
Meaty Beaty Big And Bouncy [1971]
   Kids Are Alright
(single only) [1972]
   Join Together
(single only) [1972]
   Relay, The
Quadrophenia [1973]
   5:15
   Love, Reign, O'er Me
   Real Me
The Who By Numbers [1975]
   Squeeze Box
Who Are You [1978]
   Who Are You
St: The Kids Are Alright [1979]
   Long Live Rock

WINTER, Edgar, Group
They Only Come Out At Night [1972]
    Frankenstein
    Free Ride

WRIGHT, Gary
The Dream Weaver [1975]
    Dream Weaver
    Love Is Alive

* *

YARDBIRDS, The
For Your Love [1965]
    For Your Love
Having a Rave Up with The Yardbirds [1965]
    Heart Full Of Soul
    I'm A Man
Over Under Sideways Down [1966]
    Over Under Sideways Down
(single only) [1966]
    Shapes Of Things
Little Games [1967]
    Little Games

YES
Yes [1969]
    Every Little Thing
The Yes Album [1971]
    Starship Trooper
    Your Move/All Good People
    Yours Is No Disgrace
(single only) [1972]
    America
Fragile [1972]
    Long Distance Runaround
    Roundabout
Close To The Edge [1972]
    And You And I
    Close To The Edge
Going For The One [1977]
    Going For The One

YOUNG, Neil
Everybody Knows This Is Nowhere [1969]
    Cinnamon Girl
    Cowgirl In The Sand
    Down By The River
After The Gold Rush [1970]
    After The Gold Rush
    Only Love Can Break Your Heart
    Southern Man
    When You Dance I Can Really Love
Harvest [1972]
    Heart Of Gold
    Needle And The Damage Done
    Old Man
On The Beach [1974]
    Walk On
American Stars 'N Bars [1977]
    Like A Hurricane
Comes A Time [1978]
    Comes A Time
    Four Strong Winds

Rust Never Sleeps [1979]
    Rust Never Sleeps (Hey Hey, My My)

YOUNGBLOODS, The
The Youngbloods [1967]
    Get Together

* *

ZAPPA, Frank
Hot Rats [1969]
    Peaches En Regalia
Weasels Ripped My Flesh [1970]
    My Guitar Wants To Kill Your Mama
Chunga's Revenge [1970]
    Transylvania Boogie
Over-nite Sensation [1973]
    Montana
Apostrophe (') [1974]
    Cosmik Debris
    Don't Eat The Yellow Snow
Sheik Yerbouti [1979]
    Dancin' Fool
Joe's Garage, Act I [1979]
    Joe's Garage

ZEVON, Warren
Excitable Boy [1978]
    Excitable Boy
    Lawyers, Guns And Money
    Werewolves Of London
Bad Luck Streak In Dancing School [1980]
    Certain Girl, A

ZOMBIES, The
The Zombies [1965]
    She's Not There
    Tell Her No
Odessey & Oracle [1969]
    Time Of The Season

ZZ TOP
Rio Grande Mud [1972]
    Francene
Tres Hombres [1973]
    La Grange
    Waitin' For The Bus/Jesus Just Left Chicago
Fandango! [1975]
    Heard It On The X
    Tush
Tejas [1977]
    Arrested For Driving While Blind
    It's Only Love
Deguello [1979]
    Cheap Sunglasses
    I Thank You
    I'm Bad, I'm Nationwide

* *

ORDER INFORMATION

Shipping/Handling Extra — If you do not order through our online Web site (see below), please contact us for book rates and shipping/handling rates.

Order By:

Online at our Web site: www.recordresearch.com

U.S. Toll-Free: 1-800-827-9810
(orders only please – Mon-Fri 8 AM-12 PM, 1 PM-5 PM CST)

Foreign Orders: 1-262-251-5408

Questions?:   1-262-251-5408 or **Email**: books@recordresearch.com

Fax (24 hours): 1-262-251-9452

Mail: Record Research Inc.
P.O. Box 200
Menomonee Falls, WI 53052-0200
U.S.A.

Preferred U.S. shipping of orders **via UPS**; please allow **7-10 business days** for delivery. (If only a post office box number is given, it will be shipped Media Mail which may delay delivery time; no S/H adjustment.) For faster delivery, contact us for other shipping options/rates.

Canadian and **Foreign** orders are shipped either **via Third Party Surface M-Bag** (please allow **50-90 days** for delivery) or **via Third Party Airmail M-Bag** (please allow **30-50 days** for delivery). These shipping option costs are automatically quoted online. Quotes for Priority Mail International (10-14 day for delivery) are available by phone, fax or email. Orders must be paid in U.S. dollars and drawn on a U.S. bank.

Payment methods accepted: MasterCard, VISA, American Express, Discover, Money Order, or Check (personal checks may be held up to 10 days for bank clearance). PayPal accepted online only.

Prices subject to change without notice.